ENVIRONMENTAL REGULATIONS FOR PRINTERS

ENVIRONMENTAL REGULATIONS FOR PRINTERS

How to Comply with Environmental Rules
While Making Your Printing Operations
More Productive and Profitable

by Fred Shapiro

JELMAR PUBLISHING CO., INC.
P O Box 488
Plainview, NY 11803

ON THE COVER:
FRONT COVER: Rainforest at Cairns, Australia
REAR COVER: Upper left: Roof mounted catalyitic oxidizer
                      Upper right: Bucks County barn, Doylestown, Pennsylvania
                      Center left: Water lilies and falls, Brookside Gardens,
                                       Rockville, Maryland
                      Lower left: Web flexo press by Bobst
                      Center right: Web litho press by Mitsubishi
                      Center right: Shanghai, China at dusk, (photo by
                                        Jeffrey Shapiro)
                      Bottom: Inkroom for printing plant not in compliance

Library of Congress Cataloging-in-Publication Data

Shapiro, Fred (Fred A.), 1932–
    Environmental regulations for printers: how to comply with environmental rules while making your printing operations more productive and profitable / by Fred Shapiro.
    p. cm.
    Includes bibliographical references and index.
    ISBN 1-885067-08-9
    regulations—United States. 2. Laminated materials—Safety regulations—United States. 3. Pollution—Law and legislation—United States. 4. Printing industry—Environmental aspects—United States. 5. Laminated materials—Environmental aspects—United States. I. Title.

KF1893.B57 S48 2002
344.73′04632—dc21
                                                            2002025683
                                                                CIP

I dedicate this book to my family for providing the motivation to work toward a cleaner environment. Foremost is my wife Madeline for her patience with me during the time I have spent hunched over the computer or taking photographs. Next are my children and their spouses—Jeff and Alayne, Rhonda and Mitchell, and Eileen and Cory. Last and most important are my grandchildren—Allison, Marisa, Brian, Benjamin, Frank and Jake, who were constant reminders that our generation must assure that their generation will have a world in which they can flourish.

Acknowledgements

I am indebted to a great many people who in some way, direct or indirect, were critical in the sequence of events of the past eighteen years that have culminated in this book.

On a professional level, I have been fortunate to be surrounded, from the time I started working in the printing and packaging industry in 1957, with some of the brightest and most cooperative people imaginable. I cannot even hope to thank all who have helped mold the person and intellect that I am today. I do want to acknowledge a few in particular who have contributed in one form or another over the years to the accumulation of knowledge and sources that eventually went into the making of this book: Stuart Fingerman, James Coyle of the New York State Environmental Facilities Corporation, Gary Jones of the Graphic Arts Technical Foundation, Doreen Monteleone of the Foundation of Flexographic Technical Association, Vicki Keenan of the Association of Graphic Communication, Sam Gilbert of Sun Chemical, Geoffrey Wilcox, P.Eng. of Wilcox Engineering, Stuart Cooper P.E. of Enviro-Assist Inc., Stanley Wald, P.E., Charles Martinson of CMM LLC, the members of the Air Resource Group LLC, Stephanie Bergman and Karen Chu of the USEPA Design for the Environment program, Lew Felleisen of USEPA Region III, and all the members of the Printing Sector Work Group of the USEPA Common Sense Initiative project.

As you read the book you will also see acknowledgements to companies that were very gracious in providing information and illustrations to make the text alive and complete. My thanks to each of them.

Last but not least, my thanks to Joel Shulman, publisher and editor, for having suggested that I do the book and then for keeping me on track as we progressed.

Fred Shapiro

Table of Contents

APPENDIX

Contents of Computer Disk
(included)

A. Pollution Prevention Checklist for Printers

B. Environmental Compliance Audit Form

C. Tools for Determining Air Emissions: Mass Balance—Small Printer

D. Tools for Determining Air Emissions: Mass Balance—Large Printer

E. Air Emission Report of VOCs to State Agencies

F. Add-on Control Systems: Sample Request for Proposal

G. Add-on Control Systems: Comparison Spreadsheet

H. Template for Hazardous Waste Management Program

I. Forms for Silver Halide Best Management Program

J. Spill Prevention Program

K. Model Hazard Communication Standard Program

L. OSHA Form 300 Reporting Forms

M. SARA Title III Inventory Reporting, Tier I and II Forms

N. SARA Title III List of Lists (Chemicals)

O. SARA Title III Toxic Release Inventory Forms

P. Filing and Tickler System for Environmental Management

Q. Return on Investment Worksheets

List of Illustrations

List of Tables

About the Author

Fred Shapiro is an industrial engineer and manager with considerable experience in the printing and packaging industries. Starting in 1957 with Equitable Bag Company in New York, over a 30-year period he has held manufacturing and technical management positions in the package printing industry. He has been an active member of industry trade associations, serving as an officer of the Flexographic Technical Association and as one of the founders and vice-president of the Foundation of FTA. Currently he is chairperson of the environmental committee of the PIA affiliate, Association of Graphic Communications, in New York City. The FTA honored him with its leadership award in 1991.

Mr. Shapiro has a Masters of Business Administration from Baruch College of the City University of New York and a Bachelor of Arts in Economics from Queens College of CUNY. He attended prestigious Stuyvesant High School in New York City.

In 1985 he organized his consulting network with the goal of assisting printers in improving the performance of their operations. Since his introduction, as a consultant, to the challenges of environmental regulations in 1985, he has been instrumental in bringing businesses, large and small, into compliance, and has promoted pollution prevention (source reduction) as the key strategy for confronting the regulations. His consulting group has been very active in promoting compliance through educational efforts. A series of workshops held around the country in 1987 introduced flexographic printers to the technical options available to enable them to comply with the Clean Air Law. The group conducted the first workshop for printers in the United States devoted to UV curable inks as a means of compliance. Over the years, Mr. Shapiro has been an organizer, moderator or speaker at various industry and government workshops and conferences on the subjects of printing technology, the environment and pollution prevention.

Complementing his work with environment regulations, Mr. Shapiro's activity as a consultant has included evaluation of printing operations to determine strengths and weaknesses in the organization, personnel and tooling of client firms, development of programs and selection of equipment to improve plant effectiveness, design and implementation of systems to control activity and quality, and training of supervisory and operating personnel.

He is currently one of the PIA/Graphic Arts Technical Foundation's "Solutions on Site" consultants, working with his group to handle assignments as expert witnesses for litigation and technical and manufacturing assignments with package printers.

Mr. Shapiro writes a monthly environmental column for *Printing News*, a Cygnus publication. From 1993 to 1996, he was consultant to the Flexographic Technical Association for environmental issues, conducted Town Hall meetings in various cities to promote compliance through pollution prevention, wrote a monthly column in *Flexo* magazine and produced a monthly Environmental Newsletter for FTA members. Mr. Shapiro has been organizer and coordinator of the CMM show's conference programs.

He continues to be involved in education, having taught Work Design at Baruch College of CUNY, printing at SUNY Farmingdale, and lectured at New York City Tech of the City University of New York (CUNY). He also serves on the Advisory Commission for Graphic Arts to the New York City Board of Education.

Active in state and federal efforts to reform regulations and promote pollution prevention, he has served as committee chairperson in the working groups of the Common Sense Initiative for the Printing Industries, and was a member of the steering and technical committees of the Flexo Design for the Environment project. He served as a subcontractor to Abt Associates and Western Michigan University for the Flexography DfE project, and to the Industrial Technical Assistance Corporation of New York City for the USEPA New York City Community Printer project.

He has spoken on the subject of pollution prevention for flexographic printers in Atlanta at the regional programs of the USEPA (Region IV), at the Pollution Prevention Conference in Palm Beach, sponsored by the Palm Beach County Health Department and the Southeast Air And Waste Management Association, at the NYSDEC Pollution Prevention Conferences in Albany, and, most recently, at the USEPA Region III Pollution Prevention Conference in Philadelphia and the Region IV Conference in Atlanta.

Shapiro was elected as the 2002 honoree to the Flexographic Hall of Fame, the citation stating that: "Breaking down barriers has been a 45-year passion for one noted flexographer. He insists on quality, errs on the side of safety, stands strong as a proponent of controls designed to better the workplace, and keeps a watchful eye out for new rules, regulations and compliance procedures that will mold the future practices of the printing industry."

Preface

The opening salvo in the current environmental movement was sounded by Rachel Carson with her landmark book, *Silent Spring*. It gave the environmental movement an impetus which is carrying it to ever widening circles. In the beginning, the emphasis was on major sources of pollution. The current—and likely future—efforts will be increasingly on lower volumes of air, water and land pollution, as well as health and safety in the workplace.

As the net spreads, more and more businesses are being drawn into a web of regulations. Regulations become increasingly more stringent, and enforcement becomes increasingly more rigorous. And, as often happens when more and more people become involved in any effort, the concepts and objectives are often lost sight of in the effort to enforce the reasonable rules and regulations, until some of them become unreasonable and improperly enforced.

It is our objective in this book to assist one group of businesses to find their way through the morass of legislation and enforcement. This group includes those businesses and companies that put ink, coatings and adhesives onto substrates, whether paper, plastics, textiles or whatever. These include not only commercial and in-house printers, but also those companies that produce printed circuit boards, thick film keyboards for computers, membrane switches, packaging with and without printing, product manufacturers who add adhesives to their packages when enclosing products such as foodstuffs, and any others who must meet the standards set by the various environmental laws and regulations passed by federal, state, and municipal governments, sanitary districts, and other appropriate legal entities.

If you are a small printer, for instance a "quick" printer, you have reason to be concerned with the environmental regulations as they become increasingly more rigorous and are applied to lower and lower quantities of pollutants as emitted into the air, washed into the waste streams, and as affecting the health and welfare of your employees—as well as yourself and your family. You will be affected, just as the larger printing companies have been for a number of years. No printer, small or large, using any printing process, is immune from these regulations.

Unfortunately, in this situation, the enforcement becomes more and more chaotic, and the original objectives of assisting businesses in developing plans that will meet the legal requirements often are lost in litigation, obscuration and obfuscation of the enforcement policies. Instead of help, it seems that vindictiveness, punishment and revenge have often become the true objectives of too many enforcement organizations.

If you think that because you own or operate a small printing shop, such as a quick print operation, that you are immune from enforcement and fines, think again! Likewise for printing operations that are merely ancillary to other production operations. No printer is immune, because of the nature of the materials and processes involved. Any printer, previously unaffected by these regulations, will soon find himself striving to meet the letter and spirit of the laws.

Printing, by its very nature, cannot become completely free of some environmental problems. The source of the problems lies in the materials used—in the inks and solvents used in the printing processes themselves—and no traditional printing process has yet solved the problem of how to avoid use of solvents and inks that cannot cause an environmental problem. However, these need not generate violations nor need they become sources of problems to printers and grist for the mill of unscrupulous enforcement personnel or advocacy groups with agendas of their own.

Because of the many laws and environmental regulations in this area, the material in this book is essential for attorneys who represent clients involved in environmental litigation as well as those who wish to avoid litigation, to understand the issues involved. Likewise, this material is useful for environmental regulators who labor under difficulties posed by conflicting interpretations, overlapping jurisdictions, inadequate guidance and public pressure—enabling them to seek a firm foundation for their efforts. And, of course, those members of the general public who are interested or involved in the environmental movement will welcome a clear picture of the world of regulators, regulations and of the businesses that are so essential to modern life as we know and experience it daily.

Without adequate guidance, many small entrepreneurs could easily be put out of business by massive fines that exceed their ability to pay or to manage the costs necessary to retain suitable legal counsel. Even minor infractions can become so costly as to place a business in jeopardy. This, despite the admonition of the legislators that they do not want to put people out of business and put workers out of work unless they flagrantly and continuously defy the law.

It is with the hope that this book, the first ever of its kind to assemble the appropriate regulations, procedures and concepts in one easy-to-use reference, will enable both small and large printers to help find their way through the massive accumulation of both law and practice that has arisen in the wake of efforts to recreate a greener world.

We have included not only the pertinent regulations but also some of the interpretations that usually are applied to various situations. The book is replete with caveats to printers as to appropriate steps they likely should take to meet both the letter and the intent of the regulations, and avoid the financial as well as psychological burdens that might ensue should they inadvertently overlook some "violation" that an inspector may find.

In addition to the emphasis on regulations, we have included information to aid the printer in selecting materials that will help to make compliance possible, or at least easier. Information is included on waterbase inks, less-polluting solvents, equipment that eliminates effluents, etc. These are all part of the efforts printers need to assure compliance with regulations.

One consequence of preparing to meet environmental and OSHA regulations—an unanticipated benefit—has been a reduction in the amount of materials used and stored and an increase in production efficiencies in the printing plant. In other words, an increase in productivity often takes place when a printer works toward environmental compliance, so much so that the profitability of his operations frequently increases significantly.

Because one source of non-compliance is the accumulation of old and useless inks and other materials, an internal audit frequently turns up areas where efficiencies of production, storage and materials movement can be realized. We have also emphasized these areas. Therefore, even if you believe you are fully in compliance, it will be useful to read through this book to see opportunities where additional savings may be attained.

While this book was in preparation, the George W. Bush administration altered a number of policies and regulations encompassing the environment. The federal government has softened some of the more onerous regulations as they affect small business and the energy industry.

Printers, as well as all medium and small businesses, should be aware that much of the changes would be to the advantage of large business. Energy companies run round the clock every day of the year; modification of new source rules will provide them with relief from one of the most onerous of all environmental measures—the potential to emit. Their potential is identical to the actual. Small businesses will still be handcuffed by the interpretation that it could emit every hour of the year. A shift to use of actual emissions as opposed to potential can benefit small business, but it unlikely that this will occur.

Likewise, it should be noted that while the federal government can relax its rules, state and local governments can and do pass more restrictive regulations and standards. It is unlikely that these local rules will be relaxed. Those states with the highest incidence of air, water and hazardous waste exposure will endeavor to maintain strict requirements. Increased enforcement will result in greater income by increasing the burden by permitting smaller entities and by levying higher penalties. Small businesses, which have been below the radar screen until now, can become the victims of this greater emphasis on broader enforcement.

Any change that will benefit business is portrayed by environmental advocacy groups as a loosening of the laws to the disadvantage of the environment. Emotion often takes the place of solid science and common sense. Outsiders take the stance that they have superior knowledge to that of the experienced managers and technical staff of most businesses.

Printers beware!!! What you read in the newspapers and hear on television about relaxation of the regulations seldom addresses your concerns. Make every effort to comply and go beyond compliance. Don't count on a relaxation of the rules to provide you with a margin of safety from litigation and penalties. If you are unsure about anything in the regulations, contact the appropriate industry association or small business ombudsman for confidential advice.

We bring to this effort well over 18 years of consulting with and assisting companies to conform with the regulations and working closely with all levels of governmental authorities to resolve questions of fact and interpretation. The results are presented here.

New York
February 2003

CHAPTER 1

Meeting the Challenge
of the Environment

The first question you might ask is, "Why my company?" Why is printing targeted by so many regulations and under increasing pressure to change the basic equipment and materials by which graphics are transferred from concept to print?

In a world dominated by many small businesses, what are printers doing individually or collectively that can be so bad? Don't the statistics show that while printing is one of the largest industries in the United States, it is made of a preponderance of firms that employ 20 or fewer employees? (See Table 1–1.*) Many are family owned and operated. Would printers use materials that would harm not only themselves, but wives, husbands, children and future generations?

To understand the reasons for and the impact of these questions, one must look at the contribution printing has made to the world and the chemistry that made these advancements possible. Then one must consider the confluence of recent revelations of the characteristics and the impact of chemistry on the daily lives of people in our community and ecology of the natural world in which we live. We can come to understand that printing uses

---

*"Table 5, U.S. Total Number of Plants by Press Type and Employment Size," from *Printing Industry and Use Cluster Profile*, United States Environmental Protection Agency, EPA 744-R-94-003, June 1994, p 1–16. This table is included to provide some insight into the relatively small size of the typical print shop. The data are out of date and do not account for major changes in the industry that have taken place since publication of these data nor does it contain a complete picture of the industry. Its information on flexographic, screen and letterpress printers is far from accurate.

TABLE 1-1. TOTAL NUMBER OF PRINTING PLANTS IN THE UNITED STATES BY PRESS TYPE AND EMPLOYMENT SIZE

PRESS TYPE	Number of Employees per Plant												Total Plants	Date	Source
	1-4	% of Total	5-9	% of Total	10-19	% of Total	20-49	% of Total	50-99	% of Total	100+	% of Total			
All Operating Plants\1	32158	46.1%	17068	24.5%	9800	14.1%	6204	8.9%	2448	3.5%	2036	2.9%	69714	September 1990	AFL #I-200
All In-plant Printers\2	7080	53.9%	3297	25.1%	1824	13.9%	694	5.3%	155	1.2%	84	0.6%	13134	Summer 1990	AFL #I-500
All Trade Plants\3	3281	42.8%	1791	23.4%	1187	15.5%	884	11.5%	374	4.9%	143	1.9%	7660	November 1991	AFL #I-700
All plants with presses\4	27528	46.2%	14580	24.4%	8227	13.8%	5274	8.8%	2132	3.6%	1895	3.2%	59636	November 1991	AFL #I-800
All offset presses	25435	46.7%	13385	24.6%	7498	13.8%	4676	8.6%	1883	3.5%	1575	2.9%	54452	February 1991	AFL #IIIA-100
- sheetfed	24367	48.4%	12172	24.2%	7142	14.2%	4052	8.1%	1425	2.8%	1165	2.3%	50323	August 1988	AFL #IIIA-400
- single color															
14"x20" or smaller	24186	50.6%	11974	25.1%	6562	13.7%	3430	7.2%	987	2.1%	634	1.3%	47773	March 1989	AFL #IIIA-240
20½" to 33"	4285	27.8%	4195	27.3%	3600	23.4%	2174	14.1%	690	4.5%	444	2.9%	15388	July 1987	AFL #IIIA-480
34" or larger	559	14.6%	744	19.4%	897	23.4%	912	23.8%	422	11.0%	306	8.0%	3840	July 1987	AFL #IIIA-560
- multicolor															
14"x20" or smaller	na	na	na	na	na	na	na	na	na	na	na	na	na		
20½" to 33"	785	16.1%	984	20.2%	1265	26.0%	1105	22.7%	426	8.7%	304	6.2%	4869	July 1987	AFL #IIIA-500
34" or larger	272	5.7%	523	11.0%	1018	21.4%	1413	29.6%	830	17.4%	712	14.9%	4768	July 1987	AFL #IIIA-580
- webfed	378	6.6%	707	12.3%	1248	21.6%	1510	26.2%	936	16.2%	987	17.1%	5766	February 1989	AFL #IIIA-800
26½" or smaller	223	8.4%	366	13.8%	617	23.2%	684	25.8%	409	15.4%	356	13.4%	2655	August 1989	AFL #IIIA-920
27" or larger	213	5.9%	385	10.7%	707	19.7%	938	26.1%	594	16.5%	758	21.1%	3595	August 1989	AFL #IIIA-860
- heatset	86	6.3%	111	8.1%	195	14.2%	261	19.0%	250	18.2%	473	34.4%	1376	February 1990	AFL #IIIA-820
27" or larger	18	2.7%	25	3.8%	76	11.6%	100	15.2%	123	18.7%	316	48.0%	658	July 1987	AFL #IIIA-900
- non-heatset	366	7.4%	662	13.4%	1140	23.0%	1376	27.8%	768	15.5%	638	12.9%	4950	February 1990	AFL #IIIA-880
27" or larger	205	6.9%	335	11.3%	576	19.4%	814	27.4%	535	18.0%	503	16.9%	2968	July 1987	AFL #IIIA-840
All flexographic presses	193	12.2%	238	15.0%	289	18.2%	373	23.5%	198	12.5%	296	18.7%	1587	November 1989	AFL #IIIA-1500
All letterpresses	9487	45.6%	4515	21.7%	3335	16.0%	1835	8.8%	781	3.8%	833	4.0%	20786	Fall 1982	AFL #IIIA-1520
- sheetfed	8397	44.3%	4694	24.8%	2969	15.7%	1815	9.6%	623	3.3%	463	2.4%	18961	November 1988	AFL #IIIA-1540
- rotary	na	na	na	na	na	na	na	na	na	na	na	na	na		
All gravure presses	na	na	na	na	na	na	na	na	na	na	na	na	1090	1989	GAA 1989
All screen presses	na	na	na	na	na	na	na	na	na	na	na	na	> 40000	Fall 1993	Kinter 1993

Information was collected by the Design for the Environment of the USEPA and published in *Printing Industry and Use Cluster Profile*, EPA 744-R-94-003, p 1-16 (footnote 1).

1. Operating plants include all firms primarily engaged in providing printing services including prepress, press, and postpress operations.

2. In-plant printers are firms engaged in internal, non-commercial printing performing prepress, press, and postpress operations for businesses, government, schools, and institutions.

3. Trade plants are firms which provide prepress or postpress services but do not engage in printing as their primary business.

4. Plants with presses are firms which possess any printing press or duplicator/photocopier and engage in printing as their primary business.

Sources: GAA 1989; A.F. Lewis 1991; and Kinter 1993.

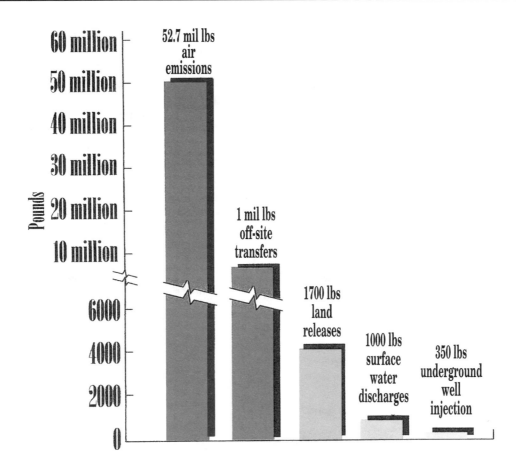

Figure 1-1. Concern for pollution caused by printing facilities is demonstrated in the charting of the volume of such wastes in 1993 from Toxic Release Inventory reports, as depicted in *Pollution Prevention Manual for Lithographic Printers*, Iowa Waste Reduction Center.

chemicals that can negatively affect the health and well being of staff, neighbors and the natural creatures in our surroundings. (See figure 1–1.*)

If the inventors and developers of the various printing processes had been faced with the environmental constraints that we know now, what would they have done differently? Would they have despaired and found another more lucrative area in which to use their energies, or would they have persevered under the restraints of government regulations to develop safer ways of communicating in print? What a calamity it would have been if the printing processes had been invented but could not be implemented and refined. Just think of our daily needs and how much the printed word or product lends to the quality of the life we lead. If printing did not exist, how would mankind have achieved much of what we take for granted in our daily lives, and in the academic and scientific communities.

*Attributed to Wayne Pferdehirt, P.E., in *Pollution Prevention Manual for Lithographic Printers*, Iowa Waste Reduction Center, University of Northern Iowa, 1995, p 3.

A Collision Course

Based on the history of the various processes, it was inevitable that printing and the environment would meet on a collision course. The characteristics and advantages of those processes that have made the quality of life so acceptable and desirable have been achieved by finding materials that would transfer, adhere and withstand various types of exposure in use. The solutions of yesterday are meeting with resistance today. The chemicals that facilitate the transfer of colorants to paper, film and other substrates, conveying information and graphics to the attention of the consumer, are loaded with risks and potential hazards to the health of workers and the community. (See figure 1–2.)

Prodded by public pressure and significant disasters, governments have taken proactive positions and enacted laws to restrict the amount and nature of pollution emanating from industrial facilities. Printing is a very large industry, considered to be one of the major sectors of industrial activity in the United States. Printing uses all sorts of chemicals, particularly solvents. Printing plants are frequently easily identified by the odor of the chemicals they use. What better or easier target for an attack on industrial activity related to pollutants in our environment?

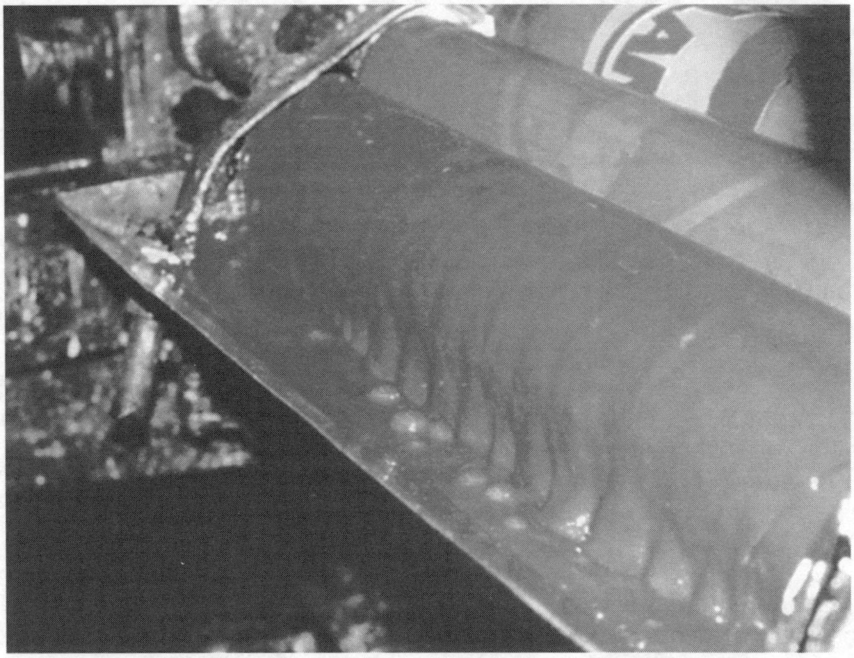

What is one to do? Give up the industry, or search to find adequate solutions that will replace or minimize the chemicals needed to prepare and print papers, films, foils and other materials that have become routine communications, packaging and decorative substrates? Compliance with regulations is mandatory, with the legal net surrounding the printing industry spreading to encompass more of the medium sized and smaller shops in places that were never regulated before.

Figure 1-2. Open fountains and rollers in printing presses are clear exhibits of the potential for air emissions and hazardous wastes.

There is no other alternative than to find the means to comply with permitting and reporting requirements, and by commencing programs to identify and use safer chemistry to reduce potential pollution. Printers can modernize their equipment, change work practices, and train their people to operate with a different, more sensitive attitude toward wastes and the community into which these wastes are disposed.

The challenge is not unrelated to the technical developments that have gripped the printing industries in the past five to 10 years. Most developments encompassing the use of computers have led to drastic changes in the way we do things and the elimination of a considerable burden of chemistry enroute to new levels of graphic achievement.

Meeting the environmental challenge is something that every printer can and must do as the market drives them to higher levels of quality and productivity.

Addressing the Environment Through Government

Private citizens were at the forefront of a vision that predicted disaster to the environment and human life on Earth. Industrial disasters, such as the underground toxic dumps which poisoned the ground and the air at Love Canal in upstate New York or the release of toxic fumes that killed and injured many in Bhopal, India, raised questions about responsibilities in an industrial society. Could industry not curtail practices that were damaging to the very ground, water and air to which all life looked for nourishment and sustenance? Public opinion, enhanced by the efforts made by these individuals, focused attention on the issues by demanding government intervention and control of the various venues by which pollutants make their presence felt in the air, water and ground.

The initial legislation and rules dealt with large facilities, capable of putting thousands of tons or gallons of pollutants into the environment. The federal government mandated criteria and standards for each of the media, and then delegated authority and responsibility to many of the states. Some local authorities—state, county and city—passed additional regulations based on the exposure to sensitive communities or ecological species. In every case, the most stringent laws and standards have taken precedence, with the local laws in no way diminishing the effectiveness of the broader federal laws, or vice versa.

There can be two ways that government can address environmental policy. The first reaction is to hit hard. The only way to show success is through litigation and the volume of penalties levied. The other approach is to educate the industry and public, and promote public participation in cooperation with industry to make changes that will clean up the environment.

Keep in mind that, historically, the heavy hand of government measures success by the number of legal cases and victories, the amount of penalties collected, and the media attention cast on the "villain." The more money claimed as the result of penalties, the greater the perceived success of an enforcement program and support of the agencies by outside lobbyists. As the span and ferocity of the programs expand, the measure of this augmentation takes form in the dollars collected as penalties and the number of firms involved. Benefits to the environment are broadly and liberally elaborated. Whether these benefits are realistic is often unknown, and might even prove to be unknowable, using normal accounting methods, and frequently is the subject matter for futurists.

One must also recognize the impact on industry from various levels of government. While federal laws may provide the framework within which the environment and worker safety are governed, state, county and local city and town governments have

The scales of environmental jurisprudence weigh heavily against industry.

taken strong stands in these areas. In most cases, the local regulations are more restrictive than those of the government levels above them. The common sense approach to compliance with the law stresses meeting the standards of the most restrictive regulations, while performing those tasks that are required by all levels of government.

Tightening Standards

As real progress has been made by the printing industry and is measured in real terms, the industry has realized both technical and human benefits that are derived from the impetus provided by the various environmental regulations. Despite all the gains made to date, increased pressure has again been brought to bear to lower the acceptable limits that have driven the progress to date. These attempts to force lower and lower levels of pollutants in the air and in the water systems have frustrated the environmental professionals in the industry. Some of these stricter standards are frequently established by rule-makers within the governing agencies, rather than being mandated by the passage of new legislation. Proposed new laws must undergo scrutiny and be approved by and be agreed to by elected officials. Industry associations are constantly on guard to build a dam or patch a hole to prevent well meaning, but not completely informed, groups from destroying the foundations upon which solutions to environmental protection have already been built.

When the Clean Air Act was first passed in the early 1970s, the pressure was on firms emitting 100 tons or more of volatile organic compounds (VOCs) per year to provide the means to reduce or destroy these emissions. Control Technology Guidelines were written in concert and with the cooperation of the industry associations and major facilities. Methods of compliance included adoption of technical solutions to reduce or eliminate the amount of volatile organic compounds in ink and coating formulations. When the ability to make a chemical change could not be achieved, the government's solution was to call for placing add-on control technology to the stacks carrying the vapors out of the plant. Destruction levels were specified for each of the different printing process. The standards became known as RACT—Reasonably Available Control Technology.

Over the years, the required levels of destruction of VOCs were raised by instituting other measurements that exceeded the standards in RACT. In a particular case with air emissions, the imposition of a concept known as Permanent Total Enclosure tightened the standards considerably. While the concept of viewing a pressroom as a total entity was of significant help to a printer with a combination of new and old machines, it raised the RACT from its reasonable level to one slightly below perfection (95%).

Attempts by the USEPA and OSHA respectively to impose stricter outdoor air emission standards and indoor level of air pollutants for worker safety were set aside by the courts. These judicial decisions were based on the failure of the regulatory agencies to test and document any real advantages in protecting the public and the workers by instituting new, more stringent standards. That their day was lost in court did not stop the regulators from implementing a movement of regulations to lower and lower emission levels. Printers must come to grips with the fact that the government will continue to press for solutions to environmental and health hazards. Inevitably, there will be more restrictive standards and more restraints on what a printer may or may not do.

The Quick Fix and Pressures to Comply

With the introduction of governmental regulations in the late 1970s, attention was turned to the process and how some of the pollutants could be controlled. Air, water and hazardous wastes drew attention, but, at the outset, only for major facilities. Smaller firms were either exempt at the time, or were not yet caught in the enforcement network of the regulatory agencies.

Unfortunately, the early emphasis of regulations was concentrated on end-of-the-pipe solutions. How do we treat and reduce the impact of wastes on the environment? To cope with air emissions, major printing firms invested in catalytic and thermal oxidizers (figure 1–3) or solvent recovery systems, where they were feasible, in line with a press. Facilities used solvent recovery stills for clean-up solvent and ink wastes to minimize hazardous wastes. Water treatment systems found homes where the volume of spent aqueous chemistry warranted the space and energy. At the time, little attention was paid to changing the basic printing processes. Printers could continue making the same product with the same materials and not risk losing a customer because of changes in the quality of product or the timeliness of deliveries. There was no need to pressure the suppliers for alternatives, at least not for most of the firms in the industry.

Figure 1-3. Catalytic oxidizers, such as this Wolverine system at MTP Industries in New York City, have been a major weapon in the rush to reduce emissions of volatile organic compounds and hazardous air pollutants.

Sustainability Through Pollution Prevention

With the passage of time, and the limited success of add-on controls to properly address multi-media chemical exposures, industry and government have embraced a new philosophy—Pollution Prevention. During the 1980s and early 1990s, some imaginative and farseeing firms worked to embrace alternatives to the petrochemical-based inks and solvents. Some did so because a few states promoted alternatives with a more holistic approach, rather than a quick fix with an incinerator. There were both successes and failures. Alternatives did not work in all circumstances, but they did work well enough to make further developments appear worthwhile.

Today, we are poised at the end of one era and the beginning of a new one. Pollution prevention efforts can help to make a difference. Small companies cannot afford the capital expense or operating costs of add-on controls. Press and material improvements can help to improve quality and productivity, and reduce chemical pollution. Incentives to plan ahead and pursue source reduction are available in some states in the form of financial support for economic development. Reduced liability and good citizenship are other less tangible forms of incentives. As new products are designed, as new presses are purchased, new inks tried, the environment will benefit.

Beware the Two-Headed Dragon

The typical outreach of government and its measure of success in enforcing environmental policy and law has been litigation, or threatened litigation, of industry and the monies collected as penalties. Small firms are generally good targets since the cost of penalties, frequently relatively high, will be less than the cost of hiring an attorney to defend against sometimes-frivolous alleged violations.

That old truism, "I'm from the government and I'm here to help you," never had a more negative tone to it than in the hands of the environmental enforcement agencies. The entire philosophy can be captured in a perversion of that old American ideal of justice; "Guilty, even though proven innocent."

In recent years, there has been an effort to find a better way. Efforts at reinventing the process have been a key factor in seeking amelioration of the atmosphere of distrust. Cooperation was seen as a way of illuminating the scene to both printers and the regulatory people sent to judge them. Representatives of the printing industry spent over four years working with the USEPA on one regulatory reinvention project—the Common Sense Initiative. Others dedicated many hours participating in the USEPA Design for the Environment programs to promote pollution prevention for three of the major printing processes. The major focus was a cooperative effort to educate both government and industry about the impact of chemicals on the community and the environment.

Foremost in both efforts was a desire to create an atmosphere of trust within which all parties could find common ground to improve the environment. Correspondingly, the methods by which government enforces the laws and by which industry understands its responsibilities could become more proactive than adversarial. In the end, this cooperative approach would reflect the need to include the local community in the regulatory process. The optimism of the reinvention programs lies in the potential to bring people together and create an atmosphere of trust among the stakeholders. Mutual respect and recognition of the needs of the other stakeholders would replace the all-too-common mistrust and disdain each held for the other.

Looking back on past efforts and then looking at present attitudes of enforcement agencies in some regions of the country, one has to wonder where all that goodwill has gone. We are faced with the two-headed dragon. On the one hand is a farsighted, well-meaning front office enforcement staff that is offering opportunities to seek better ways of doing things. On the other hand has been the more evident effort of local, regional and state enforcement agents holding the big stick and seeking extremely high penalties. Environmental success is perceived as the amount of penalties collected, even at the expense of businesses that would not be required to do anything in most venues.

In the one region in the Northeastern portion of the country, the name of the game has become "how much can we collect as fines!" Instead of showing the improvement in quality, which is due mainly to the efforts of industry, the agencies persist on using dollars collected as a measure of enforcement effectiveness.

Have we sunk to a level where the results are less important than the sums collected under circumstances that are hardly in keeping with the American tradition, innocent until proven guilty? With these agencies, it is frequently "guilty even if proven innocent."

With many of the requirements set forth in regulations, under conditions that are not elaborated in the specific documents, judgement plays a factor. Rational enforcement should always include the ability to have an inspector view the performance of a facility as a reality and in its entirety. The intent of the standards may be related to large facilities or processes that are not specifically targeted. Some judgment must be employed to apply appropriate standards to predetermined templates, or make allowances for those "round pegs" which do not fit into the "square holes."

People, mechanical and electrical systems do fail to perform adequately at times, regardless of the preventive care that is taken. Guidelines and practical approaches to these situations have to be defined and understood to be components of best management practices. A black-and-white policy of interpretation of the regulations and minor breaches can only lead to distortion of the law and its objectives, and in the ability of any facility to live up to the "letter of the law." Most certainly, black and white exists only when people are not adequately trained and have no ability to separate the obvious isolated item from the total performance and experience of the subject facility.

What better way to observe some of the inappropriate ways in which the laws are enforced than to review events that have taken place which illustrate some of the injustices of enforcement. Take note that while these cases are cited, they are not representative of enforcement in all venues. In some

Case Histories of Enforcement Actions

cases, better definition of the conditions and how they are to be handled may alleviate some of the abuses of power. In other cases a need for better definition of an industrial process and real world conditions may result in more understanding of the situation with more reasonable terms of compliance. The cases described are ones in which I served as the consultant to the printers.

Oxidizer Problems, Reasonable Policy for Repairs

As a quick fix, the USEPA has promoted the use of add-on controls to destroy pollutants in air emissions. Typical control systems are oxidizers: catalytic and thermal. As ink and solvent vapors are exhausted from drying or collection systems, the high temperatures of the oxidizer and chemical reaction caused by the catalyst convert the pollutants to carbon dioxide and nitrogen oxide. The technology is alien to that of the printing industry.

During the Spring of 1999, coinciding with a week long Jewish holiday, one company experienced a major problem with its oxidizer. The failure came at a time when the oxidizer was to commence operation, after a permitted period of shutdown. Within a day after the problem was detected, the company alerted the vendor of the problems with the system and requested assistance to repair the damages. One malfunctioning item was the temperature monitor and recorder (figure 1–4); the other malfunction was a breach in the wall of the oxidizer box. With the holiday approaching and a backlog of work in the field, the vendor agreed to send the service personnel immediately after the holiday. This did not take place, as the vendor was swamped with calls, until a week later than planned.

Figure 1-4. Temperatures of the catalytic oxidizer are monitored and recorded to assure compliance. This instrument requires the manual replacement of the circular record on a daily or weekly basis.

In the days following the holiday, in walked the inspectors from the USEPA regional office. The attitude was far from friendly, particularly after the plant management wrongly was reluctant to show them records that they requested. A search of the facility resulted in a number of violations, among which were such incidences as "one open can of ink in the inkroom," and open drums in a working solvent recovery room. The inspectors failed to take into account that the solvent recovery still was being used at the time of the visit, and that the operator had left the room to allow them to see the site. Under the regulations, a limited number of open containers are acceptable within the constraints of the process.

The printer made one drastic mistake; he did not realize that an inspector from the agency has carte blanche to enter and inspect a facility and request records. He was not aware that their authority has the effect of a search warrant. Unlike any other legal obligation, the environmental agency does not have to show cause to enter any building.

Take it for granted that the printer did have some legitimate violations; there are few places where one could claim that everything is done in perfect accord with the laws at all times. However, the actions that followed were indicative of the hard fist of the law, rather than the outreach to understand the position in which many small and medium size printers find themselves when trying to comply with the law. The ensuing search resulted in a list of violations, including one that claimed that the oxidizer was down and inoperative for a period that included the days of the holiday, a matter of about almost half of the 20 days cited.

EPA has established software formulas to compute penalties. This software was developed for use with large firms and violators. Although there are questionable areas when applied to smaller facilities, the agency uses the program as if it were a holy scripture. The penalty program has distinct tracks for different types of violations.

In this case, the agency sought penalties on two conflicting sets of data. They first claimed a penalty because the oxidizer was down; they then claimed another heavy penalty because the facility was not using compliant inks. Both are options under the regulations; it is not one or the other in the case of a malfunction of the oxidizer. If the compliant inks were available, the facility would have had no need to install and operate a costly add-on control. To the contrary, this plant had installed one of the first oxidizers in the region and had operated well beyond compliance levels for many years. The period in which the oxidizer was down was the end of the ozone period, when EPA rules that there is little threat from ozone due to diminished ozone generation by Nature. Additional emissions were less than 2.5 tons.

Meetings with the regional engineers and attorneys resulted in no accommodation. At the suggestion of the EPA attorney, the parties entered into mediation. At least two parties came to mediate—the printer and the attorney for the agency. The engineers did not; they would not agree to any compromise, even when advised by the judge, who was the mediator, that the printer and his attorney were right, and that a hearing before an administrative judge would most likely rule in favor of the printer. The engineers would not relent. The attorney could not get her superiors to override the engineers.

The cost of proceeding any further was unrealistic. The company had already spent over $20,000.00 to fight the charges. Going ahead would have meant additional fees amounting to $25,000.00 or more. It was less expensive to pay a total of $40,000.00, and let the incident become history.

The EPA region was not content to close the case. It made a point of using the example to promote the success it had with a "major polluter." Every media outlet was enlisted to paint a picture that was both unjust and questionable. One must take note that with elections that year, the case for the people was made a matter of record and accomplishment. Were it not for the legal fees, this case would have ended quite differently, much to the embarrassment of the environmental agency engineers.

Was justice served? Were our tax dollars used wisely? Was anything done to help the environment? And finally, did this incident help to precipitate a sensible procedure and time line to handle the breakdown of the add-on equipment? The answer to all questions is "No."

Moving to a New Site Within the System

Another case involved a group of small printers caught in the turmoil of the castigation of printers in one of the nations largest cities, and the expulsion of these firms from their lofts and facilities. There were three firms, two printers and one prep house, which agreed to merge and find a location that would enable them to consolidate their operations under one roof. A place was found in a neighboring county, with the three firms moving as quickly as they could to the new address.

As with their compatriots in the city, guided by the local Printing Industries of America affiliate, the major concern of the firms was a fight for their existence. It was live or die, with the need for a site that was sufficient for their operations and convenient to their customers, as well as affordable. Beyond this, everything else was a matter to be dealt with at a later date. Even in meetings with the helpful government agencies, environmental permitting was not addressed.

The principals recognized the need to comply with government regulations and arranged for the filing of permits. This took time and was not completed until the firms had all moved into the new plant. Both city and state permit preparation was delayed, as the need to locate and install exhausts was determined. But in time, the permit applications were all submitted. As a very small source of emissions, the state permit was to be a Registration Certificate, evidence of a very small source of air pollutants.

Then a sequence of events occurred which took a bizarre twist and brought the state agency down on the small printers. It took place within a few days of the delivery of the registration application to the regional office and the city agency. An invoice for regulatory fees was received for one of the closed facilities. As a good citizen, the owner of the firm contacted the state to advise them that the facility, which had been sent the invoice, was closed, and that he was in his new location. Within hours, an inspector was dispatched to the new facility and a notice of violation filed. The reason cited was failure to submit the applications prior to the move.

Despite all pleas to drop the violation in light of the precarious situation facing the city printers, the case was targeted for penalties. Why? The attorney for the state is still digging to find justification.

Everyone Knew but One Inspector

A third case developed when a printing business moved from one county to another within the same city. This firm sought a new location to react to the changing nature of the neighborhood in which it had operated. The owner recognized the changing characteristics of his site; industrial buildings were giving way to residential housing. He sought a new site, in an area that is and will remain industrial, even though it meant considerable travel for his own family and key people. The site selected was in an abandoned factory, a major concern for the economy of the neighboring county. With government assistance, the facility relocated to the new building. This move was done by the book, well in advance of the relocation and start-up of equipment and in concert with the state economic development and environmental agencies.

No one at the regional office told the inspector at the old site. One day, as the printer was in the midst of moving some of the minor equipment from the old plant to the new one, an inspector walked into the plant. A vinyl strip doorway had been opened to enable the movement of equipment from the pressroom to the new site. She interpreted this as a violation of the permit, because the vinyl strips were in place during the stack test in which the performance of the oxidizer was verified and measured. When advised of the move, she expressed a lack of knowledge of such plans or the registration certificate that had already been issued. No matter that the firm followed the rules and lived up to its commitment to the state, violations were filed and justifications commenced.

The open vinyl strips are essentially a door between the pressroom and other rooms of the facility (figure 1–5). The strips are made to be opened and closed as people, machinery and materials move into and out of the pressroom. Within the definition of the permanent closure for the pressroom, natural draft openings of up to five percent of the room area are allowable. Without the strips, the open door represents slightly more than two percent. By every definition and criterion of common sense, this is not an event that would detract from the destruction efficiency of the add-on control.

To make a case, the vinyl door opening was defined by the inspector as a major modification of the permit. Efforts have been made to denigrate the destruction of the emissions by the oxidizer. Straws were pulled to build a case under the premise that success comes only when a firm is penalized. A penalty of $55,000 to $60,000.00 was proposed to settle the case.

Once again the printer was faced with the alternative; does the printer pay the piper or defend the case in court? At what cost can a small business buck the system?

Figure 1-5. Vinyl strips cover an opening (door) through which fork lift trucks, materials and people can move into and out of the pressroom.

Every dollar in penalties exacts a burden on business. Penalties are normally levied in a manner that does not allow the business to deduct them from tax computations. The result diminishes the profits earned by the firm. The cost of confronting and resolving a notice of violation and the ensuing penalty is high. Legal counsel and technical regulatory advisors or consultants are expensive. The demands for correspondence, research and meetings can be excessive. Resources can be stretched beyond the dollars demanded in retribution by the agencies. And in the end, the money needed to be in compliance will still have to be spent.

Penalties Plunder Profits

An old industrial engineering adage claimed that for every dollar of waste, a business would have to sell at least $40 to $50 of products to make up for the loss. Consider this analogy when a fine is directed at a facility. A penalty of $10,000.00 will require sales of $500,000 to replace the earnings. A fine in the realm of $100,000.00 will require $5,000,000 in compensatory sales. Does your firm make sales that easily?

Penalties add up. To compensate for every dollar paid as a penalty, there must be an increase in sales of $40–50.

Where Do We Go From Here?

In passing legislation on a federal level, the cost and ramifications must meet a test that measures the burdens on small business. That this be done effectively must be a concern of all small businesses, of which a large majority of printers constitute the bulk of the establishments.

The printing industry, through its associations and local business organizations, must pursue lobbying initiatives to make elected officials aware of the distortions that are twisting the good intentions of the environmental laws into cash cows for the regulatory agencies. This perception has to be changed to reflect a more positive, cooperative attitude, with increased requirements for training and supervision of agency personnel. Sensitivity training and dispute resolution awareness is essential. Inclusion of all stakeholders in the establishment of these guidelines is critical to bridging differences.

On the other hand, it is incumbent on printers to know what is required of them and make sure that the rules, especially the reasonable rules, are followed. That is where outreach efforts can help. Printers should attend seminars and workshops to learn what is expected of them, learn about which developments in technology can help to defuse the issues by reducing pollution, and make the effort to train and retrain personnel to live in this new, embattled environment. Without exception, if printers cannot live by the rules, they must communicate what and when the standards are beyond their control. Where dialogue can eliminate a point of stress or conflict, the possibility of compromise and resolution can be more reasonably achieved.

In the perfect world, the environmental agencies will be there to mentor and guide the printer through his troubles, realizing the benefits of his efforts through results—cleaning the workplace and the environment.

CHAPTER **2**

The Role of Government as Protector of the Environment

We live in a nation ruled by laws. When it is in the public interest to encompass a given set of circumstances or conditions, the elected officials of the nation can see fit to place under restraints the subject in question. The bureaucracy then adds the policies, rules, standards and procedures by which the intent of the law is to be satisfied. The substance of the work by the lawmakers and regulators is subject, throughout the process, to public comment, scrutiny and legal action.

Following a period of growth and prosperity based on the introduction of ever new chemicals into the industrial and consumer processes of our society, concern was raised about the impact of the wastes (disposal) of these chemicals, as well as the use of certain specific chemicals, on the ecological fiber of our planet and the health of our communities. The boon to progress raised the specter of a threat to the continuation of life, as we know it on Earth.

Some organizations existed within the government that were dedicated to issues that had some bearing on health and safety issues, but none that specifically addressed the environment—the air we breath, the water we drink, or the ground in which we grow our food. The response from the federal government was the founding of the U.S. Environmental Protection Agency in 1970. This agency was charged with developing rules and regulations for protecting the natural resources from the excesses and carelessness of the public and industry. The organizational structure of the EPA is illustrated in figure 2–1. It is within this structure

15

that industry must now coexist and perform in a manner that is protective of the environment and the health of the community and of the nation. This concept is now accepted as applicable, to greater or lesser degree, to all countries of the world.

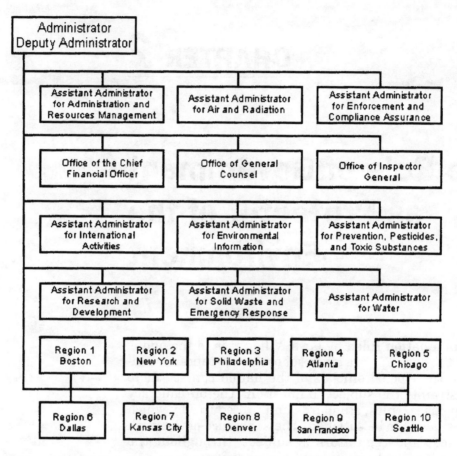

Figure 2–1. EPA organizational structure.
Source: http:/www.epa.gov/epahome/organization.htm

The Laws that Bind Us

The development of laws that set the boundaries for the activities of the USEPA is the domain of the Congress. The Senate and the House of Representatives each have a committee that oversees the environment and the workings of the EPA. Similar relationships exist in the 50 states and in many of local political entities that constitute the regions, counties, townships and cities. (See figure 2–2.)

When a law is under consideration, lawmakers meet with their constituents, listen to lobbyists for every interest group, and discuss the merits and disadvantages of the details that will become part of the law. There is ample opportunity for every interest group to have its day and help to mold the intent and details of the law. In the end, the legislators adopt what they consider to be a law whose details enforce the objective for which the law is being considered. Not everything that people want is adopted; compromises are usually necessary to obtain a winning

1. Creating a Law

Step 1: A member of Congress proposes a **bill**. A bill is a document that, if approved, will become law.

Step 2: If both houses of Congress approve a bill, it goes to the President who has the option to either approve it or veto it. If approved, the new law is called an **act**, and the text of the act is known as a public statute. Some of the better-known laws related to the environment are the Clean Air Act, the Clean Water Act, and the Safe Drinking Water Act.

Step 3: Once an act is passed, the House of Representatives standardizes the text of the law and publishes it in the United States Code. The U.S. Code is the official record of all federal laws.

2. Putting the Law to Work

So now that the law is official, how is it put into practice? Laws often do not include all the details. The U.S. Code would not tell you, for example, what the speed limit is in front of your house. In order to make the laws work on a day-to-day level, Congress authorizes certain government agencies— including EPA— to create **regulations**.

Regulations set specific rules about what is legal and what isn't. For example, a regulation issued by EPA to implement the Clean Air Act might state what levels of a pollutant—such as sulfur dioxide—are safe. It would tell industries how much sulfur dioxide they can legally emit into the air, and what the penalty will be if they emit too much. Once the regulation is in effect, EPA then works to **help Americans comply** with the law and to **enforce** it.

3. Creating a Regulation

First, an authorized agency—such as EPA—decides that a regulation may be needed. The agency researches it and, if necessary, proposes a regulation. The proposal is listed in the Federal Register so that members of the public can consider it and send their comments to the agency. The agency considers all the comments, revises the regulation accordingly, and issues a final rule. At each stage in the process, the agency publishes a notice in the Federal Register. These notices include the original proposal, requests for public comment, notices about meetings where the proposal will be discussed (open to the public), and the text of the final regulation. (The Federal Register also includes other types of notices, too.)

Twice a year, each agency publishes a comprehensive report that describes all the regulations it is working on or has recently finished. These are published in the Federal Register, usually in April and October, as the **Unified Agenda of Federal and Regulatory and Deregulatory Actions**.

Once a regulation is completed and has been printed in the Federal Register as a final rule, it is "codified" by being published in the Code of Federal Regulations (CFR). The CFR is the official record of all regulations created by the federal government. It is divided into 50 volumes, called **titles**, each of which focuses on a particular area. Almost all environmental regulations appear in Title 40. The CFR is revised yearly, with one fourth of the volumes updated every three months. Title 40 is revised every July 1.

Figure 2–2. From concept to enforcement, writing laws and regulations.

Source: http://www.epa.gov/epahome/lawintro.htm

margin. But once passed and signed by the President, the law is the law. It may seem unfair to some, but it is the document upon which the EPA will then base its rulings, processes and procedural requirements.

That is not to say that an unfair or bad bill has to become law. The President can veto the bill as presented to him. The courts may rule against the constitutionality of a law or any of its components, as well as the scope that the law allows the government to exercise control over what may appear to be offenses.

Rulemaking: The Process that Follows

Once a law has been enacted, the agency must then implement its intent. The law sets the policy for the agency. Regulations and rules provide the details of this policy and the procedures and guidance documents by which the policies will be implemented.

The EPA has a basic set of priorities within which it exercises this authority. The process may include participation by outside consultants, industry and environmental-interest organizations. Public hearings must be held at various stages to provide insight by interested parties into the proposed rules. Of concern is the objective of the rules as they meet the needs of the public to:

• Protect human health,

• Preserve and enhance the environment,

• Meet environmental goals without being unnecessarily burdensome.

Congress has stipulated a number of requirements that agencies must meet when they issue regulations. These requirements are designed to support the creation of effective regulations and protect the rights of people affected by the rules. Among the requirements that govern the procedural aspects are the Administrative Procedures Act, the Regulatory Flexibility Act as amended by the Small Business Regulatory Enforcement Fairness Act, the Unfunded Mandates Reform Act, the Paperwork Reduction Act, the National Technology Transfer and Advancement Act and the Congressional Review Act.*

The President can issue executive orders to supplement the laws passed. Orders of particular significance are Executive Order 12866 (Regulatory Planning and Review), 13045 (Children's Health Protection), 13084 (Consultation and Coordination with Indian Tribal Governments), and 13132 (Federalism).**

The public is encouraged to take part in the legislative and review process. Information on regulations, preliminary drafts of regulations, supporting testimony and research are readily available through such sources as the Library of Congress, the

---

*Information on pertinent statutes may be found at http://www.cornell.edu.uscode/.
**Details on executive orders are available at http:/library.whitehouse.gov/.

For every law there is considerable supporting documentation containing guidance and clarifications, as well as expansion of the scope of the original law.

U.S. Chamber of Commerce, and industry associations such Printing Industries of America. Drafts of proposed rules are published in the Federal Register with deadlines specified for submission of comments by the public. Comments submitted by industry, environmental organizations, unions, lobbyists and the public in general are considered, frequently summarized and published, and become a part of the process that molds the law. These comments can be addressed at an open hearing or introduced by mail or Internet. The comments are reviewed and consideration is given where the arguments are deemed plausible and will enhance the intent of the ruling. The final rule is issued with the consideration of the changes initiated by this public participation.

Delegation of Enforcement to Lower Authorities

Most laws and regulations are administered by federal agencies but are delegated to the states for enforcement. The states promulgate regulations, which parallel those of the federal government. In many cases the states may chose to set more rigid standards. In turn, some localities will either place even more stringent restraints or have a duplicate process in place for the same exposures. Enforcement takes place on all levels. At times, various agencies will work in conjunction with each other. At other times, what is acceptable to one jurisdiction may be unacceptable to another. The common sense of this situation is that the facility should identify all applicable regulations and comply with a comprehensive plan that will address all issues and satisfy the most severe requirements.

The Clean Air Act provides an excellent example of the layering of the laws. Using New York as an example, the New York State Department of Environmental Conservation (NYSDEC) submits its State Implementation Plan to the USEPA for approval, followed by each of the parts of its regulations which parallel, and in some cases are more stringent than, the federal technical guidelines.

For the Metropolitan New York Regions, the NYSDEC has established a zero threshold for every facility that uses any ozone precursors of VOCs, regardless of quantity. The DEC enforces the federal standards plus the additional tighter standards established by the state.

In addition, New York City has a Department of Environmental Protection that requires a permit for all sources of air emissions, including an application for a permit to erect, and then an inspection to obtain a certificate to operate. Westchester County also requires a separate permit to operate. Both local governments enforce their own regulations.

Enforcement in this region of the country takes place at all levels. Even though the federal threshold for permits is 25 tons for major facilities, enforcement actions will follow the stricter standards set up by the NYSDEC. The zero threshold becomes the rule, despite the fact that in most states this level of emissions is not regulated.

The Clean Water Act is an example of an opposite scenario. While federal standards have been established, local authorities set the rules, process permits, and handle enforcement actions. Federal involvement occurs in only those instances when violations are drastic or involve regional complications.

Permits: A Right or a Privilege?

The process by which the industrial community acquiesces to the law is that of obtaining a permit or a certificate to operate. This document is evidence that the facility has provided the government agency with adequate information to describe the activities or the business and the impact that it will have on the environment and the surrounding community, and that such activity is consistent with the safeguards intended by the law. The requirements can vary from jurisdiction to jurisdiction, within the letter of the law, and may vary based on the size and impact of the facility on its surroundings.

Being granted a permit is not a right accorded to the business. Rather, it is an agreement between the facility and the community to provide assurances that the business will operate in a manner that will protect the best interests of community and ecology. The type and complexity of the permit will depend on the geographic location and the size of the facility, measured by its air emissions, water waste discharges or hazardous waste disposal. Each law specifies the types of permits required and the information necessary to review and assign the appropriate status in the permits.

The permit will describe the exposure that is acceptable, and will provide for controls in the form of inspections, records and reports that must be maintained. Exceeding the permit limitations, or the special conditions under which the facility must operate, would be considered a violation of the permit. (See figure 2–3.)

Permit Review

In many areas the filing of an application for a permit is the domain of the architect or the professional engineer. The certification is considered a means of assuring the public that a competent individual with an appropriate health and safety background is reviewing the plans. The professional not only prepares the application but subjects the facility and chemistry to a review that is intended to protect the health of the community.

New York State Department of Environmental Conservation

Registration ID: Facility DEC ID:

AIR FACILITY REGISTRATION CERTIFICATE
in accordance with 6NYCRR Part 201-4

Registration Issued to: PRINTING COMPANY INC
STREET
LONG ISLAND CITY, NY 11101

Contact: COMPANY INC
STREET
LONG ISLAND CITY, NY 11101

Facility: PRINTING COMPANY INC
STREET
LONG ISLAND CITY, NY 11101

Description:
Printing is a commercial printer, utilizing lithographic printing presses. The company operates five presses utilizing alcohol free fountain solution.

Total Number of Emission Points: 1   **Cap By Rule:** Yes

Authorized Activity By Standard Industrial Classification Code:
2752 - COMMERCIAL PRINTING LITHOGRAPH

Registration Effective Date: 07/23/2001   **Registration Expiration Date:** (Not Applicable)

This registrant is required to operate this facility in accordance with all air pollution control applicable Federal and State laws and regulations. Failure to comply with these laws and regulations is a violation of the Environmental Conservation Law (ECL) and the registrant is subject to fines and/or penalties as provided by the ECL.

REGION 2 AIR POLLUTION CONTROL ENGINEER
1 HUNTER'S POINT PLAZA
4740 21ST STREET
LONG ISLAND CITY, NY 11101-5407

Figure 2-3. The most basic form of a permit is a registration. The certificate to operate for a small facility in New York State under the registration process is illustrated. Maximum emissions under the registration are 12.5 tons. Chemistry must be in compliance with RACT.
Source: P-F Technical Services Inc.

Reviewing the permit application is a critical function of the enforcement agency.

The application submitted for the permit will undergo a two-part inspection by the agency engineers. The first process checks the application for completeness. The inspectors will check the permit application for completeness; is every space occupied and are attachments enclosed? Is everything attached in accordance with the regulations?

The next phase will be a technical review of the application and assignment of applicable regulatory requirements. The supporting data will be evaluated to determine the apparent accuracy of the status of the facility based on its pollutants and quantities reported. The requirements will vary based on the nature of the permit and the controls required by the specific applicable law.

A normal review will also include a visit to the facility by an agency inspector to see the operation and to determine the accuracy of the contents of the application. Samples of ink, solvent and fountain solution may be taken to verify the technical compliance of the chemicals used or wastes leaving the facility. A note of caution is offered with regard to the sampling done by the agency. When the samples are drawn from the reservoir, it is wise to have a second sample taken at the same time and submitted by the printer for analysis by a private laboratory. The split sample and independent test will be of considerable help in the event there is a disagreement with the results of the government testing service.

Once the content of the application is confirmed, there will be discussions among the agency, the consulting engineers and the printer to include "conditions" in the permit. Pertinent conditions will address the applicability of specific restraints on the facility and its operations, limitations in the quantities of emissions, as well as to delineate what records, tests, and reports will be a component of the compliance procedures. Some conditions will be dictated by the various requirements of the law that apply to the use of identified chemicals, such as those to which special standards apply, and to the controls and records necessitated by the use of these chemicals.

When add-on controls are installed to meet compliance standards, the conditions will describe the required testing of the system and records that will be maintained. Air control systems will require stack tests, maintenance logs and usage records; wastewater treatment systems will require "before" and "after" lab analysis, etc.

The permit, as finally issued, will contain a description of the facility, the sources of emissions or discharges, the various parts of the law that apply, and the measures the facility must take to assure that it is operating within the parameters established by the authorizing agency. Since each state is designated to write its own permits, the format of the permits varies from state to state. Some can be one-page applications with the barest of details, while other localities appear to want to parallel, and sometimes outdo, the USEPA in collecting data for their files. State permits for larger, but less than major sources, can vary considerably, from letter authorizations to full-fledged permits comparable in format to a major source Title V permit.

For the federal Title V permit applicants, some measure of consistency is reflected in the content rather than the form. The Clean Air Act of 1990 set the ground rules for Title V facilities and the rulemaking that followed deals with issues on a national level. While there is latitude in the writing of the permits, specific standards have been established to delineate thresholds, control requirements, maintenance and operating recordkeeping and reports, among other issues.

Sample copies of air permit applications and permits are illustrated in Appendix XXI.

Enforcing the Law, Inspection

That knock on your door may be a representative of one of the enforcement agencies, seeking to assure that you are in compliance with both the paperwork and the technical standards. It could be a phone call or a letter requesting information. Any contact triggers the commencement of what is generally called an enforcement action. *The USEPA is bound by definition. Enforcement commences at first contact!*

Denying entry is not an option! The authority backing the inspector is tantamount to a subpoena to search the premises. Nor can one not respond to a call or ignore a mailed first class letter requesting information. The inspector is there to see the premises, the equipment in operation and all records that are required to confirm the operating conditions and emissions or discharges of the process. *Woe unto anyone who denies access, for litigation will surely follow!* See figure 2–4 for the Eight Commandments when undergoing an inspection.

A mandatory phase of the inspection will be the taking of a sample of the liquid ink, the solvent cleaner or the fountain solution to test for VOCs. The printer can put some control in place by requesting that the sample be split. Each party can then test the samples independently, assuring the printer of a control to assure that the results of the government tests are acceptable. Method 24 is the protocol for testing inks and coatings. Unfortunately, this method is not as accurate with waterborne formulations as it is with solvents. Scrutiny of the results of testing of aqueous solutions is necessary to assure that the tests reflect the composition of the actual formulation.

The condition of the pressroom and chemical storage is frequently surveyed, with specific items sought to assure compliance with regulations. Attention will be given to containers of ink and solvent relative to covers, dirty wipers in safety cans that are covered, grounding of drums of flammable liquids, smoking, etc. Unsafe conditions can lead to higher risk in the workplace and can presumably lead to pollution of the area outside the facility. Both workers and the community can be placed at risk by unsafe practices.

A clean, orderly shop is a positive factor when an inspector visits. There is nothing more reassuring than seeing things in place, all safety equipment engaged or in place, and having documents pulled

1. Never bar entry to the inspector.

2. Ask to see the inspector's credentials.

3. Be polite and respect the position of the inspector.

4. Answer all questions with a direct answer.

5. If all that is needed is a Yes or a No, do not elaborate or volunteer information.

6. Show the inspector any records he requests.

7. Do not destroy or misplace records.

8. Maintain all permits, records and reports in an organized fashion, readily available upon request.

Figure 2–4. Eight commandments for an inspection.

Source: P-F Technical Services Inc.

without hesitation from designated files as questions are asked. Permits should be posted. Reports and Material Safety Data Sheets should be on file and waiting to be reviewed on request.

The permit or permits will list specific records and reports that are required. Monthly purchases of chemicals, the VOC emissions computations and maintenance logs are major areas of concern. Other regulations will require the filing of hazardous waste manifests, water usage and treatment records, and pertinent lab tests results. The various permits that a facility must have should be readily available. These are all records that may be part of the inspection, though not specific to the particular permit.

Inspection by Requests for Information

Another means of determining how well a facility is conforming to the law is through requests for information from an agency. While seemingly innocent in its format, the request is tantamount to a warrant for all records that could lead to information that would be necessary to indict the operation.

A typical request for information will ask for submission of a summary of purchases or usage of chemicals for a year or more, Material Safety Data Sheets, equipment specifications and performance data, VOC or pollutant content, maintenance logs, records of operating conditions, etc. The responsible party at the facility must certify that the information submitted is complete and accurate. Refusal to respond or provide accurate information would constitute a failure to comply and initiate an enforcement action. Consequently, answer the questions asked directly, without elaboration or enhancement with extraneous information. Do not open the door to unasked for situations.

Notice of Violation and Confrontation

The inspector has been through the plant and taken his sample, or a request for information has been submitted. Now what?

In most cases, a review will be conducted, at which time management will be advised of deficiencies in the plant and in the paperwork. For some agencies, this is a cooperative approach, which is intended to facilitate the correction of any unsafe or unpermitted operations without penalizing the company. A prompt response with the description of the actions taken is frequently adequate to put the matter to rest. In cases where the infraction is minor, even a phone call might suffice.

The cooperative road is not the road most often taken by enforcing agencies. More frequently, firms are placed in a process that has but one objective—penalties. Let's see what happens in this scheme. A letter is mailed to announce a "Notice of Violation." This may be a simple letter indicating the offense and requesting a meeting or correspondence to review the action to be taken. Test results or a copy of the inspection report will most likely accompany this letter. The writer may refer the violator to the legal affairs officer for resolution.

A more formal "Complaint" may be issued, or may follow the Notice of Violation, which will cite all the legal requirements and infringements observed, or assumed, by the inspector. This notice will include a date for a hearing before an administrative judge. In most cases, the agency attorneys do not want a protracted case presented in a court before a sitting judge. Therefore, the Notice of Violation will typically include a recommendation that the agency would welcome a request for an informal conference prior to the hearing. The conference would be held in the hope that the issue can be settled without recourse to the courts. Settling includes, of course, an agreement to pay a penalty.

The facility has a right to object and deny allegations by the inspectors and the agency's attorneys. The meeting and/or conferences are the places to take the firm's version to the table and request that the agency justify the validity of any claim. Inspectors do not always make the correct assumptions when they observe a process with which they are not familiar; tests are not always accurate, and knowledge of the fine points of regulations are frequently as unknown to the inspector as to the printer. An accused facility should take every advantage to make its case and seek a resolution that is fair and equitable.

If the case is litigated, an attorney will be required who is knowledgeable in the law and the industry. Environmental attorneys exist whose main job is to try to reach an accord with minimum friction. Make no mistake, when a case enters full-scale litigation, the war commences. It is no longer a matter of right and wrong, but one of precedent. The government does not like to lose and can be vindictive to those who question its authority.

The Consent Order

The conclusion of any legal action taken by the agencies against a violator is the drafting of a consent order. This legal document summarizes the alleged claims against the facility, the basis of each claim under the laws and rules, and spells out in detail the exact items with which the government takes offense. The consent order describes the agreement to settle the claim and the schedules for taking corrective or remedial action. This document will be the basis for measuring compliance with the settlement of the claims. It will also specify any actions that must be taken and any penalties that will be levied. Failure to achieve the objectives by the interim dates set forth in the consent order is tantamount to failure to meet the final compliance deadline. The ultimate penalty can be levied at any point in the process as well as at the end. It is wise to have a clause in the consent order that protects the rights of the printer if any delay is caused by conditions not under or beyond his control.

Determining the Amount of Penalties

Penalties are computed by formula. USEPA has guidance documents and software programs to develop a penalty based on a given set of criteria. Specific regulations, such as those concerning air and water, may have penalty policies that are very specific to defined conditions or known variations from rules and

Penalties add up.

standards. State agencies may use the same formulas in determining the penalties they impose.

Violations are viewed from two perspectives: Gravity and Economic Benefit. The measure of damage or risk to the ecology and community are the scope of Gravity calculations. How much air pollutants were emitted during a given period? What was discharged into the river without control? Was hazardous waste buried in a backyard neighboring on a school? This perception of the damage done by non-compliance is reasonable, related as it is to the known health and other risks of certain chemicals and wastes, and the impact they may have within a given distance from the release.

Economic benefit is another matter. This is the cost that would normally have been avoided by not taking the appropriate action to eliminate or reduce risk. This could be the cost of an add-on control, or the cost of properly maintaining equipment or training personnel. The penalty levied reflects the savings in expenditures by the offender when compared to his competitors. The penalty seeks to remove the profits made by the violator which have presumably had been used by his competitors to comply with the law.

The formula is set forth in a way that the accused may be able to identify and negotiate on the point-by-point premise upon which the penalty has been based. This can serve as a means of specifically addressing the components of the alleged violations, and thereby endeavor to reduce the total amount of the penalty.

There are Only Losers

There are no winners when confronting the environmental or safety and health agencies. There are only losers.

Money spent on confronting the agencies, in and out of court, can be considerable. This money could be better spent on productive needs. Consider the selling effort that would be required to replace the profits eliminated by any financial penalty. A rule of thumb used by industrial engineers to justify improvements to reduce waste was that for every dollar of waste generated $40.00 to $50.00 of sales is needed to offset the cost. Just think how much sales a penalty will take to make up for violations in the plant. At $50 of sales per dollar of penalty, a $40,000.00 violation would require $2,000,000 in sales. How easily does the average plant develop that amount in sales?

Reputations tarnished in the courts and media are damaging to a business. Customers are exhibiting more and more concern about the environmental practices of their suppliers. Publicity about violations can do no good to the image that a company wants to project to its marketplace.

The role of government in the environment is that of the hammer. Never forget that. Even when sitting around a table to discuss how government, the public and industry can work together, the final authority rests with the agency and the law.

Keep in mind: *the law may not be fair, but IT IS THE LAW!*

CHAPTER 3

Public Participation

Every printing plant is surrounded by a community. This community may consist of the people who live in the area, people who work in the area or people who find themselves affected by the activities of the printing facility. The community will have its residences, businesses and natural resources.

With potential hazards from the industrial processes and the requisite chemistry, this community has concerns about the well-being of its inhabitants and the natural resources that provide the air they breathe, the food they eat, and the water they drink. They are interested in many aspects involving immediate concerns regarding wastes generated, as well as the long-term ramifications of exposure to these chemical wastes.

As members of the community, printers have their own interest in working in a clean environment. The typical printer employs the owners, family members, whether they be brothers, sisters, sons, daughters or parents. With most print shops employing less than 10 people, there is a great personal concern that hazardous risks be reduced and eliminated.

Cooperating with the community to achieve this goal is one of the current trends in environmental management. For the printer, this can be a familiar scenario. Many local print shops do the printing for local businesses, schools, churches, synagogues, social and fraternal groups. Their personnel participate in community activities, and attend meetings of local groups such as Kiwanis, chambers of commerce, Masons, parent-teacher associations, Little League, youth soccer leagues, etc.

How does this scenario change with environmental regulations? In many cases not one bit; in others the change can be drastic. Regulatory requirements spell out specific procedures and mechanisms for public participation. The friendly handshake and social agreement is replaced by policies and standards, with public notification and public hearings required under defined conditions and circumstances. The cooperative efforts of informal relationships have been replaced by rigid rules, regulations and enforcement activities.

Community groups have joined statewide and national advocacy groups in petitioning and filing complaints about the activities of businesses. Many groups even try to enter the management process and influence the plans and operation of a facility. In many cases, emotion rather than objective science has become the ruling characteristic, overriding efforts by industry to respond to the concerns of the local citizens.

Government has responded to this public pressure through legislation, and has obligated business to react by making changes in the manner in which regulations are enforced. In many cases, legal action is invoked where earlier a friendlier interaction between the agency and a business would have been sufficient to address the problems. Cooperative steps, taken to eliminate or reduce problems, have been replaced by legal actions and penalties. The situation has been changed so that the agencies proclaim effectiveness by demonstrating the amount of penalties collected, rather than by showing improvement in quality through the reduction of pollutants and elimination of unsafe conditions.

Environmental Advocacy Groups

During the early days of the environmental movement, individuals stood at the forefront. Determined and insatiable, these people collected data, observed effects, and brought the attention of everyone to the damages and pollution originating from the handling and disposition of chemicals in our society.

Rachel Carson was a strong proponent of environmental measures needed to reclaim that precious commodity—water, one of the pillars of human life on this planet. Her book, *Silent Spring*, keynoted the founding of the environment advocacy movement and the genesis of many environmental organizations. Others followed in her footsteps, buttressing the need to do something to save our natural resources and life chains which rely on these resources for food and sustenance. Figure 3–1 extracts bits of descriptive material on the development and motivation of the advocacy groups from the early 1900s to the end of the century, from the comments by Michael Silverstein in his book, *The Environmental Economic Revolution*.

The pioneers of the 1960s led to the development of organizations such as Greenpeace, Environmental Defense Fund, the National Environmental Defense Fund. Targets of the new advocates were broad and sweeping. Public interest groups, such as the New York Public Interest Research Group and similar organizations in other states, joined the fray. These volunteer groups all endeavor to collect data concerning damages to the environment

The first-wave twentieth century environmental economic revisionism affected only a relatively few industries, such as forest products and mining, and, to a lesser extent agriculture, stock raising and fishing. Though initially opposed by leaders within the industries, it was gradually accepted by these same people. They came to recognize its limited geographic and economic scope, its long term benefits for their business investments and its personal advantages to their lives as sportsmen and property owners.

Into a nineteenth-century fabric of environmental economics . . . was thus added turn-of-the-century conservationism and preservationism.

This century's second major revision of environmental thinking . . . began to take hold in the 1960s. It involved a process of democratization, both in terms of how it defined "the environment" and in the number and types of people attracted by the changed perspective.

The important visionary here was a marine biologist named Rachel Carson. Her 1962 best-selling book, *Silent Spring* . . . described how the entire world environment . . . was at risk because of pollution . . . To many, quality of life suddenly mattered as much as quantity of production. Our continued physical health . . . became popularly linked to the endangered health of the larger ecologies in which we dwell.

This was an era of unprecedented prosperity and optimism in the United States. The children of a widely diffused affluence were bored with "success" and "corporate conformity" and the accumulation of "things generally." The chance to join a movement that not only promised to save the world (literally), but that permitted rejection of the acquisition ethic . . . of their parents, had enormous appeal to the young people of the Sixties' generation.

The environmentalism that blossomed in the late 1960s and early 1970s, then, featured elements that combined young people's rejection of their parents' money-making values with an idealistic quest for rustic simplicity . . .

Organized environmentalism's major nod to a new environmental economics in the late 1980s and early 1990s was a push for greater "corporate social responsibility." This nebulous smorgasbord of good intentions called for big companies to treat workers well and provide day care and, yes, pollute less . . .

Language, as well as history, has long muddled the environmental . . . debate . . .

Figure 3–1. Transition of environmental advocacy organizations.
Source: Michael Silverstein, *The Environmental Economic Revolution*, St. Martins Press, New York, 1993, pp 11–18.

or to very specific forms of animal and plant life and proselytize the public. The main tools of this effort have been and are intimidation and legal suits. The object was, and remains, to collect the large sums needed to keep these sizeable organizations active in the pursuit of both government and industry. Philanthropic ecological projects are the main agenda, but a more immediate concern has become financial, to support survival.

With this in mind, many groups have maintained a steady barrage on the public, industry and government, forcing issues that may or may not have a positive impact on the environment, but that fit with their agendas. Emotion frequently replaces science and facts in the quest to influence the public.

This is not to diminish the work being done by such responsible environmental groups as the Nature Conservancy, the Sierra Club and other groups dedicated to proactive programs to preserve land, human health, animals and resources that would otherwise be destroyed by poor public or business plans and decisions. The very nature of the activities of these broader based groups tends to bring the various partners in the community together to resolve issues. Dispute resolution takes the place of adversarial confrontation.

To maintain its credibility, there is a need for industry to be on the alert in terms of compliance with the law and the requirements for recordkeeping and reporting. Public information rights to the information required by the law can provide much information to an adversary. Taken out of context, this information can appear to create an extreme danger to the public. In many cases, the drive is intended to go beyond the scope of the law, to limits that have not yet been proven to the satisfaction of the lawmakers. Such advocacy groups are ready to bring legal actions when it fits their purposes, without regard to the impact of such litigation on the operation and economic viability of a business and the welfare of employees as well as other aspects of the local community.

Environmental Justice Organizations

A recent development has been the growth and recognition of local organizations representing the neighborhoods in which people of color reside. Combining the provisions of the civil rights laws and environmental legislation, environmental organizations pursue what they perceive to be violations of the rights of minorities caused by exposure to hazardous chemicals. This movement is based on the premise that industry deliberately places facilities in areas that are populated by African-American, Hispanic and other minority residents.

The fear and major emphasis of the environmental justice groups is the cumulative negative health effects of hazardous chemicals on members of the local community. (See figure 3–2.) They make the connection with other factors that are vital to the life of a community, seeking a balance that protects not only their health but the economic and social wellbeing of the members of the community. While conventional environmental advocacy associations, as mainstream lobbyists, pursue an agenda of saving wildlife and other natural resources, environmental justice groups

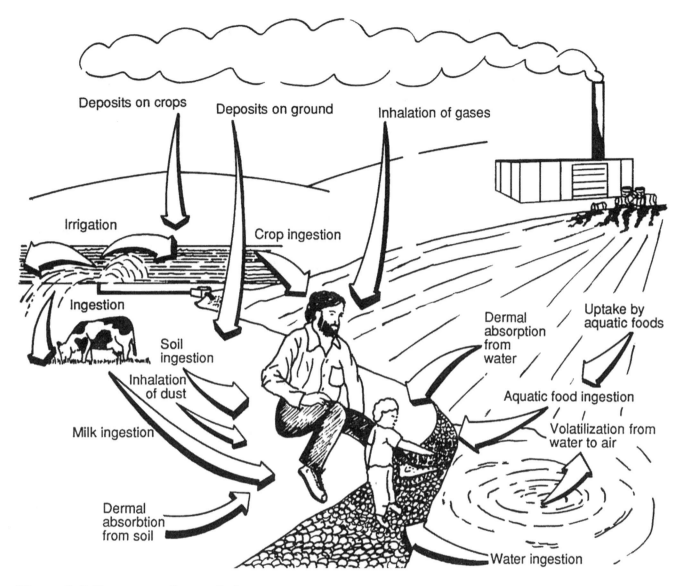

Figure 3–2. Exposure pathways for humans.

Source: United States Environmental Protection Agency, *Risk Communication About Chemicals In Your Community*, EPA 230/09-89-066, p 20.

direct their efforts to the elimination of pollutants in their communities and the education of their constituents to the dangers related to chemicals.

The strong position taken by the federal government in support of the environmental justice movement is in the form a Presidential Order to the effect that grievances by environmental justice can be litigated under Title VI of the Civil Rights Act of 1964. Executive Order No. 12898 directs the Attorney General to include discriminatory effects resulting from the issuance of pollution control permits by state and local governmental agencies that receive USEPA funding. As stated in the draft document of the *Environmental Justice Community Handbook*: "The order does not create any new enforceable rights for persons impacted by environmental justice.

Agency strategies adopted under the Executive Order, however, can influence how agencies incorporate environmental justice issues into their daily tasks."*

In the past 30 or so years, the extensive development of chemical and nuclear technologies has been accompanied by the potential to cause catastrophic and long-lasting damage to the planet and those life forms that find this planet comfortable. The mechanisms underlying these complex, and dynamic technologies are unfamiliar and incomprehensible to most people. Harmful consequences are often delayed, and therefore difficult to assess by statistical analysis in a profit/loss statement, and are not well suited to trial-and-error learning.

The elusive and hard-to-manage qualities of today's hazards provides impetus to the field of risk assessment, which is designed to aid in identifying, characterizing and quantifying risk. The dominant perception of most people is that they face greater risks today than in the past and that risks in the future will be even greater than today. This view contrasts sharply with the views of most professional risk assessors. These perceptions, and the opposition to technology that accompanies them, have frustrated industrialists and regulators.

Addressing these issues has not always been done well by government agencies or industry. Much of the anger expressed by environmental justice advocates at meetings with the other stakeholders in our society has been at the expense of the federal and state regulatory agencies, and with the accusation that these agencies have not been sufficiently harsh with industry. The typical mainline environmental advocates are seen as an extension of the white community, rather than as partners in the search for a cleaner environment.

Efforts undertaken through the auspices of the USEPA in its reinvention projects have been to convert this maze of distrust into a circle of trust and understanding. Programs such as the Common Sense Initiative and other groups addressing environmental policy have had to meet the criteria of a presidential order mandating a balanced membership, including environmental justice representatives. In areas under discussion, a consensus must be reached to finalize an issue. Participants are trained in dispute resolution, in order to better prepare the participants to be more sensitive to and aware of the needs of others, rather than mediating a settlement in which parties win and lose. The intent is to have everyone walk away from the table with respect for each other, having gained something toward their own agendas.

Risk Assessment and the Community

This brings us to a term which has been received with mixed emotions—risk assessment. In the eyes of the regulatory community, this is a scientific assessment that is elusive in its complexity and has yet to be adequately defined by methodology that would simplify the study of chemicals to a point that

---

*David S. Bailey, Esq., and Selena Mendy, Esq., *Environmental Justice Community Handbook*, The Lawyers' Committee for Civil Rights Under Law, Washington, D.C., August 1997, p 105.

valid conclusions can be reached and communicated to the layman. To the environmental justice groups, the current use of the term risk assessment does not address its concerns about cumulative health risks in the neighborhood. They feel that it is defined by environmental advocates and health experts as effects that are observed in the workplace or on the ecology. The substance of risk assessment has yet to be defined in plain language that enables the ordinary person to know the effects on his or her health, in terms that he/she can understand and in context of the total exposure that surrounds the members of the community.

What is Risk Assessment?

Very simply, a risk is a description of a chance that some hazard to health or the environment will occur. Evaluating that risk is called risk assessment. This evaluation may include information on how toxic a chemical is, what type of contact links the individual or nature to exposure to the chemical, and the likelihood that people or the environment will be exposed to any deleterious effects of the chemical. (See Table 3–1.) It is often not possible to ascertain precise estimates of risk. There has been much disagreement about the science and the results of risk assessment. The questions surrounding risk and trust are implicit in the discussion of community involvement in environmental decision-making at the local and state level. Without community involvement in these decisions, distrust and community perception of risk increase.

Who is selected to speak, who is allowed to speak (or write), the legitimacy accorded the speaker (or writer), and the types of arguments presented all contribute to the construction of "risk".

Risk is ultimately a social construction, but one that has been construed only by those allowed to meaningfully participate in environmental decision-making. Because communities of color have not been given meaningful opportunities to participate in environmental decisions, the perception exists that the construction of risk, and risk assessment, do not incorporate the legitimate concerns of these communities.

For example, models of risk in food consumption assume the consumption patterns of a healthy, white male of about 150 pounds. If the community is not made up of white males, and if they consume the food differently, then the risk assessment fails to assess risk accurately.

Risk assessment is a new and rapidly evolving way to attempt to quantify risk events. It originates from a rational, scientific and technical world view that disregards values and cultural elements in an attempt to be "objective". (See figure 3–3.)

Currently, the field of risk assessment is incorporating cultural rationality as risk assessments become used increasingly in environmental decision-making. Cultural rationality describes the

TABLE 3–1. CHARACTERISTICS OF RISK
(Factors on right increase perception of riskiness)

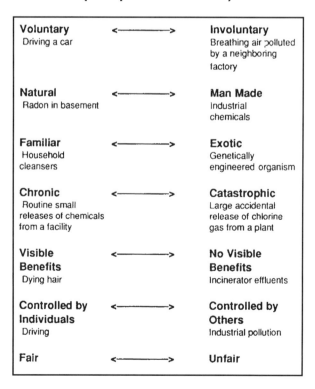

Voluntary Driving a car	<———>	Involuntary Breathing air polluted by a neighboring factory
Natural Radon in basement	<———>	Man Made Industrial chemicals
Familiar Household cleansers	<———>	Exotic Genetically engineered organism
Chronic Routine small releases of chemicals from a facility	<———>	Catastrophic Large accidental release of chlorine gas from a plant
Visible Benefits Dying hair	<———>	No Visible Benefits Incinerator effluents
Controlled by Individuals Driving	<———>	Controlled by Others Industrial pollution
Fair	<———>	Unfair

Source: United States Environmental Protection Agency, *Risk Communication About Chemicals In Your Community*, EPA 230/09-89-066, p 9.

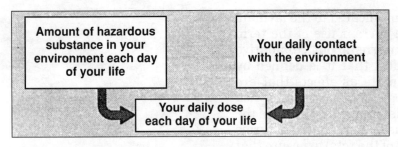

Figure 3–3. How scientists estimate daily dose of a hazardous substance.

Source: United States Environmental Protection Agency, *Hazardous Substances In Our Environment, A Citizen's Guide To Understanding Health Risks And Reducing Exposure*, EPA 230/09/90/081, September 1990, p 12.

concept that the cultural context of risk includes values, ethics, morality and qualitative judgments. As expressed by researchers in this area, cultural rationality does not separate the context to the layman from the content of risk analysis to the scientist. Technical rationality operates as if it can act independently of popular culture in constructing risk analysis. In the real world, cultural rationality seeks technical knowledge but incorporates it within a broader decision framework.

By constructing a social reality that separates facts from feelings and assessments from perceptions, sources of facts lose their credibility. Scientific assessments cannot be kept distinct from a cultural context, especially when one culture receives a disproportionate amount of risk because they do not fit the assumptions of traditional risk assessment models. For example, risk assessment requires scientists and policy makers to make value judgments concerning the impacts of risks. These impacts usually reflect mortality (risk of death), which has been judged as having greater importance than morbidity (risk of disease). (See Tables 3–2 and 3–3.) Further, impacts upon human health are judged hierarchically as more important than impacts upon wildlife (even where it is the basis of sustenance) and other environmental impacts. Therefore, scientific rationality, which supposedly has no connection to any cultural context, is actually a revealing metaphor for discussing differing world views on social issues that embrace science.

Risk and Trust

The key is to find new ways to link risk assessment, risk management, public policy and real public participation to achieve sound environmental decisions that include consideration of cultural values and other, as yet, intangible factors. In this way, trust will be developed in the ultimate decision by all partners in the community.

The time frame of the environmental decision may answer some of these questions. If the time frame is one day, for example, then a given printer may have no emissions that day, may incur no profit-eroding costs that day, and may therefore have no regulation on that day. However, if the time frame is 100 years, then cumulative emissions accrue, profit-eroding costs may accrue, and regulation, monitoring and enforcement actions may be brought to bear on that very old printer.

Communities are interested in a time frame that is longer than that related to quarterly profit reports, because they will bear the personal and monetary costs of public health concerns. If they have been excluded from this process, they simply will not trust environmental decisions.

In order to create trust in risky environmental decisions, all parties in the total community can enhance the understanding

TABLE 3–2. HEALTH RISKS LEADING TO CANCER

(1) Hazardous substance	(2) Estimated extra cases per 100,000 people at 1 mcg per day	(3) Weight-of-evidence classification	(4) Source	(5) Example daily dose	(6) Extra cancer cases per 100,000 people at example daily dose [(2) x (5)]
Asbestos	50	A	Cement-pipe factory	0.2 mcg per day in air	10
Benzene	0.04	A	Car exhaust	450 mcg per day in air	18
Carbon tetra-chloride	0.08	B2	Chemical factory	560 mcg per day in air	45
Chloroform	0.12	B2	Disinfection of drinking water	95 mcg per day in drinking water	11
Formaldehyde	0.05	B1	Chemical factory	20 mcg per day in air	1
Methylene chloride	0.02	B2	Chemical factory	2,400 mcg per day in air	50
Perchloro-ethylene	0.002	B2	Sewage treatment plant	730 mcg per day in air	2
Radon	0.011 (at 1 picocuries per day)	A	Underground deposits	16,000 pico-curies per day in indoor air	180
Tobacco smoke	0.3	A	Cigarette smokers	1,430 mcg per day in indoor air	429

Notes:
The daily doses and extra cancer cases shown here are just examples. Your extra chance of getting cancer from exposure to each of the hazardous substances may be lower or higher than the example, depending on whether your daily dose is lower or higher than the example daily dose.

Estimates assume a breathing rate of 20 cubic meters per day; water consumption of 2 liters per day; lifetime exposure (70 years), except 50 years for tobacco smoke; 154 pounds body weight; and 100% absorption of hazardous substance into body.

1 mcg per day = 1 microgram per day = 1 millionth of a gram per day.

1 gram = .035 ounces.

See page 25 for an explanation of the weight-of-evidence classification.

The extra cancer cases are in addition to the 20,000 cases of cancer expected for the 100,000 people from all other causes.

Source: United States Environmental Protection Agency, *Hazardous Substances In Our Environment, A Citizen's Guide To Understanding Health Risks And Reducing Exposure*, EPA 230/09/90/081, September 1990, p 31.

TABLE 3–3. NON-CANCEROUS HEALTH RISKS

(1) Hazardous substance	(2) Human threshold levels (mcg per day)	(3) Noncancer health effects/organ damage	(4) Source	(5) Example daily dose	(6) Estimated noncancer health effects
Benzene	820	Fetal development	Car exhaust	450 mcg per day from air	Environmental levels are lower than human threshold—health effects unlikely
Carbon tetrachloride	48 48 480	Liver Nerves/behavior Fetal development	Chemical factory	560 mcg per day from air	Possible liver, nerves/behavior, and fetal development effects
Chloroform	48 220	Fetal development Nerves/behavior	Disinfection of drinking water	95 mcg per day from water	Possible fetal development effect
Methylene chloride	13,000 13,000	Liver Fetal development	Chemical factory	2,400 mcg per day from air	Environmental levels are lower than human threshold—health effects unlikely
Perchloro-ethylene	1,400 1,400	Kidney Liver	Dry cleaning	200 mcg per day from air	Environmental levels are lower than human threshold—health effects unlikely
Xylene	1,100 1,100	Fetal development Reproduction	Car exhaust	610 mcg per day from air	Environmental levels are lower than human threshold—health effects unlikely

Notes: 1 mcg per day = 1 microgram per day = 1 millionth of a gram per day.

1 gram = 0.035 ounces.

Source: United States Environmental Protection Agency, *Hazardous Substances In Our Environment, A Citizen's Guide To Understanding Health Risks And Reducing Exposure*, EPA 230/09/90/081, September 1990, p 34.

among stakeholders of the many factors important to risk-based environmental decisions, including, but not limited to, quality of life issues such as social and cultural values and ecological impacts. On a policy level, there can be environmental impact statements that include these factors, with no marginal, unfounded claims of "findings of no significant impact." Governmental efforts can encourage the joint development of a holistic process that can be an integral part of linking risk assessment and management, policy development and implementation, and shared, tolerant communication.

Not all environmental regulations have provision for public participation. In a number of areas, governmental review is all that is required. In other areas, the regulations call for significant public activity and require participation that is imbedded in the permitting process and the compliance assurance efforts that ensue. To help its members respond to these requirements, a number of industries have established voluntary programs for the stewardship of the environment and community health concerns in partnership with the community.

Legal Requirements for Public Participation

The most comprehensive public participation has taken place as a result of the Superfund Amendment and Reauthorization Act, commonly known as SARA Title III. This legislation provides for the reporting of both inventories and releases of toxic chemicals. The reports are available for public review and have been the basis of much litigation by both government and environmental advocacy groups.

SARA Title III, Right-To-Know

The act provides lists of chemicals and thresholds for the chemicals, which require industry to report on an annual cycle. One such report (Toxic Release Inventory) asks for the amounts released to the various media and relative information with regard to recovery and recycling on-site and off-site. The second report required under SARA is an inventory of all listed chemicals that exceed listed thresholds. The thresholds are based on the relative toxicity of the chemicals. Using available information in the files of the EPA and OSHA, lists were prepared with thresholds of applicability for all chemicals that the government deemed part of the problem of pollutants being stored or released to the environment.

The process of identifying and cleaning up a site provides for considerable public participation. Public hearings, public notices and publicity are all a major part of the process. Citizens are encouraged by the Act to find and bring to government attention any facility that they feel contributes to the potential pollution of a site. The Act provides a bounty for those who identify offenders. Freedom-of-information laws have facilitated public searches of government records for company compliance actions and environmental permit files. Public school children, as a class project, can research the businesses in their neighborhood and compile a very thorough report on the firms' environmental status. The Act provides for a cash bounty when identification of a violator takes place.

Forms and further information on SARA can be found in chapter 20 and Appendices XXXV and XXXVI.

Clean Air Act of 1990

With the institution of the Federal Title V air permitting provisions, public participation has become a vital part of the permitting process. Prior to acceptance of any permit for a major source of emissions of volatile organic compounds, nitrogen dioxide, carbon dioxide, sulfur dioxide or listed hazardous air pollutants, public notice must be posted and hearings held in the event of challenges or concerns. (See figure 3–4.)

After a formal review process in which the facility and the governmental agency have discussed and agreed to the specific legal conditions in the permit, a draft is made available to all interested parties for their review and comment. This notice to the public can take place by listing in an agency bulletin, an advertisement in a local newspaper, or listing on a web site. The public is given a number of days, typically from 20 to 30, in which to notify the agency that it has concerns and request a public hearing. Requests may come from concerned citizens living in the community, environmental justice groups in the community, or state/national advocacy groups. Some address problems in the community; others address broader issues in keeping with the organization's agenda.

The federal government expects the facility to take any measures necessary to address legitimate concerns of the public prior to issuance of the permit. Pre-permit meetings with the community and the agency are encouraged to recognize the need to know and to defuse any negative reaction by taking appropriate steps to assure that the planned installation will be in accordance with the best interests of the business and the community. Some of the agreements and controls installed to assure compliance and lower risk to the public can be included in an agreement resulting from public participation. This agreement can become part of the conditions of the permit.

After a waiting period and the public hearing, if one is requested, the state agency has the authority and will issue the appropriate permit. It has the authority to recognize the validity of public concerns and incorporate them in the permit, or recognize that the concerns are not valid and issue the permit without including reference to the issues raised by the public.

Community-Based Environmental Protection

The EPA, through regulatory reinvention, is developing a new environmental system to cope with the need for a more flexible approach to place-specific problems. The objective is to encourage innovation at state and local levels that would be more user-friendly to the community. To support this philosophy, the agency has articulated operational goals for its own programs and practices:

• Integrate the delivery of services and programs on a geographic basis,

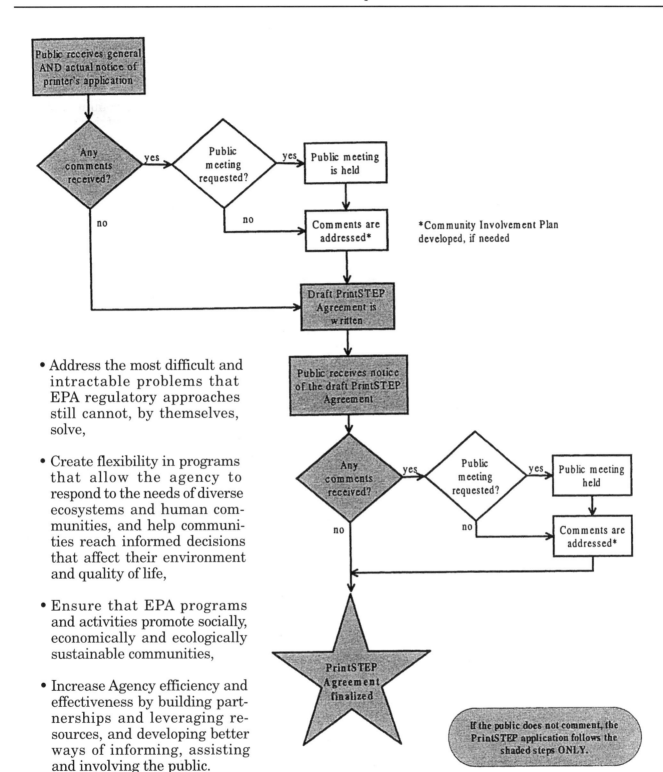

- Address the most difficult and intractable problems that EPA regulatory approaches still cannot, by themselves, solve,

- Create flexibility in programs that allow the agency to respond to the needs of diverse ecosystems and human communities, and help communities reach informed decisions that affect their environment and quality of life,

- Ensure that EPA programs and activities promote socially, economically and ecologically sustainable communities,

- Increase Agency efficiency and effectiveness by building partnerships and leveraging resources, and developing better ways of informing, assisting and involving the public.

Among the programs in which the printing industry participated as part of this new philosophy were the Design for the Environment and the Common Sense Initiative.

Figure 3–4. Flow chart depicting public participation in permit process.

Source: United States Environmental Protection Agency, *PrintSTEP Pilot Program, Community Handbook Template,* Common Sense Initiative Printing Sector Project, April 1999, p 3–16.

Voluntary Community Programs

Some industries and associations have long recognized the benefits of including representatives of the local community in its quest to attain higher levels of chemical safety. Many individual programs have been developed locally by companies and have been very successful in integrating the concerns of the community with the plans of the firm. A number of major industries have put together programs which are promoted for their members to use in their local communities. In more than one case, membership in an association requires that the potential member have an active community care program in place to qualify for membership. One such program, which is related to the printing industries, is that of the National Association of Printing Ink Manufacturers. Their program is based on that of the chemical industry, entitled "We Care."

Individual companies can make a difference. Merck & Co., Inc., for instance, has developed *A Guide to Becoming a Neighbor of Choice*, to correspond to the mission stated by its chairman and CEO Raymond V. Gilmartin as an introduction to the guide: "At Merck, our business is to respond to society's needs for life-saving medicines and vaccines. This is the foundation of everything we do. We are able to support society in other ways—through the support of programs and organizations that hold the promise of making the world in which we live and work a better place."* Merck's program helps its plants to:

- Build sustainable relationships of trust,
- Assess the pulse of the communities,
- Respond to emerging issues,
- Design and implement key community programs,
- Measure the effectiveness of their activities.

These resources assist facilities as they design and implement community relations strategies that are targeted towards meeting business objectives. Given the sensitive nature of any objective that has an impact on the environment, such programs can provide a bridge of opportunity in meeting the public participation mandates of the regulations. (See figure 3–5.)

A Final Note: Proactive Industry Response

With the dominance of small businesses in the printing industries, recognition of the community and its concerns is a matter of self-preservation. Many shops are in the midst of the community and staffed by family members of the owners. While not all employees are necessarily related as family, the close working and social relationship in small shops frequently approaches that of a feeling of family; what will affect the community will be felt within the family as well.

---

*Cover of *A Guide to Becoming a Neighbor of Choice*, published by Merck & Co. Inc., 1997. The publication was a product of The Center for Corporate Community Relations at Boston College.

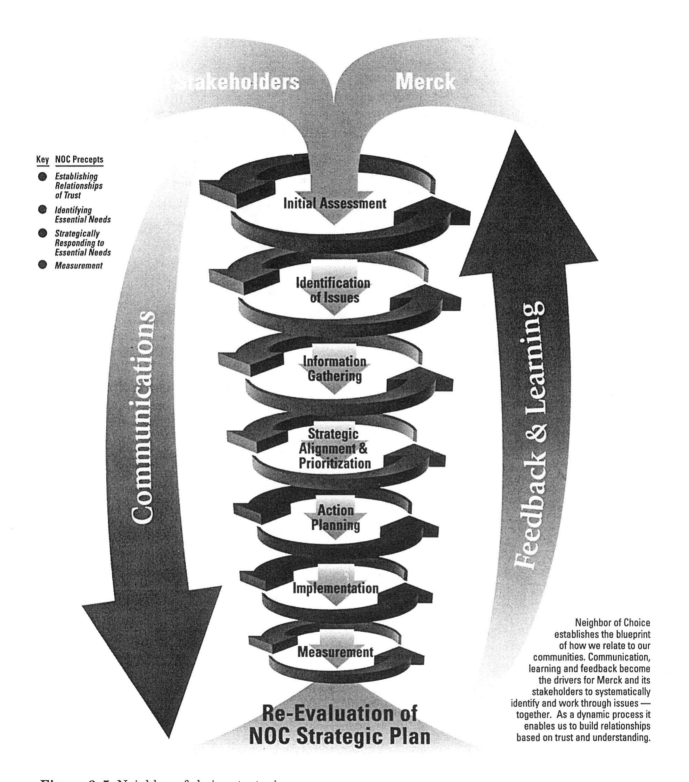

Figure 3–5. Neighbor of choice strategic process.
Courtesy of Merck & Co. Inc., *A Guide to Becoming a Neighbor of Choice*, 1997, back cover.

It's a small world; we are all members of the community.

Therefore, it would not be uncommon for the print shop personnel to have a close working and social relationship with the community and its organizations. The owners and staff may have memberships in local organizations such as Kiwanis, Craftsmen, Masons, Little League, soccer teams, etc. They may be active in the affairs of the local schools and houses of worship, as well as in the political system. The print shop cannot be viewed as an outsider in the definition of who is the community.

Environmental compliance and stewardship is just one more facet of doing business. Printers should involve the community where there is a need and a concern. Printers should have the natural desire to protect their own as well as their neighbors, a desire which can carry over to the inclusion of the community when plans are being made that might seem threatening to an outsider.

CHAPTER **4**

Overview of Environmental and Safety Regulations

With the proliferation of chemicals in industry and the concentration of regulatory efforts segregated by point of impact, it is no wonder that there are a considerable number of regulations, each addressing its own particular audience. The number of regulations, coupled with the ensuing enforcement and guidance documents for each, has led to considerable concern and confusion by industry as to what regulations are applicable in a specific situation.

The major categories of environment and health legislation include:

1. Clean Air Act of 1990 (CAA90),

2. Resource Conservation and Recovery Act (RCRA),

3. Clean Water Act (CWA),

4. CERCLA AND EPCRA—Superfund and Superfund Amendments & Reauthorization Act,

5. Toxic Substances Control Act (TSCA),

6. Occupational Safety and Health Act (OSHA).

In addition to federal regulations and technical guidelines established by the USEPA and OSHA, states and local agencies can specify more stringent requirements. This is common practice in the control of air emissions, discharges to sewer systems, storage of hazardous materials, and health-related concerns. The printer must be aware of and alert to the impact of such local ordinances and comply with the most strict regulatory standards and procedures.

This chapter will provide an overview of the regulations. Subsequent chapters will delve into the specifics of those regulations that have the greatest consequences to any industrial printing and converting facility.

Emitting Pollutants to Air

Clean Air Act (CAA) provisions, dating back to the 1970s, seek to improve the quality of air and reduce the incidence of damage to human health and the ecology by hazardous air pollutants. Among the major air emissions-related targets of the CAA are respiratory ailments and mortality rates, the ramifications of pollutants on natural resources such as acid rain, and the problem of ozone depletion in the upper atmosphere.

Air pollutants effect human health and nature.

The Clean Air Act with the 1990 amendments set the framework for air pollution in a series of sections, known as Titles. Of major interest to the printer are:

1. **National Ambient Air Quality Standards (NAAQS)** to reduce the emission of chemicals that result in the formation of ground level ozone (commonly referred to as smog). Many of the solvents used in inks and clean-up solvents fall into this category. They are grouped under the heading of VOCs (Volatile Organic Compounds). Control Technique Guidelines (CTGs) set standards/objectives for printing inks and chemistry based on the type of printing process used and the percentage of VOCs in the inks and solvents, as used at the press or as a percent destroyed through the use of add-on controls such as catalytic oxidizers or solvent recovery systems.

   Standards have also been set for allowable levels of nitrous oxide (NOx), carbon monoxide (CO), particulate (PM–10), sulfur dioxide (SO_2) and lead. Emissions of these substances can be derived from the use of natural gas or fuel oil for drying and thermal oxidation. Particulate is also found in some printing processes. (See figure 4–1).

   The nation has been divided into zones based on tested air quality, which labels them as attainment or non-attainment. An attainment area is one in which the air quality is at or better than the standards. Non-attainment areas are those that have failed the standards. Within the non-attainment definition, regions or local areas are defined at various

Figure 4–1. Industrial sites exhaust particulates and volatile organic compounds into the air.

levels of severity. Table 4–1 lists the non-attainment areas as of 1994. Some significant changes have since taken place, with some regions getting worse (Houston, TX) and others improving.

TABLE 4–1. OZONE NON-ATTAINMENT AREAS

Extreme (1 area)	Serious (16 Areas)
Los Angeles-Anaheim-Riverside, CA	Atlanta, GA
	Bakersfield, CA
Severe (8 areas)	Baton Rouge, LA
	Beaumont-Port Arthur, TX
Baltimore, MD	Boston, MA
Chicago, IL-IN-WI	El Paso, TX
Houston-Galveston-Brazoria, TX	Fresno, CA
Milwaukee-Racine, WI	Hartford, CT
Muskegon, MI	Huntington-Ashland, WV-KY-OH
New York, NY-NJ-CT	Parkersburg-Marrieta, WV-OH
Philadelphia, PA-NJ-DE	Portsmouth-Dover-Rochester, NH-ME
San Diego, CA	Providence, RI
	Sacramento, CA
	Sheboygan, WI
	Springfield, MA
	Washington, DC-MD-VA

Source: United States Environmental Protection Agency, *Federal Environmental Regulations Potentially Affecting The Commercial Printing Industry*, EPA 744B-94-001, March 1994, p 7.

2. **Hazardous air pollutants (HAPs)** are listed in the CAA (Table 4–2) and are, or will be, subject to new National Emission Standards for Hazardous Air Pollutants (NESHAPS) as they are developed. The level of control required will be called MACT (Maximum Achievable Control Technology). Use of such chemicals as toluene, hexane, methanol, ethylene glycol and ethylene glycol compounds as a generic group can place you in this category. Elimination of these chemicals from ink and solvent blend formulations will exclude you from the mandates of this regulation. Use of the HAPs will necessitate control amounting to a reduction of 95%.

3. **Ozone depleting chemicals** are listed and subject to a ban in accordance with international agreements. Among the chemicals on this list is 1,1,1, trichloroethane and other chlorinated solvents. Use of these chemicals has been discouraged by means of increasing the taxes levied on current purchases and storage of quantities of the prohibited chemicals in inventory. The cost of continued usage has been made economically prohibitive.

TABLE 4–2. CHEMICALS USED IN THE PRINTING INDUSTRY THAT ARE LISTED AS HAZARDOUS AIR POLLUTANTS IN THE CLEAN AIR AMENDMENTS

HAZARDOUS AIR POLLUTANT	
Benzene	Lead compounds
Cadium compounds	Methanol
Carbon tetrachloride	Methyl ethyl ketone
Chromium compounds	Methyl isobutyl ketone
Cobalt compounds	Methylene chloride
Cumene	Perchloroethylene
Dibutylphthalate	Polycyclic organic matter
Diethanolamine	Propylene oxide
Ethyl benzene	Toluene
Ethylene glycol	2,4-Toluene diisocyanate
Formaldehyde	1,1,2-Trichloroethane
Glycol ethers	Trichloroethylene
Hexane	Vinyl chloride
Hydrochloric acid	Xylenes
Isophorone	

Source: United States Environmental Protection Agency, *Federal Environmental Regulations Potentially Affecting the Commercial Printing Industry*, EPA 744B-94-001, March 1994, p 12.

TABLE 4–3. EXISTING SOURCE RACT REQUIREMENTS FOR EACH OZONE NON-ATTAINMENT CATEGORY

CATEGORY OF NONATTAINMENT AREA	SIZE OF VOC OR NO_x SOURCES AFFECTED (TONS/YEAR)
Extreme	10
Severe	25
Serious	50
Moderate and Marginal	100

Source: United States Environmental Protection Agency, *Federal Environmental Regulations Potentially Affecting The Commercial Printing Industry*, EPA 744B-94-001, March 1994, p 8.

4. Under **Title V permitting**, the agency levels the playing field for national permitting of major sources. States were required to file plans that provide for the issuance of the major source permits, with the assurance that the permit and permitting procedures conform to federal standards. The thresholds for major sources, as well as lesser sources, vary with the conditions of severity in the non-attainment categories. (See Table 4–3 for major source definitions.)

   Provision is made for facilities to set upper limits that will establish maximum VOC emission levels allowable under the facility permit. This is known as "capping out." The ability to cap-out can excuse the facility from the Title V process, or set a limit within the Title V permit to preclude the application of various regulatory requirements. An example for printers would lie in the use of past history to establish a baseline of emissions, let's say 20 tons, in a region that is considered "Severe," with a threshold of 25 tons for Title V permitting. The potential to emit may be as high as 60 tons. The facility would agree to limit the use of inks and solvents so that a maximum amount of emissions would be less than 24 tons. The emissions would not require a major source permit and would be granted a state facility permit that is not subject to EPA review. The facility, in essence, has agreed to only grow by a maximum of four tons; it will have to maintain records and file reports to assure that the agreement is kept.

   Clean air regulations are the major environmental challenge to printers. With the CAA90 and the drive to include smaller and smaller sources of air pollution, many more facilities are coming increasingly under the purview of the law. Local governments in severe non-attainment areas have seen the need to pass and enforce stricter regulations than those of the federal government.

   The requirement for air permits has developed into a means of adding needed funds for government activity by agencies committed to the environmental effort as well as into the general budget. Title V programs are mandated to be supported by fees elicited through the program.

5. **Industry comes under varying degrees of control**, depending on where it is and what technology is available to curtail emissions. The more severe the pollution in a non-attainment region, the more stringent the standards. New facilities face tighter controls of emissions. The following are definitions of technology used in defining status under the Clean Air Act.

   - **RACT—Reasonably Available Control Technology**: The lowest emission limitation that a particular source is capable of meeting by the application of control technology that is reasonably available considering current technological and economic feasibility.

- **BACT—Best Available Control Technology**: The USEPA or the local agency determines BACT requirements by (1) identifying all control technologies, (2) eliminating technically infeasible options, (3) ranking remaining control options by control effectiveness, (4) evaluating the most effective controls and documenting results, and (5) selecting the BACT. While this is a government-driven process, the printer will be charged with conducting the research and submitting the plan establishing BACT on a site-by-site basis.

- **MACT—Maximum Available Control Technology**: The control requirements for specific industry segments, and subdivisions within the industry processes, are to be developed over time. EPA has already released the NESHAPS for Printing by Publication Heat Set Lithography, Gravure and Flexography. The standards for Coating for Paper and Other Web Operations became effective as of April 2000.

- **LAER—Lowest Achievable Emissions Reduction**: LAER is the most stringent limitation. It is derived from either the most stringent emission limitation contained in any State Implementation Plan (SIP), or the most stringent emission limitation achieved in practice by any facility in a class or category. Any documentation by a printer in a given category of exceedingly high levels of destruction or elimination of emissions can be used as the standard for that segment of the industry.

Each of the compliance demonstrations refers to the level of attainable destruction or reduction of VOCs or HAPs by means of acceptable process technology or add-on controls. Older facilities have the benefit of reasonable controls, while new facilities must conform to the tighter standards that look to achieve maximum reductions.

6. **New major stationary sources** of air pollution and major modifications to major sources are required to obtain an air pollution permit prior to commencing construction. This process is subject to new source review (NSR), and must be conducted in both attainment and non-attainment areas.

Permits for attainment areas must meet conditions that are referred to as prevention of significant air quality deterioration (PSD) requirements. These include:

a. Installation of best available control technology (BACT),

b. A detailed air quality analysis showing there will be no violation of PSD "increments,"

c. Prediction of future air quality emissions and compliance with standards,

d. Possible monitoring of air quality for one year prior to the issuance of the permit,

e. Demonstration of standard attainment through the undertaking of an air quality analysis.

The documentation required for each of the steps above may be satisfied by means of a mass balance accumulation of all purchases during a given period and the determination of the composition and quantities of all volatiles emitted. These data can then be used to extrapolate exposure for any given period of time—day, hour, minute—as well as predict future emissions and air quality based on projections of growth.

Restrictions are more severe in non-attainment areas. NSR in these areas will also include:

- Installation of lowest achievable emission rate (LAER) technology,

- Provision for "offsets" representing emission reductions that must be made from other sources. Offsets are credits for emission tonnage that results from the quantity of reduction of emissions achieved by technology that goes beyond compliance requirements, or from the shutting down sources of emissions. Formulas for the areas, based on severity, call for the application of tons of emissions that will reduce pollution by an amount that is in excess of the tons that will now be erected. As an example, for every ton added, offset credits will remove one and a third tons from the emissions inventory.

Hazardous and Solid Wastes

RCRA (Resource Conservation and Recovery Act), governing the control and handling of hazardous and solid wastes, is the second highest priority for printers. The use of chemicals throughout the process, including a major concern with solvents in liquid inks and for clean-up, requires disposition in accordance with the hazardous waste provision of this act. The overriding concern is ground and ground water contamination, affecting agriculture, wildlife and human health (figure 4–2).

The waste substrates and converted products produced fall under provisions for the disposition and reclamation (recovery) of materials classified as solid wastes. The major concerns are conservation of resources and the problem of where such wastes can be disposed of without impacting on the environment, i.e., need for adequately designed and erected landfill facilities.

Hazardous waste must be identified, categorized in accordance with the type of hazard and/or listed hazardous chemicals, disposed of by approved and controlled methods, with a paperwork trail to monitor the quality of the process. From time of generation of the waste until it is destroyed, the generator (printer) is responsible for the waste and any damage it may cause.

Figure 4–2. Leaking drums can pollute water supplies.

Classifying Hazardous Waste

The first step toward control of hazardous wastes is identification and classification of the wastes. Material Safety Data Sheets are a beginning point. They identify the components of chemicals used and, to some extent, define the composition of the wastes. Laboratory tests of the actual wastes will enable recognition and quantification of the contents. Once the composition is known, the hazardous waste can be properly classified.

Hazardous wastes can be defined as categorical, i.e. Ignitable and Corrosive, or as a listed waste stemming from the use of specific chemicals, i.e., toluene, MEK, ethyl acetate, chlorinated solvents, etc. (See Tables 4–4 and 4–5.) Where pure surplus chemicals are being disposed of, they can be described under the Department of Transportation (DOT) U codes. (See Table 4–6 and Appendix XXVI.)

The major flammable solvents used by printers are categorized as Ignitable or D001. Prepress chemistry frequently contains alkali or acid solutions and is categorized as Corrosive, D002. Among the more common solvents in some inks and many press washes, under listed classifications such as F001, F003 and F005, are 1,1,1, trichloroethane, ethyl acetate, methanol, toluene and MEK respectively. If a drum of pure ethyl acetate is to be disposed of, it could be described as U112; as part of a mixture the solvent, based on its components, would be described as a D number with secondary F codes for the constituent chemistry. An example of this might be a solvent blend containing mineral spirits and toluene. The hazardous waste would be

TABLE 4–4. EPA TOXIC CHARACTERISTIC CONTAMINANTS THAT MAY BE FOUND IN PRINTING WASTE

Waste Code	Contaminant
D005	Barium
D007	Chromium
D019	Carbon tetrachloride
D035	Methyl ethyl ketone
D011	Silver
D040	Trichloroethylene
D043	Vinyl chloride

Source: United States Environmental Protection Agency, *Federal Environmental Regulations Potentially Affecting The Commercial Printing Industry*, EPA 744B-94-001, March 1994, p 34.

labeled D001 as flammable and carry a second designation of F005 for the toluene.

Under certain conditions, where solvent recovery has concentrated heavy metals in still bottoms and sludge, there may be adequate lead and chromium or other constituents that will require the waste to be designated in a listed waste category.

TABLE 4–5. EXAMPLES OF LISTED WASTE (F) FOUND IN THE PRINTING INDUSTRY

Waste Code	Name or Description of Waste
F001	The following spent halogenated solvents used in degreasing: Tetrachloroethylene, trichloroethylene, methylene chloride, 1,1,1-trichloroethane, carbon tetrachloride, and chlorinated fluorocarbons; all spent solvent mixtures/blends used in degreasing containing, before use, a total of ten percent or more (by volume) of one or more of the above halogenated solvents or those solvents listed in F002, F004, and F005; and still bottoms from the recovery of these spent solvents and spent solvent mixtures.
F002	The following spent halogenated solvents: Tetrachloroethylene, methylene chloride, trichloroethylene, 1,1,1-trichloroethane, chlorobenzene, 1,1,2-trichloro-1,2,2-trifluoroethane, ortho-dichlorobenzene, trichlorofluoromethane, and 1,1,2-trichloroethane; all spent solvent mixtures/blends containing, before use, a total of ten percent or more (by volume) of one or more of the above halogenated solvents or those listed in F001, F004, or F005; and still bottoms from the recovery of these spent solvents and spent solvent mixtures.
F003	The following spent non-halogenated solvents: Xylene, acetone, ethyl acetate, ethyl benzene, ethyl ether, methyl isobutyl ketone, n-butyl alcohol, cyclohexanone, and methanol; all spent solvent mixtures/blends containing, before use, only the above spent non-halogenated solvents; and all spent solvent mixtures/blends containing, before use, one or more of the above non-halogenated solvents, and, a total of ten percent or more (by volume) of one or more of those solvents listed in F001, F002, F004, and F005; and still bottoms from the recovery of these spent solvents and spent solvent mixtures.
F005	The following spent non-halogenated solvents: Toluene, methyl ethyl ketone, carbon disulfide, isobutanol, pyridine, benzene, 2-ethoxyethanol, and 2-nitropropane; all spent solvent mixtures/blends containing, before use, a total of ten percent or more (by volume) of one or more of the above non-halogenated solvents or those solvents listed in F001, F002, or F004; and still bottoms from the recovery of these spent solvents and spent solvent mixtures.

Source: United States Environmental Protection Agency, *Risk Communication About Chemicals In Your Community*, EPA 230/09-89-066, p 34.

**TABLE 4–6. EXAMPLES OF LISTED WASTES (U) FOUND
IN THE PRINTING INDUSTRY**

Waste Code	Name or Description of Waste
U002	Acetone
U019	Benzene
U211	Carbon tetrachloride
U055	Cumene
U056	Cyclohexane
U069	Dibutyl phthalate
U112	Ethyl acetate
U359	Ethanol, 2-ethoxy
U359	Ethylene glycol monoethyl ether
U122	Formaldehyde
U154	Methanol
U226	Methyl chloroform
U080	Methylene chloride
U159	Methyl ethyl ketone (MEK)
U161	Methyl isobutyl ketone
U210	Tetrachloroethylene (perchloroethylene)
U220	Toluene
U223	Toluene diisocyanate
U228	Trichloroethylene
U043	Vinyl chloride
U239	Xylene

Source: United States Environmental Protection Agency, *Federal
Environmental Regulations Potentially Affecting The Commercial
Printing Industry*, EPA 744B-94-001, March 1994, p 33.

Solid Wastes

Solid wastes that are not classified as hazardous are addressed
under Subtitle D. While not a direct issue for most printers,
many of the substrates and products manufactured fall within the
jurisdictions of communities with problems of landfills and solid
waste incineration. The printing and packaging materials industries have been very active in industrial recycling, as well as in
consumer return and recycling programs for paper and plastics, to
reduce the impact of solid waste on the community and the environment.

Some states and localities have mandatory programs for recycling and/or waste reduction. Companies are committed to reduce
waste by established percentages each year.

Hazardous waste generators are segregated by the amount of waste generated and disposed of, with varying levels of requirements based on the designated classification.

1. **Large quantity generators (LQG)** are those that generate at least 1000 kg (approximately 2,200 pounds) of hazardous waste per month, or greater than 1 kg (2.2 pounds) per month of acutely hazardous waste.

2. **Small quantity generators (SQG)** generate between 100 and 1,000 kg (approximately 220 to less than 2,200 pounds) of hazardous waste per month, or up to 1 kg of acutely hazardous waste per month.

3. **Conditionally exempt small quantity generators (CESQG)** create no more than 100 kg (220 pounds) of hazardous waste per month or less than 1 kg (2.2 pounds) of acutely hazardous waste.

Categories of Hazardous Waste Generators

The RCRA regulations specify the types of records, reports and other requirements for the printer relative to the category of generation. Many requirements are similar for all sizes and types of printers, including the application for an EPA generator identification number, manifests and landfill ban documents for shipment of wastes, testing and classification of wastes, training, storage, segregation and inspections for the waste storage areas and inventory, contingency plans in the event of crisis, plans for closing a facility, and periodic reports. The degree of applicability and requirements for the various components will vary based on the size of the generator.

A key element of the RCRA regulations calls for the shipment of waste within a given period of time that is appropriate for the quantity for that particular category of installation. Missing the regulatory deadline for that time period can move a facility into a higher category, based on the fact that the time the hazardous waste has been in storage has exceeded the prescribed limit. For large quantity generators, hazardous wastes must be disposed of within 90 days of accumulation of the waste, with a maximum inventory of 6,000 kg (13,200 pounds). Small quantity generators must ship within 180 days of attaining the 6,000-kg limit. Failing to do so in either case could result in the need to file for a permit as a treatment, storage and disposal (TSD) facility. The regulations require that a generator take responsibility for not including specified chemicals banned in shipments destined for landfills. Every manifest must be accompanied by this document. Failure to do so constitutes a violation.

Operating Requirements

A tangential issue, other than the concern as a hazardous waste, for printers stems from the federal and state regulations and standards for the operation of industrial laundries. The discharges of water used in the cleaning of wipers and garments by

Secondary Issue: Laundered Wipers

these facilities are governed by categorical effluent guidelines. Failure to adhere to contractual terms with the laundries, which require the exclusion of the containers of the soiled wipers as a means of disposing of inks or solvents, could lead to the inclusion of a printer in any legal action and penalties levied against the laundry.

Underground Storage Tanks

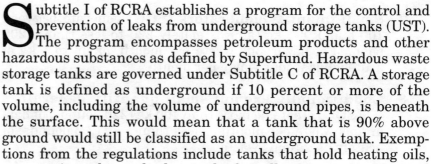

Subtitle I of RCRA establishes a program for the control and prevention of leaks from underground storage tanks (UST). The program encompasses petroleum products and other hazardous substances as defined by Superfund. Hazardous waste storage tanks are governed under Subtitle C of RCRA. A storage tank is defined as underground if 10 percent or more of the volume, including the volume of underground pipes, is beneath the surface. This would mean that a tank that is 90% above ground would still be classified as an underground tank. Exemptions from the regulations include tanks that hold heating oils, septic tanks, and other tanks for collecting wastewater and stormwater (figure 4–3).

Typical construction and operating requirements for an underground storage tank program include:

1. Design, construction, installation and notification,

2. General operations,

3. Release detection,

4. Release reporting, investigation and confirmation,

5. Release response and corrective action (for petroleum underground storage tanks),

6. Closure of underground storage tanks,

7. Financial assurance (for petroleum storage tanks).

Figure 4–3. Underground storage tanks represent a potential to leak and contaminate local ground and water resources.

Process Water Wastes

Various portions of the Clean Water Act (CWA) can impact on the printing facility, some based on the storage and potential of the used solvents and inks to leak or spill to the groundwater. The CWA covers such diverse areas as spills of oil and hazardous substances, discharge of process waters into the waterways of the United States, the standards required of publicly owned treatment works (POTW), and stormwater drains and discharges. Of primary concern to the printer are the storage conditions for his inks, solvents and other related materials and processes, as well as the handling of discharges, spills, etc.

Use of waterborne inks and coatings or other aqueous chemistry must be supervised to determine whether the wastes of these chemicals can be discharged or must be handled as hazardous or non-regulated wastes that cannot be discharged to a sewer system or to below-ground tanks.

Discharges of oil are defined as including, but not limited to, any spilling, leaking, pumping, pouring, emitting, emptying or dumping into the marine environment of quantities that violate applicable water standards or cause a film, sheen or discoloration of the surface of the water or the adjoining shoreline, or cause a sludge or emulsion to be deposited beneath the surface of the water or upon the adjoining shorelines.

The Federal Water Pollution Control Act (FWPCA) of the CWA designates hazardous substances and establishes the Reportable Quantity (RQ) for each substance. When an amount equal to or greater than the RQ is discharged, facilities not subject to an NPDES permit or discharging to a publicly owned treatment works (POTW) must provide notice to the government. Among the RQs established for the printing industries are toluene and xylene. The standards have been set by the federal government and administered under state implementation programs. Table 4–7 identifies some of the typical reportable quantities for chemicals found in the printing industry processes.

Wastewater flows from industrial plants and enters the streams and rivers to affect drinking supplies.

TABLE 4–7. CLEAN WATER ACT: REPORTABLE QUANTITIES OF HAZARDOUS SUBSTANCES THAT MAY APPLY IN THE PRINTING INDUSTRY

Hazardous Substance	RQ in Pounds
Benzene	10
Carbon tetrachloride	10
Chloroform	10
Cyclohexane	1,000
Ethylbenzene	1,000
Formaldehyde	100
Hydrochloric acid	5,000
Propylene oxide	100
Styrene	1,000
Toluene	1,000
Xylene (mixed)	1,000

Source: United States Environmental Protection Agency, *Federal Environmental Regulations Potentially Affecting The Commercial Printing Industry*, EPA 744B-94-001, March 1994, Appendix B-1.

Permits

An NPDES (National Pollutant Discharge Elimination System) permit is required if discharges are being made from any point source or simply drainage from stormwaters to navigable waters. The two sources are broadly defined by the government agencies. Therefore, a source will be required to obtain a NPDES if it discharges almost anything directly to surface waters. Discharges of stormwater associated with industrial activity may require a facility to obtain an NPDES.

Sources discharging to POTWs may be required to obtain an industrial user permit from local authorities. General pretreatment standards will apply to all facilities discharging pollutants to a POTW. There are general prohibitions for which pretreatment is forbidden and must be adhered to when treatment does take place. These include:

1. Pollutants that create a fire hazard,

2. Pollutants that can cause corrosive structural damage to the POTW,

3. Solid or viscous pollutants in amounts that will obstruct flow,

4. Any pollutant, including oxygen demanding pollutants, that will cause interference with the POTW,

5. Heated effluents that will inhibit biological activity in the POTW,

6. Petroleum oil, non-biodegradable cutting oils or mineral oils that will cause interference or pass through,

7. Pollutants that will result in the presence of toxic gases, vapors or fumes within the POTW that will subject workers to health and safety problems,

8. Any trucked or hauled pollutants, except at designated points.

Silver Halides and Aqueous Solutions

Silver halides are of specific concern for printers. Many, although not all, print shops require adherence to discharge standards. Prepress darkroom activities in the processing of films, photographic papers and printing plates use developer and fixer aqueous solutions for processing. The end result of the finished negative, print or plate is the washing off of silver halides to create the image. The silver is a hazardous pollutant that must be recovered prior to discharge or recycled off-site, being shipped as a listed hazardous waste. Best management practices have been developed for the recovery of silver halides.

Caution should be taken when employing any aqueous solutions or inks. The mere fact that they have water as the major ingredient does not render the waste non-hazardous. Alcohols, ketones, glycols and other chemical substances may lead to the classification as unacceptable discharges for the POTW and the NPDES.

Stormwater Runoff

Stormwater permits are required for areas where industrial activity or storage is exposed to stormwater which drains to either a municipal water treatment sewer system or directly to surface waters. Stormwater going to combined municipal sewer systems does not require a permit, although notification to the POTW is required. Any stormwater going to a receiving body of water must be permitted.

Applications for the stormwater permit will include a site map of the topography of the facility, including drainage and discharge structures, drainage area for each stormwater outfall, paved areas and buildings, areas used for outdoor storage or disposal, control measures, treatment and storage areas, wells, springs and other surface waters which receive the stormwater drainage. Certification of the quality of the discharges must be determined by testing. EPA issues general permits for those facilities that are not covered by NPDES, POTWs or other exclusions.

Superfund/SARA and the Printer

Commonly known as Superfund, the Comprehensive Environmental Response, Compensation and Liability Act (CERCLA) was amended in 1986 to broaden the scope to cover Emergency Planning and Community Right to Know provisions (SARA). The combined acts set up a variety of mechanisms to address risks to public health, welfare and the environment caused by the release of hazardous substances.

Title III of SARA created an emergency planning framework and established the right of local governments and the public to obtain information on the hazards posed by potential toxic substance releases. To the printer, this poses the need to comply with recordkeeping and reporting mandates. Specifically, the right-to-know regulations call for reporting of:

1. Release of CERCLA listed hazardous substances subject to reporting quantity thresholds (Toxic Release Inventory Report),

2. Presence of certain amounts of extremely hazardous substances at a facility (Tier II Inventory Report),

3. An emergency release of certain hazardous substances to state and local emergency response authorities,

4. Other toxic chemical releases.

The lists of chemicals vary for the two reports cited, as do the reportable quantities. Both have thresholds that determine whether a report has to be made, as well as quantities that trigger the requirement for reporting of releases.

Under the two reporting provisions of SARA Title III (312 and 313), printers have to maintain records that enable the filing of annual reports if the thresholds for either report is exceeded. Care must be taken to consult the lists for each section. Each report has its own list of chemicals that must be reported, and there are major differences between the two lists. See Appendices XXXV and XXXVI.

Toxic Release Inventory Report (TRI)

The Toxic Release Report, known as either the R report or the TRI report, requires an annual accounting of releases that conform to one of two basic thresholds. If a chemical is used and becomes part of the product, i.e., certain pigment chemistry, the reporting threshold is the use of 25,000 pounds per year. For chemicals that are ancillary to the process, such as solvents for dilution or cleaning, the threshold is 10,000 pounds per year. The report summarizes disposal of hazardous wastes, recycling efforts, air emissions, any emergency releases, etc. It is a major tool for promoting the implementation of pollution prevention programs.

The major waste sources leading to reporting for printers rests in the solvents used for dilution and cleaning, as well as the presence of solvents in inks and metals in pigments. In many cases, the primary contributor that triggers reporting comes from the extremely high amount of solvents used for cleaning. Among these are toluene, methyl ethyl ketone and ethylene glycols. Acetone and methylene chloride are members of this group, used primarily by lithographic printers.

A common chemical found in the flexographic and gravure processes, the frequent use of which is not always apparent and usually exceeds the threshold, is methanol. Methanol is used to denature ethyl alcohol, in percentages ranging from 14 to 17 percent. Use of a fast blend or straight ethanol, combined with any methanol for dilution and cleaning, added to that which may be in the inks, can elevate the flexographic printer to reportable levels. Table 4–8 lists some of the more commonly used chemicals listed for inclusion in TRI reporting.

TABLE 4–8. CHEMICALS USED IN THE PRINTING INDUSTRY THAT ARE LISTED IN THE TOXIC RELEASE INVENTORY

TOXIC CHEMICALS	
Acetone	Ammonia
Barium	Cadmium
Chromium	Copper*
Cumene	Cyclohexane
Methylene chloride	Ethylbenzene
Ethylene glycol	Ethylene oxide
Formaldehyde	Freon 113
Hydrochloric acid	Hydroquinone
Lead	Methanol
Methyl ethyl ketone	Methyl isobutyl ketone
Phosphoric acid	Silver
Sulfuric acid	Tetrachloroethylene
Toluene	Trichloroethylene
1,1,1-Trichloroethane	Xylene

Source: United States Environmental Protection Agency, *Federal Environmental Regulations Potentially Affecting The Commercial Printing Industry*, EPA 744B-94-001, March 1994, Appendix F-1.

TIER II Inventory Report

Emergency planning efforts require the filing of inventory reports using a standard form entitled Tier II. Any listed chemical that exceeds the threshold for that chemical must be reported. See Table 4–9 for a list of the chemicals on the list that are closely related to the printing industry. Any OSHA listed chemical stored in excess of 10,000 pounds must be reported. This information is used by local emergency planning committees

(LEPCs) to plan or react to any emergency in or near the facility. Some localities have embellished the Tier II report to include larger numbers of chemicals at lower inventory levels than those called for in the federal statute.

TABLE 4–9. CERCLA REPORTABLE QUANTITIES FOR SOME CHEMICALS USED IN THE PRINTING INDUSTRY

Chemical	Reportable Quantity (lbs)
Acetone	5,000
Ammonia	100
Benzene	10
Cadmium and compounds	1
Carbon tetrachloride	10
Chloroform	10
Chromium and compounds	1
Cumene	5,000
Cyclohexane	1,000
Dibutyl phthalate	10
Ethanol, 2-ethoxy	1,000
Ethyl acetate	5,000
Ethylbenzene	1,000
Formaldehyde	100
Hydrochloric acid	5,000
Isophorone	5000
Lead and compounds	1
Methyl chloroform	1,000
Methylene chloride	1,000
Methanol	5,000
Methyl ethyl ketone	5,000
Methyl isobutyl ketone	5,000
Perchloroethylene	100
Phosphoric acid	5,000
Propylene oxide	100
Sulfuric acid	1,000
Toluene	1,000
Toluene diisocyanate	100
1,1,1-Trichloroethane	1,000
1,1,2-Trichloroethane	100
Trichloroethylene	100
Vinyl chloride	1
Xylene (mixed)	1,000

Source: United States Environmental Protection Agency, *Federal Environmental Regulations Potentially Affecting The Commercial Printing Industry*, EPA 744B-94-001, March 1994, Appendix D-1.

The Tier II report is intended to aid local emergency responders to identify beforehand the hazards they may face upon entering the facility in the event of a fire, spill or explosion. It is also an annual accounting of in-plant chemistry that promotes analysis for pollution prevention efforts. See figure 4–4 for a representative page prepared for the New York City Right-to-Know Law annual report.

Toxic Substance Control

Protection for printers stems from the Toxic Substances Control Act of 1976 (TSCA). The law applies to manufacturers, processors, importers, distributors, users and disposers of chemical substances and mixtures. With the internationalization of industry, particularly the printing industries, TSCA provides for the protection of the public by requiring testing and reporting of the risks to health and the environment posed by any new chemical substance or mixture. The law empowers EPA to require testing to determine potential risks to health and the environment, and provides the authority to regulate the manufacture, processing, distribution in commerce, use and disposal of these chemical substances and mixtures.

New materials must pass TSCA testing requirements.

TSCA requires that a business that imports or manufactures a new chemical substance, or processes a chemical substance for a new use, must notify the EPA at least 90 days prior to manufacture, import or processing. The business must keep records and file reports as required for specific chemicals. The records will include documentation of significant adverse reactions to health or the environment. The records provide support for the need-to-know information that will help potential users determine whether a chemical poses a substantial risk of injury to health or the environment, and whether use will mandate reporting required by the EPA.

Importers of chemical substances and mixtures are responsible for ensuring that chemical importation complies with TSCA, just as chemical manufacturers assure that domestic activities comply with the law. Printers and their suppliers who import inks and cleaning formulations are subject to inventory reporting regulations and should reference the regulations for guidance. EPA is required to compile and maintain a current list of all chemical substances manufactured or processed in the United States, based on information provided to the agency by industry.

While the TSCA regulations do not impact directly on the average printer, it provides a safety net to assure that the suppliers to the industry are taking the necessary steps to assure protection to the printer for any hazards that may be posed by the products they sell.

Revised 11/99   *Important: Read all instructions before completing form*   Reporting period: From January 1 to December 31, **1999**   Page 1 of 1 pages

NEW YORK CITY Right-to-Know FACILITY INVENTORY FORM TIER TWO

Facility Identification

Name   RTK Manufacturing Co., Inc.
Street   59-17 Junction Blvd., 3rd Floor
City   Elmhurst   State   NY   Zip+4   10068-5109   County   Queens
Telephone (718) 595-5555   Dun & Brad. Number
SIC Code   5 5 9 4

For Official Use Only: ID#   1 2   3 4 5   6 7 8 9   Date Received:

Owner/Operator

Name   Nancy Doe   Phone (212)566-7264
Mail Address   346 Broadway,   New York, NY   10013

Emergency Contacts

Name   William Clark   Title   Supervisor
Day Phone (212) 566-7264   24-hr phone (718) 587-2130
Name   George Richmond   Title   Supervisor
Day Phone (212) 566-7263   24-hr phone (718) 999-8787

Chemical Description

CAS [ ] Trade Secret
Name(s) of Chemical(s): Solvent X – 50% 2-butoxyethanol (111-76-2) 14% sodium hypochlorite (768-52-9) 10% formaldehyde (50-00-0) 0.5% benzene (71-43-2)
Check all that apply: [ ] Pure [x] Mix [ ] Solid [x] Liquid [ ] Gas [ ] EHS

CAS   8 0 0 6 6 1   9 [ ] Trade Secret
Name(s) of Chemical(s): Gasoline
Check all that apply: [ ] Pure [x] Mix [ ] Solid [x] Liquid [ ] Gas [ ] EHS

CAS [ ] Trade Secret
Name(s) of Chemical(s): Batteries – 30% Sulfuric Acid (7664-93-9)
Check all that apply: [ ] Pure [x] Mix [ ] Solid [x] Liquid [ ] Gas [ ] EHS

Physical and Health Hazards *Check all that apply*

Row 1: Fire [ ]   Sudden Release Of Pressure [ ]   Reactivity [ ]   Immediate (acute) [x]   Delayed (chronic) [x]
Row 2: Fire [x]   Sudden Release Of Pressure [x]   Reactivity [ ]   Immediate (acute) [x]   Delayed (chronic) [x]
Row 3: Fire [ ]   Sudden Release Of Pressure [ ]   Reactivity [x]   Immediate (acute) [x]   Delayed (chronic) [ ]

Inventory

Max Amount (code) 0 4   Avg. Amount (code) 0 3   No. of Days Present 3 6 5
Max Amount (code) 0 4   Avg. Amount (code) 0 4   No. of Days Present 3 6 5
Max Amount (code) 0 3   Avg. Amount (code) 0 3   No. of Days Present 3 6 5

Storage Codes and Locations (Non-Confidential) *Storage Locations*

Container / Pressure / Temperature

C 1 6   Refrigerated area, 3 holding tanks – first floor
B 1 4   Parking area – North side of building
A 1 4   Batteries – Back up power Third floor

OPTIONAL — Check box if information submitted is identical to last year: [ ], [x], [ ]

Certification (*Read and sign after completing all sections*)
I certify under penalty of law that I have personally examined and am familiar with the information submitted in pages one through 1 , and that based on my inquiry of those individuals responsible for obtaining the information, I believe that the submitted information is true, accurate and complete.

Nancy Doe, President   _____ Signature   January 6, 2000 Date signed
Name and official title of owner/operator OR owner/operator's authorized representative

OPTIONAL: I have attached a site plan [x]

Figure 4–4. Sample page from a Tier II report for a printer.
Source: NYCDEP, illustration in manual for filing Right-to-Know Facility Inventory Report.

Occupational Health and Safety

Safety and health in the workplace are primary objectives of the Occupational Health and Safety Administration (OSHA). With the use and abuse of chemicals in industry and the effects on surrounding communities, OSHA has instituted and implemented many directives and standards for the safe handling, storage and use of general categories of hazardous substances as well as some very specific guidelines for individual substances. The regulations typically outline the engineering, safeguarding and educational procedures and standards that a firm must exercise to assure the safe use of its chemicals and the safety and health of its employees. Resources are made available to properly explain the issues and consequences for both employers and employees. Among the basic chemical-related requirements for the printing industry are:

1. Hazard communication standard (right to know),

2. Indoor air pollution standards,

3. Personal protective equipment,

4. Storage requirements,

5. Standards for specific chemicals, such as those for methylene chloride.

Hazard Communication Standard

The need for better communication of health and safety risks is the major goal of this regulation. Workers are entitled to have information that will enable them to work in a safe environment and protect them from exposure to the hazardous affects of a chemical substance. This is one of the major reasons that the Hazard Communication Standard is more commonly referred to as the Right-to-Know law. The regulations set forth a few basic requirements:

1. Firms must have a written program.

2. Material Safety Data Sheets (MSDSs) must be provided by suppliers and maintained in-house for reference and use by employees.

3. All containers must be properly labeled.

4. A training program must be developed.

5. All employees must be trained in the use of the MSDS and the labels, as well as the safety rules that apply to their work and the chemicals they handle.

6. If a chemical is claimed to be proprietary, the appropriate information must be made available to a proper health official of the firm to assure that appropriate protective measures are taken.

The nature of chemicals used throughout the printing process, from start to finish, dictates that OSHA Hazard Communications training is mandatory.

A positive note for the printer is that the MSDS provides information about the inks and solvent blends that were not available to him in less-regulated times. Knowing what the components and percentages of the components are present in the inks and solvent blends that the printer uses can be a vital tool for pollution prevention and production troubleshooting. A good MSDS specifies the various solvents and percentages of each. This information can provide valuable insight as to the production and quality results influenced by drying rates of inks, fountain solutions and other chemicals used in the process.

Training is the key to safety.

Ambient Indoor Air Pollutant Standards

OSHA has established air emission standards for various chemicals, indicating the limits that are acceptable in the workplace. The limits are published for short-term exposure (15 minutes) and for eight-hour periods. The limits enable users to determine which chemicals are safer to use and to be able to decide which substances are more acceptable for use in their facilities.

Where purchasing decisions and price were made previously independent of considerations of safety issues, publication of these exposure standards in MSDSs now enables the printer to select and purchase those substances that are safer for the personnel in the facility. With the publication of the standards, the enforcement arm of OSHA looks for industry to select the safer substances and then provide engineering controls to minimize or eliminate exposure by the worker. When the controls do not exclude complete exposure, steps must be taken to provide appropriate protective equipment to the exposed workers.

Personal Protective Equipment (PPE)

The use of personal protective equipment dates back to the earliest exposure of workers to dust, moisture and chemicals. Clothing, gloves, glasses and masks have been employed to eliminate exposure to the obvious hazards of the job. OSHA has mandated that employers conduct audits of the individual jobs to determine the exposure to health and safety risks, and to provide adequate protective equipment to protect the worker (figure 4–5).

Charting the process and the input of chemicals to the process will enable management to determine exactly what exposures cannot be eliminated by engineering controls. This, is turn, will identify the need for personal protective measures. Coupled with the introduction of the protective equipment is the need for adequate training in the proper care and use of the equipment. Additional precautions and training may be required for some protective measures. An example would be the need to use respiratory masks. In addition to proper fitting and training in the use of the masks, medical examinations are required to assure that the masks themselves do not pose a problem to a worker with a history of respiratory ailments.

Figure 4–5. Protective gear to guard against injury and exposure.

Storage Standards

Storage of hazardous chemicals poses problems in plants and for the community. OSHA has published standards and guidelines for the building of chemical storage rooms, for storage and handling in areas in which flammable chemicals are to be used, as well as for hazardous waste facilities. The federal rules have been supplemented by local building and fire department regulations, as well as by insurance companies.

Other Pertinent Concerns

The broad scope of OSHA regulations covers virtually every activity in a printing plant. While not a subject of this volume, it is important for the printer not to neglect these other responsibilities. Included are:

1. Lock-out/tag out—elimination of all forms of energy when maintaining or breaking down equipment,

2. Fork lift truck training,

3. Guards on equipment,

4. Noise and noise abatement measures,

5. Grounding of flammable materials when dispensing.

The list of regulations is comprehensive and quite lengthy. Information and guidance can be found at every OSHA regional office.

Summing Up

Doing business in today's world is not simply a matter of selling, producing and shipping. Compliance with environmental and safety regulations requires that every business include these factors in its normal business policies and practices. The complications derived from the vast number of laws, and the possible conflicts when comparing what one law requires versus another, requires that due consideration be given to the multiplicity of ramifications when addressing compliance. Where any action can benefit the business by making compliance simpler with a multitude of regulations rather than just one, it should be given preference. If there is a conflict, seek advice before making a final decision. Industry associations and governmental agencies all have staff available to assist the public and industry. Consult them prior to doing anything foolish.

CHAPTER 5

Preventing Pollution by Design

The advent of environmental legislation and enforcement by federal and state engineers was followed by decades of efforts to influence industry to use end-of-pipe add-on engineering controls to reduce air emissions, water discharges and hazardous wastes that were polluting the environment. Emphasis on pollution control was placed at the end of each process. Handling, collecting and disposing of the waste streams took priority. Achieving the necessary technologies to develop compliant materials and processes to accomplish the jobs required time. There was no time available for development of appropriate printing process and chemistry technology if quick results were required. Failure to comply within a rather short time frame would potentially subject business to very substantial fines.

There were some technological alternatives, but these did not always make sense. The alternative one agency selected to solve its problem was not necessarily accepted by agencies enforcing other regulations. This was the circumstance with the substitution of 1,1,1, trichloroethane for the volatile organic compounds in liquid inks and press washes. This solvent was not classified as a VOC and thus had the potential to become a solvent that would be in compliance with the air emissions regulations. At the same time, however, 1,1,1, trichloroethane was a listed (F) hazardous waste and specified in SARA Title III 312 and 313 lists as an extremely hazardous chemical. An added deterrent was the formation of hydrochloric acid when 1,1,1, trichloroethane was subjected to heat. Many presses and pressrooms were subjected to the corrosive action of the acid on the drying systems and building structure. This solvent subsequently was targeted under the 1990 Clean Air Act as an ozone-depleting chemical and destined for complete elimination by the year 2000.

Planning ahead, industry was faced with the option of developing compliant materials and process equipment, or making more investments in add-on control equipment and living with the by-product wastes in other media. As more money was being spent on controls with relatively long life expectancies, the incentives to develop new technology alternatives became less urgent. This is evidenced not only by changes in printing and ink technology, but in the lack of development of more compact and cost-effective designs for add-on controls.

Early impetus for reducing the amount and toxicity of the wastes generated came from RCRA. Waste minimization programs were promoted, and in many states placed into law that mandated steps to reduce the amount of waste that was going to landfills and solid and hazardous waste incinerators. While stressing the same hierarchy as would subsequently be pursued as pollution prevention, these efforts were directed mainly at large quantity generators of hazardous wastes, and with no recognition of the benefits of applying the same precepts to air emissions or wastewater discharges.

Under pressure from the public to reduce the number and toxicity of chemicals in the environment, Congress enacted the Pollution Prevention Act of 1990 and developed the Pollution Prevention Strategy. The national policy to ameliorate environmental degradation was now stated under Section 6602 (b) of the Act as:

- "pollution should be prevented or reduced at the source where feasible;

- "pollution that cannot be prevented should be recycled in an environmentally safe manner where feasible;

- "pollution that cannot be prevented or recycled should be treated in an environmentally safe manner whenever feasible; and

- "disposal or other release into the environment should be employed only as a last resort and should be conducted in an environmentally safe manner."

Pollution prevention means "source reduction," as defined under the Pollution Prevention Act, and other practices that reduce or eliminate the creation of pollutants through:

- "Increased efficiency in the use of raw materials, energy, water or other resources, or

- "Protection of natural resources by conservation."

The encoding philosophy, a call for pollution prevention by Congress and the USEPA, was a sign that the federal government had come to some understanding of its need to address the problems of the environment from a more proactive, positive posture. They had come to realize that it is better to solve the problems at the beginning of the process than afterward.

There was also the realization that a more comprehensive approach to pollution can be achieved through pollution prevention. One must be concerned with the "multi-media" approach, considering all ramifications of substitutions that would eliminate pollution. This calls for a search for materials, processes and methods that produce broad benefits in achieving clean air and clean water and less solid and hazardous wastes.

Source Reduction

The highest priority for action under the hierarchy of procedures for pollution prevention is Source Reduction. This encompasses the design of the products, selection of materials, design of machinery, operating practices and procedures, maintenance, housekeeping, etc. In the hierarchy of pollution prevention, the greatest emphasis lies in doing it right the first time, stopping the generation of wastes by design and planning. (See figure 5–1.) Source reduction is another way of expressing the age-old approaches taken by industrial or manufacturing engineers to plan a new facility or addition, and to improve the performance of an existing operation or plant. Successful manufacturing facilities are based on:

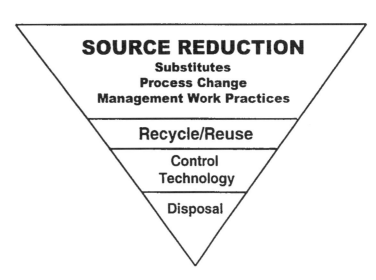

Figure 5–1. Pollution prevention hierarchy.

Source: United States Environmental Protection Agency, *Integrated Environmental Management Systems, Implementation Guide*, EPA 744-R-00-011, October 2000, p vi.

- Selection and/or design of the proper equipment,

- Use of materials and supplies that will contribute the necessary quality characteristics,

- Product performance in accordance with customer requirements, and

- Well-trained personnel with good working procedures and methods to carry out the job.

Printers have traditionally performed the same functions to improve the quality and productivity of their operations, as well as to maintain a close eye on the changes in technology that have revolutionized the way printing is conceived and transferred to paper, films and a wide variety of other materials. Within these changes are the seeds that can lead to the appropriate management of the environment and safety in the workplace. A profitable, well-managed business can only benefit by adding the improvement of the environment to its equation for success.

The Government recognized this commonality of objectives in its ongoing programs to promote pollution prevention efforts. The USEPA has conducted joint projects with the printing industry under the umbrella program, "Design for the Environment (DfE)" and in other initiatives that have come with the desire to reinvent the way the agencies do business. The programs instituted with the cooperation of leading industry associations and representatives of printers and their suppliers have endeavored to seek alternatives to process and chemistry that enable a printer to be provided with options that are safer and smarter while producing an acceptable level of product quality.

The current outlook on pollution prevention provides for a multi-media approach. Every chemical in the printing process—from design to shipment—is evaluated for its total impact on the process, the finished product and the environment, and from a total perspective of its impact on all waste streams and regulations. Selecting chemistry involves a thorough analysis of performance, economics and impact on the environment and the workplace. Once determined, the program seeks to provide tools and resources for training and retraining of personnel to cope with new developments. A great number of resources have been placed in accessible form for printers to access and use. Figure 5–2 shows the typical flow chart for the printing process activities and their interactions.

Opportunities to Reduce Pollution

Source reduction encompasses consideration of some of the basic activities of a manufacturing facility. An assessment of the three Ms of manufacturing engineering—Materials, Machinery and Manpower—will reveal the basic opportunities that are available in every segment of industry. They may be broadly defined as:

- Good operating practices,
- Technology changes,
- Input material changes,
- Product changes.

Adopting change to prevent pollution can—and should—also serve to reduce manufacturing wastes and the resulting costs of such wastes. Given the proper support by management, pollution prevention programs can parallel quality assurance efforts to improve product acceptability and profitability.

Reclamation and reuse of materials are not considered source reduction, but rather activities that can take place at the second level of the hierarchy for pollution prevention. The philosophy of recycling allows for the ability to recover pure materials from spent process wastes for reuse or to find new uses that will take the wastes of one process and channel them into a role as the raw materials for a second process.

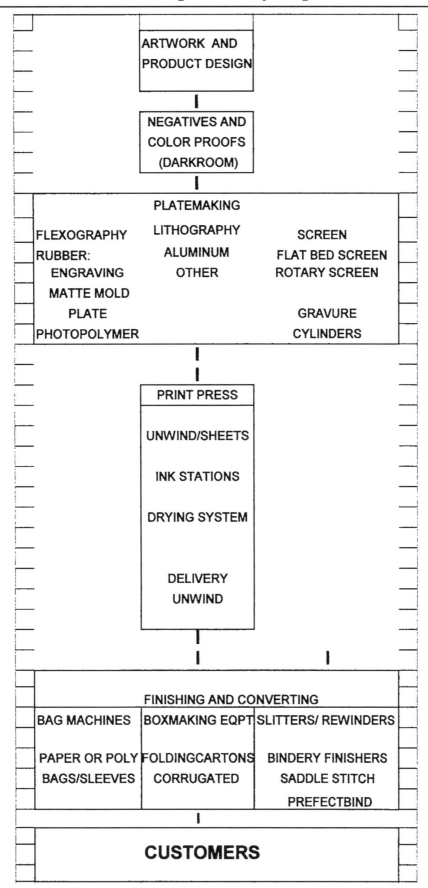

Figure 5–2. Flow chart of printing processes.

Source: P-F Technical Services Inc.

Targeting Printing Opportunities

An assessment of the operation will reveal the nature and quantities of the chemical substances and wastes in the facility. Process flow charts will place the generation of wastes at specific points in the process. Such information can be accrued during the compliance audit or from a separate audit concentrating on the process rather than on compliance issues. Brainstorming each identified problem can relate the observed end result with the possible causes. Figure 5–3 shows a typical input-output flow chart which, in this case, plots the materials that are involved in the cleaning of a printing press and the wastes that are generated.

Pollution prevention aims to identify usage that lends itself to a potential for significant reductions in toxicity and volume. There is a significant use of chemistry in just about every activity in the scenario that takes print from design to printed product. Any single project, dealing with darkroom chemistry, inks and coatings, solvents and cleaning solutions, will inevitably produce a desirable, highly visible result. All printers select and mix chemicals for a variety of prepress applications. Darkroom chemistry, platemaking, proofing are all processes that use chemicals to achieve the ultimate goal of providing an image carrier that will transfer a quality image on the printing press. Computer hardware and software play critical roles in finding non-chemical alternatives to ages-old practices.

Figure 5–3. Input-output diagram for cleaning a press.

Source: United States Environmental Protection Agency, *Integrated Environmental Management Systems, Implementation Guide*, EPA 744-R-00-011, October 2000, p 19.

Gravure and flexographic printing have a considerable impact on the environment, based on their use of engraved cylinders and plates, rubber and photopolymer printing plates, liquid inks and hydrocarbon solvents, as well as a broad range of paper, film and foil substrates. Many opportunities arise from the substitution of current hazardous chemicals for safer alternatives. Waterborne inks and coatings have made great inroads in both gravure and flexographic facilities. The use of UV curable inks and coatings is attaining more recognition and greater acceptability, particularly among narrow and mid-web press users. Less hazardous washout solvents for processing photopolymer plates, laser engraved anilox rolls and chambered doctor blade units all contribute simultaneously to superior product quality and a safer environment in a flexographic plant. Chambered blade systems have also found a place in the gravure plant, as has the use of photopolymer surfaces for exposing and etching the engraved image on the gravure cylinder (figure 5–4).

Figure 5–4. Chambered doctor blade system on a coating machine.

Courtesy of Deneka Printing Systems, Inc.

Lithographic presses employ fountain solutions to facilitate the proper transfer of paste inks from the printing plate to the sheets or web fed paper and paperboard stock. Alcohol-free fountain solutions, aqueous platemaking chemistry, less volatile press washes, and soy oil inks are key areas for source reduction (figure 5–5).

Screen printing inks are liquid and vary in volatile organic compounds based on application. Some applications require extremely high volumes of solvent, while the plasticizer inks for textiles have negligible

Figure 5–5. Lithographic printing press at Contemporary Color Graphics.

amounts of solvent. Changes in equipment and composition of solvent blends play a major role in reducing the quantity and toxicity of solvents and the resulting hazardous wastes normally encountered in the cleaning of screens (figure 5–6).

Cleaning solvents and blends are by far the greatest contributors to environmental concerns for all printing processes. Ranging from very safe aqueous cleaning solutions to solvents such as methylene chloride, MEK and toluene, cleaning is a major factor in air emissions, hazardous waste generation, and discharge of wastewater to sewer systems or off-site treatment centers. New cleaning solvents and changes in operating practices, when cleaning ink and coatings off plates and machinery, can add up to considerable reductions in usage and waste.

Process waters are discharged from darkrooms, cleaning tanks and cooling systems. Waterbase inks and coatings may result in clean-up wastes that are unacceptable for discharge to sewers and definitely are unacceptable for discharge to septic tanks. Adhesives used in converting may also contribute wastes that find their way into the water discharges. Silver halides in darkroom chemistry require best management practices to remove silver from the aqueous wastes. While post-treatment can reduce the toxicity of these water wastes and allow for discharge to sewer system treatment plants, in areas where wastes are discharged to septic tanks or natural waterways, the treated waste must still be carted off for further treatment off-site. Such wastes can be classified and labeled as non-regulated wastes, not subject to the RCRA regulations or threshold for determining the category of generator.

Figure 5–6. Screen printing.

Pollution prevention assessments make use of the same tools as are available for auditing and appraising the compliance of the facility. Material Safety Data Sheets, flow charts and mass balances help to put a face on the process of going from raw materials to products and wastes. Figure 5–7 shows a more detailed flow chart, illustrating the general flow of materials to the different stages of the printing process and illustrating the wastes that are generated from each incoming substance. The waste streams attest to the need for a management program for research and development of alternatives to current printing chemistry and equipment for the purpose of reducing pollution.

Water Ink Technology

Water-base inks are now accepted in flexographic and gravure facilities for printing on paper, film and foils. Progress had long been stymied by the preferred governmental definition of emissions control, and the early introduction of thermal and catalytic add-on controls by the larger firms in the printing industry. The policies prevalent for the first 20 years of governmental regulation leaned heavily toward end-of-pipe controls. The result is a situation that will continue as long as the market specifies a preference for solvent-based ink quality and productivity. As long as enforcement was directed at larger firms, which have elected to use thermal or catalytic incinerators, there had been little need to develop more universal and effective systems in waterborne or other ink technology.

However, spurred by regulatory pressures in California and overseas, and adopted as the wave of the future by other states, waterborne inks have been improved and have found their way beyond printing on paper into the mainstream of film and foil printing. Challenges to waterborne inks and coatings come from specific end-use quality performance characteristics rather than from the broad assumption that "water won't work."

The rationale for flexographic and gravure package printers to use water inks has many facets, all of which improve environmental performance and have the potential to add considerably to the profitability of the printing firm. Pound for pound, more substrate can be printed with waterborne inks under current air regulations, within a specified level of air emissions, than by solvent inks. Compliance will enable the printer to ship more product per ton of VOC emissions than if the ink was based on solvent formulations. At the same time, other environmental regulations will either be addressed or become inconsequential. Storage regulations, hazardous waste disposal, OSHA requirements—all may become moot with the switch to water. The added benefit will be lower costs of compliance.

Because water inks require little in the way of solvents to dilute the formulations at press-side, and with the ability to clean using aqueous products, adopting water ink technology as a compliance technique will also enable the printer to deliver more product within the same permit parameters. Given the volume of VOCs that can be emitted to the air, and working backward using the prevalent percentages of solvents in the inks and the elimination of

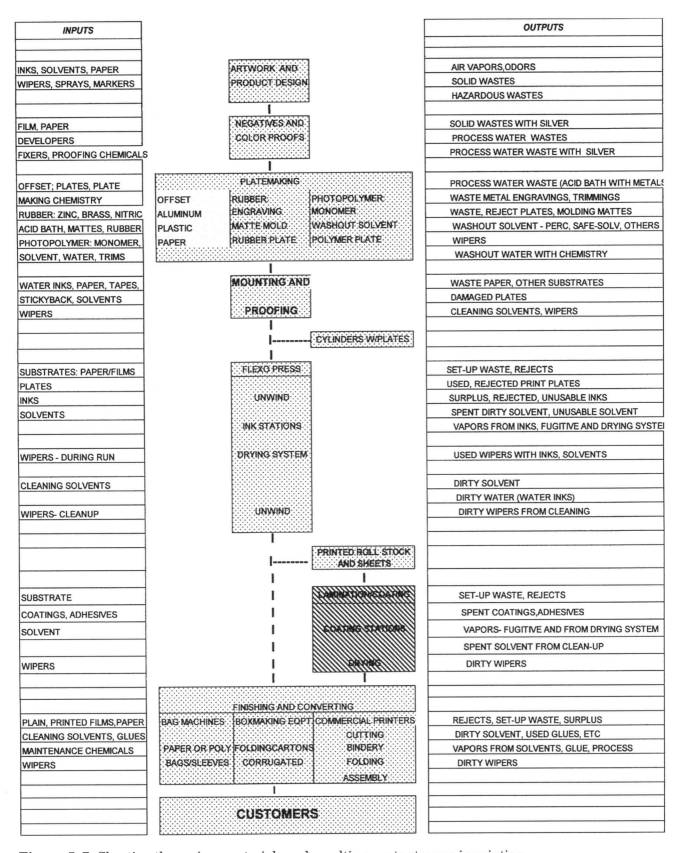

Figure 5–7. Charting the various materials and resulting waste streams in printing.
Source: P-F Technical Services Inc.

a heavy burden of solvent for dilution and cleaning, it is evident that the printer will be able to use considerably more ink with water than with solvent. More ink relates to more printed matter. This, in turn, relates to increased sales, lower costs and greater profit. Tables 5–1 and 5–2 illustrate the difference in gallons of ink that may be used within the same emissions categories for solvent- and water-base ink technologies. The tables were developed for the work sessions of the Printing Sector working committee of the Common Sense Initiative that was developing a template for a multi-media facility permit for printers. It is modeled on the translator tables that were used for the Massachusetts Printers Partnership program.

Considerable work remains for water to become the standard. This involves efforts to engineer more films that are tailored for the wetting out and adhesion of water inks. Research efforts have to find and make more universal resins and additives to films that will enhance the use of waterborne technology. Equipment manufacturers must develop inking and drying systems that can better transfer waterborne inks and remove all volatile components. Cleaning systems are needed which will facilitate the removal of dried water ink components and extend the life of anilox rolls and doctor blade systems.

Alcohol-free Fountain Solutions

A major target of the enforcement agencies is lithographic shops that use fountain solutions that have isopropyl alcohol (IPA) as a major component. Standards dictate just how much can be used, yet the method of testing is not sufficiently accurate to meet such standards. Method 24, the standard chosen by the EPA, is designed for coatings and solvents. Water content requires a more complex computation than a simple laboratory test and is fraught with errors.

Alcohol serves a very valuable purpose in wetting the plate with water to prevent the transfer of inks from those areas of the image carrier that will not transfer ink to the substrate. During hot and humid weather, IPA has become a favorite tool to facilitate the transfer of inks. Historic experience does not sit well with the standards for air emissions control. Typically, the IPA has represented over 25 percent of the fountain solution.

Substitutes have been offered to replace the IPA. Some work well; some do not. Culture plays a role as the effort is made to change the habits of years in approaching press chemistry. There has been considerable success at the same time, yet there still remain some misconceptions in the pressroom.

The change in chemistry has generated a modification in the design of the transfer system. Rubber rollers, which meter the fountain solution, have had to be substituted for rollers with different hardness and solvent resistance characteristics. Some suppliers opt for harder rolls, some for softer. There are various chemistries in use; it is best to follow the advice offered by the equipment supplier.

Caution must also be taken to not create a new situation in which the chemistry will be worse than that with the use of IPA. Earlier alternatives included ethylene glycol and glycol ethers.

TABLE 5–1. PERMIT THRESHOLD TRANSLATOR FOR SOLVENT AND WATERBORNE INKS
(Waterborne inks are assumed to be at RACT level, 25% VOCS)

Material Use Air Level Table for VOCs - "Counties C and D"

Sheetfed Offset or Nonheatset Web Lithography, or Screen Printing	Heatset Web Offset Lithography (uncontrolled), or Flexography or Rotogravure with solvent-based inks	Flexography or Rotogravure with water-based inks*		Air Level
less than 1,425 gals	less than 10,000 lbs	less than 40,000 lbs	→	Level 1
1,425 - 3,560 gals	10,000 - 25,500 lbs	40,000 - 100,000 lbs	→	Level 2
3,560 - 7,125 gals	25,500 - 50,000 lbs	100,000 - 200,000 lbs	→	Level 3
7,125 - 14,250 gals	50,000 - 100,000 lbs	200,000 - 400,000 lbs	→	Level 4
more than 14,250 gals	more than 100,000 lbs	more than 400,000 lbs	→	Level 5

* A water-based ink contains no more than 25% of the volatile fraction as VOCs.

Source: United States Environmental Protection Agency, *PrintSTEP Pilot Program, Plain Language Workbook Template*, Common Sense Initiative Printing Sector, April 1999, p A-2.

TABLE 5–2. PERMIT THRESHOLD TRANSLATOR FOR WATERBORNE INKS
(Solvent content of inks available in market is assumed to be 5%.)

CSI TRANSLATOR TABLES FOR FLEXOGRAPHY							
WATERBORNE INKS			(5% VOC'S)				
	EXTREME	SEVERE	SERIOUS	MODERATE	ATTAINMENT		PERMIT
	10 tons	25 tons	50 tons	100 tons			
							CATEGORY
	less than	more than	more than	more than	more than		
	40,600	101,500	203,000	304,500	406,000		FACILITY
Total Gallons							TITLE V
Inks							
Coatings							
Solvents							
Diluent	20,300	50,750	101,500	152,250	203,000		STATE
Cleanup							FESOP
	10,150	25,375	50,750	76,125	101,500		STATE
							CERTIFICATION
	5,075	12,688	25,375	38,063	50,750		REGISTRATION
	4,060	10,150	20,300	30,450	40,600		EXEMPT

Source: P-F Technical Services Inc., developed by the author for presentation to USEPA Common Sense Initiative PrintSTEP Working Group, to demonstrate increased sales volume possible with water ink technology under the similar air emissions permit.

Some contained butyl cellosolve. While these chemicals may be present in small quantities, the alternative chemistry can pose health hazards for plant operating personnel and for the neighboring community. Sample components of "alcohol-free" fountain solutions are illustrated in figure 5–8.

SECTION 1: PRODUCT INFORMATION
Product Name: **MILLENNIUM** (Universal Fountain Solution)
D.O.T. Designation: Cleaning Liquid. Not Regulated.
U.N. Designation: Same as D.O.T.

SECTION 2: HAZARDOUS COMPONENTS/IDENTITY INFORMATION

HAZARDOUS COMPONENT	CAS No.	% WT.	OSHA PEL	ACGIH TLV-TWA	OTHER RATINGS	OSHA STEL
Propylene Glycol	57-55-6	1-2			50ppm(AIHA)	
Dipropylene Glycol Monomethyl Ether	34590-94-8	2-6	100ppm			150ppm
Glyceritol	56-81-5	2-6	10mg/m3 5mg/m3(respirable)	10mg/m3		

SECTION 3: PHYSICAL/CHEMICAL CHARACTERISTICS
Boiling Point: 212 degrees F.
Specific Gravity: (Water = 1) 1.01
Vapor Pressure: (mmHG, calculated) None
Melting Point: N/A
Vapor Density: (Air = 1, calculated) 2
Solubility in Water: Complete
pH of Concentrate: 3.8-4.2
Appearance & Odor: Blue liquid, detergent odor.
Maximum VOC Content: .3 lbs. per gal. (40 grams per liter)
Maximum VOC% :   4%

Figure 5–8. A representative alcohol-free fountain solution formulation.
Courtesy of Tower Products, Inc.

Concerns about quality were some of the early obstacles. However, the work produced and offered for consideration in a number of printing exhibitions offer good reason to believe that with diligence, high level, top quality process printing can be achieved using alcohol-free substitutes.

Recirculation and refrigeration have also played a role in extending the life of fountain solutions and reducing air emissions. Recirculation systems will normally include filters that remove lint, dried ink particles and other solid matter from the solution, enabling continued use of the fountain solution for a longer period of time. Lowering the temperature of the solution reduces the evaporation rate of the IPA and other volatile solvents in the formulation, with the added benefit of extending the usability of the fountain solution.

emoving liquid and dried inks from rollers and parts of or adjacent to the ink transfer system and from the image carriers in each of the printing process requires a considerable quantity of solvents, blends of various solvents and cleaners and other cleaning formulations. This cleaning effort is by far the most significant contributor to both air emissions and hazardous waste in most facilities. Pollution prevention efforts should concentrate on reducing the exposure due to cleaning solvent in four major areas:

Housekeeping and Maintenance

1. Seeking alternative, safer cleaning chemicals (See figure 5–9.),

2. Seeking mechanical improvements or devices at the presses to minimize use while operating the presses, and off-press preventive maintenance techniques to improve cleaning with minimal use of chemicals,

3. Modifying the methods that are used by employees to clean plates and press parts,

4. Training of employees to gain acceptance to change and the use of new, different materials and equipment.

Every segment of the printing industry uses inks, coatings and adhesives that adhere to plates, blankets, rollers, dies and other components of the press and finishing equipment. Aggressive cleaners are frequently needed to remove the accumulated substances, many times on or in components that are critical to the transfer of measured amounts of ink to the image carriers and the substrates. Changes in on-press cleaning techniques facilitate productive operating conditions.

Off-press cleaning, directed at preventive maintenance, can frequently require machinery that enhances the cleaning ability using somewhat less traditional approaches. Use of cleaning tanks with caustic sodas or safer, high-boiling-point solvents, aided by ultrasonic waves or high-pressure air, improves cleaning. Supplies of adequate spare pumps, ink pans and reservoirs, as well as other press components, will minimize clean-up waste and presstime losses during clean-up. Use of smaller size wipers or spray bottles can minimize the amount of solvents required to do a clean-up.

Preventive maintenance programs can lead to less wear of the press and related prepress equipment and a reduction in unacceptable product quality. At the same time, preventive maintenance provides for excellent opportunities for reducing the impact of the facility on the local community resources and the environment.

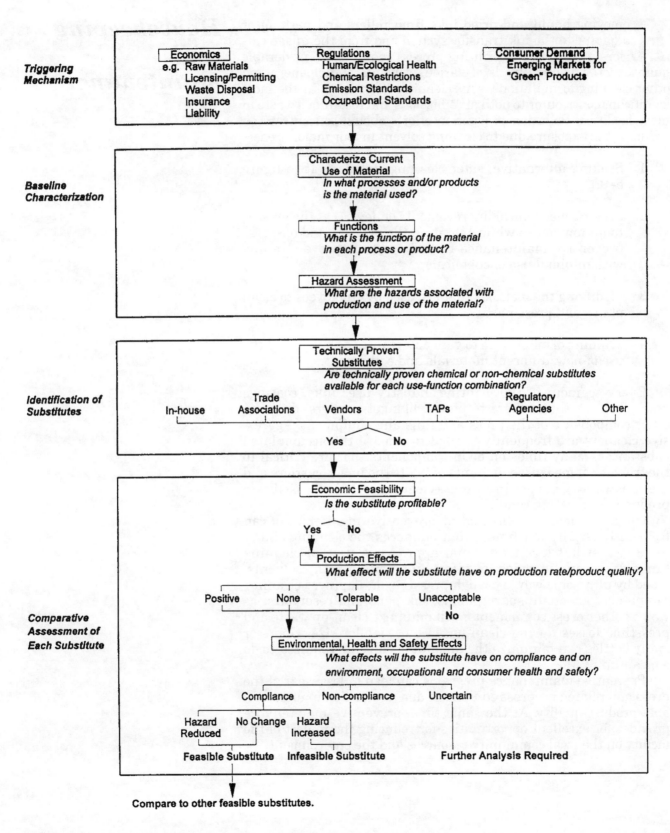

Figure 5–9. Decision framework for chemical substitution analysis.

Source: Karen Shapiro, Rebecca Little and Allen White, "To Switch or Not To Switch: A Decision Framework for Chemical Substitution," *Pollution Prevention Review*, Volume 4, Number 1, Winter 1993/94, p 4.

reative thinking can lead to innovative approaches and the development of equipment that meet the criteria of source reduction and pollution prevention. Departing from the tried and true methods dictated by custom, it is possible to approach a problem and develop solutions utilizing knowledge of processes in other industries. Many situations that are defined as typical of printing have their parallels in other industries. Utilizing lessons learned in other industries can bring innovative solutions to areas which printing and other industries have in common, and that can contribute to the amelioration of the environmental exposures of the printer.

One such development in doctor blade technology for flexographic printers meets all the objectives and criteria for pollution

Creativity and Innovation Make a Difference: The Self-Cleaning Chambered Doctor Blade System

prevention and environmental responsibility, simultaneously with the attainment of top quality output and high productivity levels. Achieving high quality on a flexographic press is a direct result of the controlled transfer of ink from the ink container to the substrate. Process printing, 100-percent coatings, as well as standard line copy, all benefit from consistent control of ink transfer. The average two-roll system with its ink fountain, fountain roller and anilox roll is a veritable open reservoir, exposing large quantities of solvents that readily evaporate. What does not evaporate into the pressroom and adjacent areas is emitted by the drying system through exhaust stacks to the community. Considerable hazardous waste is generated in the process. The average flexographic facility purchases solvents in quantities that can be three to four times the amount of ink that is used.

The chambered doctor blade puts a halt to this evaporation. Ink enters the chamber from the reservoir or ink can, moved through by a pump which maintains a constant flow. The ink is held in the manifold area with only a small area exposed to the anilox roll. A doctor blade is positioned to shear off the excess ink as the anilox roll turns, returning all excess ink to the chamber. A second plastic or metal blade retains the ink within the chamber. At each end of the chamber is a seal, which acts as a dam to contain the liquid ink. These close off the chamber completely. The seals ride on a smooth surface at the ends of the anilox roll to assure that the ink does not spread beyond the width of the unit or is ejected onto the printing cylinder or impression drum (figure 5–10).

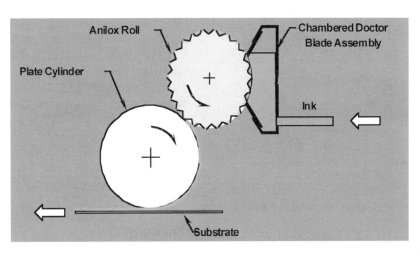

Figure 5–10. Cross-section of chambered doctor blade system.
Courtesy of Harris and Bruno Machine Company.

Figure 5–11. Built-in high pressure cleaning jets in chambered doctor blade system.
Courtesy of FIT—Flexographic Inking Technologies.

Anilox roll technology has advanced to accommodate the wear of the doctor blade. The copper-chrome-plated surfaces on steel rolls have been replaced by laser engraved ceramic surfaces. With this tough, abrasive surface, the doctor blades become an expendable component, intended to wear out, while the life of the engraved anilox roller is lengthened considerably. Coupled with the new surface material has been a move to smaller volume cells to carry a more concentrated, higher solids ink in finer bits. The higher solids inks reduce the amount of solvent or water required to transfer the inks through the ink train system, enabling the use of shallower cells in the anilox roller engraving design.

An innovative feature of the new chamber blade unit has been the design of a cleaning system into the bed of the chamber. Pressurized air directs a blast of cleaner into the anilox cells to remove any dried or partially dried ink remnants (figure 5–11). When the job is completed, ink is allowed to drain from the chamber and cleaning solution is injected. The pressurized jets then do their job.

Through use of the chambered doctor blade system and the cleaning related improvements, air emissions have been sharply curtailed, and the amount of hazardous waste generated in cleaning has been drastically reduced. A research project conducted at the USEPA's Research Triangle center estimated a reduction in the use of solvent, and the ensuing emissions, of 50 percent The project was undertaken as part of ongoing research and development into printing technology for pollution prevention. The final report was published in April 1998: "Fugitive emission reductions due to the use of the enclosed doctor blade systems in the flexographic and rotogravure printing industries," EPA-600/R-98-050.

The chamber has introduced a press component that embodies all the principles of pollution prevention. The system will meter the ink at a measured rate and provide predictability and consistency in printing high-quality process graphics. The decreased use of solvents and the restrictions placed on evaporation by the design of the chamber system have helped to reduce emissions significantly. High quality has been attained at the same time that ingenuity has resulted in a positive effort toward pollution prevention. With the proven success in flexography as a guide, some gravure printers have adapted the chamber doctor blade system for their presses.

The Role of Substrates in the Printing Environment: Boon or Barrier to Pollution Prevention?

In the rush to find compliant inks and coatings, much attention has been devoted to addressing shortcomings in the surface of the substrate to improve wetting out and adhesion. The appearance of the graphics is tantamount, including an overwhelming but questionable emphasis on gloss. Inkmakers have been deluged with demands to change formulations to accomplish these objectives. But what good are graphics if the package doesn't perform to quality standards that are acceptable to the customer or the ultimate consumer?

Surely more of the effort to come into compliance with the use of alternatives to the current solvents must dwell on the nature of the nonabsorbent substrates, the demands on the products, and how materials suppliers can develop new substrates that provide printing surfaces for the graphics as well as physical performance capabilities for the product. Problems encountered with the various ink alternatives—water, UV curable or substitute safer solvents—are very similar. Corona or flame treatment helps to increase the surface energy of film substrates, but certainly is not completely efficient when heavier doses of slip agent or additives, such as ethyl vinyl acetate (EVA), in the film bloom to the surface of plastics. Figure 5–12 illustrates the relative performance of water inks compared to solvent ink on a variety of substrates.

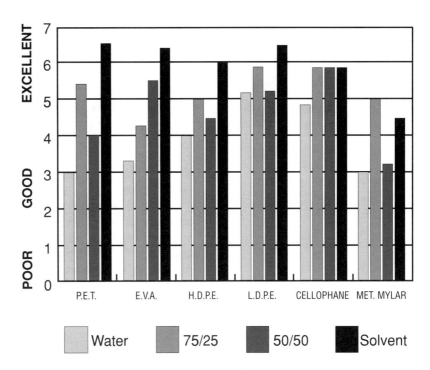

Figure 5–12. Relative performance of water and solvent inks with various films during trials with Brooklyn, NY converters.

Source: P-F Technical Services, Inc., SEP project at Supreme Poly Products; results published in *American Ink Maker*, November 1996, pp 34–43.

Coatings can play an important role in providing a more receptive foundation to which water and UV curable inks can anchor. Absorbent surfaces suck in water or UV inks, dulling their appearance and negating some of the benefits of the alternatives. In these instances, appropriate coatings are used to seal the surface and hold out the ink or coating. Water-friendly coatings can enhance the use of compliant alternatives to solvent inks that are now used to provide a glossier, stronger color. This approach applies to films as well where coatings are applied to facilitate printing and other performance requirements.

The answer has to be in spending more development time in such areas of substrate design as will benefit the printer and his customer and produce benefits for the environment. These efforts are taking place in many arenas, but not at a pace adequate for the needs of the industry or with any relationship to the benefits to the environment. One of the means to this end would be the development of new polymers or modifications of existing polymers that would be more receptive to ink alternatives. This would include the basic resins and pigments as well as additives that pose problems for printers.

The other approach would be the use of coatings or finishes that are more receptive and enhancing with alternative ink and coating systems. A number of film suppliers do have some products that are coated for use with water inks. More are needed that will provide the converter with substrates that can deliver specific and desirable physical and chemical requirements.

EVA Films: A Case in Point

Converters of plastic bags or roll stock for the packaging of ice, frozen foods and products that require exceptional strength have found a solution in the low density polyethylene films with EVA content percentages varied to accomplish specific protective features. EVA films are noted for blooming of the additive to the surface of the film, sometimes making it appear as if a layer of oil is covering the surface. The EVA provides stretch and burst strength characteristics that allow for the packaging, transportation and display on shelves, in bins or refrigerated displays of a wide variety of foods. Without the EVA content, the polyethylene packages could not withstand the packaging or handling pressures.

EVA films will not readily accept water-based inks with the same degree of success as with solvent-based inks. Most efforts to use water have been negated by the withdrawal of product liability for these applications by the ink suppliers. Ice or low temperature are immediate barriers to the use of water inks because both are based on EVA films or coextrusions which use the EVA layer as its outer component.

A water ink development project conducted in 1995 in Brooklyn, New York, provided clear evidence that EVA films available at that time could not produce an acceptable surface for use with waterborne inks of that period. The trials took standard water inks with normal amounts of VOCs and measured the effectiveness of the straight water formulation against a solvent-based ink. Alcohol was then added in two different, increasing, amounts to see if the added solvents would improve performance. While adding a small amount of alcohol to the virgin ink helped improve the performance, as measured by end-use lab tests, the improvements were insufficient to make water ink an acceptable alternative. The project was sponsored by the Industrial Technology Assistance Corporation in cooperation with the USEPA, with funding provided by NIST (National Institute of Science and Technology). The study, which ultimately enabled the participants to adopt water technology, resulted in guidelines for the successful use of waterborne inks. The project, using a variety of films, also served to identify limitations that were barriers to the use of water (figure 5–13).

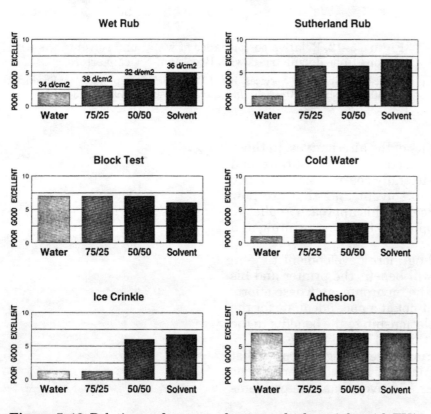

Figure 5–13. Relative performance of water and solvent inks with EVA films during SEP project at Supreme Poly Products, Brooklyn, NY.

Source: P-F Technical Services Inc., results published in *American InkMaker*, November 1996, pp 34–43.

The project led to the experimentation with different resins that were developed for strength characteristics and, coincidentally, had good slip characteristics without the need for slip additives. The key to selection of the new resins was their targeted objective—to replace the EVA films now in use. Water inks embraced the new films and endured under the stringent quality tests to which the EVA films had to be subjected. At the time of the trials, success was limited by other factors in the appearance or the processing of the new resins into film. The point was made that water could work better with appropriate engineering of the film substrates.

Metallocenes to the Rescue

During the latter part of 1995, polyolefin suppliers promoted a new process for producing polyethylene and polypropylene resins for films. The products are known as metallocenes. The name metallocene refers to the catalytic process by which the resin is produced. Dow, Exxon and Union Carbide were the three producers who, at that time, had developed the new resins. The resins can be extruded into film with the same basic equipment as is used for high-pressure, low-density polyethylene. Propylene resins have also been produced for sale in the marketplace. The combination of molecular weight, molecular weight distribution and density provides superior toughness compared to liner grade high-pressure, low-density polyethylene. Tensile strength, tear strength and dart impact strength are all superior. The films contain very low levels of extractable components, such as waxes, minimizing the amount that will exude to the surface of the film and interfere with printing. The lower wax levels reduce slip and antiblock additive requirements as compared to traditional poly-olefins. The films were targeted for marketplaces such as frozen food packaging. This is one of the major problem areas presently for printers trying to use water inks.

The new films, potentially, sound like the answer to the dilemma created by the need for an EVA film. Its properties lie in its strength, particularly for those markets in which EVA has taken the dominant position. Presentations at plastics industry forums have stated that the films will take the place of traditional films used in the marketplace where EVAs play a large role. Sample trials were conducted to see if this film could fill the void and result in benefits to the customer as well as help comply with government environmental requirements. The materials tested were extruded in two formats: one film was a straight extrusion of the metal-locenes; the second was a 50/50 blend with a linear low-density polyethylene. Waterborne inks adhered well to the treated version of the metallocene with considerable aggressiveness. Placed through two different presses, the inks adhered extremely well on the treated surfaces (figure 5–14).

Of concern for the extruder and the printer/converter was the question of machineability in the pre- and post-printing processes. Would the pure resin perform on existing equipment? Extrusion with the pure resin was a problem. The pressure that built up in the extruder was too great. A blend was preferable. But what should that blend be and who would do the blending? Bag machine performance indicated that adjustments would have to be made to accommodate this new, tougher film. Attachments and heat-sealing equipment that was adequate for normal polyethylene would not perform well because of the physical attributes of the new films. The very qualities that enabled the new resins to replace existing films proved to be challenges to standard equipment and practices. But these are not insurmountable obstacles.

Further development is needed in the area of substrates and in converting technology. If the premise is realistic, then an entirely new approach can be taken to bring compliance, via technology, into products that currently demand the use of solvent-based technology.

Coatings Can Offer Relief

In the early years of water inks, when the quality was far from the level now available, some firms resorted to the use of water coatings as a preliminary stage to printing. This approach can be very helpful in addressing substrates that are hard to print, but necessary for the package design plastics. Such coatings can enable the inks to adhere to the coating rather than to the surface of the film. This removes the need for concern about film treatment levels and stability. It also eliminates the impact of additives on the inks.

Biaxially oriented propylene films and coextrusions, as well as cellophane, come with a variety of coatings or exterior extrusion coatings. These provide physical and chemical barrier properties. There is no reason why they cannot be developed further, to provide surfaces that are more receptive to alternative ink systems.

Figure 5–14. Representatives from Dow Chemical during extrusion of metallocene films at Supreme Poly Products for pollution prevention project with waterborne inks.

The metallocenes may well present such an opportunity in these multilayer films as well as in blown or cast copolymer films.

Financial justification of proposals that will institute new management programs or procure equipment is done by evaluating the return on investment. Typical expenditures for enhancement of product productivity and quality can be defined within the normal parameters in which a business operates. Environmental investments, to the contrary, must be analyzed and evaluated in terms, both tangible and intangible, that are outside the normal realm of return on investment computations.

Pollution prevention projects require consideration of the costs of being in compliance with the law as well as the intangible potential costs of non-compliance. Permits, records, reports and operating procedures are essential elements of environmental management. Treatment or recycling equipment, whether in-line in the process or as add-on controls coping with waste products, is costly to acquire and to operate. Many companies find the need to retain consultants, engineers and attorneys to prepare, review and represent them in the many transactions or the inevitable confrontations. Each has a cost associated with its services. Non-compliance can bring penalties, conferences and legal proceedings that must be paid for. Penalties are usually paid from post-tax earnings. Off-site services add to the cost of generating wastes. The graph in figure 5–15 illustrates the relative impacts of generating waste, conducting waste pollution programs, and disposing of the waste.

In a formal pollution prevention evaluation, each of the identifiable environmental costs is assessed and allocated to product costs. When this is not possible using normal procedures, it is critical that judgments be made to identify and allocate such costs to obtain a truer picture of what the manufacturing cost is, and thence the true profitability realized in the manufacture and sale of the product.

Among the costs to be considered are:

1. Engineering and consultants' fees to maintain compliance,

2. Permit applications and renewal fees,

3. Testing of substances, wastes and control equipment,

4. Training programs,

Economics of Pollution Prevention

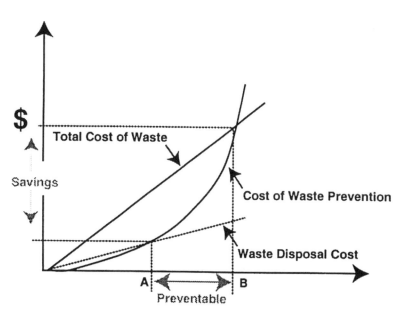

Figure 5–15. Total cost of waste generation versus cost of waste disposal only.

Source: Charles Czarnecki, Kevin F. O'Donnell and Jerry R. Perrich, "Calculating the True Cost of Waste," *Pollution Prevention Review*, Volume 7, Number 1, Winter 1997, p 119.

5. Environmental management and contingency plan,

6. Pollution insurance,

7. Maintenance of any equipment associated with the generation or control of chemicals in the process,

8. Fees to dispose of wastes, both hazardous and non-hazardous,

9. Lab fees to test wastes,

10. In-house treatment or pollution-control equipment—both acquisition and operational costs,

11. Legal fees,

12. The unpredictable cost of being out of compliance and being served a notice of violation—legal and consulting fees and government fines.

13. Penalties for not doing the right thing.

This in-depth analysis can provide justification at such times as the evaluation based on a typical ROI study (Table 5–3) would fail to properly warrant a purchase that has benefits only for environmental compliance. Rather, it is the intention of the advocates of pollution prevention to use the potential cost of non-compliance to demonstrate more fully the benefit of taking the environmentally responsible high road.

Strategy for Success

Making changes in an established operation can frequently end in failure. People have to be conditioned to change and have to be involved in the process that is being changed. Therefore, it is essential to approach pollution prevention programs in the same manner that one institutes a quality management program. Inclusion and solicitation of employee participation will be critical to success. While the common knowledge would recommend that the initial project should address the item that will result in the greatest reward, it is suggested that the first project be one that is manageable and sure to succeed. There is nothing better to build confidence than a success story.

Select a waste stream that lends itself to a quick resolution. Determine which problem has the circumstances with which analysis and evaluation of the problem and selection of a solution can readily be identified. Include all personnel in the process of identifying this problem, observing and researching the reasons for the problem, and recommending the solution(s.) Advertise the goal of the project in the plant, bringing into the process all employees who have ideas and opinions. The more participation, the better the receptivity to change.

Meeting to review results of project.

TABLE 5–3. RETURN ON INVESTMENT WORKSHEET

ROI WORKSHEET   PRIME FLEXIBLE PACKAGING LTD. (50% REDUCATION)

A. SAVINGS DUE TO REDUCTION IN WASTE

MATERIAL COST

CURRENT WASTE PERCENTAGE *(printing and converting)*	25.00%	%
CURRENT WASTE PERCENTAGE *(attributable to printing)*	10.00%	%

ANNUAL MATERIAL PURCHASES	5000000	pounds/footage
AMOUNT PRINTING WASTE GENERATED	500000	pounds/footage
COST OF MATERIAL PURCHASED	$0.75	per pound/m feet
ANNUAL COST OF WASTE MATERIAL	(amount waste x cost)	$375,000.00

PROCESSING COSTS

AMOUNT OF WASTE (POUNDS/FOOTAGE)	*PRESS*	500000	
(50% OF WASTE AFTER PRESS)	*CONVERT*	375000	
RATES TO PROCESS WASTE	*PRINTING*	700	lbs/hour
	CONVERTING	300	lbs/hour
TIME TO PROCESS WASTE	*PRINTING*	714	hours
	CONVERTING	1250	hours
MACHINE RATES FOR ESTIMATING	*PRINTING*	$400.00	
	CONVERTING	$150.00	

COST TO PROCESS WASTE	*PRINTING*	$285,714.29
	CONVERTING	$187,500.00

COST OF LABOR AND OVERHEAD DUE TO WASTE	$473,214.29

TOTAL COST - MATERIALS, LABOR & OVERHEAD	$848,214.29

B ANTICIPATED SAVINGS FROM EQUIPMENT MODIFICATION

PERCENTAGE REDUCTION IN WASTE	50%	%
AMOUNT OF WASTE SAVED (POUNDS/FEET)	437500	pounds
DOLLAR VALUE OF WASTE MATERIAL SAVED		$328,125.00

TIME SAVED THROUGH REDUCTION IN WASTE

TIME TO PROCESS WASTE (POUNDS OR FEET/HOUR)

	PRINTING	CONVERTING	TOTALS
HOURS SAVED	625	1458	2083
MACHINE COSTS	250000	218750	468750

LABOR & OVERHEAD SAVED WITH WASTE REDUCTION	$468,750.00

TOTAL SAVINGS - MATERIALS, LABOR & OVERHEAD	$796,875.00

C COST OF MACHINE MODIFICATION   2 UNITS $500,000.00

ROI (COST OF MODIFICATION VERSUS SAVINGS PER YEAR)	0.627
	year

Source: P-F Technical Services Inc., developed by author for client to demonstrate payback with waste reduction from installation of new equipment.

With a fairly limited project and objective, the need and the ability to overcome problems should be transparent. Finding the causes and identifying solutions should be readily apparent to most, if not all, participants. Moving from problem to solution should be possible in a short period of time. Success should be realized and the results obvious.

Happy environment.

Then promote the resolution of the problem and the results as a team effort. Praise the participants and recognize their contributions. There is nothing more satisfying to the average worker than the gratification of having one's work appreciated. In a formal program, this gratification can also be expressed by tangible rewards, financial or otherwise. Having succeeded in a single problem, the step up to that major problem will be on a road paved by the satisfaction of success and accomplishment.

Pollution prevention works. It can work for anyone who approaches a problem with an open mind, a keen sense of knowing what is happening in the technology, and the enthusiasm to face change and remove obstacles as they arise. Pollution prevention can bring you into a posture of environmental management that includes the profitability of the business.

CHAPTER **6**

Process Chemistry: The Foundation of Printing and Source of Printers' Environmental Concerns

The basic process chemistry in printing is very simple. Transfer colors from a design to paper or to other materials through the medium of a printing press and you are able to communicate ideas or sell products. The means to that end, however, involves the use of a variety of chemicals.

Once printed, the printed materials are subjected to finishing and converting operations. Some processes, such as coating and laminating, will add decorative or protective surface coatings or adhesive coatings to the printed substrate. Folding carton or corrugated boxmaking will use adhesives for joining of parts. Some coatings may serve as a means of closure for flexible packaging. Chemistry does the job here too.

Which chemicals and what quantities will be used depend on the materials to be printed, the process by which that printing will be accomplished, the process used for finishing and converting, as well as the end-use characteristics that are expected of the finished product. Make no mistake, there will be chemicals. And with the need for chemicals, there must be a concern for the use and disposition of the various substances and formulations before, during and after the printing process takes place. The corollary holds true for the chemicals entering the printing and converting processes. Any chemical substance that is hazardous coming into a printing facility will leave the building as a hazardous waste in one form or another. Therefore, it is important to commence any discussion of the question of compliance with environmental and safety regulations by taking a close look at the various inputs to the printing process.

Ink: The Necessary Ingredient

Without ink, there would be no way of printing most of the products we see in the marketplace, on the shelves of libraries, or in many other places vital to modern living. Ink provides the means of putting into visual form the thoughts and art developed to help convey messages, inform or simply entertain. Inks provide the means of transferring color from an image carrier to a substrate, making an image visible to the human eye.

Inks are composed of some basic building blocks, the specifics of which are modified depending upon the process, the substrate and the end use. As a general substance, the components of inks fall into very specific categories of chemicals (figure 6–1):

1. Pigment or colorant,

2. Resin,

3. Solvents/water), and

4. Additives.

Combining these substances has to result in ink that will perform well on press and in the marketplace. A variety of characteristics are needed to convey an image, protect a product, or simply inform the consumer. The colorant will convey the color(s) that project the message or images. Resins enable the inks to adhere within the formulation as well as to the substrate, in addition to being able to impart other characteristics to the performance and appearance of the dried ink. Resins and solvents or water are the vehicles that enable the inks to flow and be transferred through the press' printing ink train; for the most part they are liquids—solvents, oils, water. Additives are special agents required to provide special features or quality characteristics. Slip agents provide a more slippery surface to facilitate the movement of one package on top of another, or simply the tracking of the substrate through the press and package converting equipment. Additives can introduce potentially serious problems for the printer when facing compliance issues. (See figure 6–2 for representative ink components.)

Each of these items represents a chemical substance or mixture that has potential ramifications on the health of the community or the environmental stability of the surrounding area. The Food and Drug Administration (FDA) has not approved inks, as such, for contact with any food or, for that matter, for other contact with humans in such a form as toys. The substrate sitting between the ink and the food product is considered a barrier between the two. Therefore, with some rare exceptions, inks are usually not FDA approved. There are a limited number of inks that are available for contact with food, the approval coming from the FDA for the components of the ink, but not for the ink as a finished substance.

While pressure on the printer to comply has been significant, the need for the inkmaking companies to clean up their own houses has not been any less critical. Therefore, inks that are being made now should be much improved over the same products that were purchased only five or 10 years ago. That rationale is no reason for a printer to not continue to review formulations and request

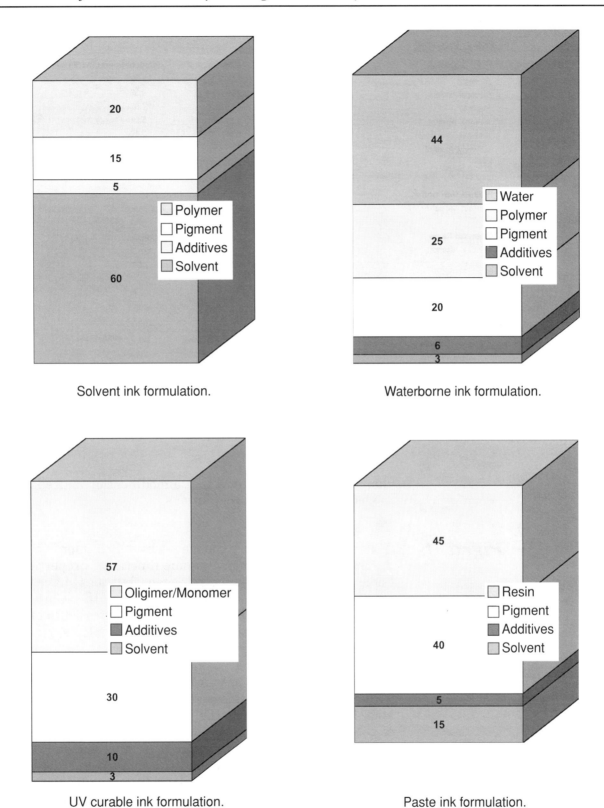

Solvent ink formulation.

Waterborne ink formulation.

UV curable ink formulation.

Paste ink formulation.

Figure 6–1. Components of ink for the four primary systems: solvent, water, UV and paste. Courtesy of Pat Laden, Atlantic Printing Ink.

Product Description SUNSHEEN PHTHALO BLUE

Chemical Name	CAS Number	Concentration (wt %)
Ethanol	64-17-5	28.62
n-Propyl Acetate	109-60-4	9.32
Heptane	142-82-5	7.87
n-Propyl Alcohol	71-23-8	5.01
Nitrocellulose Resin	9004-70-0	3.40
Isopropyl Alcohol	67-63-0	3.39

Product Description ULTRABOND PHTHALO BLUE
Product Category Solvent Flexo Film Ink

Chemical Name	CAS Number	Concentration (wt %)
n-Propyl Alcohol	71-23-8	63.10
Heptane	142-82-5	7.08

Product Description AQUASURF II G/S CYAN

Chemical Name	CAS Number	Concentration (wt %)
2-Butoxyethanol	111-76-2	5.00
n-Propyl Alcohol	71-23-8	4.00

Figure 6–2. Representative ink hazardous materials formulated for different applications for the color phthalo (cyan) blue.

MSDSs, courtesy of Sun Chemical Company.

changes when he perceives that a modification is needed in order to meet environmental regulations.

Pigments

Pigments and dyes are the means by which color is conveyed to the ink. They also convey some functional properties as well. Some colorants are known carcinogens, but these have been eliminated from inks made at this time. Much of the effort to develop environmentally friendly inks has been dedicated to eliminating colorants that pose health and ecological problems.

Many pigments are composed of materials that contain basic metals, some of which are considered heavy metals. Some of the metals are reacted to produce the pigment. In some instances, without the specific metals, some colors would simply not be available. How do we address the issue of color selection in the face of potential risks? Consider the function of heavy metals as conveyers of color. Some of the best reds, oranges and yellows resulted from the inclusion of basic lead chromate pigments. These pigments are no longer in use. Driven from use by the agreement between the inkmakers and the Conference of Northeast Governors (CONEG), heavy metals were banned from use in inks, with strict limits placed on the natural occurrence of these metals.

Other pigments were either developed or identified for use to achieve similar final colors. The new pigments and resulting inks did not contain the heavy metals. This has enabled printers to print reds, oranges and yellows very close in hue to those formerly obtained by use of the lead chromate formulations. The change has posed other problems. Blending with the same basic colors no longer produces the same new color. Any blending formula that included one of these lead chromate pigmented inks has had to be reformulated when using the new inks as substitutes.

Pressure has not decreased on the use of other metals in the inks. Public perceptions continue to pressure packaging buyers to avoid inks with any metals. Barium and copper are two major targets. Barium salts are a fundamental part of the manufacturing process of the pigments and can be found in much ink. It is a basic component, providing the hue to the mainly yellow-shade reds. Copper is a primary constituent of the greens and blues. Can they be replaced? Quite possibly, but at a fairly high cost. Would the environment benefit significantly by the removal of these metals? That is a matter of judgment, more than it is a scientific fact.

Pigment is intended to remain on the substrate. It is not intended to come into contact with any sensitive products, such as food. It is not intended to volatilize. If discarded after use, the product on which the ink is printed may find its way to a landfill. Under the best circumstances the printed products will enter a deinking and recycling cycle, or be part of the waste that is burned at a solids waste incinerator as an alternative fuel and source of energy.

Resins

The ink vehicle consists of a number of components, of which the resin is an important constituent. Resins provide the binding characteristics between the pigments and the substrates, as well as other properties that contribute to the appearance and performance of the printed image. Among these are wetting out of the pigment, solvent release, odor, gloss, transfer and printability. Resins also impart special characteristics: for example, nitrocellulose is important for heat resistance, while polyamides are excellent for adhesion to corona-treated films.

Resins have been developed for many applications and to withstand many different physical requirements. Any discussion of the particular impacts of resins with the environment and safety would have to be formulation-specific. Some may introduce styrene, which would interface with health and environmental concerns. It is best to communicate with the suppliers to identify and take cognizance of the ingredients introduced with the resins.

The resin, like the pigment, is one of the solid components of the ink. It is not expected to volatilize, but will be present in any solid wastes generated and to be disposed of during printing and finishing, and at the end of the life of the product in the hands of the consumer.

Solvents as Vehicles

The liquid and most volatile portion of the ink is the clear solvent, which conveys the pigment and resin to the substrate. This liquid can consist of alcohols, ketones, petroleum-derived hydrocarbons, glycols or simply water. Most likely, it is a combination of several of these elements.

The solvent has the primary function of converting the solid components into a fluid that is capable of being printed. The solvent must perform several tasks to achieve this goal:

- Solubilize the resin(s) to produce a rheologically suitable vehicle,

- Evaporate or be absorbed easily,

- Impart minimal odor to the dried ink film,

- Wet out and adhere to the substrate,

- Maintain stability of the components in the formulation,

- Not react with other components to create undesirable quality concerns,

- Not react with press rollers or plates to create ink transfer problems or destroy press parts, and

- Comply with customer specifications and government regulations for health and environment.

Selecting solvents for ink formulation requires the chemist to develop a balance between those that will have high solvency properties to bind the resin, pigments and additives into a viable package, and those that will simply act as diluents. The diluent will improve the liquidity of the ink without causing a change in viscosity or precipitation of the solids. That being said, what alternatives are there that are available with regard to the last item in the list of concerns for the selection of solvents, that being "satisfy customer specifications and government regulations?" (See Table 6–1 for comparative solvent weights and evaporation rates.*)

Selection of the solvent must first satisfy the requirement that it serves in the composition of the ink, with the understanding that the solvent will present the largest and most sensitive component relative to environmental and safety/health considerations. The printer's choice of inks will vary by process and end use, with major differences stemming from the amount and nature of the solvents in the formulations relative to the amounts of pigment, resins and additives. The right ink, which will satisfy both the printer and his customer, is the one that has the lowest amount of necessary solvents, in which all constituents are neither carcinogens nor constitute other health hazards. Flammability may be an unavoidable characteristic for certain end uses and processes.

Not all solvents are hazardous to health. Water is a solvent. Other solvents are used regularly in the foods we eat. Selecting some of these same solvents for the ink can make for safer inks. The key question is whether they can perform in a manner that is

---

*Table of Solvents is extracted from a handout given to participations at workshops of the Flexographic Technical Association in 1980 to accompany presentations made by Benjamin Trombetta, Sun Chemical Company, Philadelphia, PA.

TABLE 6–1. CHART OF SOLVENTS DEMONSTRATING EVAPORATION RATINGS AND WEIGHT PER GALLON

SOLVENT	EVAPORATION RATE Butyl Acetate = 1(Pounds/Gallon)	WEIGHT PER GALLON
Alcohols:		
Methanol	5.9	6.60
Ethanol	3.3	6.60
Isopropanol	2.3	6.55
N-propanol	1.1	6.71
Glycol Ethers:		
Propylene glycol monomethyl ether	0.81	7.66
Ethylene glycol monomethyl ether	0.71	8.04
Ethylene glycol monoethyl ether	0.43	7.75
Esters:		
Ethyl acetate	6.2	7.51
Isopropyl acetate	5.0	7.27
N-propyl acetate	2.7	7.39
Ketones:		
Acetone	11.5	6.59
Methyl ethyl ketone	5.7	6.71
Hydrocarbons:		
Toluene	2.1	7.25
Hexane	9.0	5.50

Source: Presented as part of a talk at an FTA workshop by Ben Trombetta, Branch Manager, Sun Chemical Company, Philadelphia, PA., talk given approximately 1980–81.

acceptable for the process and end use. Among the efforts made to comply with air emission regulations are the use of waterborne inks and radiation curable inks. Radiation curable inks should have no solvent components, but this may not be true in all cases when greater liquidity is needed.

Waterborne inks are not free of solvents. A typical formulation will include some alcohols, glycols and surfactants. The amount of volatile organic compounds may range from zero to 25 percent, often with some components at quantities of less than one percent of the solution. Amines, either as ammonia or other amines, are necessary components to maintain the proper working pH of the water ink (Table 6–2).

UV curable inks are promoted as being free of solvents (volatile organic compounds). Care must to be taken to assure that this is indeed a fact. Manufacturers can increase the fluidity of ink by adding solvent to make a particular UV ink or coating flow and transfer better. While this is not the norm, questions have been raised by state agencies when lab tests have indicated a small but accountable amount of a volatile organic compounds in some UV inks tested. It is incumbent on the printer to qualify the inks and coatings that are purchased. UV inks have other safety/health and environmental issues that have to be addressed, relative to the use of photoinitiators to activate the ink on exposure.

Lithographic inks typically use mineral spirits and oils as vehicles. There has been an increase in use of vegetable oils to replace hydrocarbon mineral oils as environmental pressures have increased. Among the most publicized are oils that have been

TABLE 6–2. REPRESENTATIVE SOLVENTS IN BLACK AND WHITE WATER INKS FROM TWO DIFFERENT SUPPLIERS AS USED AT PRESS WITH ADDITIVES

COMPONENT	BLACK 1 (lbs/gal)	BLACK 2 (lbs/gal)	WHITE 1 (lbs/gal)	WHITE 2 (lbs/gal)
Ammonium hydroxide	0.2	0.18	0.2	0.22
Isopropanol	0.1	0.08	0.1	0.14
Normal propanol	0	0.03	0.3	0.32
Ethyl alcohol	0.2	0.23	0	0
Glycols	0.5	0.53	0.6	0.56
Water	4.6	4.62	3.8	3.77
Weight per gallon of ink	9.0	9.0	10.9	10.9
Percent VOCs	9.5%	9.0%	9.3%	9.3%

Source: P-F Technical Services Inc., SEP Project at Supreme Poly Products, Brooklyn.

derived from soybeans. However, rapeseed and linseed oil have been used for many years. Based on the specific lithographic process, the percentage of these oils varies as a component of the total vehicle package.

Liquid ink systems for flexography and gravure have embraced water as the key solvent, but have only been successful in limited segments of the marketplace where printing, converting and product performance have not been compromised. Many of the more hazardous solvents in solvent-based inks have been eliminated by substitution with safer solvents. Toluene, methanol and ethylene glycol compounds are rarely found in liquid inks today, except in specific gravure markets such as publication printing.

One thing that the MSDS has revealed to most printers is the complex nature of the liquid package of their inks. With rare exceptions, liquid inks can have anywhere from four to seven or eight solvent components. Each component serves a different purpose. The key challenge for the future is to develop or identify safer substitutes for those components that continue to pose health and ecological hazards. While this development takes place, environmental compliance takes advantage of a key characteristic of the primary solvents used for inkmaking and press operations. Hydrocarbon and organic solvents have economic value due to their potential heat-carrying (BTU) values. Spent solvent and waste inks can be used as an alternative fuel in cement kilns or in the generation of energy. Passing the exhausted fumes from the printer through an oxidizer can result in a heated air stream that can be redirected for use as either process or comfort heat. Many large and medium size flexographic, gravure and lithographic printing facilities have come into compliance using this option. Figure 6–3 depicts an oxidizer with a heat recovery option.

Fountain Solutions

A primary concern for the lithographic printer is the fountain solution that coats the unexposed portion of the printing plate. This has traditionally been a mixture of isopropanol and water, with some additives. The purpose of the fountain solution is to cover the portion of the plate from which ink is to be repelled, allowing the ink to be conveyed to the exposed area for transfer to the substrate. The alcohol promotes the ability of the water and additives to wet-out on the predominantly aluminum plate.

Isopropanol (isopropyl alcohol) is a volatile organic compound. It was targeted by the government and subject to standards that would reduce the amount used. At the same time, printers were encouraged to find alcohol substitutes. Under RACT, isopropanol can be used within certain guidelines. A total of 15 percent by weight, maximum, can be used in fountain solution for presses that were installed prior to 1988. Fountain solutions for newer presses must not exceed 10 percent of the weight of the solution.

An attempt to increase control of fountain solution emissions to a higher degree was a subject of negotiation between the USEPA and industry associations and larger printers. Discussions about the publication of a Control Technology Guideline (CTG) for lithographic printing were not conclusive. The result was the

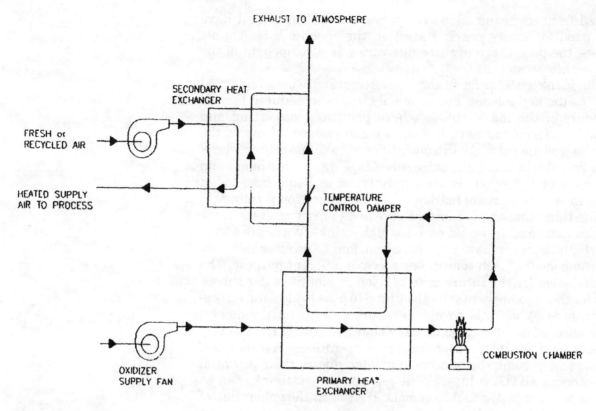

Figure 6–3. Schematic of heat recovery loop from an oxidizer that takes advantage of the hydrocarbon composition and BTU value of solvents in the printing process.

Courtesy of The CMM Group, LLC.

publication of an Advisory Technology Guidance (ATG) document. The ATG, while not as authoritative as the CTG, recommends the use of refrigeration or chilling to reduce the percentage of isopropanol to much lower, single-digit levels.

Alternatives for fountain solution have been developed. Among the chemical substances that replace the need for isopropanol are ethylene glycol, ethylene glycol ethers, propylene glycol and propylene glycol ethers, glycerine, butyl cellosolve, etc. Some of the substitutes are safe. Others are hazardous. Many of them are still volatile organic compounds (figure 6–4). The key factor is the very low percentage of the chemicals that are used in the mixing of the solution that is used on press. Another development that limits the amount of solvents present in a fountain solution has been the introduction of recirculating, chilled reservoirs on many modern web- and sheet-fed lithographic presses.

Solvents Used to Dilute Ink on Press

Liquid ink systems for flexography, gravure and screen printing will make use of solvents to modify the color density and speed of drying of inks on press. The solvents have to be compatible with the ink systems and the components of the printing press. They must also perform their function without destroying the integrity of the basic ink or coating formulation, and maintain the quality characteristics required for customer satisfaction.

MATERIAL SAFETY DATA SHEET

Tower Products, Inc., 2703 Freemansburg Ave., Easton, PA   18045

SECTION 1: PRODUCT INFORMATION
Product Name: **MILLENNIUM** (Universal Fountain Solution)
D.O.T. Designation: Cleaning Liquid. Not Regulated.
U.N. Designation: Same as D.O.T.

SECTION 2: HAZARDOUS COMPONENTS/IDENTITY INFORMATION

HAZARDOUS COMPONENT	CAS No.	% WT.	OSHA PEL	ACGIH TLV-TWA	OTHER RATINGS	OSHA STEL
Propylene Glycol	57-55-6	1-2			50ppm(AIHA)	
Dipropylene Glycol Monomethyl Ether	34590-94-8	2-6	100ppm			150ppm
Glyceritol	56-81-5	2-6	10mg/m3	10mg/m3 5mg/m3(respirable)		

SECTION 3: PHYSICAL/CHEMICAL CHARACTERISTICS
Boiling Point: 212 degrees F.
Specific Gravity: (Water = 1) 1.01
Vapor Pressure: (mmHG, calculated) None
Melting Point: N/A
Vapor Density: (Air = 1, calculated) 2
Solubility in Water: Complete
pH of Concentrate: 3.8-4.2
Appearance & Odor: Blue liquid, detergent odor.
Maximum VOC Content: .3 lbs. per gal. (40 grams per liter)
Maximum VOC% :   4%

MILLENNIUM
UNIVERSAL FOUNTAIN SOLUTION

DESCRIPTION:

Millennium is a true one-step, universal fountain solution that does not usually require the addition of alcohol or alcohol substitutes to the fountain. It is formulated to run metal, polyester and paper plates on all types of dampening systems. Millennium is a buffered product that has an expected pH of 3.8-4.2. Water hardness range is not an issue with the product.

DIRECTIONS FOR USE:

Always clean the dampening system before changing fountain solution.

METAL PLATES: Add 3-6 oz. of Millennium per gallon of water.

POLYESTER PLATES: Add 6 oz. of Millennium per gallon of water.

PAPER PLATES & ELECTROSTATIC PLATES: Add 6 oz. of Millennium per gallon of water.

Figure 6–4. Representative solvent-free fountain solution formulation. Solvent-free is usually defined as free of isopropyl alcohol.
Courtesy of Tower Products, Inc.

Typically, the solvents will be representative of the major families of solvents used in the inks to provide them with liquidity. The need to modify the drying rate of the inks will dictate the selection of solvents to add to the press ink. Slower solvents will retard drying; faster evaporating solvents will increase the speed of drying. A major concern is that adding a solvent mixture will detract from the basic balance designed for the ink. To achieve this end, blends of solvents may be used.

As the press runs and ink feeds through the system, the solvents will evaporate and leave the scene as air emissions. More solvent is added, and that too evaporates. It is an endless cycle that had been taken to heart and addressed by development of such tools as the enclosed chamber doctor blade systems and improved capture drying systems in flexographic printing.

Typical solvents found in publication gravure inks are hexane, mineral spirits, lactol spirits, napthas, heptane, toluene, xylene and alcohols. Packaging gravure inks will have the same solvents, plus a number of others, including acetone, methyl ethyl ketone, methyl isobutyl ketone, ethyl acetate, isopropyl alcohol, isopropyl acetate, butyl acetate, n-butyl acetate, ethylene glycol monoethyl ether, methanol, ethanol and tri-decanol. Selection of additive solvents would be based on which solvents will help to reduce viscosity and maintain the original chemical composition of the solution.

Flexographic inks use a slightly smaller library of solvents, and an even smaller number for use as the diluting solvent. Principal solvents are ethanol, normal propanol, isopropanol, n-propyl acetate, ethyl acetate and n-heptane. A typical solvent blend for use on press will be a fast formulation consisting of ethanol and n-propyl acetate, and a slow blend of normal propanol and n-propyl acetate. Where methanol was once the major denaturant in ethanol, environmental concerns have led to substitution with other solvents such as isopropanol.

Solvents for screen printing inks vary in the same manner as in gravure inks. Some ink, such as the plasticizer inks that are used for T-shirts, have virtually no volatile organic compounds, while others for films and plastics may have considerable amounts of solvent. The solvents are very similar to those used for gravure and flexography, but are in a much more viscous state. Similarly, solvents added to the inks during printing must be compatible with the formulation in use.

Much of the question of evaporation of the solvents and their replacement has been studied to develop ink transfer systems that can curtail evaporation and reduce the amount of solvent that must be added during press runs. At the same time, research has developed high-solids resins that achieve a more liquid state with the addition of lesser quantities of solvent. This combination can bring about a considerable reduction in emissions at an improved level of quality in ink.

Cleaning the Press and Image Carriers

Perhaps the single major factor that is common to all printing processes is the need for great quantities of solvents to clean the presses, image carriers (plates, cylinders and screens), ink transfer rollers and components of the equipment that come in contact with the inks, coatings and adhesives. No matter what the solvent, the proportion of cleaning solvent to ink usage has to be at least two to three times as much solvent as the weight of inks used. Chemistry and quantities used will vary, based on one of two concepts:

1. Do we do all cleaning on-press?

2. Do we clean adequately to continue press runs, and then do preventive maintenance periodically off-press?

The nature and the quantities of solvents used and wastes generated will vary considerably, based on which approach is taken. On-press cleaning will necessitate use of considerable amounts of solvents, and they must be quick drying to facilitate production. Off-press cleaning will reduce usage drastically and allow for the use of alternatives that are slower drying, evaporate less, and do not have to be compatible with the ink formulations.

Press washes for lithographic presses vary, but the majority are based on major percentages of aliphatic and aromatic hydrocarbons. Some still use methylene chloride, a target of OSHA, and toluene.

Flexographic and gravure printers tend to use the same solvents for cleaning that they do for diluting the inks on press. Alcohols and esters are common. For more aggressive cleaning, particularly of anilox rollers and gravure cylinders or removing plates and stickyback adhesives from cylinders, the printer may use such solvents as toluene, hexane or methyl ethyl ketone (MEK) (figure 6–5).

Off-press cleaning stations are much friendlier to the environment, both in the nature of the solvent and the amounts of solvents used. A typical cleaning tank will be used until the accumulated solids no longer provide an adequate cleaning reservoir. The amount disposed of could range from less than 300 to 500 gallons and the tank may be emptied as seldom as every other week. A solvent cleaner such as mineral spirits can be used or a caustic solution with water can be employed.

With the development of more aqueous solutions, cleaners have been developed that are water based, frequently with a butyl cellosolve component. Many have caustic chemicals at a significantly high percentage to provide a "bite" to the cleaning solution and literally "eat" dried inks out of cells or from corners of printing pans and reservoirs. Sodium hydroxide and butyl cellosolve are common chemicals found in aqueous cleaning formulations.

Prepress— Design and Image Carriers

At every stage of the printing process, chemicals come into play. Whether color is needed at the artist's desk or a reaction is needed at a given point to create a photographic image, there is a need to bring a chemical into the equation. Traditional design of graphics has been a function of the commercial arts. Markers, acrylic paints, watercolors, spray paints and coatings are used to develop a piece of art that will eventually be transformed into print. Photographic processes are used to create paper images, negatives, proofs and printing plates. Developers, fixers and washes bring specific chemical substances into play, as

Tower Products, Inc.

Product Name: **LO-VO WASH 50** One Step Low V.O.C. Press Wash

SECTION 2: HAZARDOUS INGREDIENTS/IDENTITY INFORMATION

Hazardous Component	CAS No.	%WT.	OSHA PEL	ACGIH TLV-TWA	OTHER RATINGS	OSHA STEL
Aliphatic Hydrocarbon	64742-88-7	45-55	100ppm (1)	100ppm (1)		

Tower Products, Inc.

Product Name: **EXEMPT WASH HF** and **EXEMPT WASH HF - M** (High Flashpoint Water Miscible Wash)

SECTION 2: HAZARDOUS COMPONENTS/IDENTITY INFORMATION

Hazardous Component	CAS No.	% WT.	OSHA PEL	ACGIH TLV-TWA	OTHER RATINGS	OSHA STEL
Aliphatic Hydrocarbon	64742-88-7	85-95	100ppm (1)	100ppm		
Dipropylene Glycol Monomethyl Ether	34590-94-8	5-10	100ppm	100ppm		150ppm

MANUFACTURER'S NAME: PRINTERS' SERVICE
PRODUCT NAME: RED MAGIC X

========= SECTION II - HAZARDOUS INGREDIENTS/SARA III INFORMATION ======

REPORTABLE COMPONENTS	CAS NUMBER	VAPOR PRESSURE mm Hg @ TEMP	WEIGHT PERCENT
PROPYLENE GLYCOL MONO METHYL ETHER ACETATE LD50-8.53 g/Kg	108-65-6	3.7mmHg 20 C	50 - 60%
ALIPHATIC PETRO DISTILLATE (C9 - C11) PEL 100ppm: TLV 100ppm // LD50> 25ml/kg: LC50 700ppm/4hr	64742-48-9	2.7 mmHg 25 C	20 - 30%
AROMATIC PETRO DISTILLATE (C8-C11) PEL 100 ppm // LD50 4.7g/kg: LC50 3670 ppm/8hr	64742-95-6	2.7mmHg 25 C	10 - 20%

CAS# 64742-95-6 contains approximately 5% XYLENE (CAS# 1330-20-7) which has a PEL and TLV of 100 ppm; approximately 4% CUMENE (CAS# 98-82-8), which has a PEL and TLV of 50 ppm-skin; and approximately 27% 1.2.4 TRIMETHYLBENZENE (CAS# 95-63-7), which has a PEL and TLV of 25 ppm. XYLENE. CUMENE AND 1.2.4 TRIMETHYLBENZENE are subject to the reporting requirements of section 313 OF SARA TITLE III

MANUFACTURER'S NAME: PRINTERS' SERVICE
PRODUCT NAME: MRC-F

========= SECTION II - HAZARDOUS INGREDIENTS/SARA III INFORMATION ===

REPORTABLE COMPONENTS	CAS NUMBER	VAPOR PRESSURE mm Hg @ TEMP	WEIGHT PERCENT
ACETONE PEL 750ppm: TLV 750ppm // LD50 9.75g/kg: LC50 16000ppm/4hr	67-64-1	186 mmHg 20 C	40 - 50%
* XYLENE PEL 100ppm: TLV 100ppm // LD50 5.2g/kg: LC50 6350ppm/4hr	1330-20-7	5.1 mmHg 20 C	20 - 30%
ISOPROPANOL 99% PEL 400ppm: TLV 400ppm // LD50 5.84g/kg: LC50 12000ppm/8hr	67-63-0	37 mmHg 20 C	10 - 20%
* 1-METHYL-2-PYRROLIDINONE PEL 100 ppm // LD50 4.2g/kg	872-50-4	0.29mmHg 20 C	1 - 10%

* Indicates chemical(s) subject to the reporting requirements of section 313 of Title III and of 40 CFR 372. CAS# 1330-20-7 Contain approximately 20% ETHYLBENZENE (CAS# 100-41-4). which has a PEL of 125 PPM and a TLV of 100 PPM. ETHYLBENZENE is subject to the reporting requirements of section 313 OF SARA TITLE III.

Figure 6–5. Representative components of press and blanket washes.

Compiled from MSDSs for press washes supplied to printers by Printers' Service and Tower Products Inc.

do the films, papers and plates on which emulsions have been coated to be transformed into the images we see and print.

Platemaking will vary from printing process to printing process; but with each process there is a trail of chemistry and chemical wastes:

1. Gravure printing requires engraving chemicals, such as etching solution and sulfuric acid, chromium, nickel and copper plating solutions.

2. Flexographic plates can introduce chemistry from two different applications:

    a. Rubber plates are made from metal engravings. The engraving process employs nitric acid and results in a water bath with metal residues.

    b. Photopolymer plates are exposed to light. The unexposed portion is washed out with a solvent, or water containing an additive. The basic solvent at one time was perchloroethane. The solvents have since been changed to safer substances, but the printer must still exercise vigilance when disposing of spent solvent.

3. Lithographic plates engage processing chemistry, much of it in aqueous formulations, as well as plate materials that lend themselves to recycling. In addition to handling the liquid wastes, printers have the opportunity to save and dispose of all used plates for recycling.

The computer is changing this scenario, although not entirely. One must remember that while technology brings advances, the technology of the past 50 years stays on with us in many places.

Computer graphics and typesetting have eliminated an entire family of chemicals. Computer-to-negative will do the same with darkroom chemistry. And computer-to-plate or to press will continue the trend toward less chemistry and more sophisticated results. The impact of the computer has started and will continue to impact every printing process. While the computer is the predominant tool for setting type, there are still printers who use typesetting equipment with hot lead to form the copy. Negatives will continue to be processed in open trays or with processors using typical photographic and platemaking chemistry in many small and medium size shops. Plates will continue to be made by traditional methods until obsolescence and/or more attractive costs lead to their replacement with computer driven technology.

After a substrate has been printed, the process is not at an end. Subsequent operations are needed to complete the product. Commercial printing groups these operations under the umbrella called "finishing." Package printers use the term "converting" to describe the subsequent steps in making a finished

Chemicals in Finishing Operations

product. The steps can include coating, laminating, diecutting, slitting, combining and forming the book, box or bag that is the shipped product. Many of these operations require chemicals as a component of the process or to maintain the cleanliness of the equipment.

Coatings

After an image is printed on a sheet or web, it may be necessary to apply an overall layer of a clear coating onto the surface. The coating may be protective, designed to prevent the graphics from being attacked by the elements and destroyed. The coating may be applied to add a luster to the print that is beyond the capability of the ink, perhaps for a gloss or matte appearance. Or it may be a functional coating to provide protection, such as heat resistance or adhesion capability for laminating to other substrates as used for flexible packaging or to other structures such as blister-pack cards for adhesion to plastic forms.

The commercial printer sees coating as a means of adding a gloss finish or a matte finish to the overall surface of the printed publication or package. The predominant coatings used are waterborne or UV curable formulations. While the traditional sheet-fed application has been a secondary operation, on an independent machine, lithographic presses are now being equipped with coating units at the end of the printing stations, allowing for in-line application of either an aqueous or radiation curable coating. The coating unit design is frequently based on flexographic or gravure ink transfer technology.

Traditional packaging coatings are solvent formulations. With the full coverage of the substrate, it is necessary to have a liquid that dries quickly and retains very little to no solvent. Specific applications require barrier properties to protect against chemicals in the packaged product or which are used in the packaging process. Liquid pack laminations have been more successful with solvent-based coatings. So too with blister cards which will house products that may rewet waterborne adhesive formulations. A typical solvent found in many lamination coatings is ethyl acetate.

Waterborne coatings have taken the place of solvent formulations in many applications. Typical formulations would use no solvent at all. When needed, the volatile organic compounds constitute, at the most, five percent of the formulation.

UV curable coatings have extremely high gloss and have captured a sizeable portion of the market in sheet-fed lithographic operations and the narrow web label and tag market printed by flexography. The concerns about safety of UV inks, in the workplace and to the environment, also apply to coatings. Effective curing of coatings becomes more critical as the overall coverage can lead to uncured, and potentially hazardous, chemistry in high-speed applications.

Hot melt coatings are available for appropriate applications, particularly when the coating results in a surface for laminating or adhering to other materials. While the hot melt may be non-VOC in use, the heat and, sometimes, odor may have to be exhausted to the atmosphere.

Folding and joining a sheet or web to form a package, such as a box or a bag, requires an adhesive. Binding a book or magazine requires an adhesive. Adhesives join seams and closures, top and bottom, to convert paperboard and corrugated forms to complete packages. Environmental requirements have promoted considerable changes in the nature of adhesives for the commercial printing and package converting industries.

Waterborne adhesives have become the major choice in the commercial printing and packaging sectors. Product design would normally allow for unprinted and uncoated areas of the package to prevent inks and coatings from acting as a barrier to adhesion with the waterborne glues. In many applications, where it is technically feasible, hot melt adhesives are now employed. Binding of perfect-bound publications is an effective use of hot melt adhesives.

Special applications may call for solvent adhesives. One such package is a bag formed from polystyrene film for frozen poultry. To provide a bond between the two layers of film, it is necessary to use an adhesive with a solvent blend that, in essence, dissolves and joins the films. The solvent required contains methyl ethyl ketone and methyl isobutyl ketone. To clean the machine parts, a solvent blend of the two is required to cut into and remove the dried adhesives.

Adhesives

With the introduction of substances that will harden and secure themselves, cleaning of parts and equipment requires very aggressive agents. Whether it is waterborne, solvent or radiation curable adhesives, the need to clean will require solvents that are capable of cutting into the solids and removing them completely. This presents an odd dilemma; the very chemicals that meet compliance standards may need very undesirable agents for cleaning. An example is a solvent blend sold for use in cleaning UV curable inks, and which finds its way to the diecutting operation where adhesives from pressure sensitive substrates accumulate on the dies. This blend contains toluene, methyl ethyl ketone and MIBK. Another cleaning agent found in many formulations is methylene chloride. While not impacting on the product, such chemicals are in the workplace and affect workers and the environment.

Maintenance Chemistry

As pressure has been placed on printers and coaters to comply with regulations, tremendous support has been given by ink and solvent suppliers to overcome the many obstacles in the path to success. The rapid development of waterborne inks, coatings, adhesives and cleaning formulations was a joint effort of printers working with their suppliers, who, in turn, worked with the suppliers of pigments, resins and solvents to find a better way. Suppliers of radiation curable inks, coatings and adhesives joined the effort later, but have made marked improvement in equipment and product to make UV curable inks and coatings factors in many segments of the printing industry.

Suppliers Spur Improvements

The key to finding technical alternatives to compliance lies in a partnership that the printer must form with the different suppliers who have any input to the process. This is a group effort in which every element can spell success or failure. From equipment manufacturers, ink train venders, image carrier suppliers, to the suppliers of the inks, coatings, adhesives and solvents, a group effort will address the needs of the printer and find the appropriate solution.

That is not to say that solvents will be eliminated completely from the process. There will always be a need for a solvent formulation based on end-use requirements. But that solvent need not be one with toxic characteristics. Safer solvents exist. Developing inks and coatings using the safer, non-invasive chemistry is as important as complete elimination. The products that need the solvents most likely have quality characteristics that are as active in safeguarding life and health as are the environmental and health regulations themselves.

It is imperative that all the facts be known in order to correctly formulate inks, coatings and adhesives. Given the basic parameters within which printing and finishing equipment will operate and the expectations for the product in the marketplace, chemistry can be expected to confront the problems and find an appropriate solution.

Changes in chemistry are often generated by the work done in the suppliers' laboratories. Keeping an open mind and keen eye for new developments can help the printer address his needs.

Moving to the Future

Printing technology and chemistry are constantly changing. As the industry seeks to find tools for improved productivity and quality, it is also challenging the sources of pollution and governmental regulation. The chemistry that we are working with today is a far stretch from that of 10 years ago.

Computers have removed a vast number of chemical substances that were used in the design and prepress activities. Digital and direct-to-press technology is replacing much of the chemistry used prior to the press. As ink and solvent suppliers research materials used to manufacture inks, they will develop products that are less hazardous or that eliminate the riskier chemicals from the process. The printer will contend with chemistry that is beyond compliance and will have to confront less demanding governmental regulation. Recent industry shows have demonstrated some of these developments. At such time as these developments become the norm rather than cutting edge innovation, the printer will be able to make such changes as will make the safer, cleaner chemicals his normal raw material. Until that day, every chemical used must be tracked and action taken for the safe handling, use and disposition of the resulting waste, emissions or discharges.

CHAPTER 7

Categories and Sources of Pollutants in a Typical Printing Facility

Every material and chemical that enters the printing process through the front door must depart the facility either as part of the product or as waste. In some cases, such as the paper and films on which we print, the wastes are not hazardous, and, in most cases, can be recycled for reuse. On the other hand, for the most part, the chemicals that enter the building and do not become part of the product sold to the customer leave the premises in some form that can impact on the ecology or the health of the public. The presence of chemicals in various states—solid, liquid or gas—in the workplace presents challenges to the employees and their health and well-being. (See figure 7–1.)

Consider that any chemical that evaporates, or has the ability to float in the air in small particles, is moved in and around the

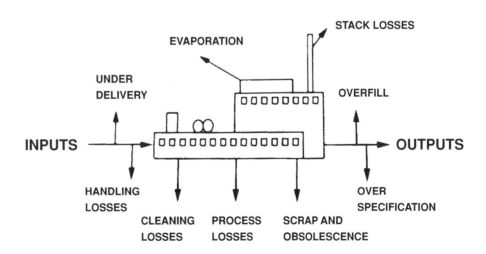

Figure 7–1. Typical plant, illustrating materials entering and product and wastes leaving the building.

Source: P-F Technical Services Inc.

107

plant by air currents and out of openings to the outside air. Most solvents evaporate readily and permeate the air with their odors as well as their presence. Powders and paper dust are carried into the air, in minute particle sizes perhaps, but are there all the same. The movement of rollers and other equipment used to move chemistry through the process can create misting, carrying droplets of liquid into the air.

Other chemicals are either dissolved in water or carried along with the waste water into the sanitary sewer system or septic tanks (in some suburban and rural areas). The use of aqueous chemical solutions sometimes lends a false sense of security as to the safety of the formulation. This can lead to discharging of chemical wastes to the publicly operated sewer system that was designed to handle primarily sanitary wastes.

A major part of the waste raw materials result from planned and unplanned solid waste generated by the printing and related processes. Rejected or used printing plates, paper trim and finishing wastes, set-up waste, and rejected finished products constitute a fairly significant part of the solid waste generated by printers. Liquids that are either spent or surplus must be disposed of; this would include inks and solvents, coatings and adhesives.

As the printer looks at his facility, he will see that, in one way or another, there are regulations stemming from federal, state or local governments that address the wastes generated.

Categories of Waste

The general categories, as illustrated in figure 7–1, into which these environmental wastes fall are:

1. **Air emissions**, emerging in the process areas and escaping from the plant through ducts and stacks or as fugitive vapors seeping through doors, windows and other openings in the building,

2. **Hazardous wastes**, collected as liquids or solids and packaged to be shipped for disposal or treatment,

3. **Wastewater**, discharged through the plumbing in the building, entering and becoming a part of the wastes in the sewer systems or septic/cesspool tanks,

4. **Defective products**, which fall outside acceptable specifications, and the **normal waste** generated as changes are made from order to order or when problems are encountered in the process,

5. **Surplus chemicals** that collect in the ink and solvent rooms or cabinets, and no longer have a practical use in the process,

6. **Indoor exposure**, to chemicals used in the process, that may cause health-related problems for workers. Primary concern is the chemicals with low exposure levels that can create ailments in body organs as well as affect the respiratory system.

Each of these categories is the subject of one or more environmental and safety regulations. Understanding the path taken and effects of each of the waste streams can enable the printer to take measures that will help reduce exposure across the board rather than for one medium at a time.

Traditionally, the different sources of pollution (air, solids and water) have been treated as individual entities by lawmakers. Each medium has its own set of laws, standards and solutions. More recent laws and revisions have been broadened to capture some of the essence of impact by more than one medium. With regard to future policy, the perception is now one of a broader based multi-media regulatory program that will address issues relative to both use and disposal, seeking to find pollution reduction opportunities in all media. The all-inclusive approach increases the need for the printer to better understand the flow of chemicals through his facility and process(es)

Air Pollution and Printing

The most significant chemical impact on the environment from printing is a consequence of air emissions. The evaporation of liquid from prepress, printing and post-printing processes results in vapors that carry a variety of pollutants into the workplace and/or out of the facility to the neighboring vicinity. (See figure 7–2.)

Environmental regulations and lists categorize these pollutants by their effect on people and ecology. The most commonly encountered descriptions are derived from the Clean Air Act and Resource Conservation and Recovery Act. OSHA standards define the allowable limits for short periods and long-term exposure of workers.

With pressrooms frequently in office and commercial buildings, or in residential areas, emissions from printing plants are often discernable by their different, foreign odors. The distinctive smell of any number of chemicals is all that is needed to initiate a complaint of environmental pollution. It is wise for the printer to take all steps necessary to identify his emissions and to prevent them from creating a potential liability. This can be accomplished by eliminating or diminishing the exposure to any questionable chemical whose characteristics can lead to a public reaction and an inspection by the authorities.

Ground Level Ozone—VOC

The major problem traceable to the use of volatile organic compounds (VOCs) at ground level is the creation of "smog, a low level form of ozone," caused by the reaction of solvent and other similar volatile organic compound vapors in the presence of sunlight. Technically, the typical solvents used in printing and related activities have been activated by heat and light to create the ozone. Ground level ozone creates havoc with people as it is inhaled. Allergic sensitivities and reactions, asthmatic attacks, eye irritation, and other respiratory ailments are common effects of exposure to ozone.

Just what are these VOCs? For the most part, they are the common solvents used in printing. Some solvents are in the inks.

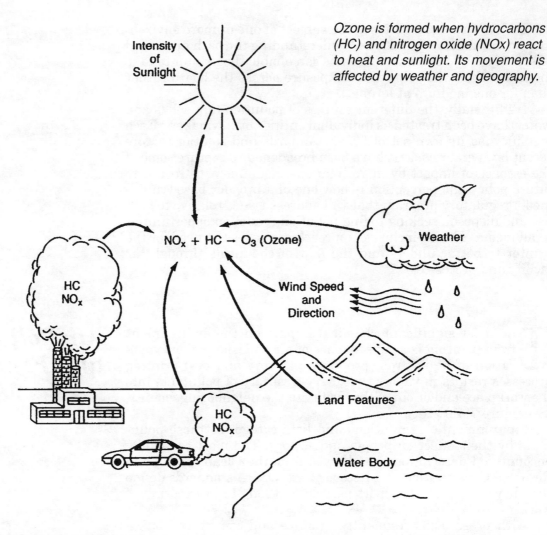

Figure 7–2. Ozone formation and movement.
Source: Kathlyn Gay, *Ozone*, Franklin Watts, 1989, p 11.

Others are there because they are required for the fountain solution or diluent during the press run. Cleaning is an essential part of the process before, during and after a job is run. A typical list of solvents used in a printing plant would include ethanol, normal-propanol, isopropanol, hexane, heptane, toluene, xylene, n-propyl acetate, ethyl acetate, as well as a number of petroleum distillates such as VM&P naptha, aromatic and aliphatic hydrocarbons and stoddard solvent.

At the opposite end of the scale, some chemicals create reactions in the upper atmosphere. Chlorinated solvents used in the printing processes and gases produced by the drying systems and add-on controls drift up into the higher levels of the upper atmosphere and deplete the ozone layer there. This depletion leads to what is commonly called the "greenhouse effect," or global warming. Included in this group are perchloroethane, 1,1,1, trichloroethane, and Freon(chlorofluorocarbons).

Figure 7–3. Smoke billowing from stack.

Hazardous Air Pollutants

While VOCs have been regulated from the outset to address respiratory health problems stemming from reactions of chemicals under climatic conditions, in 1990 the need was seen to extend this regulatory process to chemicals that are considered toxic to humans and animals. The Hazardous Air Pollutants list addresses chemicals that can be airborne and detrimental to the general health of a community.

The Clean Air Act originally listed some 190 chemicals that are considered hazardous to health. Some are VOCs; many are not. But all are carried in the air exhausted from industrial facilities. Since 1990, petitions have been made and some granted to add or delete various chemicals.

Some of the more common HAPs (Hazardous Air Pollutants) listed in the Clean Air Act of 1990, which can be found in a typical printing facility, include: ethylene glycol, hexane, methanol, MEK (methyl ethyl ketone), MIBK (methyl isobutyl ketone), toluene and the general category of glycol ethers. The list also includes other chemicals such as cumene, methylene chloride, quinone and the heavy metals typically found in ink pigments

Particulates in the Air

Some of the materials printers use consist of powders, or powders suspended in a solution, such as in inks or coatings. In some cases, the process may create dust or small particles, i.e., paper dust or Oxydry powder. Particles of microscopic size are known as particulates. They can cause respiratory ailments, as well as other diseases of the organs. Particulates can also occur in a form in which a number of HAPs enter the human or animal body. Particulates do not necessarily have to be solids. They may take the form of droplets of liquid suspended in the air. This is the case with the hydrocarbon oils used in heatset web offset lithographic ink for the printing of publications and newspapers.

Evidence of particulates can be observed at the smokestack from which the hot air and vapors are exhausted from the dryers on the presses. Emissions are evaluated based on the density of the smoke coming out of the stack. If smoke is visible, the process may be emitting objectionable particulates or vapor mist (figure 7–3).

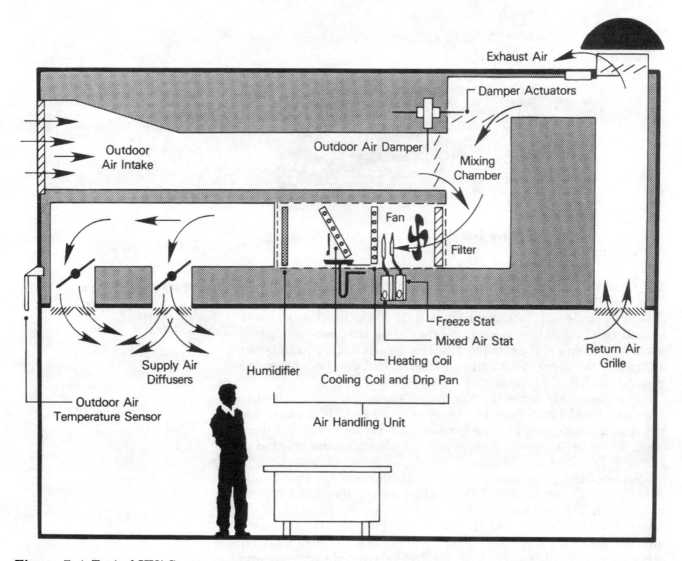

Figure 7–4. Typical HVAC system components.

Source: United States Environmental Protection Agency, Building Air Quality, *A Guide for Building Owners and Facility Managers*, EPA/400/1-91-033, December 1991, p 124.

With the use of chemical solutions that both evaporate and mist, their presence in a typical pressroom will normally be evident by their odors. The odors consist of the evaporation of the more volatile solvents and the liquid drops that splash or mist in the workplace by the rotating action of pumps, rollers and air flow, as well as through handling by personnel. Air removal systems, such as exhausts or air conditioning, may remove the fumes but might also move the irritants to another part of the building. During periods of intensive use of chemistry, such as during clean-up, excessive amounts of the chemicals may escape to other parts of the building. (See figure 7–4.)

OSHA has assigned values to the various chemicals that identify the level and extent to which airborne chemicals will affect health. These limits are expressed in parts per million over an eight-hour exposure period, and a short term of 15 minutes of intense exposure on the job.

For specific chemicals, with radical health ramifications, the agency has issued chemical-specific regulations and much tighter standards of exposure. Among these chemicals is methylene chloride, a compound frequently found in cleaning solutions. The limit of exposure is not only extremely low, but OSHA mandates that such chemicals may only be used in an area that has engineer designed controls, personal protective equipment and specific training standards.

Indoor Air Pollution

The major source of air pollution by printers stems from the cleaning process. Even in the flexographic and gravure processes, where liquid inks may appear to be the source of the problem, most air emissions originate from the clean-ups during and after jobs are run. Tough solvents are used in the cleaning procedures as pressmen look for materials that will cut into and clean off dried inks, coatings and adhesives quickly, and will evaporate with the greatest speed. For that reason, chemicals such as methylene chloride, toluene, xylene, methyl ethyl ketone and hexane usually find their way into the pressroom as the mediums to clean printing plates, ink rollers and fountains, and plate cylinders.

Considerable work is being done by the chemical industry and government pollution prevention groups to find alternative, safer cleaning solvents. Chemistry is not always the answer. Methods of cleaning, meaningful cleaning objectives, and training or retraining of personnel is also critical in altering the mindset of people who have been led by a tradition that may not be the best method to achieve both quality and environmental objectives. See what is being offered; test some of the newer cleaning solvents. There are answers out there, waiting for people to try them.

Process and work practice changes can help to minimize use of chemicals during clean-up. Off-press cleaning equipment is one area for minimizing waste. Recycling of cleaning solutions is another. The key is to reduce the amount used, either by recovering significant amounts for reuse or reducing the amount of solution needed to accomplish the purpose. One method returns the solution back to the process; environmental regulations are based

Clean-up Alternatives

on counting that material just once, not each time it is used or reused. A second method conserves the amount of the solutions needed and disposed of when completely expended.

Hazardous Wastes

At the end of each job, there is a quantity of ink and solvent left over. If the ink or solvent is contaminated, or if it is discolored in any way that renders it unusable, the printer is faced with the problem of disposing of the material properly. In every case where the initial formulation was considered hazardous, these wastes must be considered hazardous wastes.

Any chemical waste, which displays one of four characteristics, or is specifically listed because of known health hazards, is a hazardous waste:

1. **Ignitable** (D001): A liquid with a flashpoint of less than 60 degrees Celsius, 140 degrees Fahrenheit.

2. **Corrosive** (D002): A liquid with a pH less than 2.0 or greater than 12.5.

3. **Reactive** (D003): Wastes that are normally unstable and subject to violent change.

4. **Toxic** (D004–D017): Chromium, lead and silver, etc.

Specific chemicals which are considered detrimental to the welfare of the environment and the community are categorized by a series of "F" numbers, among which are F005 for toluene, F003 for acetone and F002 for perchloroethylene. Figure 7–5 delineates one of the F categories that are pertinent to printing chemistry.

F005 . . . . . . The following spent non-halogenated solvents: Toluene, methyl ethyl ketone, carbon disulfide, isobutanol, pyridine, benzene, 2-ethoxyethanol, and 2-nitropropane; all spent solvent mixtures/blends containing, before use, a total of ten percent or more (by volume) of one or more of the above non-halogenated solvents or those solvents listed in F001, F002, or F004; and still bottoms from the recovery of these spent solvents and spent solvent mixtures.

Figure 7–5. F005—A category of waste frequently found in print shops.
Source: United States Environmental Protection Agency, *Notification of Regulated Waste Activity*, Office of Solid Waste, EPA Form 8700-12 (Revised 7/90).

Once the chemical has been used and no longer has any further use in the process, it is considered a hazardous waste. If the chemical, i.e., ink or solvent, is no longer of use at the press, it is a hazardous waste. A general rule of thumb used by the environmental agencies defines any hazardous chemical that has not been used in a year as a hazardous waste. The printer who generates this waste is responsible for it from the time it is generated until it is finally destroyed. This is termed "cradle to grave" responsibility.

Any material classified as a hazardous waste must be stored, labeled and disposed of in a manner in conformity with the guidelines of the USEPA and the environmental agencies of the various states.

Locating Hazardous Wastes in the Pressroom

Pressrooms and photographic darkrooms generate many wastes which are classified as hazardous. Some enter the process as chemicals, others as a part of the product that is used during the process.

Material Safety Data Sheets (MSDS) are a major tool in the identification and quantification of hazardous chemicals. The listing of hazardous components and percentages in the body of the MSDS and the instructions for disposition of the product and its wastes will help to identify specific substances and describe the potential dangers of releases. Laboratory tests of the waste can help to specify in more detail the number, type and amount of each pollutant present. Wastes can come from any number of sources in the average printing facility.

Darkrooms generate photographic wastes. The fixer solution washes the silver off the film and paper during the developing process. If the fixer that is discharged from the developing system contains more than five parts per million of silver, that liquid is classified as a hazardous waste.

Photographic developer solution, as a corrosive, is a hazardous waste only if its pH exceeds 12.5. Photographic film and paper contain leachable silver in the emulsions. Once processed, the silver will not leach from the paper or film. Unprocessed waste papers and films can carry the silver leachate to a landfill.

Inks and solvents, used to print or to clean, contain a number of solvents which can be both flammable and health risks. Liquid ink systems, including waterborne inks, will employ solvents as the vehicle for carrying pigments and resins. The solvents used are frequently flammable and may create health hazards. Paste inks are defined as non-hazardous, but most contain oils and solvents, some of which could be considered hazardous.

Plates and plate processing chemicals may contain hazardous chemicals or be processed with the use of chemicals which are listed as hazardous. In addition to the chemicals used for processing, the plates themselves may be classified as hazardous.

Shop towels can be contaminated with solvents, inks or other chemicals used for maintaining the presses and other equipment. If disposable wipers are used with hazardous chemicals, such as ignitable alcohols, methylene chloride or MEK, the dirty wipers cannot be sent with the regular garbage for disposal in a landfill. Use of a laundry does allow for the shipment of a limited amount of solvent in the wipers. The wipers must be wrung dry, or at least as dry as is possible. Shipping solvents and inks in wipers can

Figure 7-6. Hazardous waste drums stored prior to disposal.

result in problems for the laundry; check the criteria in the agreement to use a laundry and rent towels relative to the inclusion of solvents and inks in the returns.

Containers which are not completely empty of inks, solvents or other chemicals may pose a problem as hazardous waste. Regulations allow for that portion of the chemical to remain in the drum that cannot be removed through normal use. As an example, a 55-gallon drum can have, at most, one inch of fluid remaining and still be considered RCRA empty. (See figure 7–6.)

Solid Wastes and Resource Conservation

By far the largest waste factor in any printing plant will come from the paper, film and other materials on which the printing is done. Setting up a job requires a certain amount of material. Cleaning at the end of a run can result in material waste. And then there are those orders or portions of orders that simply do not satisfy the quality specifications and must be discarded.

While these wastes do not pose hazards to the public, they do impinge on the availability of space in which they can be disposed of. Sanitary landfills around the country are reaching capacity and there is very little desire in most communities to open new ones.

Burning the wastes in incinerators does not always appeal to local communities. The NIMBY, Not In My Backyard, syndrome opposes erection and operation of incinerators in all communities. Smoke and odors coming from these facilities do not win friends in the neighborhood nor plaudits from local politicians. Environmental justice groups are very sensitive about the siting of garbage incinerators in the poorer and minority communities (figure 7–7).

The dilemma associated with handling and disposing of such solid wastes has given impetus to recovery and recycling programs around the world. The law that we most know for controlling the movement and disposal of hazardous waste also was designed to address the need to reduce the amount of solid wastes generated by our society. The regulation has been designed to be more of a motivator to education and funding of resource conservation than to be a punitive measure.

Printers can readily address one area of waste generation—that of recovering material waste prior to disposal. Paper trim can be cut to smaller sizes for in-house use. When not usable in-house, many printers donate their paper waste, cut to appropriate sizes, to schools, day care centers, community centers, hospitals and other non-profit organizations. There are always uses for paper in art, writing and other classes. Film can also be welcomed in schools and vocational

Figure 7–7. Hempstead, NY recycling center where waste is sorted for recycling and unusable solid waste is burned for energy.

centers, both for creative use in classes or when packaging materials are needed.

But what does one do with the waste that cannot be given away for reuse? This is a problem that has always been addressed by the printing industry. Recycling of paper and film is second nature to the printing and converting industry. Papers and films are made regularly using reprocessed wastes. There have always been applications with paper and film with less stringent quality characteristics for which recycled raw materials can be used. (See figure 7–8.)

Figure 7–8. Paper waste is baled for shipment to mill for recycling.

Recovery and recycling are options that are an essential component of every printing operation. A vast amount of literature exists to guide printers through these programs. Whatever can be recovered and reused avoids the need to purchase fresh stock. Whatever can be sold for recycling into a fresh material or a secondary product can produce an income stream and remove a potential problem for the community.

As a final measure, waste solids can be used as fuel for the generation of energy. Electricity generating plants have been built that can take these wastes and feed them to ovens as a source of energy. Some research and development experimentation projects have developed methods of pelletizing paper and films for use as fuels. While the materials are not being recovered in a physical state, they are serving the purpose of supplying an energy source that will conserve those fossil fuels that are normally used as fuels—coal, petroleum and natural gas.

Wastewater and Printer Discharges

Pollution of water resources is a relatively minor concern, but is nevertheless a lingering problem for many printers. Water is an inherent component of many prepress operations, as well as on-press formulations. Where water is not used, the adverse effects of petrochemicals and other materials that are used are feared in the event of spills—both in house and to the water table (figure 7–9).

Standards for clean water are used as guidelines to establish standards defining the maximum allowable amount of a chemical or category of pollutants in any water tested. The standards are typically issued as a section of the regulations of the local sewer or treatment system (POTW). Wastewater cannot be discharged into septic tanks or directly into navigational waterways.

The USEPA has established standards for specific industries. The standard is titled "Categorical," and is very specific in terms of standards and control options. None of the printing processes are defined in categorical classifications; however, prepress photographic darkroom chemistry falls under categorical status and standards for photoprocessing. In addition to defining the pollutant standards, categorical sources will have to meet pretreatment requirements prior to discharge of wastes to the POTW.

In general, the regulations concerning discharges to sewer systems will list the acceptable levels of various metals that can

Figure 7–9. Sources of drinking water have to be protected.

be discharged and percentages of other contaminants that will be accepted at the POTW. Periodic water testing by the local agency will verify the quality of the drinking water, as well as the wastewater generated by the various processes.

Key items, other than the presence of objectionable chemicals such as heavy metals, that define the quality of the water are:

- Pollutants that can create a fire hazard,

- Pollutants that will cause corrosive structural damage to the POTW, as measured by the pH of the discharged water,

- Solids that will obstruct the flow in the POTW,

- Pollutants that contain oxygen-demanding chemicals, both Biological Oxygen Demand (BOD) and Chemical Oxygen Demand (COD),

- Heated pollutants that will inhibit biological activity in the POTW,

- Petroleum and other oils or products of oils,

- Any pollutant that can result in the release of toxic gases or fumes in the POTW and affect the health of sewer system workers.

Aqueous Systems Common to Printing

A review of the printing process, commencing with prepress and ending in the finishing or converting processes, reveals a number of areas in which aqueous chemistry is dominant or common enough to require an evaluation of the wastes that are discharged.

Prepress activities frequently include the processing of photographic negatives, positives and proofing materials. The piping through which water flows contributes some element of hazardous waste to discharges from the processing equipment. Most dominant in this phase is the prevalence of silver (silver halides). Other metals—copper and lead—may enter the wastewater through the piping and solders through which the process waters must pass. Regardless of source, they are items which must be addressed prior to discharge of the waters to a POTW or to disposal off-site as hazardous waste.

On press, inks may present opportunities for discharge of water wastes. Waterborne ink formulations can carry a number of solvents, which facilitate the suspension of the pigments and resins and surfactants to improve the wetting of inks on films and coatings. At low percentages these ostensibly flammable solutions will not ignite; however, when evaporation occurs in a sewer pipe, they can accumulate and reach levels at which explosions and fires can occur. Some of the surfactants and solvents may be considered health hazards, and discharges could be limited by their presence, as for instance ethylene glycol or ethylene glycol ethers.

Metals in the pigments may also be concentrated in a waste, thereby exceeding the levels acceptable to the POTW. Such metals as barium, zinc and copper may not be heavy metals, but can frequently exceed acceptable discharge limitations.

Fountain solutions required for lithographic printing have historically called for a percentage of isopropanol (isopropyl alcohol). Isopropanol is a VOC; percentages in use can reach 25 percent, although air emission standards have called for reductions to 15 percent for older equipment and 10 percent for newer presses. With refrigeration systems, the percentages of this alcohol can run as low as 2–3 percent. For air, this reduced amount is excellent. For water discharge, the waste must pass the ignitability test before the process waste can be released to the POTW.

Substitutes for what are termed alcohol-free fountain solutions cannot be considered as readily qualified for discharge. Too frequently, the slower drying agents are present in the same or greater amounts as isopropanol, even though there may be chemicals that are more toxic in nature. Toxic chemicals are not welcome in the water system.

Cleaning the press during and after the job run may introduce some of the same problems as the inks used for the press run. A common chemical used in aqueous press washes is butyl carbitol, excellent for cleaning but a known health hazard. Many of the same concerns voiced for inks and fountain solutions are present in press washes, blanket washes, roller washes, etc.

Since many finishing and converting operations that follow printing use adhesives or coatings, care must be taken to go through the same process of identification and analysis for these wastes as well. This includes laminations, UV or water coatings, pressure sensitive adhesives, and similar materials.

Spills a Major Focus

Many print shops may have no reason to create or generate water wastes. They simply do not employ aqueous solutions and/or have their prepress done by a trade shop. This does not preclude the potential for a spill of inks and solvents, which, in turn, will penetrate the ground or exit through drains and thereby enter the water table.

Storage and pressroom use of chemicals must include provision for containment of all solutions contained in drums or large cans. Provision is made by the containment to preclude leakage of any spill into the ground and water system. (See figure 7–10.)

Multimedia Overview

With the various concerns stemming from the use of chemicals, responsible environmental and safety management will identify and evaluate the many ramifications of using any specific chemical. What will help to solve a media problem should alleviate concerns in other areas of confrontation with the community and the ecology as well as in the workplace.

Chemicals do not have one-dimensional effects. Rather, they can impact a variety of concerns. A proactive approach to reducing pollution considers all impacts. Possibly the best overall solution may be the one that compromises for the benefit of all, rather than solving one problem while transferring the hazards to another medium.

Figure 7–10. Containment barriers are aimed at restricting the flow of liquid spills. Rooms or embankments contain the liquid spills (left). Ramps facilitate the movements of drums into the contained area (right).

CHAPTER **8**

Identifying and Quantifying Hazardous Chemicals

Once we have recognized that the materials used in the typical printing plant are potentially hazardous, it is now our job to identify the specific chemicals employed, and to determine the quantities that are held in inventory. Records and reports are required by the various oversight and enforcement agencies, based on periodic usage or typical inventory levels. These records can also be of significant value in helping the printer visualize and understand how well his plant is operating.

The tools are not complex nor are they foreign to the typical plant. Computers and business software will provide the foundation for the collection of data and the analytical processes needed to interpret performance. Computer spreadsheets are easy to develop and maintain. They can be modified or used to model changes that may be contemplated, as well as to dissect the data to provide meaningful representations of how chemicals are used in the plant.

Documents with the basic information necessary to build the spreadsheets are readily available. Very often, something that was developed for one purpose finds many uses beyond the vision of the author. A number of documents and procedures, that are critical elements of work design, quality assurance and safety programs, provide value in the tracking and control of chemicals for environmental compliance and responsibility. Learning to use these tools for conformity to environment regulations requires a smaller investment than developing a completely new set of methods for coping with the measurement of chemicals used in the various printing, coating, adhesive and clean-up processes.

Material Safety Data Sheet
May be used to comply with
OSHA's Hazard Communication Standard,
29 CFR 1910.1200. Standard must be
consulted for specific requirements.

U.S. Department of Labor
Occupational Safety and Health Administration
(Non-Mandatory Form)
 Form Approved
OMB No. 1218-0072

IDENTITY *(As Used on Label and List)*	*Note: Blank spaces are not permitted. If any item is not applicable, or no information is available, the space must be marked to indicate that.*

Section I

Manufacturer's Name	Emergency Telephone Number
Address *(Number, Street, City, State, and ZIP Code)*	Telephone Number for Information
	Date Prepared
	Signature of Preparer *(optional)*

Section II — Hazardous Ingredients/Identity Information

Hazardous Components (Specific Chemical Identity; Common Name(s))	OSHA PEL	ACGIH TLV	Other Limits Recommended	% *(optional)*

Section III — Physical/Chemical Characteristics

Boiling Point		Specific Gravity (H_2O = 1)	
Vapor Pressure (mm Hg.)		Melting Point	
Vapor Density (AIR = 1)		Evaporation Rate (Butyl Acetate = 1)	
Solubility in Water			
Appearance and Odor			

Section IV — Fire and Explosion Hazard Data

Flash Point (Method Used)		Flammable Limits	LEL	UEL
Extinguishing Media				
Special Fire Fighting Procedures				
Unusual Fire and Explosion Hazards				

(Reproduce locally)   OSHA 174, Sept. 1985

Figure 8–1. Material Safety Data Sheet format as proposed by OSHA (page 1 of 2).
Source: OSHA.

Section V — Reactivity Data

Stability	Unstable		Conditions to Avoid
	Stable		

Incompatibility (*Materials to Avoid*)

Hazardous Decomposition or Byproducts

Hazardous Polymerization	May Occur		Conditions to Avoid
	Will Not Occur		

Section VI — Health Hazard Data

Route(s) of Entry: Inhalation?   Skin?   Ingestion?

Health Hazards (*Acute and Chronic*)

Carcinogenicity: NTP?   IARC Monographs?   OSHA Regulated?

Signs and Symptoms of Exposure

Medical Conditions
Generally Aggravated by Exposure

Emergency and First Aid Procedures

Section VII — Precautions for Safe Handling and Use

Steps to Be Taken in Case Material Is Released or Spilled

Waste Disposal Method

Precautions to Be Taken in Handling and Storing

Other Precautions

Section VIII — Control Measures

Respiratory Protection (*Specify Type*)

Ventilation	Local Exhaust		Special
	Mechanical (*General*)		Other

Protective Gloves		Eye Protection

Other Protective Clothing or Equipment

Work/Hygienic Practices

Figure 8–1. Material Safety Data Sheet format as proposed by OSHA (page 2 of 2).

Among the basic tools that will be used to identify and quantify chemicals and wastes in the printing processes are:

1. **Material Safety Data Sheets:** These documents will help to determine just what chemicals are in the inks, solvents and other pressroom chemistry that is used. (See figure 8–1.)

2. **Process Flow Chart:** The charting of the process will provide a visual map of what chemistry is entering the particular process(es), how it is being used, and what leaves the process as a finished product, by-product or waste. (Refer to figure 8–8.)

3. **Mass Balance Spreadsheet:** With information gained from the MSDS and the process flow chart, an analysis can be made of the purchases of inks, solvents and pertinent pressroom chemicals using the mass balance. The mass balance is an accounting for all pertinent purchases of raw materials and the extrapolation of components to determine the quantities of regulated chemicals entering the process. Provisions are made for correlating and computing air, hazardous wastes and wastewater discharges with purchases to develop a model of how the plant operates with respect to the waste streams and how the waste streams are treated. (See Appendix XVII.)

Using these basic tools, the printer will proceed from general fact-finding to data collection and the database need for compliance and problem-solving.

Material Safety Data Sheets

A major instrument of great value to the printer is the Material Safety Data Sheet (MSDS). The MSDS is designed to enable identification of the hazardous chemicals within a product, any potential physical or health hazards, precautions for safe handling, emergency fire and first aid procedures, required personal protective gear, and more. As illustrated in figure 8–1, the format designed by the government was not mandatory. Companies could modify the format, provided that all sections were represented in the final document. As a result, the printer will be faced with various formats from different suppliers. A typical MSDS is shown in figure 8–2. The more pertinent basic sections of the MSDS that are of value to the printer at this stage, for the development of a better understanding of his environmental emissions and discharges, are:

1. **Hazardous Ingredients/Health Hazard Standards:** This lists each hazardous chemical that is in the product in excess of 1% for most chemicals, greater 0.1% for extremely hazardous chemicals. The percentage by weight of the chemical in the product is listed; if not, there will usually be a range or a more than/less than symbol. For

each chemical, the table includes standards for health exposure, such as indoor air pollutants, expressed in parts per million, and limits for internal organs if ingested, typically based on animal studies.

While this section is dedicated to health standards, it has become useful in mapping environmental issues and providing data for compliance with air, hazardous waste and water issues. It is not necessarily complete because of the omission of chemicals and quantities below 1%, but that issue is easily overcome by working with suppliers. Most reputable ink, coating and solvent suppliers will provide the details needed for components under the OSHA thresholds. Some have an additional page on the MSDS for itemizing the data required for air quality compliance. This is frequently called the Air Quality Sheet (figure 8–3).

2. **Physical Characteristics:** This section itemizes the physical characteristics, which enable facilities to properly design or obtain process and safety equipment to secure the well-being of company personnel as well as the local community. Included are the boiling point, vapor pressure, vapor density, specific gravity or weight per gallon of product, percentages volatile and solid by weight and/or volume, evaporation rate, appearance and odor. In many cases, the MSDS will list percentage by weight of VOCs to facilitate air emission computations.

3. **Fire and Explosion Hazard Data:** Many chemicals used for printing can be flammable or combustible. The MSDS will include the flash point of the liquid, the minimum temperature at which the liquid will evaporate and burn, and the flammable explosion limits, which define the range within which the substance will more readily catch fire. The lower the flash point, the more flammable the substance. While this factor does not enter into the development of the mass balance, it can shed light on which solvents will evaporate faster, thereby influencing the selection process.

The other sections of the MSDS are discussed in greater detail in chapter 18, devoted to OSHA and Chemical Safety.

Every chemical must be accompanied by an MSDS when it is delivered to a facility. Suppliers are obligated by law to provide the document with, at least, the first delivery of the substance in a calendar year. This is even more specific if the chemical in its entirety or as a component of a blend or formulation is listed as a toxic chemical under the SARA Title III reporting regulations. Suppliers are well aware of these requirements and are prepared to comply.

Under the rules for providing the MSDS, any manufacturer can adopt the cover of "proprietary or confidential information" to withhold chemical composition information. Any such application must submit information and may be subjected to a rigid test by the Government. However, the company must reveal the information when requested by a health officer or for submission to the enforcement

MATERIAL SAFETY DATA SHEET

AUTOWASH 6000   Page: 1

PRODUCT NAME: AUTOWASH 6000   **HMIS CODES**: H F R P
PRODUCT CODE: A299   1 2 0 B
CHEMICAL NAME: BLANKET AND ROLLER WASH

================ SECTION I - MANUFACTURER IDENTIFICATION ================
MANUFACTURER'S NAME: PRINTERS' SERVICE
ADDRESS   : 26 Blanchard Street
                        Newark, New Jersey 07105

EMERGENCY PHONE   : 1-800-424-9300   LAST REVISION : 09/22/00
INFORMATION PHONE : 1-973-589-7800   DATE REVISED   : 01/25/01
                                            PREPARER   : ENVIRONMENTAL DEPT.

========= SECTION II - HAZARDOUS INGREDIENTS/SARA III INFORMATION =========

		VAPOR PRESSURE	WEIGHT
REPORTABLE COMPONENTS	CAS NUMBER	mm Hg @ TEMP	PERCENT

ALIPHATIC PETRO DISTILLATE (C9 - C11)   64742-48-9   2.7 mmHg   25 C   70 - 80%
     PEL 100ppm: TLV 100ppm // LD50> 25ml/kg: LC50 700ppm/4hr
AROMATIC PETRO DISTILLATE (C8-C11)   64742-95-6   2.7mmHg   25 C   20 - 30%
     PEL 100 ppm // LD50 4.7g/kg: LC50 3670 ppm/8hr
NONYLPHENOXYPOLY(ETHYLENEOXY)ETHANOL   9016-45-9   NO DATA   NO DATA 1 - 10%
     LD50 2.4g/Kg

CAS# 64742-95-6 contains approximately 5% XYLENE (CAS# 1330-20-7) an HAP reportable which has a PEL and TLV of 100 ppm: approximately 4% CUMENE (CAS# 98-82-8). an HAP reportable which has a PEL and TLV of 50 ppm-skin: and approximately 27% 1.2.4 TRIMETHYLBENZENE (CAS# 95-63-6). which has a PEL and TLV of 25 ppm. XYLENE. CUMENE AND 1.2.4 TRIMETHYLBENZENE are subject to the reporting requirements of section 313 OF SARA TITLE III.

=============== SECTION III - PHYSICAL/CHEMICAL CHARACTERISTICS ============
BOILING POINT : 313 F   SPECIFIC GRAVITY (H2O=1): 0.78
VAPOR DENSITY : 4.56 (air = 1)   VAPOR PRESSURE : 2.7 mmHg   at 20 C
DRYING RATE   : .12(n-Butyl Acet.=1) VOC   : 6.48 lb/gl   METHOD: EPA #24
PHOTOREACTIVE : YES   H2O SOLUBILITY : SLIGHT
VOLATILES   : 98%   APPEARANCE   : CLEAR
PHYSICAL STATE : LIQUID   ODOR   : SOLVENT ODOR

================ SECTION IV - FIRE AND EXPLOSION HAZARD DATA ==============
FLASH POINT   : 105 F   **METHOD USED**: TCC
FLAMMABLE LIMITS IN AIR BY VOLUME- LOWER: 0.5   **UPPER**: 6.0
EXTINGUISHING MEDIA: CARBON DIOXIDE. FOAM. OR DRY POWDER (WATER MAY BE INEFFECTIVE)
SPECIAL FIREFIGHTING PROCEDURES : KEEP CONTAINER COOL. CONTROL COOLING WATER SINCE IT MAY TEND TO SPREAD BURNING MATERIAL.
UNUSUAL FIRE AND EXPLOSION HAZARDS: IF BOILING POINT OF SOLVENT IS REACHED. THE CONTAINER MAY RUPTURE EXPLOSIVELY AND IF IGNITED. GENERATE A FIREBALL.

===================== SECTION V - REACTIVITY DATA ======================

STABILITY: YES   **IF NO CONDITIONS**:
INCOMPATIBILITY (MATERIALS TO AVOID): YES
IF YES WHICH ONES: STRONG OXIDIZER
HAZARDOUS DECOMPOSITION OR BYPRODUCTS: CARBON DIOXIDE. CARBON MONOXIDE ON IGNITION
HAZARDOUS POLYMERIZATION: NONE
================== SECTION VI - HEALTH HAZARD DATA =================
INDICATIONS OF EXPOSURE:
INHALATION HEALTH RISKS AND SYMPTOMS OF EXPOSURE: HEADACHE. DIZZINESS. NAUSEA. VERY HIGH LEVELS OF VAPORS COULD CAUSE UNCONCIOUSNESS. SLIGHT IRRITATION OF THE MUCOUS MEMBRANE
EYE CONTACT AND SYMPTOMS OF EXPOSURE: REDNESS OR BURNING SENSATION.
SKIN HEALTH RISKS AND SYMPTOMS OF EXPOSURE: REDNESS. ITCHING. IRRITATION ON OVEREXPOSURE.
INGESTION HEALTH RISKS AND SYMPTOMS OF EXPOSURE: SEVERE GASTROINTESTINAL IRRITATION. NAUSEA. VOMITING AND DIARRHEA.

Figure 8–2. A typical material safety data sheet for a press wash (page 1 of 2).

Courtesy of Printers' Service

MATERIAL SAFETY DATA SHEET

AUTOWASH 6000   Page: 2

EMERGENCY AND FIRST AID PROCEDURES
IF IN EYES: FLUSH WITH WATER FOR 15 MIN. LIFT UPPER AND LOWER EYE LIDS. SEE A DOCTOR.
IF ON SKIN: WASH WITH SOAP AND WATER.
IF INHALED: REMOVE TO FRESH AIR. IF UNCONSCIOUS. USE ARTIFICIAL RESPIRATON.
IF INGESTED: DO NOT INDUCE VOMITING. SEE DOCTOR IMMEDIATELY TO PUMP STOMACH.

HEALTH HAZARDS (ACUTE AND CHRONIC):
EFFECT OF CHRONIC EXPOSURE: PROLONGED HIGH VAPOR EXPOSURE MAY CAUSE LIVER AND KIDNEY PROBLEMS.
EFFECT OF ACCUTE EXPOSURE: NONE

IN ALL CASES OF EMERGENCY AND FIRST AID, WE STRONGLY RECOMMEND A DOCTOR BE SEEN

CARCINOGENICITY: NTP CARCINOGEN: No IARC MONOGRAPHS: No   OSHA REGULATED: No
MEDICAL CONDITIONS GENERALLY AGGRAVATED BY EXPOSURE: DERMATITIS

=========== SECTION VII - PRECAUTIONS FOR SAFE HANDLING AND USE ============
STEPS TO BE TAKEN IN CASE MATERIAL IS RELEASED OR SPILLED: VENTILATE AREA. KEEP AWAY FROM STRONG OXIDIZERS. HEAT. SPARKS OR OPEN FLAMES. PREVENT SPILL FROM SPREADING BY USING AN INERT MATERIAL. SUCH AS SAND. AS A DAM. KEEP OUT OF ALL WATERWAYS OR WATER DRAINS. DO NOT FLUSH AREA WITH WATER. FOR SMALL SPILLS USE ABSORBENT PADS. FOR LARGE SPILLS. CALL A SPILL RESPONSE TEAM. IF REQUIRED. CONTACT STATE/LOCAL AGENCIES.

WASTE DISPOSAL METHOD: PRODUCT SOAKED ABSORBENT SHOULD BE PLACED IN SEALED METAL DRUMS FOR DISPOSAL IN ACCORDANCE WITH LOCAL. STATE AND FEDERAL REGULATIONS.

PRECAUTIONS TO BE TAKEN IN HANDLING AND STORING: KEEP AWAY FROM STRONG OXIDIZERS. HEAT. SPARKS AND OPEN FLAMES. DO NOT CUT OR DRILL INTO AN EMPTY CONTAINER IN ANY WAY THAT MIGHT GENERATE A SPARK. SOLVENT RESIDUE IN THE CONTAINER COULD IGNITE AND CAUSE AN EXPLOSION. KEEP CONTAINER TIGHTLY CLOSED AND OUT OF THE WEATHER.

OTHER PRECAUTIONS: WE RECOMMEND THAT CONTAINERS BE EITHER PROFESSIONALLY RECONDITIONED FOR REUSE OR PROPERLY DISPOSED OF BY CERTIFIED FIRMS TO HELP REDUCE THE POSSIBILITY OF AN ACCIDENT. DISPOSAL OF CONTAINERS SHOULD BE IN ACCORDANCE WITH APPLICABLE LAWS AND REGULATIONS. "EMPTY" DRUMS SHOULD NOT BE GIVEN TO INDIVIDUALS.

===================== SECTION VIII - CONTROL MEASURES =======================
EXPOSURE CONTROL AND PERSONAL PROTECTION:
RESPIRATORY PROTECTION: IF TLV IS EXCEEDED USE A GAS MASK WITH APPROPRIATE CARTRIDGES. CANNISTER OR SUPPLIED AIR EQUIPMENT.
VENTILATION: IF NORMAL VENTILATION IS INADEQUATE USE ADDITIONAL SYSTEMS.ESPECIALLY LOCAL VENTILATION. IF THE VAPOR LEVEL CAN APPROACH THE LEL - LOWER EXPLOSION LIMIT. USE EXPLOSION PROOF SYSTEMS.
PROTECTIVE GLOVES: USE SOLVENT RESISTANT GLOVES.
EYE PROTECTION: USE SAFETY GLASSES OR GOGGLES.
OTHER PROTECTIVE EQUIPMENT OR CLOTHING: NONE.

WORK/HYGIENIC PRACTICES: WASH SKIN/CLOTHES IF THEY COME IN CONTACT WITH THE PRODUCT. DO NOT WEAR CLOTHING WET WITH THE PRODUCT.

========================= SECTION IX - SHIPPING INFORMATION ==================
GROUND SHIPMENT.   UN No   : NA 1993
D.O.T HAZARD CLASSIFICATION: COMBUSTIBLE LIQUID- N.O.S.

========================= SECTION X - DISCLAIMER ===========================
THE INFORMATION AND RECOMMENDATIONS HEREIN HAVE BEEN COMPILED FROM OUR RECORDS AND OTHER SOURCES BELIEVED TO BE RELIABLE. NO WARRANTY. GUARANTY OR REPRESENTATION IS MADE BY PRINTERS' SERVICE AS TO THE SUFFICIENCY OF ANY REPRESENTATION. THE ABSENCE OF DATA INDICATES ONLY THAT THE DATA IS NOT READILY AVAILABLE TO US. ADDITIONAL SAFETY MEASURES MAY BE REQUIRED UNDER PARTICULAR OR EXCEPTIONAL CONDITIONS OF USE. WITH REGARD TO THE MATERIALS THEMSELVES. PRINTERS' SERVICE MAKES NO WARRANTY OF ANY KIND WHATEVER. EXPRESSED OR IMPLIED. AND ALL IMPLIED WARRANTIES OF MERCHANTABILITY AND FITNESS FOR A PARTICULAR PURPOSE ARE HEREBY DISCLAIMED.

Figure 8–2. A typical material safety data sheet for a press wash (page 2 of 2).

VOLATILE COMPONENT INFORMATION

	US EPA Designate

A. Product Density:

1.)   7.39 LB Product /gal Product   =(Dc)s

B. Nonvolatile Content:

1.)   29.82 Weight percent of nonvolatiles in product   =(Wn)s

2.)   21.54 Volume percent of nonvolatiles in product   =(Vn)s

3.)   10.23 Density, lb nonvolatiles/gal nonvolatiles   =(Dn)s

C. Volatiles:

1.)   70.18 Weight percent of total volatiles in product   =(Wv)s

2.)   6.62 Density, lb volatiles/gal volatiles   =(Dv)s

D. Water Content:

1.)   0.00 Weight percent of water in product   =(Ww)s

2.)   0.00 Volume percent of water in product   =(Vw)s

E. Organic Volatiles, (VOCs):

1.)   70.18 Weight percent of organic volatiles in product   =(Wo)s

2.)   78.45 Volume percent of organic volatiles in product   =(Vo)s

3.)   6.62 Density, lb organic volatiles /gal organic volatiles   =(Do)s

4.)   100.00 Weight percent of VOCs in total volatiles   =(Wo)v

5.)   100.00 Volume percent of VOCs in total volatiles   =(Vo)v

F. VOC Content in Product Expressed in Other Terms:

1.) a.)   5.19 lb VOC / gal Product

1.) b.)   621.71 grams VOC / liter Product

2.) a.)   5.19 lb VOC / gal Product less water & exempt solvent

2.) b.)   621.71 grams VOC / liter Product less water & exempt solvent

3.)   24.07 lb VOC / gal total nonvolatiles

G. Volatiles: (all VOCs, HAPs, water & ammonia)

Ingredient	CAS Number	Weight Percent	Density (lb/gal)
n-Propyl Alcohol	71-23-8	63.10	6.71
Heptane	142-82-5	7.08	5.87
Non HAP/SARA Organic Volatiles		0.00	7.75
Water	7732-18-5	0.00	8.34

Figure 8–3. A more precise accounting for the hazardous chemicals in an ink formulation can be found in the Air Quality Sheet included in some material safety data sheets.

Source: MSDS for Ultrabond Phthalo Blue solvent flexo film ink, courtesy of Sun Chemical Company.

agencies This is an important condition that will be referenced when the need arises to obtain more accurate records of the individual components and the amount that is released to the environment. Such information may be critical is establishing categories of waste generation and adhering to regulations and reports whose object is to inform the agencies and the public of the condition of the environment.

Organizing MSDS for Reference

The first step in the process is to take a physical inventory of the chemistry in the plant. Include everything that is on the shelves or at the presses and prepress equipment. This will provide a comprehensive overview of everything in the building—currently used, obsolete or surplus. The inventory will provide a snapshot that can then be used to eliminate or substitute for those hazardous chemicals that are much too dangerous or which duplicate other chemicals being used. A cross-reference with purchases of the past year can help to identify which of the items are current and which are inactive.

Then match the inventory with the MSDSs on file. Do you have the MSDS? If yes, is it a relatively new MSDS or has it been in the plant for a considerable period of time? If you do not have an MSDS, get one quickly. You will need it to develop the mass balance. It is also a requirement of the OSHA hazard communication regulations.

Arrange the MSDSs that are in the facility in a logical system, filing them with a cross-reference code to make access simpler. Use a coding that will segregate the chemicals by areas or process at which used, or in a similar grouping that makes sense for your operation. Organization will facilitate updating the collection and referencing specific MSDSs. As an example, MSDSs can be segregated by function: Prepress, Platemaking, Pressroom, Finishing, Maintenance, etc. Assign an alphabetic designation to the general group, and then use numbers for the individual substances within the grouping. As an example:

Maintaining files can be overwhelming if not organized.

Inks	A—solvent-based ink	1–299
	B—water-based ink	300–499
Solvents	C—process	500–549
	D—cleaning	550–599
Fountain Solutions	E—all	600–625
Press Chemistry	F—all other	626–700
Prepress Chemistry	G—all other	701–799
Adhesives	H—all	800–849

Identifying the Hazardous Components

Once the MSDSs are organized, the next step is to review the hazardous components in the inks, coatings, press chemistry, adhesives and solvents. Accumulate data from the listed components or acquire additional formulation details from the supplier that will serve to identify the common chemicals that are subject to regulation. Using the mass balance arrange columns and a summary table to collect data and group the chemicals in regulatory categories for further use in the evaluation and determination of air emissions. (See figures 8–4 and 8–5.)

Photoreactive chemicals, particularly solvents, are classified as volatile organic compounds and subject to air emission regulations. The common acronym for a photoreactive chemical is VOC. Hazardous air pollutants are chemicals known to be toxic, and are designated as HAPs. Some HAPs are also VOCs; many are not. By the same token, only a selected number of VOCs are HAPs.

Ozone-depleting chemicals affect the ozone layer in the upper atmosphere. A list of ozone-depleting chemicals usually includes a number of chlorinated solvents, e.g., chlorofluorocarbons such as Freon, 1,1,1, trichloroethane, etc.

Pollutants in wastewater can stem from VOCs and HAPs, and can also include other factors that are more relative to aqueous technologies. Grease or grease-like substances, solids, dyes and pigments, and similar products are pollutants to drinking water systems. Photoprocessing introduces silver halides from the negative or paper coating to the wastewater stream. Other metals can be introduced by pigments in the inks as well as by metals in the incoming water. Hazardous wastes will most likely encompass chemicals previously listed for air and water contamination.

The objective at this stage is to accumulate information that will be helpful in developing the process flow charts and the mass balance. As an example, let's examine two MSDSs for press washes. The first is a Metering Roller Cleaner (MRC); the second is a general press wash that will be designated "Powerplus." The chemistry of the two is vastly different, but the intended application and effectiveness in removing dried inks and solids from the press rollers is the same.

The MRC contains methylene chloride, xylene and isopropanol. The Powerplus consists of aromatic petroleum distillates, aliphatic petroleum distillate and sorbitan monoleate. Components of the aromatic petroleum distillate include trimethylbenze, xylene, cumene, all of which are listed as toxic under SARA Title III chemicals. The VOCs are xylene, isopropanol, and the petroleum distillates including its components. The one chemical that is only HAP is the methylene chloride. Those that are both HAPs and VOCs are xylene and cumene. All fall into hazardous waste categories, some as "listed" hazardous wastes. With the exception of the methylene chloride, all are ignitable. Xylene and methylene chloride would be listed and F designated. Wastewater, which should not be affected by the two formulations however, could be of concern in the event of misuse or a spill. Then all would be undesirable pollutants, most as toxic or flammables.

As other pressroom chemistry is brought into the system, there will be many common chemicals, most hazardous, a few not hazardous. The key to environmental responsibility is in identifying the common formulations, as well as listing the specific individual chemicals and determining the total impact of each regulated chemical. Perception of a true hazard depends on both a qualitative and a quantitative measure of the impact that chemical will have in the workplace and on the environment.

COMPANY	Exquisite Printing Inc.							
ADDRESS	220 West North Street, Star, NJ							
WORKSHEET TO COMPUTE VOC EMISSIONS						YEAR: 1999		
							VOC'S EMITTED SHEETFED	HS WEB
ITEM	POUNDS PER GALLON	POUNDS VOC'S PER GALLON	PERCENT VOC'S A	GALLONS PURCHASED	POUNDS PURCHASED	VOC'S (COL A X B)		W/OXIDIZER
					B			
INKS- LITHOGRAPHIC			5.00%		50925	2546	891	1655
VARNISH			5.00%		10125	506	253	253
AQUEOUS COATINGS	9.1	0.11	1.68%	4685	42634	716	716	0
FOUNTAIN CONCENTRATES								
ANCHOR EMERALD JRNC	8.90	1.70	19.10%	237	2109	403	403	0
ANCHOR PREMIUM MXEH	8.70	0.72	8.24%	399	3471	286	0	286
55-NONPILING ADDITIVE	8.86	4.87	55.00%	385	3410	1875	1875	0
ARS-ML (ALCOHOL SUBSTITUTE)	7.7	6.48	84.16%	122	939	791	791	0
ISOPROPANOL ALCOHOL	6.55	6.55	100.00%	660	4323	4323	4323	0
PRESS WASH								
A70 NWM WASH	6.70	6.70	100.00%	110	737	737	553	184
AUTO WASH 6000- WEB	6.47	6.47	100.00%	270	1748	1748	0	1748
AUTO WASH 6000- SHEET	6.47	6.47	100.00%	440	2849	2849	2849	0
A220 ALT WASH 7662	6.70	6.70	100.00%	1330	8911	8911	8911	0
TSG EVERGREEN PRESS WASH	8.30	0.52	6.24%	395	3279	205	205	0
CLEANSALL	8.22	1.10	13.39%	42	345	46	46	0
SPEEDY	6.12	3.06	50.00%	259	1586	793	595	198
MRC F PRISCO	6.81	3.54	52.01%	180	1225	637	478	159
RED MAGIC	7.28	7.28	100.00%	207	1507	1507	1507	0
FSG	8.94	0.07	0.78%	39	349	3	2	1
LITHOTURPS	6.55	6.55	100.00%	114	747	747	560	187
TOTALS				9874	141217	29628	24957	4671
						POUNDS		
OXIDIZER WEB - 90% DESTRUCT								467
SHEET-FED							24957	
TOTAL NET VOC EMISSIONS							25424	
ANNUAL OPERATING HOURS						6000		
						HOURS		
TOTAL VOC'S PER HOUR						4.94		
						LBS VOCS/HOUR		
ANNUAL TONS VOC'S							12.71	

Figure 8–4. Summary portion of mass balance for printer to compute total VOCs emitted.
Source: P-F Technical Services Inc.

PRIME PLASTICS INC
22 Venturi Lane
Brookfield, MA

PRINTING-FLEXO
INKS

	AMOUNT PURCHASED (POUNDS)	POUNDS VOC'S BREAKDOWN	PROPANOL 71-23-8	ETHANOL 64-17-5	NP ACETATE 109-60-4	PROP GLY MONO ETHR 107-98-2	PRO GLY ETHR ACE 108-65-6	DIACETONE ALCOHOL 123-42-2	ISOPROPYL ALCOHOL 67-63-0	ISOPROPYL ACETATE 108-21-4
Label Magenta	593	409		267	18	89	12		12	12
Label Red 032	677	447		305	7	135				
CS White	865	484		346	17	87	9		17	9
Press Ready Black	1000	700		450		150	25		50	25
Orange	264	187		119	5	53			5	5
Red 185	962	673	308	87	38	221	10		10	
Green 348	1313	906	381	184	39	276			26	
Process Blue	2300	1610	552	345	46	437		230		
Yellow 109	3000	2130		1350	60	600			60	60
Red 485	2000	1400	640	220	80	340		120		
White	2000	880	520	60	40	260				
Extender	1000	700		500	50	20	50		50	30
Rubine Red	1500	1050		705	45	75	30		120	75
RLC Warm Red	2000	1400		1000	80	200			80	40
Violet	582	425		262		87	23		29	23
Reflex Blue	1050	777	347	126	21	263			21	
TOTALS FOR YEAR	21106	14179	2747	6325	547	3292	158	350	480	279

POUNDS

Figure 8-5. Portion of mass balance that segregates usage by components.
Source: P-F Technical Services Inc.

The information in the hazardous ingredients section of the MSDS also provides the printer with insight into the performance of the inks and solvents. By listing the various solvents and percentages, the MSDS has opened a window to understanding of the functioning of the ink on press and of the press washes in cleaning. Each solvent has a particular drying characteristic; some are faster, some slower. (Refer to Chapter 6, Table 6–1.)

Based on the now known solvent blend (see Table 8–1), we can determine why one ink dries differently than another ink, even when both are sold under the same brand name. The solvent blend we then use to dilute the ink can be engineered to satisfy changes required in drying speeds to achieve higher productivity and more acceptable product quality. By the same token, this portion of the MSDS allows the printer to understand what substances are being used and to take action to eliminate or reduce the amount of unwanted chemicals in the plant. Preventing potential pollution through materials substitution can be beneficial for the process and eliminate the exposure that may require permits or periodic reports to the regulatory agencies.

Two examples in flexographic inks have been methanol and toluene. Both were staples for many years for solvent blends and ink formulations. Both have been eliminated or greatly reduced as firms seek means of reducing their exposure to SARA Title II, Section 313. Any facility using 10,000 pounds of the listed chemicals is required to file an annual report every July 1 with the USEPA. During the past few years, firms using these chemicals have been asked to submit plans and institute a pollution prevention program.

Some press washes for lithographic presses have methylene chloride as a major component. A major impetus in replacing this component came with the intense program of enforcement and drastically reduced allowable air exposure in standards promulgated by OSHA.

Using the Hazard Data to Eliminate Pollution and Liability

TABLE 8–1. TYPICAL BLEND OF SOLVENTS USED TO MANUFACTURE AN INK FOR PRINTING ON THE SURFACE OF A FILM

G. Volatiles: (all VOCs, HAPs, water & ammonia)

Ingredient	CAS Number	Weight Percent	Density (lb/gal)
Ethanol	64-17-5	28.62	6.62
n-Propyl Acetate	109-60-4	9.32	7.40
Heptane	142-82-5	7.87	5.87
n-Propyl Alcohol	71-23-8	5.01	6.71
Isopropyl Alcohol	67-63-0	3.39	6.55
Light Aliphatic Solvent Naphtha	64742-89-8	0.49	6.26
Non HAP/SARA Organic Volatiles		0.00	7.75
Water	7732-18-5	0.01	8.34

Source: MSDS for Sunsheen Phthalo Blue ink, courtesy of Sun Chemical Company

Responsible for causing birth defects in expectant mothers, substitutions have been made in many presswash formulations to eliminate and replace the methylene chloride.

At this stage of the evaluation of facility chemistry it is opportune to replace the more hazardous inks, coatings, adhesives and solvents with less hazardous or non-hazardous formulations which will perform the necessary jobs. In many companies, making changes in ink and solvent blend formulations has reduced liability and actually resulted in considerable monetary savings for the printer. Knowing how to control the materials with which graphics are transferred has resulted in a better technical understanding of the environmental impact of the printing ink transfer systems and control of the physical and chemical variables.

Charting the Use of Chemicals in the Process

Now that you have identified the chemicals that you purchase and inventory, the next step is to chart the use of these materials in the process and determine what happens to them. This step is known as Process Flow Charting. Figure 8–6 has been developed to show all the steps of the various printing processes and presents a broad overview of the flow of materials into and out of most printing processes from start to finish. The materials that are used are shown at each stage, going into the particular phase of the process (input column) and what becomes of them (output column). Whatever remains as product moves to the next step in the process.

Using this general overview as a guide, a flow chart can be developed for every machine or process, commencing with the design of the artwork and proceeding through prepress and printing to the finishing or converting of the end product. Each function of the system will identify the chemicals going into the process and the wastes emerging after the materials have become part of the printed product. The flow chart illustrates the movement of the materials through the process, the operations in which the chemicals are used, and the safety and ecological hazards which dictate compliance with government regulations and standards. The flow chart for a specific process or group of similar processes will be more explicit as to which chemicals are going into the product and which are exiting as waste.

As illustrated by the flow chart, each step in the sequence, from prepress to finishing, is included. Broad categories of materials are shown entering the process and broad definitions of the resulting waste stream are itemized. This chart is an excellent starting point to identify what is happening and where, and can serve as a guide for the smaller, more concise charts of the individual processes.

Taking the charting down to the next level (figure 8–7), an analysis is made of every chemical, other than ink, which enters the pressroom. The chart identifies how the chemical is being used and depicts what happens with the remnants (waste). In this pressroom, chemicals are divided into two major categories—wastewater and other pressroom chemistry. Aqueous chemicals are destined to

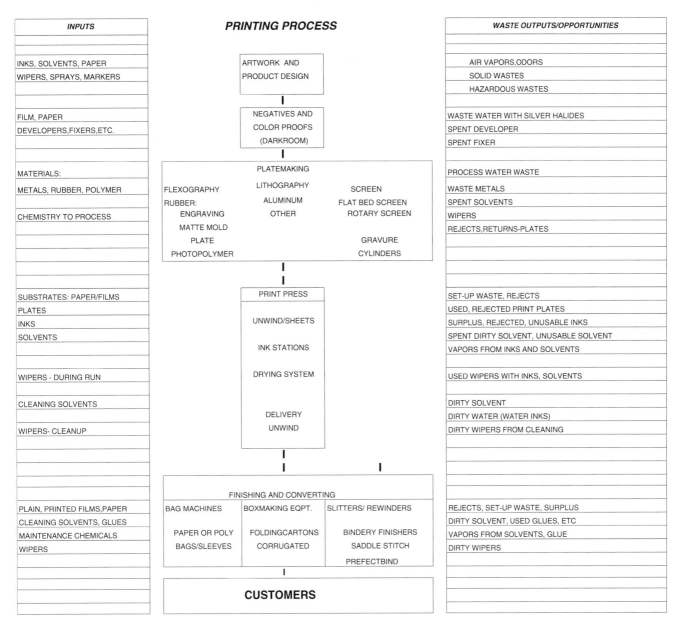

Figure 8–6. Flow chart depicting input of materials and output of wastes and product.
Source: P-F Technical Services Inc.

enter a water treatment system that will result in a non-hazardous waste stream. Each formulation is tracked to indicate how it is to be handled enroute to the treatment process, and from there out of the facility. The common thread in tracking these chemicals is how they enter the wastewater stream, as well as how the support system channels all aqueous wastes to the point at which the pollutants are removed from the effluent.

The flow chart then addresses the non-aqueous chemicals. Some are not hazardous and used with wipers, which are then laundered off-site. Others are hazardous and are destined for disposition off-site at authorized treatment and disposal facilities. On the way to

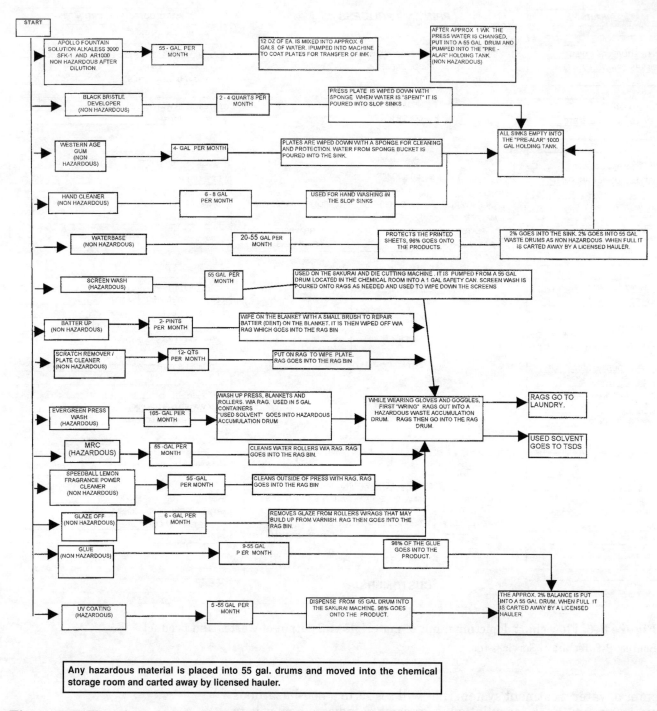

Figure 8–7. Flow chart depicting processing of chemicals in lithographic pressroom.
Courtesy of Joe Badalamenti, Disc Graphics Inc.

this disposition, the chemicals come into contact with wiping cloths. Disposal of these wipers is also addressed, involving shipping the soiled wipers to laundries that are also managing their processes to minimize impact on the environment. By following the path of the chemicals, the printing facility has been able to make changes and utilize its chemistry in safer and less polluting ways.

This flow charting process can be taken to an even more detailed level (figure 8–8) by depicting the steps taken to accomplish a job and usage of chemistry for an individual piece of equipment. This would be desirable for other reasons, one being to plan and comply with health and safety regulations.

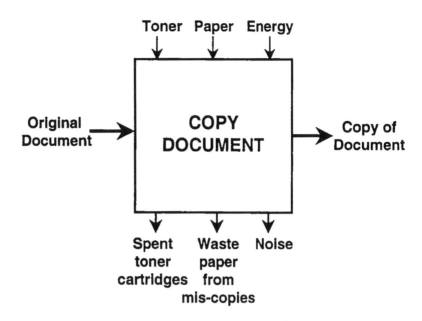

Figure 8–8. Flow chart of the input-output for a copier.

Source: United States Environmental Protection Agency, *Integrated Environmental Management Systems, Implementation Guide*, EPA 744-R-00-011, p 18.

Quantifying the Chemicals and Exposure

Compliance with environmental regulations has two aspects. One is a question of quality, laying in the nature of the chemistry and how it relates to regulated standards for compliance. The other is the quantity of the various chemicals and how much that quantity represents in terms of exposing the community and ecology to potential dangers. Given the fact that many pressroom chemicals are made of either VOCs or HAPs, both of which raise questions of health impacts, how is a printer, coater or package converter to know what type of permit he is required to have to operate a print shop? Additionally, what specific regulations address his concern about the wastes generated and their effects on public health?

The answer is a "Mass Balance" accounting in which all purchases of inks, coatings, adhesives and solvents containing chemicals classified as VOCs and HAPs are recorded and an analysis of the chemicals is evaluated to determine just how much the VOCs and HAPs represent. The size of the facility and the nature of the chemistry used will determine how extensive an accounting is required. A small firm may be able to manually compute its emissions and discharges. A larger facility, using a more extensive, variable inventory of inks, solvents and other chemicals, would need a more exacting, complex computerized spreadsheet or data-based software program (see Appendix XVII).

Using a manual or computerized spreadsheet, let's walk through a typical Mass Balance computation for a small offset printer. This can be done periodically, when the number of chemicals being used is limited and the variety of components can be easily

Computing Emissions for Small Facilities

computed. Permits may dictate the time periods that would be acceptable for such records and reports. The underlying premise in using the record of purchases is that purchases replace depletions in inventory and replicate the amounts being consumed.

Using the format illustrated in Appendix XVII, gather all Material Safety Data Sheets and purchase information and prepare to develop your emissions statement. Follow the steps below.

1. Enter the various chemical products purchased in the rows on the left side of the spreadsheet. This will entail listing the inks purchased by color, fountain solutions and concentrates, solvents and solvent blends (press washes), coatings and adhesives. Each formulation can have different components or different percentages of the same components.

2. For each chemical, enter basic information from the MSDS: pounds per gallon of the product, total percent VOCs, and pounds of VOCs per gallon of product. This information will be used to compute pounds of materials used and then to calculate the air emissions as a whole and by the various chemical components.

3. Enter pounds of product purchased, by item. The only exception will be lithographic paste inks. Enter total pounds for all inks purchased by supplier and then as a whole. For the first analysis, the entries can be for the period as a whole—year, six months or quarter. Subsequently, the records will be maintained on a monthly basis to conform with recording and reporting standards established by the USEPA. When entering by months, the data will be accumulated by quarter and by year-to-date.

4. If purchased in gallons, enter the number of gallons purchased. This will be done in a similar manner as with pounds, on a periodic basis, i.e., a quarter, or, if using a computer, on a monthly basis with a year-to-date computation. The computer formulas will convert the gallons to pounds.

5. Some chemicals, particularly thinners and press washes, may be sold by the gallon. Enter those in the Gallons Purchased column. Convert to pounds using the Pounds Per Gallon and enter in the total pounds column for that product. Others may be invoiced by pound; enter these items in the Pounds Purchased column.

6. Multiply the purchases by the appropriate factor (% VOCs when pounds are recorded; pounds per gallon when purchases are by the gallons). Enter this number in the VOCs column.

7. For lithographic inks, an average percentage has been deemed acceptable to calculate the VOCs. The percentages vary by the particular lithographic process, but these standards by process have been accepted as engineering standards by industry and the USEPA. (Refer to figure 8–9.)

8. For liquid ink systems, in gravure and flexography, every ink by color will have to be listed separately to make the computations. The MSDSs are committed to containing the total percentage or pounds of affected chemicals (VOCs). If not a percentage, the amount per gallon can be expressed as pounds per gallon.

9. Add the items in the columns for VOCs, Pounds Purchased and Gallons Purchased.

10. Divide the Total VOCs by 2,000 pounds to get the Tons Emitted.

You now have the actual air emissions that are emanating from your facility. Similar computations can be done with chemicals that enter the wastewater discharges. Hazardous waste can be accumulated and deducted, within reason, from the actual amounts departing the building as air emissions or as water waste.

Computing Emissions for Major Facilities

The simple spreadsheet shown in figure 8–9 does not satisfy the requirements for major facilities. Enforcement policies require monthly accounting for emissions; in some states the accounting period can be as short as one day. The role of the computer in maintaining records and generating reports cannot be minimized. The amount of detail and the formulas required to break out the information needed to adequately collect and analyze the data is beyond the scope of a manual process.

An expanded spreadsheet enables a facility to establish maximum reliability in charting the purchases of all chemistry and in tracking the emissions, hazardous wastes and water discharges from those purchases. This approach is viable as long as the number of items is manageable. When the volume of different chemicals increases, it is best to work with a program that is data based. The same approach would be mandated when reporting moves to shorter and shorter periods, where the number of computations would increase exponentially to account for the increased number of different items entering the printing process during the day for that number of shorter periods. The difference between the simpler mass balance illustrated above and the more comprehensive spreadsheet is reflected in Appendix XVII, which is indicative of a typical flexographic, gravure or publication lithographic facility.

Potential to Emit—A Federal Mandate

Once the emissions of VOCs have been determined, it is time to calculate the potential for your facility to emit in the course of a full year. This is known as PTE—Potential To Emit, a measure of how much will be exhausted from the facility if it ran every hour of every day of the year. That would amount to a total of 8,760 hours. The tonnage emitted as represented by the PTE will be the key factor in determining the type of permit that will be required for the facility.

7.9.1   Ink

     7.9.1.1   Heatset Ink. The annual potential emissions from the use of heatset ink is equal to the amount of ink used per year multiplied times the VOC content of the ink, minus 20 percent of this total VOC to account for retention of VOC by the substrate. The VOC content of the ink should be determined by the EPA Method 24. In lieu of using this estimate of 20 percent VOC retention, test data can be used to establish the exact amount of VOC's retained in the substrate for this type of ink.

     7.9.1.2   Non-heatset Ink. The annual potential emissions from the use of non-heatset ink is equal to the amount of ink used per year multiplied times the VOC content of the ink, and minus 95 percent of this total VOC to account for retention of VOC by the substrate. The VOC content of the ink should be determined by the EPA Method 24. In lieu of using this estimate of 95 percent VOC retention, test data can be used to establish the exact amount of VOC's retained in the substrate for this type of ink.

7.9.2   Fountain Solution

     7.9.2.1   Alcohol. In facilities where alcohol is used in the fountain solution, the annual potential to emit VOC's is equal to the amount of alcohol used per year, since alcohol is a VOC. In most cases, the alcohol will be isopropyl alcohol.

     7.9.2.2   Nonalcohol Additive or Alcohol Substitute. For facilities where a nonalcohol additive or alcohol substitute is used in the fountain solution, the potential to emit VOC's is equal to the amount of additive or substitute used per year multiplied by the VOC content of the additive or substitute, as determined by the EPA Method 24.

7.9.3   Cleaning Solution

     The potential to emit VOC's from the use of cleaning solution is equal to the amount of cleaning solution used during the year multiplied by the VOC content of the cleaning solution, as determined by the EPA Method 24.

Figure 8–9. The EPA has worked with the industry associations to develop standards for VOC emissions from lithographic presses. These percentages may be used in lieu of information provided in the MSDS.

Source: United States Environmental Protection Agency, *Guideline Series, Control of Volatile Organic Compound Emissions from Offset Lithographic Printing, Draft*, Office of Air Quality Planning Standards Research Triangle Park, September 1993, pp 7–12.

Take the quantity of VOC emissions for the year and divide that number by the hours operated during the year. Use all hours—run, clean-up, set-up and downtime. Emissions are occurring at all times when inks and solvents are present at the presses. Clean-up hours may contribute a large percentage of your emissions.

COMPANY	BLAND OFFSET LLC					
ADDRESS	2 BLANKET PLACE, ANILOX,		OHIO			
WORKSHEET TO COMPUTE VOC EMISSIONS				YEAR: 1999- SIX MONTHS		
ITEM	POUNDS PER GALLON	POUNDS VOC'S PER GALLON	PERCENT VOC'S A	GALLONS PURCHASED	POUNDS PURCHASED B	VOC'S (COL A X B)
INKS			5.00%		1700	85
FOUNTAIN CONCENTRATES						
ALKALESS P	8.47	5.20	61.42%	30	254	156
CONCENTRATE 5451	8.88	0.70	7.88%	54	480	38
CONCENTRATE 3451	8.88	0.73	8.22%	100	888	73
ISOPROPANOL ALCOHOL	6.55	6.55	100.00%	30	197	197
PRESS WASH						
NB SPECIAL BLANK & ROLLR	6.75	6.75	100.00%	330	2228	2228
CLEANSALL	8.22	1.10	13.39%	15	123	17
MRC PRISCO (Acetone)	6.80	4.00	58.82%	12	82	48
RED MAGIC	7.28	7.28	100.00%	5	36	36
LITHOTINE	6.56	5.91	90.13%	6	39	35
LITHOTURPS	6.55	6.55	100.00%	8	52	52
FEDEROID	6.81	3.71	54.51%	60	408	223
POWERKLEENE	6.71	6.71	100.00%	180	1208	1208
TOTALS				830	7695	4395
						POUNDS
ANNUAL OPERATING HOURS						4000
						HOURS
TOTAL VOC'S PER HOUR						1.10
						LBS VOCS/HOUR
ANNUAL TONS VOC'S						2.20
						TONS

Figure 8–10. Emission statement for small printer.
Source: P-F Technical Services Inc.

The printer will now have the pounds per hour. This is a measure of the product and process design for the facility. It accounts for differences from job to job of ink coverage, numbers of colors being printed, speed, and other variables that are common to the printing processes. Multiply the pounds per hour by 8,760 hours. The result will be the pounds of VOCs that could be emitted for the year. Divide by 2,000 pounds and the PTE will be expressed in tons per year.

As an example, use a plant that emits an actual amount of VOCs of 100,000 pounds over the course of two eight-hour shifts. That would result in 4,000 operating hours. The emissions divided by 4,000 equates to 25 pounds per hour. Multiplying the 25 pounds per hour by 8,760 hours yields 219,000 pounds of VOCs, or a potential to emit of 109.5 tons. This facility would require a major permit in every state of the Union. See Appendix XIX for more details in addressing site specific computation of the potential to emit.

Next Step: Where Do We Go From Here?

Now that you have a more comprehensive picture of what you use, where it goes and how much there is of each of the hazardous components, the printer can move to the next step.

1. What are the specific regulations that apply to my facility?

2. How do we satisfy the regulatory requirements, including all activities and responsibilities for a facility of our size?

3. Can steps be taken to lessen the regulatory load?

4. How can we address the nature of our chemistry and find safer, sounder alternatives without sacrificing productivity and quality?

5. Where do we turn for help to better understand the options available to better manage the environmental responsibilities and implement the necessary measures?

This book will be a guide to finding the answers to your specific questions and needs. Use it as a reference, reaching out to those resources identified to assist in general, as well as in the specific state in which the facility is located. State and local laws necessitate a close review of any mandates that may be more stringent than those of the federal government.

CHAPTER **9**

Taking a Proactive Stance: The Internal Audit

The basis for establishing and maintaining a viable environmental program is by means of the periodic internal audit. This snapshot of the status of the facility provides insight into how well compliance issues have been addressed and how effectively personnel are functioning within the constraints of regulatory limitations. What the audit does is to ascertain what the status of the facility is with regard to OSHA and the environment.

An environmental and safety compliance audit is a systematic examination of the records, the physical plant and the working practices in a facility to verify whether all are in compliance with the requirements dictated by regulations applicable to the activities taking place within the facility. The compliance audit discussed in this chapter is not to be confused with the Phase 1 or Phase 2 audits, which are conducted at the time of real estate or financial lending negotiations. The Phase 1 and 2 audits are conducted to determine the environmental status of the site and identify problems where pollution exists that may require remediation. Phase 1 and 2 audits will be required when property, including machinery, is being purchased, sold or rented and financed by banks or insurance companies.

The compliance audit is intended to identify and expose any conditions, whether physical or paperwork, that are not in compliance with existing regulations for the facility and its personnel. With knowledge of the existing conditions and practices obtained from the audit, plans can be made to provide the necessary support and resources to meet the challenges of the regulations.

Advantages of Conducting an Audit

The question may be raised as to the value of conducting an audit. Would it not open doors to inconsistencies that could be used against the company? While that outcome may be possible, there are compelling reasons for supporting the benefits that the audit will achieve.

1. An effective audit can often show areas where performance can be improved, reducing production costs by enhancing productivity.

2. An audit can often show where there can be better utilization of men, materials and machinery to create the same product at a lower cost—either by reducing the labor needed, by substituting equivalent materials that perform with less impact on the environment, or by showing more effective ways of using production equipment while generating less waste.

3. An audit may demonstrate a better means of throughput of the product, enhancing operational efficiency.

4. An audit may lead to improvements in the design of the product, enabling the company to become more competitive in the marketplace.

5. An audit can show how a change in technology will offer compliance as well as enable the introduction of advantages in the product and the costs of manufacture.

6. An audit can focus on inventory and purchase policies and procedures for use of process chemistry, such as inks, coatings, adhesives and solvents, to provide guidance for better management of these resources in light of production needs and regulatory constraints. Large quantity purchases may be self-defeating. Lack of control over internal use of chemicals may generate excessive waste. Poor color matching and control may lead to excessive quantities of unusable ink, which will eventually become waste. The introduction of internal blending and control equipment may save money up front, as well as in the consequences of current practices.

7. Non-compliance may lead to a heavy burden in penalties and legal costs. The audit can identify areas of non-compliance and remedy the lapses before the exceedances from regulatory standards become a matter of record. With some exceptions, self-audits and redeeming actions will not lead to agency penalties.

Organizing for the Internal Audit

The first challenge to generating a successful internal audit lies in the organization of the planning for a program that will have management support and appropriate personnel involvement. As in every other major effort by the corporation, management must provide a policy statement to set the stage.

This statement must be very specific in assuring every member of the organization, as well as outsiders, that the personnel, resources and the will of management will accept nothing less than complete compliance with all regulations. A good example of a corporate policy statement would say that: "Firm X respects the environment and the health of the community and will do everything appropriate to protect the ecology and residents of the community."

The next step is most crucial for establishing the basis of an environmental compliance audit. That is the composition and selection of the team that will conduct the audit. The team must reflect the various talents and expertise of the personnel who will inspect, review and interpret the actual performance of the facility with respect to the laws, rules and technical aspects for the specific processes and activities.

Accordingly, the ideal team should include a representative of manufacturing management, technical or engineering staff, legal, human resources and regulatory affairs. In a number firms, one individual may carry the burden of two or more of these disciplines. In a small firm these may all be embodied in only one or two people. The key is to be able to have a full perspective inasmuch as the audit is designed to document actual conditions and compare them with the legal and theoretical benchmarks established by the regulatory agencies.

An ideal audit team is representative of many skills and experience.

Knowledge of the production process is critical. Recognizing the validity of plant activities and acknowledging the potential for improvement will require a sound background in the technology. Improving the current level of activity will require knowledge of the latest developments in technology, and the applicability of any changes to be made, which result from the findings of the audit as to the process and the product. Without this expertise, evaluations and recommendations may sound inviting but may be impractical.

Understanding of the scope and requirements of the various environmental and safety regulations is another aspect. With the broad assortment of laws that have been passed and are being enforced, the team should include a member who is generally knowledgeable about the federal, state and local regulations. This person does not have to have expertise in all facets of the laws, but should have a general background, with in-depth knowledge of the major factors likely to be of concern for the particular facility.

Human Resources will play a major role in the safety and training aspects of the regulations. Most environmental, and certainly all safety, regulations contain provisions for specific and ongoing training of personnel. While the Human Resources staff may not do the physical training, they should be aware of and be able to document any and all training that takes place.

The legal member of the team is there to read and interpret the laws and the regulations. If there is any question as to intent and compliance, this member of the team should be able to provide guidance to all other members of the team.

Role of Consultants

Outside consultants lend a fresh viewpoint.

Once the team has been assembled, management may want to introduce a neutral party to the process. There is nothing better than seeing an operation with a fresh eye, one that has not been influenced by daily contact with the culture of the facility and yet has sufficient comprehension of the process and the constraints placed on that process by the law. That, in essence, is the role of a consultant.

The consultant may be an outsider, hired to work with the audit team, or may be engaged to fully conduct the audit with the assistance of the management and personnel of the facility. The consultant may be drawn from another facility owned by the same company or from an internal consulting department, such as the industrial or manufacturing engineering department.

The major criterion when selecting the consultant is to recognize the support that will be brought to the firm and the audit team. Whoever is selected must bring with him his own team of experts. There is so much diversity inherent in the technologies of printing, and the environmental and safety regulations that apply to the industry, that a competent consultant will necessarily be supported by a network of specialists, both technical and regulatory.

The consultant, however, is there only to help identify what is taking place and to guide the team or management in making decisions. Facility personnel must retain responsibility for providing the auditors with all pertinent information and resources, as well as taking the steps required to achieve or maintain compliance.

Conducting the Audit

An environmental audit is a step-by-step assessment of the status of the facility in all aspects of safety and environmental regulations. Legally, it can be considered as an admission by your firm that it is not in compliance with the law. In fact, and in practice, there has been considerable discussion and disagreement about the role of audits in the enforcement of the law. Prodded by Industry, the EPA has encouraged firms to conduct audits and has provided guidelines to protect them from having the contents of an audit being used against the firm in any litigation by the government. Some states have passed laws prohibiting the citing of audits in enforcement actions. Others have not and rely on federal policies. This remains a point of contention and it is wise to consider the legal implications, working with the lawyers and consultants as a team when planning and conducting the audit.

The audit should take place in stages:

1. **Plan the audit.** Know what regulations are to be part of the investigation; determine what records will be needed; ascertain the personnel in each plant who will be on the audit team to assure adequate technical and managerial input; determine if a consultant is to be utilized and what will be required of the consulting firm that will, if necessary, be hired to do the audit.

2. **Review all paperwork** relative to the regulations; insure that all files are available, that all information relating to compliance is available. This will include permits, permit applications, correspondence to and from regulatory agencies, information from associations and other firms in the industry (competitors and suppliers), internal memos.

3. **Inspect all physical aspects** of the facility with regard to process performance, materials storage and conditions, personnel practices as they reflect on the compliance requirements.

4. **Assemble all technical information** relative to chemicals used in the plant. This should include material safety data sheets (MSDS), technical bulletins and any manuals.

5. **Provide all data relative to purchase and use** of chemicals; compute a mass balance for each to determine what happens with all chemicals that are taken into the plant. How much goes into the product, how much is emitted into the air outside the plant, how much is fugitive in the plant, water discharges, solid waste disposal, etc.? Account for all material by weight and/or volume.

6. **Evaluate how effective** the facility's efforts have been to date in complying with the regulations.

7. **Summarize the findings** of the audit in a comprehensive report. The report should be presented to management and become the basis for a long-range program, with the immediate objective of bringing the operation under control and into full compliance with the laws.

In general, the audit should be a snapshot of the operation as it was observed on the day the team inspected the plant and the files and interviewed personnel. The report should reflect what was seen and heard during the day or period in which the audit was conducted.

Tools to Use in the Audit

The audit will make use of a number of tools. Some are very structured and take the shape of check-off lists to ascertain whether something is or is not taking place. Others are there to quantify pollutants and activity, to give a third dimension to the data. There are also tools which provide a basis for analysis of the data and discussion as to cause-and-effect relationships.

Audit Checklist

The audit checklist consists of a listing of the various regulations and the key elements required to comply with the particular law/regulation. The checklist will consist of groups of similar items. Some listed regulations and requirements are national or state; other regulations may be local.

A checklist helps to avoid the omission of any regulations and provisions.

It is imperative that the checklist be complete as to coverage of regulations affecting the particular regional regulations pertaining to the location of the plant and also take cognizance of the local regulations. Often, the local fire and health departments may have more stringent standards than those of the federal and state government agencies.

The checklist is used to note both physical conditions seen during the plant inspection and the completeness and accuracy of documents in the files. To facilitate inspection of the facility in a logical and structured fashion and to review appropriate records a check-off list will embody the requisite organization. The format will depend on the complexity of the particular facility and the regulations that confront that site. The basic components may change in degree of detail, but not in applicability. A typical checklist is shown in Appendix X.

MSDS, Flow Charts and Mass Balances

Using the tools set up earlier to maintain records of the chemistry and the volume of usage, observations in the audit can be quantified. The material safety data sheets provide the resources for describing the details of the chemicals used as well as the compliance issues that must be addressed for both safety and the environment. The flow charts will substantiate the paths taken by the chemicals in the production process and the wastes that will be generated. The mass balance will document the purchases of the chemistry and how these translate into the various types of pollutants and wastes in terms of pounds per hour, per minute or whatever may be the most pertinent method of measurement.

Put into the context of observations and interviews by the audit team, the three tools will provide another dimension to the capability of the operations and the measure of compliance that has been realized.

Fleshing Out the Observations and Developing an Action Plan

Once the physical inspection and paper review has been completed, a determination can be made as to whether the plant is either in or out of compliance. If the plant is in compliance, the audit represents a form of certification attesting to that fact. If the audit determines that the facility is not in compliance, completely or in part, then the audit team must concentrate its efforts on identifying cause-and-effect relationships that have led to noncompliance. It must then develop an action plan to bring the facility into compliance and take the necessary steps to reduce the pollution generated by current operations. The action plan will more likely identify subjects for further investigation than it will provide conclusive responses to any deficiencies.

It is appropriate at this stage to consider the legal ramifications of the audit report. Damaging information may be of significant use to the government in the event of an inspection or enforcement action. Therefore, all notes and reports generated by the audit team, including the action plan, should be directed to the firm's attorney. The confidential relationship between attorney and client can provide a protective shield for the contents of the audit report.

While many states have statutes protecting business from the use of self-auditing, the position of the federal government and some states is not quite as clear.

The first order of business, in the event that the facility is not in compliance, would be to develop programs and obtain permits to correct any deficiencies found that are inconsistent with the regulatory process. This could mean filing permit applications, sending in late reports, instituting needed procedures and training programs, etc.

The team can recommend the development of programs and processes to minimize or eliminate such problems as stack or fugitive air emissions, discharges of waste process water, or disposal of hazardous and solid wastes. These changes can be addressed and accomplished by following the hierarchy of pollution prevention—source reduction first and recycling/recovery efforts next, other alternatives last.

Source reduction is a process in which technology and work practices are developed to minimize or eliminate needless pollution. It can be accomplished by designing the process to minimize waste and use safer materials, by finding safer substitutes for the current chemistry as well as by altering the methods and procedures by which jobs are planned and taken through the printing and converting processes.

Recycling and recovery come into play at the end of the process, designed to reuse materials by purifying them or finding alternative uses for what would otherwise become wastes. A typical example would be the distillation of spent solvent to remove the solids and foreign agents, while allowing the clean liquid to pass through for reuse as if the solvent was virgin material.

Fishbone Brainstorming Chart

Originally developed for use by quality circles to identify cause-and-effect relationships, the fishbone chart (figure 9–1) is an excellent tool for brainstorming why wastes are caused and to motivate members of the team to derive reasons for the variances and to solicit their ideas for correcting the problems.

This tool allows a facilitator to work at a leisurely pace, or to move quickly with a group of people taken from the various disciplines in the plant through a preplanned scenario to determine what factors in the process lead to waste and what support will be needed for the effort (or for that matter for any other similar problem). The procedure is called "fishbone" because of its structure, in which each major factor leads to the main spinal column. These would include materials, equipment, methods, personnel, environment, end use specifications, etc. In some cases, management commitment and methodology may also be added as actions for consideration and possible action.

The group would then brainstorm, listing each member's perception of causes for the problem identified in the audit, attributable under each major leg of the chart. Any and all causes and effects can be listed, no matter how trivial or controversial.

Once the solicitation of contributions is exhausted, the group can then review the overall picture and decipher which causes are duplicative, which are major, which are minor or inconsequential.

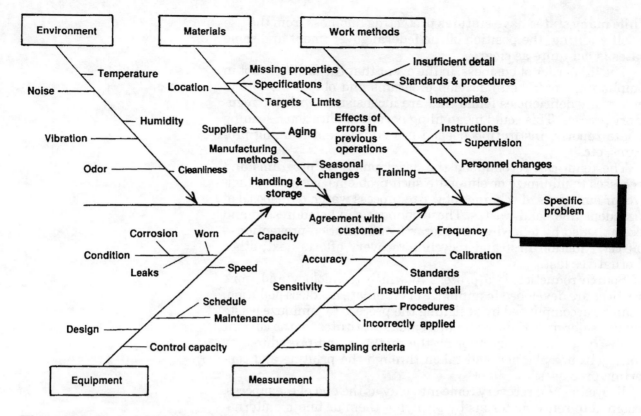

Figure 9–1. Typical dispersion analysis diagram, including possible categories and and subcategories of "causes."

Source: A.H. Jaehn, "The cause and effect diagram—a powerful tool for quality improvement," *TAPPI Journal*, December 1990, p 261.

Discussion will isolate those factors which are a result of culture and are not process related. It may be found that some factors are recognized as having no real effect on the outcome. Attention can then be brought to the major contributors and priorities assigned for further investigation and development of solutions. An example of the use of the cause and effect chart is illustrated in figure 9–2.

Making Use of Technology

Anyone looking at the speed with which technology is changing, spurred by the introduction of computers into every phase of business, can appreciate the changes that have taken place over the past 20 years. The printing and packaging industries have gone from pure craft to very highly sophisticated automated processes that have made product and graphic predictability and tight standards a normal expectation. Action plans should be heedful of the latest technology, for in it lies the path to the elimination of chemistry. Or, if not the elimination, at least the amelioration of hazardous elements in the process. Action plans should also be realistic and provide an economic benefit to the facility, from both a process and product perspective as well as the avoidance of regulatory non-compliance costs.

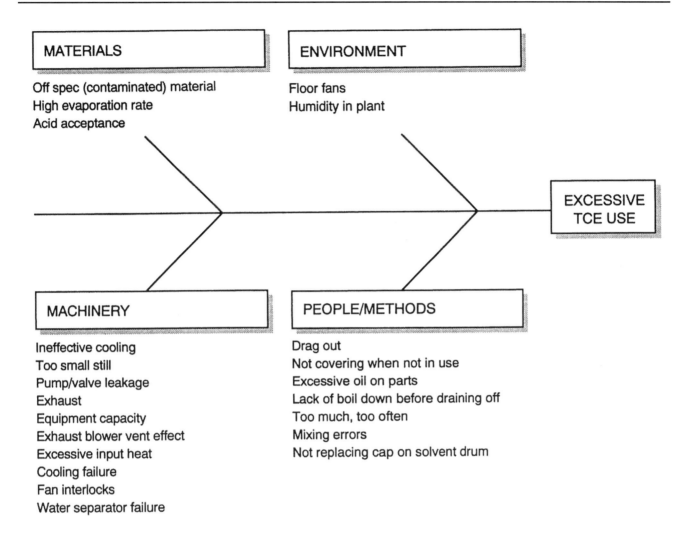

Figure 9–2. An example of the use of the cause-and-effect chart to analyze excessive use of 1,1,1, trichloroethane as a degreasing agent.

Source: John C.Houseman, "Parker Pen's Total Quality Management Strategy to Prevent Pollution from Solvents," *Pollution Prevention Review*, Spring 1993, p 188.

Lastly, action plans should be achievable. A plan that is beyond the scope of the facility or the firm is simply an academic exercise that may be more damaging to the overall goal. In many cases, it is wise to institute, as a first project, one that is readily achievable, to bolster morale and build a sense of accomplishment. Then go on to the bigger and more complex issues. The final product of the audit should be a document that plans for the future growth and well-being of the facility.

CHAPTER 10

Clean Air: Permits and Compliance Standards

The year 1990 was notable for the passage by Congress of the Clean Air Act Amendments. The revision of the original law, passed in 1970, expanded the efforts to cleanse the air of pollutants that endanger the health of the community and the ecological balance of the planet. It is an expansion of the controls introduced by the earlier law that extends regulation for an increased number of pollutants and broadens the scope to include many smaller size facilities. The CAA90 empowers the EPA to review and augment the existing guidelines, as well as to develop new guidance under the National Emission Standards for Hazardous Air Pollutants (NESHAPs) provisions. The new set of guidelines is the basis for the MACT standards (Maximum Available Control Technology).

The definition of major source has been redefined for nonattainment areas, and clarified in terms of volatile organic compounds and hazardous air pollutant thresholds. The law provides for federal permit requirements that will be more consistent nationwide. Responding to this expressed need for more comprehensive permitting and regulation guidance for all sources on the national level, many states have strengthened their permitting procedures and added emission standards to an expanded list of controlled substances and processes.

The Clean Air Act has been a source of much consternation and conflict since its inception. Both federal and state agencies have seen fit to issue periodic guidelines as inconsistencies

Smoke exhausting from stack attracts attention from enforcement agencies and public.

153

and vagaries of the law are brought to light and clarification is required. Such questions as modifications, potential to emit, temporary shutdown of control systems, and new source review have inspired in-house reviews and public comment. Many questions have been resolved by making permits site-specific. This raises the question of whether the standards established for very large sources are applicable to smaller facilities.

The Clean Air Act is a very comprehensive body of laws, rules and supporting guidance documents. The information contained in this chapter intends to provide insight into the various aspects of the law. The printer is advised to refer to the local agency regulators to review current policies, guidance and documentation for his specific needs prior to making any decision to purchase a piece of equipment, modify existing equipment, or build new facilities.

Basic Components of CAA90

The law is composed of seven basic sections, most of which may have some impact on a printing business.

Title I. National Ambient Air Quality Standards (NAAQS)

Despite the improvement in air quality in most sectors of the nation, most urban areas still register air pollutants in excess of the national ambient air quality standards and continue to be designated as non-attainment. Of the contaminants identified in the NAAQS, ozone is the most widespread and intractable. Formed by the reaction of volatile organic compounds (VOCs) and nitrogen oxide under heat and light, ozone causes havoc with the health of people if it is inhaled. Allergic sensitivities, asthmatic attacks and other respiratory ailments are typical reactions of exposure to ozone. High levels of ozone attributed to nature are present during the warmer months of the year, fostered by the photosynthesis process common to green leaf plant life.

For ozone, urban areas are now classified and permitted in categories based on the amounts and types of pollutants generated. The categories are "marginal," "moderate," "serious," "severe" and "extreme." Deadlines have been established as targets for attaining an acceptable level of emissions.

The more unacceptably forbidding the air quality, the more stringent the control measures that will be required of the non-attainment area. State and local agencies must identify and address additional measures if the mandated ones do not work.

Other contaminants addressed under NAAQS are nitrogen oxide, carbon monoxide, sulphur dioxide, lead and particulates. (See Table 10–1.)

Title II. Mobile Sources

Tailpipe emissions are by far the greatest problem for urban areas, being the source of considerable nitrogen oxide. In addition to the establishment of more stringent standards for automobiles, buses and trucks, the law calls for inspection and maintenance programs, as well as the development of clean fuel alternatives.

Title III. Hazardous Air Pollutants

Under pressure from the public, Congress expressed dissatisfaction with the small number of chemicals under control. With reason to believe that a larger number are associated with the incidence of cancer, the law issues a list of 189 chemicals that are perceived as being hazardous to the health of the human population. EPA is directed to set standards (NESHAPS) and control strategies to maximize the reduction or the destruction of the substance (MACT.)

TABLE 10–1. NATIONAL AMBIENT AIR QUALITY STANDARDS FOR CRITERIA POLLUTANTS (As of July 1, 1991)

POLLUTANT	PRIMARY STANDARDS (PROTECTIVE OF HEALTH)*
Ozone	0.120 ppm (235 μg/m^3) (1-hour average)
Carbon Monoxide	9 ppm (10 mg/m^3) (8-hour average) 35 ppm (40 mg/m^3) (1-hour average)
Particulate Matter (PM-10)	150 μg/m^3 (24-hour average) 50 μg/m^3 (annual arithmetic mean)
Sulfur Dioxide	0.140 ppm (365 μg/m^3) (24-hour average) 0.03 ppm (80 μg/m^3) (annual arithmetic mean)
Nitrogen Dioxide	0.053 ppm (100 μg/m^3) (annual arithmetic mean)
Lead	1.5 μg/m^3 (arithmetic mean averaged quarterly)

*See 40 CFR Part 50. The Clean Air Act also requires that EPA establish secondary standards, which protect against adverse effects on the environment. Secondary standards have been established for most of the listed pollutants, and, in most cases, the levels are lower than those in the primary standards.

Source: United States Environmental Protection Agency, *Federal Environmental Regulations Potentially Affecting The Commercial Printing Industry*, EPA744B-94-001, March 1994, p 4.

Vehicular emissions continue to be the major source of smog.

How acid rain is formed.

Source: United States Environmental Protection Agency, *The Plain English Guide to the Clean Air Act*, EPA 400-K-93-001, April 1993, p 15.

Burning fuels release acid pollutants. These pollutants are carried far from their sources by wind. Depending on the weather, the acid pollutants fall to Earth in wet form (acid rain, snow, mist or fog) or dry form (acid gases or dusts).

Title IV Acid Rain

Acid rain is primarily a problem stemming from the sulphur dioxide emitted by utilities and large industries in the Midwest United States, and carried to lakes, rivers and land of Canada and the Northeast United States by prevailing winds.

The law requires a reduction in emissions, and provides an economic incentive for the establishment of new facilities with compliant fuels. This incentive provides for Emission Reduction Credits to offset emissions from new or modified facilities, utilizing the emissions from processes that exceed federal compliance requirements. This concept allows for facilities to purchase credits for emissions from operations or facilities that are shut down, as well as to offset the installation of the new source. The concept of emissions offsets stems from the retirement of a percentage of emissions at such time as approval is granted for new sources. The formula calls for applying a percentage to the anticipated additional tons to determine the tons to be effectively retired, i.e., in a severe area 1.3 tons of credits are required for every ton added to capacity. In effect, the retired tonnage helps to reduce the overall potential for emissions from that area.

Title V. Permits

The permitting provisions of CAA90 were designed to reduce inconsistencies that existed from state to state. The law would now require all major sources to obtain air permits. Emission controls would be extended to thousands of sources in many areas that were not previously under regulation. The federal definition for a major source for facilities that are in attainment areas would be 100 tons per year of any of the six criteria pollutants and any entity that emits 10 tons of any one toxic air pollutant or 25 tons of a combination of toxic air pollutants. Non-attainment areas would be classified by the severity of the air quality in the region, governed by lower thresholds based on the degree of poor air quality. Permits would mandate conditions that are acceptable to the federal authorities, and provide controls and records that would make enforcement more consistent from region to region.

Title VI. Enforcement

The law provides for administrative, civil judicial and criminal penalties. EPA can issue administrative penalty orders up to $200,000 and field citations up to $5,000 for lesser infractions. Civil and criminal penalties are increased from the levels under the previous air regulations. Sources are required to certify their compliance. EPA can issue administrative subpoenas for compliance data, and can issue compliance orders with schedules of up to one year. Citizen suits allow citizens to seek penalties against violators; the penalties are deposited in a U.S Treasury fund for use in EPA compliance and enforcement activities.

Title VII. Stratospheric Ozone and Climate Protection

Provision is mandated for the phase-out of chlorofluorocarbons (CFCs), halons and methyl chloroform, and a program for the recycling of the CFCs used in air conditioners and refrigerators is established.

The Clean Air Act Amendments of 1990 also included miscellaneous provisions, among which is research and development. The primary objectives of the CAA90 have faced a bumpy road. Delays in state programs, invalidation of some segments of the law, and the overwhelming workload placed on all parties have resulted in some delays. From the vantage of industry, the law may be moving slowly, but is moving definitively in the direction of increased micromanagement of the permitted facilities. The permitting process and the interjection of New Source Review and the NESHAPS have complicated the conduct of business. Printers must learn to cope with the intricacies of the regulation and guidance documents as they seek to expand, relocate or simply grow in place.

Low level ozone causes a smog curtain over public areas.

Source: United States Environmental Protection Agency, *The Plain English Guide to the Clean Air Act*, EPA 400-K-93-001, April 1993, p 5.

Ozone Poses Major Printing Problems

The major problem traced to the use of volatile organic compounds (VOCs) at ground level is the creation of smog, caused by the reaction of the vapors in the presence of sunlight and heat. Technically, the chemical reaction forms the compound ozone. The presence of this condition can be seen as a haze that hangs over the polluted area. Allergic sensitivities, asthmatic attacks and other respiratory ailments are common results of exposure to ground-level ozone.

At the opposite end of the scale, we are faced with the reverse reaction in the upper atmosphere. Vapors from chlorinated solvents, used in manufacturing processes for cleaning, aerosols and refrigeration, drift up into the higher levels of the atmosphere and deplete the ozone layer there. This depletion leads to the erosion of the protective ozone cap over the atmosphere and results in a increase in ultraviolet rays reaching earth. The exposure to higher levels of ultraviolet rays has been linked to development of cataracts and skin cancer. Periodic monitoring of the ozone layer over the polar caps has revealed the existence of holes and relates the percentage of opening over a period of time to industrial activity on the ground.

Accordingly, the CAA90 includes provisions to reduce or eliminate the use and emissions of the harmful chemicals. The printer is faced with the need to change working habits, find alternative chemicals or processes that do not require use of these chemicals, or subject the operation to add-on control equipment to reduce emissions.

Implementation of compliance technology is guided by standards that have been established by the EPA in the form of Control Technology Guidelines (CTG) or Advisory Technology Guidelines

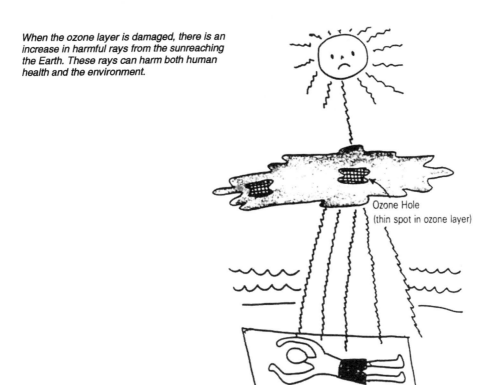

When the ozone layer is damaged, there is an increase in harmful rays from the sun reaching the Earth. These rays can harm both human health and the environment.

Ozone Hole (thin spot in ozone layer)

What happens when there are holes in the ozone layer?

Source: United States Environmental Protection Agency, *The Plain English Guide to the Clean Air Act*, EPA 400-K-93-001, April 1993, p 17.

(ATG). The guidelines have been developed through the process of a review and analysis of industry performance, based on a limited sampling of facilities and with some sharing of information with industry and industry associations. The basic premise of the control guidelines is to limit the amount of VOCs and HAPs that are exhausted to the atmosphere by requiring adherence to strict standards for inks and solvents used in the pressroom and/or the addition of control equipment to destroy a high percentage of the emissions.

Hazardous Air Pollutants

With the passage of the CAA90, the EPA was empowered to develop a comprehensive new program for the control of hazardous air pollutants (HAPs). The law included a list of 189 chemicals that were assumed to be hazardous. While some of the listed substances are also volatile organic compounds, many are not. The law mandates that the agency identify categories and sub-categories of the sources from which HAPs could be emitted. The agency was to then establish emission standards requiring the maximum degree of reduction in emissions. This emission criterion has come to be known by the acronym MACT.

A major source for HAPs is defined as having the potential to emit 10 tons of any one HAP or 25 tons of combined HAPs. Other provisions specified that construction of new sources, modifications or reconstructions would require assurance that the state has the opportunity to determine that the facility will meet the MACT standards prior to the issuance of the permit. For printers, the list of HAPs includes a number of the solvents used for ink formulation and cleaning, compounds intrinsic to pigments and resins, and other darkroom and pressroom process chemistry. These include:

Benzene	Formaldehyde	Polycyclic organic
Cadmium compounds	Glycol ethers	matter
Carbon tetrachloride	Hexane	Propylene oxide
Chromium compounds	Hydrochloric acid	Toluene
Cobalt compounds	Isophorene	2,4-toluene diisocyanate
Cumene	Lead compounds	1,1,1-trichlorethane
Dibutylphthalate	Methanol	Trichloroethylene
Diethanolamine	Methyl ethyl ketone	Vinyl chloride
Ethyl benzene	Methylene chloride	Xylenes
Ethylene glycol	Perchloroethylene	

Attainment Versus Non-Attainment Areas

To provide priorities for compliance under the NAAQS, the law defined the areas of the country that required different levels of control and emission reductions. The three pollutants upon which the classifications were based are ozone, carbon dioxide and particulate matter. The country is divided into two basic levels of air quality—attainment and non-attainment. Attainment areas are those in which the quality of the air has been better than the standards established for the basic pollutants. In these areas, the threshold of 100 tons establishes the limit above which permits and federal standards are applicable. Non-attainment areas are those that have air pollutants in excess of allowable standards set forth by the EPA. These areas are divided into distinctive zones defined by the degree of air pollution. The five defined categories and RACT thresholds for a major source follows. As the degree of non-attainment is reduced, from extreme to marginal, the RACT thresholds defining the type of permit required will rise.

Extreme:	10 tons of VOC
Severe:	25 tons of VOC
Serious:	50 tons of VOC
Moderate:	100 tons of VOC
Marginal:	100 tons of VOC

In terms of the HAPs, the threshold for a major source is 10 tons of any one pollutant, or 25 tons of any combination of HAPs.

Congress also provided for consideration of the combined effects of ozone in the Northeast corridor under a provision called a transport region. The transport region includes 11 Northeast states and the District of Columbia. Within this transport zone, any facility with a potential to emit 50 tons is considered major. The 11 states are Connecticut, Delaware, Maine, Maryland, Massachusetts, New Hampshire, New Jersey, New York, Pennsylvania, Rhode Island and Vermont.

In areas designated as attainment, a major source is required to obtain a permit. The source is defined as a single point from which emissions are released, or as an entire facility that is under the control of the same person(s). The emissions that characterize the major sources are: 10 tons per year of any hazardous air pollutant, 25 tons per year or more of any combination of hazardous air pollutants, and 100 tons per year of any air pollutant.

Clean Air Compliance Thresholds: Potential to Emit

The definition of major source and the thresholds for the various air quality regions determine the type of permit that will be required. Local permit and registration documentation vary from state to state for sources that are not considered major. With the inception of Title V, major sources are held to comparable provisions and standards in all parts of the country; format and process will vary by state.

Printers frequently misread the emissions threshold that identifies the need to have a specific type of permit. The problem arises from the mistaken idea that the actual purchases are the measure of how much they pollute. The formula used by the environmental agencies derives from the concept known as "potential to emit." This is not to be confused with the emissions that a facility or press is actually generating during the hours and days that the facility operates. Potential To Emit (PTE) is the amount that, by design, the presses will exhaust from the plant over a 365-day, 24-hours-per-day operation. The computation is one that uses the process design to determine hourly emissions and extrapolates the anticipated emissions by multiplying the hourly rate by 8,760 hours. This is tantamount to having the press operate without stop during the year.

Design Parameters for Printing

The amount of emissions that can be exhausted by a process is usually a function of the design of the equipment and the product that is made. A chemical or petroleum process is continuous and the design parameters are easily defined by the ability to move the chemicals through a pipeline. Some are batch processes in which finite activities are carried out within a specific time period and then changes are made to the process. PTE has to be determined based on the best judgment of how that process will operate over a period of one year.

Due to the variable nature of work (coverage, number of colors, line versus process) performed on printing presses, the design parameters for printing can be defined by the average actual usage over a period of time. The design parameter for printing has been interpreted as the average number of pounds of volatile organic compounds (VOCs) that are emitted in a previous baseline year(s) for the number of hours that the plant actually operated. The value derived will be expressed as pounds of VOCs or HAPs emitted per hour (see Table 10–2). This design parameter is important to note and use when discussing permits with state agencies. Lack of knowledge of the printing processes by enforcement personnel at the agency may lead to misinterpretation of how the PTE should be calculated.

There have been instances in which printers and enforcement engineers have tried to apply a formula which expected every print station to print at full coverage to determine PTE. This is a misapplication of the process, and should be avoided in such a calculation. The drying systems on most presses, unless configured for heavy coatings, will not be able to dry the inks deposited on the web or the sheet as it passes from station to station, making this an invalid calculation for a given press. The average emissions per operating hour takes into account the combination of setup, running and clean-up time, which will vary by the nature of the product mix. This is as much a part of the design of the process as the graphics of the printed products.

Computing Your PTE

Just how does one determine what the average emissions are, and how is the PTE determined for the plant? A recommended procedure follows.

Collect all the Material Safety Data Sheets (MSDSs) for the inks and solvents purchased. The MSDS should supply two pieces of information. The first will be a listing of all solvents, with a percentage by weight, that are in the inks or solvent blends. The second item would be a total percent by weight of VOCs in the formulation. If these are not listed, contact the supplier to obtain the appropriate information. Note that only VOCs and HAPs that are VOCs are used in this computation. Do not include items listed in the MSDS which are not volatile organic compounds. Items to avoid include, but are not limited to, pigments, nitrocellulose, ammonia and ammonium hydroxide. Using a spreadsheet or worksheet similar to that illustrated in Table 10–3, list all the inks and solvents purchased. If the inks have similar formulations, i.e., the percentage by weight of VOCs is the same, combine the quantities for this purpose. Enter these values in the column "Percent VOCs."

When all the ink and solvent purchases for the year are listed, multiply the Percent VOCs by the Pounds Purchased and enter the amount of VOCs in pounds in the next column. Total this column to obtain the total VOCs for the year.

Calculate the number of hours the plant has operated. This is total time, not running hours. You want to reflect the setup, clean-up and downtimes that are normally incurred. These hours, for most of the time, reflect the variations in the product mix and are part of the design parameters for the facility. As an example, the plant may run one, two, four and six-color work. Downtime to clean up and set up new jobs will be reflected in the amount of time required to make these changes. Repair time will be influenced by the wear and tear of various parts of the press due to the need to produce a variety of products. A typical plant operating one shift for eight hours, 250

TABLE 10-2. WORKSHEET TO COMPUTE EMISSION RATES AND POTENTIAL TO EMIT

PURCHASES IN POUNDS:

	POUNDS PURCHASED	PERCENT VOC	VOC EMISSIONS	VOC EMISSIONS (use add-on control)
	FROM INVOICES	FROM MSDS	PURCHASES x %VOC	AFTER CONTROL(90%)
INKS	50000	60%	30000	3000
SOLVENTS	125000	100%	125000	12500
TOTAL POUNDS	175000		155000	15500

HOURS OPERATED

1 SHIFT, 8 HOURS, 5DAYS/WEEK	2000 HOURS	
2 SHIFTS, 16 HOURS, 5DAYS/WEEK	4000 HOURS	

POUNDS PER HOUR (VOC EMISSIONS/HOURS OPERATED)

	HOURS	POUNDS PER HOUR NO CONTROL	POUNDS PER HOUR AFTER CONTROL
	2000	77.5	7.75
	4000	38.75	3.875

POTENTIAL TO EMIT (VOC EMISSIONS FOR 8760 HOURS)
(MULTIPLY LBS/HR BY 8760 HOURS)

			POUNDS	TONS
	8760	NO CONTROL, 2 SHIFTS	339450	169.73
		CONTROLS, 2 SHIFTS	33945	16.97

TABLE 10–3. COMPUTATION OF VOC EMISSIONS USING SOLVENT INK AND AN OXIDIZER AND WATERBORNE INK THAT IS COMPLIANT

SOLVENT BASED INKS	POUNDS PURCHASED	PERCENT VOC	VOC EMISSIONS	if add-on control used VOC EMISSIONS
	FROM INVOICES	FROM MSDS	PURCHASES x %VOC	AFTER CONTROL(90%)
INKS	50000	60%	30000	3000
SOLVENTS	125000	100%	125000	12500
TOTAL POUNDS	175000		155000	15500
HOURS OPERATED	2 SHIFTS, 16 HOURS, 5DAYS/WEEK	4000 HOURS		
POUNDS PER HOUR	(VOC EMISSIONS/HOURS OPERATED)	4000	38.75	3.875
POTENTIAL TO EMIT	(VOC EMISSIONS FOR 8760 HOURS)	8760	339450	33945
			POUNDS	POUNDS
			169.7	17.0
			TONS	TONS

WATERBASED INKS	POUNDS PURCHASED	PERCENT VOC	VOC EMISSIONS	VOC EMISSIONS
	FROM INVOICES	FROM MSDS	PURCHASES x %VOC	no add-on control
INKS	50000	4%	2000	2000
SOLVENTS	10000	100%	10000	10000
TOTAL POUNDS	60000		12000	12000
HOURS OPERATED	2 SHIFTS, 16 HOURS, 5DAYS/WEEK	4000 HOURS		
POUNDS PER HOUR	(VOC EMISSIONS/HOURS OPERATED)	4000	3.00	3.00
POTENTIAL TO EMIT	(VOC EMISSIONS FOR 8760 HOURS)	8760	26280	26280
			POUNDS	POUNDS
			13.1	13.1
			TONS	TONS

days a year will average 2,000 hours per year. A two-shift, 8-hour-per-shift operation for the 250 days will operate 4,000 hours.

Divide the total VOCs by the number of hours the facility has actually operated. This will determine the pounds per hour that are actually being emitted. Divide the total pounds of VOCs by 2,000 pounds. The result will be the actual tons of emissions from your plant for the year. Once the average pounds per hour of VOC emissions have been determined, multiply that number by 8,760 hours. The pounds will be your potential to emit for a year. Divide this by 2,000 pounds to obtain the calculated potential tonnage that could be emitted. As an example, if the average was 15 pounds per hour in a one-shift operation, the actual tons emitted will be documented as 30,000 pounds for the year or 15 tons. Taking the 15 pounds per hour and multiplying that by 8,760 hours results in calculated potential to emit of 131,400 pounds, or 65.7 tons.

If the facility is located in a severe non-attainment area, the threshold to comply and be permitted is 25 tons. In a moderate area the threshold is 50 tons. Even though the actual was 15 tons, the facility has a calculated potential emissions rate of 65.7 tons and thus would have to apply for a permit to be in compliance with the graphic arts provisions of the state implementation plan.

Options to Comply as a Less than Title V Source

If the PTE exceeds the threshold for the area of attainment in which the plant is located, the facility will have to do one of three things to avoid filing for a Title V permit. In each case, the ability to place a ceiling on the emissions will still be held to federally acceptable conditions but will held accountable by review of the state agency:

1. Become a synthetic minor by capping emissions at an allowable level below the threshold for the region. In this approach, the facility volunteers to maintain emissions below a specified level and thus not have to comply with more stringent rules that would be imposed, based on the PTE. The level of emissions agreed upon is considered a "cap" on actual emissions.

2. Come into compliance with the use of an add-on control and reduce emissions of both VOCs and HAPs to very low levels.

3. Adopt a new ink technology that will place the facility in compliance with the RACT regulations, i.e., waterborne inks or UV curable inks that will lower the emissions.

Capping out is the election of a ceiling beyond which the facility agrees not to emit. For example, consider a facility that is located in a severe region; if actual emissions are 19 tons and the potential to emit is 50 tons, the facility could agree to limit its emissions to 24.5 tons. This would limit the ability of the facility to add extra hours or take on work that would increase its emissions beyond the 24.5 tons. Capping out provides a 5.5-ton cushion from the actual emissions of 19 tons within which the facility can grow.

The resulting permit will not be subject to the same review by the federal agency as a Title V permit, but will contain operating conditions that are acceptable to the USEPA. The permits are commonly called FESOPs, federally enforceable state operating permits. The conditions will define monitoring, records and reports that will assure that the limits on emissions approved for the facility are not exceeded.

While this may be a good option to keep out of a Title V permit with federal conditions, the cap may be too restrictive to allow a business to grow and prosper. Capping out will require records and reports to assure that the limit in the permit is not exceeded. While seemingly a good strategy to avoid the more comprehensive major source permit, the restrictions may not make good business sense. Given the voluntary nature of the process of "capping-out" and the possibility of reacting to market conditions without regard for the cap, the printer can be assured that the environmental agencies will be monitoring these facilities as much as, if not more than, the major facilities. (See figure 10–1.)

Components of an Air Permit

Prior to the Clean Air Act of 1990, most states had regulations and procedures in place for the registration and permitting of air emission processes as stationary sources of air pollution. Practices and parameters varied from state to state and within states, depending on the severity of the air pollution and the objectives of the state program. There were many inconsistencies in what was demanded for the same basic configuration of equipment and emissions from state to state.

With the passage of the amended act in 1990, the EPA sought to standardize the manner in which major sources are permitted under the various state regulations. States are mandated to submit plans for permitting under Title V of the CAA90. The time has come for states to finalize these programs and submit them to the USEPA for approval.

Under Title V, major sources will be permitted in accordance with federal guidelines. This form of permitting will provide for all emissions in a facility. With reduction of emissions to levels under specified thresholds, companies can "cap-out" of the Title V permit. The measures taken to reduce emissions, i.e., catalytic oxidation, reduced operating hours, changes in ink or paint formulations, must all be federally enforceable. In other words, the facility must be able to substantiate what is being done on an ongoing basis.

In such cases, many states will issue their own permits for plants with lesser amounts. This will enable the agencies to maintain some form of control over air pollution. Registration programs are used in some states for very small sources to provide an inventory of all contributors to air emissions. What does this mean to the typical printer?

The typical wide web flexographic press has the potential to emit anywhere from 25 to 100 pounds an hour. Using the potential to emit, as defined by the EPA, a typical press operating for 8,760 hours a year will produce 110 tons of emissions at 25 pounds per hour. Every wide web flexography and gravure printing press has the potential to require permits. A narrow web flexographic press emitting five pounds per hour has the potential to produce 22 tons of pollutants a year. Two presses will qualify the facility as a major polluter in a Severe area of the country.

Lithographic presses, while under a RACT standard for fountain solution, will qualify for permitting as a result of the combination of the fountain solution and the press washes used. Reducing emissions will be more a factor of press wash reduction or substitution than it will be of the question of fountain solutions.

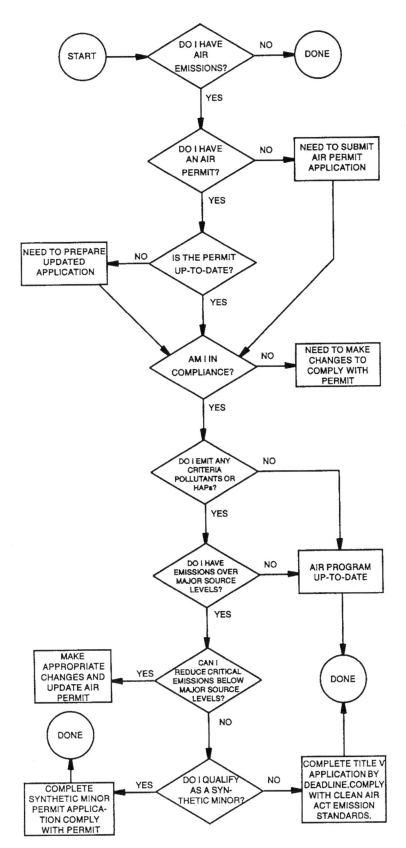

Figure 10–1. Compliance flow chart to determine permit status.

Source: *Environmental Update, Clean Air Act,* "Compliance Flow-chart," Conversion Technology Inc., Summer 1994, p 3.

Screen printers will, for a majority of medium and small operations, require permits based less on the use of liquid inks and more on the quantity of solvent-based screen washes used. The opportunity to substitute for solvent cleaning solutions and to institute changes in the process of cleaning screens can result in sharp decreases in solvent use and emissions of pollutants, as well as decreases in the hazardous nature of the emissions.

Adding or Modifying Equipment

If new equipment or emission control devices are purchased, the firm will have to file an application for a permit to erect. Under state and previous permitting regulations, once a press was installed and commenced operating in compliance with the regulations that govern the acceptable technology (compliant inks or add-on controls), a certificate to operate would be issued. Under Title V regulations, the application for the permit to erect and certificate to operate are one. Applications or notice of modification must be filed prior to the installation of any equipment. In most states, equipment should not be purchased and surely not installed prior to the receipt of a proper permit.

Under the CAA90, new sources are governed by the mandate to satisfy the New Source Review (NSR), which will require BACT (Best Available Control Technology), or LAER (Lowest Achievable Emission Reduction) analysis and adherence to these highly restrictive standards. NESHAPS standards for hazardous air pollutants have been developed for some processes at this time, applying MACT (Maximum Available Control Technology). The MACT will apply to the list of 189 hazardous air pollutants designated by the federal government in CAA90, calling for a 95-percent reduction of emissions.

For each printing technology, the Technology Control Guidelines mandate the use of specific types of inks, coatings or solvents, based on the composition of the ink as applied or chemicals used for a specific process or end use. These are considered as VOCs. The standards can be in pounds of VOCs per gallon, per hour or as a percentage of the total formulation as applied. A permit application is not considered "approvable" unless the press is operating in conformance with the Control Guidelines or operating under a waiver or variance.

The Permit Package

To prepare an application for the permit to erect or certificate to operate, certain basic information is required:

1. Description of the equipment, e.g., Brand X six-color CI with gas burner for drying (specify size of gas burner), or lithographic sheet fed six-color press with tower coater, or semi-automatic screen printer feeding heated drying tunnel.

2. Site plan of location with physical description of facility and location of press(es) in the plant, normally accompanied by blueprints or computer-generated drawings. (See figure 10–2.)

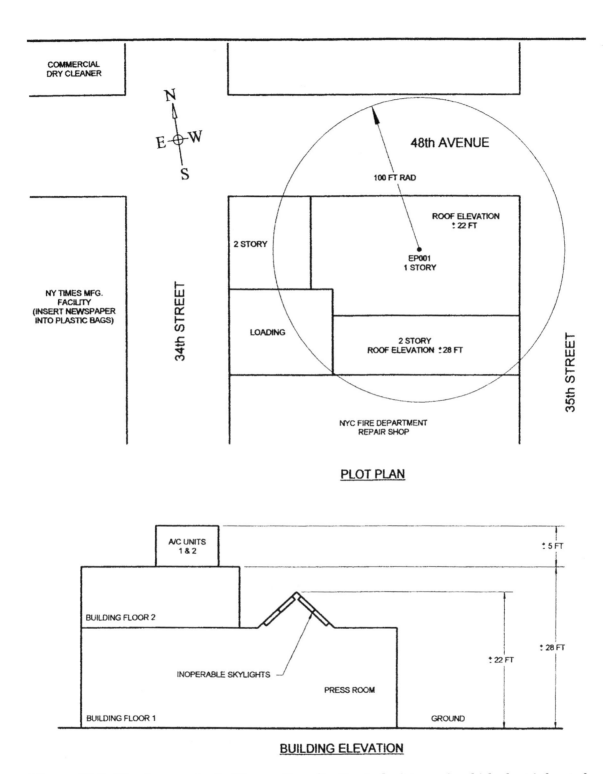

Figure 10–2. Site plan required with permit application to depict area in which plant is located and nature of surroundings.

Source: P-F Technical Services Inc.

3. System components, such as fan and motor sizes, dryer exhaust temperatures, stack heights and dimensions, exhaust air flows, etc.

4. Description of coatings, inks, other listed chemicals and the solvent components, with data supporting the amounts of emissions, by components, on an hourly and annual basis. The Material Safety Data Sheets (MSDSs) document this information.

5. Projected operating hours and days worked during year.

6. Description of any control equipment and the methods that will measure the performance of this equipment.

7. Provision for testing of the control equipment in accordance with procedures and test methods prescribed by the EPA, or certification of the volatile content of the inks, coatings, adhesives and solvents if compliant ink technology is the option selected.

Much of the information required for the application will continue to be needed for reporting of air emission data, as well as for the computation of emission fees under Title V or state regulatory fee formulas. Depending on local (state, city or county) statutes, firms may have to hire professional engineers to prepare and submit the applications. The registration and permit threshold determination forms are typically designed for ease of understanding and preparation by the printer or his engineer. If a permit has not been approved, the company may not be able to erect its press in most jurisdictions. In others, the facility may be able to put the press on the floor, but not be allowed to connect the energy sources and operate the equipment without a permit.

It is to the advantage of the facility management to check local regulations and take the necessary precautions to have permits or regulatory determination made of the need to file for a permit. Facilities that come forward, looking for assistance in filing of permits, are welcomed. When the agencies find a non-complying facility in the course of enforcement activity, the facility can expect to be penalized, and possibly have the press shut down and secured so that it cannot be run until a permit has been granted. Avoid the dilemma faced by some firms, which have had process equipment arrive at their plant, only to find that they were not allowed to operate the machinery.

In many cases the only way to comply is by the acquisition of add-on controls. Normal lead time for delivery and installation runs from 16 to 20 weeks. With the time normally required to process a permit, nine to 12 months can pass before that press will be operational.

States vary in the permitting of smaller sources. Much depends on the location of the state and the perception of the environmental impact by smaller entities. Within the transport region, states have taken measures to permit or register all facilities above a minimum threshold.

The major concern in urban areas, where ozone from vehicular traffic is most damaging, is that the combined emissions of many small entities in a given locale can equal the emissions of a major source. At one point in the deliberations in Congress on the Clean Air Act of 1990, consideration was given to inclusion of small firms in a designated area, whose total emissions would trigger the major thresholds. To avoid an onerous economic burden for small business, this was not enacted into law. However, in many states there is concern that is frequently expressed in the local regulations. New York State, for instance, has identified this need in the metropolitan downstate area by setting a ZERO threshold for VOCs. This amounts to mandating that every printer, including quick and in-plant printers, must file a permit application for a certificate to operate. New Jersey has set a limit based on a maximum number of gallons per hour and per day. Other states have established annual emission limits, below which printers do not have to file for a registration or a permit.

The formats for registration vary by state. Some allow letter notifications. Others accept only specific forms, such as illustrated for New York, which is a one-page application supported by an emission statement and a site plan to provide verification documentation of the location of the facility. (See sample application in Appendix XXI.)

The statement of emissions serves as the baseline values for the facility, and typically consists of an analysis of the ink, coatings and press chemistry purchases for two or more of the most recent years, with a computation of the resulting VOCs and HAPs. The site plan provides an accurate picture of the location of the facility and the neighboring area, the north-south axis and the real estate identification information (figure 10–2). A plant layout provides information with respect to the location within the plant of all equipment and emission points. Refer to figure 10–3 for sample plant layout.

Minor Sources: State Permits

Complete and accurate records are mandatory, no matter what the size the facility and the status of its permit. Among the records that must be maintained by a facility are:

1. **Purchase of inks, coatings and solvents (press washes):** For major sources and those which cap out, the records should be maintained monthly. Data should be collected by item—every ink (color), solvent, press wash, etc. For minor sources, this should be done periodically by calendar quarter.

2. **Computations of VOCs and HAPs based on actual purchases:** For major facilities, VOC and HAP emissions

Records and Reports

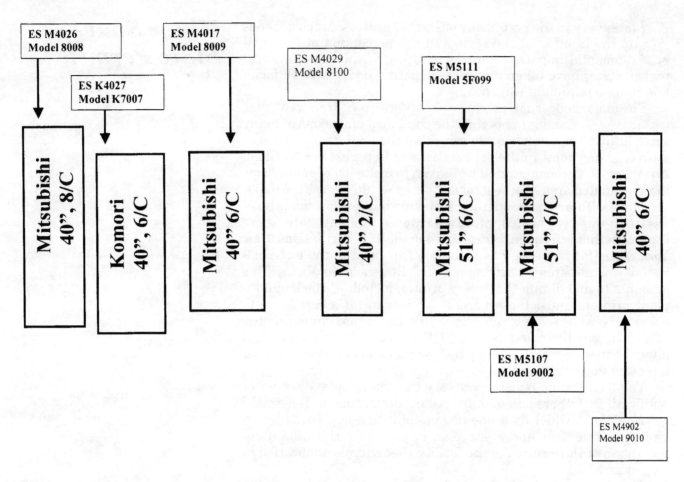

Figure 10–3. Schematic plant layout illustrating equipment and location in facility.
Source: P-F Technical Services Inc.

should be computed by item, i.e., all inks by color and all solvents. A breakdown of the components of the items, by solvent or chemical, is essential to determining the composition of the emissions, VOCs and HAPs, with the compliance status of each.

3. **Continuous recording charts** for oxidizers, which record three parameters: temperatures going into the catalyst bed, temperatures going out of the catalyst bed, and the heat of the air that is going up the stack,

4. **Maintenance log** for all equipment which emits air pollutants, particularly for add-on control equipment (figure 10–4),

5. **Opacity log**, if required: log to record daily inspections of stacks to evaluate nature of any smoke that may be exhausted (figure 10–5),

6. **Material Safety Data Sheets** for all chemicals used,

7. **Operating and maintenance manuals** for all equipment.

DATE	OCCURRENCE	WORK PERFORMED	TIME DOWN	BY WHOM
1/4/01	maintence	greased bearings and checked intake screen		
1/9/-1/12/01	no problems			
1/15/-1/19/01	no problems			
1/22-1/26/01	no problems			
1/29-2/1/01	no problems			
2/2/01	around 12noon catalyst temp. went up to 1200* on the chart and a burn out condition was registered. Oxidizer shut off.	Presses shut down	remainder of day	
2/5-2/9/01	no problems			
2/8/01	Called Megtec,they said it was a possibly a bad thermo couple	none		
2/12-2/16/01	no problems			
2/19-2/23/01	no problems			
2/26-3/2/01	no problems			
3/5-3/9/01	no problems			
2/13/01	maintenance	greased bearings and checked intake screen		
3/19-3/23/01	no problems			
3/26-27/01	no problems			
3/28/01	burner would not light	cleaned flame rod	1 hr. 6-7 am	
3/29-3/30/01	no problems			

Figure 10–4. Sample add-on control system maintenance log.

Source: P-F Technical Services Inc.

FACILITY: _____ Month:_____
ADDRESS: _____

DATE	TIME	TEMPERATURE	SEE SMOKE	NO SMOKE	NOTE ADVERSE WEATHER CONDITIONS

Where a continuous opacity monitor is not utilized for measuring smoke emissions, the facility shall be required to perform the following:

1) Observe the stack for each printing press once per day for visible emissions. This observation(s) must be conducted during daylight hours except during adverse weather conditions (fog, rain, or snow).

2) The results of each observation must be recorded in a bound logbook or other format acceptable to the Department. The following data must be recorded for each stack:
—weather condition
—was a plume observed?
This logbook must be retained at the facility for five (5) years after the date of the last entry.

3) If the operator observes any visible emissions (other than steam) for two consecutive days, then a Method 9 analysis (based upon a 6-minute mean) of the affected emission point(s) must be conducted within two (2) business days of such occurrence. The results of the Method 9 analysis must be recorded in the logbook. The operator must contact the Regional Air Pollution Control Engineer within one (1) business day of performing the Method 9 analysis if the opacity standard is contravened. Upon notification, any corrective actions or future compliance schedules shall be presented to the Department for acceptance.

Figure 10–5. Sample opacity log and instructions for daily observations.

Source: Region 1 NYSDEC relative to records and reports for Title V permits.

Risk Management Plans

Every stationary source at which regulated substances are present in more than the established threshold quantities must prepare a detailed risk management plan that will detect and minimize accidental releases of the listed toxic chemicals. The plan shall be designed to protect human health and the environment by detecting and preventing accidental releases. The risk management plan should contain three basic components: hazard assessment, program for preventing releases, and a response program. A hazard assessment is an engineering analysis of a facility or process in which an extremely hazardous substance is used, to determine the potential of any accidental release and the consequences (death, injury or property damage) that would likely occur in the event of a release.

The program to prevent releases should include provisions for back-up and interlock systems in the design of the process, substitution of less hazardous materials, reduction in process severity (temperature, pressure), storage of smaller volumes of extremely hazardous substances, process monitors to detect deviations from normal parameters, protection systems like scrubbers, and post-release containment measures.

The final requirement is for a response plan that provides for specific actions and notifications to protect human health and the environment. The plan would include procedures for responding to accidental releases, emergency health care, and employee training programs.

New Source Review

New equipment or significant modifications of the facility require a review prior to permitting to assess environmental impact of the changes. New Source Review (NSR) proposes to assure that any addition or modification will not add unreasonably to the emissions inventory of a region and also to assure that any such modification is subjected to public comment. The procedure requires a five-year look back at the actual and potential emissions for the facility and a projection of the emissions after the modification or new installation. The records maintained, of actual purchases and emissions of inks, coatings and solvents, hours worked, and the resulting emissions, will serve as the basis of this historical analysis. The computation of the effect on the emissions for agency review centers on potential to emit rather than actual quantities of emissions. In some states, the new potential is compared to the historic actual annual emissions. The added emissions will be the basis for determining the status of the modified facility and the acceptability of the modifications by the agency . Not all requests will be approved.

The NSR process will require a BACT and LAER evaluation. Since every site is considered on its own merits, the evaluations will be based on the processes and chemistry of the specific site. The agency may demand LAER as a mandate for obtaining the permit to erect and operate the new source or modification of an existing source. NESHAPS will require that a major source of HAPs comply with MACT.

Changes in emissions falling below the major source emissions threshold may take place without any compensatory tradeoff of emissions. Changes that exceed the threshold will be held responsible for offsetting the added emissions with emission reduction credits (ERCs). This method of retiring emissions was developed to facilitate the process of approving modifications that add emissions. Based on the severity of pollution in the region in which the facility is located, the application of ERCs is for an amount that is in excess of the tons to be emitted. The excess will be retired and removed from the state inventory of emissions. Every state files a state implementation plan with the USEPA in which it describes the inventory of air pollutants in the state and what measures it is taking to reduce the inventory. The policy of granting ERCs enables the state to reduce its emission inventory by the number of credits retired.

New Source Review has been under review for a number of years, primarily to make it a clearer and more easily applied rule. Revision has taken much longer than expected, due in part to the complexity of the rule and the variability of the printing processes, as well as the need to achieve acceptability by the many stakeholders in the environmental regulatory picture. Where industry seeks a looser, more flexible process, environmental advocacy organizations view any loosening as compromises affecting the quality of the environment.

There are many concerns for business in the NSR process. Use of potential rather than actual emissions places undue burdens on a business that needs upward mobility to survive in a competitive market. EPA has acknowledged this need for simplification and revision, but has yet to amend the regulations on the books. An announcement in the Federal Register of July 23, 1996 described an "EPA Proposal On New Source Review," that would streamline the preconstruction permitting process, reducing by half the number of permitting actions that new or significantly modified major sources of air pollution must endure before commencing construction. The issue is still open. It is a hot button item for industry.

Emission Reduction Credits

The concept of trading emission credits was conceived as a means of reducing air emissions while encouraging the growth and modernization of business. Sustainable development could come at a price that would, in effect, reduce the emissions of air pollutants. Initially established to foster the change from polluting technologies to newer, cleaner facilities by public utilities faced with a mandate to reduce causes of acid rain, the concept of allowances for reductions beyond compliance was applied to other pollutants and other industries. Every ton of reduction that exceeds the required emissions reduction counts as one credit.

In essence, a facility may use credits for exceeding the reduction required by RACT to offset the anticipated (or calculated) emissions from a planned growth of the source. The facility may also register the tonnage and make them available to other facilities that are expanding or erecting installations but do not have their own

TABLE 10–4. MAJOR SOURCE DEFINITIONS AND OFFSET RATIOS IN OZONE NON-ATTAINMENT AREAS

CATEGORY	SIZE OF MAJOR SOURCE (TONS/YEAR OF VOCs)	OFFSET RATIOS
Marginal	100	1.1:1
Moderate	100	1.15:1
Serious	50	1.2:1
Severe	25	1.3:1
Extreme	10	1.5:1

Source: United States Environmental Protection Agency, *Federal Environmental Regulations Potentially Affecting The Commercial Printing Industry*, EPA744B-94-001, March 1994, p 11.

credits. Shutting down a facility or a portion of a facility that has emitted pollutants can also be registered for credits.

The amount of the estimated reduction in air pollutants is derived from the formula which calculates the emission reduction credits as they are applied to the new application. The new source or modification is subjected to a new source review. If the anticipated emissions are high enough to trigger NSR, then emission reduction credits will be required. For every ton of new emissions, an additional amount of credits will be required. That additional number of credits will be retired.

As an example, in a Severe area with a threshold of 25 tons, a new facility is being built which will generate 100 tons of VOC emissions. The formula for the Severe areas calls for 1.3 tons to compensate for every ton of new emissions. The facility will have to apply, from another of its own facilities or from other plants in the region, a total 130 credits. The 30 tons in excess of the planned emissions of the plant would then be retired. Table 10–4 identifies the offsets that CAA90 requires in the various non-attainment areas.

Some of these credits may be acquired from past and planned efforts of the facility to go beyond compliance. Pollution prevention programs can bring the facility benefits beyond the anticipated safer, cleaner operation. If a facility uses safer chemistry, more effective working practices and newer, more efficient equipment, it can exceed the standards required of it by law. These excesses can be used to apply and register emission reduction credits. For example, a flexographic printer has been using solvent-base inks and is working with a limit of 20 tons per year. The printer converts to water-base inks, which have a much smaller requirement for allowable VOCs, and is able to use even lower VOC inks than required by RACT, further reducing the amount of his emissions. This is termed "going beyond compliance." The printer can file for credits for the difference between his old actual emissions and the new level of emissions. The operating air permit for the facility will be amended to reflect the new, lower emission level.

Putting Away Credits for the Future

Emission reduction credits can be "banked." The credits are registered with the state and acknowledged as certified credits. The printer can retain the credits and use them for subsequent growth, the opening of a new facility, or modifications that will add to the emissions from the plant. Use of the emission reduction credits in these cases is known as "netting." Credits are applied within the permitting application process, protected from any agency policy that would transfer a portion of the credits to the state.

More often, the credits may be acquired from other facilities that have "banked" their reductions or have shut down all or a portion of their operations. A lively commodity market has developed to handle the trading or sale of emission reduction credits. A facility may register the tonnage and make them available to other facilities that are expanding or erecting installations but do not have their own credits. Shutting down a facility or a portion of a facility that has emitted pollutants can also be registered for credits.

What are ERCs?

Emission reduction credits (ERCs) are certified reductions in air emissions of volatile organic compounds (VOCs), nitrogen oxide (NOx), and in some areas particulates and carbon monoxide (CO), in quantities which are over and above the current regulatory standards. They are part of an economic incentive approach to reduce pollutants as an alternative to traditional command and control methods. ERCs are aimed at giving industry more choices for compliance, opportunities for economic savings, achievement of better environmental protection, and an encouragement to engage innovative pollution prevention alternatives.

The emissions must be real, permanent and enforceable to the satisfaction of the government agencies, and have occurred within the five years prior to the date of submittal for certification. Only reductions which lower actual air emissions and come from a source beyond levels prescribed by the applicable emission standards of the regulations can be used as offsets.

How do You Quantify ERCs?

Emission reduction credits are calculated as the difference between prior actual annual emissions and future potential emissions, using a baseline established from actual experience in the most recent five years. The spreadsheets that each firm must maintain to verify its status under an existing air permit will provide the data necessary for computation of emission reductions.

The emissions will be based on either purchases or usage of ink, solvent, cleaning materials, etc. Emissions will be computed using:

- Stack tests for any add-on control system,

- Manufacturers' guarantees,

- Published emission rates, such as the EPA's AP-42,

- Material Safety Data Sheets/Air Quality Data Sheet,

- Continuous emissions monitoring,

- Other environmental reports, such as hazardous waste or SARA Title III,

- Best engineering judgement.

Of the five years reviewed, the two most representative years will be selected as the basis for applying for the emission reduction credits. Once registered, the ERCs represent an asset to the business, a reserve that can be tapped to raise funds for growth and development.

Other than Over-control, How are ERCs Created?

Given the current changes in the printing industry, there are a number of avenues to generate ERCs, other than by efforts to go beyond compliance:

- Shutdown of a facility: Many businesses that have had to close due to the pressures of landlords and real estate agents are no longer emitting air pollutants.

- Shutdown of equipment, reducing the production and emission of air pollutants,

- Replacement of traditional equipment with non-polluting equipment,

- Source reduction and pollution prevention.

There's Gold in Them Thar Hills

At one time, the cost of registering credits versus the value of the credits in the marketplace was a disincentive for printers to consider filing. That scenario has changed. Registering can be done at a lower cost, and the value of the credits is moving upwards. The current proposals by commodity brokers for VOC ERCs, to be used in the states of New York, Pennsylvania and Connecticut, suggest that credits can command from $3,500 to $5,500 per ton. The cost of registering can run as low as $2,500.00 per application. Even for a firm that closed down or curtailed an operation with emissions of three to four tons, ERCs can represent a significant amount of money.

While the concept has received a mixed reception by the various stakeholders having an interest in the environment, it has provided a means for allowing facilities to be expanded or built. The credits have also created a new investment market, where credits can be registered and held as an asset for sale in a commodity marketplace.

Technology Control Guidelines

The standards used by the agency engineers are derived from a process that evaluates the state of the art of technology and potential developments that will reduce emissions by modification of the formulation or of the process. The methods are no more than a sampling, based on a maximum universe of seven facilities. Selection of any more than that number would require application of the project to the Office of Management and Budget (OMB) for approval. This approach is used because the application to OMB would require more time and detailed justification.

Described below are the major technology control guidelines for rotogravure, flexography and heatset web offset printers, and the advisory guideline for lithographic printing. The original guidelines were researched and developed for large, major sources. As smaller businesses are brought into the regulated community, questions have been raised in a number of jurisdictions, and less stringent requirements have been considered and established for smaller size emission sources.

a. **OAQPS Guideline Series**
   (EPA-450/2-78-033, OAQPS No. 1.2-109, December 1978)
   Control of Volatile Organic Emissions from Existing Stationary Sources
   Volume VIII: Graphic Arts—Rotogravure and Flexography
   The document states that the graphic arts industry encompasses printing operations which fall into four principal categories, namely: letterpress, offset lithography, rotogravure and flexography. This guideline is applicable to both the flexography and rotogravure processes as applied to both publication and package printing. It does not apply to offset lithography or letterpress printing. This Technology Control Guideline (TCG) is intended for large major sources. It encourages the development of high solids and waterborne inks, preferring the addition of add-on controls. The report concludes that add-on controls would not be feasible for smaller flexographic operations. The conclusions for add-on controls state that a reduction efficiency of 90% of the VOC delivered to the devices can and should be achieved, with a capture efficiency of 75–85 percent as a reasonable condition.

b. **Graphic Arts, An AP-42 Update**
   (EPA-450/4-79-014, September 1979)
   This report was written for inclusion in EPA Publication No. AP-42, "Compilation of Air Pollutant Emission Factors." The report describes the various printing processes, including schematics of the major processes. It includes a statement that has caused consternation for both government and industry, which equates printing with coating. This is obviously a document written by an environmental engineer with little practical knowledge of the printing industries.

c. **Procedure for Certifying Quantity of Volatile Organic Compounds Emitted by Paint, Ink, and Other Coatings**
   (EPA-450/3-84-019 dated December 1984, revised 1986)
   This manual was conceived as simple step-by-step instructions for certifying the quantity of volatile organic compounds that will be released by a coating. In fact, it has been anything but simple, but still represents a procedure that can standardize the computations needed.

d. **Best Demonstrated Control Technology for Graphic Arts (EPA-450/3-91-008, February 1991)**
This study documents the reported overall control efficiency for VOCs at a number of rotogravure and flexographic printing facilities. The facilities contacted exhibited 90 percent or greater destruction efficiency. The objective was to provide state and local agencies with information relative to BACT and LAER. The introduction indicates that information at the facilities was not always available or was of limited availability. Of the facilities visited, all were very large operations, and primarily rotogravure. Two were only flexographic (of which one extruded and used waterborne inks) and one was a combined flexographic/rotogravure plant. Two used catalytic incinerators; three used regenerative incinerators; one was thermal and one used carbon adsorption methods.

e. **Guideline Series: Control of Organic Compound Emissions from Offset Lithographic Printing (DRAFT TCG, September 1993)**
This document is a draft addressing the offset lithographic printing industry as a source of volatile organic compounds. The draft was never accepted as a final TCG, but is in the workplace as a reference for enforcement agencies. It discusses, among many subjects, the process, model plants, emission control strategies, costs of control technologies, and emission estimation techniques. The draft elicited considerable concern by industry. While not a formal TCG, the document contains much that would be of interest to the printer in looking ahead at potential curtailment of chemistry in the process and allow for insightful planning for the future.

f. **Alternative Control Techniques Document: Offset Lithographic Printing (EPA 453/R-94-054, June 1994)**
Supplemental information based on public comment of draft control techniques guideline announced in the Federal Register of November 8, 1993. The purpose of this document is to provide information that would amplify and clarify some of the concerns with the draft TCG for lithography. It specifically states that the draft should not be used as a source of guidance without reference to this additional information.

g. **National Emission Standards for Hazardous Air Pollutants from the Printing and Publishing Industry, (40CFR Parts 9 and 63, Federal Register, Volume 61, No. 105, Thursday May 30, 1996, pp 27132-27159)**
In accordance with the provisions of CAA90, MACT standards were established for major sources in publication rotogravure, product or packaging rotogravure and wide web flexography. Major sources are defined as any source over 10 tons of any one HAP or 25 tons of combined HAPs. Control

will require 95 percent destruction efficiency. Monitoring, recordkeeping and reporting requirements are intensified.

h. **NESHAPS for Source Categories—Paper and Other Web Coating Operations—Background Information for Proposed Standards (EPA-453/R-00-002, April 2000)**

This document is the proposed rule to establish MACT standards for the web coating industries, described by the EPA as "Paper and Other Web Coating Operations (POWC)." It was published in the Federal Register, September 13, 2000 (Volume 65, Number 178). The definition used to describe the applicability of the rule is for "processes that apply a uniform layer of coating across essentially the entire length and/or width of a continuous substrate (web) to provide a covering, finish, or functional or protective layer to a substrate, to saturate a substrate or to provide adhesion between two substrates for lamination. This definition serves to distinguish the POWC from the printing and publishing source category, which can be described as processes that apply words, designs, or pictures to a substrate."

Sources that use HAPs and qualify for the NESHAP are required to operate control technologies that will achieve a 95-percent reduction of the air emissions. Once a facility has been identified as subject to the NESHAP, it will always be under surveillance by the federal agency.

What Next? Reactivity Research

Where the regulations and the standards of compliance will go next is a matter of conjecture by the agency and its scientists, as pressured by industry and environmental advocates. Considerable work with regard to what is happening in the air at ground level air has been done by the few scientists in the field who work on ozone reactivity scales for volatile organic compounds. As data become available that identify safer solvents, industry may anticipate efforts to delist or give more favorable treatment to those substances that are less reactive and therefore less hazardous as air emissions.

According to one of the leading scientists in the specialty, William P.L. Carter of the University of California; "Many different types of VOCs are emitted into the atmosphere, each reacting at different rates and with different reaction mechanisms. Because of this, VOCs can differ significantly in their effects on ozone formation ... Such differences have often been neglected in the past and all non-exempt VOCs have been regulated equally."* Some of the values determined by Dr. Carter, for solvents frequently used in the printing processes, are abstracted in Chapter 24, Table 24–1.

---

*Carter, William P.L., "Development of Ozone Reactivity Scales for Volatile Organic Compounds," *Air Waste*, Volume 44, July 1994, p 881.

In the name of pollution prevention as a process modifier, the identification and use of solvents (VOCs) that are reacting at safer levels can do much to expedite progress in areas where water and radiation curable technology is not effective or applicable. An example of one such delisting is acetone, which has been removed from the list of solvents categorized as VOCs. While acetone remains hazardous as a flammable substance, it is no longer considered a precursor of ozone.

How many more common solvents can be identified in the same manner and delisted to fill the need when only a solvent ink can perform adequately in the market, and where add-on controls are not cost-effective? Reactivity provides a rational means of determining what happens when any solvent reacts under the conditions that create ozone. Given a safety zone, formulators can develop inks, coatings, adhesives and cleaning solutions that will satisfy the needs of the printer. Minor sources, as well as major, could benefit from this form of source reduction.

Avoiding the High Price of Non-Compliance

The speed and complexity of decisions made by printers is necessary for doing business in a very dynamic industry. Playing by the rules sometimes gets sidetracked in haste to meet the objectives of immediate business pressures. Attracting new business or satisfying the increasingly higher standards of quality and productivity of a major customer may require the acquisition of new presses. Relocating under the pressure of eviction by a landlord involves the transfer of equipment to a new site. Both scenarios subject the facility to legal obligations in the form of permits or notifications. Unfortunately, one of the major areas that becomes sidetracked as the physical processes move ahead is the need to comply with the administrative side of environmental regulations.

Permits and Reports

A permit is to some degree a privilege granted to a business to conduct its affairs. In the case of environmental issues, the permit agrees to allow a printer to emit air comprising a percentage of the chemistry used, to discharge water from its process within certain limitations, and to dispose of its hazardous wastes in an authorized manner. Environmental permits are merely an extension of other permits necessitated by government to protect the public interest when a business opens its doors. When a printer opens a facility, adds equipment to that facility, or modifies the equipment in a way that adds emissions or discharges, he must file an appropriate permit application. When a facility is closed, it is equally important to notify the agencies and cancel the permits.

In some segments of regulation, it is not a permit but notifications and periodic reports that are mandated. This would apply to filing for an EPA hazardous waste identification number and periodic reports, and to reports required for New Jersey and New York City Right to Know Law notifications and annual reports.

Filing periodic reports requires records of purchases of inks, solvents, fountain solution and other pertinent chemistry. For some reports, the printer must collect logs of maintenance, tests of wastewater discharges, hazardous waste manifests, etc. The accumulated information, maintained to corroborate the performance of the firm in accordance with its permit, is subject to review during a visit from a representative of one of the agencies. It is essential that in responding to the questions raised that the support documents be readily available and accessible.

Punishment by Penalties

Not having a permit, or not filing a report in a timely manner can lead to considerable distress, time spent and penalties paid by the offending business once caught. Unfortunately, the environmental agencies often measure the success of their efforts in terms of dollars collected from offending businesses.

The sums are not the $50 to $100 fines one assumes, based on those levied by other local agencies, but considerable thousands and hundreds of thousands of dollars. The Department of Environmental Conservation for the State of New York can penalize offenders up to $10,000 for each violation of environmental regulations (Article 19), plus an additional $10,000 per day for each day the violation persists. Where appropriate, criminal actions may be sanctioned. For second offenders, the penalty can increase to $15,000 per violation and an additional $15,000 for each day during which the violation continues.

The amounts levied are aimed at penalizing offenders based on the severity of the violation, the length of time involved, as well as consideration of any economic benefit that the firm would experience against its competitors. Among the cases with which I have been involved recently, the lowest penalty was settled at $25,000, the highest was $135,000. In relatively few cases, with knowledge of the fine points of the regulations, adequate evidence and much persistence, were we were able to have the violations canceled.

The penalties are only a part of the cost; hiring a consultant or an attorney can be as expensive as the amount of the penalty. The initial phase of any violation offers the possibility of resolving the violation at a more limited cost. Engaging a competent consultant can facilitate negotiations with the agency. A conference can be scheduled as a cooperative means of meeting and resolving any issues and coming to an agreement. Litigation for more serious violations can involve the need for an attorney and the costs that accompany any legal procedure.

Firms that have experienced the process and paid penalties have learned the lesson the hard way. It was an expensive lesson, and, in most cases, not a pleasant experience. The burden of proof of innocence falls on the accused. The agency is not sympathetic to your account of events that may have led to the violation; they have heard the same stories over and over, and find it hard to separate the facts presented by an aggrieved innocent party from the webs woven by willful violators. What seems like common sense and is apparent to you may be swept aside with an unconcerned attitude. There are times when the alleged violator can be made to feel guilty even when he is confident that he has been proven innocent. In the words of a former supervisor in a state agency;

"The law may not be fair, but it is the law and I have to carry it out to the letter."

How Does One Get Into Trouble?

The key to avoiding violations and penalties lies in the recognition by management that adherence to environmental regulations is a necessary concern if one is to stay in business. It is then the job of everyone to conduct themselves responsibly and recognize any activities that are not in compliance with the appropriate environmental and safety regulations. There is a general similarity in the violations that are encountered by all printers. Listed below are some of the major causes of confrontations with the agencies:

Lack of a permit. This is probably the major omission in many regions. Have you opened a new business? Moved to a new location? Added a press to your pressroom? All these and more are good reason for you to have filed an application for a permit to erect the equipment and a certificate of operation to confirm that the installation is in compliance. Or more basically, have you neglected to get a permit because you are unaware of the need to make this application? A challenge to both government and industry associations is creating the vehicles that will get the message to the vast numbers of printers in the region. Outreach programs are a necessary means of closing this gap. While some programs were organized in the early days, the extent of the outreach has not been adequate.

The Hazardous Waste Division of the NYSDEC has cooperated in the past with the printing associations and local printing technology consultants to conduct pollution prevention workshops in which regulations, including air, were discussed. The New York City Department of Environmental Protection conducts workshops for printers and other industries. However, workshops are effective only in that they attract printers who are already in compliance and looking to further improve their procedures, or are there because their consultants persisted in advocating that they attend. The owners of many small shops do not attend, in part because they are busy operating the presses or out getting sales to keep the presses moving. This situation puts many printers in danger of not knowing that they have to file for permits. It also hinders a printer by not having information in hand which is pertinent to his status when he makes changes in location, equipment or chemistry. Once the violation is in place, the cost to perform the basic requirements remains the same, but the additional cost of dealing with the violation escalates and impinges on the finances of the firm.

Non-compliance with the standards of the Reasonably Available Control Technology (RACT) for your process. The government has established baseline maximum quantities of volatile organic compounds (VOCs) that are acceptable in the inks and fountain solutions used at press-side. If the inspector samples your inks and/or fountain solutions for lab testing, a determination will be made of the VOC content and to determine if it is in conformity with the rules. If the VOC content exceeds the mandatory limits, the source is then out of compliance.

Lithographic printers using fountain solutions must assure that the percentage of VOCs does not exceed 15 percent if the press has been operated at its current location prior to a date that has been grandfathered under the regulations. For newer equipment, if installed and operating since that date, the percentage of allowable VOCs is 10 percent. Heatset web lithographic presses must exhaust to add-on controls.

Flexographic and gravure printers, using liquid inks, are allowed one of three options, two of which center on solvent (VOC) content. Allowable inks can be high solids or waterborne. High solids inks must have no more than 40 percent by volume of VOCs, while water inks must have VOC content at no more than 25 percent by volume of the volatile portion of the solution. The third alternative would be the use of add-on controls.

Screen printers, in some localities, must have no more that 3.3 pounds of VOC per gallon of ink as applied, except for the category of "serigraph/fine arts" for which 5.0 pounds per gallon of VOC is permitted. In many locations, large sources are subject to add-on controls, while most small screen printers are below the enforceable thresholds for permits.

How is this monitored by the agencies? An inspector will visit the plant to do a routine inspection and take representative samples from the ink pans or fountain solution reservoirs. The samples will be sent to a licensed or state laboratory for testing in accordance with USEPA Method 24. The lab will report the pounds per gallon and percentage of VOCs and note whether they are in compliance with the standards. After some time, the report will be reviewed at the agency and an appropriate letter will be mailed to the facility. The letter will indicate if the facility is in or out of compliance. If the determination is that the test failed and the facility is in violation, an opportunity will be offered to meet with the agency and correct the offense. A typical inspection report is illustrated in figure 10–6.

It is important for printers to note that this letter provides them with the opportunity to challenge the findings. The testing procedure is not always accurate, or the sample may not be truly representative of the normal usage of inks and fountain solutions. A retest can be requested, with an opportunity for the taking of split samples. The agency retains one sample, while a lab designated by the printer can do an analysis on the second, identical sample. In some cases, there can be an overstatement of VOCs by the test method. Method 24 has been challenged at USEPA level as not being accurate with waterborne and radiation curable ink formulations, resulting in misleading measurements of the VOC content. At other times, the sample may not be consistent with the use of inks and fountain solutions in the plant. An irregularity can be contested as not being representative of the usage in the facility. A challenge is a right of the facility and should be exercised if the test results do not ring true.

New York State Department of Environmental Conservation
Facility DEC ID : 2610100150

CERTIFIED MAIL RETURN RECEIPT REQUESTED   Date : 07/20/2001

NOTICE OF VIOLATION

Owner :

          BROOKLYN, NY 11222

Facility :

          BROOKLYN, NY 11222

Contact :

          BROOKLYN, NY   11222

PLEASE TAKE NOTICE THAT YOU ARE IN VIOLATION OF NEW YORK STATE AIR POLLUTION CONTROL LAW,
Article 19 of the Environmental Conservation Law ('ECL'), and applicable regulations as set forth herein, in connection
with operation of the above named Facility.

Inspected On :   05/01/2001   2:30 PM

Inspection Performed By :

                    NYSDEC - REGION 2
                    47-40 21 ST
                    LONG ISLAND CITY, NY 11101
                    (718) 482-4944

Reason(s) for Inspection :   Follow Up Inspection   From 11/16/2000
                               Sample Collection

Inspection for :   Issued Permits   Type   Effective
                    2-6101-00150/00005   Air Title V Facility   01/12/2000 - 01/11/2005

Comments :

     The sample results of the sample ID 24964 collected on 5/1/2001 shows content of volatile matter of
     4.60 lbs/gallon in violation of the allowable of 3.5 lbs/gallon as specified in permit condition 24, Item
     24.2 of the Title V Permit Issued on 1/13/00.

     Sample results are attached.

     This case was previously referred to the Division of Legal Affairs. For questions regarding this matter,
     contact   , Assistant Regional Attorney at (718) 482-4965.

Figure 10–6. Notice of violation sent to facility based on inspection report by enforcement agency engineer.
Source: P-F Technical Services Inc.

Failure to operate an add-on control system properly and maintain records of the activity of the control system. For those printers who must use oxidizers, solvent recovery systems or carbon absorption units, operation of the systems must be within definable conditions supported by the maintenance of specific records. Not adhering to the standards or failing to keep records to support the historical performance of the system can constitute a major violation.

The most common add-on control for printers is the thermal or catalytic oxidizer. The regulations specify minimum acceptable levels of VOC destruction for each of the printing processes. Other conditions, and the use of actual stack tests, can tighten the standards. A facility that is subject to MACT (Maximum Achievable Control Technology) will require 95-percent destruction of its hazardous air pollutants. The equipment is required to be functioning at all times that the printing presses are in operation. Failure to operate at the specified conditions is grounds for citation of violations.

Records must be maintained to demonstrate compliance. Temperature records, maintenance logs and correspondence are all required references that must be available to any inspector. Failure to have the records and make them available is a violation.

Poor housekeeping around the press. Regulations mandate that all containers in press areas must be closed. Drums without covers or bung holes open, ink cans without covers, rags in open drums or on top of machinery—all are invitations for an inspector to file a finding of a violation.

Open containers invite evaporation. Both workers and the surrounding community feel the safety and environmental impacts. Specific rules call for them to be closed and to be maintained under safe conditions. While seemingly minor, the existence of these open containers and loose wipers/rags are a cause for concern during many inspections. While they may be overlooked in citing a plant with an otherwise good compliance effort, the inspector will be sure to note such conditions when other violations are cited. Poor housekeeping tends to support the claim of lack of management concern for safety and the environment. Some Title V programs require daily housekeeping inspections and logs to verify the observations and actions taken.

Failure to allow an inspector to enter your premises. Many firms suspect anyone who wishes to enter their premises. It is not unusual for customers to wait in a conference room or office to approve a set-up sheet for the purpose of assuring color and copy. Many printers confer with suppliers in the office, not in the plant. Therefore, it is not unusual for an employee to challenge the right of entry to someone who shows up, claiming to be a government agent, and simply walks into a plant via the employees' entrance or the shipping dock.

Representatives of the environmental agencies have subpoena powers when entering a facility. They have the right to enter unannounced and conduct an inspection. This does not mean that they do not have to identify themselves properly, not does it exclude the right of employees to request that the inspector return at a later date for good cause, i.e. management is not there and the standard operating procedure for security does not allow the employee to let anyone enter the building except in the event of an emergency.

If an inspector does come to the plant door, allow him to enter, but request that he meet with the owner or manager of the firm. A manager or supervisor should accompany him during the visit at all times. Answer all questions within the scope of the questions raised.

Failure to allow an inspector into a facility has been a contrite cause of violations. It is difficult for people to understand that anyone can walk through a facility without some form of permission. But in this case, it is a fact. The element of surprise is intended to catch people off guard and doing something wrong. The key here is to make sure that the normal process is to follow standard, acceptable procedures and work habits. Then an inspector can come in at any time and not find anything with which to find fault. By all means, ask for identification, and then let the legitimate inspector in to see the facility.

Violations, Penalties and Common Sense

In the end, if you have not followed the letter of the law, you are a violator and subject to punishment handed down by attorneys for the agencies or by administrative judges. The question then becomes one of common sense. What is good for the environment? What is acceptable for business to survive without having a major impact on the health of the community? What is a reasonable compromise that benefits both objectives? Penalties for small businesses do not solve the problem. The big stick may do more to bring about an end to the business community than it does to improve the quality of our environment. With that end comes an impediment to the opportunity for members of the community to earn a living.

The moneys exacted by penalties could be better spent in upgrading personnel knowledge and skills and improving technology to reduce pollution. At the federal level, this can be done under a program entitled Supplemental Environmental Projects. Money intended as a penalty can be used as a partial settlement, under specific conditions and a defined program, to benefit a broader base and provide greater impact on the reduction of pollution in the community.

First and foremost, the message is not in how to defer penalties. Avoiding non-compliance is the responsibility of the printer. Taking the necessary actions to assure that permits are in place and that all standards of compliance are addressed is a necessity when doing business in today's world. Printers have the responsibility of doing it right the first time, not as a consequence of being found out.

CHAPTER 11

Add-On Controls for Cleaner Air

From the outset, government agencies established a preference for the use of control systems at the end of the process. Using exceedingly high temperatures, the vapors would be destroyed. What better way to deal with the problem? Once incinerated, the volatile organic compounds and hazardous air pollutants would no longer exist. In a memorandum to the Florida Department of Environmental Protection, the USEPA Research Triangle manager, who negotiated the CTG with the flexographic and gravure industry representatives, admitted that the only solution they sought was the add-on control. Ink formulation solutions were not a favored alternative but were included only as a means of mollifying the industry ink specialist who participated in the regulatory process (figure 11–1). No other means, such as performance-based reductions, were even considered as viable strategies.

Thus the RACT, and later the BACT, MACT and LAER strategies, set the stage for printers, large and small, to divert the emissions from the press stacks to an oxidizer or solvent recovery system. The contemplated chemical replacement ink solutions cannot come close to the 99 percent elimination of the pollutants claimed for add-on controls. With the more recent adoption of the total enclosure concept, thermal oxidation emerged as the ultimate destroyer. Experience over the years has demonstrated that the positive impact on air emissions overlooks negative multi-media impacts. Solvent usage leads to hazardous wastes, potential spill contaminants, and workplace health exposure. A responsible decision for air

The following inquiries were posed to EPA by a representative of the Florida Department of Environmental Regulations concerning graphic arts RACT limitations. The questions raised and EPA responses are as follows:

Question: In what ways were the emissions from two RACT technologies (low-solvent inks vs. add-on controls) considered comparable?

Response: "We assume that the question arose largely because the limit for low-solvent inks on packaging rotogravure and flexography operations is sometimes more stringent than if abatement equipment is used. The difference is intentional. To clarify the reason for the differences, we must briefly explain our program for analysis of emissions from a variety of sources as it took place in the late 1970's.

"The printing industry was one of the last industries studied by EPA. More than a year earlier, we had published a guideline for paper-coating that required essentially 81 percent control. This control level was recommended as a result of analyzing the capabilities and cost of suitable abatement equipment for a variety of web-coating industries. The guideline also would allow compliance via adoption of low-solvent coatings whose allowable solvent content was calculated to have emissions equivalent to the discharge from a complying abatement device.

"Equipment used for printing on webs is very similar to that used to coat webs. There are two main differences. First, unlike a coating operation where the entire web is usually coated, the 'coverage' or portion of the exposed web on which printing is performed can vary dramatically, from as little as 1 or 2 percent to as much as 300 to 400 percent. This affects the solvent emission rate, makes it far more difficult to maximize solvent concentration in the dryer exhaust, and thereby increases the cost of abatement. The second major difference is the physical arrangement of the ink fountains which varies by type of printing operation rendering some less susceptible to efficient containment of evaporative losses.

"We concluded that the physical constraints of printing machinery and operations would likely preclude retrofitting such equipment to achieve the same levels of control possible with similar equipment used to coat a web. The ink industry subsequently asked that we write the guidance in a fashion that provided incentive for developing low-solvent inks, even though such inks did not exist (and the printing industry had little hope that they could be developed).

"We subsequently accommodated the request but saw no reason why the physical constraints of different types of printing equipment should predetermine the characteristics of its 'complying inks.'

"To set the VOC value for complying inks and coats for the web-printing industry identical to that for web-coating industry (81 percent) seemed inappropriate inasmuch as that would effect better VOC reduction than an abatement device could reasonably achieve on the most easily-controlled type of printing operation (publication rotogravure). Hence, we selected 75 percent (a figure recommended by an ink supplier) as the reduction for compliance by low-solvent inks for all printing operations regardless of the type of press.

"It might be of interest to note that, at the time the guideline was prepared, although we recognized the overall desirability of low-solvent inks, abatement was the only control option which appeared likely to be available within the time constraints mandated by the Clean Air Act. The low-solvent target was a concession (which we willingly made) to one ink manufacturer who, although he had previously invested considerable research in waterborne inks, had been unable to find printers willing to investigate and experiment with his product."

Figure 11–1. USEPA comments relative to preference for add-on control when establishing RACT.

Source: Memorandum from James Barry, USEPA Research Triangle, to the Florida Department of Environmental Protection, explaining the basis for the Graphic Arts TCG for flexography, date unknown (believed to be in the year or two following issuance of the guidance document).

requires a total assessment of compliance alternatives to forestall the transfer of one pollutant waste stream for others.

Alternatives for Add-On Control

Each of the printing processes poses a different challenge for the application of add-on controls. Based primarily on the volume of emissions and the nature of the solvent(s) used, some systems are more effective than others. Airflow from the press exhausts is a key sizing factor, related to the dwell time required within the control system. Economics plays a key role in the selection of appropriate technology from both the initial capital expenditure and the impact of the operating costs on the profitability of the final product.

The basic systems available for reducing the volume of air pollutants are:

• Thermal oxidation,

• Catalytic oxidation,

• Solvent recovery,

• Carbon absorption (zeolites),

• Bioremediation.

Selection of the technology that best suits the printing process will hinge on the nature of the solvents and other pollutants that are being exhausted and the energy that they bring to the add-on control process. Water-laden fumes are not particularly conducive to the efficient operation of some systems, while specific solvents will pass through or destroy other systems. The major capital investment represented by the control system necessitates thorough and competent evaluation of all factors.

Basic Types of Add-On Controls

Thermal oxidation exposes the emissions to very high temperatures—1400 to 1500 degrees Fahrenheit (760–815 degrees Celsiuis). Different designs provide for the pass-through or collection of the emissions in tanks packed with ceramic pieces to oxidize the vapors at these high temperatures. Turbulence assures the proper mixing of the components in the air stream. Destruction is frequently close to 99 percent. Maintaining the temperature can be costly, depending on the level of flammable solvent vapors in the emissions. There are few restrictions in the types of chemicals that will be adequately processed in such a system. (See figures 11–2, 11–3 and 11–4.)

Catalytic oxidation is similar to thermal oxidation, but engages the emissions with a catalyst to chemically decompose the vapors at considerably lower temperatures. Two popular catalytic materials are noble metals (platinum and iridium) and manganese dioxide, available in pellet form that can be placed in trays within the oxidizer bed. The noble metal catalyst can be wash-coated on a metal block configured as a honeycomb. The blocks are arrayed to form a wall through which the vapors must pass to exit the system. Typical destruction levels, at temperatures varying from 500 to 650 degrees Fahrenheit (260–343 degrees Celsius), would range from 90 to 97 percent. Potential poisoning of the catalyst

Figure 11–2. Regenerative thermal oxidizer.
Courtesy of Anguil Environmental System Inc.

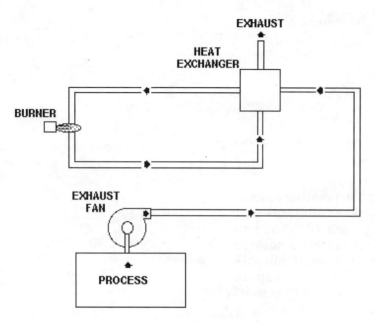

Figure 11–3. Schematic of recuperative thermal oxidizer.
Courtesy of MEGTEC Systems.

Figure 11–4. Recuperative thermal oxidizer.
Courtesy of Anguil Environmental System Inc.

puts some limits on the universality of the catalytic system. (See figures 11–5 and 11–6.)

Solvent recovery systems are in-line adsorption/desorption installations, which remove solvent vapors from the exhaust and recover the solvents for reuse. This type of system works best when the solvent blend is simple and the distillate will not retain water in the purified solvent. Retention of water could be injurious in reuse of the distillate from the inks, lest there be precipitation or congealing of the solids content of the inks. The complex solvent blend of flexographic inks, as well as those solvents that are aquaphobic, precludes the use of solvent recovery systems in flexography. Gravure ink systems are frequently less complex, consisting of a limited number of basic solvents, making the recovery system outflow more acceptable. The key to success is the ability to reuse the recycled solvent for cleaning and as a diluent. (See figure 11–7.)

Carbon absorption is available but is not very effective under many printing facility conditions. The system provides for the passage of the emissions into a container packed with carbon. The principle is that the solvent is retained in the absorbent carbon, to be disposed of as a hazardous waste or from which the solvents can subsequently be removed for destruction. This function lacks reliability as various solvents either can pass through, are only partially absorbed, or may destroy the carbon.

Another form of absorbent material is **zeolite**, which is configured as a rotating wheel into which the air flows. The advantages of zeolite are its ability to perform well with most solvents—whereas carbon has mixed results with different solvents—and elimination of the need to dispose of the absorbent as a hazardous waste. The major value of the zeolites lies in their ability to pull high airflows into the zeolite and desorb at a later date to a much smaller, more economically feasible thermal oxidizer. (See figure 11–8.)

Bioremediation utilizes microbes to ingest the pollutants and break them down to safer compounds, such as carbon dioxide and water. The microbes require a natural, humid biomass to which they can cling and obtain nourishment. The microbes produce enzymes, which, in turn, digest the pollutants in the exhaust air stream. The selection of the microbe will be conditioned by the nature of the pollutant. For every compound, there appears to be a match with a microbe in nature that can digest it. This technology is still in a developmental stage, with systems in place in Europe and the United States. Two major drawbacks have been: 1) the requirement for a large area occupied by a system and, 2) the structure needed to contain the water required to maintain the humidity that sustains the microbes. The biomass varies from cow manure to peat moss to synthetic plastics. A major advantage is the minimum amount of energy required to sus-tain the system. Bioremediation may find its place as water ink technology takes hold, which though containing small percentages relatively, generates significant amounts of volatile organic compounds. (See figure 11–9.)

Figure 11–5. Catalytic oxidizer at printing plant in New York City.

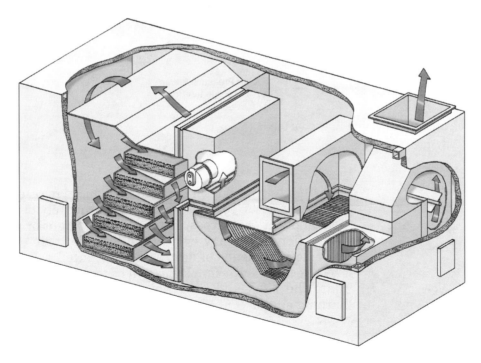

Figure 11–6. Cross-section of catalytic oxidizer.
Courtesy of MEGTEC Systems.

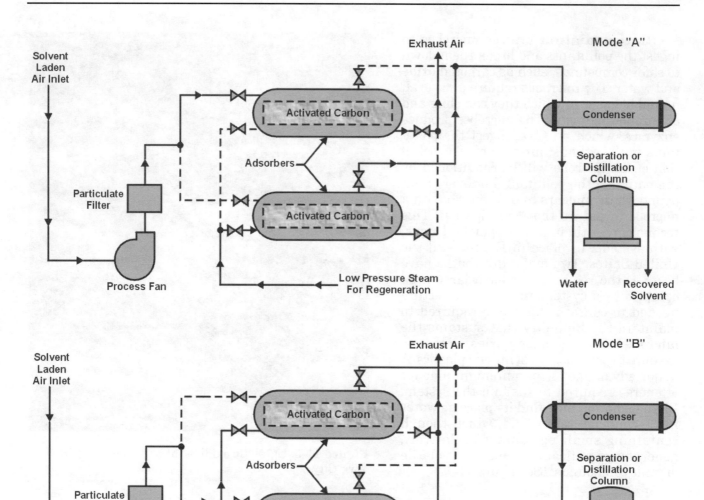

Figure 11–7. Solvent recovery system flow charts.

Courtesy of MEGTEC Systems.

Other technologies have been introduced in research and development projects, some of which may ultimately develop into practical applications. Exposure to ultraviolet light or microwaves are two options that may evolve and provide more energy-efficient, cost-effective means of destroying unwanted pollutants. It is conceivable that new technologies will be fostered by the desire to eliminate the NOX and CO_2 that are currently generated by fuel-burning add-on control systems.

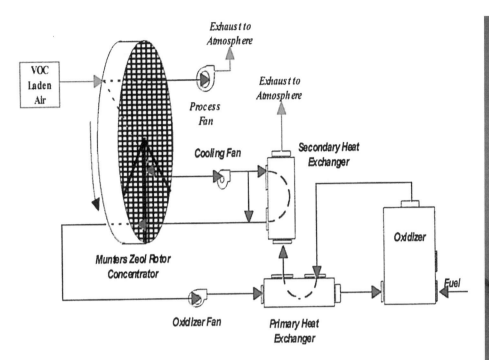

Figure 11–8. Complete Munters zeol rotor concentrator system.
Courtesy of Munters Corporation, Zeol Division.

Figure 11–9. Portable air treatment unit by SRE Inc. uses bioremediation systems with bacteria to digest chemical compounds and eliminate hazardous substances.

It is quite obvious that some systems will work well under most conditions; others will fare better under very specific, more limited scenarios.

By far, thermal oxidation systems have captured the bulk of the printing marketplace. Both thermal and catalytic oxidizers are functioning across a broad spectrum of printing processes. Solvent recovery has proven viable in many gravure facilities. Bioremediation has been introduced at a few sites where there has been considerable space and sufficient grounds to house a large acreage system. Carbon absorption has had more limited success in print shops, mostly in the role of indoor air cleaners for odors.

Thermal oxidation provides the maximum insurance for compliance. With temperatures of 1400 to 1500 degrees Fahrenheit (760–815 degrees Celsius), there are very few substances that will withstand the exposure in such a system. Volatile hydrocarbon compounds are broken down into water and carbon dioxide. When asked to destroy in excess of 95 percent of the emissions, the obvious answer would appear to be to employ a thermal system.

Advantages and Disadvantages— Which Do We Select?

Thermal Oxidation

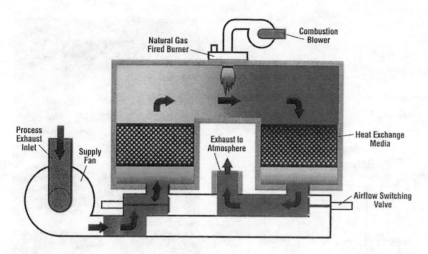

Figure 11–10. Regenerative thermal oxidizer system schematic.
Courtesy of The CMM Group, LLC.

The three elements required for success are high temperatures, turbulence and dwell time. Lacking any one of these elements will tend to reduce the efficiency of the burn. Turbulence assures a proper mix of the clean air with the solvent laden air. A poor mix will require much higher temperatures and dwell time. The amount of time that the air stream is maintained at a high temperature will generally determine the effectiveness of the system. Typical dwell times range from 0.5 seconds and up. This facilitates the mixing of the vapor-laden stream with clean air. There are two basic concepts in thermal oxidation: regenerative and recuperative.

The **regenerative system** consists of two or more vertical columns in which a ceramic stoneware medium has been placed to retain heat. The process air is passed through a column as it enters the oxidizer. The burner in the central combustion chamber heats the incoming air to oxidation temperature. The heated air stream then exits to the next media column, in which the energy from the hot air is stored. By constantly alternating the air stream from one chamber to the next, the alternating incoming air stream is heated by the energy stored from the previous cycle. As the column cools, it becomes a receptor of heat. (See figure 11–10.) The cost of a regenerative system is considered moderate to high for the tooling and installation. Operating costs are deemed to be low. Thermal destruction efficiencies are high. It is a system recommended for low concentrations of VOCs with high volume air flows.

The disadvantages are primarily based on economics and space. To run at such high temperatures requires metals that will withstand the heat and the expansion and contraction as the unit heats up and cools down. The initial cost of such systems is high and the physical dimensions quite large compared to the size of a typical print shop. The heavy weight of the unit requires ground-level installation. If space is not available at ground level, it may be necessary to place the unit on the roof. Such installation can generate costly structural improvements. It may not be practical to place a system on the roof. From an operating perspective, if the system is not running continuously the cost of starting up and idling can negate the intended benefits in fuel savings.

The **recuperative thermal oxidizer** also carries out its mission by heating the process air to a very high temperature. The incoming air passes through an air-to-air heat exchanger to be preheated before it enters the burner chamber. In the chamber, the process exhaust air is heated to a sufficiently high temperature for a period of time during which some degree of turbulence is introduced to ensure VOC destruction. Operating at a temperature in excess of 1200 degrees Fahrenheit (650 degrees Celsius) will destroy over 99 percent of the VOCs and HAPs and will release carbon monoxide and carbon dioxide.

The cost of purchasing and erecting a recuperative system ranges from moderate to high. The cost reflects the nature of the materials needed to sustain the high temperatures. The stack will require high quality materials to withstand the high temperature of the exhaust air stream.

Operating costs are high, as natural gas or propane is needed to maintain the very high temperatures, particularly with low solvent loads. The high temperatures are needed to minimize carbon monoxide levels. In addition to the formation of carbon dioxide, nitrogen dioxide will be generated at these very high temperatures. On the positive side, destruction efficiency will exceed 99 percent, more than ample to demonstrate BACT and LAER.

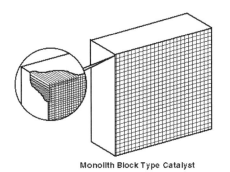
Monolith Block Type Catalyst

Bead Type Catalyst

Advantages of Bead Catalyst Systems
- High surface area.
- High mass-transfer efficiency between reactants and catalyst.
- Improved poison resistance due to high volume fraction of catalyst in reactor.
- Durability under conditions of thermal cycling.
- A portion of the catalyst can be easily replaced, if necessary.

Disadvantages of Bead Catalyst Systems
- Higher bed pressure drop.
- High cost due to large volume.
- Larger oxidizer sizing.

Advantages of Monolith Catalyst Systems
- Small combustion chamber size.
- Easy to install/hold catalyst into the chamber.
- Low pressure drop.

Disadvantages of Monolith Catalyst Systems
- Smaller surface area easily poisoned or deactivated.
- Susceptible to thermal cycle cracking.

Figure 11–11. Catalysts—advantages and disadvantages.

Courtesy of MEGTEC Systems.

Catalytic Oxidizers

Catalysts provide an alternative to thermal oxidation for the destruction of gaseous combustible pollutants into carbon dioxide and water. Catalytic units offer considerable savings in fuel consumption in the destruction of volatile organic compounds, but will be more limited in the types of applications for which they will be suited. (See figure 11–11.)

The key element of the catalytic oxidizer is the reaction between the solvent laden air and the catalyst to break down the bond of the carbon, hydrogen and oxygen molecules that compose the volatile organic compounds. This reaction can take place at considerably lower temperatures than are experienced in thermal oxidizers. Temperatures will vary based on the type of catalyst utilized, typically oxidizing the vapors in the range of 300 to 900 degrees Fahrenheit (150–480 degrees Celsius). Among the more common catalysts employed are the noble metals (platinum and iridium) and manganese dioxide. (See figure 11–12.)

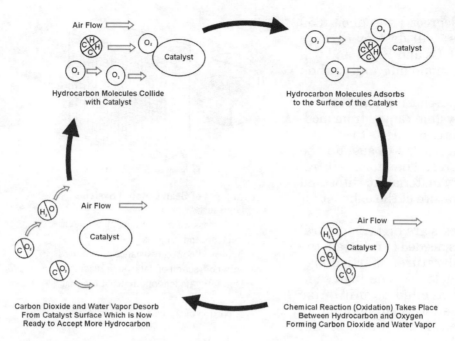

Air Flow

Hydrocarbon Molecules Collide
with Catalyst

Hydrocarbon Molecules Adsorbs
to the Surface of the Catalyst

Air Flow

Carbon Dioxide and Water Vapor Desorb
From Catalyst Surface Which is Now
Ready to Accept More Hydrocarbon

Chemical Reaction (Oxidation) Takes Place
Between Hydrocarbon and Oxygen
Forming Carbon Dioxide and Water Vapor

Figure 11–12. Molecular reaction of air emissions with catalyst.

Courtesy of MEGTEC Systems.

Catalytic systems are designed to allow for the dwell time, temperature and turbulence parameters similar to the pattern of the thermal oxidizers:

1. Requires sufficient time for oxidation to occur,
2. Must be maintained at a minimum temperature to facilitate destruction, and
3. Turbulence must be adequate to assure uniform temperature across the catalyst bed.

In addition, the catalyst should be configured to provide a high surface area for better contact between the catalyst and the process air stream. The more contact surface, the higher the efficiency of the reaction with the process exhaust air stream.

The catalysts themselves also pose problems to the user. Particulate matter can coat or clog the catalyst, reducing its ability to maintain a high surface area for reaction. Some waste streams will "poison" the catalyst, preventing it from functioning effectively. Among these "poisons" are silicon, phosphorus, halogens such as chlorine, and sulfur. The oxidation activity can be reduced by the loss of active components of the catalyst. Catalyst activity can also be reduced by the deposition of unreacted VOCs on the surface (called coking), by attrition as the catalyst ages, or by sintering—the collapse of the catalytic structure at high temperatures. The testing of catalysts to ascertain their ability to function properly is described in Appendix XXIII.

Performance of the catalytic unit can be maintained, in light of some of the problems noted, by compensating for the anticipated decline in efficiency in the design of the system. The quantity of catalyst can be planned in excess of actual needs, allowing for a portion of the catalyst to become deactivated and still maintain destruction efficiency. Increasing the temperature over time can also compensate for the decline in the vitality of the catalyst. Of course, periodic replacement of the catalyst will return the unit to original operating conditions. This replacement schedule will depend on the poisons in the process exhaust stream.

One of the advantages of the ability to run at lower temperatures is the cost of fabricating the unit. The materials need not be as demanding and rugged as when facing thermal temperatures of 1400–1500 degrees. This reflects in the size and weight of the units and, thereby, in the cost of installation. The lower operating temperatures also conserve on the use of natural gas to maintain destruction temperatures. With high air flow, low solvent loading, the input of fuel to maintain temperatures averaging between 500–600 degrees will be considerably less than maintaining temperatures of 1400–1500 degrees.

Specifying Control Systems

The first step in selecting an add-on control system is to know your own printing and coating equipment and chemistry. Certain basic information is required to establish the parameters within which a system must operate:

1. **Define the airflow** that the presses and coating lines will exhaust to the control system. The size and the destruction capability of the control system will depend on the amount of air that must be taken in and manipulated. Every press has a specified air volume coming in to its drying system, as well as a higher rated exhaust to evacuate the solvent-laden air. The add-on control must have adequate capacity to handle the total airflow from all sources in the pressroom.

2. **Determine if the airflow can be redirected** to reduce the volume that will enter the control system. Recirculation of air in the drying systems can frequently bring the airflow down by 50 to 60 percent. Output from a typical flexographic six-color central impression press can be reduced from a theoretical value of 8,000 cfm to approximately 3,000 cfm. In a plant with four identical printing presses, it is possible to reduce the total airflow from 32,000 cfm to 12,000 cfm. The savings in capital expenditures can be significant. The cost of installation would also be considerably lower, taking into account the weight of a larger system that would otherwise be needed for the facility.

   In addition to reducing the airflow, to minimize the initial capital cost, recirculating the air at the press dryers will bring the added benefit of virtually doubling the amount of vapor in the air. Remember that the solvent is a fuel. The more fuel provided by the solvents to burn at adequate destruction efficiency, the less natural gas that has to be pumped into the oxidizers. Using the average pounds per hour of solvent moving through the system, recirculation can just about double that capacity. As an example, the typical flexographic press may exhaust at a 5–7 percent LEL (Lower Explosion Limit). With recirculation, the LEL will rise to 10–14 percent.

3. **Evaluate the composition of the exhausted vapors** and the amount that will pass into the control system. The assignment of adequate catalyst or thermal capacity will be vital to properly sizing the oxidation system; solvent composition and the nature of the solvents can determine whether the choice can be controlled by solvent recovery or absorption techniques.

    The mass balance developed for the audit and usage management of the chemicals purchased for the printing and coating operations is the primary source of this information. Based on the material safety data sheets and other competent formulation breakdowns, the mass balance reduces purchases to its volatile components and distributes these volatiles among the pieces of equipment and ultimately through the oxidizer. Identification of process rates, based on hours of operation, provides a guide to minimum, average and maximum pounds of volatiles per hour which the system must control.

    Identification of the components also defines the limitations that will be placed on system selection due to lack of adequate capability to properly react with the chemistry and achieve acceptable levels of destruction. Some chemicals will not be effectively destroyed by oxidation or at temperatures within the range of the thermal or catalytic system. Other avenues must be researched for these compounds.

4. **Evaluate the energy requirements** for each of the competing systems. How much natural gas or propane is needed to maintain a temperature level that will maximize destruction? How much pressure must be in the gas lines? Many units must operate on high pressures. How much electricity is required for operating the system? Is cooling required by means of heat exchangers prior to sending the clean air up the stack?

    The cost of purchasing the equipment is a one-time occurrence. Operating the system will be a variable that must be absorbed in the cost of producing product. If the day-to-day cost of any system is prohibitive, that will not likely be the proper system for the facility.

5. **Where will the system be located?** Space requirements and weight considerations can dictate whether a particular system can be installed. Consider the need to erect a 50,000-pound system on top of a 10- or 20-story building. Or, where do you locate a unit with a space requirement that is too large in a plant and for which there is insufficient space outside the walls of the building?

Figure 11–13. Rooftop installation of ductwork from multiple presses to one oxidizer.

In the case of rented facilities, will the landlord allow the erection of a system on the roof or in an area next to the building? Will the landlord approve penetration of the roof to make room for the ductwork? (See figure 11-13.) Will the local authorities approve an installation on the particular site?

6. **Which catalyst or thermal system will be most effective** for ridding the plant of the pollutants in the air stream? Will the facility have to satisfy normal standards, or have to conform to a NESHAP (National Emission Standard for Hazardous Air Pollutants) standard? Will the system selected provide for adequate destruction efficiencies?

7. With the **expenditure being made for energy** and the high temperatures at which both thermal and catalytic systems operate, can the heated exhaust air be utilized for energy recovery in heating the facility or in other processes, as well as for air conditioning during summer months? Is this cost effective?

There are other technical considerations in the configuration and tooling of a control system. The key is to propose the basic information cited above and then compare, in detail, the proposals that are submitted in response to the specifications by various venders of similar or competing technologies.

See Appendix XXII for a typical request for proposals for add-on control systems and a checklist for comparison of the proposal details submitted by vendors.

Stack Tests

Once the add-on control is installed and operational, a stack test must be conducted to confirm the performance of the system. The test is performed by a qualified independent party, equipped to monitor the airflow and volatiles into the system and out of the exhaust, and to analyze the composition of the exhaust. The object of the test is determine capture and destruction efficiencies and ascertain if the system will meet the compliance standard for the particular printing process. Tests are run in accordance with approved EPA test standards which are confirmed beforehand by the submission of a stack test protocol to the Agency.

Typically, the test is conducted in a one-day period, consisting of three one-hour runs of all the presses under the oxidizer. The runs are to be uninterrupted and representative of the maximum ink coverage that would be applied. Our recommendation would be to identify a job for each press that has the maximum number of colors and coverage, and that is large enough to run all day without making any copy or color changes. Roll changes and normal stoppages to clean plates are acceptable conditions during the runs.

If there are no jobs from which to select the stack test runs, then use a dummy job that will maximize coverage and use waste materials. With a six-color press printing on four stations, our suggested sequence would be plates on the first station that are close to 100 percent, 50 percent on the third station, and 25 percent each on the fourth and fifth stations. The plates can be overall color or some pattern. The intent is to maximize volatiles entering the oxidizer. Waste or rejected film can be used, as well as press return inks to minimize the cost of conducting the test. The instrumentation will be set up to monitor airflows, temperatures, the concentration of volatiles entering the chamber, and the concentration of the carbon in the outgoing stack (figure 11–14). As the test proceeds, all data will be processed into a computer for analysis and documentation.

All inks and solvents entering the pressroom will be weighed and entered into a log for each press. At the conclusion of the test (day), all inks and solvents will be removed from the press and weighed. This will provide a basis for determining what went into the machine and how much went up the stack, as illustrated in Table 11–1. The VOC computations from the actual consumption can be compared to the data collected at the oxidizer. A final report is submitted to the agency and, based on the successful results of the test, a permit is issued. A sample of a final report is part of Appendix XXIII.

Permanent Total Enclosure

To assure the capture of fugitive emissions and the exhausting of these emissions through the control devices, EPA has established standards for the permanent total enclosure of either the source of the emissions, the pressroom or the facility. Meeting the conditions of the design of the room, the claim can be made for 100 percent capture of all emissions from the process. See figure 11–15 for a schematic of a typical permanent total enclosure for a flexographic facility.

Figure 11–14. Instrumentation used for monitoring emissions during stack test.

There has been much concern over the concept of a Permanent Total Enclosure (PTE) as a means of increasing control over the capture and destruction of volatile organic compounds (VOCs) and hazardous air pollutants (HAPs). To the average printer, a total enclosure presents both advantages and disadvantages. The total enclosure concept came into being as a means of improving the ability of printers to capture a higher percentage of the vapors evaporating and escaping during operation of a typical flexographic or rotogravure press. The concept of RACT (Reasonable Available Control Technology) for flexography is based upon an anticipated 30 percent of the vapors escaping as fugitives. With the goal of destroying much higher percentages of VOCs and HAPs, the need arises to capture almost all of the fugitive emissions.

Envisioning the improvement of capture as a function for the individual press, this approach has led to many enclosure designs that have been viewed as restrictive for normal working procedures and the health of the press personnel. Armor plate, metal or glass,

TABLE 11–1. INK AND SOLVENT COLLECTION FORM USED DURING STACK TEST

COMPANY:	VITAL POLYETHELENE MFG. CO. INC.
ADDRESS:	8 EAST 100TH STREET, BROADSIDES, NY
DATE OF TEST:	DECEMBER 20,2000
PRESS NO.	A DESCRIPTION: KIDDER 6 COLOR CI
PRESS SPEED:	450 FPM OVEN TEMPERATURE: 125

COLOR/SOLVENT	IN PRESS START TEST	ADDED DURING TESTS	DEDUCT END OF TEST	AMOUNT USED	PERCENT VOC'S	POUNDS VOC'S
INKS						
1 WHITE	50 50	50	35	115	42%	48
2 YELLOW	45 45	45	40	95	50%	48
3 BLUE	39 39		28	50	57%	29
4 RED	39 39		27	51	57%	29
5						
6 BLACK	40 40		15	65	59%	38
TOTAL INKS	213 213	95	145	376		192
SOLVENTS						
NORMALPROPANOL	45 45	45	25	155	100%	155
NP ACETATE	35 35		30	40	100%	40
TOTAL SOLVENTS	80 80	45	55	195		195
TOTAL VOC'S						387

Source: P-F Technical Services Inc.

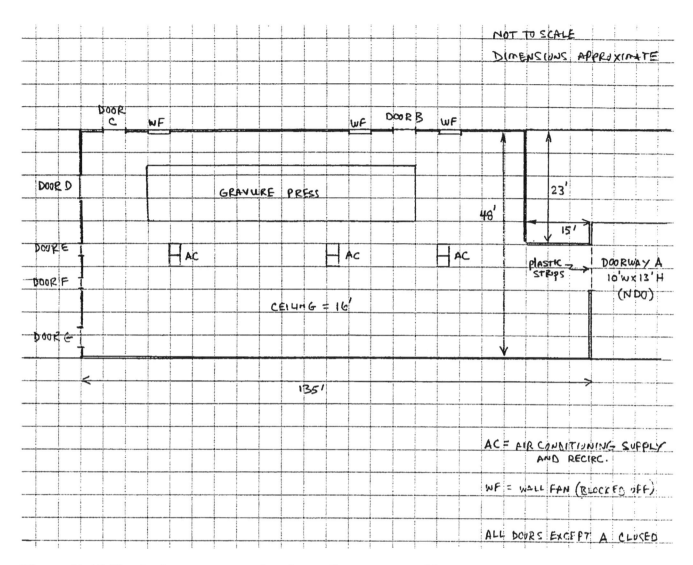

Figure 11–15. Sketch of permanent total enclosure for pressroom with one gravure press.
Source: Eric Pearson, P.E., Environmental Science Services.

placed around printing stations have fostered negative impressions on operating management and press crews. Rooms built around the press have negative implications due in part to the sharp rise in air pollutants in the enclosed area and the need for extreme personal protective equipment to cope with OSHA health and safety standards. Press personnel do not want to be constrained by respiratory equipment. On a practical note, materials handling with a closed portion of the press can be time consuming and costly as well as extremely difficult.

Enclosing the pressroom as a whole provides a number of benefits to the operation. With a variety of older and newer presses in the plant, the enclosure can insure a higher level of capture and destruction efficiency for pieces of equipment that, on their own, may not qualify. Locating the pressroom in the total enclosure can provide the facility with much greater flexibility in setting up and running the presses, while greatly enhancing the ability to remove and destroy solvent vapors. A key element in a successful permanent total enclosure is provision for maintenance of the quality of the air in the room. This may result in the need for air conditioning the pressroom, which, in turn, will provide a benefit in more consistent conditions in which to produce more predictable quality in the printed product.

Definition of a Total Enclosure

To summarize the USEPA guidelines for a permanent total enclosure in layman's terminology, a PTE consists of a closed area which has no more than five percent of its area that are natural draft openings (NDOs) and has a negative draft measured by an air flow into the pressroom that can be measured at, or in excess of, 200 feet per minute.

Picture an average pressroom with at least two openings through which materials are moved by forklift trucks, plus doors, windows and exhausts from fans or other operations. The room openings can be closed by using vinyl strips; fans can be shut down and covered. Exit doors can be kept closed, other than opening and closing for entry. Plate cylinders, anilox rollers, inks, etc. can be moved into the presses and back to storage without encumbrances. People work in their normal work clothes using only the minimum of personal protective equipment. The oxidizer exhausts all air from the room.

The cubic volume of the room is computed (length × width × height). The area represented by any of the natural draft openings, including the volume of air moved out of the room by other exhaust systems, is measured and calculated. If the NDOs are in excess of five percent, steps must be taken to reduce the openings or airflow.

The viability of the total enclosure is measured and verified during the stack test of the add-on control system. The principal measurement, once the NDO percentage has been verified, is the flow of air into the room. The negative pressure will be obvious, as observed from the vinyl strips at the door being pulled into the room. The flow meter reads in excess of 200 fpm. A visual smoke bomb test wafts into the room. The total enclosure has been affirmed.

Disadvantages of PTE

The negative aspects of the total enclosure are cost, movement of materials and equipment in and out of the room, health exposures, as well compliance with other regulations.

1. The cost of building a permanent total enclosure for the pressroom will vary depending on the materials selected and the building codes of the locality.

2. Building walls around an operation places restrictions on the movement of materials into and out of the area, requiring the planning of a layout which adequately evaluates the effective utilization of space, equipment and labor. For an existing pressroom, the placement of equipment and the permanent features of the structure may not be

conducive to an efficient flow. Moving the presses could be a costly and problematic solution.

3. Enclosing the presses can, and will, restrict airflow and raise the level of air pollutants in the room. If the add-on control exhaust fan is not sized properly, and if make-up air is not adequately brought into the room, there could be an imbalance which results in increased concentrations of solvents remaining in the closed confines of the pressroom. OSHA concerns for indoor air pollutants may require the use of respiratory equipment by press personnel.

4. Building and fire codes in states, cities or other localities may specify construction codes and air movement standards that will be contradictory to the dictates for the permanent total enclosure. The materials that can be used to construct the enclosure may be tightly regulated by fire codes. Property owners may not allow the erection of a permanent structure based on these legal restrictions.

5. Considering the above, a facility may be tempted to size an add-on control to completely exhaust the pressroom. The resulting airflow would be considerably higher than that required to service the drying systems of the presses. The capital cost of the equipment and the cost to feed large quantities of fuel into the system to maintain the high destructive temperatures may render this approach economically infeasible.

Is There a Future for Add-on Controls?

The negative impacts of the introduction of oxidizers to the printing industry were not foreseen at the time that such systems were first introduced in the 1970s. While oxidation was the preferred control method at that time, subsequent concerns about the effects of carbon dioxide on the upper atmosphere brought a new evaluation concerning the use of fossil fuels. Coupled with the desire of environmental advocates to move away from solvent-based technologies in the future, there may very well be a move to the use of the more energy-cost-effective application of bioremediation technology. Other, less costly alternatives, may promote energy efficient systems as well as promote the use of waterborne and radiation cured inks and coatings.

Natural gas is a resource that calls for conservation measures. Using this natural resource without some control can dissipate the major weapon this country has against the cartel supplying crude oil for fuel and gasoline. Some few states recognized this need for conservation and enacted seasonal shutdown provisions in their regulations. During months when ground level ozone is not being generated by the forces of nature, printers can apply for the right to print without use of the oxidizers.

Coming out of the stacks of the add-on control systems could be the very things that have negative impacts on other aspects of the environment. Carbon dioxide is a major by-product of oxidation, as is nitrous oxide. CO_2 is a major culprit in the decrease in ozone in the upper stratosphere and a contributor to global warming. NOx is a precursor of low level ozone, and is most certainly generated by thermal oxidizers.

Bioremediation provides an intriguing option for control of air pollutants; however, there are issues to be addressed. Two major concerns are the amount of space needed to house the biomass on which the microorganisms will live, and the problem of maintaining a moist environment in which the microorganisms can sustain themselves. Secondary is the issue of maintaining the microorganisms at such time as the plant is closed for vacation, holidays or maintenance.

Most certainly, add-on controls perform effectively, but are they the real long-term solution to the problem of air emissions? Looking at the future, will add-on controls be viewed as a temporary measure until alternative ink technology can be found, or will they be here to stay? Can technology redesign the add-on controls to be more effective at a lower cost? As the nation and world move to a virtually solventless society, innovative technologies will have to serve as controls where a substitute ink or coating can not.

CHAPTER 12

Inks: Meeting the Demands of Quality and the Environment

Propelled by the dual forces of customer demand for higher quality graphics and the challenge of the environment, inkmakers and their suppliers have been under pressure to develop ink technologies that will respond to these influences. Changes that have taken place to bring printers into environmental compliance, have, in turn, required new disciplines on the part of the printer and his equipment. Sometimes this has been for the good, producing both superior quality products and environmental responsibility. In other instances, the environmental challenges have resulted in major production and quality concerns and problems that have acted as deterrents to change. (See figure 12–1.)

These challenges have changed the relationships among substrate suppliers, printers and inkmakers in today's marketplace. Never before has it been more critical for the printer and his suppliers to work together. Making a marriage between ink and substrate has become highly sensitive to the basic chemistry of both materials, both becoming victims to changes in the basic process and both necessarily becoming responsive to any changes.

Conditions that were routine in years gone by, when the only function of ink was to put an image onto paper is no longer the case. Papermaking has had to change to meet the demands of environmental regulations, putting some new barriers in the way of the ink. Titanium dioxide is now used as a filler for some grades of

Market Forces Work Against Each Other

Figure 12–1. Inks are critical to print the graphics for packaging and commercial products.

paper; chlorine-free paper produces a new pH level; recycled paper introduces both known and unknown chemistry into the texture of the fibers; hydrogen peroxide is now being used as a brightener.

New resins, developed for physical characteristics, present new surfaces on which the ink must anchor and withstand the abuse of handling, temperature changes, light and processing. Additives change the reaction of ink to film and foil, as well as introduce the possibility of interaction with the ink itself.

For lithographers, changes in plate chemistry stemming from direct-to-plate systems, have altered the traditional relationship between plate and fountain solution. This too has ramifications in the formulation of the ink.

Add these changes to the removal of isopropanol as a major component of fountain solution, and there arise some critical questions relative to the pH of the various materials and how they come together to make the ink adhere to paper, film or foil substrates. Can the inks now endure whatever wear is intended for the particular printed product? Making a universal ink that can run on multiple substrates becomes more of a quest than a reality.

Contending with these changes in chemistry requires a new approach to ordering inks. Without a sharing of information, a partnership between the substrate maker, the printer and the inkmaker, routine work of yesteryear will become the problem of today. Each partner must be concerned with the problems of the other as paper or film is made, ink is formulated and the two are mated on the press.

Soy and Vegetable Oil Inks

With lithographic printers facing the need to reduce air emissions and hazardous waste, while at the same time striving for more color and more sophisticated graphics, there have been many developments that have yielded positive results. Soy and vegetable oil inks have taken a firm hold in the making of lithographic inks. More product lines are embracing the natural oils and replacing the hydrocarbons that were the older standards. Sheetfed process inks are composed of soy and vegetable oils at percentages ranging from 25 to 35 percent. Said oil content of web inks are higher, with 40 to 50 percent of the formulation consisting of the natural oils. Typical oils used come from soy beans, rape seed, walnuts and corn. The quality of these inks has been excellent and has been well received by print buyers. (See figure 12–2.)

Radiation Curing Finds Niches

Ultraviolet radiation curable inks and coatings have made inroads in the lithographic and narrow web flexographic markets as well as in screen printing. With pressures to reduce air emissions based on the solvents and oils inherent to the lithographic and flexo solvent inks and press washes, UV inks offer a no-solvent liquid which cures to a solid film on exposure to controlled UV radiation. If not exposed to UV light, the inks remain liquid and easy to remove from a press ink fountain for reuse. Primary products printed with UV inks at this time are labels, business forms, publication and book covers, and paperboard packaging.

The lack of solvents provides environmental acceptance. Without solvents, there are no emissions to the air. As long as the inks remain in the fountains, waste is minimal and the environmental impact is significantly reduced. This situation is perfect for the printer of four-color process work. Since the basic colors are the same from job to job, the inks do not have to be removed from the fountains. In essence there is minimal downtime for clean-up and marginal waste since the ink fountains and rollers do not have to be washed down with solvents.

Nevertheless, printing of line copy with screen inks when matching standard color systems can pose a problem. The removal of UV ink and subsequent cleaning of the print station presents the printer with a problem. When one ink must be removed from the press and replaced with another ink, the time and chemistry required to do a proper cleaning entails a considerable amount of a fairly aggressive and toxic solvent blend. Toluene, methyl ethyl ketone and xylene are fairly common components of a press wash for UV curable inks.

Installation of the UV ink system on an existing press involves major modification of the press. The primary additions are the UV curing lamps (figure 12–3) and other necessary auxiliary equipment. A major concern for printers is the high cost of equipping a press to use UV inks and coatings.

Figure 12–2. Lithographic printing station at Contemporary Color Graphics, Edgewood, NY.

Figure 12–3. Ultraviolet curing system mounted on existing flexographic printing press.

Courtesy of Prime UV.

In specialty markets, this cost can be more readily absorbed into the selling price of the products. Commodity and highly competitive packaging markets may not be able to overcome the capital and daily operating costs.

UV inks have given the forms printer the ability to use color freely. These printers have also been able to realize higher productivity and more consistent quality. Turnaround time for printing and shipping a job has been reduced from days (or weeks) to hours. A case cited was an in-plant financial printer, who can print, fold and cut a finished brochure and have it shipped to the customer within three hours from time of plating.

Packaging with coated carton board also lends itself to the use of UV inks. Process printing becomes much easier and more predictable. The inks remain stable throughout the run. After printing, high gloss UV coatings are critical as a marketing tool and for product protection.

Labels printed flexographically benefit materially from UV ink systems, particularly in the printing of four-color process jobs. Laying down exact dots of highly concentrated ink without gain allows for the transfer of graphics that compete in quality with gravure. The intensive markets for electronic games and videos have enabled narrow web printers to capitalize on the advantages of radiation curable inks. (See figure 12–4.)

Printing line color by flexography has not been as efficient as four-color process work. When a Pantone color ink is specified and provided by the inkmaker, there is little room for toning at the average print shop. The inks are too viscous for color to be modified simply by stirring with a stick. As a result, printers have had to change anilox rollers to see if different screens and volumes will achieve the colors desired. This is costly both in time and in the need for a press cleanup with each change of rollers.

The clarity and high gloss of UV has also made an impact on coatings. Solvent-based coatings have given way, for the most part, to aqueous and UV curable coatings, both spot and total coverage. The highest gloss is attainable only with UV curable coatings. In addition to overall coatings, very effective design components now consist of the intelligent placement of UV coatings in shapes (pattern coating) to highlight segments of the graphics.

Screen printers can more readily adapt to the use of radiation curable inks and coatings. Conveyer curing units, such as illustrated in figure 12–5, allow manual, semi-automatic and automatic screen equipment to channel printed product under a UV lamp system. Many lithographic pressrooms employ conveyer systems for the coating of printed sheets with UV curable high gloss finishes.

Printers are cautioned to exercise extreme care in the handling of UV inks. Strict adherence to safety and health precautions will protect workers from undue exposure to the deleterious effects of the lights and the abusive chemistry of the UV inks.

Regular lithographic and flexo-graphic inks are not compatible with UV curable inks, thereby requiring either dedicated presses or extremely well-cleaned machines when switching from one system to the other. This has changed somewhat in recent days as one of the major ink companies has intro-duced a hybrid UV-traditional litho-graphic ink.

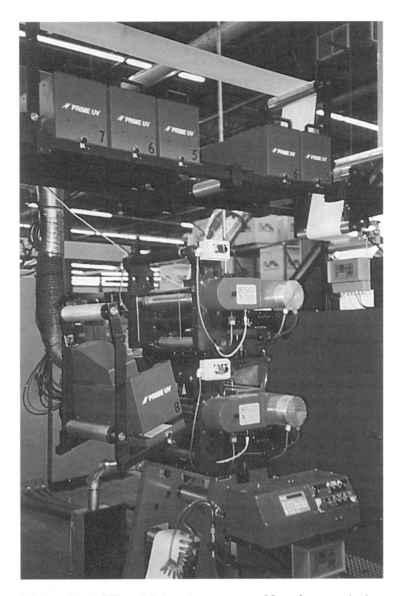

Figure 12–4. Ultraviolet curing system adds value to printing of narrow webs.

Courtesy of Prime UV.

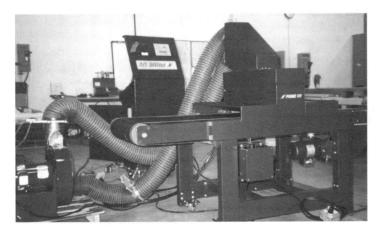

Figure 12–5. Conveyer configuration facilitates use of radiation curable inks and coatings by screen printers.

Courtesy of Prime UV.

Waterborne Inks and Flexographic Printing

Despite the preference for add-on controls of solvent emissions, the long-range outlook for liquid ink printers—gravure or flexographic—is for the development of more effective waterborne inks, capable of meeting the quality characteristics needed for the packaging and miscellaneous products marketplace. Film and foil packages are made to withstand considerable exposure to the elements and to chemicals in the processing of the foods and other packaged products. Success with water will come when the inks can meet the arduous requirements for such items as frozen foods, ice cubes and food products packaged in EVA film structures. (See figure 12–6.)

Waterborne inks have been used for flexographic printing of papers and paperboard since the invention of the process. Printing on these substrates with water was readily successful because of the absorbent nature of the paper fibers. The inks and solvents (water included) are partially absorbed into the surface of the substrate, and partially vaporized into the surrounding air.

With the advent of the environmental regulations, notably the Clean Air Act, work commenced on the development and use of waterborne inks for printing on films, foils and similar nonabsorbent substrates. Advancements have been slow as industry has had to develop the means of overcoming the innate problems

Figure 12–6. Printing with waterborne ink on films and metallic surfaces poses problems for flexographic and gravure printers.

posed by this combination of materials. A number of primary characteristics of films and laminates intended for automatic packaging equipment require additives that are counterproductive to the acceptance of water as a vehicle for the ink. This includes slip and ethyl vinyl acetate additives.

Perhaps the most contentious and argumentative ink formulation to meet the environmental issues has been the development, or lack of adequate development, of high-performance waterborne inks. Barriers and challenges have been recognized, and some erected, to stall the development of the best response to environmental responsibility for those processes which use liquid inks. As with many environmental issues, both science and emotions played a part in the picture.

Printing with solvents on films and foils is relatively easy. The surface tension of the inks and the films are relatively similar. The solvent can dissolve additives on the surface and bite into the film. With some exceptions, comparable but rival brand solvent inks can be mixed without any major consequences. If a problem arises, the solvent ink can be easily manipulated and adjusted. Solvent can also be used to remove any ink that has dried.

Waterborne inks are different. They are not all compatible and brands cannot be mixed unless specified by the supplier. When dried, water inks are unmovable, almost like cement. Surface energy plays a role, measured in units called "dynes". The surface energy of water is in the range of 60 dynes versus the high 36–38 dynes for corona-treated films. It is difficult to make one material attract the other with such obvious differences. Drying is complicated by the fact that for every volume of solvent evaporated, water will be 10 times the volume. Proper drying may slow down the process. To some, the gloss of the water inks is not as good as that of solvent inks, but does that make the gloss of the water ink totally unacceptable? The observer can surmise that there is much to be considered when making the choice to convert to waterborne inks.

Basically, placing a waterborne solution on a film or foil is similar to placing water on a newly waxed car; the water beads up and slides around the surface. The surface of the film is similar to the wax coating. Furthermore, the slip agent, which is added to the film to enable it to slide easily during filling operations, blooms to the surface and adds an additional impediment to the wetting out and adhesion of the inks. Overcoming these characteristic tendencies has been one of the major tasks facing package printers when using waterborne ink and coating formulations.

Basic Requirements for Waterborne Inks

Other problems arose with regard to the technological development of the flexographic printing press and its functional components. The ink transfer system required attention to the metering capabilities of the components and, from a structural perspective, the materials of which the rollers are manufactured. Changes in the rollers are required because of the nature of the water ink (it tends to act somewhat like a high-solids ink), as well

Flexographic Equipment Limitations

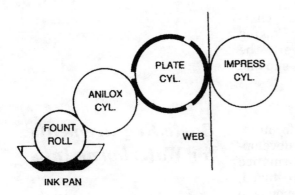

Figure 12–7. Schematic of a traditional flexographic printing station.

Source: *Flexography: Principles and Practices,* Fourth edition, p 23.

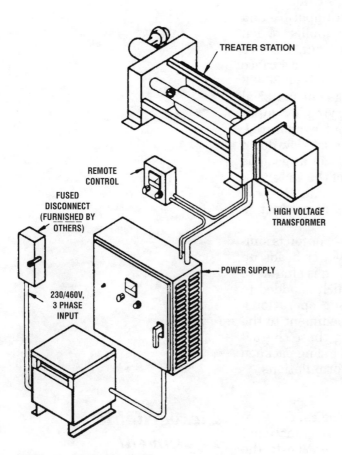

Figure 12–8. Typical corona treating system prepares the surface of films to accept inks.

Source: Enercon Industries Corporation, "Corona Treating for Water-Based Technology," Water-Based Technology Seminar.

as the need to use less solvent (water) to facilitate drying.

It is imperative that the metering rollers are in continuous motion when the water inks are in the print station. Rewetting of all surfaces is critical; dried water ink is like cement. Continuous circulation of the inks is most important during press stoppages. Older press configurations and in-line units, designed for solvent inks, do not always have this continuous circulation feature and must be modified. At the same time, provision must be made to automatically move the plate cylinder away from the anilox roll when the press stops or the ink will act as an adhesive, bonding the plates to the anilox roll and solidifying in the anilox cells and on the fountain roller as the ink dries. (See figure 12–7.)

Drying systems which were more than adequate with hydrocarbon solvents can be totally inadequate for water. The typical flexo dryer box has air flowing into the constrained area, bouncing off the walls and through slots or holes onto the web. This was very adequate with a solvent that evaporated quickly into the air, and which could be removed by a slightly higher exhaust air flow.

Water inks pose two drying problems. One is the actual volume of the vapors from the water—essentially 10 times the volume of solvent given the same liquid measurement as a starting point. The second problem arises from amines, which are required in the formulations to hold the resins and pigments in suspension. If the amines are not completely removed by a scrubbing action, they can remain in the ink layer to soften subsequent layers of inks that may be printed in succession.

Therefore, to use waterborne ink formulations, certain basic requirements are mandatory for the printer:

1. Post-treating units (corona) are required to bombard the surface of the film and make it more receptive to the waterborne inks. The corona treatment not only raises the surface tension of the film surface, making it more receptive to ink wetting out and adhesion but it either causes the slip compound to retreat into the film surface temporarily or moves the slip compound adequately to facilitate wetting out of the inks. (See figure 12–8.)

2. Fountain (ink) and anilox rollers in the ink transfer systems have to be replaced with new rollers that have properties that will facilitate the use of the water formulated inks.

The fountain roller carries the ink from the ink reservoir (pan) to the metering roller (anilox). The harder the rubber covering of the roll (higher durometer), the less ink the roller will transfer. Solvent ink runs with a standard rubber covering that is typically between 65–75 durometer, Shore A. A harder roll has been found to more adequately meter water inks, the durometer measured in the range of 85–90 durometer.

The anilox roller is engraved with cells which serve to meter and transfer the inks. The finer the screen (more cells per inch), the less ink that is transferred. For example, a 360 screen would deliver a much finer layer and smaller quantity of ink and solvents than would a 200 screen. In addition to the screen count, the three-dimensional volume of the cells must also be considered. For every screen count, there is a range of acceptable shapes and depths, each delivering a different volume of ink. With the higher strength waterborne inks, the screens and volumes required for transfer are considerably lower than with the typical alcohol-based ink. The actual layer of ink that is metered to the printing plate contains the same amount of pigment and resin, but considerably less diluent (water) to be dried. (See figure 12–9.)

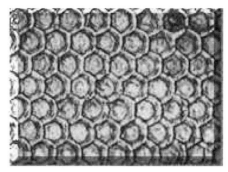

Figure 12–9. With higher solids inks and for better control of ink deposit, smaller volume anilox and gravure cells are required.

Courtesy of Micro Clean International.

3. The printing station rollers must also be capable of rotating at all times with inks present in the system, even when the press is down. Water inks dry extremely hard and are not rewettable. They are very similar to water-base latex paints. Any ink that dries in an anilox roller cell will be impossible to remove and will destroy the usefulness of the roller. Therefore, any press which does not have continuously rotating rubber ink and anilox rollers will have to be retrofitted to assure that the ink train is always in motion, except when it is down for cleaning.

Personnel must be trained to utilize new methods in the setting up and cleaning of presses to assure that inks do not dry on the rollers, on plates, or other parts of the machinery.

4. Drying systems have to be rebuilt or installed with better control of the action of the air and with much higher exhaust rates. Drying efficiency is also a factor of speed. A very slow press will not require as much air flow. A high-speed press will be limited if the air flow is not adequate. A general finding with water inks on existing high-speed presses is the loss of 25 to 30 percent of the speed which is otherwise achievable when run with standard drying systems.

Another factor in the development of the newer generation dryer boxes has

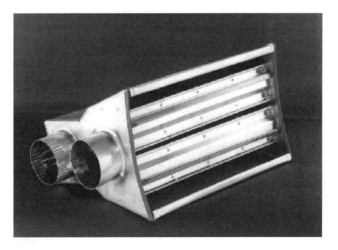

Figure 12–10. Between-color drying elements have been designed to more effectively exhaust water vapors.

Courtesy of DriTec, Inc.

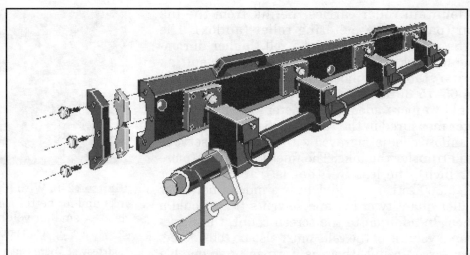

- Multiple Push Points with HydroComp™ (hydraulic) Cylinders
- Easy loading with optional air cylinder tilt
- Easy seal removal & chamber removal
- Automatic Blade Wear Compensation

Figure 12–11. Chambered doctor blade system for controlled ink delivery.
Courtesy of Harris and Bruno Machine Company.

been a more engineered approach to the nozzles and the type of air flow created. The best designs have sought to produce a scrubbing action to remove the amines and water, and high velocity to evacuate the vapors. (See figure 12–10.)

5. Coupled with these major mechanical changes in equipment are those necessitated in auxiliary systems:

   a. Ink pumps that were used with solvent inks are not good with water. The fast impeller speed promotes foaming of the water inks. New pumps must be obtained.

   b. Printing plates may have to be changed to rubber or photopolymer materials that will accept and transfer inks more adequately.

   c. Solvent recovery equipment, normally distillation units, which were used for solvents, are not feasible for reclamation of water inks. New technology, i.e., evaporation or ultrafiltration, or carting away of this waste, may be required.

6. A major development in flexographic press design has become a major consideration for the printer using water. This involves the replacement of the traditional two-roll ink transfer system with the enclosed (chambered) doctor

blade system. Further refinement of the chambered doctor blade system now enables the flexo printer to automatically clean the chamber at the end of a run.

Instead of having the ink fed from an open fountain to the anilox roller by a rubber roller, ink in a doctor blade system is injected into a cavity which comprises the space enclosed by the anilox roller, a retaining blade and a cutting blade (or anilox blade). The cutting blade shears off all unwanted ink from the rotating surface of the roller just before the ink is transferred to the printing plate. (See figure 12–11.)

Not only does this system improve the quality of the printing, it eliminates a major area of both captured and fugitive emissions by eliminating the open fountain. By controlling the layer of ink (and water) being transferred more positively, the system reduces the amount of diluent that will vaporize when the press is in operation. As a result, the ink will retain its components and be more consistent in printing and in performing its graphic and physical roles on the substrate.

The chambered doctor blade provides considerable advantages to the flexographic printing process. More consistent viscosity and ink solids provides for both consistency and predictability of graphic colors. The doctor blade system eliminates variation in color found with the changing hydraulic dynamics as ink flows through a two-roll system, resulting in the feeding of greater or lesser volumes of ink. The higher solids inks require less solvent as a diluent and to maintain viscosity and pH without the constant addition of solvent being added during a run. The chamber and blades contain the fluids and minimize evaporation. This is turn reduces the need to add solvent to maintain liquidity.

A recent innovation provides for an air-powered wash cycle that cleans out the chamber and blades and the anilox roller, minimizing the amount of waste ink and washwater (or solvent) required for cleaning. (See figure 12–12.)

7. A major effort has to be made to improve methods used in setting up, operating and breaking down presses. The transfer characteristics of waterborne inks are such that the workforce has to be completely trained in the use and troubleshooting of the new inks. Solvent inks are very forgiving, water inks are not.

   The drying of waterborne inks results in a solid that is difficult to remove. To avoid loss of rollers and gears, as well as damage to cylinders and impression drums (cylinders), pressroom personnel have to be indoctrinated concerning the need to clean any spills, as well as all rollers and plates, when the press is down for changes or any extended downtime.

8. Obtain a complete technical profile of the substrate to be printed. Various polymers, coatings and additives, e.g.,

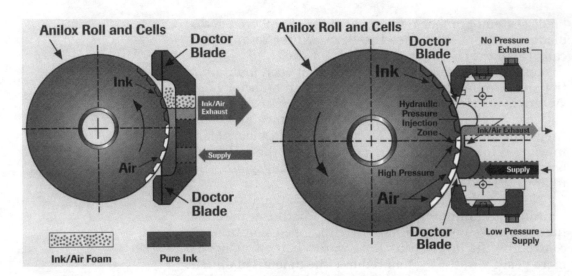

Figure 12–12. Chambered doctor blade system employs pressure to facilitate delivery of ink to anilox roller.

Courtesy of Deneka Printing Systems.

slip agents, may be more or less receptive to water inks. Knowing the limitations can help you to use the appropriate substrates or treat the materials in a manner which will facilitate wetting out and adhesion of the inks.

It is this area in which research and development efforts are most needed. Little has been done and published concerning waterborne inks with regard to various slip agents and anti-block additives and the ramifications of their use in films. The same can be said of coatings used to promote adhesion to films and foils.

Case History— Firm X Coating Mills; Water Inks and Multi-media Pollution Prevention

Firm X Coating Mills represents a classic example of how a firm confronted its past and planned its future through pollution prevention. They have achieved admirable success in reducing their exposure and liability by avoiding environmental incidents. The study is a classic case of finding viable alternatives to solvent-based ink technology.

Firm X is a coater of spun polyolefin for use in the manufacture of stationery items. The firm was privately held for many years and developed a leadership role as a supplier to its industry. The owner's knowledge of environmental regulations and their applicability to his firm was limited. Because of the size of the firm, many regulations were thought not to apply.

The firm was purchased by an investment fund to be a part of its portfolio of profitable ventures. One of the initial management dictates was to order an environmental audit of the facility. A consultant knowledgeable in printing and in environmental regulations was engaged to conduct the audit and develop an action plan to assure that the firm would be brought into compliance. From the outset, the technical knowledge of the industry by the consultants enabled the firm to view compliance from the perspective of pollution prevention. The concept was to do it right at the start and not have to worry about taking remedial actions later on.

When first audited, the plant was emitting a total of 145 tons of volatile organic compounds into the atmosphere. Storage of hazardous materials comprised a large collection of partially used, as well as new, drums and kits of inks and solvents. Dirty solvent was used to clean parts in open 55-gallon drums, and then put into the black inks for disposal. Hazardous waste generation was not being addressed. The plant used inks that consisted primarily of isopropyl alcohol and isopropyl acetate. Other solvents were present in smaller concentrations.

The audit identified the critical areas that required immediate attention, as well as assigning priorities to less critical items. A management team was assigned to implement the plan. The immediate task was to come into compliance with New York State air regulations for the graphic arts, 6NYCRR Part 234. The options available dictated a change to either high solids inks or waterborne inks, or the installation of an incineration system.

Specification packages were sent to four manufacturers of incineration systems. The resulting proposals involved costly capital expenditures that were also costly to operate. The firm was dealing with an airflow in excess of 40,000 cfm and a relatively low solvent loading per hour.

There were no viable high-solids solvent-based ink formulations. The only other alternative was to switch to waterborne inks. To do this Firm X had to consider the various factors that would make water work for them.

The typical flexographic printing station is wide open, with a large ink fountain into which the ink roller dips, and then carries the ink to the engraved anilox roll. The ink train is conducive to the evaporation of solvents, exhausted as fugitive emissions.

One of the traditional advantages of flexography has been the liquid, easy to blend, and use, ink. One need not have a very experienced and well-trained technician to mix and match colors. A pressman or helper with minimal instructions can mix and match the inks to customer samples or standard color systems.

Drying systems were very rudimentary in design since liquid solvent inks are very fast drying. The typical flexo solvent ink, when applied, may have VOCs ranging from 55 to 85 percent of the formulation. Utilizing an obviously non-compliant ink under these conditions demands the use of control technology, either thermal or catalytic oxidation.

Waterborne inks could comply with the regulations, if one planned appropriately and put them to work with proper preparation. Finding the right combination of components that would work was the key to success. Efforts were made to minimize the amount of VOCs, and reduce the liquid volatiles to as low a level as possible, while increasing the percentage of solids (pigments, resins, additives.)

However, this might not have been the right approach for achieving more universality in the application of the waterborne inks, nor would it help to achieve higher gloss. Working within the formula provided by the USEPA, of solvent comprising 25 percent of the volatile portion of the ink as applied, it was essential that the maximum, not the minimum, amounts of solvent be used in the calculations for the applications that required a higher loading to respond to use characteristics.

One obstacle, that was to be addressed by the resin suppliers, was the development of a water ink resin that would be compatible with a higher level of solvents. Existing high performance resins for waterborne inks have low compatibility tolerance for solvents. New resin technology could provide higher solids that would facilitate the development of inks that could convey a higher level of gloss. This technology was available for coatings and is expected to be extended to inks in the near future.

A number of changes had to be made in the machinery. The key to good flexo quality is the selection of the right anilox roll configuration and volume. The anilox roll is an engraved roller that transfers the ink to the printing plates from the rubber roll that dips into the ink fountain. A typical solvent ink may use a 200-line screen etching with a volume of 7 to 14 billion cubic microns (BCM) per square inch.

Water inks present problems when applied in excess. In addition to drying problems, the physical characteristics of water ink demand less space between cells as applied. Water does not wet as well as solvents, and therefore water inks do not flow together as easily as solvent-based inks. To use water, the etching must be changed to a finer, lower volume configuration. The example above would be altered from a 160-line screen with volumes of 5.6 to 7.8 BCM to a 300-line screen with volumes of anywhere from 2.5 to 4.0 BCM (billion cubic microns), depending on the color and the coverage desired.

With the steps taken to improve metering of the ink, as well as to eliminate the wide open ink fountain and roller train, the flexo printer has advanced the technology of ink transfer by moving to doctor blades. The blades are housed in a chambered system that becomes the method for feeding and applying the ink to the anilox roller.

A typical doctor blade system has a closed loop between the can or reservoir of ink and the chamber of the system. The ink flows to the unit and returns to the reservoir, with the anilox roller taking away a measured amount of ink. Firm X addressed this modification initially to the gravure stations and then to the flexographic units.

Drying was the next critical factor. Water vapors represent 10 times the volume of the equivalent solvent emissions. Removing that moisture from the web and out through the exhaust system necessitated a more effective dryer. The function of the drying system now required an effective redesign. The old blast of air to clear the solvent would not work. To completely remove the water and solvent vapors, as well as the amines that are an essential part of the water ink formulation, the dryer system had to be engineered. Higher volume capability and a scrubbing action on the web were required. They replaced the drying system on the older press. The newer press had more than adequate airflow, having

TABLE 12–1. EMISSIONS AT FIRM X USING SOLVENT-BASED INKS ON FILM

FIRM X		1990						
VOLATILE EMISSIONS FROM INKS AND SOLVENTS:						PERCENTAGES BASED ON 1991		
	CAS NUMBER	TOTAL	SOLVENT	WATER		ALL INKS	SOLVENT	WATER
ISOPROPYL ACETATE	108-21-4	199,472	196,832	0		65.65%	67.65%	
NITROTHANE	79-24-3	19,812	19,552	0		6.52%	6.72%	
KETONE ALCOHOL	123-42.2	35,036	33,547	0		11.53%	11.88%	
NORMALPROPANOL	71-23-8	91	116	0		0.03%	0.04%	
ETHYL ALCOHOL	64-17-5	9,481	9,340	26		3.12%	3.21%	0.20%
METHANOL	67-56-1	365	349	0		0.12%	0.13%	
ETHYL ACETATE	141-78-6	3,403	3,259	0		1.12%	1.15%	
N-PROPYL ACETATE	109-60-4	14,889	14,257	0		4.90%	5.05%	
ALIPHATIC HYDROCARBONS		1,003	989	0		0.33%	0.34%	
1METOXY 2PROPANOL	108-65-6	3,768	3,608	0		1.24%	1.28%	
MIBK	108-10-1	1,246	1,251	0		0.41%	0.43%	
ISOPROPYL ALCOHOL	67-63-0	5,014	3,637	1,898		1.65%	1.25%	14.71%
PM GLYCOL ETHER	107-98-2	517	524	0		0.17%	0.18%	
BUTYL CELLOSOLVE	111-76-2	0	(6)	6		0.00%	0.00%	0.05%
AMMONIUM HYDROXIDE	1336-21-6	243	(96)	339		0.08%	0.00%	2.63%
WATER		9,511	2,008	10,638		3.13%	0.69%	82.42%
TOTAL VOLATILES		303,865	290,957	12,908		100.00%	100.00%	100.00%
TOTAL VOC'S		290,382	288,934	1,448				
VOC'S PER YEAR (TONS)		145.19 tons	144.47 tons	0.72 tons				

Source: P-F Technical Services Inc.

been designed for gravure printing. All this, including retraining of personnel to handle the new inks, was undertaken by the firm.

It took nine months to achieve the major modifications for the conversion to water, and almost a year and a half to completely convert to water. But without question, and with many hurdles to leap, it was done.

The result was dramatic. From the 145 tons in 1990, the firm had total VOC emissions of 11.75 tons in 1994 and 11.43 tons in 1995. Tables 12–1 and 12–2 illustrate the difference, not only in tons, but in the composition of the emissions from the plant.

One last aspect had to be tackled. The one critical area of the conversion of flexo presses to water, that was not addressed earlier, was the substrate. Spun polyolefin has a surface that closely

TABLE 12–2. EMISSIONS AT FIRM X USING WATERBORNE INKS DEVELOPED TO BE IN COMPLIANCE WITH ALL REGULATIONS

FIRM X

VOLATILE EMISSIONS FROM INKS AND SOLVENTS: YEAR   1997
 (INCLUDES FIRE RETARDANT COATINGS)

	CAS NUMBER	TOTAL	FUGITIVES 30.00%	STACK 70.00%
ETHYLENE GLYCOL	107-21-1	34	10	24
ETHYL ALCOHOL	64-17-5	1,010	303	707
N-PROPYL ACETATE	109-60-4	66	20	46
ISOPROPYL ALCOHOL	67-63-0	3,294	988	2,306
MONOPROPYL GLYCOL	107-98-2	425	128	298
PM GLYCOL ETHER	111-76-2	1,103	331	772
2-AMINO-2-METHYL-PR	124-68-5	588	176	412
NORMALPROPANOL	71-23-8	1	0	1
ETHANOLAMINE	141-43-5	366	110	256
GLYCOL ETHER DE	111-90-0	1,918	575	1,343
PROPYL GLYCOL	57-55-6	1,485	446	1,040
HEXL CELLOSOLVE	112-25-4	92	28	64
AMMONIUM HYDROXIDE	1336-21-6	4,789	1,437	3,352
WATER		150,622	45,187	105,435
TOTAL VOLATILES		165,793	49,738	116,055
TOTAL VOC'S		10,382	3,115	7,267
VOC'S PER YEAR 1997 (TONS)		5.19	1.56	3.63

Source: P-F Technical Services Inc.

resembles a wax coating. The supplier of the film treats the material during manufacture. In the early stages of conversion to water, it was believed that treatment at the supplier's plant was adequate. The printing plant personnel soon came to question this presumption; some problems with adhesion and ruboff continued to arise as complaints from customers.

The decision was made at Firm X to add corona-treating systems to the presses. Corona treating is employed as a means of assuring better adhesion to the films by waterborne inks. The treater raises the surface energy of the substrate, making it more receptive to the water and promoting wetting out and adhesion. Determined to use only water-based inks, tests were conducted with the trial corona treater. The improvement in ink appearance and end-use wear characteristics was remarkable. The treater units were ordered and installed.

Firm X Coating Mills has been delivering a quality product at normal rates of production. Their customers are happy with the results. In addition, there are many regulations which no longer apply to the firm, including those of the local regulatory agencies.

1. Hazardous materials storage permits. By imposing a strict specification for a flashpoint in excess of 200 degrees Fahrenheit (93 degrees Celsius), the firm was able to avoid having to erect an ink room or modify their building to serve as an acceptable containment perimeter. A permit was not needed under Nassau County (NY) Article 11.

2. Process water discharges from clean-up were tested. The results were below the standards set by Nassau County. That enabled the firm to discharge such wastes into the sewer system. Tests of water samples provided to the local sewer authority verified this condition.

3. OSHA exposure has been improved considerably. The strong odor of solvents in the press area is no longer present and pressroom personnel are not exposed to heavy concentrations of isopropyl acetate and alcohol.

4. There is no need to be concerned about filing a TRI (Toxic Release Inventory) report under SARA Title III.

5. Awareness of all regulations and the need to maintain programs and records has made this company a model for compliance issues.

6. With the "greening" of Firm X, sales increased and profits were realized. The cost of compliance and the potential cost of liability due to the use of hazardous substances was reduced. The ability to produce quality products at competitive prices while protecting the environment was confirmed. The key factor was the capability of the water-borne ink to provide adequate graphics at a lower delivered cost per unit when compared with the total cost of using solvent inks.

Pollution prevention worked as a means of eliminating air pollutants and reducing the regulatory burdens to Firm X. The process required the printer and his suppliers to look beyond what they were doing at the point of contact, and visualize what they could be doing with the resources that were available to them. Alternatives to solvent-based inks are possible. It just takes management commitment and resolve, and the cooperation and support of the suppliers, who are almost always very willing to help.

Success comes at the end of another pollution-free day.

CHAPTER 13

Managing Hazardous Waste Streams

Articles and presentations concerning landfills, ground and water pollution and clean-up efforts by the USEPA appear regularly in newspapers, magazines and on television. Hazardous waste dumping has been depicted in both factual and fictional settings. The concerns of the public highlight a major area in which the printer can act to assure compliance with governmental regulations and exhibit a positive proactive responsible concern for the health of the community.

Every chemical entering the printing plant must find a way out. If the chemicals do not become part of the printed product, they become wastes—exhausted as vapors, discharged to the wastewater streams, or disposed of as solid or hazardous wastes.

The chemicals, which enter the process with known hazardous characteristics, leave as hazardous wastes. When they leave the process as either a liquid waste or as solid wastes going to a landfill, the waste components have the ability to leach into the ground. Pollutants can enter the soil and the drinking water system, and ultimately contaminate plant life, fish and animals. Managing the hazardous waste streams to avoid ground and water pollution is the responsibility of the generator—the print shop and its management.

The USEPA and the state governing agencies define this responsibility as "cradle to grave." From the time a firm generates a hazardous waste until it is totally destroyed or converted to another use, the initial generator is legally responsible for the existence of that waste in all its forms. (See figure 13–1.)

Figure 13–1. The life cycle of a typical printing waste.

Source: United State Environmental Protection Agency, *RCRA IN FOCUS, Printing,* EPA530-K097-007, p 4–5.

IDENTIFY WASTE

By running tests or using your knowledge of the waste, identify whether your waste is hazardous. Based on these analyses, determine the appropriate waste code for your solvents; in this case, it is F001. File all records of test results, waste analyses, and other determinations made in the hazardous waste identification process and keep them for at least 3 years.

COUNT WASTE

As a second step, determine how much solvent waste you have produced in a calendar month. Do not count solvent placed directly into a solvent recovery still. Count the solvent still bottoms when they are removed from the still, however.

DETERMINE GENERATOR STATUS

Based on waste counting, determine your generator status. In this case, you have produced more than 25 gallons, but less than 200 gallons, of hazardous waste in the past month, which means you are an SQG in this calendar month period.

OBTAIN EPA IDENTIFICATION NUMBER

To identify your business as a hazardous waste generator, obtain an EPA identification number by submitting Form 8700-12 (Notification of Regulated Waste Activity), which is obtained from your state hazardous waste agency. Remember, your state requirements might be different.

PLACE WASTE IN ACCUMULATION UNIT

When the waste is generated, place it in an accumulation unit. Mark accumulation tanks and containers with the date the waste was placed in the unit as well as mark the words "Hazardous Waste." Ensure that containers are not rusty or leaking, are stored in areas with adequate ventilation and drainage, and are kept closed except to add or remove waste.

IMPLEMENT LOG PREPAREDNESS AND PREVENTION REQUIREMENTS

Check to be sure that emergency preparedness and prevention requirements are met. These include adequate emergency response systems and notification to local emergency response authorities.

PREPARE CONTINGENCY PLAN

Next, ensure that a contingency plan is prepared in accordance with standards. The contingency plan is designed to minimize hazards from fires, explosions, and unplanned releases. Keep a copy of the contingency plan on site, and assign a facility emergency coordinator to be on site or on call at all times.

IMPLEMENT PERSONNEL TRAINING

Be sure that your personnel are familiar with hazardous waste handling and emergency procedures.

CONTRACT WITH HAZARDOUS WASTE TRANSPORTER

To send waste off site to a TSDF, contract with a registered hazardous waste transporter. To locate a reliable transporter, contact a colleague to obtain a reference.

FOLLOW U.S. DEPARTMENT OF TRANSPORTATION (DOT) PACKAGING STANDARDS

Before shipping waste off site for treatment, storage, or disposal, package, label, and mark waste containers in accordance with all applicable DOT requirements. Call the DOT Hotline at 800 467-4922.

PREPARE HAZARDOUS WASTE MANIFEST

Send a manifest along with all hazardous waste sent off site to a TSDF, and keep your copy on site for 3 years. The manifest contains a certification stating that you have a program in place to reduce the volume and toxicity of waste generated to the degree economically practicable, and that you have selected a treatment, storage, or disposal method currently available that minimizes current and future threats from the waste.

PREPARE APPROPRIATE NOTIFICATION AND CERTIFICATION

Ensure that all hazardous waste sent off site for treatment, storage, or disposal is accompanied by appropriate notifications and certifications (initial shipments only).

SEND WASTE OFF SITE FOR TREATMENT, STORAGE, OR DISPOSAL

Using a registered hazardous waste transporter, send the waste to a RCRA hazardous waste TSDF accompanied by the appropriate manifest and land disposal restrictions notifications and certifications. You can choose from any permitted or interim status TSDF. Optional destinations for solvents include a hazardous waste incinerator that will landfill the incinerator ash, a hazardous waste fuel blender who will blend the solvents with other wastes and then burn them for energy recovery in a boiler or or industrial furnaces, or a facility that will recycle the solvents.

The printer utilizes many chemicals in the pressroom. Darkroom and platemaking chemistry, proofing techniques—even the art design process—will contribute to the waste stream, in addition to the wastes generated at the presses. Recognizing which chemicals are hazardous and disposing of the resulting wastes in an authorized manner will avoid costly mistakes. Failure to do so can lead to penalties and litigation, as well as unfavorable media attention. The regulation controlling the handling of hazardous waste is known as RCRA, the Resource Conservation and Recovery Act.

What is a Hazardous Waste?

Any chemical waste which displays one of four characteristics, or is specifically listed as creating known health hazards, is a hazardous waste:

1. **Ignitable (D001):** i.e., a liquid with a flashpoint of less than 60 degrees Celsius, 140 degrees Fahrenheit. Typical examples would be the solvents used in inks or for cleaning (figure 13–2).

2. **Corrosive (D002):** i.e., a liquid with a pH of less than 2.0 or greater than 12.5. Aqueous coatings, inks and cleaners will contain hydroxides that are caustics (figure 13–3).

3. **Reactive (D003):** i.e., wastes that are normally unstable and subject to violent change. It is unusual to see any reactive chemicals in a printing facility; however, they might enter the building as maintenance products such as drain pipe cleaners (figure 13–4).

4. **Toxic (D004–D017):** i.e., chromium, lead and silver. A most common metal found in prepress operations is silver, in the form of silver halide coatings on film and paper. The designation for silver is D011 (figure 13–5).

Specific chemicals that are considered detrimental to the welfare of the environment and the community have been assigned a series of F-numbers, i.e. F005 for toluene, F003 for acetone and F002 for perchloroethylene.

Among the more common chemicals used in printing processes, and their F numbers are:

F002: methylene chloride, 1,1,1, trichloro-ethane

F003: xylene, acetone, ethyl acetate, methyl isobutyl ketone, n-butyl alcohol, methanol

It is easily combustible or flammable. This is called an *ignitable* waste. Examples are paint wastes, certain degreasers, or other solvents.

Figure 13–2. Ignitables.

Source: United State Environmental Protection Agency, *Understanding the Small Quantity Generator Hazardous Waste Rules: A Handbook for Small Business,* EPA/530-SW-86-019, September 1986, p 2.

It dissolves metals, other materials, or burns the skin. This is called a *corrosive* waste. Examples are waste rust removers, waste acid or alkaline cleaning fluids, and waste battery acid.

Figure 13–3. Corrosive.

Source: United State Environmental Protection Agency, *Understanding the Small Quantity Generator Hazardous Waste Rules: A Handbook for Small Business,* EPA/530-SW-86-019, September 1986, p 2.

It is unstable or under-goes rapid or violent chemical reaction with water or other materi-als. This is called a *reactive* waste. Exam-ples are cyanide plating wastes, waste bleaches, and other waste oxidizers.

Figure 13–4. Reactive.

Source: United State Environmental Protection Agency, *Understanding the Small Quantity Generator Hazardous Waste Rules: A Handbook for Small Business*, EPA/530-SW-86-019, September 1986, p 2.

A waste sample is tested and shows EP (extraction procedure) toxicity. Wastes are *EP toxic* if an extract from the waste is tested and found to contain high concentrations of heavy metals (such as mer-cury, cadmium, or lead) or specific pesticides that could be released into the ground water.

Figure 13–5. Toxic.

Source: United State Environmental Protection Agency, *Understanding the Small Quantity Generator Hazardous Waste Rules: A Handbook for Small Business*, EPA/530-SW-86-019, September 1986, p 3.

F005: toluene, methyl ethyl ketone, isobu-tanol, pyridine, benzene, 2-ethoxy-ethanol

When chemicals are discarded in their pure or commercial form, the waste will take on a P or a U number assigned for shipment by the Department of Transportation. Examples would be U239 for xylene, U031 for n-butyl alcohol, and P028 for benzene. Other categories of hazardous waste are designated as K numbers, indicative of wastes generated by specific industries. Ink for-mulation wastes can be shipped under the cate-gory K086. A full listing of the various waste numbers appears in Appendix XXVI.

Hazardous waste characterization does not stop with the chemicals and chemical wastes. Materials that have been in contact with the chemicals can also be classified as hazardous wastes. This includes wipers that are used for cleaning, as well as materials and filters that absorb or separate the vapors or liquids of haz-ardous chemicals. Spill containment pads and filters, once they have absorbed the chemicals, are subject to disposal as hazardous wastes. All hazardous wastes must be accurately docu-mented by classification in the shipping mani-fest and in any subsequent reports.

Once the chemical has been used and no longer has any further use in the process, it is considered a hazardous waste. If the chemical, i.e., ink or solvent, is no longer of use at the press, it is a hazardous waste. A rule of thumb used by the regulatory agencies defines any chemical that has not been used in the past year as a hazardous waste. (See figure 13–6.)

Any material classified as a hazardous waste must be stored, labeled and disposed of in a manner conforming to the guidelines of the USEPA and the environmental agencies of the various states. In its simplest form, this means that all hazardous wastes must be controlled from the time they are generated until the time of their ultimate destruction. The continued existence of the waste poses a responsibility and liability for the generator.

Classifying Generators by Activity

The RCRA laws are very specific in the classification of levels at which generators are to be held responsible for the gen-eration of hazardous wastes (figure 13–7).

Large Quantity Generators (LQG) are those who generate over 1,000 kilograms (2,200 pounds) of hazardous waste in a month. This definition changes in the event that the waste is an acute sub-stance, in which case from 1 kg or 2.2 pounds of the material is con-sidered hazardous waste.

A Small Quantity Generator (SQG) is one which generates more than 100 kg but less than 1,000 kg of non-acute waste during a period of a month, and less than 1 kg of acute waste in a month.

A conditionally exempt small quantity generator is one who accumulates less than 100 kg in a month.

The responsibilities assigned to each of the three classes differ greatly, in keeping with the relative potential for greater damage from larger generators than from smaller facilities.

Locating Hazardous Wastes in the Pressroom

Pressrooms and photographic darkrooms generate wastes, which are classified as hazardous. Some enter the process as pure, single element chemicals, others as a part of mixture within the product that is used during the process.

Material Safety Data Sheets (MSDS) are a major tool for the identification and quantification of hazardous chemicals. The listing of hazardous components and percentages in the MSDS, and the instructions for disposal of the product and its wastes, will help to identify specific substances and describe the potential dangers of releases.

Laboratory tests of the wastes help to specify in more detail the number, type and amount of each pollutant present. The test is known as TCLP (Toxic Chemical Leaching Profile). The law requires that the generator maintain copies of the results of the lab tests in its files to support the categorization of shipments in the manifest. For large quantity generators, periodic testing is mandatory.

Figure 13–6. Drum of hazardous waste with appropriate label.

Lab tests identify composition of hazardous waste.

KEY: = *1 barrel = about 200 kilograms of hazardous waste which is about 55 gallons*

Generators of No More Than 100 kg/mo

If you generate no more than 100 kilograms (about 220 pounds or 25 gallons) of hazardous waste and no more than 1 kg (about 2 pounds) of acutely hazardous waste in any calendar month, you are a conditionally-exempt small quantity generator and the federal hazardous waste laws require you to:

▶ Identify all hazardous waste you generate.

▶ Send this waste to a hazardous waste facility, or a landfill or other facility approved by the state for industrial or municipal wastes.

▶ Never accumulate more than 1000 kg of hazardous waste on your property. (If you do, you become subject to all the requirements applicable to 100-1000 kg/mo generators explained in this handbook.)

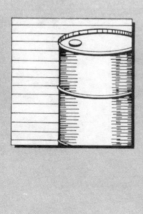

100-1000 kg/mo Generators

If you generate more than 100 and less than 1000 kg (between 220 and 2,200 pounds or about 25 to under 300 gallons) of hazardous waste and no more than 1 kg of acutely hazardous waste in any month, you are a 100-1000 kg/mo generator and the federal hazardous waste laws require you to:

▶ Comply with the 1986 rules for managing hazardous waste, including the accumulation, treatment, storage, and disposal requirements described in this handbook.

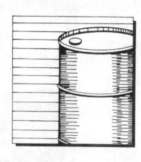

Generators of 1000 kg/mo or More

If you generate 1000 kg (about 2,200 pounds or 300 gallons) or more of hazardous waste, or more than 1 kg of acutely hazardous waste in any month, you are a generator of 1000 kg/mo or more and the federal hazardous waste laws require you to:

▶ Comply with *all* applicable hazardous waste management rules.

Figure 13-7. Classification of generators by monthly accumulation of hazardous waste.

Source: United State Environmental Protection Agency, *Understanding the Small Quantity Generator Hazardous Waste Rules: A Handbook for Small Business*, EPA/530-SW-86-019, September 1986, p 7.

Wastes can come from any number of sources in the average graphic arts/printing facility.

Darkrooms generate photographic wastes. Fixer solution washes the silver off the film and paper during developing. If the fixer that is discharged from the developing system contains more than five parts per million of silver, that liquid is now considered a hazardous waste. Photographic developer solution, as a corrosive, is a hazardous waste, but only if its pH exceeds the waste range of 12.5 or more. Photographic film and paper contain leachable silver in their emulsions. Once processed, the silver will not leach from the paper or film. Unprocessed waste papers and films can carry the silver with a potential to leach out into the ground in a landfill. (See figure 13–8.)

Printing plates and plate processing chemicals for all printing processes may contain hazardous chemicals or be processed by means of such chemicals.

Printing inks, depending on the printing process and the concentration when disposed, will constitute hazardous waste. Lithographic inks are classified as non-hazardous. Care should be taken not to include any other press chemistry when disposing of such inks. Mixing non-hazardous waste with hazardous waste alters the profile of that waste. (See figure 13–9.)

Sources of Waste in a Printing Facility

Figure 13–8. Darkroom and plate-making processes contribute to water wastes.

Figure 13–9. Accumulated inks eventually wind up in the waste drum.

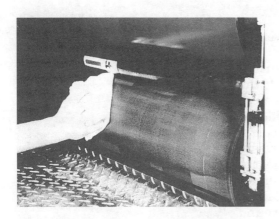

Figure 13–10. Solvents generate the most waste when used for cleaning presses and plates.

Solvents, in inks or as a diluent when printing, are usually hazardous because of their flammable or combustible nature. Some are toxic and are accountable as listed F number hazardous wastes. Press washes for cleaning contain a number of solvents, some of which can be flammable and pose toxic health risks. (See figure 13–10.)

Shop towels can be contaminated with solvent, ink or other chemicals used for maintaining the press and other equipment. There are differences in the regulatory rules pertaining to the disposition of reusable and disposable towels. If using disposable towels, the used wipers must be shipped to a hazardous waste treatment facility as a hazardous waste. If the press wash contains listed chemicals, such as methylene chloride, butyl cellosolve or MEK, the wipers should not be sent for disposal in a landfill. The best route for disposal would be a facility that will use the hazardous waste as an alternative fuel. Wipers that are used without any listed chemicals but exhibit ignitability would lend themselves, as well, to use as an alternative fuel. (See figure 13–11.)

Reusable wipers are sent to a laundering service for cleansing and are returned to the printing facility. To minimize the potential for transporting and laundering excessive amounts of solvents in the wipers, federal and state guidelines specify that the wipers should be wrung dry before being sent for laundering. In some states, a "one drop" test is applied to assure that wipers do not leave the pressroom with excessive solvent absorbed in the cloth. If the printer does not take preventive measures to restrict the shipment of soaked wipers, the laundry may be held liable for carting illegal hazardous wastes. Any such violation and enforcement action would also fall on the shoulders of the facility that generated the wastes.

Containers which are not completely empty of the inks, solvents or other chemicals, within the legal definition set forth in the regulations, may pose a problem as hazardous waste. A container is deemed empty if the contents are removed by normal means, allowing for specified maximum retention amounts that are not easily extracted. A rule of thumb has been that a 55-gallon drum may be considered RCRA acceptable if there is a maximum of one inch of liquid retained in the bottom of the drum. Neverthe-less, it is in the facility's best interest to empty the drum of as much of the material as possible beyond that one inch. It is not only in the interest of protecting the environment, but in minimizing losses due to excessive wastes of all kinds.

Figure 13–11. Wipers (rags) used to clean press with solvents become hazardous wastes.

By observation during a brief walk through the printing facility, it would appear that most chemistry used in the pressroom or in prepress departments could potentially be hazardous waste. Following prescribed procedures, the collection, handling, storage and disposition of all hazardous wastes can be done safely and with due consideration for legal liability.

A firm is required to do specific things to be in compliance, based on the amount of wastes generated.

1. **Obtain a USEPA Identification Number:** Every facility must have its own hazardous waste identification number. These are easily obtained from the regional office of the USEPA. A telephone call is all it takes.

2. **Follow rules and accepted procedures** for identifying, managing and minimizing hazardous waste on site. The facility must have an established procedure for testing and identifying the waste streams to determine what constitutes the waste and what areas or categories identify the hazardous nature of the waste.

3. **Follow standards for storing waste during accumulation.** All containers of hazardous waste materials should be stored in accordance with safety and health regulations specified in RCRA and by local authorities. They will require fire protection, spill containment berms, explosion-proof fixtures and fire rated doors, and all the necessary equipment and supplies in the event of a spill, fire or explosion.

   Waste streams should be kept separate, so as not to mix any wastes that may react with one another. Within a chemical/waste storage room distinct areas should be designated for the various waste streams.

4. **Label all waste appropriately.** Containers of hazardous waste are required to have complete information on them that will indicate compliance. The first and foremost rule of collecting hazardous waste is that every drum should identify to an observer what chemical or family of chemicals is in the drum. This can include a generic description but must include the waste category, such as "Ignitable," "Corrosive," etc. The final note is the written dates that tell when accumulation of the wastes started and at what date the drum was completely full, sealed and moved to the storage area. (See figure 13–12.)

5. **Develop a contingency plan to deal with emergencies.** What happens in the event of a fire, explosion or major spill? How are personnel notified of the emergency? What steps are to be followed by management and by line and staff personnel at the time of an incident? Who in the government is to be notified and what information is required? This information is all part of the contingency plan for the facility. It is a comprehensive plan as to what is expected during and after an incident, and with whom the plant should have contact.

Managing the Hazardous Wastes

Training is critical to handling of hazardous wastes.

6. **Train all employees** involved to be "familiar with proper waste handling and emergency procedures." Records are extremely important in documenting the nature of the training and proof of training. Nothing should be taken for granted. A comprehensive (written) training program is required to educate personnel about the RCRA requirements and to train them in the procedures that must be followed to assure compliance with the law. Such personnel should include anyone who generates and collects the wastes, handles the paperwork and record files, or submits reports to the agencies. Larger facilities, such as those that encompass more storage and treatment activities than the normal generator, may require personnel to take OSHA training as a hazardous waste site.

7. **Select an approved hazardous waste hauler** and have records to verify the manner and site at which the waste is disposed. It is imperative that the firm(s) engaged to transport and dispose of the hazardous waste be subjected to a thorough inspection of their permits, insurance and the performance of their facilities. Since the generator is ultimately responsible for the waste until it ceases to exist (cradle to grave), the generator has responsibility for determining that the off-site transportation/storage/disposition contractors are duly permitted and operate within the parameters established for their activities under RCRA.

    Without this background check, many generators have found themselves subject to Superfund clean-up litigation and sued for the cost of removing illegal dump sites in which their drums have been uncovered. Two major sites in New York State, in which products from many printers were found, were traced to the solvent supplier, Mattiace Industries and its subsidiaries. Drums were unearthed at the first, a leased site known as Garvey's Point on Long Island, and a major suit was filed against all customers of the firm. Clean-up costs were recouped by the USEPA. Even the smallest customer was obligated for legal fees in the thousands of dollars. Improper disposal at a second site was more recently the cause of a wave of information collected by the agency as a preliminary to filing a suit against those it considered primary responsible parties. Penalties suggested in a settlement agreement offered by the agency for past costs of clean-up ranged from a high, for a utility, of $1,999,000 to a low, for a group of very small alleged polluters, at $2,500 each. This does not include the potential for additional levies as the clean-up continues. A high percentage of the firms are printers. Even if a firm were able to have itself excluded with good cause, there would still be a significant cost for legal or consulting fees to accomplish this feat.

8. **Complete manifests for each shipment** and submit copies to states as required. Maintain in files for a period of at least three years. Cradle to grave is also descriptive of the paperwork which tracks the waste as it is handled from the

Figure 13–12. Typical hazardous waste label.

Courtesy of Prime Environmental Inc.

time it is shipped until ultimate recovery, recycling or destruction. The manifest (figure 13–13) and an attached land-ban document are signed at such time as the transporter picks up the waste. A copy is sent immediately to the state of residence and the state to which the waste is being transported. Subsequently, the operator of the site of destruction will return a copy indicating that the waste has been destroyed in accordance with the specified end destination. This could be a landfill, incinerator, alternative fuel consumption, cement kiln, etc.

This paperwork should be maintained for a period of no less than three years, and should be available for inspection or the filing of reports. Many attorneys recommend keeping the paperwork for much longer periods.

9. **Submit reports as required** by the EPA and state agencies. The USEPA requires a biennial report by Large Quantity Generators (figure 13–14). The report summarizes the waste streams for the year, disposition and any waste minimization activities. Some states will require this report on an annual basis, and may even request reports from smaller generators.

A representative sample Hazardous Waste Management Program has been included as Appendix XXV, which can be used as a template in preparing a program for your own facility.

Minimizing All Wastes

A key factor in managing hazardous wastes is a program to eliminate or minimize as many of the contributing chemicals or processes. This philosophy is known as pollution prevention.

When signing the hazardous waste manifest, the generator attests to the fact that the facility has embarked on a program of pollution prevention to reduce or lessen the hazards of its wastes. Some states require annual or biennial reports of pollution prevention activity and results from major sources, i.e., large quantity generators. In some jurisdictions, there has been talk of targets for waste reduction.

Finding safer substitutes or using lesser quantities of chemicals while accomplishing acceptable productivity and quality can help to reduce the quantities and the toxicity of the waste generated. This is known as source reduction. If source reduction is not possible, steps to recycle or recover reusable chemicals from the wastes can help to conserve raw materials. This can be done on or off site. A good example is the return of negatives, plates, etc, for recovery of silver in the emulsions.

Both efforts can reduce wastes entering the ecosystem and help to safeguard against the potential for health risks to the community. The materials recovered or recycled represent a by-product, and could bring income to supplement the normal sales of the firm. Any material that still has commercial value can be sold and converted into a new product. Reuse within the facility or firm can reduce the cost of purchases.

State of New Jersey
Department of Environmental Protection
Hazardous Waste Regulation Program
Manifest Section
P.O. Box 421, Trenton, NJ 08625-0421

Please type or print in block letters. (Form designed for use on elite (12-pitch) typewriter.) *Form Approved.* OMB No. 2050-0039.

UNIFORM HAZARDOUS WASTE MANIFEST	1. Generator's US EPA ID No.	Manifest Document No.	2. Page 1 of	Information in the shaded areas is not required by Federal law.

3. Generator's Name and Mailing Address

A. State Manifest Document Number
NJA 3275057
B. State Generator's ID-(Gen. Site Address)

4. Generator's Phone (   )

5. Transporter 1 Company Name	6. US EPA ID Number	C. State Trans. ID-NJDEP
		Decal No. -
7. Transporter 2 Company Name	8. US EPA ID Number	D. Transporter's Phone ( )
		E. State Trans. ID-NJDEP
9. Designated Facility Name and Site Address	10. US EPA ID Number	Decal No. -
		F. Transporter's Phone ( )
		G. State Facility's ID
		H. Facility's Phone ( )

11. US DOT Description (Including Proper Shipping Name, Hazard Class or Division, ID Number and Packing Group)		12. Containers		13. Total Quantity	14. Unit Wt/Vol	I. Waste No.
HM		No.	Type			
a.						
b.						
c.						
d.						

J. Additional Descriptions for Materials Listed Above		K. Handling Codes for Wastes Listed Above	
a.	c.	a.	c.
b.	d.	b.	d.

15. Special Handling Instructions and Additional Information

16. **GENERATOR'S CERTIFICATION:** I hereby declare that the contents of this consignment are fully and accurately described above by proper shipping name and are classified, packed, marked, and labeled, and are in all respects in proper condition for transport by highway according to applicable international and national government regulations.

If I am a large quantity generator, I certify that I have a program in place to reduce the volume and toxicity of waste generated to the degree I have determined to be economically practicable and that I have selected the practicable method of treatment, storage, or disposal currently available to me which minimizes the present and future threat to human health and the environment; **OR**, if I am a small quantity generator, I have made a good faith effort to minimize my waste generation and select the best waste management method that is available to me and that I can afford.

Printed/Typed Name	Signature	Month	Day	Year

17. Transporter 1 Acknowledgement of Receipt of Materials

Printed/Typed Name	Signature	Month	Day	Year

18. Transporter 2 Acknowledgement of Receipt of Materials

Printed/Typed Name	Signature	Month	Day	Year

19. Discrepancy Indication Space

20. Facility Owner or Operator: Certification of receipt of hazardous materials covered by this manifest except as noted in Item 19.

Printed/Typed Name	Signature	Month	Day	Year

EPA Form 8700-22

SIGNATURE AND INFORMATION *MUST* BE LEGIBLE ON ALL COPIES

NJA 3275057

In case of an emergency or spill immediately call the state the emergency occurred in and the N.J. Dept. of Environmental Protection. (609) 292-7172

Figure 13–13. Manifest documents shipment and route taken of hazardous waste.
Courtesy of Prime Environmental Inc.

BEFORE COPYING FORM, ATTACH SITE IDENTIFICATION LABEL OR ENTER:

SITE NAME ______________________

EPA ID NO.

U.S. ENVIRONMENTAL PROTECTION AGENCY

Hazardous Waste Report

FORM **GM**

WASTE GENERATION AND MANAGEMENT

INSTRUCTIONS: Read the detailed instructions beginning on page 14 of the 1989 Hazardous Waste Report booklet before completing this form.

Sec. I

A. Waste description
Instruction Page 15

B. EPA hazardous waste code
Page 15

C. State hazardous waste code
Page 16

D. SIC code
Page 16

E. Source code
Page 16
A

F. Form code
Page 16
B

G. Origin
Page 16
Code
System type M

H. TRI constituent
Page 17

I. CAS numbers
Page 17
1. 2. 3. 4. 5.

Sec. II

A. Quantity generated in 1988
Instruction Page 17

B. Quantity generated in 1989
Page 17

C. UOM
Page 18

D. Density
Page 18
☐ 1 lbs/gal ☐ 2 sg

E. Was this waste treated, disposed or recycled on site or discharged to a sewer/POTW?
Page 18
☐ 1 Yes (CONTINUE TO SYSTEM 1)
☐ 2 No (SKIP TO SEC. III)

SYSTEM 1
System type
Page 18
M
Quantity treated, disposed or recycled in 1989
Page 18

SYSTEM 2
System type
Page 18
M
Quantity treated, disposed or recycled in 1989
Page 18

Sec. III

A. Was this waste shipped off site?
Instruction Page 19
☐ 1 Yes (CONTINUE TO BOX B)
☐ 2 No (SKIP TO SEC. IV)

Site 1
B. EPA ID No. of facility to which waste was shipped
Instruction Page 19
C. System type
Page 19
M
D. Total quantity shipped in 1989
Page 19

Site 2
M

Sec. IV

A. Waste minimization results in 1989
Instruction Page 20
☐ 1 Yes (CONTINUE TO BOX B)
☐ 2 No (THIS FORM IS COMPLETE)

B. Activity
Page 21
W W
W W

C. Other effects
Page 21
☐ 1 Yes
☐ 2 No

D. Quantity recycled in 1989 due to new activities
Page 21

E. Activity/Production Index
Page 21

F. Source Reduction Quantity
Page 22

Comments:

Page ____ of ____

Figure 13–14. Waste stream reporting page from biennial hazardous waste report required by USEPA of large quantity generators.

Source: USEPA.

CHAPTER **14**

Understanding and Managing Your Inks for Environmental Compliance

Take a good look at your inkroom and then visit your press-room. Are you happy with the way it looks? Just think how a stranger, notably a government inspector, would react if that person was entering your facility to check on the storage and use of what they perceive to be "dangerous chemicals."

Are the inks stored in an orderly and clean manner? Do you have an excessive number of kits sitting on shelves or pallets piled high with kits of press return colors mixed for jobs you have not run in the past two to three years (figure 14–1)? Is your pressroom cluttered with open ink cans, unlabeled ink and solvent cans and press parts dirty from lack of good working practices? Are rags stored in appropriate safety cans ?

To the outsider, this conglomeration will certainly spell inefficiency, waste and, from the point of an inspector's visit, a candidate for closer inspection to record poor environmental and safety practices. Managing your ink and pressroom are critical to compliance with most, if not all, safety and environmental regulations.

The government has provided industry with an excellent tool upon which to build an ink management system. That tool is the Material Safety Data Sheet (MSDS). An MSDS is the key to unlocking the critical information pertinent to understanding what is in an ink and how to handle the ink safely. The MSDS also provides information that can be most helpful to an

Another Look at the MSDS

Figure 14–1. An inkroom in disarray.

understanding of the performance of the inks on the printing press. Keep copies of the MSDSs in the vicinity of the pressroom, for better understanding of how any ink is performing relative to those in other stations/presses.

The second section of the MSDS normally lists the ingredients of the ink, subject to a deminimus level of one percent or less. Companies are not required to list anything for components comprising less than the 1 percent, other than some extremely hazardous chemicals at small quantities above 0.1 percent. However, this information is available on request, for use in determining air emission data as required by the permitting authorities. A typical breakdown section is illustrated.

<u>Product Name:</u>   Cyan Blue

<u>Identification Number:</u>   CB102-2000

Ingredient	CAS Number	Weight %
Isopropyl alcohol	67-63-0	4.0
n-Propyl alcohol	71-23-8	10.3
Ethyl alcohol	64-17-5	31.8
n-Propyl acetate	109-60-4	4.5
Heptane	142-82-5	13.7
Dibutyl phthalate	84-74-2	1.0

Judging from the composition and relative drying speeds of these components, it is relatively easy to determine what solvent blends are needed to increase, maintain or reduce drying times on press. Each of the solvents in the mixture is listed, providing you with a reasonable measure for determining how fast the particular ink may dry.

You may also prefer reviewing the MSDS as a means of identifying "rogue" chemicals, with the objective of replacing them with safer products. The basis for the movement to cleaner chemistry lies with the ability of the individual worker, as well as management, to evaluate the action of chemicals in the workplace and seek out safer alternatives. The safer the solvent you are using, the better chance you may have of getting your personnel involved in seeking alternatives to other hazardous conditions in the plant. A good example would be an ink that contains a high percentage of toluene or methyl ethyl ketone (MEK). Substituting less hazardous solvents, when possible, in the formulation can reduce the potential for health and ecological repercussions.

The MSDS collection should be located in the inkroom for ready reference, to be used by all press personnel when seeking an answer to a problem. It should act as a guide to safe practices, precautions to take when the product is in use, and to provide directions in the event that an incident does occur with exposure to the workers or to the environment.

T he quantity of ink in storage is a matter of concern for many reasons. Practical decisions relate the quantities to availability, lead time when ordering and price. Permits and local regulations may place constraints on the quantities stored. Exposure to hazards may pose yet another limitation on the volume that may be allowed to be maintained in the plant.

Ordering Ink to Maximize Capacity

The key to a successful ink management program is the establishment of a logical ordering system. Purchase only those quantities of any one color that will provide an adequate supply for a given period. That period will be based on the lead time required to place an order and have it shipped by the inkmaker.

The first step is to establish the basic colors required to satisfy both printing out of the can, and blending of matched colors from standard single pigmented inks. Using a library of 10 to 12 colors, press personnel will possess the ability to mix most matched colors. The list would usually include white, black, cyan blue, reflex blue, purple, rubine red, rhodamine red, warm red, primrose yellow, chrome yellow, orange and cyan green. An extender would also be a standard inventory item. If the firm prints four-color process, these inks would be a part of the basic inventory.

Having established the standard colors, purchasing can make use of traveling requisitions (figure 14–2) and historical records to provide insight as to the pattern by which each of the basic colors is ordered. This, in turn, can provide insight into the quantities needed within any given period. Minimum inventory levels can be established for ordering the standard inks. Automatic orders can be placed to obtain the major stock colors at appropriate intervals, the amount and time lag based on usage history. Less frequently used colors can be ordered on a need-to-have basis, triggered by periodic inventory inspections of the raw stock and orders in-house. Guidelines should be established to define when a color-matched ink should be mixed in-house or purchased from the inkmaker. This will depend on the quantity required, as well as the fidelity with which the new color must be matched and maintained.

In both cases—whether colors are blended in-house or purchased from the ink supplier—care should be taken to accurately determine the quantities needed. Order what is needed, with only a small overage that would account for any foreseen set-up waste or order overrun. Avoid ordering excess quantities that will add to the collection of mixed press returns in the inkroom.

One custom previously practiced in print shops has changed with the intervention of safety and environmental concerns. The practice of buying inks and solvents in quantity was prevalent to

PRODUCT							

SOURCE	BRAND NAME	FORMULATION	%VOC	%SOLIDS	MSDS #	PRICE	

PURCHASES			RECEIPTS		WEEKLY	WEEKLY	WEEKLY
DATE	SOURCE	QUANTITY	DATE	AMOUNT	INVENTORY	USAGE	VOCs

Figure 14–2. Traveling purchase requisition provides a tool for ordering inks and solvents based on historical usage. It can serve as a method of computing air emissions for small plants.
Source: P-F Technical Services Inc.

obtain price concessions. This could amount to no more than pennies per pound or gallon. With the costs—real and intangible—of compliance, such price differentials may be self-defeating. The larger quantities ordered may save a small sum compared to the cost of compliance and the possibility of penalties for exceeding legal limits. The penny saved may cost dollars in retribution.

Color Management and Storage Challenges

Ink management requires a controlled plan for using inks and solvents, and maintaining a minimum inventory on the shelf (or floor). If the plant operates on the basis that the inks that are purchased replace the ones that have been used from inventory, then the inks in the inkroom should represent a safe buffer to maintain a suitable level of your press activities from shipment to shipment.

The problem with this practice lies with matched colors. If press personnel are continually mixing matched colors for use on the press and have no inventory control plan, the result will be an inkroom full of kits holding obsolete color matches. The question arises, "are we blending fresh colors each time the schedule calls for that color, or is it routine practice to check the inventory and mix from the old inks that are the same or close enough to use in blending and matching the color that is now needed?"

The most efficient companies, using manual or computer systems, work off all inks as they come off the press. Aggressive efforts are needed to maintain an ink inventory listing and to use the surplus inks within the facility. Computer software is available to enable pressroom ink blending with the press returns to match a wide variety of colors. Tracking systems using bar codes take this control to an even higher and more precise level. (See figure 14–3.) At the core of computer-driven systems is the ability to monitor and evaluate press returns for color and strength, and determine what combination of other inks (colors) have to be added to move the old color to a new color.

Manual systems are more limited in effective reuse of colors, and, in most plants, limit reuse only within color families, for example reds, oranges, blues, etc. As a last resort a manual system will place press returns into black ink. Every gallon of reused ink represents one less gallon that has to be purchased and stored in the plant. Pantone and other color swatch systems provide the printer with the means to determine what color combinations will produce a desired color match. Formulas provide the percentages or weights of the various components that will produce the required color. Using this information enables the printer to meet new requirements by using existing stock (fresh and press returns) to mix the new color. Trained ink technicians can use seemingly diverse inks to mix a third new, apparently unrelated color. A good example would be the blending of excess inventories of orange and purple. The result will be an excellent chocolate brown.

The objective is to minimize the amount of inks you have in storage. Do it by training ink and press personnel to use the resources at their command to find a way to work off any and all inks left at the end of a job. One outgrowth of the desire to minimize inventory, rework press returns, and operate a cost-effective program has been the development and installation of in-plant ink blending systems. Driven by computer-based ink formulations and spectrophotometers for color management and control, these blending systems utilize drums or kits of basic colors, and a selection of the varnishes with different chemical and physical properties, to satisfy color and specific end-use characteristics (figure 14–4.) Color matching can be more precise lot to lot. Product will be predictable from order to order, as well as throughout the range of larger orders. Press returns can be assimilated with fresh ink to work off potential inventory into new colors or more of the same. Inventory and waste can be kept to a minimum.

The growing dependence on color standards and the need for graphic predictability has provided a rationale for managing inks by more objective means. The human eye continues to act as a safeguard, but color measurement has become a valuable aspect of press instrumentation. The spectrophotometer (figure 14–5) has given printers the ability to "read" the ink and

Color Standard Systems and Automated Ink Blending

Figure 14–4. Ink blending system aims at minimizing waste and assuring predictability.

Courtesy of *Ink Maker*, Feb. 2002.

derive a graphic image of the color and the shift within limits of acceptable tolerances.

The spectrophotometer depicts a color in terms of a graphic display of the relationship among the three primary colors, charting a curve that describes that particular color (figure 14–6). Every color has a curve that is peculiar to that one hue. Shifts in the color of any of the contributing pigments will change the curve. From another perspective, an instrument reading of a color sample can identify the curve that will have to be matched to achieve an exact duplication of that sample color.

The ability to depict the characteristics of a color enables an automatic blending system to be consistent and accurate in the duplication of an ink to convey the desired color. This consistency will carry over from order to order. This feature affords the opportunity to control the quantities blended and eliminate unnecessary over-ordering that is typical of a conservative, cautious production planning department.

The ink blending system will provide for storage of a limited number of inks, and the capability of reworking press returns into usable product for orders that are in the schedule. With software and know-how built into the system, color combinations to satisfy most requirements will be blended from just eight basic colors plus black, white and extender.

Process Printing; The Ultimate Goal

Ink inventories reflect the many colors currently printed as line copy, more often a result of the promotion of "new colors" and fashionable color trends. Despite all efforts to conserve, there are always colors that cannot be blended or that defy good judgment. Inks tinted with white or darkened by black are extremely difficult to rework into color. Dark or otherwise unmixable colors can always be blended into a black, but the tints often defy sensible reclamation.

Process printing, using the four primary colors or the hexachrome configurations, will enable the printer to achieve the ultimate in environmental responsibility. The only inks required will be limited to the basic colors. A wide variety of colors can be reproduced as a combination of the screened images of these basic colors. The introduction of stochastic screens has further extended the ability of all printing processes to do a commendable job with four-color process graphics. With a limited number of inks, there can be minimal waste and no need to have any rework ink inventories. Solvent usage can be reduced since there are fewer stations to which diluents will be added, and less clean-up that has to be done from time to time.

Figure 14–5. The spectrophotometer is used in the inkroom and at the press.

Courtesy of X-Rite Inc.

This is one of the principal advantages of radiation curable ink systems. When UV inks are used for process printing, there is no need to empty and clean ink fountains and rollers. Ink usage is maximized and diluent solvent usage is virtually unknown. There is no need for press wash except for cleaning the print-ing plates or other image carriers at the end of a run. With a decrease in usage comes a sharp reduction in the emissions exhausted and the wastes generated.

Probably the best measure of good ink management will not be recognized as an improved environment. What will be obvious is the reduction in the expense for inks and solvents and the space occupied by old, unused press returns. Less ink will be coming into the receiving area at any one time and the space required for inventory will be reduced considerably. Mass balances based on ink and solvent purchases will show a decline in the computed VOCs and HAPs for the month, the quarter and the year. Simultaneously, hazardous waste storage space will be reduced, as will shipments off-site for disposal. Permits and reports triggered by thresholds may no longer be necessary, along with the elimination of regulatory demands based on the amounts stored and/or used.

Potential safety and environmental problems can be avoided. Lower exposures will reduce the potential for accidents, health incidents or other unexpected occurrences. Insurance rate benefits can ensue from this more limited exposure.

Air emissions will drop somewhat if inks and solvents are properly stored in reasonable quantities. Every open can or drum invites evaporation of the solvents. The result is higher levels of fumes, odors, and, at times, an increased potential for dangerous fire and explosion conditions. Potential spills and accidental discharges of ink and solvent wastes into floor drains or wash tubs can be prevented by having more manageable quantities stored under more effective control.

What Does Ink Management Do for You?

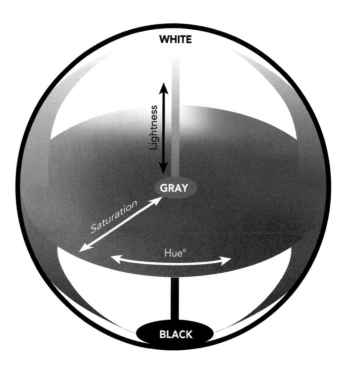

Figure 14–3. The CIELAB color system is a means of matching and controlling color in the lab and on press to assure predictable delivered graphics.

Courtesy of X-Rite Inc.

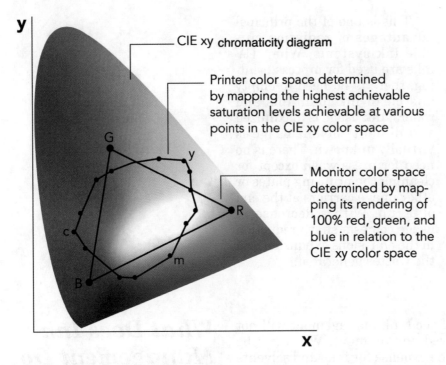

y

CIE xy **chromaticity diagram**

Printer color space determined by mapping the highest achievable saturation levels achievable at various points in the CIE xy color space

Monitor color space determined by mapping its rendering of 100% red, green, and blue in relation to the CIE xy color space

x

Figure 14–6. CIE xy diagram allows for charting a color with specific reference points and a color space.

Courtesy of X-Rite Inc.

Managed use of solvents can lead to lowering inventory levels to a point that will assure adequate supplies for the work on hand. Smaller, more frequent shipments can reduce potential hazards in the plant, and reduce the number and types of permits and other enforcement measures. Substituting the packaging of the solvents by ordering tote tanks to replace larger accumulations of drums of the same solvents is a measure that relates to efficiency in handling and storage and minimization of exposure for safety and the environment.

Controlled usage and materials substitution can lead to a reduction in the use of any listed chemicals, i.e., chemicals on the SARA Title III listing under Section 313, the source of the TRI annual report. With lower usage and inventory quantities comes the opportunity to avoid record-keeping and reports based on threshold quantities. Accompanying the obvious regulatory relief will be a reduction in the potential liability for accidents or incidents that could occur under less controlled conditions.

Starting the Program

The best place to seek help in developing an ink management program will be with current ink suppliers. Many have already established relationships with the manufacturers of ink handling, blending and monitoring equipment. Many have access to appropriate computer software and hardware to enable better control the inks you use and manage the excesses that are typical. No one knows your inks better than the people who make them. Use the suppliers as the backbone of your program.

Include your other suppliers too. Inks must be compatible and perform well with anilox rollers, fountain solutions, gravure cylinders, printing plates, screens and substrates. Every printing process has its own needs and experts are available in every segment of the industry to assist the printer with ink management solutions. The input from each of these sources can help to produce a three-dimensional model of your needs. Getting them all together in one room can help to eliminate the need to go from one to the other as one tries to work his way into the ideal program to suit the needs of your operation.

Read the publications produced for the ink, printing and packaging industries. There are articles every month about new developments or applications, new products and other material and equipment information that can help you identify the solutions to your particular needs.

Attend industry shows to see the latest technology advancements. Large firms announce new products at the shows. Small, innovative firms use shows to find an audience for products and equipments they have developed. Many benefits have been derived from the interaction that takes place at printing and packaging expositions.

Partnerships are the key to success.

CHAPTER 15

Reducing Pollution by Addressing Press Clean-up

Solvents of all types are the major source of many of the environmental problems faced by printers in the normal conduct of their business. Whether the solvent is a petroleum derivative or water, the manner in which it is used on press and disposed of after use brings the printer into the jurisdiction of the various regulatory agencies.

The largest amount of solvent or water used in any operation is normally incurred during clean-up of the printing stations and printing image carriers. Traditionally, printers purchase and use considerably more solvent for cleaning than they purchase inks or fountain solutions. Table 15–1 illustrates the relative percentages of ink to solvent purchases, based on records of printers in different printing processes.

A flexographic or gravure printer may buy three to four times more solvent than inks. While a portion of this solvent is used to dilute inks to operating viscosity and to maintain that viscosity, the greater percentage is applied to cleaning the inking fountains, rollers, plates, cylinders and doctor blade systems.

Screen printers may use little solvent in the printing process, but they can use significant amounts to clean screens for reuse with new copy or to salvage the screens for reorders. Different solvents and approaches are taken based on whether or not an image is to be saved. Less aggressive but effective solutions are used

Clean-up Spews Wastes

TABLE 15–1. SOLVENT PURCHASES BY FLEXOGRAPHERS

Solvent purchases far exceed that of inks for flexographic printers and the emissions from ink for lithographic printers. The table summarizes usage by a number of printing plates, with information demonstrating the impact that solvents have on plant emissions. Primary reason for the disparity with ink usage can be attributed to use of solvents for cleaning image carriers and press parts.

TYPE OF COMPANY	SIZE	INKS - LIQUID POUNDS	VOCs IN INK POUNDS	SOLVENTS POUNDS	TOTAL PURCHASES INKS AND SOLVENT	% SOLVENT PURCHASED
Flexography	Large	307,266	153,633	380,322	687,588	55.3%
	Medium	71,312	35,656	136,955	208,267	65.8%
	Medium	52,424	26,212	88,017	140,441	62.7%
	Medium	24,546	12,273	92,977	117,523	79.1%
	Medium	23,529	11,765	83,759	107,288	78.1%
	Small	15,651	7,826	54,260	69,911	77.6%
	Small	7,264	3,632	28,171	35,435	79.5%
Total Flexography		501,992	250,996	864,461	1,366,453	63.3%

	PRODUCT	INKS - PASTE POUNDS	VOCs IN INK POUNDS	PRESSWASH POUNDS	TOTAL PURCHASES INKS AND SOLVENT	% SOLVENT PURCHASED
Lithographic	Packaging	105,814	5,291	38,159	143,973	26.5%
	Commercial	61,050	3,053	23,281	84,331	27.6%
	Commercial	25,958	1,298	31,427	57,385	54.8%
	Commercial	20,374	1,019	45,458	65,832	69.1%
Total Lithographic		213,196	10,660	138,325	351,521	39.4%

Source: P-F Technical Services Inc.

when a screen with an image is to be saved and reused, with work practices limited by the need to not disturb the image. Destruction of the image so that the screen may be reused for other orders can require very aggressive solvents.

Offset lithographic printers use blanket washes, press washes and plate cleaners. Where the ink is paste and emits only a small amount of VOCs, the cleaning solutions can comprise some very toxic solvents, defined as both VOCs and HAPs. It is not unusual to find that pressmen have their preferences and more than one press wash is used in a pressroom.

Solvent and Aqueous, Both Pose Hazards

Compounding the volume of solvent or aqueous cleaners used for cleaning is the question of toxicity and other hazards. When ink dries, the hardened residue can be difficult to break down and remove thoroughly. Water inks and coatings formulations, when dry, are almost impossible to remove without very aggressive cleaning agents. Adhesives and glues can be extremely difficult for traditional cleaning formulations to remove.

To compensate for the need to attack these difficult, hard deposits, aggressive cleaners are employed. Blends used for cleaning solvent-based inks and adhesives may include toluene, methyl ethyl ketone, methyl isobutyl ketone, xylene, hydrocarbons including a high percentage of trimethyl-benzene, and acetone. Methylene chloride has been a favorite as a fast evaporating, aggressive solvent. Chlorinated solvents have been favored for cleaning metal surfaces. All leave much to be desired from the standpoint of the environment and health issues (figure 15–1).

Figure 15–1. Drums of spent press wash sit on containment pallets next to the virgin wash, awaiting disposal off-site.

Aqueous solutions tend to be corrosive in nature, containing significant percentages of caustic sodas. While much safer for the environment, these cleaning agents pose safety risks to the workers. Proper procedures for cleaning and the need to wear appropriate personal protective equipment are essential.

Resolving Cleaning Issues at the Press

With or without new chemistry, a number of simple, easy-to-institute measures can be taken to minimize most of the typical emissions, discharges and hazardous wastes when disposing of the spent cleaning solvent or water. More difficult situations may require more innovative and complex solutions.

Basic to all remedies is the need to train personnel to be receptive of change. New attitudes and the need to understand the negative ramifications of past practices may be required if there is to be proper use of the new materials, equipment or methods. Habits and expectations of the past may have to give way to a new reality.

Any, or all, of the measures cited below will make a positive contribution to the productivity and quality of your work. They will also contribute to a more positive approach to the management of the quality of your printing operation, as well as to the stewardship of the environment.

Why Do We Produce Excess Clean-Up Waste?

There are a number of reasons why printers use large volumes of cleaning solvents. Most of this usage stems from several common in-plant practices. Take a step back and observe your facility to see if any of these conditions exist:

1. **Use of continuously running water or freely dispensed solvent to clean parts.** This can be done on or off press, but the result is the same. More fluid is used than is required to do the job. Are parts cleaned in a sink with continuously running water, as opposed to allowing the parts to soak in a tub which has been plugged and which has been partially filled with water, into which the press parts are then placed for cleaning?

A few years back, a project involved a flexographic printer in New Jersey, who was rinsing parts in a sink and collecting the running water in drums. The drums of waste were then shipped to the local sewer system treatment plant for disposal. At one point, the company was advised that they could not continue to ship the drums of wash-up water waste to the sewer treatment facility. They requested consulting assistance. An audit found that the press department was generating over a thousand gallons of water waste each day. The presses waited for all parts to be cleaned as the workers moved from one job to the next. Almost every job was scheduled by need, not by color sequence, and the number of changes per day was excessive. The obvious control technology was a water treatment system. Installing the water treatment system would cost upwards of $100,000, plus the additional costs for labor and overhead to operate the unit on a daily basis.

Changes were made in scheduling of the work and in the inventory of parts that typically had to be cleaned as one job followed the other. The need to make so many changes was reduced. The wait between jobs was eliminated, with clean parts ready at the time the previous job ended, rather than wait for the time it took to clean the parts.

Installing a wash tank, in which the water with a cleaning agent could be used until no longer effective, was a correct and appropriate solution. Periodically, the solids were removed from the tank and fresh caustic chemicals were added to restore the strength of the cleaning solution. When the spent water was no longer clean enough for the purpose, the workers would empty the tank into drums for disposal. The firm was able to reduce its water usage and its water bill drastically, while cutting the amount of waste that had to be disposed. A treatment system was not needed (figure 15–2).

Figure 15–2. Wash tanks can minimize use of solvent or water cleaning solutions.

Courtesy of Graymills Corporation, Chicago, IL.

2. **Are solvents in an open can** into which rags or wipers are dipped to use for cleaning? Or is the solvent kept in a spray bottle or pressure release safety dispenser to minimize both the amount of solvent dispensed and the possibility for evaporation?

In a situation where solvents are used to clean the press and plates, air emissions pose another problem for the environment and health of the workers. Free use of solvents to clean parts on the press adds to the fumes in the air as the solvents evaporate. In many printing plants there is no hazardous waste stream because the cleaning solvent simply flashes off and exits through exhaust ducts, window fans, windows and doors.

Solvents are selected primarily because of the speed with which they attack the dried residues and the speed at which the parts dry. Production people look for fast action to avoid delays in the printing process. The faster the rate of evaporation, the quicker the press can recommence operations. By the same token, the faster the evaporation rate, the more solvent that will be used. See Table 6–1 for a listing of the various solvents used in printing, with their relative evaporation rates.

One solution to the problem of having excess solvents evaporate to the ambient air is to modify the method of using solvents for cleaning. One company substituted spray bottles and safety cans for five-gallon buckets that were being used to hold the solvent. As a pressman needed a wet rag, he would either spray the solvent onto the rag or depress the plunger on the safety can. In either case, a minimum of solvent was dispensed and cleaning was accomplished without deterioration in the quality of the work. The results were quite obvious as purchases and use of solvent declined (figure 15–3).

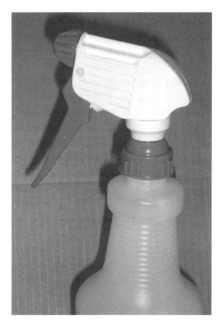

Figure 15–3. Use of spray bottle can reduce amount of solvents or press wash used when cleaning ink rollers and plates.

3. **Lack of proper working methods** complicates the matter. Press personnel do not have an established procedure and the proper tools with which to do the job. They do the best of their ability or ingenuity.

A common clue as to whether proper methods are being used is provided by simple observation. Just what are the pressmen doing as they go about cleaning the press? Why does each pressman have a different preferred cleaning agent? Just how much more chemistry than necessary is used because each person has his own favorite cleaner?

A simple example is the cleaning of ink trays and rollers. Good practice requires removal of all, or almost all, ink solids before commencing with cleaning the pans or rollers. The cleaning solvent should remove a minimum amount of residual ink solids, not a significant quantity of usable ink. On-press cleaning should be done when needed, not on a fixed schedule or set interval. Allowing cleaning to be put off until it is convenient—according to a preset schedule—may require more time and materials. Delays in cleaning may also cause damage to printing plates and press components.

Use of wipers/rags purchased by the bale leaves something to be desired. If not made up of a standard size, the baled rags will come in various sizes and porosity. Oversized wipers or rags simply bunch up more and absorb considerably more cleaning solvent than needed. This, in turn, is evaporated into the air or winds up as liquid wastes dripping from or wrung out of the wipers. Wipers should be the smallest size that will facilitate cleaning.

4. **Lack of adequate preventive maintenance cleaning tools and wash-up tanks** on-press during runs or off-press. Some facilities and ink systems lend themselves to clean-up in the press; others require an off-press system to clean parts adequately. Without the right tools, more waste is generated as personnel try to clean the parts.

Just how are the parts in your pressroom best handled? Do you accomplish the job adequately on press, or would your operation benefit by use of an off-press cleaning tank? Can you visualize greater productivity and more consistent quality if the parts in the press are always clean, having been cleaned away from the machine?

Cleaning on press helps to maintain quality during the run. Having the right tools and cleaning agents is critical. An effective cleaning agent should be able to remove ink, paper dust and grease. However, do we sacrifice cleaning when the demand for output outweighs the cost of shutting down the press to remove dried ink, paper dust and grease? Automatic on-press cleaning systems are becoming increasingly more common. These systems prevent buildup of ink residues but require more effective cleaning solutions. Automatic systems have been praised for reducing downtime and waste. Does your equipment have automatic cleaning systems?

5. **Lack of an adequate inventory of printing station parts** to maximize use of off-press cleaning and maximize printing operations. Extra ink pans and rollers can be easily replaced, leaving the cleaning to be done off press. Press time can be productive and can easily offset the cost

of the extra parts. As you observe your press crews, would they benefit from being able to make a quick change to new, cleaned parts, as opposed to cleaning, and recleaning, and recleaning in the press until they get it right?

6. **Improper scheduling**, calling for many clean-ups as colors change from job to job. Proper placement of orders in the schedule minimizes the need to do thorough cleaning, as colors are sequenced by family. Variations within a color family will not necessitate thorough cleaning. Hopping from job to job without color consideration will necessitate clean-ups between all, or most, jobs.

Do you have a plan and schedule for your presses? Or do you place jobs on the press strictly to meet dates, without consideration for the sequences in which one ink will replace another in the change of jobs? The time you may think you are saving may be lost as press crews clean dirty stations to make way for lighter colors. Perhaps a schedule that looks at what takes place in a change, which minimizes those factors that create lost time and generate wastes, makes more sense in the total picture.

Positive Steps in the Pressroom

Remedies to all of the above are common knowledge and common sense. All that is required is top management support and good line supervision to make sure that the pressroom is properly tooled and managed effectively.

The objective of daily activity is to keep the presses running. In pursuit of this objective, cleaning a press must be approached with the proper perception. The main interest of management and supervision is the time required between jobs. What transpires between the end of one job and the start of the next must be planned and managed and not left to the devices of the operator at the machine. Just as a job to be printed is planned and proofed against standards, the manner in which cleaning operations are conducted in a pressroom should be done with specific objectives. Hurried cleaning procedures, utilizing inordinate amounts of liquid (solvent or water), may accomplish the job, but at what price in time and excessive waste? Consider the liability and higher costs that accompany the hazardous wastes.

There is a proper way to clean an inking station, one that will maximize the use of inks purchased and minimize the amount of solvent or water required to remove all traces of the inks being replaced. Proper training and supervision is required to assure that the methodology is maintained or improved. There is no substitute for good training, nor for repetition of training to assure that work practices do not regress.

There is also logic for cleaning such parts as fountain pans, rollers and pumps in a separate wash-up tank while the press is running the next job. Every hour released from press downtime for productive output results in increased sales and income. The cost of the extra parts may pale by comparison with the added productivity and profits.

Innovative Approaches

Consideration should be given to many of the newer techniques and materials that are coming into the marketplace for other processes. Such things as safer solvents or aqueous-based cleaning products, automated cleaning equipment, laundry services, etc. should be evaluated as the facility looks to reduce the amount and toxicity of its waste streams.

Dry Ice Does the Job

A good example of transferring technology from one industry to another is the use of high-pressure air with particles of dry ice (solid carbon dioxide) to clean inks and coatings off metal parts. First seen at a pollution prevention conference in Albany, New York in 1997, the equipment has since been demonstrated at the Graph Expo show. The vender showed a system that cleans paint and ink on machine parts by utilizing an air blast containing particles of dry ice. The unit can be used at the press or as a separate operation. The dry ice bombards the dried inks and coatings, abrading the solids off the metal surfaces. The solids are removed, leaving a clean surface. No chemistry is used and no wastes result, except for the particles that are stripped from the equipment. The dry ice evaporates and constitutes no threat to workplace or community air quality (figure 15–4).

Safe Press Washes Replace Traditional Solvents

Every month there are at least one or more articles in the printing trade magazines citing the environmental benefits of a new ecologically safe cleaning solution. Many are aqueous, and contain such chemicals as sodium hydroxide and butyl cellosolve.

Figure 15–4. Dry ice blasting of ink from transfer rollers and machine frame eliminates need for chemicals to remove dried ink, oil and dust; before (left), after (right).
Courtesy of Alpheus, A CAE Company.

Some are solvents, with high boiling points, that evaporate at extremely slow rates. At the press, some work better than others. Part of the problem with trying the new formulations is the lack of adequate perception of the potential benefits of the new cleanser. Too frequently, performance is compared to the solvent press wash, without due consideration as to whether the attributes of the solvent currently being used are really necessary. Time must be taken to consider just how long it takes to clean a part, for the cleaning solution to dry, and enable the press to run. The fastest solvent may not be necessary if there is sufficient lapse of time when the press is down to allow even the slowest drying press wash to dry.

A good example is a series of new cleaning formulations, solvent and aqueous, produced by one company, which are safer and environmentally responsible. The vapor pressure of the liquids is such that a quantity spread over an area for a period of a month demonstrated an evaporation rate that was negligible. In practical terms, when this solvent is used in most plants, there will be as much left when you are finished as when you start.

Cleaning solutions must be selected based on the job they have to do and the ramifications to worker safety and health and the environment. Sacrificing any one for the benefit of the others must be done with an eye towards the total impact on product and the regulatory requirements. (See figure 15–5.)

Formulation Number 14:	Fatty acid derivatives Propylene glycol ethers Water
	VOC content: 12%, 0.97 lbs/gal Flashpoint: 230+degrees F pH: 5.0
	Test Performance — good
Formulation Number 25:	Terpenes Esters/lactones
	VOC content: 55%, 4.1 lbs/gal Flashpoint: 220+ degrees F pH: 4.3
	Not tested during trials.
Formulation Number 26:	Fatty acid derivatives Esters/lactones
	VOC content: 18%, 1.3 lbs/gal Flashpoint: 230+ degrees F pH 7.8 (fluctuates)
	Test Performance — good

Figure 15–5. The Design for the Environment blanket wash project evaluated many different formulations. The above are representative of washes with high boiling temperatures that are less likely to evaporate.

Source: United States Environmental Protection Agency, *Cleaner Technologies Substitutes Assessment: Lithographic Blanket Washes*, EPA 744-R-97-006, September 1997.

In-Line Cleaning Equipment

Automatic cleaning equipment has been developed for use on a number of presses. Some systems are set in place and are activated when needed. Other units can be brought to the press and utilized on the print station without disrupting the press. Some work with cleaning solutions, either solvent or aqueous, while others do not utilize any liquids.

Lithographic presses have had automatic cleaning units with liquids for some time. Alternative concepts have been introduced to eliminate the liquids and the resulting waste stream. One such unit contains a cleaning roller coated with a proprietary polymer. The roller removes surface contaminants by simply rolling over the surface of the ink or coating roller. The coating removes the debris from the process roller (see figure 15–6). More than one roller can be used to assure the transfer of the ink and dust from the prime roller. Another version of the automatic cleaner uses a roll of cloth which is brushed up against the process roll to wipe off dried ink, coating or dust. The cloth advances as the cleaning is accomplished.

In a more dramatic fashion for flexographic presses, one manufacturer has designed an enclosed chambered doctor blade system that has built-in nozzles that pressure sprays cleaning solution into the anilox cells from a small reservoir. The unit also is made of an alloy that is not receptive to the ink, thus limiting drying in its cavities. The object is to reduce cleaning time and fluid, while maximizing the performance of the unit (figure 15–7).

Off-Press Cleaning Equipment

While proper cleaning procedures and chemicals are needed to keep the presses rolling, preventive maintenance will require the use of off-press cleaning equipment. Much of this type of equipment will depend on the type of printing being done.

Screen printers traditionally wash the screens off press to either preserve the screen itself or the screen with the copy intact. When preserving the copy, the use of solvents is preferred, typically in a washtub from which the spent solvent can be drained to a drum for disposition as a hazardous waste. To render the screen perfectly clean, equipment is available to reduce the dependency on chemicals and solvents in particular. Recirculating wash tanks allow the screens to be placed in a vertical position and for the water cleanser to constantly be reused. A power-blaster discharges the water with an additive cleaning agent at approximately 3,000 fpm. The result is the complete destruction of the copy

Three Roll Turret Configuration
This configuration provides flying replacement for continuous operations, with the expired rolls accessible for cleaning.

Figure 15–6. Patented contact web cleaner removes contamination deposits on printing roll using a cleaning roll or cloth that works continuously while the press is running. Rollers are kept clean without chemicals and downtime.

Courtesy of R.G. Egan Equipment, Inc.

Figure 15–7. Chambered doctor blade system has cleaning jets built into floor of ink cavity.

Courtesy of FIT—Flexographic Inking Technologies.

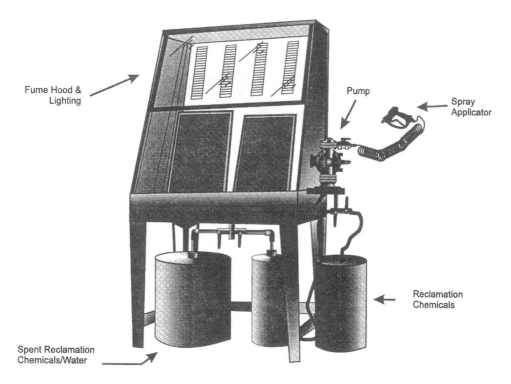

Figure 15–8. Recirculating wash tank combined with power blaster for cleaning screens reduces waste water discharges and minimizes hazardous waste.

Source: United States Environmental Protection Agency, *Cleaner Technologies Substitutes Assessment , Screen Reclamation*, EPA 744-R-94-005, September 1994, p vi–17.

portion and the recycling of the screen for yet another job. With a filter on the discharge to collect solids, the cleaning water can be discharged into the sewer system (figure 15–8).

Flexographic and gravure printers have had a choice of equipment for cleaning their machine parts and engraved anilox and printing rollers. Cleaning tanks have been equipped to use either safer solvent or caustic water solutions, with some turbulence introduced to provide for more active exposure of the dirty surface to the cleaning agents. Some cleaning tanks have introduced ultrasonics to enhance the breakdown of the ink residues.

Two versions of solids used for cleaning the rollers have emerged. One uses bicarbonate of soda particles; the other uses polyethylene beads. In both cases, the solid particles bombard the surface and cells of the rollers, chipping away the dried inks (figure 15–9). Adherents speak well of both methods. Of concern to suppliers of the engraved rollers is the potential damage to

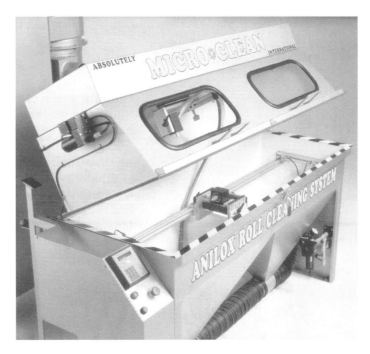

Figure 15–9. Minute solid particles, in this case polyethylene beads, bombard anilox roll cells and remove dried ink residues.

Courtesy of Micro Clean International.

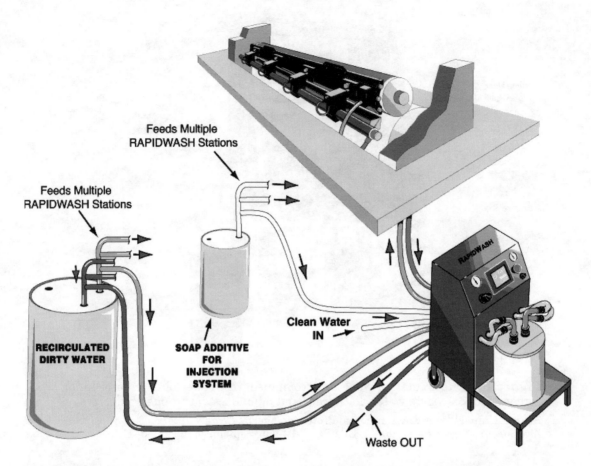

Figure 15–10. Portable unit is brought to press and connected to water lines for cleaning chambered doctor blade system and anilox roller, and then to drums to collect dirty water for treatment or disposal.

Courtesy of Harris and Bruno Machine Company.

the thin walls of the cells. As anilox rolls are engraved with finer and finer screens (700–900 lines per inch), the walls of the cells become increasingly thinner and more susceptible to damage.

As an outcome of the development of the off-line cleaning equipment, suppliers of chambered doctor blade units have developed equipment that can be used off-press or wheeled to the press for cleaning the rollers in their operating positions. A solvent or water liquid cleaning solution is used depending on the ink system in use. One such cleaning system, working with either water or solvent cleaning agents, is depicted in figures 15–10 and 15–11, respectively.

Case Studies with New Cleaning Solutions

With new solutions appearing on the market, trials were scheduled to test the adequacy of the new chemistry. Simply leaving samples for testing does not always get the results one would desire. Using both an aqueous and a hydrocarbon solvent with a high boiling temperature, trials were conducted at a few sites. The results are described in the following narratives.

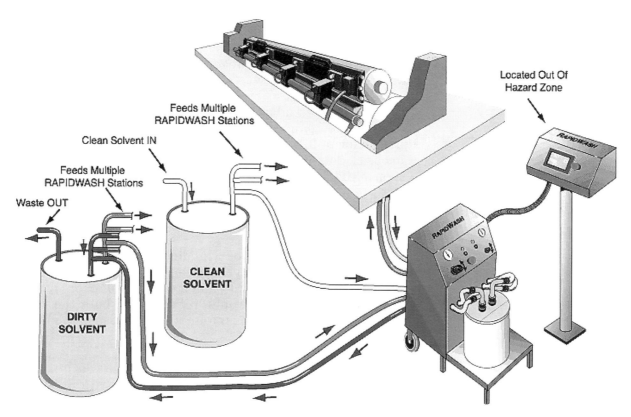

Figure 15–11. Portable unit is brought to press and connected to solvent drum for cleaning chambered doctor blade system and anilox roller, and then to drums to collect dirty solvent for treatment or disposal.

Courtesy of Harris and Bruno Machine Company.

Faced with the need to operate a clean facility and produce newspapers with predictable ink density and graphic quality, the general manager of a regional newspaper printing facility elected to employ a two-pronged attack on ink and other collected residues in the newspaper pressroom. A chance visit by the cleaning manufacturer's sales manager opened the door to consideration of a variety of pressroom cleaners developed to satisfy the need for aggressive, yet environmentally safe, cleaning chemicals. The newspaper is a member of a major publishing corporation, operating two presses, one letterpress and one flexographic. The letterpress uses traditional oil-based inks; the flexographic press depends on waterborne inks. Each condition requires its own cleaning solution.

The general manager had set a goal for his pressroom to be a clean operation. This goal was intended for the presses and their components, as well as the impact that chemical usage could have on the workplace and environment of the neighboring community. If the plant were to be clean, it would have to eliminate wastes and pollutants that have characterized the printing processes. Existing cleaning products generated hazardous wastes. The

Water Flexo Newspaper Seeks Cleaner Environment

major cleanser, offered as a package with cleaning tanks, was a mineral spirit-based solvent which was delivered periodically by the supplier's truck. Spent solvent was taken off premises by the supplier for disposal as a hazardous waste. Secondary cleaners included a citrus-based solvent and an aqueous cleaner. Waste from all three cleansers categorized the newspaper printer as a generator of hazardous waste and air pollutants.

With two ink transfer systems and different ink chemistry, there was need to adapt two approaches to the cleaning of the presses and its components. The supplier offered both solvent and aqueous formulations from which choices could be made. An aqueous cleaner was selected as the answer to the waterborne ink system of the flexo press. A high boiler solvent blend was the alternative to the mineral-based blend for cleaning the letterpress inks and the general accumulation of all types of residues on both presses and such parts as static bars. The letterpress parts are cleaned in a tank.

The results have been outstanding. Both presses have been maintained at a very high level of cleanliness. Recycling of the high boiler solvent blend has resulted in a drastic reduction in the purchase of fresh cleaning solvents, reflecting on both the reusable nature of the cleaner and the minimal evaporation of the liquid.

Folding Cartons in North Carolina

The objective at a box plant in North Carolina was primarily to meet the increasing demand for high quality graphics. Environmental regulations were not a driving force, but the conditions in the workplace were a factor. The plant manager supervised the change for the facility, using the aqueous formula for the normal automatic on-press cleaning. For more aggressive action with ink dried in the anilox roller cells, cleaning was done with a second solution that contained a higher percentage of caustic soda.

Prior to developing a program with the new solvent cleaners, plant personnel used a variety of solutions and adopted a hit-or-miss attitude towards the cleaning process. Weekly preventive maintenance employed both automatic and manual cleaning methods. The major cleaner used prior to the change was a powder, which required mixing. The press crew was never happy with the need to mix the cleaning solution, nor was there consistency in the solution when it was mixed. They appreciated use of an effective liquid cleaner that came into the plant ready to use.

Since the introduction of the new aqueous formula, all cleaning is performed automatically. When asked about the effectiveness of the cleansing agent, the response was that parts were 100 percent cleaner. The crews were amazed when they first started using the new product. Anilox rollers they considered beyond hope were delivering measured amounts of ink within 45 minutes. The new cleaner was easier to use and produced high quality results. The real answer came on the press. The challenge of printing high quality graphics had been met. Quality has been dramatically improved. (See figure 15–12.)

Remedies to all of the problems cited above are common knowledge, but most require management support and good line supervision to make sure that the pressroom is properly tooled and operating effectively. The objective of daily activity is to keep the presses running. In the pursuit of this objective, cleaning of presses must be approached with the proper perspective. The main interest of management and supervision is to minimize the time required between jobs. What transpires between the end of one job and the start of the next must be planned and managed, and not left to the devices of the man at the machine. Rushed cleaning procedures, utilizing inordinate amounts of liquid (solvent or water), may accomplish the job. But at what price in time and excessive wastes, with the liability and higher costs that accompany the hazardous wastes?

There is a proper way to clean an inking station, one that will maximize the use of inks purchased and minimize the amount of solvent or water required to remove all traces of the inks being replaced. Proper training and supervision is required to assure that the methodology is maintained or improved.

There is also logic for cleaning such parts as fountain pans, rollers and pumps in a separate wash-up tank or system while the press is running the next job. Extra fountain pans, ink pumps and even doctor blade assemblies can enable press personnel to effect a job change in minimum time and then clean the parts while the press is producing another job. Selection of an appropriate system for doing off-press cleaning will enhance the quality and productivity of the presses, while minimizing the impact on health and the environment.

Solving the Problem of Clean-Up Wastes

Figure 15–12. Environmentally safe aqueous cleaning solutions are coming into the market every day as seen in the Allied Pressroom Chemistry exhibit at Print 2001.

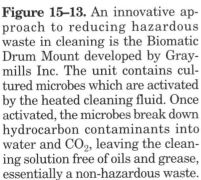

Figure 15–13. An innovative approach to reducing hazardous waste in cleaning is the Biomatic Drum Mount developed by Graymills Inc. The unit contains cultured microbes which are activated by the heated cleaning fluid. Once activated, the microbes break down hydrocarbon contaminants into water and CO_2, leaving the cleaning solution free of oils and grease, essentially a non-hazardous waste.

Courtesy of Graymills Inc.

Don't get stuck in the mentality of modifying an existing tool or method by patching it up as a means of moving ahead. Look for new tested and untested approaches (figure 15–13); they can and will work for you, the printer, just as they are working in other industries. All it takes is the fortitude to withstand pressures to avoid changing from the existing, less safe practices and chemistry.

CHAPTER 16

The Digital Revolution in Prepress Operations: Pollution Prevention Partners with Technology

In order to appreciate where the printing industry is now and where it is headed, one must go back to its roots and see how printing was done previously. Only then, with this historical perspective, can the tremendous progress in printing technology be appreciated. This is particularly impressive when one reviews the status of prepress activities. The changes have had great impact on every phase of the science and art of printing, bringing it ever closer to being an industrial, virtually automated technology.

It must be remembered that printing and the activities preceding the operation of the printing press have always been considered as graphic arts, not a science nor a technology. Graphic design is taught at art schools; artists are the people who have traditionally initiated the process and bring the graphics to the point of printing on press. Craftsmen, people who took pride in their skills, brought the printed product to life by operating manually set and run printing presses. All told, printing has always had an element of human contribution that recognized the skill of the person as being more of a controlling factor than that exercised by the machine.

That perception, and the reality of the technology, is changing rapidly as computers become integrated with the process, both prior to and on the printing press. With the introduction of the computer, the creation of art has become a mix of both computer skills and artistic perception; some would even say it is more of the former than of the latter. Operation of the printing press has been assisted by a marriage of electronics and traditional printing

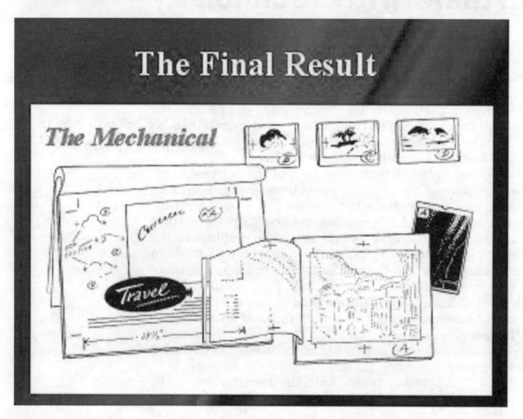

Figure 16–1. Traditional method of developing art for printing.
Courtesy of Tom Cernera, Graphix Press.

technology to provide the craftsman with tools that enable him to reach higher levels of printing quality. At the same time that electronic creation and communication has become the norm, there has been considerable elimination of much chemistry from the process. Progress in technology has also benefited the environment and safety in the workplace.

Traditional Art and Plate Preparation

A concept can be born anywhere. It could be a marketing idea. A salesman could bring in a request from a customer. Production people may see enhanced capabilities in the process. Trends in the marketplace may create demands for new concepts, better graphics. When all is said and done, an artist has had to put all this into a form that would both be printable and also satisfy the customer. Once this objective has been established, the design has to be transferred to an image carrier from which the image could be printed.

A graphic and product design would start life as thumbnail sketches. The artist would try to cover a broad range of ideas in individual small sketches that could be reviewed by a client. Sketches were frequently made with charcoal pencils, solvent-based markers, gouache paintings or watercolors. More subtle effects might be made using air brush techniques. Then, overcoat varnishes and adhesives would be sprayed from aerosol cans. Thinners would be used for clean-up of paints and adhesives.

From these sketches, the client would select the one or more designs that would be created in full size for transition to the image carriers of the particular printing process or processes. Changes in copy or graphics would be made at this stage. Each variation would require its own "mechanical" art. (See figure 16–1.) Variations in the copy that would print in any particular color could be done by means of overlays within that color rendition. Components of a design could include, in addition to copy, photographs, art boards, paintings and sketches. All the materials would be brought together and assembled by hand. The copy would be set with hot lead on a typesetting machine or by hand (figure 16–2). The paintings, art boards and sketches would be done full scale using watercolor, oil paint, acrylic, gouache and the appropriate solvents and other chemicals required with each medium. Illustrations would be separated into the basic process colors using cameras, using color filters and the photographic process to produce negatives.

The mechanical art would then be assembled by hand, using separate acetate sheets for each color to be printed. Process sections would be inserted in areas that were masked for the purpose, delineating the space in which the process screen would print. The mechanical would be examined to assure fidelity of the copy separation by color and the accuracy of both content and placement of all components of the graphics. A color proof would be made of each acetate sheet and combined, which would then be sent to the customer for his approval.

Figure 16–2. Ludlow typesetting machine at Precise Corporate Printing in Brooklyn, NY uses hot lead to set type.

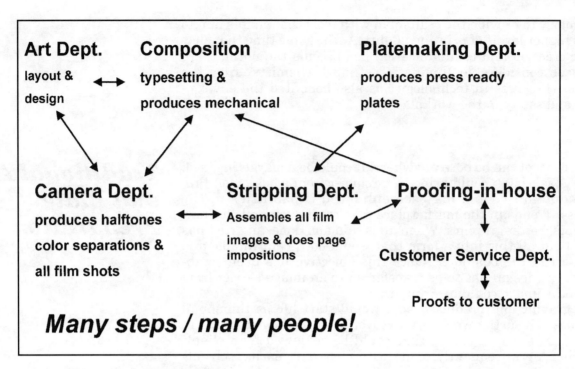

Figure 16–3. Workflow of yesterday.
Courtesy of Tom Cernera, Graphix Press.

The approved mechanical would then be photographed and processed using basic chemicals to reproduce the images on film. When more than one impression of a copy was to be printed on the same sheet, or print repeat, multiple negatives would be produced. In turn, the individual negatives would then be assembled in appropriate positions on a form called a "flat." This would be done manually by a craftsman known as a "stripper." A master negative would then be made with every component or repetition of the copy in position. The resulting negative would be ready for transfer of the graphics to the printing plate or other image carrier. The process for producing the image carrier would vary by the printing process.

Visualize this complex series of processes and it is easy to see the many points at which personnel and the environment are affected by chemistry (figure 16–3). The materials used for the initial design frequently contained pigments and solvents that were toxic. Many of the solvents used for thinning, retarding or cleaning were toxic. The photographic process to make negatives or proofs resulted in hazardous wastes from the development and fixing of the silver emulsion. Platemaking, in every process, used chemistry that was hazardous. And with this mélange of activity there was a degree of compromise in the ability to produce quality work. The human and material variables took time and generated wastes during the prepress processes and at the press.

T he words and numerical content of any design start with a writer. An editor then reads and corrects errors or rewrites cumbersome sentences and paragraphs. The copy is then set and a proofreader reviews the proofs and makes any necessary corrections. This brings the process back to the point at which the type was set and corrections are made. This is a long and cumbersome sequence of events, particularly when type was set by hand or by typesetting machines.

The first major breakthrough out of this complex process came with the development of computer phototypesetting in the late 1970s (figure 16–4). The computer of the time was able to use a limited number of fonts and produce "acceptable" quality copy for the typical printed product. The type characters were carried on photographic disks, drums, strips or grids. High quality was still consigned to the realm of the traditional lead typesetter. The new process required extensive training and was not as accessible as the desk-top computer of today, nor was the composing equipment in these systems of a quality that could compete on an acceptable basis with traditional typeset copy. The equipment was massive and required special environmental conditions for the room in which it operated. Personnel had to be highly trained. The library of type styles and fonts was limited. On a positive note, the computerized typesetting did eliminate one of the more hazardous chemicals in the prepress process—lead.

Copy was produced in a galley proof, which would be proofread to assure the accuracy of the typesetting. Corrections could be noted and the proof returned to the computer typesetter for correction. The computer file could be brought to the screen and adjustments made. When the copy was corrected and reprinted on galleys, the computer-generated printed copy would be assembled on an art board or in a mechanical by a commercial artist.

Tradition led to some reservations about the quality of the type as set by computer and printed using the best quality in-line printers of the time. Many computers transferred type to paper by means of a carbon ribbon. Lead typesetting equipment continued to be used for more exacting end uses or customers. Culture played a part in the acceptance of the computer-set type. As time progressed, these objections lessened and most typesetting was done by computers.

Time has brought considerable progress and refinement in the ability of computers to set type and the quality of the assorted printers that transfer the electronic images to paper. The development of compact, highly effective desktop computers and printers has enabled designers and writers to work in an electronic mode that allows for considerable flexibility in the design and refinement of copy, as well as redefining the types of people that could be employed as operators. The computer

Setting Copy Comes of Age

Courier New	AAAaaaBBBbbbCCCccc
Incised 901 Bd BT	**AAAaaaBBBbbbCCCccc**
Jester	AAAaaaBBBbbbCCCccc
Long Island	**AAAaaa BBBbbbCCCccc**
Poster	**AAAaaaBBBbbbCCCccc**
Rockwell	AAAaaaBBBbbbCCCccc
Storybook	**AAAaaaBBBbbbGGGccc**
Tahoma	AAAaaaBBBbbbCCCccc
Times New Roman	AAAaaaBBBbbbCCCccc

Figure 16–4. Computers facilitate selection of type fonts.

opened the way for women and handicapped people to enter the field, as hot type and the accompanying harsh factory working conditions were replaced by an office atmosphere. Files are now stored electronically in the typesetting unit itself as digital information or as electronic data in imagesetters. Changes can be made and files of copy saved with minimal repetition of any part or all of a design. Copy can be checked for spelling and grammar or reviewed for language deficiencies at the time of creation. Copy can be printed as a preliminary proof or, in many cases, as the finished copy that will be replicated by the printing press (figure 16–5).

Software Leads the Way

The electronic media has given the computer the capability to generate and transmit copy directly from the writer/designer to other departments within the same building or over vast intervening distances among customer, designer, prepress house and printer. Computer disks and e-mail have enabled communication over large distances, from a customer to one or more printers working on the same project. Electronics can communicate the basic copy for review or to generate a product by either the negative or the platemaking processing equipment. Ink jet and laser printers have elevated the quality of the printed copy for proofs when hard copy is required. Imagesetters convert electronic impulses to exposure of copy for film negatives. Laser and thermal equipment serve as plate processing activators.

Software has been the critical element in the success of the electronic age for printers. Basic features such as spelling checks and language searches have reduced the need for the scrupulous proofreading of the past and the reworking of copy at a typesetter. More advanced skills are complemented by software that covers the broad range of skills and expertise previously performed by mechanical artists, strippers and darkroom personnel. Competency with computer programs is more easily attained than the years of training and apprenticeship that had been part of the culture in the past. The time needed to write, prepare and go to press has been considerably reduced, with many of the previous prepress transactions now compressed into the space of a computer screen.

The ability of the computer to deliver high quality, almost instantaneous product came about with the development of software to bring together the various entities that compose the graphics (figure 16–6). Today's prepress needs only produce

Figure 16–5. Working on graphic computers at Technopak in Tver, Russia with some of the graphics designed.

digital files that cap-ture all the elements of the concept and the design, in a format that is usable by the printer. The digital workflow eliminates many steps and the vagaries of hand assembly found in earlier traditional process. Changes can be made with minimal upset of the original design and copy. Color separation can be done by computer for direct transmission to the imagesetter or platemaker.

Among the major categories of software available on the market, developed specifically for graphic design and prepress activities, are products that provide for:

- Electronic design of graphics or packaging,

- Drawing programs to create shapes and images,

- Word processing programs,

Barco display at Print 2001 demonstrating the broad scope of software available for computer graphics for commercial and package printing.

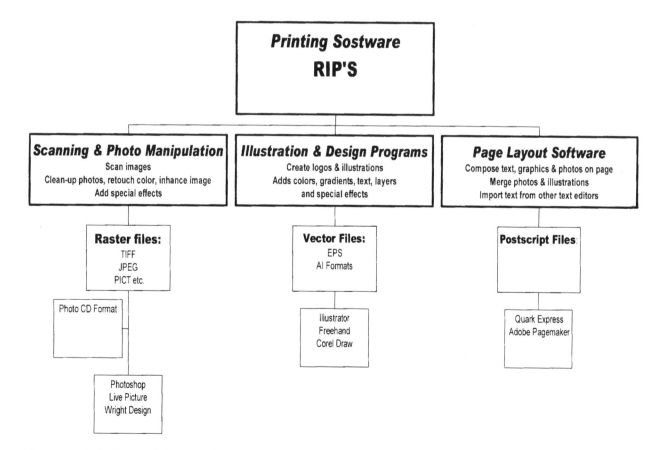

Figure 16–6. Types of front-end software.
Courtesy of Tom Cernera, Graphix Press.

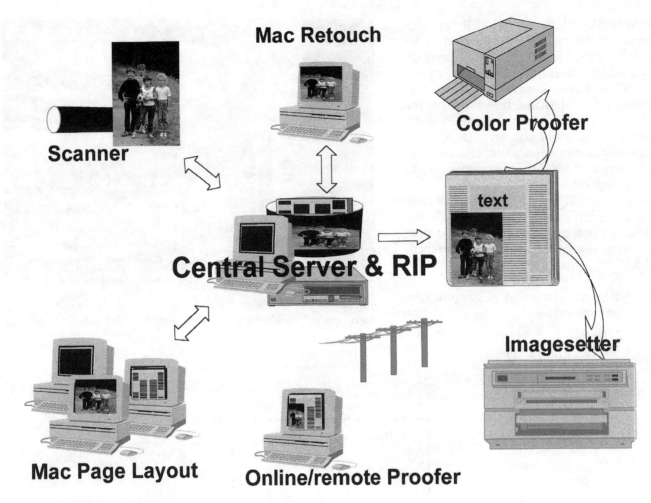

Figure 16–7. Flow chart with digital technology.
Courtesy of Tom Cernera, Graphix Press.

- Proofreading systems,
- Electronic page layout,
- Scanning,
- Computer illustration, and
- Preflight programs to check incoming disks for accuracy of design, copy and fonts on file.

Designs can be initiated and saved on disk, brought forward to the stage of a mechanical using the same file as a starting point, and then modified to make changes wanted by the customer or corrections found on examination. Modifications on repeat jobs can be accomplished by pulling up the file from the disk to the monitor, using the mouse and keyboard to do the work. (See figure 16–7.)

The use of chemicals to produce an end result has diminished significantly as electronic impulses, imagesetting and platemaking technologies have paralleled the development of the computer.

Darkroom chemistry can be eliminated. Technological developments in prepress operations have proven to be critical contributors to the safekeeping of the ecology and health of workers and the public.

Electronic Prepress Production

The transition from manual to computer prepress benefits the printer in many ways. The four major identifiable operational benefits come from:

1. A reduction in production costs,

2. A substantial decrease in production time,

3. Quick verification and revision of copy, and

4. Superior security and supervision of information.

Of equal consequence in the total picture is the reduction of exposure, and the ensuing cost, to hazardous chemicals and wastes, adding to both the health and welfare of the workers and a reduction in the release of pollutants to the neighboring environment. The various process steps and chemistry required in the mostly manual systems that predated the introduction of the computer represented industrial activities that were heavy consumers of disposable substances. The introduction of electronic communication has changed all that.

Making Plates a Safer Way

While the design and darkroom operations are very similar for all printing processes, the materials and processing required to produce image carriers varies from process to process. In virtually every printing process progress has been made in altering the materials, the process and the chemistry at the same time as the quality and repeatability of the graphic images have been improved. Since the major printing processes vary significantly, it is appropriate to discuss each in light of its own history. As a broad statement, it is safe to say that processing today is far safer and more environmentally responsible than it was as little as five or 10 years ago.

Lithographic Platemaking, Then and Now

The lithographic plate has a base material and an emulsion that is light sensitive to serve as the coating that becomes the image area of the plate. The base material may be metal, plastic or paper (figure 16–8). The plate is exposed to light through the negative or from a paper positive taken from the form prepared by the strippers. This is normally done in a vacuum frame to assure a tight fit between negative and plate. The exposed plate will consist of two areas—the image area, which will transfer ink to the substrate, and the non-image area—which accepts water and

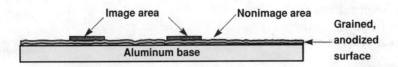

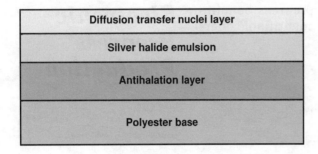

Figure 16–8. Cross-section of lithographic plate.

Source: Nelson R. Eldred, *Chemistry for the Graphic Arts*, Third edition, GATF Press, Pittsburgh, p 145.

repels the ink. Variations in the contact between the negative and the plate can lead to distortions in the transfer of the image and ultimately the ink.

There are many variations in the chemistry of lithographic plates. The most frequently used plates are pre-sensitized, with a number of coating materials employed, based on end use. The most common emulsions are bichromated coatings and photopolymers. Plate exposure can be made in both positive and negative formats. Other coatings come into play for very specific applications, such as silver halides for camera exposed plates.

Processing can be done manually or in an automatic processor, using chemistry that will remove the emulsion from those areas that will not print. Coatings used for lithographic plates are soluble in either oil-based solvents or water. After exposure, the negative-working plates are developed and the unexposed coating is removed from the base plate using an appropriate liquid. Positive plate coatings are insoluble in the unexposed areas. Aqueous developers will frequently contain a corrosive substance, such as sodium hydroxide or potassium hydroxide, to facilitate the removal of the emulsion in appropriate areas. Photo-processed plates will release silver compounds into the wash water.

The computer can and does change the manner in which plates are made. Directly driven by the computer memory, impulses will activate a laser or heat source to expose the plate and prepare it for removal of all unwanted, unprintable surface. Planned and operated properly, computer-driven lasers can etch out the unwanted parts of the plates. (See figure 16–9.) At this time there is still need to use chemicals to process negatives or positives as the means of developing the plates. With the move to more water-based processing chemistry for platemaking, there has been a definite reduction and, in many instances, elimination of pollutants in the workplace and those exiting to the environment.

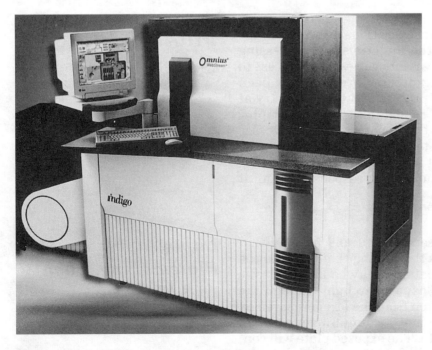

Figure 16–9. Indigo Omnius web digital press.

Courtesy of Indigo.

Where the computer will make a big difference is in direct-to-press technology. The ability to move a graphic image from the computer directly to an image-setter (figure 16–10) eliminates darkroom chemistry. Going directly to a cylinder on the press eliminates both darkroom and platemaking chemicals in the process. Introduced in the mid 1990s, direct-to-press has gained momentum in the short-run market and is moving into longer run markets. Improvements in printing presses and the imaging process have demonstrated that better quality and longer run capability are within the scope of this technology. With computer-driven prepress and platemaking in place, gone are all chemicals employed to generate the negatives and then develop a plate. The cutting edge technology has not only provided the printer with a profitmaker, but has eliminated all of the hazardous chemicals that would previously have been present in his facility.

Figure 16–10. Agfa imagesetter at Prestige Corporate Printing, Brooklyn, NY.

The development of more effective image carriers has enabled flexography to leap into a high quality future from its meager beginnings. Within a short time span, flexography has moved from a "rubber stamp," mediocre quality process to a level that is qualitatively competitive with gravure and lithography. This change has been fueled by improvements in plate materials and processing technology. Flexography started with a molded rubber plate and has moved through a series of developments with photopolymer and rubber plates, including direct-to-plate using laser technology.

Flexographic Image Carriers

The earlier rubber plates created a number of unfavorable environmental impacts, including both hazardous and solid wastes. The process started with the typical design and darkroom work, followed by the making of a metal engraving in an acid etch bath. The engraving would be used to make a matrix, which in turn would be used to mold the plate. The mold and plate processes involved vulcanizing molding presses that utilized heat and pressure to produce the relief images (figure 16–11). Aside from the broad tolerances needed to accommodate the variations in the plates due to the multiple steps and the shrinkage and stretch of the rubber plate, this process had a direct impact on the environment, resulting from the acid bath and the metals removed from the engraving bases as the copy was etched into the surface.

Photopolymers appeared in the early 1960s, and became commercial in the 1970s, as an alternative to rubber plates. Economics and practicality were barriers for wider web and sheet printers in the early days. Photopolymer plates were readily accepted by narrow web tag and label printers, who were, at that time, just getting started as flexographic printers.

Figure 16–11. Vulcanizer uses heat and pressure to make moulds from engravings and rubber plates from the moulds for flexographic printing.

Courtesy of Anderson & Vreeland, Inc.

Figure 16–12. Water washable photopolymer exposure and processing equipment.

Courtesy of Anderson & Vreeland, Inc.

The photopolymer plate starts with a master sheet or liquid that is a monomer (which may appear to be a solid but in reality is a liquid), that is exposed to light through a negative. The exposed portion reacts to form the polymer; the unexposed monomer is then washed away. The relief image that remains is the image carrier. The wash-out liquid used in the early days was perchloroethane, a carcinogen and ozone-depleting chemical. The process had many open areas from which evaporation could take place (figure 16–12.). In this process, used plates and plate wastes have to be boxed and shipped as hazardous wastes. The impact on health and the environment was recognized and solutions sought.

With the opportunity to improve graphic quality, and as photopolymer technology provided other advantages, the photopolymer plates became more extensively used in the wider web equipment as well as with narrow presses. Safer solvents were tried, ranging from extractions from citric fruits to other chlorinated, less hazardous hydrocarbon solvents. Many printers resorted to having spent solvent distilled and recovered on-site or off-site to minimize purchases and hazardous wastes. Equipment was developed to reduce fugitive emissions and to move the spent solvents directly into solvent recovery systems for reuse in the process. With safer solvents, solid wastes could go directly to public waste incinerators or landfills. The flexographic printing plate became more environmentally acceptable.

Photopolymers also provided a means of salvaging the rubber plate. Not all ink and coating transfers are as effective with photopolymer as with rubber. The release characteristics are different, as is the ability to pull ink off the anilox roll for transfer to the plate. The availability of harder (durometer) photopolymers provided printers with a replacement for the engraving and chemical process used for engraving. The new process could expose and develop the hard photopolymer to serve as master for molding rubber plates. The master is processed in the same manner as the photopolymer plate. Releases of corrosive liquid acid waste and particles of metals from the engraving could be avoided. The solid waste created, when engravings are rejected or outdated, could be eliminated. (See figure 16–13.)

The introduction of the computer has also had its effect on flexography. Direct-to-plate technology first appeared in the laser engraving of rubber plates. It has been adapted for continuous printing rollers, and is now marketable for the flat photopolymer plate user. With direct-imaged printing plates, the digital image in the graphics computer is exposed directly to a masking material that is a basic part of the print surface on the monomer. The laser evaporates the monomer in the unexposed areas, leaving the exposed areas as the relief image for transfer of the graphics. The plate is then processed by conventional chemistry. Quality of product improves as the laser engraved image has better definition and restricts ink transfer to the maximum limits of high quality printing. The ability to process plates without the need for some of the more hazardous materials resolves the various issues

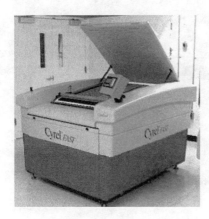

Cyrel First thermal photopolymer platemaking equipment.

Courtesy of Dupont Imaging Technologies.

associated with the more traditional chemistry used in the making of flexographic image carriers. The direct-imaged plate eliminates the photoprocessing chemicals, but retains the need to use wash-out solvents.

DuPont Imaging Technologies has introduced the latest development in a high quality, environmentally responsible photopolymer platemaking system with the launch of its thermal platemaking system. Thermal technology has added a new dimension to clean platemaking. The proprietary monomer has a unique formulation that can be heat-processed. With a strictly controlled heat source and contact pressure from a treated developer roll, the unexposed portions of the plate are removed, leaving the relief image for flexographic printing. Once the plate is "developed," it is ready for post-exposure and finishing, just as in processing of conventional solvent-processed plates. The system is completely dry and eliminates the need for any washout solution—solvent or water, and the resulting waste streams.

- Outstanding thickness uniformity — dry processing eliminates plate swell completely. Provides faster make-ready and excellent print quality.

- Excellent ink transfer for uniform printing of images and solids on tag and label, envelopes, business forms and folding carton.

- Ozone-resistant.

- Good flexibility.

- Aqueous, UV and solvent ink compatibility.

Shore Hardness

	Shore A
.045 mils/1.14mm	75
.067 mils/1.70mm	67

Image Reproduction

Halftone	2-95%	120-line screen/inch
		48-line screen/cm
Isolated Dots	.01 inch in diameter	
	.25 millimeter	
Fine Lines	.007 inches in width	
	.17 millimeters	
Relief Depth	.020-.030 inches recommended	
	0.5-0.8 millimeters	
Ink Compatibility	Aqueous, UV and solvent	

Figure 16–13. Description of Cyrel "FAST."
Courtesy of Dupont Imaging Technologies.

Gravure Cylinders

Gravure graphics are transferred from an image that is engraved in a cylinder the width of the press and the circumference of the printing length of the product. Environmental considerations in the preparation of gravure cylinders are as important as the etching of the graphics.

A gravure roller is made by depositing a layer of copper on a steel cylinder, and engraving the image into the copper coating. A chromium layer is then plated onto the copper skin. Copper is a soft substance, easily damaged; the chromium plating provides a hard shield to protect the copper image as the doctor blade cleans ink off the roller. At the end of an order or the use of the particular set of graphics, the chromium skin can be removed and the copper replated for reuse. The de-chroming process adds to environmental concerns about traditional gravure cylinder use, releasing process water waste with metal content that is regulated in pretreatment standards. (See figure 16–14.)

The gravure roller engraving process bears many of the environmental concerns of any plating operation. Air, water and hazardous waste issues abound from the chemistry, the waste by-products and the general exposure of pollutants to the environment.

The computer has long played a role in the transfer of graphics to the gravure roller. The chemical process for etching an image uses a ferric chloride solution, either directly or with a carbon tissue transfer of the image to be printed. The gelatin layer on the carbon tissue is exposed to the negative and then transferred to the roller surface. The etching liquid then removes the exposed portions and etches cells into the copper at depths that vary with the amount of ink to be transferred.

Figure 16–14. Laser engraving of cylinder for gravure or flexographic anilox roller.

Courtesy of Pamarco Incorporated.

Photographic photopolymer films were introduced in the 1950s, replacing the carbon tissue transfer method. The photopolymer films enabled direct transfer of the images to the roller. This development improved the quality of the engraving. More recently, laser engraving of the film has facilitated the more precise transfer of graphics to the roller.

A competing technology for cutting the image into the gravure roller is electronic engraving. It is an electromechanical process that takes places on equipment similar to a lathe. A diamond stylus creates the cells, driven by a scanning cylinder that reads the copy mounted on the scanner cylinder. Analog signals are transformed to digital signals for use in the image processor. A multitude of engraving heads can be working simultaneously to create the etched roller. The computer enters this process, feeding digital data to the engraving heads directly from disks. The computer thus eliminates the need to generate film positives, and the accompanying chemistry and hazardous waste streams.

The chemical process for etching the rollers has many advantages. It is a quick process, taking minutes to engrave the cells into the metal surface. It offers a wider variety of cell configurations than electromechanical systems. Future developments with new roller coatings may place the computer at an advantage to the chemical process; the benefits of laser engraving could do for gravure what it has done for the flexographic anilox roll process, with the elimination of the plating baths and the potential hazards from plating chemistry.

Screen and Digital Printing

Traditional screen printing employs a woven fabric screen which is stretched tightly on a frame. A stencil or sensitized emulsion is placed on the screen and the image is developed by blocking out those portions that are not to be printed, enabling the unblocked areas to allow ink to pass through onto the substrate. The ink is then placed in the frame and drawn across the screen by means of a squeegee. The ink passes through the openings and is deposited as a replication of the design image. There are many types of screens and stencils or emulsions that can be used to produce a printable image, but the various concepts are basically the same. (See figure 16–15.)

In those cases where the graphics are transferred by photographic exposure, typical photoprocessing chemistry is required, with resulting waste streams. A liquid light-sensitive coating is applied to the screen. The negative is placed in contact with the coating and exposed to light. When the non-image area is exposed, it hardens. The unexposed image area of emulsion is then washed away (developed), leaving the hardened non-image area to act as the stencil.

The environmental impact comes not so much from making the screen, but from the process of cleaning it for reuse of the graphics on subsequent jobs, or the removal of the stencil from the screen for reuse of the screen for other jobs. A considerable volume of solvent cleaners can be used and may have components that are very hazardous in nature. The ability to control the amounts of the screen cleaning fluids can be addressed when the image is to be completely removed from the screen. High-pressure air and water can be used to literally blast the stencil or film from the screen. Reuse of the screen with its graphics employs a more subtle approach, usually resolved by hand cleaning with wipers soaked in solvent.

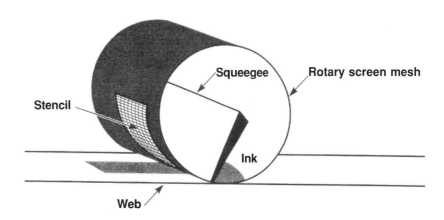

Figure 16–15. Rotary screen printing.

Source: Nelson Eldred, *Chemistry for the Graphic Arts*, Third edition, GATF Press, Pittsburgh, p 213.

Figure 16–16. Wide format digital printer at Nomad Worldwide LLC, in Jersey City, NJ, replaces large screen printers.

Digital technology has entered this field in two modes. One is to transfer the images from the computer to the screen film emulsion. The second is as a substitute printing process for jobs that would have traditionally been done using screens. The latter has replaced screen printing and the chemistry that screen printing required.

Large format digital printers capable of printing materials as wide as 16 feet, using ink jet technology, have captured a considerable part of the market for billboards and stage backdrops, posters and similar end uses. One need only look at the huge billboards and smaller hanging street signs to see evidence of the impact digital printing has had. The versatility in printing stage backdrops for shows in the theatre is evidence of the move to wide format digital printing (figure 16–16). The market for fine art prints, which thrived on the serigraph process (another term for screen printing), is now being served by narrower digital wide-format printers. With time, other screen applications will succumb to the technical and economic advantages of digital technology, as well as enabling printers to meet environmental requirements that currently identify screen printers as potentially hazardous emitters of VOC and HAP chemicals.

The computer has begun to play a key role in specific areas that were traditionally done by screen printing. Wide-format digital printers are using ink jet and ion deposition technology to print the large posters and banners that were in the mainstream of screen printing. The need to make stencils has been replaced by computer-driven ink engines that move across a substrate, depositing the graphics as they go (figure 16–17). Ink usage is minimized and cleaning is almost eliminated, at least in comparison with the volume of solvents required when using screens. The ability to use the computer and eliminate steps in the process, as well as to minimize environmental exposure, can be a driving force in adapting digital

Figure 16–17. Computer to large format ink jet printer demonstrated by AB Dick at Print 2001.

printing to some of the automatic and semiautomatic screen printing lines now in production. With direct-to-press engineering taking place in lithography, it is not beyond reason to expect similar advancements to be made in the screen printing industry.

Labels and Tags

A market segment that can benefit greatly from the introduction of digital technology and the elimination of prepress chemistry is the label printer. Not only can the printer forego the need to make negatives; he can eliminate the need to make any form of plate. Printing technology directly from the computer has been accompanied by similar engineering to include reformatting of the diecutting operation as the patterns change. Complete label printing and converting lines are in the field and producing product (figure 16–18).

An advantage that comes with the digital printing of labels and narrow webs on any substrate is the added value of printing distinct images on every label in the order. By having unique features, such as bar codes or identification codes, producers of food products and pharmaceuticals can clearly identify each and every package. Recalls of questionable packaged product quality can be reduced from the millions, that are normal, to a much more limited number. Consider the overall impact on the environment if such wastes can be limited and public safety and health improved.

Digital efforts have to be closely monitored in label printing. The tremendous advantage has to be maintained by intensive quality management to assure that the digital image conveyed to the press is always correct. There is no room for error in this application.

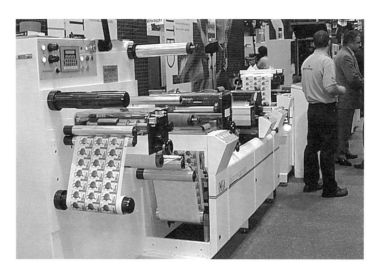

Figure 16–18. Label printing with digital input provides a new dimension to added value. For markets with risks due to product failure, digital labels can provide a safety zone by bar-coding each label with its own distinctive code. Recalls of pharmaceuticals and food products can be limited to small quantities, compared to the millions that are prevalent at this time.

Digital: A Means, Not an End

The concept of direct feed from a computer into which information is placed to manufacture a finished product is most attractive to the printer. What better way to serve a customer well than by eliminating many of the steps that have placed barriers in the way of productivity and product quality? The computer can be a tremendous tool in attaining that goal, but only if the person doing the planning and implementation gives due respect to the talents and judgments that are necessary. (See figure 16–16.)

One precaution to be observed involves the need for the computer to be programmed with due recognition of the capabilities and limitations of the equipment for which it is preparing image carriers. The vast and almost infinite potential characteristics of the computer may design graphics that are too complex, registration too fine, color renditions too subtle for the typical press to print. Realistic specifications and parameters must be a part of the process. Review of design, including proofreading, is essential. Direct-to-plate or to press allows little margin for error. Digital is the future, but mishandled it can lead to disaster. There can be no environmental benefits if the results are waste.

CHAPTER **17**

Process Water Waste: Protecting Our Drinking Supply

The pressure to maintain the quality of water has been with civilization since man learned to live in communities. That is not to say that man has always acted responsibly for his own best interests. It does confirm the history of human contamination of its drinking resources and the continuing battle to find the means to satisfy the needs of a growing population and the sustenance of the food chain that is dependent on a source of potable water. History has recorded all too many periods tainted by plagues, disease and hunger, all stemming from pollution or lack of adequate pure water. Many states and localities have passed laws and regulations to protect water resources, commencing in the earliest days of the establishment of reservoir systems for major cities.

The current system of standards and controls came onto the scene with the passage by Congress of the Clean Water Act in 1972. This law codified many of the standards already enacted by a number of the states. The law called for the restoration and maintenance of the chemical, physical and biological integrity of the nation's water. The law also established a national permitting system for point sources, called the National Pollutant Discharge Elimination System (NPDES). States adopted the permit provision in their own local legislation. Areas which are serviced by septic tanks or which allow discharges directly to streams, rivers or lakes, are very sensitive to the discharge of any pollutants to the water which not only come back through the water tap, but adversely affect plants, fish and animals that provide us with food and drink.

Water resources require care to prevent pollutants from entering and damaging vital organs of human, animal and plant life.

Subsequent regulations were enacted to provide for the treatment of process water that was being discharged to publicly owned treatment works (POTW), commonly known as sewer system treatment facilities. To reduce the amount of pollutants entering the POTW and, in any number of cases, passing through into the drinking supply as treated water, the federal and state governments added pretreatment standards for specific industrial processes. These standards limit the amount of specific pollutants that may enter the POTW. Sewer discharge permits for process water place limits on each pollutant or category of pollutants entering the treatment facility. Some standards are purposely established at very low levels to prevent specific pollutants from contaminating the water; others are to prevent contaminants, that may prevent the POTW from performing its job properly, from flowing into the system. (See figure 17–1.)

What Concerns Affect Printers?

Water has been a contributor to printing technologies from the inception of the photographic image process and the use of the developer/fixer technology for prepress activities, to the fountain solution for offset lithography, to the development of waterborne inks and coatings in recent years for flexography, gravure and screen printing.

Passage of the CONEG (Conference of North East Governors) regulations to restrict the use of the heavy metals in inks and coatings was instrumental in reducing sharply the amount of heavy metals that traditionally entered the printing processes in the form of colorants and pigments. A key objective was the elimination lead chromates, which gave the industry its rich reds, yellows and oranges. However, other metals, not defined as heavy metals, continue to play a significant role in the pigments that allow our eyes to see greens, blues, and other less esoteric colors. Some metal salts are by-products of the metals that are intrinsic to the pigment-making process. Many other metals, although not classified as "heavy metals," have also been targeted by public officials and environmental advocacy groups.

Photographic images are based on the exposure of silver halides to light and then developed to leave a silver image on the negative film or positive print paper. The silver and silver halides

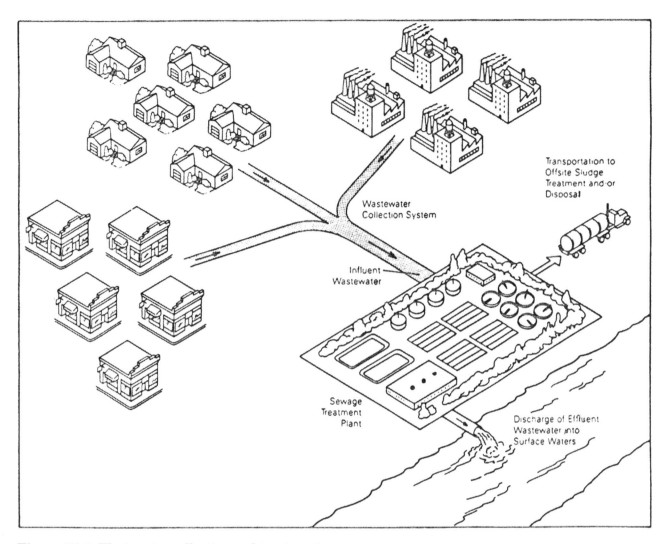

Figure 17–1. Wastewater collection and treatment.

Source: United States Environmental Protection Agency, *Environmental Regulations and Technology, The National Pretreatment Program*, EPA/625/10-86/006, July 1986.

that are removed from the films and discharged from the processors can exceed pollutant standards for metallic silver. Waterborne inks and coatings may contain pigments that have metals and compounds that can pass elevated amounts of copper, zinc, barium and other undesirable materials to the water system. Older inks that have lost a portion of their liquid may concentrate the amount of the metals found in the remaining sludge. Cleaning of press parts with water can generate a collection of solids that may take very insignificant volumes of metal components and concentrate the remnants into a more viable and objectionable sludge.

Of lesser consequence in normal practice, but ever threatening from its potential as an unintentional release in the form of a spill, are the many solvents and inks that could enter the water stream directly by accident. Spill prevention is a very critical requirement for just about every printer, large and small. Large or small spills can impact on the environment of the workplace and the area just beyond the walls of the facility.

Standards for Pretreatment

Clean water standards are very specific and call for very clear limits on a number of general categories of pollutants, as well as for individual chemicals. These are repeated in the standards that are promulgated for any treated water re-entering the main stream through a sewer system or directly into surface waters.

Some processes are very strictly regulated and there are directives that address them specifically. One such related process is photoprocessing. The process-specific regulations are termed "categorical." Printing is not addressed by a categorical standard. However, the silver halide regulations, which are a critical component of the photoprocessing process, do have a direct impact on prepress operations.

Among the pollutants addressed in the general standards for pretreatment of water are:

- BOD—limits on chemicals that affect Biological Oxygen Demand,

- COD—limits on chemicals that affect Chemical Oxygen Demand,

- Grease (oil),

- Flammable hydrocarbon solvents,

- Color,

- Solids,

- pH (Is a solution too acidic or too alkaline?),

- Turbidity,

- Metals:
    Barium
    Chromium
    Copper
    Iron
    Lead
    Manganese
    Silver
    Zinc

- Other chemicals:
    Chlorides
    Fluorides
    Nitrates
    Sodium
    Sulfates

Periodic sampling of the outgoing water wastes, either by the printer or the government, will determine whether a facility is in compliance. The rules and standards are fairly clear cut, leaving little room for deviation, variances or misinterpretations. In some jurisdictions, periodic self-monitoring reports are required to substantiate compliance. In addition to monitoring the water discharges, surveillance of the disposal of hazardous wastes may be an intrinsic element of self-preservation for the printer.

Of major concern to most printers is the currently inescapable disposal of the silver halides that are a given characteristic of the photographic process (figure 17–2). Rather than specifying a standard for the silver content of a facility's waste water, the regulatory agencies have developed a plan to effectively reduce pollution by employing current recovery technology and periodic self-monitoring. This approach is less burdensome for smaller size facilities, and eases testing and reporting procedures that would accompany a formal permit.

Best Management Practices (BMP) are typically schedules of activities, prohibitions, management and maintenance procedures that are implemented to reduce the discharge of pollutants to sewer systems. To restrict the discharge of silver, BMPs are regulated in proportion to the size of the facility as determined by the amount of water discharged on a daily basis to the sewer system by the processing machinery. It is anticipated that most graphic arts firms will fall into the following categories, which will mandate 90 percent collection of the silver. Some of the larger firms may fall into the more stringent categories. Larger users of water, and thereby larger dischargers of wastewater, will have more stringent requirements for control and monitoring than smaller users of water. The efficiency with which the control equipment removes silver from the wastewater increases with the volume discharged.

Best Management Practices— Silver Halides

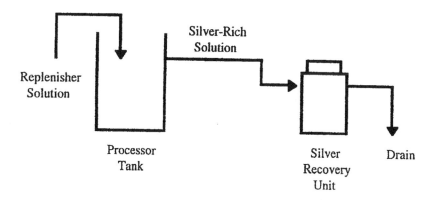

Figure 17–2. Flow-through system using electrolytic treatment unit common in small print shops.

Source: New York City Department of Environmental Protection, New York City Best Management Practices *Workbook*, November 1995, p 48.

Components of a Silver BMP

The BMP consists of six major activities:

1. Install appropriate silver reclamation/water treatment systems. The two smaller categories, from 0 to 999 gallons per day, must meet a standard of 90 percent recovery of silver by the silver recovery system. Discharges in excess of 1,000 gallons per day must install systems which will recover at least 95 percent of the silver discharged.

2. Test for the silver concentrate from the solution prior to entry to the treatment equipment and the effluent discharged to the sewer. This can be done with relatively simple test strips or kits for small facilities, or lab testing services by the larger firms. The testing must be done at least once a month, on what would be an average day. The simplest test uses specially treated strips of paper. Immersion of the paper into the solution will result in varying shades of color, which identify the concentration of silver. The most accurate method, required for larger dischargers, would be to use the services of an independent laboratory.

3. Measure the daily quantities of silver halide process waste water that are discharged to the public sewer. This must be done individually for each system operating within the facility. If you have three film processors, and each has its own silver recovery filter, then the measurement has to be made for each unit. This measurement can take place on a day that is considered representative during the month.

4. Maintain written records of the pretreatment technology.

5. Maintain written records of the date that new pretreatment technology is brought into service.

6. Keep records of all measurements and testing required by the regulations.

As the volume of the discharges increases, so too does the intricacy and magnitude of the requirements. Key elements that will make the BMP work well are engendered in the training of personnel, the housekeeping and maintenance of the operation, and the support of management.

What Methods Are Available to Reclaim Silver?

There are three popular methods for recovering silver from silver halide laden wastewater in print shops. Recovering the silver is good business; reclaimed silver can add to profits or reduce the cost of treatment.

1. **Metallic Replacement:** This method involves a chemical reaction during which the silver in the solution is replaced by the iron in the filter. The metals change places, with the silver becoming a sludge in the filter cartridge. To engage the two

chemicals in a reaction, the wastewater solution is passed through a container packed with steel wool. This method is found in many pre-press and print shops. The filter is placed between the processing equipment and the discharge pipe to the sewer system. The cost of such systems is low. Frequently, two or more filter cartridges may be placed in line to improve the efficiency of silver removal. The silver is collected as a sludge, which must then be treated to extract the usable metal (figure 17–3).

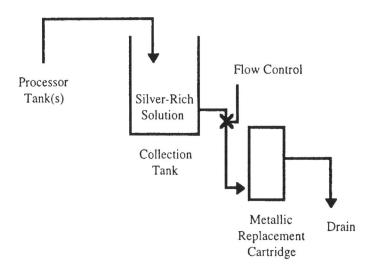

Figure 17–3. Metallic replacement treatment units, cartridge system with gravity flow.

Source: New York City Department of Environmental Protection, New York City Best Management Practices *Workbook*, November 1995, p 49.

2. **Electrolytic Silver Recovery:** In this method, the silver-laden solution passes between two electrodes with a controlled current. The silver is plated on the cathode in a form that is almost pure metal. The most obvious advantage of this method is the purity and ease of removal of the silver from the cathode. The electrolytic recovery method is more expensive to purchase and has a higher operating cost than the metallic replacement method, but may be cost effective because of the higher purity of the salvaged silver. (See figure 17–4.)

3. **Coupling the two methods for the most effective silver recovery system:** Metallic replacement and electrolytic recovery units are placed in line to obtain a high efficiency recovery rate. The electrolytic unit removes a high percentage of silver; the replacement filter removes the remainder.

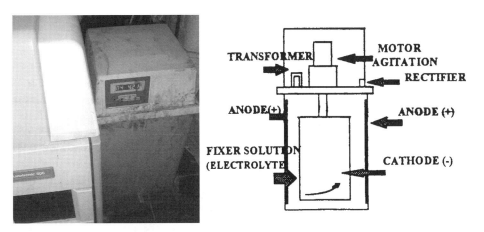

Figure 17–4. Elements common to all electrolytic units, similar to unit connected to film processor at R.S. Rosenbaum in New York City.

Source: New York City Department of Environmental Protection, New York City Best Management Practices *Workbook*, November 1995, p 61.

No Sewers: Have Septic Tank

In regions of the country where there are no sewer systems, the most likely places into which water wastes are discharged are underground tanks or natural bodies of water such as streams, rivers or lakes. Contaminated wastewater should not be discharged directly into the ground, nearby bodies of water, or underground cesspools or septic tanks. In water-sensitive regions, these practices would be contrary to regulations. Discharging to septic tanks, cesspools or to natural bodies of water is virtually forbidden in most localities.

The only solution for facilities that do not empty into sewer systems is to collect the wastes in storage tanks or drums. The wastes can then be carted away as either a hazardous waste or non-regulated non-hazardous waste, as appropriate for offsite treatment (figure 17–5).

Figure 17–5. Drum of water waste awaiting shipment off site for treatment.

Periodic testing will confirm whether the process water waste is hazardous or can be handled as a non-hazardous waste. This distinction is important from a regulatory perspective as well as cost. One cannot simply state that a waste is not hazardous. Documentation in the form of laboratory tests must confirm the composition of the waste and quantify its ingredients. The cost of transporting and disposing of the waste will be determined in part by the classification of the waste and the liability assumed by the Transportation, Storage and Disposal (TS&D) facility.

Traditional Methods of On-site Wastewater Treatment

Water treatment that will return clean water to the drinking water supply requires a process that will eliminate all undesirable pollutants from the waste stream. The expectation of the public and government is a quality treated water that in many cases may exceed that of the water fresh from the tap. Such systems may prove to be economic burdens to the average business. Reusing the treated water internally by means of a recirculating system, or manually in its raw state as a vehicle for other purposes, can allow for alternatives for which the quality of the water is not critical. Reuse of the water can provide economic alternatives that are beneficial to the operation of the facility.

Selecting an appropriate system involves evaluating the composition of the waste against the quality of the end-product clean water and waste by-products. The technical means of accomplishing the treatment must be evaluated in terms of the cost of

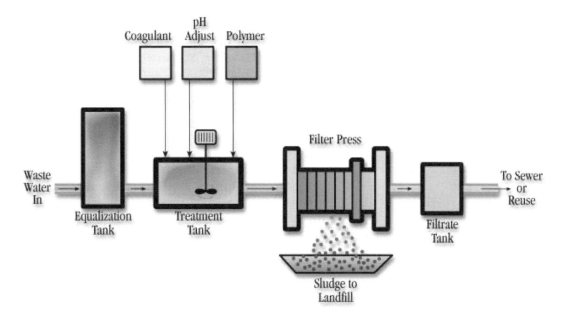

Figure 17–6. Schematic of water treatment system used in flexographic or lithographic printing plants.

Courtesy of Beckart Environmental, Inc.

installing and operating the treatment system, including the disposition of any wastes.

Among the most practical methods for processing production water waste streams are:*

1. **Chemical splitting** in continuous or batch process. After adjustment of the pH, the solids (pigments and resins) are precipitated via flocculation into an encapsulated sludge. The sludge is then separated from the water through paper filtration for dewatering and easy disposal. A filter press further removes water

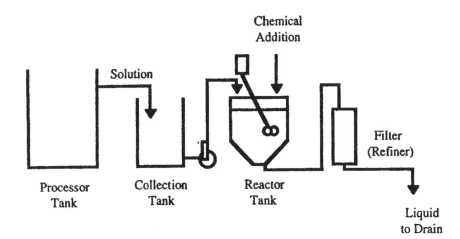

Figure 17–7. Flow of waste process water to drain using precipitation and filter press to remove contaminants.

Source: New York City Department of Environmental Protection, New York City Best Management Practices *Workbook*, November 1995, p 51.

and the "cake" is disposed of. Typically, a band filter can process 0.1 to 2 cubic meters per day, while a chamber filter press can process 0.5 to 20 cubic meters per day (figures 17–6 and 17–7).

*Monteleone, Doreen Ph.D., "How To Dispose of Aqueous Wastes From Flexographic Printing Process," *Printing News* with permission of PNEAC, Oct. 2, 2000, pp 16–17.

2. **Continuous effluent treatment.** A process similar to chemical splitting described above, continuous effluent treatment systems are designed to handle wastewater flows from 15 to 200 cubic meters per day.

3. **Microfiltration, ultrafiltration, nanofiltration and reverse osmosis.** These processes work like kidneys in mammals. By passing wastewater through organic and inorganic membranes, 0.1 to 5000 liters per hour can be processed. The processes basically take water (or anything else with the same or smaller molecular weight) out of the process solution. Post-membrane carbon filters remove ammonia. There are no secondary disposal costs of the spent membranes with this type of filtration. The clean water can be used in other areas (e.g., as the liquid part of an adhesive in corrugated box or envelope manufacturing).

   Although these process terms are sometimes used interchangeably, they differ in membrane size. Microfiltration (0.7 to 2.0 micrometers) separates out paint pigment and bacteria; ultrafiltration (0.007 to 0.2 micrometers) will remove carbon black and viruses); nanofiltration (0.0009 to 0.009 micrometers) will remove sugar and synthetic dyes), and reverse osmosis (0.00009 to 0.002 micrometers) will remove aqueous salt and metal ions.

4. **Biologically-absorptive treatment** using activated brown carbon; recycling with part or full stream desalination and reactivation of the carbon (mixed slope-reactors, flotation, filtration, softening, reverse osmosis, revolving cylindrical furnace).

5. **Oxidation technology** through modular systems, offering oxidation, ozone/UV oxidation, UV/H_2O_2 oxidation.

A sixth technology that has been introduced to printers is the use of bioremediation. Bacteria are maintained in a biomass through which the contaminated water must pass. The microorganisms digest the pollutants and cleanse the water. The key to success has been the tailoring of the bacteria to the type of pollutant that is prevalent in the press and prepress waste streams. Conditions must be maintained to provide an adequate environment for the microorganisms to live. When units are idle, provision must be made to "feed" the biomass or the bacteria will die. (figure 17–8.)

The quality and quantity of wastewater to be treated are generally the determining criteria for choosing which method is best for a particular production scenario. For nearly all printers generating wastewater, chemical splitting is the least expensive short- and long-term solution for reducing or eliminating wastewater problems. The step up from a band filter process to filter press process is based on consideration of the quantity and quality of wastewater. The resulting quality of treated water will have to conform to local discharge limits and any plans by the printer to reuse the treated water in his process.

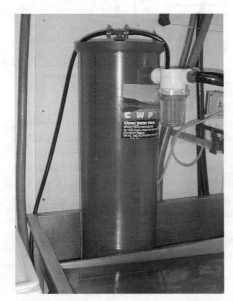

Figure 17–8. SRE Inc. bioremediation system treats photographic process waste water with bacteria to destroy hazardous components.

Courtesy of SRE Inc.

While many printers elect to process only their wastewater, and handle waste ink, coatings and adhesives disposal as a separate component of waste management, some opt to add waste inks, coatings and adhesives to their wastewater. This will increase the volume of suspended solids, frequently forming an emulsion in the waste stream, requiring a more effective and costly way to process the sludge resulting from the chemical treatment. In the end, more wastewater may need to be processed.

Many companies are being offered simple filtration as a means of handling their printing, coating and adhesive wastewaters and remove solids and some coloration. The following should be understood: Most wastewaters resulting from printing, coating and finishing operations create an emulsion through the addition of the liquid inks, coatings, adhesives and cleaning solutions. Processing this wastewater effectively can only be accomplished by first breaking the emulsion through chemical splitting, then physically filtering the resulting material.

Different chemistries are available for breaking this emulsion; all will accomplish the following:*

1. **Neutralization.** Adjustment of pH level back to neutral range,

2. **Absorption.** Absorbing selected chemicals and suspended solids from the water,

3. **Coagulation.** Continued chemical additions resulting in flocculants—filterable material,

4. **Encapsulation.** Permanent entrapment of selected chemicals in solid form suitable for disposal in a non-hazardous industrial landfill,

5. **Physical filtration.** Through band filter or filter press operation.

Most commercially available splitting agents operate best in a pH range of 6.5 to 9.0. Pretreatment monitoring and adjustment of pH is recommended when wastes are outside that range to achieve more effective performance of the agent. The pH of the discharge water may need to be adjusted prior to discharge to meet effluent limits.

Minimizing Wastewater Output

The use of water is so widespread that it is taken for granted; it is seemingly inexpensive to obtain and use. When the entire cost of its acquisition, use and disposal are fully taken into account, it is often surprising how expensive water can be. By minimizing water use, a facility can reduce the cost of acquiring water, as well as its disposal. Decreasing water usage consists of

---

*Monteleone, Doreen Ph. D., *Printing News* op. cit.

Figure 17–9. Graymills Lift-Kleen tank is specifically designed for handling and cleaning anilox rolls.
Courtesy of Graymills Corporation.

source reduction and recycling. Of the two approaches to waste minimization, source reduction is considered preferable.

Employ cleaning tanks as opposed to using free-running water. Wash tanks can be fitted to run with a caustic solution or detergent, depending on the cleaning activity required. Where the cost of free-running water would mount up quickly, the volume in the tank will place a maximum on the amount that could be used in a given period. Solids and sludge can be removed and pH adjusted when needed. Emptying the tank can be done on a weekly, biweekly or monthly schedule, based on the use and accumulation in the tank (figure 17–9).

Personnel should be trained to minimize use of water on press. This can be accomplished by addressing the following work practices.

1. Drain as much ink as possible into containers at the end of a job. Ink has value and can be reused.

2. Use filters in the system to recover as much usable chemistry as possible. Filters in fountain solution reservoirs can remove paper dust, lint and ink solids to increase the working lifetime of the solution. Flexographic inks can be filtered as they return to the ink reservoirs and their usability can be increased. Filters increase the life cycle of chemicals and minimize the need to be cleaned as frequently.

3. Thoroughly scrape press parts before placing them in a wash tank or when cleaning on press.

4. Decrease waste solids by cleaning ink stations before the ink dries.

5. Use low-flow spray nozzles or plastic spray bottles when cleaning at the press.

On-press cleaning wastes can be reduced by an organized three-phase process:

- **Phase 1:** Most ink, adhesives and press chemistry is removed at the end of a run or shift.

- **Phase 2:** Ink, adhesives and press chemistry remaining, are removed using water previously used in the same color family.

- **Phase 3:** Any remaining ink and other materials are then cleaned using fresh water, which is then used for cleaning in Phase 2.

A key consideration when dealing with water discharges and regulations is to be prepared by knowing exactly what it is that you are discharging. The various regulations and standards enforced by all agencies are virtually all black and white. There are few gray areas. You are either in compliance or out of compliance. Penalties for not being in compliance can be high. The cost of not being in compliance and contaminating the soil or water in your area can add considerable expenditures to clean the area and remove all contaminants from the site.

If water wastes are a by-product of your printing and finishing processes, then laboratory tests of representative samples are essential. The tests will serve to protect the facility if the discharges are within limits. Results of the tests identify problems before the facility gets into an adversarial confrontation with the authorities. The tests also provide the information and the opportunity to correct a situation before trouble starts.

If the answer is not waste reduction, then it will be controls.

When in Doubt Test First

CHAPTER **18**

Chemical Safety in the Pressroom

C hemistry has made our world a better place in which to live. Coincidentally, the very same chemicals that have improved our lives have created hazards in the workplace. While the printed finished product may be deemed safe for the user, the inks, solvents and other components used along the way can pose potential harm to the people working in the pressroom, both when handling and using the materials, some of which are considered hazardous.

The need for controls to safeguard workers was brought to the forefront by environmental incidents that became international disasters. The accidental release of toxic gases in Bhopal, India; the poisoning of the Rhine river by an accidental discharge of chemicals in Switzerland; the fires and explosions in facilities in the United States—all examples of accidents that gave rise to public awareness of the dangers that chemicals pose. They highlighted the need to take action on a federal level to protect both workers and the public.

Responsibility for overseeing the establishment of safeguards in the workplace lies with the government agency known as OSHA—Occupational Safety and Health Administration, an agency within the Department of Labor. OSHA was created in 1970 to assure, insofar as possible, that every worker has safe and healthful working conditions and to preserve the human resources of the nation. The role outlined for the new agency included its responsibility to:

- Encourage employers and employees to reduce workplace hazards and to implement new or improved safety and health programs,

- Provide for research to develop innovative ways of dealing with safety and health conditions,

- Establish separate but dependent responsibilities and rights for employers and employees for the achievement of better health and safety conditions,

- Maintain a reporting and recordkeeping system to monitor job-related injuries and illnesses,

- Establish training programs to increase the number and competence of occupational and health personnel,

- Develop mandatory job safety and health standards and enforce them effectively, and

- Provide for the development of competent state occupational safety and health programs.

OSHA is supported in its efforts by the research activities of the National Institute for Occupational Health and Safety (NIOSH). NIOSH provides technical assistance to OSHA, recommending standards and investigating toxic substances for the purpose of developing criteria for the use of such substances in the workplace.

Inasmuch as OSHA reviews and promulgates regulations and standards for every aspect of the workplace, it would be awesome to present the printer with a total picture of all the regulations that impact on the printing environment. Rather, this chapter will deal only with a number of subjects that involve the use of chemicals and the role of the printer in these limited subjects.

The printer is cautioned to make every effort to research the broad scope of regulations that apply to all manufacturing facilities and be especially alert for those that are very specific to the activities in the printing plant.

The regulations that are delineated in this chapter include:

1. The Hazardous Communication Standard,

2. Process Safety Management (PSM),

3. Personal protective equipment,

4. Respiratory protection, and

5. Access to medical and exposure records.

Safety in the print shop goes hand in hand with good quality and high productivity. Personnel who do their jobs right will do them with knowledge of why things happen and how to make them happen in the right sequences. This should include those working practices and tools that are in place to safeguard them and their fellow workers from injury or exposure to hazardous conditions.

Compliance with the OSHA regulations requires an understanding of the exposures in the plant and the steps that must be taken to conform to the law. The essential ingredients of a program are:

1. Commitment by top management and labor,

2. A plan for hazard anticipation, recognition, evaluation and abatement,

3. Written statement of objectives, policies and procedures; a plan for implementation,

4. Plans for monitoring and auditing the program to evaluate progress and correct deficiencies,

5. An active, regularly scheduled training and education program,

6. An effective recordkeeping system for workplace and employee health and safety records,

7. Emergency procedures to assure prompt action in the event of fire, spill or explosion,

8. Prescribed work practices and engineering controls, and

9. Compliance with existing health and safety standards.

A Safety Committee is an excellent group to set up to start and maintain a safety program. The Safety Committee will make certain to include input from people who work on the line in the evaluation of the safety of their operations and who will make suggestions that will enhance the ability of workers to avoid exposure to hazardous conditions and materials.

Essentials of a Safety Program

The purpose of the Hazard Communication Standard (HAZCOM) is to ensure that the hazards of all chemicals received in the workplace are documented, and that the information pertaining to potential hazards is communicated to employees. Formats have been established for the communication of basic information about the chemistry of a product, the hazards of its components, as well as precautions to assure that the product is handled, stored and used in a safe manner.

Printers, regardless of the particular process, utilize materials that contain hazardous chemicals as essential ingredients in the prepress, printing and postpress operations. The finished product, with rare exception, does not result in exposure to any hazardous materials under normal conditions of use or in any foreseeable emergency. As such, printers are classified as "employers" of chemicals, not as chemical manufacturers. (See figure 18–1.)

Hazard Communication Compliance Program

Figure 18–1. Open cans of ink are out of compliance and are an invitation for fire, potential health problems and violation citations from government inspectors.

HAZCOM recognizes the need for hazard training and education and dictates that the communication of this information be performed on a periodic basis to assure a reasonable level of understanding by employees of the potential dangers posed by the chemicals in their workplace. All employees, new and old, are to be told of their rights under HAZCOM. Employees have the right to know about the substances with which they work and to which they are exposed. They should be trained in the safe handling and precautions to take to protect themselves. Basic to HAZCOM are the responsibilities of the employer to conduct specific activities and make them available to the employees:

1. Conduct a chemical inventory, listing all substances found in the facility and the workplace.

2. Receive and maintain an accessible library of Material Safety Data Sheets.

3. Reference copies of the Chemical Inventory and the MSDSs are to be available to employees.

4. Labels are to be on all containers and are to be explicit in describing the contents and the potential hazards of the product.

5. Training programs are to be conducted periodically, and at any time the chemistry changes.

6. New employees are to be informed as part of the initial training and orientation to the company and the job.

7. A written program will be prepared to describe the program.

8. Records will be maintained of training and other safety requirements addressed during any safety or health training relative to the use of chemicals.

The safety manual prepared for the Hazard Communication Standard compliance program should include procedures which will provide for better compliance with the handling of chemicals or reacting to hazards in the event of an incident such as fire, explosion or spill. The manual should include documents that describe emergency contingency plans, personal protective equipment, storage precautions, etc. A sample manual is included as Appendix XXX, which can be used as a guide in preparing your own documentation (figure 18–2).

Figure 18–2. Written manuals are required by many safety regulations.

The OSHA Hazard Communication Standard is intended to provide for the improved processing of information related to chemical consumption in a plant. Other manufacturing, operating and maintenance procedures that exist should be included in the program and manual as a total commitment to the safety and health of the employees.

Equally important is making the appropriate information available to any visitors or contractors working in the plant to ensure that they are aware of any hazards present in the facility and of the measures required for protection from these hazards. By the same token, any hazards introduced into the plant by outsiders should be properly addressed to protect the employees of both the contractor and the facility.

Material Safety Data Sheets

OSHA established the format of the Material Safety Data Sheet (MSDS) to assure that every chemical brought into a facility will incorporate basic information. This information will be of use to an employee when preparing to use a product or in the event there is an incident that requires a protective reaction. Designed by OSHA as a means of providing information to safeguard workers using chemicals, the MSDS opens the door to many opportunities for the printer to know more about his process.

By understanding the contents of the MSDS, the printer can have a better appreciation of the composition of his various inks, solvent/thinner blends, and other chemicals used in the plant. The use for safety and environmental compliance is obvious; having a better understanding of the behavior of the various components can help the printer in his effort to improve productivity and quality. While the information is already provided to the reader in chapter 8, related to environmental concerns, this chapter is concerned with the safety aspects for which the MSDS was intended by its designers.

Format of MSDS

The Materials Safety Data Sheet, as conceived by OSHA (and illustrated in figure 18–3), has eight basic sections. ANSI expanded the scope to include additional breakout sections.

Material Safety Data Sheet

May be used to comply with
OSHA's Hazard Communication Standard,
29 CFR 1910.1200. Standard must be
consulted for specific requirements.

U.S. Department of Labor

Occupational Safety and Health Administration
(Non-Mandatory Form)
Form Approved
OMB No. 1218-0072

IDENTITY *(As Used on Label and List)*	*Note: Blank spaces are not permitted. If any item is not applicable, or no information is available, the space must be marked to indicate that.*

Section I

Manufacturer's Name	Emergency Telephone Number
Address *(Number, Street, City, State, and ZIP Code)*	Telephone Number for Information
	Date Prepared
	Signature of Preparer *(optional)*

Section II — Hazardous Ingredients/Identity Information

Hazardous Components (Specific Chemical Identity; Common Name(s))	OSHA PEL	ACGIH TLV	Other Limits Recommended	% *(optional)*

Section III — Physical/Chemical Characteristics

Boiling Point		Specific Gravity (H$_2$O = 1)	
Vapor Pressure (mm Hg.)		Melting Point	
Vapor Density (AIR = 1)		Evaporation Rate (Butyl Acetate = 1)	
Solubility in Water			
Appearance and Odor			

Section IV — Fire and Explosion Hazard Data

Flash Point (Method Used)		Flammable Limits	LEL	UEL
Extinguishing Media				
Special Fire Fighting Procedures				
Unusual Fire and Explosion Hazards				

(Reproduce locally)

OSHA 174, Sept. 1985

Figure 18–3. Material Safety Data Sheet format recommended by OSHA (page 1 of 2).

Section V — Reactivity Data

Stability	Unstable		Conditions to Avoid
	Stable		

Incompatibility (*Materials to Avoid*)

Hazardous Decomposition or Byproducts

Hazardous Polymerization	May Occur		Conditions to Avoid
	Will Not Occur		

Section VI — Health Hazard Data

Route(s) of Entry: Inhalation?   Skin?   Ingestion?

Health Hazards (*Acute and Chronic*)

Carcinogenicity: NTP?   IARC Monographs?   OSHA Regulated?

Signs and Symptoms of Exposure

Medical Conditions Generally Aggravated by Exposure

Emergency and First Aid Procedures

Section VII — Precautions for Safe Handling and Use

Steps to Be Taken in Case Material Is Released or Spilled

Waste Disposal Method

Precautions to Be Taken in Handling and Storing

Other Precautions

Section VIII — Control Measures

Respiratory Protection (*Specify Type*)

Ventilation	Local Exhaust	Special
	Mechanical (*General*)	Other

Protective Gloves	Eye Protection

Other Protective Clothing or Equipment

Work/Hygienic Practices

Figure 18–3. Material Safety Data Sheet format recommended by OSHA (page 2 of 2).

SECTION 1: PRODUCT INFORMATION

Product Name: **MILLENNIUM SILVER** (One-Step Fountain Solution for Polyester Plates)

D.O.T. Designation: Cleaning Liquid. Not Regulated.

U. N. Designation: Same as DOT.

SECTION 2: HAZARDOUS COMPONENTS/IDENTITY INFORMATION

HAZARDOUS COMPONENT	CAS No.	% WT.	OSHA PEL	ACGIH TLV-TWA	OTHER RATINGS	OSHA STEL
Propylene Glycol	57-55-6	2 - 4			50ppm(AIHA)	
Dipropylene Glycol Monomethyl Ether	34590-94-8	10 - 15	100ppm	100ppm	150ppm(ACGIH) STEL	150ppm
Tripropylene Glycol Methyl Ether	25498-49-1	10 - 15	100ppm	100ppm	150ppm(ACGIH) STEL	150ppm

Figure 18–4. The hazardous components section of the MSDS lists the various chemicals in the mixture, CAS numbers, percentages in the formulation and related health standards. Material Safety Data Sheet for Millenium Silver (One-Step Fountain Solution for Polyester Plates).

Courtesy of Tower Products, Inc.

1. The heading describes the company which manufactured or repacked the product and wrote the MSDS, with contact information, including an emergency phone number and the date the MSDS was prepared.

2. Section 1 identifies the chemical name and/or common name of the product/chemical, the scientific name and CAS number and any other pertinent description or classification.

3. Section 2 lists the hazardous ingredients in the product, including CAS numbers of the ingredients, the percentage by weight of each component and may include data relative to the impact on health by each component. The description could list the maximum parts per million to which a worker may be safely exposed over a continuous eight-hour period. Other information may be included at the discretion of the manufacturer to provide guidance for the protection the worker. The only exception to full disclosure allowed by OSHA is for any chemical that passes a rigid test for a claim to proprietary knowledge (figure 18–4).

4. Section 3—Physical Characteristics: Lists such items as boiling points, freezing point, vapor pressure and density, pH, reactivity in water, appearance and odor, etc. This information is pertinent to planning for identification of the chemical and its releases, and to provide criteria for providing engineering controls in the process to limit or contain releases from the chemicals (figure 18–5).

5. Section 4—Fire and Explosion Data: Identifies flashpoints, conditions that could result in fire or explosion, and the means to contain any incident.

SECTION 1: PRODUCT INFORMATION
Product Name: **EXEMPT WASH HF** and **EXEMPT WASH HF - M** (High Flashpoint Water Miscible Wash)
D.O.T. Designation: Cleaning Liquid (Non-Regulated Combustible) (1)
U.N. Designation: Flammable Liquids, N.O.S. (Contains Naphtha, Solvent), 3, Un1993, PGIII
 (1) Contact manufacturer for designation for bulk domestic ground shipments.

SECTION 3: PHYSICAL/CHEMICAL CHARACTERISTICS
Boiling Point: 355 degrees F. (estimated)
Specific Gravity: (Water=1) 0.801
Vapor Pressure: (mmHG, calculated) <1 at 68 degrees F, 20 degrees C.
Melting Point: N/A
Vapor Density: (Air=1, calculated) Not calculated.
Solubility in Water: Miscible
Appearance & Odor: Light colored liquid, petroleum odor
Maximum VOC Content: 6.6 lbs. per gallon (792 grams per liter)
Maximum VOC%: 99% (EPA Method 24)
Non Photochemically Reactive

Figure 18–5. The MSDS provides a summary of the physical characteristics of the product. Material Safety Data Sheet for Exempt Wash HF.

Courtesy of Tower Products, Inc.

6. Section 5—Reactivity Data: Stability and compatibility characteristics are detailed, with precautions given for the handling of reactive chemicals.

7. Section 6—Health Hazards: Identifies if materials are irritants, sensitizers, corrosives or carcinogens. Describes signs and symptoms of overexposure, routes of exposure, medical conditions recognized as due to exposure, OSHA and ACGIH limits of exposure.

8. Section 7—Emergency and first aid procedures are outlined in the event of exposure and reaction to the chemical.

9. Section 8—Toxicity data.

10. Section 9—Special Protection Information: Describes the use of protective equipment, safe handling procedures and engineering control requirements.

11. Section 10—Special Precautions and Spill/Leak Procedures.

Since OSHA specified the content of MSDSs, but not a standard format, the documents provided by different suppliers will vary in style and detail, but should include all the basic information required by law. Any deviations can be questioned; the information must be provided, even if only to a qualified health official of the chemical manufacturer's customer.

Every chemical manufacturer with whom a printer deals, which falls into the appropriate group, must supply an MSDS for

Figure 18–6. OSHA requires that MSDS collections be readily available to workers.

every product sold, usually with the first sale of the product. Any change in the formulation or composition of the product will require a new MSDS. For chemicals that have been listed in the SARA Title III Toxic Release Inventory category, a new MSDS should be received at the start of each new year. Sample MSDSs can be seen in Appendix XXXI.

Location of MSDS Books in Facility

Material Safety Data Sheets are required to be accessible to all employees. A copy of the chemical inventory and the appropriate MSDS collection should be maintained in a central location in or in an office adjacent and accessible to plant personnel. Separate sets may be maintained in the departments in which the chemicals are stored and/or used (figure 18–6). The collection should be kept up to date with regard to all chemicals used in the facility or in the particular department. Where the number of chemicals used and the situation allows, MSDSs may be posted on the bulletin board for easy access by employees.

Any employee who wants to read an MSDS will have that opportunity. If there are any questions or a need for explanation, that would be accomplished in accordance with company procedures. If a suitable answer cannot be found in the plant, the question can be directed to the supplier for an adequate response. The request and the response should be kept on file for future reference. No employee should be discouraged or refused the opportunity to see any MSDS used by the company.

O ne of the more obvious things a printer should take notice of when a package arrives is an item printed every day in print shops around the country—the label. Under one regulation or another, the label is one of the most regulated pieces of paper or film that the printer must be aware of (figure 18–7).

Food regulations are very specific about the terminology and contents described in the label. Safety regulations for various products require easy-to-understand language as well as approved inks. Transportation rules specify labels that must appear on hazardous containers. And, of course, environmental and safety regulations require their own set of necessary information.

Choosing the right label and information for the labels for a chemical may at first seem confusing. Based on the labels that exist on products used by printers, it would be easy to come to the conclusion that it is confusing to some manufacturers and, more so, to many consumers. It is not easy to cope with the thousands of chemical products in the marketplace, each one with its own identity and composition, and with varying approaches to defining flammability, explosiveness and health risks.

Since the label is the first point of contact by a user with a chemical product, let's take the time to review why we need the information on the label and how we should look to labels for guidance in doing our jobs safely. The need for accuracy and simplicity in our labels is critical to safety in the workplace as well as in protecting the community in which we work.

T he use of chemicals is quite obvious in the printing industry. Every phase of the process, from design to finished product, involves chemistry. Developers and fixers are in the darkroom and platemaking, inks and solvents are in the pressrooms, adhesives and coatings are in the finishing operations. The plates and materials on which we print are composed of substances we would also classify as chemicals.

The prevalence of chemicals in the workplace has exposed workers to hazards that affect their safety and health, as well as having the potential to affect the public in communities in which the plants are located. Any provision that will inform workers of the hazards and cautions will help to reduce the potential impact of improperly handled chemicals.

Labels provide the first line of identification when a worker places his hands on a product that will be used in the plant. It provides the first warning that care must be taken in the use and handling of that particular product, as well as the disposition of the wastes of that product. Training personnel to read and acknowledge, by their actions, the information that is provided by the label is the first step in assuring a safer, healthier work environment.

Labels: Up-Front Key to Safety in the Workplace

Role of the Label in the Use of Industrial Chemicals

ISOPROPYL ALCOHOL 99%
ISOPROPANOL

CUST. CODE #

FLAMMABLE LIQUID
UN1219   HMIS #

CAUTION
FLAMMABLE. HARMFUL IF INHALED.
CAUSES EYE AND SKIN IRRITATION.
Keep away from heat, sparks, and flame.
Avoid breathing vapor.
Avoid contact with eyes.
Keep container closed.
Use with adequate ventilation.
Wash thoroughly after handling.

FIRE
SMALL FIRES - Dry chemical, CO2, water spray or foam.
LARGE FIRES - Water spray, fog or foam.
SPILL
Flush with water or cover with absorbent. Prevent runoff.
Collect and dispose. Observe government regulations.

C.A.S. #
FIRST AID
SKIN - Wash immediately with plenty of soap and
water. Immediately contact physician.
EYES - Flush promptly and thoroughly with clear water
for at least 15 minutes. Immediately contact physician.
INHALATION - If inhaled, remove to fresh air. If not
breathing, give artificial respiration. If breathing is
difficult, give oxygen. Call a physician.

WARNING
This container may be hazardous when empty. May contain explosive or harmful vapors or product residue.
Do not cut, weld, or expose this container to any
source of ignition. Empty drums should be properly

LOT #   NET WT:361

FOR INDUSTRIAL USE ONLY

Figure 18–7. A typical label for a drum of solvent containing isopropanol.

OSHA Hazcom Labeling

The basic OSHA regulation for safety in the use of chemicals is the Hazardous Communication Standard, known more commonly as HAZCOM or the Right-to-Know law. One of the key provisions of HAZCOM is the requirement for all chemicals to be labeled with the appropriate information to provide safe use in the workplace. In essence, the label is a condensed version of the material safety data sheet that must be on every container in which the chemical is shipped.

The OSHA labeling guidelines require:

- Identification of the hazardous chemical or chemicals,
- The name and address of the manufacturer,
- A telephone hot line for questions in the event of an emergency,
- Appropriate hazard warnings, and
- Suggested actions to be taken in the event of exposure.

Since OSHA has not spelled out the exact definition of appropriate warnings for all chemicals and exposures, various manufacturers may have different interpretations. The writer of the label must rely on his or her experience and judgment in deciding what is appropriate. Where OSHA or another agency has been specific, the language of the label must be consistent from one source to another.

An example of very specific requirements is the listing of key hazardous chemicals in the product. Some states, California and New Jersey included, require a listing and percentages of the more prominent hazardous ingredients, in some cases limited to a specific number of the components. These may be either environmental or safety related.

If chemicals are transferred from one container to another, for example taking solvent blend from a 55-gallon drum and dispensing it into one-gallon safety cans, the new container must be appropriately labeled. "Appropriate" means that the new label will contain adequate information to satisfy the basic requirements of OSHA.

The label is but one of the items covered by the Hazardous Communication Standard. Material Safety Data Sheets (MSDS), signs, tags and warnings are all inherent to the communication of safety and health hazards. All fit into a comprehensive program to provide workers with the information they need to protect themselves on the job.

HMIS Labels— Hazard Material Identification System

Given the diversity of the workforce and the universal use of chemicals manufactured in all parts of the world, the HMIS labels provide an excellent tool for immediate identification of hazards with minimal language difficulty or conception of how hazardous a particular chemical may be. Developed by PPG Industries and assigned to the National Paint and Coatings Association, the Hazard Material Identification System utilizes four-color spaces and a numerical system of 0 to 4 to designate the level of hazard (figure 18–8). Easy to use for employee recognition and training, the key element is the appropriate designation by the manufacturer of the chemical by use of the numerical designations for the hazards.

The four basic color areas are:

• Red—Flammability

• Blue—Health

• Yellow—Reactivity

• White—field used to illustrate personal protective equipment and for product description.

The hazard indices are printed in the color area for each category. Assignment of the classification is based on guidance developed for the HMIS:

Severe hazard   4

Serious hazard   3

Moderate hazard   2

Slight hazard   1

Minimal hazard   0

Personal protective equipment symbols consist of illustrations of a worker with the designated protective items—glasses, gloves, respirator, etc.

The labels can be either a diamond broken down into four-color diamonds or the more popular four-color bars printed horizontally. They come in all sizes, ranging from one inch by one inch, to larger, depending on the size of the container or the judgment of the manufacturer. Labels are available in English and with Spanish translations.

A major advantage of using labels is the ease with which they can be applied for the in-house labeling of containers to which chemicals have been transferred, or for containers whose labels have been destroyed or damaged.

DOT Hazardous Materials Labels

The Department of Transportation (DOT) requires shipments of hazardous materials and wastes to display cautionary placards, labels and markers with written and numerical classifications (figure 18–9). DOT has mandated the design of its labels. They are diamond shaped (square on point) and have pictorial elements as well as specific colors to designate the classification of the hazard. The labels must be at least four inches on a side. The required color must bleed to the edge of the label and have a black solid border one-quarter inch from the edge. The labels must pass a 72-hour fadeometer test and be able to endure 30 days of exposure to climatic conditions.

The prescribed colors are:

Orange—Explosive

Red—Flammable

Blue—Don't mix with water

Yellow—Caution

White—Poisonous (designated routes only)

Green—Non-flammable gas under high pressure.

The hazard description is clearly identified by a United Nations class number or an NA four-digit identification. Typical DOT labels seen on printing facility chemicals are Flammable Liquid and Corrosive.

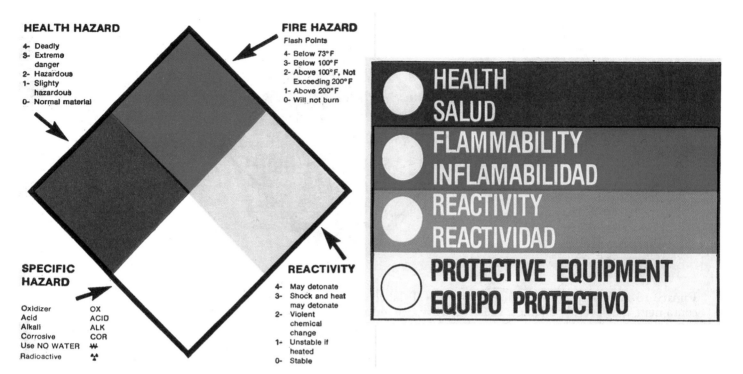

Figure 18–8. HMIS labels feature bars of color and numeric designation blocks to describe level of hazards and are produced by many label printers. A similar concept is the NFPA label which uses four diamonds of color and overprint number to designate hazard levels.

Hazardous Waste Labels

Hazardous waste labels are required by law for all wastes that are collected, stored and shipped for disposal. The shipping label is a format that satisfies the regulatory requirements and is usually provided by the firm that will be handling the disposition. The hazardous waste label carries a distinctive yellow background with black and red copy. It contains a very precise and detailed description of the waste, when it was generated, the hazardous designations that describe the waste category(ies), and the facility that generated the waste (figure 18–10).

While the waste is being collected, the drums that will contain the waste should be labeled with some basic information. The format and colors used are not mandated. Some firms offer printed labels for hazardous waste prior to shipment. Simple blank, pressure-sensitive labels can be used, provided the appropriate information describes the contents of the containers in lettering both large enough and legible to meet regulations (figure 18–11).

The label should be clearly marked as Hazardous Waste, and have a description of the waste in the container, the date that accumulation of the waste was started, and the date the drum was placed in storage. The last date is important. At every level of hazardous waste generation, there is a quantity threshold and time limits that waste can be held in storage.

Empty drums, particularly those from solvents or press washes that are flammable, should carry an empty drum label. The vapors which remain in the empty drums after all liquid has been emptied

Figure 18–9. Department of Transportation (DOT) labels and placards are found are containers, trucks and buildings. Illustrated are two formats for flammable liquids.

Source: DOT.

Figure 18–10. The hazardous waste label placed on all drums in transit must comply with RCRA regulations and contain very specific information.

Source: USEPA.

present an easy source of explosion. Empty drums should be handled with the same concern and care as full drums of flammable and explosive chemicals.

As a final note for safety, and to guard against unwarranted suspicion during an inspection, every container at the press and prepress areas should have a label. To protect against any misconceptions about the contents of any drum, if not a drum containing raw material and labeled, every drum of in-process waste should be appropriately labeled. This will also mean placing labels on wastes that are not hazardous and that will be shipped off site for disposal or recycled or treated in-plant for reuse.

The possibility of someone picking up a container and using the contents, without knowing what the contents are, is an invitation to an accident. Whether the exposure will be damaging to humans, the equipment or the product, there is no excuse for it happening. The rationale that the particular pressman knows what is in the containers at his press is no excuse for not labeling containers, nor is the need to constantly replace labels that get covered with ink or loosen from exposure to solvents an acceptable excuse.

Proper labels will assure that everyone has full knowledge of the chemicals stored, handled and used in the facility. With this knowledge, proper methods should be used in handling the chemicals on the press, to treat an injury if anyone is negatively exposed to the chemistry, and to disposing of the wastes properly.

No Container Without a Label

Figure 18–11. Label on in-process drum for accumulation of hazardous waste in the pressroom.

The major objective of process safety management of highly hazardous chemicals is to prevent unwanted releases that will expose employees and others to serious hazards. An effective program requires a systematic approach to evaluating the whole chemical process to design safeguards into the process to prevent or mitigate a release. The program will identify, evaluate and mitigate or prevent chemical releases that could occur as a result of failure of the process, working procedures or equipment. The challenge to the printer is to develop the necessary expertise by the press personnel that will result in a properly developed and maintained program.

Process Safety Management

A complete and accurate assessment of all chemistry used in the process and the hazards posed by this chemistry is essential in light of specific process technology and equipment. The information compiled will be a necessary resource for performing the process hazard analysis required by the regulations which outline the process safety management procedures. This information will be invaluable to staff when setting up training programs and developing operating procedures.

As the hazards become documented, management will realize the benefits of making this information available to outside contractors who work in the plant, as well as to local emergency response

Hazards Assessment

agencies. Insurance companies are increasingly requesting this information to use as a basis for underwriting decisions and rate setting. In general, the better the documentation, the more likely there will be an opportunity for lower insurance rates.

The information to be compiled about the chemicals, including by-product intermediates and wastes, needs to be comprehensive enough for an accurate assessment of the fire and explosion characteristics, reactivity hazards, safety and health hazards to workers, and the corrosion and erosion effects on the equipment and monitoring tools. Current material safety data sheets can be used to meet this requirement, but must be complemented with technical process chemistry information, including potential hazards under extraordinary conditions.

Technology of the Process

With chemistry in hand, the information relative to the process technology becomes essential to an understanding of the relationships of the components and the conditions under which the process operates effectively. This will include employer-established criteria for maximum inventories of process chemicals, limits of activity that can result in upset conditions, and qualitative estimates of the consequences of operating beyond established process limits.

A major tool for charting the process technology is the process flow diagram (Appendix XI). The diagram is a complex depiction showing all main flow streams, including valves, to enhance the understanding of the process, as well as all pressures and temperatures on all feed and product lines, showing all major vessels and points of pressure and temperature control. Information is shown relative to construction materials, pump capacities and pressure heads, compressor horsepower and vessel design pressures and temperatures. In addition, process flow diagrams usually show major components of control loops and key utilities.

The block diagram (figure 18–12) is a simplified representation of the more detailed flow chart, depicting the major process equipment and interconnecting process flow. The diagram is a pictorial relationship of the major process equipment and controls, and the movement to and from each by materials and products in the process. The diagram illustrates flow and flow rates, stream composition, temperatures and pressures.

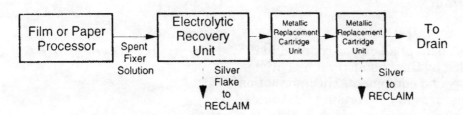

Figure 18–12. Block diagrams help to visualize material usage and waste in specific processes, as an example silver recovery from film or paper processing.

Source: Institute of Advanced Manufacturing Sciences Inc. and Printing Industries Association of Southern Ohio, *Improve Efficiency and Reduce Waste Through Process Control in the Lithographic Industry*, 1997, p 23.

Section 302 of the Clean Air Act Amendments requires that employers consult with their employees and their representatives regarding the development and implementation of process safety management programs and hazard assessments. Employers are required to train and educate employees, informing them of incident investigations.

A key recommendation is the formation of safety committees, something many firms may already have done, to establish methods of keeping employees informed about relevant health and safety issues. Such a committee can play a significant role in implementing and maintaining an effective process safety program.

Employee Involvement

OSHA regulations warrant a review of the protective clothing and equipment supplied or required by printers for their personnel. With greater concern for exposure to chemicals in the workplace, the implementation of a program is essential to study the risks and provide adequate safeguards for the employees.

Every plant management has to ascertain the extent of personal exposure based on the nature of the processes, the chemicals (inks, solvents, adhesives, etc.) used in the plant, and the risk to employees based on the equipment and methods employed. Personnel who have daily contact with chemicals and other hazards will require training and fitting for protective equipment (figure 18–13). Provision should also be made to provide the proper equipment, training and other requirements for those employees who would take part in emergency response activities.

In general, a chemical protective clothing program should include the following steps:

1. Conduct an assessment of exposure potentials.

2. Evaluate control options prior to considering protective clothing.

3. Define the characteristics required for adequate performance.

4. Determine any restraints stemming from the ergonomics of the job.

5. Research and evaluate decontamination requirements.

6. Select the proper protective clothing to fit the specified restraints.

7. Develop and implement a training program.

8. Establish supervisory responsibility for enforcing compliance with wear regulations and policies.

Rules for Personal Protective Gear

9. Promote safety records based on adherence to the rules.

The two critical steps that precede selection of any clothing are the evaluation of the risk of the chemical in question and the ability of the firm to institute engineering controls. Exactly what hazards do the chemicals represent in the workplace? An evaluation of the chemical and potential exposures identifies chemical, biological, physical or combined hazards. Are the materials toxic, flammable; do they react immediately or are the effects felt after a period of time? At what stage of the printing and its related processes does exposure take place? How does this exposure take place?

Control options raise other questions. Can exposure to chemicals be avoided by imposing engineering solutions? Can equipment be purchased and methods developed which do not expose workers to chemicals? Can methods be developed which minimize handling of chemicals? If the protective equipment should fail, will the controls be adequate to minimize damaging consequences to the workers?

Selection of protective clothing must deal with resistance to different types of chemicals. The five major distress areas to be considered are:

1. **Degradation:** A detrimental change in the physical properties of the material by physical contact with the chemical.

2. **Penetration:** Imperfections in the material that permit the passage of the chemicals through the material and into contact with the skin.

3. **Permeation:** Diffusion of the chemical through the protective layer provided by the clothing.

4. **Breakthrough time:** Elapsed time from initial contact until detection on skin surface.

5. **Permeation rate:** The rate of movement through the barrier after equilibrium is established.

The printing plant utilizes a wide variety of chemicals in its various related processes. Exposure, however, is greatest when press personnel are working in close quarters, either cleaning or setting up in the area of the press ink transfer system, engaged in blending or cleaning up in an inkroom, or cleaning up an ink or solvent spill. The material safety data sheets are excellent sources of information about the chemical properties; technical service representatives of ink and solvent companies can be helpful. Many resources are there for the asking from industry and government.

Ergonomic restraints deal with clothing and the restrictions they may place on job performance. Of importance are such things as ability to feel, to handle with ease, not to limit movement in doing any task. The optimum situation is to select the

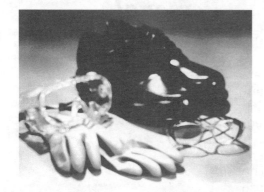

Figure 18–13. Personal protective equipment is critical in safeguarding workers with exposure to chemicals.

Figure 18–14. Respiratory masks are vital in areas with heavy concentrations of air pollutants.

least amount of clothing that will afford the greatest protection to safely perform the job. Making the selection will take into account all elements of the program. Cost will be a factor, but should not be such a factor as to impair performance and safety standards. Any compromises should be made in a manner that will be both cost effective and performance oriented.

Respiratory Protection Program

Workplaces where employees are exposed to airborne hazardous materials are required by OSHA's Respiratory Protection Standard to assure that all employees whose specific tasks require them to wear, or who may benefit from the wearing of, respiratory protective equipment be given training in the selection, proper fitting, use and maintenance of said respiratory equipment (figure 18–14).

Who is affected by this regulation? Ink technicians, pressroom personnel, shipping and receiving workers when designated to take part in handling incoming and outgoing bulk shipments, clean-up activities at such time as a spill occurs, or other conditions during which the vapor level of the chemical will be higher than normal. Persons shall not be assigned tasks that require the use of respirators unless it has been determined that they are physically able to use the equipment properly and perform the work while using the equipment.

Nature of Respiratory Hazards

In the event of a spill or other leak in the ink and solvent storage areas or in the solvent recovery room, the volume of solvents evaporating will be much greater than normal. Under such conditions, it is possible that the vapor levels may exceed the allowable parts per million designated under OSHA regulations.

Under normal working conditions, the employee is exposed intermittently to low levels of solvent vapors. The MSDS will indicate the allowable parts per million during an eight-hour period, as well as a 15-minute exposure limitation, for the specific substances. Under an emergency condition, when the vapor level rises above the standard, the employee should wear a respirator for his comfort and health. The respirator will screen out the objectionable fumes. Many solvents used in printing inks and for cleaning blankets and press rollers can pose respiratory problems. If an employee voluntarily elects to use a respiratory mask in a safe area to satisfy his personal preference, management is charged with the responsibility to assure that the individual adheres to the same program prescribed for all persons who don the masks as a function of their jobs.

Training Includes:

- **Selection of correct type of respiratory equipment:** For this application, the correct type of protection is defined as an NIOSH/MSHA approved half-face mask equipped with an Organic Vapors Cartridge.

- **Proper fitting of equipment:** The pressroom supervisor or his designee will conduct a fit test of all respiratory protective equipment, exercising due care to see that a proper seal with the face is achieved. The trainer will evaluate the effect of facial hair as it may affect proper fit. The trainer will demonstrate how the employee can continue to check for proper fit each time the equipment is to be used.

- **Use of respiratory equipment:** The employee will be instructed on how and when to use the respiratory equipment.

- **The pressman or ink technician** will store the equipment in a plastic bag with a zipper closure in a metal storage cabinet in the inkroom work area. The operator will, each week, clean all surfaces of the facemask with an alcohol wipe. Once per month, or sooner if the operator should detect loss of performance, the proper cartridges (for organic vapors) will be replaced with new cartridges. Any other defect suspected or actual, in the mask and/or cartridges, will be immediately brought to the attention of the pressroom supervisor.

- **Medical follow-up** for users of respirator equipment. The respirator user's medical status will be reviewed periodically (annually). The physician shall determine what health and physical conditions are pertinent.

- **Inspection of equipment:** The operator will inspect his respirator equipment prior to each use, and will maintain a log of weekly inspection, cleaning and periodic changes of cartridges. That log will be kept in a secure location near a location at which the respirators will be needed, available for plant supervision to inspect.

Upon completion of the program, written acknowledgements shall be signed and placed in the personnel file of the individual worker.

Medical Records— A 30-Year Responsibility

Each of the regulations pertaining to chemical usage, safety and health requires records pertaining to the individual's health, tests and training; the nature of the hazards in the workplace, and standard documents that relate potential health hazards to which the employee may have been exposed. OSHA regulations require that any record that may be deemed "medical," should be maintained in the company files for a period of not less than 30 years. The employee and health officials shall have access to such records to determine if exposure and/or lack of adequate training in the handling of the substance was a direct cause of any resulting disability or death. The time period of 30 years was derived from the statistical determination of the working life of the typical worker.

In the event there is a need to substantiate the cause of an illness or fatality following the retirement or termination of the employee, it is mandated that records be accessible to ascertain

Medical records must be saved for 30 years.

the cause of any potentially damaging disease or medical condition that may have resulted from that person's previous employment. A request from a physician or attorney may be required, in writing, specifying the need and reasons why alternative information will not suffice. A confidentiality agreement may be required of the recipient to prevent the use of the information for any use or for any purpose other than the health need stated at such time as the documents were requested. Refusal of a request by an employer requires the employer to satisfy a set procedure established at the behest of OSHA to encourage full disclosure by an employer, while providing a legal basis to protect the rights of the employer.

At the time of employment, and annually thereafter, employees are to be told of the existence, location and availability of their medical and exposure records. The ideal time to do this is during the annual HAZCOM training sessions.

An Annual Responsibility— Forms 200 and 300

Every February of the year, employers are required to post the record of injuries that require medical treatment during the previous year. The procedure has called for posting Form 200, a summary of the accident reports filed during the year. A new form and procedure has been designed by OSHA to be effective for reporting as of the experience in 2001. The designation for the revised format is Form 300 (figure 18–15). Instructions for this new, easier-to-administer procedure are in Appendix XXXII.

The report is posted for the entire month from the first of February to the first day of March. Form 200 and Form 300 are logs that compile the details for all injuries that result in medical care

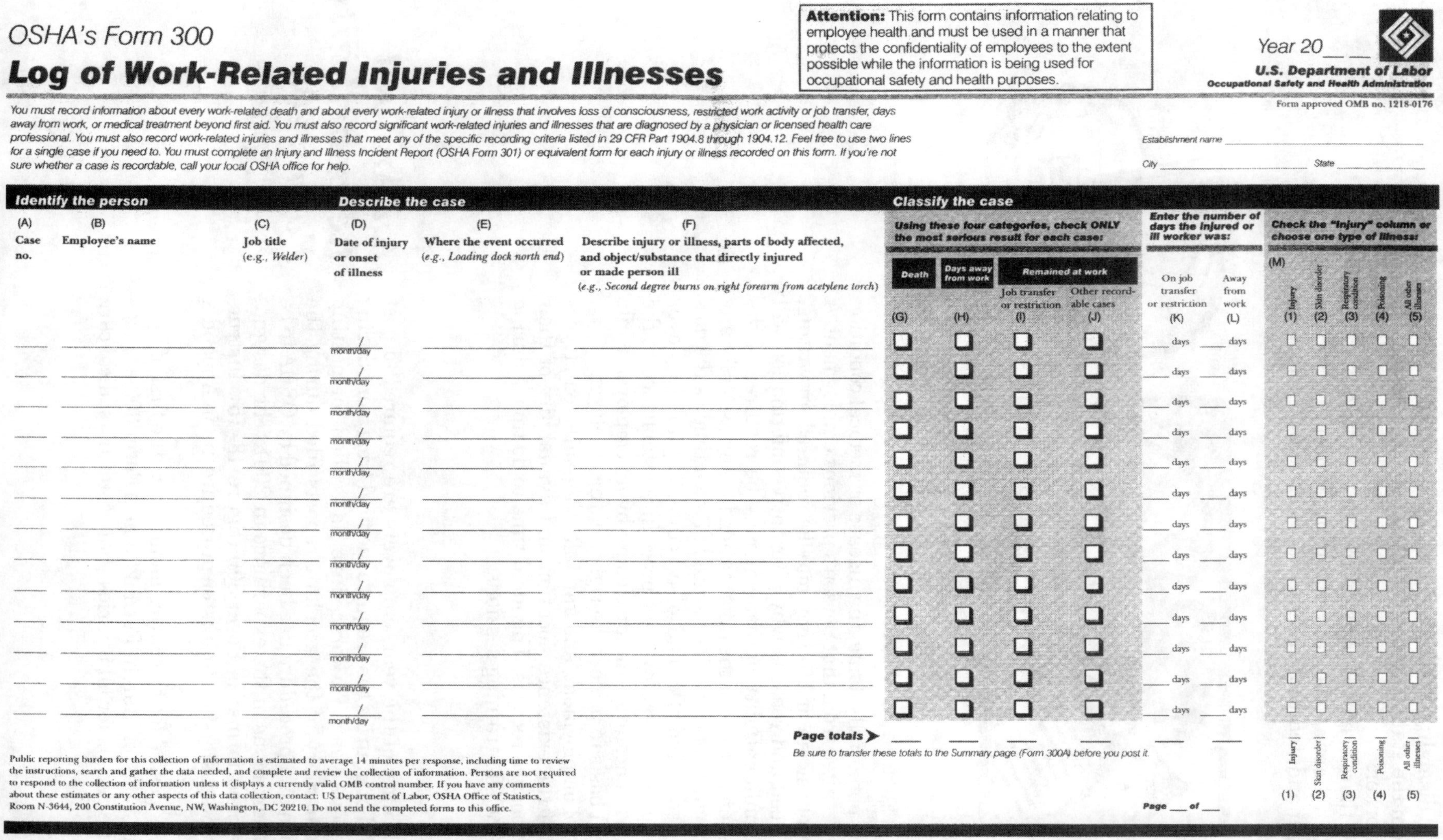

Figure 18–15. Form 300 is the new ongoing record of lost time accidents, which is posted annually during the month of February for employees to see.

Source: OSHA Regulations (Standard-29 CFR) 1904.43.

OSHA's Form 301
Injury and Illness Incident Report

Attention: This form contains information relating to employee health and must be used in a manner that protects the confidentiality of employees to the extent possible while the information is being used for occupational safety and health purposes.

This *Injury and Illness Incident Report* is one of the first forms you must fill out when a recordable work-related injury or illness has occurred. Together with the *Log of Work-Related Injuries and Illnesses* and the accompanying *Summary*, these forms help the employer and OSHA develop a picture of the extent and severity of work-related incidents.

Within 7 calendar days after you receive information that a recordable work-related injury or illness has occurred, you must fill out this form or an equivalent. Some state workers' compensation, insurance, or other reports may be acceptable substitutes. To be considered an equivalent form, any substitute must contain all the information asked for on this form.

According to Public Law 91-596 and 29 CFR 1904, OSHA's recordkeeping rule, you must keep this form on file for 5 years following the year to which it pertains.

If you need additional copies of this form, you may photocopy and use as many as you need.

Completed by _____

Title _____

Phone (___) ___ - ___   Date ___/___/___

Information about the employee

1) Full name _____
2) Street _____
   City _____ State ___ ZIP ___
3) Date of birth ___/___/___
4) Date hired ___/___/___
5) ☐ Male ☐ Female

Information about the physician or other health care professional

6) Name of physician or other health care professional _____
7) If treatment was given away from the worksite, where was it given?
   Facility _____
   Street _____
   City _____ State ___ ZIP ___
8) Was employee treated in an emergency room? ☐ Yes ☐ No
9) Was employee hospitalized overnight as an in-patient? ☐ Yes ☐ No

Information about the case

10) Case number from the Log _____ (Transfer the case number from the Log after you record the case.)
11) Date of injury or illness ___/___/___
12) Time employee began work ___ AM / PM
13) Time of event ___ AM / PM ☐ Check if time cannot be determined
14) What was the employee doing just before the incident occurred? Describe the activity, as well as the tools, equipment, or material the employee was using. Be specific. *Examples:* "climbing a ladder while carrying roofing materials"; "spraying chlorine from hand sprayer"; "daily computer key-entry."
15) What happened? Tell us how the injury occurred. *Examples:* "When ladder slipped on wet floor, worker fell 20 feet"; "Worker was sprayed with chlorine when gasket broke during replacement"; "Worker developed soreness in wrist over time."
16) What was the injury or illness? Tell us the part of the body that was affected and how it was affected; be more specific than "hurt," "pain," or sore." *Examples:* "strained back"; "chemical burn, hand"; "carpal tunnel syndrome."
17) What object or substance directly harmed the employee? *Examples:* "concrete floor"; "chlorine"; "radial arm saw." *If this question does not apply to the incident, leave it blank.*
18) If the employee died, when did death occur? Date of death ___/___/___

Figure 18–16. Form 301, Injury and Illness Incident Report.
Source: OSHA Regulations (Standard-29 CFR) 1904.43.

and lost time. While the OSHA requirement is not exclusive to injuries and illnesses related to exposure to chemicals, it is worth including, in this chapter, a brief synopsis of the reporting requirements for the new format devoted to safety and health issues.

OSHA mandates employee involvement and information, with no exceptions, in just about every area of health and safety. Publicizing the Forms 200 and 300 is the culmination of the yearly health and safety record of the facility. It is management's message to its employees, as well as a report card of the efforts during the year, that safety is a priority in the business of the company.

The posting of Forms 200 and 300 expresses management's desire for employees to recognize any patterns of injuries or unsafe exposures, and uphold their responsibility, as well, to prevent carelessness and disregard of safety precautions that lead to injuries and illness.

The new format has endeavored to simplify the process and to eliminate the broad interpretations that accompanied Form 200. Accidents and illness are better defined to determine what is and what is not reportable. This includes definitions of first aid and medical treatment and a list of illnesses and conditions that can be excluded or included. It defines the conditions that render an injury or illness "work-related." Guidelines are provided for accurately counting the days away from work. Specific circumstances are described that would not require reporting of an injury or illness.

Records of the incidents are as important as the final document in which the experiences of the facility are described. An injury and illness incident (Form 301) report is part of the total procedure prescribed by OSHA (figure 18–16). Supervisors and management personnel should be trained in the proper completion and submission of all reports relative to injuries and illnesses and the actions that are initiated by any such occurrences.

OSHA Consultation Services

Printers can avail themselves of a service that OSHA offers at no cost to the facility. A corps of experienced engineers, typically retired, is on call to help audit a facility and highlight deviations from safety and health practices and standards. The OSHA consultants are bound by confidentiality unless they observe an extremely hazardous situation. All inspection notes and recommendations are between the consultant and the printer. The printer agrees, when making the contact, to correct and eliminate any deficiencies.

This is an excellent program that can enlighten the printer at the same time as it protects the facility from penalties. Appendix III is a list of the contacts for the consulting services by state.

CHAPTER 19

Storing Chemicals: Precautions and Limitations

Storage of chemicals is a major concern. With the exception of OSHA standards for the safeguards that must be taken when storing hazardous chemicals and the EPA requirements for hazardous wastes and storage tanks, the questions of how much can be stored and under what conditions are primarily addressed by local agencies and insurance companies. The local fire and health departments and the insurance carriers each have vested interests in the way a printer stores the chemical substances that are required for the various printing processes. The concern lies not only with the hazardous chemicals, but with the basic substrates which are printed on. Papers, paperboard, corrugated paperboard and films can and do burn. The safety of the workers and the neighboring community are essential ingredients of concern of firefighters and insurance company engineers. (See figure 19–1.)

The construction of new buildings, as well as the installation of printing presses and control equipment in older buildings, may frequently require approval by a town or city building department or zoning commission. Printers must be aware of all these entities and requirements long before a move is made. The time to start interacting with these agencies is when you first start to make your plans, up to two or three years in advance of a move. Preparing applications, filing them and then undergoing any public or departmental review can take time; the printer will be the only party in a rush to get the plans approved and to start making the move or commence building.

Figure 19–1. Typical ink storage racks in flexographic (left) and lithographic (right) facilities.

OSHA Regulations Relative to Storing Chemicals

The characteristics of fire, explosion and toxicity are the primary concerns for storing chemicals under OSHA regulations. Precautions are mandated to keep chemicals that can react with each other separate, to assure that flammable materials are not activated by electric sparks or static electricity. Regulations require appropriate containment provisions to restrict the free movement of any liquid spill outside the storage room or area. These are pretty much the same concerns that any fire marshal or insurance company engineer would have relative to risk exposure and liability coverage.

Flammability and Explosion

Appropriate storage of flammable liquids is normal for printing facilities. Precautions are mandated for small as well as large volume consumers of inks, solvents, press washes, etc., depending on the quantities stored at any given time.

The incidence of static electricity in a printing operation mandates that provision be made for grounding of all drums containing solvents and for solvent dispensing equipment. Electrical equipment within a radius of 20 feet from the point of usage or chemical storage should be explosion-proof. (See figure 19–2.)

The storage room should have adequate ventilation exhausts to remove any vapors from the room. A certain amount of air movement is required, based on the size of the room, to forestall the build-up of vapors that will explode if ignited or heated. (See figure 19–3.) Indoor air quality standards may also dictate that any work being done in a solvent and ink storage room may require that personnel performing such work wear respirator masks, with the appropriate fitting, medical examination and training.

All drums within the room should be grounded, if in use. Alligator clips on electrical wires can be attached to the drums and to any cold water pipe running through the room (figure 19–4). Sparks

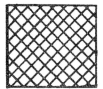

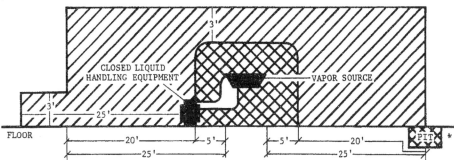

CLASS I DIVISION 1

Division 1 area shall extend 5 feet in all directions from all points of vapor liberation. All areas within pits shall be classified Division 1 if any part of the pit is within a Division 1 or 2 classified area, unless the pit is provided with mechanical ventilation.

HAZARDOUS AREA

*ANY PORTION OF A FLOOR

PIT THAT FALLS IN THE

HAZARDOUS AREA MAKES

ENTIRE PIT CLASS I DIV. 1

CLASS I DIVISION 2

Division 2 locations include an area within 20 feet horizontally, 3 feet vertically beyond a Division 1 area, and up to 3 feet above floor or grade level within 25 feet, if indoors, or 10 feet, if outdoors, from any pump, bleeder, withdrawal fitting, meter, or similar device handling Class I liquids. Pits provided with adequate mechanical ventilation within a Division 1 or 2 area shall be classified Division 2.

Figure 19–2. Extent of hazardous areas protected from vapor sources by explosion-proof electrical equipment and outlets.

Source: OSHA.

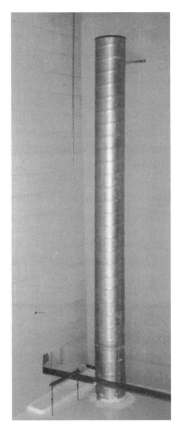

Figure 19–3. Air duct (left) and low level sweep (right) remove vapors from inkroom.

Figure 19–4. Alligator clips ground metal drums and cans during transfer of flammable liquids.

Figure 19–5. Fire extinguishers hang in key areas at R. S. Rosenbaum & Co. Inc., New York, NY.

can ignite solvent vapors as the solvents are pumped from the drums into safety cans or other process containers. There have been untold numbers of deaths and injuries caused by random sparks igniting solvent in the process of being dispensed from a drum to a pail or safety can.

Adequate safeguards must be taken with respect to fire extinguishers, sprinkler systems, spill containment, etc. Fire extinguishers must be hung at arm level height, with appropriate signage to designate from a distance where the extinguishers are located (figure 19–5). Nothing should be placed in front of the extinguishers, blocking immediate access to them. Sprinklers and extinguishers must be inspected and maintained on a regular schedule. (See figure 19–6.)

Based on the equipment and layout of the facility, any exposure with a safety or health risk should be evaluated to determine what the corresponding regulation(s) require to assure compliance with the law.

Storing Toxic and Reactive Chemicals

Not all storage regulations deal with fire and explosion. Some specify air quality, others the need to isolate and/or segregate some chemicals to prevent fatal reactions between them or to workers.

Pressurized gas tanks containing oxygen, hydrogen, propane, acetylene, etc. should be stored in secure areas where they can be chained to be prevented from falling, and at least 10 feet from each other to prevent the fumes must mixing and reacting. Tanks with gases that may not be flammable or explosive may have the propensity to exclude oxygen from the area and lead to suffocation of anyone in the vicinity. Signage should be very obvious to warn personnel in the area of the hazard.

All toxic chemicals should be properly labeled and stored on a containment pallet (figure 19–7) or in a room that has been properly sealed. Safety of workers and the public is at risk should any toxic chemical permeate the cement or concrete flooring, spill into a drain, or otherwise find its way into the drinking water system.

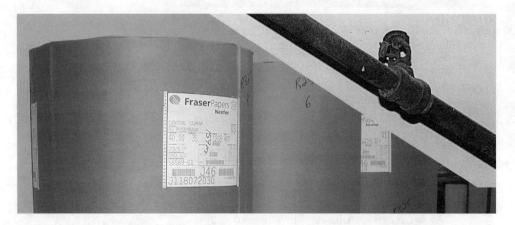

Figure 19–6. Sprinkler systems are required to contain and extinguish fire in material storage areas at R. S. Rosenbaum & Co. Inc., New York, NY.

Storage should be segregated and well marked with appropriate warning signs. Plumbing used to carry chemicals from one tank to another should be adequately marked with the appropriate color labels or tapes. (See figure 19–8.)

Fire Departments and NFPA Standards

The agency that has the most immediate and frequent interaction with printers is the local fire department. Periodic visits by inspectors or fire marshals monitor the nature, quantities and safety precautions taken in the storage of flammable and explosive chemical substances. The standards against which performance is measured are those developed by the National Fire Protection Association (NFPA.) Permits issued by fire departments will typically include limits on the amount of flammable chemicals that may be stored, as well as prevention and containment provisions.

Storage Rooms

Construction details for the storage of flammable materials are very clearly defined in the NFPA standards utilized by fire departments. Among the more notable NFPA rules for an inside liquid storage room are:

"4.4.2 Design and Construction Requirements.

"4.4.2.1 All storage areas shall be constructed to meet the specified fire resistance ratings ... Such construction shall comply with the test specifications given in NFPA 251, *Standard Methods of Tests of Fire Endurance of Building Construction and Materials.*

"4.4.2.2 Openings in interior walls to adjacent rooms or buildings and openings in exterior walls with fire resistance ratings shall be provided with normally closed, listed fire doors with fire protection ratings corresponding to the fire resistance rating of the wall specified ... Such doors shall be permitted to be arranged to stay open during material handling operations if the doors are designed to close automatically in a fire emergency in provision of list closure devices. Fire doors shall be installed in accordance with NFPA 80, *Standard for Fire Doors and Fire Windows.*

"4.4.2.3 Communicating openings in fire walls separating liquid warehouses from adjacent building areas shall be protected by 3 hr. fire doors on each side of the wall.

"4.4.2.4 Construction design of exterior walls shall provide ready accessibility for fire-fighting operations through access openings, windows or lightweight noncombustible wall panels.

Figure 19–7. Drums, properly labeled. stored on containment pallet.

"4.4.2.5 Where Class 1A or 1B liquids or unstable liquids are dispensed or where Class 1A liquids or unstable liquids are stored in containers larger than 1 gal.(4L), the exterior wall or roof construction shall incorporate deflagration vents.

"4.4.2.6 Effective January 1,1997, and where required . . . containment of drainage shall be provided for all new construction.

"4.4.2.7 When containment or drainage is required. . . . Means shall be provided to prevent the flow of burning liquid under emergency conditions into adjoining building areas, property, or critical natural resources.

"4.4.2.8 Where automatic sprinkler protection is provided . . . means shall be provided to prevent burning liquids from exposing other storage piles or racks and from exposing other important buildings, adjoining property, or critical natural resources.

> Exception No. I: This requirement shall not apply to areas where only the following are stored:
>
> (a) Class III liquids;
>
> (b) Liquids that are heavier than water;
>
> (c) Water-miscible liquids;
>
> (d) Liquids having viscosities greater than 10,000 centipoise.
>
> Exception No. 2: This requirement shall not apply to areas where fire protection is provided by non-water extinguishing systems, such as total flooding CO_2, high expansion foam, or aqueous filmforming foam (AFFF).

"4.4.2.9 Electrical equipment and wiring in inside rooms used for storage of Class I liquids shall be suitable for Class I, Division 2, classified locations. Electrical equipment and wiring in inside rooms for the storage of only Class II and Class III liquids shall be for general purpose use. All electrical equipment and wiring must be explosion-proof within twenty feet of the source of ignition.

"4.4.2.10 Where Class I liquids are dispensed or where Class II or Class III liquids at temperatures at or above their flash points are dispensed, electrical equipment and wiring shall be suitable . . . In addition, electrical equipment and wiring located within 3 ft. (0.9m) of dispensing nozzles shall be suitable . . ."

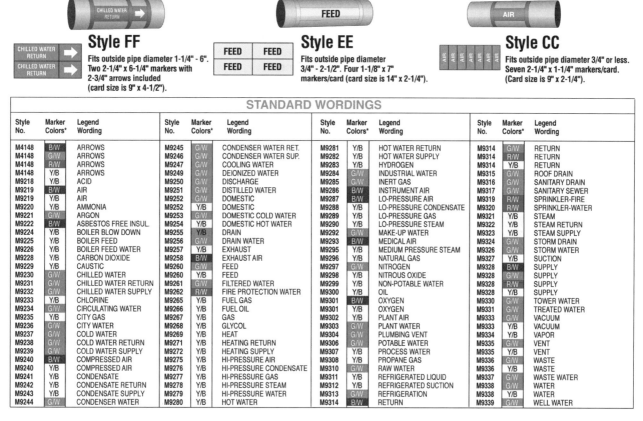

Style FF
Fits outside pipe diameter 1-1/4" - 6".
Two 2-1/4" x 6-1/4" markers with 2-3/4" arrows included (card size is 9" x 4-1/2").

Style EE
Fits outside pipe diameter 3/4" - 2-1/2". Four 1-1/8" x 7" markers/card (card size is 14" x 2-1/4").

Style CC
Fits outside pipe diameter 3/4" or less.
Seven 2-1/4" x 1-1/4" markers/card.
(Card size is 9" x 2-1/4").

STANDARD WORDINGS

Style No.	Marker Colors*	Legend Wording	Style No.	Marker Colors*	Legend Wording	Style No.	Marker Colors*	Legend Wording	Style No.	Marker Colors*	Legend Wording
M4148	B/W	ARROWS	M9245	G/W	CONDENSER WATER RET.	M9281	Y/B	HOT WATER RETURN	M9314	G/W	RETURN
M4148	G/W	ARROWS	M9246	G/W	CONDENSER WATER SUP.	M9282	Y/B	HOT WATER SUPPLY	M9314	R/W	RETURN
M4148	R/W	ARROWS	M9247	G/W	COOLING WATER	M9283	Y/B	HYDROGEN	M9314	Y/B	RETURN
M4148	Y/B	ARROWS	M9249	G/W	DEIONIZED WATER	M9284	G/W	INDUSTRIAL WATER	M9315	G/W	ROOF DRAIN
M9218	Y/B	ACID	M9250	Y/B	DISCHARGE	M9285	G/W	INERT GAS	M9316	G/W	SANITARY DRAIN
M9219	B/W	AIR	M9251	G/W	DISTILLED WATER	M9286	B/W	INSTRUMENT AIR	M9317	G/W	SANITARY SEWER
M9219	Y/B	AIR	M9252	G/W	DOMESTIC	M9287	B/W	LO-PRESSURE AIR	M9319	R/W	SPRINKLER-FIRE
M9220	Y/B	AMMONIA	M9252	Y/B	DOMESTIC	M9288	Y/B	LO-PRESSURE CONDENSATE	M9320	R/W	SPRINKLER-WATER
M9221	G/W	ARGON	M9253	G/W	DOMESTIC COLD WATER	M9289	Y/B	LO-PRESSURE GAS	M9321	Y/B	STEAM
M9222	B/W	ASBESTOS FREE INSUL.	M9254	Y/B	DOMESTIC HOT WATER	M9290	Y/B	LO-PRESSURE STEAM	M9322	Y/B	STEAM RETURN
M9224	Y/B	BOILER BLOW DOWN	M9255	Y/B	DRAIN	M9292	G/W	MAKE-UP WATER	M9323	Y/B	STEAM SUPPLY
M9225	Y/B	BOILER FEED	M9256	G/W	DRAIN WATER	M9293	B/W	MEDICAL AIR	M9324	G/W	STORM DRAIN
M9226	Y/B	BOILER FEED WATER	M9257	Y/B	EXHAUST	M9295	Y/B	MEDIUM PRESSURE STEAM	M9326	G/W	STORM WATER
M9228	Y/B	CARBON DIOXIDE	M9258	B/W	EXHAUST AIR	M9296	Y/B	NATURAL GAS	M9327	Y/B	SUCTION
M9229	Y/B	CAUSTIC	M9260	G/W	FEED	M9297	G/W	NITROGEN	M9328	B/W	SUPPLY
M9230	G/W	CHILLED WATER	M9260	Y/B	FEED	M9298	Y/B	NITROUS OXIDE	M9328	G/W	SUPPLY
M9231	G/W	CHILLED WATER RETURN	M9261	G/W	FILTERED WATER	M9299	Y/B	NON-POTABLE WATER	M9328	R/W	SUPPLY
M9232	G/W	CHILLED WATER SUPPLY	M9262	R/W	FIRE PROTECTION WATER	M9300	Y/B	OIL	M9328	Y/B	SUPPLY
M9233	Y/B	CHLORINE	M9265	Y/B	FUEL GAS	M9301	B/W	OXYGEN	M9330	G/W	TOWER WATER
M9234	Y/B	CIRCULATING WATER	M9266	Y/B	FUEL OIL	M9301	Y/B	OXYGEN	M9331	G/W	TREATED WATER
M9235	Y/B	CITY GAS	M9267	Y/B	GAS	M9302	Y/B	PLANT AIR	M9333	G/W	VACUUM
M9236	G/W	CITY WATER	M9268	Y/B	GLYCOL	M9303	G/W	PLANT WATER	M9333	Y/B	VACUUM
M9237	Y/B	COLD WATER	M9269	Y/B	HEAT	M9304	G/W	PLUMBING VENT	M9334	Y/B	VAPOR
M9238	G/W	COLD WATER RETURN	M9271	Y/B	HEATING RETURN	M9306	G/W	POTABLE WATER	M9335	G/W	VENT
M9239	G/W	COLD WATER SUPPLY	M9272	Y/B	HEATING SUPPLY	M9307	Y/B	PROCESS WATER	M9335	Y/B	VENT
M9240	B/W	COMPRESSED AIR	M9275	Y/B	HI-PRESSURE AIR	M9308	Y/B	PROPANE GAS	M9336	G/W	WASTE
M9240	Y/B	COMPRESSED AIR	M9276	Y/B	HI-PRESSURE CONDENSATE	M9310	G/W	RAW WATER	M9336	Y/B	WASTE
M9241	Y/B	CONDENSATE	M9277	Y/B	HI-PRESSURE GAS	M9311	Y/B	REFRIGERATED LIQUID	M9337	G/W	WASTE WATER
M9242	Y/B	CONDENSATE RETURN	M9278	Y/B	HI-PRESSURE STEAM	M9312	Y/B	REFRIGERATED SUCTION	M9338	G/W	WATER
M9243	Y/B	CONDENSATE SUPPLY	M9279	Y/B	HI-PRESSURE WATER	M9313	G/W	REFRIGERATION	M9338	Y/B	WATER
M9244	G/W	CONDENSER WATER	M9280	Y/B	HOT WATER	M9314	B/W	RETURN	M9339	G/W	WELL WATER

Figure 19–8. Plumbing must be color coded and identified. Extract from catalog lists various chemicals and the marker colors designated by OSHA.

Courtesy of Seton Identification Products, Fall 2001 Catalog, Code BR-23, (BR-PM-1).

Alligator-clip cables must be in place for attachment to the grounding pipe near all drum usage areas. The ground must be to a cold water pipe. It cannot be attached to the hot water or sprinkler plumbing. All open or dispensing drums and other container of the flammable solvents must be grounded at all times. (Refer to figure 19–4.)

"4.4.2.11 Liquid storage areas where dispensing is conducted shall be provided with either a gravity or a continuous mechanical exhaust ventilation system. Mechanical ventilation shall be used if Class I liquids are dispensed within the room."

An exhaust must be in place to remove vapors from the room. This is usually in one corner, or two in a larger area, of the storage room, with the sweep at the floor level (figure 19–9). NFPA calls for the exhaust air to be taken from a point near a wall on one side of the room, within 12 inches from the floor. The location of the exhaust and any inlet air openings shall be arranged to provide for practical air movement across the floor to prevent accumulation of vapors.

Figure 19–9. Solvent storage pallet bins with low floor sweep and exhaust duct.

Storage Cabinets

Flammable storage cabinets are treated as miniature storage rooms. They are well suited for the storage of a minimum amount of flammable chemicals, in drums or in small cans and containers. The cabinet acts as containment for both spills and fires. Taken in perspective, the rules for storage rooms apply to the cabinets. Exhausts, grounding and proximity to electrical equipment are equally important (figure 19–10).

Local Laws to Restrict Storage of Chemicals

Local governments can regulate the conditions under which hazardous materials are stored and used. Building codes and standards provide one avenue to contain or restrict the volume of chemicals and the conditions of storage. Sanitary codes come into play in regions with sensitive ecological exposures. Using some example jurisdictions should enable the reader to relate to the regulations in other locales.

Suffolk County on Long Island, New York exemplifies the application of permitting and standards under sanitary codes to keep storage of chemicals at a minimum. Articles 12 and 7 in Suffolk County set the stage for maintaining limits on the volume of chemicals that can be stored on site and the conditions under which the chemicals will be stored.

Suffolk County, New York

Suffolk County is located at the east end of Long Island, between the salt water bodies of the Atlantic Ocean and Long Island Sound. The drinking water supply is from deep wells placed at various points in the county. The aquifer level is rather low. In a relatively few areas sewers have been installed and remove water wastes for treatment. However, for the greater area of the county wastewater is discharged to septic tanks and cesspools. Regulations are in place to restrict the use of underground tanks for industrial wastes to protect against contamination of the wells and streams that constitute the water supply for the population.

Storage of hazardous chemicals to safeguard groundwater supplies is governed under two separate and distinct codes. Article 12 addresses "Toxic and Hazardous Materials Storage and Handling Controls." Article 7 protects water supplies by more severe "Water Pollution Control" limitations on inventories of chemicals in a more limited area of the county. Both articles include virgin toxic and hazardous chemicals and hazardous chemical wastes in the computation of inventory levels acceptable in any given facility.

Article 12 encompasses all of the territory governed by Suffolk County. The article includes:

1. Toxic or hazardous materials as defined, "any substance, solution or mixture which, because of its quality, quantity, concentration, physical, chemical or infectious characteristics, or any combination. . . , presents or may present an actual or potential hazard to human health or to the drinking water supply if such substance . . . is discharged

to the land or waters of the County . . ."

2. "All toxic and hazardous wastes are toxic or hazardous materials."

The regulation covers all forms of storage—tanks below and above ground, drums and other containers. Outside oil storage tanks of 1,100 gallons or less and all indoor storage tanks come under the regulations. Construction of facilities and modifications of existing facilities cannot be undertaken without appropriate permits. Standards itemize the requirements for underground storage facilities, outdoor aboveground storage facilities, transfer of toxic or hazardous materials, and indoor storage facilities. Other provisions pertain to reporting, records, clean-up and maintenance, and posting and labeling. The code allows for waivers and variances.

Figure 19–10. Storage cabinets contain smaller quantities or single drums of flammable chemicals.

Article 12 discusses standards for construction, operating methodology, inspection routines, as well as handling of leaks and spills. An additional guidance was issued in 1995 to address the removal of underground storage tanks.

Article 7 is limited to deep discharge areas and water supply sensitive areas to protect them from discharges of sewage, industrial and other wastes, toxic or hazardous materials and stormwater runoff. The rather erratic zone of compliance follows the path of the Long Island Expressway and other major east-west roads encompassing the industrial complexes that abut the roads.

The article has a very specific list of chemicals and limitations on the amount of chemicals that can be stored in this zone. A typical facility that is housed in a building with 20,000 or less square feet is limited to a total of 250 gallons of liquid capacity and 2,000 pounds of dry storage. This includes wastes as well as virgin chemicals. Capacity for large facilities is determined based on a formula of 0.0125 gallons per square foot of gross floor area. In addition to codifying the conditions for storage of materials, Article 7 provides requirements for monitoring and reporting the composition of all discharges allowable under the facility permit.

Local governments within the county play a role through the zoning laws and building permits. Localities may place restrictions of the location of storage rooms or facilities and on the nature and quantity of the chemicals to be stored. They will also require landscaping to conceal outdoor equipment such as oxidizers and storage tanks.

The threat of leaks and spills has been a major concern of the public and environmental agencies. Much publicized hazardous conditions in homes and drinking water wells exposed to leaks from gasoline stations and industrial facilities has led to a high level of concern relative to the stability of tanks as they age

Above- and Below-Ground Storage Tanks

and provisions for containment in the event of leaks or spills. This concern has been manifested in regulations for both underground and aboveground storage tanks promulgated by federal and state agencies. Local governments have also passed legislation, placing restrictions on the installation and use of storage tanks.

The regulations specify the acceptable materials for fabrication based on the nature of the chemical, the containment that will be required in the event of a breach in the tank, monitoring instrumentation if warranted, testing procedures, as well as exemptions from the rules. Facilities must either register or permit the tanks with the local or state agency and maintain records relative to the maintenance and performance of the tanks.

Underground Storage Tanks

Leaks from underground storage tanks (UST) have made them a particular target for regulation and enforcement actions. In 1996, the USEPA estimated that there were over one million underground storage tanks in the United States, and that many were leaking.* Gasoline tank leaks have decimated residential areas and have been highly publicized in the newspapers. Underground oil tanks have been replaced in many areas by aboveground tanks to avoid leaks. The tanks that remain in the ground or are being installed must meet stringent standards to avoid these leaks.

Federal Regulation 40CFR Part 280 provides the "Technical Standards and Corrective Action Requirements for Owners and Operators of Underground Storage Tanks (UST)," which specifies that "no person may install an UST system . . . for the purpose of storing regulated substances unless the system . . . 1. Will prevent releases due to corrosion or structural failure for the operational life of the UST system; 2. Is cathodically protected against corrosion, constructed of noncorrodible material . . . or designed in a manner to prevent the release or threatened release of any stored substance: and 3. Is constructed or lined with material that is compatible with the stored substance."*

Performance standards for new UST systems under Part 280.20 require the prevention of releases due to structural failure, corrosion, spills and overfills. UST systems must meet the specific provisions:

1. Tanks must be properly designed and constructed and protected from corrosion in accordance with codes of practice developed by a recognized national association** or independent testing laboratory. Consideration is given to specifications based on the materials from which the tank will be fabricated—steel or fiberglass-reinforced plastic or any combination. Steel tanks must be cathodically protected to prevent or limit corrosion. Records must be kept that demonstrate compliance with regulations.

Storage tanks require provisions against overflow and spills.

*Musts for USTs, A Summary of Federal Regulations for Undergound Storage Tank Systems, USEPA, EPA510K-95-002, pg. 1.

2. Piping that is handling the chemicals, and may be in contact with the ground, must also meet stringent requirements relative to materials used and protection against corrosion. Piping must also be conformance with NFPA and local fire regulations. The two concerns for piping are flammability of the chemicals and, again, the propensity to corrode when exposed to corrosive forces in the environment.

3. Precautions must be taken to design the piping to prevent actual or threatened overfills and spills. Overfill equipment will prevent the accidental release of chemicals by shutting off the flow into a tank when it has reached 95 percent of its capacity. Spill prevention will contain any releases to avoid any the impact on the environment.

Aboveground Storage Tanks

The conditions for fabrication and installation of aboveground tanks are very similar to those for underground tanks. A major difference is the need to erect a containment area which will hold a given amount of "released" liquids. The containment will typically be required to hold 110% of the liquids stored in the tank(s).

Certification of UST Installation

Owners of facilities with UST must ensure that installations meet one or more of the methods of certification, in accordance with the local agencies:

1. Installer has been certified by the tank and piping manufacturers,

2. Installer has been certified or licensed by the implementing agency,

3. The installation has been inspected by a registered professional engineer with credentials in UST system installation,

4. Installation has been inspected and approved by the local agency, or

5. All work listed by the manufacturer has been completed.

---

*Code of Federal Regulations 40 CFR, Part 280, *Technical Standards and Corrective Action Requirements for Owners and Operators of Underground Storage Tanks (UST)*, Part 280.11 "Interim prohibition for deferred UST systems."

**Based on Note in Part 280.20, industry codes acceptable for UST systems are Underwriters Laboratories Standard 1316, "Standard for Glass-Fiber-Reinforced Plastic Underground Storage Tanks for Petroleum Products" and Standard 1746, "Corrosion Protection Systems for Underground Storage Tanks," American Society of Testing and Materials Standard D4021-86, "Standard Specification for Glass-Fiber-Reinforced Polyester Underground Storage Tanks," Steel Tank Institute, "Specification for STI-P3 System of External Corrosion Protection of Underground Steel Storage Tanks."

Spill Prevention Programs

A major requirement, given that construction standards are met, is the development of a spill prevention and response plan for the facility. A typical plan, as outlined for facilities in New York State, includes:

1. General information about the tanks, registration or permit status and a management certification,

2. Facility map with location of tanks and piping,

3 Summary of releases in previous five years,

4. Identification and assessment of causes of release (if any occurred),

5. Compliance status,

6. Inspection procedure and log,

7. Spill response plan,

8. Site assessment and findings,

9. Spill Reporting Form.

Appendix XXIX is a template for a spill prevention program.

Checklist for site assessment and findings.

Housekeeping and Maintenance

The most critical factor in storage of chemicals is the need to enforce safety regulations. Given the most compliant installation, poor housekeeping or disregard for safe practices can negate the precautions taken to provide deterrents to accidents and incidents. A periodic inspection routine must accompany the construction and use of any storage facility for hazardous chemicals. This must be a documented inspection with provisions for the remedial actions needed to correct any observed infractions. Training of personnel is crucial in the proper handling and use of chemicals and in the steps to be taken in the event of an incident.

Production and inventory management is vital to assure that remnants of previously used chemicals do not accumulate in storage rooms and that purchases are made within the limits established as acceptable quantities for a given area. Orderliness and cleanliness are necessary ingredients. Housekeeping must make sure that everything is in its place, that aisles are not blocked, and that dirt and debris are removed. Personnel using the chemicals must conform to safety standards and avoid spills or littering of the chemical storage room or area. Areas around drums and tanks should be kept accessible and not blocked by pallets or other drums.

Proper storage is not just the building of an edifice. It is the sum total of the room and how it is being used and not abused by the people in the facility.

CHAPTER 20

EPCRA: Motivation for Pollution Prevention

The intention of the law commonly known as Superfund, and technically under the acronyms CERCLA and EPCRA (Comprehensive Environmental Response, Compensation and Liability Act and Emergency Planning and Community Right-to-Know Act), was to set up a variety of mechanisms to address and ameliorate risks to public health, welfare, and the environment caused by hazardous substance releases. Since its inception, citations to businesses, which have contributed directly or indirectly to the creation of polluted sites, have led to litigation and high penalties.

When amended by SARA (Superfund Amendments and Reauthorization Act), the amendments known as SARA Title III added new dimensions to the process. Records and reports were required to provide guidance to local emergency response agencies and to develop an inventory of the releases of the list of additional hazardous substances. Title III of SARA created an emergency planning framework, which established the rights of local governments and members of the public to obtain information on the hazards posed by potential toxic substance releases and participate in the regulatory process.

The activities required to comply with SARA Title III have become the best motivators and incentives for the application of pollution prevention principles. Identifying the toxic chemicals, that are reason to come under the surveillance of EPCRA, is the first step to reducing usage or eliminating them completely from process and product. The Emergency Planning and Community Right to Know Act contains four major provisions:

1. Planning for chemical emergencies,

2. Emergency notification of chemical accidents and releases,

3. Reporting of hazardous chemical inventories,

4. Toxic chemical release reporting.

The law also deals with questions of trade secrets, disclosure of information to health professionals, and public access to the information gathered under the law.

Emergency Planning

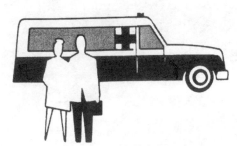

Emergency agencies, such as fire departments and hospitals, must be prepared to handle any release of chemicals in the event of an accident.

Source: USEPA booklet, "Chemicals in Your Community."

A key feature of the law provides for information collection that will enable community emergency response agencies to better confront incidents involving hazardous substances. States are empowered to appoint a State Emergency Response Commission. Existing agencies, such as environmental, health, commerce, emergency or other departments, can be given responsibility for developing comprehensive plans, distributed at the local level in the form of Local Emergency Planning Committees (LEPC). Committees at both levels can comprise representatives of government, law enforcement officers, civil defense workers, firefighters, health, hospital and transportation workers. Members of community groups, news media and local industry owners and operators can join them.

The initial task of the LEPCs was to set up its organization, collect information, analyze the potential hazards in the community and proceed to prepare plans to prepare for and respond to chemical emergencies in their districts. These analyses would identify the location of chemicals, the hazards posed by these chemicals and the vulnerable areas and populations. It could further explore the risk of accidents and their effect on the community.

Once the hazards have been analyzed, the LEPC develops a local emergency response plan. The plan lays out potential hazards, response capabilities and procedures to follow in the event of an emergency. The emergency plan must:

1. Use information provided by industry to identify facilities and transportation routes where hazardous substances are present,

2. Establish emergency response procedures including evacuation plans on and off site,

3. Set up notification procedures for personnel who will respond to emergencies,

4. Establish methods for determining the cause of the occurrence and severity of a release, the areas and populations most likely to be affected,

5. Establish means of notifying the public of a release,

6. Inventory the emergency equipment available in the community, including those at industrial facilities,

7. Provide for programs and schedules to train local emergency response personnel and medical workers who will respond to chemical emergencies,

8. Conduct exercises to test elements of the emergency response plans, and

9. Designate a community coordinator and facility coordinators to carry out the plans.

The exercise of this planning function for emergencies is as important at the level of the printing plant as it is for the community. A logical plan of action, with designated responsibilities, is equally as important for addressing fires, explosions and spills if they occur in or in the vicinity of the plant. With the growing number of regulations for the various environmental media that are calling for emergency contingency and risk management plans, it behooves the printing plant management to parallel the actions of the LEPC within its own walls. A sample contingency plan based on RCRA requirements is shown in Appendix XXV.

The law requires that facilities notify the local emergency planning committee if there is a release of a listed hazardous chemical. Thresholds have been established for a list of hazardous substances, and reportable quantities have been established to act as triggers for reporting of releases. An initial listing of over 400 chemicals was generated as extremely hazardous substances, plus substances that are subject to the emergency notification requirements of CERCLA Section 103(a). The initial notification can be by telephone, radio or in person. These requirements can be satisfied by dialing 911, or in the absence of 911, dialing the operator.

The emergency notification must include:

Emergency Notification

• The chemical name,

• An indication if the substance is extremely hazardous,

• An estimate of the quantity released to the environment,

• The time and duration of the release,

• The medium into which the release occurred (e.g., air, water, soil),

• Any known or anticipated acute or chronic health risks associated with the emergency and where to obtain appropriate advice regarding medical attention for exposed individuals,

• Proper precautions including evacuations, and

• Name and the telephone number of contact person in the plant.

The procedure carries forward to a follow-up after the incident, which updates the information from the initial notice and provides information on actual response actions taken, any known data on health risks associated with the release, and advice regarding the medical attention required for individuals who have been exposed to the release.

Reporting Chemicals Stored on Site

The regulations provide for a number of reporting techniques to assure that LEPCs have the information required to adequately plan for emergencies. These reports serve a dual purpose in providing a facility with a snapshot of the number and volume of hazardous chemicals that are being used or simply held on the shelves and in storage areas of the building.

The required reports initially conform to Section 301, requiring any facility in the region of an LEPC to transmit basic information indicating hazardous materials that are stored above the listed threshold for that chemical. Section 312 requires an annual, fairly detailed report, which describes the chemical nature of the substances, the hazards, quantities stored, types of containers, and conditions of storage for temperature and pressure.

SARA Title III has a unique listing of chemicals for which data must be filed annually, based on specific thresholds by chemical. The minimum for many chemicals is 500 pounds. Extremely hazardous chemicals have lower thresholds; less hazardous chemicals have thresholds up to 1,000 pounds. As a general catchall for large inventories, the regulations call for the reporting of any OSHA regulated chemical that is stored in quantities in excess of 10,000 pounds.

The format of the report is quite simple and is available in commercial software packages. A sample is illustrated in figure 20–1. The form consists of blocks to check or codify the appropriate classifications that describe the materials, and codes to relate actual inventories to ranges indicative of the quantity of materials stored in the facility. The Tier II report asks the printer to identify the SIC code (Standard Industrial Classification) for the particular process or market that is being served. SIC codes are discussed in the following descriptive information for the Toxic Release Inventory report.

The report is based on an actual inventory of the facility, listing all chemicals that are sitting on the shelves or on the floor. The average inventory is noted, as well as the maximum on any given day during the year. The information is taken from the material safety data sheets. Take note that in the event an MSDS provides an inadequate picture of the hazards inherent to that chemical, the supplier/manufacturer must supply that information in confidence to an authorized health official of the company.

Revised 11/99   *Important   Read all instructions before completing form*   Reporting period: From January 1 to December 31, 1999   Page 1 of 1 pages

NEW YORK CITY Right-to-Know FACILITY INVENTORY FORM TIER TWO

Facility Identification

Name: RTK Manufacturing Co., Inc.
Street: 59-17 Junction Blvd., 3rd Floor
City: Elmhurst   State: NY   Zip+4: 10068-5109   County: Queens
Telephone (718) 595-5555
SIC Code: 5 5 9 4
Dun & Brad. Number: 1 2 3 4 5 6 7 8 9
For Official Use Only: ID# ____   Date Received: ____

Owner/Operator
Name: Nancy Doe   Phone (212) 566-7264
Mail Address: 346 Broadway, New York, NY 10013

Emergency Contacts
Name: William Clark   Title: Supervisor
Day Phone (212) 566-7264   24-hr phone (718) 587-2130
Name: George Richmond   Title: Supervisor
Day Phone (212) 566-7263   24-hr phone (718) 999-8787

Chemical Description

CAS ____   [ ] Trade Secret
Name(s) of Chemical(s): Solvent X – 50% 2-butoxyethanol (111-76-2), 14% sodium hypochlorite (768-52-9), 10% formaldehyde (50-00-0), 0.5% benzene (71-43-2)
Check all that apply: [ ] Pure [x] Mix [ ] Solid [x] Liquid [ ] Gas [ ] EHS

Physical and Health Hazards (Check all that apply): [ ] Fire [ ] Sudden Release Of Pressure [ ] Reactivity [x] Immediate (acute) [x] Delayed (chronic)

Inventory: Max Amount (code) 0 4; Avg. Amount (code) 0 3; No. of Days Present 3 6 5

Storage Codes and Locations (Non-Confidential) — Storage Locations: Container C, Pressure 1, Temperature 6 — Refrigerated area, 3 holding tanks – first floor
OPTIONAL: Check box if information submitted is identical to last year [ ]

CAS 8 0 0 6 | 6 1 | 9   [ ] Trade Secret
Name(s) of Chemical(s): Gasoline
Check all that apply: [ ] Pure [x] Mix [ ] Solid [x] Liquid [ ] Gas [ ] EHS

Physical and Health Hazards: [x] Fire [ ] Sudden Release Of Pressure [ ] Reactivity [ ] Immediate (acute) [x] Delayed (chronic)

Inventory: Max Amount (code) 0 4; Avg. Amount (code) 0 4; No. of Days Present 3 6 5

Storage: Container B, Pressure 1, Temperature 4 — Parking area – North side of building
OPTIONAL: Check box if information submitted is identical to last year [x]

CAS 7 6 6 4 | 9 3 | 9   [ ] Trade Secret
Name(s) of Chemical(s): Batteries – 30% Sulfuric Acid (7664-93-9)
Check all that apply: [ ] Pure [x] Mix [ ] Solid [x] Liquid [ ] Gas [ ] EHS

Physical and Health Hazards: [ ] Fire [x] Sudden Release Of Pressure [x] Reactivity [x] Immediate (acute) [ ] Delayed (chronic)

Inventory: Max Amount (code) 0 3; Avg. Amount (code) 0 3; No. of Days Present 3 6 5

Storage: Container A, Pressure 1, Temperature 4 — Batteries – Back up power, Third floor
OPTIONAL: Check box if information submitted is identical to last year [ ]

Certification (Read and sign after completing all sections)
I certify under penalty of law that I have personally examined and am familiar with the information submitted in pages one through 1, and that based on my inquiry of those individuals responsible for obtaining the information, I believe that the submitted information is true, accurate and complete.

Nancy Doe, President   ____ Signature   January 6, 2000 Date signed
Name and official title of owner/operator OR owner/operator's authorized representative

OPTIONAL: I have attached a site plan [x]

Figure 20–1. Sample New York City Facility Inventory Report form that is submitted every year in compliance with the SARA Title III, Section 312 requirements, although with a more comprehensive list of chemicals and lower thresholds.

Source: NYCDEP Right to Know Law.

TABLE 20–1. INVENTORY RANGES FOR TIER II ANNUAL REPORTS

Weight Range in Pounds		
From	To	Code
0	99	01
100	999	02
1,000	9,999	03
10,000	99,999	04
100,000	999,999	05
1,000,000	9,999,999	06
10,000,000	49,999,999	07
50,000,000	99,999,999	08
100,000,000	499,999,999	09
500,000,000	999,999,999	10
billion	higher	11

An example of a reportable item would be isopropanol, The Tier II report would note that it is a liquid, pure (as opposed to a blend), flammable, and an acute or chronic health hazard, stored in drums or cans at ambient temperature and pressure, and where the containers are stored. The quantities (maximum and average) would be in code, indicative of the range rather than the exact quantity, i.e., 2 would represent a range from 100 to 999 pounds, and 3 would indicate 1000 to 9,999 pounds (Table 20–1).

At the time the report is first filed to notify the state and local LEPC, most jurisdictions will require a complete set of MSDSs. Subsequently, in general, the only requirement is to submit the report, accompanied only by any new MSDS. Some localities, such as New York City, will require submission of a fresh set of MSDS every time the report is submitted.

A second form that is required by some agencies as part of this law is the Tier I report (figure 20–2). The Tier I report assembles the ingredients by chemical from the various substances used and accumulates them to a single total number for that chemical. As an example, the facility may have a few solvent blends, all of which contain a percentage of toluene. On the Tier I report, the quantity reported would be the total of all the toluene in the various solvent blends used. The report would also list the same basic information as the Tier II report to describe the hazards and storage data. The State of New Jersey requires filing of the Tier I form annually.

Process for Filing a TIER II Report

The report of listed chemicals in the facility provides a snapshot of the average and maximum stores on the premises that may be encountered by emergency response personnel answering a call for help. It also puts some dimensions on the potential hazards to workers and the public from any incident that may release these chemicals to the environment.

The systematic inventorying of all chemicals in the building is an essential element to completing the Tier II report (figure 20–3). While a review of current purchases may reveal substances used in the previous period, it in no way takes into account any chemicals that remain in the facility as remnants of previous orders and practices, or as samples supplied for trials by well-meaning sales personnel. The physical inventory lists names of the product, quantities, types of containers used, and the physical conditions under which the substances are stored: temperature and pressure. The location of the storage areas should also be noted.

The process of preparing the report provides an excellent annual review of the chemistry used or of chemicals sitting on the shelves in the plant (figure 20–4), highlighting the possible duplication of effort or potential danger of misuse that can arise from

Tier One — EMERGENCY AND HAZARDOUS CHEMICAL INVENTORY

Aggregate Information by Hazard Type

FOR OFFICIAL USE ONLY: ID # ______ Date Received ______

Important: Read instructions before completing form

Reporting Period From January 1 to December 31, 19____

Facility Identification

Name ______
Street ______
City ______ County ______ State ______ Zip ______
SIC Code [ ][ ][ ][ ] Dun & Brad Number [ ][ ]-[ ][ ][ ]-[ ][ ][ ][ ]

Emergency Contacts

Name ______
Title ______
Phone ( ) ______
24 Hour Phone ( ) ______

Name ______
Title ______
Phone ( ) ______
24 Hour Phone ( ) ______

Owner/Operator

Name ______
Mail Address ______
Phone ( ) ______

[ ] Check if information below is identical to the information submitted last year.

[ ] Check if site plan is attached

	Hazard Type	*Max Amount**	*Average Daily Amount**	*Number of Days On-Site*	*General Location*
Physical Hazards	Fire	[ ][ ]	[ ][ ]	[ ][ ][ ]	______
	Sudden Release of Pressure	[ ][ ]	[ ][ ]	[ ][ ][ ]	______
	Reactivity	[ ][ ]	[ ][ ]	[ ][ ][ ]	______
Health Hazards	Immediate (acute)	[ ][ ]	[ ][ ]	[ ][ ][ ]	______
	Delayed (Chronic)	[ ][ ]	[ ][ ]	[ ][ ][ ]	______

Certification *(Read and sign after completing all sections)*

I certify under penalty of law that I have personally examined and am familiar with the information submitted in pages one through ______, and that based on my inquiry of those individuals responsible for obtaining the information, I believe that the submitted information is true, accurate and complete.

______
Name and official title of owner/operator OR owner/operator's authorized representative

______ Signature ______ Date signed

* **Reporting Ranges**

Range Code	Weight Range in Pounds From...	To...
01	0	99
02	100	999
03	1000	9,999
04	10,000	99,999
05	100,000	999,999
06	1,000,000	9,999,999
07	10,000,000	49,999,999
08	50,000,000	99,999,999
09	100,000,000	499,999,999
10	500,000,000	999,999,999
11	1 billion	higher than 1 billion

Figure 20–2. Sample Tier I report complies inventory information by chemical rather than product. Source: USEPA.

Figure 20–3. Physical inventory of chemicals is annual chore.

Figure 20–4. Inks stored on shelves in chemical storage room.

employing more chemistry than is needed to accomplish the work in progress. The process is a constant reminder of wastes that arise from lack of training and motivation stemming from oversight by management of its role to monitor all line activities when purchasing and using chemicals. Management is afforded a means of reducing costs by controlling this inventory in a more effective and profitable manner.

The list of substances is compiled and an evaluation is made of the quantities in-house against the thresholds for inclusion. The inventory can be narrowed down to those items that qualify for reporting. At this point, the collection of MSDSs should be assembled for the items that will be reported. The MSDSs will reveal the nature of the physical and health hazards. Does the chemical cause chronic effects? Are there more immediate acute ramifications? Is it flammable or reactive? These are questions that have to be satisfied in the Tier II format.

A common practice at the time of the Tier II inventory data collection is to perform housecleaning. If the process does not use a particular product anymore, ship it out as a hazardous waste if the chemistry is hazardous. If there are inks, thinners, fountain solutions, developers and fixers that are no longer in use, pack them up and ship them out. Find out if friends who print or local schools with printing courses can put the chemistry to use. Give it to them, but don't keep it. Don't build an inventory of worthless hazardous products. A rule of thumb used by the regulatory agencies is that any chemical that has not been used for the past 12 months is a waste, a hazardous waste in most cases.

Information and forms for the Tier I and II reports are included as Appendix XXXV.

The Toxic Release Report— TRI

Probably the most critical report required by the regulation is known alternately as the Form R or TRI report. The formal name is Toxic Release Inventory report. Filed annually by July 1st, the TRI provides the basis for much of the information that is provided to the public and the press about the presence of chemicals in our environment.

This report is the most comprehensive summary of where the waste products of manufacturing go. Every medium is covered as to quantity and destination of any hazardous chemical waste. Air emissions, water discharges, off site disposal of hazardous wastes, and accidental releases are encompassed in this eight-page summation of a year's activities. On-and-off site recovery, recycling and energy usage are included, as are efforts at pollution prevention.

The major objective of this report is to inform the government and the public of the volume of pollutants that are entering the environment and to encourage pollution prevention by industry. When the EPA first started to collect data, it issued periodic publicity releases for the nation and by area, describing the chemicals and volumes. This placed considerable pressure on major sources of such pollution. Topographical maps with levels of pollutants released, depicted as mountains above a plain tended to highlight cities and towns with abnormal quantities. The city of Rochester, New York, was typical, where releases from a few major companies towered above the pollution levels of any of the other cities in the state, metropolitan New York City included. Needless to say, industries in Rochester did not particularly appreciate being singled out by this physical depiction of their area or the negative image associated with the chart.

A more recent development has been the posting of the reports on the Internet, making the information available to anyone. Large multinational companies, on the assumption that making such reported data readily accessible would provide damaging information to vandals and terrorists, opposed this action. Of equal concern was posting of information that would not be easily understood by community groups.

The list of toxic chemicals that trigger reporting under this provision of the law is not the same as for the Section 312 Tier 2 report, nor are the quantities that trigger reporting the same. There is no provision for reporting OSHA chemicals based on usage. It is important to reiterate that the TRI is not a function of purchases; it is based on usage. An accurate inventory should be taken of the listed chemicals and used to adjust the purchase figures for the year. Table 20–2 lists TRI chemicals and sources typical of print shops.

The next question is whether a facility has to report definitions and thresholds under TRI. Figure 20–5 outlines the step-by-step considerations to determine applicability.

The threshold for any listed chemical that becomes a component of the product is 25,000 pounds used per year. Let's assume that the most popular ink used to produce a line of products contains a 10-percent loading of lead chromate. If total usage for a year of this ink is 100,000 pounds and the lead contents amounts to 10,000 pounds, the facility does not have to report the substance for that year. On the other hand, chemicals that facilitate or are otherwise used in the process but do not become part of the product, i.e., as a diluent or as a cleaning agent, will require reporting if the quantity used exceeds 10,000 pounds. If a solvent such as toluene is used for cleaning the press rollers, and the volume amounts to 10,000 or more pounds, then the facility must file a TRI report.

TABLE 20–2. CHEMICALS AND CHEMICAL CATEGORIES COMMONLY ENCOUNTERED IN PRINTING OPERATIONS

Process	Chemical
Ink solvent Cleaning	Toluene, MEK, Methanol, Xylene, Ethylbenzene
Fountain solution Cleaning	Certain Glycol Ethers
Cleaning	Xylene (mixed), MIBK
Acrylic coatings, gravure inks	Zinc Compounds
Copper plating	Copper
Red ink pigments	Barium Compounds
Green ink pigment	Copper Compounds
Adhesive solvent	n-Hexane
Ink solvent	n-Butyl Alcohol
Fountain solution cleaning	Ethylene Glycol
Plasticizer	Dibutyl Phthalate
Cleaning solvent	Ethylbenzene, 1,2,4-Trimethylbenzene, Hexane
Water-based inks and coatings	Ammonia
Cleaning Etching	Nitric Acid

Source: USEPA, *Emergency Planning and Community Right-To-Know Act Section 313 Reporting Guidance for the Printing, Publishing, and Packaging Industry*, EPA 745-B-00-005, p 2–9.

Another qualifier is the number of employees. If the facility employs less than 10 people, it does not have to file a report. However, it must be noted that simply not reporting does not satisfy the intent of the law. The facility must conduct a summation of the data for the year for the listed chemicals and have the analysis available for inspection by the agency.

Once the basic information has been collected, it is necessary to determine what releases have occurred and where the releases went. Figure 20–6 outlines the various releases and other waste management alternatives that are reported in the TRI. Documentation will come from hazardous waste manifests, bills of lading, mass balances, engineering standards, as well as from internal records. Individual processes and chemicals may be analyzed using flow charts, as in figure 20–7, assure that all releases are accounted for.

Once this information has been gathered, it is time to complete the form. Using the codes provided in the instructions, the name of each substance is entered and the components of the product listed. CAS numbers and percentages of the formulation are entered in the descriptive box provided for each chemical product. See Appendix XXXVI for form and codes used when preparing the TRI report.

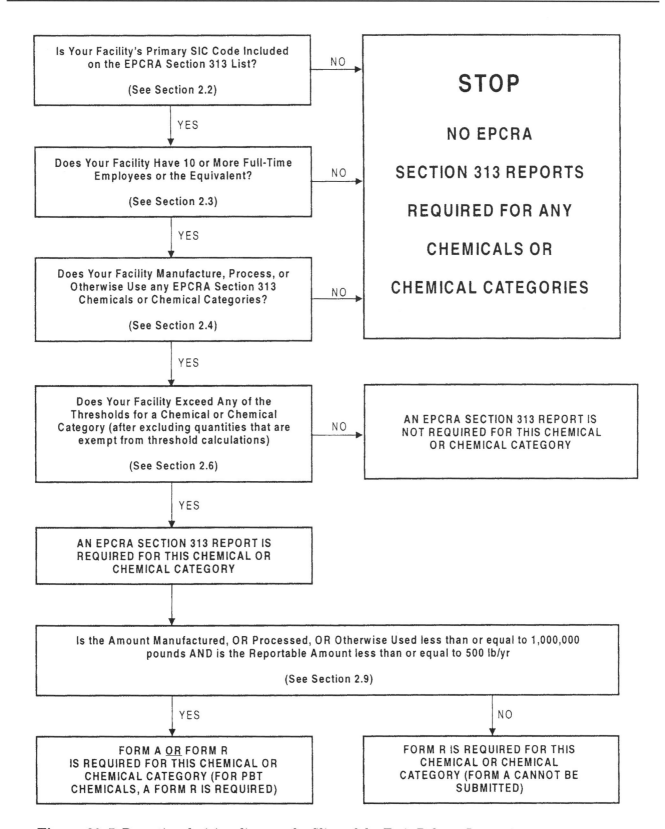

Figure 20–5. Reporting decision diagram for filing of the Toxic Release Inventory report.

Source: USEPA, *Emergency Planning and Community Right-To-Know Act Section 313 Reporting Guidance for the Printing, Publishing, and Packaging Industry*, EPA 745-B-00-005, p 2–3.

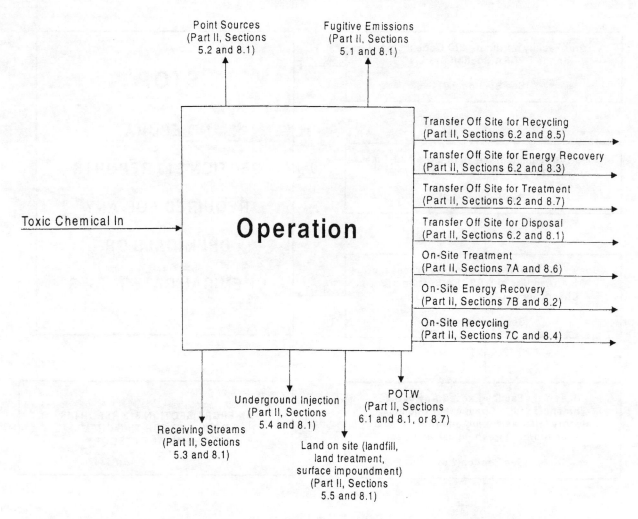

Figure 20–6. Possible release and other waste management types for EPCRA Section 313 chemicals and other chemical categories.

Source: USEPA, *Emergency Planning and Community Right-To-Know Act Section 313 Reporting Guidance for the Printing, Publishing, and Packaging Industry*, EPA 745-B-00-005, p 4–5.

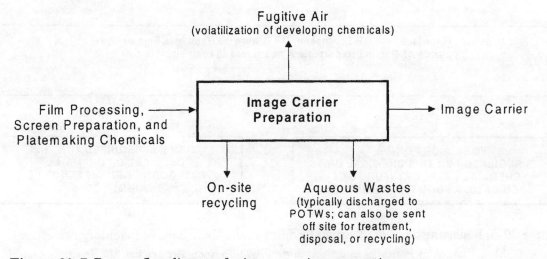

Figure 20–7. Process flow diagram for image carrier preparation.

Source: USEPA, *Emergency Planning and Community Right-To-Know Act Section 313 Reporting Guidance for the Printing, Publishing, and Packaging Industry*, EPA 745-B-00-005, p 4–40.

The TRI may not be as lengthy as many Tier II reports, but it contains a more detailed analysis of the sources and destinations of the various waste streams and where they go after leaving the facility. The combination of the information collected for the Tier II report and the mass balance of air emissions and hazardous waste disposal will provide a portion of the information needed for this report. Manifests for the hazardous waste, waste- water disposal manifests and sewer/water records will provide information needed for their respective portions of the report. Purchasing records and inventories are required, since this is a usage report.

Keep in mind the fact that EPA has developed a relationship with industry, and has developed guidelines to assist printers (and other processes) in the computation of data and the completion of the report. This cooperative effort has resulted a document, "Emergency Planning and Community Right-To-Know Act, Section 313 Reporting Guidance for the Printing, Publishing and Packaging Industry," (EPA 745-B-00-005, May 2000).

The first thing one must do is determine if the facility must submit a TRI report. Key data are as follows:

1. How many employees are there in total in the facility? If the number is 10 full-time employees or more, as determined by number of hours worked, then TRI must be reported.

2. The SIC code for the business conducted. Manufacturing includes SIC codes with the first two numbers beginning with 20 and ending at 39. Table 20–3 lists SIC codes that perform printing operations. Since other businesses may print product whose SIC codes do not fall into these categories, facility management should consider secondary SIC activities in the plant. Caution should be exercised with businesses that have a primary SIC code that is not covered, but in which printing contributes at least 50 percent of the sales value of the product. As a secondary SIC, the facility may have to report. An example could be the case of a firm that produces advertising displays. The primary SIC code would be 3993, but the printing by the screen process would also require a secondary SIC of 2759, Commercial Printing, n.e.c. (not elsewhere classified).

3. Does the facility use any chemicals that are listed for Section 313 reporting? Consult the MSDSs and the mass balance breakout of chemicals in the inks, coatings, solvents and other chemistry used in the facility.

4. The next two questions relate to the amounts of the chemicals used and the thresholds for reporting. Does the facility use a listed chemical that becomes part of the product, such as a pigment containing lead chromate, of which usage exceeds 25,000 pounds for the year? If the mass balance, developed for evaluating the environmental components of the inks and coatings reveals the existence

Completing a TRI Report

TABLE 20–3. REPRESENTATIVE SIC CODES FOR FACILITIES THAT MAY PERFORM PRINTING OPERATIONS

SIC Code	SIC Description
2653	Corrugated and solid fiber boxes
2657	Folding paperboard boxes, including sanitary
2672	Coated and laminated paper, n.e.c.*
2673	Plastics, foil, and coated paper bags
2674	Uncoated paper and multiwall bags
2677	Envelopes
2678	Stationary, tablets, and related products
2679	Converted paper and paperboard products, n.e.c.*
2711	Newspapers: publishing, or publishing and printing
2721	Periodicals: publishing, or publishing and printing
2731	Books: publishing, or publishing and printing
2732	Book printing
2741	Miscellaneous publishing
2752	Commercial printing, lithography
2754	Commercial printing, gravure
2759	Commercial printing, n.e.c.*
2761	Manifold business forms
2771	Greeting cards
2782	Blankbooks, looseleaf binders and devices
2789	Bookbinding and related work
2791	Typesetting
2796	Platemaking and related services
3999	Manufacturing Industries, n.e.c.*

* n.e.c. - not elsewhere classified

of this quantity of the lead chromate, then the facility has to report. The key is the 25,000-pound threshold.

5. Does the facility use any listed chemical as an ancillary material in making the product? Cleaning solvents, solvents that add liquidity to an ink or coating, maintenance—these are all uses that are governed by a threshold of 10,000 pounds per year.

Having determined that the facility must submit a report, there is one more qualifier that the EPA has added in recent years. If a facility qualifies to report, but the sum of the on-site amounts released, treated, recycled or combusted for energy, combined with the disposition off site is less than 500 pounds for the chemical, then a shorter form (Form A) can be substituted for the lengthier TRI report. This requires completion of that portion of the report which describes the facility, but not the detail of releases.

I t has been determined that the facility must complete a report for each of the listed chemicals. Proceed to follow the procedure for completing the report.

Getting Started

1. Summarize all purchases for the year of any products that include listed chemicals. This may have been done already in the audit or the annual mass balance for air emissions and water discharges. The amount that counts is that percentage of the product purchased that is the listed chemical; it is not the entire amount of the total product. For example, if an ink has a 20 percent component that is listed, i.e., methanol, only 10 percent of the purchased amount will be counted toward the accumulation that will trigger the threshold quantity.

2. Accumulate the material safety data sheets to confirm the inclusion of the listed chemistry. The Tier I and II reports will provide additional insight into what must be reported.

3. Consult the process flow chart that was developed during the audit of the facility. This will identify what is happening to the chemicals and where records will be needed to account for the different releases that are accountable in the TRI report.

4. Accumulate the hazardous waste manifests and annual report, and any documentation on the discharge of wastes into the sewer system or other wastewater discharge points.

5. Obtain records of any treatment, recovery or recycling activity of the listed chemistry.

6. Any other documentation that tracks the purchase, use and disposition of "waste" by-products and sheds light on the life cycle of the listed chemicals will be of value.

All documentation used to develop the reports should be maintained in a manner that will be available in the event of an inspection or audit. Once the facility has all the information necessary to identify and quantify the listed chemicals, it is relatively simple to isolate those substances that must be reported.

There are rare cases in which printers use a chemical in excess of 25,000 pounds in the course of the printing process that becomes part of the product. It is possible that such chemicals may enter the facility in the course of other industrial activities that precede or follow the printing of the product. In most cases, printers will exceed the threshold of 10,000 pounds due to the use of listed solvents. Whether used as a diluent or for cleaning, there are many listed chemical substances that wind up as a liquid component of the process. With the need for aggressive cleaning action and "fast drying cycles," some of the major solvents used are listed. Typical examples are toluene, methyl ethyl ketone, xylene and glycol ethers.

For each chemical, determine the usage, amount disposed as hazardous waste, discharged legally to a public sewer system or recycled for reuse in the plant. The computation of the amount released can be function of a stack test, lab testing of waste solvent or water samples, or calculations using equations that have been developed for the purpose.

Completing The Form—Part I: Facility Identification

The first part of the report contains facility identification information and is similar for each chemical submission. Included are the name and address, contact persons, phone numbers, permit numbers as they apply to the disposition of waste products, etc. An authorized member of management signs the form. While the basic form may be copied for each of the chemicals reported, the signature must be an original for each chemical reported. (See figure 20–8.)

Perhaps the most troublesome feature in this part is the determination of the latitude and longitude of the facility. Maps are available from a limited number of sources, but the actual location must be extrapolated using the degrees, minutes and seconds of the closest printed lines of either dimension. This can best be done by a physical tracing of the location in the closest box of known numbers and using the measured proportions to come to a more exact determination of the latitude and longitude of the facility. It has not been uncommon for errors in calculations or perception to place a facility in the middle of a body of water. If in doubt, seek knowledgeable assistance.

Completing the Form: Chemical Specific Information

Using the information gathered in the fact-finding process, a determination will be made of the quantity of each chemical that exits the building in a specific form or category. Actual numbers based on shipments, stack tests, lab tests, etc. can be used. Where actual numbers are not available, engineering factors have been determined which can be used to estimate releases. These are available from the EPA, many in documents that are industry and process specific. As summarized in Section 8 of the report (figure 20–9), the specific releases reported in detail are:

1. Air emissions that are fugitive or non-point specific,

2. Air emissions that are exhausted from stacks or specified points (fans, etc.),

3. Discharges to streams or bodies of water,

4. Discharges to underground injection wells,

 **EPA**

United States
Environmental Protection
Agency

FORM R

Section 313 of the Emergency Planning and Community
Right-to-Know Act of 1986, also known as Title III of the Superfund
Amendments and Reauthorization Act

TOXIC CHEMICAL RELEASE
INVENTORY REPORTING FORM

WHERE TO SEND COMPLETED FORMS:
1. EPCRA Reporting Center
P.O. Box 3348
Merrifield, VA 22116-3348
ATTN: TOXIC CHEMICAL RELEASE INVENTORY

2. APPROPRIATE STATE OFFICE
(See instructions in Appendix F)

Enter "X" here if this
is a revision

For EPA use only

IMPORTANT: See instructions to determine when "Not Applicable (NA)" boxes should be checked.

PART I. FACILITY IDENTIFICATION INFORMATION

SECTION 1. REPORTING YEAR 19 ——

SECTION 2. TRADE SECRET INFORMATION

| 2.1 | Are you claiming the toxic chemical identified on page 2 trade secret? ☐ **Yes** (Answer question 2.2; Attach substantiation forms) ☐ **No** Do not answer 2.2; go to Section 3 | 2.2 | Is this copy ☐ Sanitized ☐ Unsanitized (Answer only if "YES" in 2.1) |

SECTION 3. CERTIFICATION (Important: Read and sign after completing all form sections.)

I hereby certify that I have reviewed the attached documents and that, to the best of my knowledge and belief, the submitted information is true and complete and that the amounts and values in this report are accurate based on reasonable estimates using data available to the preparers of this report.

Name and official title of owner/operator or senior management official:	Signature:	Date signed:

SECTION 4. FACILITY IDENTIFICATION

TRI Facility ID Number

4.1	Facility or Establishment Name	Facility or Establishment Name or Mailing Address (if different from street address)
	Street	Mailing Address
	City/County/State/Zip Code	City/County/State/Zip Code

4.2	This report contains information for: (**Important**: check a **or** b; check c if applicable)	a. ☐ An entire facility	b. ☐ Part of a facility	c. ☐ A Federal facility

4.3	Technical Contact Name		Telephone Number (include area code)
4.4	Public Contact Name		Telephone Number (include area code)

4.5	SIC Code (s) (4 digits)	a.	b.	c.	d.	e.	f.

4.6	Latitude	Degrees	Minutes	Seconds	Longitude	Degrees	Minutes	Seconds

4.7 Dun & Bradstreet Number(s) (9 digits)	4.8 EPA Identification Number(s) (RCRA I.D. No.) (12 characters)	4.9 Facility NPDES Permit Number(s) (9 characters)	4.10 Underground Injection Well Code (UIC) I.D. Number(s) (12 digits)
a.	a.	a.	a.
b.	b.	b.	b.

SECTION 5. PARENT COMPANY INFORMATION

5.1	Name of Parent Company	☐ NA	
5.2	Parent Company's Dun & Bradstreet Number	☐ NA	(9 digits)

EPA Form 9350-1 (Rev. 04/97) - Previous editions are obsolete.

Figure 20–8. Sample TRI IC page with description of facility.
Source: USEPA.

5. Discharges to a publicly owned treatment works (sewer system),

6. Transfers to other off-site locations for the purpose of disposal, treatment, energy recovery or recycling. Disposal off-site would include landfill, underground injection or transfer to a waste broker.

The information is requested in individual sections, requesting very specific information as to quantity, disposition on site and off, where the off-site facilities are located and their EPA identification numbers.

The final section (8) summarizes the releases for the current year in comparison with the previous year and projection of the releases in future years. This table represents a history of the use of the particular chemical and the success of the facility in reducing

SECTION 8. SOURCE REDUCTION AND RECYCLING ACTIVITIES				
All quantity estimates can be reported using up to two significant figures.	Column A Prior Year (pounds/year)	Column B Current Reporting Year (pounds/year)	Column C Following Year (pounds/year)	Column D Second Following Year (pounds/year)
8.1 Quantity released *				
8.2 Quantity used for energy recovery on-site				
8.3 Quantity used for energy recovery off-site				
8.4 Quantity recycled on-site				
8.5 Quantity recycled off-site				
8.6 Quantity treated on-site				
8.7 Quantity treated off-site				
8.8 Quantity released to the environment as a result of remedial actions, catastrophic events, or one-time events not associated with production processes (pounds/year)				
8.9 Production ratio or activity index				
8.10 Did your facility engage in any source reduction activities for this chemical during the reporting year? If not, enter "NA" in Section 8.10.1 and answer Section 8.11.				

	Source Reduction Activities [enter code(s)]	Methods to Identify Activity (enter codes)		
8.10.1		a.	b.	c.
8.10.2		a.	b.	c.
8.10.3		a.	b.	c.
8.10.4		a.	b.	c.
8.11	Is additional optional information on source reduction, recycling, or pollution control activities included with this report? (Check one box)		YES ☐ NO ☐	

* Report releases pursuant to EPCRA Section 329(8) including "any spilling, leaking, pumping, pouring, emitting, emptying, discharging, injecting, escaping, leaching, dumping, or disposing into the environment." Do not include any quantity treated on-site or off-site.

Figure 20–9. Sample Section 8 of TRI with listing of release media and chronological history.

Source: USEPA.

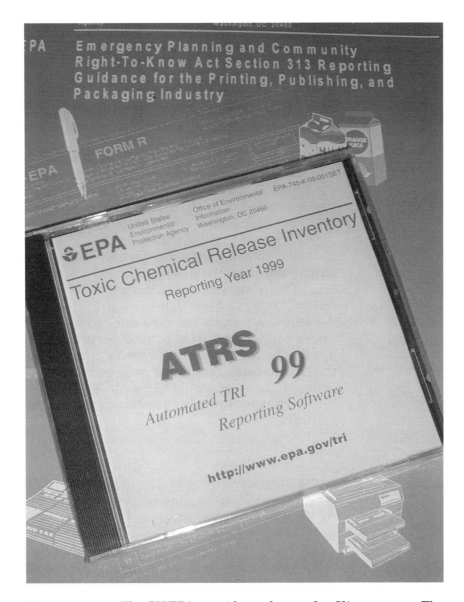

Figure 20–10. The USEPA provides software for filing reports. The current CD is much improved over earlier editions.

the quantities used, as well as a projection of the intentions for the next two years.

Information on pollution prevention activities is solicited but it is not mandatory to provide any details of the pollution prevention program or its results. To some extent, the impact of pollution prevention is made obvious by the experience summarized as actual releases and the projections for the coming years. If a facility has an active pollution prevention program, documentation of the activities of the program can be most advantageous should the TRI report be reviewed as part of a citizen's surveillance effort of industrial environmental impacts by a community or environmental advocacy organization.

Submission of the report can be done by hard copy or by use of specially designed software provided by the agency. The USEPA developed software for electronic or disk submission of the TRI report (figure 20–10). Each year, the report booklet is accompanied by a disk with the current version of the software. Over the years, the program has been improved considerably and only the latest version should be used. When submitting a disk with an annual report, it is also necessary to provide the printed facility identification (IC) page with the authorized signature. The report, when completed, should be reviewed for accuracy. If done using the software, a validation process checks the information prior to copying to a disk or printing a hard copy. Keep in mind that this is to check for completion only, not for accuracy of the numerical data pertinent to the facility releases.

Upon submission to the EPA, the report will be reviewed and a computer checklist will be returned for confirmation of the accuracy of the report. If any errors are detected, a request for correction of the submitted information will be sent. There will be a deadline for making the necessary changes, Be alert that not all errors can be attributed to your preparation of the report; some are due in part to the software or changes in the programming that are not apparent to the preparer of the report. In any case, it is important to communicate with the agency and make the necessary changes to conform to the current version of the reporting software.

Lesson to be Learned from SARA Title III Reports

Given a list of chemicals that subjects a business to the process described in this chapter, it would indeed be desirable to take whatever actions are appropriate to avoid the need to file this report. There are costs and liabilities accompanying the need to maintain records, prepare reports and withstand inspections and audits. The facility could face the prospect of being subjected to government and public scrutiny that entails the need for engaging legal and consulting services. In other words, wouldn't life be simpler if the targeted chemicals could be eliminated from the process by being replaced by safer, unlisted substances? If not eliminated completely, could we restrict use to limits well below the thresholds? These are the immediate questions that result from facing the facts with regard to use of any listed chemicals.

The answer is a management-driven program of pollution prevention. Use technology to eliminate the need to use the listed chemicals. Use working practices to minimize the use of those that cannot be replaced. Don't take no for an answer, when it is apparent that change is necessary.

At such time as the actual usage is below the threshold, some activities to meet the regulations will still be necessary. Records will be required for a period of time to substantiate that the usage has either ceased or declined. This can be accomplished at the same time that records are being maintained for other media, specifically

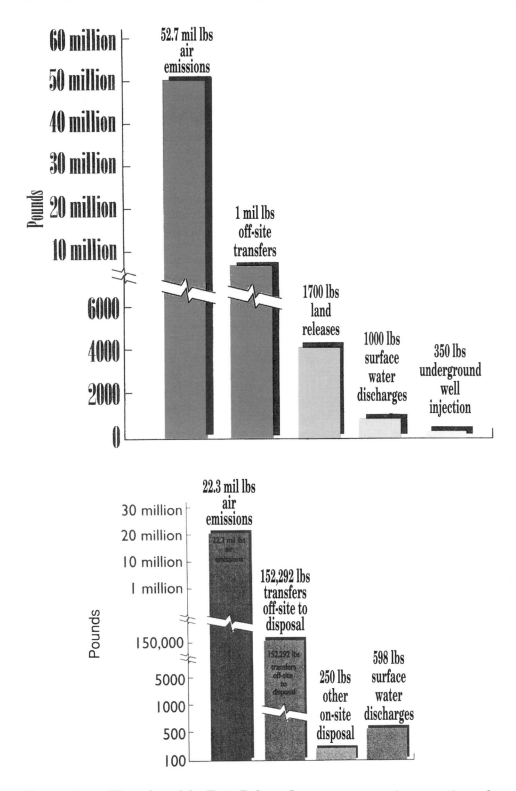

Figure 20–11. The value of the Toxic Release Inventory reports in promoting pollution prevention in the printing industry can be seen in the improvement demonstrated by the comparative bar charts for the years 1993 (top) and 1998 (bottom).

Source: Information provided to the Waste Reduction Center at the University of Northern Iowa by PNEAC for publications describing pollution prevention opportunities for lithographic printers.

for the mass balance maintained to comply with air emission regulations. Once a facility falls below the threshold or for other reasons that required filing the reports, it is not unusual for either the federal or state agencies to monitor the facility to confirm the reason for ceasing to file a report. All told, the reduction in usage of extremely hazardous chemicals that require compliance with SARA Title III will result in a safer, more environmentally responsible and more profitable operation. Figure 20–11 depicts printing releases for two years (1993 and 1998), demonstrating the extent to which printing chemistry has declined with the attention brought to releases and toxicity of pollutants by the SARA reports.

CHAPTER 21

Environmental Management Systems

The traditional approach to compliance with environmental issues has been piecemeal. Every regulation has its own set of rules and standards and is dealt with individually. The scope of activity is driven by the intent of the individual regulation and the activity necessary to technically comply with the mandates set forth by the code or rule. The objective has been, and for many firms continues to be, compliance. In many cases this means reacting to conditions after they have occurred.

As the move to pollution prevention programs and sustainable development philosophy has taken root, emphasis has shifted to a more comprehensive approach to the environment and a state "beyond compliance." Programs endeavor to bring a broader dimension to cleansing the environment. Multi-media perception takes the place of single mode compliance. The objective shifts from merely complying with the law to a more intensive effort to reduce or eliminate pollutants before they instigate intolerable conditions (figure 21–1).

The systematic approach to the environment embodies the need for a management system to bring together all facets of the process with environmental regulation and compliance with a mandate to take a more holistic, systematic

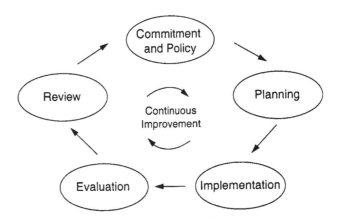

Figure 21–1. The continuous improvement cycle of a management system.

Source: United States Environmental Protection Agency, Design for the Environment, *Integrated Environmental Management Systems, Implementation Guide*, EPA 744-R-00-011, October 2000, p 3.

approach to managing the business and the environment. Environmental management systems (EMS) are designed to address the life cycles of the products made and materials used. An EMS is designed to weigh the broader impacts of chemistry on all facets of doing business—the public at large, the ecology, the neighboring community, the insurers, the workers and the government.

The EMS should be designed to encompass specific activities. It should provide for:

1. Identification and assessment of environmental impacts arising from the business' present and future activities, products and services,

2. Identification and evaluation of potential incidents and accidents that will impact on the environment,

3. Identification of all relevant environmental and safety/health regulatory mandates,

4. Establishment of objectives and priorities relative to environmental issues,

5. Provision for a full range of management activities to ensure that the policies and objectives are attained, including planning, controls, monitoring, auditing and review,

6. Fostering an attitude of acceptance to change and evolution as conditions and circumstances change.

The key factors in developing the environmental management system must be tempered by perspective. Smaller businesses do not require the intricate systems and documentation required of larger firms. The number and intensity of regulations will vary as a function of the size of the operation and the volume of its chemical usage. An effective EMS will be developed to best utilize the resources available, and not create procedures and paperwork for the sake of meeting artificial criteria that merely suggest that control has been achieved.

In other words, even the more sophisticated ISO 14000, in proportion, may be appropriate for the family firm in which every member wears two or more hats of responsibility. The importance of the EMS is the ability of the system to provide owners and managers with adequate, consistent information to control and improve their efforts to reduce pollution in its many forms. The EMS should not be evaluated by a measure of the volumes of printed policies and procedural documents and performance records. It should be viewed on the basis of the effectiveness with which it provides information to management for performance improvement.

The Challenge of the EMS

A management system can look only to see if there are indications that things are not going right, or it can become effective in seeking out and curing the causes of problems. An environmental management system must address the causes, not simply the symptoms of any given problem. To do so may require modification of the behavioral patterns of the individuals who work in the business as well as the group dynamics. There are three avenues to meet these challenges:

1. Advisory
2. Economic (fiscal)
3. Regulatory.

The advisory approach involves education, demonstration projects, use of the media, and use of all types of outreach products or systems. This approach makes people aware of the opportunities and rewards of managing the environment, and retrains them to modify both attitude and performance towards environmental wastes and incidents.

The programs should have an economic foundation. Providing adequate budget is a key within the business. External encouragement can come from having support from government in the form of low interest loans, grants, reduced energy costs, or the abatement of taxes. Avoidance of negative incentives posited by government,

Negative incentives frequently call for taxes on hazardous products.

ISO 14001 COMPONENTS	ENVIRONMENTAL MANAGEMENT SYSTEMS ACTIVITIES
Commitment and Policy	Laying the groundwork
	Creating an environmental policy
Planning	Laying the groundwork
	Determining significant environmental aspects
	Setting objectives
Implementation	Evaluating alternatives
	Setting targets and measuring success
	Developing operational controls
	Implemeneting the EMS
	Building organizational support
Evaluation	Setting targets and measuring success
	Building organizational support
Review	Establishing continuing improvement

Figure 21–2. Components of ISO 14001 and how they relate to a typical environmental management system.

Source: United States Environmental Protection Agency, Design for the Environment, *Integrated Environmental Management Systems, Implementation Guide*, EPA 744-R-00-011, October 2000, p xi.

such as taxes on toxic materials, is an economic reason for promoting management beyond strict compliance.

Regulatory standards have a two-fold purpose in the environment management scenario. The first is complying with the regulations. Simply complying with regulatory restraints on business is a not a solution for motivating change and control. What better way to meet the demands of the regulations than by not having them apply to your business? Meeting standards brings a facility into compliance. Operating at levels below the regulatory standards may be grounds for removing a facility from the regulatory screen. Operating beyond compliance objectives can result in performance that will be below the radar of the legal thresholds. This can effectively remove the facility from the need to institute myriad procedures and practices necessary to comply with each of the regulations.

The underlying program will require standards of operation and performance. In essence, meeting the regulatory standards will be a primary objective, but it will not be the sole purpose for developing the EMS. The EMS will set the standards for internal action and performance that will support the need to be in or go beyond compliance. ISO14000 is a formal, certifiable program which reviews and evaluates adherence to standards of performance by an organization (figure 21–2).

Components of an EMS

Basically, the EMS is a system in which documentation tracks the activity and materials through a process to assure that procedures and standards are upheld. In the case of the environment, this would mean evaluation of: incoming materials and chemicals, in-process production and wastes, finished products and by-product wastes, as well as the processes through which they flow. The objective would be to eliminate, at every stage, sources that could contribute to environmental and health impacts on workers, the community and the ecology.

The management system will be a combination of programs designed to contribute to the overall plan to reduce or eliminate pollution, including but not limited to:

- Programs to address the environmental policies and procedures,

- Programs to establish accountability through job training,

- Regulatory tracking system,

- Review of environmental impact of new activities,

- Waste reduction planning,

- Plans for accidental release prevention and emergency response,

- Audits of environmental compliance and non-compliance, including follow-up activities,

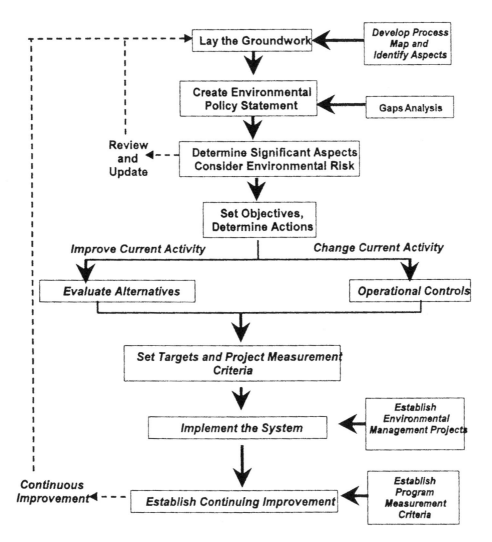

Figure 21–3. The environmental management system process.

Source: United States Environmental Protection Agency, Design for the Environment, *Integrated Environmental Management Systems, Implementation Guide*, EPA 744-R-00-011, October 2000, p x.

• Provisions for outreach to the community, including a complaint procedure,

• Product stewardship,

• Plans for relationships with contractors—on and off site.

Each of the programs must consist of meaningful components that can be individually observed and evaluated. These include organization, policy, procedures, staffing, documentation in records and reports, and implementation. In every instance, standards are required as measuring sticks for evaluating performance. The standards may be very specific with a numerical measurement, or descriptive of the activity and the intended level of performance. (See figure 21–3.)

A Basic System for the Smaller Facility

Figure 21–4. The computer is a valuable tool in bringing together the many subjects that are part of the EMS, providing opportunity to analyze and model process inputs and outputs, to plan for both compliance and the reduction of pollutants in all media.

Consider putting a system into a small family-owned firm that has only two basic files—paid bills in one drawer, unpaid bills in the second. Then think about how complex one would want to make a system, or conversely, how simple should a system be to encourage this small business to embrace and participate in this effort to manage its impact, if any, on the environment? This is the challenge in developing an EMS that will make a difference for the typical small print shop.

Perhaps the most important tool for management in the small business is the computer. Using this tool as the focal point of an EMS can ease the introduction and acceptance by the owners of the shop. Personal computers have opened the door to a degree of sophistication that can easily be translated into easy-to-use documentation of environmental and health activity. Spreadsheets, databases and word processing software are readily available that can be used as the foundation for the EMS. The most popular of the software packages are Microsoft's Excel, Lotus 123, and Quattro-Pro. (See figure 21–4.)

Organization and ease of access to information pertinent to all aspects of the environmental laws are critical to the small business EMS. Anyone who wears more than one hat needs to be able to find the regulations, permit or any related materials and correspondence without difficulty. The computer and an accompanying hard document filing system can provide this ease of access and follow-up.

A regulatory calendar and filing system can be organized using any of the more popular spreadsheets. The spreadsheet can include an inventory of permits with appropriate dates for renewal, reporting deadlines, and other dates that trigger activities such as training, inspections, emergency drills, etc. The flow of information relative to usage and inventory can help to present the opportunities for change and reduced pollution, a key to commencing an effective pollution prevention program.

A recommended filing and tickler system would include the following:

I.   Permits:
     a.   Air—state or federal
     b.   Air—local
     c.   Hazardous Waste Identification Number
     d.   Wastewater Discharge Permits (SPEDES, etc.)
     e.   Fire department
     f.   Local storage of hazardous materials
     g.   Underground and aboveground storage tanks
     h.   Other miscellaneous permits

II.   Clean Air Act:
     a.   Back-up for permits—applications, correspondence
     b.   Inspections and tests (stack test reports)
     c.   Reports—quarterly and annual
     d.   Maintenance logs
     e.   Performance records (i.e., charts for add-on control activity)

f. Violations

g. Regulations and advisory notices

h. Industry association information, correspondence

i. Miscellaneous information

j. Other pertinent information and correspondence

III. Hazardous Waste (RCRA):

    a. Back-up for ID number—application, correspondence

    b. Manifests for shipments of hazardous waste

    c. Reports—quarterly and annual

    d. Inspection logs

    e. Maintenance logs

    f. Lab sample reports

    g. Violations

    h. Regulations and advisory notices

    i. Industry association information, correspondence

    j. Miscellaneous information

    k. Other pertinent information and correspondence

IV. Wastewater:

    a. Back-up for discharge permit—application, correspondence

    b. Manifests for shipments of hazardous or non-hazardous waste

    c. Reports

    d. Inspection logs

    e. Maintenance logs

    f. Lab sample reports

    g. Violations

    h. Regulations and advisory notices

    i. Industry association information, correspondence

    j. Miscellaneous information

    k. Other pertinent information and correspondence

V. Storage of Hazardous Materials:

    a. Fire department correspondence, regulations

    b. Local, town or county storage permit applications

    c. Local, town or county storage permit correspondence

    d. Local, town or county notices of violations

    e. State storage tank applications and correspondence

    f. Local storage tank applications and correspondence

    g. OSHA related storage information and correspondence

    h. Industry association information, correspondence

    i. Miscellaneous information

    j. Other pertinent information and correspondence

VI. OSHA:
a. Training records
b. Material Safety Data Sheet collection
c. Inspection reports and follow-up correspondence
d. Hazard Communication Standard program
e. Emergency Response Program and contacts
f. Personal Protective Equipment program
g. Respiratory mask program
h. Hearing loss (noise) program
i. Medical surveillance program
j. Lock-out/tag-out program
k. Other pertinent programs relative to site specific regulations such as guard, grounding, explosion-proof electrical installations, etc.
l. Industry association information, correspondence
m. Miscellaneous information
n. Other pertinent information and correspondence

VII. Superfund (SARA Title III) Chemical Use and Releases:
a. Tier II or Local Inventory reports
b. TRI—Toxic Release reports and correspondence (annual)
c. Regulations
d. Miscellaneous information
e. Other pertinent information and correspondence

VIII. Other regulations and concerns

IX. Pollution Prevention and Waste Reduction Programs:
a. Mandated program by regulation
b. Voluntary
c. Regulations
d. Miscellaneous information
e. Other pertinent information and correspondence

Within each of the sections noted, particularly permits and reports, a tickler file can be set up on the computer to identify when the permit renewal or report is due, when work should commence and what information will be need, who will do work (on-site or consultant), etc. The data from the computer is physically supported by the documents in the filing system, as well as other reference materials (figure 21–5).

ISO 14000: International Certification

The international system of standards developed for the management of the environment is known as ISO 14000. Based on the popular ISO 9000 system for managing quality, the standard was published by the International Organization for Standards (ISO) in 1996. The standards bring together the varying and complementary interests of compliance, exceeding compliance through pollution prevention and sustainable development. ISO 14000 establishes a coordinated scenario of policy, procedure and controls to manage the environmental protection efforts of the business.

ISO 14000 is a series of documents addressing various aspects of the management system. Standards are not set according to a single yardstick, but rather developed for each facility or firm in accordance with its resources. Adherence to the ISO standards is thus based on the objectives and performance of the facility as projected versus achieved in practice. The segments of the ISO program for which a firm registers includes such components of its ISO 14000 as:

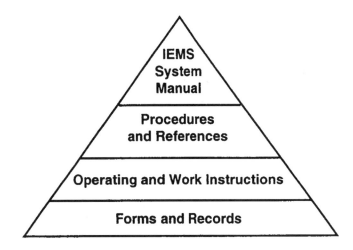

Figure 21–5. Documentation levels in an EMS.

Source: United States Environmental Protection Agency, Design for the Environment, *Integrated Environmental Management Systems, Implementation Guide*, EPA 744-R-00-011, October 2000, p 15.

- Environmental policy,

- Human resources skills and responsibilities,

- Establishing environmental risk priorities,

- Setting objectives for environmental stewardship,

- Compliance with the legal requirements,

- Pollution prevention; going beyond compliance,

- Continual improvement of facility performance and impact on community.

Signing onto the program commits a company to comply with all laws and regulations, to practice pollution prevention, and to assure that there is a continuing effort to address environmental issues and challenges. The means of assuring compliance lies in the establishment and maintenance of documented procedures for many of the requirements. ISO 14000 encompasses the main principles of professional management. The environmental process is similar to that of work improvement and quality management, based on moving through the cyclical process: plan, implement, check, review and modify.

Within each section, ISO 14000 endeavors to define areas of concern, policies to address the concerns, and procedures to assure conformance with the objectives of the program. Auditing measures compliance with the components of the program, as well as the overall objective of the ISO 14000.

A key factor for the small and medium size printer is the ability to develop an ISO program that fits within the scope of its resources, human and financial. If there is good reason to have an ISO program to promote the sale of your products and services, then by all means do it in a way that will be beneficial to your operations and the profitability of the business.

ISO 14000 is a global effort to improve and manage the environment.

ISO14001: An Integrated Environmental Management System

ISO 14001 is that component of the ISO14000 series which provides for a management program that primarily sets up guidelines for establishing a meaningful sequence of events. This sequence of events leads to a continuous loop in which management plans, implements, reviews and corrects the conduct and products of its business. Each firm can plan the desired sequence of events and the acceptable organizational requirements to conduct business in accordance with this plan. Thus, ISO14001 will contain the necessary elements to commit to the concept of an environmental management system, to plan the program and to implement it, and finally, to evaluate the fidelity and success of the various components and review this evaluation to institute changes that will improve the system.

Commitment

An environmental management system provides a systematic way of reviewing and improving operations for better environmental performance. This will require that top management commit to a policy of environmental improvement and provide the company with a firm statement delineating that objective. Without the implicit support and encouragement of management, there will not be a positive reaction from lower level supervision and personnel.

Productivity and quality are the major concerns of the pressroom and finishing personnel. Too frequently, the need to deliver an order takes precedence over the obligation to observe safety and environmental requirements. Many a firm has suffered penalties as a result of needless lapses in the conduct of its business due to breaches of safety standards; many have found themselves in litigation due to breaches in environmental regulations.

A firm policy by top management, for example, as part of its mission statement, will set the tone for an organization that is committed to compliance and to improving the environment. A typical mission statement taken from the USEPA manual on Integrated Environmental Management Systems (EPA 744-R-00-011) is illustrated in figure 21–6.

Planning for the EMS

The only way in which a management plan is going to work is by effective planning of the work to be done. The plan will serve as a template for the company and will serve as a measuring device to evaluate progress in the implementation of the management policy for environmental improvement.

The plan should include provision for:

1. Establishing the level of management involvement at which implementation will take place, and determining what decisions will be needed from the various levels of management,

2. Setting a deadline for developing the EMS and establishing a schedule for implementing the elements of the program.

```
┌──────────────────────────────────────────────────────────────┐
│                    YOUR COMPANY (ABC)                          │
│          HEALTH, SAFETY AND ENVIRONMENTAL POLICY               │
│                                                                │
│          This is a sample policy. Adapt for your company.      │
│                                                                │
│ ABC Company is committed to managing health, safety and        │
│ environmental (HS&E) matters as an integral part of our        │
│ business. In particular, it is our policy to assure the HS&E   │
│ integrity of our processes and facilities at all times and at  │
│ all places. We will do so by adhering to the following         │
│ principles:                                                    │
│                                                                │
│ COMPLIANCE                                                     │
│ We will comply with applicable laws and regulations and will   │
│ implement programs and procedures to assure compliance.        │
│ Compliance with HS&E standards will be a key ingredient in     │
│ the training, performance reviews, and incentives of all       │
│ employees.                                                     │
│                                                                │
│ RISK REDUCTION, PREVENTION, RESOURCE MANAGEMENT                │
│ We will seek opportunities, beyond regulatory compliance       │
│ requirements, for reducing risk to human health and the        │
│ environment, and we will establish and meet our own HS&E       │
│ quality standards where appropriate.                           │
│                                                                │
│ We will employ management systems and procedures               │
│ specifically designed to prevent activities and / or           │
│ conditions that pose a threat to human health, safety, or the  │
│ environment. We will look for ways to minimize risk and        │
│ protect our employees and the communities in which we          │
│ operate by employing clean technology, including safe          │
│ technologies and operating procedures, as well as being        │
│ prepared for emergencies.                                      │
│                                                                │
│ We will strive to minimize releases to the air, land, or water │
│ through use of cleaner technologies and the safer use of       │
│ chemicals. We will minimize the amount and toxicity of waste   │
│ generated and will ensure the safe treatment and disposal of   │
│ waste.                                                         │
│                                                                │
│ We will manage scarce resources, such as water, energy, land,  │
│ forests, in an environmentally sensitive manner.               │
│                                                                │
│ COMMUNICATION                                                  │
│ We will communicate our commitment to HS&E quality and to      │
│ our company s environmental performance to our employees,      │
│ vendors, and customers. We will solicit their input in meeting │
│ our HS&E goals and in turn will offer assistance to meet their │
│ goals.                                                         │
│                                                                │
│ CONTINUOUS IMPROVEMENT                                         │
│ We will measure our progress as best we can. We will review    │
│ our progress at least on an annual basis. We will continuously │
│ seek opportunities to improve our adherence to these           │
│ principles and to improving our environmental performance,     │
│ and we will periodically report progress to our stakeholders.  │
│                                                                │
│ {Signature}              President                    Date     │
└──────────────────────────────────────────────────────────────┘
```

Figure 21–6. A sample policy statement that demonstrates the objectives of the company for a cleaner and safer environment.

Source: United States Environmental Protection Agency, Design for the Environment, *Integrated Environmental Management Systems, Implementation Guide*, EPA 744-R-00-011, October 2000, p 33.

3. Establishing a budget for the program,

4. Determining the costs of developing and implementing the program and establishing a budget.

The USEPA Design for the Environment program has developed an excellent worksheet for guidance in the planning stages of an EMS. It outlines the major components of a development schedule and provides for assignment of personnel, a budget, and deadlines for completion (figure 21–7).

Understanding the Implications Within the Company

In order to properly plan, one must understand the implications based on the prevailing conditions in the plant and the regulations that govern activities of the business. Using information and tools described in other chapters of this book, a printer can identify the exposures that affect safety and the environment in the process as used within a plant. The key issues will be:

1. Identifying the activities and processes in the facility,

2. Charting the flow of materials into and out of the processes that occur in the various phases of the operations performed by the print shop,

3. Identifying the environmental implications of every process material,

4. Connecting activities to the pertinent regulations and requirements.

It is important to note that many printers work with processes and materials that require attention as related to regulations. This is not to be misconstrued to imply that every printer has an impact on the environment. An environmental impact presupposes that changes will occur in the environment due to the nature of the exposure from the facility. While there may be constraints on the business due to the nature of the printing processes, it does not follow that all printers generate an impact on the condition of the environment. One of the major objectives of the EMS is to address the environmental aspects and limit environmental impact. See figure 21–8 for an illustration of items that reflect environmental aspects and related impacts.

Evaluating and Implementing Alternatives

When the program team has assembled the documentation that identifies the process, the rules and the significant areas of exposure, it is time to evaluate alternatives to address the significant environmental aspects of the facility. The previous step in the process will have already reviewed the process and highlighted items of significance. The time has come to review the information collected and determine whether an alternative approach or materials would have less impact on the environment. The tools are described in previous chapters relative to recognizing hazards in

IEMS Development Schedule and Resources Worksheet			
Module	**Participants**	**Budget**	**Target Completion**
Laying the Groundwork: Identifying Environmental Aspects			
Intermediate steps: (As appropriate)			
Making the Commitment: Creating a Policy Statement and Determining the Scope			
Intermediate steps: (As appropriate)			
Determining Significant Environmental Aspects and Setting Objectives			
Intermediate steps: (As appropriate)			
Setting Targets and Measuring Success			
Intermediate steps: (As appropriate)			
Developing Operational Controls			
Intermediate steps: (As appropriate)			
Evaluating Alternatives			
Intermediate steps: (As appropriate)			
Implementing Your IEMS			
Intermediate steps: (As appropriate)			
Setting Up Environmental Management Projects			
Intermediate steps: (As appropriate)			
Establishing Continuing Improvement			

Figure 21–7. IEMS development schedule and resources worksheet.

Source: United States Environmental Protection Agency, Design for the Environment, *Integrated Environmental Management Systems, Implementation Guide*, EPA 744-R-00-011, October 2000, p 10.

Environmental Aspects	Potential IMPACTS of Each Aspect
Metals discharged to POTW	Contamination of aquatic habitat and drinking water supply
VOC emissions	Contribution to smog; worker or community exposure to volatile organic compounds (VOCs)
Scrap generation	Degradation of land, habitat, water supply
Solid waste generation	Habitat destruction, drinking water contamination from landfills, wasted land resources
Fresh water use	Depletion of natural resources
Electricity use	Contribution to global warming; degradation of air quality by electric generating plants
Exposure to chemicals during business activities	Harm to health of workers, neighbors, wildlife or plant life

How an Activity Becomes an Impact

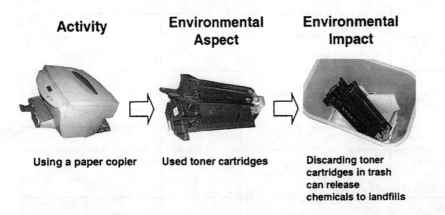

Activity　　　　**Environmental Aspect**　　　　**Environmental Impact**

Using a paper copier　　Used toner cartridges　　Discarding toner cartridges in trash can release chemicals to landfills

Figure 21–8. Examples of environmental aspects and associated inputs.

Source: United States Environmental Protection Agency, Design for the Environment, *Integrated Environmental Management Systems, Implementation Guide*, EPA 744-R-00-011, October 2000, p 13.

the process (Chapter 7) and identifying and quantifying them (Chapter 8).

Using the information collected, it would be desirable to select a given period and use the information from that period as a baseline against which performance and results can be measured. The baseline would be the quantities of materials used or purchased in a period representative of the activity of the facility (or process).

Define the function of the process or the material used in terms that describe the work performed and the reasons for the chemistry used, as well as the exposures to environmental regulations. This will help to draw perimeters around the problem areas and lead to constructive discussion of alternative methods, substitute materials, or the use of controls. Consider alternatives that will produce similar product characteristics and rates of production. Substitutions can be made of inks, adhesives, coatings, etc., with more desirable components, as well as the formulations that are used to clean equipment. Changes may be made in the way work is performed, or in the equipment being used to manufacture the product, or in the design of the product itself.

Once the alternatives have been considered from process and regulatory perspectives, budgets should be developed to ascertain the cost effectiveness of any given project. This will help to assign a priority to the project in the full scheme of the program. It will also provide a financial basis for measuring progress and success of the project.

The key is to develop strategies that will enhance the business of the company, at the same time that improvements are made to reduce or eliminate impacts on the environment. The program will provide for testing and implementation of alternative solutions that are deemed worthwhile.

It is not enough to plan for changes. A procedure must be put in place to provide for evaluation of these efforts, and to measure progress against the deadlines, budget and environmental impact expectations of the projects. In the planning stage, criteria would have been drawn up to use as guidelines for evaluating alternatives.

Evaluating Efforts and Progress

One measure of progress will be observation and feedback from personnel. Improvement due to absence of odors, reactions, irritations, or other manifestations from the replaced chemicals are quickly noticed by people on the line. Ease of use and the removal of objectionable barriers in the workplace are evident to those who perform the physical work in prepress, press and finishing activities. Anecdotal evidence is strong support for progress or lack of progress. This information should be sought and summarized by the evaluation team.

Usage is another measure of progress. Just what ramifications can be seen in the pattern of purchases and the ensuing releases to the environment? How much have potential problems been relieved as seen in reductions in amounts of chemicals procured? What are the impacts of the replacement chemicals and/or process changes?

Impact on personnel and the environment can be deduced from analysis of the usage of chemistry. Breaking down the purchases into components and evaluating the amounts of critical substances, in total and on a hourly basis, provides insight into the potential impact on health and the ecology. This analysis can also be used to determine the extent to which compliance efforts are made with respect to the various regulations.

Financial considerations can be computed using comparisons of the current results against the project budget and baseline statements. Figures 21–9 and 21–10 illustrate typical worksheets comparing the cost of investment and operating for various alternatives.

The efforts of team and plant personnel should be recognized. An incentive program may be desirable. Most certainly, posted notices of recognition will help to boost employee morale and support for the program.

An essential part of the management loop has to be a periodic review of the plans and the progress in meeting the objectives of the program. Changes may have to be made in any number of components of the EMS. Discussions at the periodic reviews will foster change where no progress is being made or if any portion of the program is bogged down and failing to make headway. Where progress is being made and the efforts have been successful, lessons learned can be translated into adjustments to projects or portions of projects which still exhibit problems.

Review and Revision

It is not critical for every project to succeed. Some projects may fall by the wayside for the lack of an adequate solution. Some may

Worksheet: Initial Investment Costs*

Significant Environmental Aspect: Press Cleaning

Baseline: Manual cleaning of press using a chemical press cleaner (a blend of acetone, toluene, methyl ethyl ketone, and isopropyl alcohol) and cloth wipers to wipe down the press, with no restrictions on the amount of cleaner or number of wipers used. Chemicals and soiled wipers are kept in uncovered containers during the work day and closed containers during after hours. Waste ink/solvent mixture is collected in drums and disposed of as hazardous waste. Wipers are collected and sent to laundry.

Alternative	Purchased Equipment	Utility Systems/ Connection	Planning/ Engineering	Site Preparation	Construction/ Installation	Start-up/ Training	Permitting	Other**	Total Inv. Costs
Products Blend A or B	none	none	none	none	none	none	none	none	none
Technologies									
Work Practices									
Recycle/Reuse									
Treatment: Centrifuge	$15,000	0	$2,000	$500	0	$200	Depends on local regulations	0	$17,700
Disposal									

Contact Person: Date:

*Typically there are no investment costs for your "business as usual" baseline.

**"Other" costs potentially include land or building purchases, contingency to cover unforeseen expenses, and investment in initial inventory (also known as working capital). For further description of these costs, see Appendix F.

Figure 21-9. Spreadsheet to evaluate the cost of investment when considering alternatives to an existing situation.

Source: United States Environmental Protection Agency, Design for the Environment, *Integrated Environmental Management Systems, Implementation Guide*, EPA 744-R-00-011, October 2000, p 101.

Worksheet: Annual Operating Costs

Significant Environmental Aspect: Press Cleaning

Baseline: Manual cleaning of press using a chemical press cleaner (a blend of acetone, toluene, methyl ethyl ketone, and isopropyl alcohol) and cloth wipers to wipe down the press, with no restrictions on the amount of cleaner or number of wipers used. Chemicals and soiled wipers are kept in uncovered containers during the work day and closed containers during after hours. Waste ink/solvent mixture is collected in drums and disposed of as hazardous waste. Wipers are collected and sent to laundry.

Alternative	Materials	Direct Labor	Utilities	Waste Management	Regulatory Compliance	Insurance	Future Liability	Total Operating Costs
Products								
Blend A: Baseline	$24,320	$2,075	n/a	$7,000	$2,100	$0	possible medical suits	$35,495
Blend B	$6,320	$2,500		$0	$0	$0		$8,820
Technologies								
Work Practices								
Recycle/ Reuse								
Treatment: Centrifuge	n/a	$420	$200	$6,200	$2,100	$200	$0	$9,120
Disposal								
Contact person:				Date:				

Figure 21-10. Spreadsheet to evaluate the cost of operating for alternatives to an existing situation.

Source: United States Environmental Protection Agency, Design for the Environment, *Integrated Environmental Management Systems, Implementation Guide,* EPA 744-R-00-011, October 2000, p 97.

encounter problems due to cultural perceptions that may hinder progress and success. Recognizing these problems may be critical to maintaining the impetus of the program. Pressure to implement an unworkable solution may damage the entire effort. On the other hand, lessons learned can be used to sharpen the goals and plans for projects that are enjoying success.

If there is no review and reaction to successes and failures, the program will fail to gain the support of personnel affected by these programs. There is nothing more devastating than the attitude that the written policy is what management says, not what it does. The success of an EMS, whether it be ISO14000 or a similar format, is the follow-up and proactive management of the facility to assure a more effective program for saving resources and the environment.

Proactive Rather than Enforced Compliance

Management succeeds in business because it sets up the mechanisms and guidance for producing a product or service that has a sales and profit value. Given that a printing operation works within established productivity and quality standards, it is equally important to note that success in business now and for the future also requires a similar commitment to the sustainability of our resources and environment. An environmental management system aims to do just that. It provides for the same policies, plans, methodology and controls that are needed to produce quality work at a profit to the company. An effective program will enable the implementation and monitoring of changes that will provide a safety net for the workers and the community, will protect the environment, and will add to the overall profits of the business.

In its 2000 report *The Environment, Health and Safety*, The Gillette Company describes its program for environmental management systems as follows:

> "As environmental issues have become more complex and interconnected, traditional reactive ways of addressing them have proved inefficient. Not only is competition increasing within the expanding global market, but environmental laws and regulations are setting new standards for businesses in every region of the world.
>
> "Good environmental issues pose a variety of risks. The most obvious is damage to the environment. Other risks include damage to a company's reputation and a resulting loss of confidence among customers, neighbors and shareholders, loss of market share, and, of course, legal liabilities.
>
> "Such risks cannot be dealt with on an ad hoc basis. As with any financial or commercial risk, only a well founded and properly implemented management approach can provide a measure of confidence that good performance is the result of good planning, and that poor performance can be identified and rectified. By properly implementing an appropriate environmental management system, any company, large or small, can ensure that it effectively manages

environmental risks while identifying the myriad opportunities that proper environmental management can bring."

The results at Gillette are quite obvious when one recognizes the decline in pollutants emitted by the company since 1990. As illustrated in figure 21–11, facilities in the Gillette family have reduced worldwide emissions from a level in excess of 10 million pounds in 1990 to under three million in 2000. This includes a rise in the overall materials used with the acquisition of Duracell in 1997. The decrease amounts to a drop of 73% in the course of 10 years.

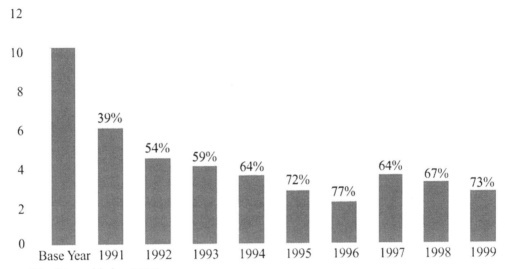

Note: Duracell facilities added in 1997

Figure 21–11. The Gillette Company pollution prevention program worldwide emissions with percent reductions from base year.

Source: *The Environment, Health and Safety, 2000 Report*, The Gillette Company, p 7.

Being at the forefront can be a sales value-added feature. Larger companies, the government, and ISO oriented firms will look favorably on a company that protects the environment and its workers. In many cases, an EMS is required before business can be conducted with a business in an industry thus impacted. The EMS, as well as ISO14000, provides the wherewithall to manage the effects on the environment. The printer must look at his current market, evaluate where his company is heading, and then plan for the future. That will include the adoption of an EMS.

An effective environmental management program will contribute to the sales and profitability of the business.

As in all business undertakings, the more one knows about the ingredients that can provide for the success or failure of a process or product, the greater one can control one's own destiny. Greater involvement stemming from the environmental management system will provide printers with the wherewithall to determine what the greatest concerns are in their operations and how to best cope with making the process more environmentally responsible. The key to success will be developing a program that reflects the ability of management to plan, monitor and control their resources—people, machinery and chemistry.

CHAPTER **22**

Economics of Compliance and Non-Compliance

For every action there is a reaction. That is a basic law of science. When dealing with government and environmental or safety regulations, business has a choice to either comply or not to comply. The consequences in either case will establish the economics of that choice.

When compliance is either very expensive or virtually unattainable and enforcement is lax with negligible penalties, there may be a tendency to look the other way. Pay the penalty and continue doing business as usual. If the damages are minor and the risks are not critical, this may be a business approach that some printers may want to take. However, when the stakes are high; when issues move from civil court to criminal court; when penalties are beyond the comprehension of the average small businessman, it is time to look at the issues from the perspective of compliance. The question is: Just what does it cost to comply? And conversely: What will the damages for non-compliance be? Do we pay the piper now, or do we pay much more later?

Many factors have to be examined when accounting for the cost of the environment to a business.

The most advantageous response to compliance is to ascertain if advancements in technology can serve two purposes—improve the capabilities and physical performance of the operation, and bring the facility or process into compliance. Printing and associated graphic arts technologies have been revolutionized in the past 10 years. The introduction of the computer

Investing in Technology to Comply

into all levels of activity has given printers the ability, in many areas, to do away with traditional chemistry and the associated hazardous wastes. There are many instances in which the printer has realized considerable profits from the physical achievements of the new process, as well as benefit from the opportunity to avoid compliance requirements and their related costs. Technology could amount to a simple change of chemistry within the process, or it may mean a complete change in the equipment and methodology to achieve a particular result. The chemistry may be a small part of a big solution.

Large Format Digital Printing

Consider the advent of digital printing of posters and billboards. This was a job that had been done in one of two ways: by lithography, using fountain solutions and cleaning press washes, or by screen printing, using liquid inks and many gallons of screen wash to salvage the screens with or without the image. Either way was a road to air pollution in a significant quantity, as well as the creation of hazardous wastes.

Figure 22–1. Wide format printer for billboards and posters at Nomad Worldwide LLC, Jersey City, NJ.

With the use of ink jet printers and other digital ink deposition technologies, the printer can eliminate a considerable amount of solvents evaporating into the air and hazardous waste drums of spent solvent shipped off-site for disposal. Safety and health issues related to the concentration of some very toxic solvents in the air can be alleviated in both the workplace and in the public space just outside the printing plant. At the same time, a whole new world has opened to decorate billboards, the sides of buildings, hang posters from overhead streetlights, and print the backdrops for Broadway shows and local theatres (figure 22–1).

The copy never sees a darkroom or generates an ounce of silver halide discharge. Developed as an artistic concept on a computer, transferred from one place to another by disk or over the Internet, and fed into the printer without ever seeing the light of day, the image appears first and only as a printed product. The quality is hard to beat; a whole new market has opened for the printer and his customers, one that reduces the use and release of pollutants to the workplace and the environment.

Direct to Plate or Press

The computer is revolutionizing the lithographic process in many ways. Considerable quantities of wastes are no longer generated following the elimination of the need to process film and paper in a darkroom and the platemaking processor in order to obtain a printing plate. Direct-to-press imaging has cut through a whole body of technology that always created environmental wastes. Direct-to-plate technology has eliminated some, but not all, of the chemistry required in the past. Direct-to-press has yet to be perfected for all end uses or for long runs. The advantages best suit the sheet-fed press with short runs. That could change with time and experience. Direct-to-plate was introduced in a format and at a cost that was prohibitive to many. That is changing each month, as more equipment is being developed to bring this technology to smaller formats and at lower costs (figure 22–2).

Figure 22–2. Indigo direct-to-press lithography at Beau Label in New York City avoids considerable use of chemicals.

Source: *Printing News*, January 8, 2001.

Just as every technical advance has its benefits, it may also have disadvantages. The printer must weigh one against the other to decide which alternative best suits his operation and the challenge. In time, the technology should become more economical. Or it may be replaced by another advancement that will be feasible in a given situation. The key to making any investment or change is the result of an evaluation of the benefits and the economics of making the investment in money, time and other resources. The tool to help put things into financial perspective is the computation of the return on investment.

Water-base Inks Replace Solvent

Flexographic and gravure printers have considerable exposure to regulation as a result of the liquid solvent inks that are used for printing of film, foil and, to some extent, paper. The technology options suggested in government guidelines call for one option that does not exist—high-solids solvent inks, and one that does—waterborne inks. Ink formulations for the liquid ink market cannot meet the mandatory 60-percent solids standard and have a ink whose rheology will allow it to be transferred in the traditional ink trains. There is no question that with management direction and support, the transition to water can be accomplished. Consideration of the economics can be a major factor in deciding whether this change is to the advantage of the printer and the end user. (See figure 22–3.)

The concept of higher solids percentages in inks, while difficult to achieve in solvent-base inks, does approach the limits with waterborne formulations. A greater portion of the liquid content of the ink, as used at the press, will be water. The percentage of highly volatile solvents is minimal, well below any of the trigger standards set by government.

The transition in not an easy one; economics is a major component of the decision. At what point does it make sense to take the route of waterborne inks?

Figure 22–3. Polyethylene converter prints with waterborne inks (Supreme Poly Products, Brooklyn, NY).

Changing to water inks requires equipment modifications that can carry a significant cost to retrofit a press. The cost of a new press would not be significantly affected. Changing an older press to the new technology can cost upwards of $60,000 for a six-color press for modifications to the ink train and drying system, as well as the installation of substrate treating equipment. To this must be added the cost of altering the culture of the workplace through retraining. This will involve a period of time during which production levels could suffer, quality could become marginal, and problems might lead to customer concern about the end-use quality characteristics of packaged products.

There is no question that with management dedication, direction and support, the transition to water can be accomplished. The financial benefits can be there. Consideration of the economics of the total regulatory commitments of the facility can be a major factor in deciding whether this change is to the advantage of the specific printer.

Eliminating the Alcohol from Fountain Solution

The primary operating exposure addressed in the regulations for air emissions in lithography is the isopropyl alcohol used in fountain solution. The role of the alcohol is to help wet out the printing plate with a solution that is primarily water. The water prevents oil-base ink from sticking to the unexposed portion of the plate and transferring to the paper substrate. It also serves other roles in maintaining the electrolytic values needed for the transfer of inks. Isopropyl alcohol has been the standard component since the outset of commercial lithography. Its value is more pronounced during hot, humid days, when an extra amount is typically added by pressmen to maintain proper performance of the fountain solution. Culture maintained that the more isopropyl alcohol, the better the performance and quality of the print.

Efforts to create replacements for the alcohol-free fountain solution have taken three routes:

1. **Waterless printing:** in which the printing plate has a silicone film on the metal surface, into which the printing image is etched. With the silicone acting as a release agent, there is no need for any fountain solution (figure 22–4). The ink is carried by an etched image, while the silicone coating rejects ink in the unwanted portions of the plate. The challenge to greater popularity lies in the higher equipment cost and the increase in operating costs for new presses. If the equipment has to be retrofitted from traditional offset, cost may pose an even greater barrier.

2. **Dry offset:** Uses relief printing plates, similar to those for letterpress, which are used to print the images in a traditional lithographic

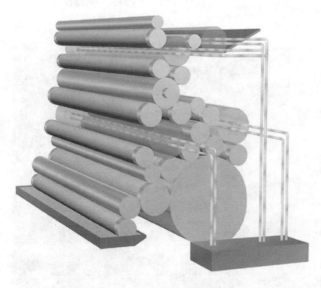

Figure 22–4. Schematic of waterless offset process on Mitsubishi press, which does not require fountain solution, indicates cooling necessary for ink transfer to occur.

Courtesy of MLP U.S.A. Inc.

press. This has been used for many years, but is not evident as a solution for most commercial printers due to the limits and mechanics of plate preparation and operating systems in normal lithographic presses.

3. **Alcohol-free fountain solution:** Chemical suppliers have worked with different solvents, that have low evaporation rates, and other substances to achieve the same effects as isopropyl alcohol and not release the volume of emissions caused by the alcohol. As with water inks for flexography, the transition requires mechanical changes to the ink train, an understanding of how to use the new solutions, and retraining of personnel. By far the greatest obstacle is the culture of change that is called for in the pressroom.

The most economic solution for the typical commercial printer is the substitution of the fountain solution formulation (figure 22–5). Any other alternative requires capital expenditures for new equipment. Retrofitting older equipment may come at a price that will not provide an adequate return on investment.

Comparing the Economic Options to Compliance

The cost of converting to new technology can be compared to the cost of installing add-on equipment. At what point does it not pay to modify equipment to use new technology? Or, are the costs justified by other economic and environmental factors? One way of weighing the values of new technology versus add-on controls is to look at the basic costs of modification versus the cost of installing an oxidizer. Consideration would then be given to the relative costs of operating the equipment. At a given

```
          M A T E R I A L   S A F E T Y   D A T A   S H E E T
FOUNTAIN CONCENTRATE 2351                                    Page:    1

PRODUCT NAME: FOUNTAIN CONCENTRATE 2351            HMIS CODES: H F R P
PRODUCT CODE: C110                                             1 0 0 B
CHEMICAL NAME: FOUNTAIN SOLUTION

=========  SECTION II  -  HAZARDOUS INGREDIENTS/SARA III INFORMATION  =========
                                                 VAPOR PRESSURE   WEIGHT
REPORTABLE COMPONENTS                    CAS NUMBER   mm Hg @ TEMP  PERCENT
------------------------------------------------------------------------------
* MAGNESIUM NITRATE                      10377-60-3  NO DATA  NO DATA  10 - 20%
     LD50-5.44g/Kg
* 2-BUTOXYETHANOL                        111-76-2    0.6 mmHg  20 C   10 - 20%
     PEL 25ppm: TLV 25ppm // LC50 800ppm/8hr: LD50 1.746g/kg //HAP reportable
* ETHYLENE GLYCOL                        107-21-1    <0.1mmHg  20 C    1 - 10%
     PEL 50 ppm. TLV 50 ppm  //  LD50 5.84g/kg  // HAP reportable
* 1-METHYL-2-PYRROLIDONE                 872-50-4    0.29mmHg  20 C    1 - 10%
     PEL 100 ppm  // LD50 4.2g/kg
* Indicates toxic chemical(s) subject to the reporting requirements of section 313 of Title III and of 40 CFR 372.
```

Figure 22–5. Typical components of an alcohol-free fountain solution concentrate.
Courtesy of Printers' Service.

point, based on the number of presses that have to be converted versus the size of the add-on control, it becomes possible to make a suitable comparison that would justify the cost of purchasing the control system over the cost of the change in technology.

There is still another dimension to the economics of such changes. If a facility can be permitted to exhaust a total amount of volatile organic compounds, just how does that relate to the amount of finished printed product that can be shipped to customers? Given a set amount of emissions, the calculation can be made of pounds of ink that will go into product by the two routes. The economic consideration would factor in this economic benefit with the analysis of the cost to install and operate under the two scenarios.

An illustration can be the example of one printer with three flexographic printing presses who had to balance the need to use solvents versus waterborne inks. The cost to modify the presses for use of water technology was compared to the cost of installing a catalytic oxidizer. Each of the three presses would require modifications to the ink train, the drying system and the addition of a corona-treating unit. The cost per press would be in the range of $60,000 to $100,000. A catalytic oxidizer to handle the recirculated airflow of the three presses would cost in the vicinity of $350.000. It would seem apparent, at face value, that given the other costs—tangible and intangible—of converting to water, that the facility would spend the same basic amount of money for either option. Table 22–1 illustrates the difference in cost between conversion to water and installation of a catalytic oxidizer for a flexographic printer with three wide-web presses.

A decision could be made to opt for the add-on control since it would allow the facility to continue operating without any change in its equipment or the culture of its working force. Operating costs might be equal for either option, given the changes that would occur in production speeds, increased drying by use of natural gas, using water, as opposed to the energy needed to fuel the oxidizer. The need for retraining and a learning curve period of time needed for water would not be necessary for the oxidizer, when using existing solvent inks.

However, consider the volume of work and sale of product that can be processed by using a low-solvent technology versus that of add-on controls. As an example, let us look at a facility that has approval to exhaust 60,000 pounds (30 tons) of volatile organic compounds per year. Using waterborne inks that have a percentage of solvents of approximately four percent, the allowable emissions would involve a total usage of 1,500,000 pounds of ink. The emissions would include a negligible amount of clean-up solvents. With 40 percent solids, ink solids transferred to product would amount to 600,000 pounds. The ink solids can be translated into shippable product and sales dollars. Another reduction in cost to be considered will be that of disposing of the water waste from the ink clean-ups. Disposition of water wastes for treatment is considerably lower as a hazardous waste, and there is a possibility that the cost will be even lower if the waste is considered non-hazardous. Tables 22–2 summarizes the translator table for compliance status that uses pounds of waterborne ink to determine the type of permit required.

TABLE 22-1. COMPARISON OF COST TO CHANGE TO WATER VERSUS INSTALLATION OF A CATALYTIC OXIDIZER

A. Cost to install 7,500 CFM catalytic oxidizer for three flexographic presses.

ITEM	TOTAL COST INSTALLATION
1. Cost of unit installed	350,000.00
2. Less Down Payment	35,000.00
3. Financed Amount	315,000.00
4. Interest at 10% annually	184,529.79
TOTAL COST TO INSTALL OXIDIZE	534,529.79

B. Conversion to waterborne inks

EQUIPMENT REQUIRED:	ESTIMATED COST PER ITEM (1995)	MINIMUM COST			MAXIMUM COST		
		PRESS 434 4 STATIONS	PRESS 660 6 STATIONS	FILMPRINTER 6 STATIONS	PRESS 434 4 STATIONS	PRESS 660 6 STATIONS	FILMPRINTER 6 STATIONS
A. CORONA TREATER	$30,000.00	$30,000.00	$30,000.00	$30,000.00	$30,000.00	$30,000.00	$30,000.00
B. ANILOX ROLL CHANGES							
1. RE-ETCH EXISTING ROLLERS	$1,000.00	$4,000.00	$6,000.00	$6,000.00			
2. LASER ENGRAVED ROLLERS	$3,000.00				$3,000.00	$18,000.00	$18,000.00
C. RUBBER ROLL REPLACEMENT	$1,000.00	$4,000.00	$6,000.00	$6,000.00			
D. DRYING EQUIPMENT							
1. REPLACE BCD'S	$1,000.00	$3,000.00	$5,000.00	$5,000.00	$4,000.00	$5,000.00	$5,000.00
2. REPLACE BURNER PACKS	$20,000.00				$20,000.00	$60,000.00	$60,000.00
E. CHAMBER DOCTOR BLADES	$10,000.00				$40,000.00	$60,000.00	$60,000.00
F. INK PUMPS	$2,000.00	$8,000.00	$12,000.00	$12,000.00	$8,000.00	$12,000.00	$12,000.00
G. MISC CONTINGENCY PARTS		$10,000.00	$10,000.00	$10,000.00	$10,000.00	$10,000.00	$10,000.00
TOTALS - PER PRESS		$59,000.00	$69,000.00	$69,000.00	$115,000.00	$195,000.00	$195,000.00
FACILITY TOTAL COST - 3 PRESSES				$197,000.00 MINIMUM	$505,000.00 MAXIMUM		

CONCLUSION: Cost of equipment, if done to maximum, would be equal between water conversion versus add-on control. Savings would result from lower operating costs.

The same computation for solvent-base ink would require a division of the emissions into inks and solvents that have been added to the ink or used as cleaning agents. Of the 60,000 pounds of allowable emissions, perhaps one-third would come from the inks purchased. The balance will result from the solvents that enter the process as diluents or cleaning solutions. The 20,000 pounds of emissions from inks, considering that the solvents represent approximately 50 percent of the weight of the ink formulation, relates to ink entering the process at a total weight of 40,000 pounds. Ink solids deposited on the printed product would amount to 20,000 pounds. This amount of ink solids can be related to shippable sales

TABLE 22–2. MATERIAL USE AIR LEVEL TABLES FOR VOCS IN A SEVERE NON-ATTAINMENT AREA TO DETERMINE PERMIT DESIGNATION BASED ON USE OF INKS AND SOLVENTS

Sheetfed Offset or Nonheatset Web Lithography, or Screen Printing	Heatset Web Offset Lithography (uncontrolled), or Flexography or Rotogravure with solvent-based inks	Flexography or Rotogravure with water-based inks		Air Level
less than 710 gals	less than 5,000 lbs	less than 20,000 lbs	→	Level 1
710 - 1,775 gals	5,000 - 12,500 lbs	20,000 - 50,000 lbs	→	Level 2
1,775 - 3,550 gals	12,500 - 25,000 lbs	50,000 - 100,000 lbs	→	Level 3
3,550 - 7,100 gals	25,000 - 50,000 lbs	100,000 - 200,000 lbs	→	Level 4
more than 7,100 gals	more than 50,000 lbs	more than 200,000 lbs	→	Level 5

Source: United States Environmental Protection Agency, Common Sense Initiative Printing Sector, *PrintSTEP Pilot Program, State Guide to PrintSTEP*, p 1–25.

TABLE 22–3. MATERIAL USE AIR LEVEL TABLES FOR VOCS IN A SERIOUS NON-ATTAINMENT AREA TO DETERMINE PERMIT DESIGNATION BASED ON USE OF INKS AND SOLVENTS

Sheetfed Offset or Nonheatset Web Lithography, or Screen Printing	Heatset Web Offset Lithography (uncontrolled), or Flexography or Rotogravure with solvent-based inks	Flexography or Rotogravure with water-based inks		Air Level
less than 1,425 gals	less than 10,000 lbs	less than 40,000 lbs	→	Level 1
1,425 - 3,560 gals	10,000 - 25,000 lbs	40,000 - 100,000 lbs	→	Level 2
3,560 - 7,125 gals	25,000 - 50,000 lbs	100,000 - 200,000 lbs	→	Level 3
7,125 - 14,250 gals	50,000 - 100,000 lbs	200,000 - 400,000 lbs	→	Level 4
more than 14,250 gals	more than 100,000 lbs	more than 400,000 lbs	→	Level 5

Source: United States Environmental Protection Agency, Common Sense Initiative Printing Sector, *PrintSTEP Pilot Program, State Guide to PrintSTEP*, p 1–24.

dollars. Tables 22–2, 22–3 and 22–4 summarize the translator table for compliance status that uses pounds of solvent-base ink to determine the type of permit required. There can be no question but that the water inks will deliver a higher volume of saleable product.

If an add-on control was installed, the 20,000 pounds of emissions, using a net destruction rate of 90 percent, would come from a gross exhaust of solvents from the ink formulations and solvents weighing approximately 200,000 pounds. 200,000 pounds of emissions would equate to approximately 67,000 pounds of ink, with

TABLE 22–4. MATERIAL USE AIR LEVEL TABLES FOR VOCS IN A MODERATE NON-ATTAINMENT AREA TO DETERMINE PERMIT DESIGNATION BASED ON USE OF INKS AND SOLVENTS

Sheetfed Offset or Nonheatset Web Lithography, or Screen Printing	Heatset Web Offset Lithography (uncontrolled), or Flexography or Rotogravure with solvent-based inks	Flexography or Rotogravure with water-based inks		Air Level
less than 2,855 gals	less than 20,000 lbs	less than 80,000 lbs	→	Level 1
2,855 - 7,135 gals	20,000 - 50,000 lbs	80,000 - 200,000 lbs	→	Level 2
7,135 - 14,275 gals	50,000 - 100,000 lbs	200,000 - 400,000 lbs	→	Level 3
14,275 - 28,550 gals	100,000 - 200,000 lbs	400,000 - 800,000 lbs	→	Level 4
more than 28,550 gals	more than 200,000 lbs	more than 800,000 lbs	→	Level 5

Source: United States Environmental Protection Agency, Common Sense Initiative Printing Sector, *PrintSTEP Pilot Program, State Guide to PrintSTEP*, p 1–24.

33,500 pounds of solids that would have been deposited on the substrate. The solvent vapors entering the add-on control will require the expenditure of natural gas to burn off the chemicals. This could amount to anywhere from $10.00 to $20.00 per hour of operation of the oxidizer. Total sales dollars that can be realized compared to that of water inks is considerably lower. In addition, one has also to consider the very real costs of the other ramifications of using solvent inks; that is the costs of collection, storage and disposal of waste inks and spent solvents as hazardous wastes.

The difference between the deliverable product printed with water inks compared to those formulated for solvents is quite significant. This fact alone should give the printer pause to think about his ability to ship more profitable product based on the selection of a less polluting technological resource, such as water, to address environmental compliance. As previously mentioned, the difference in the cost of handling waste from the process represents another tangible cost benefit. The cost of disposal, regulatory fees, administrative requirements and periodic reports could represent a sizeable sum.

Return on Investment

Investments in manufacturing are frequently subject to the determination of the ratio of savings or profits to the cost of the equipment and/or other process modifications. A rule of thumb calls for any capital expenditure to pay for itself in a period of, let's say, three years. If the equipment is to cost a total of $200,000, the savings accrued over the three-year period would have to amount to at least the capital cost and installation. Measurement, therefore, is in terms of the time it will take to pay back the capital and operating expense of the change. If the equipment cost is $200,000, and the savings per year amounted to $70,000, the ROI would be

Potentially Hidden Costs		
Regulatory	**Upfront**	**Voluntary (Beyond Compliance)**
• Notification • Reporting • Monitoring/testing • Studies/modeling • Remediation • Recordkeeping • Plans • Training • Inspections • Manifesting • Labeling • Preparedness • Protective equipment • Medical surveillance • Environmental insurance • Financial assurance • Pollution control • Spill response • Stormwater management • Waste management • Taxes/fees	• Site studies • Site preparation • Permitting • R&D • Engineering and procurement • Installation **Conventional Costs** Capital equipment Materials Labor Supplies Utilities Structures Salvage value **Back-End** • Closure/ decommissioning • Disposal of inventory • Post-closure care • Site survey	• Community relations/ outreach • Monitoring/testing • Training • Audits • Qualifying suppliers • Reports (e.g., annual environmental reports) • Insurance • Planning • Feasibility studies • Remediation • Recycling • Environmental studies • R & D • Habitat and wetland protection • Landscaping • Other environmental projects • Financial support to environmental groups and/or researchers
Contingent Costs		
• Future compliance costs • Penalties/fines • Response to future releases	• Remediation • Property damage • Personal injury damage	• Legal expenses • Natural resource damages • Economic loss damages
Image and Relationship Costs		
• Corporate image • Relationship with customers • Relationships with investors • Relationship with insurers	• Relationship with professional staff • Relationship with workers • Relationship with suppliers	• Relationship with lenders • Relationship with host communities • Relationship with regulators

Figure 22–6. Examples of environmental costs incurred by firms.

Source: United States Environmental Protection Agency, *An Introduction to Environmental Accounting as a Business Management Tool: Key Concepts and Terms*, EPA 742-R-95-001, June 1995, p 9.

just less than three years. In a normal review for ROI, the accounting would be fairly basic: machinery, materials, human resources and overhead. The ramifications of the costs in each of these areas would apply to the formula that computes how fast the financial investment that is expended will be returned.

Environmental cost accounting is quite different. It involves more than the obvious costs of doing business. Tangible items are easy enough to define and target, much as are the basic costs of making a product. In addition to those costs that we can define, the intangible costs are what are needed to define the return on any add-on control, process control modification or other environmental program. Refer to figure 22–6 for a broad picture of the many elements of cost that are influenced by the environment.

Some are real costs faced by the facility in the normal course of doing business:

1. Hazardous waste shipments and the ensuing paperwork,
2. Recordkeeping and reports,
3. Engineers and consultants,
4. Permitting fees,
5. Equipment and supplies for fire suppression, spill control, etc.,
6. Maintenance of environmental and safety systems,
7. Training, and
8. Insurance.

Other costs may be less tangible and not relative to any one period of time. They may have been a factor in the past and might still pose problems in the future or are something down the road that may or may not ever happen. These are the things that you cannot foresee or even project with any degree of reliability.

1. Legal fees,
2. Penalties, most after taxes,
3. Tests and lab fees,
4. Site remediation (clean-up and legal) costs,
5. Public notices and hearings,
6. Customer reaction to negative publicity, and
7. Lost time and morale due to employee illness or injury.

While ROI is a complicated accounting procedure, the printer can use a simple format to determine the economic benefits and return on investment for any project that is being considered. The following is one approach to the justification of an investment that is intended to reduce solid waste by 50 percent. The printing presses are to be equipped with monitoring devices that will scan a printing web and detect defects. A printing problem can be detected early and remedied. Waste can be significantly reduced. At the same time, the press can be operated at higher speeds with the automatic sensing and control of quality. This format can be applied to any modification or addition of equipment.

A sample spreadsheet is illustrated in Appendix XLI. The format is one that can be adapted to standard spreadsheet software such as Microsoft Excel, Lotus 1,2,3, QuattroPro, etc. More comprehensive software to compute return on investment for environmental pollution prevention projects has been developed for each of the printing processes and is available at the USEPA Design for the Environment web site.* The software was developed for screen, lithographic and flexographic printing with peer review by members of industry and industry associations. The various versions are available on-line from the EPA web site.

Add-on Controls: A Question of Feasibility

If compliance is attainable only by the acquisition of control equipment, how does one measure the cost and validity of using control? The government has conducted studies that established guidelines for the economic feasibility of purchasing and operating an add-on control system. In 1980 dollars, control was considered feasible if the cost per ton destroyed did not exceed $2,500 per ton. This standard has been updated for inflation or by some other rule of thumb by individual states. Where states have regulations that allow for variances based on the excessive cost of destruction for smaller sources, the computation of the cost of adding a control system is important to understand.

Federal and state environmental protection agencies work on the premise that the cost of destroying a ton of hazardous air emissions can be related to the ability of a business to pay for the investment in a control system as well as the cost to operate the system. Using basic accounting guidelines, the system can be depreciated over its useful life, as would be the cost of replacing catalyst or other vital parts of the system. For purposes of this example, it is anticipated that the oxidizer will have a lifetime of 10 years, with replacement of the catalyst periodically in the course of seven years.

Operating costs should be based on actual costs. Theoretical factors are normally used in the preparation of proposals but the actual costs may be far different from those in any other location than the location used by the vender. It is not unusual for the proposal to be based on very low utility rates. Labor and overhead rates should be used as representative of the costs factored into the estimating of selling prices or the standards from the facility cost accounting system.

The spreadsheet, as illustrated in figure 22–7, is relatively simple. The format provides spaces to fill in the pertinent information to determine the annual cost of operating a control system and the cost per ton destroyed. The capital cost of purchasing and installing the control system is amortized over a period of years, in many jurisdictions, over a 10-year period. Cost of maintenance, including the replacement of components, is also allocated over the 10-year period. Utility supply of fuels (natural gas, propane, etc.) and facility labor for upkeep and operation of the system can be based on actual expenditures. The objective of the computation is to ascertain what it costs to operate the system on an annual basis.

Having determined the cost per year, then computing the cost per ton destroyed, is a matter of using the actual emissions, multiplied by the percentage of destruction efficiency confirmed by

---

*The web site for the USEPA Design for the Environment program is www.epa.gov/dfe.

ECONOMIC ANALYSIS - AIR EMISSIONS CONTROL EQUIPMENT			
ANNUAL OPERATING COSTS	TOTAL COSTS		ANNUAL COSTS (over 10 year period)
1. Cost of unit (3,000 CFM Catalytic Oxidizer)	$137,655.00		
Installation and Testing (estimated)	$37,000.00		
Total Cost of System	$174,655.00		
2. Less Down Payment	$17,465.50		
3. Financed Amount	$157,189.50		$15,719
4. Interest	$135,685.54	0.14	$13,569
5. Operating Costs			
a. Electricity			$7,500
b. Natural Gas			$14,060
c. Catalyst	$16,000.00		$2,286
d. Maintenance			$5,000
e. Indirect costs			$2,000
Total Operating Costs			$30,846
TOTAL ANNUAL COST OF CONTROL			$60,133
VOC REDUCTIONS			
A. Tons emitted per projection for permit			20.00
B. Percent required destruction (RACT)			60%
C. Tons Reduced			12.00
TOTAL COST PER TON OF TON REDUCED			$5,011.10
Notes: 1. Equipment amortized over 10 year period.			
2. Interest accrued over 10 year period			
3. Electrical based on vender data - $3.75 per hour			
4. Natural gas based on vender data - $7.03 per hour			
5. Catalyst replacement based on attrition in 7 years.			
6. Maintenance - estimated labor and parts, PM by vender.			

Figure 22-7. Worksheet to compute the cost of operating an oxidizer.

the stack test, or the percentage required by law. The tons that will be destroyed are divided into the annual cost of operating the control system. For example:

Annual tons of VOC emissions .... 100 tons

Percentage destruction efficiency 95%

Tons of VOCs destroyed .... 95 tons

Cost of operating the system $95,000

Cost per ton destroyed $1,000/ton

If the cost per ton destroyed is greater than the current standard of feasibility, the facility can apply for a variance or relief from RACT requirements. Such a provision is available only in those states that have enacted latitude in their regulations for business to conserve on energy during the time of year when nature is not generating ozone by photosynthesis. The original standard of feasibility published by the USEPA in the late 1980s was $2,500 per ton. This number has been increased using inflation rates, as well as arbitrary restrictive percentages in some states. In New York, for instance, the number used in their Air Guide 20 for filing variances is $5,000 per ton, with adjustments for inflation.

From a practical, ongoing perspective, the operating information can be channeled into the cost accounting system of the plant and used to properly estimate the cost of environmental compliance as a component of estimating the manufacturing and selling prices of printed products.

Cost of Non-compliance: Litigation and Penalties

There is no question that coming to grips with compliance can be a costly affair. Equipment, operating costs, retraining—all add to the cost of doing business. However, the cost of not coming into compliance can be dramatic and drastic. And when the entire unpleasant process has come to a conclusion, the business will still have to invest in the same solutions that it failed to pursue earlier. The USEPA considers penalties as a deterrent to non-compliance and a means of leveling the playing field among competitors. Penalties seek to collect any benefits that a violator may have gained over its competitors and thus penalize the firm for not taking proactive stances.

Non-compliance opens a Pandora's box. Penalties are based on formulas that take into account the impact on the environment by the failure to adhere to requirements and the cost benefits that accrued by not being in compliance. The wealth of the business can be used as a multiplier to increase the amount of the penalty. Suggested daily penalties are significant. And the penalties are payable after taxes, eliminating any offset that a business might normally take for any expenditures.

EPA has developed a number of penalty formulas. Some are integrated with the specific regulations; others are more general in application. To illustrate the impact of the penalties for non-compliance, let's consider some of the major documents that determine penalties for violations of the Clean Air Act. The USEPA has developed a number of policies which are followed when facilities are in violation and in litigation. A good example is the Stationary Source Civil Penalty Policy for the Clean Air Act. Examples of policies designed to help mitigate the impact of penalties are the Supplemental Environmental Projects Policy and the Small Business Incentive Program.

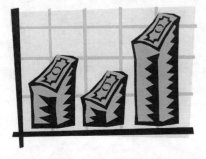

To make up for every dollar of penalty, the printer must sell $40 to $50 of new sales.

The Clean Air Act Stationary Source Civil Penalty Policy was issued in October 1991, it consists of a number of sections dealing with the various concerns in developing and applying penalties for violations leading to the emission of hazardous air pollutants to the atmosphere. The introductory statement updates the policy from the initial EPA penalty policy issued in 1984, and revised in 1987, to the present with the passage of the Clean Air Act and the need to integrate the experience of the agency since the inception of the air program.

The CAA90 provided for penalty orders in the amount of up to $25,000 per day of violation, generally assessed in "cases where the penalty sought is not over $200,000 and the first alleged violation occurred no more than 12 months prior to the initiation of the administrative action." The new policy seeks to provide guidance for more uniform calculation of the administrative penalties levied under the Act. The policy states: "In calculating the penalty amount which should be sought under an administrative complaint, the economic benefit of non-compliance and a gravity component should be calculated under this penalty policy using the most aggressive assumptions supportable."

For the printer with a violation in hand, this presents a formidable challenge. In an industry with narrow margins of profit, an aggressive penalty policy can wipe out the profits of considerable effort and productivity. Even with provisions for lowering the "aggressive" penalty in the policy, the printer is faced with the prospects of a still weighty penalty and the costs of legal advisors to confront the agency.

The policy is subdivided into sections that discuss:

* Preliminary Deterrence Amount (Economic and Gravity Components),

* Litigation Risk,

* Ability to Pay,

* Offsetting Penalties Paid . . . for the Same Violations,

* Supplemental Environmental Projects,

* Calculating a Penalty in Cases With More Than One Violation,

* Apportionment of the Penalty Among Multiple Defendants, and

* Examples, Conclusion and Appendixes.

Some portions of the policy have been included as Appendix XXXVIII to demonstrate the factors that will come into play as the agency develops its proposed penalty, and which are the basis for finding areas in which a compromise can be reached. The economic benefit component weighs such factors as the benefits from delayed costs, from avoided costs, if the component is insignificant, and compelling public concerns. The gravity component

Clean Air Civil Penalty Policy

assesses the penalty in light of actual or possible harm, importance to the regulatory scheme, and size of the violator, balanced against the history of the violator and the degree of cooperation in resolving the issues. The policy provides avenues for compromise and relief for portions of the penalty. Good faith and a clean record can help to minimize the damage of a financial assessment—but keep in mind, there will be a penalty to pay!

Supplemental Environmental Projects (SEPs)

A section of the CAA penalty policy that warrants consideration is that which provides for the use of supplemental environmental projects as a means of mitigating a portion of a penalty. In the settlement of enforcement cases, the agency can approve projects which will address one or more of the violations and provide greater benefit to the public health. The cost of the project can be made a component of the penalty, reducing the amount the violator must pay to the government.

One emphasis of SEPs is the selection of projects based on the principles and hierarchy of pollution prevention in the communities where environmental justice can be served. Reduction or elimination of pollution in the minority communities is not a category within the SEP definitions, but is an overarching goal for communities in which low income and minority populations are disproportionately burdened by pollution exposure.

SEP projects must meet the following criteria:

1. Ensure that the project meets the basic definition of an SEP,

2. Ensure that all legal guideline are satisfied,

3. Ensure that the project fits within one (or more) of the designated categories of SEPs,

4. Determine the appropriate amount of penalty mitigation, and

5. Ensure that the project satisfies all of the implementation and other criteria.

SEP projects are defined as environmentally beneficial projects which a defendant agrees to undertake in settlement of an enforcement action, but which the defendant is not otherwise legally required to perform. The SEP cannot put the violator into compliance; it must be a project that will go beyond compliance. The project cannot be inconsistent with existing statutes and it must advance at least one of the objectives of the environmental statutes that are the basis of the enforcement action.

EPA is restricted from playing an active role in the project, but may perform oversight to ensure that the project is implemented in accordance with the provisions of the settlement. Among the categories of projects that would properly come under the SEP program are:

- Public health,
- Pollution prevention,
- Pollution reduction,
- Environmental restoration and protection,
- Assessments and audits,
- Environmental compliance promotion,
- Emergency planning and preparedness.

Certain types of projects are not acceptable. These include general public seminars or public awareness projects, contributions to environmental research at a college or university, community based projects that are not related to the environment, studies or assessments without a requirement to address the problems identified in the study, and projects which are funded by federal contracts, grants or other forms of financial assistance. If a penalty is unavoidable, an SEP is an excellent means of spending money where it will do good on a local level and enhance the image of the company.

The basis for much of the background (research and guidance) for environmental compliance stems from agency experience with larger sources of emissions. Consequently, the cost of compliance could be a major concern for a small printer. Compliance with RACT standards may be beyond the capability of the smaller printer. Even the awareness by the small printer of the requirements may be limited or nonexistent, depending on the amount and quality of any outreach program by the agencies to promote awareness.

Recognizing these factors, the EPA developed a program that would encourage self-evaluation or the use of outside consultants to audit a facility, with the provision of relief from some of the penalties if the facility voluntarily admitted its lack of compliance and took action to come into compliance. Small business is defined as any firm with 100 or fewer employees. The policy calls for a business to self-audit its operations, and reveal the findings to the agency within a 30-day period. The facility must then provide a plan to come into compliance. This must all be done within a very limited time span. In return, the agency will waive a portion of the penalties. The gravity portion of any penalty determination is waived completely, and the other components are viewed in a more favorable light.

While the policy has many values, it does not forego the levying of penalties. The threat of monetary punishment remains a key factor in enforcement of compliance with environmental law. The small business also commits itself to whatever consequences of demonstrated non-compliance may arise from the self-audit process.

Small Business Incentive Program

It Pays to Comply

Confronting the demands of the environment is costly. Changes in operations to comply with safer standards for the emission, discharge or disposal of hazardous waste by-products come with both financial commitments and intangible costs. On the other hand, non-compliance can only add more to the cost of doing business in the form of penalties, legal and consulting fees, and other remedial expenses, after which the facility will still have to pay the price that it would have cost to come into compliance in the first place. Non-compliance is a losing proposition.

Taking a proactive stance, by developing plans to steward the environmental impact of the products, the workplace and the process will conserve the financial resources of the business. Promoting pollution prevention as a component of the economics of environmental stewardship will produce profits where at first glance there were only prohibitive costs. The final message is that old adage—do you want to spend the money now, or will you do it later at greater expense?

CHAPTER 23

The Environment in the International Arena

The impression that the environment is more a source of concern for the United States than for other nations is a fallacy. Global efforts have addressed many issues, some with more success than others. Nations and regional groups of nations have addressed specific issues and set regulations to stem environmental pollution. What separates the United States and nations that follow its lead from those who lag behind are conditions that each country or region must face with its political structure, economy and culture. There are few conditions that are universal. The level of industrial development, the status of agricultural ventures, population growth, as well as the natural resources that influence the ecology and humankind, differ from region to region, from people to people. But the message is clear in many venues: nations must address environmental issues or face the consequences.

One observation, made by a friend, who is the environmental manager for one of the largest ink companies in the world, is worth mentioning. While the United States and western European countries have moved at a fast pace to address environmental problems, most of the other regions have been slower and more casual about coming to grips with their situations. This approach is changing, and he has observed more intensive efforts to legislate and enforce environmental restrictions on previously unbridled sources of pollution. Looking ahead to retirement, he sees a very fertile and active source of work assisting branches in foreign countries with their environmental rules and standards.

This chapter is not a litany of regulations, but rather an overview of concerns and activities relative to the environment, based on information gathered through research in the library, on the Internet and in discussions with colleagues. Volumes would be required to summarize the laws of the various nations and regional organizations. This modest chapter can only hope to enlighten us as to the global potential for identifying and curing some of the problems caused by hazardous chemicals in our daily lives.

Treaties and Agreements

During the period from 1970 to the present, global conferences and top leadership meetings have addressed major concerns for the environment that have been considered universal. Among the issues are:

- Global warming,
- Ozone depletion,
- Deforestation,
- Water pollution,
- Agricultural production,
- Population growth,
- Industrial air contamination, and
- Preservation of species.

Global environmental problems require universal solutions.

A search of the internet brought me to a Columbia University site that listed a menu of treaties, dealing with environmental related subjects, agreed upon between the years 1940 and 2000. The list contains a total of 196 international agreements dealing with these issues. A total of 170 treaties were negotiated between 1960 and 1999. The majority of the treaties deal with oceans and marine life, 104. Conservation of biological diversity numbered 43 agreements, and trade/industry and the environment 21 covenants. Some issues were controversial, while others have met with universal approval. Implementation has not always been as forthcoming as good intentions.

Environmental regulations exist in most of the industrialized nations. Permitting appears to have become a norm in most nations. Just how strong the regulations and enforcement are varies considerably. Cultural, political and economic priorities may determine the degree of effectiveness of enforcement of the law.

In some regions of the world, the United States serves as a model. The United Kingdom and Germany serve as models in Europe, while Japan is the archetype in Asia and the Pacific Rim. Preservation of the environment for the benefit of the public and nature is the objective in many regions, while safety of the working population is foremost in other countries.

Most notable of the agreements was the Montreal Protocol on Substances that Deplete the Ozone Layer. Signed in September 1987, and amended in June 1990 and November 1992, this protocol has served as a model of what works. The protocol had definite objectives. It provided adequate time periods for replacement of the chemicals and incentives for those nations which required financial support. Major international corporations had economic motivation to eliminate the ozone depleters from their production facilities. Progress made in eliminating pollutants, while not 100 percent, was sizable and contributed to movement toward the resolution of one major challenge to industrial society. Complete evaluation of the success of the protocol remains, since developing countries' contributions will not be evident until 10 years after they became parties to the pact.

An important factor on the international scene is the heavy involvement of non-governmental organizations (NGOs). Research and scientific organizations work closely with or against governments to determine cause and effect patterns and to measure changes in environmental and health conditions. Groups such as Greenpeace and the Green political parties place considerable pressure on governments by stirring public demonstrations and emotions to address their own agendas. These groups play an important role in international gatherings, hoping to bring attention to the failings of governments to act in good faith to stem pollution and the threat to human, plant and animal life.

Non-governmental organizations monitor the activities of industry and govern-

Considering the number of international accords for environmental issues, how does one measure the success with which individual nations are complying with the law? This was a subject addressed by Edith Brown Weiss in an article found at FINDarticles.com, a looksmart service. She focuses on five specific treaties and takes a look at a random number of countries to see what they have done and rationalizes why some have not accomplished as much as they had agreed to. She postulates on four broad categories of interrelated factors:

1. Characteristics of the activity,

2. Characteristics of the accord,

3. The international environment, and

4. Factors involving the country.

"Important characteristics of the activity target by the agreement include the number of participants involved, the significance of the markets and trade to the activity, the location of the activity (whether centralized or dispersed) and the degree of concentration of the activity in major countries.

"The characteristics of an accord, such as the perceived equity of the obligations, the precision of the obligations, provisions for obtaining scientific and technical advice, monitoring and reporting requirements, implementation

Gathering the Nations to do Good

and non-compliance procedures, incentives, and sanctions, are important to compliance.

"The international community's increasing attention to international environmental issues, including international environmental accords, is one of the most important factors explaining the acceleration in the trend toward improved implementation and national compliance . . . The prominence of environmental issues mobilized worldwide media, roused public opinion and energized national and international NGOs and the public to put increased pressure on governments to deal with environmental issues. This enhanced implementation and compliance.

"Countries are at the center of the compliance process and must take required actions to fulfill their obligations under the treaties . . . A country's administrative capacity is crucial to compliance. Strong administrative capacity generally leads to better implementation and compliance . . . Economic factors are important but only indirectly . . . The effect of political systems and institutions is complex and mixed . . . Multiple levels of political authority must be coordinated, which is often difficult . . . The authority of a central government . . . does not reach deeply into local areas . . . Political stalemates can bring about a decline in implementation and compliance."*

She stresses three strategies to motivate and stimulate countries:

1. The sunshine methods which are intended to bring behavior into the open for scrutiny,

2. Positive incentives to induce countries to join and comply,

3. Coercive measures in terms of sanctions, penalties, etc. which pose negative incentives for non-compliance.

The key to success on an international level is to engage the relevant parties to promote compliance and the benefits that compliance has brought to their constituents.

Aggressive options to force compliance may include sanctions, penalties and other actions which cause hardships for the non-compliant country.

Challenge of Population Growth

Population growth has an enormous impact on the state of natural resources in any given region. The demands on natural resources to feed and maintain growing populations are sure to deplete local availability of food, water and shelter. Satisfying this great appetite can only lead to searches for more sources in an ever-growing area beyond the locality. Destruction of resources accompanies this effort and leads to the depletion of natural resources. Where do people live? How do they move from place to place to work, get an education or simply spend leisure time? How do they weather the seasons, confronting hot and cold

*Edith Brown Weiss, "Getting countries to comply with international agreements," *Environment*, July–August 1999 (www.findarticles.com) p 3–5.

extremes? These are questions which are answered by engaging natural resources and/or destroying some of the resources in the process.

In earlier times, when the amount of available land far exceeded the needs of the population, tribes could move from their current sites to new ones with ease. As a campsite became polluted from human waste or arid for agriculture or hunting, the tribe could pick up its tents and travel a short distance to the new location. Archeologists move from site to site to trace the patterns of tribal movement and the development of society. As populations grew and cities replaced campsites, the ability to transport people became more difficult and eventually impossible. Natural resources frequently gave way to "progress." Pollution then became a problem, whether coming from fires to heat and cook or sanitary wastes flowing into the nearby streams. Society had to learn how to cope with its environment.

As population growth makes demands for products for subsistence, economies shift from agriculture to industry. Manufacturing replaces farmland. Forests fall to make room for agriculture or manufacturing. The disappearance of natural habitats leads to loss of species. Then farms make way for homes. The by-products of development reduce the areas from which natural resources come and replace them with sites that are devastated, barren or polluted. Unbridled, developers take advantage of the needs of population growth to destroy the very fiber that has sustained that population. Urbanization brings its pressures on the resources that facilitate rural society and destroy many of them in the process. In many of the developed countries, public pressure has been brought to bear to pass legislation that will control and limit the activities of developers and protect the environment. Restrictions have been harder to legislate and enforce in the less developed nations.

Industrialization seeks to develop an economic foundation for a growing population by producing products for use within the boundaries or for export to other nations of the world. With proper planning and design, such efforts can make use of natural resources in a manner that will sustain the existing ecology and not impact on the health of the population. This has not always been the case, with developers of industry in less developed countries raping the landscape and poisoning the resources. Concerted pressure from within and outside a country has led to public demands for a better way to do things.

Pollution prevention has become a theme for environmental programs in all corners of the globe. The more acceptable term on a global level is "sustainable development." Efforts at sustainable development operate on the premise that there is a better way to accomplish our goals without destroying the world around us and by minimizing the impact of industrialization on natural resources and the public. Reuse of resources is a common thread in paving the way for new developments.

Efforts are ongoing around the world to teach and practice the basics of sustainable development. International conferences provide opportunities for exchange of ideas and promotion

As conditions change, decisions have to be made.

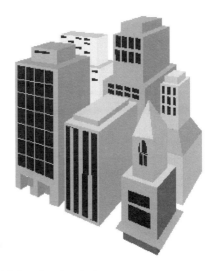

Urbanization brings pressures on natural resources.

of successful projects and programs. The basic elements of sustainability embrace the concepts of environmental management systems (ISO14000) and pollution prevention.

Energy Poses Challenges

Population growth, industrialization and urbanization all make demands on the environment. The need for energy to fuel and protect all three influences poses an environmental challenge. Beyond the intrinsic ability to contribute to the pollution of our air, soil and water resources, energy poses the question of availability. Conservation of natural resources is as important a factor for the coal, natural gas and oil that we exploit as is the pollution that is derived from them. The use of nuclear energy is a point of confrontation based on the fear of health problems stemming from exposure to radiation from accidents and the disposal of the spent nuclear fuel rods.

Modern technology requires considerable sources of energy.

"Energy has long been a basic requirement of human societies. Archeological evidence from caves in Africa suggest that fire was used by early humans, the hominids, as long ago as 1.5 million years BP, and fire has since fueled the technologies on which civilized societies have been built . . . Through time, the ability of human cultures to access energy, and the amounts of energy used, are often indicators of society's level of development and resource use."*

Modern society places a great demand on all forms of energy to fuel the high technology world in which we live. Automobiles, trucks and all forms of transportation soak up a major part of these resources and, in turn, emit an enormous level of pollution. The industrial base upon which we count for the necessities of life, including large scale agricultural and aquacultural endeavors,

---

*Nick Middleton, *The Global Casino, An Introduction to Environmental Issues*, Edward Arnold, London, 1995, p 224.

consumes considerable amounts of energy, as well as materials that generate wastes. Much of the efforts in the industrial and the developing nations is aimed at handling and disposing of such wastes in a manner that will create reusable sources of energy or new sources of materials from the waste, rather than stockpiling wastes and the potential hazards they pose. Reuse of resources reduces the need for the energy required to produce them in the first place.

The need to use energy more effectively has led to the drive by NGOs to make society aware of and a part of the movement to practice energy conservation and efficiency and to promote sustainable development.

Nuclear energy has continued to pose problems for the NGOs. As economic and supply pressures have been exerted on nations using oil as the basis for their energy needs, research into alternative methods has not yet come up with a system that is as effective as nuclear reactors. Safety cautions have been taken but public sentiment continues to object to old installations, let alone the building of new nuclear plants. The movement of spent fuel from reactors to safe havens is fought to ostensibly protect the public and nature on the route from reactor to cemetery cell. Many studies have been conducted to relate the incidence of cancer in a community that houses a nuclear plant. "While studies of adults suggested that no such effect is associated with nuclear installations. . . , the situation is less clear-cut for children."*

The situation with respect to nuclear power has taken on more emotional impact with the lagging behind of provisions to handle and store the wastes of the energy reactors. No one wants nuclear waste rolling through the streets or on railroad tracks in proximity of their homes. No one wants to have safe facilities for storage of wastes in their backyard. No one wants to pay the price for energy wastes that are not of their own making. Chernobyl provided impetus to this public concern, with the spreading of radiation to untold areas surrounding the world and debilitating the population, especially children, within the immediate region (Table 23–1).

All forms of energy fuel modern society.

Atmospheric Concerns

Concerns about air quality are largely aimed at ozone depletion and global warming. Of primary concern is the impact of changes in the atmosphere that will result in major changes in climate. In the one case, chemicals used for refrigeration, air conditioning, and as an industrial degreaser rise to the upper atmosphere and destroy the layer of ozone that surrounds the earth. In the second case, gases rising from surface of the earth are trapped under the atmospheric shield around the planet, resulting in an increase in temperature that alters climatic conditions and ecological balances.

---

*Ibid., p 233.

TABLE 23–1. MAIN BIOLOGICAL EFFECTS OF THE CHERNOBYL CATASTROPHE

Level	Short-term response	Long-term response
Biosphere	Global and local changes in radionuclide accumulation and dispersion	Global and local disturbances in genetic and phenetic structure of the biosphere
Ecosystem	Changes in ecosystem diversity, stability and development patterns	Changes in co-evolution process and ecosystem succession
Human population	Changes in birth and mortality rates	Changes in mutation rate, natural selection intensity and adaptive reaction
Human individual	Disturbances in physiology and behaviour	Changes in probability of cancer, hereditary abnormalities and other diseases

Source: Nick Middleton, *The Global Casino, An Introduction To Environmental Issues*, Edward Arnold, London, 1995, p 235.

The Montreal Protocol addressed the proliferation of chlorinated fluorocarbons and their effect on the upper atmospheric shield. Monitoring flights and satellite photographs over the two poles revealed an increase in the size of the holes (lack of ozone) over the poles, particularly the South Pole. Measurements of polar ozone in recent decades has contributed to our knowledge of this phenomena and the dangers inherent in allowing greater amounts of ultraviolet rays to penetrate through to the earth. Skin cancers accelerate under the glow of the ultraviolet rays that reach earth.

Global warming has been a more contentious environmental football. Lack of agreement in the science community and between political entities has resulted in rejection of broad-based agreements at the international level. While all concerned agree to the persistence of global warming, not all agree as to its cause and means of resolution. A recent display of the lack of consensus took place at the meeting in Kyoto, Japan, at which the United States refused to agree to the covenant based on a claim of "flaws" in the agreement. A more promising report was issued by Reuters November 7, 2001, describing the successful negotiations at a meeting in Marrakesh, Morocco stating that, "government ministers from around the world moved a step closer today to bringing a treaty to combat global warming into force after their officials reached agreement on a crucial sticking point."* The new treaty includes binding sanctions on the countries that do not comply, a shortcoming in previous discussions.

"The Earth is comfortably warm because it is surrounded by a blanket of air . . . it is a suitable home for life; since water is an essential ingredient of life . . . that requires average temperatures on our globe to be in the range that liquid water can exist,

---

*"Global-Warming Talks Gain With Accord on Compliance," *The New York Times*, November 8, 2001, p A5.

between 0 degrees C and 100 degrees C." Compare this to the atmosphereless Moon which orbits the Earth with temperatures ranging from 100 degrees C on the sunlit surface and –150 degrees C at night.* In a normal greenhouse effect, "about forty percent of incoming solar radiation is reflected back into space, fifteen percent is absorbed by the atmosphere, and about forty five percent reaches the Earth's surface. The warm surface of the Earth radiates at infrared wavelengths, and some of the radiation is absorbed in the atmosphere and re-radiated back to the surface, making it warmer than it would otherwise be."** This natural phenomenon keeps the Earth in an equilibrium that sustains life as we know it.

Global warming upsets this normal balance, increasing the temperature ranges on Earth and altering the normal conditions in which various forms of flora and animal life flourish. Among the causes of this imbalance is a growing presence of carbon dioxide, methane, nitrous oxide and other gases in the atmosphere. The gases act as impediments to the normal pattern of radiation and reflection, increasing the ambient temperature of the Earth. (See figure 23–1.)

In his book *Hothouse Earth*, John Gibbons ends with a chapter entitled "What To Do." With the understanding that climatic

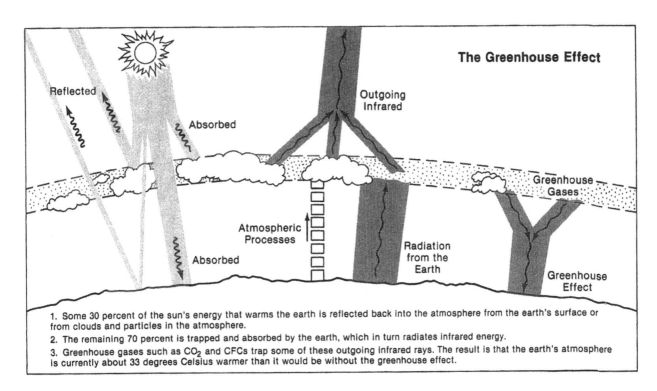

The Greenhouse Effect

Reflected

Absorbed

Outgoing Infrared

Greenhouse Gases

Atmospheric Processes

Absorbed

Radiation from the Earth

Greenhouse Effect

1. Some 30 percent of the sun's energy that warms the earth is reflected back into the atmosphere from the earth's surface or from clouds and particles in the atmosphere.

2. The remaining 70 percent is trapped and absorbed by the earth, which in turn radiates infrared energy.

3. Greenhouse gases such as CO_2 and CFCs trap some of these outgoing infrared rays. The result is that the earth's atmosphere is currently about 33 degrees Celsius warmer than it would be without the greenhouse effect.

Figure 23–1. Global warming is caused by trapped gases which trap outgoing infrared rays and increase temperature of the atmosphere.

Source: Kathryn Gay, *Air Pollution*, Franklin Watts, New York, 1991.

*John Gribben, *Hothouse Earth*, Grove Weidenfeld, New York, 1990, pp 24–25.
**Ibid., pp 24–25.

changes are in progress, what can we do to slow down the conditions that lend impetus to global warming. "The most direct way to reduce emissions of greenhouse gases . . . is to burn less fossil fuel—more realistically, we should aim to minimize the increase in the rate at which such fuels are being consumed . . . we could gain some breathing room by changing the mixture of fuels being burnt. Coal produces more carbon dioxide than oil, and oil much more than natural gas . . . Synthetics derived from coal . . . produce even more carbon dioxide than coal itself. Reforestation is being taken seriously as a policy option, not only because every little bit helps in our efforts to slow the growth of the greenhouse effect,"* but for all the other ecological benefits stemming from forests.

Governmental action to stem global warming will inevitably require reductions in those chemicals and processes that add to the problem. Compliance issues will deal with the degree to which levels of the gases are reduced. Among the issues that are being addressed are targets for specific greenhouse gases, protection and enhancements of reservoirs of greenhouse gases, transfer of sound environmental technologies, and the establishment of funding mechanisms to provide incentives for developing countries to comply with the covenants. Overriding the process must be a means of economically pressuring the non-compliers to take action and contribute to the improvement of the environment.

International Law and Regulation

The United Nations Centre on Transnational Corporations issued a report in 1992 covering emerging trends in the development of international environmental law. The study considered contemporary international environmental law and policy at the global and regional level, with reference to intergovernmental agreements, non-binding intergovernmental declarations, and acts of intergovernmental organizations. "It is clear from this general survey that the relationship between environmental protection and international law has undergone a significant transformation in recent years. The evidence clearly points to a continued and sustained increase in the nature and scope of international regulation after UNCED, irrespective of the outcome. Growing concern about global and regional environmental issues is now reflected in a dramatic and almost overwhelming increase in the number of international agreements, policy declarations, resolutions, decisions, guidelines, and codes of conduct, which relate directly, or indirectly, to the protection of the environment."**

Among the general conclusions drawn from the survey of developments at that time were:

1. The increase in international environmental regulation will continue to grow significantly.

---

*Ibid., pp 233–245.
**Phillipe Sands, "Emerging Trends in the Development of International Environmental Law at the Regional and Global Level: Implications for Transnational Corporations," United Nations Centre on Transnational Corporations, February 1992, p 7.

2. The standards developed by international regulations are becoming less general and increasingly specific in nature.

3. As the standards become more specific and detailed, they are becoming more stringent in the nature of obligations which they establish.

4. There are wide disparities from region to region in the nature and extent of the regulations.

5. Environmental law and policy has now entered mainstream economic regulation.*

The 1991 Tunis Declaration of Francophone Ministers of the Environment affirmed a basic set of principles with relevance to industry:

- "the obligation of prevention and precaution;

- the need to evaluate environmental impacts, including transboundary impacts, at each stage of development;

- the responsibility of those who damage the environment;

- the application of the "polluter pays" principle;

- placing responsibility on the user of natural resources;

- seeking to ensure respect for international and regional conventions. . . ;

- establishing procedure for notification and consultation in cases where the environment of another state is likely to be affected by development projects;

- improving the conditions of participation for non-governmental organizations. . ."**

The differences in environmental law and regulations between regions and nations reflects the general attitudes of the different populations concerning the relationship between a government and its public. Countries with histories of strong central governments will differ from those with weak central governments and strong local administrations. Autocratic countries will have less difficulty in pressing issues than democratic nations, or perhaps it may be reversed by strong opinions by the public in a democratic country pressing for solutions that may be swept aside as inconsequential by a strong centralized ruler.

Regional and National Approaches to the Environment

*Ibid., p 7.
**Ibid., pp 8–9.

Addressing the issue of national environmental protection in Australia at a conference in Sydney, Australia in 1991, Donald K. Anton, Jennifer Kohout and Nicola Pain noted; "As the scope and coverage of international environmental law progressively widens, the coordinated operation of treaty rights and obligations will be crucial in establishing an effective international legal order for the protection of the environment. Without an integrated application of effective national regulations, international environmental law is likely to become superfluous . . . At the domestic level, the implications of an effective structure of international environmental law are considerable . . . The power to enact laws implementing a treaty is meaningless in the absence of a means of enforcement and a method of intra- and inter-government coordination. The most efficient method of enforcement and coordination is through a dedicated centralized authority."*

Attempts at finding common denominators for international approaches are evident in the many international, global and regional conferences that have been held since 1991. A major ingredient addressed by the discussions, both for and against international regulations, has been the critical, essential need for enforcement, as well as stipulated punishment/penalties for non-compliance.

To illustrate some of the environmental activities taking place in various parts of the world, we conducted a search of library resources and the internet. Some of the information obtained is described below.

Western European Community

After the United States, there is no region that has more laws and more specific regional regulations than the nations of western Europe. With the European Union bringing together most of the countries in the region, there are both regional and national environmental laws. Germany and the United Kingdom have led the way in setting the standards for Europe, with most countries following either of the two in modeling their own legislation and setting standards for compliance. The earliest laws dealt with safety and health issues in the workplace, which set the tone for the environmental laws and compliance.

The United Kingdom passed the Health and Safety at Work etc. Act in 1974. This was a broad, sweeping law to cover the many aspects of safety in the plant. At the time, the Act was described as "the most significant statutory advance in Health and Safety since Shaftesbury's Acts of 1883. The new Act aims to radically change not only the scope of these provisions, but also the way that Health and Safety provisions are enforced and administered."** In 1992 the Management of Health & Safety at Work Regulations added additional provisions, including risk assessment

---

*D.D. Anton, J. Kohout, and N. Pain, "Nationalizing Environmental Protection in Australia: The International Dimensions," *Environmental Law* 23, 1993, pp 763–83, from Internet http:www.ciesin.org/docs/010-567/010-567.html.

**H.E. McDermott, "Health and Safety in the Flexographic Workshop," European Flexographic Technical Association, September 16, 1975.

to assure the monitoring of the workplace to improve worker safety and health.

Concerns for air emissions were addressed in the 1973 Environmental Action Program of the European Community, drawn up by the European Commission and approved by the Council of Ministers. Subsequent action programs were enacted in 1977 and 1982. The fourth such program was undertaken in period 1987–1992, with five main goals:

- "to identify pollutants (both indoor and outdoor),

- to determine the most appropriate focus for control instruments (the pollutants themselves or the source of the pollution),

- "to set and implement EC-wide objectives for substantial emission reductions in order to combat acid deposition and forest die-back,

- "in the longer term, to reduce ambient air concentrations of pollutants to levels acceptable for sensitive ecosystems,

- "To develop appropriate management techniques (such as pollution modeling, monitoring networks and economic control instruments). "*

The fifth framework program is now in progress, with eight institutes that constitute the Joint Research Centre of the European Commission. The Environment Institute is located in Ispra, Italy. "The Institute supports the development of effective policies by seeking to create a sound scientific and technical basis and, in the longer term, the preservation of the Earth's natural resources . . . The new structure of the Institute, in place since October 1998, covering all compartments of the environment—air, water, soil, energy and life—is proving very efficient in coping with the vast variety of environmental issues in which the European Institutions have a strategic role."**

Individual member nations of the European Community have enacted their own local regulations that address air quality standards, product standards for fuels and vehicles, and standards for industrial plants. A representative example is seen in Table 23–2, illustrating the ambient air quality standards that were established in the Federal Republic of Germany. Note the differences between health and environmental standards for a few of the similar substances, i.e., lead and cadmium.

Formal compliance with the directives varies. The most aggressive action was taken by the Federal Republic of Germany, France, Luxembourg and the Netherlands; this group of countries had completed their mission by 1991. At that time, Belgium, Denmark, Ireland, Italy and the United Kingdom had a good legal record, but specific measures had to be resolved. Substantial failures of

---

*Graham Bennett, *Air Pollution Control in the European Community, Implementation of the EC Directives in the Twelve Member States*, Graham & Trotman, London, pp 1–2.
**Jean-Marie Martin, "A Word from the Director," EI website http://www.ei.jrc.it/ overview/director/content.html, June 2001.

TABLE 23–2 AMBIENT AIR QUALITY STANDARDS IN THE FEDERAL REPUBLIC OF GERMANY

| SUBSTANCE | UNIT | AMBIENT AIR QUALITY STANDARD (TA-LUFT, 1986) | | | |
| | | HEALTH STANDARDS | | ENVIRONMENTAL STANDARDS | |
		Long term	Short term	Long term	Short term
Suspended particulates	mg	0.15	0.30	—	—
Inorganic lead compounds in suspended particulates	g/m³	2.0	—	—	—
Inorganic cadmium compounds in suspended particulates	g/m³	0.04	—	—	—
Chlorine	mg/m³	0.10	0.30	—	—
Hydrochloric acid	mg/m³	0.10	0.20	—	—
Carbon monoxide	mg/m³	10	30	—	—
Sulphur dioxide	mg/m³	0.14	0.40	—	—
Nitrogen dioxide	mg/m3	0.08	0.20*	—	—
Non-hazardous dust deposits	g/m²	—	—	0.35	0.65
Inorganic lead in dust deposits	mg/m²	—	—	0.25	—
Inorganic cadmium in dust deposits	g/m²	—	—	5	—
Inorganic thallium in dust deposits	g/m²	—	—	10	—
Inorganic gaseous fluorine compounds	g/m³	—	—	1.0	3.0

*0.30 mg/m³ where hydrochloric acid cannot be measured and clearly separated from chlorides.

Source: Graham Bennett, *Air Pollution Control in the European Community, Implementation of the EC Directives in the Twelve Member States*, Graham & Trotman, London 1991, p 13.

compliance were found in Greece, Spain and Portugal. A common problem was the setting of standards for vehicular emissions, including lead in petrol.*

Central and Eastern Europe

Commencing in 1989, with the transition from the Soviet Union domination to that of independent nations, assistance was forthcoming from the United States and the European Community. With the passage of time, it has been possible to see that the current state of the environment demonstrates some victories and a number of disappointments. "Some early emission reductions were more directly related to declines in economic activity rather than improved environmental regulation. But even in some countries where the economy has picked up, emissions have stayed stable, or even dropped . . . The air in some cities has improved . . . and wastewater treatment plants are being built or improved. Overall, however, many environmental laws, including new ones written since 1989, continue to sit on the books unimplemented."**

While the initial impetus for environmental investment was in response to citizen protest and rage about damage to health and nature by the old regime, today's governments pay attention to the environment as part of the commitment to membership in the European Union. In part, investment in the environment mirrors the economic needs, with weaker countries using their resources to build their economies and deferring the cost of an environmental infrastructure. This is not too different from the

*Graham Bennett, op. cit., p 197.
**Ruth Greenspan Bell, "Environmental Policy, Legislation, and Regulation in Central and Eastern Europe," Internet web page http:/www.envirodialogue.net/legpol.shtml (9/25/01), p 1.

period in which Soviet form of communism favored full employment and maximal economic production, frequently elevating the
party goals over the environmental requirements found in the
laws. The current debate about change addresses the desire for a
cleaner environment as a possible catalyst to demonstrate how civil
society works and for building faith in the legitimacy of laws.*

"The goal of the renewed Canadian Environmental Protection
Act (CEPA) is to contribute to sustainable development
through pollution prevention and to protect the environment,
human life and health from the risks associated with toxic substances. CEPA also recognizes the contribution of pollution prevention and the management and control of toxic substances and
hazardous waste to reducing threats to Canada's ecosystems and
biological diversity. It acknowledges for the first time the need to
virtually eliminate the most persistent toxic substances that
remain (in) the environment for extended periods of time before
breaking down and bioaccumulative toxic substance that accumulate within living organisms. Health Canada works in partnership
with Environment Canada to assess potentially toxic substances
and to develop regulations to control toxic substances."**

As expressed by the Honourable David Anderson, P.C., M.P.,
Minister of the Environment: "The need for more innovative ways
of protecting our natural heritage is increasingly evident. Although
we have achieved considerable environmental progress over the
years, we face increasing demands on our natural resources from a
growing population and an expanding economy . . . We must
rethink old methods, use new tools, and forge stronger partnerships
if we are to better protect our environment and conserve our quality
of life. We need stronger science and more reliable information to
help us know where we are, where we want to be, and how we are
going to get there . . ."***

Our Neighbor to the North

Environmental concerns arose early for the Japanese, when
copper mining began to damage the environment near Ashio.
This began in 1868 with government protective measures, but
with little enforcement. The modern era began with the end of
World War II and the rehabilitation and industrialization of the
country. People regarded pollution as a local government concern
with authority coming from the Local Autonomy System created
in the Japanese Constitution of 1946. Several large local governments enacted ordinances for pollution control.**** The national
approach to environmental regulation came as a response to
crisis. Seemingly isolated events prompted a move to a more centralized approach to protecting the environment.

Japan

---

*Ibid., pp 1–5.

**Environment Canada, "Acts Administered by the Minister of the Environment: Cana-
dian Environmental Protection Act (1999)" Internet web page http:/www3.ec.gc.ca/
EnviroRegs/ENG/SearchDetail.cfm?intact=1001, 10/23/01, p 1.

***Environment Canada, "Minister's Message to Canadians," Internet web page
http://www.ec.gc.ca/tkei/main e.cfm, 8/19/01.

****Harashima, Yohei, "Effects of Economic Growth on Environmental Policies in North-
east Asia," Internet web page http://www.findarticles.com/m1076/6_42/63993858/
p1/article.jhtml, 6/1/01, p 1.

The Basic Law for Environmental Pollution Control was passed in 1967 and is the foundation of national environmental law in Japan. "It was enacted to protect human health and the living environment and allows the government to set environmental quality standards for air, water, soil and noise pollution. It also empowers the government to conduct research and monitoring and to create environmentally beneficial subsidies. The law originally had a clause for harmonizing the environment with economic development, which was removed in 1970. The Air Pollution Control Law was amended in 1974; the Water Pollution Control Law was amended in 1983, 1989 and 1990; and the Law for Compensation of Pollution-Related Health Injuries was amended in 1987. The Nature Conservation Law was the first law to allow coordinated action of nature conservation in Japan.*

China

"Chemical companies in China are facing environmental regulations that are akin to those of Western nations. Ultimately, these regulations could benefit Western companies that are already well-versed in pollution control technologies. China's environmental laws are also opening new markets for U.S. pollution control products and expertise.

"The NEPA (National Environmental Protection Agency) measures air and water pollution and solid wastes. Air pollution measurements focus on soot, industrial dust and sulfur dioxide; water pollution measurements focus on chemical oxygen demand, oil pollutants, cyanide, arsenic, mercury, lead, cadmium and hexavalent chromium and solid waste is measured in actual discharge amounts." (See figure 23–2.)

"'China is targeting heavy polluting industries—the chemical, metallurgy, papermaking, electrical industries,' says Wang Yuqing, minister of China's NEPA." "We have plans to contain the total amount of pollution, but we may defer some of the standards for the inland regions, according to their economies. The coastal cities can try to reduce pollution; the inland areas can try to control their pollution."**

ISO 14000 Expected to Boost Environmental Compliance

With many multi-national corporations doing business in all parts of the world, environmental awareness and the need to sustain the environment have become more accepted responsibilities for management. Compliance is not a question; it is a way of doing business. Environmental costs and obligations have grown substantially, fostered by the growing awareness of the public to the influences on their quality of life. Laws and regulations are being expanded and are encompassing more businesses and activities. Businesses are being held more and more accountable for their actions and obligations.

*Japan: Policy Instruments, Important Legislation, Internet web page http://www.rri.org/envatlas/asia/japan/jp-inst.html, p 1.
**Gail Dutton, "Chinese Environmental Laws a Plus for the West." *Chemical Market Reporter*, Jan. 19, 1998, on Internet web site http:/www.findarticles.com.

Figure 23–2. Air pollutants hang low at dusk in Shanghai, China.
Photograph by Jeffrey Shapiro.

ISO 14000 provides an excellent foundation for communication and management of the environment beyond the borders of the parent company. It provides a basis for responding to local needs within an international program, maintaining conformity with corporate targets and objectives while confronting differing conditions and laws. ISO 14000 fits in with the voluntary, proactive programs that are industry conceived and driven to improve the environment. Since the success of any program begins with top management, the ISO program will assure the communication of management's desire to operate a sustainable environment to its personnel with positive results. (See Chapter 21 for details on ISO 14000 and environmental management systems.)

International Efforts to Control Chemicals

Just as the United States enacted the Toxic Substances Control Act, nations worldwide are moving to legislation that calls for registration of chemicals. A chemical is considered "registered" if it appears on the chemical inventory list of the appropriate official government agency. Chemicals listed may include those used in manufacturing a product, a commercial product within the country, or products that are exported and imported for commercial purposes. The lists of registered chemicals will not be the same from country to country (Table 23–3).

Chemical registration requires testing. Various tests will be conducted to ascertain the impact of the particular substance on health and the ecology. The tests may include biodegradation, bioaccumulation, chromosomal aberration, ignition, ecotoxicity and oral/dermal toxicity. Some regions may require heavy-metal analysis. Requirements may differ by country and by the nature and use of the substance. The registration process can be time-consuming and costly.

TABLE 23–3 COUNTRIES WITH WORLDWIDE CHEMICAL LEGISLATION WHICH INCLUDES CHEMICAL REGISTRATION

North America	Europe	Asia / Pacific / Africa
Canada USA Mexico*	European Community (EU) Switzerland Eastern Europe e.g.: Hungary* Poland * Czech Republic*	Australia Japan South Korea Peoples Republic of China Philippines New Zealand Taiwan* Malaysia* Thailand* Singapore* South Africa *

* Inventory in preparation / to be established
Status: January 2000.

Source: Terry Moretti, and Andrew Zarnoyski, Clariant Corporation, from presentation made at Non-Impact Printing Conference.

TABLE 23–4 "BLUE ANGEL" ECO LABEL FOR LASER PRINTERS, INK-JET PRINTERS AND MATRIX PRINTERS
Scope: Laser Printers, Ink-Jet Printers, Matrix Printers ≤ 25 pages/minute

Requirements:

1.	Longevity of the Devices	10.	Device Safety
2.	Recyclable Design	11.	Electromagnetic Compatibility
3.	Reduction of the Number of Plastics	12.	Printing Paper
4.	Material Requirements for the Plastics forming Cases and Case Parts of Printers	13.	Inked-Ribbon Cartridges, Toner Cartridges and Ink Cartridges
5.	Marking of Plastics	14.	Packaging
6.	Acceptance of the Return of Used Devices	15.	User Manual
		16.	Substance-related Standards for Toners and Inks
7.	Noise Emissions	17.	Pollutant Emissions of Electrophotographic Printers
8.	Batteries / Accumulators		
9.	Power Draw	18.	Quality of the Photoconductor Drum of Electrophotographic Printers

Source: Terry Moretti, and Andrew Zarnoyski, Clariant Corporation, from presentation made at Non-Impact Printing Conference.

TABLE 23–5. "BLUE ANGEL" ECO LABEL FOR INK/TONER REQUIREMENTS FOR PRINTER AND COPIER

Inks and toners must not contain:

Part 1	Part 3
Heavy Metals	**Other Hazardous Substances**
Substances based on: - mercury - lead - cadmium - chromium VI	Substances classified as carcinogenic or suspected carcinogenic: MAK[1] III A1, MAK III A2, MAK III B and marked with the risk phrases: R26: very toxic when inhaled R40: possible irreversible damage R42: possible sensitization by inhalation R45: may cause cancer R46: may cause genetic damage R49: may cause cancer if inhaled R62: may possibly impair reproduction R63: may possibly be harmful to embryo R64: may be harmful to the infant via the mother's milk
Part 2	- MAK III 1, MAK III 2, MAK 3 (EC-Cat.)
Azo Colorants	- TRGS 905
Azo colorants (dyes and pigments) based on amines classified as carcinogenic or suspected carcinogenic: MAK III A1, MAK III A2, MAK III B	- entire product R43 (skin sensitization)

[1] MAK Listing = Maximum concentration at the place of work and biological tolerance values for working materials

Source: Terry Moretti, and Andrew Zarnoyski, Clariant Corporation, from presentation made at Non-Impact Printing Conference.

Several countries, or environmental advocacy groups in those countries, have adopted special labels for environmentally friendly products and practices. These "seals of approval" are used to promote products. Typical are "Green Seal" in the United States, "Eco Mark" in Japan, "White Swan" in Scandanavia, "Blue Angel" in Germany, and "Flower" in Europe. A sample of requirements for classifying an ink-jet printer for the Blue Angel label is illustrated in Table 23–4, and for the ink in Table 23–5.

Chemical registration may be the key to long term pollution prevention efforts, as countries measure the need for environmental compliance and review the lists with the aim of eliminating any chemical that poses health risks or ecological damage. It may become the ultimate tool in international efforts to attain source reduction and sustainability.

CHAPTER **24**

Looking Back to Look Ahead

The condition of the ecology and public health and the challenges to regulate the environment by government interference are always in a state of flux. Politics change and agendas shift. Economic stresses place demands on what we can or cannot do. Science changes, as new research supports some contentions and debunks others. The needs of the public wax and wane, shifting under the influence of real hard evidence, anecdotal science and organized appeals to the emotions. International balance in attacking the causes of pollution hinges on the response to all these considerations.

This was most evident in the year 2001, as a new administration in Washington came to grips with the legacy and executive orders of the previous administration. Decisions to uphold some environmental and safety orders and regulations were in disagreement with the previous administration. Other decisions upheld or slightly modified those directives. The reception of these decisions by the general public and advocacy groups in the United States and by the international community was disbelief and dismay, since the decisions were often at odds with the generally accepted science, policies and remedies accepted by governments in all parts of the world.

It would therefore appear timely to write the final chapter of this book in review of the past and, based on current EPA initiatives, look at what might be the future.

417

30 Years in the Working

Now that the USEPA has celebrated 30 years of existence, it is a good time to look back to put some perspective on what the future likely holds in store. Each of the nation's regions was asked to publish a review of the efforts made and accomplishments realized during those 30 years. It is interesting to see what the EPA regions present in their vision of accomplishments and challenges.

In the Region III publication *Remember the Past, Protect the Future*, regional administrator Bradley M. Campbell says:

"The 30 years of environmental progress highlighted in this report chart a remarkable success story: In one generation, we have reversed the effects of more than a century of industrial pollution and environmental degradation, and we have begun the effort to restore and protect our treasured natural resources. We have done this and at the same time built the strongest economy in our history." (See figure 24–1.)

"This remarkable progress is a tribute to the work of thousands of dedicated and talented EPA employees, to the cooperation of other federal agencies and state and local governments, to the efforts of scores of nonprofit organizations and their volunteers, to the tenacity of dedicated community activists and to the enlightened leadership of many in business and industry.

"This leadership, joined by that of environmental leaders in communities across the country, offers the promise that we may fulfill Theodore Roosevelt's mandate that we leave this nation 'a better land for our descendants than it is for us.'"

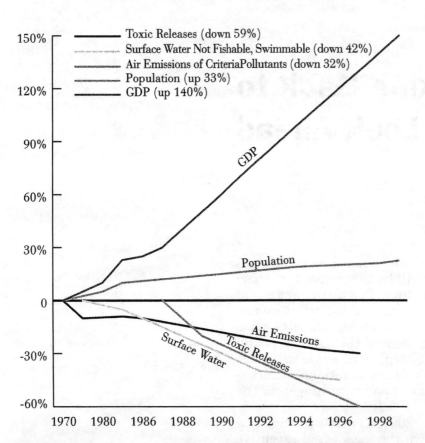

Figure 24–1. National environmental improvements/economics and population growth.

Source: United States Environmental Protection Agency Region III, "30 Years of Environmental Progress," *Remember the Past, Protect the Future*, EPA-903-R-00-004, p 31.

The ensuing chapters of the report cite the horror stories of the past and the results of efforts to clean the air, the waters and the land of pollutants that affect the ecology and public health. Buried in paragraphs are hints of present and future concerns, some of them dealing with nature itself.

By and large, there has been considerable change in air quality for the better, as illustrated by the graphs (figure 24–2) showing the significant reduction made in this region, of four of

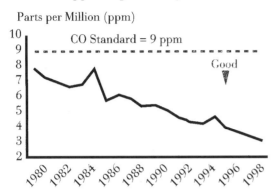

Carbon Monoxide Air Levels Have Dropped Significantly

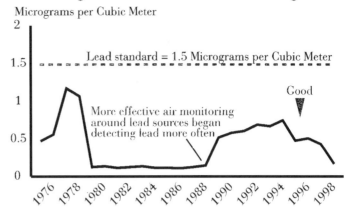

Regional Lead Air Levels are Declining

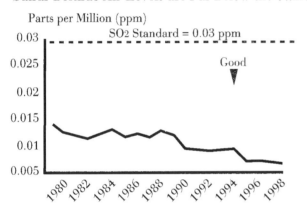

Sulfur Dioxide Air Levels are Far Below the Standard

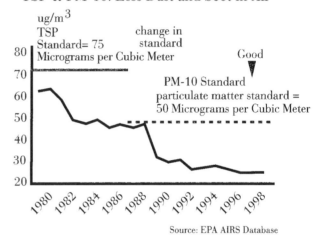

TSP & PM-10: Less Dust and Soot in Air

Source: EPA AIRS Database

EPA's efforts to reduce air pollution began with six criteria air pollutants:carbon monoxide (CO), sulfur dioxide (SO2), particulate matter which is dust and soot (PM-10), lead (Pb), ozone, and nitrogen dioxide. Progress has been made in reducing all six of these criteria pollutants. Utilities and industry's compliance with the Clean Air Act have brought about serious air quality improvements by reducing CO, SO2, and PM-10. Removing lead from from gasoline has brought about more air quality gains.

Figure 24–2. Considerable reductions have been made in four of six most common air pollutants affecting public health in the Mid-Atlantic region.

Source: United States Environmental Protection Agency Region III, "30 Years of Environmental Progress," *Remember the Past, Protect the Future*, EPA-903-R-00-004, p 6.

the six common air pollutants. At the same time, concern comes with the introduction of the changing population and use of vehicles for transportation. As seen in figure 24–3, the number of vehicles on the road and miles traveled will continue to increase. Just how will the emissions of these vehicles impact on the demands for industry to reduce its relatively smaller contribution to pollution?

Water quality has also shown a marked improvement over the 30 years. Rivers and streams, once polluted, are now home to considerable edible fish populations. Drinking water is cleaner than ever. Yet over the horizon there are clear challenges with increasing population. This is illustrated by the anticipated growth of sewage

Automobiles and trucks contribute heavily to air pollution.

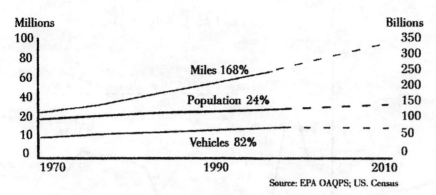

Source: EPA OAQPS; US. Census

During the past 30 years, air quality has improved significantly while the GDP grew by 140 percent, the population grew by 24 percent, and the number of motor vehicle miles driven increased by 168 percent.

Figure 24–3. Number of vehicles (in millions) and vehicle miles traveled (in billions) increase dramatically.

Source: United States Environmental Protection Agency Region III, "30 Years of Environmental Progress," *Remember the Past, Protect the Future*, EPA-903-R-00-004, p 7.

to be flushed daily in the Mid-Atlantic states (figure 24–4). Agricultural run-off is a major concern, as should be the activities of the public in discharges from private residences.

In the final chapter of the 30-year report, discussing future challenges, Region III indicates; "EPA has progressed from reducing human health threats to improving human and ecological health. The agency's direction is long-term habitability and global sustainability. Many of the obvious, visible sources of pollution are largely under control, but pollution from past years still must be cleaned up, and many subtler pollution problems are equally pernicious. We also are moving to control pollution from smaller businesses and runoff, which cumulatively causes environmental and health problems."

The experience and projections for the future of this region, which encompasses Delaware, Maryland, Pennsylvania, Virginia, West Virginia, and the District of Columbia, can be seen as typical of most regions of the country. As pressures build to reduce the impact of pollution, the focus of the environmental enforcement programs has been to expand to include ever-smaller size sources of emissions.

To the printing industry, this last statement has to be a call for action. Printers are normally small businesses, frequently with fewer than 10 people in an installation. They are also congregated in urban and suburban areas. The case for addressing more small firms can be made from a perspective of cumulative effects rather than those from a single facility. An escalation of enforcement will reach down to facilities, which, in many states, currently are below the threshold requiring permits and compliance with technical standards.

Population in the mid-Atlantic states has increased significantly and is projected to be 31 million by 2025. 30 billion gallons of human waste is flushed every day, and will grow with the population. The water we flush today may be the water we drink tomorrow. That's why sewage treatment and drinking water standards are so important.

Figure 24–4. Regionally 30 billion gallons of sewage will be flushed daily by 2025.

Source: United States Environmental Protection Agency Region III, "30 Years of Environmental Progress," *Remember the Past, Protect the Future*, EPA-903-R-00-004, p 10.

In a recent ruling by the U.S. Supreme Court concerning the lowering of air emission standards, the Court ruled that the standards needed more substantiation prior to implementation; however, the Court verified the right of the Agency to set standards without regard for cost effectiveness. This becomes a major challenge to small businesses, which cannot afford to purchase and operate add-on controls or modify their operations to accept less-polluting inks and coatings.

Growth of population centers and urban sprawl poses problems as nature surrenders to the need for roads, homes and shopping centers. Vehicular travel dominates life in America, as do the weekly or more frequent visits to the malls. One will frequently find printing establishments in the strip malls or larger shopping malls. Quick printers and small offset shops are part of the way of life in the suburbs. The printers bring with them the chemistry of their trade, and with the chemistry come odors to trigger reaction from the public. Here again, the printer has to be aware of the regulations that require him to be permitted and in compliance, and take steps to satisfy both the paper and technical requirements.

Carol Browner, former administrator of the EPA, in the *Agenda for 2000*, states: "We must inform and involve those who must live with the decisions we make—the communities, the industries, the people of this country." She continues by saying: "EPA believes that if the people affected by the rules take part in developing them, we will produce rules that are clearer, less burdensome, and more effective." Just how this message will carry over to other administrations is yet to be seen. For their part, printers must support the efforts of the associations that represent them in Washington, D.C. and the various state capitals, in pressing this approach forward. There is nothing more critical to the future than having credibility in the demands made on the industry by the government.

Reinvention of the Agency and its Tools

Early in the Clinton administration, under the tutelage of Vice President Al Gore, a program was started to reinvent the ways things were being done and improve on performance and the quality of the efforts made by all parties to environmental protection. A number of initiatives addressed different approaches to the objective of making government slimmer and more effective, at the same time that a more effective plan of action was taken to improve the quality of the environment.

A basic premise of the reinvention program was to streamline government by removing redundancy from the regulations and bringing more accessibility into the way regulations were written and enforced. The Federal Advisory Committee Act provided the ground rules for bringing outsiders into the process, to promote the concept of consensus, and, thereby, to critically evaluate and rewrite or recommend changes to the current methods and policies.

One of the organizational arrangements that were brought to the table was the concept of sectors. Regulations too often covered a wide range of activities, causing much conflict and frustration in efforts by industry to determine exactly what applied to a particular industry. Square pegs were forced into round holes, triangles into diamonds. The sector approach enables the participants to talk about related problems, challenges and regulations.

Cleaner, Cheaper, Smarter

The slogan for the Common Sense Initiative was simply put: "How can we do things cleaner, cheaper and smarter?" One of the seven sectors established was for printing and related technologies. The diversity of the printing industry, when all technologies were considered, was itself an eye opener for the government personnel. Within the regulations written for the sector, round pegs were being forced into square holes. Recognition of the variety of technical conditions within the printing and finishing/converting industry came as representatives from the various printing technologies outlined the uniqueness of the particular processes and the markets each served. However, sufficient significant similarities existed to enable the sector members to work together as a group for the benefit of all.

The group had representatives from the various interested parties—government (federal, state and local), industry, labor, environmental advocates and environmental justice. The concept was to develop consensus on the various issues that would come before the group, each stakeholder relating his/her needs to those of the others. The consensus agreement would bridge the agendas and allow each party to meet, to some extent, their individual objectives. Facilitators engaged the group using dispute resolution techniques to draw out the ideas, opinions, misgivings, etc. from the participants.

Initial discussions were introductory, letting the various representatives acquaint the other members with the organization and goals, as well as the technology differences and needs, for the industry participants. Frequent reviews of the charts led to distillation of some ideas and consolidation of others. In the end, an agenda was drafted to deal with the two major areas that encompassed all, or at least most, of the miscellaneous items suggested.

The two projects endorsed by the group were the New York City Education Project and a multi-media flexible permitting process.

The New York City Education Project provided valuable lessons in working with local community groups on environmental outreach. The project resulted in the publication of a guide to resources in the city for technical assistance. It included visitations to a group of small, storefront printers for the purpose of auditing the facilities and provided a brief education on pollutants, compliance and the pertinent local, state and city regulations. The project provided considerable insight to EPA for development of future efforts to work with the community groups in providing outreach to technical assistance for the small printers in their neighborhoods. At the same time, it provided the community groups with a better understanding of environmental issues and the role that pollution prevention can play in reducing exposure to the community.

The permitting project was renamed in its final stages to Print-STEP (the Printers Simplified Total Environmental Partnership).

PrintSTEP is a multi-media process for evaluating the exposure at the facility in all areas of regulation, providing adequate public participation by community leaders. The committee produced three manuals to implement the project. One was developed for the state agencies that enforce the regulations. A second was developed to acquaint community leaders with the process. The third volume was the workbook for the printer. Each volume provides basic information, tailored to fulfill the needs of the particular stakeholder.

The PrintSTEP project will provide EPA and the other stakeholders with an opportunity to test the effectiveness of a multi-media permit, with enhanced public participation, greater flexibility for facility modifications, and increased environmental protection. All this will be accomplished within a streamlined governmental process. A number of states applied to conduct pilot trials, and work is now in progress. With data that is being collected from the pilot projects, EPA will be better able to make decisions relative to the permitting process and the application of the concept to other sectors.

Project XL stands for "eXellence and Leadership," a program that allows states and local governments, businesses and federal facilities to develop innovative strategies to test better or more cost-effective ways of achieving environmental and public health protection. In exchange, the EPA offers flexibility in the enforcement of regulations, programs, policies, and procedures and to conduct the experiment. The project is aimed at new approaches to old problems.

The eight criteria* outlined for Project XL selection are:

1. "produce superior environmental results beyond those that would have been achieved under current and reasonably anticipated future regulations or policies;

2. "produce benefits such as cost savings, paperwork reduction, regulatory flexibility or other types of flexibility that serve as an incentive to both project sponsors and regulators;

3. "supported by stakeholders;

4. "achieve innovation/pollution prevention;

5. "produce lessons or data that are transferable to other facilities;

6. "demonstrate feasibility;

7. "establish accountability through agreed upon methods of monitoring, reporting, and evaluations;" and

Project XL

---

*Web Site, USEPA, http://www.epa.gov/ProjectXL/file2.htm, July 17, 2001.

8. "avoid shifting the risk burden, i.e., do not create worker safety or environmental justice problems as a result of the experiment."

Since most XL projects require state as well as federal regulatory flexibility, EPA works with the state government to assess merits of the proposals. The assessment is then referred to EPA's senior management for review and selection. After the experiment begins, the regulators will periodically monitor and evaluate the project. Observations are recorded and integrated into the system to assist EPA administrators to integrate lessons learned into agency policy, guidance and regulations.

Design for the Environment (DfE)

This program was developed as a joint government-industry effort to gather information and test premises in the field to recognize pollution prevention opportunities and alternatives. The Design for the Environment staff worked with industry associations to identify areas of concern in each of the major printing processes, and then proceeded to testing and analysis of information with technical committees composed of personnel from the EPA and representatives of the applicable industry associations, printers and suppliers. The result of these efforts was the publication of a library of documents and working tools to educate printers and to provide information that will guide them in making decisions for compliance relative to changes in technology and working practices (figure 24–5).

The projects that have been completed for the printing industries include:

1. Lithography: a study of blanket washes for safer formulations,

2. Screen printing: screen reclamation chemistry and methodology,

3. Flexography: ink options: solvent, water or UV curable,

4. Gravure: the effect of ink temperature on solvent losses and print quality,

5. Environmental Management Systems.

In addition to presentations at conferences and forums held annually by the various printing associations and EPA regions, DfE has authorized parallel studies and projects, and published reports on the findings of the studies. Educational materials have been developed for distribution to printers, including videos to demonstrate pollution prevention in the specific printing process and software for economic analysis of a pollution prevention project. The outreach products are all available from EPA; some products, such as the videos, are available through the industry associations. A full listing of all literature and tools is available through the Internet at the EPA web site, www.epa.gov/dfe or the PNEAC web site, www.pneac.org.

The information collected and disseminated by the DfE program is intended to help printers make intelligent choices in the approaches they may take to achieve or go beyond compliance requirements. At the same time, the trials have helped the Agency to better understand real world conditions that challenge the printer in his quest to comply. This, in turn, can lead to standards for compliance that are more realistic and attainable.

The traditional practice for developing rules and regulations has not always been a transparent process. In many cases, neither industry nor the public has had an opportunity to voice their concerns and state their "facts" at the outset of the deliberations.

Consensus for Regulatory Reform

By the time government opens its doors to receive comment, the damage may have been done in the eyes of the parties left out of the initial process. In an effort to broaden the base for changes in regulations and the manner in which they are enforced, the concept of dispute resolution and consensus was invoked.

Dispute resolution, resulting in consensus decision-making, brings together all the parties (stakeholders) to air common concerns in question and to arrive at a solution that will benefit and satisfy everyone. This concept requires that each stakeholder recognize the needs of the other members of the group in addition to those in their own agenda. Compromise is achieved by trade-offs that recognize the need for all stakeholders to bring some accomplishments back to their constituents. Consideration of the multi-media ramifications of any environmental policy or rulemaking decision allows consensus to bridge the harmful gaps and make compromises that will benefit all.

All members of the community feel the pressures of environmental decisions in rulemaking and enforcement. Safety and health are concerns of the local community. Advocacy groups address ecological impact. Industry has an equal stake in the health of the community, because the same factors effect workers, and in the ecology because the owners and employees

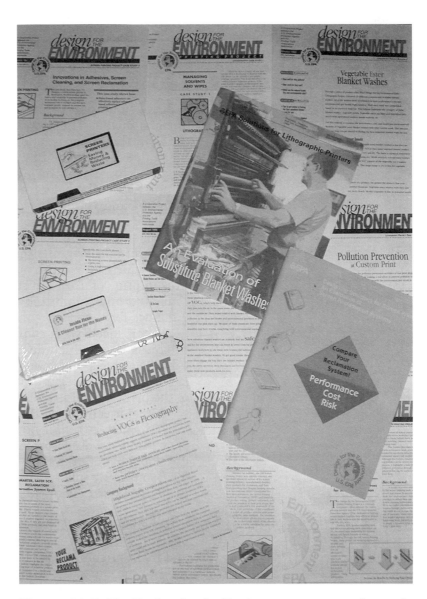

Figure 24–5. The Design for the Environment program has published many booklet and pamphlets to promote pollution prevention in the printing industry.

Consensus comes from group discussion and agreement.

of the businesses live in the area. Economics and jobs can have a relatively high priority in the local community. Transportation needs and the impact of transportation on the environment and public health is a key issue. Bringing people together to discuss these issues before any law or rule is contemplated can only result in a more effective means of addressing the issues brought on by the use of chemicals in industry and in the home.

Consensus provides a vehicle for recognizing the local interests and concerns, rather than the broader and more global aspects of pollution prevention. Facilitators rather than regulators conduct these sessions. The approach has to be broad based and fair. The ability to compromise is a key to success. Everyone in the process must walk away with a positive achievement from participation. Done right, consensus can be a win/win situation for everyone.

How Effective is Reinvention?

There are two concerns with the effectiveness of reinvention of the system. One deals with the premises that have been used for determining the many rules and regulations in the various media. The second is the ability of any positive changes made in the upper echelons to reach and modify the work that is being done in the field by federal and state employees.

Working with the agencies on any major project, one is impressed by the talent and capabilities of the people working at the EPA and the state agencies. They are intelligent, dedicated people who are able to listen and absorb information as well as take into consideration emotional concerns of people involved. But there are limits that are imposed by a rigidity that comes from the laws under which they must operate and a mindset that precludes the presumption of errors in rules and evaluations that have been promulgated and committed to writing as reports which are used as guidance for their decisions.

When faced with contradictory information that refutes the premises upon which decisions have been made, there is a reluctance to go back and change the basic structure. Some of these decisions, and the criteria that have evolved, are critical to the ability of the printing industry to continue to grow in the United States.

A major concern is the negative approach taken in all venues. With the history that is now known and the science of the chemistry of printing, it would appear that the government could just as easily develop a list of preferred chemicals, i.e., solvents that can be used for formulating ink and cleaning solvent blends. Is it not preferable to identify those chemicals that have the least effects on health and ecology and encourage the use of these safer substances? Wouldn't it be beneficial to allow the use of safer chemicals when the products for which they are used play a role in the well-being of citizens and their surroundings?

The matter of getting the message down to the lower levels is one that professionals in the field see all the time. Field personnel are often not adequately informed or trained, and therefore frequently make judgments that are not consistent with the facts. This applies to the processes they are asked to monitor as well as the regulations themselves. When a government engineer or inspector enters a plant, he/she should have at least enough training to know the difference between a light box and a printing press, a bucket of water and a can of solvent. Every rule has guidance documents and explanations, but the field inspector often does not know the pertinent documents and policies. Some criteria are misapplied when an inspector employs rules established for one set of conditions in circumstances that have no reason to be so considered.

If reinvention or redirection of the efforts of the EPA and the state environmental agencies is to succeed, more effort must be made in the development of appropriate guidelines and training of personnel to enforce the regulations properly and with a sense of concern for the interests of the facility. Enforcement staff should be viewed with trust based on the knowledge of the law and the process, and the ability to view the workings of a facility in proper perspective. A capable, sensitive representative of the government can bridge gaps by projecting a positive image that looks to achieving results that will be beneficial to the business and to a cleaner environment. This requires an investment in training, supervision and, foremost, management of the Agency.

Tantamount to the success of future policies and rules will be the recognition of the need to validate the scientific claims of conflicting camps and plot a course which recognizes the factual data while addressing the emotional concerns of the public.

Technical Challenges to the Current System

Are We Tackling the Real Issues?

A major concern for industry is whether the EPA and other, international, agencies are putting the issues under scrutiny to discern the real from the unreal, the truth from the dramatic, the achievable from pure fantasy. If each solvent or chemical is analyzed and tested on its own, the knowledge that we gain is biased. We live in a complex environment, in which chemicals play roles both on their own and in either reaction or co-existence with other chemicals.

True progress in pollution prevention can come only when we are able to categorize the chemicals as acceptable, marginal and unacceptable. Given a set of solvents, pigments, resins and additives that come from a list of acceptable chemicals, inkmakers and solvent suppliers can generally provide a full range of products that can meet the quality requirements of the printer and his customer. There would be no need for complex add-on control systems, except for those products for which marginal chemicals have to be used. A list of totally unacceptable chemicals can be published and use discouraged by negative incentives, such as were used in eliminating the use of the ozone-depleting solvents. When a chemical is identified as extremely hazardous and printers are advised accordingly, it can be eliminated completely, as was the case with cellosolve when it was discovered to be a carcinogen. Today, we only hear of lists chemicals that are hazardous, but little attempt is made by enforcement agencies to differentiate between those VOCs that infringe significantly on our health and those that do not.

Ozone Reactivity Scales

One of the leading researchers in the testing of photochemical ozone formation of volatile organic compounds is William P.L. Carter of the University of California. Dr. Carter wrote of his experiments in *Air & Waste* magazine in July 1994, explaining that; "Many different types of VOCs are emitted into the atmosphere, each reacting at different rates and with different reaction mechanisms. Because of this, VOCs can differ significantly in their effects on ozone formation. These differences of ozone formation are referred to as the ozone 'reactivities of the VOCs.'"

The question raised by Dr. Carter's work is, how does the EPA delist some solvents while others with relatively the same reactivities are not delisted?

His work also addresses the means of determining a list of safer solvents, while providing the basis for banning significantly hazardous chemicals. This can be done in a gradual process with tax disincentives. The tax on such ozone destroying chemicals as 1,1,1, trichloroethane was instrumental in developing acceptable, less harmful solvents as alternatives.

A good example is the solvent acetone. Acetone was delisted as an ozone precursor and unacceptable VOC. Many formulations for cleaning solvents and coatings substituted acetone for other solvents to reach acceptable VOC limits. But acetone continues to be a hazardous waste, a flammable safety problem and indoor air pollutant. Carter rates acetone with a Maximum Incremental Reactivity (MIR) of 0.56, toluene has an MIR of 2.7, normal propanol has an MIR of 2.3, and isopropanol has an MIR of 0.54. It would appear that isopropanol should be given the same consideration as acetone, but that is not the case. Excerpts of typical printing solvents from Dr. Carter's tables are illustrated in Table 24–1.

Dr. Carter's data supports an analogy I make when trying to motivate my peers in discussions about pollution prevention. I have a penchant for challenging the hygienists and environmental engineers when sitting around the table for a project, with the following dilemma: When I read the newspapers I frequently read articles in which it is stated that the quality of the air in major cities has improved dramatically. Within the same newspaper, I also read that asthma is on the rise in the very same cities. I pose the question: "Could it be that in cleaning the air we are taking out some components, such as solvents, which would have dissolved the particles that are causing the rise in asthma?" You can read the consternation on their faces. "Are you trying to say that pollution should be acceptable?" My response is clear: "Perhaps you are not looking at the total picture. Each item on its own may represent a threat, but under the wider scheme of nature, some things balance others. In legislating cleaner air, you may have given asthma an opportunity to flourish."

TABLE 24–1. RELATIVE REACTIVITY OF SOLVENTS COMMON TO PRINTING
Based on the research of Dr. William P.L. Carter of the University of California

COMPOUND	MIR Inc.Rct.	OZONE YIELD MIR	MOIR	EBIR		RELATIVE REACTIVITY INTEGRATED ZONE (b) MIR	MOIR	EBIR
Alkanes:	(a)							
n-Hexane	0.980	0.310	0.550	0.650		0.280	0.350	0.380
n-Heptane	0.810	0.260	0.450	0.490		0.220	0.260	0.250
Aromatics:								
Toluene	2.700	0.880	0.530	-0.023		0.770	0.710	0.540
Ethylbenzene	2.700	0.860	0.520	0.007		0.770	0.720	0.540
o-Xylene	6.500	2.100	1.600	1.260		2.000	2.000	1.800
Alcohols/ethers								
Methanol	0.560	0.180	0.230	0.280		0.149	0.180	0.190
Ethanol	1.340	0.430	0.610	0.720		0.330	0.360	0.370
n-Propyl Alcohol	2.300	0.720	0.950	1.070		0.600	0.630	0.610
Isopropyl Alcohol	0.540	0.170	0.270	0.350		0.170	0.220	0.270
n-Butyl Alcohol	2.700	0.860	1.090	1.250		0.740	0.770	0.760
Ketones								
Acetone	0.560	0.180	0.170	0.180		0.160	0.142	0.134

Notes:
(a) Incremental activities in units of grams ozone formed per gram VOC emitted for the ozone reactivity scale for the MIR scale.
(b) Incremental activities of the VOCs (in units of ozone per gram VOC divided by incremental reactivities of the base ROG (Reactive Organic Gases) mixture.

Source: William P.L.Carter, "Development of Ozone Reactivity Scales for Volatile Organic Compounds," *Air & Waste*, Volume 44, July 1994, pp 881–899.

You can be sure that this is not an acceptable posture for die-hard environmentalists, but it is a point that warrants experimentation. Working with one solvent at a time can be misleading. The tests may be more complex, but that is not the issue. The issue is determining the factual basis for making better decisions on how to arrive at a cleaner environment and improved public health. One should not be sacrificed at the expense of the other.

Dr. Carter's work may provide a basis for promoting research to better explore the reactions of various solvents to identify those which can lead to a cleaner environment and improved public health. What better way for source reduction than to provide the ink chemists with tools with which they can work, rather than lists of chemicals that have problems.

Multimedia and Performance-based Standards

Another approach to reducing air pollution and promoting source reduction across the broad spectrum of regulations is to abandon the current VOC content or add-on control destruction efficiency as the sole measures of compliance. Substitute a measure that every printer can understand, one of performance-based improvements. Any printer can tell you that a reduction in waste

Figure 24–6. Industry shows and conventions bring the latest technology to the printer. PRINT and CMM are shows where the latest in equipment, materials and methodology to improve quality, productivity and the environment are demonstrated.

of 1 or 2 percent is added profits. Why not use the same approach with environmental compliance? Give a printer a target for improvement determined by using a representative year as the baseline. Then set targets for reduction of air emissions, hazardous waste shipments, water discharges, etc. as percentages of total usage.

Let's say that air emissions are now 100 tons. A target is set for a 10-percent reduction over the next three years. The printer can approach this target in any way that he sees fit. Solvent usage can be studied and reduced by mechanical means. Using solvents that have higher boiling points and will not evaporate as quickly can reduce emissions. Or, the printer may elect to adopt a new set of inks and ink transfer system. How he does this is his concern. If he meets the targeted reductions, he is in compliance. If he does not, he must present a defense of the performance and of his plans to accelerate reductions in the next period. In the process of reducing air emissions, the printer will also seek solutions that will have positive ramifications in the generation and disposition of hazardous wastes and discharges of process wastewater.

Performance standards can accelerate the progress a printer can make by taking advantage or spurring technology developments. It can build on the natural instinct of the entrepreneur in each printer to do better and build the business. It is a positive motivation that can surpass the accomplishments forced by negative pressures.

Technology Advances the Cause

Looking beyond the law and the barriers to compliance, the printer has vast resources at his service to meet the need for a cleaner environment. Printing today is a vastly different business than it was even five years earlier. New, radical developments are the norm rather than the exception.

Technological advancements in all phases of the printing process are leading to the use of less chemistry, the elimination of all chemistry or the substitution of safer chemicals. Improved mechanics and materials for the transfer of inks can reduce ink usage and waste. Chambered doctor blade systems are finding their way into the gravure and lithographic pressrooms. Automatic video/computer monitoring systems are narrowing the range in which out-of-specification product is printed and reducing the wastes that are generated by poor quality. New raw materials have enhanced the ability of inkmakers to develop radiation curable inks and coatings, and water-base or water-miscible formulations for liquid and paste ink systems. Aqueous pressroom solutions are becoming more available and being used successfully. A leading manufacturer of pressroom chemistry has plans to follow the lead of detergent companies and sell fountain solution concentrates and press washes in their powder state, to be mixed with water in the pressroom. Why pay for water and the added shipping costs when an effective product can be made from the powder?

Trade shows open the door to the latest in technology. The CMM shows for packaging printers and converters, Graph Expo and the periodic PRINT shows are comprehensive displays and conferences of the latest developments in the technology of printing. Association shows, large or small, add to this wealth of resources for the printer. Take advantage and spend a few days wandering the aisles, picking brains and making connections (figures 24–6 and 24–7).

The relationship a printer has with his suppliers becomes extremely critical in dealing with new developments. Every change is accompanied by modifications in other elements of the process, without which change is doomed to failure. A key factor will be the training and retraining that accompanies the use of new materials or process. Suppliers can be excellent sources of assistance as the printer plans and executes his plans. There is nothing worse than to make changes and see them negated by neglect or outright lack of cooperation.

Figure 24–7. Small and large printers find new technology at industry shows such as PRINT and CMM.

At the end of the day, it is difficult to relegate everyone to a particular side of the issues with the environment. We are all environmentalists. If we are not, then we have no regard for our own health or that of our families. The printing industry should be more sensitive than most to this claim. Strangers do not run the average firm; it provides jobs for family and friends. The person we may injure may be ourselves or our loved ones.

Every printer lives and works in a community. Many rely on community groups to earn a living. Many provide jobs for the young and the old in the community. They belong to Chambers of Commerce, Kiwanis, Elks, Masons and Knights of Pythias. They are at Little League, Pop Warner football and junior soccer games. The environment is not the sole possession of a group that advocates environmental issues nor is it a business dominated by the government. Every printer has the opportunity and responsibility to do things safer and healthier. This is the road to be taken. Comply with the law, practice pollution prevention, be a good neighbor.

As a concluding statement for this book, let us take guidance from the American Forest & Paper Association's "Code to Live By: Environmental, Health and Safety Principles."*

Facing Up to the System

Community encompasses us all.

---

*American Forest & Paper Association, Environmental, Health & Safety Principles, Washington D.C., January 1996.

A Code to Live By: Environmental, Health, and Safety Principles

America's major producers of paper and wood products are commited to environmental quality and the protection of natural resources. To carry forward this commitment, AF&PA members publicly pledge to adhere to a comprehensive code of Environmental, Health, and Safety Principles. This pledge means members will:

1 Make environmental, health, and safety considerations priorities in operating existing facilities, as well as in planning new operations.

2 Recognize, in developing and designing products to meet customer needs, the environmental, health, and safety effects of product manufacture, distribution, use, and disposal.

3 Monitor their environmental, health, and safety performance and report regularly on these matters to their Boards of Directors, as well as confirm their adherence to these principles annually to AF&PA.

4 Train employees in their environmental, health and safety responsibilities and promote awareness and accountability on these matters.

5 Improve environmental, health, and safety performance through support of research and development that advance the frontiers of knowledge.

6 Communicate with employees, customers, suppliers, the community, public officials, and shareholders to build greater understanding on environmental, health, and safety matters.

7 Participate constructively in the development of public policies on environmental, health, and safety matters.

8 Continue to pursue energy conservation, increased energy efficiency, greater utilization of alternatives to fossil fuels, and opportunities for cogeneration of electricity.

In the end we all want to be good neighbors.

APPENDICES

APPENDIX I

SOURCE:

United States Environmental
Protection Agency

Environmental Protection Agency Regional Offices

Regions

Each EPA Regional Office is responsible within selected states for the execution of the Agency's programs, considering regional needs and the implementation of federal environmental laws.

Select a region by clicking within the area of the map covered by the region, or use the links located below the map to go directly to a region.

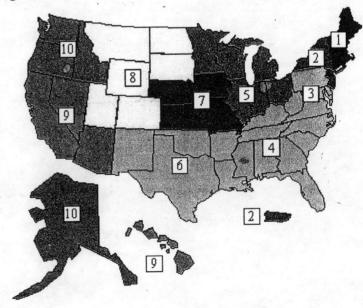

Region 1 - responsible within the states of Connecticut, Maine, Massachusetts, New Hampshire, Rhode Island, and Vermont.

Region 2 - responsible within the states of New Jersey, New York, Puerto Rico and the U.S. Virgin Islands.

Region 3 - responsible within the states of Delaware, Maryland, Pennsylvania, Virginia, West Virginia, and the District of Columbia.

Region 4 - responsible within the states of Alabama, Florida, Georgia, Kentucky, Mississippi, North Carolina, South Carolina, and Tennessee .

Region 5 - responsible within the states of Illinois, Indiana, Michigan, Minnesota, Ohio, and Wisconsin .

Region 6 - responsible within the states of Arkansas, Louisiana, New Mexico, Oklahoma, and Texas.

Region 7 - responsible within the states of Iowa, Kansas, Missouri, and Nebraska.

Region 8 - responsible within the states of Colorado, Montana, North Dakota, South Dakota, Utah, and Wyoming.

Region 9 - responsible within the states of Arizona, California, Hawaii, Nevada, and the territories of Guam and American Samoa.

Region 10 - responsible within the states of Alaska, Idaho, Oregon, and Washington.

Postal Addresses to Contact the US EPA

To contact individuals and offices within the U.S. Environmental Protection Agency, you can address all correspondence to them using the following addresses and their Mail Code. To find an individual's mail code, search for that person using the EPA People Locator.

EPA Headquarters

Environmental Protection Agency
Ariel Rios Building
1200 Pennsylvania Avenue, N.W.
Washington, DC 20460
(202) 260-2090
www.epa.gov

Region 1 (CT, MA, ME, NH, RI, VT)
Environmental Protection Agency
1 Congress St. Suite 1100
Boston, MA 02114-2023
http://www.epa.gov/region01/
Phone: (617) 918-1111
Fax: (617) 565-3660
Toll free within Region 1:
(888) 372-7341

Region 2 (NJ, NY, PR, VI)
Environmental Protection Agency
290 Broadway
New York, NY 10007-1866
http://www.epa.gov/region02/
Phone: (212) 637-3000
Fax: (212) 637-3526

Region 3 (DC, DE, MD, PA, VA, WV)
Environmental Protection Agency
1650 Arch Street
Philadelphia, PA 19103-2029
http://www.epa.gov/region03/
Phone: (215) 814-5000
Fax: (215) 814-5103
Toll free: (800) 438-2474
Email: r3public@epa.gov

Region 4 (AL, FL, GA, KY, MS, NC, SC, TN)
Environmental Protection Agency
Atlanta Federal Center
61 Forsyth Street, SW
Atlanta, GA 30303-3104
http://www.epa.gov/region04/
Phone: (404) 562-9900
Fax: (404) 562-8174
Toll free: (800) 241-1754

Region 5 (IL, IN, MI, MN, OH, WI)
Environmental Protection Agency
77 West Jackson Boulevard
Chicago, IL 60604-3507
http://www.epa.gov/region5/
Phone: (312) 353-2000
Fax: (312) 353-4135
Toll free within Region 5:
(800) 621-8431

Region 6 (AR, LA, NM, OK, TX)
Environmental Protection Agency
Fountain Place 12th Floor,
Suite 1200
1445 Ross Avenue
Dallas, TX 75202-2733
http://www.epa.gov/region06/
Phone: (214) 665-2200
Fax: (214) 665-7113
Toll free within Region 6:
(800) 887-6063

Region 7 (IA, KS, MO, NE)
Environmental Protection Agency
901 North 5th Street
Kansas City, KS 66101
http://www.epa.gov/region07/
Phone: (913) 551-7003
Toll free: (800) 223-0425

Region 8 (CO, MT, ND, SD, UT, WY)
Environmental Protection Agency
999 18th Street Suite 500
Denver, CO 80202-2466
http://www.epa.gov/region08/
Phone: (303) 312-6312
Fax: (303) 312-6339
Toll free: (800) 227-8917
Email: r8eisc@epa.gov

Region 9 (AZ, CA, HI, NV)
Environmental Protection Agency
75 Hawthorne Street
San Francisco, CA 94105
http://www.epa.gov/region09/
Phone: (415) 744-1305
Fax: (415) 744-2499
Email: r9.info@epa.gov

Region 10 (AK, ID, OR, WA)
Environmental Protection Agency
1200 Sixth Avenue
Seattle, WA 98101
http://www.epa.gov/region10/
Phone: (206) 553-1200
Fax: (206) 553-0149
Toll free: (800) 424-4372

Other Locations
U.S. EPA
26 Martin Luther King Drive
Cincinnati, Ohio 45268

U.S. EPA
Research Triangle Park, North
Carolina 27711
http://www.epa.gov/rtp/

U.S. EPA National Health and
Environmental Effects Research
Laboratory (NHEERL)
Mid-Continent Ecology Division
6201 Congden Boulevard
Duluth, MN 55804
http://www.epa.gov/med/
Fax: (218) 720-5703

U.S. EPA National Health and
Environmental Effects Research
Laboratory (NHEERL)
Western Ecology Division
200 SW 35th Street
Corvallis, OR 97333
http://www.epa.gov/wed/
Voice: 541-754-4600
Fax: 541-754-4799

National Risk Management
Research Laboratory
26 Martin Luther King Drive
Cincinnati, Ohio 45268
http://www.epa.gov/ordntrnt/ORD/N
RMRL/
Fax: 513-569-7680

Satellite Locations and Laboratories

U.S. EPA National Air and Radiation
Environmental Laboratory (NAREL)
540 South Morris Avenue
Montgomery, AL 36115-2601
http://www.epa.gov/narel/
Phone: (334) 270-3400
Fax: (334) 270-3454

U.S. EPA National Enforcement
Investigations Center Laboratory
Box 25277, Bldg. 53
Denver Federal Center
Denver, CO 80225
http://es.epa.gov/oeca/oceft/neic/
Phone: (303) 236-5132

U.S. EPA National Exposure
Research Laboratory (NERL)
Mail Code: MD-75
Research Triangle Park, NC 27711
http://www.epa.gov/nerl/
Phone: (919) 541-2106
Fax: (919) 541-0445

U.S. EPA National Exposure
Research Laboratory (NERL)
Ecosystems Research Division
960 College Station Road
Athens, GA 30605-2700
http://www.epa.gov/AthensR/
Phone: (706) 355-8005

U.S. EPA National Exposure
Research Laboratory (NERL)
Environmental Sciences Division
P.O. Box 93478
Las Vegas, Nevada 89193-3478
http://www.epa.gov/crdlvweb/
Phone: (702) 798-2100
Fax: (702) 798-2637

U.S. EPA National Health and
Environmental Effects Research
Laboratory (NHEERL)
Mail Code: MD-51
Research Triangle Park, NC 27711
http://www.epa.gov/nheerl/
Phone: (919) 541-2281
Fax: (919) 541-4324

U.S. EPA National Health and
Environmental Effects Research
Laboratory (NHEERL)
Atlantic Ecology Division
27 Tarzwell Drive
Narragansett, RI 02882
http://www.epa.gov/aed/
Phone: (401) 782-3001
Fax: (401) 782-3030

U.S. EPA National Health and
Environmental Effects Research
Laboratory (NHEERL)
Gulf Ecology Division
Sabine Island Drive
Gulf Breeze, FL 32561
http://www.epa.gov/ged/
Phone: (850) 934-9200
Fax: (850) 934-9201

National Risk Management
Research Laboratory (NRMRL)
Subsurface Protection and Remedi-
ation Division
P.O. Box 1198
Ada, OK 74820
http://www.epa.gov/ada/
Phone: (580) 436-8500

National Risk Management
Research Laboratory (NRMRL)
Water Supply and Resources
Division
Urban Watershed Management
Branch
2890 Woodbridge Avenue (MS-104)
Edison, NJ 08837
http://www.epa.gov/ednnrmrl/

U.S. EPA National Vehicle and Fuel
Emissions Laboratory (NVFEL)
2000 Traverwood Drive
Ann Arbor, MI 48105
Phone: (734) 214-4200

U.S. EPA Radiation and Indoor
Environments National Laboratory
P.O. Box 98517
Las Vegas, NV 89193-8517
http://www.epa.gov/radiation/rienl/
Phone: (702) 798-2476

APPENDIX ▌▌

Small Business Ombudsman Contacts for EPA and by States

SOURCE:
United States Environmental
Protection Agency

Karen V. Brown, EPA SBO
Ariel Rios Building
1200 Pennsylvania Ave., NW (1808)
Washington, DC 20460

Phone: 800-368-5888 or 202-260-1211 (in DC Area)
Fax: 202-401-2302

Established in 1982, the Office of the Small Business Ombudsman serves as an effective conduit for small businesses to access EPA and facilitates communications between the small business community and the Agency. The Office reviews and resolves disputes with EPA and works with EPA personnel to increase their understanding of small businesses in the development and enforcement of environmental regulations.

The SBO's primary customer group is the nation's small business community. Significant secondary customer groups include state and EPA regional small business ombudsmen and national trade associations serving small businesses.

In response to the identified needs of the Office's target customer groups, the SBO has undertaken a variety of major outreach efforts including:

437

- Serving as liaison between small businesses and the EPA to promote understanding of Agency policy and small business needs and concerns.
- Staffing a small business hotline that provides regulatory and technical assistance information.
- Maintaining and distributing an extensive collection of informational and technical literature developed by the various EPA program offices.
- Making personal appearances as a speaker or panelist at small business related meetings.
- Interfacing on an ongoing basis with over 45 key national trade associations representing several million small businesses and with state and regional ombudsmen who serve businesses on the local level. Also in contact with over 400 additional national organizations that represent millions of small businesses.
- Providing guidance on the development of national policies and regulations that impact small business.
- Tracking development and implementation of regulations affecting small business in support of the Regulatory Flexibility Act.

The SBO actively seeks feedback on its responsiveness to small business inquiries and ever evolving needs, primarily in the areas of technical assistance and advocacy. The SBO can "package" relevant information for the most effective and efficient delivery through training seminars, fact sheets, or position papers to a targeted audience.

Individual outreach activities are tracked and reported by the SBO on a monthly basis. Key statistics include numbers and types of hotline calls and written inquiries; nature and results of small business advocacy efforts; and personal appearances at conferences, seminars, and training sessions. Random, informal quality checks of customer satisfaction ensure that program performance meets or exceeds customer expectations.

The SBO also began serving as the Agency's Asbestos Ombudsman in 1986. In this role, the Office focuses on asbestos-in-schools requirements and handles questions and complaints.

Information concerning asbestos management may also be obtained through the small business toll-free hotline at (800) 368-5888.

TOLL-FREE HOTLINE SERVICE

The Ombudsman operates a toll-free hotline for the convenience of small businesses, trade associations, and others seeking free, confidential help. A member of the Ombudsman's staff will answer between 8:30 AM and 4:30 PM EST. Message-recording devices for calls during non-business hours and overload periods are provided. All calls are personally handled on a fast turn-around basis. The toll-free hotline number is:

(800) 368-5888 or (202) 260-1211 (in DC area)

Callers request information on a variety of topics including:

- Explanation of regulatory requirements
- Lists of reports and documents
- Names and telephone numbers of liaisons
- Clean Air Act regulations
- Underground storage tank notification
- Small quantity generator requirements
- Effluent standard guidelines
- Used oil
- Asbestos compliance
- Waste minimization/pollution prevention
- Pesticide registration fees

Increases in the number of direct-dial calls and hotline calls (from 4,000 calls per year in the early 1980s to the current level of 1,100–1,500 calls monthly) and the associated distribution of technical and informational literature, growth in requests for personal appearances at conferences and workshops, and an expansion in participation in policymaking activities are evidence of the customer groups' confidence in the integrity and proactive stance of the SBO.

REGULATORY TRACKING AND ANALYSIS

The SBO performs a careful review of all proposed regulatory actions published in the biannual regulatory agenda to make a prima facia determination of small business impact. From the agenda, certain proposed regulations are selected that appear to have the potential for adverse impact on small businesses. In 1995, the SBO reviewed and monitored 22 regulatory actions. In all instances, the SBO endeavored to minimize the requirements (especially reporting and recordkeeping) on small businesses. Equally significant is the level of voluntary compliance with DPA regulations by the small business community as a result of the rapport established between the Ombudsman and trade associations during the developmental phase of the regulations.

How do you spell relief from the EPA?

IFRA, RCRA, CERCLA, NEPA. Do these and the many other environmental rules and regulations have you confused?

Dial 800-368-5888 for relief.

You'll reach Karen Brown, small business ombudsman for the United States Environmental Protection Agency (EPA). It's Brown's job to facilitate communication between the EPA and small business owners such as NFSA dealers.

Brown, in turn, calls on a staff of individual experts, including three engineers and an economist, to answer specific questions. There's a chemical engineer to handle toxic substances and hazardous materials concerns; a civil engineer dealing with asbestos, radon and air pollution; and a mechanical engineer to answer questions regarding waste water and pollution problems.

EPA's staff economist assists with general regulation matters. "We want to ensure the public has access to all the EPA rules and regulations that affect them," says Brown. "We're an information source as well as a facilitator for regional programs for environmental compliance."

Dealers looking for funds to expand or remodel fertilizer and pesticide facilities can also turn to the EPA hotline for information or assistance.

Even when an agricultural facility looks good on paper, many lenders are balking at funding such projects due to liability concerns. This has been the experience of several NFSA members trying to finance updated bulk fertilizer and chemical handling facilities recently.

The Small Business Administration (SBA) 7(a) loan program might provide the necessary financial assistance, suggests Brown. This program provides loans of up to $1 million to businesses with fewer than 500 employees that meet their criteria.

For information on this program, start with the EPA hotline. They'll provide the address and phone numbers of the nearest SBA field office to call for an appointment.

In all, the EPA hotline handles over 1000 calls per month on issues as diverse as hazardous waste disposal, pesticide registrations and toxic inventory release reports. Specifically pertaining to agriculture, inquires to the toll-free number have covered underground storage tank notification, waste minimization and registration fee schedules. Most inquiries seek information to aid in compliance with specific regulations.

The office also serves as an advocate for small businesses facing EPA regulations and works towards voluntary compliance with existing rules. Cursory reviews of all proposed regulatory actions impacting small businesses are performed by this office and, in at least eight to ten instances, the ombudsman has made significant input benefiting small businesses.

So next time you've got an environmental or regulatory question, call the EPA at (800) 368-5888. It's toll-free and confidential.

Just tell them *SOLUTIONS* sent you.

STATE	OMBUDSMAN	SBAP	OTHER SBAP
ALABAMA	Gary Ellis, Ombudsman Office of Education and Outreach AL Department of Environmental Management P.O. Box 301463 Montgomery, AL 36130-1463 334-394-4352 334-394-4383 (F) 800-533-2336 (N) gle@adem.state.al.us	Mike Sherman Air Division AL Department of Environmental Management P.O. Box 301463 Montgomery, AL 36130-1463 334-271-7873 334-279-3044 (F) 800-533-2336 (N) mhs@adem.state.al.us	
ALASKA	Bill Smyth AK DEC 610 University Avenue Fairbanks, AK 99709 907-451-2177 907-451-2188 (F) 800 520-2332 (S) Bill_smyth@envircon.state.ak.us		
ARIZONA			Ira Domsky AZ DEQ - Air Program 3033 N. Central Avenue Phoenix, AZ 85012 602-207-2365 800-234-5677 (S) domsky.ira@ev.state.az.us
ARIZONA - Maricopa County		Richard Polito Maricopa County SBEAP 1001 N. Central, Suite 500 Phoenix, AZ 85004 602-506-5102 602-506-7303 (F) rpolito@mail.maricopa.gov	Maggie Bathory Environmental Compliance Specialist 1001 N. Central, Suite 500 Phoenix, AZ 85004 602-506-5149 602-506-7303 mbathory@mail.maricopa.gov
ARKANSAS		Ron Alexander Department of Environmental Quality P.O. Box 8913 8001 National Drive Little Rock. AR 72219-8913 501-682-0866 501-682-0880 (F) 888-233-0326 (N) alexander@adeq.state.ar.us	Darren Morrissey (501) 682-0824 Gena Hoenle (501) 682-0709 *Note: Same Address, fax and State 800 Number for all.
CALIFORNIA	Kathleen Tschogl Ombudsman Air Resources Board 1001 I St P.O. Box 2815 Sacramento, CA 95814 916-323-6791 916-322-4737 (F) 800-272-4572 (S) ktschogl@arb.ca.gov	Robert White, RG, REA II Manager Business Environmental Resource Center Sacramento County - Dept of Economic Dev. 10425 Norden Avenue Mather, CA 95655-4130 916-364-4106 916-364-4115 (F) rwhite@sacberc.org	

STATE	OMBUDSMAN	SBAP	OTHER SBAP
CALIFORNIA - South Coast		Larry Kolczak, Community Relations Manager South Coast Air Management District Small Business Assistance Office 21865 E. Copley Drive Diamond Bar, CA 91765 909-396-3215 909-396-3638 (F) 800-388-2121 (S) 800-CUT-SMOG (S) Lkolczak@aqmd.gov	Kevin Heiss Small Business Assistance Specialist San Diego County Air Pollution Control District 9150 Chesapeake Drive San Diego, CA 92123 858-650-4549 858-650-4659 (F) heiss@sdconty.ca.gov
COLORADO	Nick Melliadis CDPHE OCS-INF-A1 4300 Cherry Creek Drive, South Denver, CO 80246-1530 303-692-2135 303-691-1979 (F) 800-886-7689 (S) nick.melliadis@state.co.us	Chuck Hix CDPHE APCD/55/B-1 4300 Cherry Creek Drive, South Denver, CO 80246-1530 303-692-3148 303-782-0278 (F) chuck.hix@state.co.us	Joni Canterbury CDPHE 4300 Cherry Creek Dr, So. Denver, CO 80246-1530 303-692-3175 303-782-0278 (F) joni.canterbury@state.co.us
CONNECTICUT	Tom Turick, Small Business Assistance Air Program Department of Environmental Protection 79 Elm Street Hartford, CT 06106-5127 860-424-3003 860-424-4063 (F) 800-760-7036 (S) thomas.turick@po.state.ct.us	(Dual Role as SBO/SBAP)	Tracy Babbidge Small Business Assistance Program Department of Environmental Protection 79 Elm Street Hartford, CT 06106-5127 860-424-3382 860-424-4063 (F) 800-760-7036 (S) tracy.babbidee@po.state.ct.us
DELAWARE	Kim Finch DE DNRC 89 Kings Highway Dover, DE 19901 302-739-6400 302-739-6242 (F) kfinch@dnrec.state.de.us		
DISTRICT OF COLUMBIA	Sandra Handon. SBO DC Dept of Health/EHA Air Quality Division 51 N Street, N.E., 5th Floor Washington, DC 20002 (202) 535-1722 (202) 535-1371(F) sandra.handon@dc.gov	Olivia Achuko Air Quality Division EHA/Department of Health 51 N Street, NE, 5th Floor Washington, DC 20002 (202) 535-2997 (202) 535-1371(F) olivia.achuko@dc.gov	

STATE	OMBUDSMAN	SBAP	OTHER SBAP
FLORIDA	Bruce Thomas Environmental Administrator Florida Department of Environmental Protection Office of Air Programs Communication & Outreach 2600 Blair Stone Road, MS-5500 Tallahassee, FL 32399-2400 850-921-7744 850-922-6979 (F) 800-722-7457 (S) bruce.thomas@dep.state.fl.us	(Dual Role as SBO/SBAP)	Stephen McKeough (850) 921-9584 Kim Tober (850) 488-1348 *Note: Same Address, fax and State 800 Number for all.
GEORGIA	Anita Dorsey-Word GA SBAP DNR/EPD 4244 International Parkway, Suite 120 Atlanta, GA 30354 404-362-4842 1-877-427-6255 (Toll Free) 404-363-7100 (F) adword@mail.dnr.state.ga.us		Lee Tate, PE GA SBAP DNR/EPD 4244 International Parkway, Ste 120 Atlanta, GA 30354 404-362-4854 404-363-7100 (F) lee_tate@mail.dnr.state.ga.us
HAWAII	Patrick Felling Environmental Ombudsman Compliance Assistance Office Hawaii Department of Health PO Box 3378 Honolulu, HI 96801 808-586-4528 808-586-7236 (F) cao@emd.health.state.hi.us	Robert Tam HI Department of Health Clean Air Branch PO Box 3378 Honolulu, HI 96801 808-586-4200 808-586-4359 (F) rtam@emd.health.state.hi.us	Willie Nagamine HI Department of Health Clean Air Branch P.O. Box 3378 Honolulu, HI 96801 808-586-4200 808-586-4359 (F)
IDAHO	Sally Tarowsky Small Business Liaison Idaho DEQ 1410 N Hilton Boise, Idaho 83706 208-373-0472 208-373-0342 (F) starowsk@deq.state.id.us	Dual Role as (SBAP)	
ILLINOIS	Donald Squires Illinois EPA/DAPC Small Business Ombudsman P.O. Box 19276 Springfield, IL 62794-9276 217-785-1625 217-785-8346 (F) 888-372-1996 (S) don.squires@epa.state.il.us	Roslyn Jackson Illinois Department of Commerce and Community Affairs 620 East Adams, 4th Floor Springfield, IL 62701 217-524-0169 217-557-2853(F) 800-252-3998 (S) rjackson@commerce.state.il.us	Jackie Neuber IEPA Bureau of Air 1021 N. Grand Ave East Springfield, IL 62794 (217) 782-9333 (217) 782-1875 (F) jackie.neuber@epa.state.il.us

STATE	OMBUDSMAN	SBAP	OTHER SBAP
INDIANA	Erika Seydel Cheney IDEM - OB&LR 100 N. Senate P.O. Box 6015 Indianapolis, IN 46206-6015 317-232-8598 317-233-6647 (F) 800-451-6027 (press 0, request X 2-8598) eseydel@dem.state.in.us	Marc Hancock IDEM - CTAP Ista Building 150 W. Market Street Suite 703 Indianapolis, IN 46204-2811 317-232-6663 317-233-5627 (F) 800-988-7901 (S) mhancock@dem.state.in.us	Marc Hancock IDEM - CTAP Ista Building 150 W. Market Street Suite 703 Indianapolis, IN 46204-2811 317-232-6663 317-233-5627 (F) 800-988-7901 (S) mhancock@dem.state.in.us
IOWA	Wendy Walker Small Business Air Quality Liaison Iowa Department of Economic Development 200 E. Grand Avenue Des Moines, IA 50309 515-242-4761 or 800-351-4668 (N) 515-242-4776 (F) wendy.walker@ided.state.ia.us	John Konefes IA Waste Reduction Center University of Northern Iowa 1005 Technology Parkway Cedar Falls, IA 50613-0185 319-273-8905 319-268-3733 (F) 800-422-3109 (S) konefes@uni.edu	Dan Nickey IA Waste Reduction Center University of Northern Iowa 1005 Technology Parkway Cedar Falls, IA 50614-0185 319-273-8905 319-268-3733 (F) 800-422-3109 (S) nickey@uni.edu
KANSAS	Theresa Hodges Environmental Ombudsman Kansas Dept of Health and Environment 1000 SW Jackson Street, Suite 430 Topeka, KS 66612 785-296-6603 785-291-3266 (F) 800-357-6087 (N) thodges@kdhe.state.ks.us	Hamdy El Rayes PPI Director Kansas State University 133 Ward Hall Manhattan, KS 66506-2508 785-532-3246 785-532-6952 (F) 800-578-8898 (N) elrayes@ksu.edu	Sherry Davis Industrial P2 Specialist Pollution Prevention Institute 133 Ward Hall Manhattan, KS 66506-2508 800-578-8898 (N) 785-532-4998 785-532-6952 (F) sbd@ksu.edu
KENTUCKY	Rose Marie Wilmoth Air Quality Representative for Small Business Office of Commissioner Department for Environmental Protection 14 Reilly Road Frankfort, KY 40601 502-564-2150, x128 502-564-4245 (F) 800-926-8111 (N) RoseMarie.Wilmoth@mail.state.ky.us	Gregory C. Copley, Director Kentucky Business Environmental Assistance Program Gatton College of Business and Economics University of Kentucky Lexington, KY 40506-0034 859-257-1131 859-323-1907 (F) 800-562-2327 (N) gccopl1@uky.edu	Susan Weaver Division for Air Quality KY DNR&EP 803 Schenkel Lane Frankfort, KY 40601 502-573-3382 502-573-3787 (F) susan.weaver@mail.state.ky.us
LOUISIANA	Jim Friloux, Small Business Ombudsman LA DEQ P.O. Box 82263 Baton Rouge, LA 70884 225-765-0735 225-765-0746 (F) 800-259-2890 (S) jim_f@deq.state.la.us	Dick Lehr Environmental Assistance Division Small Business Assistance Program P.O. Box 82135 Baton Rouge, LA 70884-2135 225-765-2453 225-765-0921 (F) 800-259-2890 (S) richard_l@deq.state.la.us	Beth Altazan-Dixon Environmental Assistance Division Small Business Assistance Program P.O. Box 82135 Baton Rouge, LA 70884-2135 225-765-2450 225-765-0921 (F) 800-259-2890 (S) beth_a@deq.state.la.us

STATE	OMBUDSMAN	SBAP	OTHER SBAP
MAINE	Ron Dyer Department of Environmental Protection Office of Innovation and Assistance State House Station 17 Augusta, ME 04333 207-287-4152 207-287-2814 (F) 800-789-9802 (S) ron.e.dyer@state.me.us	Julie M. Churchill Small Business Assistance Program State House Station 17 Augusta, ME 04333 207-287-7881 207-287-2814 (F) 800-789-9802 (S) julie.m.churchill@state.me.us	Jim Brooks Department of Environmental Protection Bureau of Air Quality State House Station 17 Augusta, ME 04333 207-287-2437 207-287-7641 (F) james.p.brooks@state.me.us
MARYLAND	Don Jackson MD Department of the Environment 1800 Washington Boulevard Suite 735 Baltimore, MD 21230-1720 410-537-3772 410-537-4477 (F) djackson@mde.state.md.us	Andrew Gosden MD Department of the Environment 1800 Washington Boulevard Suite 735 Baltimore, MD 21230-1720 410-537-4158 410-537-4477 (F) agosden@mde.state.md.us	
MASSACHUSETTS			
MICHIGAN	Susan Holben Business and Community Services Michigan Economic Development Corporation 300 North Washington Square Lansing, Michigan 48913 517-335-5883 holbens@michigan.org	Dave Fiedler MDEQ Environmental Assistance Division P.O. Box 30457 Lansing, MI 48909 517-373-0607 517-335-4729 (F) 800-662-9278 (N) fiedlerd@michigan.gov	
MINNESOTA	Charlie Kennedy MPCA/PPRF/SBO 520 Lafayette Road St. Paul, MN 55155-4194 651-297-8615 651-297-8676 (F) 800-985-4247 (S) charlie.kennedy@pca.state.mn.us	Troy Johnson MPCA/MAR/SBAP 520 Lafayette Road St. Paul, MN 55155 651-296-7767 651-297-8701 (F) 800-657-3938 (S) troy.johnson@pca.state.mn.us	
MISSISSIPPI	Jesse Thompson Small Business Ombudsman MS DEQ 2380 Hwy. 80 West P.O. Box 20305 Jackson, MS 39289-1305 601-961-5167 601-961-5541 (F) 800-725-6112 (N) jesse_thompson@deq.state.ms.us	Randy Wolfe Small Business Technical Assistance Dir. MS DEQ 2380 Hwy. 80 West P.O. Box 20305 Jackson, MS 39289-1305 601-961-5166 601-961-5541 (F) 800-725-6112 (N) randy_wolfe@deq.state.ms.us	Jennifer Kimbrough SBAP MS DEQ 2380 Hwy. 80 West P.O. Box 20305 Jackson, MS 39289-1305 601-961-5676 601-961-5541 (F) 800-725-6112 (N) jennifer_kimbrough@deq.state.ms.us

STATE	OMBUDSMAN	SBAP	OTHER SBAP
MISSOURI		Byron Shaw Missouri DNR 1659 E. Elm Street P.O. Box 176 Jefferson City, MO 65102 573-526-6627 573-526-5808 (F) 800-361-4827 (N) nrshawb@mail.dnr.state.mo.us	Nancy Morgan MO. DNR St Louis Urban Outreach 4030 Chouteau 6th Floor St. Louis, MO 63110 314-340-5900 314-340-5904 (F) nrmorgn@mail.dnr.state.mo.us
MONTANA	Bonnie Rouse MT Deq P.O. Box 200901 1520 E. 6th Avenue Helena, MT 59620-0901 406-444-3641 406-444-6836 (F) 800-433-8773 (N) brouse@state.mt.us	(Dual Role as SBO/SBAP)	
NEBRASKA	Tom Franklin Small Business & Public Assistance NE DEQ PO Box 98922 Lincoln, NE 68509-8922 402-471-8697 402-471-2909 (F) 877-253-2603 (N) tom.franklin@ndeq.state.ne.us	(Dual Role as SBO/SBAP)	Melissa Woolf Air Program Compliance Assistance NE DEQ PO Box 98922 Lincoln, NE 68509-8922 402-471-6624 402-471-2909 (F) melissa.woolf@ndeq.state.ne.us
NEVADA	Marcia Manley NV Division of Environmental Protection 333 West Nye Lane Carson City, NV 89706-0851 775-687-4670, x3162 775-687-5856 (F) 800-992-0900, x4670 (S) mmanley@govmail.state.nv.us	Cory Chang Small Business Air Quality Technical Assistance NV Division of Environmental Protection 333 West Nye Lane Carson City, NV 89706-6851 775-687-4670, x3067 775-687-6396 (F) 800-992-0900, x4670 (S) chang.cory.ann@govmail.state.nv.us	Kevin Dick Business Environmental Program NV Small Business Development Ctr, UNR 6100 Neil Rd., Ste 400 Reno, NV 89511 775-689-6677 775-689-6689 (F) (800) 882-3233 (N) dick@unr.edu
NEW HAMPSHIRE	Rudolph Cartier Air Resources Division Department of Environmental Services 6 Hazen Drive Concord, NH 03301-2033 603-271-1379 603-271-1381 (F) 800-837-0656 (S) rcartier@des.state.nh.us	(Dual Role as SBO/SBAP)	

STATE	OMBUDSMAN	SBAP	OTHER SBAP
NEW JERSEY	Joe Constance Small Business Ombudsman NJ Commerce and Economic Growth Commission 20 West State Street P. O. Box 820 Trenton, NJ 08625-0820 609-984-6922 609-777-4097 (F) 800-643-6090 (N) ceacons@commerce.state.nj.us	Ky Asral Small Business Assistance Program Manager NJ DEP P. O. Box 423 Trenton, NJ 08625-0423 609-292-3600 609-777-1330 (F) 877-753-1151 (S) kasral@dep.state.nj.us	Jeanne Mroczko Pollution Prevention-Permit Director SBAP NJ DEP P.O. Box 423 Trenton, NJ 08625-0423 609-292-3600 609-777-1330 (F) jmroczko@dep.state.nj.us
NEW MEXICO	Rita Trujillo NMED AQB 2048 Galisteo Street P.O. Box 26110 Santa Fe, NM 87505 505-955-8091 505-827-1523 (F) 800-224-7009 (N) rita_trujillo@nmenv.state.nm.us	Steve Dubyk NMEDAQB 2044 Galisteo Santa Fe, NM 87505 505-955-8025 505-827-1543 (F) 1-800-224-7009 (N) steve_dubyk@nmenv.state.nm.us	
NEW YORK	Keith Lashway Environmental Service Unit SBEO Director Environmental Ombudsman Unit 30 S Pearl Street Albany, NY 12245 (518) 292-5340 (518)-292-5886 (F) 800-782-8369 (N) klashway@empire.state.ny.us	Marian J. Mudar, PhD. Environmental Program Manager Small Business Assistance Program NYS Environmental Facilities Corporation 625 Broadway Albany, NY 12207 518-402-7462 518-402-8562 (F) 800-780-7227 (S) mudar@nysefc.org	
NORTH CAROLINA	Edythe McKinney NC DENR Customer Service Center Small Business Assistance Program 1640 Mail Service Center Raleigh, NC 27699-1640 919-733-0823 919-715-7468 (F) 877-623-6748 (N) edythe.mckinney@ncmail.net	Tony Pendola NC DENR Customer Service Center Small Business Assistance Program 1640 Mail Service Center Raleigh, NC 27699-1640 919-733-0824 919-715-7468 (F) 877-623-6748 (N) tony.pendola@ncmail.net	Karen Davis NC DENR Customer Service Center Small Business Assistance Program 1640 Mail Service Center Raleigh, NC 27699-1640 919-733-0951 919-715-7468 (F) 877-623-6748 (N) karen.davis@ncmail.net
NORTH DAKOTA	Dana Mount ND Dept of Health 1200 Missouri Avenue P.O. Box 5520 Bismarck, ND 58506 701-328-5150 701-328-5200 (F) 800-755-1625 (S) dmount@state.nd.us	Tom Bachman ND Dept. of Health 1200 Missouri Avenue Division of Air Quality P.O. Box 5520 Bismarck, ND 58506 701-328-5188 701-328-5200 (F) 800-755-1625 (S)	Terry O'Clair ND Dept. of Health 1200 Missouri Avenue Division of Air Quality P.O. Box 5520 Bismarck, ND 58506 701-328-5188 701-328-5200 (F) 800-755-1625 (S)

STATE	OMBUDSMAN	SBAP	OTHER SBAP
		tbachman@state.nd.us	toclair@state.nd.us
OHIO	Mark Shanahan Clean Air Resource Center 50 West Broad Street, Room 1901 Columbus, OH 43215-5985 614-728-3540 614-752-9188 (F) 800-225-5051 (S) mark.shanahan@aqda.state.oh.us	Rick Carleski Ohio EPA/DAPC Lazarus Government Center P.O. Box 1049 Columbus, OH 43216 614-728-1742 614-644-3681 (F) rick.carleski@epa.state.oh.us	
OKLAHOMA	Steve Thompson Deputy Executive Director Department of Environmental Quality P.O. Box 1677 Oklahoma City, OK 73101-1677 405-702-7100 405-702-7101 (F) steve.thompson@deq.state.ok.us	Dave Dillon Customer Services Division Department of Environmental Quality P.O. 1677 Oklahoma City, OK 73101-1677 405-702-1000 405-702-1001 (F) 800-869-1400 (N) dave.dillon@deq.state.ok.us	
OREGON	Rich Grant Small Business Ombudsman Office of Compliance and Enforcement OR Dept. of Environmental Quality 811 SW 6th Avenue Portland, OR 97204 503-229-6839 800-452-4011 (S) grant.richard@deq.state.or.us		
PENNSYLVANIA	Bruce McLanahan Small Business Ombudsman PA Department of Environmental Protection Office of Pollution Prevention and Compliance Assistance RCSOB, 15th Floor P.O. Box 8772 Harrisburg, PA 17105-8772 717-772-5942 717-783-2703 (F) bmclanahan@state.pa.us	Gerald Laubach PA Department of Environmental Protection Bureau of Air Quality P.O. Box 8468 Harrisburg, PA 17105-8468 717-772-2333 717-772-2303 (F) glaubach@state.pa.us	Cecily Beall Tetra Tech EM, Inc 1800 JFK Boulevard, 6th Floor Philadelphia, PA 19103 215-656-8709 215-972-0484 (F) 800-722-4743 (N) cecily.beall@ttemi.com
PUERTO RICO		Mr. Angel O. Berrios-Sivestre Environmental Quality Board Air Quality Program Director PO Box 11488 Santurce, PR 00919 787-767-8025 787-756-5906	Maria Rivera PREQB - SBAP Coordinator HC 91. Box 9197 Vega Alta, PR 00692 787-767-8181 x2721 787-620-9554 (F) pr_sbap@hotmail.com

STATE	OMBUDSMAN	SBAP	OTHER SBAP
RHODE ISLAND		Office of Customer Assistance 401-222-6822, 401-222-3810 (F)	
SOUTH CAROLINA	Phyllis T. Copeland, SBO Small Business Ombudsam SCDHEC – EQC Administration 2600 Bull Street Columbia, SC 29201-1708 803-896-8982 803-896-8999 (F) 800-819-9001 (N) copelapt@columb30.dhec.state.sc.us	James Robinson Technical Assistance Engineer SCDHEC – EQC Administration 2600 Bull St Columbia, SC 29201-1708 803-896-8984 800-819-9001 (N) 803-896-8999 (F) robinsjc@columb30.dhec.state.sc.us	Willie Morgan SCDHEC – EQC Administration 2600 Bull Street Columbia, SC 29201-1708 803-896-8983 803-819-9001 (N) 803-896-8999 (F) morganwj@columb30.dhec.state.sc.us
SOUTH DAKOTA	Joe D. Nadenicek Small Business Ombudsman Department of Environment & Natural Resources Joe Foss Building 523 East Capitol Pierre, SD 57501 605-773-3836 605-773-6035 (F) 800-438-3367 (S) joe.nadenicek@state.sd.us	Rick Boddicker SBAP Department of Environment & Natural Resources Joe Foss Building 523 East Capitol Pierre, SD 57501 605-773-6706 605-773-5286 (F) 800-438-3367 (S) rick.boddicker@state.sd.us	
TENNESSEE	Ernest C. Blankenship TN Department of Environment & Conservation L&C Annex 8th Floor 401 Church Street Nashville, TN 37243-1551 615-741-5262 615-532-8007 (F) (800) 734-3619 (N) eblankenship@mail.state.tn.us	Linda Sadler Small Business Environmental Assistance Prog. L&C Annex, 8th Floor 401 Church Street Nashville, TN 37243-1551 615-532-0779 615-532-8007 (F) 800-734-3619 (N) lsadler@mail.state.tn.us	
TEXAS	Israel Anderson Small Business Advocate TNRCC (Mail Code 112) P.O. Box 13087 Austin, TX 78711-3087 512-239-5319 512-239-3165 (F) 800-447-2827 (N) ianderso@tnrcc.state.tx.us	Tamra Shae-Oatman Small Business & Local Govt Asst Section Mgr TNRCC (Mail Code 106) P.O. Box 13087 Austin, TX 78711-3087 512-239-1066 512-239-1065 (F) 800-447-2827 (N) toatman@tnrcc.state.tx.us	Daphne McMurrer Small Business & Local Govt Assist TNRCC (Mail Code 106) P.O. Box 13087 Austin, TX 78711-3087 512-239-5920 512-239-1055 (F) 800-447-2827 (N) dmcmurre@tnrcc.state.tx.us

STATE	OMBUDSMAN	SBAP	OTHER SBAP
UTAH	Renette Anderson UT Department of Environmental Quality Office of the Small Business Ombudsman 168 North 1950 West Salt Lake City, UT 84114-4810 801-536-4478 801-536-0061 (F) 800-458-0145 (N) randerso@deq.state.ut.us	Ron Reece, Environmental Engineer UT Department of Environmental Quality Division of Air Quality 150 North 1950 West P.O. Box 144820 Salt Lake City, UT 84114-4820 801-536-4091 801-536-4099 (F) (800) 270-4440 (N) rreece@utah.gov	
VERMONT		Judy Mirro VT DEC Environmental Assistance Division Laundry Building 103 South Main Street Waterbury, VT 05671 802-241-3745 802-241-3273 (F) 800-974-9559 (S) judym@dec.anr.state.vt.us	
VIRGINIA	John Daniel, Director Air Programs Coordinator VA Department of Environmental Quality 629 E. Main Street P.O. Box 10009 Richmond, VA 23240 804-698-4311 804-698-4510 (F) 800-592-5482 (S) jmdaniel@deq.state.va.us	Richard Rasmussen Director Office of Small Business Assistance VA Department of Environmental Quality 629 E. Main street P.O. Box 10009 Richmond, VA 23240 804-698-4394 804-698-4510 (F) 800-592-5482 Ext 4394 (S) rgrasmusse@deq.state.va.us	Gordon Kerby Senior Engineer Office of Small Business Assistance VA Department of Environmental Quality 629 E Main Street PO Box 10009 Richmond, VA 23240 804-698-4305 804-698-4264 (F) 800-592-5482 Ext 4305 (S) egkerby@deq.state.va.us
VIRGIN ISLANDS		Marylyn A. Stapleton, SBTAP Program Adm. V.I. Department of Planning & Natural Resources Environmental Protection Division, SBAP Terminal Bldg, 2nd Fl Cyril E. King Airport St. Thomas, VI 00802 (340) 774-3320, X5167 (340) 714-9528-9549 (F) 340-714-9529 (S) envproj@viaccess.net	Jasmine A. Blyden, Small Business Assistant V.I. Department of Planning & Natural Resources Environmental Protection Division, SBAP Terminal Bldg, 2nd Fl Cyril E. King Airport St. Thomas, VI 00802 (340) 774-3320, X5119 (340) 714-9528-9549 (F) envproj@viaccess.net
WASHINGTON	Bernard Brady WA Department of Ecology Air Quality Program P.O. Box 47600 Olympia, WA 98504-7600 360-407-6803 360-407-7534 (F) bbra461@ecy.wa.gov	(Dual Role as SBO/SBAP)	

STATE	OMBUDSMAN	SBAP	OTHER SBAP
WEST VIRGINIA	Terry L. Polen PE, QEP WV Department of Environmental Protection 10 McJunkin Road Nitro, WV 25143 304-759-0510 ext 341 tpolen@dep.state.wv.us	Gene M. Coccari, Technical Specialist Small Business Assistance Program WV DEP, Division of Air Quality 7012 MacCorkle Avenue, SW Charleston, WV 25304 304-926-3731 304-926-3637 (F) 800-982-2474 (S) gcoccari@mail.dep.state.wv.us	
WISCONSIN	Pam Christenson WI Small Business Clean Air Assistance Program P.O. Box 7970 - 6TH FLOOR 201 West Washington Avenue Madison, WI 53707-7970 608-267-9384 608-267-0436 (F) 800-435-7287 (N) pchristenson@commerce.state.wi.us	Renee Lesjiak Bashel WI Department of Commerce PO Box 7970 6th FL 201 West Washington Avenue Madison, WI 53707-7970 608-264-6153 608-267-0436 (F) 800-435-7287 (N) rlesjiakbashel@commerce.state.wi.us	Tom Coogan SBCAAP PO Box 7970 6th FL 201 West Washington Avenue Madison, WI 53707-7970 608-267-9214 608-267-0436 (F) 800-435-7287 tcoogan@commerce.state.wi.us
WYOMING	Dan Clark Department of Environmental Quality Small Business Ombudsman Herschler Bldg. 4-W 122 W. 25th Street Cheyenne, WY 82002 307-777-7388 307-777-3610 (F) dclark@state.wy.us	Charles Raffelson Department of Environmental Quality Technical Assistant Program Coordinator Herschler Bldg. 4-W 122 W. 25th Street Cheyenne, WY 82002 307-777-7347 307-777-3610 (F) craffie@state.wy.us	Tina Jenkins Department of Environmental Quality Air Toxics Sheridan Field Office 1043 Coffeen Ave, Ste D Sheridan, WY 82801 307-672-6457 307-674-6050 (F) cjenki@state.wy.us

APPENDIX III

Directory of OSHA Consultation Offices

SOURCE:
Occupational Safety and
Health Administration

Updated 12 July 2001

ALABAMA
Safe State Program
University of Alabama
432 Martha Parham West
P.O. Box 870388
Tuscaloosa, Alabama 35487
(205) 348-3033
(205) 348-3049 FAX
E-mail:
mailto:%20bweems@ccs.ua.edu
Website:
http://scripts.osha-slc.gov/cgi-bin/
redirect2state?url=http://bama.ua.edu/
~deip/safest.html

ALASKA
Consultation Section, ADOL/AKOSH
3301 Eagle Street
P.O. Box 107022
Anchorage, Alaska 99510
(907) 269-4957
(907) 269-4950 FAX
E-mail:
mailto:%20timothy_bundy@labor.state.
ak.us
Website:
http://scripts.osha-slc.gov/cgi-bin/
redirect2state?url=http://www.labor.
state.ak.us/lss/oshhome.htm

ARIZONA
Consultation and Training
Industrial Commission of Arizona
Division of Occupational Safety &
Health
800 West Washington
Phoenix, Arizona 85007-9070
(602) 542-1695
(602) 542-1614FAX
E-mail:
pat.ryan@osha.gov

ARKANSAS
OSHA Consultation
Arkansas Department of Labor
10421 West Markham
Little Rock, Arkansas 72205
(501) 682-4522
(501) 682-4532 FAX
E-mail:
mailto:%20clark.thomas@osha.gov
Website:
http://scripts.osha-slc.gov/cgi-bin/
redirect2state?url=http://www.state.ar.
us/
labor/serv01.htm

CALIFORNIA
CAL/OSHA Consultation Service
Department of Industrial Relations
455 Golden Gate Avenue, 10th Floor
San Francisco, California 94102
(415) 703-5270
(415) 703-4596 FAX
E-mail:
mailto:%20InfoCons@hq.dir.ca.gov
Website:
http://scripts.osha-slc.gov/cgi-bin/
redirect2state?url=http://www.dir.ca.
gov/DOSH/consultation.html

COLORADO
Colorado State University
Occupational Safety and Health
Section
115 Environmental Health Building
Fort Collins, Colorado 80523
(970) 491-6151
(970) 491-7778 FAX
E-mail:
mailto:%20rbuchan@lamar.colostate.
edu
Website:
http://scripts.osha-slc.gov/cgi-bin/
redirect2state?url=http://www.
bernardino.colostate.edu/enhealth/
7c1.html

CONNECTICUT
Connecticut Department of Labor
Division of Occupational Safety &
Health
38 Wolcott Hill Road
Wethersfield, Connecticut 06109
(860) 566-4550
(860) 566-6916 FAX
E-mail:
mailto:%20donald.heckler@osha.gov
Website:
http://www.ctdol.state.ct.us/osha/
osha.htm

DELAWARE
Delaware Department of Labor
Division of Industrial Affairs
Occupational Safety and Health
4425 Market Street
Wilmington, Delaware 19802
(302) 761-8219
(302) 761-6601 FAX
E-mail:
mailto:%20ttrznadel@state.de.us
Website:
http://scripts.osha-slc.gov/cgi-bin/
redirect2state?url=http://www.state.
de.us/labor/aboutdol/industrialaffairs.h
tml

DISTRICT OF COLUMBIA
*Program available only for
employers within the District
of Columbia*
DC Department of Employment
Services
Office of Occupational Safety and
Health
950 Upshur Street, N.W.
Washington, D.C. 20011
(202) 576-6339
(202) 576-7579 FAX
E-mail:
mailto:%20jcates3@aol.com

FLORIDA
University of South Florida—Consulta-
tion Program
Department of Environmental and
Occupational Health
College of Public Health
3500 East Fletcher Avenue
Suite 105
Tampa, Florida 33613
Phone: 866-273-1105
E-mail: Charlene Vespi:
mailto:%20cvespi@hsc.usf.edu
Website:
http://scripts.osha-slc.gov/cgi-bin/
redirect2state?url=http://publichealth.
usf.edu/consult

GEORGIA
Georgia Institute of Technology
7(c)(1) Onsite Consultation Program
151 6th Street, NW
O'Keefe Building, Room 22
Atlanta, Georgia 30332-0837
(404) 894-2643
(404) 894-8275 FAX
E-mail:
mailto:%20daniel.ortiz@gtri.gatech.edu
Website:
http://scripts.osha-slc.gov/cgi-bin/
redirect2state?url=http://www.oshainfo.g
atech.edu/

GUAM
OSHA Onsite Consultation
Dept. of Labor, Government of Guam
107 F Street
Tiyam, Guam 96931
011 (671) 475-0136
011 (671) 477-2988 FAX
E-mail:
mailto:%20tpbadl@ns.gov.gu
Website:
http://scripts.osha-slc.gov/cgi-bin/
redirect2state?url=http://mail.admin.
gov.gu/webdol/oshacompl.htm

HAWAII
Consultation & Training Branch
Dept of Labor and Industrial Relations
830 Punchbowl Street
Honolulu, Hawaii 96813
(808) 586-9100
(808) 586-9099 FAX
E-mail:
ellen.kondo@osha.gov
Website:
http://scripts.osha-slc.gov/cgi-bin/
redirect2state?url=http://www.state.hi.
us/dlir/hiosh/consult.htm

IDAHO
Boise State University Occupational
Safety and Health Program
Risk Management and Audit Services
1910 University Drive
Boise, Idaho 83725-1825
(208) 426-3283
(208) 426-4411 FAX
E-mail:
mailto:%20lhill@boisestate.edu
Website:
http://www2.boisestate.edu/rmas/
environ_&_occup_health.htm

ILLINOIS
Illinois Onsite Consultation
Industrial Service Division
Department of Commerce &
Community Affairs
State of Illinois Center, Suite 3-400
100 West Randolph Street
Chicago, Illinois 60601
(312) 814-2337
(312) 814-7238 FAX
E-mail:
mailto:%20sfryzel@commerce.state.il.us
Website:
http://scripts.osha-slc.gov/cgi-bin/
redirect2state?url=http://www.
commerce.state.il.us/Services/
SmallBusiness/OSHA/OSHAhome.htm

INDIANA
Bureau of Safety, Education and
Training
Division of Labor, Room W195
402 West Washington
Indianapolis, Indiana 46204-2287
(317) 232-2688
(317) 232-3790 FAX
E-mail:
mailto:%20jon.mack@osha.gov
Website:
http://scripts.osha-slc.gov/cgi-bin/
redirect2state?url=http://www.state.in.
us/labor/book$.html

IOWA
7(c)(1) Consultation Program
Iowa Bureau of Labor
1000 East Grand
DesMoines, Iowa 50309-0209
(515) 281-7629
(515) 281-5522 FAX
E-mail:
mailto:%20steve.slater@osha.gov
Website:
http://scripts.osha-slc.gov/cgi-bin/
redirect2state?url=http://www.state.ia.
us/iwd/labor/index.html

KANSAS
Kansas 7(c)(1) Consultation Program
Kansas Dept. of Human Resources
512 South West 6th Street
Topeka, Kansas 66603-3150
(785) 296-7476
(785) 296-1775 FAX
E-mail:
mailto:%20rudy.leutzinger@osha.gov

KENTUCKY
Kentucky Labor Cabinet
Division of Education and Training
1047 U.S. Highway 127, South
Frankfort, Kentucky 40601
(502) 564-6895
(502) 564-6103 FAX
E-mail:
mailto:%20arussell@mail.lab.state.ky.us
Website:
http://scripts.osha-slc.gov/cgi-bin/
redirect2state?url=http://www.state.ky.
us/agencies/labor/oshcons.htm

LOUISIANA
7(c)(1) Consultation Program
Louisiana Department of Labor
1001 N. 23rd Street, Room 230
P.O. Box 94094
Baton Rouge, Louisiana 70804-9094
(225) 342-9601
(225) 342-5158 FAX
E-mail:
mailto:%20shart@ldol.state.la.us

MAINE
Division of Industrial Safety
Maine Bureau of Labor Standards
Workplace Safety & Health Division
State House Station #45
Augusta, Maine 04333-0045
(207) 624-6460
(207) 624-6449 FAX
E-mail:
david.e.wacker@state.me.us
Website:
http://scripts.osha-slc.gov/cgi-bin/
redirect2state?url=http://janus.state.
me.us/labor/consult.htm

MARYLAND
MOSH Consultation Services
312 Marshall Avenue, Room 600
Laurel, Maryland 20707
(410) 880-4970
(301) 483-8332 FAX
E-mail:
virginia.anklin@osha.gov
Website:
http://scripts.osha-slc.gov/cgi-bin/
redirect2state?url=http://www.dllr.state.
md.us/labor/mosh.html

MASSACHUSETTS
Div. of Occupaional Safety & Health
Dept. of Workforce Development
1001 Watertown Street
West Newton, Massachusetts 02165
(617) 727-3982
(617) 727-4581 FAX
E-mail:
joe.lamalva@state.ma.us
Website:
http://scripts.osha-slc.gov/cgi-bin/
redirect2state?url=http://www.state.ma.
us/dos/Consult/Consult.htm

MICHIGAN
Department of Consumer and Industry
Services
7150 Harris Drive
Lansing, Michigan 48909
(517) 322-1809
(517) 322-1374 FAX
E-mail:
mailto:%20ayalew.kanno@cis.state.
mi.us
Website:
http://scripts.osha-slc.gov/cgi-bin/
redirect2state?url=http://www.cis.state.
mi.us/bsr/divisions/set/set_con.htm

MINNESOTA
Department of Labor & Industry
Consultation Division
443 LaFayette Road
Saint Paul, Minnesota 55155
(612) 297-2393
(612) 297-1953 FAX
E-mail:
james.collins@state.mn.us
Website:
http://scripts.osha-slc.gov/cgi-bin/
redirect2state?url=http://www.doli.
state.mn.us/wsc.html

MISSISIPPI
Mississippi State University
Center for Safety and Health
2906 North State Street
Suite 201
Jackson, Mississippi 39216
(601) 987-3981
(601) 987-3890 FAX
E-mail:
kelly.tucker@osha.gov
Website:
http://scripts.osha-slc.gov/cgi-bin/
redirect2state?url=http://www.msstate.
edu/dept/csh/

MISSOURI
Onsite Consultation Program
Division of Labor Standards
Dept. of Labor & Industrial Relations
3315 West Truman Boulevard
Post Office Box 449
Jefferson City, Missouri 65109
(573) 751-3403
(573) 751-3721 FAX
E-mail:
rsimmons@dolir.state.mo.us
Website:
http://scripts.osha-slc.gov/cgi-bin/
redirect2state?url=http://www.dolir.
state.mo.us/ls/onsite/index.html

MONTANA
Dept. of Labor and Industry
Bureau of Safety
PO Box 1728
Helena, Montana 59624-1728
(406) 444-6418
(406) 444-4140 FAX
E-mail:
mailto:%20sstapler@state.mt.us
Website:
http://scripts.osha-slc.gov/cgi-bin/
redirect2state?url=http://erd.dli.state.
mt.us/Safety/SBhome.htm

NEBRASKA
Division of Safety & Labor Standards
Nebraska Department of Labor
State Office Building, Lower Level
301 Centennial Mall, South
Lincoln, Nebraska 68509-5024
(402) 471-4717
(402) 471-5039 FAX
E-mail:
mailto:%20ediedrichs@dol.state.ne.us
Website:
http://scripts.osha-slc.gov/cgi-bin/
redirect2state?url=http://www.dol.state.
ne.us/safety/7c1.htm

NEVADA
Safety Consultation and Training
Section
Division of Industrial Relations
Department of Business and Industry
1301 Green Valley Parkway
Henderson, Nevada 89014
(702) 486-9140
(702) 990-0362 FAX
E-mail:
gary.sloop@osha.gov
Website:
http://scripts.osha-slc.gov/cgi-bin/
redirect2state?url=http://www.state.nv.
us/b&i/ir/index.htm

NEW HAMPSHIRE
New Hampshire Dept of Health &
Human Services
6 Hazen Drive
Concord, New Hampshire 03301-6527
(603) 271-2024
(603) 271-2667 FAX
E-mail:
mailto:%20stephen.beyer@osha.gov
Website:
http://scripts.osha-slc.gov/cgi-bin/
redirect2state?url=http://www.state.nh.
us/dhhs/ohm/dphs.htm#I.
HEALTHRISKASSESSMENT

NEW JERSEY
New Jersey Department of Labor
Division of Public Safety and
Occupational Safety and Health
225 E. State Street
8th Floor West
P.O. Box 953
Trenton, New Jersey 08625-0953
(609) 292-3923
(609) 292-4409 FAX
E-mail:
mailto:%20carol.farley@osha.gov
Website:
http://scripts.osha-slc.gov/cgi-bin/
redirect2state?url=http://www.state.nj.
us/labor/consult.htm

NEW MEXICO
New Mexico Environment Department
Occupational Health and Safety
Bureau
525 Camino de Los Marquez, Suite 3
PO Box 26110
Santa Fe, New Mexico 87502
(505) 827-4230
(505) 827-4422 FAX
E-mail:
mailto:%20Debra_McElroy@nmenv.
state.nm.us
Website:
http://scripts.osha-slc.gov/cgi-bin/
redirect2state?url=http://www.nmenv.
state.nm.us/env_prot.html

NEW YORK
Division of Safety and Health
State Office Campus
Building 12, Room 130
Albany, New York 12240
(518) 457-2238
(518) 457-3454 FAX
E-mail:
mailto:%20james.rush@osha.gov
Website:
http://scripts.osha-slc.gov/cgi-bin/
redirect2state?url=http://www.labor.
state.ny.us/html/employer/p469.html

NORTH CAROLINA
Bureau of Consultative Services
NC Department of Labor—
OSHA Division
4 West Edenton Street
Raleigh, North Carolina 27601-1092
(919) 807-2905
(919) 807-2902 FAX
E-mail:
mailto:%20wjoyner@mail.dol.state.nc.us
Website:
http://scripts.osha-slc.gov/cgi-bin/
redirect2state?url=http://www.dol.state.
nc.us/osha/consult/consult.htm

NORTH DAKOTA
Division of Environmental Engineering
1200 Missouri Avenue, Room 304
Bismarck, North Dakota 58504
(701) 328-5188
(701) 328-5200 FAX
E-mail:
agilliss@state.nd.us
Website:
http://scripts.osha-slc.gov/cgi-
bin/redirect2state?url=http://www.ehs.
health.state.nd.us/ndhd/environ/ee/
oshc/index.htm

OHIO
On-Site Consultation Program
Bureau of Occupational Safety and
Health
LAWS Division / Ohio Dept. of
Commerce
50 W. Broad Street, Suite 2900
Columbus, Ohio 43215
1-800-282-1425 or 614-644-2631
614-644-3133 FAX
E-mail:
mailto:%20owen.wagner@perrp.com.
state.oh.us
Website: http://www.osha.gov/oshdir/
ohio-stateweb-redirect.html

OKLAHOMA
Oklahoma Department of Labor
OSHA Division
4001 North Lincoln Boulevard
Oklahoma City, Oklahoma 73105-5212
(405) 528-1500
(405) 528-5751 FAX
E-mail:
mailto:%20leslie.stockel@osha.gov
Website:
http://scripts.osha-slc.gov/cgi-bin/
redirect2state?url=http://www.state.ok.
us/~okdol/osha/index.htm

OREGON
Oregon OSHA
Department of Consumer & Business
Services
350 Winter Street, N.E., Room 430
Salem, Oregon 97310
(503) 378-3272
(503) 378-5729 FAX
E-mail:
mailto:%20steve.g.beech@state.or.us
Website:
http://scripts.osha-slc.gov/cgi-bin/
redirect2state?url=http://www.orosha.
org/

PENNSYLVANIA
Indiana University Pennsylvania
Room 210 Walsh Hall
302 East Walk
Indiana, Pennsylvania 15705-1087
(724) 357-2396
(724) 357-2385 FAX
E-mail:
mailto:%20john.engler@osha.gov
Website:
http://scripts.osha-slc.gov/cgi-bin/
redirect2state?url=http://www.iup.edu/
sa/osha/index.html

PUERTO RICO
Occupational Safety and Health Office
Department of Labor & Human
Resources, 21st Floor
505 Munoz Rivera Avenue
Hato Rey, Puerto Rico 00918
(787) 754-2171
(787) 767-6051 FAX
E-mail:
mailto:%20alopez@osha.gov

RHODE ISLAND
OSH Consultation Program
Division of Occupational Health &
Radiation Control
Rhode Island Department of Health
3 Capital Hill
Providence, Rhode Island 02908
(401) 222-2438
(401) 222-2456 FAX
E-mail:
mailto:%20safesite@doh.state.ri.us
Website:
http://scripts.osha-slc.gov/cgi-bin/
redirect2state?url=http://www.state.ri.
us/dohrad.htm

SOUTH CAROLINA
South Carolina Department of Labor,
Licensing and Regulation
3600 Forest Drive
P.O. Box 11329
Columbia, South Carolina 29204
(803) 734-9614
(803) 734-9741 FAX
E-mail:
bob.peck@osha.gov
Website:
http://scripts.osha-slc.gov/cgi-bin/
redirect2state?url=http://www.llr.state.
sc.us/oshavol.htm

SOUTH DAKOTA
Engineering Extension
Onsite Technical Division
South Dakota State University
West Hall, Box 510
907 Harvey Dunn Street
Brookings, South Dakota 57007
(605) 688-4101
(605) 688-6290 FAX
E-mail:
mailto:%20don_froehlich@sdstate.edu

TENNESSEE
OSHA Consultation Services Division
Tennessee Department of Labor
3rd floor
710 James Robertson Parkway
Nashville, Tennessee 37243-0659
(615) 741-7036
(615) 532-2997 FAX
E-mail:
mailto:%20jcothron@mail.state.tn.us
Website:
http://scripts.osha-slc.gov/cgi-bin/
redirect2state?url=http://www.state.tn.
us/labor/toshcons.html

TEXAS
Workers' Health and Safety Division
Texas Workers' Compensation
Commission
Southfield Building
4000 South I H 35
Austin, Texas 78704
(512) 804-4640
(512) 804-4641 FAX
OSHCON Request Line: 800-687-7080
E-mail:
mailto:%20jharper@twcc.state.tx.us
Website:
http://scripts.osha-slc.gov/cgi-bin/
redirect2state?url=http://twcc.state.tx.
us/services/oshcon.html

UTAH
State of Utah Labor Commission
Workplace Safety and Health
Consultation Services
160 East 300 South
Salt Lake City, Utah 84114-6650
(801) 530-6901
(801) 530-6992 FAX
E-mail:
mailto:%20icmain.nanderso@state.ut.us
Website:
http://scripts.osha-slc.gov/cgi-bin/
redirect2state?http://www.labor.state.
ut.us/Utah_Occupational_Safety_Hea/
Consultation_Services/consultation_
services.html

VERMONT
Division of Occupational Safety &
Health
Vermont Department of Labor and
Industry
National Life Building, Drawer 20
Montpelier, Vermont 05602-3401
(802) 828-2765
(802) 828-2195 FAX
E-mail:
mailto:%20robert.mcleod@labind.state.
vt.us
Website:
http://www.state.vt.us/labind/vosha.htm

VIRGINIA
Virginia Department of Labor and
Industry
Occupational Safety and Health
Training and Consultation
13 South 13th Street
Richmond, Virginia 23219
(804) 786-6359
(804) 786-8418 FAX
E-mail:
NLJ@doli.state.va.us
Website:
http://scripts.osha-slc.gov/cgi-bin/
redirect2state?url=http://www.dli.state.
va.us/programs/consultation.htm

VIRGIN ISLANDS
Division of Occupational Safety and
Health
Virgin Islands Department of Labor
3021 Golden Rock
Christiansted
St. Croix, Virgin Island 00840
(340) 772-1315
(340) 772-4323 FAX
Website:
http://scripts.osha-slc.gov/cgi-bin/
redirect2state?url=http://www.gov.
vi/vild/

WASHINGTON
Washington Dept of Labor and
Industries
Division of Industrial Safety and
Health
P.O. Box 44643
Olympia, Washington 98504
(360) 902-5638
(360) 902-5459 FAX
E-mail:
mailto:%20jame235@lni.wa.gov
Website:
http://scripts.osha-slc.gov/cgi-
bin/redirect2state?url=http://www.wa.
gov/lni/wisha/wisha.htm#intro

WEST VIRGINIA
West Virginia Department of Labor
Capitol Complex Building #3
1800 East Washington Street, Room 319
Charleston, West Virginia 25305
(304) 558-7890
(304) 558-9711 FAX
E-mail:
mailto:%20jburgess@labor.state.wv.us
Website:
http://scripts.osha-slc.gov/cgi-bin/
redirect2state?url=http://www.state.wv.
us/labor/sections.htm

WISCONSIN (Health)
Wisconsin Department of Health and
Human Services
Division of Public Health
Section of Occupational Health,
Room 112
1414 East Washington Avenue
Madison, Wisconsin 53703
(608) 266-8579
(608) 266-9383 FAX
E-mail:
mailto:%20moente@dhfs.state.wi.us
Website:
http://scripts.osha-slc.gov/cgi-bin/
redirect2state?url=http://www.dhfs.stat
e.wi.us/dph_boh/OSHA_Cons/index.htm

WISCONSIN (Safety)
Wisconsin Department of Commerce
Bureau of Marketing, Advocacy and
Technology Development
Bureau of Manufacturing and
Assessment
N14 W23833 Stone Ridge Drive
Suite B100
Waukesha, Wisconsin 53188-1125
(262) 523-3040   1-800-947-0553
(262) 523-3046 FAX
E-mail:
mailto:%20jim.lutz@osha.gov
Website:
http://scripts.osha-slc.gov/cgi-bin/
redirect2state?url=http://www.commerce.
state.wi.us/MT/MT-FAX-0928.html

WYOMING
Wyoming Department of Employment
Workers' Safety and Compensation
Division
Herschler Building, 2 East
122 West 25th Street
Cheyenne, Wyoming 82002
(307) 777-7786
(307) 777-3646 FAX
E-mail:
mailto:%20sfoste1@missc.state.wy.us
Website:
http://scripts.osha-slc.gov/cgi-bin
redirect2state?url=http://wydoe.state.
wy.us/wscd/osha/evtap.htm

APPENDIX **IV**

Converting, Printing and Publishing Associations and Organizations

SOURCE:
NPES and
Jelmar Publishing Co., Inc.

UNITED STATES

ADHESIVES AND SEALANTS COUNCIL
7979 OLD GEORGETOWN RD, #500
BETHESDA, MD 20814
TEL: 301-986-9700
FAX: 301-986-8795

ADHESIVES MANUFACTURERS ASSN
OF AMERICA
2300 N. BARRINGTON ROAD, SUITE 400
HOFFMAN ESTATES, IL 60195
TEL: 847-490-5377
FAX: 847-884-9423

AMERICAN FOREST AND PAPER
ASSOCIATION (AFPA)
1111 19TH STREET NW, SUITE 800
WASHINGTON, DC 20036
TEL: (202)463-2700
FAX: (202)463-2785

AMERICAN INSTITUTE OF GRAPHIC
ARTS (AIGA)
164 FIFTH AVENUE
NEW YORK, NY 10010
TEL: 212-255-4004
FAX: 212-255-4410

AMER SOCY FOR TESTING AND
MATERIALS
100 BARR HARBOR DRIVE
WEST CONSHOHOCKEN, PA 19428
TEL: 610-832-2500
FAX: 610-832-9555

ASEPTIC PACKAGING COUNCIL
2111 WILSON BLVD., SUITE 700
ARLINGTON, VA 22201
TEL: (703) 351-5062
FAX: (703) 351-9750

ASSN FOR GRAPHIC ARTS TRAINING
ONE SHENANDOAH VALLEY DRIVE
STRASBURG, VA 22657
TEL: 540-405-6663
FAX: 800-214-1120

ASSN OF COLLEGE & UNIV PRINTERS
WAKE FOREST UNIV, SCHOOL OF
MEDICINE
1920 WEST FIRST STREET
WINSTON-SALEM, NC 27104
TEL: 336-716-9907
FAX: 336-716-7201

ASSN OF EASTERN CORRUGATED BOX
MANUFACTURERS
P. O. BOX 307
TEANECK, NJ 07666
TEL: 201-692-9600
FAX: 201-801-9007

ASSN OF GRAPHIC COMMUNICATIONS
330 SEVENTH AVENUE, 9TH FL
NEW YORK, NY 10001
TEL: 212-279-2100
FAX: 212-279-5381

ASSN OF INDEPENDENT
CORRUGATED CONVERTERS
113 S. WEST ST., P O BOX 25708
ALEXANDRIA, VA 22313
TEL: 703-836-2422
FAX: 703-836-2795

ASSN OF INDUSTRIAL METALLIZERS,
COATERS & LAMINATORS (AIMCAL)
2166 GOLD HILL ROAD
FORT MILL, SC 29708
TEL: 803-802-7820
FAX: 803-802-7821

BINDERS & FINISHERS ASSOCIATION
(BFA)
408 EIGHTH AVENUE, SUITE 10A
NEW YORK, NY 10001-1816
TEL: (212)629-3232
FAX: (212)465-2012

BINDING INDUSTRIES OF AMERICA
(BIA)
70 EAST LAKE STREET
CHICAGO, IL 60601
TEL: 312-372-7606
FAX: 312-704-5025

BOOK MANUFACTURERS INSTITUTE
(BMI)
65 WILLIAM STREET, SUITE 300
WELLESLEY, MA 02181-4007
TEL: (617) 239-0103
FAX: (617) 239-0106

BUSINESS FORMS MGMT ASSOC (BFMA)
319 S.W. WASHINGTON ST., SUITE 710
PORTLAND, OR 97204
TEL: 503-227-3393
FAX: 503-274-7667

CALIFORNIA FILM EXTRUDERS &
CONVERTERS ASSN
2402 VISTA NOBLEZA
NEWPORT BEACH, CA 92660-3545
TEL: 949-640-9901
FAX: 949-640-9911

CONTRACT PACKAGING ASSOCIATION
519 NORTH HIGHLAND AVE.
JACKSON, TN 38301-4824
TEL: 731-422-7994

CONVERTING EQUIPMENT
MANUFACTURERS ASSOC
66 MORRIS AVENUE
SPRINGFIELD, NJ 07081
TEL: 201-379-1100
FAX: 201-379-6507

DIGITAL PRINTING & IMAGING ASSN
10015 MAIN STREET
FAIRFAX, VA 22031-3489
TEL: 703-359-1328
FAX: 703-273-0469

DOCUMENT MANAGEMENT
INDUSTRIES ASSN
433 EAST MONROE AVENUE
ALEXANDRIA, VA 22301-1693
TEL: 703-836-6226
FAX: 703-836-2241

EDUCATION COUNCIL OF THE
GRAPHIC ARTS INDUSTRIES
1899 PRESTON WHITE DRIVE
RESTON, VA 22091-4367
TEL: 703-648-1768
FAX: 703-620-0994

ELECTRONIC PREPRESS SOLUTIONS
GROUP
PO BOX 40
MEDFORD, NJ 08055-0040
TEL: (609)714-1812
FAX: (609)714-1805

ENVELOPE MANUFACTURERS ASSOC
(EMA)
360 NO. WASHINGTON ST., SUITE 500
ALEXANDRIA, VA 22314-2530
TEL: 703-739-2200
FAX: 703-739-2209

THE ENVIRONMENTAL GROUP
1899 PRESTON WHITE DRIVE
RESTON, VA 20191-4367
TEL: (703)648-3218
FAX: (703)648-3219

FIBRE BOX ASSOCIATION
2850 GOLF ROAD
ROLLING MEADOWS, IL 60008
TEL: 847-364-9600
FAX: 847-364-9639

FLEXIBLE PACKAGING ASSN
971 CORPORATE BLVD, SUITE 403
LINTHICUM, MD 21090
TEL: 410-694-0800
FAX: 410-694-0900

FLEXOGRAPHIC PREPRESS
PLATEMAKERS ASSOCIATION
111 SOUTH CALVERT ST, SUITE 2700
BALTIMORE, MD 21202
TEL: 401-385-5301
FAX: 401-385-5201

FOIL STAMPING & EMBOSSING ASSN
536 NW TYLER CT, SUITE 204
TOPEKA, KS 66608
TEL: 785-232-8776
FAX: 785-232-8747

GLASS PACKAGING INSTITUTE
515 KING STREET, STE 420
ALEXANDRIA, VA 22314
TEL: 703-684-6359
FAX: 703-684-6048

GRAPHIC ARTS TECHNICAL
FOUNDATION (GATF)
200 DEER RUN ROAD
SEWICKLEY, PA 15143-2600
TEL: (412)741-6860
FAX: (412)741-2311

GRAPHIC COMMUNICATION
INTERNATIONAL UNION (GCIU)
1900 L STREET NW
WASHINGTON, DC 20036-5002
TEL: (202)462-1400
FAX: (202)721-0600

GRAVURE ASSN OF AMERICA (GAA)
1200-A SCOTTSVILLE RD
ROCHESTER, NY 14624
TEL: 716-436-2150
FAX: 716-436-7689

HIGH DEFINITION FLEXO
CONSORTIUM
322 SO PATTERSON BLVD.
DAYTON, OH 45402
TEL: 937-293-8381
FAX: 937-299-9604

HOUSTON ASSN OF IN-PLANT PRINTING
1324 WEST CLAY STREET
HOUSTON, TX 77019
TEL: 713-522-2046
FAX: 713-522-8342

IDEALLIANCE
100 DAINGERFIELD ROAD
ALEXANDRIA, VA 22314
TEL: 703-837-1070
FAX: 703-548-2867

INSTITUTE OF PACKAGING
PROFESSIONALS
1601 NORTH BOND STREET
NAPERVILLE, IL 60563
TEL: 630-544-5050
FAX: 630-544-5055

INSTITUTE OF PAPER SCIENCE &
TECHNOLOGY
500 10TH STREET, N.W.
ATLANTA, GA 30318-5794
TEL: 404-894-9523
FAX: 404-894-4778

INTL ASSN OF DIEMAKERS &
DIECUTTERS (IADD)
P O BOX 1587
CRYSTAL LAKE, IL 60039-1587
TEL: 815-455-7519
FAX: 815-455-7510

INTERNATIONAL ASSOCIATION FOR
DOCUMENT AND INFORMATION
MANAGEMENT SOLUTIONS (IBFI)
100 DAINGERFIELD ROAD
ALEXANDRIA, VA 22314
TEL: (703)684-9606
FAX: (703)684-9675

INTL ASSN OF PRINTING HOUSE
CRAFTSMEN
7042 BROOKLYN BLVD.
MINNEAPOLIS, MN 55429
TEL: 800-466-4274
FAX: 763-560-1350

INTERNATIONAL CORRUGATED CASE
ASSN
2850 GOLF ROAD
ROLLING MEADOWS, IL 60008
TEL: 847-364-9600
FAX: 847-364-9639

INTERNATIONAL CORRUGATED
  PACKAGING FOUNDATION
113 SOUTH WEST ST, P O BOX 25708
ALEXANDRIA, VA 22314
TEL: 703-549-8580
FAX: 703-549-8670

INTERNATIONAL DIGITAL IMAGING
  ASSOCIATION (IDIA)
PO BOX 81261
CHAMBLEE, GA 30366
TEL: (770)452-8119
FAX: (770)234-9058

IPA — INTERNATIONAL PREPRESS
  ASSN
7200 FRANCE AVE SOUTH, SUITE 223
EDINA, MN 55435
TEL: 952-896-1908
FAX: 952-896-0181

INTL REPROGRAPHIC ASSN (IRgA)
800 ENTERPRISE DR., SUITE 202
OAX BROOX, IL 60523
TEL: 630-571-4685
FAX: 630-571-4731

INTERNATIONAL THERMOGRAPHERS
  ASSOCIATION (ITA)
100 DAINGERFIELD ROAD
ALEXANDRIA, VA 22314
TEL: (703)519-8122
FAX: (703)548-3227

MARKING DEVICE ASSOCIATION INTL
222 WISCONSIN AVENUE, SUITE 1
LAKE FOREST, IL 60045
TEL: 847-283-9810
FAX: 847-283-9808

NATIONAL ASSOCIATION OF
  PRINTING INK MANUFACTURERS
  (NAPIM)
581 MAIN STREET
WOODBRIDGE, NJ 07095-1104
TEL: (732)855-1525
FAX: (732)855-1838

NATIONAL ASSN OF PRINTING
  LEADERSHIP (NAPL)
75 WEST CENTURY BLVD.
PARAMUS, NJ 07652-1408
TEL: 201-634-9606
FAX: 201-643-0327

NATIONAL METAL DECORATORS ASSN
  (NMDA)
9616 DEERECO ROAD
TIMONIUM, MD 21093
TEL: 410-252-5205
FAX: 410-628-8079

NATIONAL PAPERBOX ASSOCIATION
801 NORTH FAIRFAX ST, SUITE 211
ALEXANDRIA, VA 22314
TEL: 703-684-2212
FAX: 703-683-6920

NATIONAL PAPER TRADE
  ASSOCIATION (NPTA)
500 BICOUNTY BLVD., SUITE 200
FARMINGDALE, NY 11735-3931
TEL: 631-777-2223
FAX: 631-777-2224

NATIONAL PRINTING EQUIPMENT
  SHOW
1899 PRESTON WHITE DRIVE
RESTON, VA 20191-4367
TEL: 703-264-7200
FAX: 703-620-0994

NATIONAL SOY INK INFORMATION
  CENTER
4554 NW 114TH STREET
URBANDALE, IA 50322-5410
TEL: (515)251-8640
FAX: (515)251-8657

NEWSPAPER ASSOCIATION OF
  AMERICA (NAA)
1921 GALLOWS ROAD, SUITE 600
VIENNA, VA 22182
TEL: (703)902-1600
FAX: (703)917-0636

NORTHERN CALIFORNIA LABEL MFRS
  ASSN
665 THIRD STREET, SUITE 500
SAN FRANCISCO, CA 94107-1990
TEL: 415-495-8242
FAX: 415-543-7790

PACIFIC COAST PAPER BOX
  MANUFACTURERS
6360 VAN NUYS BLVD., SUITE 220
VAN NUYS, CA 91401
TEL: (818) 781-3378
FAX: (818) 787-6206

PACIFIC PRINTING & IMAGING ASSN.
5319 SW WESTGATE DRIVE, SUITE 117
PORTLAND, OR 97221-2488
TEL: 503-297-3328
FAX: 503-297-3320

PACKAGE DESIGN COUNCIL
4350 FAIRFAX DRIVE, LBBY 600
ARLINGTON, VA 22203-1632
TEL: 703-318-7225
FAX: 703-318-0310

PACKAGING AND LABEL GRAVURE
  ASSN
6200 PLATEAU DRIVE
SPRINGFIELD, OH 45502
TEL: 937-390-2528
FAX: 937-390-2385

PAPER SHIPPING SACK MFRS ASSN
505 WHITE PLAINS ROAD
TARRYTOWN NY 10591
TEL: 914-631-0909
FAX: 914-631-0333

PAPERBOARD PACKAGING COUNCIL
201 NORTH UNION STREET, SUITE 220
ALEXANDIA, VA 22314
TEL: 703-836-3300
FAX: 703-836-3290

PMMI-PACKAGING MACHINERY MFRS
  INST
4350 NORTH FAIRFAX DRIVE, SUITE 600
ARLINGTON, VA 22203
TEL: 703-243-8555
FAX: 703-243-8556

PRINTING AND GRAPHIC
  COMMUNICATIONS ASSOCIATION
6411 IVY LANE, SUITE 700
GREENBELT, MD 20770
TEL: (301)474-8911
FAX: (301)474-2937

PRINTING & IMAGING ASSN OF TEXAS
910 W MOCKINGBIRD LANE, #200
DALLAS, TX 75247
TEL: 214-630-8871
FAX: 214-688-1176

PRINTIMAGE INTERNATIONAL
70 EAST LAKE STREET, NO. 333
CHICAGO, IL 60601-5907
TEL: 312-321-6886
FAX: 312-234-0040

PRINTING INDUSTRIES OF AMERICA
  (PIA)
100 DAINGERFIELD ROAD
ALEXANDRIA, VA 22314
TEL: (703)519-8100
FAX: (703)548-3227

PRINTING INDUSTRIES ASSOCIATION
  OF ARIZONA — PIAZ
4315 N 12TH STREET, SUITE 200
PHOENIX, AZ 85014
TEL: 602-265-7742
FAX: 602-365-8259

PRINTING INDUSTRIES ASSOCIATION
  OF THE SOUTH
305 PLUS PARK BLVD, P O BOX 290249
NASHVILLE, TN 37229
TEL: 615-366-1094
FAX: 615-368-4192

PRINTING INDUSTRIES OF
  ILLINOIS/INDIANA ASSOCIATION
70 EAST LAKE STREET
CHICAGO, IL 60601
TEL: 312-704-5000
FAX: 312-704-5025

PRINTING INDUSTRIES OF THE
    CAROLINAS, INC. (PICA)
3601 ROSE LAKE DR, P O BOX 19889
CHARLOTTE, NC 28219
TEL: 704-357-1150
FAX: 704-357-1154

PRINTING INDUSTRIES OF THE GULF
    COAST
1324 WEST CLAY STREET
HOUSTON, TX 77019
TEL: 713-522-2046
FAX: 713-522-8342

PRINTING INDUSTRIES ASSOCIATION
420 ARMOUR ROAD, SUITE 20267
NORTH KANSAS CITY, MO 64116-3541
TEL: 816-421-7677
FAX: 816-421-7072

PRINTING INDUSTRIES ASSOCIATION
    OF NEW YORK
636 NORTH FRENCH ROAD
AMHERST, NY 14228
TEL: 716-691-3211
FAX: 716-691-4249

PRINTING INDUSTRIES ASSN OF
    NORTHERN CALIFORNIA
330 ROSITA AVE
PASADENA, CA 91105
TEL: 818-792-9818

PRINTING INDUSTRIES OF MICHIGAN
23815 NORTHWESTERN HWY, STE 2700
SOUTHFIELD, MI 48075
TEL: 313-354-9200

PRINTING INDUSTRIES OF
    NEW ENGLAND (PINE)
5 CRYSTAL POND RD
SOUTHBOROUGH, MA 01772-1868
TEL: 508-804-4100
FAX: 508-804-4119

PRINTING INDUSTRIES OF ST. LOUIS
1790 S BRENTWOOD BLVD.
ST LOUIS, MO 63144
TEL: 314-962-6780
FAX: 314-962-4490

PRINTING INDUSTRIES OF WISCONSIN
13005 W BLUEMOUND ROAD
BROOKFIELD, WI 53211
TEL: 262-785-7040
FAX: 262-785-7043

PRINTING INDUSTRY ASSOCIATION
    OF GEORGIA
5020 HIGHLANDS PARKWAY
SMYRNA, GA 30082
TEL: 404-433-3050
FAX: 404-433-3062

PRINTING INDUSTRY OF MINNESOTA
    FOUNDATION
2829 UNIVERSITY AVENUE SE
MINNEAPOLIS, MN 55414-3222
TEL: 615-379-3360
FAX: 612-379-6030

PRINTING INDUSTRIES ASSOCIATION
    OF SOUTHERN CALIFORNIA
5800 SOUTH EASTERN AVE, SUITE 400
LOS ANGELES CA 90040
TEL: 323-728-9500
FAX: 323-724-2327

PRINTING INDUSTRIES OF
    CONNECTICUT &
    WESTERN MASSACHUSETTS
4 RESEARCH PARKWAY
WALLINGFORD, CT 06492-1929
TEL: 203-294-0202
FAX: 203-294-0249

RADTECH INTERNATIONAL
3 BETHESDA METRO CIR, SUITE 700
BETHESDA, MD 20814
TEL: 301-664-8408
FAX: 301-657-9776

RESEARCH AND ENGINEERING
    COUNCIL OF THE GRAPHIC ARTS
P O BOX 1086
WHITE STONE, VA 22578-1066
TEL: 804-436-9922
FAX: 804-436-9511

SCREENPRINT & GRAPHIC IMAGING
    ASSN
10015 MAIN STREET
FAIRFAX, VA 22031-3489
TEL: 703-385-1335
FAX: 703-273-0456

SCREEN PRINTING TECHNICAL
    FOUNDATION
10015 MAIN STREET
FAIRFAX, VA 22031-3489
TEL: 703-385-1417
FAX: 703-273-0456

SOCIETY OF THE PLASTICS
    INDUSTRY
1801 K STREET NW, SUITE 600K
WASHINGTON, DC 10006-1301
TEL: 202-974-5246
FAX: 202-296-7005

TAG & LABEL MANUFACTURERS
    INSTITUTE
40 SHUMAN BLVD, SUITE 295
NAPERVILLE, IL 60563
TEL: 630-357-9222
FAX: 630-357-0192

TECHNICAL ASSOCIATION OF THE
    PULP AND PAPER INDUSTRY
    (TAPPI)
PO BOX 105113
NORCROSS, GA 30348-5113
TEL: 770-446-1400
FAX: 770-446-6947

TECHNICAL ASSOC OF THE GRAPHIC
    ARTS (TAGA)
68 LOMB MEMORIAL DRIVE
ROCHESTER, NY 14623-5604
TEL: 716-475-7470
FAX: 716-475-2250

UNIFORM CODE COUNCIL INC
1009 LENOX DRIVE, SUITE 202
LAWRENCEVILLE, NJ 08648
TEL: 609-620-0200
FAX: 609-620-1200

WATERLESS PRINTING ASSOC (WPA)
P O BOX 59800
CHICAGO, IL 60659
TEL: 773-743-5677
FAX: 773-743-5756

WEB OFFSET ASSOCIATION (WOA)
100 DAINGERFIELD ROAD
ALEXANDRIA, VA 22314
TEL: (703)519-8142
FAX: (703)548-3227

WOMEN IN PACKAGING INC.
4290 BELLS FERRY RD, STE 106-17
KENNESSAW, GA 30144-1400
TEL: 770-924-3563
FAX: 770-928-2338

ARGENTINA

ARGENTINE ASSOCIATION OF THE
    GRAPHIC ARTS (FAIGA)
RL FALCON 1657/59
BUENOS AIRES, 1406, ARGENTINA
TEL: +54 1 6315120
FAX: +54 1 6327924

AUSTRALIA

AFTA-AUSTRALIAN FLEXOGRAPHIC
    TECHNICAL ASSN
P O BOX 1540
NEUTRAL BAY, NSW 2089 AUSTRALIA
TEL: +61-2-9972-3466
FAX: +61-2-9972-3466

GAMAA
PO BOX 1051
CROWS NEST, NSW 2065, AUSTRALIA
TEL: +61 29 439 1675
FAX: +61 29 439 1675

PRINTING INDUSTRIES ASSOCIATION
   OF AUSTRALIA
LEVEL 10. 99 YORK STREET
SYDNEY, NSW 2000 AUSTRALIA
TEL: +61-2-9248-7300
FAX: +61-2-9299-0087

AUSTRIA

AUSTRIAN FEDERATION OF GRAPHIC
   ARTS
GRUNANGERGASSE
VIENNA, A-1010, AUSTRIA
TEL: +43 1 512 49 85
FAX: +43 1 513 28 26/19

VERBAND INDUSTRIELLER
   BUCHBINDER
BRUCKNERSTRASSE 8
VIENNA, A-1041, AUSTRIA
TEL: +43 1 505 53 82
FAX: +43 1 505 90 18

BELGIUM

ALLIANCE FOR BEVERAGE CARTONS
   AND THE ENVIRONMENT
15-17 RUE BELLIARD
BRUSSELS, 1040 BELGIUM
TEL: 32 2 504 07 10
FAX: 32 2 504 07 19

EUROPEAN CARTON MAKERS ASSOCI-
   ATION
715 CHAUSSEE DE WATERLOO 715
   BUS 25
B-1180, BRUXELLES, BELGIUM
TEL: +32 2 343 64 74
FAX: +32 2 344 86 61

EUROPEAN ORGANIZATION FOR
   PACKAGING AND THE
   ENVIRONMENT (EUROPEN)
LE ROYAL, TERVUREN
AVENUE DE L'ARMEE 6
BRUSSELS, 1040 BELGIUM
TEL: +32-2-736-3600
FAX: +32-2-736-3521

FEBELGRA
RUE BELLIARD 20, BTE 16
BRUSSELS, B-1040, BELGIUM
TEL: +32 2 512 36 38
FAX: +32 2 513 56 76

FEFCO/PROBOX
AVENUE LOUISE 250
BRUSSELS B-1050 BELGIUM
TEL: +32-2-646-40-70
FAX: +32-2-646-64-60

INTERGRAF
INTERNATIONAL CONFEDERATION
   FOR PRINTING AND ALLIED
   INDUSTRIES
SQUARE MARIE-LOUISE 18, BTE 27
B-1000 BRUSSELS, BELGIUM
TEL: +32 2 230 86 46
FAX: +32 2 231 14 64

BRAZIL

AB FLEXO/FTA (BRAZIL)
RUA DOMINGOS DE MORAES Nº 2243
CJS 24, BAIRRO DE VILA MARIANA
   SAO PAULO 04035-0006, BRAZIL
TEL: +55-11-5085-0033 x25
FAX: +55-11-9910-0482

ABIGRAF
BRAZILIAN PRINTING INDUSTRIES
   CONFEDERATION
RUA DO PARAÍSO 533
SÃO PAULO, 04103 BRAZIL
TEL: +55 11 5087 7777
FAX: +55 11 5087 7733

ABIMEG
RUA GUATEMOZIM 77
SÃO PAULO-SP, 02054, BRAZIL
TEL: +55 11 9483455
FAX: +55 11 2645783

BRAZILIAN ASSOCIATION OF
   CORRUGATED BOARD
   MANUFACTURERS
RUA BRIGADEIRO GAVIAO PEIXOTO 646
SAO PAULO, SP 05078-000 BRAZIL
TEL: +55-11-3831-9844
FAX: +55-11-3836-6801

CANADA

ASSOCIATION DES ARTES
   GRAPHIQUE DU QUEBEC
65 RUE DE CASTELNAU OUEST
BUR 101
MONTREAL, PQ, H2R 2W3, CANADA
TEL: 514 274 7446
FAX: 514 274 7482

ASSN QUEBECOISE DE LA
   FLEXOGRAPHIE
999 AV EMILE-JOURNAULT EAST
MONTREAL H2M 2E2 CANADA
TEL: 514-389-5840
FAX: 514-389-5840

CANADIAN CORRUGATED CASE ASSN
NO YORK SQ, 45 SHEPPARD AVE E #900
NORTH YORK, ONT M2N 5W9 CANADA
TEL: 416-590-9471
FAX: 416-590-9812

CANADIAN PAPER BOX
   MANUFACTURERS ASSN
701 EVANS AVENUE, SUITE 400
TORONTO, ONT M9C 1A3 CANADA
TEL: 416-626-7056
FAX: 416-626-7054

CANADIAN PLASTICS INDUSTRY ASSN
5925 AIRPORT ROAD, SUITE 500
MISSISSAUGA, ONT L4V 1W1 CANADA
TEL: 905-678-7405
FAX: 905-678-0774

CANADIAN PULP & PAPER
   ASSOCIATION
1155 METCALFE STREET, 19TH FLOOR
MONTREAL, QUEBEC, CANADA H3B 4T6
TEL: (514) 866-6621

PACKAGING ASSOCIATION OF
   CANADA
2255 SHEPPARD AVENUE EAST, STE 330
WILLOWDALE, ONT M2J 4YI CANADA
TEL: 416-490-7860
FAX: 416-490-7844

SOCIETY OF PLASTICS INDUSTRY OF
   CANADA
399 LEO-PARISEAU, SUITE 2210
MONTREAL, PQ H2W 2N1 CANADA
TEL: 514-499-0500
FAX: 514-499-0258

CHILE

ASIMPRES
CANADÁ 253, 2 PISO
SANTIAGO, CHILE
TEL: +56 2 225 7706
FAX: +56 2 204 7299

CHINA

ASIAN CORRUGATED CASE ASSN
15F KIU KIN BLDG, 568 NATHAN ROAD
KOWLOON HONGKONG, CHINA
TEL: +85 2-2385-6894
FAX: +85 2-2770-4727

BEIJING PRINTING INSTITUTE
POSTAL CODE 102600
DAXING, BEIJING, CHINA
TEL: +86-21-924-3024

CHINA PACKAGING TECHNOLOGY
   ASSN
RM 1115, 99 JIANGUO ROAD
BEIJING 100 020 CHINA
TEL: +86-10-6581-2361
FAX: +86-10-6581-3489

CHINA PACKAGING TECHNOLOGY
   ASSOCIATION (CHN)
4-F STANHOPE HOUSE, 734 KING'S
   ROAD
NORTH POINT, HONG KONG, CHINA
TEL: +85 2-2811-8897
FAX: +85 2-2576-5719

FLEXO TECHNOLOGY COMMITTEE
   OF CHINA PRINTING ASSN
NO. 60, LANE 1209, XINZHA ROAD
SHANGHAI 200 041
CHINA
TEL: +86-21-627-11329
FAX: +86-21-625-53562

GRAPHIC ARTS ASSOCIATION OF
   HONG KONG
BLK. C, 16/F., ROOM 1625,
   METROPOLE BLDG.
416 KING'S ROAD, NORTH POINT
HONG KONG, CHINA
TEL: +85 2 408 1515

HONG KONG PRINTERS ASSOCIATION
1/F 48-50 JOHNSTON ROAD
WANCHAI
HONG KONG, CHINA
TEL: +85 2 527 5050
FAX: +85 2 861 0463

THE HONG KONG PRINTERS
   ASSOCIATION
THE GREEN PAGODA PRESS LIMITED
655 KING'S ROAD, 9TH FLOOR
HONG KONG, CHINA
TEL: +85 2 561 2324, 561 7548
FAX: +85 2 811 0946

PEIAC
LANGJIYUAN, JIANGUOMEN, WAI
INSIDE BEIJING PRT. 2 FACTORY
BEIJING, 100022, CHINA
TEL: +86 10 650 76422
FAX: +86 10 650 65592

SHANGHAI PRINTING MATERIALS
   ASSOCIATION
226 QINGYUN ROAD
SHANGHAI, 200 081, CHINA
TEL: +86 10 662 4700

SHANGHAI PUBLISHERS
   ASSOCIATION
5 SHAOXING ROAD
SHANGHAI, 200 020, CHINA
TEL: +86 10 433 9268
FAX: +86 10 433 2452

YINSHUA ZAZHI/PRINTING FIELD
NO. 60, LANE 1209, XINZHA LU
SHANGHAI 200 041
CHINA
TEL: +86-1-841-2026
FAX: +86-1-841-2048

ZHONGGUO ZAOZHI
12 GUANGHUA LU, CHAOYANG-QU
BEIJING 100 020
CHINA
TEL: +86-10-6506-0072
FAX: +86-10-6500-5677

COLOMBIA

ANDIGRAF
ASOCIACIÓN COLOMBIANA DE
   INDUSTRIAS GRÁFICAS
CARRERA 4A, NO. 25B-46
AA 45243, BOGOTA, COLOMBIA
TEL: +57 1 341 3129
FAX: +57 1 281 8442

COSTA RICA

ACCCSA-ASSOCIATION OF
   CARIBBEAN, CENTRAL AND SOUTH
   AMERICAN CORRUGATORS
P O BOX 04-6155
SANTA ANA, SAN JOSE, COSTA RICA
TEL: +506-204-7201/7202
FAX: +506-204-7203

CROATIA

HRVATSKA UDRUGA POLODAVACA
PRASKA 5/III
ZAGREB, HR -10000, CROATIA
TEL: +385 01 42 42 84
FAX: +385 01 42 42 86

CYPRUS

CYPRUS MASTER PRINTERS ASSOCIA-
   TION
C/O CYPRUS EMPLOYERS,
   CHARALAMBIDES BUILDING
30 GRIVAS DIGENIS AVE.
NICOSIA, CYPRUS
TEL: +357 2 445102
FAX: +357 2 459459

CZECH REPUBLIC

SVAZ POLYGRAFICKYCH
   PODNIKATELU
HÁLKOVA 2
PRAGUE 2, 120 00
CZECH REPUBLIC
TEL: +42 2 2421 62 21
FAX: +42 2 2422 24 75

SVOBADA GRAFICKÉ ZAVODY
SAZECSKA 8
PRAGUE, 108 25
CZECH REPUBLIC
TEL: +42 2 703414
FAX: +42 2 702788

DENMARK

DANSK FLEXO FORUM
SVANEMOSEVEJ 2
VARNDRUP 6580 DENMARK
TEL: +45-75-59-49-09
FAX: +45-75-59-49-09

MASTER PRINTERS IN THE
   PROVINCES OF DENMARK
BOGTRYKERNES HUS, HELGAVEJ 26
ODENSE, DK-5100, DENMARK
TEL: +45 9 130601

SCANDINAVIAN PACKAGING
   ASSOCIATION (SPA)
P O BOX 141
2630 TAASTRUP, DENMARK
TEL: +45-7220-3185

ECUADOR

ASSOCIATION DE INDUSTRIALES
   GRAFICOS DE PINCHINCHA
EDIFICOS LAS CAMARAS
AVE. REPUBLICA Y AMAZONES
QUITO, ECUADOR

GRUPO IMPRENTA MARISCAL
6 DE DICIEMBRE 7015 E ISLA ISABELA
QUITO, ECUADOR
TEL: +593 2 449 710
FAX: +593 2 449 713

FINLAND

FINNISH PACKAGING ASSOCIATION
SUOMEN PAKKAUSYHDISTYS
RITARIKATU 3 B.A.
HELSINKI 00170 FINLAND
TEL: +358-1-9-684-0340
FAX: +358-1-9-6840-3410

GRAAFISEN TEOLLISUUDEN LIITTO
LONNROTINKATU 11A
HELSINKI 12, SF - 00120, FINLAND
TEL: +358 1 9 228 77200
FAX: +358 1 9 603 527

KIRJAPAINOTEOLLISUUDEN
   LIITTO R.Y.
ARKADIANKATU 19 D 49
HELSINKI, SF-00100, FINLAND
TEL: +358 1 9 445 152
FAX: +358 1 9 492 172

FRANCE

ASSOCIATION OF PRINTING
COMPANIES AND THE GRAPHICS
INDUSTRIES
11 BOULEVARD DES RECOLLETS
TOULOUSE CEDEX, F-31078
FRANCE

ATF (FRANCE)
15, RUE L' ABBE GREGOIRE
PARIS, 75006 FRANCE
TEL: +33-1-45-44-13-37
FAX: +33-1-45-48-44-74

FEDERATION FRANÇAISE DE
L'IMPRIMERIE ET DE LA
COMMUNICATION GRAPHIQUE
68, BOUL ST. MARCEL
PARIS, 75005 FRANCE
TEL: +33 1 44 08 64 46
FAX: +33 1 43 36 09 51

SIPG
18, CHAMPS-ELYSEES
PARIS, 75008 FRANCE
TEL: +33 1 41 11 60 09
FAX: +33 1 41 11 60 01

GERMANY

DFTA (GERMANY)
NOBELSTRASSE 58
STUTTGART 70569 GERMANY
TEL: +49-0711-679 600
FAX: +49-0711-679 6020

FEDERAL ASSOC. OF THE PRINTING
INDUSTRY
BUNDESVERBAND DRUCK E.V.
BIEBRICHERALLEE 79
WIESBADEN, D-65187, GERMANY
TEL: +49 611 80 30
FAX: +49 611 3113

IFRA
WASHINGTONPLATZ 1
DARMSTADT, 64287 GERMANY
TEL: +49 6151 733-6
FAX: +49 6151 733-800

INSTITUT OF SURFACE MODIFICATION
PERMOSERSTRASSE
LEIPZIG D-04303 GERMANY
TEL: +49-341-2400
FAX: +49-341-3400

GREECE

HELLENIC FEDERATION OF
PRINTING INDUSTRIES
245 SYNGROU AVENUE
ATHENS, GR-171 22, GREECE
TEL: +30 1 93 00 440
FAX: +30 1 94 25 091

HUNGARY

FEDERATION OF HUNGARIAN
PRINTERS
EÖTVÖS U.12
BUDAPEST, H-1067, HUNGARY
TEL: +36 1 1 352 1788
FAX: +36 1 1 352 1791

ICELAND

FEDERATION OF ICELANDIC
INDUSTRIES
PO BOX 1450
REYKJAVIK, 121, ICELAND
FAX: +354 511 5566

INDIA

ALL INDIA FEDERATION OF MASTER
PRINTERS
A-370, 2ND FLOOR, DEFENSE COLONY
NEW DELHI, 110 024, INDIA
TEL: +91 11 2460 1571
FAX: +91 11 2460 1570

FED OF CORRUGATED BOX MFRS
138, MITTAL INDUSTRIAL ESTATE, NO. 3
M. VASANJI ROAD, ANDHERI (EAST)
MUMBAI 400 059, INDIA
TEL: +91-22-2850-0687
FAX: +91-22-2850-4523

INDORE FLEXO GRAPHERS
ASSOCIATION
43/4 B.L.C. MARG
INDORE 452 009 INDIA
TEL: +91-7-2-31-282 933
FAX: +91-7-2-31-476 833

IPAMA
B-51, 2ND FLOOR, SEC 7, NOIDA
NEW DELHI, 101 301, INDIA
TEL: +91 11 28 535 191
FAX: +91 11 28 535 191

INDONESIA

ASSOCIATION OF INDONESIAN
PHOTOGRAVURE INDUSTRIES
23/F GAJAH MADA TOWER
JL GAJAH MADA
JAKARTA PUSAT, 12-26, INDONESIA
TEL: +62 21 36 6070 EXT.2301

ASSOCIATION OF INDONESIAN
PRINTERS
JL BANGKA 2-C/3
JAKARTA, SLATTERN, INDONESIA
TEL: +62 21 799 1320

INDONESIAN GRAPHIC COMPANIES
ASSOCIATION
C/O SUMBER BAHAGIA PT IND.
ESTATE
PULONGADUNG 6, JL RAWATERATE II
JAKARTA 13930, INDONESIA
TEL: +62 21 489 0200

INDONESIA MASTER PRINTING
ASSOCIATION
C/O PT SUMBER BAGHAGIA
GEDUNG, KRAMAT CENTRE, BLK D,
NO. 5
JAKARTA PUSAT, RAYA NO. 7
INDONESIA

INDONESIAN PACKAGING INSTITUTE
JL. CIKINI IV/8
JAKARTA 10330 INDONESIA
TEL: +62-21-314-3641
FAX: +62-21-314-3663

IRELAND

IRISH MASTER PRINTER'S
ASSOCIATION
33 PARKGATE STREET
DUBLIN, 8, IRELAND
TEL: +353 1 679 3679
FAX: +353 1 677 9144

IRISH PRINTING FEDERATION
BAGGOT BRIDGE HOUSE
84-86 LOWER BAGGOT STREET
DUBLIN, 2, IRELAND
TEL: +353 1 601011
FAX: +353 1 601717

NATIONAL GRAPHICAL ASSOCIATION
107 CLONSKEAGH ROAD
DUBLIN, 6, IRELAND

ISRAEL

BOOK PUBLISHERS ASSOCIATION OF
    ISRAEL
29, CARLEBACH STREET
PO BOX 20123
TEL AVIV, 67132, ISRAEL
TEL: +972 3 561 4121
FAX: +972 3 561 1996

MANUFACTURING ASSN. OF
    ISRAEL/PRINTING DEPT.
29 HAMERED STREET
PO BOX 50022
TEL AVIV, ISRAEL
TEL: +972 3 512 8846
FAX: +972 3 66 2026

ITALY

ACIMGA
ITALIAN MANUFACTURERS
    ASSOCIATION OF MACHINERY FOR
    THE GRAPHIC, CONVERTING AND
    PAPER INDUSTRY
C.SO SEMPIONE 4
MILAN, 20154 ITALY
TEL: +39 02 3191 091
FAX: +39 02 3450 647

ATIF-ASSOC TECNICA ITALIANA PER
    LO SVIL D FLESSOGRAFIA
CORSO SEMPIONE 4
20154 MILAN, ITALY
TEL: +39-02-319-1091
FAX: +39-02-345-0647

ISTITUTO POLIGRAFICO E ZECCA
    DELLO STATO
PIAZZA GIUSEPPE VERDI, 10
00198 ROME, ITALY
TEL: +39-06-85081
FAX: +39-06-854-2192

ITALIAN PRINTING AND PAPER
    CONVERTING INDUSTRIES
    ASSOCIATION (ASSOGRAFICI)
PIAZZA CONCILIAZIONE 1
MILAN, 20123 ITALY
TEL: +39 02 498 10 51
FAX: +39 02 481 69 47

TECHNICAL ASSOCIATION OF
    ITALIAN GRAPHIC ARTS
VIA SANDRO BOTTICELLI 19
MILAN, I-20133, ITALY
TEL: +39 02 236 4558

JAPAN

ASSOCIATION FOR GRAPHIC ARTS
    AND MATERIALS
3-21-4 MINAMI-OHI, SHINAGAWA-KU
TOKYO, 140, JAPAN
TEL: +81 3 37 63 4141

FTAJ-FLEXOGRAPHIC TECH ASSN
    OF JAPAN
3-16 SHINOGAWA-MACHI,
    SHINJUKI-KU
TOKYO 162-0841 JAPAN
TEL: +81-3-3267-6231
FAX: +81-3-3268-5265

JAPAN ASSOCIATION OF GRAPHIC
    ARTS TECHNOLOGY
1-29-11 WADA, SUGINAMI
TOKYO , 166, JAPAN
TEL: +81 3 3384 3111
FAX: +81 3 3384 3116

JAPAN CORRUGATED CASE ASSN
KAMI-PARUPU KALKAN, 9-11, 3-CHOME
GINZA, CHUO-KU,
TOKYO 104-8139 JAPAN
TEL: +81-3-3248-4851
FAX: +81-3-5550-2101

JAPAN FEDERATION OF PRINTING
    INDUSTRIES
1-16-8 SHINTOMI, 1-CHOME
CHUO-KU, TOKYO, 104, JAPAN
TEL: +81 33 553 6501
FAX: +81 33 553 6079

JAPAN LIGHT-PRINTING INDUSTRIES
    ASSOCIATION
7-16 NIHONBASHI, KODEMA-CHO
CHOU-KU, TOKYO, JAPAN
TEL: +81 33 667 2271

JAPAN PRINTING INK MAKERS
    ASSOCIATION
TOKYO CLUB BUILDING, 2-6
    KASUMIGASEKI
3-CHOME, CHIYODA-KU
TOKYO, 100, JAPAN
TEL: +81 33 580 0876
FAX: +81 33 580 0857

JAPAN PRINTING MACHINERY MANU-
    FACTURERS ASSOCIATION
KIKAI SHINKO KAIKAN BLDG
3-5-8 SHIBAKOEN, MINATO-KU
TOKYO, 105, JAPAN
TEL: +81 33 434 4661
FAX: +81 33 434 0301

JAPANESE SOCIETY OF PRINTING
    SCIENCE & TECHNOLOGY
1-16-8 SHINTOMI, CHUO-KU
TOKYO 104-0041 JAPAN
TEL: +81-3-3551-1808
FAX: +81-3-3552-7206

NATIONAL CORRUGATED CASE ASSN
ANWA-TAKARA-CHO, BDG 5F,
    1-3,4-CHOME
HACCHOBORI, CHUO-KU
TOKYO 104-0032 JAPAN
TEL: +81-3-3551-6111
FAX: +81-3-3551-6113

TOKYO PRINTING INDUSTRY
    ASSOCIATION
NIHON INSATSU KAIAN, 16-8
    SHINTOMI
1-CHOME, CHUO-KU
TOKYO, 104, JAPAN
TEL: +81 33 552 4042

KOREA

KOREA BOOKBINDING INDUSTRY
    COOPERATIVE
614-7 AHYON-DONG, MAPO-GU
SEOUL, KOREA
TEL: +82 2 362 7182

KOREA CORRUGATED PACKING CASE
    INDUSTRY ASSN
6F, SEONGSAN BLDG, 1669,
    BANGBEE-DONG
SEOCHU-GU, SEOUL, KOREA
TEL: +82-2-594-0381-4
FAX: +82-2-594-1310

KOREA FEDERATION OF PRINTING
    INDUSTRY COOPERATIVES
C/O KOREAN PRINTING CULTURAL
    CENTER
352-26 SOGYO-DONG, MAPO-GU
SEOUL, KOREA
TEL: +82 2 335 6161
FAX: +82 2 334 6773

KOREAN INSTITUTE OF PACKAGING
    INDUSTRY
2F SOMON BLDG 699-21 YOKSAMDON
KANHNAMKU, SEOUL VA5-080 KOREA
TEL: +82-2-540-428-2092
FAX: +82-2-540-814-4961

KOREAN PRINTERS ASSOCIATION
352-26 SOGYO-DONG, MAPO-GU
SEOUL, KOREA
TEL: +82 2 335 5881 EX 3
FAX: +82 2 338 9801

KOREAN PUBLISHERS ASSN
105-2 SAGAN-DONG,
SEOUL, 100 190, KOREA
TEL: +82 2 735 2701
FAX: +82 2 738 5414

KOREAN PUBLISHERS COOPERATIVE
448-6 SHINSU-DONG, MAPO-GU
SEOUL, 100 KOREA
TEL: +82 2 716 5621
FAX: +82 2 716 2995

LUXEMBOURG

ASSOCIATION DES MAITRES
    IMPREMEURS DE GRAND-DUCHE
    DE LUXEMBOURG
2 CIRCUIT DE LA FOIRE
    INTERNATIONALE
BP 1604, LUXEMBOURG, L-1604
LUXEMBOURG
TEL: +352 42 451122
FAX: +352 42 4525

MEXICO

ASOCIACIÓN NACIONAL DE
    INDUSTRIALES Y DISTRIBUIDORES
    PARA LA INDUSTRIA GRÁFICA, A.C.
    (ANIDIGRAF)
INDIANA NO. 57-59, COL. NÁPOLES,
CP 03810, MEXICO DF, MEXICO
TEL: +52 5 536 2533
FAX: +52 5 536 2340

ASSN TECNICA MEXICANA DE
    FLEXOGRAFIA
RIO MIXCOAC Nº 36, DEPT 301-B
COL ACTIPAN, MEXICO DF MEXICO
TEL: +52-5-534-9351
FAX: +52-5-534-2884

CANAGRAF
AV. RIO CHURUBUSCO NO. 428
COL. DEL CARMEN, DEL. COYOACAN
MEXICO DF, 04100, MEXICO
TEL: +52 5 659 1520
FAX: +52 5 554 3545

UNION DE INDUSTIALES
    LITOGRAFOS DE MEXICO, A.C.
CERRO DE LAS TORRES 265
CAMPESTRE CHURUBUSCO
MEXICO DF, 04200, MEXICO
TEL: +52 5 549 2597
FAX: +52 5 549 2637

NETHERLANDS

EFTA BENELUX (HOLLAND)
LAAN COPES VAN CATTERBURCH 79
THE HAGUE, 2585 EW, NETHERLANDS
TEL: +31-70-312-3918
FAX: +31-70-363-6348

EUROPEAN FEDERATION FOR THE
    FLEXIBLE PACKAGING INDUSTRY
LAAN COPES VAN CATTENBURCH 79
2585 EW, THE HAGUE, NETHERLANDS
TEL: +31-70-312-3913
FAX: +31-70-363-6348

KVGO
STARTBAAN, 10
POSTBUS 220
AMSTERDAM, NL-1180 AE
NETHERLANDS
TEL: +31 20 547 5678
FAX: +31 20 547 5475

VEREINIGING VAN LEVERANCIERS
    VOOR DE GRAFISCHE EN
    AANVERWANTE INDUSTRIE (VLGA)
ADRIAAN GOEKOOPLAAN 5
2517 JX DEN HAAG
POSTBUS 29822
2502 LV DEN HAAG, NETHERLANDS
TEL: +31-070 338 46 63
FAX: +31-070 351 27 77

VEREINIGEN VAN NEDERLANDSE
    FABRIKANTEN VAN
    KARTONNAGES EN FLEXIBLE VER-
    PAKKINGEN
POSTBUS 220
AMSTELVEEN 1180 AE,
    NETHERLANDS
TEL: +31-20-547-5678
FAX: +31-20-547-5475

NEW ZEALAND

FLEXIBLE PACKAGING ASSOCITION
    OF NEW ZEALAND
P O BOX 76-378, MANUKUA CITY
AUCKLAND 1701 NEW ZEALAND
TEL: +64-9-262-3773
FAX: +64-9-262-3850

NEW ZEALAND PAPERBOARD
    PACKAGING ASSOCIATION
P O BOX 28245
REMUERA, AUCKLAND, NEW
    ZEALAND
TEL: +64-9-520-2044

PRINTING INDUSTRIES OF NEW
    ZEALAND
HUDDART PARKER BUILDING
POST OFFICE SQUARE 6001
WELLINGTON, 6001, NEW ZEALAND
TEL: +64 4 472 3497
FAX: +64 4 472 3534

NORWAY

GRAFISKE BEDRIFTER
    LANDSFORENING HAVNELAGERET
LANGKAIA, 1
OSLO, N-0150, NORWAY
TEL: +47 22 41 2180
FAX: +47 22 33 6972

NORSK FLEXO FORUM
KARENSLYSTALLE 9A
POSTBOKS 442 SKOYEN
OSLO N-0212 NORWAY
TEL: +47-2212-1760
FAX: +47-2212-1761

NORWEGIAN FEDERATION OF
    GRAPHIC ENTERPRISES
AKERSGATAN 16
OSLO 1, NORWAY
TEL: +47 22 41 2180

PAKISTAN

PAKISTAN ASSOCIATION OF GRAPHIC
    ARTS INDUSTRY
16-A MOHAMMED ALI ROAD
KARACHI, 0812, PAKISTAN

PARAGUAY

ASOCIACION DE INDUSTRIALE
    GRAFICOS DEL PARAGUAY
AYOLAS NO 1627
ASUNCIÓN, PARAGUAY
TEL: +59 5 21 71 163

CENTRO DE CAPACITACION EN ARTES
    GRAFICAS
PARIS 1018 ESQ. COLON
ASUNCION, PARAGUAY
TEL: +59 5 21 83 038
FAX: +59 5 21 83 038

PERU

ASOCIACION PARA LA
    INVESTIGACION Y TECHNICAS
    GRAFICA (APITG)
AV. COLONIAL 2140
LIMA 1 PERU
TEL: +51-1-452-3759
FAX: +51-1-452-4473

PHILIPPINES

PHILIPPINE PRINTING TECHNICAL
    FOUNDATION
2ND FL SCC CHEVELIER CENTER
    BLDG.
3892 R. MAGSAYSAY BLVD.
MANILA , PHILIPPINES

PRINTING INDUSTRIES ASSOCIATION
    OF THE PHILIPPINES, INC.
SUITE 212 DELA ROSA CONDOMINIUM
7648 DELA ROSA STREET
MAKATI CITY, PHILIPPINES
TEL: +632 894 5224
FAX: +632 894 5224

POLAND

ABIX
UL. WYNALAZEK 2
WARSAW, 02-672, POLAND
TEL: +48 22 43 85 11

INSTITUT FUR DRUCK
UL KONWIKTORSKA 2
WARSAW, 00-217, POLAND
TEL: +48 22 635 47 98
FAX: +48 22 635 50 44

POLISH CHAMBER OF PRINTING
UL. MIEDZIANA 11
WARSAW, 00-835, POLAND
TEL: +48 22 624 87 49
FAX: +48 22 620 02 81 (497)

PLFTA
ZRZESENIE POLSKICH
    FLEKSOGRAFOW
UL STAWRI 14
WARSZAWA 00-178 POLAND
TEL: +48-22-644-76-30
FAX: +48-22-644-76-30

PORTUGAL

APIGTP
LARGO DO CASAL VISTOSO,
    2/D-ESC. B.
LISBON, 1900, PORTUGAL
TEL: +351-1-849 1020
FAX: +351-1-847 0778

ROMANIA

OPTR
STR. ION BREZOLANU NR 23-25
SECTOR 1, BUCHAREST, ROMANIA
TEL: +40 1 616 1701
FAX: +40 1 312 7039

RUSSIA

RUSSIAN RESEARCH INSTITUTE FOR
    GRAPHIC ARTS
STAROPETROVSKY PR. 11
MOSCOW, 125130, RUSSIA
TEL: +7 095 153 8280
FAX: +7 095 159 4723

SERBIA

CELULOZE, PAPIRNE I GRAFICKE
    INDUSTIJE I
IZDAVACKE DELATNOSTI,
    TERAZIJE 23
BEOGRAD, 11000, SERBIA

SIERRA LEONE

SIERRA LEONE ASSOC. OF MASTER
    PRINTERS
C/O ODUNTOR PRINTING PRESS
61 SOLDIER STREET
FREETOWN, SIERRA LEONE
TEL: +232-22 5706

SINGAPORE

MASTER PRINTERS ASSOCIATION
68 LORONG 16 GAYLAND #04-02
ASSOCIATION BUILDING
SINGAPORE, 1439, SINGAPORE
TEL: +65 6 745 6913
FAX: +65 6 745 6916

SINGAPORE BOOK PUBLISHERS'
    ASSOCIATION
C/O OCTOPUS PUBLISHING ASIA PTE.
    LTD
37 JL, PEMIMPIN #07-04
BLOCK B, UNION IND. BUILDING
SINGAPORE, 2057, SINGAPORE
TEL: +65 6 258 3255
FAX: +65 6 258 8279

SLOVAK REPUBLIC

PRINTING INDUSTRIES OF THE
    SLOVAK REPUBLIC
DRIENOVA 24, BRATISLAVA, 82603
SLOVAK REPUBLIC
TEL: +42 7 2997 330
FAX: +42 7 2335 42

SOUTH AFRICA

CORRUGATED AND PAPERBOARD
    INDUSTRIES ASSOCIATION OF
    SOUTH AFRICA
P O BOX 1084
HONEYDEW 2040 SOUTH AFRICA
TEL: +27-11-794-3810/8
FAX: +27-11-794-3964

FTASA SOUTH AFRICA
PRIVATE BAG X2
ST FRANCIS BAY 6312 SOUTH AFRICA
TEL: +27-42-298-0014
FAX: +27-42-298-0014

INSTITUTE OF PACKAGING
P O BOX 2271
CLAREINCH 7740 SOUTH AFRICA
TEL: +27-21-611-140
FAX: +27-21-611-384

PRINTING IND FED OF SOUTH AFRICA
PRINTECH AVENUE/LASER PARK
HONEYDEW 2040 SOUTH AFRICA
TEL: +27-11-794-3810
FAX: +27-11-794-3964

SPAIN

ANFEC-ASOCIACION NACIONAL
    FABRICANTES ETIQUERAS
    CONTINUO
GRAN VIA CORTS CATALANES, 645
BARCELONA 08025 SPAIN
TEL: +34-93-481-3163
FAX: +34-93-481-3173

ATEF (SPAIN), ASSOC GRAPHICPACK
PLAZA DE ESPANA s/n
FIRA DE BARC, BARCELONA 08004
    SPAIN
TEL: +34-93-233-2250
FAX: +34-93-233-2252

FEDERACION EMPRESARIAL DE
    INDUSTRIAS GRAFICAS DE ESPANA
BARQUILLO 11, 4 D
MADRID, E-28004, SPAIN
TEL: +34 1 522 9084
FAX: +34 1 532 6745

GRAPHISPACK
PLAZA D'ESPANYA S/N°
    (FIERA DE BARCELONA)
BARCELONA, 08004 SPAIN
TEL: +34 932 332 250
FAX: +34 932 332 252

NATIONAL ASSOCIATION OF PAPER
    AND GRAPHIC ARTS
FERNANDEZ DE LA HOZ 12
MADRID, 28004 SPAIN

SPANISH ASSOCIATION FOR THE
    DEVELOPMENT OF THE
    GRAPHIC ARTS
JESUS MAESTRO S/N
MADRID, 28003 SPAIN
TEL: +34-1-234 5359

SUDAN

SUDANESE PRINTERS AND
  PUBLISHERS ASSOCIATION
PO BOX 136, KHARTOUM, SUDAN

SWEDEN

GRAFISKA FORETAGENS FÖRBUND
BOX 16 383
STOCKHOLM, S- 103 27, SWEDEN
TEL: +46 8 762 6800
FAX: +46 8 611 0828

GRUPPEN GRAFISKA MASKINER
C/O SVERIGES MEKANFORBUND
BOX 5506
STOCKHOLM, S-114 85, SWEDEN
TEL: +46 8 783 8200
FAX: +46 8 660 3378

SWEDISH PRINTING INDUSTRIES
  FEDERATION
SANKT ERIKSGATAN 26 111
PO BOX 12069
STOCKHOLM, S-102 22, SWEDEN
TEL: +46 8 598 99097

SVENSK FLEXOGRAFIFORENING
c/o BROBY GRAFISKA
SUNNE S-686 00 SWEDEN
TEL: +46-565-17900
FAX: +46-565-17901

SVENSKA FORPACKINGSFORENINGEN
POSTBOKS 9038
DRAKENBERGSGATAN 61
STOCKHOLM S-102 71 SWEDEN

WORLD PACKAGING ORGANIZATION
  (WPO)
P O BOX 9
SE-16493
KISTA, SWEDEN

SWITZERLAND

ASAG
POSTFACH 39, CARMENSTRASSE 6
ZURICH, CH-8030 SWITZERLAND
TEL: +41 1 252 1440
FAX: +41 1 252 1743

ASSOCIATION OF THE SWISS
  PRINTING INDUSTRY
SCHOSSHALDESTRASSE 20
POSTFACH 3000
BERN, CH-3000, SWITZERLAND
TEL: +41 31 43 1515
FAX: +41 31 44 3738

DIVISION OF TRADE SERVICE, INTL
TRADE CENTER, UNCTAD, PAL DES
  NATIONS
GENEVA, CH-1211 SWITZERLAND
TEL: +41-22-907-1234
FAX: +41-22-907-0043

EMPA
POSTFACH 977
ST GALLEN, CH-9001, SWITZERLAND
TEL: +41 71 209 141
FAX: +41 71 227 220

SWISS ASSOCIATION FOR VISUAL
  COMMUNICATION
CARMENSTRASSE 6
ZURICH, CH-8030, SWITZERLAND
TEL: +41 1 266 2424
FAX: +41 1 266 2425

VERBANDES DER SCHWEIZER
  DRUCKINDUSTRIE
BERN 32
CH-3000 SWITZERLAND

VFI (SWITZERLAND)
BERGSTRASSE 110
POSTF 134, ZURICH 8030 SWITZERLAND
TEL: +41-1-266-99-30
FAX: +41-1-266-99-49

TAIWAN

CHINA PRINTING TECHNOLOGY
  ASSOCIATION ROC
165 HSING-AN ROAD
PEITUN DISTRICT
TAICHUNG, TAIWAN
TEL: +886 4 236 7217
FAX: +886 4 236 4564

TAIPEI COMMERCIAL PRINTING
  ASSOCIATION
7F 220 KUNMING ST.
TAIPEI, TAIWAN
TEL: +886 2 505 5206

TAIPEI COMMERCIAL PUBLISHERS
  ASSOCIATION
1/F 6 LANE 168
CHUNG HUA ROAD, SEC. 1
TAIPEI, 10817, TAIWAN
TEL: +886 2 371 8325

TAIWAN PAPER CONTAINERS
  INDUSTRY ASSN
10-1 FL 33, MIN SHENG RD,
  SEC 1, PAN CH
TAIPEI, HSIEN TAIWAN
TEL: +886-2-3959-9394
FAX: +886-2-2959-9395

TAIWAN PRINTING INDUSTRIAL
  ASSOCIATION
RM. A 6/F 71, JEN AI ROAD
SEC. 4, TAIPEI, TAIWAN
TEL: +886 2 391 9274
FAX: +886 2 391 9294

TAIWAN PRINTING INDUSTRY
  ASSOCIATION
64 CHUNG-HSIAO ROAD
TAICHUNG, TAIWAN
TEL: +886 4 287 1181
FAX: +886 4 287 1066

THAILAND

THAI COLOR SEPARATION
  ASSOCIATION
C/F 111/10-12 RACHADAMNOEN
  CONDOMINIUM
NAKORNSAWAN ROAD, POMPRAB
BANGKOK, 10200, THAILAND
TEL: +66 2 282 0148
FAX: +66 2 217 9580

THAI PRINTING ASSOCIATION
158/2-4 NEW RAMA VI ROAD
PRATUMWAN
BANGKOK, 10330, THAILAND
TEL: +66 2 214 3982
FAX: +66 2 254 6151

UKRAINE

UFTA (UKRAINE)
ORLOVSKAYA STR 16-21
KYIV 252 060 UKRAINE
TEL: +380-44-516-5261
FAX: +380-44-516-5785

UNITED KINGDOM

BRITISH BOX & PACKAGING
  ASSOCIATION
64 HIGH STREET
KIRKINTILLOCH
GLASGOW, G66 1PR, UNITED KINGDOM
TEL: +44-141-777-7272
FAX: +44-141-777-7747

BRITISH PRINTING INDUSTRIES
  FEDERATION
11 BEDFORD ROW
LONDON WC1R 3DX UNITED KINGDOM
TEL: +44 171 242 6904
FAX: +44 171 405 7784

CORRUGATED PACKAGING
    ASSOCIATION
2 SAXON COURT, FREESCHOOL
    STREET
NORTHAMPTON NN1 1ST, UNITED
    KINGDOM
TEL: +44-1604-621-002
FAX: +44-1604-620-636

EUROPEAN FTA (UNITED KINGDOM)
4/5 BRIDGE BARNS, LANGPORT RD
LONG SUTTON, SOMERSET
UNITED KINGDOM
TEL: +44-1458-241 455
FAX: +44-1458-241 684

INDUSTRY COUNCIL FOR PACKAGING
    AND THE ENVIRONMENT
TENTERDEN HOUSE, 3 TENTERDEN
    STREET
LONDON W1R 9AH UNITED KINGDOM
TEL: +44-207-409-0949
FAX: +44-207-409-0161

INSTITUTE OF PACKAGING
SYSONBY LODGE, NOTTINGHAM ROAD
MELTON MOWBRAY, LEICS LE13 0NU
UNITED KINGDOM
TEL: +44-1664-500-055
FAX: +44-1664-64164

INSTITUTE OF PRINTING
THE MEWS, HILL HOUSE,
    CLANRICADE ROAD
TONBRIDGE WELLS, KENT
TN1 1PJ, UNITED KINGDOM
TEL: +44-1892-535-118
FAX: +44-1892-518-028

PIRA
RANDALLS ROAD, LEATHERHEAD,
SURREY KT22 7RU UNITED KINGDOM
TEL: +44-1372-802-000
FAX: +44-1372-802-239

SOCIETY OF MASTER PRINTERS OF
    SCOTLAND
48 PALMERSTON PLACE
EDINBURGH, EH12 5DE
UNITED KINGDOM
TEL: +44 31 220 4353
FAX: +44 31 220 4344

VENEZUELA

AIGES
CONGLOMERADO DE MELENDEZ,
    GALPON 13-A
CUMANA - EDO SUCRE DEL ESTADO
    SUCRE
CARACAS, VENEZUELA
TEL: +58 93 66 3923
FAX: +58 93 66 2359

CAINGRA
AV. 4 BELLA VISTA C/CALLE 67,
    CECILIO ACOSTA
EDIF TORRE SOCUY, 2DO PISO,
    MARACAIBO
EDO. ZULIA, CARACAS, VENEZUELA
TEL: +58 61 92 0762
FAX: +58 61 92 3057

VIETNAM

PRINTEXIM
16-32 PHAN VAN DAT ST.
DIST. 1
HO CHI MINH CITY, VIETNAM
TEL: +84 8 29 6151

ZAMBIA

PRINTERS ASSOCIATION OF ZAMBIA
C/O THE SCHOOL OF PRINTING
EVELYN HONE COLLEGE
PO BOX 33850
LUSAKA, 10101, ZAMBIA

APPENDIX **V**

Printing Industry and
Environmental Publications

SOURCE:
Jelmar Publishing Co., Inc.

Printing and Packaging publications are included in this listing. Most publications concerned with packaging also editorially cover the printing of such packaging, whether performed by separate packaging converters or performed inplant where the product is actually packaged.

This list includes most major trade publications throughout the world, verified insofar as possible, from the latest information available. It has not been possible to obtain all the data that are appropriate, e.g., telephone and fax numbers, without making contact with each and every publication. This would be an unrealistic undertaking for this purpose, in view of the fact that there are several hundred publications listed here.

We have attempted to avoid listing publications which are of such a specialized mature that they are of interest to only a very small segment of the printing/packaging industry. The people who are involved in the technologies covered by such specialized publications (peer-reviewed issues, government publications, newsletters, proceedings of meetings and conventions, and the like) are usually well aware of them. The listings here, therefore, are for the generalist, not the specialist, designed to be of assistance to those persons in the printing field who require non-specialized information about the industry and its technologies.

*Printing and
Package
Printing
Publications*

469

UNITED STATES

ADHESIVES & SEALANTS
NEWSLETTER
7979 OLD GEORGETOWN RD, STE 500
BETHESDA, MD 20814
TEL: 301-986-9700
FAX: 301-986-9795

AMERICAN PRINTER
29 NORTH WACKER DRIVE
CHICAGO, IL 60606
TEL: 312-726-2802
FAX: 312-726-3091

ARTES GRAFICAS
901 PONCE DE LEON BLVD, SUITE 901
CORAL GABLES, FL 33134-3073
TEL: 561-879-6666
FAX: 561-879-7388

BOARD CONVERTING NEWS
43 MAIN STREET
AVON ON THE SEA, NJ 07717
TEL: 732-502-0500
FAX: 732-502-9606

BOXBOARD CONTAINERS
29 NORTH WACKER DRIVE
CHICAGO, IL 60606
TEL: 312-726-2802
FAX: 312-726-4100

BRAND PACKAGING
210 SOUTH 5TH STREET, STE 202
ST. CHARLES, IL 60164
TEL: 630-377-0100
FAX: 630-377-1678

BUSINESS FORMS, LABELS AND
SYSTEMS
401 NORTH BROAD STREET
PHILADELPHIA, PA 19108
TEL: 215-238-5300
FAX: 215-238-5457

CANDY INDUSTRY
155 PFINGSTEN ROAD, SUITE 205
DEERFIELD , IL 60015
TEL: 847-205-5660
FAX: 847-205-5680

COATINGS WORLD
17 SOUTH FRANKLIN TURNPIKE
RAMSEY, NJ 07446
TEL: 201-825-5225
FAX: 201-825-0553

CONVERSION Y EMPAQUES
901 PONCE DE LEON BLVD
CORAL GABLES, FL 33134
TEL: 561-879-6666
FAX: 561-879-7388

CONVERTING MAGAZINE
1350 EAST TOUHY AVENUE
DES PLAINES, IL 60018-3358
TEL: 847-390-2405
FAX: 847-390-2460

CORRUGATING INTERNATIONAL
TECHNOLOGY PARK/ATLANTA
BOX 105113,
ATLANTA, GA 30348
TEL: 770-446-1400
FAX: 770-209-7517

COSMETIC/PERSONAL CARE
PACKAGING
11444 WEST OLYMPIC BLVD.
LOS ANGELES, CA 90064
TEL: 310-445-4200
FAX: 310-445-4269

DOCUMENT PROCESSING
TECHNOLOGY
2424 AMERICAN LANE
MADISON, WI 53704-3102
TEL: 608-241-8777
FAX: 608-241-8666

EMPAQUE PERFORMANCE
8508 PLUM CREEK DR.
GAITHERSBERG, MD 20882
TEL: 301-869-6610
FAX: 301-869-6611

FLEXIBLE PACKAGING
210 SOUTH 5TH ST, STE 202
ST. CHARLES, IL 60174
TEL: 630-377-0100
FAX: 630-377-1678

FLEXO
900 MARCONI AVENUE
RONRONKOMA, NY 11779
TEL: 516-737-6023
FAX: 516-737-6813

FLEXO MARKET NEWS
43 MAIN STREET
AVON ON THE SEA, NJ 07717
TEL: 847-498-5850
FAX: 847-498-1187

FOOD & DRUG PACKAGING
210 SOUTH 5TH STREET, SUITE 202
ST CHARLES, IL 60174
TEL: 630-377-0100
FAX: 630-377-1678

GATF WORLD
200 DEER RUN ROAD
SEWICKLEY, PA 15743-2600
TEL: 412-621-6941
FAX: 412-621-3049

GRAPHIC ARTS MONTHLY
360 PARK AVENUE SOUTH
NEW YORK, NY 10010
TEL: 646-746-7321
FAX: 646-746-7489

GRAPHIC COMMUNICATIONS WORLD
P O BOX 1126
PORT ORCHARD, WA 98366
TEL: 360-769-5617
FAX: 360-769-5622

GRAPHIC NETWORK
729 WASHINGTON AVENUE
PITTSBURGH, PA 15228
TEL: 412-341-3741
FAX: 412-341-6344

GRAPHIC NEWS
2829 UNIVERSITY AVE, S.E., SUITE 750
MINNEAPOLIS, MN 55410-3230
TEL: 612-369-6003
FAX: 612-379-6030

GRAPHICS UPDATE
P O BOX 170 010
HIALEAH, FL 33017-0010
TEL: 305-558-4855
FAX: 305-823-8965

GRAVURE
1200-A SCOTTSVILLE RD
ROCHESTER, NY 14624
TEL: 585-436-2150
FAX: 585-436-7689

HIGH VOLUME PRINTING
PO BOX 7280
LIBERTYVILLE, IL 60048-7280
TEL: 847-816-7900
FAX: 847-247-8855

INK MAKER
445 BROADHOLLOW ROAD, SUITE 21
MELVILLE, NY 11747-3601
TEL: 631-845-2700
FAX: 631-845-7109

INK WORLD
17 SOUTH FRANKLIN TURNPIKE
RAMSEY, NJ 07446
TEL: 201-825-2552
FAX: 201-825-0553

INPRO LATINA
2666 TIGERTAIL AVE., STE 108
MIAMI, FL 33133
TEL: 303-285-3133
FAX: 303-285-3134

INSTANT AND SMALL COMMERCIAL
    PRINTER
P O BOX 7280
LIBERTYVILLE, IL 60048-7280
TEL: 847-816-7900
FAX: 847-247-8855

IN-PLANT GRAPHICS
401 NORTH BROAD STREET
PHILADELPHIA, PA 19108
TEL: 215-238-5300
FAX: 215-238-5457

IN-PLANT PRINTER
P O BOX 7280
LIBERTYVILLE, IL 60048-7280
TEL: 847-816-7900
FAX: 847-247-8855

INTL METAL DECORATOR MAGAZINE
9616 DEERECO ROAD
TIMONIUM, MD 21093
TEL: 410-252-5205
FAX: 410-628-8079

INTERNATIONAL PAPERBOARD
    INDUSTRY
43 MAIN STREET
AVON-ON-THE-SEA NJ 07717
TEL: 732-502-0500
FAX: 732-502-9606

LABEL & NARROW WEB
17 SOUTH FRANKLIN PIKE
RAMSEY, NJ, 07446-0555
TEL: 201-825-2552
FAX: 201-825-0553

LABELS AND LABELING MAGAZINE
16985 WEST BLUEMOUND ROAD,
    SUITE 210
BROOKFIELD, WI 53005
TEL: 262-782-1900
FAX: 262-782-8474

MARI
43 MAIN STREET
AVON ON THE SEA, NJ 07717
TEL: 732-502-0500
FAX: 732-502-9606

MARI/PAPEL
2666 TIGERTAIL AVE. #198
MIAMI, FL 33133
TEL: 305-285-3133
FAX: 305-285-3134

MODERN REPROGRAPHICS
445 BROADHOLLOW ROAD, SUITE 21
MELVILLE, NY 11747
TEL: 631-845-2700
FAX: 631-845-7109

NEW ENGLAND PRINTER
5 CRYSTAL POND ROAD
SOUTHBOROUGH, MA 01772-1758
TEL: 508-804-4170
FAX: 508-804-4119

NPTA MANAGEMENT NEWS
500 BICOUNTY BLVD., SUITE 200
FARMINGDALE, NY 11735-3921
TEL: 631-777-2223
FAX: 631-777-2224

OFFICIAL BOARD MARKETS
100 WEST MONROE ST., SUITE 1100
CHICAGO, IL 60603-1905
TEL: 312-553-8922
FAX: 312-553-8926

OFFICIAL BOARD MARKETS
7500 OLD OAK BOULEVARD
CLEVELAND, OH 44130
TEL: 440-891-2730
FAX: 440-891-2675

PACKAGE PRINTING & CONVERTING
401 NORTH BROAD STREET
PHILADELPHIA, PA 19108
TEL: 215-238-5300
FAX: 215-238-5457

PACKAGING DIGEST
2000 CLEARWATER DRIVE
OAK BROOK, IL 60523
TEL: 630-320-7429
FAX: 630-320-7457

PACKAGING HORIZONS
4290 BELLS FERRY RD, STE 106-17
KENNESAW, GA 30144-1300
TEL: 770-928-3563
FAX: 770-928-2238

PACKAGING MANAGEMENT
31408 NARRAGANSETT LANE
BAY VILLAGE, OH 44140
TEL: 216-892-0998
FAX: 216-892-0208

PACKAGING STRATEGIES
901 SOUTH BOLMER STREET
WEST CHESTER, PA 19382
TEL: 610-436-4220
FAX: 610-436-6277

PACKAGING TECHNOLOGY &
    ENGINEERING
401 NORTH BROAD STREET
PHILADELPHIA, PA 19108
TEL: 215-238-5300
FAX: 215-238-5457

PACKAGING WORLD
330 NORTH WABASH, SUITE 3131
CHICAGO, IL 60611
TEL: 312-222-1010
FAX: 312-222-1310

PACKINFO
4143 WEEKS DRIVE
P O BOX 861588
WARRENTON, VA 20187
TEL: 540-428-2092
FAX: 504-814-4961

PAPER AGE
77 WALDRON AVENUE, SUITE 5
GLEN ROCK, NJ 07452-2830
TEL: 201-666-2262
FAX: 201-666-9046

PAPERBOARD PACKAGING
7500 OLD OAK BOULEVARD
CLEVELAND, OH 44130
TEL: 440-891-2730
FAX: 440-891-2675

PAPER, FILM & FOIL CONVERTER
29 NORTH WACRER DRIVE
CHICAGO, IL 60606
TEL: 312-726-2802
FAX: 312-726-2574

PAPERLOOP NEW YORK
1250 BROADWAY
NEW YORK, NY 10001
TEL: 212-268-4160
FAX: 212-268-4178

PERSONAL CARE PACKAGING
3 PAOLI PLAZA, SUITE A
PAOLI, PA 19301
TEL: 610-647-8585
FAX: 610-647-8565

PRESHIPMENT TESTING
1400 ABBOTT ROAD, SUITE 310
EAST LANSING, MI 48823-1900
TEL: 519-333-3437
FAX: 517-333-3813

PRINT AND GRAPHICS
445 BROADHOLLOW ROAD, SUITE 21
MELVILLE, NY 11747
TEL: 631-845-2700
FAX: 631-845-7109

PRINTING IMPRESSIONS
401 NORTH BROAD STREET
PHILADELPHIA, PA 19108
TEL: 215-238-5300
FAX: 215-238-5457

PRINTING JOURNAL
445 BROAD HOLLOW ROAD
MELVILLE, NY 11747
TEL: 631-845-2700
FAX: 631-845-7109

PRINTING MANAGER
75 WEST CENTURY ROAD
PARAMUS NJ 07652-1408
TEL: 20I-634-9600
FAX: 201-634-0324

PRINTING NEWS
445 BROADHOLLOW ROAD, STE 21
MELVILLE, NY 11747-3601
TEL: 516-845-2700
FAX: 516-845-7109

PRINTMEDIA
401 NORTH BROAD STREET
PHILADELPHIA, PA 19108
TEL: 215-238-5300
FAX: 215-238-5457

PULP & PAPER MAGAZINE
600 HARRISON STREET
SAN FRANCISCO, CA 94107
TEL: 415-905-2200
FAX: 415-905-2232

QUICK PRINTING
445 BROADHOLLOW ROAD, SUITE 21
MELVILLE, NY 1747-3601
TEL: 631-845-2700
FAX: 631-845-7109

RADTECH REPORT
60 REVERE DRIVE, SUITE 500
NORTHBROOK, IL 60062
TEL: 847-480-9080
FAX: 847-480-9282

SCREEN PRINTING
407 GILBERT AVENUE
CINCINNATI, OH 45302
TEL: 513-421-2050
FAX: 513-421-5144

SCREEN PRINTING TODAY
3300 NORTH CENTRAL AVENUE,
    SUITE 2500
PHOENIX, AZ 85012

SCREEN & DISPLAY GRAPHICS
2880 WEST MIDWAY BLVD
BROOMFIELD, CO 80020
TEL: 303-469-0424
FAX: 303-469-5730

SIGNS OF THE TIMES
407 GILBERT AVENUE
CINCINNATI, OH 45202
TEL: 513-421-2050
FAX: 513-421-5144

SOLUTIONS!
15 TECHNOLOGY PARKWAY SOUTH
NORCROSS, GA 30092
TEL: 770-446-1400
FAX: 770-446-6947

SOUTHERN GRAPHICS
1818 POT SPRING RD, #102
TIMONIUM, MD 21093
TEL: 410-628-7826
FAX: 410-628-7829

TEXAS PRINTER
910 WEST MOCKINGBIRD LANE
DALLAS, TX 75247-5174
TEL: 817-332-8236
FAX: 817-877-1862

THE PREPRESS BULLETIN
552 WEST 167TH STREET
SOUTH HOLLAND, IL 60473
TEL: 708-596-5110
FAX: 708-596-5112

TLMI ILLUMINATOR
40 SHUMAN BLVD, SUITE 295
NAPERVILLE, IL 60563
TEL: 630-357-9222
FAX: 630-357-0192

ARGENTINA

ENVASIEMENTO
TALCAHUANO 342 PD 4
CP, BUENOS AIRES, ARGENTINA
TEL: +54-1 14-375-4458
FAX: +54-1 14-375-4458

OFICIO GRAFICO
PARAN 123, 6 PISO OF 139
BUENOS AIRES 1017 ARGENTINA

PACKAGING
    ARGENTINO-IBERAMERICA
ESTADOS UNIDOS 2796 1A
BUENOS AIRES 1227 ARGENTINA

REV DE LA ASSN FABRICANTES DE
    PAPEL
BELGRANO 2852
BUENOS AIRES, ARGENTINA

AUSTRALIA

AUSTRALIAN LITHO, PTR & PKGR
P O BOX 5158, GPO SYDNEY
SYDNEY NSW 2001 AUSTRALIA

AUSTRALIAN PRINTER
P O BOX 1316, NORTH SYDNEY
NSW 2059 AUSTRALIA
TEL: +61-2-9922-6133
FAX: +61-2-9922-4734

NEW ZEALAND PRINTER
P O BOX 1313
NORTH SYDNEY, NSW 2059
    AUSTRALIA
TEL: +61-2-9922-6133
FAX: +61-2-9922-4734

PACKAGING
LOCKED BAG 2999
CHATSWOOD, NSW, 2067 AUSTRALIA

PACKAGING NEWS
17-21 BELLUM V.
SURREY HILLS NSW 2010 AUSTRALIA
TEL: +61-2-9281-2333
FAX: +61-2-9281-2750

PRINT ASIA PACIFIC
P O BOX 112
PRABAN, VICTORIA 3181
AUSTRALIA
TEL: +61-3-9245-7606
FAX: +61-3-9245-7777

AUSTRIA

DAS OESTERREICHISCHE
    GRAPHISCHE GEWERBE
GRUENANGERGASSE 4
A-1010 WEIN, AUSTRIA
TEL: +43-1-512-4985
FAX: +43-1-5132-82619

GRAPHISCHE REVUE OSTERREICHS
SEIDENGASSE 15-17
WIEN A-1070 AUSTRIA
TEL: +43-1-523-8231

BELGIUM

M & C GRAFIEK
VAN DE HAUTLEI 195
ANTWERP DEUME 2100, BELGIUM
TEL: +32-3-366-0886
FAX: +32-3-366-1672

NOUVELLES GRAPHIQUES
LEUVENSESTEENWEG 262
VILVOORDE 1800 BELGIUM
TEL: +32-2-253-0000
FAX: +32-2-257-8972

PRINTING & PACKAGING
AVENUE LOUISE 149
BRUSSELS B-1050 BELGIUM

BRAZIL

ABIGRAF REVISTA
RUA DU PARADISO 533
SAO PAULO 04103 BRAZIL
TEL: +55-11-50877-777
FAX: +55-11-50877-733

EMBALAGEM
AV GOMES FREIRE, 663 GR 1102
RIO DE JANIERO 20231 BRAZIL

EMBANEWS
AV FRANCISCO MATARAZZO 999-2°
SAO PAULO 05001-350 BRAZIL
TEL: +55 11 864 2390
FAX: +55 11 262 9518

INFORFLEXO
RUA DOMINGOS DE MORAES 2243,
    cjs 24e25
SAO PAULO, SP
BRAZIL 04035 000
TEL: +55-11-5085-0033

NOTIPACK-PACKNEWS
CAJAIBA 520
SAO PAULO 05025 BRAZIL

CANADA

CANADIAN PACKAGING
777 BAY STREET, 6TH FL
TORONTO, ONT M5W 1A7 CANADA
TEL: 416-596-5745
FAX: 416-596-5905

CANADIAN PRINTER
777 BAY STREET, 16TH FLOOR
TORONTO, ONTARIO M5W 1A7
    CANADA
TEL: 416-596-5898
FAX: 416-596-5905

GRAPHIC MONTHLY
1606 SEDLESCOMB DRIVE, UNIT 8
MISSISSAUGA, ONT L4X 1M6 CANADA
TEL: 905-625-7070
FAX: 905-625-4856

LE MAITRE IMPRIMEUR
644 BOUL CURE-POIRIER
    QUEST, BUR 100
LONGUEUIL PQ J4J 2H9
CANADA
TEL: +450-670-9311
FAX: +450-670-8762

PULP & PAPER CANADA
1 HOLIDAY ST, EAST TOWER, #705
POINTE-CLAIRE, PQ H9R 5N3 CANADA
TEL: 800-363-1327
FAX: 514-630-5980

PRINTACTION
2240 MIDLAND AVENUE, SUITE 201
SCARBOROUGH, M1P 4R8 CANADA

THE GRAPHIC ARTS MAGAZINE
1180 KINGDALE ROAD, SUITE 202
NEWMARKET, ONTARIO L3Y 4W1
    CANADA
TEL: 905-513-3999
FAX: 905-830-9345

CHILE

VAS PACKAGING MAGAZINE
MERCED 346 / F3
SANTIAGO, CHILE
TEL: +56-2-632-5440
FAX: +56-2-638-2622

CHINA

PACKAGING PRO
4/F STANHOP E HOUSE, 734 KING'S RD
NORTH PT, HONGKONG, CHINA
TEL: +852 2811-8897
FAX: +852 2516-5119

COLOMBIA

INPRA LATINA
APDO POST 67 252
MEDELLIN, ANT COLOMBIA
TEL: +57-4-262-4037
FAX: +57-4-262-8005

CROATIA

ACTA GRAPHICA
GETALDICEVA 2, P O BOX 225
ZAGREB, 41001 CROATIA
TEL: +385-1-216-4444
FAX: +385-1-233-5397

DENMARK

AGI DENMARK
HOLBERGSGADE 14
COPENHAGEN 1057, DENMARK
TEL: +45-33-32-71-72
FAX: +45-33-32-62-73

DE GRAFISKE FAG
HELGAVEJ 26
ODENSE, DK-5230 DENMARK
TEL: +45-66-13-06-01
FAX: +45-33-24-07-88

IN-PACK
SKELBAEKGADE 4
COPENHAGEN V 1780 DENMARK
TEL: +45-53-48-28-60
FAX: +45-53-48-22-05

PAK & PAPIR
LYGTEN 16
COPENHAGEN DK-1790 DENMARK
FAX: +45-35-82-02-07

FINLAND

GRAPHIC ARTS IN FINLAND
TEKNIIKANTIE 3
ESPOO SF-02150 FINLAND

PAINOMPMAAILMA
LONNROTINKATU 11A
HELSINKI SF-00120 FINLAND
TEL: +358-9-2287-7242
FAX: +358-9-603-914

PAKKAUS
RITARIKATU 3 B A
HELSINKI SF-00170 FINLAND
TEL: +358-9-684-0340
FAX: +358-9-6840-3410

FRANCE

CARACTERE
26 RUE D'ORADOU-SUR-GLANE
PARIS CEDEX 15, 75504 PARIS FRANCE
TEL: +33-1-4425-3131
FAX: +33-1-4557-3506

CARTONNAGES & EMBALLAGES
    MODERNES
31 PLACE ST. FERDINAND
PARIS 75017 FRANCE
TEL: +45-1-74-67-43
FAX: +45-1-72-63-21

CIRCULAIRE DES PRUTES
64, RUE TUITBOUT
PARIS 75009 FRANCE

COMMUNICATIONS IMPRIME
31 PLACE ST. FERDINAND
PARIS 75017 FRANCE
TEL: +45-1-74-67-43
FAX: +45-1-72-63-21

EL PAPEL
34 RUE DE BAGNEAUX
ST JEAN DELA RUELLE 45140 FRANCE
TEL: +33 2 38 704017
FAX: +33 2 38 721772

EMBALLAGES MAGAZINE
26, RUE D'ORADOUR-SUR-GLANE
PARIS, CEDEX 15 F-77504 FRANCE
TEL: +33-1-44-25-0600
FAX: +33-1-44-25-0734

FLEXO-GRAVURE EUROPE
31 PLACE ST. FERDINAND
PARIS 75017 FRANCE
TEL: +45-1-74-67-43
FAX: +45-1-72-63-21

GUIDE DES PAPIER CARTON
16 RUE SAINT FIACRE
PARIS 75002 FRANCE
TEL: +45-1-4236-9559
FAX: +45-1-4233-8324

INNOVATIVE PACKAGING
42, AVENUE DE VERSAILLES
PARIS F-75016 FRANCE

LABELS ETIQUETTES INFO
31 PLACE SAINT-FERDINAND
PARIS, 75017 FRANCE
TEL: +33-1-45-74-67-43
FAX: +33-1-45-72-63-21

PRINTING & GRAPHIC ARTS
8, RUE DES ETANGS
COIGNIERES F-78310 FRANCE

GERMANY

A. P. R.
BORSIGSTRASSE 1-3
HEUSENSTAMM 63150 GERMANY
TEL: +49-6104-606-216
FAX: +49-6104-606-333

CREATIV VERPACKEN
HAUPSTRASSE 6
WILMERSDORF 16278 GERMANY
TEL: +49-33334-7504
FAX: +49-33334-7505

DEUTSCHER-DRUCKER
POSTFACH 4124, SENEFELDERSTR 12
OSTFILDERN D-73744 GERMANY
TEL: +49-711-448-170
FAX: +49-711-442-099

DRUCK U MEDIEN MAGAZINE
ANTON SCHMIDTSTR 6
WAIBLINGEN 71332 GERMANY
TEL: +49-7151-95809-0
FAX: +49-7151-958 0910

DRUCKSPIEGEL
BORSIGSTR 1-3
HEUSENSTAMM 63150 GERMANY
TEL: +49-6104-606-216
FAX: +49-6104-606-333

ETIKETTEN- LABELS
AM STOLLEN, 6/1
GUTACH-BLEIBACH D-79261
　　GERMANY
TEL: +49-7685-918-110
FAX: +49-7685-909-011

EUROPAEISCHER WIRTSCHAFFSD
BLEICHSTRASSE 22
GERNSBACH 76593 GERMANY
TEL: +49-7224-9397-0
FAX: +49-7224-937-750

FARBE & LACKE
SCHIFFGRABEN 43
HANNOVER D-30175 GERMANY
TEL: +49 511 991 021550
FAX: +49 511 991 02099

FLEXO & GRAVURE ASIA PACIFIC
AM STOLLEN, 6/1
GUTACH-BLEIBACH D-79261
　　GERMANY
TEL: +49-7685-918-110
FAX: +49-7685-909-011

FLEXO & GRAVURE INTERNATINAL
AM STOLLEN, 6/1
GUTACH-BLEIBACH D-79261
　　GERMANY
TEL: +44-1379-741-844
FAX: +44-1379-741-844

FLEXOPRINT
INDUSTRIESTRASSE 2
HEUSENSTAMM D-63150 GERMANY
TEL: +49-6104-606-216
FAX: +49-6104-606-333

GRAFLEX
POSTFACH 1869
WIESBADEN 65200 GERMANY
TEL: +49-611-803112
FAX: +49-611-803113

I G MEDIEN FORUM
POSTFACH 102451
STUTTGART, 70020 GERMANY
TEL: +49-711-2018-0
FAX: +49-711-2018-8262

INNOVATION UND TECHNIK
POSTFACH 700 450
STUTTGART 70574 GERMANY
TEL: +49-711-97617-0
FAX: +49-711-97667-49

INTERNATIONALE
　　PAPIERWIRTSCHAFT
BORSIGSTRASSE 1-3 10
HEUSENSTAMM 63150 GERMANY
TEL: +49-6104-606-216
FAX: +49-6104-606-317

NARROWEB TECH
AM STOLLEN 6/1
GUTACH-BLEIBACH D-79261
　　GERMANY
TEL: +49-7685-918110
FAX: +49-7685-909011

NV NEUE VERPACKUNG
POSTF 10 28 69
HEIDELBERG 69018 GERMANY
TEL: +49-6221-489-298
FAX: +49-6221-489-480

O P DRUCKMAGAZIN
HOEHENSTRASSE 17, POSTFACH 1329
FELLBACH 70736 GERMANY
TEL: +49-711-5206-256
FAX: +49-711-5281-424

PACKAGING PRODUCTION INTL
POSTF 10 28 69
HEIDELBERG 69121 GERMANY
TEL: +49-6221-489-280
FAX: +49-6221-489-279

PAPIER UND KUNSTOFF
　　VERARBEITER
MAINZER LANDSTRASSE 251
FRANKFURT-AM-MAIN 60326
　　GERMANY
TEL: +49-69-7595-01
FAX: +49-69-7595-2999

PAPIERMACHER MAGAZIN
BACHSTRASSE 14-16
HEIDELBERG 69121 GERMANY
TEL: +49-6221-6446-0
FAX: +40-6221-644-640

PHANOMEN FARBE
NOERDINGERSTR 15
DUSSELDORF 40597 GERMANY
TEL: +49 211 718 2314
FAX: +49 211 718 2366

POLYGRAPH
HERFORDERSTR 74
BIELEFELD 33602 GERMANY
TEL: +49-521-966-0522
FAX: +49-521-966-0530

PRINT UND PRODUCTION
OSTRING 13
WIESBADEN 65205 GERMANY
TEL: +49-611-770-9223
FAX: +49-611-770-9233

WORLD WIDE PRINTER
POSTFACH 4124
OSTFILDERN 73744 GERMANY
TEL: +49-711-444-005
FAX: +49-711-442-099

GREECE

THE NEWS OF GRAPHIC ARTS
157 SOKRATOUS STREET
KALLITHEA, ATHENS 176-73 GREECE

HUNGARY

MAGYAR GRAFIKA
P O BOX 433
BUDAPEST H-1371 HUNGARY

PAPIRIPAR
FO.U. 68, P O BOX 433
BUDAPEST 1371 HUNGARY

INDIA

FOUR P NEWS
22 CONGRESS EXHIBITION ROAD
CALCUTTA, W. BENGAL-700 017 INDIA
TEL: +91-33-2247-8718
FAX: +91-33-2247-8718

INDIAN PRINTER & STATIONER
OPP SHARDA BAUGH
RAJKOT-SAURASHTRA 350 000 INDIA

INDIAN PRINT & PAPER
95 PARK STREET
KOLKATA
WEST BENGAL 700 016 INDIA

INTELPACK
BLDG 2,113 SONAL LINK IND EST
LINK RD, MALAD W, MUMBAI 400064
    INDIA
TEL: +91-22-2880-3977
FAX: +91-22-2881-9008

JOURNAL OF PACKAGING
FLAT NO. 7, 201 SARAT BOSE RD
CALCUTTA 700 039 INDIA

PACKAGING INDIA
E-2, MIDC, BX 9432, ANDHERI(E)
MUMBAI 400 093 INDIA
TEL: +91-22-2821-9803
FAX: +91-22-2837-5302

PACKAGING TECHNOLOGY
8947/229-A KANNANWAR NAGAR,
VIKHROLI E, MUMBAI 400 083 INDIA
TEL: +91-22-2259-6907

PAPERPRINTPACK INDIA
7-104, VEER NARIMAN ROAD
    PRABHA DEVI P.O.
MAHARASHTRA, MUMBAI, 400 025
    INDIA
TEL: +91-22-2422-0906

PRINTING TIMES
A-370, 2ND FL., DEFENCE COLONY
NEW DELHI, 110 024 INDIA
TEL: +91-11-2460-1571
FAX: +91-11-2462-4808

THE CORRUGATOR
H4/2, JANKALYAN
BANGUR NAGAR, GOREGAN (WEST)
MUMBAI, 400 090 INDIA
TEL: +91-22-2877-2890
FAX: +91-22-2877-2702

YOUNG PRINTING
1786 SADASHIV BETH
PUNE 411 030 INDIA

INDONESIA

GRAFIKA INDONESIA
JALAN KEBON SIRIH NO. 34
JAKARTA 10110 INDONESIA

IRELAND

IRISH PRINTER
52 GLADTHULE ROAD, SANDYCOVE,
SANDYCOVE, COUNTY DUBLIN
    IRELAND
TEL: +353-1-280-0000
FAX: +353-1-280-1818

ITALY

CORRUGATED & CARTONBOARD BOX
VIA FRUILI, 16
MILANO I-20135 ITALY
TEL: +39 02.54.65.990
FAX: +39 02.54.65.990

FLEXO, GRAVURE & CONVERTING
VIA FRUILI, 16
MILANO I-20135 ITALY
TEL: +39 02.54.65.990
FAX: +39 02.54.65.990

GRAFICA
9 VIA ANDREA SABATINO
SALERNO I-84100 ITALY

GRAPHICUS
VIA ODDINO MORGARI 36/B
TORINO I-10125 ITALY
TEL: +39-11-6690-577
FAX: +39-11-6689-200

IL POLIGRAFICO ITALIANO
VIA KOLBE 8
MILANO I-20137 ITALY
TEL: +39-02-752-9101
FAX: +39-02-752-91039

IMBALLAGGIO
VIA GORKI 69
CINISELLO BALSAMO (MI) 20092 ITALY
TEL: +39-02-6603-4327
FAX: +39-02-6603-4333

ITALIA IMBALLAGGIO
VIA BENIGNO CRESPI, 30-32
MILAN 20159 ITALY
TEL: +39-02-6900-7733
FAX: +39-02-6900-7664

L'ITALIA GRAFICA
PIAZZA DELLA CONCILIAZIONE 1
MILANO I-20123 ITALY
TEL: +39-02-498-10 51
FAX: +39-02-481-69 47

PACK
VIA CIRO MENOTTI, 14
MILAN (MI) 20129 ITALY
TEL: +39-02-757-0330
FAX: +39-02-757-0332

PACKAGING & BOTTLING INTL
VIA CIRO MENOTTI NO. 14
MILANO, 20129 ITALY
TEL: +39-02-757-0330
FAX: +39-02-757-0332

RASSEGNA DELL 'IMBALLAGGIO
VIA CASELLA, 16
MILANO I-20156 ITALY
TEL: +39-02-3922-81
FAX: +39-02-3921-4341

RASSEGNA GRAFICA ARTI POLIGRAF
VIA CASELLA 16,
MILANO I-20156 ITALY
TEL: +39-02-392281
FAX: +39-02-3921-4341

JAPAN

INSATSUKA/PRINTING WORLD
16-8 SHINTOMI, 1-CHOME, CHUO-KU
TOKYO 104-0041 JAPAN
TEL: +81-3-3553-5681
FAX: +81-3-3553-5684

JAPAN GRAPHIC ARTS
16-8,1-CHOME
SHINTOMI, CHUO-KU TOKYO 104
    JAPAN
TEL: +81-3-3553-5681
FAX: +81-3-3543-5684

JAPAN PRINTER
INSATU GAKKAI SHUPPANBU 2-5,
4-HATCHOBORI TOKYO 104 JAPAN

PACKAGING JAPAN
3-1-5, MISAKI-CHO, 3-CHOME
CHIYODA-KU, TOKYO 101 0061 JAPAN
TEL: +81-3-3661-7458
FAX: +81-3-3667-9646

PRINTING NEWS
3-16 SHINJUKU-SHIN-OGAWAMCHI
TOKYO, 162 JAPAN

KOREA

GRAPHICS WORLD MONTHLY
3F, 45-1 KYONAM-DONG,
    CHONGRO-KU
SEOUL 110 100 KOREA
TEL: +92-2-734 3473 EX 6
FAX: +92-2-733-5895

MEXICO

EL TLACUILO
DR OLVERA NO. 205-A, ZP 7
COL DOCTORES, MEXICO, DF MEXICO

EL IMPRESOR
STA MA LA RIVERA 9-103
MEXICO DF 06400 MEXICO
TEL: +52-5-546-8725
FAX: +52-5-566-1038

PLASTICO EMPAQUE
INSURGENTES SUR NO 590-1
COL DEL VALLE, MEXICO, DF, MEXICO

NETHERLANDS

GRAFICUS
P O BOX 1860,
NL-1112 CD DIEMAN NETHERLANDS
TEL: +31-20-660-3300
FAX: +31-20-660-3303

GRAFISCH NEDERLAND
POSTBUS 220
AMSTELVEEN 1180 AE NETHERLANDS
TEL: +31-20-547-5678
FAX: +31-20-547-5475

HET CARTONNAGEBEDRIFF
SPORTLAAN 42,
VLAARDINGEN, NETHERLANDS

KARTOFLEX MAGAZINE
POSTBUS 55
LEIDEN, 2300 AB NETHERLANDS
TEL: +31-71-161-515
FAX: +31-71-121-550

MISSETS PAKBLAD
P O BOX 4
DOETINCHEM NL-7000 BA
    NETHERLANDS
TEL: +31-314-349-371
FAX: +31-314-363-638

VERPAKKEN
POSTBUS 1932
HILVERSUM, NL-1200 BX
    NETHERLANDS
TEL: +31-35-623-2756
FAX: +31-35-623-2401

NIGERIA

NIGERIAN PACKAGING NEWS
1 OBASA ROAD
IKEJA, NIGERIA
TEL: +234-82-221-782

NIGERIAN PRINTER
1 OBASA ROAD
IKEJA, NIGERIA
TEL: +234-82-221-782

NORWAY

EMBALLERING
P O BOX 9070, VATERLAND
N-0134 OSLO NORWAY
TEL: +47-22 36 4440
FAX: +47-22 36 0550

IN-PUBLISH
POSTBOKS 9076, GROENLAND
OSLO 0133 NORWAY
TEL: +47-22-20-80-90
FAX: +47-22-20-89-68

MAT & PACKMARKEDET
POSTBOX 156
OSLO N-1203 NORWAY
TEL: +47-22-61-0006
FAX: +47-22-62-4917

POLAND

OPAKOWANIE
P O BOX 1004
WARSAW 00950 POLAND
TEL: +48-22-8180918
FAX: +48-22-6192187

PREZGLAD PAPIERNICZY
RATUSZOWA 11, PO BOX 1004
WARSAW 00-950 POLAND
TEL: +48-22-818-091
FAX: +48-22-619-21871

PORTUGAL

EMBALAGEM
PRACA DAS INDUSTRAIALES
LISBON, 1300 PORTUGAL

NOTICIAS POLIGRAFICAS
RAMAHLO ORTIGAO 20-3D
LISBOA P-1000 PORTUGAL

ODITECNICA-REVIPACK
PETA DE DEZEMBRO 55/C, APDO 30
ODIVELAS CODEX, P-2676 PORTUGAL

RUSSIA

NOVOSTI POLIGRAPHII
UL PETROVKA 26, K 302-304
MOSCOW, 101-429 RUSSIA
TEL: +7-095-923-7640
FAX: +7-095-923-7640

POLIGRAFIST I IZDATEL
SUSHCHEVSKII VAL U 64
MOSCOW, 129 272 RUSSIA
TEL: +7-095-288-9317
FAX: +7-095-288-9444

TARA I UPAKOVKA
SADOVAYA-SPASSKAYA 18
MOSCOW, 107 807 RUSSIA
TEL: +7-095-207-2141
FAX: +7-095-975-3731

SINGAPORE

ASIAN PRINTER
12 AILJUNIED RD, Nº. 03-02
SCN CENTER 389801 SINGAPORE
TEL: +65-6-842-3678
FAX: +65-6-842-3616

SINGAPORE PRINTER
21 KIM KEAT ROAD,#07-01
SINGAPORE 328 803 SINGAPORE
TEL: +65-6-336-4227
FAX: +65-6-336-1401

SOUTH AFRICA

AFRICAN PRINTER
P O BOX 8147
JOHANNESBURG 2000 SOUTH AFRICA
TEL: +27-11-496-22 60
FAX: +27-11-496-2266

GRAPHIX
P O BOX 751 119
GARDENVIEW 2047 SOUTH AFRICA
TEL: +27-11-622-4800
FAX: +27-11-622-2480

PACKAGING REVIEW, SOUTH AFRICA
P O BOX 2271
CLAREINCH 7740 SOUTH AFRICA
TEL: +27-21-611-140
FAX: +27-21-611-384

SPAIN

ALABRENT EDICIONES S.A.
SOSPIR, 32, 2° 1A
BARCELONA 08026 SPAIN
TEL: +34-93-436-3255
FAX: +34-93-455-5601

CARTIFLEX
SOSPIR 32, 2°, 1A
BARCELONA 08026 SPAIN
TEL: +34-93-436-3255
FAX: +34-93-455-5601

EL PAPEL
PASAGE MEDIODIA, 2, APDO 101
PALAFRUGE 11 (GERONA) E-17200
    SPAIN

EN SERIGRAFIA
SOSPIR 32, 2° 1A
BARCELONA 08626 SPAIN
TEL: +34-93-436-3255
FAX: +34-93-455-5601

GRAFICAS
BIASCO DE GARAY, 76 1°
MADRID E-28015 SPAIN
TEL: +34-1-445-25-64

IMPREMPRES
GOYA 115 4 TO DCHA
MADRID 28009 SPAIN
TEL: +34-91-309-6310
FAX: +34-91-401-9025

NOTICIAS TECNIAS
PIO FELIPE 12
MADRID E-28038 SPAIN

PRENSA DE LA INDUSTRIA GRAFICA
DOCTOR ESQUERDO 105
MADRID 28007 SPAIN
TEL: +34-91-573-7400
FAX: +34-91-409-6452

SWEDEN

AKTUELL GRAFISK INFORMATION
SKEPPSBRON 13B
S-211 20 MALMO, SWEDEN
TEL: +46-40-12-7840
FAX: +46-40-12-5820

GRAFISKT MEDIA FORUM
BOX 601
25106 HELSINGBORG, SWEDEN
TEL: +46-31-62-94-00
FAX: +46-31-80-27-54

MEDIA GRAFICA
SANKT ERIKSGATAN 26, FACK 12069
STOCKHOLM S-102 22 SWEDEN
TEL: +46-8-598-99097

NORD-EMBALLAGE
BANKVAGAN 30
262 70 STROVELSTORP
SWEDEN
TEL: +46-42-20-71-66
FAX: +46-42-20-71-96

PACKMARKNADEN NORDICA
P O BOX 127817
STOCKHOLM S-115 93 SWEDEN
TEL: +46-8-620-41-29
FAX: +46-8-661-64-55

TRADE PRESS SERVICE
P O BOX 5
S-260 42 MOLLE, SWEDEN

SWITZERLAND

COATING
BANKGASSE 8
ST GALLEN CH-9001 SWITZERLAND
TEL: +41-71-222-3239
FAX: +41-71-222-8761

DRUCK- BULLET IN
POSTFACH 1116
ZURICH 8048 SWITZERLAND
TEL: +41-1-928-5631
FAX: +41-1-928-5630

FACHHEFTE BULLETIN TECHNIQUE
BASLERSTR 30
ZURICH 8048 SWITZERLAND
TEL: +41-1-522-500
FAX: +41-1-491-2922

SWISSPACK INTERNATIONAL
STAMPFENBACHSTR 61
ZURICH 8048 SWITZERLAND
TEL: +41-1-431-6445
FAX: +41-1-431-6497

VISICOM
FUERSTENLANDSTR 122,
CH-9001 ST. GALLEN, SWITZERLAND
TEL: +41-71-272-7298
FAX: +41-71-272-7244

TAIWAN

GRAPHIC COMMUNICATIONS
    MONTHLY
7F 159, 2 SKI TA ROAD, 100
TAIPEI, TAIWAN, REP OF CHINA
TEL: 886-2-365-6268
FAX: 886-2-365-6521

THAILAND

ASIAN PACKAGING BULLETIN
ISD BLDG, 4TH FL, KLUAYNAMTHAI
RAMA IV RD, BANGKOK 1011
    THAILAND

THE THAI PRINTER
487/42 SOI VATTANASILIP
PRATUNAM, BANGKOK 10400
    THAILAND

TURKEY

AMBALAJ DERGISI
BES YOL FABRIKALAR CAD 21
TR-SEFAKOY/ISTANBUL, TURKEY

MATBAA & TEKNIK
BINASI 29 EKIM CAD, 23
YENIBOSNA-ISTANBUL 34530,
    TURKEY
TEL: +90-212-454-2530
FAX: +90-212-454-2555

UKRAINE

FLEXODRUCK REVUE
ORLOVSKAYA STR 16-21
KYIV 252060 UKRAINE
TEL: +380 44 516-5785
FAX: +380 44 516-5262

UNITED KINGDOM

BRITISH PRINTER
SOVEREIGN WAY, TONBRIDGE,
KENT, TN9 1RW UNITED KINGDOM
TEL: +44-1732-364422
FAX: +44-1732-361534

CONVERTER
232A ADDINGTON RD, S. CROYDON
SURREY CR2 8CE UNITED KINGDOM
TEL: +44-181-651-7100
FAX: +44-181-651-7117

CONVERTING TODAY
361 CITY ROAD
LONDON EC1V 1PG UNITED KINGDOM
TEL: +44-1-20-7417-7400
FAX: +44-1-20-7417-7500

CORRUGATED AND CARTON
    BULLETIN
P O BOX 14
DORKING, SURREY RH5 4YN
UNITED KINGDOM
TEL: +44-1306-884-473

DISPOSABLE PAPER PRODUCTS
60-61 BRITTON STREET
LONDON EC1M 5NA
UNITED KINGDOM
TEL: +44-171-252-8024
FAX: +44-171-608-3149

FLEXO TECH
30 LONDON RD, SOUTHBOROUGH,
TONBRIDGE, KENT TN4 0RE
UNITED KINGDOM
TEL: +44-1892-542-099
FAX: +44-1892-546-693

FOLDING CARTON INDUSTRY
THRUXTON HOUSE, THRUXTON
    DOWN
ANDOVER, HANTS SP11 8PR
UNITED KINGDOM
TEL: +44-1264-889-533
FAX: +44-1264-889-524

GRAPHIC NETWORK
1 EASTGATE, NORK, BARNSTEAD
SURREY SM7 1 RN UNITED KINGDOM

GRAPHIC REPRO
99 BURY ROAD, WOKING
SURREY GU21 5HX,
UNITED KINGDOM
TEL: +44-1483-740-271
FAX: +44-1483-740-397

INK & PRINT
PEMBROKE HOUSE
CAMPSBOURNE RD
LONDON N8 7PT
UNITED KINGDOM
TEL: +44-181-340-3291
FAX: +44-181-341-4840

LABELS & LABELLING MAGAZINE
COMMONWEALTH HOUSE,
    2 CHALK HILL RD.,
HAMMERSMITH, LONDON W6 8DW
UNITED KINGDOM
TEL: +44 208 846 2700
FAX: +44 208 846 2801

NEW IN PRINTING
38/42 HAMPTON ROAD, TEDDINGTON,
MDSX, TW11 0JE
UNITED KINGDOM
TEL: +44-(0)-1732-768-611
FAX: +44-(0)-1737-885-469

PACKAGE PRINT & DESIGN
COMMONWEALTH HOUSE, 2 CHALK
    HILL ROAD
HAMMERSMITH, LONDON W6 8DW
UNITED KINGDOM
TEL: +44 208-846-2700
FAX: +44 208-846-2801

PACKAGING
38 MARKET SQUARE
UXBRIDGE, MIDDX UB8 1TG
UNITED KINGDOM
TEL: +44-1895-454-545
FAX: +44-1895-454-647

PACKAGING MAGAZINE
SOVEREIGN WAY,
TONBRIDGE, KENT TN9 1RW
UNITED KINGDOM
TEL: +44-1732-377-486
FAX: +44-1732-353-328

PACKAGING NEWS
19 SCARBROOK ROAD, CROYDEN
SURREY CR9 1QH UNITED KINGDOM
TEL: +44-181-271-5000
FAX: +44-181-277-5560

PACKAGING TECH & SCIENCE
BAFFINS LN, CHICHESTER
W SUSSEX PO19 IUD
UNITED KINGDOM
TEL: +44-1243-779-7777
FAX: +44-1212-850-6695

PACKAGING TECHNICAL BULLETIN
PIRA, RANDALLS ROAD,
    LEATHERHEAD
SURREY KT22 7RU UNITED KINGDOM
TEL: +44-1372-602-630
FAX: +44-1372-802-239

PACKAGING TODAY
361-363 CITY ROAD
LONDON EC1V 1PQ UNITED KINGDOM
TEL: +44-20-7417-7400
FAX: +44-20-7417-7500

PAINT & INK INTERNATIONAL
2 QUEENSWAY
REDHILL, SURREY RH1 1QS
UNITED KINGDOM
TEL: +44 1737 855-485
FAX: +44 1737 855-470

PRINTING AND CONVERTING
    DECISIONS INTERNATIONAL
BRUNEL HSE, 55-57 N WHARF RD
LONDON, W2 1LA
UNITED KINGDOM
TEL: +44-1-20-7915-9560
FAX: +44-1-20-7724-2089

PRINTING WORLD
SOVEREIGN WAY, TONBRIDGE
KENT TN9 1RW UNITED KINGDOM
TEL: +44-1732-364-422
FAX: +44-1732-301-534

PRINTLINK INTERNATIONAL
BOX 923
MILTON KEYNES, MK8 0AY
UNITED KINGDOM
TEL: +44-1908-561-444
FAX: +44-1908-569-564

PRINTWEAR & PROMOTION
PEMBROKE HSE, CAMPSBOURNE RD,
LONDON N8 7PE UNITED KINGDOM
TEL: +44-181-340-3291
FAX: +44-181-341-4840

PRINT WEEK
174 HAMMERSMITH ROAD
LONDON W6 7JP UNITED KINGDOM
TEL: +44-181-943-5000
FAX: +44-171-413-4013

PROFESSIONAL PRINTER
THE MEWS, HILL HSE,
    CLANRICADE RD
TONBRIDGE WELLS, KENT TB1 1PJ
UNITED KINGDOM
TEL: +44-1892-538-118
FAX: +44-1892-518-028

QP
P O BOX 75, CRANBROOK
KENT TN17 3ZN
UNITED KINGDOM
TEL: +44-1580-714449
FAX: +44-1580-714449

THE EUROPEAN SCREEN PRINTER &
    DIGITAL IMAGES MAGAZINE
74 WEST STREET, RELGATE, SURREY
]RH2 9BL UNITED KINGDOM
TEL: +44-1737-240 788
FAX: +44-1737-240 770

VENEZUELA

REVISTA EMPAQUE
APTO DE CORR 68530
CARACAS, VENEZUELA

ADDENDUM

UNITED STATES

INSIDE FINISHING
536 NORTHWEST TYLER CT, SUITE 204
TOPEKA, KS 66606
TEL: 785-232-8776
FAX: 785-232-8747

MODERN PLASTICS
TWO PENN PLAZA
NEW YORK, NY 10121
TEL: 212-621-4900
FAX: 212-621-4800

The vast number of publications concerned with environmental affairs in all its ramifications makes it impossible to list even some of the most prestigious ones here. They run into the many hundreds and are issued in numerous countries throughout the world. As a result, we have attempted to list only those few publications which enjoy widespread general circulation in the Untied States, Canada, and the United Kingdom, and which are not issued by governmental units. Omitted are newsletters, publications which are issued on a variable or infrequent basis, and those publications which are designed only for scholarly, scientific and research purposes. Every effort has been made to assure the accuracy of these lists of publications.

We suggest, therefore, that anyone who needs access to specialized publications in the field refer to Ulrich's Periodicals Directory, issued annually by R. R. Bowker Company, and available in most public and institutional libraries. The "Environmental" categories under which one may seek information include, but are not limited to, the following

Environmental Publications

- Abstracting and Bibliographies, Statistics
- Computer Applications
- Pollution
- Studies
- Toxicology and Safety
- Waste Management

UNITED STATES

AMERICAN ENVIRONMENTAL
LABORATORY
P O BOX 870, 30 CONTROLS DRIVE
SHELTON, CT 06484-0870
TEL: 203-926-9300
FAX: 203-926-9310

EM
ONE GATEWAY CENTER, 3rd FLOOR
PITTSBURGH, PA 15222
TEL: 412-232-3444
FAX: 412-232-3450

ENVIRONMENT
1319 18th STREET NW
WASHINGTON, DC 20036-1802
TEL: 202-296-6267
FAX: 202-296-5149

ENVIRONMENTAL FORUM
1616 P STREET SW, SUITE 200
WASHINGTON, DC 20036
TEL: 202-939-3800
FAX: 202-939-3868

ENVIRONMENTAL MANAGEMENT
BETHEL VALLEY RD, BLDG 1505, RM
200
OAK RIDGE, TN 37831-6036
TEL: 865-576-0000
FAX: 865-576-8543

ENVIRONMENTAL PROTECTION
5151 BELTLINE ROAD, SUITE 1010
DALLAS, TX 75254
TEL: 972-687-6700
FAX: 972-687-6799

ENVIRONMENTAL QUALITY
MANAGEMENT
605 THIRD AVENUE
NEW YORK NY 10158
TEL: 212-850-6645
FAX: 212-850-6021

ENVIRONMENTAL SCIENCE &
TECHNOLOGY
1155 16th STREET NW
WASHINGTON, DC 20009-1749
TEL: 202-332-5544
FAX: 202-332-4559

ENVIRONMENTAL TESTING &
ANALYSIS
P O BOX 5244
GLENDALE, CA 91221-1081
TEL: 818-842-4777
FAX: 818-842-0578

GEORGIA & SOUTHEAST
ENVIRONMENTAL NEWS
7457 ALOMA AVENUE, SUITE 202
WINTER PARK, FL 32792
TEL: 407-761-7777
FAX: 407-761-7757

IIE SOLUTIONS
25 TECHNOLOGY PARK
NORCROSS, GA 30092-2988

INDUSTRIAL WASTEWATER
601 WYTHE STREET
ALEXANDRIA, VA 22314-1994
TEL: 703-684-2400
FAX: 703-684-2492

ISN, INDUSTRIAL SAFETY & HYGIENE
NEWS
755 W. BIG BEAVER RD, SUITE 1000
TROY, MI 48084
TEL: 248-362-3700
FAX: 248-362-0317

JOURNAL OF ENVIRONMENTAL
   HEALTH
720 S COLORADO BLVD, STE 970, S TOW
DENVER, CO 80246
TEL: 303-756-9090
FAX: 303-691-9490

OCCUPATIONAL HAZARDS
1300 EAST NINTH ST,
CLEVELAND, OH 44144
TEL: 216-696-7000
FAX: 216-696-7658

POLLUTION ENGINEERING
2000 CLEARWATER DRIVE
OAK BROOK, IL 60523-8809
TEL: 630-320-7154
FAX: 630-320-7150

POLLUTION ENGINEERING
   INTERNATIONAL
20Q0 CLEARWATER DRIVE
OAK BROOK, IL 60523
TEL: 630-320-7154
FAX: 630-320-7150

POLLUTION EQUIPMENT NEWS
8650 BABCOCK BLVD
PITTSBURGH, PA 15237
TEL: 412-364-5366
FAX: 412-369-9720

SOIL & GROUNDWATER CLEANUP
204 WEST RANSAS, SUITE 103
INDEPENDENCE, MO 64050
TEL: 816-254-8735
FAX: 816-254-2128

WASTE AGE
6151 POWERS FERRY ROAD
ATLANTA, GA 30339-2941
TEL: 770-955-2500
FAX: 770-955-0400

CANADA

CANADIAN ENVIRONMENTAL
   PROTECTION
2323 BOUNDARY ROAD, SUITE 201
VANCOUVER, BC, V5M 4V8 CANADA
TEL: 604-291-9900
FAX: 604-291-1906

MUNICIPAL & INDUSTRIAL WATER &
   POLLUTION CONTROL
11966 WOODBINE AVENUE
GORMLEY, ONTARIO LOH 1G0, CANADA
TEL: 905-887-5048
FAX: 905-887-0764

UNITED KINGDOM

EUROPEAN PACKAGING AND WASTE
   LAW
80 CALVERLEY ROAD
TUNBRIDGE WELLS, KENT TN1 2UN
UNITED KINGDOM
TEL: +44-1892-533 813
FAX: +44-1892-544 895

INDUSTRY COMM FOR PACKAGING
   AND ENVIRONMENT
FOUNTAIN HSE, 1A ELM PK,
   STANMORE,
MIDDLESEX HA7 4BZ UNITED KINGDOM
TEL: +44-01-954-6277

APPENDIX **VI**

Major Environmental Laws

SOURCE:
United States Environmental
Protection Agency

More than a dozen major statutes or laws form the legal basis for the programs of the Environmental Protection Agency (EPA).

National Environmental Policy Act of 1969 (NEPA); 42 U.S.C. 4321-4347
NEPA is the basic national charter for protection of the environment. It establishes policy, sets goals, and provides means for carrying out the policy.

Chemical Safety Information, Site Security and Fuels Regulatory Relief Act
Public Law 106-40, Jan. 6, 1999; 42 U.S.C. 7412(r)
Amendment to Section 112(r) of the Clean Air Act

The Clean Air Act (CAA); 42 U.S.C. s/s 7401 et seq. (1970)

The Clean Water Act (CWA); 33 U.S.C. ss/1251 et seq. (1977)

Comprehensive Environmental Response, Compensation, and Liability Act (CERCLA or Superfund) 42 U.S.C. s/s 9601 et seq. (1980)

The Emergency Planning & Community Right-To-Know Act (EPCRA); 42 U.S.C. 11011 et seq. (1986)

The Endangered Species Act (ESA); 7 U.S.C. 136;16 U.S.C. 460 et seq. (1973)

Federal Insecticide, Fungicide and Rodenticide Act (FIFRA); 7 U.S.C. s/s 135 et seq. (1972)

Federal Food, Drug, and Cosmetic Act (FFDCA) 21 U.S.C. 301 et seq.

Food Quality Protection Act (FQPA) Public Law 104-170, Aug. 3, 1996

The Freedom of Information Act (FOIA); U.S.C. s/s 552 (1966)

The Occupational Safety and Health Act (OSHA); 29 U.S.C. 651 et seq. (1970)

The Oil Pollution Act of 1990 (OPA); 33 U.S.C. 2702 to 2761

The Pollution Prevention Act (PPA); 42 U.S.C. 13101 and 13102, s/s et seq. (1990)

The Resource Conservation and Recovery Act (RCRA); 42 U.S.C. s/s 321 et seq. (1976)

The Safe Drinking Water Act (SDWA); 42 U.S.C. s/s 300f et seq. (1974)

The Superfund Amendments and Reauthorization Act (SARA); 42 U.S.C.9601 et seq. (1986)

The Toxic Substances Control Act (TSCA); 15 U.S.C. s/s 2601 et seq. (1976)

A more comprehensive list of laws administered by EPA is available.

Please note that most of the full text versions below are those available at Cornell University.

This collection was generated from the most recent version of the Government Printing Office CD-ROM. The Government Printing Office maintains the official government version of the laws through the GPO Access database structure.

The U.S. Code is the official record of all federal laws and contains the general and permanent laws of the United States. The most recent version of the U.S. Code released in electronic form contains the laws in effect as of January 16, 1996. For more recent laws one must turn to the uncompiled Public Laws as passed by Congress available through the Thomas Legislative Information Website.

APPENDIX VII

Typical Regulations Encountered by Printers in Lower New York State

SOURCE:
P-F Technical Services, Inc.

	APPLIED BY AGENCY:		
REGULATION	FEDERAL	STATE	LOCAL
SARA TITLE III			
TIER II, INVENTORY	Only if meet threshold levels with listed chemicals.	Submit only if meet threshold . quantities in Federal listings.	LEPC's in Nassau and Suffolk if thresholds met.
			NYCDEP RTK is same as Tier II, only very low levels to qualify and report.
TRI, Section 313	Only if thresholds are met	Copy of Federal TRI goes to NYSDEC	none
PROCESS WATER DISCHARGES		Issue permits and monitor.	NYCDEP monitors and requires semi-annual reports and water lab tests.
			NYCDEP new BMP program for Silver Halides started 9/96. Require on site tests, logs to record and report maintenance.
			Nassau and Suffolk Counties Sewer Depts. are localized;

REGULATION	APPLIED BY AGENCY: FEDERAL	STATE	LOCAL
			testing required at times. Do monitor and test septic tanks, discharges to sewers, etc.
OSHA/HEALTH	Yes	Yes	Yes
SIZE OF FIRM AND LEVEL OF REGULATION:			
CLEAN AIR	NYC METROPOLITAN AREA	VOC'S - ZERO THRESHOLD	
	UPSTATE - LOWER LEVELS		
HAZARDOUS WASTE	Exempt small quantity generator		
	Small quantity generator		
	Large quantity generator		
SARA TITLE III Tier II	Listed as chemical with threshold; OSHA 10,000 pounds.		
Tri report	Listed as chemical; Part of Product 25,000 #/yr; used 10,000 pounds		
NYCDEP FIF	extended list of chemicals, some with thresholds of ZERO, others 50 pounds		
	or more		
CLEAN AIR	EPA enforces federal law,rules. EPA enforces NY Part 200, 201, 234 and other pertinent parts of State law.	6NYCRR Air laws: Part 200 General Provisions Part 201 Construction and Operating Permits	NYCDEP - air permit to erect and certificate to operate. Local fee and regulations.
	Visits and inspects.	Part 234 Graphic Arts Part 231 New Source Review Part 621 Uniform Procedures	Westchester - local codes to erect and operate. consistent with NYSDEC.
	Requests 114 Letters	Part 212 Air Toxics other parts as applicable	Nassau County Health Dept.
	Issues violations.		contract with state but no authority to issue permits.
	Will meet and enforce with legal action, fines	Reviews and issues permits, inspects facilities.	Local authorities will visit and inspect facilities.
		Annual Fuel & Air Emissions report.	
		Periodic reports based on records maintained (have accepted monthly records)	

REGULATION	APPLIED BY AGENCY: FEDERAL	STATE	LOCAL
HAZARDOUS WASTE	Issues ID Numbers	DEC acts as agent for EPA; rules follow Federal rules.	NYCDEP enters HW area in RTK inspections, Waste Process Water discharge tests and reports.
	Will make inspections, sample not regular routine.	Must have HW Mgt program incl Training, Contingency,	
	Issues violations.	Sampling, Closure Plans	Nassau and Suffolk have hazardous storage regs
	Will meet and enforce with legal action, fines	If over 25 tons generated (not disposed), must file HW Reduction Program and file biennial reports.	which could impact on HW storage.
		Annual HW Report	
HAZARDOUS MATERIAL STORAGE	Storage tanks regulation	Storage tank registration.	All areas - Fire Dept permits
		Tanks tests.	Nassau - Article 11 permit and annual report
		Spill Prevention Program	Suffolk County Article 12 & 7 permit.
			NYCDEP RTK facility report inspect for safety.

APPENDIX **VIII**

SOURCE:

Terms of Environment, Glossary, Abbreviations and Acronyms, USEPA, revised December 1997

Abbreviations and Acronyms Used by Environmental Agencies

Terms of Environment defines in non-technical language the more commonly used environmental terms appearing in EPA publications, news releases, and other Agency documents available to the general public, students, the media, and Agency employees. The definitions do not constitute the Agency's official use of terms for regulatory purposes, and nothing in this document should be constructed to alter or supplant any other federal document. Official terminology may be found in the laws and related regulations as published in such sources as the *Congressional Record*, *Federal Register*, and elsewhere.

The terms selected for inclusion are derived from previously published lists, internal glossaries produced by various programs and specific suggestions made by personnel in many Agency offices. The chemicals and pesticides selected for inclusion are limited to those most frequently referred to in Agency publications or that are the subject of major regulatory or program activities.

Definitions or information about substances or program activities not included herein may be found in EPA libraries or scientific/technical reference documents, or may be obtained from various program offices.

Those with suggestions for future editions should write to the Office of Communications, Education, and Public Affairs, 1704, USEPA, Washington, DC 20460-0001.

Also available on http://www.epa.gov/OCEPAterms.

A

A&I: Alternative and Innovative (Wastewater Treatment System)

AA: Accountable Area; Adverse Action; Advices of Allowance; Assistant Administrator; Associate Administrator; Atomic Absorption

AAEE: American Academy of Environmental Engineers

AANWR: Alaskan Arctic National Wildlife Refuge

AAP: Asbestos Action Program

AAPCO: American Association of Pesticide Control Officials

AARC: Alliance for Acid Rain Control

ABEL: EPA's computer model for analyzing a violator's ability to pay a civil penalty.

ABES: Alliance for Balanced Environmental Solutions

AC: Actual Commitment. Advisory Circular

A&C: Abatement and Control

ACA: American Conservation Association

ACBM: Asbestos-Containing Building Material

ACE: Alliance for Clean Energy

ACE: Any Credible Evidence

ACEEE: American Council for an Energy Efficient Economy

ACFM: Actual Cubic Feet Per Minute

ACL: Alternate Concentration Limit. Analytical Chemistry Laboratory

ACM: Asbestos-Containing Material

ACP: Agriculture Control Program (Water Quality Management); ACP: Air Carcinogen Policy

ACQUIRE: Aquatic Information Retrieval

ACQR: Air Quality Control Region

ACS: American Chemical Society

ACT: Action

ACTS: Asbestos Contractor Tracking System

ACWA: American Clean Water Association

ACWM: Asbestos-Containing Waste Material

ADABA: Acceptable Data Base

ADB: Applications Data Base

ADI: Acceptable Daily Intake

ADP: AHERA Designated Person; Automated Data Processing

ADQ: Audits of Data Quality

ADR: Alternate Dispute Resolution

ADSS: Air Data Screening System

ADT: Average Daily Traffic

AEA: Atomic Energy Act

AEC: Associate Enforcement Counsels

AEE: Alliance for Environmental Education

AEERL: Air and Energy Engineering Research Laboratory

AEM: Acoustic Emission Monitoring

AERE: Association of Environmental and Resource Economists

AES: Auger Electron Spectrometry

AFA: American Forestry Association

AFCA: Area Fuel Consumption Allocation

AFCEE: Air Force Center for Environmental Excellence

AFS: AIRS Facility Subsystem

AFUG: AIRS Facility Users Group

AH: Allowance Holders

AHERA: Asbestos Hazard Emergency Response Act

AHU: Air Handling Unit

AI: Active Ingredient

AIC: Active to Inert Conversion

AICUZ: Air Installation Compatible Use Zones

AID: Agency for International Development

AIHC: American Industrial Health Council

AIP: Auto Ignition Point

AIRMON: Atmospheric Integrated Research Monitoring Network

AIRS: Aerometric Information Retrieval System

AL: Acceptable Level

ALA: Delta-Aminolevulinic Acid

ALA-O: Delta-Aminolevulinic Acid Dehydrates

ALAPO: Association of Local Air Pollution Control Officers

ALARA: As Low As Reasonably Achievable

ALC: Application Limiting Constituent

ALJ: Administrative Law Judge

ALMS: Atomic Line Molecular Spectroscopy

ALR: Action Leakage Rate

AMBIENS: Atmospheric Mass Balance of Industrially Emitted and Natural Sulfur

AMOS: Air Management Oversight System

AMPS: Automatic Mapping and Planning System

AMSA: Association of Metropolitan Sewer Agencies

ANC: Acid Neutralizing Capacity

ANPR: Advance Notice of Proposed Rulemaking

ANRHRD: Air, Noise, & Radiation Health Research Division/ORD

ANSS: American Nature Study Society

AOAC: Association of Official Analytical Chemists

AOC: Abnormal Operating Conditions

AOD: Argon-Oxygen Decarbonization

AOML: Atlantic Oceanographic and Meteorological Laboratory

AP: Accounting Point

APA: Administrative Procedures Act

APCA: Air Pollution Control Association

APCD: Air Pollution Control District

APDS: Automated Procurement Documentation System

APHA: American Public Health Association

APRAC: Urban Diffusion Model for Carbon Monoxide from Motor Vehicle Traffic

APTI: Air Pollution Training Institute

APWA: American Public Works Association

AQ-7: Non-reactive Pollutant Modelling

AQCCT: Air-Quality Criteria and Control Techniques

AQCP: Air Quality Control Program

AQCR: Air-Quality Control Region

AQD: Air-Quality Digest

AQDHS: Air-Quality Data Handling System

AQDM: Air-Quality Display Model

AQMA: Air-Quality Maintenance Area

AQMD: Air Quality Management District

AQMP: Air-Quality Maintenance Plan.

AQSM: Air-Quality Simulation Model

AQTAD: Air-Quality Technical Assistance Demonstration

AR: Administrative Record

A&R: Air and Radiation

ARA: Assistant Regional Administrator; Associate Regional Administrator

ARAC: Acid Rain Advisory Committee

ARAR: Applicable or Relevant and Appropriate Standards, Limitations, Criteria, and Requirements

ARB: Air Resources Board

ARC: Agency Ranking Committee

ARCC: American Rivers Conservation Council

ARCS: Alternative Remedial Contract Strategy

ARG: American Resources Group

ARIP: Accidental Release Information Program

ARL: Air Resources Laboratory

ARM: Air Resources Management

ARNEWS: Acid Rain National Early Warning Systems

ARO: Alternate Regulatory Option

ARRP: Acid Rain Research Program

ARRPA: Air Resources Regional Pollution Assessment Model

ARS: Agricultural Research Service

ARZ: Auto Restricted Zone

AS: Area Source

ASC: Area Source Category

ASDWA: Association of State Drinking Water Administrators

ASHAA: Asbestos in Schools Hazard Abatement Act

ASHRAE: American Society of Heating, Refrigerating, and Air-Conditioning Engineers

ASIWCPA: Association of State and Interstate Water Pollution Control Administrators

ASMDHS: Airshed Model Data Handling System

ASRL: Atmospheric Sciences Research Laboratory

AST: Advanced Secondary (Wastewater) Treatment

ASTHO: Association of State and Territorial Health Officers

ASTM: American Society for Testing and Materials

ASTSWMO: Association of State and Territorial Solid Waste Management Officials

AT: Advanced Treatment. Alpha Track Detection

ATERIS: Air Toxics Exposure and Risk Information System

ATS: Action Tracking System; Allowance Tracking System

ATSDR: Agency for Toxic Substances and Disease Registry

ATTF: Air Toxics Task Force

AUSM: Advanced Utility Simulation Model

A/WPR: Air/Water Pollution Report

AWRA: American Water Resources Association

AWT: Advanced Wastewater Treatment

AWWA: American Water Works Association

AWWARF: American Water Works Association Research Foundation.

B

BAA: Board of Assistance Appeals

BAC: Bioremediation Action Committee; Biotechnology Advisory Committee

BACM: Best Available Control Measures

BACT: Best Available Control Technology

BADT: Best Available Demonstrated Technology

BAF: Bioaccumulation Factor

BaP: Benzo(a)Pyrene

BAP: Benefits Analysis Program

BART: Best Available Retrofit Technology

BASIS: Battelle's Automated Search Information System

BAT: Best Available Technology

BATEA: Best Available Treatment Economically Achievable

BCT: Best Control Technology

BCPCT: Best Conventional Pollutant Control Technology

BDAT: Best Demonstrated Achievable Technology

BDCT: Best Demonstrated Control Technology

BDT: Best Demonstrated Technology

BEJ: Best Engineering Judgement. Best Expert Judgment

BF: Bonafide Notice of Intent to Manufacture or Import (IMD/OTS)

BID: Background Information Document. Buoyancy Induced Dispersion

BIOPLUME: Model to Predict the Maximum Extent of Existing Plumes

BMP: Best Management Practice(s)

BMR: Baseline Monitoring Report

BO: Budget Obligations

BOA: Basic Ordering Agreement (Contracts)

BOD: Biochemical Oxygen Demand. Biological Oxygen Demand

BOF: Basic Oxygen Furnace

BOP: Basic Oxygen Process

BOPF: Basic Oxygen Process Furnace

BOYSNC: Beginning of Year Significant Non-Compliers

BP: Boiling Point

BPJ: Best Professional Judgment

BPT: Best Practicable Technology. Pest Practicable Treatment

BPWTT: Best Practical Wastewater Treatment Technology

BRI: Building-Related Illness

BRS: Bibliographic Retrieval Service

BSI: British Standards Institute

BSO: Benzene Soluble Organics

BTZ: Below the Treatment Zone

BUN: Blood Urea Nitrogen

C

CA: Citizen Act. Competition Advocate. Cooperative Agreements. Corrective Action

CAA: Clean Air Act; Compliance Assurance Agreement

CAAA: Clean Air Act Amendments

CAER: Community Awareness and Emergency Response

CAFE: Corporate Average Fuel Economy

CAFO: Concentrated Animal Feedlot; Consent Agreement/Final Order

CAG: Carcinogenic Assessment Group

CAIR: Comprehensive Assessment of Information Rule

CALINE: California Line Source Model

CAM: Compliance Assurance Monitoring rule; Compliance Assurance Monitoring

CAMP: Continuous Air Monitoring Program

CAN: Common Account Number

CAO: Corrective Action Order

CAP: Corrective Action Plan. Cost Allocation Procedure. Criteria Air Pollutant

CAPMoN: Canadian Air and Precipitatiion Monitoring Network

CAR: Corrective Action Report

CAS: Center for Automotive Safety; Chemical Abstract Service

CASAC: Clean Air Scientific Advisory Committee

CASLP: Conference on Alternative State and Local Practices

CASTNet: Clean Air Status and Trends Network

CATS: Corrective Action Tracking System

CAU: Carbon Adsorption Unit; Command Arithmetic Unit

CB: Continuous Bubbler

CBA: Chesapeake Bay Agreement. Cost Benefit Analysis

CBD: Central Business District

CBEP: Community Based Environmental Project

CBI: Compliance Biomonitoring Inspection; Confidential Business Information

CBOD: Carbonaceous Biochemical Oxygen Demand

CBP: Chesapeake Bay Program; County Business Patterns

CCA: Competition in Contracting Act

CCAA: Canadian Clean Air Act

CCAP: Center for Clean Air Policy; Climate Change Action Plan

CCEA: Conventional Combustion Environmental Assessment

CCHW: Citizens Clearinghouse for Hazardous Wastes

CCID: Confidential Chemicals Identification System

CCMS/NATO: Committee on Challenges of a Modern Society/ North Atlantic Treaty Organization

CCP: Composite Correction Plan

CC/RTS: Chemical Collection/ Request Tracking System

CCTP: Clean Coal Technology Program

CD: Climatological Data

CDB: Consolidated Data Base

CDBA: Central Data Base Administrator

CDBG: Community Development Block Grant

CDD: Chlorinated dibenzo-p-dioxin

CDF: Chlorinated dibenzofuran

CDHS: Comprehensive Data Handling System

CDI: Case Development Inspection

CDM: Climatological Dispersion Model; Comprehensive Data Management

CDMQC: Climatological Dispersion Model with Calibration and Source Contribution

CDNS: Climatological Data National Summary

CDP: Census Designated Places

CDS: Compliance Data System

CE: Categorical Exclusion. Conditionally Exempt Generator

CEA: Cooperative Enforcement Agreement; Cost and Economic Assessment

CEAT: Contractor Evidence Audit Team

CEARC: Canadian Environmental Assessment Research Council

CEB: Chemical Element Balance

CEC: Commission for Environmental Cooperation

CECATS: CSB Existing Chemicals Assessment Tracking System

CEE: Center for Environmental Education

CEEM: Center for Energy and Environmental Management

CEI: Compliance Evaluation Inspection

CELRF: Canadian Environmental Law Research Foundation

CEM: Continuous Emission Monitoring

CEMS: Continuous Emission Monitoring System

CEPA: Canadian Environmental Protection Act

CEPP: Chemical Emergency Preparedness Plan

CEQ: Council on Environmental Quality

CERCLA: Comprehensive Environmental Response, Compensation, and Liability Act (1980)

CERCLIS: Comprehensive Environmental Response, Compensation, and Liability Information System

CERT: Certificate of Eligibility

CESQG: Conditionally Exempt Small Quantity Generator

CEST: Community Environmental Service Teams

CF: Conservation Foundation

CFC: Chlorofluorocarbons

CFM: Chlorofluoromethanes

CFR: Code of Federal Regulations

CHABA: Committee on Hearing and Bio-Acoustics

CHAMP: Community Health Air Monitoring Program

CHEMNET: Chemical Industry Emergency Mutual Aid Network

CHESS: Community Health and Environmental Surveillance System

CHIP: Chemical Hazard Information Profiles

CI: Compression Ignition. Confidence Interval

CIAQ: Council on Indoor Air Quality

CIBL: Convective Internal Boundary Layer

CICA: Competition in Contracting Act

CICIS: Chemicals in Commerce Information System

CIDRS: Cascade Impactor Data Reduction System

CIMI: Committee on Integrity and Management Improvement

CIS: Chemical Information System. Contracts Information System

CKD: Cement Kiln Dust

CKRC: Cement Kiln Recycling Coalition

CLC: Capacity Limiting Constituents

CLEANS: Clinical Laboratory for Evaluation and Assessment of Toxic Substances

CLEVER: Clinical Laboratory for Evaluation and Validation of Epidemiologic Research

CLF: Conservation Law Foundation

CLI: ConsumerLabelling Initiative

CLIPS: Chemical List Index and Processing System

CLP: Contract Laboratory Program

CM: Corrective Measure

CMA: Chemical Manufacturers Association

CMB: Chemical Mass Balance

CME: Comprehensive Monitoring Evaluation

CMEL: Comprehensive Monitoring Evaluation Log

CMEP: Critical Mass Energy Project

CNG: Compresed Natural Gas

COCO: Contractor-Owned/ Contractor-Operated

COD: Chemical Oxygen Demand

COH: Coefficient Of Haze

CPDA: Chemical Producers and Distributor Association

CPF: Carcinogenic Potency Factor

CPO: Certified Project Officer

CQA: Construction Quality Assurance

CR: Continuous Radon Monitoring

CROP: Consolidated Rules of Practice

CRP: Child-Resistant Packaging; Conservation Reserve Program

CRR: Center for Renewable Resources

CRSTER: Single Source Dispersion Model

CSCT: Committee for Site Characterization

CSGWPP: Comprehensive State Ground Water Protection Program

CSI: Common Sense Initiative; Compliance Sampling Inspection

CSIN: Chemical Substances Information Network

CSMA: Chemical Specialties Manufacturers Association

CSO: Combined Sewer Overflow

CSPA: Council of State Planning Agencies

CSRL: Center for the Study of Responsive Law

CTARC: Chemical Testing and Assessment Research Commission

CTG: Control Techniques Guidelines

CTSA: Cleaner Technologies Subsitutes Assessment

CV: Chemical Vocabulary

CVS: Constant Volume Sampler

CW: Continuous working-level monitoring

CWA: Clean Water Act (aka FWPCA)

CWAP: Clean Water Action Project

CWTC: Chemical Waste Transportation Council

CZMA: Coastal Zone Management Act

CZARA: Coastal Zone Management Act Reauthorization Amendments

D

DAPSS: Document and Personnel Security System (IMD)

DBP: Disinfection By-Product

DCI: Data Call-In

DCO: Delayed Compliance Order

DCO: Document Control Officer

DDT: DichloroDiphenylTrichloroethane

DERs: Data Evaluation Records

DES: Diethylstilbesterol

DfE: Design for the Environment

DI: Diagnostic Inspection

DMR: Discharge Monitoring Report

DNA: Deoxyribonucleic acid

DNAPL: Dense Non-Aqueous Phase Liquid

DO: Dissolved Oxygen

DOW: Defenders Of Wildlife

DPA: Deepwater Ports Act

DPD: Method of Measuring Chlorine Residual in Water

DQO: Data Quality Objective

DRE: Destruction and Removal Efficiency

DRES: Dietary Risk Evaluation System

DRMS: Defense Reutilization and Marketing Service

DRR: Data Review Record

DS: Dichotomous Sampler

DSAP: Data Self Auditing Program

DSCF: Dry Standard Cubic Feet

DSCM: Dry Standard Cubic Meter

DSS: Decision Support System; Domestic Sewage Study

DT: Detectors (radon) damaged or lost; Detention Time

DU: Decision Unit. Ducks Unlimited; Dobson Unit

DUC: Decision Unit Coordinator

DWEL: Drinking Water Equivalent Level

DWS: Drinking Water Standard

DWSRF: Drinking Water State Revolving Fund

E

EA: Endangerment Assessment; Enforcement Agreement; Environmental Action; Environmental Assessment;. Environmental Audit

EAF: Electric Arc Furnaces

EAG: Exposure Assessment Group

EAP: Environmental Action Plan

EAR: Environmental Auditing Roundtable

EASI: Environmentl Alliance for Senior Involvement

EB: Emissions Balancing

EC: Emulsifiable Concentrate; Environment Canada; Effective Concentration

ECA: Economic Community for Africa

ECAP: Employee Counselling and Assistance Program

ECD: Electron Capture Detector

ECHH: Electro-Catalytic Hyper-Heaters

ECL: Environmental Chemical Laboratory

ECOS: Environmental Council of the States

ECR: Enforcement Case Review

ECRA: Economic Cleanup Responsibility Act

ED: Effective Dose

EDA: Emergency Declaration Area

EDB: Ethylene Dibromide

EDC: Ethylene Dichloride

EDD: Enforcement Decision Document

EDF: Environmental Defense Fund

EDRS: Enforcement Document Retrieval System

EDS: Electronic Data System; Energy Data System

EDTA: Ethylene Diamine Triacetic Acid

EDX: Electronic Data Exchange

EDZ: Emission Density Zoning

EEA: Energy and Environmental Analysis

EECs: Estimated Environmental Concentrations

EER: Excess Emission Report

EERL: Eastern Environmental Radiation Laboratory

EERU: Environmental Emergency Response Unit

EESI: Environment and Energy Study Institute

EESL: Environmental Ecological and Support Laboratory

EETFC: Environmental Effects, Transport, and Fate Committee

EF: Emission Factor

EFO: Equivalent Field Office

EFTC: European Fluorocarbon Technical Committee

EGR: Exhaust Gas Recirculation

EH: Redox Potential

EHC: Environmental Health Committee

EHS: Extremely Hazardous Substance

EI: Emissions Inventory

EIA: Environmental Impact Assessment. Economic Impact Assessment

EIL: Environmental Impairment Liability

EIR: Endangerment Information Report; Environmental Impact Report

EIS: Environmental Impact Statement; Environmental Inventory System

EIS/AS: Emissions Inventory System/ Area Source

EIS/PS: Emissions Inventory System/ Point Source

EKMA: Empirical Kinetic Modeling Approach

EL: Exposure Level

ELI: Environmental Law Institute

ELR: Environmental Law Reporter

EM: Electromagnetic Conductivity

EMAP: Enviornmental Mapping and Assessment Program

EMAS: Enforcement Management and Accountability System

EMR: Environmental Management Report

EMS: Enforcement Management System

EMSL: Environmental Monitoring Support Systems Laboratory

EMTS: Environmental Monitoring Testing Site; Exposure Monitoring Test Site

EnPA: Environmental Performance Agreement

EO: Ethylene Oxide

EOC: Emergency Operating Center

EOF: Emergency Operations Facility (RTP)

EOP: End Of Pipe

EOT: Emergency Operations Team

EP: Earth Protectors; Environmental Profile; End-use Product; Experimental Product; Extraction Procedure

EPAA: Environmental Programs Assistance Act

EPAAR: EPA Acquisition Regulations

EPCA: Energy Policy and Conservation Act

EPACASR: EPA Chemical Activities Status Report

EPACT: Environmental Policy Act

EPCRA: Emergency Planning and Community Right to Know Act

EPD: Emergency Planning District

EPI: Environmental Policy Institute

EPIC: Environmental Photographic Interpretation Center

EPNL: Effective Perceived Noise Level

EPRI: Electric Power Research Institute

EPTC: Extraction Procedure Toxicity Characteristic

EQIP: Environmental Quality Incentives Program

ER: Ecosystem Restoration; Electrical Resistivity

ERA: Economic Regulatory Agency

ERAMS: Environmental Radiation Ambient Monitoring System

ERC: Emergency Response Commission. Emissions Reduction Credit, Environmental Research Center

ERCS: Emergency Response Cleanup Services

ERDA: Energy Research and Development Administration

ERD&DAA: Environmental Research, Development and Demonstration Authorization Act

ERL: Environmental Research Laboratory

ERNS: Emergency Response Notification System

ERP: Enforcement Response Policy

ERT: Emergency Response Team

ERTAQ: ERT Air Quality Model

ES: Enforcement Strategy

ESA: Endangered Species Act. Environmentally Sensitive Area

ESC: Endangered Species Committee

ESCA: Electron Spectroscopy for Chemical Analysis

ESCAP: Economic and Social Commission for Asia and the Pacific

ESECA: Energy Supply and Environmental Coordination Act

ESH: Environmental Safety and Health

ESP: Electrostatic Precipitators

ET: Emissions Trading

ETI: Environmental Technology Initiative

ETP: Emissions Trading Policy

ETS: Emissions Tracking System; Environmental Tobacco Smoke

ETV: Environmental Technology Verification Program

EUP: End-Use Product; Experimental Use Permit

EWCC: Environmental Workforce Coordinating Committee

EXAMS: Exposure Analysis Modeling System

ExEx: Expected Exceedance

F

FACA: Federal Advisory Committee Act

FAN: Fixed Account Number

FATES: FIFRA and TSCA Enforcement System

FBC: Fluidized Bed Combustion

FCC: Fluid Catalytic Converter

FCCC: Framework Convention on Climate Change

FCCU: Fluid Catalytic Cracking Unit

FCO: Federal Coordinating Officer (in disaster areas); Forms Control Officer

FDF: Fundamentally Different Factors

FDL: Final Determination Letter

FDO: Fee Determination Official

FE: Fugitive Emissions

FEDS: Federal Energy Data System

FEFx: Forced Expiratory Flow

FEIS: Fugitive Emissions Information System

FEL: Frank Effect Level

FEPCA: Federal Environmental Pesticide Control Act; enacted as amendments to FIFRA.

FERC: Federal Energy Regulatory Commission

FES: Factor Evaluation System

FEV: Forced Expiratory Volume

FEV1: Forced Expiratory Volume—one second; Front End Volatility Index

FF: Federal Facilities

FFAR: Fuel and Fuel Additive Registration

FFDCA: Federal Food, Drug, and Cosmetic Act

FFF: Firm Financial Facility

FFFSG: Fossil-Fuel-Fired Steam Generator

FFIS: Federal Facilities Information System

FFP: Firm Fixed Price

FGD: Flue-Gas Desulfurization

FID: Flame Ionization Detector

FIFRA: Federal Insecticide, Fungicide, and Rodenticide Act

FIM: Friable Insulation Material

FINDS: Facility Index System

FIP: Final Implementation Plan

FIPS: Federal Information Procedures System

FIT: Field Investigation Team

FLETC: Federal Law Enforcement Training Center

FLM: Federal Land Manager

FLP: Flash Point

FLPMA: Federal Land Policy and Management Act

F/M: Food to Microorganism Ratio

FMAP: Financial Management Assistance Project

FML: Flexible Membrane Liner

FMP: Facility Management Plan; Financial Management Plan

FMS: Financial Management System

FMVCP: Federal Motor Vehicle Control Program

FOE: Friends Of the Earth

FOIA: Freedom Of Information Act

FOISD: Fiber Optic Isolated Spherical Dipole Antenna

FONSI: Finding Of No Significant Impact

FORAST: Forest Response to Anthropogenic Stress

FP: Fine Particulate

FPA: Federal Pesticide Act

FPAS: Foreign Purchase Acknowledgement Statements

FPD: Flame Photometric Detector

FPEIS: Fine Particulate Emissions Information System

FPM: Federal Personnel Manual

FPPA: Federal Pollution Prevention Act

FPR: Federal Procurement Regulation

FPRS: Federal Program Resources Statement; Formal Planning and Supporting System

FQPA: Food Quality Protection Act

FR: Federal Register. Final Rulemaking

FRA: Federal Register Act

FREDS: Flexible Regional Emissions Data System

FRES: Forest Range Environmental Study

FRM: Federal Reference Methods

FRN: Federal Register Notice. Final Rulemaking Notice

FRS: Formal Reporting System

FS: Feasibility Study

FSA: Food Security Act

FSS: Facility Status Sheet; Federal Supply Schedule

FTP: Federal Test Procedure (for motor vehicles)

FTS: File Transfer Service

FTTS: FIFRA/TSCA Tracking System

FUA: Fuel Use Act

FURS: Federal Underground Injection Control Reporting System

FVMP: Federal Visibility Monitoring Program

FWCA: Fish and Wildlife Coordination Act

FWPCA: Federal Water Pollution and Control Act (aka CWA): Federal Water Pollution and Control Administration

G

GAAP: Generally Accepted Accounting Principles

GAC: Granular Activated Carbon

GACT: Granular Activated Carbon Treatment

GAW: Global Atmospheric Watch

GCC: Global Climate Convention

GC/MS: Gas Chromatograph/ Mass Spectograph

GCVTC: Grand Canyon Visibility Transport Commission

GCWR: Gross Combination Weight Rating

GDE: Generic Data Exemption

GEI: Geographic Enforcement Initiative

GEMI: Global Environmental Management Initiative

GEMS: Global Environmental Monitoring System; Graphical Exposure Modeling System

GEP: Good Engineering Practice

GFF: Glass Fiber Filter

GFO: Grant Funding Order

GFP: Government-Furnished Property

GICS: Grant Information and Control System

GIS: Geographic Information Systems; Global Indexing System

GLC: Gas Liquid Chromatography

GLERL: Great Lakes Environmental Research Laboratory

GLNPO: Great Lakes National Program Office

GLP: Good Laboratory Practices

GLWQA: Great Lakes Water Quality Agreement

GMCC: Global Monitoring for Climatic Change

G/MI: Grams per mile

GOCO: Government-Owned/ Contractor-Operated

GOGO: Government-Owned/ Government-Operated

GOP: General Operating Procedures

GOPO: Government-Owned/ Privately-Operated

GPAD: Gallons-per-acre per-day

GPG: Grams-per-Gallon

GPR: Ground-Penetrating Radar

GPS: Groundwater Protection Strategy

GR: Grab Radon Sampling

GRAS: Generally Recognized as Safe

GRCDA: Government Refuse Collection and Disposal Association

GRGL: Groundwater Residue Guidance Level

GT: Gas Turbine

GTN: Global Trend Network

GTR: Government Transportation Request

GVP: Gasoline Vapor Pressure

GVW: Gross Vehicle Weight

GVWR: Gross Vehicle Weight Rating

GW: Grab Working-Level Sampling. Groundwater

GWDR: Ground Water Disinfedtion Rule

GWM: Groundwater Monitoring

GWP: Global Warming Potential

GWPC: Ground Water Protection Council

GWPS: Groundwater Protection Standard; Groundwater Protection Strategy

H

HA: Health Advisory

HAD: Health Assessment Document

HAP: Hazardous Air Pollutant

HAPEMS: Hazardous Air Pollutant Enforcement Management System

HAPPS: Hazardous Air Pollutant Prioritization System

HATREMS: Hazardous and Trace Emissions System

HAZMAT: Hazardous Materials

HAZOP: Hazard and Operability Study

HBFC: Hydrobromofluorocarbon

HC: Hazardous Constituents; Hydrocarbon

HCCPD: Hexachlorocyclo-pentadiene

HCFC: Hydrochlorofluorocarbon

HCP: Hypothermal Coal Process

HDD: Heavy-Duty Diesel

HDDT: Heavy-duty Diesel Truck

HDDV: Heavy-Duty Diesel Vehicle

HDE: Heavy-Duty Engine

HDG: Heavy-Duty Gasoline-Powered Vehicle

HDGT: Heavy-Duty Gasoline Truck

HDGV: Heavy-Duty Gasoline Vehicle

HDPE: High Density Polyethylene

HDT: Highest Dose Tested in a study. Heavy-Duty Truck

HDV: Heavy-Duty Vehicle

HEAL: Human Exposure Assessment Location

HECC: House Energy and Commerce Committee

HEI: Health Effects Institute

HEM: Human Exposure Modeling

HEPA: Highly Efficient Particulate Air Filter

HERS: Hyperion Energy Recovery System

HFC: Hydrofluorocarbon

HHDDV: Heavy Heavy-Duty Diesel Vehicle

HHE: Human Health and the Environment

HHV: Higher Heating Value

HI: Hazard Index

HI-VOL: High-Volume Sampler

HIWAY: A Line Source Model for Gaseous Pollutants

HLRW: High Level Radioactive Waste

HMIS: Hazardous Materials Information System

HMS: Highway Mobile Source

HMTA: Hazardous Materials Transportation Act

HMTR: Hazardous Materials Transportation Regulations

HOC: Halogenated Organic Carbons

HON: Hazardous Organic NESHAP

HOV: High-Occupancy Vehicle

HP: Horse Power

HPLC: High-Performance Liquid Chromatography

HPMS: Highway Performance Monitoring System

HPV: High Priority Violator

HQCDO: Headquarters Case Development Officer

HRS: Hazardous Ranking System

HRUP: High-Risk Urban Problem

HSDB: Hazardous Substance Data Base

HSL: Hazardous Substance List

HSWA: Hazardous and Solid Waste Amendments
HT: Hypothermally Treated

HTP: High Temperature and Pressure

HVAC: Heating, Ventilation, and Air-Conditioning system
HVIO: High Volume Industrial Organics

HW: Hazardous Waste

HWDMS: Hazardous Waste Data Management System

HWGTF: Hazardous Waste Groundwater Task Force; Hazardous Waste Groundwater Test Facility

HWIR: Hazardous Waste Identification Rule

HWLT: Hazardous Waste Land Treatment

HWM: Hazardous Waste Management

HWRTF: Hazardous Waste Restrictions Task Force

HWTC: Hazardous Waste Treatment Council

I

I/A: Innovative/Alternative

IA: Interagency Agreement

IAAC: Interagency Assessment Advisory Committee

IADN: Integrated Atmospheric Deposition Network

IAG: Interagency Agreement

IAP: Incentive Awards Program. Indoor Air Pollution

IAQ: Indoor Air Quality

IARC: International Agency for Research on Cancer

IATDB: Interim Air Toxics Data Base

IBSIN: Innovations in Building Sustainable Industries

IBT: Industrial Biotest Laboratory

IC: Internal Combustion

ICAIR: Interdisciplinary Planning and Information Research

ICAP: Inductively Coupled Argon Plasma

ICB: Information Collection Budget

ICBN: International Commission on the Biological Effects of Noise

ICCP: International Climate Change Partnership

ICE: Industrial Combustion Emissions Model. Internal Combustion Engine

ICP: Inductively Coupled Plasma

ICR: Information Collection Request

ICRE: Ignitability, Corrosivity, Reactivity, Extraction

ICRP: International Commission on Radiological Protection

ICRU: International Commission of Radiological Units and Measurements

ICS: Incident Command System. Institute for Chemical Studies; Intermittent Control Strategies.; Intermittent Control System

ICWM: Institute for Chemical Waste Management

IDLH: Immediately Dangerous to Life and Health

IEB: International Environment Bureau

IEMP: Integrated Environmental Management Project

IES: Institute for Environmental Studies

IFB: Invitation for Bid

IFCAM: Industrial Fuel Choice Analysis Model

IFCS: International Forum on Chemical Safety

IFIS: Industry File Information System

IFMS: Integrated Financial Management System

IFPP: Industrial Fugitive Process Particulate

IGCC: Integrated Gasification Combined Cycle

IGCI: Industrial Gas Cleaning Institute

IIS: Inflationary Impact Statement

IINERT: In-Place Inactivation and Natural Restoration Technologies

IJC: International Joint Commission (on Great Lakes)

I/M: Inspection/Maintenance

IMM: Intersection Midblock Model

IMPACT: Integrated Model of Plumes and Atmosphere in Complex Terrain

IMPROVE: Interagency Monitoring of Protected Visual Environment

INPUFF: Gaussian Puff Dispersion Model

INT: Intermittent

IOB: Iron Ore Beneficiation

IOU: Input/Output Unit

IPCC: Intergovernmental Panel on Climate Change

IPCS: International Program on Chemical Safety

IP: Inhalable Particles

IPM: Inhalable Particulate Matter. Integrated Pest Management

IPP: Implementation Planning Program. Integrated Plotting Package; Inter-media Priority Pollutant (document); Independent Power Producer

IRG: Interagency Review Group

IRLG: Interagency Regulatory Liaison Group (Composed of EPA, CPSC, FDA, and OSHA)

IRIS: Instructional Resources Information System. Integrated Risk Information System

IRM: Intermediate Remedial Measures

IRMC: Inter-Regulatory Risk Management Council

IRP: Installation Restoration Program

IRPTC: International Register of Potentially Toxic Chemicals

IRR: Institute of Resource Recovery

IRS: International Referral Systems

IS: Interim Status

ISAM: Indexed Sequential File Access Method

ISC: Industrial Source Complex

ISCL: Interim Status Compliance Letter

ISCLT: Industrial Source Complex Long Term Model

ISCST: Industrial Source Complex Short Term Model

ISD: Interim Status Document

ISE: Ion-specific electrode

ISMAP: Indirect Source Model for Air Pollution

ISO: International Organization for Standardization

ISPF: (IBM) Interactive System Productivity Facility

ISS: Interim Status Standards

ITC: Inovative Technology Council; Interagency Testing Committee

ITRC: Interstate Technology Regulatory Coordination

ITRD: Innovative Treatment Remediation Demostration

IUP: Intended Use Plan

IUR: Inventory Update Rule

IWC: In-Stream Waste Concentration

IWS: Ionizing Wet Scrubber

J

JAPCA: Journal of Air Pollution Control Association

JCL: Job Control Language

JEC: Joint Economic Committee

JECFA: Joint Expert Committee of Food Additives

JEIOG: Joint Emissions Inventory Oversight Group

JLC: Justification for Limited Competition

JMPR: Joint Meeting on Pesticide Residues

JNCP: Justification for Non-Competitive Procurement

JOFOC: Justification for Other Than Full and Open Competition

JPA: Joint Permitting Agreement

JSD: Jackson Structured Design

JSP: Jackson Structured Programming

JTU: Jackson Turbidity Unit

L

LAA: Lead Agency Attorney

LADD: Lifetime Average Daily Dose; Lowest Acceptable Daily Dose

LAER: Lowest Achievable Emission Rate

LAI: Laboratory Audit Inspection

LAMP: Lake Acidification Mitigation Project

LC: Lethal Concentration. Liquid Chromatography

LCA: Life Cycle Aassessment

LCD: Local Climatological Data

LCL: Lower Control Limit

LCM: Life Cycle Management

LCRS: Leachate Collection and Removal System

LD: Land Disposal. Light Duty

LD L0: The lowest dosage of a toxic substance that kills test organisms.

LDC: London Dumping Convention

LDCRS: Leachate Detection, Collection, and Removal System

LDD: Light-Duty Diesel

LDDT: Light-Duty Diesel Truck

LDDV: Light-Duty Diesel Vehicle

LDGT: Light-Duty Gasoline Truck

LDIP: Laboratory Data Integrity Program

LDR: Land Disposal Restrictions

LDRTF: Land Disposal Restrictions Task Force

LDS: Leak Detection System

LDT: Lowest Dose Tested. Light-Duty Truck

LDV: Light-Duty Vehicle

LEL: Lowest Effect Level. Lower Explosive Limit

LEP: Laboratory Evaluation Program

LEPC: Local Emergency Planning Committee

LERC: Local Emergency Response Committee

LEV: Low Emissions Vehicle

LFG: Landfill Gas

LFL: Lower Flammability Limit

LGR: Local Governments Reimbursement Program

LHDDV: Light Heavy-Duty Diesel Vehicle

LI: Langelier Index

LIDAR: Light Detection and Ranging

LIMB: Limestone-Injection Multi-Stage Burner

LLRW: Low Level Radioactive Waste

LMFBR: Liquid Metal Fast Breeder Reactor

LMOP: Landfill Methane Outreach Program

LNAPL: Light Non-Aqueous Phase Liquid

LOAEL: Lowest-Observed-Adverse-Effect-Level

LOD: Limit of Detection

LQER: Lesser Quantity Emission Rates

LQG: Large Quantity Generator

LRTAP: Long Range Transboundary Air Pollution

LUIS: Label Use Information System

M

MAC: Mobile Air Conditioner

MAPSIM: Mesoscale Air Pollution Simulation Model

MATC: Maximum Acceptable Toxic Concentration

MBAS: Methylene-Blue-Active Substances

MCL: Maximum Contaminant Level

MCLG: Maximum Contaminant Level Goal

MDL: Method Detection Limit

MEC: Model Energy Code

MEI: Maximally (or most) Exposed Individual

MEP: Multiple Extraction Procedure

MHDDV: Medium Heavy-Duty Diesel Vehicle

MOBILE5A: Mobile Source Emission Factor Model

MOE: Margin Of Exposure

MOS: Margin of Safety

MP: Manufacturing-use Product; Melting Point

MPCA: Microbial Pest Control Agent

MPI: Maximum Permitted Intake

MPN: Maximum Possible Number

MPWC: Multiprocess Wet Cleaning

MRF: Materials Recovery Facility

MRID: Master Record Identification number

MRL: Maximum-Residue Limit (Pesticide Tolerance)

MSW: Municipal Solid Waste

MTD: Maximum Tolerated Dose

MUP: Manufacturing-Use Product

MUTA: Mutagenicity

MWC: Nachine Wet Cleaning

N

NAA: Nonattainment Area

NAAEC: North American Agreement on Environmental Cooperation

NAAQS: National Ambient Air Quality Standards

NACA: National Agricultural Chemicals Association

NACEPT: National Advisory Council for Environmental Policy and Technology

NADP/NTN: National Atmospheric Deposition Program/National Trends Network

NAMS: National Air Monitoring Stations

NAPAP: National Acid Precipitation Assessment Program

NAPL: Non-Aqueous Phase Liquid

NAPS: National Air Pollution Surveillance

NARA: National Agrichemical Retailers Association

NARSTO: North American Research Strategy for Tropospheric Ozone

NAS: National Academy of Sciences

NASDA: National Association of State Departments of Agriculture

NCAMP: National Coalition Against the Misuse of Pesticides

NCEPI: National Center for Environmental Publications and Information

NCWS: Non-Community Water System

NEDS: National Emissions Data System

NEPI: National Environmental Policy Institute

NEPPS: National Environmental Performance Partnership System

NESHAP: National Emission Standard for Hazardous Air Pollutants

NIEHS: National Institute for Environmental Health Sciences

NETA: National Environmental Training Association

NFRAP: No Further Remedial Action Planned

NICT: National Incident Coordination Team

NIOSH: National Institute of Occupational Safety and Health

NIPDWR: National Interim Primary Drinking Water Regulations

NISAC: National Industrial Security Advisory Committee

NMHC: Nonmethane Hydrocarbons

NMOC: Non-Methane Organic Component

NMVOC: Non-methane Volatile Organic Chemicals

NO: Nitric Oxide

NOA: Notice of Arrival

NOAA: National Oceanographic and Atmospheric Agency

NOAC: Nature of Action Code

NOAEL: No Observable Adverse Effect Level

NOEL: No Observable Effect Level

NOIC: Notice of Intent to Cancel

NOIS: Notice of Intent to Suspend

N_2O: Nitrous Oxide

NO_x: Nitrogen Oxides

NORM: Naturally Occurring Radioactive Material

NPCA: National Pest Control Association

NPDES: National Pollutant Discharge Elimination System

NPHAP: National Pesticide Hazard Assessment Program

NPIRS: National Pesticide Information Retrieval System

NPTN: National Pesticide Telecommunications Network

NRD: Naural Resource Damage

NRDC: Natural Resources Defense Council

NSDWR: National Secondary Drinking Water Regulations

NSEC: National System for Emergency Coordination

NSEP: National System for Emergency Preparedness

NSPS: New Source Performance Standards

NSR: New Source Review

NTI: National Toxics Inventory

NTIS: National Technical Information Service

NTNCWS: Non-Transient Non-Community Water System

NTP: National Toxicology Program

NTU: Nephlometric Turbidity Unit

O

O_3: Ozone

OCD: Offshore and Coastal Dispersion

ODP: Ozone-Depleting Potential

ODS: Ozone-Depleting Substances

OECD: Organization for Economic Cooperation and Development

OF: Optional Form

OLTS: On Line Tracking System

O&M: Operations and Maintenance

ORM: Other Regulated Material

ORP: Oxidation-Reduction Potential

OTAG: Ozone Transport Assessment Group

OTC: Ozone Transport Commission

OTR: Ozone Transport Region

P

P2: Pollution Prevention

PAG: Pesticide Assignment Guidelines

PAH: Polynuclear Aromatic Hydrocarbons

PAI: Performance Audit Inspection (CWA); Pure Active Ingredient compound

PAM: Pesticide Analytical Manual

PAMS: Photochemical Assessment Monitoring Stations

PAT: Permit Assistance Team (RCRA)

PATS: Pesticide Action Tracking System; Pesticides Analytical Transport Solution

Pb: Lead

PBA: Preliminary Benefit Analysis (BEAD)

PCA: Principle Component Analysis

PCB: Polychlorinated Biphenyl

PCE: Perchloroethylene

PCM: Phase Contrast Microscopy

PCN: Policy Criteria Notice

PCO: Pest Control Operator

PCSD: President's Council on Sustainable Development

PDCI: Product Data Call-In

PFC: Perfluorated Carbon

PFCRA: Program Fraud Civil Remedies Act

PHC: Principal Hazardous Constituent

PHI: Pre-Harvest Interval

PHSA: Public Health Service Act

PI: Preliminary Injunction. Program Information

PIC: Products of Incomplete Combustion

PIGS: Pesticides in Groundwater Strategy

PIMS: Pesticide Incident Monitoring System

PIN: Pesticide Information Network; Procurement Information Notice

PIP: Public Involvement Program

PIPQUIC: Program Integration Project Queries Used in Interactive Command

PIRG: Public Interest Research Group

PIRT: Pretreatment Implementation Review Task Force

PIT: Permit Improvement Team

PITS: Project Information Tracking System

PLIRRA: Pollution Liability Insurance and Risk Retention Act

PLM: Polarized Light Microscopy

PLUVUE: Plume Visibility Model

PM: Particulate Matter

PMAS: Photochemical Assessment Monitoring Stations

PM2.5: Particulate Matter Smaller than 2.5 Micrometers in Diameter

PM10: Particulate Matter (nominally 10m and less)

PM15: Particulate Matter (nominally 15m and less)

PMEL: Pacific Marine Environmental Laboratory

PMN: Premanufacture Notification

PMNF: Premanufacture Notification Form

PMR: Pollutant Mass Rate; Proportionate Mortality Ratio

PMRS: Performance Management and Recognition System

PMS: Program Management System

PNA: Polynuclear Aromatic Hydrocarbons

PO: Project Officer

POC: Point Of Compliance

POE: Point Of Exposure

POGO: Privately-Owned/ Government-Operated

POHC: Principal Organic Hazardous Constituent

POI: Point Of Interception

POLREP: Pollution Report

POM: Particulate Organic Matter. Polycyclic Organic Matter

POP: Persistent Organic Pollutant

POR: Program of Requirements

POTW: Publicly Owned Treatment Works

POV: Privately Owned Vehicle

PP: Program Planning

PPA: Planned Program Accomplishment

PPB: Parts Per Billion

PPE: Personal Protective Equipment

PPG: Performance Partnership Grant

PPIC: Pesticide Programs Information Center

PPIS: Pesticide Product Information System; Pollution Prevention Incentives for States

PPMAP: Power Planning Modeling Application Procedure

PPM/PPB: Parts per million/ parts per billion

PPSP: Power Plant Siting Program

PPT: Parts Per Trillion

PPTH: Parts Per Thousand

PQUA: Preliminary Quantitative Usage Analysis

PR: Pesticide Regulation Notice; Preliminary Review

PRA: Paperwork Reduction Act; Planned Regulatory Action

PRATS: Pesticides Regulatory Action Tracking System

PRC: Planning Research Corporation

PRI: Periodic Reinvestigation

PRM: Prevention Reference Manuals

PRN: Pesticide Registration Notice

PRP: Potentially Responsible Party

PRZM: Pesticide Root Zone Model

PS: Point Source

PSAM: Point Source Ambient Monitoring

PSC: Program Site Coordinator

PSD: Prevention of Significant Deterioration

PSES: Pretreatment Standards for Existing Sources

PSI: Pollutant Standards Index; Pounds Per Square Inch; Pressure Per Square Inch

PSIG: Pressure Per Square Inch Gauge

PSM: Point Source Monitoring

PSNS: Pretreatment Standards for New Sources

PSU: Primary Sampling Unit

PTDIS: Single Stack Meteorological Model in EPA UNAMAP Series

PTE: Potential to Emit

PTFE: Polytetrafluoroethylene (Teflon)

PTMAX: Single Stack Meteorological Model in EPA UNAMAP series

PTPLU: Point Source Gaussian Diffusion Model

PUC: Public Utility Commission

PV: Project Verification

PVC: Polyvinyl Chloride

PWB: Printed Wiring Board

PWS: Public Water Supply

PWSS: Public Water Supply System

Q

QAC: Quality Assurance Coordinator

QA/QC: Quality Assistance/ Quality Control

QAMIS: Quality Assurance Management and Information System

QAO: Quality Assurance Officer

QAPP: Quality Assurance Program (or Project) Plan

QAT: Quality Action Team

QBTU: Quadrillion British Thermal Units

QC: Quality Control

QCA: Quiet Communities Act

QCI: Quality Control Index

QCP: Quiet Community Program

QL: Quantification Limit

QNCR: Quarterly Noncompliance Report

QUA: Qualitative Use Assessment

QUIPE: Quarterly Update for Inspector in Pesticide Enforcement

R

RA: Reasonable Alternative; Regional Administrator; Regulatory Alternatives; Regulatory Analysis; Remedial Action; Resource Allocation; Risk Analysis; Risk Assessment

RAATS: RCRA Administrate Action Tracking System

RAC: Radiation Advisory Committee. Raw Agricultural Commodity; Regional Asbestos Coordinator. Response Action Coordinator

RACM: Reasonably Available Control Measures

RACT: Reasonably Available Control Technology

RAD: Radiation Adsorbed Dose (unit of measurement of radiation absorbed by humans)

RADM: Random Walk Advection and Dispersion Model; Regional Acid Deposition Model

RAM: Urban Air Quality Model for Point and Area Source in EPA UNAMAP Series

RAMP: Rural Abandoned Mine Program

RAMS: Regional Air Monitoring System

RAP: Radon Action Program; Registration Assessment Panel; Remedial Accomplishment Plan; Response Action Plan

RAPS: Regional Air Pollution Study

RARG: Regulatory Analysis Review Group

RAS: Routine Analytical Service

RAT: Relative Accuracy Test

RB: Request for Bid

RBAC: Re-use Business Assistance Center

RBC: Red Blood Cell

RC: Responsibility Center

RCC: Radiation Coordinating Council

RCDO: Regional Case Development Officer

RCO: Regional Compliance Officer

RCP: Research Centers Program

RCRA: Resource Conservation and Recovery Act

RCRIS: Resource Conservation and Recovery Information System

RD/RA: Remedial Design/ Remedial Action

R&D: Research and Development

RD&D: Research, Development and Demonstration

RDF: Refuse-Derived Fuel

rDNA: Recombinant DNA

RDU: Regional Decision Units

RDV: Reference Dose Values

RE: Reasonable Efforts; Reportable Event

REAP: Regional Enforcement Activities Plan

RECLAIM: Regional Clean Air Initiatives Marker

RED: Reregistration Eligibility Decision Document

REDA: Recycling Economic Development Advocate

REE: Rare Earth Elements

REEP: Review of Environmental Effects of Pollutants

ReFIT: Reinvention for Innovative Technlogies

REI: Restricted Entry Interval

REM (Roentgen Equivalent Man)

REM/FIT: Remedial/Field Investigation Team

REMS: RCRA Enforcement Management System

REP: Reasonable Efforts Program

REPS: Regional Emissions Projection System

RESOLVE: Center for Environmental Conflict Resolution

RF: Response Factor

RFA: Regulatory Flexibility Act

RFB: Request for Bid

RfC: Reference Concentration

RFD: Reference Dose Values

RFI: Remedial Field Investigation

RFP: Reasonable Further Programs. Request for Proposal

RHRS: Revised Hazard Ranking System

RI: Reconnaissance Inspection

RI: Remedial Investigation

RIA: Regulatory Impact Analysis; Regulatory Impact Assessment

RIC: Radon Information Center

RICC: Retirement Information and Counseling Center

RICO: Racketeer Influenced and Corrupt Organizations Act

RI/FS: Remedial Information/ Feasibility Study

RIM: Regulatory Interpretation Memorandum

RIN: Regulatory Identifier Number

RIP: RCRA Implementation Plan

RISC: Regulatory Information Service Center

RJE: Remote Job Entry

RLL: Rapid and Large Leakage (Rate)

RMCL: Recommended Maximum Contaminant Level (this phrase being discontinued in favor of MCLG)

RMDHS: Regional Model Data Handling System

RMIS: Resources Management Information System

RNA: Ribonucleic Acid

ROADCHEM: Roadway Version that Includes Chemical Reactions of BI, NO_x and O_3

ROADWAY: A Model to Predict Pollutant Concentrations Near a Roadway

ROC: Record Of Communication

RODS: Records Of Decision System

ROG: Reactive Organic Gases

ROLLBACK: A Proportional Reduction Model

ROM: Regional Oxidant Model

ROMCOE: Rocky Mountain Center on Environment

ROP: Rate of Progress; Regional Oversight Policy

ROPA: Record Of Procurement Action

ROSA: Regional Ozone Study Area

RP: Radon Progeny Integrated Sampling. Respirable Particulates. Responsible Party

RPAR: Rebuttable Presumption Against Registration

RPM: Reactive Plume Model. Remedial Project Manager

RQ: Reportable Quantities

RRC: Regional Response Center

RRT: Regional Response Team; Requisite Remedial Technology

RS: Registration Standard

RSCC: Regional Sample Control Center

RSD: Risk-Specific Dose

RSE: Removal Site Evaluation

RTCM: Reasonable Transportation Control Measure

RTDF: Remediation Technologies Development Forum

RTDM: Rough Terrain Diffusion Model

RTECS: Registry of Toxic Effects of Chemical Substances

RTM: Regional Transport Model

RTP: Research Triangle Park

RUP: Restricted Use Pesticide

RVP: Reid Vapor Pressure

RWC: Residential Wood Combustion

S

S&A: Sampling and Analysis. Surveillance and Analysis

SAB: Science Advisory Board

SAC: Suspended and Cancelled Pesticides

SAEWG: Standing Air Emissions Work Group

SAIC: Special-Agents-In-Charge

SAIP: Systems Acquisition and Implementation Program

SAMI: Southern Appalachian Mountains Initiative

SAMWG: Standing Air Monitoring Work Group

SANE: Sulfur and Nitrogen Emissions

SANSS: Structure and Nomenclature Search System

SAP: Scientific Advisory Panel

SAR: Start Action Request. Structural Activity Relationship (of a qualitative assessment)

SARA: Superfund Amendments and Reauthorization Act of 1986

SAROAD: Storage and Retrieval Of Aerometric Data

SAS: Special Analytical Service. Statistical Analysis System

SASS: Source Assessment Sampling System

SAV: Submerged Aquatic Vegetation

SBC: Single Breath Cannister

SBS: Sick Building Syndrome

SC: Sierra Club

SCAP: Superfund Consolidated Accomplishments Plan

SCBA: Self-Contained Breathing Apparatus

SCC: Source Classification Code

SCD/SWDC: Soil or Soil and Water Conservation District

SCFM: Standard Cubic Feet Per Minute

SCLDF: Sierra Club Legal Defense Fund

SCR: Selective Catalytic Reduction

SCRAM: State Consolidated RCRA Authorization Manual

SCRC: Superfund Community Relations Coordinator

SCS: Supplementary Control Strategy/System

SCSA: Soil Conservation Society of America

SCSP: Storm and Combined Sewer Program

SCW: Supercritical Water Oxidation

SDC: Systems Decision Plan

SDWA: Safe Drinking Water Act

SDWIS: Safe Driking Water Information System

SEA: State Enforcement Agreement

SEA: State/EPA Agreement

SEAM: Surface, Environment, and Mining

SEAS: Strategic Environmental Assessment System

SEDS: State Energy Data System

SEGIP: State Environmental Goals and Improvement Project

SEIA: Socioeconomic Impact Analysis

SEM: Standard Error of the Means

SEP: Standard Evaluation Procedures

SEP: Supplementary Environmental Project

SEPWC: Senate Environment and Public Works Committee

SERC: State Emergency Planning Commission

SES: Secondary Emissions Standard

SETAC: Society for Environmental Toxicology and Chemistry

SETS: Site Enforcement Tracking System

SF: Standard Form. Superfund

SFA: Spectral Flame Analyzers

SFDS: Sanitary Facility Data System

SFFAS: Superfund Financial Assessment System

SFIREG: State FIFRA Issues Research and Evaluation Group

SFS: State Funding Study

SHORTZ: Short Term Terrain Model

SHWL: Seasonal High Water Level

SI: International System of Units. Site Inspection. Surveillance Index. Spark Ignition

SIC: Standard Industrial Classification

SICEA: Steel Industry Compliance Extension Act

SIMS: Secondary Ion-Mass Spectrometry

SIP: State Implementation Plan

SITE: Superfund Innovative Technology Evaluation

SLAMS: State/Local Air Monitoring Station

SLN: Special Local Need

SLSM: Simple Line Source Model

SMART: Simple Maintenance of ARTS

SMCL: Secondary Maximum Contaminant Level

SMCRA: Surface Mining Control and Reclamation Act

SME: Subject Matter Expert

SMO: Sample Management Office

SMOA: Superfund Memorandum of Agreement

SMP: State Management Plan

SMR: Standardized Mortality Ratio

SMSA: Standard Metropolitan Statistical Area

SNA: System Network Architecture

SNAAQS: Secondary National Ambient Air Quality Standards

SNAP: Significant New Alternatives Project; Significant Noncompliance Action Program

SNARL: Suggested No Adverse Response Level

SNC: Significant Noncompliers

SNUR: Significant New Use Rule

SO$_2$: Sulfur Dioxide

SOC: Synthetic Organic Chemicals

SOCMI: Synthetic Organic Chemicals Manufacturing Industry

SOFC: Solid Oxide Fuel Cell

SOTDAT: Source Test Data

SOW: Scope Of Work

SPAR: Status of Permit Application Report

SPCC: Spill Prevention, Containment, and Countermeasure

SPE: Secondary Particulate Emissions

SPF: Structured Programming Facility

SPI: Strategic Planning Initiative

SPLMD: Soil-pore Liquid Monitoring Device

SPMS: Strategic Planning and Management System; Special Purpose Monitoring Stations

SPOC: Single Point Of Contact

SPS: State Permit System

SPSS: Statistical Package for the Social Sciences

SPUR: Software Package for Unique Reports

SQBE: Small Quantity Burner Exemption

SQG: Small Quantity Generator; Sediment Quality Guidelines

SR: Special Review

SRAP: Superfund Remedial Accomplishment Plan

SRC: Solvent-Refined Coal

SRF: State Revolving Fund

SRM: Standard Reference Method

SRP: Special Review Procedure

SRR: Second Round Review. Submission Review Record

SRTS: Service Request Tracking System

SS: Settleable Solids. Superfund Surcharge. Suspended Solids

SSA: Sole Source Aquifer

SSAC: Soil Site Assimilated Capacity

SSC: State Superfund Contracts

SSD: Standards Support Document

SSEIS: Standard Support and Environmental Impact Statementt; Stationary Source Emissions and Inventory System.

SSI: Size Selective Inlet

SSMS: Spark Source Mass Spectrometry

SSO: Sanitary Sewer Overflow; Source Selection Official

SSRP: Source Reduction Review Project

SSTS: Section Seven Tracking System

SSURO: Stop Sale, Use and Removal Order

STALAPCO: State and Local Air-Pollution Control Officials

STAPPA: State and Territorial Air Pollution

STAR: Stability Wind Rose. State Acid Rain Projects

STARS: Strategic Targeted Activities for Results System

STEL: Short Term Exposure Limit

STEM: Scanning Transmission-Electron Microscope

STN: Scientific and Technical Information Network

STORET: Storage and Retrieval of Water-Related Data

STP: Sewage Treatment Plant. Standard Temperature and Pressure

STTF: Small Town Task Force (EPA)

SUP: Standard Unit of Processing

SURE: Sulfate Regional Experiment Program

SV: Sampling Visit; Significant Violater

SW: Slow Wave

SWAP: Source Water Assesment Program

SWARF: Waste from Metal Grinding Process

SWC: Settlement With Conditions

SWDA: Solid Waste Disposal Act

SWIE: Southern Waste Information Exchange

SWMU: Solid Waste Management Unit

SWPA: Source Water Protection Area

SWQPPP: Source Water Quality Protection Partnership Petitions

SWTR: Surface Water Treatment Rule

SYSOP: Systems Operator

T

TAD: Technical Asssistance Document

TAG: Technical Assistance Grant

TALMS: Tunable Atomic Line Molecular Spectroscopy

TAMS: Toxic Air Monitoring System

TAMTAC: Toxic Air Monitoring System Advisory Committee

TAP: Technical Assistance Program

TAPDS: Toxic Air Pollutant Data System

TAS: Tolerance Assessment System

TBT: Tributyltin

TC: Target Concentration. Technical Center. Toxicity Characteristics. Toxic Concentration:

TCDD: Dioxin (Tetrachlorodibenzo-p-dioxin)

TCDF: Tetrachlorodi-benzofurans

TCE: Trichloroethylene

TCF: Total Chlorine Free

TCLP: Total Concentrate Leachate Procedure. Toxicity Characteristic Leachate Procedure

TCM: Transportation Control Measure

TCP: Transportation Control Plan; Trichloropropane;

TCRI: Toxic Chemical Release Inventory

TD: Toxic Dose

TDS: Total Dissolved Solids

TEAM: Total Exposure Assessment Model

TEC: Technical Evaluation Committee

TED: Turtle Excluder Devices

TEG: Tetraethylene Glycol

TEGD: Technical Enforcement Guidance Document

TEL: Tetraethyl Lead

TEM: Texas Episodic Model

TEP: Typical End-use Product. Technical Evaluation Panel

TERA: TSCA Environmental Release Application

TES: Technical Enforcement Support

TEXIN: Texas Intersection Air Quality Model

TGO: Total Gross Output

TGAI: Technical Grade of the Active Ingredient

TGP: Technical Grade Product

THC: Total Hydrocarbons

THM: Trihalomethane

TI: Temporary Intermittent; Therapeutic Index

TIBL: Thermal Internal Boundary Layer

TIC: Technical Information Coordinator. Tentatively Identified Compounds

TIM: Technical Information Manager

TIP: Technical Information Package; Transportation Improvement Program

TIS: Tolerance Index System

TISE: Take It Somewhere Else

TITC: Toxic Substance Control Act Interagency Testing Committee

TLV: Threshold Limit Value

TLV-C: TLV-Ceiling

TLV-STEL: TLV-Short Term Exposure Limit

TLV-TWA: TLV-Time Weighted Average

TMDL: Total Maximum Daily Limit; Total Maximum Daily Load

TMRC: Theoretical Maximum Residue Contribution

TNCWS: Transient Non-Community Water System

TNT: Trinitrotoluene

TO: Task Order

TOA: Trace Organic Analysis

TOC: Total Organic Carbon/ Compound

TOX: Tetradichloroxylene

TP: Technical Product; Total Particulates

TPC: Testing Priorities Committee

TPI: Technical Proposal Instructions

TPQ: Threshold Planning Quantity

TPSIS: Transportation Planning Support Information System

TPTH: Triphenyltinhydroxide

TPY: Tons Per Year

TQM: Total Quality Management

T-R: Transformer-Rectifier

TRC: Technical Review Committee

TRD: Technical Review Document

TRI: Toxic Release Inventory

TRIP: Toxic Release Inventory Program

TRIS: Toxic Chemical Release Inventory System

TRLN: Triangle Research Library Network

TRO: Temporary Restraining Order

TSA: Technical Systems Audit

TSCA: Toxic Substances Control Act

TSCATS: TSCA Test Submissions Database

TSCC: Toxic Substances Coordinating Committee

TSD: Technical Support Document

TSDF: Treatment, Storage, and Disposal Facility

TSDG: Toxic Substances Dialogue Group

TSI: Thermal System Insulation

TSM: Transportation System Management

TSO: Time Sharing Option

TSP: Total Suspended Particulates

TSS: Total Suspended (non-filterable) Solids

TTFA: Target Transformation Factor Analysis

TTHM: Total Trihalomethane

TTN: Technology Transfer Network

TTO: Total Toxic Organics

TTY: Teletypewriter

TVA: Tennessee Valley Authority

TVOC: Total Volatile Organic Compounds

TWA: Time Weighted Average

TWS: Transient Water System

TZ: Treatment Zone

U

UAC: User Advisory Committee

UAM: Urban Airshed Model

UAO: Unilateral Administrative Order

UAPSP: Utility Acid Precipitation Study Program

UAQI: Uniform Air Quality Index

UARG: Utility Air Regulatory Group

UCC: Ultra Clean Coal

UCCI: Urea-Formaldehyde Foam Insulation

UCL: Upper Control Limit

UDMH: Unsymmetrical Dimethyl Hydrazine

UEL: Upper Explosive Limit

UF: Uncertainty Factor

UFL: Upper Flammability Limit

ug/m3: Microgrms Per Cubic Meter

UIC: Underground Injection Control

ULEV: Ultra Low Emission Vehicles

UMTRCA: Uranium Mill Tailings Radiation Control Act

UNAMAP: Users' Network for Applied Modeling of Air Pollution

UNECE: United Nations Economic Commission for Europe

UNEP: United Nations Environment Program

USC: Unified Soil Classification

USDA: United States Department of Agriculture

USDW: Underground Sources of Drinking Water

USFS: United States Forest Service FS:

UST: Underground Storage Tank

UTM: Universal Transverse Mercator

UTP: Urban Transportation Planning

UV: Ultraviolet

UVA, UVB, UVC: Ultraviolet Radiation Bands

UZM: Unsaturated Zone Monitoring

V

VCM: Vinyl Chloride Monomer

VCP: Voluntary Cleanup Program

VE: Visual Emissions

VEO: Visible Emission Observation

VSI: Visual Site Inspection

VSS: Volatile Suspended Solids

VOC: Volatile Organic Compounds

VOS: Vehicle Operating Survey

VOST: Volatile Organic Sampling Trair

VP: Vapor Pressure

W

WAP: Waste Analysis Plan

WAVE: Water Alliances for Environme tal Efficiency

WB: Wet Bulb

WDROP: Distribution Register of Organic Pollutants in Water

WENDB: Water Enforcement National Data Base

WERL: Water Engineering Research Laboratory

WET: Whole Effluent Toxicity test

WHO: World Health Organization

WHP: Wellhead Protection Program

WHPA: Wellhead Protection Area

WHWT: Water and Hazardous Waste Team

WICEM: World Industry Conference or Environmental Management

WL: Warning Letter; Working Level (radon measurement)

WLA/TMDL: Wasteload Allocation/ Total Maximum Daily Load

WLM: Working Level Months

WMO: World Meteorological Organiza tion

WP: Wettable Powder

WPCF: Water Pollution Control Federa tion

WQS: Water Quality Standard

WRC: Water Resources Council

WRDA: Water Resources Development Act

WRI: World Resources Institute

WSF: Water Soluble Fraction

WSRA: Wild and Scenic Rivers Act

WSTB: Water Sciences and Technology Board

WSTP: Wastewater Sewage Treatment Plant

WWEMA: Waste and Wastewater Equipment Manufacturers Association

WWF: World Wildlife Fund

WWTP: Wastewater Treatment Plant

WWTU: Wastewater Treatment Unit

Z

ZEV: Zero Emissions Vehicle

ZHE: Zero Headspace Extractor

ZOI: Zone Of Incorporation

ZRL: Zero Risk Level

APPENDIX **IX**

Pollution Prevention Opportunities: Flexography, Lithography, Screen

SOURCE:

Flexography, *Flexographic Ink Options: A Cleaner Technologies Substitutes Assessment*, USEPA Document EPA 744-R-00-004a; Lithography, *Fit to Print*, An Environmental Prevention Manual for New England Lithographers, USEPA, Document EPA-903-B-97-001; Screen, *Cleaner Technologies Substitutes Assessment*, USEPA, Document EPA 744-R-94-005

Opportunities for reducing or eliminating pollution exist in every printing process. Ink and solvents present many opportunities for substitution, better usage and ultimately elimination of the chemicals that result in wastes in various forms. We have selected lists from a few sources to demonstrate, by process, some of the very obvious means of attacking pollution. There are duplications between the lists but this should only confirm the fact that printers, regardless of process, face some of the same challenges. This is seen in the general flow chart for materials going into and wastes coming out of the generic printing process flow chart.

The flexography list was developed as part of an internal document written to guide the Design for the Environment staff in the flexography ink alternatives project (Part 1) (pp 502–506).

The lithographic pollution prevention opportunities is excerpted from *"Fit to Print, An Environmental Compliance and Pollution Prevention Manual for New England Lithographers,"* published by USEPA Region I (EPA-901-B-97-001, May 1997) (Part 2) (pp 506–509).

The screen printers opportunities are taken from the CTSA of the Design for the Environment project for screen reclamation. (EPA744R-94-005, September 1994) (Part 3) (pp 511–512).

While each format is different, the content and objectives are consistent. The question is universal. How do we pinpoint activities and usage that can lend themselves to a safer environment?

Do your pollution prevention audit and then compare the existing conditions in your plant with the opportunities listed in this appendix. How many experiences are reflected in both? What can you learn from the test that will help you create a safer workplace.

PART 1 — FLEXOGRAPHY

GUIDE FOR IDENTIFICATION OF POTENTIAL POLLUTION PREVENTION OPPORTUNITIES

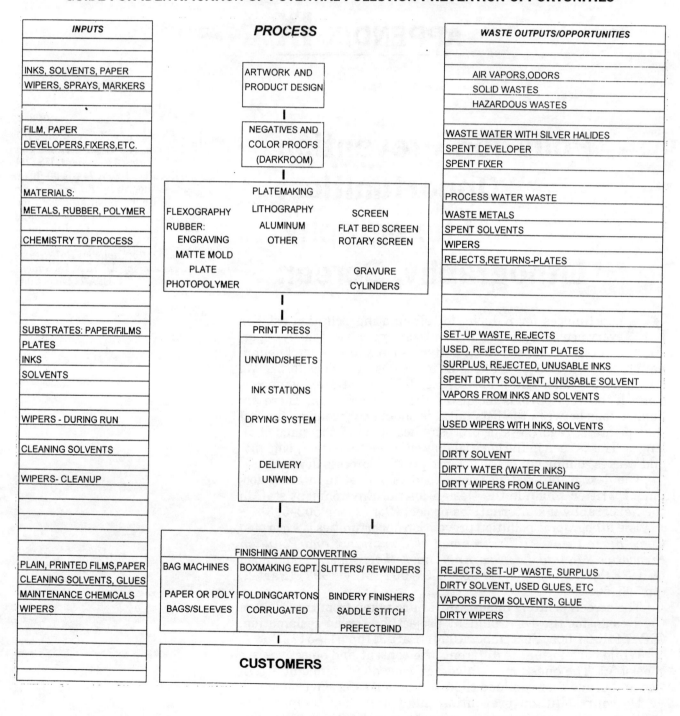

INPUTS	PROCESS	WASTE OUTPUTS/OPPORTUNITIES
INKS, SOLVENTS, PAPER WIPERS, SPRAYS, MARKERS	ARTWORK AND PRODUCT DESIGN	AIR VAPORS, ODORS SOLID WASTES HAZARDOUS WASTES
FILM, PAPER DEVELOPERS, FIXERS, ETC.	NEGATIVES AND COLOR PROOFS (DARKROOM)	WASTE WATER WITH SILVER HALIDES SPENT DEVELOPER SPENT FIXER
MATERIALS: METALS, RUBBER, POLYMER CHEMISTRY TO PROCESS	PLATEMAKING FLEXOGRAPHY LITHOGRAPHY SCREEN RUBBER: ALUMINUM FLAT BED SCREEN ENGRAVING OTHER ROTARY SCREEN MATTE MOLD PLATE GRAVURE PHOTOPOLYMER CYLINDERS	PROCESS WATER WASTE WASTE METALS SPENT SOLVENTS WIPERS REJECTS, RETURNS-PLATES
SUBSTRATES: PAPER/FILMS PLATES INKS SOLVENTS WIPERS - DURING RUN CLEANING SOLVENTS WIPERS- CLEANUP	PRINT PRESS UNWIND/SHEETS INK STATIONS DRYING SYSTEM DELIVERY UNWIND	SET-UP WASTE, REJECTS USED, REJECTED PRINT PLATES SURPLUS, REJECTED, UNUSABLE INKS SPENT DIRTY SOLVENT, UNUSABLE SOLVENT VAPORS FROM INKS AND SOLVENTS USED WIPERS WITH INKS, SOLVENTS DIRTY SOLVENT DIRTY WATER (WATER INKS) DIRTY WIPERS FROM CLEANING
PLAIN, PRINTED FILMS, PAPER CLEANING SOLVENTS, GLUES MAINTENANCE CHEMICALS WIPERS	FINISHING AND CONVERTING BAG MACHINES BOXMAKING EQPT. SLITTERS/ REWINDERS PAPER OR POLY FOLDINGCARTONS BINDERY FINISHERS BAGS/SLEEVES CORRUGATED SADDLE STITCH PREFECTBIND	REJECTS, SET-UP WASTE, SURPLUS DIRTY SOLVENT, USED GLUES, ETC VAPORS FROM SOLVENTS, GLUE DIRTY WIPERS
	CUSTOMERS	

DEPARTMENT ACTIVITY	POLLUTANT/WASTE	REGULATIONS	OPTIONS/ACTIONS
PRE-PRESS			
Art preparation	Solvents in sprays, markers, adhesives, thinners.	OSHA,	1. Water based products, hot melt adhesives.
			2. Air cleaning devices, hoods. Innovative - Ozone reactors to reduce pollutants to harmless compounds.
			3. Computer graphics and design.
Negative process for platemaking	Silver halides in films,paper. Removed by developer and fixer and wash for discharge to waste water system.	Wastewater- Silver standards RCRA - HW	1. Silver recovery systems 2. Recirculation systems. 3. Computer generated graphics and negatives.
PLATEMAKING			
RUBBER:			
Engravings	Magnesium, zinc, copper	RCRA, HW SARA TRI if over threshold.	1. Replace with photopolymers 2. Eliminate zinc and copper 3. Laser engraved rubber plates
	Nitric Acid bath	Wastewater - corrosive acids heavy metals	Neutralize and filter out metal. Dispose as non-regulated water waste for further treatment; HW if metal levels exceed standards.
Mattes	Board	Solid Waste in landfills	Consider use as alternate fuel. Break down to pellets for feed
Rubber plates	Rubber compounds	Solid Waste in landfills	Consider use as alternate fuel. Break down to pellets for feed
PHOTOPOLYMER			
SOLVENT WASH			
Monomers	Monomers and solids in washout solvents, sludges from solvent recovery.	RCRA HW OSHA	1. Alternate fuel (special kiln) 2. Controlled landfill 3. Change to safer solvent

DEPARTMENT ACTIVITY	POLLUTANT/WASTE	REGULATIONS	OPTIONS/ACTIONS
Washout Solvents	Perchloroethylene	RCRA HW	1. Solvent recovery, reuse clean
	1,1,1 Trichloroethane		solvent; dispose sludge as HW.
			2. Replace solvent with non-HW
			solvent, recycle, landfill sludge.
Reject/Used Plates	Plates with solvent absorbed	RCRA HW	1. Alternate fuel (special kiln)
	during processing and while		2. With safer solvent, can be
	cleaning during printing.		alternate fuel or landfill.
PHOTOPOLYMER			
WATER WASH			
Monomers	Monomers and solids in	Waste Water	Clarification treatment, reclaim
	water discharges.	solids in effluent.	water for process; sludge to
			landfill.
Washout Solvents	Water plus any chemical	Waste Water	Clarification treatment, reclaim
	additives and solids in	solids in effluent.	water for process; sludge to
	discharges.	? chemicals and	landfill, unless above limits
		amount in water.	for POTW.
Reject/Used Plates	Plastic plates	Solid waste in	1. Alternate fuel
		landfills.	2. Landfill
MOUNT/PROOF			
Clean cylinders	Toluene, Hexane	RCRA HW, OSHA	Replace with less volatile solvent
and used plates	Wipers with solvents	RCRA HW, OSHA	Laundry, or disposable (incinerate)
PRESSROOM			
Solvent Based Ink	Alcohols, Esters, Ketones	CAA - VOC's	1. Add-on control, catalytic oxidize
	Other Hydrocarbon solvents	RCRA - HW	2. Rework used inks, dirty solvent
	Pigments - traces of metals	Storage Hazmat	3. Reuse inks, control inventory.
	Pigments - Heavy Metals	Transport Hazmat	4. Ink management
		OSHA	5. Select and modify/purchase new
		SARA RTK, TRI	presses to use ink alternatives -
			high solids, water, UV curable.
		MACT, CAA90	(see below)
		Listed HW-RCRA	
	Other solvents - HAPS:		
	Methanol	MACT, CAA90	Denaturant in ethanol -replace
	Ethyl Glycols	Listed HW-RCRA	Replace with Propylene Glycols
	Toluene		Replace with safer cleaning agent

DEPARTMENT ACTIVITY	POLLUTANT/WASTE	REGULATIONS	OPTIONS/ACTIONS
Alternatives:			
High Strength	Alcohols, Esters, Ketones	CAA - VOC's	1. Re-etch anilox rollers, less volum
(High Solids)	Other Hydrocarbon solvents	RCRA - HW	2. Recover rubber roller- harder
	Pigments - traces of metals	Storage Hazmat	3. Replace 2 roll with chamber
		Transport Hazmat	doctor blade system, proper anilox
		OSHA	roller with proper screen/volumes.
		SARA RTK	
Water	Ethylene Glycols, Ethers	CAA - VOCs	1. Replace with Propylene Glycols
	Alcohols	CAA - VOCs	2. Re-etch anilox rollers, less volum
		OSHA	3. Recover rubber roller- harder
	Cleaning water and agents	Waste Water	4. Replace 2 roll with chamber
			doctor blade system, proper anilox
			roller with proper screen/volumes.
			5. Modify drying system
			6. Add corona treater for films
			7. Water treatment (if necessary)
Alternatives			
UV Curable	UV Lights	RCRA - HW	Press retro-fit, if possible.
	Photoinitiator (sensitizes)	OSHA	Preferred - new press for UV
	Waste inks/cleaning solvent		
Set-up & Run Press			
Substrates	Film,paper waste due to set-up	Solid Waste	Recycle off-site.
	Splices, top and core waste		If mixed substrates, alternative fuel
Inks	Rejected color matches	CAA	Adjust or rework inks.
	Air emissions	RCRA - HW	Add-on or alternative ink
		OSHA	
Solvents	Cleaning wipers	RCRA - HW	Laundry or disposable (incinerate)
	Air emissions	OSHA	Add-on or alternative ink
Quality Controls	Rejected product	Solid Waste	Salvage or get customer waiver.
			Recycle discards off-site
Clean-up Job			
Solvents	Alcohols, Esters, Ketones	CAA - VOC's	1. Safer cleaning solvents
And Inks	Other Hydrocarbon solvents	RCRA - HW	2. Cleaning tank
	Pigments - traces of metals	OSHA	3. New cleaning equipment/Borax
	Pigments - Heavy Metals	SARA RTK, TRI	4. New cleaning agents
			5. Use spray bottle to dispense.

DEPARTMENT ACTIVITY	POLLUTANT/WASTE	REGULATIONS	OPTIONS/ACTIONS
			6. Automatic cleaning equipment
			7. Solvent recovery
Wipers	Dirty wipers with ink and solvent	RCRA - HW	1. Launder and reuse
		OSHA	2. Disposable wipers (incinerate)
Solvent Recovery	Dirty solvent, unusable inks	RCRA - HW	1. Reclaim solvent for reuse.
			2. Sludge, still bottoms - incinerate.
Water Treatment	Dirty water ink cleanup, inks	Waste Water	1. Filtration
			2. Clarification
			3. Evaporation
			4. Reuse in darker or same colors
CONVERTING			
LAMINATING	Solvent based adhesives	CAA - VOC's	1. Water based adhesives
AND COATING	and coatings	RCRA - HW	2. Solventless laminations
	Cleaning solvents	OSHA	3. Extrusion lamination
		SARA RTK, TRI	4. Add-on controls
	Substrates	Solid Waste	1. Recycle off-site.
			2. Mixed substrates - alternate fuel
SLITTING/REWIND	Substrates	Solid Waste	1. Recycle off-site.
			2. Mixed substrates - alternate fuel
BAG MAKING	Substrates	Solid Waste	1. Recycle off-site.
BOX MAKING			2. Mixed substrates - alternate fuel

PART 2 — LITHOGRAPHY

PREPRESS WASTE

Wastewater	Hazardous Waste*	Air Emissions	Solid Wastes

• Used, treated fixers
• Used developers
• Used activators/ stabilizers
• Plate developer
• Rinse water
	• Chrome-based system cleaners
	• Non-empty aerosol cans
	• Discarded, unused, or outdated chemicals
	• Used, untreated fixers
	• Used shop towels contaminated with hazardous waste**
	• Proofing system chemicals
		• Volatile Organic Compounds (VOCs) or toxics emitted from
		  -Film cleaner
		  -Proofing systems solvents
			• Empty containers
			• Developed or out-dated film
			• Out-dated materials
			• Used or damaged plates
			• Used, empty aerosol cans
			• Used shop towels**

PRESS WASTE

Wastewater	Hazardous Wastes*	Air Emissions	Solid Wastes

• Spent fountain solution
• Rinse water
	• Waste ink containing solvents
	• Waste lubricating oil (if defined as hazardous waste by your state)
	• Used blanket or roller wash
	• Spent cleaning solvent
	• Used shop towels contaminated with hazardous waste**
	• Used parts washer solvent
		• VOCs or toxics emitted from
		  - Solvents from heatset inks/ink oils
		  - Isopropyl alcohol
		  - Cleaning solvents
		  - Coatings
		  - Solvent-saturated shop towels
		  - Fountain solution additives
			• Ink containers
			• Used plates
			• Used blankets
			• Off-spec printings
			• Paper wrappings
			• Paper roll ends
			• Unprinted paper roll cores
			• End caps
			• Used shop towels**

POSTPRESS WASTE

Wastewater	Hazardous Wastes*	Air Emissions	Solid Wastes

• Water-based inks from ink jet operations
• Water-based coatings
• Water-based adhesives
	• Used shop towels contaminated with hazardous waste**	• VOCs or toxics emitted from
		  - Adhesives
		  - Coatings
			• Waste paper
			• Waste shipping materials
			• Scrap board
			• Excess adhesives
			• Used shop towels**
			• Non-recyclable paper
			• Empty containers

HOUSEKEEPING WASTE

Wastewater	Hazardous Wastes	Air Emissions	Solid Wastes

• Cleaning wastewater	• Waste oil (if defined as hazardous waste by your state)
	• Absorbent materials used to pick up residual oils (if defined as hazardous waste by your state) or solvents
	• Used shop towels contaminated with hazardous waste**
		• VOCs or toxics emitted from
		  - Miscellaneous cleaners
		  - Paints
		  - Parts washers
			• Empty containers
			• Used shop towels**
			• Pallets

* A waste is a "hazardous waste" if it is listed in federal or state regulations or if it exhibits hazardous characteristics. (See Section 5.1 for the definition.) The list of hazardous waste here assumes that the waste meets one of these criteria.

** Check with your state's hazardous waste office (see the information presented in the pocket at the end of this manual) to help you determine whether your shop towels are hazardous.

GOOD ENVIRONMENTAL MANAGEMENT PRACTICES

Here are some tips on good environmental management practices that could help you save money and improve your operations:

- Document all actions you take to reduce or eliminate emissions.

- Keep good records of product purchases and use so you can accurately calculate your emissions.

- Do appropriate reporting and keep important records of waste disposal.

- Document your actual and potential VOC and HAP emissions calculations as well as your operating time.

- Educate your customers on the environmental impacts of their product choices.

- Conserve and reuse inks.

- Handle solvents carefully to minimize spills.

- Avoid use of products containing VOCs and chlorinated solvents (e.g., benzene, 1,1,1-trichloroethylene, methylene chloride, toluene, and xylene).

- Choose solvents with a low VOC content or low vapor pressure or that are water-miscible when possible.

- Reuse shop towels for low quality cleaning needs in the shop prior to proper disposal.

- Use solvents conservatively by using plunger cans to dispense solvents with meters and using only the amount necessary. Appoint one person to store and distribute solvents.

- Do not leave shop towels out in the open; use a metal container with a lid that can be closed using a foot pedal.

- Do not leave product containers open.

- Switch to alcohol-free fountain solution — today.

POLLUTION PREVENTION OPPORTUNITIES FOR AIR EMISSIONS

This section describes pollution prevention (P2) opportunities that can limit air emissions. Information on whether the technique is easy or more difficult to use is included next to each listing, followed by a description of the technique and its benefits Each discussion provides information on the relative cost of the technique and the waste streams that can be reduced using each technique, where possible.

Cover Photoprocessing Chemical Container — Easy

Technique: This is a simple P2 technique that can be implemented at your shop to:

- Reduce or eliminate air emissions generated by chemical evaporation.
- Reduce purchases of virgin photoprocessing chemicals.

Developers evaporate very quickly, while fixers evaporate at a slightly slower rate. The containers should always be sealed or covered to prevent evaporation. Many print shops use floating lids, caps, or other devices to do this. You should also cover trays overnight if tray processing is done.

Benefits:
- Your photoprocessing costs are reduced because there is minimal loss of the product through evaporation.
- Your working environment will be safer because of the reduction and/or elimination of air emissions from the solutions.

Costs:
- This technique may require you to purchase covers and lids. Special tanks/containers can be purchased for $20 to $250.

Alternative Fountain Solution — Easy/Moderate

Technique: The use of alternative fountain solution will reduce or eliminate your facility's VOC emissions. Fountain solutions traditionally contain isopropyl alcohol (IPA). Non-IPA fountain solutions that use glycol ether are typically used as a replacement for IPA.

Benefits:
- Substitutes may help you meet VOC emission limits for your printing shop.
- Since substitutes are used at much lower concentrations, you will incur cost savings by using less product.
- Substitutes will improve the indoor air quality of your shop because VOC emissions will be significantly reduced or eliminated.
- Substitutes eliminate the use of highly flammable, dangerous products.

Costs:
- Non-IPA fountain solutions cost approximately $18 to $20 per gallon, while IPA solutions cost around $10 per gallon.
- Non-IPA fountain solutions perform differently on the press than IPA solutions. Generally, their operating range is smaller, and the viscosity can vary with temperature resulting in inconsistent wetting.

Alternative Cleaning Solutions — Moderate

Technique: The use of alternative blanket washes and cleaners that are less toxic and flammable will reduce your facility's VOC emissions. Typical press-cleaning solutions contain aliphatic and aromatic hydrocarbons. Alternative blanket washes, which contain mixtures of glycol ethers and other heavier hydrocarbons, have higher flash-points and low toxicities, which are formulated to produce lower VOC emissions. These glycol ether solutions clean comparably to conventional solvents.

These alterative cleaning solutions do not evaporate as rapidly as other solvents and may require a substantially longer drying time. Because of the environmental and safety benefits of these materials, however, they are gaining in popularity. Cleanup should be done with detergents or soap solutions wherever possible. Solvents should be used only for cleaning up inks and oils.

Water miscible solvents are another alternative worth exploring. They contain 100percent VOCs when purchased, but are cut to 50 percent with water, so at press contain only 50 percent VOCs by content.

Benefits:
- The benefit of using lower VOC solvents is the reduced VOC emissions, which improves indoor and regional air quality.

Costs: Many alternative cleaning solutions require a substantially longer drying time. Extra time is required for cleaning presses.

Water-Based Adhesives for Postpress Operations — Moderate

Technique: Water-based adhesives have long been used in printing shop operations in addition to using solvent-based adhesives. However, an important trend in postpress operations is the increasing use of water-based adhesives in place of solvent-based adhesives, which contain toluene and methyl ethyl ketone, two highly toxic chemicals.

Benefits:
- Reduces VOC and HAP emissions from solvent-based adhesives.
- Reduces worker exposure to hazards.

Reduce Fountain Solution Temperature — Moderate/Challenging

Technique: This P2 technique is a good operating practice that will minimize waste paper and ink generated from poor press runs, as well as significantly reduce VOC emissions. Whether you use IPA or non-lPA fountain solution, you can maximize the efficiency of the fountain solutions by maintaining them at their optimum operating temperature through cooling or refrigeration. The optimum temperature may vary for different solutions.

Refrigeration units can be installed for large presses. The smallest press that can typically accommodate a refrigeration unit is a 26-inch one-color press.

Benefits:
- A refrigeration unit with a filtration system can significantly extend the life of non-IPA fountain solutions by removing ink and paper particles. Fountain solution life may be extended to months instead of days.
- Reduced fountain solution losses.
- Increased employee safety by reduced exposure to VOC emissions.

Costs:
- They do not work well in open fountains.
- A fairly significant capital expenditure is required for the refrigeration unit and the replumbing. A 5-gallon refrigeration unit costs approximately $2,400, and the plumbing can cost approximately $1,000.

PART 3 — SCREEN PRINTING

BENEFITS OF WORKPLACE PRACTICES TO RAISE EMPLOYEE AWARENESS

Workplace Practices	Benefits
Prepare a written environmental policy	Establishes environmental management goals; illustrates management commitment to pollution prevention and environmental goals
Prepare written procedures on equipment operation and maintenance, materials handling and disposal	Better informs employees of the proper procedures for using and disposing of materials
Provide employee training on health and safety issues, materials handling and disposal	Ensures that employees have proper training to understand benefits of proper materials handling and disposal, and potential consequences of improper workplace practices to their health and safety, the environment, and company profitability
Seek employee input on pollution prevention activities	Encourages the persons closest to the process, the operators, to develop the best, most creative approach to pollution prevention; employee involvement and ownership of the program is essential to a successful program
Make employees accountable for waste generation and provide incentives for reduction	Encourages employees to be aware of ways they can prevent pollution; rewards active involvement in pollution prevention activities
Provide feedback to employees on materials handling and disposal and pollution prevention performance	Re-emphasizes management commitment to pollution prevention; encourages employees to continue to improve

BENEFITS OF WORKPLACE PRACTICES FOR MATERIALS MANAGEMENT AND INVENTORY CONTROL

Workplace Practices	Benefits
Manage inventories on a first-in, first-out basis	Reduces materials and disposal costs of expired materials
Maintain accurate logs of chemical and materials stock, chemicals and materials use, and waste generation rates	Understanding materials flow and how it relates to waste generation rates provides insights into pollution prevention opportunities
Minimize the amount of chemicals kept on the floor at any time	Gives employees an incentive to use less materials
Centralize responsibility for storing and distributing chemicals	Gives employees an incentive to use less materials
Segregate waste by waste stream and keep in marked, easily accessible, closed containers	Allows for more effective reuse or recycling of waste materials; prevents nonhazardous waste from becoming contaminated with hazardous waste; minimizes evaporation of VOCs; reduces worker exposure
Keep spent solvents in marked, easily accessible, closed containers	Promotes waste segregation, recovery and reuse; minimizes evaporation of VOCs; reduces worker exposure

BENEFITS OF PROCESS IMPROVEMENTS TO PREVENT POLLUTION

Workplace Practices	Benefits
Keep chemicals in safety cans or covered containers between uses	Reduces materials loss; increases worker safety; reduces worker exposure
Use plunger cans, squeeze bottles or specialized spraying equipment to apply chemicals to the screen	Reduces potential for accidental spills; reduces materials use; reduces worker exposure
Consider manual, spot-application of chemicals, where applicable	Reduces materials use; reduces worker exposure if aerosol mists are avoided
Use a pump to transfer cleaning solutions from large containers to the smaller containers used at the work station	Reduces potential for accidental spills; reduces worker exposure
Reduce the size of the towel or wipe used during clean-up	More efficient use of the towel; reduces solvent use; reduces worker exposure
Reuse shop towels on the first pass with ink remover	Reduces material (shop towel and ink remover) use; reduces worker exposure
Evaluate alternative chemical: water dilution ratios (increase the amount of water)	Reduces chemical usage with no loss of efficiency; reduced worker exposure
Only apply chemicals where necessary	Reduces chemical usage; reduces worker exposure
Avoid delays in cleaning and reclaiming the screen	Simplify ink and emulsion removal; less potential for haze on the screen
Gravity-drain, wring, or centrifuge excess solvent from rags	Recovers solvent for reuse
Place catch basins around the screen during the screen cleaning/reclamation process	Captures chemical overspray for recovery and reuse
Use appropriate personal protective equipment (gloves, barrier cream, respirator, etc.)	Reduces worker exposure

APPENDIX X

Pollution Prevention Checklist for Printers

SOURCE:

P-F Technical Services, Inc.

An audit for pollution prevention requires an in-depth analysis of the materials, process and working practices that take place from the time an order is entered until the final product is shipped. This checklist encompasses every activity that takes place in the making of a printed product. The audit team can pursue the materials that enter the facility and the ensuing use or disposal as waste of the various components.

The checklist provides for discussion and planning for source reduction, materials substitution or recycling and recovery of materials for reuse. Pertinent regulations are noted, to serve as a guide when multimedia solutions to release of wastes are addressed.

The checklist will be supported by use of other tools described in this book, such as flow charts and mass balances. Arriving at recommendations for reduction or elimination of pollutants will be facilitated by use of the cause-and-effect fishbone chart.

Start when an order is written and artwork has to be developed. Follow the processes from artwork to image carrier to press to finishing/converting. At each step, note the materials/chemicals that enter the process and what happens to the components of the materials. Do they remain in the product? Does some evaporate and mix with the room air, or is the vapor exhausted through a stack or a fan? Is waste collected for disposal? Is any of the chemistry discharged into drains that empty into the sewer system?

Having assembled this information, the question can then be asked at each stage: Is this step necessary or is there a better, less waste-producing or less toxic way of making this printed product?

(EXPAND ROWS TO SUIT NEEDS OF FACILITY)

	POTENTIAL FOR: SOURCE REDUCTION	MATERIALS SUBSTITUTION	RECYCLING	PERTINENT REGULATIONS								
				AIR	HW	WATR	STOR	SARA	RTK	SLID	OSHA	OTHER
A. PREPRESS												
1. ARTWORK - TRADITIONAL												
a. Materials												
b. Solvents												
c. Equipment												
d. Methods												
e. Wastes												
2. ARTWORK - COMPUTER												
a. Materials												
b. Solvents												
c. Equipment												
d. Methods												
e. Wastes												
3. ARTWORK - DIRECT TO PLATE												
a. Materials												
b. Solvents												
c. Equipment												
d. Methods												
4. DARKROOM												
a. Materials												
b. Machinery												
c. Methods												
d. Waste s												
5. COLOR SEPARATION												
a. Materials												
b. Machinery												
c. Methods												
d. Wastes												
B. PLATE MAKING												
1. RUBBER PLATES												
a. Materials												
Acid Bath												
b. Machinery												
c. Methods												
d. Wastes												
2. PHOTOPOLYMERS - SOLVENT WASHOUT												
a. Materials												
b. Machinery												
c. Methods												
d. Wastes												
3. PHOTOPOLYMERS - WATER WASHOUT												
a. Materials												
b. Machinery												
c. Methods												
d. Wastes												

(EXPAND ROWS TO SUIT NEEDS OF FACILITY)	POTENTIAL FOR: SOURCE REDUCTION	RECYCLING	MATERIALS SUBSTITUTION	PERTINENT REGULATIONS AIR	HW	WATR	STOR	SARA	RTK	SLID	OSHA	OTHER
4. LASER ENGRAVING - RUBBER AND PHOTOPOLYMER												
a. Materials												
b. Wastes												
5. LITHOGRAPHIC PLATES												
a. Materials												
b. Machinery												
c. Methods												
d. Wastes												
6. SCREEN PRINTING												
a. Materials												
b. Machinery												
c. Methods												
d. Wastes												
C. MOUNTING AND PROOFING												
1. OPTICAL MOUNTING AND PROOFING												
a. Materials												
b. Machinery												
c. Methods												
d. Waste s												
2. PIN REGISTER MOUNTING SYSTEMS												
a. Materials												
b. Machinery												
c. Methods												
d. Wastes												
3. DIRECT TO PRESS												
a. Materials												
b. Machinery												
c. Methods												
d. Wastes												
D. SET-UP PRESS												
1. ROLL TO ROLL PRESSES												
a. Materials												
b. Machinery												
INK TRAIN												
DRYING												
ANILOX												
c. Methods												
d. Wastes												
2. IN-LINE PRINTING PRESSES												
a. Materials												
b. Machinery												
c. Methods												
d. Wastes												
E. RUN PRESS												
1. ROLL TO ROLL PRESSES												
a. Materials												

(EXPAND ROWS TO SUIT NEEDS OF FACILITY)

POTENTIAL FOR: SOURCE REDUCTION — MATERIALS SUBSTITUTION — RECYCLING — PERTINENT REGULATIONS (AIR | HW | WATR | STOR | SARA | RTK | SLID | OSHA | OTHER)

- b. Machinery
  - INK TRAIN
  - DRYING
  - ANILOX
- c. Methods
- d. Waste Streams

2. IN-LINE PRINTING PRESSES
   - a. Materials
   - b. Machinery
   - c. Methods
   - d. Waste Streams

3. QUALITY MANAGEMENT AT PRESS

F. CLEAN-UP PRESS
1. ROLL TO ROLL PRESSES
   - a. Materials
   - b. Machinery
   - c. Methods
   - d. Wastes

F. CLEAN-UP PRESS
2. IN-LINE PRINTING PRESSES
   - a. Materials
   - b. Machinery
   - c. Methods
   - d. Wastes

3. AUTOMATION IN CLEAN-UP

PROCESS AND FINISHING
1. LAMINATING
   - a. Materials
   - b. Machinery
   - c. Methods
   - d. Wastes

2. COATING
   - a. Materials
   - b. Machinery
   - c. Methods
   - d. Wastes

3. SLITTING AND REWINDING
   - a. Materials
   - b. Machinery
   - c. Methods
   - d. Wastes

4. BAG MAKING
   - a. Materials
   - b. Machinery
   - c. Methods
   - d. Wastes

5. BOX MAKING
   - a. Materials
   - b. Machinery

(EXPAND ROWS TO SUIT NEEDS OF FACILITY)

	POTENTIAL FOR:			PERTINENT REGULATIONS								
	SOURCE REDUCTION	MATERIALS SUBSTITUTION	RECYCLING	AIR	HW	WATR	STOR	SARA	RTK	SLID	OSHA	OTHER
c. Methods												
d. Wastes												
6. LABELS AND TAGS												
a. Materials												
b. Machinery												
c. Methods												
d. Wastes												
7. COMMERCIAL PRINTING												
BINDERY/FINISHING												
a. Materials												
b. Machinery												
c. Methods												
d. Wastes												
8. OTHER PRODUCTS												
a. Materials												
b. Machinery												
c. Methods												
d. Wastes												

APPENDIX **XI**

SOURCE:
Joseph Badalamenti, Disc Graphics

Flow Diagram,
Chemical Usage at Presses

The flow chart is a tool for depicting the steps on a process, leading to the final outcome. In a study of work practices, the flow chart will itemize the motions or activities that take place in order to accomplish a job. As used in environmental studies, the flow chart maps the route taken by chemicals and the various byproducts that result from the use of these chemicals.

The development of the flow chart starts with observation of the specific process. Note what is happening and why in the sequence that events take place. Then consult the mass balance to determine amount of the products used and disposition of waste streams. Waste disposal manifests and bills of lading will provide information as to quantities of waste disposed and the ultimate destination and method of processing the waste.

Flow charts can be developed using spreadsheet software such as Excel or Lotus 123 or software designed for the purpose. The physical depiction of the process allows for the understanding of interrelationships between materials used and the waste streams that are created. This relationship is critical when considering materials substitutions or source reductions that will alter the way the process works.

This example plots the various chemical products used at the press in conjunction with lithographic ink, the amounts used, the purpose that is served by the product, and the disposition of wastes from the process. It was used to develop a template for removing or replacing unnecessary or duplicative chemistry with safer products. See Chapter 9 for other examples.

518

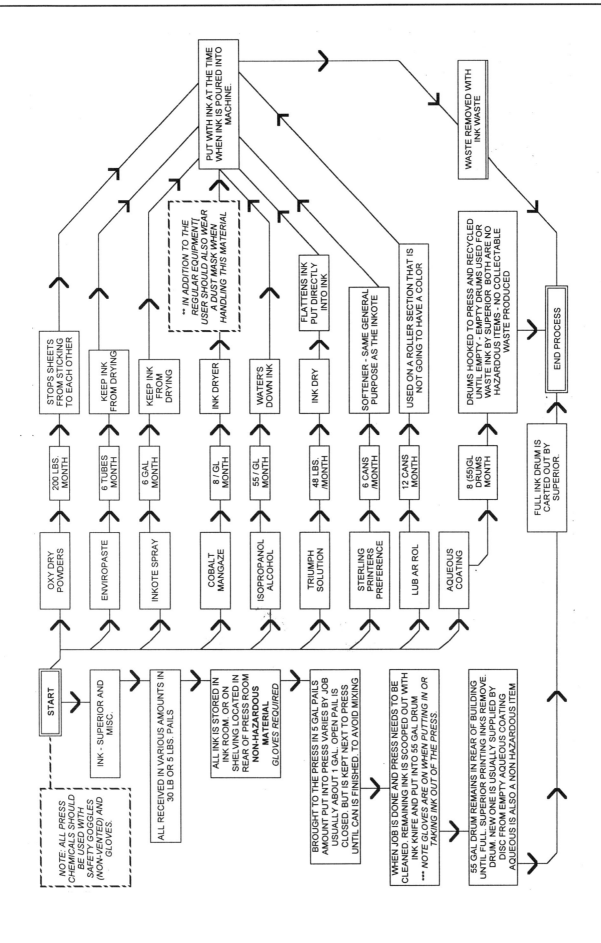

APPENDIX **XII**

SOURCE:
USEPA, EPA 310-R-95-014

EPA's Industrial Process Description of the Printing Industry

Industrial Process Description

This section describes the materials and equipment used, and the processes employed within the printing and publishing industry. The section is designed for those interested in gaining a general understanding of the industry, and for those interested in the inter-relationship between the industrial process and the topics described in subsequent sections of this profile—pollutant outputs, pollution prevention opportunities, and Federal regulations. This section does not attempt to replicate published engineering information that is available for this industry.

This section specifically contains a description of commonly used production processes, associated raw materials, the byproducts produced or released, and the materials either recycled or transferred off-site. This discussion, coupled with schematic drawings of the identified processes, provide a concise description of where wastes may be produced in the process. This section also describes the potential fate (via air, water, and soil pathways) of these waste products.

Industrial Processes in the Printing and Publishing Industry

The diversity of technologies and products in the printing industry makes it difficult to characterize the processes and the environmental issues facing the industry as a whole. These process differences can lead to distinct environmental concerns and are critical when developing compliance assistance programs. It is estimated that 97 percent of all printing activities can be categorized within five different printing processes: lithography, gravure, flexography, letterpress, and screen printing. The equipment, applications, and chemicals for each of these processes differ; however, they all print an image on a substrate following the same basic sequence. The fundamental steps in printing are referred to as imaging, pre-press, printing, and post-press operations. The type of printing technology that is used depends on a variety of factors, including the substrate used (e.g., paper, plastic, metal, ceramic, etc.), the length and speed of the print run, the required print image quality, and the end product produced.

The first step in the printing process, imaging, produces an image of the material to be printed. Traditionally, this image is produced photographically, but with increasing frequency the image is produced electronically. The production of a photographic image involves a variety of chemicals similar to those used in other fields of photography. The image on the film is transferred to the image carrier or plate. In pre-press operations, an image carrier is produced that can transfer the ink in the image area and can repel the ink in non-image areas. In printing, ink is applied to the plate and the image is transferred to the substrate. In the post-press step, the printed material may receive any one of numerous finishing operations, depending on the desired form of the final product.

Each of the five predominant printing technologies differs significantly in how the image is transferred from the image carrier to the substrate in the printing step. In general, the imaging and post-press operations are fairly similar for all printing technologies. Therefore, imaging and post-press procedures are discussed for all printing technologies, and the platemaking and press operations are discussed separately for each technology.

Imaging Operations

Imaging operations begin with composition and typesetting, and are followed by the production of a photographic negative or positive. Composition involves the arrangement of art and text into the desired format. This composition task was performed manually. Today, however, computer systems are commonly used to accomplish the task. Computers can be equipped with both optical character recognition and photographic image scanners and digitizers so that pre-typed material and images can be incorporated into the document being composed.

Once the desired format and images are assembled, they are photographed to produce transparencies. The printing industry photographic process uses input materials very similar to those used in other fields of photography. The purpose of this step is to produce a photographic negative (for lithography and letterpress) or a positive (for gravure, screen printing, and other lithographic processes). Input materials for the process include paper, plastic film, or a glass base covered with a light-sensitive coating called a photographic emulsion. This emulsion is usually composed of silver halide salts and gelatin. The desired image is projected onto the film to produce a film negative or a film positive. When the exposed photographic emulsion is developed, the silver halide in the emulsion is converted to metallic silver, in proportion to the amount of exposure it has received. The developing action is stopped by immersing the film in a fixing bath, which is mainly composed of sodium thiosulfate ("hypo"). The fixed photographic emulsion is then rinsed. If an image is to be printed as a color reproduction, transparencies are made for each of the colors to be used on the press. Multi-color printing is done by passing the same substrate through several single-color printing operations. Three or four basic colors are combined on the final product to yield any color desired.

Platemaking and Printing

From photographic negative or positive, a plate is produced that is used in each printing process to carry or transfer ink in the form of the image to the substrate. The plate must pick up ink only in the areas where ink is to be applied to the final image on the substrate. The five basic printing technologies employ five different types of plates. The platemaking step and the printing operations summaries are described below for each technology.

Lithography

In lithography, a planographic plate is used where the image areas and the non-image areas are on the same plane (they are neither raised nor depressed) and are defined by differences in their physiochemical properties. There are several types of lithographic printing, but they all use a planographic plate and they all rely on the fundamental property that oil and water do not mix. As a result, lithographic inks are oil-based and traditionally the ink oils are petroleum based. A metal or paper or plastic printing plate is coated with a light-sensitive chemical which becomes ink receptive when exposed to light. Through the photographic negative, the coating is exposed to light chemically changing the exposed areas, making the image areas ink-receptive. The non-image areas remain water-receptive. Water-based mixtures, referred to as fountain solution, are applied to enhance the non-image area's ability to repel ink. Fountain solutions may contain five to 10 percent isopropyl alcohol or they may contain alcohol substitutes that meet the same needs but with a lower VOC content. Through the use of inking rollers, ink is applied to the plate, adhering only to the image areas. The image is transferred or offset from the plate to a rubber roller (the blanket), which then transfers the image to the substrate

being printed. To accelerate drying and control ink flow characteristics, lithographic inks contain solvents. There are lithographic inks that are curable using ultraviolet energy or electron beam, and do not contain solvents.

Depending on the type of substrate or the products printed, the lithographic process is further divided into subprocesses: sheet-fed, heatset web, and non-heatset web. In lithography, as in most printing technologies, presses are available as sheet-fed or as web-fed. On a sheet-fed press, the substrate is fed into the press one sheet at a time. A web-fed press prints on a continuous roll of substrate, known as a web, which is later cut to size. "Offset" lithography refers to the use of a rubber blanket to transfer the image from the plate to the substrate. Within the category of web offset lithography, there is heatset web offset and non-heatset web offset. In the heatset process, the ink is dried by evaporating the ink oil with indirect hot air dryers. This process is potentially the most significant source of VOC emissions in lithography.

Sheet-fed offset lithography is typically used for printing books, posters, brochures, and artwork. Web-fed offset lithography is commonly used for high speed production of magazines, catalogs, and other periodicals, newspapers, and magazines.

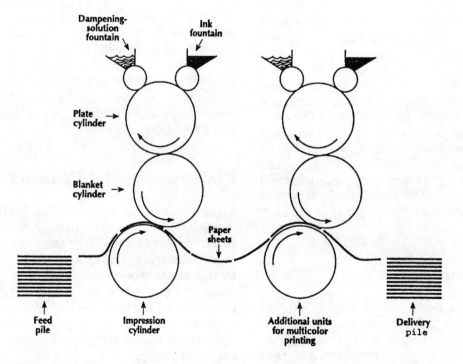

Simplified lithographic press layout.

Gravure

Gravure printing uses almost exclusively electro-mechanically engraved copper image carriers to separate the image area from the non-image area. Typically, the gravure image carrier is a cylinder. It consists of a steel or plastic base which is plated with copper or a special alloy. The electro-mechanical engraving is accomplished by the electronic impulses driving the diamond stylus which engraves minute cells at the rate of over 3,000 per second. Today, most of the gravure cylinders are engraved directly from digital files. Chemical etching, which is a dominant technology for the gravure cylinder imaging in the past, represents a very small percentage of the total engravings done today. It is used for special applications only. Gravure was the first printing process capable of direct imaging from electronic data.

In gravure printing, ink is applied to the engraved cylinder, then wiped from the surface by the doctor blade, leaving ink only on the engraved image area. The printing substrate is brought into contact with the cylinder with sufficient pressure so that it picks up the ink left in the depressions on the cylinder. Low viscosity inks are required for gravure printing in order to fill the tiny depressions on the plate. To dry the ink and drive off the solvents, drying ovens are placed in the paper path. The solvent-laden air can be passed through carbon beds to trap and condense the solvent. Most of the ink solvents are recaptured using this process, and can either be reused or destroyed by incineration. Also, low VOC inks can be used making carbon beds unnecessary.

The cost of a gravure cylinder is still considered higher compared to other types of printing plates; however, today gravure is the most mature process in "digital data/direct to plate" technology. Also, gravure cylinders have a very long useful life. Several million impressions can be printed before a cylinder needs to be replaced. Gravure printing is capable of producing high-quality, continuous tone images on a variety of substrates. It is most commonly used for large circulation catalogs, magazines, Sunday supplements, and advertising inserts. Also, gravure printing is used for a variety of packaging materials, postage stamps, greeting cards, currency, resilient floor coverings, and wallpaper. As in lithography, the two basic types of gravure presses are sheet-fed and web. In the US, almost all commercial gravure printing is done on web fed rotogravure presses.

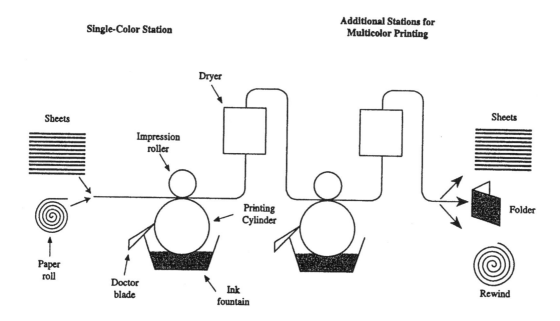

Rotogravure press.

Flexography

Flexographic and letterpress plates are made using the same basic technologies. Both technologies employ plates with raised images and only the raised images come in contact with the substrate during printing.

The traditional method of making these plates begins with the exposure of a metal plate through a negative and processing of the exposed plate using an acid bath. The resulting metal engraving may be used directly for letterpress (flatbed), or alternatively used to mold a master using a bakelite board. The board, under pressure and heat, fills the engraving and, when cooled, becomes a master for molding a rubber plate with a raised area that will transfer the graphics. The second method of making plates employs photopolymers in either a solid or liquid state. The photopolymer sheet (consisting of monomers) is exposed to light through a negative and the unexposed areas washed out by means of a solvent or water wash. The result is the relief plate.

Typically, flexographic plates are made of plastic, rubber, or some other flexible material, which is attached to a roller or cylinder for ink application. Ink is applied to the raised image on the plate, which transfers the image to the substrate. There are three basic configurations of flexographic press—stack, central impression and in-line. (Presses can be configured to print both sides of the web.* In the typical flexographic printing sequence, the substrate is fed into the press from a roll. The image is printed as the substrate travels through a series of stations with each station printing a single color. Each station is made up of four rollers where the first roller transfers the ink from an ink pan to the second roller, the meter roller. The meter roller (also known as an Anilox Roll) meters the ink to a uniform thickness onto the third roller, the plate cylinder. The substrate moves between the plate cylinder and fourth roller. The plate is attached to the third roller (the plate cylinder) and the fourth roller (the impression cylinder) applies pressure to the plate cylinder, thereby forming the image on the substrate. The printed web proceeds through an overhead dryer section to dry the ink before the next station. Upon completion of the printing of the last color, the web may then move through an overhead tunnel dryer to remove all residual solvents. The finished product is rewound onto a roll. The width of flexography presses ranges from 4.5 inches up to 115 inches. The ink tray used on larger flexographic presses is very long, allowing for significant evaporation of ink (which may have a high alcohol content).

---

*Information on other flexographic printing configurations, such as, the wide web common impression press and the wide web stack type press is available from the Flexographic Technical Association.

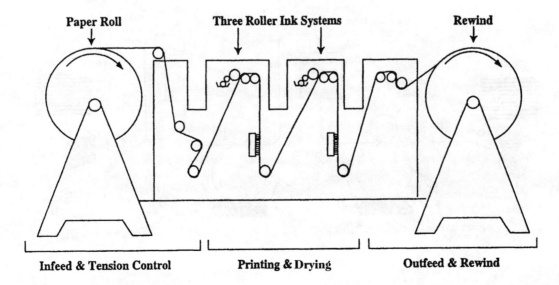

Webfed rotary flexographic press.

Modern presses are now equipped with enclosed doctor blade systems which eliminate the fountain roller and fountain, thereby reducing evaporation losses. Printers with the more narrow presses (for tags, labels and tapes) generally use water based inks and UV coatings. Using UV inks reduces the volatility of the ink.

As in gravure, fast-drying, low-viscosity inks are used. These inks lie on the surface of non-absorbent substrates and solidify when solvents are removed, making flexography ideal for printing on impervious materials such as polyethylene, cellophane and other plastics and metallized surfaces. The soft plates allow quality printing on compressible surfaces such as cardboard packaging.

With low cost plates and a relatively simple two roller press, flexography is one of the least expensive and fastest growing printing processes. According to the Flexographic Technical Association, 85 percent of packaging is printed with flexography. It is used primarily for packaging, such as plastic wrappers, corrugated boxes, milk cartons, labels, and foil and paper bags.

Letterpress

Like flexography, letterpress uses a plate with a raised image on a metal or plastic plate. The three types of letterpresses in use today are the platen, flat-bed, and rotary presses. On the platen press, the raised plate is locked on a flat surface. The substrate is placed on another flat surface and pressed against the inked plate. The flat-bed cylinder press prints as the substrate passes around an impression cylinder on its way from the feed stack to the delivery stack. These presses are often very slow relative to lithographic, flexographic or gravure presses. The most popular letterpress is the web-fed rotary letterpress. Designed to print both sides of the web simultaneously, these presses are used primarily for printing newspapers.

Letterpress was once the predominant printing method, but its prevalence has declined dramatically. It now accounts for an estimated 11 percent of the total value of the U.S. printing industry. Lithographic printing, gravure, and flexography have all begun to replace letterpress.

Rotary letterpress presses configurations.

Web letterpress, traditionally used to print newspapers, is being replaced by lithography and flexography. Gravure has largely replaced letterpress for printing long-run magazines and catalogs, while flexography is replacing it for printing paperbacks, labels, and business forms. Today, letterpress is primarily used for printing books, business cards, and advertising brochures.

Screen Printing

Unlike the impervious plates used in the other four printing processes, the screen printing process uses a porous polyester mesh. The mesh is stretched tightly over a frame, and a stencil, which defines the image to be printed, is applied to the mesh. The squeegee applies pressure to the ink thereby forcing the ink through the open areas of the screen. The thread count and diameter determine the amount of ink deposited onto the substrate below.

The major chemicals used in screen printing process include organic solvents, adhesives and inks. The chemical composition of the ink used varies depending on the substrate printed and the end product produced. There are five main categories of inks used within the screen printing process: UV-curable, solvent-based, and water-based for graphic applications, plastisols for textile applications, and water-based for textile applications. Screen printing is an extremely versatile printing process, and can be used to print on a wide variety of substrates including paper, plastics, glass, metals, nylon and cotton to produce a wide variety of products including, but not limited to, posters, labels, fleet decals, signage, all types of textile garments and membrane circuits.

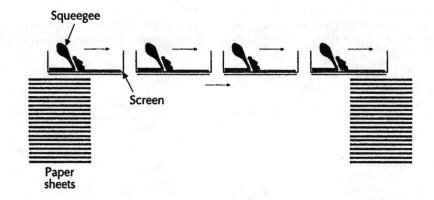

Schematic drawing of a flat-screen type press.
Screens lift after each application, as substrate advances.

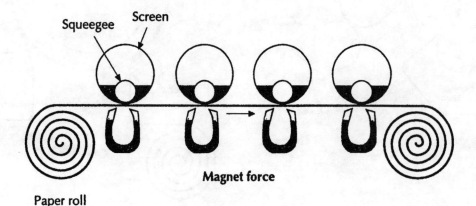

Rotary-screen printing press. Magnet force is applied to control the squeegee pressure.

Two methods of screen printing.

Plateless Technologies

Plateless technologies include electrostatic and laser printing, and other printing methods which do not rely upon the use of a separately developed or prepared plate or screen. Although currently used primarily for low-volume applications, these methods are likely to see increased use as the technologies continue to develop.

Post-press Operations

Post-press processes include cutting, folding, collating, binding, perforating, drilling, and many others. From an environmental impact viewpoint, binding is the most significant of the post-press operations. Liquid glue used for binding is typically a water-based latex that becomes impervious to water when it dries.

Raw Material Inputs and Pollution Outputs in the Production Line

Printing operations use materials that may adversely affect air, water, and land: certain chemicals involved in printing volatilize, which contributes to air emissions from the facility and to smog formation; other chemicals may be discharged to drains and impact freshwater or marine ecosystems; and solid wastes contribute to the existing local and regional disposal problems. The five printing processes outlined in the previous section have many common wastes; however, they also each have outputs that are process specific. Thus, it is important to note that wastes do differ from process to process and the solutions identified to reduce waste in one printing process do not necessarily apply to other printing processes. The following charts outline potential outputs for each of the five printing processes.

LITHOGRAPHY PROCESS: INPUTS AND OUTPUTS

Process	Inputs	Outputs
Imaging	Film	Used film and out-of-date film.
	Paper	Scrap paper.
	Developer	May be volatile and contribute to air emissions. Spent developer (sent to POTW).
	Fixer	May be volatile and contribute to air emissions. Silver from film is often electrolytically recovered from the fixer prior to discharge of spent fixer to POTW.
	Wash Water	Used rinse water.
	Cleaning Solutions	Rags containing solvents (sent to laundry service or disposed of as hazardous waste).
	Chemical Storage Containers	Empty containers (disposed of or returned to suppliers).
Platemaking	Plates	Used plates.
	Water	Used rinse water (discharged to POTW).
	Developer	Spent developer (may contain alcohol; contributes to air emissions).
Printing	Fountain Solution	May contain VOCs and contribute to air emissions.
	Ink	Waste oil based ink disposed of as hazardous waste. Solvent-based inks contribute to air emissions.
	Paper	Waste paper from bringing press up to required print quality and from rejected prints.
	Cleaning Solutions	Solvents used to clean press and remove excess ink contribute to air emissions.
	Rags	Ink and solvent-laden rags (sent to laundry service, disposed of as hazardous waste, or treated to recover solvents).
Finishing	Paper	Reject prints and edges from trimming.
	Adhesives	Possible losses to the air.
	Shipping boxes	Waste issue.

GRAVURE PROCESS: INPUTS AND OUTPUTS

Process	Inputs	Outputs
Imaging	Digital Data	Film or engraved image carrier (cylinder)
	Film	Used film and out-of-date film.
	Paper	Scrap paper.
	Photographic processing solution	May be volatile and contribute to air emissions. Waste solution.
	Wash Water	Used rinse water.
	Cleaning Solutions	Rags containing solvents (sent to laundry service, disposed of as hazardous waste, or treated to recover solvents).
	Chemical Storage Containers	Empty containers (disposed of or returned to suppliers).
Cylinder Making	Copper-clad Cylinder	Used cylinders.
	Acid etching solution	Waste solution.
Printing	Ink	Solvent-based inks (toluene-based for mass-circulation printing and alcohol-based for packaging) maintain the required low viscosity and contribute to air emissions. Waste ink disposed of as hazardous waste.
	Heat	Ovens are used to drive off the solvents to dry the ink. Ink solvents are recaptured through chillers and other equipment.
	Paper	Waste paper from bringing press up to required print quality and from rejected prints.
	Cleaning Solutions	Solvents used to remove excess ink contribute to air emissions.
Finishing	Paper	Reject prints and edges from trimming.
	Adhesives	Possible losses to the air.
	Shipping boxes	Waste issue.

FLEXOGRAPHY PROCESS: INPUTS AND OUTPUTS

Process	Inputs	Outputs
Imaging	Film	Used film and out-of-date film.
	Paper	Scrap paper.
	Developer	May be volatile and contribute to air emissions. Spent developer (to POTW).
	Fixer	May be volatile and contribute to air emissions. Silver from film is often electrolytically recovered from the fixer prior to disposal of spent fixer to POTW).
	Wash Water	Used rinse water.
	Cleaning Solutions	Rags containing solvents (sent to laundry service, disposed of as hazardous waste, or treated to recover solvents).
	Chemical Storage Containers	Empty containers (disposed of or returned to suppliers).
Platemaking	Plate mold	Used molds, engravings and washes.
	Rubber plate	Used plates, defective plates and photopolymer.
	Etching and wash-out solutions	Waste solution and spent solvents.
Printing	Ink	Waste ink disposed of as hazardous waste. Solvent-based inks contribute to air emissions.
	Paper/film	Waste paper and film from bringing press up to required print quality and from rejected prints.
	Heat	Exhaust heat and odor. High alcohol content of some inks contribute to air emissions as ink dries. Water-based inks are used for paper and some films.
	Cleaning Solutions	Solvents used to remove excess ink contribute to air emissions and hazardous wastes.
Finishing	Paper/film	Reject prints, edges from trimming, box and bag-making wastes.
	Adhesives	Possible losses to the air.
	Shipping boxes	Waste issue.

LETTERPRESS PROCESS: INPUTS AND OUTPUTS

Process	Inputs	Outputs
Imaging	Film	Used film and out-of-date film.
	Paper	Scrap paper.
	Developer	May be volatile and contribute to air emissions. Spent developer to POTW.
	Fixer	May be volatile and contribute to air emissions. Spent fixer (silver from film is often electrolytically recovered from the fixer prior to disposal of spent fixer to POTW).
	Wash Water	Used rinse water.
	Cleaning Solutions	Rags containing cleaning solvents (sent to laundry service, disposed of as hazardous waste, or treated to recover solvents).
	Chemical Storage Containers	Empty containers (disposed of or returned to suppliers).
Platemaking	Plate mold	Used molds.
	Plate	Used plates.
	Plate developer solution	Waste solution.
Printing	Ink	Waste ink disposed of as hazardous wastewater. Solvent-based inks contribute to air emissions.
	Paper	Waste paper from bringing press up to required print quality and from rejected prints.
	Cleaning Solutions	Solvents used to remove excess ink contribute to air emissions.
Finishing	Paper	Reject prints and edges from trimming.
	Adhesives	Possible losses to the air.
	Shipping boxes	Waste issue.

SCREEN PRINTING PROCESS: INPUTS AND OUTPUTS

Process	Inputs	Outputs
Imaging and Screen Making	Emulsion	Waste emulsion and out-of-date product.
	Photosensitization solution (needed for unsensitized films only)	Waste solution.
	Screen (polyester, nylon or wire mesh)	Excess screen trimmings; used screens.
	Frame	Reused.
	Developer	Spent developer (sent to POTW).
	Fixer	Spent fixer.
	Chemical Storage Containers	Empty containers.
Printing	Ink	Waste ink usually disposed of as hazardous waste. Solvent-based inks contribute to air emissions.
	Paper or other printing substrate	Waste paper from bringing press up to required print quality and from rejected prints.
	Blockout	Removed during screen reclamation and disposed with screen reclaim chemicals.
	Screen Reclamation Chemicals	Screen reclamation chemicals and ink are disposed of in rags and in clean-up wastewater.
	Water	Water used for screen reclamation is discharged to POTW; sometimes it is filtered prior to discharge.
Finishing	Paper or other printing substrate	Reject prints and edges from trimming.
	Adhesives	Possible losses to the air.
	Shipping boxes	Waste issue.

APPENDIX XIII

Printing Industry Chemistry: Flexography Lithography, Screen

SOURCE:

USEPA, *Design for the Environment, A Cleaner Technologies Substitutes Assessment*; Flexography, EPA 744-R-00-004a, Sept. 2000, pp 3-30 – 3-32; Lithography, EPA 744-R-95-008, July 1996, pp 2-8 – 2-10; Screen, EPA 744-R-94-005, pp II-2 – II-5

Each printing process has its own chemistry. While ink is basic to every printing process, the chemistry that carries the pigment to its ultimate destination on a substrate will vary based on the process, the nature of the substrate and the purpose for which the final product is intended. The major use of chemicals is in the cleaning of ink from the image carriers and presses. To demonstrate the nature of the chemistry of three of the major processes, this appendix includes listings of chemicals that were developed in three different USEPA Design for the Environment projects. They illustrate the basic chemicals that are encountered when addressing environmental and work safety issues.

The flexography project addressed ink system alternatives: solvent, water and radiation curable inks. Since solvents used for cleaning flexographic presses are frequently some of the same solvents as are used in formulating, the chart of chemicals is fairly inclusive (pp 534–536).

The lithographic project sought safer blanket washes. Lithographic inks are paste formulations made with oils and mineral spirits with relatively low emission rates and hazardous ingredients. Lithographic cleaning solutions are composed of highly volatile and hazardous chemicals. The project evaluated commercially available blanket washes and proposed safer alternatives. This list is representative of the chemistry that is prevalent in the lithographic printing plant (pp 536–539).

The screen project was devoted to alternatives for cleaning screens of the film emulsion that comprised the image carrier. Screen inks will vary depending on the material to be printed and the end use. They are more liquid than lithographic inks and more similar to paints than the thinner flexographic or gravure inks. The cleaning solutions are used in much larger quantities than the ink printed. This chart itemizes the various chemicals found in current commercial screen washes (pp 539–542).

533

CATEGORIZATION OF INK CHEMICALS—FLEXOGRAPHY

Category	Chemicals in category	CAS number
Acrylated polyols	Dipropylene glycol diacrylate	57472-68-1
	1,6-Hexanediol diacrylate	13048-33-4
	Hydroxypropyl acrylate	25584-83-2
	Trimethylolpropane triacrylate	15625-89-5
Acrylated polymers	Acrylated epoxy polymer[c]	NA[a]
	Acrylated oligoamine polymer[c]	NA
	Acrylated polyester polymer (#'s 1 and 2)[c]	NA
	Glycerol propoxylate triacrylate	52408-84-1
	Trimethylolpropane ethoxylate triacrylate	28961-43-5
	Trimethylolpropane propoxylate triacrylate	53879-54-2
Acrylic acid polymers	Acrylic acid-butyl acrylate-methyl methacrylate-styrene polymer	27306-39-4
	Acrylic acid polymer, acidic (#'s 1 and 2)[c]	NA
	Acrylic acid polymer, insoluble[c]	NA
	Butyl acrylate-methacrylic acid-methyl methacrylate polymer	25035-69-2
	Styrene acrylic acid polymer (#'s 1 and 2)[c]	NA
	Styrene acrylic acid resin[c]	NA
Alcohols	Ethanol	64-17-5
	Isobutanol	78-83-1
	Isopropanol	67-63-0
	Propanol	71-23-8
	Tetramethyldecyndiol	126-86-3
Alkyl acetates	Butyl acetate	123-86-4
	Ethyl acetate	141-78-6
	Propyl acetate	109-60-4
Amides or nitrogenous compounds	Amides, tallow, hydrogenated	61790-31-6
	Ammonia	7664-41-7
	Ammonium hydroxide	1336-21-6
	Erucamide	112-84-5
	Ethanolamine	141-43-5
	Hydroxylamine derivative	NA
	Urea	57-13-6
Aromatic esters	Dicyclohexyl phthalate	84-61-7
	Ethyl 4-dimethylaminobenzoate	10287-53-5
Aromatic ketones	2-Benzyl-2-(dimethylamino)-4'-morpholinobutyrophenone	119313-12-1
	1-Hydroxycyclohexyl phenyl ketone	947-19-3
	2-Hydroxy-2-methylpropiophenone	7473-98-5
	2-Isopropylthioxanthone	5495-84-1
	4-Isopropylthioxanthone	83846-86-0
	2-Methyl-4'-(methylthio)-2-morpholinopropiophenone	71868-10-5
	Thioxanthone derivative[c]	NA

CATEGORIZATION OF INK CHEMICALS—FLEXOGRAPHY (continued)

Category	Chemicals in category	CAS number
Ethylene glycol ethers	Alcohols, C11-15-secondary, ethoxylated Butyl carbitol Ethoxylated tetramethyldecyndiol Ethyl carbitol Polyethylene glycol	68131-40-8 112-34-5 9014-85-1 111-90-0 25322-68-3
Hydrocarbons — high molecular weight	Distillates (petroleum), hydrotreated light Distillates (petroleum), solvent-refined light paraffinic Mineral oil Paraffin wax	64742-47-8 64741-89-5 8012-95-1 8002-74-2
Hydrocarbons — low molecular weight	n-Heptane Solvent naphtha (petroleum), light aliphatic Styrene	142-82-5 64742-89-8 100-42-5
Inorganics	Barium Kaolin Silica	7440-39-3 1332-58-7 7631-86-9
Organic acids or salts	Citric acid Dioctyl sulfosuccinate, sodium salt Methylenedisalicylic acid	77-92-9 577-11-7 27496-82-8
Organophosphorus compounds	Diphenyl (2,4,6-trimethylbenzoyl) phosphine oxide 2-Ethylhexyl diphenyl phosphate Phosphine oxide, bis(2,6-dimethoxybenzoyl) (2,4,4-trimethylpentyl)-	75980-60-8 1241-94-7 145052-34-2
Organotitanium compounds	Isopropoxyethoxytitanium bis(acetylacetonate) Titanium diisopropoxide bis(2,4-pentanedionate) Titanium isopropoxide	68586-02-7 17927-72-9 546-68-9
Pigments — inorganic	C.I. Pigment White 6 C.I. Pigment White 7	13463-67-7 1314-98-3
Pigments — organic	C.I. Pigment Blue 61 C.I. Pigment Red 23 C.I. Pigment Red 269 C.I. Pigment Violet 23 C.I. Pigment Yellow 14 C.I. Pigment Yellow 74	1324-76-1 6471-49-4 67990-05-0 6358-30-1 5468-75-7 6358-31-2
Pigments — organometallic	C.I. Basic Violet 1, molybdatephosphate C.I. Basic Violet 1, molybdate-tungstatephosphate C.I. Pigment Blue 15 C.I. Pigment Green 7 C.I. Pigment Red 48, barium salt (1:1) C.I. Pigment Red 48, calcium salt (1:1) C.I. Pigment Red 52, calcium salt (1:1) C.I. Pigment Violet 27 D&C Red No. 7	67989-22-4 1325-82-2 147-14-8 1328-53-6 7585-41-3 7023-61-2 17852-99-2 12237-62-6 5281-04-9

CATEGORIZATION OF INK CHEMICALS—FLEXOGRAPHY (continued)

Category	Chemicals in category	CAS number
Polyol derivatives	Nitrocellulose Polyol derivative A	9004-70-0 — [b]
Propylene glycol ethers	Dipropylene glycol methyl ether Propylene glycol methyl ether Propylene glycol propyl ether	34590-94-8 107-98-2 1569-01-3
Resins	Fatty acid, dimer-based polyamide Fatty acids, C18-unsatd., dimers, polymers with ethylenediamine, hexamethylenediamine, and propionic acid Resin acids, hydrogenated, methyl esters Resin, acrylic Resin, miscellaneous Rosin, fumarated, polymer with diethylene glycol and pentaerythritol Rosin, fumarated, polymer with pentaerythritol, 2-propenoic acid, ethenylbenzene, and (1-methylethylenyl)benzene Rosin, polymerized	NA 67989-30-4 8050-15-5 NA NA 68152-50-1 NA 65997-05-9
Siloxanes	Silanamine, 1,1,1-trimethyl-N-(trimethylsilyl)-, hydrolysis products with silica Silicone oil Siloxanes and silicones, di-Me, 3-hydroxypropyl Me, ethers with polyethylene glycol acetate	68909-20-6 63148-62-9 70914-12-4

[a] No data or information available.
[b] Actual chemical name is confidential business information.

CHEMICALS IN BLANKET WASH FORMULATIONS—LITHOGRAPHY

Chemical Name	CAS Number	Synonym
Alcohols, C_{12}-C_{15}, ethoxylated[c]	68131-39-5	EMUL/Mix[b]
Benzene, 1,2,4-trimethyl-	95-63-6	Pseudocumene
Benzenesulfonic acid, dodecyl-[c]	27176-87-0	Dodecyl benzene sulfonic acid[b]
Benzenesulfonic acid, dodecyl-, compounds with 2-aminoethanol	26836-07-7	Dodecylbenzenesulfonic acid, ethanolamine salt
Benzenesulfonic acid, dodecyl-, compounds with 2-propanamine[c]	26264-05-1	Isopropylamine salt of dodecylbenzenesulfonic acid[b]
Benzenesulfonic acid, (tetrapropenyl)-, compounds with 2-propanamine	157966-96-6	Isopropylamine salt of (tetrapropenyl) benzenesulfonic acid

CHEMICALS IN BLANKET WASH FORMULATIONS—LITHOGRAPHY (continued)

Chemical Name	CAS Number	Synonym
Benzenesulfonic acid, C_{10}-C_{16}- alkyl derivatives, compounds with 2-propanamine[c]	68584-24-7	Benzenesulfonic acid, C_{10}-C_{16}- alkyl derivatives, compounds with isopropylamine
Butyrolactone	96-48-0	2(3H)-Furanone, dihydro[b]
Cumene[a]	98-82-8	Benzene, (1-methylethyl)-[b]
Diethanolamine[a]	111-42-2	Ethanol, 2,2'-iminobis-[b]
Diethylene glycol monobutyl ether	112-34-5	Ethanol, 2-(2-butoxyethoxy)-[b]
Dimethyl adipate	627-93-0	Dimethyl hexanedioate; methyl adipate; dimethyl ester adipic acid
Dimethyl glutarate	1119-40-0	Glutaric acid, dimethyl ester; pentanedioic acid, dimethyl ester
Dimethyl succinate	106-65-0	Succinic acid, dimethyl ester; butanedioic acid, dimethyl ester; methyl succinate
Dipropylene glycol monobutyl ether	29911-28-2	2-Propanol, 1-(2-butoxy-1-methylethoxy)-[b] DGMBE
Dipropylene glycol methyl ether	34590-94-8	DPGME
Distillates (petroleum), hydrotreated middle[c]	64742-46-7	Hydrotreated middle distillate[b]
Ethoxylated nonylphenol	9016-45-9 26027-38-3 68412-54-4	Ethoxylated nonylphenol[b], Poly(oxy-1,2-ethanediyl), α-(nonylphenyl)-ω-hydroxy-, branched and unbranched isomers[c]; NP-6[b]; NP-9[b]
Ethylenediaminetetraacetic acid, tetrasodium salt	64-02-8	Tetrasodium EDTA
Fatty acids, C_{16}-C_{18}, methyl esters[c]	67762-38-3	Fatty acid methyl esters[b]
Fatty acids, C_{16}-C_{18} and C_{18}-unsatd, compounds with diethanolamine[a]	68002-82-4	Diethanolamine tallate[b]
Fatty acids, tall oil, compounds with diethanolamine	61790-69-0	Diethanolamine tallate
Hydrocarbons, terpene processing by-products[c]	68956-56-9	
d-Limonene[a]	5989-27-5	Cyclohexene, 1-methyl-4-(1-methylethenyl)-[b]; Terpenes[b]
Linalool[a]	78-70-6	1,6-Octadien-3-ol, 3,7-dimethyl-[b]
Mineral spirits (light hydrotreated)	64742-47-8	Petroleum distillate[b]
N-Methylpyrrolidone	872-50-4	NMP

CHEMICALS IN BLANKET WASH FORMULATIONS—LITHOGRAPHY (continued)

Chemical Name	CAS Number	Synonym
Naphtha (petroleum), hydrotreated heavy[c]	64742-48-9	Aliphatic petroleum distillate C_9-C_{11}[b]
Nerol[a]	106-25-2	2,6-Octadien-1-ol, 3,7-dimethyl-[b]
Oxirane, methyl, polymer with oxirane, monodecyl ether[c]	37251-67-5	Linear alkyl ethoxylate[b]
2-Pinanol[a]	473-54-1	Bicyclo[3.1.1]heptan-2-ol, 2,6,6-trimethyl-[b]
Plinols[b]	72402-00-7	Cyclopentanol, 1,2-dimethyl-3-(1-methylethenyl)-[c]
Polyethoxylated isodecyloxypropylamine[b]	68478-95-5	Poly(oxy-1,2-ethanediyl), α,α'-(iminodi-2,1-ethanediyl)bis[ω-hydroxy]-, N-[3-(branched decyloxy)propyl] derivatives[c]
Poly(oxy-1,2-ethanediyl), α-hexyl-ω-hydroxy-[c]	31726-34-8	Ethoxylated hexyl alcohol
Propanoic acid, 3-ethoxy-, ethyl ester[a]	763-69-9	Ethyl-3-ethoxy propionate
Propylene glycol	57-55-6	1,2-Propanediol
Propylene glycol monobutyl ether	5131-66-8	2-Propanol, 1-butoxy-[b]
Sodium bis(ethylhexyl) sulfosuccinate[b]	577-11-7	Butanedioic acid, sulfo-, 1,4-bis(2-ethylhexyl) ester, sodium salt[c]
Sodium hydroxide	1310-73-2	Caustic soda
Sodium xylene sulfonate[b]	1300-72-7	Benzenesulfonic acid, dimethyl-, sodium salt[c]
Solvent naphtha (petroleum), heavy aromatic	64742-94-5	Aromatic 150[b]
Solvent naphtha (petroleum), light aliphatic	64742-89-8	VM&P naphtha[b]
Solvent naphtha (petroleum), light aromatic	64742-95-6	Aromatic petroleum distillate C_8-C_{11}[b]
Solvent naphtha (petroleum), medium aliphatic[c]	64742-88-7	Solvent 140[b]
Sorbitan, mono-9-octadecenoate[c]	1338-43-8	Sorbitan mono-oleate (crillet 4)[b]
Sorbitan, monododecanoate, poly(oxy-1,2-ethanediyl) derivatives[c]	9005-64-5	Laurate of polyoxyethylenic sorbitan[b]
Sorbitan, monolaurate	5959-89-7	D-Glucitol, 1,4-anhydro-, 6-dodecanoate[b]
Sorbitan, tri-9-octadecenoate, poly(oxy-1,2-ethanediyl) derivatives[c]	9005-70-3	Ethoxylated sorbitan tri-oleate (crillet 45)[b]

CHEMICALS IN BLANKET WASH FORMULATIONS—LITHOGRAPHY (continued)

Chemical Name	CAS Number	Synonym
Soybean oil, methyl ester[c]	67784-80-9	Soybean based methyl esters[b]
Soybean oil, polymerized, oxidized[c]	68152-81-8	Oxidized soybean oil[b]
Stoddard solvent[a]	8052-41-3	Mineral spirits
Tall oil, special	68937-81-5	Special tall oil[b] methyl stearate, methyl oleate
α-Terpineol[a]	98-55-5	3-Cyclohexene-1-methanol, α,α, 4-trimethyl-[b]
Terpinolene[a]	586-62-9	Cyclohexene, 1-methyl-4-(1-methylethylidene)-[b]
Tetrapotassium pyrophosphate[b]	7320-34-5	Diphosphoric acid, tetrapotassium salt[a]
Xylene	1330-20-7	Dimethyl benzene

[a] Indicates that the name was chosen from the CHEMID Files.
[b] Indicates name supplied by industry.
[c] Indicates that the name was chosen from the TSCA Inventory.

SUMMARY OF SCREEN RECLAMATION CHEMICALS AND THEIR FUNCTIONS

Chemical	CAS Number	Ink Remover	Emulsion Remover	Haze Remover	Possible Substitutes	Page Number
Acetone	67-64-1	X	X	X		II-7
Alcohols, C_8-C_{10}, ethoxylated	71060-57-6	X				II-8
Alcohols, C_{12}-C_{14}, ethoxylated	68439-50-9	X				II-10
Benzyl alcohol	100-51-6	X				II-11
2-Butoxyethanol	111-76-2	X				II-13
Butyl Acetate	123-86-4	X	X			II-14
Butyrolactone	96-48-0	X	X			II-16
Cyclohexanol	108-93-0	X				II-17
Cyclohexanone	108-94-1	X	X	X		II-19
Diacetone alcohol	123-42-2	X	X			II-20
Dichloromethane	75-09-2	X				II-22

SUMMARY OF SCREEN RECLAMATION CHEMICALS AND THEIR FUNCTIONS (continued)

Chemical	CAS Number	Ink Remover	Emulsion Remover	Haze Remover	Possible Substitutes	Page Number
Diethyl adipate	141-28-6				X	II-23
Diethyl glutarate	818-38-2				X	II-25
Diethylene glycol	111-46-6	X				II-26
Diethylene glycol monobutyl ether	112-34-5	X	X	X		II-28
Diethylene glycol butyl ether acetate	124-17-4	X	X	X		II-29
Diisopropyl adipate	6938-94-9				X	II-31
Dimethyl adipate	627-93-0	X		X		II-32
Dimethyl glutarate	1119-40-0	X		X		II-34
Dimethyl succinate	106-65-0	X		X		II-35
Dipropylene glycol methyl ether	34590-94-8	X	X			II-36
Dodecyl benzene sulfonic acid, triethanol amine salt	27323-41-7			X		II-39
Ethyl acetate	141-78-6	X	X			II-41
Ethyl lactate	97-64-3				X	II-42
Ethyl oleate	111-62-6				X	II-44
Ethoxylated castor oil	61791-12-6	X		X		II-45
Ethoxylated nonylphenol (np 4-9.5)	9016-45-9	X	X	X		II-47
Ethoxypropanol	52125-53-8	X				II-48
Ethoxypropyl acetate	54839-24-6	X				II-50
Furfuryl alcohol	98-00-0			X		II-51
Isobutyl isobutyrate	97-85-8	X				II-53
Isobutyl oleate	10024-47-2				X	II-54
Isopropanol	67-63-0	X	X			II-55
d-Limonene	5989-27-5	X				II-57
Methanol	67-56-1	X				II-58
Methoxypropanol acetate	84540-57-8	X				II-60

SUMMARY OF SCREEN RECLAMATION CHEMICALS AND THEIR FUNCTIONS (continued)

Chemical	CAS Number	Ink Remover	Emulsion Remover	Haze Remover	Possible Substitutes	Page Number
Methyl ethyl ketone	78-93-3	X	X			II-61
Methyl lactate	547-64-8				X	II-62
Mineral spirits (straight run naphtha)	64741-41-9	X		X		II-64
Mineral spirits (light hydrotreated)	64742-47-8	X		X		II-66
N-methylpyrrolidone	872-50-4	X	X	X		II-68
2-Octadecanamine, N,N-dimethyl-, N-oxide	71662-60-7	X				II-69
Periodic acid	13444-71-8		X			II-70
Phosphoric acid, mixed ester w/ispropanol and ethoxylated tridecanol	68186-42-5			X		II-72
Potassium hydroxide	1310-58-3	X	X	X		II-73
Propylene carbonate	108-32-7				X	II-75
Propylene glycol	57-55-6	X		X		II-76
Propylene glycol methyl ether	107-98-2 1320-67-8	X	X			II-78
Propylene glycol methyl ether acetate	108-65-6	X	X			II-79
Silica	7631-86-9		X			II-81
Silica, fumed (amorphous, crystalline-free)	112945-52-5		X			II-82
Sodium bisulfate	10034-88-5		X			II-84
Sodium hexametaphosphate	10124-56-8		X	X		II-85
Sodium hydroxide	1310-73-2	X	X	X		II-87
Sodium hypochlorite	7681-52-9		X			II-88
Sodium lauryl sulfate	151-21-3			X		II-90
Sodium metasilicate	6834-92-0			X		II-91
Sodium periodate	7790-28-5		X			II-93
Sodium salt, dodecyl benzene sulfonic acid	25155-30-0			X		II-94

SUMMARY OF SCREEN RECLAMATION CHEMICALS AND THEIR FUNCTIONS (continued)

Chemical	CAS Number	Ink Remover	Emulsion Remover	Haze Remover	Possible Substitutes	Page Number
Solvent naphtha (petroleum), light aliphatic	64742-89-8	X				II-96
Solvent naphtha (petroleum), light aromatic	64742-95-6	X				II-98
Solvent naphtha (petroleum), heavy aromatic	64742-94-5	X				II-100
Tall oil, special	68937-42-5			X		II-101
Terpineols	8000-41-7	X	X			II-103
Tetrahydrofurfuryl alcohol	97-99-4			X		II-104
Toluene	108-88-3	X				II-106
1,1,1-Trichloroethane	71-55-6	X				II-107
1,2,4-trimethylbenzene	95-63-6	X				II-109
Tripropylene glycol methyl ether	25498-49-1	X		X		II-110
Trisodium phosphate	7601-54-9	X	X			II-112
Xylenes (dimethyl benzene)	1330-20-7	X		X		II-114

APPENDIX **XIV**

Environmental Compliance Audit Form

SOURCE:
P-F Technical Services, Inc.

An environmental and safety audit is conducted to determine the status of compliance with the regulations that govern a specific site. It encompasses regulations enforced by all levels of government. The format is designed to address each regulation and the specific requirements set forth in each of the regulations. It is a checklist of the regulations with room for observations and assessments by the auditor, as well as notes for remedial action.

The form is designed to enable the auditor to follow a listing of regulations as they apply to the facility as a whole or to specific departments or areas within a facility. Each regulation is then subjected to the collection of data pertinent to compliance exposure and fulfillment.

The basic elements are: (1) Air emissions, (2) Hazardous waste, (3) Water waste, (4) Storage regulations, (5) SARA Title III, (6) Hazmat transportation, (7) Other environmental regulations, and (8) OSHA safety and health regulations.

The audit inspector or team will do a physical inspection of the facility, including interviews of supervisory and line personnel. Conditions will be noted. A review will be conducted of all files pertinent to permits, violations, written programs, training records, etc. The results of this search will be noted in the audit form. The members of the audit team will compare notes and discuss any discrepancies in their observations.

After the audit inspection and paper search has been concluded, an action plan can be developed to remove deficiencies or plan for projects to eliminate non-compliant conditions. Where possible, budgets should be developed for each of the corrective actions. The resulting report to management will highlight items in need of corrective action, as well as identify areas of accomplishment.

ENVIRONMENTAL AUDIT		
DATE		
FIRM		
ADDRESS		PHONE
		FAX
	INSPECTION	ACTION PLAN
AIR EMISSIONS:		
PERMITS		
AMOUNT OF VOC'S		
SPECIATE		
AMOUNT OF HAP'S		
SPECIATE		
EQUIPMENT		
EXHAUSTS		
CONTROL EQUIPMENT OR TECHNOLOGY		
AGENCY INSPECTIONS AND COMMUNICATIONS		
INCIDENTS/RELEASES		
HAZARDOUS WASTE		
EPA ID NUMBER		
AMOUNT PER MONTH		
DISPOSED YEAR:		
SIZE GENERATOR		
(BI)ANNUAL REPORTS		

MANIFESTS/LAND BAN FORMS		
DESIGNATED STORAGE AREA		
OPERATING LOG		
INSPECTION LOG		
CONTAINER CONDITION		
CONTAINER LABELS/DATED		
WASTE CLASS DETERMINATION		
TRAINING/DOCUMENTATION		
CONTINGENCY/SPILL PLANS		
ALARM/COMMUNICATION		
AGENCY INSPECTIONS/NOV'S ACTION REQUIRED		
COMMENTS		

WATER WASTE:

NATURE OF DISCHARGES FROM PROCESS:		
PROCESS DESCRIPTION		
IN-HOUSE TREATMENT		
DISPOSITION OFF-SITE (POTW)		
PERMIT (IF NEEDED)		

AGENCY INSPECTIONS/NOV'S

REPORTS TO AGENCY

INCIDENTS/RELEASES

STORMWATER CONCERNS

ON-SITE WLLS, LAGOONS

STORAGE
REGULATION APPLICABLE
Nassau County ART 11
Suffolk County ART 7,12
Fire Department

CHEMICAL STORAGE ROOM

BUILDING AS BERMED AREA

TANKS: PETROLEUM

TANKS: CHEMICALS

COMPATABILE MATERIALS

EMERGENCY VENTING

SECONDARY CONTAINMENT

GROUNDING

AGENCY INSPECTIONS/NOV'S		
COMMENTS		
SARA TITLE III		
Tier II - LEPC (NYC RTK)		
Does facility qualify?		
Has it complied?		
TRI Report		
Does facility qualify?		
What chemicals?		
Has it complied?		
SARA 302 - LIST OF HAZMATS (sent to LEPC)		
HAZMAT TRANSPORTATION		
SHIP HAZMATS		
REGISTRATION		
TRAINING/DOCUMENTATION		
OTHER ENVIRONMENT REGULATIONS/CONCERNS		

OSHA REQUIREMENTS		
OSHA 200 FORM		
HAZCOM:		
MSDS		
TRAINING/DOCUMENTATION		
FIRE DRILLS		
LABELS		
WRITTEN PROGRAM		
MSDS AVAILABILITY		
CONTINGENCY PLAN SPILL CONTROL PLANS		
OTHER		
PERSONAL PROTECTIVE EQUIPMENT		
JOB ASSESSMENTS/EVALUATION		
PROGRAM		
TRAINING/DOCUMENTATION		
SIGNS		
RESPIRATORY EQUIPMENT		
FORMAL PROGRAM		
CHEMICALS OF CONCERN		
EQUIPMENT AVAILABILITY		

MONITORING/DOCUMENTATION		
MEDICALS/DOCUMENTATION		
FIT TESTING/DOCUMENTATION		
TRAINING/DOCUMENTATION		
SIGNS		
HEARING PROTECTION		
MONITORING/DOCUMENTATION		
FORMAL PROGRAM		
EQUIPMENT AVAILABLE		
SIGNS		
MEDICALS/DOCUMENTATION		
TRAINING/DOCUMENTATION		
GUARDING		
MACHINES		
OPENINGS		
STORAGE:		
FLAMMABLES GROUNDED		
HAZMAT CONTAINMENT		
STACK STABILITY		

CONTAINER CONDITIONS		
HOUSEKEEPING		
OTHER		

LOCK-OUT/TAG-OUT

FORMAL PROGRAM		
TRAINING/DOCUMENTATION		
AUDITS/DOCUMENTATION		

FORK-LIFT TRAINING

PROPER EQUIPMENT FOR JOB		
DRIVER TRAINING/DOCUMENTATION		
DRIVER EVALUATION/DOCUMENTS		

ELECTRICAL

PROPER CLASS		
BARE WIRES/OPEN BOXES		
GROUNDED EQUIPMENT		
EXTENSION CORDS		
OTHER		

CONFINED SPACE

FORMAL PROGRAM

TRAINING/DOCUMENTATION

EQUIPMENT

HOUSEKEEPING

NEAT AND ORDERLY

CLEAN

OTHER

FIRE EXTINGUISHERS

TESTED REGULARLY

PROPERLY MOUNTED

PROPERLY SIGNED/LABELLED

CONDITION

TRAINING/DOCUMENTATION

FREE OF OBSTABLES

EXITS

ACCESSIBLE

OBSTRUCTIONS

ILLUMINATED SIGNS

EMERGENCY LIGHTING

DIRECTIONAL SIGNS

OPERATIONAL FROM INSIDE

AISLES		
ACCESSIBLE		
UNOBSTRUCTED		
MARKED		
FLOOR CONDITION		
SPRINKLERS		
BLOOD PATHOGENS		
FORMAL PROGRAM		
TRAINING		
MEDICALS/DOCUMENTATION		
INCIDENT INVESTIGATIONS		
FORMS		
PROCESS		
PERIODIC EVALUATIONS		
SAFETY & HEALTH POLICY		
FORMAL COMPANY PROGRAM		
WRITTEN STATEMENT(MISSION)		
SAFETY COMMITTEE		
PRACTICE FOLLOWS PREACHING		
STANDARD OPERATING PROCEDURES		
FORMAL OR UNWRITTEN		
FOR WHAT OPERATIONS		
TRAINING/DOCUMENTATION		

OTHER

APPENDIX XV

SOURCE:

Georgia Department of Natural
Resources, Air Protection Branch

Glossary of
Air Pollution Terms

Acid rain — Air pollution produced when acid chemicals are incorporated into rain, snow, fog or mist. The "acid" in acid rain comes from sulfur oxides and nitrogen oxides, products of burning coal and other fuels and from certain industrial processes. The sulfur oxides and nitrogen oxides are related to two strong acids: sulfuric acid and nitric acid. When sulfur dioxide and nitrogen oxides are released from power plants and other sources, winds blow them far from their source. If the acid chemicals in the air are blown into areas where the weather is wet, the acids can fall to Earth in the rain, snow, fog, or mist. In areas where the weather is dry, the acid chemicals may become incorporated into dusts or smokes. Acid rain can damage the environment, human health, and property.

Alternative fuels — Fuels that can replace ordinary gasoline. Alternative fuels may have particularly desirable energy efficiency and pollution reduction features. Alternative fuels include compressed natural gas, alcohols, liquefied petroleum gas (LPG), and electricity. The 1990 Clean Air Act encourages development and sale of alternative fuels.

Attainment area — A geographic area in which levels of a criteria air pollutant meet the health-based primary standard (national ambient air quality standard, or NAAQS) for the pollutant. An area may have on acceptable level for one criteria air pollutant, but may have unacceptable levels for others. Thus, an area

554

could be both attainment and non-attainment at the same time. Attainment areas are defined using federal pollutant limits set by EPA.

BACT — Best available control technology. It is an emission limitation that considers the cost of energy, environment, and economics in developing a degree of emission reduction that is achievable through application of good production processes, control systems, and techniques. In no event can BACT allow emissions of a pollutant in excess of a NSPS or a NESHAPS. BACT is determined on a case-by-case basis, is applied to each pollutant regulated under the Clean Air Act (federal) and is used mostly in PSD permit work.

Carbon monoxide (CO) — A colorless, odorless, poisonous gas, produced by incomplete burning of carbon-based fuels. including gasoline, oil, and wood. Carbon monoxide is also produced from incomplete combustion of many natural and synthetic products. For instance, cigarette smoke contains carbon monoxide. When carbon monoxide gets into the body, the carbon monoxide combines with chemicals in the blood and prevents the blood from bringing oxygen to cells, tissues, and organs. The body's parts need oxygen for energy, so high-level exposures to carbon monoxide can cause serious health effects. Massive exposures to CO can cause death. Symptoms of exposure to carbon monoxide can include vision problems, reduced alertness, and general reduction in mental and physical functions. Carbon monoxide exposures are especially harmful to people with heart, lung, and circulatory system diseases.

CFCs (chlorofluorocarbons) — These chemicals and some related chemicals have been used in great quantities in industry, for refrigeration and air conditioning, and in consumer products. CFCs and their relatives, when released into the air, rise into the stratosphere, a layer of the atmosphere high above the Earth. In the stratosphere, CFCs and their relatives take part in chemical reactions which result in reduction of the stratospheric ozone layer, which protects the Earth's surface from harmful effects of radiation from the sun. The 1990 Clean Air Act includes provisions for reducing releases (emissions) and eliminating production and use of these ozone-destroying chemicals.

Clean Air Act (CAA) — The original Clean Air Act was passed in 1963, but our national air pollution control program is actually based on the 1970 version of the law. The 1990 Clean Air Act Amendments are the most far-reaching revisions of the 1970 law. In this glossary, we refer to the 1990 amendments as the 1990 Clean Air Act.

Clean fuels — Low-pollution fuels that can replace ordinary gasoline. These are alternative fuels, including gasohol (gasoline-alcohol mixtures), natural gas, and LPG (liquefied petroleum gas).

Combustion — Burning. Many important pollutants, such as sulfur dioxide, nitrogen oxides, and particulates (PM-10) are combustion products, often products of the burning of fuels such as coal, oil, gas, and wood.

Compliance Advisory Panel (CAP) — A seven member panel appointed by the governor state legislature and the Air permitting agency. The panel is composed of 4 small business owners, one permitting representative, and two people to represent the public at large. The CAP provides oversight to the Small Business Assistance Program (SBAP).

Continuous emission monitoring systems (CEMS) — Machines which measure, on a continuous basis, pollutants released by a source. The 1990 Clean Air Act requires continuous emission monitoring systems for certain large sources.

Control technology; control measures — Equipment, processes, or actions used to reduce air pollution. The extent of pollution reduction varies among technologies and measures. In general, control technologies and measures that do the best job of reducing pollution will be required in the areas with the worst pollution. For example, the best available control technology/best available control measures (BACT, BACM) will be required in serious non-attainment areas for particulates, a criteria air pollutant. A similar high level of pollution reduction will be achieved with maximum achievable control technology (MACT) which will be required for sources releasing hazardous air pollutants.

Criteria air pollutants — A group of very common air pollutants regulated by EPA on the basis of criteria (information on health and/or environmental effects of pollution). Criteria air pollutants are widely distributed all over the country. A National Ambient Air Quality Standard exists for each criteria pollutant (particulate matter, sulfur dioxide, nitrogen dioxide, ozone, carbon dioxide, and lead).

Emission — Release of pollutants into the air from a source. We say sources emit pollutants. Continuous emission monitoring systems (CEMS) are machines, which some large sources are required to install, to make continuous measurements of pollutant release.

Enforcement — The legal methods used to make polluters obey the Clean Air Act. Enforcement methods include citations of polluters for violations of the law (citations are much like traffic tickets), fines, and even jail terms. EPA and the state and local governments are responsible for enforcement of the Clean Air Act, but if they don't enforce the law, members of the public can sue EPA or the states to get action.

Hazardous air pollutants (HAPs) — Toxic chemicals that cause serious health and environmental effects. Health effects include cancer, birth defects, nervous system problems, and death due to massive accidental releases such as occurred at the pesticide plant in Bhopal, India. Hazardous air pollutants are released by sources such as chemical plants, dry cleaners, printing plants, and motor vehicles (cars, trucks, buses, etc.)

Inspection and maintenance program (I/M program) — Auto inspection programs are required for some polluted areas. These periodic inspections, usually done once a year or once every two years, check whether a car is being maintained to keep pollution down and whether emission control systems are working properly. Vehicles which do not pass inspection must be repaired. Under the 1990 Clean Air Act, some especially polluted areas will have to have enhanced inspection and maintenance programs, using special machines that can check for such things as how much pollution a car produces during actual driving conditions.

Interstate air pollution — In many areas, two or more states share the same air. We say these states are in the same air basin defined by geography and wind patterns. Often, air pollution moves out of the state in which it is produced into another state. Some pollutants, such as the power plant combustion products that cause acid rain, may travel over several states before affecting health, the environment, and property. The 1990 Clean Air Act includes many provisions, such as interstate compacts, to help states work together to protect the air they share. Reducing interstate air pollution is very important since many Americans live and work in areas where more than one state is part of a single metropolitan area.

LAER — Lowest achievable emission rate. Considered to be the lowest rate of emissions from a source category which is contained in the State Implementation Plan, or which is achieve in practice by such category of sources. This term is most often associated with a nonattainment area.

Major source — Under the PSD regulations it is a facility, belonging to one or more of 28 source categories, having the potential to emit 100 tons per year of a pollutant regulated under the federal Clean Air Act (CAA). For categories other than the 28 sources, the potential emission level can not exceed 250 tons per year.

A major source for the purpose of Title V in the CAA is a stationary source that has the potential to emit 100 tons per year a pollutant regulated under the CAA and/or a source that has the potential to emit 10 tons per year for a single hazardous air pollutant or 25 tons per year of a combination of all hazardous air pollutants.

Material safety data sheets (MSDSs) — Product safety information sheets prepared by manufacturers and marketers of products containing toxic chemicals. These sheets can be obtained by requesting them from the manufacturer or marketer. Some stores, such as hardware stores, may have material safety data sheets on hand for products they sell.

Mobile sources — Motor vehicles and other moving objects that release pollution; mobile sources include cars, trucks, buses, planes, trains, motorcycles and gasoline-powered lawn mowers. Mobile sources are divided into two groups: road vehicles, which includes cars, trucks, and buses, and non-road vehicles, which includes trains, planes, and lawn mowers.

Monitoring (monitor) — Measurement of air pollution is referred to as monitoring. EPA, state, and local agencies measure the types and amounts of pollutants in community air. The 1990 Clean Air Act requires states to monitor community air in polluted areas to determine if the areas are being cleaned up according to schedules set by law.

NAAQS — National ambient air quality standards. Ambient standards developed by EPA that must be attained and maintained to protect public health. "Secondary" NAAQS are necessary to protect the public welfare. NAAQS exist for particulate matter, sulfur dioxide, nitrogen dioxide, ozone, carbon dioxide, and lead.

Nitrogen oxides (NOx) — A criteria air pollutant. Nitrogen oxides are produced from burning fuels, including gasoline and coal. Nitrogen oxides are smog formers, which react with volatile organic compounds to form smog. Nitrogen oxides are also major components of acid rain.

Non-attainment area — A geographic area in which a criteria air pollutant level is higher than allowed by the federal standards. A single geographic area may have an acceptable level for one criteria air pollutant, but have unacceptable levels of one or more other criteria air pollutants. Thus, an area can be both an attainment and non-attainment area at the same time. Sixty percent of Americans are estimated to live in non-attainment areas.

NSR — New source review. NSR typically means any new source locating in a, e.g., ozone nonattainment area that will emit volatile organic compounds (VOCs) and/or oxide of nitrogen (NO) in certain amounts. These sources must: undergo a new source review that provides for offsetting emissions for any increases in the emissions of these two pollutants; use the lowest achievable emissions technology to control emissions; apply for a construction permit; and meet other state requirements before the new emission from the source can be permitted. Existing sources, located in the ozone nonattainment area, that emit these two pollutants and plan to change

their operational methods that will cause an increase in the emissions of these two pollutants must apply for a modification permit and under go a review similar to a new source.

NSPS — New source performance standards. These are federal EPA emission standards for certain air pollutants that are emitted from new, modified, or reconstructed stationary emission sources which reflect the use of best available control technology

NESHAPS — National emission standards for hazardous air pollutants.

Offset — A method used in the 1990 Clean Air Act to give companies, which own or operate large (major) sources in non-attainment areas, flexibility in meeting overall pollution reduction requirements when changing production processes. If the owner or operator of the source wishes to increase releases of a criteria air pollutant, an offset (reduction of a somewhat greater amount of the same pollutant) must be obtained either at the same plant or by purchasing offsets from another company.

Ozone — A gas which is a variety of oxygen. The oxygen gas found in the air consists of two oxygen atoms stuck together; this is molecular oxygen. Ozone consists of three oxygen atoms stuck together into an ozone molecule. Ozone occurs in nature; it produces the sharp smell you notice near a lightning strike. High concentrations of ozone gas are found in a layer of the atmosphere — the stratosphere — high above the Earth. Stratospheric ozone shields the Earth against harmful rays from the sun, particularly ultraviolet B. Smog's main component is ozone; this ground-level ozone is a product of reactions among chemicals produced by burning coal, gasoline and other fuels, and chemicals found in products such as solvents, paints, and hair sprays.

Particulates: particulate matter (PM-10) — Particulate matter is a criteria air pollutant and is a finely divided particle with an aerodynamic diameter of 10 micrometers or less. Particulate matter includes dust, soot and other tiny bits of solid materials that are released into and move around in the air. Particulates are produced by many sources, including burning of diesel fuels by trucks and buses, incineration of garbage, mixing and application of fertilizers and pesticides, road construction, industrial processes such as steel making, mining operations, agricultural burning (field and slash burning), and operation of fireplaces and wood stoves. Particulate pollution can cause eye, nose, and throat irritation and other health problems.

Permit — A document that resembles a license that is required by the Clean Air Act for big (major) sources of air pollution, such as power plants, chemical factories and, in some cases, smaller polluters. Usually permits are issued by states, but if EPA has disapproved part or all of a state permit program, EPA will issue the permits in that state. The 1990 Clean Air Act includes requirements for permit applications, including provisions for members of the public to participate in state and EPA reviews of permit applications. Permits contain information on all the regulated pollutants at a source. Permits include information on which pollutants are presently released, how much pollution the source is allowed to release, and the control measures necessary to meet pollutant release requirements. Permits are required both for the operation of plants (operating permits) and for the construction of new plants. The 1990 Clean Air Act introduced a nationwide permit system for air pollution control.

Permit fees — Fees paid by businesses required to have a permit. Permit fees are like the fees drivers pay to register their cars. Money from permit fees helps pay for state air pollution control activities.

Pollutants (pollution) — Unwanted chemicals or other materials found in the air. Pollutants can harm health, the environment and property. Many air pollutants occur as gases or vapors, but some are very tiny solid particles: dust, smoke, or soot.

Primary standard — A pollution limit based on health effects. Primary standards are set for criteria air pollutants.

PSD — Prevention of significant deterioration. This term refers to regulations that requires a major new source or an existing source making majoring modifications to be permitted by the state before construction is started if they are located in an attainment area.

RACT — Reasonably available control technology. It is usually an emission limit set by a state air program and is the basis for emission rates used in their SIP. It usually applies to sources in attainment areas and in most cases is less stringent than the NSPS level of control.

Reformulated gasoline — Specially refined gasoline with low levels of smog-forming volatile organic compounds (VOCs) and low levels of hazardous air pollutants. The 1990 Clean Air Act requires sale of reformulated gasoline in the nine smoggiest areas. Some reformulated gasolines were sold in several smoggy areas before passage of the 1990 Clean Air Act.

SBA — Small Business Administration

SBAP — Small Business Assistance Program

SBDC — Small Business Development Center

Secondary standard — A pollution limit based on environmental effects such as damage to property, plants, or visibility. Secondary standards are set for criteria air pollutants.

State Implementation Plan (SIP) — A detailed description of the programs a state will use to carry out its responsibilities under the Clean Air Act. This includes such things as rules and regulations, plans to control ozone, and ambient air standards used by a state to reduce air pollution. The Clean Air Act requires that EPA approve each state implementation plan.

Smog — A mixture of pollutants, principally ground-level ozone, produced by chemical reactions in the air involving smog-forming chemicals. A major portion of smog-formers comes from burning petroleum-based fuels such as gasoline. Other smog-formers, volatile organic compounds, are found in products such as paints and solvents. Smog can harm health, damage the environment and cause poor visibility. Major smog occurrences are often linked to heavy motor vehicle traffic, sunshine, high temperatures and calm winds, or temperature inversion (weather condition in which warm air is trapped close to the ground instead of rising).

Source — Any place or object from which pollutants are released. A source can be a power plant, factory, dry cleaning business, gas station, or a farm. Cars, trucks, and other motor vehicles are sources. Consumer products and machines used in industry can also be sources.

Stationary source — A place or object from which pollutants are released which stays in place. Stationary sources include power plants, gas stations, incinerators, and houses.

Sulfur dioxide — A criteria air pollutant. Sulfur dioxide is a gas produced by burning coal, most notably in power plants. Some industrial processes, such as production of paper and smelting of metals, produce sulfur dioxide. Sulfur dioxide is closely related to sulfuric acid, a strong acid. Sulfur dioxide plays an important role in the production of acid rain.

Synthetic minor permit — A permit with practically, enforceable conditions issued to a facility. These conditions limit the amount of regulated pollutant emissions so the permitted amount of actual emissions from the facility is below potential major source emission levels. These major source thresholds are usually 100 tons per year under Title V, 50 tons per year VOC/NO in the nonattainment area for ozone; 100/250 tons per year for P.D; 10 tons per year for a single hazardous air pollutant; 25 tons per year for a combination of all hazardous air pollutants; and 50 tons per year for a new source review.

Title V permit — Is a federal operating permit program adopted and implemented by the state. The basic program elements typically specify that major sources will submit an operating application to the specified state environmental regulatory agency according to a schedule. EPA and the affected states will review the permit issuance. The pubic also has an opportunity to comment on the permit, which is renewable every five years. Minor changes to the permit can be made without opening the permit for public participation.

Ultraviolet B (UVB) — A type of sunlight. The ozone in the stratosphere filters out ultraviolet B rays and keeps them from reaching the Earth. Ultraviolet B exposure has been associated with skin cancer, eye cataracts, and damage to the environment. Thinning of the ozone layer in the stratosphere results in increased amounts of ultraviolet B reaching the Earth.

Vapor recovery nozzles — Special gas pump nozzles that reduce the release of gasoline vapor into the air as gas is pumped into car tanks. There are several types of vapor recovery nozzles. Therefore, nozzles may not look the same at all gas stations. The 1990 Clean Air Act requires the installation of vapor recovery nozzles at gas stations in smoggy areas.

Volatile organic compounds (VOCs) — Organic chemicals all contain the element carbon (C). Organic chemicals are the basic chemicals found in living things and in products derived from living things, such as coal, petroleum, and refined petroleum products. Many of the organic chemicals we use do not occur in nature, but were synthesized by chemists in laboratories. Volatile chemicals readily produce vapors at room temperature and normal atmospheric pressure. Vapors escape easily from volatile liquid chemicals. Volatile organic chemicals include gasoline, industrial chemicals such as benzene, solvents such as toluene and xylene, and tetrachloroethylene (perchloroethylene, the principal dry cleaning solvent). Many volatile organic chemicals, such as benzene, are also hazardous air pollutants.

APPENDIX XVI

SOURCE:
USEPA, *Fit to Print* manual

List of Federal Hazardous Air Pollutants (HAPs)

CAS Number	Chemical Name
75070	Acetaldehyde
60355	Acetamide
75058	Acetonitrile
98862	Acetophenone
53963	2-Acetylaminofluorene
107028	Acrolein
79061	Acrylamide
79107	Acrylic acid
107131	Acrylonitrile
107051	Allyl chloride
92671	4-Aminobiphenyl
62533	Aniline
90040	o-Anisidine
1332214	Asbestos
71432	Benzene (including benzene from gasoline)
92875	Benzidine
98077	Benzotrichloride
100447	Benzyl chloride
92524	Biphenyl
117817	Bis(2-ethylhexyl)phthalate (DEHP)
542881	Bis(chloromethyl)ether
75252	Bromoform
106990	1,3-Butadiene
156627	Calcium cyanamide
133062	Captan
63252	Carbaryl

CAS Number	Chemical Name
75150	Carbon disulfide
56235	Carbon tetrachloride
463581	Carbonyl sulfide
120809	Catechol
133904	Chloramben
57749	Chlordane
7782505	Chlorine
79118	Chloroacetic acid
532274	2-Chloroacetophenone
108907	Chlorobenzene
510156	Chlorobenzilate
67663	Chloroform
107302	Chloromethyl methyl ether
126998	Chloroprene
1319773	Cresols/Cresylic acid (isomers and mixture)
95487	o-Cresol
108394	m-Cresol
106445	p-Cresol
98828	Cumene
94757	2,4-D, salts and esters
3547044	DDE
334883	Diazomethane
132649	Dibenzofurans
96128	1,2-Dibromo-3-chloropropane
84742	Dibutylphthalate
106467	1,4-Dichlorobenzene(p)

CAS Number	Chemical Name
91941	3,3-Dichlorobenzidene
111444	Dichloroethyl ether (Bis(2-chloroethyl)ether)
542756	1,3-Dichloropropene
62737	Dichlorvos
111422	Diethanolamine
121697	N,N-Diethyl aniline (N,N-Dimethylaniline)
64675	Diethyl sulfate
119904	3,3-Dimethoxybenzidine
60117	Dimethyl aminoazobenzene
119937	3,3'-Dimethyl benzidine
79447	Dimethyl carbamoyl chloride
68122	Dimethyl formamide
57147	1,1-Dimethyl hydrazine
131113	Dimethyl phthalate
77781	Dimethyl sulfate
534521	4,6-Dinitro-o-cresol, and salts
51285	2,4-Dinitrophenol
121142	2,4-Dinitrotoluene
123911	1,4-Dioxane (1,4-Diethyleneoxide)
122667	1,2-Diphenylhydrazine
106898	Epichlorohydrin (1-Chloro-2,3-epoxypropane)
106887	1,2-Epoxybutane
140885	Ethyl acrylate
100414	Ethyl benzene
51796	Ethyl carbamate (Urethane)
75003	Ethyl chloride (Chloroethane)
106934	Ethylene dibromide (Dibromoethane)
107062	Ethylene dichloride (1,2-Dichloroethane)
107211	Ethylene glycol
151564	Ethylene imine (Aziridine)
75218	Ethylene oxide
96457	Ethylene thiourea
75343	Ethylidene dichloride (1,1-Dichloroethane)
50000	Formaldehyde
76448	Heptachlor
118741	Hexachlorobenzene
87683	Hexachlorobutadiene
77474	Hexachlorocyclopentadiene
67721	Hexachloroethane
822060	Hexamethylene-1,6-diisocyanate
680319	Hexamethylphosphoramide
110543	Hexane
302012	Hydrazine
7647010	Hydrochloric acid
7664393	Hydrogen fluoride (Hydrofluoric acid)
7783064	Hydrogen sulfide
123319	Hydroquinone
78591	Isophorone
58899	Lindane (all isomers)
108316	Maleic anhydride
67561	Methanol
72435	Methoxychlor
74839	Methyl bromide (Bromomethane)
74873	Methyl chloride (Chloromethane)
71556	Methyl chloroform (1,1,1-Trichloroethane)
78933	Methyl ethyl ketone (2-Butanone)

CAS Number	Chemical Name
60344	Methyl hydrazine
74884	Methyl iodide (Iodomethane)
108101	Methyl isobutyl ketone (Hexone)
624839	Methyl isocyanate
80626	Methyl methacrylate
1634044	Methyl tert butyl ether
101144	4,4-Methylene bis(2-chloroaniline)
75092	Methylene chloride (Dichloromethane)
101688	Methylene diphenyl diisocyanate (MDI)
101779	4,4'-Methylenedianiline
91203	Naphthalene
98953	Nitrobenzene
92933	4-Nitrobiphenyl
100027	4-Nitrophenol
79469	2-Nitropropane
684935	N-Nitroso-N-methylurea
62759	N-Nitrosodimethylamine
59892	N-Nitrosomorpholine
56382	Parathion
82688	Pentachloronitrobenzene (Quintobenzene)
87865	Pentachlorophenol
108952	Phenol
106503	p-Phenylenediamine
75445	Phosgene
7803512	Phosphine
7723140	Phosphorus
85449	Phthalic anhydride
1336363	Polychlorinated biphenyls (Arochlors)
1120714	1,3-Propane sultone
57578	beta-Propiolactone
123386	Propionaldehyde
114261	Propoxur (Baygon)
78875	Propylene dichloride (1,2-Dichloropropane)
75569	Propylene oxide
75558	1,2-Propylenimine (2-Methyl aziridine)
91225	Quinoline
106514	Quinone
100425	Styrene
96093	Styrene oxide
1746016	2,3,7,8-Tetrachlorodibenzo-p-dioxin
79345	1,1,2,2-Tetrachloroethane
127184	Tetrachloroethylene (Perchloroethylene)
7550450	Titanium tetrachloride
108883	Toluene
95807	2,4-Toluene diamine
584849	2,4-Toluene diisocyanate
95534	o-Toluidine
8001352	Toxaphene (chlorinated camphene)
120821	1,2,4-Trichlorobenzene
79005	1,1,2-Trichloroethane
79016	Trichloroethylene
95954	2,4,5-Trichlorophenol
88062	2,4,6-Trichlorophenol
121448	Triethylamine
1582098	Trifluralin
540841	2,2,4-Trimethylpentane

CAS Number	Chemical Name
108054	Vinyl acetate
593602	Vinyl bromide
75014	Vinyl chloride
75354	Vinylidene chloride (1,1-Dichloroethylene)
1330207	Xylenes (isomers and mixture)
95476	o-Xylenes
108383	m-Xylenes
106423	p-Xylenes
0	Antimony Compounds
0	Arsenic Compounds (inorganic including arsine)
0	Beryllium Compounds
0	Cadmium Compounds
0	Chromium Compounds

CAS Number	Chemical Name
0	Cobalt Compounds
0	Coke Oven Emissions
0	Cyanide Compounds[1]
0	Glycol ethers[2]
0	Lead Compounds
0	Manganese Compounds
0	Mercury Compounds
0	Fine mineral fibers[3]
0	Nickel Compounds
0	Polycyclic Organic Matter[4]
0	Radionuclides (including radon)[5]
0	Selenium Compounds

Note: For all listings above which contain the word 'compounds' and for glycol ethers, the following applies: Unless otherwise specified, these listings are defined as including any unique chemical substance that contains the name chemical (i.e., antimony, arsenic, etc.) as part of that chemical's infrastructure.

[1] X'CN where X=H' or any other group where a formal dissociation may occur. For example KCN or $Ca(CN)_2$.

[2] Includes mono- and di-ethers or ethylene glycol, diethylene glycol, and triethylene glycol $R-(OCH_2CH_2)_n-OR'$ where n=1, 2, or 3; R=alkyl or aryl groups; R'=R ,H, or groups which, when removed, yield glycol ethers with the structure: $R-(OCH_2CH)_n-OH$. Polymers are excluded from the glycol category.

[3] Includes mineral fiber emissions from facilities manufacturing or processing glass, rock, or slag fibers (or other mineral derived fibers) of average diameter 1 micrometer or less.

[4] Includes organic compounds with more than one benzene ring, and which have a boiling point greater than or equal to 100°C.

[5] A type of atom which spontaneously undergoes radioactive decay.

APPENDIX **XVII**

Tools for Determining Air Emissions: Spreadsheets, Worksheets, Guidance

SOURCE:
P-F Technical services, Inc.

Compliance for printers is determined by two measures: 1. the amount of volatile organic compounds emitted to the atmosphere; 2. the amount of volatile organic compounds in the inks or fountain solution as they are applied on the press.

This appendix has three components:

1. A mass balance (worksheet) that computes the amount of air emissions for a small printer based on periodic purchases, i.e. annually (p 564).

2. A mass balance for a medium to large printer that requires monthly records and itemization of every ink and chemical used. This spreadsheet is quite large and is depicted in sections to illustrate the information either entered or computed (pp 565–569).

3. USEPA document describing "Procedures for Certifying Quantity of Volatile Organic Compounds Emitted by Inks." This document contains forms and describes the mathematics of computing the emissions for inks as supplied to the printer and as used at the press after addition of solvents or other additives (pp 570–573).

The mass balances are developed using the Material Safety Data Sheets for data that is descriptive of the composition of the ink or other chemistry used and for percentages or basic information that can be used to compute emissions. Formulas are placed in all cells that will develop the information required for compliance records and reports, as well as controls to assure the quality of the information. Physical postings will be limited to amounts purchased by month or period, whichever is suitable, and other items such as hazardous waste shipments, energy usage, etc.

The small printer is required to know the extent of emissions and how they relate to regulatory permit limits. The larger facility is required to itemize usage and the resulting emissions. Model mass balances are included in the enclosed disk for use in developing one for your site.

563

SMALL PRINTER—LITHOGRAPHER
RECORD PURCHASES AND COMPUTE VOC EMISSIONS

COMPANY: BLAND OFFSET LLC

ADDRESS: 2 BLANKET PLACE, ANILOX, OHIO

WORKSHEET TO COMPUTE VOC EMISSIONS

YEAR: 1999- SIX MONTHS

ITEM	POUNDS PER GALLON (MSDS)	POUNDS VOC'S PER GALLON (MSDS)	PERCENT VOC'S (MSDS)	GALLONS PURCHASED (SUM MONTHS)	POUNDS PURCHASED (COL E X B)	VOC'S (COL A X B) (COL F X D)	JAN	FEB	MAR	APR	MAY	JUN
INKS			5.00%		1700	85	250	300	150	200	300	500
				SUM MONTHS	(COL E X B)							
FOUNTAIN CONCENTRATES												
ALKALESS	8.47	5.20	61.42%	30.0	254.0	156	5	5	5	5	5	5
CONCENTRATE 451	8.88	0.70	7.88%	54.0	479.6	37.8			10	19	15	10
CONCENTRATE 345	8.88	0.73	8.22%	100.0	888.1	73	30	20	5	15	10	20
ISOPROPANOL ALCOHOL	6.55	6.55	100.00%	30.0	196.5	196.5	5	5	5	5	5	5
PRESS WASH												
SPECIAL BLANKT & ROLLER	6.75	6.75	100.00%	330.0	2227.5	2227.5	55	55	55	55	55	55
CLEANSUP	8.22	1.10	13.39%	15.0	123.3	16.5	5	0	5	0	5	0
MRC (Acetone)	6.80	4.00	58.82%	12.0	81.6	48	4	0	4	0	4	0
PURPLE MAGIC	7.28	7.28	100.00%	5.0	36.4	36.4	5	0	0	0	0	0
LITHOTINE	6.56	5.91	90.13%	6.0	39.3	35.46	0	0	6	0	0	0
LITHOTURPS	6.55	6.55	100.00%	8.0	52.4	52.4	4	0	0	0	0	4
FEDEROID	6.81	3.71	54.51%	60.0	408.4	222.6	10	10	10	10	10	10
POWERCLEAN	6.71	6.71	100.00%	180.0	1207.8	1207.8	30	30	30	30	30	30
TOTALS				830.0	7694.8	4395.0						
					POUNDS	POUNDS						
ANNUAL OPERATING HOURS	5 DAYS	2 SHIFTS	8 HOURS	250 DAYS		4000 HOURS						
TOTAL VOC'S PER HOUR						1.10 LBS VOCS/HOUR						
ANNUAL TONS VOC'S						2.20 TONS						

MASS BALANCE FOR LARGE PRINTER/LAMINATOR PURCHASES OF INKS, ADHESIVES AND SOLVENTS COMPUTATION OF VOC EMISSIONS (Sheet 1 of 5)

** Specific Gravity X 8.3= Pounds Per Gallon

FUNNYBONE FLEXIBLE PACKAGING — 2000 — YEAR:1999 — YEAR:1999

INK AND SOLVENT PURCHASES — INK**

INKS/COATINGS/SOLVENT	FORMULATION	DENSITY LBS/GAL (MSDS)	WEIGHT % VOC'S MSDS	VOC ANNUAL POUNDS (COL G x D)	INK ANNUAL GALLONS (COL G / C)	INK ANNUAL POUNDS (SUM MONTHS)	COMBINED SOLVENTS (SUM SOLVENTS)	ETHANOL 64-17-5 (%MSDS x G)	NORMAL PROPANOL 71-23-8 (%MSDS x G)	NP ACETATE 109-60-4 (%MSDS x G)	ISOPROPNL 67-63-0 (%MSDS x G)	HEXANE (%MSDS x G)	N-HEPTANE 142-82-5 (SUM MSDS x G)	TOLUENE 108-88-3 (%MSDS x G)	ISOPROPYL ACETATE 108-21-4 (%MSDS x G)
PRESSES															
ORION HT PROCESS MAGENTA	TN10155P	7.7	66.50%	1264	247	1900	828	21	659	93	55				
ORION HT PROCESS CYAN	TN10156P	8.8	62.30%	766	140	1230	766	14	405	80	48				
ORION HT BALANCED EXTENDER	TN10158D	8.5	70.00%	3990	669	5700	3990	63	2092	319	308				
ORION BLEND VEHICLE	TN10809	7.9	48.70%	14561	3804	29900	14561	4844	8671	1047					
ALFALAM BLEND VEHICLE	TN13089	7.2	69.59%	14753	2957	21200	13844	9095		3816	933				
ALFALAM WHITE	TN13090	10.2	46.17%	50328	10685	109000	48287	31937	4360	5123	4360				
ALFALAM EXTENDER	TN13092	7.0	75.92%	3712	702	4890	3912	1570	1340	460	42				
OHT HI STRENGTH BLACK	TN13117P	8.0	61.93%	935	190	1510	939	17	683						132
ORION P/A G GOLD	TN13450	7.4	42.44%	3242	1026	7640	3239	1490	1536	122	92				
ORION DIARYLIDE YELLOW	TN13710	7.2	59.78%	2367	547	3960	2348	1348	578	123	178				123
ORION Y/S NAPTHOL	TN13712	7.3	59.21%	983	226	1680	983	508	242	48	58				126
ORION RUBINE RED	TN13714	7.3	59.91%	803	184	1340	803	485	196	43	55				24
ORION CYAN BLUE	TN13718	7.4	58.56%	773	179	1320	766	408	193	38	53				74
ORION GREEN	TN13719	7.6	55.89%	755	178	1350	757	369	197	38	66				88
ORION BLACK	TN13720	7.4	56.62%	2950	701	5210	2959	1730	761	162	182				125
ORION WHITE	TN14041	10.4	30.49%	29458	9322	96600	31878	16712	9274		1932				
ALFALAM HIGH OPACITY WHITE	TN14172	9.7	37.92%	4740	1295	12500	4688	2500		738	388				875
POLYGLOSS SILVER	RYN05552	9.0	50.89%	588	128	1155	588	180		135	170		103		
SPECIALTY HIGH OPACITY WHITE	RYW10245	10.0	27.10%	4282	1580	15800	4282	2162	632	133	186		1169		
TOTALS - INK PURCHASED				141249 POUNDS	34761 GALLONS	323865 POUNDS	140418	75448	31817	12516	9389	0	1272	0	1567

AMOUNT VOC CONTENT	141249		
SOLVENT IN INK	141249		43.6%
SOLIDS IN INK	182816		56.4%
TOTAL WEIGHT INKS	323865		100.0%

SOLVENTS:		DENSITY LBS/GAL	PERCENT VOC'S	VOC ANNUAL POUNDS	ANNUAL GALLONS	ANNUAL POUNDS	COMBINED SOLVENTS	ETHANOL	NORMAL PROPANOL	NP ACETATE	ISOPROPNL	HEXANE	N-HEPTANE	TOLUENE	ISOPROPYL ACETATE
NORMAL PROPANOL	71-23-8	6.7	100.0%	531309	79182	531309.0	531309		531309						
ETHANOL		6.6	100.0%	734	111	734.0	734	734							
ISOPROPANOL		6.6	100.0%	18476	2821	18476.0	18476				18476				
N-PROPYL ACETATE		7.4	100.0%	86758	11740	86758.0	86758			86758					
DOW PM GLYCOL ETHER		7.7	100.0%	15653	2045	15653.0	15653								
SLOW BLEND X-785		6.8	100.0%	114133	16770	114133.0	114133		97013	17120					
HEXANE		5.5	100.0%	112	20	112.0	112					112			
TOTAL SOLVENTS PURCHASED				767175.0 POUNDS	112689.1	767175.0	767175.0	734	628322	103878	18476	112	0	0	0
TOTAL VOC EMISSIONS: - PRINTING PRESSES				908424 POUNDS / 454.21 TONS		1091040 POUNDS	907593	76182 / 8.4%	660139 / 72.7%	116394 / 12.8%	27865 / 3.1%		1272 / 0.1%	0	1567 / 0.2%
NET EMISSIONS AFTER INCIN				45421 POUNDS / 22.71 TONS											
NUMBER DAYS				356											
POUNDS VOC'S PER DAY				2551.8 POUNDS/DAY											

MASS BALANCE FOR LARGE PRINTER/LAMINATOR PURCHASES OF INKS, ADHESIVES AND SOLVENTS COMPUTATION OF VOC EMISSIONS (Sheet 2 of 5)

FUNNYBONE FLEXIBLE PACKAGIN 2000

INK AND SOLVENT PURCHASES   YEAR:1999

** Specific Gravity X 8.3= Pounds Per Gallon

INKS/COATINGS/SOLVENT	FORMULATION	INK** DENSITY LBS/GAL	INK % VOC'S WEIGHT	VOC ANNUAL POUNDS	INK ANNUAL GALLONS	INK ANNUAL POUNDS	COMBINED SOLVENTS	ETHANOL 64-17-5	NORMAL PROPANOL 71-23-8	NP ACETATE 109-60-4	ISOPROPNL 67-63-0	HEXANE	N-HEPTANE 142-82-5	TOLUENE 108-88-3	ISOPROPYL ACETATE 108-21-4
POUNDS VOC PER DAY AFTER INCINERATION				127.6 LBS/DAY AFTER INCIN											
LAMINATION															
LAMAL CR 1-8002	1424-1-5	9.25	20.00%	2160	1168	10800.0	2160	2160							
SERFINE 2022AA	1562-1-6	10.41	0.00%	0	16134	168000.0	0	0							
ADCOTE 532BB	1723-1-7	8.83	39.64%	5827	1665	14700.0	2940	2940							
ADCOTE 532DD	1889-1-6	9.41	25.00%	1250	531	5000.0	1000				860				
LAMAL HR2	75505-1-2	8.16	30.62%	18803	7521	61400.0	18420	17560							
LIOFOL LA1192		10.60	0.00%	0	5537	59800.0	0	0							
TOTAL COATINGS/ADHESIVES				28040	32557	319700	24520	17560		0	860		0	0	0
SOLVENTS															
ETHYL ACETATE		7.5	100.0%	66000	8800	66000.0	66000								
TOTAL SOLVENTS				66000	8800	66000	66000		0	0	0	0	0	0	0
TOTALS - LAMINATION				94040	41357	385700	90520	17560		0	860		0	0	0
NET EMISSIONS AFTER INCIN				4702											
NUMBER DAYS				356											
POUNDS VOC'S PER DAY				264.2											
POUNDS VOC PER DAY AFTER INCINERATION				13.2											
				VOC'S POUNDS											
FACILITY EMISSIONS															
PRINTING				908424											
LAMINATION				94040											
TOTAL POUNDS				1002464											
TOTAL TONS				501.23											
LESS HAZARDOUS WASTE				19.56											
NET TONS EMISSONS				481.67											
NET TONS VOC'S AFTER OXIDIZER				24.08											

MASS BALANCE FOR LARGE PRINTER/LAMINATOR PURCHASES OF INKS, ADHESIVES AND SOLVENTS COMPUTATION OF VOC EMISSIONS (Sheet 3 of 5)

FUNNYBONE FLEXIBLE PACKAGING   2000   1999

INK AND SOLVENT PURCHASES

INKS/COATINGS/SOLVENT	FORMULATION	1ST QTR	2ND QTR	3RD QTR	4TH QTR	JAN INK	JAN VOC	FEB INK	FEB VOC	MAR INK	MAR VOC	APR INK	APR VOC	MAY INK	MAY VOC	JUNE INK	JUNE VOC
PRESSES																	
ORION HT PROCESS MAGENTA	TN10155P	600	500	300	500	200	133	200	133	200	133	200	133	200	133	100	67
ORION HT PROCESS CYAN	TN10156P	300	300	300	330	100	62	100	62	100	62	100	62	100	62	100	62
ORION HT BALANCED EXTENDER	TN10158D	1425	1425	1425	1425	475	333	475	333	475	333	475	333	475	333	475	333
ORION BLEND VEHICLE	TN10809	7400	7500	7500	7500	2400	1169	2500	1218	2500	1218	2500	1218	2500	1218	2500	1218
ALFALAM BLEND VEHICLE	TN13089	5100	5100	5500	5500	1700	1183	1700	1183	1700	1183	1700	1183	1700	1183	1700	1183
ALFALAM WHITE	TN13090	28000	27000	27000	27000	10000	4617	9000	4156	9000	4156	9000	4156	9000	4156	9000	4156
ALFALAM EXTENDER	TN13092	1190	1200	1100	1400	400	304	390	296	400	304	400	304	500	380	300	228
OHT HI STRENGTH BLACK	TN13117P	350	350	410	400	100	62	150	93	100	62	100	62	150	93	100	62
ORION P/A G GOLD	TN13450	1960	1960	1970	1750	660	280	600	255	700	297	660	280	700	297	600	255
ORION DIARYLIDE YELLOW	TN13710	970	1030	950	1010	340	203	340	203	290	173	350	209	340	203	340	203
ORION Y/S NAPTHOL	TN13712	360	360	480	460	120	71	120	71	120	71	120	71	120	72	120	71
ORION RUBINE RED	TN13714	300	340	400	300	100	60	100	60	100	60	100	60	120	72	120	72
ORION CYAN BLUE	TN13718	330	330	330	330	110	64	110	64	110	64	110	64	110	64	110	64
ORION GREEN	TN13719	300	300	300	450	100	56	100	56	100	56	100	56	100	56	100	56
ORION BLACK	TN13720	1310	1360	1210	1330	430	243	430	243	450	243	430	255	500	283	430	243
ORION WHITE	TN14041	24200	24400	24000	24000	8100	2470	8100	2470	8000	2440	8200	2440	8000	2440	8200	2501
ALFALAM HIGH OPACITY WHITE	TN14172	3100	3200	3000	3200	1000	379	1100	417	1000	379	1100	379	1000	379	1100	417
POLYGLOSS SILVER	RYN05552	380	235	315	225	95	48	95	48	190	48	0	0	190	97	45	23
SPECIALTY HIGH OPACITY WHITE	RYW10245	4000	3800	4200	3800	1400	379	1400	379	1200	379	1200	325	1400	379	1200	325
		0	0	0	0		0		0		0		0		0		0
TOTALS - INK PURCHASED		81575	80690	80690	80910	27830	12118	27010	11740	26735	11667	26845	11676	27205	11898	26640	11537

AMOUNT VOC CONTENT

SOLVENT IN INK

SOLIDS IN INK

TOTAL WEIGHT INKS

SOLVENTS:		PRIDE			4TH QTR *	PRIDE		ELCO									
		1ST QTR	2ND QTR	3RD QTR	4TH QTR	JAN	VOC	FEB	VOC	MAR	VOC	APR	VOC	MAY	VOC	JUNE	VOC
NORMAL PROPANOL	71-23-8	531309	0	0	0	99582	99582	431727	431727	0	0	0	0	0	0	0	0
ETHANOL		734	0	0	0	734	734	0	0	0	0	0	0	0	0	0	0
ISOPROPANOL		18476	0	0	0	367	367	18109	18109	0	0	0	0	0	0	0	0
N-PROPYL ACETATE		86758	0	0	0	17120	17120	69638	69638	0	0	0	0	0	0	0	0
DOW PM GLYCOL ETHER		15653	0	0	0	425	425	15228	15228	0	0	0	0	0	0	0	0
SLOW BLEND X-785		114133	0	0	0	114133	114133	0	0	0	0	0	0	0	0	0	0
HEXANE		112	0	0	0	0	0	112	112	0	0	0	0	0	0	0	0

MASS BALANCE FOR LARGE PRINTER/LAMINATOR PURCHASES OF INKS, ADHESIVES AND SOLVENTS COMPUTATION OF VOC EMISSIONS (Sheet 4 of 5)

	FORMULATION	1ST QTR	2ND QTR	3RD QTR	4TH QTR	JAN INK	JAN VOC	FEB INK	FEB VOC	MAR INK	MAR VOC	APR INK	APR VOC	MAY INK	MAY VOC	JUNE INK	JUNE VOC
FUNNYBONE FLEXIBLE PACKAGING		2000			1999												
INK AND SOLVENT PURCHASES																	
INKS/COATINGS/SOLVENT																	
TOTAL SOLVENTS PURCHASED		767175	0.0	0.0	0.0	232361*	232361	534814	534814	0		0	0	0	0	0	0
TOTAL VOC EMISSIONS: - PRINTING PRESSES							244479		546554		11667		11676		11898		11537
NET EMISSIONS AFTER INCIN							12224		27328		583		584		595		577
NUMBER DAYS																	
POUNDS VOC'S PER DAY																	
POUNDS VOC PER DAY AFTER INCINERATION																	
LAMINATION																	
LAMAL CR 1-8002	1424-1-5	2700	2700	2700	2700	900	180	900	180	900	180	900	180	900	180	900	180
SERFINE 2022AA	1562-1-6	42000	42000	42000	42000	14000	0	14000	0	14000	0	14000	0	14000	0	14000	0
ADCOTE 532BB	1723-1-7	3600	3600	3700	3800	1200	476	1200	476	1200	476	1200	476	1200	476	1200	476
ADCOTE 532DD	1889-1-6	1000	2000	2000	0	1000	250	0	0	1000	250	0	0	1000	250	0	0
LAMAL HR2	75505-1-2	16200	15000	15000	15000	5100	1562	5000	1531	5100	1562	5100	1562	6100	1868	5000	1531
LIOFOL LA1192		14400	14800	14800	16200	4800	0	4800	0	4800	0	4800	0	4800	0	4800	0
TOTAL COATINGS/ADHESIVES		79900	80200	80200	79700	27000	2468	25900	2187	27000	2468	26000	2218	28000	2774	25900	2187
SOLVENTS																	
ETHYL ACETATE		14600	18000	15800	17600	5000	5000	4800	4800	4800	4800	6000	6000	6000	6000	6000	6000
TOTAL SOLVENTS		14600	18000	15800	17600	5000	5000	4800	4800	4800	4800	6000	6000	6000	6000	6000	6000
TOTALS - LAMINATION		94500	97900	96000	97300	32000	7468	30700	6987	31800	7268	32000	8218	34000	8774	31900	8187

MASS BALANCE FOR LARGE PRINTER/LAMINATOR PURCHASES OF NKS, ADHESIVES AND SOLVENTS COMPUTATION OF VOC EMISSIONS (Sheet 5 of 5)

** Specific Gravity X 8.3 = Pounds Per Gallon

FUNNYBONE FLEXIBLE PACKAGING — 2000 — YEAR: 1999

INK AND SOLVENT PURCHASES

(Purchases column subtotals — Printing: 88942 / 26653; Lamination: 51959 / 12470)

Emissions by Solvent	CAS Number	Facility Annual Pounds	Percent of Total	Purchases: Printing Pounds	Lamination Pounds	Hazrd Waste Presses	Hazrd Waste Laminators	Net Emissions After HW-Press	Net Emissions Lamination	Presses Oxidizer 95%	Laminators Oxidizer 95%	Total Emissions	Alloc. 6 Color CI 23.08%	Alloc. 6 Color CI 23.08%	Alloc. 8 Color CI 30.77%	Alloc. 6 Color CI 23.08%	Alloc. 6 Color CI 23.08%
ETHANOL	64-17-5	93742.4	9.39%	76182.0	17560	2503		73679	17560	3684	878	4562	17005	17005	22671	17005	17005
NORMAL PROPANOL	71-23-8	660139.2	66.14%	660139.2	0	17828		642511	0	32126	0	32126	148292	148292	197701	148292	148292
NP ACETATE	109-60-4	116394.4	11.66%	116394.4	0	3106		113286	0	5664	0	5664	26146	26146	34858	26146	26146
ISOPROPANOL	67-63-0	28724.8	2.88%	27865.0	860	767	359	27098	907	1355	45	1400	6254	6254	8338	6254	6254
TOLUENE	108-88-3	0.0	0.00%	0.0	0	0		0	0	0	0	0	0	0	0	0	0
HEPTANE	142-82-5	1272.0	0.13%	1272.0	0	34	16	1238	-15	62	-1	61	286	286	381	286	286
HEXANE	110-54-3	112.0	0.01%	112.0	0	3		109	0	5	0	5	25	25	34	25	25
ISOPROPYL ACETATE	108-21-4	1566.8	0.16%	1566.8	0	42	20	1525	138	76	7	83	352	352	469	352	352
ETHYL ACETATE	8030-30-6	78862.2	7.90%	6762.2	72100	2108	12072	4676	60028	234	3001	3235	1079	1079	1439	1079	1079
N-BUTYL ACETATE	123-86-4	311.9	0.03%	311.9	0	8	4	304	0	15	0	15	70	70	93	70	70
DIPRO GLYC METH ETHER	34590-94-8	15653.0	1.57%	15653.0	0	0		15653	0	783	0	783	3613	3613	4816	3613	3613
METHANOL	67-56-1	0.0	0.00%	0.0	0	0		0	0	0	0	0	0	0	0	0	0
METHYL ETHYL KETONE	78-93-3	0.0	0.00%	0.0	0	0		0	0	0	0	0	0	0	0	0	0
BUTYL CELLOSOLVE	111-76-2	0.0	0.00%	0.0	0	0		0	0	0	0	0	0	0	0	0	0
TRIPROPYLENE GLYCOL ETHER	25498-49-1	0.0	0.00%	0.0	0	0		0	0	0	0	0	0	0	0	0	0
ETHOXY PROPANOL	52125-53-8	197.8	0.02%	197.8	0	5		193	0	10	0	10	44	44	56	44	44
1-METHOXY 2-PROPANOL	107-98-2	1116.7	0.11%	1116.7	0	30		1087	0	54	0	54	251	251	334	251	251
LACTOL SPIRIT		0.0	0.00%	0.0	0	0		0	0	0	0	0	0	0	0	0	0
TOTAL EMISSIONS		998113.1	100.00%	907563.1	90520.0	26235.0	12470.0	881358.1	78619.0	44067.9	3930.9	47998.9	203417.4	203417.4	271193.9	203417.4	203417.4
ANNUAL TONS (TO DATE)		499.06		453.80	45.26	13.12	6.24	440.68	39.31	22.03	1.97	24.00	101.71	101.71	135.60	101.71	101.71
ANNUAL TONS AFTER OXIDIZER (95% DEST)													5.09	5.09	6.78	5.09	5.09

<u>VOC DATA SHEET:</u>

<u>PROPERTIES OF THE COATING "AS SUPPLIED" BY THE MANUFACTURER</u>

Coating Manufacturer: _____

Coating Identification: _____

Batch Identification: _____

Supplied To: _____

Properties of the coating as supplied[1] to the customer:

    A.   Coating Density $(D_c)_s$: _____ lb/gal _____ kg/l

           ☐ ASTM D1475   ☐ Other[2]

    B.   Total Volatiles $(W_v)_s$: _____ Weight Percent

           ☐ ASTM D2369   ☐ Other[2]

    C.   Water Content: 1. $(W_w)_s$ _____ Weight Percent

           ☐ ASTM D3792   ☐ ASTM D4017   ☐ Other[2]

                       2. $(V_w)_s$ _____ Volume Percent

           ☐ Calculated   ☐ Other[2]

    D.   Organic Volatiles $(W_o)_s$: _____ Weight Percent

    E.   Nonvolatiles Content $(V_n)_s$: _____ Volume Percent

    F.   VOC Content $(VOC)_s$: 1. _____ lb/gal coating less water

                       or _____ kg/l coating less water

                       2. _____ lb/gal solids

                       or _____ kg/l solids

Remarks: (use reverse side)

---

[1]The subscript "s" denotes each value is for the coating "as supplied" by the manufacturer.

[2]Explain the other method used under "Remarks".

                       Signed: _____ Date _____

<u>VOC DATA SHEET</u>

<u>PROPERTIES OF THE COATING "AS APPLIED" TO THE SUBSTRATE</u>

Coating Manufacturer:_____

Coating Identification:_____

Batch Identification:_____

User:_____

User's Coating Identification:_____

_____

Properties of the coating as applied[1] by the User:

A. Coating Density $(D_c)_a$: _____ kg/l, or _____ lb/gal

   | ____ | ASTM D1475 | ____ | Other[2]

B. Total Volatiles $(W_v)_a$: _____ Weight Percent

   | ____ | 40 CFR 60, App. A, Meth. 24A[4] | ____ | Other[2]

C. Water Content: 1. $(W_w)_a$ _____ Weight Percent

   | ____ | ASTM D3792 | ____ | ASTM D4017 | ____ | Other[2]

          2. $(V_w)_a$ _____ Volume Percent

   | ____ | Calculated | ____ | Other[2]

D. Weighted Average Density of the dilution solvent (D_d)[3]: _____ lb/gal

   | ____ | ASTM D1475 | ____ | Handbook | ____ | Formulation.

(Continued on Reverse Side)

---

[1]The subscript "a" denotes each value is for the coating "as applied" to the substrate.
[2]Explain the other method used.
[3]The subscript "d" denotes values are for the dilution solvent.
[4]40 CFR 60, App. A, Meth. 24A uses W_o to refer to total volatiles in the coating, whereas this document uses the notation W_v.

[6]Weighted Average Density of the negligible photochemically reactive dilution solvent: $(D_w)_d$ _____ lb/gal

|☐| ASTM D1475 |·| Handbook |☐| Formulation

E.   [6]Dilution Organic Solvent Ratio: 1. (R_d) _____ · $\dfrac{\text{gal organic diluent}}{(\text{gal coating})_s}$ [4]

     [6]Dilution Water Solvent Ratio: 2. $(R_w)_d$ _____ $\dfrac{\text{gal water diluent}}{(\text{gal coating})_s}$ [4]

F.   Organic Volatiles Content[5] $(W_o)_a$: _____ Weight Percent

G.   Non-Volatiles Content $(V_n)_a$: _____ Volume Percent

Remarks:

---

[4]The subbscript "s" denotes values are for the coating "as supplied" by the manufacturer.

[5]This terminology is used to be consistent with Method 24. It refers to all photochemically reactive organic compounds emitted from the coating including reactive by-products of the cure reaction, exactly the same matter as indicated in Paragraph H, i.e., volatile organic compounds, or VOC.

[6]If Method (3) on Pg. III-4 is being used to calculate A., B., and C., then parts D. and E. of the VOC DATA SHEET do not have to be filled out.

LOCAL SAMPLE #_____
STATE SAMPLE #_____

<u>PAINT/INK SAMPLE COLLECTION SHEET</u>

1. Bottle Filled By:_____Region:_____

2. Regional Representative who Collected Sample:_____

3. Facility Name and Address:_____

   _____

   _____

4. Date and Time of Sample Collection:_____

5. Type of Sample (check one) Sample I.D. #

   ( ) High Solids Paint (228)   ( ) High Solids Ink (234)

   ( ) Solvent-Borne Paint (228)   ( ) Solvent-Borne Ink (234)

   ( ) Low Solvents Paint (228)   ( ) Water-Borne Ink (234)

   ( ) Water-Borne Paint (228)   ( ) Excluded Solvent Ink (234)

   ( ) Excluded Solvent Paint (228)   Ex Solvent_____

       Ex Solvent_____

6. Paint or Ink Trade Name and Color:_____

   _____

7. Sampling Point Description (Include Emission Point #):

   _____

   _____

   _____

8. Method of sampling (check one):

   ( ) From Spray Gun   ( ) From Pot Connected to Spray Gun

   ( ) From Paint Cans   ( ) From Ink Well

   ( ) From Pot or Drum that Supplies Ink to Well/<u>Who said so?</u>_____

   ( ) Other (Describe)_____

   _____

   _____

   _____

_____
SIGNATURE   DATE

APPENDIX **XVIII**

SOURCE:
P-F Technical Services, Inc.

Air Emission Reports to State Agencies

Reports are a necessary part of the enforcement of environmental regulations. Periodic reports of air emissions may be required of the printer to confirm compliance. The reports will be a condition of the air permit. This appendix illustrates two sample forms of air emission reports. One is for the smaller state-regulated facility; the second is a report that certifies compliance with the USEPA enforceable Title V permit.

For the smaller print shop, the concern is maintaining emissions of VOCs and HAPs below the threshold that defines the facility as a registration or state facility permit. This report will confirm that the shop is operating in accordance with regulations and quantify the usage of ink and chemistry and the emissions from plant. In the event that an add-on control is used, assurances are given that the system has been operating normally and in accordance with the standards of the regulations.

The Title V printer must do more than report emissions and indicate that the control system has been performing adequately. This report is submitted biannually and is a certification that every condition of the permit has been satisfied. The spreadsheet illustrated is a representation of the types of conditions included in a Title V permit and the nature of the response required in semiannual and annual reports.

Reports are available to the public. Every admission and certification made in the reports must be substantiated by accurate records, if requested by the government agency or the public.

Every state may have its own report form. If none is available and required, follow the examples given here.

TYPICAL REPORT OF QUARTERLY AIR EMISSIONS

July 30, 2001

Maryland Dept. of the Environment
2500 Broening Highway
Baltimore, MD 21224

Re. Branded Packaging, Emissions Report for 2001- 2ND Quarter

Dear Sir:

This is to report the emissions from the Branded Packaging facility during the three months of the Second Quarter of 2001. Emissions are for three flexographic printing presses and one laminator.

The attached summary of emissions of volatile organic compounds is based on purchases for the three months of the Quarter. Hazardous waste disposed has been factored into the overall totals.

There was one shipment of hazardous waste generated during this period for the printing presses and the lamination operation. The shipments amounted to 2,739 pounds, of which 2,082 pounds were solvents (VOC's).

The catalytic oxidizer operated normally during the period, at standard or higher temperatures. The presses are in a permanent total enclosure and destruction efficiency was demonstrated during the stack test at an efficiency of 99.6%. For purposes of the reports, net destruction is computed at a net 90%.

Total VOC emissions, after oxidation, for the three months amounted to 7,173 pounds, 3.6 tons.

Total emissions for the cumulative year to date, reduced for hazardous waste shipped off-site for treatment, was 7.87 tons.

Natural gas consumption, based on invoices from BGE, during this 2nd Quarter amounted to 8,477 Therms, or 8,136 CC Feet.

Detailed spreadsheets are attached for your review.

Sincerely,
Joe Someone
President

TYPICAL REPORT OF QUARTERLY AIR EMISSIONS

BRANDED PACKAGING

100 WEST OUTSIDE STREET
ANYWHERE, MARYLAND 21250

YEAR 2001 - SECOND QUARTER

MONTHLY REPORT OF VOC EMISSIONS

	MONTH	VOC EMISSIONS (HW not deducted):				
		PRESSROOM	LAMINATIONS	PLANT	VOC'S BY QUARTER	12 MONTH CUMULATIVE
2001	JANUARY	1108	1261	2369	6141	27831
2001	FEBRUARY	403	1343	1746		27972
2001	MARCH	526	1500	2026		27741
2001	APRIL	1074	2640	3714	7173	30060
2001	MAY	584	660	1244		29255
2001	JUNE	565	1650	2215		27084
2000	JULY	454	1338	1792	8360	24864
2000	AUGUST	1254	3351	4605		27960
2000	SEPTEMBER	574	1389	1963		28331
2000	OCTOBER	1105	1358	2463	5406	29658
2000	NOVEMBER	715	1739	2454		31666
2000	DECEMBER	489	0	489		27081
					POUNDS	
	CUMULATIVE YEAR	8851	18229	27080		
	July 2000-June 2001	POUNDS	POUNDS	POUNDS		
		4.43	9.11	13.54		
		TONS	TONS	TONS		
	LESS HW EMISSIONS	0.3424	5.33	5.67		
	NET TONS VOC'S	4.08	3.78	7.87		

AUTHORIZED REPRESENTATIVE: JOE SOMEONE, PRESIDENT   _____

SIGNATURE OF REPRESENTATIVE   _____

DATE_____ _____

SPREADSHEET OF PURCHASES OF INK, ADHESIVES AND SOLVENTS

MATERIAL	FORMULA NUMBER	APR INK	VOC	MAY INK	VOC	JUNE INK	VOC
BRANDED PACKAGING 2001 2ND QUARTE							
SOLVENT/INK USEAGE-AIR EMISSIONS							
INKS:							
polyethylene inks		0	0	0	0	0	0
WHITE		2650	848	2650	848	1060	339
BLACK		0	0	195	98	0	0
REFLEX BLUE		0	0	160	82	135	69
CYAN BLUE		0	0	0	0	0	0
072 BLUE		0	0	120	84	0	0
PURPLE C		0	0	0	0	72	50
VIOLET PANTONE		0	0	144	83	0	0
RED 485		0	0	0	0	0	0
RED 485 HI STR		179	94	228	120	152	80
RHODAMINE RED		0	0	0	0	0	0
THERMO RED LAKE C		193	112	0	0	0	0
RED 185 HI STR		195	66	195	66	0	0
ORANGE 021		168	94	0	0	0	0
BROWN 490		190	105	0	0	152	84
GREEN 347		0	0	216	121	0	0
CYAN GREEN		206	114	0	0	0	0
YELLOW 116		533	266	0	0	164	82
DIARYLIDE YELLOW		0	0	190	95	0	0
YELLOW 1235		0	0	155	83	0	0
EXTENDER VARNISH		0	0	0	0	0	0
NO-TOX WHITE		0	0	0	0	0	0
ORANGE*		0	0	150	100	0	0
NO-TOX BLACK		0	0	150	100	0	0
TOTAL INKS		4314	1699	4553	1879	1735	705
Inventory adjustment (based on gallons)							
NET INKS		4314	1698.9759	4553	1879.3487	1735	704.6
SOLVENTS:							
NORMAL PROP ALCOHOL		7920	7920	3960	3960	3960	3960
ETHANOL ANHYDROUS		0	0	0	0	0	0
DUPLICATING FLUID #5		990	990	0	0	990	990
NORMAL BUTYL ALCOHOL		0	0	0	0	0	0
TOTAL SOLVENTS		8910	8910	3960	3960	4950	4950
inventory adjustment							
NET SOLVENTS		8910	8910	3960	3960	4950	4950
TOTAL INKS & SOLVENTS		13224	10609	8513	5839	6685	5655
TONS EMISSIONS INCL HAZARD WASTE			10609		5839		5655
NET EMISSIONS AFTER OXIDIZER (90%)			1061		584		565

TITLE V. COMPLIANCE CERTIFICATION

FACILITY IDENTIFICATION

COMPANY NAME:				
FACILITY NAME:				
MAILING ADDRESS;				
STREET ADDRESS:	Same			
CITY:		**STATE:** NY	**ZIP:** 122.	
PERMIT ID:	2-.?..?i..?i	**ISSUE DATE:**	01/1./2C00	
DESCRIPTION:	Article 19: Title V Facility Permit			
SIC:	**MAJOR POLLUTANTS:**			

FACILITY CONTACTS

Person	Name	Phone	Fax	E-mail
Responsible Official				N/A
Technical Contact				N/A

CERTIFICATION

I,   ., Responsible Official, certify under penalty of law that, based in information and belief formed after reasonable inquiry, the statements and information contained in the attached compliance certification are true, accurate and complete. I am aware that there are significant penalties for any person who knowingly makes a false material statement, representation or certification in any notice, application records, report plan or other document pursuant to the Clan Air Act including the possibility of fine or imprisonment. See 42 USC 7401 Title I, Part A, Sec 113.

Signature	
Title	
Date	

Reporting Period: 01/12/2000 to 01/11/2001

COMPLIANCE CERTIFICATION: RECORD KEEPING/MAINTENANCE PROCEDURES

Brooklyn, NY 11222
Title V Permit ID: 2-...
Reporting Period: 01/12/2000 to 01/11/2001

Item	Point	Monitoring Type	Monitoring Description	Reporting Requirements	Method	Limit	Monitoring Frequency	Compliance Status
28.2	Not Appl.	Record Keeping/ Maintenance Procedures	Emission Statement	Annual – April 15th	Not Appl.	Not Appl.	Annual	Not required this reporting period.
32.2	Not Appl.	Record Keeping/ Maintenance Procedures	HAP: Ink and solvent purchases recorded on a computer spreadsheet monthly...	Upon request by regulatory agency	Spreadsheet	Not Applicable	Monthly	Record keeping was performed as required. See attachment 1.
33.2	Not Appl.	Record Keeping/ Maintenance Procedures	VOC: Ink and solvent purchases recorded on a computer spreadsheet monthly....	Upon request by regulatory agency	Spreadsheet	Not Applicable	Monthly	Record keeping was performed as required. See attachment 1.
38.2	U-00001	Monitoring of Process or Control Device Parameters as Surrogate	Opacity	Upon request by regulatory agency	6 Minute Average	20%	As required	Monitoring and record keeping were performed as required.
40.2	U-00002	Monitoring of Process or Control Device Parameters as Surrogate	Opacity	Upon request by regulatory agency	6 Minute Average	20%	As required	Monitoring and record keeping were performed as required.
41.2	U-00002	Record Keeping/ Maintenance Procedures	Coating supplier/manufacturer certification verifying parameter used to determine actual VOC content of as applied coating for each coating used at the facility....	Upon request by regulatory agency	Not Specified	Not Specified	Not Specified	No requests this period.
42.2	U-00002	Work Practice Involving Specific Operations	Extreme performance coatings may contain a max of 3.5 lbs of FOC per gallon of coating as applied...	Upon request by regulatory agency	Method 24	3.5 lbs/gallon	Single Occurrence	No requests this period.
48.2	Not Appl	Work Practice Involving Specific Operations	Sulfur quantity limitation for distillate fuel oil.	Upon request by regulatory agency	Maximum	0.2% by weight	As required	No requests this period.

ANNUAL VOC REPORT

2000

MONTH	Monthly VOC (lbs.)	Cumulative VOC (lbs)
January 12-31, 2000	3,268	3,268
February 2000	7,401	10,669
March 2000	4,932	15,601
April 2000	12,302	27,904
May 2000	7,651	35,555
June 2000	9,244	44,799
July 2000	9,629	54,428
August 2000	4,277	58,705
September 2000	6,418	65,123
October 2000	6,014	71,137
November 2000	6,917	78,054
December 2000	6,072	84,126
January 1-11, 2001	36	84,162

CUMULATIVE 12 MONTHS ENDING DECEMBER 2000

84,162 POUNDS

42.1 TONS

PAINT AND SOLVENT PURCHASES INDIVIDUAL SOLVENTS	CAS NUMBER	POUNDS	TONS
TOLUENE - HAP	108-88-3	32,265	16.1
XYLENE - HAP	1330-20-7	9,622	4.8
ACETONE	67-64-1	1,241	0.6
MIBK - HAP	108-10-1	0.0	0.0
METHANOL - HAP	67-56-1	0.0	0.0
VM&P NAPTHA	64742-89-8	2,962	1.5
MINERAL SPIRITS	64742-88-7	12	0.0
N-BUTYL ALCOHOL	71-36-3	0.92	0.0
LEAD DRIER	301-8-6	0.00	0.0
STODDARD SOLVENT	8052-41-3	10,250	5.1
SOLVESSO 150	64742-95-6	4,419	2.2
ETHYL BENZENE - HAP	100-41-4	1,247	0.6
DIOCTLY PHTHALATE - HAP	117-81-7	33.47	0.0

APPENDIX **XIX**

Potential to Emit: A Guide to Small Businesses

SOURCE:
USEPA, EPA-456/B-98-003

How do I determine the potential to emit for my business:

Your maximum capacity determines your potential to emit. So, once you've identified your maximum capacity (or have chosen alternatives, such as permit limits or other state limits), as described above, you can determine your potential to emit. The steps involved in determining your emissions are presented in Box 1. Specific methods for figuring out your potential to emit are described below.

BOX 1. BASIC STEPS FOR DETERMINING EMISSIONS

1. Identify all sources of emissions.

2. Identify all criteria pollutants and hazardous air pollutants (HAPs) that your business emits. (Note that other types of pollutants may also be regulated and require a Title V permit; check with your state air pollution control agency or state small business assistance program for a list of all regulated air pollutants. For who to contact, see "Where can I get more information?").

3. Select a method to use from Table 2 below to determine your emissions.

4. For each criteria and hazardous air pollutant, determine the maximum amount that each production process or piece of equipment in your business can emit in one year.

5. For each criteria and hazardous air pollutant, add the maximum emissions from all production processes/equipment.

581

Does a screening method exist that can easily tell me if I am a major or minor source before I try to determine my potential to emit?

Yes. EPA has developed guidance that you can use to quickly determine if you are a major or minor source (see EPA, 1998a in the Reference section [Appendix C]). The screening method covers pollutants and materials that are of the greatest concern for different types of businesses. The method includes cutoff levels for materials that you may use (e.g., solvents, etc.). If you use less than the cutoff level for a certain material, then you are probably a minor source. In all cases, you should confirm your results with your state air pollution control agency. If the screening method does not apply to you, then you can use the procedures described below to determine your potential to emit.

What methods can I use to determine my emissions?

You can use one of the following four methods to determine your emissions:

- Use test data (onsite measurements).

- Use a material-balance approach (comparing inputs and outputs).

- Use source-specific models (based on information about your business's operations).

- Use emission factors (based on industry-average emission rates).

Table 2 describes these methods in more detail.

Which method should I use to calculate emissions?

It depends on the type of business and types of emissions you have, what information and resources are available, and the degree of accuracy required. Consult your state air pollution control agency or your state small business assistance program before choosing a particular method (for who to contact, see "Where can I get more information?"). Different methods may be used for different types of emissions. Whichever method you use, when you determine your potential to emit, assume that no pollution controls are in place.

What are fugitive emissions, and do they need to be considered when calculating my potential to emit?

Fugitive emissions refer to air pollutant emissions that enter the atmosphere from a business without first passing through a stack or duct designed to direct or control their flow. While air emissions often do pass through a stack or duct (or are otherwise captured) before being discharged to the atmosphere, some fugitive emissions typically escape the system without being captured.

Depending on the purpose of your potential to emit calculation, you may or may not be required to include fugitive emissions. Also, some regulations require certain types of businesses to include fugitive emissions when determining their potential to emit. Contact your state air pollution control agency or state small business assistance program for guidance on whether to include fugitive emissions in your potential to emit.

TABLE 2. EMISSIONS CALCULATION METHODS

Method	Description
Test data	Onsite measurement of emissions.
Material-balance calculations	Estimate emissions by comparing types and quantities of inputs to types and quantities of outputs.
Source-specific models	Formulas for emissions using source-specific parameters such as types and quantities of inputs, operating hours, and physical characteristics of equipment.
Emission factors	Uses average pollutant emission rates (provided by EPA, other agencies, or equipment vendors), multiplied by time or frequency of operation, to obtain emissions. Emission factors specific to your business can be used but should be approved by the state air pollution control agency.

How does the number of hours my business operates affect my emission estimates?

As discussed earlier, in determining potential to emit you should assume that equipment operates every hour of the year (8,760 hours per year), unless certain limitations affect how much your business can operate (see the earlier question, "What is maximum capacity?" which describes these limitations). If such limitations are present, you should assume that your equipment operates for the maximum number of hours allowed by the limitations. In the case of batch operations, when emissions are not continuous in time, determine your potential to emit by multiplying the emissions per batch by the maximum number of batches per year.

If after calculating my potential to emit my business is above major source levels, what do I do?

If your potential to emit is just above major source levels, carefully check and document any assumptions used in your calculation. If your numbers are correct, you might still qualify as a minor source if you limit your operations in certain ways.

Example: Potential to Emit of a Sheetfed Offset Lithographic Printing Operation

A small printing company operates several sheetfed offset lithographic presses. Instead of figuring out its maximum capacity, the company has accepted an operating limit from the state of 16,000 pounds of ink per year, and 1,350 gallons of total solvent per year with an average VOC content of 6.6 pounds per gallon. These limits are based on the company's best estimate of the maximum amounts of inks and solvents that will be used. (If the business owner were to determine maximum capacity instead of accepting a predetermined limit from the state, he or she would need to determine the maximum operating schedule, line speed, and drying time, which might be difficult to figure out.)

What is my maximum capacity?

* For ink: 16,000 pounds of ink per year, which is the operating limit you accepted from the state.
* For solvents: 1,350 gallons of total solvents per year with an average VOC content of 6.6 pounds per gallon, which you also accepted as a limit from the state.

What pollutants do I emit?

The ink, cleaning solvent, blanket wash solvent, and fountain solution you use all contribute to VOC and HAP emissions. You can get some of the information you need from your state air pollution control agency, state small business assistance program, and Material Safety Data Sheets (MSDS) located at your business, including:

* Find out from your state air pollution control agency or state small business assistance program what the major source level for VOCs is. (For this example, according to the state agency, the major source level for VOCs is 50 tons per year.)
* Comparing your MSDS with the list of HAPs in Appendix B of this document tells you that you emit the following HAPs from your inks and solvents:

    toluene

    ethylene glycol

* Look at your MSDS to determine the specific VOC and HAP content of the inks and solvents you use.

Table 5 lists the relevant input materials, their maximum usage rates, and their VOC and HAP content based on the MSDS.

Can I use EPA's screening method to determine if I am a major or minor source?

Yes. According to EPA's screening method (see EPA, 1998a in Appendix C), if your printing business:

* Uses less than 7,125 gallons of cleaning solvent and fountain solution per year, you are probably a minor source for VOCs.

TABLE 5. MAXIMUM USAGE AND POLLUTANT CONTENT OF INPUTS

Material	Usage	VOC Content	HAP Content
Ink	16,000 lbs/year	10% by weight (which = 10 lb VOC per 100 lb ink)	0 lb/gal
Cleaning Solvent	600 gal/year	6.9 lb/gal	0 lb/gal
Blanket Wash Solvent	500 gal/year	6.2 lb/gal	2.3 lb/gal toluene
Fountain Solution	250 gal/year	6.8 lb/gal	1.2 lb/gal ethylene glycol

• Uses less than 3,333 gallons of all materials that contain hazardous air pollutants and less than 1,333 gallons of material containing any one HAP, you are probably a minor source for HAPs.

Since, in this example, you have accepted a limit of 1,350 gallons of total solvent per year, you are probably a minor source for VOCs and total HAPs. Based on the solvent data in Table 5, the maximum solvent usage for any one HAP is the 500 gallons per year blanket wash solvent, which contains toluene. Because this is less than 1,333 gallons, you are probably also a minor source for any individual HAP. You should confirm this information with your state air pollution control agency or state small business assistance program (for who to contact, see "Where can I get more information?"). If the screening process is not sufficient to determine whether you are a major or minor source, use the procedures described in Box 4.

What is my total potential to emit for VOCs?

To find the total VOC emissions from this printing business, add up all of the individual VOC emissions above as shown in Box 5.

This result shows that this printing company could be only a minor source of VOC emissions (which can contribute to criteria pollutants), since the maximum VOC emissions are less than the major source level of VOCs, which is 50 tons per year.

What is my potential to emit HAPs emissions?

Determine your potential to emit for HAP emissions in the same way you did for VOC emissions. That is, for a particular kind of HAP, first figure out separately the maximum HAPs that could be emitted from each individual input material used (in this case, the blanket wash solvent and fountain solution). Determine your potential HAP emissions from each of these materials by using the following steps:

• Determine the potential to emit HAPs from each material used (e.g., solvents, solutions). To do this, multiply a material's usage by its HAP content (see Table 5 for usage and HAP content).

• Change each individual HAP emission from pounds of HAP per year to tons of HAP per year. Do this by dividing the result you have by 2,000 (because there are 2,000 pounds in 1 ton).

• Add the individual HAP emissions together to get total HAPs emissions.

You can use the equations summarized in Box 6 to carry out the above steps.

BOX 4. HOW TO DETERMINE POTENTIAL TO EMIT VOC EMISSIONS

VOC emissions, in tons/year =

Step 1: Determine potential to emit VOCs from the ink, solvents, and solution:

Ink usage (from Table 5)	×	VOC content (from Table 5)
(in lbs per year)		(in lb of VOC per lb of ink)

and also

Solvent and solution usage (from Table 5)	×	VOC content (from Table 5)
(in gal per year)		(in lb of VOC per gal of solvents and solution)

Step 2: Add together the individual results for the ink, solvents, and solution:

lb VOC per yr	+	lb VOC per yr	+	lb VOC per yr	+	lb VOC per yr
(from ink)		(from the cleaning solvent)		(from the blanket wash solvent)		(from the fountain solution)

Step 3: Change from lb per year to tons per year:

total lb VOC per year	÷	2000	=	tons total VOCs per year

Thus the VOC emissions from the ink are:

Ink:

16,000 lb per yr of ink	×	10 lb of VOC per 100 lb of ink	=	**1,600 lb of VOCs per year from ink**
(usage)		(VOC content)		

The VOC emissions from the solvents and solution are:

Cleaning Solvent:

600 gal per yr of cleaning solvent	×	6.9 lb VOC per gal of cleaning solvent	=	**4,140 lb per year of VOCs from the cleaning solvent**
(usage)		(VOC content)		

Blanket Wash Solvent:

500 gal per yr of blanket wash solvent	×	6.2 lb VOC per gal of blanket wash solvent	=	**3,100 lb per year of VOCs from the blanket wash solvent**
(usage)		(VOC content)		

Fountain Solution:

250 gal per yr of fountain solution	×	6.8 lb VOC per gal of fountain solution	=	**1,700 lb per year of VOCs from the fountain solution**
(usage)		(VOC content)		

(Note that changing from pounds to tons per year will be done later.)

BOX 5. TOTAL POTENTIAL TO EMIT VOCs

Total Potential to Emit VOCs:

1,600 lb VOC per yr	+	4,140 lb VOC per yr	+	3,100 lb VOC per yr	+	1,700 lb VOC per yr	=	10,540 lb of total
(from ink)		(from cleaning solvent)		(from blanket wash solvent)		(from fountain solution)		VOC per year

Now, change from lb of VOCs to tons of VOCs by dividing by 2,000: 10,540 ÷ 2,000 = **5.27 tons per year of total VOCs**

BOX 6. POTENTIAL TO EMIT HAP EMISSIONS

Potential to Emit HAP Emissions

Step 1:   Determine potential to emit HAPs from the solvents and solution:

Solvent and solution usage in gal per year HAP content of the material in lb per gal of solvents and solution

Step 2:   Change each HAP emission from lb per year to tons per year:

lb HAP per year   ÷   2000   =   tons HAP per year

Step 3:   Add together the individual results for the solvents and solution:

| tons HAP per yr (from the blanket wash solvent) | + | tons HAP per yr (from the fountain solution) | = | tons of total HAPs per year |

From this example, first figure out the potential to emit for the individual HAPs: toluene and ethylene glycol, listed in Table 5, as follows:

Toluene from the blanket wash solvent:

| 500 gal per yr of blanket wash solvent (usage) | × | 2.3 lb of toluene per gal of blanket wash solvent (HAP content) | = | *1,150 lb of toluene per year from the blanket wash solvent* |

Change from pounds to tons: 1,150 lb of toluene per year + 2000 = **0.575 ton toluene per year**

Ethylene glycol from the fountain solution

| 250 gal per yr of fountain solution (usage) | × | 1.2 lb of ethylene glycol per gal of fountain solution (HAP content) | = | *300 lb of ethylene glycol per year from the fountain solution* |

Change from pounds to tons: 300 lb of ethylene glycol per year ÷ 2000 = **0.15 ton ethylene glycol per year**

What is my total potential to emit HAPs?

To find the total HAP emissions from this printing business, add up all of the individual HAP emissions above, as follows:

Total Potential to Emit HAPs:

| 0.575 ton per yr (of toluene from the blanket wash solvent) | + | 0.15 ton per yr (of ethylene glycol from the fountain solution) | = | **0.725 tons per year of total HAPs** |

This result shows that the printing company could be only a minor source of HAP emissions, since its individual HAP emissions all lie below 10 tons per year (which is the major source level for individual HAPs), and its total HAP emissions are less than 25 tons per year (which is the major source level for total HAPs).

Am I a major source of either VOC or HAP emissions?

No, the printing business in this example is not a major source, it is a minor source of both VOC and HAP emissions because its emissions fall below the major source levels for both VOCs and HAPs.

APPENDIX **XX**

New Source Review Requirements

SOURCE:
USEPA, EPA 300-N-99-002

Under the Clean Air Act (CAA), companies must obtain a major new source review ("major NSR") permit for new construction or major modifications that substantially increase a facility's emissions of certain regulated air pollutants.

Because air pollution control requirements in these major NSR permits reduce emissions of nitrogen oxides (NOx), particulate matter (PM) and other pollutants by as much as 95 percent, compliance is key to achieving the nation's air quality goals. One U.S. Environmental Protection Agency (EPA) action to enforce these requirements reduced NOx emissions at one facility by more than 400 tons per year, which is equivalent to removing about 60,000 cars from the road. NOx and PM exacerbate asthma, lower resistance to respiratory disease and harm vegetation, including crops and forests.

In addition to excess emissions of air pollutants, violations of NSR requirements can result in inequities. First, noncompliance shifts the burden of pollution control to law-abiding facilities, which are effectively forced to compensate for illegal unpermitted emissions by meeting more stringent control standards in State Implementation Plans. Moreover, because NOx and other criteria pollutants can be transported long distances, violations in one state can impact air quality in another state. Finally, as the State of Iowa has pointed out in a recent letter to EPA, lax implementation in some states can make it more difficult for others to insist that permit standards be met.

587

Evidence suggests that violations of the major NSR requirements are widespread. Thus, EPA has made enforcement of the CAA's New Source Review requirements a priority for the coming year. EPA encourages regulated industries to take affirmative steps to improve compliance by meeting their obligation to obtain permits and reduce air emissions.

This issue of 'Enforcement Alert':

• Summarizes the New Source Review requirements

• Presents evidence that noncompliance is widespread

• Identifies common types of violations to be avoided

What is New Source Review?

In areas not meeting the national ambient air quality standards (NAAQS) and in the Ozone Transport Region, NSR requirements are implemented through the "nonattainment" NSR program. In areas either meeting the NAAQS (attainment areas) or for which there is insufficient information to determine whether they meet the NAAQS (unclassifiable areas), the prevention of significant deterioration (PSD) program applies.

Both programs require preconstruction review and permitting of new or modified existing major stationary sources of certain regulated air pollutants. A new "greenfield" source in a nonattainment area is subject to major NSR if its potential to emit exceeds 100 tons per year (tpy); the threshold can be as low as 10 tpy for some pollutants in extreme ozone nonattainment areas. In attainment areas, the major source threshold is 250 tpy, except for 28 identified source categories, which have a threshold of 100 tpy.

In addition, an existing major source that makes a modification which increases emissions above significance levels (e.g., 15 tpy for PM10) triggers NSR review. In other words, if an existing facility changes or expands its operations in a manner that increases its emissions of air pollution above certain levels, it must undergo NSR. As the D.C. Circuit stated, "[t]he statutory scheme intends to 'grandfather' existing industries; but the provisions concerning modifications indicate that this is not to constitute a perpetual immunity from all standards under the PSD program." Alabama Power v. Costle, 636 F.2d 323, 400 (D.C.

Cir. 1979). A source may "net" out of NSR, however, if it generates enough emissions decreases to offset its emissions increases.

What are NSR Requirements?

The NSR permitting process has several elements. Generally, there is a control technology component and an air quality component. In nonattainment areas, the control technology requirement is the application of the lowest achievable emission rate (LAER), which is the most stringent emissions rate limitation required in any State Implementation Plan (SIP) or otherwise achievable in practice.

In addition, a new major source or major modification must offset its emissions increases, generally at a ratio of 1:1; for certain ozone nonattainment areas, however, the ratio can reach 1.5:1. There are some additional nonattainment NSR requirements related to alternative site analysis and company compliance.

In attainment and unclassifiable areas, the control technology requirement is the application of best available control technology (BACT), which is an emissions limitation based on the maximum degree of emissions reduction achievable considering economic, environmental and energy factors. In addition, the PSD review includes an air quality impact analysis to determine whether the source's emissions will violate the NAAQS or any air quality increments. Moreover, in some instances, a consultation must occur regarding the impact of emissions on national parks and other pristine areas.

The installation and operation of LAER and BACT can achieve significant emissions reductions. LAER can achieve emission reductions in excess of:

VOC — 95%	SO2 — 90-95%
PM — 99%	NOx — 85-90%

BACT controls can achieve emissions reductions in excess of:

VOCs — 85-95%	SO2 — 90-95%
PM — 99%	NOx — 85%

What is the Rate of Compliance?

The relatively low numbers of NSR permits issued per year raises serious NSR compliance concerns.

For instance, after the 1990 CAA Amendments tightened the definition for "major source," EPA anticipated that approximately 900 NSR permit applications would be filed per year. Despite an economy that has been expanding at an annual rate of about 4.2 percent, applications for major NSR permits (both new sources and modifications) have remained relatively steady at about 200 per year.

When EPA looks closely at an industry sector, usually it discovers a high rate of noncompliance. For example, in its Wood Products Initiative, EPA found NSR violations at approximately 70-80 percent of the facilities investigated. Moreover, EPA continues to find high rates of noncompliance despite several successful enforcement actions. In an EPA Region 3 Pulp & Paper Initiative, initial results show a potential 80 percent rate of noncompliance. In addition, other databases indicate a substantial increase in the capacity at existing facilities, and a series of modifications that may have triggered NSR permit and pollution control requirements.

What Types of Violations Has EPA Found?

Violations may occur at the front and back of the NSR permitting process. "Front-end" violations lead to avoidance of NSR review altogether. Some common examples of front-end violations are:

- Improper use of exemptions: The EPA has seen sources inappropriately apply certain exemptions from the NSR regulations. For example, the "routine maintenance, repair and replacement" exemption was meant to cover frequent, traditional and comparatively inexpensive repairs to maintain existing equipment. Some sources, however, have tried to extend it to activities that are infrequently performed in the industry, alter the design or function of the equipment, or involve a significant capital cost. In other instances, sources have failed to recognize that the alternative fuels exemption, which allows a source to switch fuels without triggering NSR under certain circumstances, requires that the entire facility, not just the combustion unit, have been capable of accommodating the alternative fuel since approximately 1975. Moreover, the alternative fuel should have been contemplated by the facility as a potential fuel during that time period.

- Failure to recognize a change as a "modification": The EPA has discovered that some sources failed to treat certain activities as modifications under the NSR regulations (e.g., removal of flue gas recirculation at utilities; catalyst changes that significantly increase capacity).

- Improper emission estimates: The EPA has uncovered permit applications that failed to list all pollutants emitted at the facility, or failed to correctly total emissions from all emission points at the facility (e.g., several wood products facilities failed to report VOC emissions). In other cases, sources failed to include "debottlenecked" emissions in their calculations (i.e., the modification at Unit A removed a bottleneck at Unit B). The emissions at all debottlenecked units should be considered when determining whether the emissions from a modification are significant.

- The EPA has also come across sources that relied on AP-42 factors to estimate emissions because they lacked source-specific emissions information. As EPA cautions, however, AP-42 factors should not be used for source-specific permitting decisions because they can underestimate emissions. Thus, the source assumes the risk that its emissions estimate may be inaccurate.

- Some facilities also failed to apply the "actual-to-potential" test when measuring the emissions increase from a modification. Under EPA regulations, post-change actual emissions for units that have "not begun normal operations . . . equal the potential to emit (PTE) of the unit on that date." (See, e.g., 40 CFR 52.21(b)(21)(iv)). Some sources have taken the position that a modified unit has "begun normal operations" and thus its post-change emissions should not be based on its potential to emit. It is EPA's position, however, that changes to a unit at a major stationary source that are non-routine or not subject to one of the other major source NSR exemptions are deemed to be of such significance that "normal operations" of the modified unit have not begun and, therefore, post-change emissions should equal the modified unit's potential to emit.

- Improper netting: EPA has discovered netting calculations that involved emissions decreases already relied on in an earlier netting exercise; double counting of emissions decreases is prohibited. In addition, EPA has seen netting calculations that used emissions decreases which were not enforceable (e.g., permitted), a requirement of the NSR regulations.

"Back-end" violations and/or permitting issues usually involve sources that go through the NSR process, but provide inaccurate or insufficient information. Some back-end violations include applications that:

• Provided an incorrect LAER analysis (e.g., failure to consider technology transfer).

• Failed to obtain sufficient offsets due to a low estimate of the emissions increase, perhaps due to improper reliance on AP-42 factors.

• Provided an inaccurate BACT analysis. EPA has discovered that when performing the economic feasibility portion of the BACT analysis, sources sometimes use inflated capital and operating and maintenance costs, include improper interest rates, or underestimate the life-expectancy of the control equipment, all of which increase the perceived cost of the controls. Also, some sources seem to be under the impression that there are bright line costs above which BACT is considered too expensive; this is not the case. If sources in the same source category have adopted a control technology as BACT, there is a general presumption that the cost is acceptable unless the source can demonstrate unique circumstances. Finally, EPA has seen BACT analyses that failed to consider all available control technology alternatives.

What Emissions Reductions Does EPA Get From NSR Enforcement?

Correcting NSR violations can lead to significant emissions reductions. For example, in the Wood Products Initiative, emission reductions were as high as 500 tons of VOCs for a single facility. Estimated total emissions reductions from the entire industry could exceed 100,000 tons of VOCs.

Other NSR cases have led to emissions reductions in the thousands of tons per year. For example:

• California Almond Growers Exchange (Region 9): Approximately 5750 tpy of CO (which, when uncontrolled, contributed to NAAQS exceedances)

• Kelco (Region 9): Approximately 1,700 tpy of VOCs in an ozone nonattainment area

• Pro-Tec (Region 5 - pending): About 400 tpy of NOx

• Region 10 Idaho Panhandle Wood Products Initiative: About 1,400 tpy of PM and 240 tpy of VOCs

• Arco/Snyder Riverton Dome (Region 8): Approximately 160 tpy of NOx

What's Next?

Given the significance of the excess emissions that result from NSR noncompliance, EPA has been increasing its emphasis on enforcement of NSR requirements. In particular, EPA has been looking at industry efforts to expand capacity and analyzing whether such activities triggered NSR.

Finally, in a recent NSR enforcement guidance, EPA clarified that it will generally be seeking significant emissions reductions (e.g., equivalent to BACT or LAER) from companies that improperly bypass the NSR permit process. This guidance should not only result in significant environmental benefit, but also ensure consistency in the resolution of these important cases.

APPENDIX **XXI**

Air Permits

SOURCE:
New York State Department of
Environmental Conservation

Permit application forms vary from state to state. The enclosed forms are representative of two levels of permitting based on the amount of emissions exhausted:

1. *Application for registration certificate – New York:* (pp 592–593)

   Facilities with VOC emissions of less than 12.5 tons file this one page form with two attachments: a. Site plan, b. Representative emissions statement based on most current year.

2. *Application for Title V permit – New York:* (pp 594–608)

   Facilities which exceed the threshold for a major source will have to file a fairly complex application with references to the operations, the emission points, a qualification of the solvents being emitted, and regulatory references that are applicable to the process and the facility (federal and state).

NEW YORK STATE
REGISTRATION APPLICATION INSTRUCTIONS

Stationary sources subject to the requirements set forth in 6 NYCRR Part 201-4 will be required to register with the Department of Environmental Conservation. Instructions for completing the New York State registration application are provided below.

OWNER/FIRM: Enter the name of the owner of the facility for which this application is being prepared. For individual owners, list the full name (last, middle initial, first). For multiple ownership, where no legal business partnership exists provide the name and mailing address, if different, of each individual owner using a backslash (/) to separate data for each owner. For corporations, include division or subsidiary name, if any. Enter the mailing address of the owner. Include the COUNTRY if foreign owned (otherwise leave blank) and the appropriate ZIP/MAIL CODE (zip code + extension may also be entered). Enter the business TAXPAYER ID number (no personal Social Security #, should be listed).

OWNER/FIRM CONTACT: List the name and telephone number of the owner/firm representative responsible for answering any air permit inquiries regarding this source.

FACILITY: Enter the name and the correct physical location of the facility (e.g. Acme Rd. or Building 3, XYZ Industrial Park). Check the appropriate box and enter the name of the CITY, TOWN, or VILLAGE, and ZIP CODE for the primary jurisdiction of the facility. For instances where a facility is located in multiple jurisdictions (i.e., across city, town, village or county lines) list all jurisdictions using a backslash (/) to separate data for each location, with the primary jurisdiction listed first.

FACILITY INFORMATION

TOTAL NUMBER OF EMISSION POINTS: Enter the total number of emission points located at this facility. Do not include any emission points which vent emissions exclusively from exempt or trivial activities as defined in 6 NYCRR Part 201-3.

CAP BY RULE: Check this box if the potential to emit for the facility is to be capped by rule pursuant to 6 NYCRR Part 201-7.3.

DESCRIPTION: Provide an overview description of the facility referred to in this application in terms of its primary function and/or business activity, principal industrial or manufacturing processes including the primary item(s) being manufactured (if applicable), and any other information supporting the SIC codes that are listed below. Mention any specific regulations (i.e., NSPS or New Source Performance Standards, MACT rules) that apply to the facility and provide the rule citation to the subpart level (i.e., Subpart Dc - small boiler NSPS).

STANDARD INDUSTRIAL CLASSIFICATION (SIC) CODES: Enter all SIC codes that apply to the facility with the principle SIC code listed first.

HAP CAS NUMBERS: Specify the Chemical Abstract Series or CAS numbers for any HAP's emitted from the facility (up to a maximum of 12) in order of emission quantity. HAP's refer to hazardous air pollutants as defined in 6 NYCRR Part 200.1(af).

APPLICABLE FEDERAL and NEW YORK STATE REQUIREMENTS (Part Nos): List the rule citations of all applicable federal and New York state regulations as they pertain to this facility. The rule citation should be listed to the "Part" level (i.e., Part 201, 212, 60 (for federal NSPS rules)) only. If a regulation is further identified by a subpart citation, the subpart citation and rule title should be listed in the facility description.

CERTIFICATION: Enter the name, official title, signature and date of signature of the responsible official accountable for the compliance of this facility with the applicable regulations. Certification is required by a representative of the firm or applicant responsible for demonstrating the truth, accuracy and completeness of the information contained in this application. The responsible official should be aware that significant penalties could result in submitting false information, including the possibility of fines and imprisonment for knowing violations.

New York State Department of Environmental Conservation
Air Facility Registration

DEC ID
·			·				

Owner / Firm   Taxpayer ID

Name
Street Address

City / Town / Village	State or Province	Country	Zip/Mail Code

Owner/Firm Contact

Name	Phone No. ( )

Facility

Name
Location Address

☐ City / ☐ Town / ☐ Village	Zip

Facility Information

Total Number of Emission Points: _____   ☐ Cap by Rule

Description

_____
_____
_____
_____
_____

Standard Industrial Classification Codes

HAP CAS Numbers

· ·	· ·	· ·	· ·	· ·	· ·
· ·	· ·	· ·	· ·	· ·	· ·

Applicable Federal and New York State Requirements (Part No.s)

Certification

I certify that this facility will be operated in conformance with all provisions of existing regulations.

Responsible Official	Title
Signature	Date ____ / ____ / ____

New York State Department of Environmental Conservation
Air Permit Application

DEC ID	APPLICATION ID	OFFICE USE ONLY
☐-☐☐☐☐-☐☐☐☐	☐-☐☐☐☐-☐☐☐☐☐/☐☐☐☐	☐/☐/☐☐☐

Section I - Certification

Title V Certification

I certify under penalty of law that this document and all attachments were prepared under my direction or supervision in accordance with a system designed to assure that qualified personnel properly gather and evaluate the information submitted. Based on my inquiry of the person or persons directly responsible for gathering the information [required pursuant to 6 NYCRR 201-6.3(d)] I believe the information is, true, accurate and complete. I am aware that there are significant penalties for submitting false information, including the possibility of fines and imprisonment for knowing violations.

Responsible Official	Title
Signature	Date _____ / _____ / _____

State Facility Certification

I certify that this facility will be operated in conformance with all provisions of existing regulations.

Responsible Official	Title
Signature	Date _____ / _____ / _____

Section II - Identification Information

Title V Facility Permit	State Facility Permit
☐ New ☐ Significant Modification ☐ Administrative Amendment	☐ New ☐ Modification
☐ Renewal ☐ Minor Modification General Permit Title:	General Permit Title:
☐ Application involves construction of new facility	☐ Application involves construction of new emission unit(s)

Owner / Firm

Name			
Street Address			

City	State	Country	Zip

Owner Classification	☐ - Federal ☐ - Corporation/Partnership	☐ - State ☐ - Individual	☐ - Municipal	Taxpayer ID ☐☐☐☐☐☐☐☐☐

Facility   ☐ Confidential

Name
Location Address

☐ City / ☐ Town / ☐ Village	Zip

Project Description   ☐ Continuation Sheet(s)

_____

_____

_____

Owner / Firm Contact Mailing Address

Name (Last, First, Middle Initial)		Phone No. ( )
Affiliation	Title	Fax No. ( )
Street Address		

City	State	Country	Zip

Facility Contact Mailing Address

Name (Last, First, Middle Initial)		Phone No. ( )
Affiliation	Title	Fax No. ( )
Street Address		

City	State	Country	Zip

10/31/96

New York State Department of Environmental Conservation
Air Permit Application

	DEC ID								

Section III - Facility Information

Classification

☐ Hospital   ☐ Residential   ☐ Educational/Institutional   ☐ Commercial   ☐ Industrial   ☐ Utility

Affected States (Title V Only)

☐ Vermont ☐ Massachusetts ☐ Rhode Island ☐ Pennsylvania Tribal Land: _____
☐ New Hampshire ☐ Connecticut ☐ New Jersey ☐ Ohio Tribal Land: _____

SIC Codes

Facility Description   ☐ Continuation Sheet(s)

Compliance Statements (Title V Only)

For all emission units at this facility that are operating <u>in compliance</u> with all applicable requirements including any compliance certification requirements under section 114 (a) (3) of the clean air act amendments of 1990, complete the following:

☐ This facility will continue to be operated and maintained in such a manner as to assure compliance for the duration of the permit, except those units referenced in the compliance plan portion of Section IV of this application.

☐ For all emission units, subject to any applicable requirements that will become effective during the term of the permit, this facility will meet all such requirements on a timely basis.

☐ Compliance certification reports will be submitted at least once a year. Each report will certify compliance status with respect to each requirement, and the method used to determine the status.

Facility Applicable Federal Requirements   ☐ Continuation Sheet(s)

Title	Type	Part	Sub Part	Section	Sub Division	Parag.	Sub Parag.	Clause	Sub Clause

Facility State Only Requirements   ☐ Continuation Sheet(s)

Title	Type	Part	Sub Part	Section	Sub Division	Parag.	Sub Parag.	Clause	Sub Clause

10/31/96

New York State Department of Environmental Conservation
Air Permit Application

	DEC ID								
-					-				

Section III - Facility Information (continued)

Facility Compliance Certification ☐ Continuation Sheet(s)

Rule Citation

Title	Type	Part	Sub Part	Section	Sub Division	Parag.	Sub Parag.	Clause	Sub Clause

☐ Applicable Federal Requirement ☐ State Only Requirement	☐ Capping	CAS No. - -	Contaminant Name

Monitoring Information

☐ Ambient Air Monitoring   ☐ Work Practice Involving Specific Operations   ☐ Record Keeping/Maintenance Procedures

Description

_____

_____

_____

Work Practice Type	Code	Process Material Description	Reference Test Method

Parameter			Manufacturer Name/Model No.
Code	Description		

Limit				Limit Units	
Upper	Lower		Code	Description	

Averaging Method		Monitoring Frequency		Reporting Requirements	
Code	Description	Code	Description	Code	Description

Facility Emissions Summary ☐ Continuation Sheet(s)

CAS No.	Contaminant Name	PTE (lbs/yr)	Range Code	Actual (lbs/yr)
NY075 - 00 - 5	PM-10			
NY075 - 00 - 0	PARTICULATES			
7446 - 09 - 5	SULFUR DIOXIDE			
NY210 - 00 - 0	OXIDES OF NITROGEN			
630 - 08 - 0	CARBON MONOXIDE			
7439 - 92 - 1	LEAD			
NY998 - 00 - 0	VOC			
NY100 - 00 - 0	HAP			
- -				
- -				
- -				
- -				
- -				

New York State Department of Environmental Conservation
Air Permit Application

DEC ID
-						-					

Section IV - Emission Unit Information

Emission Unit Description ☐ Continuation Sheet(s)

EMISSION UNIT | - | | | | |

_____

_____

_____

Building ☐ Continuation Sheet(s)

Building	Building Name	Length (ft)	Width (ft)	Orientation

Emission Point ☐ Continuation Sheet(s)

EMISSION PT. | | | | |

Ground Elev. (ft)	Height (ft)	Height Above Structure (ft)	Inside Diameter (in)	Exit Temp. (°F)	Cross Section Length (in)	Width (in)

Exit Velocity (FPS)	Exit Flow (ACFM)	NYTM (E) (KM)	NYTM (N) (KM)	Building	Distance to Property Line (ft)	Date of Removal

EMISSION PT. | | | | |

Ground Elev. (ft)	Height (ft)	Height Above Structure (ft)	Inside Diameter (in)	Exit Temp. (°F)	Cross Section Length (in)	Width (in)

Exit Velocity (FPS)	Exit Flow (ACFM)	NYTM (E) (KM)	NYTM (N) (KM)	Building	Distance to Property Line (ft)	Date of Removal

Emission Source/Control ☐ Continuation Sheet(s)

Emission Source ID	Type	Date of Construction	Date of Operation	Date of Removal	Control Type Code	Description	Manufacturer's Name/Model No.

Design Capacity	Code	Design Capacity Units Description		Waste Feed Code	Description	Waste Type Code	Description

Emission Source ID	Type	Date of Construction	Date of Operation	Date of Removal	Control Type Code	Description	Manufacturer's Name/Model No.

Design Capacity	Code	Design Capacity Units Description		Waste Feed Code	Description	Waste Type Code	Description

10/31/96

New York State Department of Environmental Conservation
Air Permit Application

DEC ID
☐ - ☐ ☐ ☐ ☐ ☐ - ☐ ☐ ☐ ☐ ☐

Section IV - Emission Unit Information (continued)

Process Information   ☐ Continuation Sheet(s)

EMISSION UNIT ☐ - ☐ ☐ ☐ ☐ ☐   PROCESS ☐ ☐ ☐

Description

_____
_____
_____
_____
_____
_____
_____
_____
_____

Source Classification Code (SCC)	Total Thruput		Thruput Quantity Units	
	Quantity/Hr	Quantity/Yr	Code	Description

☐ Confidential ☐ Operating at Maximum Capacity ☐ Activity with Insignificant Emissions	Operating Schedule		Building	Floor/Location
	Hrs/Day	Days/Yr		

Emission Source/Control Identifier(s) (continued)

EMISSION UNIT ☐ - ☐ ☐ ☐ ☐ ☐   PROCESS ☐ ☐ ☐

Description

_____
_____
_____
_____
_____
_____
_____
_____
_____

Source Classification Code (SCC)	Total Thruput		Thruput Quantity Units	
	Quantity/Hr	Quantity/Yr	Code	Description

☐ Confidential ☐ Operating at Maximum Capacity ☐ Activity with Insignificant Emissions	Operating Schedule		Building	Floor/Location
	Hrs/Day	Days/Yr		

Emission Source/Control Identifier(s) (continued)

New York State Department of Environmental Conservation
Air Permit Application

		DEC ID			
-				-	

Section IV - Emission Unit Information (continued)

Emission Unit	Emission Point	Process	Emission Source	Emission Unit Applicable Federal Requirements ☐ Continuation Sheet(s)									
				Title	Type	Part	Sub Part	Section	Sub Division	Parag.	Sub Parag.	Clause	Sub Clause
-													
-													
-													
-													
-													
-													

Emission Unit	Emission Point	Process	Emission Source	Emission Unit State Only Requirements ☐ Continuation Sheet(s)									
				Title	Type	Part	Sub Part	Section	Sub Division	Parag.	Sub Parag.	Clause	Sub Clause
-													
-													
-													
-													
-													
-													

Emission Unit Compliance Certification ☐ Continuation Sheet(s)
Rule Citation

Title	Type	Part	Sub Part	Section	Sub Division	Parag.	Sub Parag.	Clause	Sub Clause

☐ Applicable Federal Requirement   ☐ State Only Requirement   ☐ Capping

Emission Unit	Emission Point	Process	Emission Source	CAS. No.	Contaminant Name
-				- -	

Monitoring Information

☐ Continuous Emission Monitoring   ☐ Monitoring of Process or Control Device Parameters as Surrogate
☐ Intermittent Emission Testing   ☐ Work Practice Involving Specific Operations
☐ Ambient Air Monitoring   ☐ Record Keeping/Maintenance Procedures

Description

Work Practice		Process Material	Reference Test Method
Type	Code	Description	

Parameter		Manufacturer Name/Model No.
Code	Description	

Limit			Limit Units	
Upper	Lower	Code	Description	

Averaging Method		Monitoring Frequency		Reporting Requirements	
Code	Description	Code	Description	Code	Description

PAGE 6

10/31/96

New York State Department of Environmental Conservation
Air Permit Application

DEC ID
-         -

Section IV - Emission Unit Information (continued)

Determination of Non-Applicability (Title V Only) ☐ Continuation Sheet(s)

Rule Citation

Title	Type	Part	Sub Part	Section	Sub Division	Parag.	Sub Parag.	Clause	Sub Clause

Emission Unit	Emission Point	Process	Emission Source	
				☐ Applicable Federal Requirement ☐ State Only Requirement

Description

_____
_____
_____
_____

Rule Citation

Title	Type	Part	Sub Part	Section	Sub Division	Parag.	Sub Parag.	Clause	Sub Clause

Emission Unit	Emission Point	Process	Emission Source	
				☐ Applicable Federal Requirement ☐ State Only Requirement

Description

_____
_____
_____
_____

Process Emissions Summary ☐ Continuation Sheet(s)

EMISSION UNIT	-									PROCESS	

CAS No.	Contaminant Name	% of Thruput	% Capture	% Control	ERP (lb/hr)	ERP How Determined
- -						

PTE			Standard Units	PTE How Determined	Actual	
(lb/hr)	(lb/yr)	(standard units)			(lb/hr)	(lb/yr)

EMISSION UNIT	-									PROCESS	

CAS No.	Contaminant Name	% of Thruput	% Capture	% Control	ERP (lb/hr)	ERP How Determined
- -						

PTE			Standard Units	PTE How Determined	Actual	
(lb/hr)	(lb/yr)	(standard units)			(lb/hr)	(lb/yr)

EMISSION UNIT	-									PROCESS	

CAS No.	Contaminant Name	% of Thruput	% Capture	% Control	ERP (lb/hr)	ERP How Determined
- -						

PTE			Standard Units	PTE How Determined	Actual	
(lb/hr)	(lb/yr)	(standard units)			(lb/hr)	(lb/yr)

New York State Department of Environmental Conservation
Air Permit Application

DEC ID
-					-				

Section IV - Emission Unit Information (continued)

EMISSION UNIT			
-				

Emission Unit Emissions Summary

☐ Continuation Sheet(s)

CAS. No.	Contaminant Name			
- -				

ERP (lb/yr)	PTE Emissions		Actual	
	(lb/hr)	(lb/yr)	(lb/hr)	(lb/yr)

CAS. No.	Contaminant Name			
- -				

ERP (lb/yr)	PTE Emissions		Actual	
	(lb/hr)	(lb/yr)	(lb/hr)	(lb/yr)

CAS. No.	Contaminant Name			
- -				

ERP (lb/yr)	PTE Emissions		Actual	
	(lb/hr)	(lb/yr)	(lb/hr)	(lb/yr)

CAS. No.	Contaminant Name			
- -				

ERP (lb/yr)	PTE Emissions		Actual	
	(lb/hr)	(lb/yr)	(lb/hr)	(lb/yr)

Compliance Plan

☐ Continuation Sheet(s)

For any emission units which will <u>not be in compliance</u> at the time of permit issuance, complete the following:

☐ This facility meets all applicable requirements <u>except</u> for those units listed below. This facility will achieve compliance for those units according to the following schedule:

Consent Order	Certified progress reports are to be submitted every 6 months beginning __/__/__

			Applicable Federal Requirement								
Emission Unit	Process	Emission Source	Title	Type	Part	Sub Part	Section	Sub Division	Parag.	Sub Parag.	Clause	Sub Clause
-												

Remedial Measure/Intermediate Milestones	R/I	Date Scheduled

10/31/96

New York State Department of Environmental Conservation
Air Permit Application

	DEC ID	
-		-

Section IV - Emission Unit Information (continued)

Request for Emission Reduction Credits   ☐ Continuation Sheet(s)

EMISSION UNIT [ ] - [ ][ ][ ][ ]

Emission Reduction Description

_____

_____

_____

Contaminant Emission Reduction Data

Baseline Period ___ / ___ / ___ to ___ / ___ / ___

		Reduction	
		Date	Method
		__ / __ / __	
CAS No.	Contaminant Name	ERC (lbs/yr)	
		Netting	Offset
- -			
- -			
- -			

Facility to Use Future Reduction

Name _____

APPLICATION ID

[ ] - [ ][ ][ ][ ][ ] - [ ][ ][ ][ ][ ][ ] / [ ][ ][ ][ ]

Location Address

☐ City / ☐ Town / ☐ Village   State   Zip

Use of Emission Reduction Credits   ☐ Continuation Sheet(s)

EMISSION UNIT [ ] - [ ][ ][ ][ ]

Proposed Project Description

_____

_____

_____

Contaminant Emissions Increase Data

CAS No.	Contaminant Name	PEP (lbs/yr)
- -		

Statement of Compliance

☐ All major facilities under the ownership of this "ownership/firm" are operating in compliance with all applicable requirements and state regulations including any compliance certification requirements under section 114 (a) (3) of the clean air act amendments of 1990, or are meeting the schedule of a consent order.

Source of Emission Reduction Credit-Facility

Name _____

PERMIT ID

[ ] - [ ][ ][ ][ ][ ] - [ ][ ][ ][ ] / [ ][ ][ ][ ]

Location Address

☐ City / ☐ Town / ☐ Village   State   Zip

Emission Unit	CAS No.	Contaminant Name	ERC (lbs/yr)	
			Netting	Offset
-	- -			
-	- -			
-	- -			

New York State Department of Environmental Conservation
Air Permit Application

DEC ID

```
| - |   |   |   |   |   | - |   |   |   |   |   |
```

Supporting Documentation

❑ P.E. Certification (form attached)

❑ List of Exempt Activities (form attached)

❑ Plot Plan

❑ Calculations

❑ Air Quality Model (__ / __ / __)

❑ Confidentiality Justification

❑ Ambient Air Monitoring Plan (__ / __ / __)

❑ Stack Test Protocols/Reports (__ / __ / __)

❑ Continuous Emissions Monitoring Plans/QA/QC (__ / __ / __)

❑ MACT Demonstration (__ / __ / __)

❑ Operational Flexibility: Description of Alternative Operating Scenarios and Protocols

❑ Title IV: Application/Registration

❑ ERC Quantification (form attached)

❑ Use of ERC(s) (form attached)

❑ Baseline Period Demonstration

❑ Analysis of Contemporaneous Emission Increase/Decrease

❑ LAER Demonstration (__ / __ / __)

❑ BACT Demonstration (__ / __ / __)

❑ Other Document(s): _____
_____ (__ / __ / __)
_____ (__ / __ / __)
_____ (__ / __ / __)
_____ (__ / __ / __)
_____ (__ / __ / __)
_____ (__ / __ / __)
_____ (__ / __ / __)
_____ (__ / __ / __)
_____ (__ / __ / __)
_____ (__ / __ / __)
_____ (__ / __ / __)
_____ (__ / __ / __)
_____ (__ / __ / __)
_____ (__ / __ / __)
_____ (__ / __ / __)

New York State Department of Environmental Conservation
Air Permit Application

DEC ID
☐ - ☐ ☐ ☐ ☐ ☐ - ☐ ☐ ☐ ☐ ☐

P.E. Certification

I certify under penalty of law that I have personally examined, and am familiar with, the statements and information submitted in this document and all its attachments as they pertain to the <u>practice of engineering</u>. This is defined as the performance of a professional service such as consultation, investigation, evaluation, planning, design or supervision of construction or operation in connection with any utilities, structures, buildings, machines, equipment, processes, works, or projects wherein the safeguarding of life, health and property is concerned, when such service or work requires the application of engineering principles and data. Based on my inquiry of those individuals with primary responsibility for obtaining such information, I certify that the statements and information are to the best of my knowledge and belief true, accurate and complete. I am aware that there are significant penalties for submitting false statements and information or omitting required statements and information, including the possibility of fine or imprisonment.

Name of P.E.

Signature of P.E.

Date _____ / _____ / _____

NYS License No.

Phone ( )

10/31/96

New York State Department of Environmental Conservation
Air Permit Application

DEC ID
-					-				

List of Exempt Activities (from 6 NYCRR Part 201)

<table>
<tr><td colspan="2">

Instructions for Completing Table

Applicants for Title V permits are required to provide a list of exempt activities in the application form. This includes all process or production units and other emission generating activities which are considered <u>exempt</u> as defined by 6 NYCRR Part 301-3.2. Completion of this table fulfills that requirement.

To complete the table, provide the following information for each exempt activity that occurs at the facility defined by this application:

    a. The <u>approximate</u> number of each listed activity, and,

    b. For location of the activity enter the building ID(s) used in the main application form. Use the building name if a building ID(s) has not been assigned.

If a listed activity does not occur at the facility, leave <u>blank</u>.

</td></tr>
</table>

Combustion

Rule Citation 201-3.2(c)	Description	No. of Activities (approx.)	Building Location
(1)	stationary or portable combustion installations where the furnace has a maximum rated heat input capacity <10mmBtu/hr burning fossil fuels, other than coal, and coal and wood fired stationary combustion units with a maximum heat input <1mmBtu/hr. - this includes unit space heaters, which burn waste oil as defined in 6 NYCRR Part 225-2 and generated on-site, alone or in conjunction with used oil generated by a do-it-yourself oil changer as defined in 6 NYCRR Subpart 374-2		
(2)	stationary or portable combustion installations located outside of any severe ozone non-attainment areas, where the furnace has a maximum rated heat input capacity <20 mmBtu/hr burning fossil fuels other than coal, where the construction of the combustion installation commenced before 6/8/89		
(3)(i)	diesel or natural gas powered stationary or portable internal combustion (IC) engines within any severe ozone non-attainment area having a maximum mechanical power rating <225bhp		
(3)(ii)	diesel or natural gas powered stationary or portable IC engines located outside of any severe ozone non-attainment areas having a maximum mechanical power rating <400bhp		
(3)(iii)	gasoline powered IC engines having a maximum mechanical power rating <50bhp		
(4)	stationary or portable IC engines which are temporarily located at a facility for a period ≤30 days/calendar year, where the total combined maximum mechanical power rating for all affected units is <1000bhp		
(5)	gas turbines with a heat input at peak load <10mmBtu/hr		
(6)	emergency power generating units installed for use when the usual sources of heat, power, water and lighting are temporarily unobtainable, or which are installed to provide power <500 hrs/yr and excluding those units under contract w/ a utility to provide peak shaving generation to the grid		

Combustion - Related

Rule Citation 201-3.2(c)	Description	No. of Activities (approx.)	Building Location
(7)	non-contact water cooling towers and water treatment systems for process cooling water and other water containers designed to cool, store or otherwise handle water that has not been in direct contact with gaseous or liquid process streams		

10/31/96

New York State Department of Environmental Conservation
Air Permit Application

DEC ID

\[_ \[_ \[_ \[_ \[_ \[- \[_ \[_ \[_ \[_ \[_ \[_

List of Exempt Activities (from 6 NYCRR Part 201)

Agricultural			
Rule Citation 201-3.2(c)	Description	No. of Activities (approx.)	Building Location
(8)	feed and grain milling, cleaning, conveying, drying and storage operations including grain storage silos, where such silos exhaust to an appropriate emission control device, excluding grain terminal elevators with permanent storage capacities over 2.5 million US bushels, and grain storage elevators with capacities above 1 million bushels		
(9)	equipment used exclusively to slaughter animals, but not including other equipment at slaughterhouses, such as rendering cookers, boilers, heating plants, incinerators and electrical power generating equipment		
Commercial - Food Service Industries			
(10)	flour silos at bakeries, provided all such silos are exhausted through an appropriate emission control device		
(11)	emissions from flavorings added to a food product where such flavors are manually added to the product		
Commercial - Graphic Arts			
(12)	screen printing inks/coatings or adhesives which are applied by a hand-held squeegee (i.e. one that is not propelled thru the use of mechanical conveyance and is not an integral part of the screen printing process)		
(13)	graphic arts processes at facilities located outside the NYC metropolitan area whose facility-wide total emissions or VOC's from inks, coatings, adhesives, fountain solutions and cleaning solutions does not exceed 20 lbs/day		
(14)	graphic label and/or box labeling operations where the inks are applied by stamping or rolling		
(15)	graphic arts processes which are specifically exempted from regulation under Part 234 with regard to emissions of VOC's which are not given an A rating		
Commercial - Other			
(16)	gasoline dispensing sites with an annual thruput <120,000 gal located outside any severe non-attainment areas		

(17)	surface coating related operations which use less than 25 gal/mo of coating materials (paints) and cleaning solvents, combined, subject to the following:
	  - the facility is located outside of severe ozone non- attainment area
	  - all abrasive cleaning and surface coating operations are performed in an enclosed building where such operations are exhausted into appropriate emission control devices		

(18)	abrasive cleaning operations which exhaust to an appropriate emission control device		
(19)	ultraviolet curing operations		
Municipal/Public Health Related			
(20)	ventilating systems for landfill gases, where the systems are vented directly to the atmosphere, and the ventilating system has been required by, and is operating under, the conditions of a valid Part 360 permit, or Order on Consent		

10/31/96

New York State Department of Environmental Conservation
Air Permit Application

DEC ID
☐ - ☐☐☐☐☐ - ☐☐☐☐☐

List of Exempt Activities (from 6 NYCRR Part 201)

Storage Vessels			
Rule Citation 201-3.2(c)	**Description**	**No. of Activities (approx.)**	**Building Location**
(21)	distillate and residual fuel oil storage tanks with storage capacities <300,000 bbls		
(22)	pressurized fixed roof tanks which are capable of maintaining a working pressure at all times to prevent emissions of VOC's to the outdoor atmosphere		
(23)	external floating roof tanks which are of welded construction and are equipped with a metallic-type shoe primary seal and a secondary seal from the top of the shoe seal to the tank wall		
(24)(i)	external floating roof tanks which are used for the storage of a petroleum or volatile organic liquid with a true vapor pressure < 4.0 psi(27.6 kPa), are of welded construction and are equipped with *a metallic-type shoe seal*		
(24)(ii)	external floating roof tanks which are used for the storage of a petroleum or volatile organic liquid with a true vapor pressure < 4.0 psi(27.6 kPa), are of welded construction and are equipped with *a liquid-mounted foam seal*		
(24)(iii)	external floating roof tanks which are used for the storage of a petroleum or volatile organic liquid with a true vapor pressure < 4.0 psi(27.6 kPa), are of welded construction and are equipped with *a liquid-mounted liquid-filled type seal*		
(24)(iv)	external floating roof tanks which are used for the storage of a petroleum or volatile organic liquid with a true vapor pressure <4.0 psi(27.6 kPa), are of welded construction and are equipped with *a control equipment or device equivalent to those previously listed in items (24)(i) thru (iii)*		
(25)	storage tanks, with capacities <10,000 gal, except those subject to either Part 229 or Part 233		
(26)	horizontal petroleum storage tanks		
(27)	storage silos storing solid materials, provided all such silos are exhausted thru an appropriate emission control device		
Industrial			
(28)	processing equipment at existing sand and gravel and stone crushing plants which were installed or constructed before 8/31/83 , where water is used other than for dust suppression, such as wet conveying, separating and washing .		
(29)(i)	all processing equipment at sand and gravel mines or quarries that *permanent or fixed installations with a maximum rated processing capacity ≤25 tph of minerals*		
(29)(ii)	all processing equipment at sand and gravel mines or quarries that *are mobile (portable) installations with a maximum rated processing capacity ≤150 tph of minerals*		
(30)	mobile (portable) stone crushers with maximum rated capacities ≤150 tph of minerals which are located at nonmetallic mineral processing operations		
(31)	surface coating operations which are specifically exempted from regulation under Part 228, with regard to emissions of VOC's which are not given an A rating		
(32)	pharmaceutical tablet branding operations		
(33)	thermal packaging operations, including but not limited to, therimage labelling, blister packing, shrink wrapping, shrink banding, and carton gluing		

10/31/96

New York State Department of Environmental Conservation
Air Permit Application

DEC ID
·				·				

List of Exempt Activities (from 6 NYCRR Part 201)

Rule Citation 201-3.2(c)	Description	No. of Activities (approx.)	Building Location
	Industrial (continued)		
(34)	powder coating operations		
(35)	all tumblers used for the cleaning and/or deburring of metal products without abrasive blasting		
(36)	presses used exclusively for molding or extruding plastics except where halogenated carbon compounds or hydrocarbon solvents are used as foaming agents		
(37)	concrete batch plants where the cement weigh hopper and all bulk storage silos are exhausted thru fabric filters, and the batch drop point is controlled by a shroud or other emission control device		
(38)	cement storage operations where materials are transported by screw or bucket conveyors		
(39)(i)	non-vapor phase cleaning equipment with an open surface area $\leq$11 sq ft and an internal volume $\leq$93 gal or, having an organic solvent loss $\leq$3 gal/day		
(39)(ii)	non-vapor phase cleaning equipment using only organic solvents with an initial boiling point $\geq$300°F at atmospheric pressure		
(39)(iii)	non-vapor phase cleaning equipment using materials with a VOC content $\leq$2% by volume		
	Miscellaneous		
(40)	ventilating and exhaust systems for laboratory operations		
(41)	exhaust or ventilating systems for the melting of gold, silver, platinum, and other precious metals		
(42)	exhaust systems for paint mixing, transfer, filling, or sampling and/or paint storage rooms or cabinets, provided the paints stored within these locations are stored in closed containers when not in use		
(43)	exhaust systems for solvent transfer, filling or sampling, and/or solvent storage rooms provided the solvent stored within these locations are stored in closed containers when not in use		
(44)	research and development activities, including both stand-alone and activities within a major stationary source, until such time as the Administrator completes a rulemaking to determine how the permitting program should be structured for these activities		
(45)	the application of odor counteractants and/or neutralizers		

10/31/96

APPENDIX XXII

Add-On Control Systems: Sample Request for Proposal, Checklist to Compare Proposals, Computation of Cost of Control, Simplified Approach to VOC Control

SOURCE:
P-F Technical Services, Inc.

Purchasing an add-on control system requires careful planning to delineate the requirements that must be met by the system, a means of evaluating the proposals, and a method of computing the cost of operating each system. This appendix includes sample documents that will enable the printer to approach add-on controls with assurance that the system purchased will perform effectively.

1. *Sample request for a proposal:* This sample document outlines the mechanical and physical requirements of the system and the guarantees that are needed to assure performance, destruction efficiency and service. Preparation of the specifications will require the analysis of air emissions in terms of composition and rates of emissions per hour (normal and maximum), the air flows of the presses, and any desired recirculation loops to reduce air flow, as well as the temperatures of the exhausted air (pp 610–613).

2. *Checklist to compare proposals:* Not all proposals are identical. Some are very detailed,

others sketchy. To assure that you are comparing "apples to apples," the checklist itemizes key components and performance requirements to which all proposals must respond. Omissions can be mitigated by contacting the vendor. The key is to make sure that price is not the sole consideration. You want to make sure that if there is a price differential, you can pinpoint the reason and determine if the cost savings are worth the risk of potential costs later (pp 614–618).

3. *Cost to operate worksheet:* The price of the system is one factor. Another is the cost of running the unit and its impact on the financial structure of the company. This spreadsheet allows you to take data provided by the vendor of the equipment and determine what it will cost your facility to operate annually, based on a 10 year life expectancy for the system. It is critical to assign operating costs that reflect the cost of doing business at your site (p 619).

4. *Simplified approach to a VOC control:* Provides a means of undertaking this task (pp 620–622).

609

MR. CAT ALYST
ADD-ON ENVIRONMENTAL SYSTEMS, INC.
9085 North 127ᵗʰ Street
OPEN FIELDS, WI 53228

Attention: Sales

Re. Request for Proposal - Catalytic or Thermal Oxidizer
    Flexographic Printing Facility

Dear Bob:

    We are requesting a proposal for a Catalytic or Thermal Oxidizer System to service the three Flexographic Presses of Flexible Packaging Inc. at the facility at 2540 West Austrian Street. The three presses are on the First floor; the incineration system will be on the ground next to the building and adjacent to the press area.
    Consideration of the systems proposals will be to determine whether capital cost and operating expenses are more feasible with either a catalytic or thermal system. If you manufacture both types, two proposals would be appreciated, as well as your recommendation as to which method you advocate for flexographic printing facilities.

    The proposal is requested as a Turnkey Installation.

    The vendor selected will have full responsibility for the manufacture and the installation of the system and all its components, and the sub-contractors who will perform such jobs as deemed necessary by our client and the vendor.
    Proposals should include financial terms relative to the purchase and payment of the system.
    The system should be installed and in operation nine months after the purchase order has been placed. All meetings, engineering evaluations and preliminary planning must be expedited to accomplish this timetable.
    The estimated exhaust air flow of the three presses are as follows:

Victory Kidder Model 660	8,000 CFM
Kidder Model 434	6,000 CFM
Kidder Filmprinter to be replaced by Model 660	8,000 CFM
Total Air Flow	22,000 CFM
Recirculated to approximately 60%	estimate 9,000 CFM

    Based on the recirculation of the presses, we would anticipate that the size of the Catalytic Oxidizer will be based on an air flow of 9,000 to 10,000 CFM.
    As noted in the opening paragraph, the unit will be installed on the ground next to the plant, behind the building and adjacent to the press area. A pad may be required and should be included in the proposal.
    In your initial visits to the facility, it would be desirable to have hand-held air flow measurements taken to determine the actual exhaust air flows from the presses.
    Based on 1997 purchases of solvents and inks, Flexible Packaging can anticipate annual solvent emissions of 80,000 pounds or 40 tons per year. This would equate to emissions of 20 pounds per operating hour for a two shift operation. Maximum normal loading would be estimated at 40 pounds per running hour.
    To protect the company from premature failure of the system, or any of its components, we request an extended warranty of four years for the catalyst and the manufactured components of the system.
    I have attached a more detailed listing of specifications required for the system. Please advise me if you have any questions or comments.
    If it would facilitate the submission of your proposal, you will want to visit the site. Please contact Mr. John Doe at the Flexible Packaging facility to make an appointment (505-689-5018).
    We would like to have the proposals submitted by the middle of of August, so that a decision can be made without delay.
    Thank you for your prompt consideration and response.

                    Sincerely,

SPECIFICATIONS FOR FLEXIBLE PACKAGING CATALYTIC OR THERMAL OXIDIZER

NUMBER: ONE (1)

TYPE: PRECIOUS METAL

APPLICATION: Three Flexographic Printing Presses

    1. Kidder Stacy   Model 660 45" CI, 6 colors
    Two exhausts: BCD...4,000 CFM, Oven..4,000 CFM

    2.* Kidder Stacy   Model 660 45" CI, 6 colors
    Two exhaust: BCD   4,000 CFM, Oven 4,000 CFM

    3. Kidder Stacy   Model 434 45" CI, 4 colors
    Two exhaust: BCD   2,500 CFM, Oven 3,500 CFM

*Current press is Film Kidder - total CFM 2,700 CF.
Will be replaced in future with press equal to Model 660.

SYSTEM SIZE: 10,000 TO 12,000 CFM, to be confirmed by air tests

VOC LOADING:

Average for three presses	20 pounds per operating hour
High for three presses	40 pounds per run hour
Maximum for three presses	80 pounds per hour (theoretical)

System must be designed to operate at average solvent loadings for optimum cost of operation.

High and theoretical maximum are provided to enable proper design and fabrication of the system to assure safety during operation.

Loading is based on amount of inks and solvents purchased during the year 1997.

Average is based on operational hours - 4,000 hrs for two shifts for year (four twenty hour days/week.)

High is based on assumption presses are down 50% for changes and downtime; is representative of load while both presses are running.

Maximum is a theoretical based on doubling the coverage during running time.

SOLVENTS ANTICIPATED IN VOC EMISSIONS:

Normalpropanol	63.8%
Ethanol	30.1%
N-Propyl Acetate	1.9%
Heptane	1.9%
Isopropanol	0.9%
Other Miscellaneous	1,4%
TOTAL	100.0%

DESTRUCTION EFFICIENCY

Must remain at 95% or better for period of seven years.

LOAD REQUIREMENTS:

Turndown capability ratio and necessary air flow sensors and circuitry to permit system to compensate for press that is not running, as well as during period of changes and downtime. Effective operation of the system is required to minimize the use of natural gas and the cost of operation.

VARIABLE SPEED FAN

INLET TEMPERATURE: 90 to 120 degrees F

T-DAMPERS: as required for the three presses.

ADDED DAMPERS: for incinerator by-pass when using water based inks. These dampers must be controlled by keyed switches, and should not be readily accessible to personnel without the permission of management.

DRYER RECIRCULATION:

Required for both presses to reduce air flow up to 60%.

CATALYST REQUIREMENTS:

Performance will be guaranteed for a minimum of three years.

Can be either Monolith or Pelletized Noble metal composition.

Catalyst should be tested once every six months for contamination during the first year, and annually thereafter.

Vendor is requested to provide safeguards to prevent masking of catalyst by any potential chemicals, i.e., Silicone, Oxi-Dry powder, etc.

THERMAL OXIDIZER:

Vender will fully describe system and method of destruction with all necessary details relating to the effectiveness of the system.

INSTRUMENTATION:

Press interlocks for purging and press operation with incinerator on.

Inlet, outlet and bed temperatures.

Air flow detectors for NFPA requirements

Two point recorder for temperature rise over catalyst bed, and other recordings as required by the State of _____. A strip recorder is preferred. (Note - some states ask for the temperature going out the stack; a few venders provide this as a normal monitoring feature.)

CAPTURE EFFICIENCY:

Vender will be required to evaluate and recommend modification of the equipment and press room to facilitate capture of the fugitive vapors; assist in design of encapsulating covers, hoods, collection sweeps, exhaust ductwork, etc.

Evaluate and make recommendations with reference to total enclosure requirements.

EXTERIOR COATING:

Standard to prevent oxidation and destruction by exposure to the rain, sun and elements.

UTILITIES:

Advise requirements to be provided by Poly Plastic.

LOCATION OF SYSTEM:

On concrete pad outside plant.

INSTALLATION:

To be shipped as completely assembled as possible on skids. Vendor is requested to advise facility of plans and schedule for Installation, to facilitate all preparations prior to shipment and erection of the equipment.

CONTRACT TYPE:

Complete turnkey installation.

ACCEPTANCE BASIS:

Acceptance according to the testing procedures of the State of _____.

Vendor will conduct FID test upon completion of installation and will have representative present prior to and during stack test at site.

Flexible Packaging will contract for stack test with an authorized laboratory for testing in accordance with USEPA and State of _____ Department of the Environment standards.

APPLICABLE RULES AND REGULATIONS:

The system, installation and operating performance must all comply with the regulations set forth by the State of _____ and the local community.

CHECKLIST TO COMPARE PROPOSALS FOR CATALYTIC OXIDATION SYSTEMS

Supplier Qualifications	SAMPLE		
Years in business	~185 years		
Company size	600 employees		
Annual sales volume	>100 million		
Primary industries served	Web/Food Industries		
Total # of installations	>10,000		
Total # of countries served	90 countries		
Oxidizer supplier since	1975		
Number of oxidizers operating	>100+		
System Proposed			
Model	C-10000		
Maximum air flow	10,000 SCFM		
Volumetric turndown	5 to 1		
Minimum air flow	2000		
Maximum solvent loading	200#/hr @ 13,969 btu/lb.		
Min. operating temperature	600 Deg. F		
Max. operating temperature	1100 Deg. F		
Destruction efficiency guaranteed	98%+		
Destruction efficiency test method	EPA Method 25A		
Heat Exchanger			
% Effectiveness	70%		
Heat exchanger design	Plate Type		
Exchanger material	304 Stainless Steel		
Expansion joint design	S.S. Rolled Bellows		
Heat exchanger bypass	Not Required		
Automatic	N/A		
Actuator Control	N/A		
Catalyst Design	Monolith / Pelleted		
Manufacturer	JMI/Prototech		
Type	Precious Metals		
Catalyst substrate	S.S. Monolith/Pelleted		
Quantity	12 cu. ft./50 cu. Ft.		
History in flexo	>12 yrs. +		
Expected life	>12 yrs. +		

CHECKLIST TO COMPARE PROPOSALS FOR CATALYTIC OXIDATION SYSTEMS (continued)

Materials/Construction			
Internal components	14 ga. #304 S.S.		
External cladding	14 ga. Carbon Steel		
Insulation type	Ceramic/Fiberglass		
Insulation thickness	6"		
Unitized construction	Yes		
Prepiped	Yes		
Prewired	Yes		
Number of major pieces	One		
Burner Assembly			
Type	Nozzle Mix		
Manufacturer	Maxon		
Turndown ratio	20 to 1		
Insurance approval	IRI or FM		
Max. btu/Hr. output	2,600,000 Btu/Hr		
System Supply Fan			
Manufacturer	New York Blower		
Spark proof construction	Yes (Type "C")		
Drive arrangement	Arrangement 9		
Clean-out doors	Yes		
System Fan Motor			
Manufacturer	Baldor or Equal		
Horsepower	60 Monolith/75 Pelleted		
Design	TEFC		
Local disconnect	Included		
Volumetric Control			
A.C. drive	Yes		
Drive manufacturer	ABB		
Control cabinet	NEMA 1 (Indoors)		
Combustion Blower			
Manufacturer	New York Blower		
Horsepower	3 H.P.		
Spark proof construction	Yes (Type "C")		

CHECKLIST TO COMPARE PROPOSALS FOR CATALYTIC OXIDATION SYSTEMS (continued)

Drive arrangement	Arrangement 1		
Local disconnect	Included		
Purge/Start-up/Idle Damper			
Included	Yes		
Actuator manufacturer	Keystone		
Actuator type	Electric		
Visual indication/Manual Operation	Included		
Process Tee-dampers			
Quantity included	3		
Damper design	3 Blade Butterfly		
Damper material	12 Gauge C.S.		
Actuator manufacturer	Keystone		
Actuator type	Electric		
Position confirmation	Yes		
Process interlocks	Yes		
Bypass control	Interlock w/Key Switch		
Visual indication/Manual Operation	Included		
Manual Dampers Included			
Exhaust balancing dampers	3		
Maximum volume control	Included		
Combustion air balancing	One (1)		
Purge/idle balancing damper	One (1)		
Control Cabinets			
Rating	NEMA 12		
Main Panel	Indoors		
Remote status panel	One (1)		
Electronics/Controls			
Type of PLC	Allen-Bradley SLC-5/03		
Type of message display	AB PanelView 550		
First-out indication	Included		
Flame safeguard	Flame Rod		
Temperature controllers	Allen Bradley		
Control transformer	120 Volt Included		
Temperature recorder	3 Pen 30 Day Strip		

CHECKLIST TO COMPARE PROPOSALS FOR CATALYTIC OXIDATION SYSTEMS (continued)

Motor starters	(3) Included		
Local disconnects	(3) Included		
Communication Modem	Included		
Dimensions	Monolith/Pelleted		
Width	5.25' / 9'		
Height	9.1' / 10'		
Length	27.25' / 34.25'		
Weight (lbs.) total	23,000lbs./32,000lbs.		
Utilities Required			
Supply voltage required	240 Volt / 3 Phase / 60HZ		
Total KVA required	75/90		
Max. natural gas required	2,600 cu. ft./hr		
Gas pressure required	2.0 to 5.0 PSIG		
Compressed air	Not Required		
460 V Step up transformer	Included		
Warranty			
Life expectancy	>15 to 20 years +		
Total system warranty	2 yrs.		
Catalyst warranty	4 yrs.		
Heat exchanger warranty	4 yrs.		
Drive warranty	4 yrs.		
Temperature recorder	3 yrs.		
Labor included	Yes		
Parts included	Yes		
All expenses included	Yes		
Nearest authorized service facility	city		
Number of service people	>15+		
24 hour service / 800 # available	Yes		
Price as Quoted	$357,000 / $380,600		
Add cost for items not included	Add $	Add $	Add $
Temperature recorder	Included		
Shipping	Included		
Collection system design	Included		
PLC/PanelView Controls	Included		
Spare parts	Included		
Start-up/training	Included		

CHECKLIST TO COMPARE PROPOSALS FOR CATALYTIC OXIDATION SYSTEMS

4 year catalyst warranty	Included		
4 year catalyst test core program	Included		
Motor starters & disconnects	Included		
Turnkey installation	Included		
Power feeder	Included		
Gas piping	Included		
Test Platform/ladder	Included		
75/112 KVA Transformer	Included		
Total Cost Monolith:	$357,000		
Total Cost Pelleted:	$380,600		
This concept of the worksheet was developed by P-F Technical Services and then enhanced and enlarged by Charles Martinson, President, The CMM Group, LLC., DePere, Wisconsin.			

COMPUTATION OF COST TO OPERATE OXIDIZER

	TOTAL COSTS		ANNUAL COSTS
POLY BAG MANUFACTURING INC.			
150 WEST 36TH STREET, BROOKLYN, NY 11210			
ECONOMIC ANALYSIS - AIR EMISSIONS CONTROL EQUIPMENT			
ANNUAL OPERATING COSTS	TOTAL COSTS		ANNUAL COSTS
			(over 10 year period)
1. Cost of unit (3,000 CFM Catalytic Oxidizer)	$137,655.00		
Installation and Testing (estimated)	$37,000.00		
Total Cost of System	$174,655.00		
2. Less Down Payment	$17,465.50		
3. Financed Amount	$157,189.50		$15,719
4. Interest	$135,685.54	0.14	$13,569
5. Operating Costs			
a. Electricity			$7,500
b. Natural Gas			$14,060
c. Catalyst	$16,000.00		$2,286
d. Maintenance			$5,000
e. Indirect costs			$2,000
Total Operating Costs			$30,846
TOTAL ANNUAL COST OF CONTROL			$60,133
VOC REDUCTIONS			
A. Tons emitted per projection for permit			20.00
B. Percent required destruction (RACT)			60%
C. Tons Reduced			12.00
TOTAL COST PER TON OF TON REDUCED			$5,011.10
Notes: 1. Equipment amortized over 10 year period.			
2. Interest accrued over 10 year period			
3. Electrical based on vender data - $3.75 per hour		(use rates applicable to your lo	
4. Natural gas based on vender data - $7.03 per hour		(use rates applicable to your lo	
5. Catalyst replacement based on attrition in 7 years.			
6. Maintenance - estimated labor and parts, PM by vender.			

Simplified Approach to a VOC Control

by Eric Pearson, P.E. and Chris Rein, P.E.,
    Environmental Science Services
    Providence, Rhode Island

1.0 INTRODUCTION

This article presents a stepwise approach to a complex situation facing many printers. The printing industry is a significant contributor to emissions of volatile organic compounds (VOC) to the atmosphere. There are several regulatory initiatives currently in progress that present the opportunity for a printer to choose to control VOC emissions from its facility. These initiatives are motivated at both the federal and state level.

There are several steps in a successful control program. The first is to assess the regulatory issues facing your operations. What VOCs are being emitted? How much of each compound is being emitted? What is the facility's potential-to-emit (PTE)? Which regulatory programs are applicable to your operations? What level of reductions is required or desired? Can you generate offsets or bank emissions for internal use or sale to others?

Once you understand the regulatory requirements you can begin to choose from several control strategies. VOC fume oxidizers are often the most appropriate choice for the printing industry given the nature of the VOC used. Because of this, this article will focus on the process of selecting a fume oxidizer, but the general approach is used to select adsorption, condensation, or scrubbing equipment as well. Because of the many different vendors available, selection of the right vendor can be more difficult than choosing the right technology, but help is available from other experienced printing shops and air quality consultants.

The design of the capture system is as important as the design of the control device, so it is important that you get a total package. The most efficient oxidizer available cannot control VOC that does not get to the control device. While many oxidizer vendors will design and provide capture systems, some do not. You may need to assemble a team for the project that includes a mechanical engineer to design the capture and ventilation system.

Do not forget, in most instances you will need a permit to construct the control device from the state. That effort should start with sufficient lead time to allow time for agency approval that is consistent with the delivery lead time for the oxidizer. Depending on the reason for installing the control device, you may be required to demonstrate the performance of the oxidizer through testing. The final step in the process is to obtain a permit to operate the source based on the successful demonstration of compliance.

2.0 DISCUSSION

2.1 Regulatory Aspects

Why are you considering a program to control VOC? Perhaps you are a "major source" and you are preparing to meet the proposed federal MACT standard for the printing and publishing industry. The USEPA is proposing 95% control of organic hazardous air pollutants (HAP) or limits based on the amount of HAP emitted per unit of applied inks or other materials as MACT. Oxidizers with a properly designed capture system typically have overall control efficiencies exceeding 95%.

An oxidizer and fugitive capture system might be designed to "overcontrol" certain sources. This approach may allow other sources to remain uncontrolled in a facility wide RACT program. This approach is generally effective where a facility has several presses of varying sizes physically located such that separate control devices or ducting all units to a common device are impractical. Furthermore, installing controls may allow you to expand your operations without exceeding the thresholds that would make you bear the administrative burden of New Source Review (NSR) or the Title V operating permit program.

Before you can determine whether a VOC control device should be part of your air quality management program, you need to know which compounds you are emitting and in what quantities. If you have not yet performed a detailed facility emission inventory, now is the time. You will need a baseline tally of facility emissions to assess whether MACT, RACT, Title V, NSR, or other regulatory requirements are applicable. Once you evaluate your emissions against the regulatory criteria, you can assess the statutory requirements for control, as well as voluntary implementation of controls to avoid certain regulatory burdens or add flexibility to your operations. Your plant environmental manager should keep the inventory up-to-date.

2.2 Add-on Emission Control Equipment

VOC fume emissions from a flexographic printing line, or from most any VOC-emitting industrial process, can be controlled with a variety of technologies. They include carbon adsorption, oxidation (incineration), a combination of carbon adsorption and oxidation, and adsorption and condensation. Note that the terms incineration or incinerator tend to be avoided these days—oxidation is a much cleaner sounding concept. For a variety of reasons, oxidation is often the only technically feasible control technology for this application. This technology has made great advances in the past 20 years, so that a source requiring control can choose between several types of oxidation technology, each of which is extremely reliable, can achieve high removal or destruction efficiencies, and when properly applied to a source can be operated for a reasonable cost.

Oxidizer Operating Principles

All fume oxidizers operate in the same basic way: The solvent laden air from the press (say at 200°F) is drawn by a fan through a heat exchanger, then into a combustion chamber where it is heated by a supplemental fuel (often natural gas) to a temperature at which 95 to 99% of the solvents burn (oxidize) to carbon dioxide and water. Exhaust gas then passes back through the heat exchanger where the hot combustion gases (ranging from 700°F to 1,500°F) heat the incoming air stream from the press, which is then vented to the atmosphere.

The three basic types of fume oxidizers are catalytic, thermal and regenerative. These terms describe how the VOC combustion takes place or how the heat exchanger works. In a catalytic oxidizer, the combustion chamber has two sections: a preheat section where the supplemental fuel heats the air stream to 400 to 700°F, followed by a catalyst section in which the now hot VOC combust aided by the catalyst material. The catalyst operates in the same way as a catalytic converter on your car. An advantage of the catalytic oxidizer is that the combustion process occurs at a relatively low temperature, thus requiring less supplemental fuel and this yielding lower operating costs. A disadvantage of a catalytic oxidizer is that the catalyst can be poisoned or rendered inactive by certain substances (such as chlorine, phosphorous, metals), and thus you must ensure that these types of substances are not in the exhaust air from your press.

In a thermal oxidizer, the press exhaust air is heated in the combustion chamber to 1,400 to 1,500°F, a temperature at which most solvents will readily oxidize without the aid of a catalyst. These high temperatures require higher supplemental fuel usage to achieve, compared to a catalytic oxidizer, though this usage can be compensated for in part by improving the degree of heat recovery obtained by the heat exchanger. A thermal oxidizer is preferred when there are contaminants in the exhaust gas stream that would damage a catalyst, or when the VOC concentration in the exhaust air stream is high enough so that the inherent heat content of the solvents will contribute significantly to achieving the 1,400-1,500°F temperature, thus counterbalancing the lower temperature/lower fuel usage advantages of a catalytic oxidizer.

A regenerative oxidizer is a thermal oxidizer (no catalyst) but with a special type of heat exchanger that operates with a very high degree of heat recovery. The heat exchanger consists of two or more stoneware beds which alternate between receiving the hot combustion chamber air or the cool exhaust air from the process. The process air first passes through a hot bed and is preheated to near the required 1,400-1,500°F combustion temperature, then enters the combustion chamber where only a small amount of fuel is needed to finally reach the combustion temperature, then passes through a cool stoneware bed which soaks up the heat and cools the gas stream. Regenerative oxidizers will typically have a higher capital cost than a catalytic or thermal oxidizer, but this is balanced by a lower operating cost because of the reduced fuel usage.

Selecting an Oxidizer

There are many oxidizer vendors offering a wide range of quality and design. Your situation is unique and therefore, you need to obtain the best available advice when selecting an oxidizer to ensure that what you buy is the most cost-effective and will meet your needs. The best way to start is to make contact with others in your industry who have oxidizers: who did they buy from and why; how well has it operated; what other vendors did they solicit bids from? An experienced consultant will also be a valuable source of information, especially since they will have experience with many printers and other industrial facilities who have installed oxidizers. You will want to solicit bids from at least three vendors who have a track record for providing high quality product and who will support you and their product throughout purchase, installation and operation.

Once the specific vendors have been identified, the process will include the following steps:

• Invite the vendors to visit your facility— Most vendors will want to do this in order to prepare a proper quote, and this gives you an opportunity for a first-hand assessment of them and to explain your needs.
• Have capture, ductwork and stacks been included in the bid.
• Receive the bids.
• Review the bids—Some of the important points to consider are price, guarantees of destruction efficiency and workmanship, operating costs, spare parts, lead times, and flexibility. This last item would address how to obtain a higher DE, how to improve heat recovery, and how to plan for future process expansion.
• Select the desired vendor for your project.

Most oxidizers today will easily achieve 95% DE and many can achieve 99%. In general the higher the DE, the higher the capital and operating cost. The trade off between higher DE and higher cost should be carefully considered, especially in light of current and possible future regulatory requirements—for example, major/minor source status, and air toxics emissions.

The heat exchanger makes up a large fraction of the initial capital cost. The higher degree of heat recovery achieved, the high the capital cost, but the lower the operating costs.

The lead time for purchasing an oxidizer, from issuing a purchase order to final installation, can typically range from three months to eight months, depending on the size and complexity of the oxidizer, and will vary from vendor to vendor. This should be carefully considered in light of your time constraints and permitting requirements.

2.3 Capture Efficiency

Capture efficiency (CE) is defined as the degree to which the VOC applied at the process is directed to the control device. VOC that escapes being collected by the control device is termed fugitive emissions. Within the past five years overall control efficiency (OCE) has become the important consideration for regulatory agencies,

rather than just DE, because of the following relationship:

$$OCE = DE \times CE$$

Thus if your oxidizer operates at 95% DE, but only 60% of your VOC applied is <u>directed to</u> the oxidizer (60% CE), your OCE is only $0.95 \times 0.60 = 0.57 = 57\%$.

There are several simple process improvements you can make to minimize fugitive losses and thus improve CE. These include exercising good housekeeping, placing lids on open containers, installing covers on coating pans, and maintaining a proper air balance in your drying oven. Even with these improvements, it is difficult to quantify exactly what your CE is. Therefore, the current regulatory approach to CE is the use of permanent total enclosures to achieve 100% CE by design. This means that if your press or presses are surrounded by a well-defined enclosure that meets certain EPA design criteria, and all air exhausted from the enclosure is directed to a control device, then your CE is defined to be 100%. With this approach CE need never be addressed again, and you have absolutely minimized your VOC emissions, at least with regard to fugitive (non-stack) emissions.

A total enclosure can be designed as an integral part of the press, or can be constructed about the press. This latter approach can be achieved by erecting one or more walls and making use of a portion of the room or building, or using the entire room or building as the enclosure. As noted above, the enclosure must meet certain design criteria, specified in EPA Method 204. These criteria include the distance of make-up air openings from sources of VOC emissions, the size of the openings, and the speed of the make-up air passing into the enclosure through the openings. An experienced consultant is often needed to help determine the feasibility of a total enclosure for your situation and to properly design the enclosure so that the design criteria are met and so that the enclosure is properly integrated into your process and production operations.

APPENDIX **XXIII**

Sample Stack Test Documents for Add-on Controls, Protocol for Test, Report of Concluded Test, Testing of Catalysts

SOURCE:
Environmental Science Services, Inc.

Operation of an add-on control must be confirmed upon installation and subsequently during the lifetime of the system. The mechanisms for measuring the performance of the system are a stack test and laboratory evaluation of the catalyst.

Stack tests are conducted in accordance with established USEPA test methods, the most common being Methods 25, 25A and 18. To assure that the stack test will be done in conformance with these and other methods, a protocol must be submitted for approval by the enforcement agency. The protocol will describe the facility, the test parameters and the methodology that will be employed (pp 624–633).

The test is conducted in a one day period, if all goes well, and the results are analyzed by the testing organization. The test will consist of three periods of one hour each, during which measurements are made of chemical and physical parameters. The field results are analyzed on-site and back in the engineering office. Any lab analyses required, for which samples are collected during the stack test, are conducted in accordance with appropriate USEPA test methods. A summary is then prepared with conclusions of both field and lab tests, supported by complete documentation of the testing process. The report is submitted for review by the enforcement agency and approval for issuance of the facility permit (pp 634–643).

Catalyst testing is a means of assuring destruction efficiency in the periods between stack tests. Permits can require testing on an annual or other schedule to certify the adequate destruction of the volatile pollutants. A procedure developed by Degussa Corporation describes the objectives of the tests and a sample report (pp 644–647).

Protocol for Test

TEST PROTOCOL
FOR A
VOC COMPLIANCE TEST
at
Four Printing Presses and
Associated Catalytic Oxidizer

Prepared For:

Name of Company
Street Address
City, State, Zip

Prepared By:

Environmental Science Services, Inc.
272 West Exchange Street, Suite 101
Providence, Rhode Island 02903

ESS Project No. xxxx-000.0

June 1, 2000

TABLE OF CONTENTS

PROTOCOL REVIEW CERTIFICATION

I, the undersigned, hereby certify that I have personally reviewed this protocol and to the best of my knowledge all information and calculations contained herein are true, accurate, and complete.

Prepared by: _____

Reviewed by: _____

PROTOCOL SUMMARY

Facility Name: Name of Company
                        Street Address
                        City, State, Zip
                        (999) 999-9999 (tel)
                        (999) 999-9999 (fax)

Facility Project Manager: Name of person

Testing Organization: Environmental Science Services, Inc.
                      272 West Exchange Street, Suite 101
                      Providence, Rhode Island 02903
                      (401) 421-0398 (tel.)
                      (401) 421-5731 (fax)

Project Manager: Don Deed, P.E.

Unit to be Tested: Catalytic Oxidizer
                        Controlling VOC Emissions from Four
                        Flexographic Printing Presses

Proposed Test Date: July 2000

Protocol Date: June 1, 2000

TEST PROTOCOL
FOR A VOC COMPLIANCE TEST AT
FOUR PRINTING PRESSES AND
ASSOCIATED CATALYTIC OXIDIZER

1.0 INTRODUCTION

Environmental Science Services, Inc. (ESS) has been retained by (Name of Company). (Name of Testing Organization or Technician) to perform a volatile organic compound (VOC) emission test program at the (Name of Company) facility in (City), New York. The purpose of this program is to measure the VOC destruction efficiency (DE) of a catalytic oxidizer that controls VOC emissions from four flexographic printing presses, and to evaluate the VOC capture efficiency (CE) of these presses and their room enclosure. At each press, solvent-based inks are applied to plastic film. This program is being performed in conformance with a permit to construct issued by the New York State Department of Environmental Conservation (NYSDEC).

Testing is tentatively scheduled for one day in (month, year) and will be supervised by (name of person) of ESS. (Name of person) of (Name of Company) will coordinate the test program and provide process and logistical support. A representative of the NYSDEC is expected to be on site to observe the test program.

Section 2.0 of this protocol summarizes the proposed measurement program; Section 3.0 describes the process and associated control equipment; Section 4.0 details the sampling and analysis methods; Section 5.0 describes the quality control plan for this program. Field data sheets and ink and solvent usage information are shown in the Appendices.

2.0 SCOPE OF WORK

2.1 Oxidizer Destruction Efficiency

The procedure for determining the VOC DE of a fume oxidizer is to measure the VOC concentration and volumetric flow rate of gases at the oxidizer inlet and outlet. To accomplish this, ESS proposes to conduct three 1-hour tests concurrently at each location.

VOC concentrations will be measured in accordance with the United States Environmental Protection Agency (US EPA) Methods 25A and 18. With Method 25A, gas samples will be analyzed on site with total hydrocarbon (THC) flame ionization detection (FID) analyzers calibrated with propane compressed gas standards. The Method 25A concentrations will be recorded on a data logger and strip chart, thus yielding continuous real-time data. With Method 18, an integrated bag sample collected from the oxidizer stack will be analyzed on site with a gas chromatograph for methane, and this non-VOC methane concentration will be subtracted from the Method 25A THC concentration. These methods are described in detail in Section 4.5.

Volumetric flow rate measurements will be made at each location during each 1-hour test using a pitot tube and water manometer, in accordance with US EPA Methods 1 and 2.

2.2 Capture Efficiency

The VOC CE of the room permanent total enclosure (PTE) about the printing presses will be assessed by measuring the face velocity at the enclosure natural draft openings, measuring the static pressure within the enclosure, and making smoke tube observations of air movement at the natural draft openings. These measurements and observations will serve to verify that 100 percent CE is being achieved by the enclosure, in accordance with the design criteria of EPA Method 204.

2.3 Report

The final emission test report will be submitted to the NYSDEC for review and approval. The following test data for each sampling location will be presented in tabular form:

- VOC concentration in parts per million by volume (ppmv);
- Volumetric flow rate in standard cubic feet per minute (scfm);
- Mass emission rate in pounds per hour (lb/hr).

The oxidizer DE will be calculated from the inlet and outlet mass emission rates. Pertinent air velocity, static pressure and smoke tube measurements will be presented to verify CE. Process data will also be included with the emission data. The test report will include a description of the sampling and analysis methods, process operations, and quality control procedures. All data sheets, strip charts, calibration data, and data reduction summaries will be included in the test report.

3.0 PROCESS DESCRIPTION

3.1 General

(Name of Company) operates four flexographic printing presses at their (City), New York facility. These presses apply solvent-based inks to plastic films producing materials for a variety of commercial and industrial applications. VOC emissions from the presses are controlled by the combined application of a permanent total enclosure and one 9,000 scfm catalytic oxidizer. A schematic layout of the presses, print room enclosure, oxidizer and associated ductwork is shown in Figure 3.1.

3.2 Printing Presses

(Name of Company) operates four flexographic printing presses:

- one Bielloni 6-color central impression press;
- one Carraro 6-color central impression press;
- one Hudson Sharp 4-color central impression press; and,
- one Kidder Stacey 6-color stack press.

At the stack press, the color stations and interstation nozzle dryers are positioned vertically with 2 stations on the ascending side of the stack and 2 stations on the descending side. At the press, plastic film from a supply roll passes through each color station and then through an overhead gas-fired drying oven maintained at between 90°F and 120°F, and then is rerolled. Maximum web width is 36 inches.

At the central impression presses, the color stations and interstation nozzle dryers are positioned around one large steel impression cylinder, which supports the plastic film or web. At the press, plastic film from a supply roll passes to the impression cylinder where inks are applied. The web then passes through an overhead gas heated drying oven maintained between 90°F and 120°F. After emerging from the oven, the web is re-rolled. The maximum web widths are approximately 54 inches, 36 inches, and 32 inches at the Bielloni, Carraro and Hudson Sharp presses, respectively.

At the Bielloni press, the color stations are equipped with enclosed chamber doctor blade systems. Ink is pumped from a covered can into the chamber and drains back to the can. While in the chamber, the ink is metered onto a roller by a doctor blade, and transferred to the printing plate and then to the web. At the other presses, the color stations are standard four roll inking systems. Ink is pumped from covered cans to an ink pan where it is transferred by rollers to the web. Ink drains from the pan back to the can.

Drying between color stations is achieved with nozzle dryers that direct air onto the web and also collect the air and duct it to the overhead drying oven, thus achieving a high degree of capture efficiency. In addition, the ink reservoirs are fitted with covers to minimize evaporative losses.

(Name of Company) uses 15 to 20 different solvent-based inks, with solvent contents ranging from approximately 35% to 65% by weight. Among all the ink formulations, more than 10 different solvents are used, with two solvents accounting for approximately 90% of the total solvent usage. These two solvents are ethanol and n-propanol. The total uncontrolled emission rate from the presses is approximately 40 pounds/hour on an annual average basis. Representative data on ink and solvent usage are contained in Appendix B.

3.3 Catalytic Oxidizer

The solvent-laden air from the drying ovens is collected by local centrifugal fans and manifolded into one duct and directed to a Model 9K-98 catalytic oxidizer through one 50 HP centrifugal fan. The oxidizer has a capacity of 9,000 scfm and is fired with natural gas.

An air-to-air plate type heat exchanger preheats the process exhaust, while cooling the incinerator exhaust. Constructed of stainless steel, it is designed for a heat transfer efficiency of approximately 70%.

The preheated process exhaust stream passes by the Maxon burner assembly, which has a gross heat release capacity of 0.8 MMBTU/hr. Here the process exhaust is heated to at least 550°F before entering the catalyst bed.

The catalyst bed contains 1/4" spherical precious metal pellets. The exothermic destruction of the VOC increases the temperature of the exhaust stream by an amount that depends on the number of presses running and the ink and solvent loading.

The hot exhaust stream from the catalyst passes through the primary heat exchanger where heat is transferred to the cooler gas stream coming from the process. The exhaust gases are vented through the stack at a temperature of approximately 250°F.

As noted in Section 3.2, the averaging VOC loading to the oxidizer is approximately 40 pounds/hour. Assuming an average molecular weight of the solvent mix of 60, and a volumetric flow rate of 9,000 scfm, the VOC loading is equivalent to an inlet VOC concentration of 475 ppmv. The oxidizer destruction efficiency may range from 94 to 96%, yielding a stack VOC concentration ranging from 19 to 29 ppmv.

3.4 Process Operation During the Test

Testing will be conducted during one day with the four printing presses operating at normal production (ink application) rates, reflecting normal maximum ink coverages. (Name of technician or organization) will monitor and record pertinent process parameters, including ink and solvent application rates and oxidizer temperatures. Process data will be included in the test report.

3.5 Enclosure Description

As shown in Figure 3.2, the flexographic presses are contained within a room with two contiguous areas: Area 1 contains the Carraro and Kidder presses with approximate dimensions of 72 feet long by 45 feet wide by 17 feet high; Area 2 contains the Hudson Sharp and Bielloni presses with approximate dimensions of 130 feet long by 45 feet wide by 36 feet high. Air flows into the room from other parts of the building through three doorways (A, B, and C) that represents natural draft openings (NDO), and by general infiltration. The three doorways are fitted with tightly overlapping vertical vinyl strips that extend to within two inches of the floor. Approximately 9,000 scfm of air is exhausted from the room to the oxidizer through the drying ovens associated with the presses. The room is maintained at a negative static pressure relative to the rest of the building. The total surface area of the room enclosure is approximately 30,000 square feet. The total area of the three open doorways (without the plastic strips in place) is approximately 300 square feet or approximately 1% of the total surface area.

Periodically during the test program, air speed at the gaps near the floor at each NDO will be monitored with a portable hot wire anemometer and air flow direction into the room will be monitored with a smoke tube. In addition, a sensitive water manometer will be used to measure the negative static pressure in the room enclosure. Because of the tightly overlapping structure of the vinyl strips at the doorways, there will be little free open area at which to measure a true face velocity characteristic of a normal NDO. The test report will present these measurements and observations to verify that 100% capture efficiency is being achieved by the room enclosure, in accordance with the criteria of EPA Method 204.

4.0 SAMPLING AND ANALYSIS METHODS

The following US EPA reference test methods will be used for this test program.

US EPA Method 1 - Sampling and Velocity Traverse Points for Stationary Sources

US EPA Method 2 - Determination of Stack Gas Velocity and Volumetric Flow Rate

US EPA Methods 3 and 3A - Gas Analysis for Carbon Dioxide, Oxygen, Excess Air, and Molecular Weight

US EPA Method 4 - Determination of Moisture Content in Stack Gases

US EPA Method 18 - Measurements of Gaseous Organic Compound Emissions by Gas Chromatography.

US EPA Method 25A - Determination of Total Organic Concentration Using a Flame Ionization Analyzer

US EPA Method 204 - Criteria for and Verification of a Permanent Total Enclosure

4.1 Sampling Points and Locations

All sampling locations are shown in Figure 4.1. Individual locations are described below.

The oxidizer inlet sampling location is in a vertical section of a 20-inch circular duct approximately 0.7 duct diameters upstream from a duct bend leading to the oxidizer fan and approximately 12 duct diameters downstream from where the duct leading from the presses descends to the oxidizer. The location is shown schematically in Figure 4.2. Flow rate measurements will be made at 16 traverse points through two ports (8 points per port). The Method 25A THC sampling probe will be positioned approximately at the center of the duct.

The oxidizer outlet sampling location is in the 28-inch circular vertical oxidizer stack, approximately 0.5 duct diameters upstream from a 30-degree bend in the duct and approximately 1.3 duct diameters downstream from the oxidizer heat exchanger. The location is shown schematically in Figure 4.3. Flow rate measurements will be made at 16 traverse points through two ports (8 points per port). The THC sampling probe will be positioned approximately at the center of the duct.

4.2 Flow Rate Measurements

A pitot tube connected to an inclined manometer will be used to determine the velocity head pressure of the stack gasses at each traverse point as specified in US EPA Reference Method 2. Temperature will be measured at each point with a thermocouple. Pitot tube leak checks will be performed for each test run.

4.3 Molecular Weight Determination

The oxygen (O_2) and carbon dioxide (CO_2) composition of the oxidizer outlet gas stream will be determined by analyzing an integrated sample of stack gas collected during each test run in accordance with US EPA Reference Method 3. During each sampling period, an integrated sample of stack gas will be collected in a Tedlar® bag attached to the bypass of the Method 25A stack analyzer. Each bag sample will be analyzed for CO_2 and O_2 using analyzers calibrated and operated in accordance with US EPA Method 3A.

4.4 Moisture

The oxidizer inlet moisture concentration will be documented by measuring the room air dry bulb temperature and relative humidity. The moisture content of the oxidizer outlet gas stream will be measured with a chilled mini-impinger sampling train following US EPA Method 4. The sampling train consists of a length of tubing, four mini-impingers in series immersed in an ice bath, and a calibrated pump. The first two impingers each contain 10 milliliters of water, the third impinger is empty, and the fourth impinger contains silica gel. During each 1-hour test run, the impinger weight gains are measured and used with the pump sampling rate and sampling duration to calculate the moisture content.

4.5 US EPA Methods 25A and 18

VOC emission measurements at the oxidizer inlet and outlet will be performed following US EPA Methods 25A and 18. At each location the Method 25A sampling train consists of a short, stainless-steel probe, a Teflon®, heated sample line, and a TECO Model 51 FID THC analyzer. A schematic of this sampling train is shown in Figure 4.4. Analyzer outputs are continuously recorded on a data logger and a strip chart recorder. The analyzers are calibrated with propane-in-air compressed gas standards at three points plus zero at the beginning of the test day and at one point plus zero at the end of each test run.

If warranted by a sufficiently high THC concentration at the oxidizer outlet, the integrated bag samples collected for CO_2 and O_2 analyses will also be analyzed for methane concentration following US EPA Method 18, using an HNU Model 321 gas chromatograph with FID (GC/FID). The GC/FID is calibrated with one or more methane standards (depending on the magnitude of the methane concentration in the oxidizer outlet), and the stack Method 25A THC analyzer is also calibrated with methane to establish a methane/propane response factor. Total non-methane hydrocarbon concentration is calculated by subtracting the methane concentration measured by the GC/FID from the THC concentration measured by the continuous THC analyzer.

4.6 Calculations

VOC emission rates are calculated using the following equations:

$$E(lb/hr) = C(ppm) \times Q(scfm) \times MW \times K$$

    Where: E = Emission Rate
             C = Concentration of VOC in parts per million (volume/volume)
             Q = Volumetric Flow Rate in standard cubic feet per minute
             K = Constant (conversion factor) = 15.58×10^{-8}
             MW = Molecular Weight of Calibration Gas (propane = 44)

The DE calculation compares the inlet VOC emission rate and the outlet VOC emission rate as follows: $DE(\%) = 100 \times [E(in) - E(out)]/E(in)$

      where: DE = Destruction Efficiency
               E(in) = Inlet Emission Rate
               E(out) = Outlet Emission Rate

5.0 QUALITY ASSURANCE PROCEDURES

ESS' emissions testing teams are committed to providing high quality testing services. To meet this commitment, ESS follows applicable US EPA sampling procedures and implements applicable quality assurance/quality control procedures with all test programs. These procedures ensure that all sampling is performed by competent, trained individuals and that all equipment used is operational and properly calibrated before and after use.

The ESS QA program generally follows the guidelines of the US EPA **Quality Assurance Handbook for Air Pollution Measurement Systems:** Volume III Stationary Source - Specific_Methods (EPA-600/R-94-038c - September 1994).

5.1 Sampling

The ESS measurement devices, thermocouples, and portable gas analyzers are uniquely identified and calibrated with documented procedures and acceptance criteria. Records of all calibration data are maintained in ESS' files. Copies of pertinent calibration data are available on site during testing. Field data are recorded on standard forms. Field notebooks are used to record observations and information that may affect data quality.

5.2 Analytical

Field blanks of all applicable sampling reagents are taken in accordance with the respective sampling methods. All samples requiring off-site laboratory analysis are accompanied to the laboratory with chain-of-custody documentation. All applicable compressed gas/calibration standards used are always US EPA Protocol No. 1-certified. Other gas standards and analytical laboratory support gases used are directly traceable to the National Institute of Standards and Technology. The certifications of the gas standards used during testing are available on site and are included in the final test· report.

5.3 Reporting

All reports undergo a tiered review. The initial review of the report and calculations is made by the project manager or field manager. A final review is then made by a senior member of the Air Measurements and Technology Group prior to issuing the final report. Signatures on a Report Review Certification contained in each report are used to document the review process.

TABLES

FIGURES

APPENDIX A. Field and Calibration Data Sheets

APPENDIX B. Ink and Solvent Usage

APPENDIX C. Site Plans and Pressroom Layout

Report of Conducted Test

TEST REPORT
FOR A
VOC COMPLIANCE TEST
at
Four Printing Presses and
Associated Catalytic Oxidizer
xxxx Manufacturing Co., Inc.
Test Date: June 30, 2000

Prepared For:

Name of Company
Street Number
City, State, Zip

Prepared By:

Environmental Science Services, Inc.
272 West Exchange Street, Suite 101
Providence, Rhode Island 02903

ESS Project No. xxxx-000

August 28, 2001

TABLE OF CONTENTS

TABLES

FIGURES

APPENDICES

REPORT REVIEW CERTIFICATION

I, the undersigned, hereby certify that I have personally reviewed this report and to the best of my knowledge all information and calculations contained herein are true, accurate, and complete.

Prepared by: _____

Reviewed by: _____

TEST SUMMARY

Facility Name: (Name of) Manufacturing Co., Inc.
                            Street Number
                            City, State, Zip
                            (999) 999-9999 (tel)
                            (999) 999-9999 (fax)

Facility Project Manager: (Name of person)

Testing Organization: Environmental Science Services, Inc.
                            272 West Exchange Street, Suite 101
                            Providence, Rhode Island 02903
                            (401) 421-0398 (tel)
                            (401) 421-5731 (fax)

Project Manager: Don Deed, P.E.

Unit Tested: Catalytic Oxidizer
                            Controlling VOC Emissions from Four
                            Flexographic Printing Presses

Test Date: June 30, 2000

TEST REPORT
FOR A VOC COMPLIANCE TEST AT
FOUR PRINTING PRESSES AND
ASSOCIATED CATALYTIC OXIDIZER

1.0 INTRODUCTION

Environmental Science Services, Inc. (ESS) was retained by (name of company), Inc. to perform a volatile organic compound (VOC) emission test program at the (plant name) facility in (plant location), New York. The purpose of this program was to measure the VOC destruction efficiency (DE) of an catalytic oxidizer that controls VOC emissions from four flexographic printing presses, and to evaluate the VOC capture efficiency (CE) of these presses and their room enclosure. At each press, solvent-based inks are applied to plastic film. This program was performed in conformance with a permit to construct issued by the New York State Department of Environmental Conservation (NYSDEC).

Testing was conducted on June 30, 2000 by (name of personnel) of ESS. (Name of project manager) of (name of firm) coordinated the test program and provided process and logistical support. (Name of person) of the NYSDEC was on site to observe the test program.

Section 2.0 of this report summarizes the results of this measurement program; Section 3.0 describes the process and associated control equipment; Section 4.0 details the sampling and analysis methods; and Section 5.0 presents the Quality Control plan for this program. Field data sheets, calibration documents, process data and other pertinent documentation are contained in the appendices.

2.0 SUMMARY OF RESULTS

2.1 Oxidizer Destruction Efficiency

Three 1-hour test runs were performed at the inlet and outlet of this fume oxidizer following United States Environmental Protection Agency (US EPA) Reference Test Method 25A. During each run, VOC concentration and volumetric flow rate of gases were measured at each location.

The results of the oxidizer DE measurements are summarized in Table 2.1. Over the three test runs, the DE ranged from 91.44 to 93.04 percent, averaging 92.22 percent. During the test program, all presses were operating except for occasional routine roll changes and press adjustments.

2.2 Capture Efficiency

The VOC CE of the room permanent total enclosure (PTE) about the presses was assessed by measuring the face velocity at the room enclosure natural draft openings (NDOs), making smoke tube observations of air movement at the NDOs, and measuring the negative static pressure within the room. These measurements and observations are discussed in Section 3.5, and verify that 100 percent CE is being achieved by the room enclosure.

3.0 PROCESS DESCRIPTION

3.1 General

(Name of company) operates four flexographic printing presses at their (location), New York facility. These presses apply solvent-based inks to plastic films producing materials for a variety of commercial and industrial applications. VOC emissions from the presses are controlled by the combined application of a permanent total enclosure and one 9,000 scfm catalytic oxidizer. A schematic layout of the presses, print room enclosure, oxidizer and associated ductwork is shown in Figure 3.1.

3.2 Printing Presses

(Name of company) operates four flexographic printing presses:

- one Bielloni 6-color central impression press;
- one Carraro 6-color central impression press;
- one Hudson Sharp 4-color central impression press; and,
- one Kidder Stacey 6-color stack press.

At the stack press, the color stations and interstation nozzle dryers are positioned vertically with three stations on the ascending side of the stack and three stations on the descending side. At the press, plastic film from a supply roll passes through each color station and then through an overhead gas-fired drying oven maintained at between 90°F and 120°F, and then is rerolled. Maximum web width is 36 inches.

At the central impression presses, the color stations and interstation nozzle dryers are positioned around one large steel impression cylinder, which supports the plastic film or web. At the press, plastic film from a supply roll passes to the impression cylinder where inks are applied. The web then passes through an overhead gas heated drying oven maintained between 90°F and 120°F. After emerging from the oven, the web is re-rolled. The maximum web widths are approximately 54 inches, 36 inches, and 32 inches at the Bielloni, Carraro and Hudson Sharp presses, respectively.

At the Bielloni press, the color stations are equipped with enclosed chamber doctor blade systems. Ink is pumped from a covered can into the chamber and drains back to the can. While in the chamber, the ink is metered onto a roller by a doctor blade, and transferred to the printing plate and then to the web. At the other presses, the color stations are standard four roll inking systems. Ink is pumped from covered cans to an ink pan where it is transferred by rollers to the web. Ink drains from the pan back to the can.

Drying between color stations is achieved with nozzle dryers that direct air onto the web and also collect the air and duct it to the overhead drying oven, thus achieving a high degree of capture efficiency. In addition, the ink reservoirs are fitted with covers to minimize evaporative losses.

(Name of company) uses 15 to 20 different solvent-based inks, with solvent contents ranging from approximately 35% to 65% by weight. Among all the ink formulations, more than 10 different solvents are used, with two solvents accounting for approximately 90% of the total solvent usage. These two solvents are ethanol and n-propanol.

3.3 Catalytic Oxidizer

The solvent-laden air from the drying ovens is collected by local centrifugal fans and manifolded into one duct and directed to an (name of manufacturer) Model 9K-98 catalytic oxidizer through one 50 HP centrifugal fan. The oxidizer has a capacity of 9,000 scfm and is fired with natural gas.

An air-to-air plate type heat exchanger preheats the process exhaust, while cooling the oxidizer exhaust. Constructed of stainless steel, it is designed for a heat transfer efficiency of approximately 70%.

The preheated process exhaust stream passes by the Maxon burner assembly, which has a gross heat release capacity of 0.8 MMBTU/hr. Here the process exhaust is heated to at least 550°F before entering the catalyst bed.

The catalyst bed contains ¼" spherical precious metal pellets. The exothermic destruction of the VOC increases the temperature of the exhaust stream by an amount that depends on the number of presses operating and the ink and solvent loading.

The hot exhaust stream from the catalyst passes through the primary heat exchanger where heat is transferred to the cooler gas stream coming from the process. The exhaust gases are vented through the stack at a temperature of approximately 250°F.

3.4 Process Operation During the Test

Testing was conducted during one day with the four printing presses operating at normal production (ink application) rates, reflecting normal maximum ink coverages. (Name of person at organization) monitored and recorded pertinent process parameters, including ink and solvent application rates and oxidizer temperatures before and after the catalyst bed. Process data are included in Appendix D of this test report.

3.5 Enclosure Description

As shown in Figure 3.2, the flexographic presses are contained within a room with two contiguous areas: Area 1 contains the Carraro and Kidder presses with approximate dimensions of 72 feet long by 45 feet wide by 17 feet high; Area 2 contains the Hudson Sharp and Bielloni presses with approximate dimensions of 130 feet long by 45 feet wide by 36 feet high. Air flows into the room from other parts of the building through three doorways (A, B, and C) that represent natural draft openings (NDOs), and by general infiltration. The three doorways are fitted with tightly overlapping vertical vinyl strips that extend to within two inches of the floor. Approximately 9,000 scfm of air is exhausted from the room to the oxidizer through the drying ovens associated with the four presses. The room is maintained at a negative static pressure relative to the rest of the building. The total surface area of the room enclosure is approximately 30,000 square feet. The total area of the three open doorways (without the plastic strips in place) is approximately 300 square feet or approximately 1% of the total surface area.

During the test program, the face velocity at the three NDOs was monitored (where practical) with a portable hot wire anemometer and air flow direction into the room was monitored with a smoke tube. The plastic strips billowed into the room due to the negative static pressure, and velocity measurements were made at gaps between the strips as they moved. Smoke tube observations indicated a strong air movement into the room at all three NDOs. In addition, the negative static pressure in the room was monitored with a sensitive water manometer positioned inside the room enclosure near NDO A and connected to the air outside the room with a length of tubing inserted through NDO A. The velocity and pressure measurements are summarized in Table 3.1. These measurements and observations verify that the room enclosure is achieving 100 percent capture efficiency, in accordance with the criteria of US EPA Method 204.

4.0 SAMPLING AND ANALYSIS METHODS

The following US EPA reference test methods were used for this test program.

US EPA Method 1 - Sampling and Velocity Traverse Points for Stationary Sources

US EPA Method 2 - Determination of Stack Gas Velocity and Volumetric Flow Rate

US EPA Methods 3A - Determination of Oxygen and Carbon Dioxide Concentration in Emissions from Stationary Sources (Instrumental Analyzer Procedure)

US EPA Method 4 - Determination of Moisture Content in Stack Gases

US EPA Method 18 - Measurements of Gaseous Organic Compound Emissions by Gas Chromatography.

US EPA Method 25A - Determination of Total Organic Concentration Using a Flame Ionization Analyzer

US EPA Method 204 - Criteria for and Verification of a Permanent Total Enclosure

4.1 Sampling Points and Locations

All sampling locations are shown in Figure 4.1. Individual locations are described below.

The oxidizer inlet sampling location is in a vertical section of a 20-inch circular duct approximately 0.8 duct diameters upstream from a duct bend leading to the oxidizer fan and approximately 9 duct diameters downstream from where the duct leading from the presses descends to the oxidizer. The location is shown schematically in Figure 4.2. Flow rate measurements were made at 16 traverse points through two ports (8 points per port). The Method 25A THC sampling probe was positioned approximately at the center of the duct.

The oxidizer outlet sampling location is in the 27-inch circular vertical oxidizer stack, approximately 0.6 duct diameters upstream from a 30-degree bend in the duct and approximately 1.4 duct diameters downstream from the oxidizer heat exchanger. The location is shown schematically in Figure 4.3. Flow rate measurements were made at 16 traverse points through two ports (8 points per port). The THC sampling probe was positioned approximately at the center of the duct.

4.2 Flow Rate Measurements

A pitot tube connected to an inclined manometer was used to determine the velocity head pressure of the stack gasses at each traverse point as specified in US EPA Reference Method 2. Temperature was measured at each point with a thermocouple. Pitot tube leak checks were performed for each test run. A cyclonic flow angle check was conducted at each location following the pitot-nulling technique of EPA Method 1, and indicated an acceptable average flow angle at each location.

4.3 Molecular Weight Determination

The oxygen (O_2) and carbon dioxide (CO_2) composition of the oxidizer outlet gas stream was continuously measured using analyzers calibrated and operated in accordance with US EPA Method 3A.

4.4 Moisture

The oxidizer inlet moisture concentration was documented by measuring the room air dry bulb temperature and relative humidity. The moisture content of the oxidizer outlet gas stream was measured with a chilled mini-impinger sampling train following US EPA Method 4. The sampling train consisted of a length of tubing, four mini-impingers in series immersed in an ice bath, and a calibrated pump. The first two impingers each contained 10 milliliters of water, the third impinger was empty, and the fourth impinger contained silica gel. After each 1-hour test run, the impinger weight gains were measured and used with the pump sampling rate and sampling duration to calculate the moisture content.

4.5 US EPA Methods 25A and 18

VOC emission measurements at the oxidizer inlet and outlet were performed following US EPA Methods 25A and 18. At each location the Method 25A sampling train consisted of a short stainless-steel probe, a Teflon® heated sample line, and a TECO Model 51 FID THC analyzer. A schematic of this sampling train is shown in Figure 4.4. Analyzer outputs were continuously recorded on a data logger and a strip chart recorder. The analyzers were calibrated with propane-in-air compressed gas standards at three points plus zero at the beginning of the test day and at one point plus zero at the end of each test run.

During each test run, an integrated bag sample collected in a Tedlar bag attached to the by-pass of the Method 25A outlet analyzer was analyzed for methane concentration following US EPA Method 18, using an HNU Model 321 gas chromatograph with FID (GC/FID). The GC/FID was calibrated with methane standards, and the outlet Method 25A THC analyzer was also calibrated with methane to establish a methane/propane response factor. Total non-methane hydrocarbon (TNMHC) concentration was calculated by subtracting the non-VOC methane concentration measured by the GC/FID from the THC concentration measured by the continuous THC analyzer.

4.6 Calculations

VOC emission rates are calculated using the following equations:

E(lb/hr) = C(ppm) x Q(scfm) x MW x K
    Where: E = Emission Rate
             C= Concentration of VOC in parts per million (volume/volume)
             Q = Volumetric Flow Rate in standard cubic feet per minute
             K = Constant (conversion factor) = 15.58 x 10^{-8}
             MW = Molecular Weight of Calibration Gas (propane = 44)

The DE calculation compares the inlet VOC emission rate and the outlet VOC emission rate as follows:

DE(%) = 100 x [E(in) - E(out)]/E(in)

       where: DE = Destruction Efficiency
                E(in) = Inlet Emission Rate
                E(out) = Outlet Emission Rate

5.0 QUALITY ASSURANCE PROCEDURES

ESS' emissions testing teams are committed to providing high quality testing services. To meet this commitment, ESS follows applicable US EPA sampling procedures and implements applicable quality assurance/quality control procedures with all test programs. These procedures ensure that all sampling is performed by competent, trained individuals and that all equipment used is operational and properly calibrated before and after use.

The ESS QA program generally follows the guidelines of the US EPA **Quality Assurance Handbook for Air Pollution Measurement Systems**: Volume III Stationary Source - Specific_Methods (EPA-600/R-94-038c - September 1994).

5.1 Sampling

The ESS measurement devices, thermocouples, and portable gas analyzers are uniquely identified and calibrated with documented procedures and acceptance criteria. Records of all calibration data are maintained in ESS' files. Copies of pertinent calibration data are available on site during testing. Field data are recorded on standard forms. Field notebooks are used to record observations and information that may affect data quality.

5.2 Analytical

Field blanks of all applicable sampling reagents are taken in accordance with the respective sampling methods. All samples requiring off-site laboratory analysis are accompanied to the laboratory with chain-of-custody documentation. All applicable compressed gas/calibration standards used are always US EPA Protocol No. 1-certified. Other gas standards and analytical laboratory support gases used are directly traceable to the National Institute of Standards and Technology. The certifications of the gas standards used during testing are available on site and are included in the final test report.

5.3 Reporting

All reports undergo a detailed review. The first review of the report and calculations is made by the project manager or field manager. A final review is then made by a senior member of the Air Measurements Group prior to issuing the final report. Signatures on a Report Review Certification contained in each report are used to document the review process.

TABLES

FIGURES

APPENDIX A. Field Data Sheets

APPENDIX B. THC Strip Chart and GC Data

APPENDIX C. Calibration Documents

APPENDIX D. Process Data

Testing of Catalysts

**DEGUSSA SEC CATALYST
FIELD SAMPLE ANALYSIS PROCEDURES**

Analysis of catalyst samples from the field is a valuable tool for determining the activity level of the catalyst and to alert the user of the presence of contaminants which degrade the performance of the catalyst. This document gives a brief outline of the procedures used to evaluate both monolithic and pelleted catalyst samples. A copy of a typical analysis report is attached to the end of this document.

Activity Level

The key test among the battery of tests to which the sample is subjected is a test of the activity level of the catalyst on a reference hydrocarbon. The catalyst sample is loaded into a stainless steel reactor chamber and placed inside an electric mantle furnace. Samples taps both upstream and downstream of the sample are connected to either an FID detector of a gas chromatograph. These detectors will monitor the change in concentration of the reference VOC, normally n-Hexane, from which the performance of the catalyst is calculated Hexane is a fairly tough VOC to destroy and as such if the catalyst has been damaged it will easily be seen in the performance data. The choice of n-Hexane can be likened to a doctor having a patient walk on a treadmill in order to check for damage to the efficiency of the heart.

A gas mixture composed of air, water and ppm levels of n-Hexane flows through the sample as the temperature is raised from 200°F to 1,000°F in 100°F increments. At each step in the temperature profile the catalyst is allowed to "soak" for 45 minutes in order to reach equilibrium before the performance data is recorded; The flow rate of gas through the catalyst is such that the gas hourly space velocity is higher than normal in the actual catalyst bed Again this is done to stress the catalyst and reveal the effects of damage.

On completion of the test cycle the destruction efficiency of the test sample is calculated from the concentration data and this information is plotted against the results from testing fresh catalyst under the same conditions. Changes in the efficiency curve relative to the baseline data indicate whether the catalyst is performing properly or if it has been poisoned, masked or overheated. While this test cannot predict the actual performance level of the users catalyst on other VOCs it can show the extent of catalyst damage and thus enables the user to initiate measures to protect the catalyst bed from further damage.

Poison Scan

The deposition of contaminants on the catalyst results in a range of effects depending on the specific elemental contaminant and the amount of material deposited. A poison scan determines the elemental chemical composition of the sample via the X-ray florescence technique. A portion of the sample is ground to a powder and compressed into a wafer. The wafer is loaded into a chamber in the instrument where it is bombarded by x-rays over a range of wavelengths. As the wavelength of the x-ray bombardment changes, each chemical element has a characteristic wavelength for which it will not absorb the x-rays, but will reflect them instead. Detectors in the chamber record the intensity of the reflection and it is recorded by computer along with the wavelength value.

The data log for a given wafer is then analyzed by specialized software to identify the elements present in the sample by comparing the recorded emission wavelengths to the expected wavelengths for the elements. The intensity of the emission is then used to calculate the approximate concentration of the individual elements. The concentration of the expected elements is then subtracted from the test data. This results in a listing of the contaminants and their concentration on the catalyst.

The presence of elemental contamination can have a profound effect on the performance of the catalyst Catalyst poisons such as phosphorus, silicon and heavy metals deactivate the catalyst by combining with either the support material or the precious metal coating which prevents them from oxidizing the VOCs.

Surface Area Analysis

The surface of a catalyst is a rough and jumbled landscape filled with cracks and pores over which the precious metal coating is distributed. This roughened state produces a very large surface area in a small volume of material. This surface is subject to degradation to exposure to high temperatures. At temperatures higher than those recommended by the catalyst manufacturer changes occur in the crystal structure of the support which collapse the pores and in general smoothes out the surface. This traps the precious metals such that the VOCs cannot reach them and thus the activity level of the catalyst is degraded.

The surface area measurement is made through a technique developed by Brunauer, Emmett and Teller and is referred to a the BET isotherm analysis. This technique involves placing a portion of the sample in a vacuum chamber, evacuating the air and immersing the chamber in a liquid nitrogen bath Once the temperature of the sample has reached that of liquid nitrogen a measured amount of gaseous nitrogen is introduced into the sample chamber. A single layer of nitrogen atoms will condense on the surface of the sample and this causes a reduction in the pressure inside the chamber. The value of this lowered pressure is entered into a series of equations which results in a calculation of the surface area per unit mass of the sample. This result is normally reported in the units of square meters/gram of sample. Comparing the calculated results to that of fresh catalyst gives and indication of the degree of degradation of the catalyst and whether or not it plays a significant role in any loss of catalyst activity.

Degussa Stationary Emission Control Catalyst
Field Sample Analysis

For:	Company A	Installation:	Oxidizer 115
Attn:	Supervisor		
Fax #:			

Catalyst:	Product 1	Type:	Ceramic Monolith
Manufacturer:	Superior Catalyst Co.		

Poison Scan

Element	Concentration (g/ft^3)	Element	Concentration (g/ft^3)
Aluminum	n/d	Phosphorus	24.85
Arsenic	n/d	Potassium	n/d
Calcium	n/d	Silicon	17.09
Cerium	n/d	Silver	n/d
Chrome	1.55	Sodium	n/d
Cobalt	n/d	Sulfur	3.11
Copper	n/d	Tin	n/d
Iron	3.57	Titanium	n/d
Lead	n/d	Tungsten	n/d
Magnesium	n/d	Vanadium	n/d
Manganese	n/d	Zinc	n/d
Nickel	4.66		

Surface Area

		Noble Metal Analysis		
Measured	28.65 m^2/g	Platinum	98.33	% Remaining
Reference	32 m^2/g	Palladium	n/a	% Remaining
Reduction	10.5 %	Rhodium	n/a	% Remaining

Conclusions

The catalyst activity level shows the effects of the elemental contamination. In particular the phosphorus and the silicon cause the worst damage to the catalyst. Continued deposition of these materials will continue to degrage the performance of the catalyst.

The surface area shows a small amount of loss. This is most likely due to high temperature excursions. Please check the high temperature shutdown setting and equipment to see if it is in good working order.

Catalyst Performance on n-Hexane

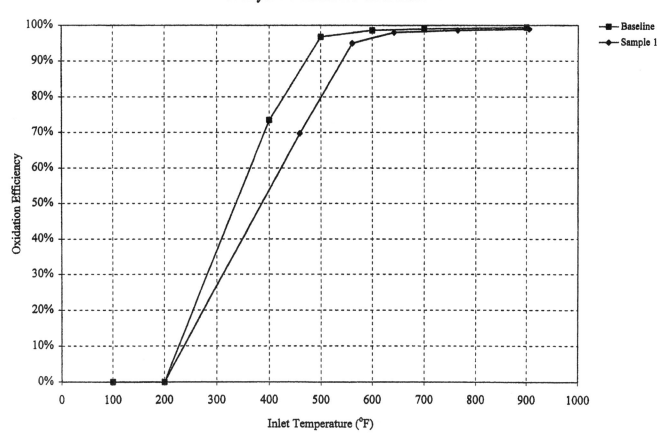

APPENDIX **XXIV**

SOURCE:
New York State Department of
Environmental Conservation

Hazardous Waste Generation for a Small Business

ARE YOU A SMALL QUANTITY GENERATOR?

If you generate between 100 and 1000 kilograms of non-acute hazardous waste per month and store less than 6000 kilograms at any time, you are a Small Quantity Generator (SQG).

A waste is hazardous if it is listed in Part 371 of the NYS Codes, Rules and Regulations (6NYCRR Part 371). Even if a waste is not listed, it is still considered to be hazardous if it has one or more of the following characteristics:

Ignitability (D001)

It catches fire easily. **Ignitable wastes** include many organic solvents and some paint wastes and strong oxidizing agents. A liquid waste is ignitable if it has a flash point of less than 60°C (140°F).

Corrosivity (D002)

It dissolves metals and other materials, or burns the skin. **Corrosive wastes** include waste rust removers, waste acid or alkaline cleaning fluids, and waste battery acid. Any liquid that has a pH of 2.0 or lower or a pH 12.5 or higher is corrosive.

Reactivity (D003)

It undergoes violent chemical reaction spontaneously or reacts violently with air or water. **Reactive wastes** include those which can generate toxic gases or vapors.

Toxicity Characteristic Leaching Procedure (TCLP) (D004–D017)

A waste sample is tested and analyzed, using the TCLP. TCLP toxic wastes contain high concentrations of heavy metals such as mercury, cadmium, lead or certain organics, including pesticides, that could contaminate groundwater.

TABLE 1. TOXICITY CHARACTERISTIC LEACHING PROCEDURE (TCLP)

The following are substances covered by the TCLP. The concentrations are not total amounts of the chemical in the waste, but concentrations in the TCLP leachate after the specific test is carried out.

D004	Arsenic	5.0	mg/l
D005	Barium	100.0	mg/l
D006	Cadmium	1.0	mg/l
D007	Chromium	5.0	mg/l
D008	Lead	5.0	mg/l
D009	Mercury	0.2	mg/l
D010	Selenium	1.0	mg/l
D011	Silver	5.0	mg/l
D012	Endrin	0.02	mg/l
D013	Lindane	0.4	mg/l
D014	Methoxychlor	10.0	mg/l
D015	Toxaphene	0.5	mg/l
D016	2,4-Dichlorophenoxyacetic acid	10.0	mg/l
D017	2,4,5-Trichlorophenoxypro-pionic acid	1.0	mg/l
D018	Benzene	0.50	mg/l
D019	Carbon Tetrachloride	0.50	mg/l
D020	Chlordane	0.03	mg/l
D021	Chlorobenzene	100.0	mg/l
D022	Chloroform	6.0	mg/l
D023	o-cresol	200.0	mg/l*
D024	m-cresol	200.0	mg/l*
D025	p-cresol	200.0	mg/l*
D026	cresol	200.0	mgl/*
D027	1,4-Dichlorobenzene	7.5	mg/l

D028	1,2-Dichloroethane	0.50	mg/l
D029	1,1-Dichloroethylene	0.70	mg/l
D030	2,4-Dinitrotoluene	0.13	mg/l*
D031	Heptachlor (and its hydroxide)	0.008	mg/l
D032	Hexachlorobenzene	0.13	mg/l**
D033	Hexachloro-1,3-Butadiene	0.5	mg/l
D034	Hexachloroethane	3.0	mg/l
D035	Methyl ethyl ketone	200.0	mg/l
D036	Nitrobenzene	2.0	mg/l
D037	Pentachlorophenol	100.0	mg/l***
D038	Pyridine	5.0	mg/l**
D039	Tetrachloroethylene	0.7	mg/l
D040	Trichloroethylene	0.5	mg/l
D041	2,4,5-Trichlorophenol	400.0	mg/l
D042	2,4,6-Trichlorophenol	2.0	mg/l
D043	Vinyl Chloride	0.20	mg/l

*   If o-,m- and p-cresol cannot be differentiated, the total cresol concentration is used. The regulatory level for total cresol is 200.0 mg/l.

**   Quantitation limit is greater than the calculated regulatory level. The quantitation limit, therefore, becomes the regulatory level.

***   The agency will propose a new regulatory level for this constituent, based on the latest toxicity information.

These TCLP standards were published by the United States Environmental Protection Agency (USEPA) on March 29, 1990. The standards were effective for fully regulated hazardous waste generators on September 25, 1990. Since March 29, 1991, small quantity generators are also required by the USEPA to handle wastes that fail the TCLP as hazardous wastes. New York State adopted the TCLP, effective January, 1995.

To obtain a copy of the test procedures, you may call the USEPA RCRA/Superfund Hotline at 1-800-424-9346.

Wastes exhibiting one or more hazardous characteristics are called **characteristic hazardous wastes;** those listed in the regulations are referred to as **listed hazardous wastes.**

COUNTING YOUR HAZARDOUS WASTE

one 55 gallon drum = about 200 kilograms of hazardous waste

1000 kilograms = 2,200 pounds = about 275 gallons

100 kilograms = 220 pounds = about 28 gallons

To determine the quantity of hazardous waste you generate per month, you must identify which wastes must be included in your monthly tally and which wastes may be excluded from your monthly total.

Do Count

You do count all quantities of "Listed" and "Characteristic" hazardous wastes (defined on page 1) that you:

* Accumulate on-site for any period of time prior to subsequent management.

* Package and transport off-site.

* Place directly in a regulated on-site treatment or disposal unit.

* Generate as still bottoms or sludges and remove from product storage tanks.

Don't Count

You do not have to count wastes that:

* Are specifically exempted from counting. Examples of these exempted wastes are:

  • spent lead-acid batteries that will be sent off-site for reclamation.

  • used oil that has not been mixed with hazardous waste.

* May be left in the bottom of containers that have been completely emptied through conventional means, for example, by pouring or pumping. Containers that held an acute hazardous waste must be more thoroughly cleaned.

* Are left as residue in the bottom of product storage tanks, if the residue is not removed from the product tank.

* You reclaim continuously on-site without storing the waste prior to reclamation.

CATEGORIES OF HAZARDOUS WASTE GENERATORS

The three categories of hazardous waste generators are:

1. **Conditionally Exempt Small Quantity Generators(CESQG)** who meet **all** of the following conditions:

    a. Generate less than 100 kilograms per month of listed and/or characteristic hazardous waste.

    b. Generate less than 1 kilogram per month of acutely hazardous waste.

c. Store less than 1000 kilograms of listed and/or characteristic hazardous waste.

d. Store less than 1 kilogram of acutely hazardous waste.

2. **Category 2 Small Quantity Generators** who do not meet CESQG conditions but meet **all** of the following conditions:

a. Generate less than 1000 kilograms per month of listed and/or characteristic hazardous waste.

b. Generate less than 1 kilogram per month of acutely hazardous waste.

c. Store less than 6000 kilograms of listed and/or characteristic hazardous waste.

d. Store less than 1 kilogram of acutely hazardous waste.

3. **Category 3 Large Quantity Generators** meet any of the following conditions:

a. Generate more than 1000 kilograms per month of listed and/or characteristic hazardous waste.

b. Generate more than 1 kilogram per month of acutely hazardous waste.

c. Store more than 1 kilogram of acutely hazardous waste.

Fully regulated generators are not covered in this manual. Fully regulated generators can obtain a copy of the regulations by calling (518) 485-8988.

CATEGORY 1:CONDITIONALLY EXEMPT SMALL QUANTITY GENERATORS

If your business is classified as conditionally exempt, there are only three things to keep in mind:

1. Identifying Your Hazardous Waste: Conditionally exempt generators are responsible for knowing which of their wastes would be classified as hazardous and what the correct waste codes are for the hazardous wastes.

2. Disposal: Conditionally exempt generators have several disposal options:

a. Recycling or treating the waste yourself. Please call the Small Quantity Generator/Household Hazardous Waste (SQG/HHW) Hotline at 1-800-462-6553 if you need more information on hazardous waste treatment.

b. Take or send the waste to an authorized hazardous waste treatment, storage or disposal (TSD) facility. You can get a list of TSD facilities that do business in New York State by calling the SQG/HHW Hotline at 1-800-462-6553 (in the Albany area or out of State, call 518-457-4105).

c. Take or send the waste to a permitted, licensed or registered municipal or industrial solid waste facility if they can take it. For example, some landfills will take dry paints and still bottoms. Sewage treatment plants may be willing and able to treat many print shop wastes. Municipal incinerators may be able to take waste materials such as paint thinners, and some solvent formulations. Prior approval from the facility is needed.

3. Transportation: Conditionally exempt generators have two options for getting their wastes to a disposer or recycler:

a. Use a NYS Part 364 Permitted Hauler

Part 364 haulers must meet certain conditions in order to receive permits: they must have a certain amount of liability insurance to cover cleanup of spills or accidents; the permits specify the types of waste that can be hauled and where the wastes may be hauled. The permits are renewed annually. You can call 518-457-3254 to find out if your hauler is permitted to haul your waste. Your local DEC office or the SQG/HHW Hotline can also help you to locate a hauler in your area.

b. Haul The Waste Yourself

If your company is a conditionally exempt generator, then you can legally haul the waste yourself within New York State. Some localities have additional requirements.

You can haul up to 220 pounds of listed and/or characteristic hazardous waste per month without having to obtain a NYS Part 364 permit.

NOTE: It is both illegal and dangerous to put hazardous waste in the trash dumpster. This practice can harm the people who unknowingly handle the waste.

CATEGORY 2 SMALL QUANTITY GENERATORS

Category 2 Small Quantity Generators must comply with all of the following requirements:

1. Accumulation limitations.

2. Storage requirements.

3. Emergency Preparedness and Response.

4. Obtain an EPA Identification Number.

5. Manifest their hazardous waste.

6. Use a licensed transporter.

7. Have waste sent only to TSDFs authorized to accept hazardous waste.

8. Pre-arrange waste transport and disposal.

9. Land disposal restrictions.

ACCUMULATION LIMITATION

Category 2 Small Quantity Generators may store up to 6000 kilograms (13,200 pounds) of listed and/or characteristic hazardous waste on-site for up to 180 days or for up to 270 days if the waste must be shipped to a treatment, storage or disposal facility that is located over 200 miles away. Small quantity generators may store no more than 1 kilogram of acutely hazardous waste on-site for any length of time.

If a Category 2 Small Quantity Generator exceeds the 180 or 270 day limit for accumulating waste, he may request an extension. Extensions of up to 30 days may be granted by this Department if the waste must remain on-site due to unforeseen, temporary, or uncontrollable circumstances.

STORAGE REQUIREMENTS

Category 2 Small Quantity Generators who generate 100 to 1000 kilograms (220 to 2,200 pounds) of hazardous waste per month and who store waste on-site must follow certain common sense rules to protect human health and the environment and to reduce the likelihood of damages or injuries caused by leaks or spills of hazardous wastes.

If you store hazardous waste in containers, you must:

1. Clearly mark each container with the words "HAZARDOUS WASTE," and with the date you began collecting waste in that container.

2. Keep containers in good condition, handle them carefully, and replace any leaking ones.

3. Not store hazardous waste in a container if it may cause rupture, leaks, corrosion, or other failure.

4. Keep containers closed except when you fill or empty them.

5. Inspect containers for leaks and corrosion every week.

6. Separate and protect reactive or ignitable waste from sources of ignition or reaction.

7. Ensure that the waste being placed in a container will not react with the container itself or with any residue of waste previously held in the container.

8. Never store in the same container wastes that could react together to cause fires, leaks, or other releases.

9. Separate by a dike, berm, wall or other device containers of waste which are incompatible with other containers of waste stored nearby.

10. Have secondary containment if you are located over a sole source aquifer and store more than 185 gallons (about 700 kilograms) of Liquid hazardous waste.

If you store waste in tanks, you must make sure the following requirements are met:

1. Never store hazardous waste in a tank if it may cause rupture, leaks, corrosion or otherwise cause the tank to fail.

2. Uncovered tanks must be operated to ensure at least 60 centimeters (two feet) of space at the top of the tank, unless the tank is equipped with a containment structure, a drainage control system, or a diversion structure with a capacity that equals or exceeds the volume of the top 60 centimeters of the tank.

3. Where hazardous waste is continuously fed into a tank, the tank must be equipped with a means to stop the inflow, such as a waste feed cut-off system or a by-pass system to a stand-by tank.

4. Discharge control equipment must be inspected once each operating day to ensure that it is in good working order.

5. Data from monitoring equipment must be gathered once each operating day to ensure that the tank is being operated according to its design.

6. To ensure compliance with number two above, the level of waste in the tank must be inspected once each operating day.

7. The construction materials of the tank must be inspected at least once a week to detect corrosion or leaking of fixtures or seams.

8. The construction material of discharge confinement structures and the area immediately surrounding discharge confinement structures must be inspected weekly to detect erosion or obvious signs of leakage.

9. Incompatible wastes, or incompatible wastes and materials must not be placed in the same tank.

10. Hazardous waste must not be placed in an unwashed tank which previously held an incompatible waste or material.

11. Have secondary containment if you store more than 110 gallons of liquid hazardous waste in underground storage tanks or more than 185 gallons of liquid hazardous waste in above ground storage tanks.

EMERGENCY PREPAREDNESS AND RESPONSE

Category 2 Small Quantity Generators who generate 100 to 1000 kilograms (220 to 2,200 pounds) of hazardous waste per month must also comply with the following requirements:

1. At least one employee must be designated as the Emergency Coordinator. The Emergency Coordinator must be on call or on the premises at all times to coordinate all emergency response measures.

2. The generator must post the following information next to the telephone:

   a.   the name and telephone number or the Emergency Coordinator;

   b.   the location of fire extinguishers and spill control material, and if present, the fire alarm; and

   c.   the telephone number of the fire department, unless the facility has a direct alarm.

3. Employees must be familiar with proper waste handling and emergency response procedures relevant to their responsibilities during normal facility operation and emergencies.

4. In the event of a fire, the Emergency Coordinator or his designee must call the fire department or attempt to extinguish the fire with a fire extinguisher.

5. In the event of a spill, the Emergency Coordinator or his designee must attempt to contain the spill and, as soon as is practicable, to clean up any resultant contamination.

6. In the event of an emergency threatening public health outside the facility or when the generator is aware that a spill has reached surface water, the generator must immediately notify the National Response Center at (800) 424-8802 and the Department at (518) 457-7362 with the following information:

   a.   the name, address and EPA identification number of the generator;
   b.   the date, time and type of incident;
   c.   the quantity and type of hazardous waste involved;
   d.   the extent of injuries, if any; and
   e.   the estimated quantity and disposition of recovered materials.

YOUR EPA IDENTIFICATION NUMBER

If your business generates more than 100 kilograms (220 pounds) of non-acute hazardous waste in any calendar month, you will need to obtain an EPA Identification Number. Transporters and facilities that store, treat or dispose of regulated quantities of hazardous waste must also have EPA Identification Numbers. **These twelve-character identification numbers uniquely identify hazardous waste generators, transporters, and TSDFs.** They allow tracking of hazardous waste from its point of origin to its ultimate point of disposal.

To obtain your EPA Identification Number, call or write the EPA Region II Office at the address given below and ask for a copy of EPA Form 8700-12, "Notification of Hazardous Waste Activity." You will be sent a booklet containing the two-page form and instructions for filling it out. Figure 1 is a sample copy of the notification form to show you the kinds of information required.

To complete item IX of the form, you need to identify your hazardous waste number. Appendix B contains some common hazardous waste numbers. If you do not understand the information in Appendix B, or if you cannot match your wastes with those listed, contact the Small Quantity Generator/Household Hazardous Waste Hotline at 1-800-462-6553.

Complete one copy of the form for each of your plant sites or business locations where you generate or handle hazardous wastes. Each site or location will receive its own EPA Identification Number.

Lastly, make sure your form is filled out completely and correctly and sign the certification in item X. Submit the form to the EPA Region II office. You will be assigned an EPA Identification Number unique to the site identified on your form. Use this number on all hazardous waste shipping papers. You should notify EPA at the address given below if the plant site or business location is moved or if the name of the facility changes.

THE MANIFEST SYSTEM

The hazardous waste manifest is a multicopy shipping document that you must fill out and use to accompany your hazardous waste shipments.

All generators, except conditionally exempt generators, must generally manifest their hazardous waste shipments. The manifest form is designed so that shipments of hazardous waste can be tracked from their point of generation to their final destination.

The hazardous waste generator, the transporter and the designated facility must each sign this document and keep a copy. The designated facility operator must also send a copy back to you, the generator, so that you can be sure that your shipment arrived. You must keep this copy, which bears the signatures of the transporter and the designated facility operator, on file for three years.

Figure 2 illustrates where the eight pages of the hazardous waste manifest are distributed. The hazardous waste manifest should be properly filled out and signed by the generator. When the transporter signs and dates the manifest he gives copy 3, 4 and 8 to the generator. The generator mails copy 3 to the state where the designated facility is located and copy 4 to the state where he is located. He keeps copy number 8 for his records. The transporter takes copies 1,2,5,6 and 7 with him to the designated facility where someone will verify acceptance of the shipment and sign and date the manifest. The representative from the designated facility will then give copy 7 to the transporter for his records. He keeps number 6 for his own records. He then mails copy 1 to the state where the designated facility is located, copy 2 to the state where the generator is located, and copy 5 is mailed back to the generator, who must retain it along with the copy 8 he already has for a period of three years.

If you do not receive a signed copy from the designated hazardous waste management facility within 35 days of the date of shipment, you must contact the transporter and/or the disposal facility to find out why. **It is important to remember that just because you have shipped the hazardous waste off your site and it is no longer in your possession, your liability has not ended. You are potentially liable for any mismanagement of your hazardous waste.** The manifest will help you to track your waste during shipment and make sure it arrives at the proper destination.

You can obtain blank copies of the manifest from several sources. To determine which source you should use, use this system:

Please print or type with ELITE type (12 characters per inch) in the unshaded areas only

Form Approved. OMB No. 2050-0028. Expires 10-31-91
GSA No. 0246-EPA-OT

Please refer to the *Instructions for Filing Notification* before completing this form. The information requested here is required by law *(Section 3010 of the Resource Conservation and Recovery Act).*	♻ EPA	Notification of Regulated Waste Activity	Date Received (For Official Use Only)
		United States Environmental Protection Agency	

I. Installation's EPA ID Number *(Mark 'X' in the appropriate box)*

☐ **A. First Notification**   ☐ **B. Subsequent Notification** *(complete item C)*   **C. Installation's EPA ID Number**

II. Name of Installation *(Include company and specific site name)*

III. Location of Installation *(Physical address not P.O. Box or Route Number)*

Street

Street (continued)

City or Town   State   ZIP Code

County Code   County Name

IV. Installation Mailing Address *(See Instructions)*

Street or P.O. Box

City or Town   State   ZIP Code

V. Installation Contact *(Person to be contacted regarding waste activities at site)*

Name *(last)*   *(first)*

Job Title   Phone Number *(area code and number)*

VI. Installation Contact Address *(See Instructions)*

A. Contact Address   Location ☐   Mailing ☐   B. Street or P.O. Box

City or Town   State   ZIP Code

VII. Ownership *(See Instructions)*

A. Name of Installation's Legal Owner

Street, P.O. Box, or Route Number

City or Town   State   ZIP Code

Phone Number *(area code and number)*   B. Land Type   C. Owner Type   D. Change of Owner Indicator   (Date Changed) Month Day Year

Yes ☐   No ☐

EPA Form 8700-12 (07-90) Previous edition is obsolete.   - 1 -

Please print or type with ELITE type (12 characters per inch) in the unshaded areas only

Form Approved. OMB No. 2050-0028. Expires 10-31-91
GSA No. 0246-EPA-OT

ID – For Official Use Only

VIII. Type of Regulated Waste Activity (Mark 'X' in the appropriate boxes. Refer to instructions.)

A. Hazardous Waste Activity

1. Generator (See Instructions)
   - a. Greater than 1000kg/mo (2,200 lbs.)
   - b. 100 to 1000 kg/mo (220 - 2,200 lbs.)
   - c. Less than 100 kg/mo (220 lbs.)
2. Transporter (Indicate Mode in boxes 1-5 below)
   - a. For own waste only
   - b. For commercial purposes

   Mode of Transportation:
   1. Air
   2. Rail
   3. Highway
   4. Water
   5. Other - specify

3. Treater, Storer, Disposer (at installation)
   Note: A permit is required for this activity; see instructions.
4. Hazardous Waste Fuel
   - a. Generator Marketing to Burner
   - b. Other Marketers
   - c. Burner - indicate device(s) - Type of Combustion Device
     1. Utility Boiler
     2. Industrial Boiler
     3. Industrial Furnace
5. Underground Injection Control

B. Used Oil Fuel Activities

1. Off-Specification Used Oil Fuel
   - a. Generator Marketing to Burner
   - b. Other Markerer
   - c. Burner - indicate device(s) - Type of Combustion Device
     1. Utility Boiler
     2. Industrial Boiler
     3. Industrial Furnace
2. Specification Used Oil Fuel Marketer (or On-site Burner) Who First Claims the Oil Meets the Specification

IX. Description of Regulated Wastes (Use additional sheets if necessary)

A. Characteristics of Nonlisted Hazardous Wastes. Mark 'X' in the boxes corresponding to the characteristics of nonlisted hazardous wastes your installation handles. (See 40 CFR Parts 261.20 - 261.24)

1. Ignitable (D001) 2. Corrosive (D002) 3. Reactive (D003) 4. Toxicity Characteristic (D000)

(List specific EPA hazardous waste number(s) for the Toxicity Characteristic contaminant(s))

B. Listed Hazardous Wastes. (See 40 CFR 261.31 - 33. See instructions if you need to list more than 12 waste codes.)

1 2 3 4 5 6
7 8 9 10 11 12

C. Other Wastes. (State or other wastes requiring an I.D. number. See instructions.)

1 2 3 4 5 6

X. Certification

I certify under penalty of law that I have personally examined and am familiar with the information submitted in this and all attached documents, and that based on my inquiry of those individuals immediately responsible for obtaining the information, I believe that the submitted information is true, accurate, and complete. I am aware that there are significant penalties for submitting false information, including the possibility of fines and imprisonment.

Signature	Name and Official Title (type or print)	Date Signed

XI. Comments

Note: Mail completed form to the appropriate EPA Regional or State Office. (See Section III of the booklet for addresses.)

1. If the state to which you are shipping your waste has its own manifest form, use that manifest form.

2. If the state to which you are shipping your waste does not have its own manifest, use the manifest of the state in which your waste was generated.

New York State has its own manifest form. A sample NYS Hazardous Waste Manifest form is presented in Figure 3. When you sign the certification in item 16 you are personally confirming that:

1. The manifest is complete and accurately describes the shipment.

2. The shipment is ready for transport.

3. You have considered whether, given your budget, your waste management arrangements are the best to reduce the amount and hazardous nature of your wastes.

If you are a generator in New York State, you may obtain NYS manifest forms from the NYS Environmental Conservation Regional Office nearest to you, see Appendix A. If you are a generator outside NYS who wishes to ship to a facility in NYS, you may obtain manifest forms from the Central Office of the NYS Environmental Conservation Department by calling (518) 457-6858.

TRANSPORT REQUIREMENTS

Category 2 Small Quantity Generators in NYS may accumulate up to 6000 kilograms (13,200 pounds) of hazardous waste for up to 180 days or for up to 270 days if they must ship to a TSDF over 200 miles away. Transporters of hazardous waste in NYS must possess NYS Part 364 Waste Transporter Permits and may only transport hazardous wastes to TSDFs which are authorized to accept hazardous waste. Since generators of hazardous waste may be held responsible for mismanagement of their waste after it has left their premises, it is advisable for generators to ensure that they use only duly authorized transporters and TSDFs.

One of the best ways to select a permitted waste transporter is to contact the Waste Transporter Permit Section of the NYSDEC at (518) 457-3254. Section personnel will be able to provide you with computer generated listings of currently permitted waste transporters of designated types of hazardous waste from which you may select the transporter who is best able to fulfill your specific needs.

You should contact the hauler and the TSDF to verify that they have EPA Identification Numbers and that they can and will handle your waste. Also, make sure that they have current permits, adequate insurance, and that the hauler's vehicles are in good condition. Choosing a transporter and a TSDF may take some time, therefore try to begin your search well ahead of the time you will need to ship your waste.

When you prepare hazardous waste for shipment, you must put the waste in containers acceptable for transportation. Make sure the containers are properly labelled and in compliance with applicable NYS DOT Regulations. To determine labelling requirements for your wastes, contact this Department, your transporter, or your TSDF.

48-14-1 (3/89)—7f

Please print or type. Do not Staple.

STATE OF NEW YORK
DEPARTMENT OF ENVIRONMENTAL CONSERVATION
DIVISION OF HAZARDOUS SUBSTANCES REGULATION

HAZARDOUS WASTE MANIFEST
P.O. Box 12820, Albany, New York 12212

Form Approved. OMB No. 2050-0039. Expires 9-30-94

In case of emergency or spill immediately call the National Response Center (800) 424-8802 and the N.Y. Dept. of Environmental Conservation (518) 457-7362.

UNIFORM HAZARDOUS WASTE MANIFEST	1. Generator's US EPA No.		Manifest Document No:	2. Page 1 of	Information in the shaded areas is not required by Federal Law.

3. Generator's Name and Mailing Address	A. State Manifest Document No.
	NY B 555983 1
4. Generator's Phone ( )	B. Generator's ID
5. Transporter 1 (Company Name)	6. US EPA ID Number	C. State Transporter's ID
		D. Transporter's Phone ( )
7. Transporter 2 (Company Name)	8. US EPA ID Number	E. State Transporter's ID
		F. Transporter's Phone ( )
9. Designated Facility Name and Site Address	10. US EPA ID Number	G. State Facility's ID
		H. Facility's Phone ( )

GENERATOR

11. US DOT Description (Including Proper Shipping Name, Hazard Class and ID Number)	12. Containers		13. Total Quantity	14. Unit Wt/Vol	I. Waste No.
	No.	Type			
a.					EPA
					STATE
b.					EPA
					STATE
c.					EPA
					STATE
d.					EPA
					STATE

J. Additional Descriptions for Materials listed Above	K. Handling Codes for Wastes Listed Above
a c	a c
b d	b d

15. Special Handling Instructions and Additional Information

16. GENERATOR'S CERTIFICATION: I hereby declare that the contents of this consignment are fully and accurately described above by proper shipping name and are classified, packed, marked and labeled, and are in all respects in proper condition for transport by highway according to applicable international and national government regulations and state laws and regulations.

If I am a large quantity generator, I certify that I have program in place to reduce the volume and toxicity of waste generated to the degree I have determined to be economically practicable and that I have selected the practicable method treatment, storage, or disposal currently available to me which minimizes the present and future threat to human health and the environment; OR if I am a small generator, I have made a good faith effort to minimize my waste and select the best waste management method that is available to me and that I can afford.

Printed/Typed Name	Signature	Mo. Day Year

TRANSPORTER

17. Transporter 1 (Acknowledgement of Receipt of Materials)

Printed/Typed Name	Signature	Mo. Day Year

18. Transporter 2 (Acknowledgement or Receipt of Materials)

Printed/Typed Name	Signature	Mo. Day Year

FACILITY

19. Discrepancy Indication Space

20. Facility Owner or Operator: Certification of receipt of hazardous materials covered by this manifest except as noted in Item 19.

Printed/Typed Name	Signature	Mo. Day Year

EPA Form 8700-22 (Rev. 9-88) Previous editions are obsolete.

NY B 555983 1

COPY 1–Disposer State–Mailed by TSD Facility

LAND DISPOSAL RESTRICTIONS

New York State has adopted Land Disposal Restrictions (LDRs) which Congress passed into law in 1984. The LDRs require treatment of hazardous wastes before disposal. Examples of wastes that must treated include used solvents, metal wastes, cyanide-containing wastes, and other types of hazardous wastes.

Since November 1988, small quantity generators that generate more than 100 kilograms of hazardous waste in any calendar month have been affected by the LDRs. The LDRS include:

1. **Notification/Certification to Treatment, Storage or Disposal Facility**

    The notification must include:

    ● the hazardous waste code(s) and constituent to be monitored (F001-F005, F039, D001, D002, and D012-D043) or the treatment standard;
    ● any subcategories;
    ● the manifest number associated with the waste shipment;

    The certification must include:

    ● all of the above;
    ● the waste analysis data (if available);
    ● a signed certification statement.

2. **Record Keeping**

    Maintain the following for at least five (5) years:

    ● waste analysis records;
    ● notifications/certifications to treatment, storage and disposal facilities, waste analysis data, if available, tolling agreement (reclamation exemption) and any other documents associated with your waste management;
    ● any constituent monitoring.

    Some commonly asked questions are:

    ● Is my hazardous waste subject to the LDRs?
    - Yes, unless specifically exempt or excluded.

    ● Is my hazardous waste subject to the LDRs even if it is not being land disposed (e.g. recycled waste)?
    - Yes.

    ● Do I need a laboratory analysis done on my hazardous waste?
    - No, if contents are known, and waste can be classified by a generator's knowledge (analysis may be necessary initially, but not every time waste is generated).

    ● How long do I need to keep my paperwork?
    - 5 years.

    ● What types of paperwork do I need?
    - Notifications/certifications; waste analysis, if available, tolling agreement (reclamation agreement) and any other documents associated with your waste management practices.

    If a broker, hauler or facility handles your paperwork for you, use the above section as a checklist to ensure that all LDR requirements are met. Keep copies of all paperwork that you sign.

APPENDIX **XXV**

Template for Hazardous Waste Management Program

SOURCE:

P-F Technical Services, Inc.

HAZARDOUS WASTE MANAGEMENT PROGRAM TABLE OF CONTENTS

662

A. FACILITY DESCRIPTION

This section should contain a description of the location of the facility, the length of time the firm has been in business, the products it makes, the processes used to make the product and a brief generic description of the materials used and wastes generated.

B. JOB DESCRIPTION HAZARDOUS WASTE OPERATOR/MANAGEMENT

The firm does not maintain formal job descriptions at this time. Job titles and responsibilities are generally acknowledged to cover the duties and requirements as commonly defined in general manufacturing industries.

The following job description was written to provide for the communication of RCRA/hazardous waste information pertaining to the duties and requirements of individuals designated to take part in the management and handling of Hazardous Materials and Wastes.

DUTIES

In addition to other responsibilities designated by the company, the Hazardous Waste Operator/Manager will perform the following functions:

1. Inspect hazardous waste facilities.
2. Maintain operating records, manifests, etc. as required.
3. Tally, inspect and record waste placed into the container storage area.
4. Transport waste in the plant.
5. Assure that all waste is segregated by category.
6. Provide for the safe handling and storage of the hazardous waste.
7. All other activities as they relate to hazardous waste.

JOB REQUIREMENTS

Must be a high school graduate, or possess a high school equivalency certificate, or have demonstrated the ability to do the work required.

Must be physically able to perform the work.

Must have a working knowledge of the work and be familiar with the materials generally handled. Must demonstrate the ability, integrity and intelligence necessary to fulfill the requirements of the job.

Must complete initial hazardous waste management training program and an annual training update.

C. HAZARDOUS WASTE MANAGEMENT TRAINING PROGRAM

OBJECTIVES:

The Hazardous Waste Management Training Program is intended to provide a positive, motivational learning experience for employees and foster a cooperative attitude in the workplace.

The program is designed to:

Provide an overview as to the nature of hazardous waste and the waste stream.

Inform as to the required identification, segregation, labeling, packaging, storage and shipping of hazardous wastes.

Identify the equipment and procedures to be followed in the event of an emergency involving hazardous materials and/or wastes.

Familiarize with the company's Contingency Plan.

In general, the program is planned to develop an appreciation for the RCRA (Resource Conservation and Recovery) regulations and the safety requirements imposed on the generator of hazardous wastes.

WHO SHOULD ATTEND

All supervisors and employees who work at jobs that use or produce hazardous wastes.

After the initial training program, an annual update will be scheduled for the subject personnel.

Any new employee who will be involved with hazardous waste will receive a training session prior to commencing work.

RECORDS

All participants in the training program will sign a roster and a statement acknowledging the subjects discussed in the program. A copy of the statement and roster is attached.

FORMAT

The program will be conducted in a classroom setting for all supervisors and key personnel. They will be trained in subject matter as outlined below.

All employees having work which involves the handling, storage, shipping or record maintenance of hazardous waste will participate.

Visual aids, posters, blackboard and hand-outs will be utilized to reinforce the training program.

OUTLINE OF PROGRAM

1. Overview of the basic elements of RCRA and state regulations.

2. Definition of hazardous waste.

3. Description of waste generated on site.

4. Hazardous waste minimization and storage facilities.

5. Packaging requirements; segregation of wastes.

6. Labeling requirements.

7. Manifests; record keeping.

8. Contingency and evacuation plans.

9. Emergency alarm and containment equipment (systems).

10. General safety rules when working with hazardous materials/wastes.

D. LABELING HAZARDOUS WASTE CONTAINERS

All drums of hazardous waste generated and packaged will be labeled in accordance with the applicable regulations of the US Department of Transportation (49 CFR 172), as referenced in NYS DEC 6 NYCRR Part 372.2(a)(5).

At the start of a new drum, the attached label will be adhered to the outside of the container. It must be visible at all times.

Complete the following items at this time on the label:

1. Name of company

2. Address

3. EPA ID Number

4. EPA Waste No.

5. Accumulation Start Date (date hazardous material is first placed in the drum).

When the drum is placed into the storage area, make sure that the label is visible at all times.

ATTACHMENT: HAZARDOUS WASTE LABEL

E. HAZARDOUS MATERIALS AND WASTE INSPECTION PROGRAM

The purpose of the inspection program is to detect any condition or malfunction of equipment that could result in the release of hazardous waste to the environment. Once identified these conditions can be promptly corrected.

The hazardous Materials and Waste Storage areas are to be inspected weekly to detect leaks or other deterioration caused by corrosion or other factors. Compliance with labeling and safety regulations are part of the inspection.

Attached is a copy of the INSPECTION LOG used in the weekly evaluation of the storage area. The log is designed to detect any problem or condition that could cause a spill or unpermitted discharge from the containers.

The inspection also allows for the notation or recommended (required) remedial action, and follow-up on previous recommendations.

Inspection Logs will be maintained by the company for a period of not less than three years minimum.

EMPLOYEE ACKNOWLEDGEMENT OF TRAINING PROGRAM

I, the undersigned employee of   have
received information and training regarding the nature and
management of Hazardous Waste which is generated in our
operations.

I have been informed of the following items as they pertain to
the handling, storage and shipment of hazardous wastes:

1. Nature of Hazardous Wastes.

2. The Waste Stream (Cradle to Grave).

3. Importance of identifying, segregating and storing
    hazardous wastes.

4. Proper maintenance of containers and storage area.

5. Labeling of hazardous waste as required.

6. Shipping of hazardous waste by authorized carriers.

7. Procedure for inspection of storage area and drums.

8. Procedure for inspection and use of emergency response
    equipment and supplies.

9. Operation of communications and alarm systems.

10. Responses to fires and explosions.

11. Responses to spills.

12. Evacuation and shutdown of operations (drills).

My training has been supplemented by additional information
relative to the recognition and handling of hazardous materials
in the workplace, including precautions to be taken in the
event of exposure or an emergency occurrence.

DATE . . . .   NAME   . . . .

                                        SIGNED   . . . .

HAZARDOUS MATERIALS AND WASTE INSPECTION LOG

DATE.....

INSPECTION ITEMS	YES	NO	YES	NO	YES	NO	YES	NO
STORAGE AREAS								
QUANTITY IN HOUSE								
1. Any visible drum leaks								
2. Any signs of drum deterioration								
3. Is area clear of obstructions								
4. Are fire extinguishers in place								
5. Have minor spills been cleaned up								
6. Are all drums labeled properly								
7. Is absorbent material available								
OPERATING AREAS								
8. Are there signs of spilled materials around equipment								
9. Are all containers labeled properly								
10. Is safety gear used and in proper place								
11. Have previous action items been completed								
12. GENERAL COMMENTS								
15. REQUIRED ACTION ITEMS								

INSPECTED BY: _____

RECEIVED BY: _____

DATE: _____

F. OSHA/HAZARDOUS WASTE CONTINGENCY PLAN

I. OBJECTIVE

To outline the responsibilities and procedures to be taken in the event of fire, explosion or spills of hazardous materials or wastes.

II. EMERGENCY COORDINATORS

A. Primary Coordinator

Home Phone Number

B. Secondary Coordinator

Home Phone Number

C. After business hours, contact

Home Phone Number

III. GENERAL PLAN OF ACTION

A. FIRE OR EXPLOSION

1. Evacuate building (shut all power to equipment).
Employees are to assemble at entrance to

2. Call Fire and Police Departments.
3. Call Primary Coordinator.
4. Call Secondary Coordinator.
5. Contain fire within limits set for plant personnel until arrival of Fire Department; abandon efforts if limit is exceeded.

B. CHEMICAL SPILLAGE

1. Evacuate building (shut all power to equipment and stop any flow of solvents or inks)
2. Call Police and Fire Departments.
3. Call Primary Coordinator
4. Call Secondary Coordinator
5. Contain spill within limits of in-plant personnel and emergency equipment
6. Call emergency environmental agency to arrange for containment and clean-up in accordance with DEP regulations.

IV. EMERGENCY ALARM AND EXTINGUISHING SYSTEMS

A. Location of all emergency alarm and containment equipment is indicated on the enclosed plant layout.

Terminology and codes are as follows:

FP – Fire Extinguishers-ABC Powder
FW – Fire Extinguishers-Water
A – Alarm bells or loudspeakers
Tel – Telephones accessible to plant
Exit – Exits from various departments and building (arrows indicate directions)
First Aid – location of first aid supplies.
Bathroom facilities noted.
Manufacturing and storage areas indicated.

B. Fire Extinguishers

1. Number in building – First Floor

ABC Powder (quantity)
CO_2 Water (quantity)
Other (quantity)

2. Service and inspection performed by:

C. Alarm System

1. Telephones located in administrative office and plant offices.

2. Loudspeakers(intercom) located at central points in plant.

3. Loudspeakers (intercom) can be activated by contacting receptionist or by dialing designated loudspeaker or paging intercom number. Speak clearly into mouthpiece and message will be transmitted over the intercom loudspeakers.

4. Alarm bells for sprinkler system will be sounded when sprinklers are activated.

Sprinkler system is serviced by:

Fire Alarm System is contracted to:

D. CHEMICAL SPILLAGE EQUIPMENT

1. Adequate supply of absorbent rags or materials to contain and absorb minor spills will be maintained in operating departments and storage areas.

2. Respiratory equipment, gloves and goggles are maintained in designated operating departments for normal operations requiring protective gear, as well as for any emergency which may arise.

3. In the event of a major spill, outside emergency support for containment and clean-up will be provided by an authorized clean-up contractor, who will perform in accordance with NYSDEC regulations.

IV. EMERGENCY PROCEDURES

A. GENERAL EVACUATION PROCEDURE

When fire, explosion or spillages alarm is activated, all personnel are to leave their stations and walk to the closest exit from the plant, via the assigned route from their departments to the assigned exits.

Should the assigned route and/or exit be blocked by the fire, explosion or spill, alternative means of departure will be designated by the supervisor (foreman) in the area.

The employees will assemble in the designated areas outside and away from the building for the purpose of a head count to assure that all personnel are present. This will assure that employees have not been left in the plant.

Simultaneously with the evacuation of the plant, designated personnel will man the emergency equipment to contain or eliminate the emergency condition. All power will be shut off and the flow of liquid chemicals stopped.

At such time as the Fire Department arrives, or the emergency conditions exceed the ability of the personnel to contain it, the plant emergency brigades will withdraw from the scene of the incident and the building.

B. EMERGENCY ENVIRONMENTAL PROCEDURES

The specific emergency procedures as related to the exposure of chemical hazards and/or hazardous wastes are as follows:

1. Whenever there is an imminent or actual emergency situation, the Emergency Coordinator (or a designee when the Emergency Coordinator is on call) shall immediately:

   a. Identify the character, exact source, amount and real extent of any discharged materials.

   b. Activate internal facility alarms or communications systems, where applicable, to notify all facility personnel.

   c. Notify appropriate State or Local Agencies with designated response rolls if their help is needed.

2. Concurrently, the Emergency Coordinator shall assess possible hazards to human health or the environment that may result from the discharge, fire or explosion. This assessment shall consider both direct and indirect effects of the discharge, fire or explosion.

3. If the Emergency Coordinator determines that the facility has had a discharge, fire or explosion which would threaten human health or the environment outside the facility, the Emergency Coordinator shall:

   a. Immediately notify appropriate local authorities if an assessment indicates that evacuation of local areas may be advisable. This will include the Fire Department, Local Environmental Planning Committee of the NYCDEP, and any other agencies required.

   The Emergency Coordinator shall be available to help appropriate officials decide whether local areas should be evacuated.

b. Immediately notify the New York Department of Environmental Conservation — (518) 457-7362 and the Nassau County Spill Hotline.

c. When notifying the Department of Environmental Conservation pursuant to subsection 373-3.4g (4)(ii) report:

(1) Name and telephone number of reporter

(2) Name and address of facility

(3) Time and type of incident

(4) The type of substance and the estimated quantity discharged (if known)

(5) The location of the discharge

(6) The extent of injuries, if any

(7) The possible hazards to human health, or the environment outside the facility.

4. During the emergency, the Emergency Coordinator shall take all reasonable measures necessary to ensure that fire, explosion and discharge do not occur, recur, or spread to other chemical materials or hazardous wastes at the facility. These measures must include, where applicable, stopping processes and operations, collecting and containing released chemicals and/or waste, and removing or isolating containers of chemicals and wastes.

5. If the facility stops operations in response to a fire, explosion or discharge, the Emergency Coordinator shall monitor for leaks, pressure build-ups, gas generation, or ruptures in valves, pipes or other equipment, wherever this is appropriate.

6. Immediately after an emergency, the Emergency Coordinator shall provide for treating, storing or disposing of recovered waste, contaminated soil or surface water, or any other material that results from a discharge, fire or explosion at the facility.

All hazardous wastes produced by the incident shall be disposed in accordance with the applicable requirements of Part 372 and Subpart 373-2 of the NYSDEC Hazardous Waste Management Regulations (6NYCRR).

7. The Emergency Coordinator shall insure that in the affected areas of the facility:

a. No waste that may be incompatible with the discharge materials is treated, stored or disposed of until clean-up procedures are completed.

b. All emergency equipment listed in the contingency plan is cleaned and fit for its intended use before operations are resumed.

8. The owner and operator shall notify the Department of Environmental Conservation and appropriate local authorities that the facility is in compliance with subparagraph 373-3.4(g)(8) before operations are resumed in the affected areas of the facility.

9. The owner and/or operator shall note in the operating record, the time, date and details of any incident that require implementing the contingency plan. Within fifteen (15) days after the incident, the owner/operator shall submit a written report on the incident to the Department.

The report shall include but not be limited to:

a. Name, address and telephone number of the owner or operator.

b. Name, address and telephone number of the facility.

c. Date, time and type of incident.

d. Name and quantity of material involved.

e. The extent of injuries (if any).

f. An assessment of actual or potential hazards to human health or the environment, where this is possible.

g. Assessment of the scope and magnitude of the problem(s).

h. Description of the immediate actions that have been taken and the estimated quantity and disposition of recovered material that resulted from the incident.

i. Provide implementation schedule for under taking suggested measure(s) to eliminate the problem(s).

CONTACTS FOR EMERGENCY SERVICE IN THE EVENT OF FIRE, EXPLOSION OR SPILLS OF HAZARDOUS MATERIALS OR WASTES

IN-PLANT EMERGENCY COORDINATORS:

  PRIMARY COORDINATOR - (name and telephone number)

  SECONDARY COORDINATOR - (name and telephone number)

  AFTER BUSINESS HOURS - (name and telephone number)

  FIRST AID SUPPLIES/SERVICES - (name and telephone number)

OUTSIDE AGENCIES

  EMERGENCY HOTLINE: 911

  FIRE DEPARTMENT:

  POLICE DEPARTMENT:

  HOSPITAL:

  FIRE EXTINGUISHERS:

  SPRINKLER SYSTEM:

  ENVIRONMENTAL CLEANUP:

  NASSAU COUNTY - SPILL HOTLINE:

  POISON CONTROL:

  NY STATE DEC, SPILL RESPONSE: 1-800-457-7362

  FEDERAL EPA NATIONAL RESPONSE CENTER: 1-800-424-8802

G. SAMPLE LETTERS TO EMERGENCY AGENCIES

To Fire and Police Departments and Hospital.

Dear   :

In accordance with the OSHA Hazard Communication Standard and other
Federal, City and State of New York environmental regulations concerning
the use and storage of Hazardous Materials and Wastes, we are advising
you of the materials used and stored by   at its
manufacturing facilities, located at

(address of facility)

is a manufacturer of

(description of product, processes)

Our products are not hazardous if used properly, but we do employ metals,
paints, thinners, compressed gases and other materials in the process that
are, or could be, considered hazardous.

A complete collection of Material Safety Data Sheets and a Chemical
Inventory is maintained on our premises, and is available for review by
your personnel.

The emergency contingency plan which has been developed for the facility is
attached for your information.

This letter is to advise you of the chemicals we use in the event that you
are called upon to assist in the care of an employee who has been exposed,
or in the event that your personnel respond to an emergency in our building.

We would be pleased to meet with representatives of your agency to tour our
facility, review our program and suggest any modifications to make our
program more effective.

Sincerely,

President

copies to Fire Dept., Police and Hospital

CLEAN-UP CONTRACTOR

```
Cleanup Contractor
7 Crag Road
Someplace, NJ 07001

Attention: James F. Handy

Dear Mr. Handy:

     This is to request your support in environmental emergencies which may
result in potential chemical spills of hazardous chemicals or wastes in or
near our plants at:

     (address in full)

     In the event of an emergency, we will notify you immediately and will
contain the spill to the best of our ability until the arrival of emergency
equipment and personnel from your firm.

     The containment and clean-up will be the responsibility of

     (name of supervisor in plant and his telephone number)

     A copy of our plant layout indicating the location of manufacturing areas
and storage of chemicals and other materials is attached. A complete Chemical
Inventory and set of Material Safety Data Sheets is available at the plant for
review by your personnel.

     It would be appreciated if you would verify this arrangement for our
records.

                                        Sincerely,
```

H. HAZARDOUS WASTE MANAGEMENT FILES

The following files will be maintained in the offices to document all activities and actions relative to the generation, storage, treatment and disposition of hazardous wastes.

> 1. Hazardous Waste Management Program including the Training and Emergency Contingency Plans.
>
> 2. Periodic Reports to New York State DEC and other agencies.
>
> 3. Manifests of all shipments of hazardous wastes.

4. Inspection reports of storage area.

5. Training records.

6. All miscellaneous correspondence relating to the generation, minimization, testing and shipment of hazardous wastes.

I. WASTE ANALYSIS PLAN

I. Waste Analysis Requirements

Before disposition, storage or treatment of a hazardous waste, its chemical and physical characteristics must be known. These characteristics may be determined through analysis or from knowledge of waste composition. This should include all information needed to store and treat the wastes in compliance with RCRA and New York State regulations.

II. Waste Analysis Plan

The firm produces a consistent hazardous waste stream composed of the solvents utilized in the following operations:

Based on analysis by an authorized laboratory, the hazardous waste consists of:

The waste is now transported for incineration (as a fuel substitute) or solvent recovery under the designations:

Any deviations due to mixed or new materials will be tested to characterize and classify them. If it is suspected that a waste may contain a listed hazardous substance (included in paragraphs 261.31-.33 of the RCRA regulations), an analytical method appropriate to that chemical will be employed.

Any waste of unknown composition may be analyzed to determine whether it exhibits any of the four characteristics of hazardous waste. Sampling will be conducted in accordance with the methods outlined in 40 CFR 261, Appendix I.

Actual analysis of the waste may not be required if sufficient data is available to determine its characteristics. If the waste has the same composition as a well known and long used product or raw material, its known properties are used to ensure proper on-site handling and storage.

Testing will be done by an independent outside laboratory to determine whether an unknown waste meets any of the following criteria:

CHARACTERISTIC	CRITERION	TEST
Ignitable Waste	1. Liquid with a flash point below 140 degrees F (60 C) except liquids containing less than 24% alcohol.	ASTM D-93-79
	2. Non-liquid that can cause fires through friction, absorption of moisture, or spontaneous chemical changes.	
	3. Ignitable compressed gas, per 49 CFR 173.300.	
	4. An oxidizer, per 49 CFR 173.151.	
Corrosive Waste	1. Aqueous liquid with pH of 2.0 or less.	NBS–Method 150.1
	2. Aqueous liquid of pH 12.5 or greater.	
	3. Corrodes steel (SAE 1020) at a rate greater than .250 inch (6.35 mm) per year at 130 degrees F.	

CHARACTERISTIC	CRITERION	TEST
Reactive Waste	1. Normally unstable; readily undergoes violent chemical change without detonation; reacts violently with water; forms potentially explosive mixtures with water; generates toxic gases, vapors or fumes when mixed with water; is a cyanide or sulfide bearing waste which can generate toxic gases, vapors or fumes when exposed to mild basic or acidic conditions.	
	2. Capable of detonation or explosive reaction on exposure to a strong initiating source.	
	3. Capable of detonation, explosive decom-position or reaction at normal temperatures and pressures.	
	4. Forbidden explosive per 49 CFR 173.51.	
	5. Class A explosive per 49 CFR 173.53.	
	6. Class B explosive per 49 CFR 173.88.	
EP Toxic Waste	The extract obtained from applying the RCRA extraction procedure has a concen-tration of a listed contaminant exceeding the limit given in the following table:	RCRA EP Toxicity Test

Contaminant	Concentration Limit (mg/l)
Arsenic	5.0 mg/1
Barium	100.00
Cadmium	1.0
Chromium(+6)	5.0
Lead	5.0
Mercury	0.2
Selenium	1.0
Silver	5.0
Endrin	0.02
Lindane	0.4
Methoxychlor	10.0
Toxaphene	0.5
2,4 D	10.0
2,4,5-TP Silvex	1.0

If it is believed that the unknown waste contains a RCRA listed chemical, an appropriate screening method will be used. For example, an analysis by gas chromatography (GC/mass spectrometry (MS)) may be used to identify volatile and non-volatile extractable organics.

III. Sampling Methods

Representative "grab" samples will be taken from drums in storage and placed in jars provided by the laboratory. This will be done in accordance with Appendix 19 of 6NYCRR or by use of an equivalent sampling method.

IV. Waste Analysis Records

A permanent file will be maintained of all analyses performed. It will be under the custody of the member of management designated to be responsible for compliance with Environmental Regulations.

Data generated by any testing will be used in determining:

A. Suitable conditions for storage.

B. Compatibility of waste with other materials in storage.

C. Proper setting for recycling equipment during distillation.

D. Proper methods of transportation and disposal.

The analyses become part of the facility's Operating Record.

V. Frequency of Waste Analysis

Waste analysis is conducted routinely and when wastes not previously generated at the facility are introduced into the waste stream, and are suspected to be hazardous.

Routine analysis of all hazardous wastes is to be repeated by (name of company) annually to assure that the analysis is accurate and up-to-date.

VI. Laboratory conducting analysis at present time is:
(name of laboratory)

Prepared: (date)

J. CLOSURE PLAN

1.0 INTRODUCTION AND BACKGROUND INFORMATION

1.1 Introduction

(Name of company) operates a manufacturing plant at

(address of facility)

As part of its activities,
generates, stores and disposes wastes which are classified as Hazardous by the United States Environmental Protection Agency (USEPA) and the New York State Department of Environmental Conservation (NYSDEC).

(Name of company) operates as a generator under an EPA identification number NYD

This closure plan has been prepared under the provisions of New York State Regulations 6NYCRR Subpart 373- 3.7, and constitutes the provisions for closing the facility at any such time in the future as determined by management. Any decision to this effect will be communicated to the NYSDEC in accordance with the provisions set forth in the regulations.

The purpose of this plan is to minimize the need for further maintenance of the facility after closure, and to ensure the maximum effort to control, minimize, and eliminate exposure of the plant personnel and community to health and environmental hazards.

1.2 Site History and Description of Activities

(Name of company) has occupied the facility at (street, city, state) since (year of operation).

Total space occupied by the building amounts to (quantity) square feet.

The company is engaged in the manufacture of (product, processes)

The equipment used includes (list of equipment)

Under the definitions of the RCRA and 6NYCRR regulations, the wastes generated by the printing operations are defined as hazardous.

Various chemicals are used in the process, including:
     (listing)

The waste is classified under current regulations as
     (to be provided)

RCRA Wastes are generated, drummed and stored in the hazardous waste area or the hazardous storage room.

The hazardous storage area is located
     (street, city, state)

The room has an impermeable concrete floor and walls that are designed to fully contain any spillage of hazardous wastes. Doorways are built up to retain any spillage or discharge of sprinkler water. The room is built in accordance with Fire Department and insurance codes for Ink Rooms/Vaults.

2.0   CLOSURE PROCEDURES

This section describes procedures to be followed in the event that the plant or any waste generating department is to be closed.

2.1   Waste Inventory

A maximum of (quantity) drums of hazardous waste is assumed in the storage area at the time of closure. It is anticipated that the drums will contain spent solvents.

2.2   Removal of Inventory

All hazardous waste is currently being inspected to ensure proper identification, packaging and labeling. Manifests will be prepared and the drums containing the hazardous waste will be transported by a licensed transporter to an off-site permitted Treatment, Storage and Disposal (TSD) facility.

(Name of company) has contracted with:
(Name of hazardous waste company)
to dispose of its hazardous wastes.

2.3   Decontamination Procedures

Following the removal of the containers from the storage area, procedures to decontaminate the area will be initiated. The source and quantity of labor required for the task will be contracted to an outside vendor at least 90 days prior to the closure.

Subsequent to the removal of wastes, the decontamination steps will be carried out for the floor slab, walls and miscellaneous fixtures such as supports and shelves.

Decontamination will be accomplished by cleaning the storage area with a biodegradable non-solvent based detergent wash, followed by high pressure steam cleaning. The wash operations will be conducted using an industrial washer equipped with rotating nylon and suction pick-up of wash/rinse waters. The steam cleaning operation will be repeated a minimum of three times.

The Decontamination Procedures will be repeated until visual inspection indicates that the storage area is clean.

After decontamination is completed, the resulting wash water will be collected in containers for treatment off-site. The third steam cleaning rinsate will be collected in a separate container for sampling purposes.

Equipment in contact with the hazardous waste will either be decontaminated or disposed of at an off-site facility. The procedures used for decontamination will be consistent with the procedures outlined above.

2.4   Closure Certification

Following the completion of the steps outlined in this plan, closure will be certified by a representative of (   ) and an independent registered Professional Engineer.

Certification will state that closure has been completed in accordance with the procedure outlined in the approved plan, with any deviation from the plan noted on the certification. It is expected that one inspection will be conducted by the Engineer.

2.5   Closure Cost Estimate and Schedule

Table I presents the estimated cost and schedule for closure of the hazardous waste storage area in accordance with the procedures presented in the plan. It is estimated that it will cost $10,125 to close the storage area.

TABLE I. HAZARDOUS WASTE STORAGE AREA
CLOSURE COST ESTIMATE AND SCHEDULE

CLOSURE STEP	COST	SCHEDULED DAYS (ELAPSED TIME)
1. Agency notification	—	—
2. Stop making waste		0
3. Remove drums of Hazardous Waste – 10 drums @ $500/drum	$ 5,000	10
4. Wash/steam clean floors, walls and miscellaneous equipment. Off-site disposal of rinse water.	5,000	25
5. Laboratory Analysis Fees	1,000	
6. Closure certification	2,000	35
7. Contingency cost (20%)	4,000	
8. Administrative cost (15%)	2,500	
CLOSURE COST ESTIMATE	$19,500	

3.0 SAMPLING AND ANALYSIS PLAN

The objective of the sampling and analysis plan is to document the hazardous waste storage area closure and to evaluate the effectiveness of the decontamination.

3.1 Sampling Location

A sample will be collected from the third rinsate collected during decontamination.

3.2 Analytical Parameters

The sample will be submitted to a NYSDEC certified laboratory for analysis of the parameters of concern:

EP Toxic Metals

Volatile Organics (US EPA 624)

It is anticipated that the test will be conducted by   in accordance with approved NYSDEC/USEPA analytical methods.

3.3 Sampling Methodology

The sample will be collected utilizing a dedicated Glass Open Tube (Thief) sampler and placed in laboratory cleaned sample containers. The sample containers will have the required preservatives originating from the laboratory.

3.4 Sample Documentation and Chain of Custody Procedures

Sample documentation and chain-of-custody procedures will include: sample labels, analysis request sheet, chain-of-custody forms, field log book and sample seals. A copy of the chain-of-custody form is attached.

The sample labels will contain the following information:

Sample Identification

Time and Date of Collection

Place of Collection

Initials of Collector

A sample seal will be placed on each sample container in such a way as to detect any unauthorized tampering. The sample seal will have the signature of the collector across the likely point of breakage.

A bound field log book will be used to record all field activities.

The chain-of-custody procedures will be initiated in the field and maintained by the laboratory.

3.5 Health and Safety Considerations

It is anticipated that the project personnel will be utilizing appropriate personnel protection equipment, and working in accordance with safe operating procedures. Detection monitors will be used to determine levels of Volatile Organics, and caution personnel to increase personal protection when levels rise.

4.   AMENDMENTS TO CLOSURE PLAN

The contents of this plan are subject to amendment at such time as the operation and its resulting hazardous waste stream(s) change, or prior to such time as Management makes the decision to close the facility and implement the plan.

All such amendments will be made and posted with the Commissioner of the New York State Department of Environmental Conservation, in accordance with the regulations 6NYCRR Subpart 373-3(c)(3).

NOTE: Substitute or supply appropriate information that pertains to your state and local contacts and regulations.

APPENDIX **XXVI**

Hazardous Waste Classifications

SOURCE:
USEPA, "Notification of Regulated
Waste Activity"

§ 261.20 General.

(a) A solid waste, as defined in § 261.2, which is not excluded from regulation as a hazardous waste under § 261.4(b), is a hazardous waste if it exhibits any of the characteristics identified in this subpart.

(b) A hazardous waste which is identified by a characteristic in this subpart, but is not listed as a hazardous waste in Subpart D, is assigned the EPA Hazardous Waste Number set forth in the respective characteristic in this subpart. This number must be used in complying with the notification requirements of section 3010 of the Act and certain recordkeeping and reporting requirements under Parts 262 through 265, 268, and Part 270 of this chapter.

(c) For purposes of this subpart, the Administrator will consider a sample obtained using any of the applicable sampling methods specified in Appendix I to be a representative sample within the meaning of Part 260 of this chapter.

[*Comment*: § 262.11 of this chapter sets forth the generator's responsibility to determine whether his waste exhibits one or more of the characteristics identified in this subpart]

[*Comment*: Since the Appendix I sampling methods are not being formally adopted by the Administrator, a person who desires to employ an alternative sampling method is not required to demonstrate the equivalency of his method under the procedures set forth in §§ 260.20 and 260.21.]

679

§ 261.21 Characteristic of ignitability.

(a) A solid waste exhibits the characteristic of ignitability if a representative sample of the waste has any of the following properties:

(1) It is a liquid, other than an aqueous solution containing less than 24 percent alcohol by volume and has flash point less than 60°C (140°F), as determined by a Pensky-Martens Closed Cup Tester, using the test method specified in ASTM Standard D-93-79 or D-93-80 (incorporated by reference, see § 260.11), or a Setaflash Closed Cup Tester, using the test method specified in ASTM Standard D-3278-78 (incorporated by reference, see § 260.11), or as determined by an equivalent test method approved by the Administrator under procedures set forth in §§ 260.20 and 260.21.

(2) It is not a liquid and is capable, under standard temperature and pressure, of causing fire through friction, absorption of moisture or spontaneous chemical changes and, when ignited, burns so vigorously and persistently that it creates a hazard.

(3) It is an ignitable compressed gas as defined in 49 CFR 173.300 and as determined by the test methods described in that regulation or equivalent test methods approved by the Administrator under §§ 260.20 and 260.21.

(4) It is an oxidizer as defined in 49 CFR 173.151.

(b) A solid waste that exhibits the characteristic of ignitability, but is not listed as a hazardous waste in Subpart D, has the EPA Hazardous Waste Number of D001.

§ 261.22 Characteristic of corrosivity.

(a) A solid waste exhibits the characteristic of corrosivity if a representative sample of the waste has either of the following properties:

(1) It is aqueous and has a pH less than or equal to 2 or greater than or equal to 12.5, as determined by a pH meter using either an EPA test method or an equivalent test method approved by the Administrator under the procedures set forth in §§ 260.20 and 260.21. The EPA test method for pH is specified as Method 5.2 in "Test Methods for the Evaluation of Solid Waste, Physical/Chemical Methods" (incorporated by reference, see § 260.11).

(2) It is a liquid and corrodes steel (SAE 1020) at a rate greater than 6.35 mm (0.250 inch) per year at a test temperature of 55°C (130°F) as determined by the test method specified in NACE (National Association of Corrosion Engineers) Standard TM-01-69 as standardized in "Test Methods for the Evaluation of Solid Waste, Physical/Chemical Methods" (incorporated by reference, see § 260.11) or an equivalent test method approved by the Administrator under the procedures set forth in §§ 260.20 and 260.21.

(b) A solid waste that exhibits the characteristic of corrosivity, but is not listed as a hazardous waste in Subpart D, has the EPA Hazardous Waste Number of D002.

§ 261.23 Characteristic of reactivity.

(a) A solid waste exhibits the characteristic of reactivity if a representative sample of the waste has *any* of the following properties:

(1) It is normally unstable and readily undergoes violent change without detonating.

(2) It reacts violently with water.

(3) It forms potentially explosive mixtures with water.

(4) When mixed with water, it generates toxic gases, vapors or fumes in a quantity sufficient to present a danger to human health or the environment.

(5) It is a cyanide or sulfide bearing waste which, when exposed to pH conditions between 2 and 12.5, can generate toxic gases, vapors or fumes in a quantity sufficient to present a danger to human health or the environment.

(6) It is capable of detonation or explosive reaction if it is subjected to a strong initiating source or if heated under confinement.

(7) It is readily capable of detonation or explosive decomposition or reaction at standard temperature and pressure.

(8) It is a forbidden explosive as defined in 49 CFR 173.51, or a Class A explosive as defined in 49 CFR 173.53

or a Class B explosive as defined in 49 CFR 173.88.

(b) A solid waste that exhibits the characteristic of reactivity, but is not listed as a hazardous waste in Subpart D, has the EPA Hazardous Waste Number of D003.

§ 261.24 Characteristic of EP toxicity.

(a) A solid waste exhibits the characteristic of EP toxicity if, using the test methods described in Appendix II or equivalent methods approved by the Administrator under the procedures set forth in §§ 260.20 and 260.21, the extract from a representative sample of the waste contains any of the contaminants listed in Table I at a concentration equal to or greater than the respective value given in that Table. Where the waste contains less than 0.5 percent filterable solids, the waste itself, after filtering, is considered to be the extract for the purposes of this section.

(b) A solid waste that exhibits the characteristic of EP toxicity, but is not listed as a hazardous waste in Subpart D, has the EPA Hazardous Waste Number specified in Table I which corresponds to the toxic contaminant causing it to be hazardous.

TABLE I—MAXIMUM CONCENTRATION OF CONTAMINANTS FOR CHARACTERISTIC OF EP TOXICITY

EPA hazardous waste number	Contaminant	Maximum concentration (milligrams per liter)
D004	Arsenic	5.0
D005	Barium	100.0
D006	Cadmium	1.0
D007	Chromium	5.0
D008	Lead	5.0
D009	Mercury	0.2
D010	Selenium	1.0
D011	Silver	5.0
D012	Endrin (1,2,3,4,10,10-hexachloro-1,7-epoxy-1,4,4a,5,6,7,8,8a-octahydro-1,4-endo, endo-5,8-dimethano-naphthalene.	0.02
D013	Lindane (1,2,3,4,5,6-hexa- chlorocyclohexane, gamma isomer.	0.4
D014	Methoxychlor (1,1,1-Trichloro-2,2-bis [p-methoxyphenyl]ethane).	10.0
D015	Toxaphene ($C_{10}H_{10}Cl_8$, Technical chlorinated camphene, 67–69 percent chlorine).	0.5

TABLE I—MAXIMUM CONCENTRATION OF CONTAMINANTS FOR CHARACTERISTIC OF EP TOXICITY—Continued

EPA hazardous waste number	Contaminant	Maximum concentration (milligrams per liter)
D016	2,4-D, (2,4-Dichlorophenoxyacetic acid).	10.0
D017	2,4,5-TP Silvex (2,4,5-Trichlorophenoxypropionic acid).	1.0

Subpart D—Lists of Hazardous Wastes

§ 261.30 General.

(a) A solid waste is a hazardous waste if it is listed in this subpart, unless it has been excluded from this list under §§ 260.20 and 260.22.

(b) The Administrator will indicate his basis for listing the classes or types of wastes listed in this Subpart by employing one or more of the following Hazard Codes:

Ignitable Waste	(I)
Corrosive Waste	(C)
Reactive Waste	(R)
EP Toxic Waste	(E)
Acute Hazardous Waste	(H)
Toxic Waste	(T)

Appendix VII identifies the constituent which caused the Administrator to list the waste as an EP Toxic Waste (E) or Toxic Waste (T) in §§ 261.31 and 261.32.

(c) Each hazardous waste listed in this subpart is assigned an EPA Hazardous Waste Number which precedes the name of the waste. This number must be used in complying with the notification requirements of Section 3010 of the Act and certain recordkeeping and reporting requirements under Parts 262 through 265, 268, and Part 270 of this chapter.

(d) The following hazardous wastes listed in § 261.31 or § 261.32 are subject to the exclusion limits for acutely hazardous wastes established in § 261.5: EPA Hazardous Wastes Nos. FO20, FO21, FO22, FO23, FO26, and FO27.

§ 261.31 Hazardous wastes from non-specific sources.

The following solid wastes are listed hazardous wastes from non-specific sources unless they are excluded under §§ 260.20 and 260.22 and listed in Appendix IX.

Industry and EPA hazardous waste No.	Hazardous waste	Hazard code
Generic:		
F001..........	The following spent halogenated solvents used in degreasing: Tetrachloroethylene, trichloroethylene, methylene chloride, 1,1,1-trichloroethane, carbon tetrachloride, and chlorinated fluorocarbons; all spent solvent mixtures/blends used in degreasing containing, before use, a total of ten percent or more (by volume) of one or more of the above halogenated solvents or those solvents listed in F002, F004, and F005; and still bottoms from the recovery of these spent solvents and spent solvent mixtures.	(T)
F002..........	The following spent halogenated solvents: Tetrachloroethylene, methylene chloride, trichloroethylene, 1,1,1-trichloroethane, chlorobenzene, 1,1,2-trichloro-1,2,2-trifluoroethane, ortho-dichlorobenzene, trichlorofluoromethane, and 1,1,2-trichloroethane; all spent solvent mixtures/blends containing, before use, a total of ten percent or more (by volume) of one or more of the above halogenated solvents or those listed in F001, F004, or F005; and still bottoms from the recovery of these spent solvents and spent solvent mixtures.	(T)
F003..........	The following spent non-halogenated solvents: Xylene, acetone, ethyl acetate, ethyl benzene, ethyl ether, methyl isobutyl ketone, n-butyl alcohol, cyclohexanone, and methanol; all spent solvent mixtures/blends containing, before use, only the above spent non-halogenated solvents; and all spent solvent mixtures/blends containing, before use, one or more of the above non-halogenated solvents, and, a total of ten percent or more (by volume) of one or more of those solvents listed in F001, F002, F004, and F005; and still bottoms from the recovery of these spent solvents and spent solvent mixtures.	(I)*
F004..........	The following spent non-halogenated solvents: Cresols and cresylic acid, and nitrobenzene; all spent solvent mixtures/blends containing, before use, a total of ten percent or more (by volume) of one or more of the above non-halogenated solvents or those solvents listed in F001, F002, and F005; and still bottoms from the recovery of these spent solvents and spent solvent mixtures.	(T)
F005..........	The following spent non-halogenated solvents: Toluene, methyl ethyl ketone, carbon disulfide, isobutanol, pyridine, benzene, 2-ethoxyethanol, and 2-nitropropane; all spent solvent mixtures/blends containing, before use, a total of ten percent or more (by volume) of one or more of the above non-halogenated solvents or those solvents listed in F001, F002, or F004; and still bottoms from the recovery of these spent solvents and spent solvent mixtures.	(I,T)
F006..........	Wastewater treatment sludges from electroplating operations except from the following processes: (1) Sulfuric acid anodizing of aluminum; (2) tin plating on carbon steel; (3) zinc plating (segregated basis) on carbon steel; (4) aluminum or zinc-aluminum plating on carbon steel; (5) cleaning/stripping associated with tin, zinc and aluminum plating on carbon steel; and (6) chemical etching and milling of aluminum.	(T)
F019..........	Wastewater treatment sludges from the chemical conversion coating of aluminum........	(T)
F007..........	Spent cyanide plating bath solutions from electroplating operations....................	(R, T)
F008..........	Plating bath residues from the bottom of plating baths from electroplating operations where cyanides are used in the process.	(R, T)
F009..........	Spent stripping and cleaning bath solutions from electroplating operations where cyanides are used in the process.	(R, T)
F010..........	Quenching bath residues from oil baths from metal heat treating operations where cyanides are used in the process.	(R, T)
F011..........	Spent cyanide solutions from salt bath pot cleaning from metal heat treating operations.	(R, T)
F012..........	Quenching waste water treatment sludges from metal heat treating operations where cyanides are used in the process.	(T)
F024..........	Wastes, including but not limited to, distillation residues, heavy ends, tars, and reactor clean-out wastes from the production of chlorinated aliphatic hydrocarbons, having carbon content from one to five, utilizing free radical catalyzed processes. [This listing does not include light ends, spent filters and filter aids, spent dessicants, wastewater, wastewater treatment sludges, spent catalysts, and wastes listed in § 261.32.].	(T)
F020..........	Wastes (except wastewater and spent carbon from hydrogen chloride purification) from the production or manufacturing use (as a reactant, chemical intermediate, or component in a formulating process) of tri- or tetrachlorophenol, or of intermediates used to produce their pesticide derivatives. (This listing does not include wastes from the production of Hexachlorophene from highly purified 2,4,5-trichlorophenol.).	(H)

Industry and EPA hazardous waste No.	Hazardous waste	Hazard code
F021	Wastes (except wastewater and spent carbon from hydrogen chloride purification) from the production or manufacturing use (as a reactant, chemical intermediate, or component in a formulating process) of pentachlorophenol, or of intermediates used to produce its derivatives.	(H)
F022	Wastes (except wastewater and spent carbon from hydrogen chloride purification) from the manufacturing use (as a reactant, chemical intermediate, or component in a formulating process) of tetra-, penta-, or hexachlorobenzenes under alkaline conditions.	(H)
F023	Wastes (except wastewater and spent carbon from hydrogen chloride purification) from the production of materials on equipment previously used for the production or manufacturing use (as a reactant, chemical intermediate, or component in a formulating process) of tri- and tetrachlorophenols. (This listing does not include wastes from equipment used only for the production or use of Hexachlorophene from highly purified 2,4,5-trichlorophenol.).	(H)
F026	Wastes (except wastewater and spent carbon from hydrogen chloride purification) from the production of materials on equipment previously used for the manufacturing use (as a reactant, chemical intermediate, or component in a formulating process) of tetra-, penta-, or hexachlorobenzene under alkaline conditions.	(H)
F027	Discarded unused formulations containing tri-, tetra-, or pentachlorophenol or discarded unused formulations containing compounds derived from these chlorophenols. (This listing does not include formulations containing Hexachlorophene sythesized from prepurified 2,4,5-trichlorophenol as the sole component.).	(H)
F028	Residues resulting from the incineration or thermal treatment of soil contaminated with EPA Hazardous Waste Nos. F020, F021, F022, F023, F026, and F027.	(T)

*(I,T) should be used to specify mixtures containing ignitable and toxic constituents.

Pretreatment Standards for Process Waste Water

SOURCE:

USEPA, EPA/625/10-86/005

Restrictions on the pollutant content of wastewaters discharged by industry into municipal sewage systems have existed in some localities for many years. The Milwaukee Metropolitan Sewerage District, for example, has regulated pH, oil and grease, and temperature levels in industrial wastewaters since the 1920s . Such regulations are the predecessors of modern pretreatment programs, which include both national standards and local programs to control industrial pollutants.

National Standards

The federal government's role in pretreatment began with the passage of the Clean Water Act in 1972. The Act called for the EPA to develop national pretreatment standards to control industrial discharges into sewage systems. The standards are uniform national requirements which restrict the level of certain pollutants in the sewage from industries. All POTWs must enforce the federal standards. The standards in effect today consist of two sets of rules: "categorical pretreatment standards" and "prohibited discharge standards."

Categorical pretreatment standards are organized by type of industry, and different requirements are mandated for each specific industry. For example, there is a categorical standard for the iron and steel industry which limits the concentration of ammonia, cyanide, and other specific toxic pollutants that may be present in the wastewater discharged into sewage systems by any firm in that industry.

Prohibited discharge standards prohibit any discharge to sewer systems of certain types of wastes from all sources. For example, the release of any wastewaters with a pH lower than 5.0 is

forbidden, since such wastes may corrode the sewer system. Chapter 4 of this document describes the prohibited discharge standards and the categorical pretreatment standards in detail.

Local Programs

The overall framework for the National Pretreatment Program is contained in the General Pretreatment Regulations that EPA published in 1978 and modified in 1981 (Figure 7). These regulations require all large POTWs—those designed to accommodate flows of more than 5 million gallons (19 million liters) per day—and smaller POTWs with significant industrial discharges to establish local pretreatment programs. Approximately 1,500 POTWs are participating in the National Pretreatment Program by developing local programs. The local programs, which are described in detail in Chapter 5, must enforce all national pretreatment standards. The local POTWs also may enforce more stringent discharge requirements (i.e., local limits) to prevent disruption of the sewage treatment system, adverse environmental impacts, or disruption of sludge use or disposal. Thus, the National Pretreatment Program consists of approximately 1,500 local programs designed to meet federal requirements and to accommodate unique local concerns.

Delegation to the Local Level

The decision to delegate enforcement authority for the pretreatment program to the local level was based on several factors. First, POTW officials are familiar with their industrial users. They usually know the location, wastewater flow, and pollutant loadings of the industries they serve. They may already have mechanisms to regulate their industrial clients, such as permits or contracts. These documents may contain agreements con-

---

Figure 7. The General Pretreatment Regulations

The General Pretreatment Regulations define the National Pretreatment Program. These regulations are published in Volume 40, Part 403 of the *Code of Federal Regulations* (40 CFR 403). This document is available in many libraries and government offices. The General Pretreatment Regulations contained in 40 CFR 403 are divided into 16 subparts — 403.1 through 403.16.

403.1   *Purpose and Applicability*
403.2   *Objectives of General Pretreatment Regulations*
403.3   *Definitions*
403.4   *State or Local Law*
403.5   *National Pretreatment Standards: Prohibited Discharge*
403.6   *National Pretreatment Standards: Categorical Standards*
403.7   *Revision of Categorical Pretreatment Standards to Reflect POTW Removal of Pollutants*
403.8   *POTW Pretreatment Programs: Development by POTW*
403.9   *POTW Pretreatment Programs and/or Authorization to Revise Pretreatment Standards: Submission for Approval*
403.10 *Development and Submission of NPDES State Pretreatment Programs*
403.11 *Approval Procedures for POTW Pretreatment Programs and POTW Revision of Categorical Pretreatment Standards*
403.12 *Reporting Requirements for POTWs and Industrial Users*
403.13 *Variances from Categorical Pretreatment Standards for Fundamentally Different Factors*
403.14 *Confidentiality*
403.15 *Net/Gross Calculation*
403.16 *Upset Provision*

As of July 1986, the EPA was in the process of revising certain definitions and other technical components of the regulations.

---

cerning both the nature and volume of industrial discharges and fees for the service. Thus, POTWs already have administrative mechanisms and client relationships in place on which to base enforcement of the pretreatment program.

A second reason for delegating pretreatment authority to the local level is that the POTWs are in the best position to understand and to correct problems within their own treatment systems. Therefore, they can tailor discharge requirements in pretreatment permits to preclude interference with their particular treatment system. The POTW is also in the best position to understand other problems that must be considered in formulating pretreatment permits, such as the hazard of explosions or corrosion in the sewage system and the treatment plant.

Finally, the POTW is the logical level of government to respond to emergencies in the treatment system. The unexpected discharge of pollutants by an industrial user could result in the discharge of untreated wastes by the POTW itself, violating federal standards and presenting an environmental hazard. In many cases, the POTW can quickly pinpoint the cause of the problem and take corrective action.

Although a strong case can be made for POTW control of pretreatment programs, the states of Vermont, Connecticut, and Mississippi have elected to direct the program at the state level. Several other states, such as Nebraska and New Jersey, delegate authority to some POTWs but retain authority in other sewer districts. The reasons for this approach include the lack of funding, technical resources, or administrative structure at the POTW level or the preference by some states for centralized control of environmental programs. In most states, however, approved pretreatment programs are or will soon be implemented by POTWs.

Approval of Pretreatment Programs

Federal, state, and local government agencies are all involved in establishing pretreatment programs. In general, the federal government requires that states develop pretreatment programs; the states, in turn, review, approve, and oversee the programs of local POTWs. The specifics of pretreatment program development and approval, however, vary from state to state, depending on the status of the state's program to control direct discharges—the National Pollutant Discharge Elimination System (NPDES).

NPDES Programs

The National Pollutant Discharge Elimination System (NPDES) regulates the direct discharge of wastewaters to surface waters (Figure 8). Under this program, industrial facilities and POTWs must receive an NPDES permit before discharging wastewater directly to surface waters. The permits require compliance with all federal standards and may also require additional controls based on local conditions.

Because POTWs are direct dischargers, they must obtain and comply with an NPDES permit. This permit limits the amount of pollutants the sewage treatment plant may discharge. If the concentration of pollutants is too high, or if its discharges endanger public health or the environment, it violates its permit and can be fined and/or forced to upgrade its operation.

A POTW may have trouble meeting its NPDES permit conditions if the concentration of toxics in the wastewater flowing into the treatment plant (the influent wastewater) is too high. One way to control the concentration of toxics in the influent wastewater is to require pretreatment. Thus, the conditions of a POTW's discharge permit might dictate the need for pretreatment. Since the implementation of the National Pretreatment

Program in 1981, a pretreatment program is, in fact, *required* of many POTWs for permit renewal.

The authority to issue NPDES permits in a given state rests either with the state's environmental agency or with the U.S. EPA. States can gain approval to administer the NPDES program by demonstrating that their state program meets all federal requirements. To date, 36 states and 1 territory have been given NPDES authority (Figure 9). These states are commonly referred to as NPDES states. In NPDES states, permits for direct discharge are issued by the state; in non-NPDES states, permits for direct discharge are issued by the EPA regional office.

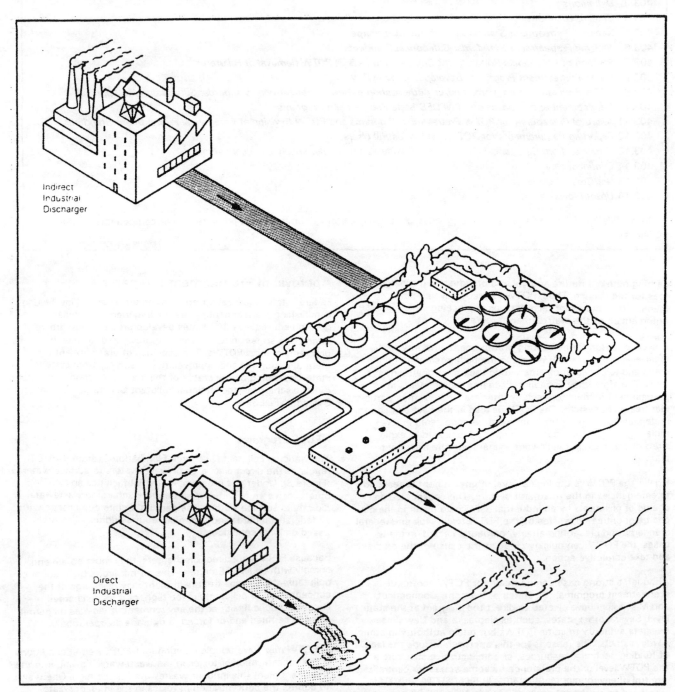

Figure 8. Direct and Indirect Industrial Dischargers. Industrial or municipal sewage treatment facilities that discharge their wastewaters directly into rivers, streams, lakes, bays, estuaries, and oceans are referred to as direct dischargers. Industrial facilities that discharge their wastewaters into a municipal sewer system are referred to as indirect dischargers; it is these indirect dischargers that the National Pretreatment Program aims to regulate.

Pretreatment Programs

States that have NPDES authority are required to develop pretreatment programs for EPA approval (40 CFR 403.10). States are granted pretreatment authority by the EPA if they show that their program meets all federal requirements. States with pretreatment authority are referred to as pretreatment-delegated states. To date, 22 states have been given approval to operate pretreatment programs (Figure 9). In these states, implementation of the National Pretreatment Program is the responsibility of the state; in the remaining states, the EPA implements the National Pretreatment Program.

The POTWs develop local pretreatment programs which are approved either by the state (in pretreatment-delegated states) or by the EPA. Once a program is approved, the state or the EPA conducts periodic checks to ensure that the program is operating properly. As noted above, a small number of states retain authority for all aspects of pretreatment programs and, therefore, do not delegate any authority to the POTW.

If a POTW does not have an approved pretreatment program, national pretreatment standards and requirements are enforced by the EPA (in nonpretreatment-delegated states) or the state (in pretreatment-delegated states). Thus, pretreatment regulations may be enforced by either the EPA, the state, or the POTW, depending upon the status of program approvals for a given community.

Industry's Role and Responsibilities

As the generator of toxic pollutants, industry is responsible for the removal of contaminants present in quantities that might

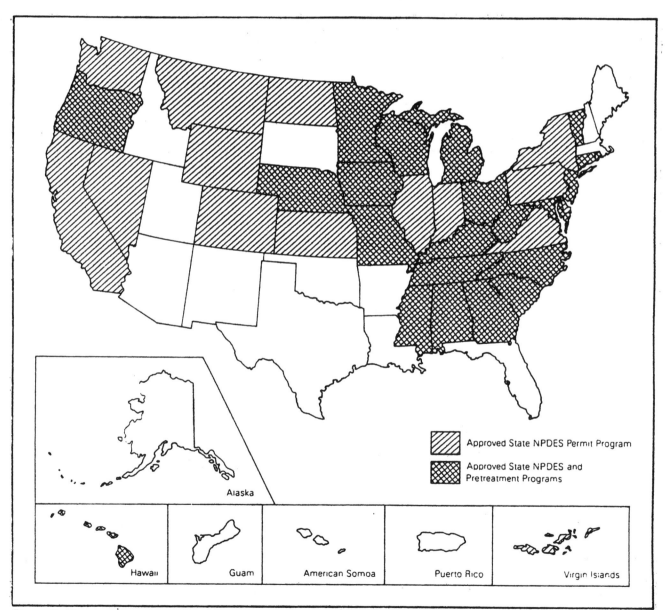

Figure 9. Status of State NPDES and Pretreatment Program Delegation (July 1986). Thirty-six states and one territory have approved NPDES programs. Twenty-two states have approved pretreatment programs.

cause problems in the collection system, the treatment plant, or the outside environment. Industry must finance, construct, and operate any pollution control equipment or facilities necessary to comply with pollutant discharge limits required under federal pretreatment regulations or local pollution control rules. Compliance by industry ensures that industrial toxic pollutants will not damage human health or the environment.

National Pretreatment Standards

The federal government has developed national regulations or "standards" that restrict the quantity of toxic industrial pollutants discharged into sewage systems. Individual POTWs can impose limitations stricter than the national standards, but cannot allow less stringent levels of control except under certain special circumstances.

Rationale for National Standards

Although POTWs have the legal authority to develop discharge limitations for their industrial users, there are several reasons for having national standards. First, there are many long-term health and environmental impacts of industrial pollutants that are not immediately apparent to local communities. Because of these potential long-term impacts, Congress required in the Clean Water Act that national effluent standards for industrial facilities be established based on the best pollution control technology that can be economically achieved. It is logical that the federal government (EPA) develops these technology-based standards since it has access to the technical resources needed to assess the industrial processes utilized by each industry and to identify the best economically achievable pollution control technology.

A second reason for federal standards is to ensure that all sewage districts control the toxic discharges of industrial facilities to certain minimum levels. Without these standards, some POTWs would not implement a pretreatment program which effectively controls toxic pollutants. In some communities, for example, there is political pressure to relax pollution control requirements for facilities that provide a large number of local jobs. Federal standards ensure that all POTWs will provide a minimum level of control, thus making a contribution to the goal of reducing toxic pollution of the nation's waters.

Finally, national pretreatment standards assure a degree of equity within each industry regarding expenses for pollution control. If pollution control requirements were established solely by POTWs, then two firms producing the same product in different sewage districts might be subject to widely different pollution limitations and costs. This could lead to an unfair competitive advantage for one of the firms. The national standards ensure that firms in the same industry are subject to the same minimum requirements throughout the country.

The national pretreatment standards consist of two sets of rules, *prohibited discharge standards* and *categorical pretreatment standards*.

Prohibited Discharge Standards

The national prohibited discharge standards forbid certain types of discharges by any sewage system user (40 CFR 403.5). The prohibited discharge standards apply to all sewage system users, regardless of whether or not they are covered by categorical pretreatment standards.

These standards have both general and specific prohibitions. The general prohibitions forbid pollutants to be discharged into the sewage system if they pass through the POTW untreated or if they interfere with POTW operations. The specific prohibitions outlaw the discharge of five categories of pollutants:

- Pollutants that create a fire hazard or explosion hazard in the collection system or treatment plant.
- Pollutants that are corrosive, including any discharge with a pH lower than 5.0, unless the POTW is specifically designed to handle such discharges.
- Solid or viscous pollutants in amounts that will obstruct the flow in the collection system and treatment plant, resulting in interference with operations.
- Any pollutant discharged in quantities sufficient to interfere with POTW operations.
- Discharges with temperatures above 104°F (40°C) when they reach the treatment plant, or hot enough to interfere with biological treatment processes at the sewage treatment plant.

The POTWs must enforce these general and specific prohibitions as a condition for approval of their pretreatment programs. POTWs must establish limits on specific pollutants from certain facilities to ensure that the prohibited discharge standards are not violated. For example, if an industrial plant discharges a pollutant that could cause interference, the POTW would have to set limits on that pollutant in the plant's pretreatment permit.

Categorical Pretreatment Standards

Categorical pretreatment standards are pollution control regulations for specific industries. The standards regulate the level of pollutants in the wastes discharged into the sewage system from an industrial process (Figure 10). Each categorical standard covers one industrial category. Within the industrial category, separate pollution control requirements might be established for distinct industrial processes or "subcategories" (Figure 11).

Categorical standards place restrictions on 126 toxic pollutants identified by EPA as having the greatest potential to harm human health or the environment (Table 1). The categorical standards may require that industrial facilities reduce their discharges of these toxic substances by 80 percent or more. Some of the categorical standards also regulate industrial discharges of certain *non-conventional* pollutants which are not included in the list of 126 toxic pollutants but which nevertheless present a threat to the aquatic environment or to human health. Categorical standards have been or are being developed for industrial categories that generate the bulk of toxic industrial pollutants (Table 2).

Development of Categorical Standards

The Industrial Technology Division within the EPA Office of Water Regulations and Standards develops the federal categorical pretreatment standards. This is done in conjunction with the development of pollution control regulations for *direct dischargers*. The process begins with the collection of a

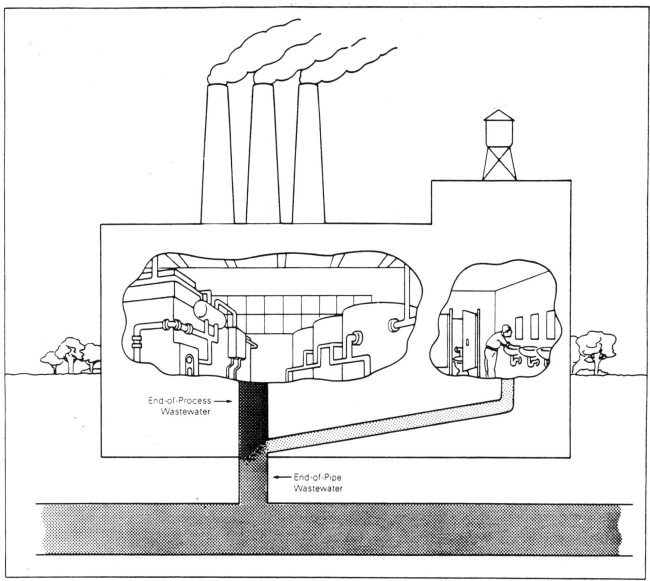

Figure 10. End-of-Process Versus End-of-Pipe Wastewaters. A manufacturing facility covered by a categorical standard generates wastewater within the industrial process, and may also generate other wastewaters (e.g., sanitary wastes from bathrooms and shower facilities). The categorical standard regulates the wastewater coming out of the industrial process (i.e., the *end-of-process* wastewater). In some cases, end-of-process wastewater combines with other wastewaters (e.g., sanitary wastes) prior to discharge into the sewer. Wastewater discharged into the sewer, which may consist of several types of wastewater from within the manufacturing facility, is referred to as *end-of-pipe* wastewater. Individual POTWs may monitor the wastewater at an end-of-process or an end-of-pipe location. If the POTW monitors at an end-of-pipe location, it must perform certain calculations to translate the end-of-process pollutant limitations in the standard into end-of-pipe requirements for the entire facility. A mathematical formula, termed the *combined waste stream formula*, has been developed for this purpose (40 CFR 403.6[e]).

variety of process engineering and environmental data concerning the regulated industry. EPA reviews these data to determine the types and quantities of effluents generated by the industry.

The EPA next identifies the best available technology economically achieveable (BAT) to control the industry's effluents (Figure 12). BAT technology performance is then analyzed to determine how much of each pollutant the technology can remove from the effluent (the numerical pollution control limits). The EPA standard for direct dischargers is based on

these limits. Although industrial discharges must meet EPA numerical pollution control limits, EPA does not require industries to use any specific treatment processes to comply with the standard.

The pollution control capabilities of BAT technology are also used to establish pretreatment standards for *indirect dischargers*. Before establishing pretreatment standards based on BAT, however, EPA considers the pollution removal capabilities of sewage treatment plants (Figure 13). If treatment plants using secondary treatment processes typically remove any of an industry's pollutants to the same extent as BAT technology, then pretreatment standards for those pollutants are generally not promulgated for that industry. If any of an industry's pollutants typically pass through the treatment plant, discharging a higher level of pollutants than would occur if the industry's facilities were direct dischargers using BAT technology, then pretreatment standards equivalent to BAT technology are promulgated for those pollutants for that industry. Thus,

pretreatment standards are set using BAT technology as a reference point, with some pollutants excluded based on the performance capabilities of sewage treatment plants.

Figure 11. Industrial Categories and Subcategories

An *industrial category*, sometimes referred to as an industry, is a broad classification of establishments involved in an industrial activity. For example, the battery manufacturing industrial category refers to establishments engaged in the manufacture of all types of storage batteries. Within an industrial category, EPA might define a number of *subcategories* to distinguish firms using different processes. In the battery manufacturing industry, for example, EPA has set pollutant discharge limitations for six separate subcategories.

Figure 12. Categorical Standards Development

In identifying BAT technology for a given industry, EPA considers a number of alternative pollution control systems. Technical and economic analyses are performed to determine whether the systems will work and whether they are economically achievable for the industry. These analyses are described in the *Federal Register* notice of the proposed rule. EPA also publishes a "development document" concerning each industry's pretreatment standard. These documents expand on the discussions in the *Federal Register* and provide more detail concerning the technologies that were considered in establishing BAT. In some cases, EPA also publishes a summary manual concerning an industry's pretreatment standard. To obtain copies of the development documents or summary manuals, contact the U.S. Environmental Protection Agency, Office of Water Regulations and Standards, Industrial Technology Division, Washington, DC.

Table 1. Toxic Pollutants Regulated Under Categorical Standards

1. acenaphthene
2. acrolein
3. acrylonitrile
4. benzene
5. benzidine
6. carbon tetrachloride
7. chlorobenzene
8. 1,2,4-trichlorobenzene
9. hexachlorobenzene
10. 1,2-dichloroethane
11. 1,1,1-trichloroethane
12. hexachloroethane
13. 1,1-dichloroethane
14. 1,1,2-trichloroethane
15. 1,1,2,2-tetrachloroethane
16. chloroethane
17. bis(2-chloroethyl) ether
18. 2-chloroethyl vinyl ether (mixed)
19. 2-chloronaphthalene
20. 2,4,6-trichlorophenol
21. parachlorometa cresol
22. chloroform (trichloromethane)
23. 2-chlorophenol
24. 1,2-dichlorobenzene
25. 1,3-dichlorobenzene
26. 1,4-dichlorobenzene
27. 3,3-dichlorobenzidine
28. 1,1-dichloroethylene
29. 1,2-trans-dichloroethylene
30. 2,4-dichlorophenol
31. 1,2-dichloropropane
32. 1,2-dichloropropylene (1,3-dichloropropene)
33. 2,4-dimethylphenol
34. 2,4-dinitrotoluene
35. 2,6-dinitrotoluene
36. 1,2-diphenylhydrazine
37. ethylbenzene
38. fluoranthene
39. 4-chlorophenyl phenyl ether
40. 4-bromophenyl phenyl ether
41. bis(2-chloroisopropyl) ether
42. bis(2-chloroethoxy) methane
43. methylene chloride (dichloromethane)
44. methyl chloride (chloromethane)
45. methyl bromide (bromomethane)
46. bromoform (tribromomethane)
47. dichlorobromomethane
48. chlorodibromomethane
49. hexachlorobutadiene
50. hexachlorocyclopentadiene
51. isophorone
52. naphthalene
53. nitrobenzene
54. 2-nitrophenol
55. 4-nitrophenol
56. 2,4-dinitrophenol
57. 4,6-dinitro-o-cresol
58. N-nitrosodimethylamine
59. N-nitrosodiphenylamine
60. N-nitrosodi-n-propylamine
61. pentachlorophenol
62. phenol
63. bis(2-ethylhexyl) phthalate
64. butyl benzyl phthalate
65. di-n-butyl phthalate
66. di-n-octyl phthalate
67. diethyl phthalate
68. dimethyl phthalate
69. benzo(a)anthracene (1,2-benzanthracene)
70. benzo(a)pyrene (3,4-benzo-pyrene)
71. 3,4-benzofluoranthene (benzo(b)fluoranthene)
72. benzo(k)fluoranthene (11,12-benzofluoranthene)
73. chrysene
74. acenaphthylene
75. anthracene
76. benzo(ghi)perylene (1,12-benzoperylene)
77. fluorene
78. phenanthrene
79. dibenzo(ah)anthracene (1,2,5,6-dibenzanthracene)
80. indeno (1,2,3-cd)pyrene (2,3-o-phenylenepyrene)
81. pyrene
82. tetrachloroethylene
83. toluene
84. trichloroethylene
85. vinyl chloride (chloroethylene)
86. aldrin
87. dieldrin
88. chlordane (technical mixture & metabolites)
89. 4,4-DDT
90. 4,4-DDE (p,p-DDX)
91. 4,4-DDD (p,p-TDE)
92. Alpha Endosulfan
93. Beta Endosulfan
94. endosulfan sulfate
95. endrin
96. endrin aldehyde
97. heptachlor
98. heptachlor epoxide (BHC-hexachlorocyclohexane)
99. Alpha-BHC
100. Beta-BHC
101. Gamma-BHC (lindane)
102. Delta-BHC (PCB-polychlorinated biphenyl)
103. PCB-1242 (Arochlor 1242)
104. PCB-1254 (Arochlor 1254)
105. PCB-1221 (Arochlor 1221)
106. PCB-1232 (Arochlor 1232)
107. PCB-1248 (Arochlor 1248)
108. PCB-1260 (Arochlor 1260)
109. PCB-1016 (Arochlor 1016)
110. toxaphene
111. antimony (total)
112. arsenic (total)
113. asbestos (total)
114. beryllium (total)
115. cadmium (total)
116. chromium (total)
117. copper (total)
118. cyanide (total)
119. lead (total)
120. mercury (total)
121. nickel (total)
122. selenium (total)
123. silver (total)
124. thallium (total)
125. zinc (total)
126. 2,3,7,8-tetrachlorodibenzo-o-dioxin (TCDD)

Figure 13. Removal Capabilities of POTWs

Categorical standards regulate only pollutants that are not controlled by POTW treatment systems. To assess the removal capabilities of POTWs, EPA has developed extensive data on the performance of 50 representative facilities. This data is available in the EPA publication titled *Fate of Priority Pollutants in Publicly Owned Treatment Works*. The information on POTW pollutant removal contained in this document is used to determine whether a given pollutant in an industry must be covered under categorical standards. Copies of the document can be obtained by contacting the U.S. Environmental Protection Agency, Office of Water Regulations and Standards, Industrial Technology Division, Washington, DC.

Implementation of Federal Categorical Standards

Once a categorical standard is promulgated, POTWs or industrial officials might be unsure whether or not a given facility is subject to the new regulation. The POTW or the industrial user can request a ruling by the EPA concerning the industrial category of the facility in question (i.e., a category determination). The Water Division Director in the EPA regional office where the facility is located makes the final decision.

If an industrial facility is subject to a categorical standard, it must submit a report to the POTW documenting the plant operations and discharges. In these reports, referred to as baseline monitoring reports, the industrial facility must also indicate whether applicable pretreatment standards currently are being met. If the standards are not being met, the facility must submit a description of the facilities and operating procedures

Table 2. Status of Categorical Pretreatment Standards

Industry Category	Date Standard was Issued in *Federal Register*	Effective Date	Compliance Date for Existing Sources[a]
Timber Products	1-26-81	3-30-81	1-26-84
Electroplating	1-28-81	3-30-81	4-27-84 (Non-integrated)[b]
			6-30-84 (Integrated)[b]
	7-15-83	8-29-83	7-15-86 (TTO)[b]
Iron and Steel	5-27-82	7-10-82	7-10-85
Inorganic Chemicals I	6-29-82	8-12-82	8-12-85
Textile Mills	9-2-82	10-18-82	—[c]
Petroleum Refining	10-18-82	12-1-82	12-1-85
Pulp, Paper, Paperboard	11-18-82	1-3-83	7-1-84
Steam Electric	11-19-82	1-2-83	7-1-84
Leather Tanning	11-23-82	1-6-83	11-25-85
Porcelain Enameling	11-24-82	1-7-83	11-25-85
Coil Coating I	12-1-82	1-17-83	12-1-85
Electrical and Electronic Components I	4-8-83	5-19-83	7-1-84 (TTO)[d]
			11-8-85 (As)[d]
Metal Finishing	7-15-83	8-29-83	6-30-84 (Part 433, TTO)[e]
			7-10-85 (Part 420, TTO)[e]
			2-15-86 (Final)[e]
Copper Forming	8-15-83	9-26-83	8-15-86
Aluminum Forming	10-24-83	12-7-83	10-24-86
Pharmaceuticals	10-27-83	12-12-83	10-27-86
Coil Coating (Canmaking)	11-17-83	1-2-84	11-17-86
Electrical and Electronic Components II	12-14-83	1-27-84	7-14-86
Non-Ferrous Metals I	3-8-84	4-23-84	3-9-87
Battery Manufacturing	3-9-84	4-23-84	3-9-87
Inorganic Chemicals II	8-22-84	10-5-84	6-29-85 (CuSO₄, NiSO₄)
			8-22-87
Plastics Molding and Forming	12-17-84	1-30-85	—[c]
Non-Ferrous Metals Forming	8-23-85	10-7-85	8-23-88
Non-Ferrous Metals II	9-20-85	11-4-85	9-20-88
Pesticides	10-4-85	11-18-85	11-18-88
Metal Molding and Casting (Foundries)	10-30-85	12-13-85	10-31-88
Organic Chemicals and Plastics and Synthetic Fibers	12/86	2/87	2/90

[a] The compliance date for any new source is the same date as the commencement of the discharge.

[b] Integrated electroplators are establishments involved both in electroplating and in other activities that are regulated by other EPA categorical pretreatment standards. Non-integrated electroplators are establishments involved in electroplating only. The compliance date for removal of total toxic organics (TTO) is July 15, 1986.

[c] No numerical pretreatment limits have been established for these industrial categories, and there is no final compliance date for categorical pretreatment standards. Firms in these categories are required to comply only with the General Pretreatment Regulations in 40 CFR 403.

[d] The compliance date for existing Phase I Electrical and Electronic Components manufacturers for TTO is July 1, 1984. The compliance date for arsenic is November 8, 1985.

[e] Existing sources that are subject to the metal finishing standards in 40 CFR Part 433 must comply only with the interim limit for Total Toxic Organics (TTO) by June 30, 1984. Plants also covered by 40 CFR Part 420 must comply with the interim TTO limit by July 10, 1985. The compliance date for metals, cyanide, and final TTO is February 15, 1986, for all sources.

SOURCE: U.S. Environmental Protection Agency, July 1986.

required for compliance and a schedule showing when these compliance measures will be implemented. If an industrial plant has already submitted the required information as part of its existing pretreatment permit application, it need not resubmit the information in a baseline monitoring report.

All industrial facilities included in a category are responsible for installing any pollution control equipment and instituting any operations and maintenance procedures that might be required for compliance with the standard. The effective date of a categorical standard is usually several weeks after the standard is promulgated in the *Federal Register* as a final regulation. In most cases, new facilities must comply with the regulation for any discharges occurring after the effective date of the regulation; existing plants must comply within 3 years of the effective date of the regulation.

Modifications of Categorical Pretreatment Standards

Although categorical standards apply throughout the country, they may be modified in three specific circumstances. If the water coming into a particular industrial facility already contains a pollutant regulated by the categorical standard for that facility, a *net/gross adjustment* may be authorized (40 CFR 403.15). Net/gross adjustments allow the facility to discharge a particular pollutant at a level in excess of the federal standard, but such an adjustment is allowed only to the degree that the pollutant is present in the incoming water.

A second type of adjustment, termed a *removal credit*, allows a categorical standard to be modified for a particular pollutant at a particular facility if the sewage treatment plant serving the facility removes the pollutant effectively (40 CFR 403.7). If a POTW demonstrates to the EPA Regional Administrator that a pollutant is removed by its sewage treatment process, then the categorical pretreatment standards for that pollutant can be adjusted accordingly for industries served by that POTW.

Categorical standards can also be adjusted if a POTW, an industrial firm, or an interested party can show that a factor or factors exist that were not considered in the development of the standards. For example, a firm or industry might apply for a change in the standard because it is using a process that was not considered by EPA when the Agency developed the categorical standard. Such adjustments are termed *fundamentally different factor(s)* variances (40 CFR 403.13).

Local Pretreatment Programs

Program Components

The POTWs develop local pretreatment programs which implement federal standards and protect local interests. They prepare detailed pretreatment program documents which are reviewed by the state, in pretreatment-delegated states, or by the EPA. To gain approval, these submissions must meet the requirements for local pretreatment programs contained in 40 CFR 403 (Figure 14).

> ### Figure 14. EPA Manuals Describing POTW Pretreatment Programs
> In addition to obtaining copies of 40 CFR 403, a person interested in understanding the components of local POTW programs should obtain the EPA publication entitled *Guidance Manual for POTW Pretreatment Program Development*. This document explains in lay terms the elements that must be included in a local pretreatment program to gain EPA or state approval. Separate chapters of the document explain the requirements for legal authority, technical information, industrial waste surveys, monitoring, implementation procedures, and program staffing. The document's appendices contain sample forms such as a sample pretreatment permit for an industrial discharger, a checklist for POTW pretreatment program submissions, and a sample compliance schedule.

To be successful, the local pretreatment programs must have the following elements:

- *Building Blocks* — Local pretreatment programs require legal authority, a professional staff, funding, and an information base on the industrial dischargers.
- *Effluent Limits* — For industrial users of the sewage system, effluent limitations that enforce federal standards and protect local interests must be established.

- *Implementation Activities* — POTWs must undertake a number of activities to implement their effluent limits including notification, permit administration, inspection, monitoring, and enforcement.
- *Information Handling and Public Access* — Pretreatment programs must include a data management system and must provide mechanisms to allow the public to have access to information about the program and to comment on program elements.

Figure 15 provides an overview of the critical components of a local pretreatment program.

POTW Pretreatment Program Building Blocks

A local pretreatment program must have four major building blocks in order to succeed. First, the POTW must have the legal authority to implement the program. This legal authority usually is based on state law and local ordinances. State law authorizes the municipality to regulate industrial users of municipal sewage systems. The municipality, in turn, establishes a local ordinance that sets forth the components of its pretreatment program and identifies the director of the POTW as the person empowered to implement the program.

The legal authority granted by state and/or local law must authorize the POTW to limit the pollution levels in discharges from industrial users of the sewage system. It must be authorized to enforce national pretreatment standards and to implement local limits in addition to or in excess of the standards. It also must be empowered to issue permits or enter into contracts with industrial users which set forth all applicable pollution control requirements. Finally, the POTW's legal authority also must include the right to inspect and monitor industrial facilities without prior notice, and to take enforcement action against violators.

In addition to obtaining legal authority, the POTW must develop

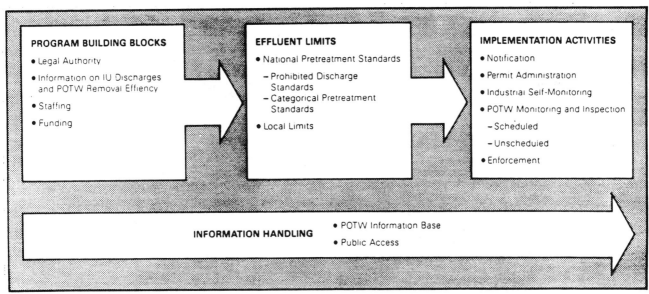

Figure 15. POTW Pretreatment Programs.

a comprehensive data base describing its industrial dischargers. An industrial waste survey is commonly used to obtain data identifying the volume and pollutant concentration of industrial effluents. This survey provides a data base that allows the POTW to identify the major sources of toxic effluents within the sewage system.

A successful pretreatment program also requires adequate staffing. Personnel are required for sampling and inspection, laboratory analysis, technical assistance, legal assistance, and program administration. The resources required for each activity depend upon the size of the sewage district, the number of industrial users, and POTW policies.

The final key building block of a successful pretreatment program is funding. Funding for the program may be included in the municipal budget for the POTW or recovered through charges to the industrial facilities. These charges can be incorporated into a facility's basic fees for sewage services, or levied as a separate pretreatment charge. The size of the charges can be based on the amount of POTW services (e.g., monitoring) required by a facility, the facility's wastewater flow, or the toxicity of its pollutants.

Effluent Limits

A POTW with adequate legal authority, a sound data base, and adequate staffing and funding can proceed to develop effluent limitations for each industrial plant. At a minimum, all facilities are required to comply with federal prohibited discharge standards. The industries covered by federal categorical standards also must comply with the appropriate discharge limitations.

The POTW may also establish local limits in excess of or in addition to the federal standards for some or all of its industrial users. To identify the need for and the nature of such limits, the POTW determines whether any public health or environmental problems related to POTW operations will exist, even with full enforcement of the federal standards. This assessment addresses the following issues:

- *Interference*—Even with full implementation of federal standards, will the remaining pollutant loadings interfere with the sewage treatment system? To answer this question, the POTW must analyze its treatment system's susceptibility to various problems and its history of breakdowns.

- *Sludge Contamination*—Will any of the pollutants contaminate the municipal sludge? To answer this question, the POTW must determine the concentration of contaminants in its sludge after full enforcement of federal standards and analyze the environmental residuals associated with each possible sludge disposal method.

- *NPDES Permit Violations*—Will the pass-through of any pollutants cause an NPDES permit violation? To answer this question, the POTW must determine whether any of the pollutants that remain in the system after full enforcement of federal standards will pass through the treatment plant in quantities significant enough to cause a permit violation.

- *Surface Water Impacts*—Will any of the pollutants that pass through the treatment plant adversely affect the receiving water body? To answer this question, the POTW must examine the environmental condition of the receiving water body and determine whether the pass-through of any pollutants might have a substantial impact.

- *Worker Safety*—Will any of the pollutants create a safety hazard for municipal employees? To answer this question, the POTW must review the design and operation of its treatment system and the chemical composition of its pollutant inflow to determine whether any of the pollutants individually, or in combination, will create a worker hazard.

If the answer to any of the above questions is "yes," the POTW will have to establish local limits to be incorporated into the discharge limitations of some or all of the industrial plants that it serves. To determine these limits, the POTW must estimate the maximum concentration of each pollutant in the incoming wastewater that will not cause any of these problems. It can then calculate the maximum pollutant loading of each user that can be allowed without exceeding the maximum concentration of pollutants arriving at the treatment plant. These calculations must consider such factors as the level of pollutants already present in the water supply, the chemical decomposition of pollutants within the sewage system, and the need to accommodate future industrial growth. Based on these calculations, local limits for each pollutant are established for each industrial facility.

Implementation Activities

The POTWs must take a number of steps to implement the effluent limits established in their programs. First, the industrial plants must be notified of the effluent limitations that apply to them. These limitations might be based on categorical pretreatment standards, prohibited discharge standards, or local limits. The effluent limits are then incorporated in a permit, contract, or other agreement between the POTW and the industrial facility.

POTWs must then ensure that the industrial facilities comply with the effluent limits in their pretreatment permits. They require industrial plants to submit self-monitoring reports in which they report the total volume and pollutant concentrations of their wastewater discharges. Federal regulations require that these reports be submitted semi-annually, at a minimum. The industrial facility's pretreatment permit might also require the submittal of additional information such as a description of any accidental discharges into the sewage system.

The POTW cannot rely solely on the information supplied by industry in self-monitoring reports. It must, therefore, conduct its own inspection and monitoring activities. POTWs identify locations within the industrial facility for collecting samples of wastewater for chemical analysis. Sampling locations might be at the end of the industrial process or at the point of connection to the public sewer. The effluent concentrations considered acceptable at each sampling location are based on the facility's pretreatment permit.

Municipal personnel periodically visit each industrial site to collect wastewater samples at the designated sampling locations within the facility. Some of these inspections are held on a regularly scheduled basis. There are also unannounced monitoring visits to ensure that the information collected during scheduled visits or submitted in self-monitoring reports truly represents the character of the plant's wastewater discharge. Monitoring also may occur in response to a suspected violation of a pretreatment permit, a public complaint, the suspected presence of explosive or corrosive materials, operating difficulties in the sewage treatment plant, or violation of the POTW's NPDES permit. Monitoring is generally undertaken immediately following the onset of a serious problem.

The frequency and extensiveness of monitoring and inspection by the POTW depends on the facility's potential impact on the sewage system and the environment. In general, major industrial facilities such as those covered by categorical standards are subject to at least one scheduled and one unscheduled monitoring visit per year; more if resources allow. The volume of wastewater discharges, the toxicity of the discharge, or the variability of monitoring results are used by sewer districts to determine the frequency of monitoring visits.

When an industrial plant violates its permit conditions, the POTW takes enforcement action. Before taking this step, however, the POTW verifies the violation. In most cases, verification involves sampling and laboratory analysis of the plant's effluent to confirm that a violation has occurred.

In emergency situations, the sewer district may take immediate action to halt all discharges from a facility that is discharging hazardous pollutants. In less serious cases, however, the POTW

will immediately inform the violator verbally of the violation, then later will do so in writing. The facility is required to meet its permit conditions within a specified period of time. Monitoring of the facility's discharges is then instituted to ensure that these compliance deadlines are met.

When compliance deadlines are not met, civil and/or criminal proceedings may be initiated against the violator. In some cases, violations can be handled without litigation. However, when a facility persists in violations that endanger public health and the environment, the POTW may take strong enforcement action. It may levy fines and/or seek injunctions to force the violating facility to come into compliance.

Information Handling and Public Access

POTW pretreatment programs require comprehensive data management systems. Large POTWs that serve many industrial facilities and operate several sewage treatment plants generally will have a computerized data management system. The computer stores records of the pollutant discharges allowed in a facility's permit, and it records the actual pollutant levels detected in wastewater samples. This allows for a rapid comparison of observed and allowed discharges and the automatic detection of violations. The computerized data base can also be used to assist the POTW to determine the source of problems, to calculate local limits, and to plan for system expansion.

In general, information and data that the POTW collects on industrial dischargers is available to the public and to government agencies without restriction. The public owns the POTW and, therefore, has the right to review the information it maintains, including any data showing evidence of detrimental effects on the collection system or the treatment plant. Restrictions are made, however, when the industrial facility is able to demonstrate that the release of such material would divulge information, processes, or methods of production entitled to protection as trade secrets. In these cases, information in a facility's file that might disclose trade secrets or secret processes is not made available for public inspection. However, industrial effluent data always remains available to the public without restriction.

Upon written request to government agencies, non-disclosed portions of a facility's file are made available for uses related to the pretreatment program. For example, a state agency may request confidential information for use in judicial review or enforcement proceedings. The company affected should be notified whenever confidential information is released to a government agency or to the general public.

The pretreatment program is a public service designed to protect the public health and environmental quality of a community. In large part, public support for the program will depend on public participation in the program and public access to the information used in developing and administering the program. The POTW staff is responsible for working with industries and the community to define the objectives and benefits of the pretreatment program. The POTW can hold public meetings during the development of its pretreatment program and during the program's implementation. These meetings open a formal channel for public comment on the program and for dialogue with local industries and environmental groups. When local limits are developed or revised, all interested parties must be notified and invited to comment on these actions.

Public access to non-confidential information regarding the pretreatment program must be maintained at a convenient location. At this place, interested people can read or copy documents, permits, monitoring reports, and records of violations. Local libraries, the city or town hall, and public works offices are usually good locations for public access.

Another aspect of providing information to the public is mandated by federal regulations: the POTW must inform the public whenever a significant violation occurs (40 CFR 403.8 [f][2]). The POTW is required to publish in the area's largest daily newspaper, on at least an annual basis, the names of industries that have significantly violated pretreatment standards during the previous 12 months.

APPENDIX **XXVIII**

Source:
P-F Technical Services, Inc.

Silver Halide
Best Management Program

NASSAU COUNTY AND NYCDEP REGULATE SILVER HALIDES; REDUCE WATER POLLUTION BY BEST MANAGEMENT PRACTICES

Nassau County Department of Public Works unveiled its program to eliminate or reduce the level of silver entering its sewer treatment plants. The plan is based on use of the best management practices (BMP) available, mirroring the same approach developed for New York City by the Silver Council and related industry associations and governmental agencies.

The regulations are performance based rather than test standard limits. By utilizing appropriate control technologies, primarily to remove the silver from the outgoing processing solution, the printer can comply. Mandated are recordkeeping and the use of simple testing strips to measure the efficiency of the silver removal systems.

Why Silver is a Hazardous Pollutant?

Silver is a common precious metal, crafted in jewelry and watches that adorn the wrists, ears, throats and fingers of many men and women. Silver halides are used extensively in the graphic arts as a component of the film and paper necessary to photographically capture images for reproduction.

In its normal metallic form, silver is not considered hazardous. However, ionic silver has toxic characteristics.

Developing the film or prints releases the silver halides from their solid form into the wastewater system of the process equipment, and then into the water lines that carry the waste into the public sewer systems. Many printers, pre-press shops and photofinishers have the potential to discharge silver-laden wastes to the sewers.

The danger is directly related to the preservation of marine life in the surrounding waters, as well as the protection of the memebrs of the community. Fish and seafood transmit the Silver to humans when caught by fishermen. The sludge can wind up as fertilizer for farms, thereby contaminating the vegetables and fruits grown, as well as the drinking water supply drawn from areas where such farming takes place.

Best Management Practices

Rather than specifying a standard for the Silver content of a facility's wastewater, the agencies have developed a program to effectively reduce pollution by employing current recovery technology, less burdensome testing for smaller size facilities, and reporting mechanisms.

Best Management Practices (BMP) are typically schedules of activities, prohibitions, management and maintenance procedures that are implemented to reduce the discharge of pollutants to the sewer system.

To restrict the discharge of silver, BMP's are regulated in proportion to the size of the facility determined by the amount of water discharged on a daily basis to the sewer system by the processing machinery.

It is anticipated that most graphic arts firms will fall into the categories, which will mandate 90% collection of the silver. Some of the larger firms may fall into the more stringent categories.

What do we have to do?

The BMP will consist of six major activities:

1. Install appropriate silver reclamation/ water treatment systems. The two smaller categories, from 0 to 999 gallons per day, must meet a standard of 90% recovery of silver by the silver recovery system. Discharges in excess of 1,000 gallons per day must install systems which will recover at least 95% of the silver discharged.

2. Test for the silver concentrate from the solution prior to entry to the treatment equipment and the effluent discharged to the sewer. This can be done with relatively simple tests strips or kits for the small facilities, or lab testing services by the larger firms. The testing must be done at least once a month, on what would be an average day.

The simplest test uses specially treated strips of paper. Immersion of the paper into the solution will result in varying shades of color, which identify the concentration of silver.

The most accurate method, required for larger dischargers, would be the use of an independent laboratory.

3. Measure the daily quantities of silver halide process wastewater that is discharged to the public sewer. This must be done individually for each system operating in the facility. If you have three film processors, and each has it's own silver recovery filter, then the measurement has to be for each unit. This measurement can take place on a day that is considered representative during the month.

4. Maintain written records of the pretreatment technology.

5. Maintain written records of the date that new pretreatment technology is brought into service.

6. Keep records of all measurements and testing required by the regulations.

As the volume of the discharges increases, so too does the intricacy and magnitude of the requirements.

Key elements that will make the BMP work well are engendered in the training of personnel, the housekeeping and maintenance of the operation, and the support of management.

What Methods Are Available to Reclaim Silver?

There are three popular methods for recovering silver from silver halide laden wastewater in print shops. Recovering the silver is good business; reclaimed silver can add to profits or reduce the cost of treatment.

1. Metallic Replacement — This method involves a chemical reaction, during which the silver in the solution is replaced by the iron in the filter. The metals change place with the silver, becoming a sludge in the filter cartridge. To engage the two chemicals in a reaction, the wastewater solution is passed through a container packed with steel wool.

This method is found in many pre-press and print shops. The filter is placed between the processing equipment and the discharge pipe to the sewer system. The costs of the systems are low. Frequently two or more filter cartridges may be placed in line to improve the efficiency of silver removal.

The silver is collected as a sludge, which must then be treated to extract the usable metal.

2. Electrolytic Silver Recovery — In this method, the silver laden solution passes between two electrodes with a controlled current. The silver is plated on the cathode in a form that is almost pure metal. The most obvious advantage of this method is the purity and ease of removal of the silver from the cathode.

Of course, this method is more expensive to purchase and has a higher operating cost.

3. For a more effective silver recovery system, couple the two systems: metallic replacement and electrolytic recovery. The electrolytic unit removes a high percentage of silver; the replacement filter removes the remnants.

Vendors of this type of equipment will provide technical and logistical support for your programs.

No Sewers; Have Septic Tank

Contaminated wastewater cannot be discharged directly into the ground or underground storage/septic tanks

The only solution for facilities that do not empty into sewer systems is to drum and cart away the waste for offsite treatment.

SAMPLE LETTER TO AGENCY

June 14, 1999

Philip J. Grande, P.E. Chief
Division of Drainage Basin Management
New York City DEP
96-05 Horace Harding Expressway
Corona, NY 11368

Re.   Silver Halide Compliance Program

Dear Mr. Grande:

The   Printing Group, at   Avenue, Queens, NY 11373, is a commercial printer. The contact person at our facility is Jeff Risque.

The company has installed an image-setter for the processing of black and white negatives. The wastewater discharges through a cartridge filter system, designed to reclaim silver in the waste.

In accordance with the NYCDEP silver halide wastewater processing regulations, we have instituted a program to comply with the best management program required to reduce the levels of silver discharging from our facility.

The average daily quantity of total silver-halide process wastewater will amount to _____ gallons.

The silver is being reduced by means of a cartridge manufactured by   , Model Number   . All wastewater from our darkroom flows through this cartridge to the local sewer system and treatment plant. Our tests indicate that the efficiency of the system is adequate to meet the 90% destruction required by the NYCDEP.

If you have any questions, please contact me at 718-896-9000.

Sincerely,

Jeff Risque

SAMPLE TRAINING PROGRAM

SUBJECT: SILVER HALIDE PROGRAM; TRAINING OF EMPLOYEES

I.   OSHA/RIGHT TO KNOW TRAINING

All employees engaged in work in the photographic darkroom will be receive training in the equipment and materials used in the process, the health and physical hazards and ramifications of the darkroom chemistry, precautions to prevent exposure in the workplace and to the outside environment, as well as proper disposition of the wastes from the process.

II.   NYCDEP WASTE WATER DISCHARGE PROGRAM

All employees will, in addition to the OSHA mandated training, receive training in the mandates of the NYCDEP regulations as they impact on the discharge of wastewater from the darkroom processes, containing silver halide.

This training will include the nature of the pollutants, the recovery process to remove silver from the water discharges, and the necessary procedures to assure the quality of the recovery process and the discharged water including maintenance of the recovery equipment.

III. RECORD OF TRAINING

A log will be used to record all employees trained, the date of the training and any comments on the nature of the training or the employee reaction to the training.

The employee will sign to verify that training was conducted.

All training records will be retained for a period of not less than three year.

COMPANY NAME

SITE CATEGORY PROFILE

DATE: _____

CONTACT NAME; _____

PROFILE BY: _____

UNIT: _____	EFFLUENT FLOW	usage time	total effluent
	gal/min X	_____min/day = _____	
DRAIN LOCATION: _____			gal/day

INLUENT BASELINE: _____ PPM   CATEGORY:_____

UNIT: _____	EFFLUENT FLOW	usage time	total effluent
	gal/min X	_____min/day = _____	
DRAIN LOCATION: _____			gal/day

INLUENT BASELINE: _____ PPM   CATEGORY:_____

UNIT: _____	EFFLUENT FLOW	usage time	total effluent
	gal/min X	_____min/day = _____	
DRAIN LOCATION: _____			gal/day

INLUENT BASELINE: _____ PPM   CATEGORY:_____

UNIT: _____	EFFLUENT FLOW	usage time	total effluent
	gal/min X	_____min/day = _____	
DRAIN LOCATION: _____			gal/day

INLUENT BASELINE: _____ PPM   **CATEGORY:_____**

SITE CATEGORY KEY:	TOTAL EFFLUENT FLOW GAL/DAY	REQUIRED REC LEVEL	SITE CATEGORY
	<99	90%	I
	100-999	90%	II
	1000-9999	95%	III
	>10,000	99%	IV

SILVER RECOVERY SYSTEM
'INSPECTION LOG FOR

MFG NAME/MODEL   **SERIAL NO.**

COMPANY NAME

The (company name) is required to perform regular inspections of our silvery recovery system. If any spills or leaks are noticed, please indicate on this log and immediately notify your supervisor. Please wear proper personal protective equipment Before checking the performance of the silver recovery system with silver test papers.

Record results below:

DATE OF INSPECTION	NAME OF PERSON CONDUCTING INSPECTION	SPILLS/LEAKS YES/NO	COMPLIANCE YES/NO	SILVER TEST PAPER READINGS
				INFLUENT
				EFFLUENT
				% RECOVERY
				INFLUENT
				EFFLUENT
				% RECOVERY
				INFLUENT
				EFFLUENT
				% RECOVERY
				INFLUENT
				EFFLUENT
				% RECOVERY
				INFLUENT
				EFFLUENT
				% RECOVERY
				INFLUENT
				EFFLUENT
				% RECOVERY

SILVER RECOVERY SYSTEM
RECORD OF ANALYSIS LOG

UNIT: _____

COMPANY NAME

ANALYTICAL

Total photoprocessing wastewater silver concentration - annual or biennial sample. If analysis shows that the treatment equipment is not effectively removing silver, indicate the steps taken to change the equipment or return it to proper operation.

SAMPLE DATE: _____   **Sample Taken By** _____

  % Silver Recovery _____   **Sampling Site** _____

Means of Analysis _____   **Certified Lab:** _____

Comments _____

_____

_____

_____

SAMPLE DATE: _____   **Sample Taken By** _____

  % Silver Recovery _____   **Sampling Site** _____

Means of Analysis _____   **Certified Lab:** _____

  Comments _____

_____

_____

_____

SAMPLE DATE: _____   **Sample Taken By** _____

  % Silver Recovery _____   **Sampling Site** _____

Means of Analysis _____   **Certified Lab:** _____

Comments _____

_____

_____

_____

SILVER RECOVERY SYSTEM
SERVICE/MAINTENANCE LOG

UNIT: _____

COMPANY NAME

SILVER RECOVERY CARTRIDGE INSTALLATION, ROTATION AND REPLACEMENT LOG

Cartridge Number	_____	**Date of Replacement**	_____
Date of Installation	_____	**Replaced By:**	_____
DAte of Rotation	_____	**Cartrdige Sent To:**	_____

Cartridge Number	_____	**Date of Replacement**	_____
Date of Installation	_____	**Replaced By:**	_____
DAte of Rotation	_____	**Cartrdige Sent To:**	_____

Cartridge Number	_____	**Date of Replacement**	_____
Date of Installation	_____	**Replaced By:**	_____
DAte of Rotation	_____	**Cartrdige Sent To:**	_____

Cartridge Number	_____	**Date of Replacement**	_____
Date of Installation	_____	**Replaced By:**	_____
DAte of Rotation	_____	**Cartrdige Sent To:**	_____

Cartridge Number	_____	**Date of Replacement**	_____
Date of Installation	_____	**Replaced By:**	_____
DAte of Rotation	_____	**Cartrdige Sent To:**	_____

Comments _____

_____

SILVER RECOVERY SYSTEM
SERVICE/MAINTENANCE LOG

UNIT: _____

COMPANY NAME

ELECTROLYTIC SILVER RECOVERY SYSTEM SERVICE LOG

Date of Service _____ Serviced By _____
Date of Silver Harvest_____ Harvested By_____
Comments _____ Flake Sent To_____

Date of Service _____ Serviced By _____
Date of Silver Harvest_____ Harvested By_____
Comments _____ Flake Sent To_____

Date of Service _____ Serviced By _____
Date of Silver Harvest_____ Harvested By_____
Comments _____ Flake Sent To_____

Date of Service _____ Serviced By _____
Date of Silver Harvest_____ Harvested By_____
Comments _____ Flake Sent To_____

Date of Service _____ Serviced By _____
Date of Silver Harvest_____ Harvested By_____
Comments _____ Flake Sent To_____

Date of Service _____ Serviced By _____
Date of Silver Harvest_____ Harvested By_____
Comments _____ Flake Sent To_____

Date of Service _____ Serviced By _____
Date of Silver Harvest_____ Harvested By_____
Comments _____ Flake Sent To_____

APPENDIX **XXIX**

SOURCE:
Stuart Cooper, PE, Enviro-Assist

Spill Prevention Programs

A number of regulations require plans to prevent, as well as react to, unplanned incidents. Spills are a major concern of water, air and hazardous waste environmental regulations, as well as OSHA for safety and health. The plans provide information about the facility and procedures for identifying sources of problems that can lead to incidents, plans to react to an incident and any requirements that will enhance safety and the prevention of widespread pollution due to a spill.

The program is designed to prevent or contain spills. While the spill may seem to be of limited exposure, the object of the program is to make sure that all media are considered. A spill will most likely effect water quality if it drains into a well, spring or into a sewer system. The spill of a liquid will evaporate, adding to the fugitive emissions that can increase the level of exposure to workers and community within the area of the spill. Increased vapors can result in a higher possibility of a fire or explosion. Cleanup of the spill results in the generation of hazardous waste.

The table of contents is an important element in this book, in that it itemizes all the components of a spill prevention program and the attachments that are needed to finalize the written program. The attachments are not included in this appendix.

Use the sample program and the disk as a guide to developing your program. All things will not apply. Select those that do and make use of the template to describe your facility, your community and emergency agencies, the local and state regulations that apply to your site, and the procedures that are applicable to your operations. The sample program illustrates a plan that is now being used and is acceptable to the enforcement agencies.

PRINT CHEMICALS STEEL DRUM CO., INC.
3205 Division Avenue
BROOKLYN, NY 11208

TABLE OF CONTENTS

(Note: Appendices to this document not included.)

1   INTRODUCTION & GENERAL INFORMATION

Printing Chemicals Steel Drum Co., Inc. (PCSDI) operates a steel drum reconditioning facility in a one story, masonry building at 3205 Division Avenue, Brooklyn, NY 11208. It is located between Dumont Street and Pitkin Place. The building is basically a one story building, two stories high, that is used for the cleaning and reconditioning of steel drums. A 5000 gallon fiberglass reinforced plastic storage tank for hydrochloric acid is located within a concrete diked area facing Richardson Street. Two 1100 gallon underground fuel oil tanks are present on the site, one outside the building on Richardson Street and the second under the building at Division Place.

Deliveries of hydrochloric acid are made by bringing the tank truck onto the parking area to unload. The fuel oil delivery truck for the Dumont Street tank is brought to the same unloading area. The fuel oil delivery truck for the Pitkin Place tank parks on the street while unloading.

1.1   Name and Address of Owner/Operator

The names and addresses of responsible persons are provided in Appendix 11.

1.2   Current Registration Applications and Certificates

A copy of the current registration applications and certificates for those tanks covered by the Spill Prevention regulations are provided in Appendix 4.

1.3   Approval Of Management

This Spill Prevention Report has been reviewed and approved by the management of PCSDI and is being implemented as witnessed by the signature below.

Shimshon Nudnick,	Date
Vice President	

1.4   Name & Signature of qualified person who prepared the report

I certify that I have acquired, through education and/or related practical experience, knowledge of the physical sciences, technology and principles of storing and handling hazardous substances as it relates to this facility.

I have examined the facility, and being familiar with the provisions of 6NYCRR Parts 595, 596, 597, 598, and 599, attest that this spill prevention report has been prepared in accordance with requirements therein.

Professional Engineer	Date
Registration No.	State

2 FACILITY MAP: The Site Map is provided in Appendix 1 and the Site Plan is provided in Appendix 2.

3 SUMMARY OF SPILLS WHICH HAVE OCCURRED AT THIS SITE OVER THE PAST FIVE YEARS: There have been no known spills to the environment from this site over the past five years.

4 IDENTIFICATION & ASSESSMENT OF CAUSES OF SPILLS, LEAKS AND RELEASES AT THIS FACILITY: While there have been no releases outside this facility, there are potential areas where spills and leaks can occur. These include the following:

Description	Potential Problems	Precautions
Outdoor Tank Filling	Overfill	Level gauging Overfill containment Unloading area containment
	Tank or hose failure or leak	Unloading area containment (buckets) Examination of fittings Refusal of leaking trucks
Indoor Tank Filling	Overfill	Level gauging Automatic level controls Overfill containment (building)
Filling underground tanks	Overfill	Level gauging (manual & gauges) Overfill containment (building at Pitkin Place; pavement at Dumont Street) Unloading area containment (None at Pitkin Place, Parking Area at Dumont Street) Inventory control (when tanks are not in use)
	Tank or hose failure or leak	Unloading area containment Examination of fittings Refusal of leaking trucks Spill cart
Transfers from tanks	Pump leaks	Do not use leakers Tag out Floor will contain
Shipping/receiving drums of paint, etc.	Container falls	Use loading dock

5 COMPLIANCE STATUS: With the production of this Report, the facility is in compliance with 6NYCRR 598, with the exception of upgrading above ground storage tank. The latter will be completed by December 21, 1999. The storage tanks are in compliance with 6NYCRR 596. Since there are no new or substantially modified hazardous substance storage tanks at this facility, compliance with 6NYCRR 599 is not required. The completed checklist is provided in Appendix 11.

6 TESTING AND INSPECTIONS

6.1 Underground Storage Tanks

Vents, gauges, monitoring equipment, piping and valves are visually inspected for cleanliness, leakage, corrosion and operability monthly (See Appendix 5 for Inspection Report). Since automatic line leak detectors and cathodic systems are not required for fuel oil tank smaller than 2000 gallon capacity, and fuel oil tanks are exempt from the Spill Prevention Report regulations, none are in place and no testing can be performed. Leak detection by inventory control, as discussed under Equivalent Technology following, is done on a monthly basis. No piping leak detection inspections are required for the suction piping located at this facility.

6.2 Above Ground Storage Tanks

Each day, the above ground tank at this facility is visually inspected for spills, leaks, cracks, areas of wear, corrosion, etc., and that valves are properly positioned. No records are kept of these inspections as they are part of the normal routine of the Plant Manager and employees. Since the tank is above ground, no monthly or annual release inspections are performed. While no five year inspections have been done in the past, future ones will be done by an outside contractor. Inspection forms are provided in Appendix 5.

7 FINANCIAL RESPONSIBILITY

No financial responsibility has been requested by the NYSDEC for this site. Thus, no special arrangements have been made or are required at this time.

8 SPILL RESPONSE PLAN

Evaluation of the site topography indicates that any external spill from a truck unloading hydrochloric acid in the parking lot at Division Street would be contained by the "speed bump" curbing at the street and the paved parking lot. In the event of such a spill, an outside cleanup contractor would be called to remediate the situation.

The bottom of the tank itself rests on a block of poured concrete, about three feet high, that is within a diked containment area. The dike walls are poured concrete topped by three courses of brick for a total height of about three feet. The floor of this area is also concrete. The walls and floor are surfaced with asphalt.

All tank truck unloading will follow the procedure provided in Appendix 7.

A list of the equipment and materials on hand to contain a spill and where they are stored is provided in the Contingency Plan in Appendix 3. The same Contingency Plan contains the NYS Hotline phone numbers, emergency contacts, reporting procedures, communications, and training and drills programs.

8.1 SITE SPECIFIC PROCEDURES

8.1.1 Release Reporting

The Contingency Plan in Appendix 3 specifies who is the site Emergency Coordinator and that he shall direct all actions in the event of a release. The Coordinator will determine what reporting is required and ensure that it is done.

8.1.2 Spill Prevention at pumps and valves

Currently, pump and valve leaks are repaired by in-house personnel when they occur. A formal maintenance and repair program will be prepared by December 22, 1999. However, since all pumps and valves are located within the building, any spills would be contained by the facility's concrete floor acting as the catchment basin specified in paragraph 598.5(e)(3).

8.1.3 Internal Coating of tanks

The acid tank at this site is not coated as it is compatible with the material it contains. There are no plans to coat this tank.

8.1.4 Corrosion protection of ASTs and ancillary equipment

The above ground storage tank at this facility is outdoors, and its material of construction (fiberglass reinforced plastic) is compatible with the material in use at the facility, no additional internal corrosion protection is present or required. However, the facility is investigating replacement of this tank as it has been negatively effected by ultraviolet light.

8.1.5 Replacement of rupture discs

None of the equipment at this facility has or has need of rupture discs. Thus, no replacement policy is present or required.

8.2 Substance transfers

Since only one tank receives hydrochloric acid, and hydrochloric acid is the only material received in bulk (other than fuel oil), the fill line connection for the tank is readily visible. For receiving bulk deliveries, the facility has a formal procedure for Receiving Tank trucks (Appendix 7) which specifies that a company employee directs which tank is to be filled and where the hose is to be connected. The appropriate spill containment precautions are provided in Section 8 above. All valves and tanks are labeled with tank contents and identification numbers.

8.3 Maintenance and repair

Any equipment found in disrepair is immediately taken out of service and not returned to service until repaired or replaced.

9 EQUIVALENT TECHNOLOGY

9.1 Secondary containment for ASTs

Secondary containment for the outdoor above ground storage tanks is provided by the asphalt coated concrete dike and floor. Consequently, as noted in Section 8 above, the diked area will contain the contents of the tank. Thus, no equivalent technology to provide secondary containment for above ground tanks is present or required.

9.2 Spill prevention at pump and valves

Currently, pump and valve leaks are repaired by in-house personnel when they occur. A formal maintenance and repair program will be prepared by December 22, 1999. However, since all pumps and valves are located within the building, any spills would be contained by the facility's concrete floor acting as the catchment basin specified in paragraph 598.5(e)(3). Thus, no equivalent technology to provide spill prevention at pumps and valves is present or required.

9.3 Proximity between non-stationary tanks containing incompatible substances

This facility receives Sodium Hydroxide which is incompatible with hydrochloric acid if mixed in an uncontrolled situation. However, since the sodium hydroxide is received in drums inside the building and the hydrochloric acid is stored in an outdoor tank, there is sufficient separation between them. The only "mixing" of the two is that one is used to neutralize the other as part of the facility processing. Thus, no additional equivalent technology to provide separation is present or required.

9.4 Leak detection for USTs

Since the underground tanks at this site are exempt from the Spill Prevention Report and Underground Storage Tank regulations, no equivalent technology leak detection methods are required. However, since one of the tanks has contained product for an extended period with no withdrawals, the inventory levels have been compared and found to match, thus indicating no leakage. The other tank has been in use, so that no inventory comparison could be done.

9.5 Painting of exterior tank surfaces

Since the exterior tank at this site is fiberglass reinforced plastic for which painting would serve no purpose, no equivalent technology for painting them is present or required.

9.6 Monitoring leakage between the tank bottom and secondary containment systems for new ASTs

Since there are no new above ground storage tanks since 1994 at this site, no equivalent technology for monitoring leakage for a tank sitting directly upon the secondary containment floor is present or required. Although the above ground hydrochloric acid storage tank bottom rests on a raised concrete block so that the tank bottom is not visible, any leakage or deterioration of the block would be readily visible during routine inspections and would be contained by the diked area.

9.7   Spill and overfill prevention

Since there are no new above ground storage tanks since 1994 at this site, this requirement does not apply to this site.

9.8   Preventing a siphon or backflow

Since there are no new above ground storage tanks since 1994 at this site, this requirement does not apply at this site.

10   SITE ASSESSMENT AND FINDINGS

While no discharges from this facility occurred in the past five years, a visual inspection was made and no evidence of a discharge was apparent. Thus, no site assessment of the site was warranted.

11   SPILL REPORTING FORM

The spill reporting form is provided in Appendix 3.

12   PROCEDURE FOR PREVENTION OF MIXING INCOMPATIBLE SUBSTANCES

No formal procedures are necessary for this site regarding mixing of incompatible substances, as the sodium hydroxide is received in drums in one area of the building and the hydrochloric acid is received in a bulk tank outside the building.

Since the incompatible substances at this site are received in different manners in different locations on the site, and the two are not connected to each other by piping or similar means, no equivalent technology to prevent the mixing of incompatible substances is present or required.

13   CONSENSUS CODES

13.1   Design and manufacture of non-stationary tanks

Although there are no existing non-stationary tanks in use, any new tanks installed after December 22, 1999 will meet the requirements of the consensus code. However, since the only non-stationary tanks used at this site are non-bulk containers and totes for waste petroleum oil, it is not likely that the code will apply. These no-bulk containers are not used for incompatible substances, are inside a closed building and are maintained in stable positions.

13.2   Five year inspection of above ground pipe systems and ASTs

Because the outdoor above ground tank is an atmospheric tank that is above grade, any leakage can be immediately seen. However, in accordance with the regulations, it will be tested every five years beginning in December 1999.

13.3   Repair of fiberglass-reinforced plastic tanks

There have been no repairs to the fiberglass-reinforced plastic tank at this site in at least the past ten years. However, records will be kept of any future repairs in compliance with a consensus standard.

13.4   Corrosion protection of ASTs, its associated piping and ancillary equipment

Since the above ground storage tank at this facility is outdoors, and its materials of construction are compatible with the material in use at the facility, no additional internal corrosion protection is present or required. However, it does require regular inspection regarding deterioration from sunlight. This will be part of the routine monthly inspections. However, the rules do not require any protection until December 22, 1999. It is anticipated that a replacement tank in conformance with the consensus codes will be in place by that date.

13.5   Tank design, construction and installation

Since no new above or underground tanks have been installed since 1994, no consensus code design or installation was required. Any new installations will be in conformance with such code. The facility will comply with the design, alarm, gauge, secondary containment and piping criteria for above ground storage tanks by December 22, 1999.

13.6   Corrosion protection of new UST

Since no new above or underground tanks have been installed since 1994, no consensus code design or installation was required. Any new installations will be in conformance with such code.

13.7   Secondary containment of USTs

Since there are no underground tanks at this site, and the present tank are exempt due to their size and contents, no secondary containment of underground storage tanks have been designed or installed in accordance with a consensus code. Any new installations will be in conformance with such code.

13.8   Installation of USTs

It is expected that the underground storage tanks at this site were designed and installed in accordance with the standards in effect at the time of their installation. Since there are no underground tanks at this site, current consensus codes could not be used. However, any new installations will be designed and installed in accordance with such code.

13.9   Cathodic protection of new AST bottoms

Since no new above or underground tanks have been installed since 1994, no cathodic protection has been used. In addition, although the present tank rest directly on the concrete block, any leakage would be immediately visible, thus precluding the need for such protection.

13.10   Secondary containment for ASTs

Since no new aboveground tanks have been installed since 1994, no secondary containment of above ground storage tanks have been designed or installed in accordance with a consensus code. However, the above ground tank is enclosed in asphalt coated concrete dikes and floor which are designed to serve as secondary containment for any spill. Any new installations will be in conformance with such code.

13.11   Installation of new piping system

New piping from the hydrochloric acid tank has been installed since 1994. Thus it was installed in accordance with the consensus code for pvc pipe that was current at the time of installation. Any new installations will also be in conformance with such code.

13.12   Corrosion protection for piping systems

New piping from the hydrochloric acid tank has been installed since 1994. In conformance with consensus codes, pvc pipe which is resistant to corrosion from hydrochloric acid was used. Corrosion protection in conformance with consensus code will be considered in the installation of any additional new piping systems.

13.13   Secondary containment for on-ground and underground piping systems

No new on-ground or underground piping has been installed since 1994. Any such new piping will be installed with secondary containment in accordance with consensus code.

13.14   Inspection of new piping prior to covering and placing in use

No applicable new piping has been installed since 1994. Any new piping will be inspected prior to covering and placing in use.

14   ACCESS TO RECORDS

All storage tanks and their records are available and accessible to any designated employee of the NYSDEC during normal business hours as required under Section 596.1(e). All onsite tanks have been registered (See Appendix 4).

15   OTHER RECORDS

The listing of tanks is found in Appendix 6.

There is one permanently out of service underground storage tank at this facility. A 500 gallon diesel fuel tank and dispensing pump on the Dumont Street side of the facility were closed in accordance with the underground storage tank regulations. Documentation of this closure is provided in Appendix 12.

No synthetic liners have been used for secondary containment of above and below ground tanks.

This rule applies to tanks installed after August 1994, of which this facility has none.

There are no inspector's statements or

records of repairs/tests/deficiencies to installed underground and above ground storage tanks and piping systems. These will be available for any tanks installed after August 1994, of which there presently are none.

Since there are no above ground horizontal tanks supported by saddles and installed after 1994 at this facility, engineering design and approval was not required. However, such design and approval will be obtained for any tanks installed in the future.

The life expectancy for the hydrochloric acid piping systems is estimated to be at least 10 years. Such determination will also be made for any systems installed in the future.

Appendices to be attached.

Prepared by: Enviro-Assist Inc.
Livingston, New Jersey

APPENDIX **XXX**

SOURCE:
P-F Technical Services, Inc.

Model Hazard Communication Program

(Name of facility)
(Address)

CORPORATE POLICY STATEMENT

WORKPLACE HAZARD COMMUNICATION

It has been our Company's policy to minimize, in whatever manner possible, the exposure of our employees to the potentially hazardous materials in the workplace.

This has been accomplished through the selection of alternate materials which pose less of a risk, careful control and documentation of the chemical substances required in our operation, and through employee training programs which stress the safe handling of all such materials.

The nature of our process and products requires that a significant number of our employees be exposed to some hazardous chemicals. We require inks, solvents, cleaners, and other products for production and maintenance that contain potentially hazardous chemicals.

Because our Company believes that the well-informed employee is more likely to use and handle hazardous materials with appropriate care, we have adopted a comprehensive "Right To Know" program designed to comply with Federal safety and health regulations.

As described in this manual, the OSHA HAZARD COMMUNICATION COMPLIANCE PROGRAM requires plant management to educate employees regarding potentially hazardous materials that are stored or used in their workplace, so that they may be better prepared to appreciate any hazards that may exist and respect the need for taking appropriate precautions to minimize exposure. We firmly believe that disclosure and candor in this potentially sensitive area will minimize worker apprehension, and that our policy is consistent with the Company's existing commitment to the welfare of its employees.

_____

PRESIDENT

DATE:_____

714

HAZARD COMMUNICATION COMPLIANCE PROGRAM

This manual represents the Company's Hazard Communication Compliance Program as mandated by the publication by OSHA of its Hazard Communication Standard in the Federal Register on November 25, 1983. The written sections describe the ingredients of the communication, training and education program that has been developed for its employees.

The purpose of the OSHA Federal Standard is to ensure that the hazards of all chemicals received in the workplace are documented, and that the information pertaining to potential hazards is communicated to our employees.

As manufacturers of products, we now utilize materials that contain hazardous chemicals as essential ingredients in our manufacturing and maintenance processes. However, the use of our products by customers does not result in exposure to any hazardous materials under normal conditions of use, or in any foreseeable emergencies. As such, our firm is classified as an "employer" within the meaning of the OSHA Standard, not that of a "chemical manufacturer."

No single document can fully define or describe how our employees are trained and educated for their jobs. However, the need for hazard training and education has dictated that this program be outlined to ensure that the communication of the information is performed with the resulting understanding by the employees of the potential dangers posed by the chemicals in their workplace.

All employees, new and old, are told of their rights under the OSHA Standard. They are told that they have the right to know about the substances with which they work and to which they are exposed. They will be trained in the safe handling and precautions to take to protect themselves. They are told about the Chemical Inventory—a list of the substances in the workplace—and where it is kept in the workplace, the hazards presented by the chemicals used in our plant, the existence and availability of the Material Safety Data Sheets, and where the MSDS's are located for reference. Copies of the Chemical Inventory and the MSDS's will be made available to any employee on request. The contents of the Material Safety Data Sheets are also utilized to train and educate our employees.

This manual is our company's written Hazard Communication Compliance Program. It includes other procedures that will provide for better compliance with the OSHA Standard as well as provide for the improved processing of information related to chemical consumption in our plant. Other plant operating and maintenance procedures exist that are not included here but are included in our commitment to the safety and health of our employees. Elements of this documentation will be made available to any contractors working in our plants to ensure that their employees are adequately trained and warned of the particular hazards that are present in our facility, and of the measures required for protection from these hazards.

Our employees receive instructions on how to read and identify labels on containers of hazardous substances in the workplace. They are told how to reference an item in the workplace with the corresponding Material Safety Data Sheet that is filed and accessible for more detailed information. Most of the substances entering the plant and any equipment that requires it are labeled to identify the substance(s) and the hazards. Where no visible markings exist, employees will have access to operating instructions, charts, placards, etc. to give them the necessary health and safety instructions and information.

Our employees are told about the methods and observations used to detect the presence of hazardous substances in the workplace. They are told what personal protective equipment is available, where it is located, and how to use it to protect them. They will be informed with regard to the protective equipment and procedures required on the equipment and the proper procedures to assure that these precautions are in effect. Special emergency procedures exist in the plant that are explained to all employees, in addition to the data which is available on the individual MSDS, including evacuation and fire emergency procedures.

As expressed in the Corporate Policy Statement that preceded this introduction, we have conscientiously planned this program to implement the intent of the OSHA Standard: the communication of information about the hazards of substances in the workplace to our employees. Any evaluations of our program should be focused on our overall success in providing such training and education, and in having warnings and information readily available to our employees.

The materials, which follow, provide a more detailed description of the corporate policy and the elements that help us to implement the Hazard Communication Compliance Standard in our facility.

_____

PRESIDENT

OSHA HAZARD COMPLIANCE PROGRAM

PROCEDURE FOR COMPILING AND USING THE OSHA CHEMICAL INVENTORY LISTING

OBJECTIVE: To make available for the plant and for the individual departments a listing of chemicals used in the workplace with such pertinent information as is required by the OSHA Hazard Communication Standard, 29CFR S 1910.1200.

This listing will be posted in each department, in a format and place that is accessible to all employees.

CONTENT OF INVENTORY LISTING

1. Number – assigned in order to be used as a reference to the appropriate Material Safety Data Sheets.
2. Common Name – will indicate the source (company name) and common name or brand name of the substance. Could be the generic name of the chemical.
3. Chemical names or the listing of chemical components of the substance.
4. Storage – indicate site in which chemical is stored when not in use.

   Below the site, indicate average usage of the chemical over a given period of time, i.e. per day, week, or month.

   Below that indicate maximum amount stored at any given time.

   For example: Chemical Storage Room
                    5 gal/week; 10 gal max.

5. Used At – indicates area of building in which chemical is used and number of employees who will have contact with the chemical.

6. Hazard – indicates the general categories of hazards posed by the particular chemical or its components.

   Use the following to describe hazards:

   Flammable
   Reactive
   Pressure
   Health Hazard – Acute
   Health Hazard – Chronic

CONDUCTING THE INVENTORY

1. Each department supervisor or foreman will compile a list of the chemicals used in his or her area, including the amounts used on a regular basis and the maximum stored.
2. Purchasing will review the lists to assure that all chemicals are listed and that the quantities are relevant.
3. Each chemical on the list will be cross-referenced with its appropriate MSDS and a number assigned.
4. The listing should be typed and organized by department.
5. A master list of all departments will be maintained in Purchasing and the Plant Manager's Office.
6. Departmental lists will be maintained in a viable location in each department.

REVISION/UPDATING THE CHEMICAL INVENTORY LISTING

At such time as a new chemical is introduced to the company or any deleted, changes will be made to update the Chemical Inventory Lists.

An annual review should be made for the purpose of assuring that all information including usage numbers is current.

MATERIALS SAFETY DATA SHEETS

OBJECTIVE: To assure that every chemical brought into the building has a Material Safety Data Sheet on file, and available in the departments of use.

DESCRIPTION

The Materials Safety Data Sheet—commonly called the MSDS—may consist of eleven sections including the heading.

1. Heading describes the company who prepared the information including an emergency phone number, and the date the MSDS was prepared.
2. Section 1 – Identity: the chemical name or common name of the substance, the scientific name and formula, and pertinent classifications.
3. Section 2 – Hazardous Ingredients: lists all the dangerous ingredients that make up the materials. Only exception is when chemical composition is a trade secret.
4. Section 3 – Physical Characteristics: lists such items as boiling points, freezing point, vapor pressure and density, pH, reactivity in water, appearance and odor, etc.
5. Section 4 – Fire and Explosion Data
6. Section 5 – Reactivity Data: stability, compatibility, etc.
7. Section 6 – Health Hazards: associated with materials such as irritants, sensitizers, corrosive, or carcinogen. Describes signs and symptoms of overexposure, routes of exposure, medical conditions recognized as due to exposure, OSHA and ACGIH limits of exposure.
8. Section 7 – Emergency and First Aid Procedures
9. Section 8 – Toxicity Data
10. Section 9 – Special Protection Information: describes the use of protective equipment, safe handling procedures, and engineered control requirements.
11. Section 10 – Special Precautions and Spill/Leak Procedures

Every section of the MSDS must be completed. If the information is not available, it should be so indicated (N/A).

MSDS may vary in style but all information above will be there.

AVAILABILITY OF MSDS'S

Every manufacturer with whom you deal must supply an MSDS for the products he sells you. You may have received copies and have them in your purchasing files.

If you do not have MSDS for any product, send a letter requesting it. A sample letter is attached for your information.

In the event a supplier will not send an MSDS, contact the local OSHA office. They have a procedure [CPL2-2, 38 (I) 8 (d) (4)] to call the manufacturer and obtain the necessary MSDS for you.

LOCATION OF MSDS BOOKS IN FACILITY

The Material Safety Data Sheets are required to be accessible to all employees.

A copy of the chemical inventory and the appropriate MSDS collection will be maintained in a central location in or adjacent to the plant. Separate sets may be maintained in the departments in which the chemicals are stored and/or used.

The collection will be kept up to date with regard to all chemicals used in the facility, or in the particular department.

In cases where the situation allows, MSDS's may be posted on the bulletin board for easy access by employees.

Any employee who wants to read an MSDS will have that opportunity. If there are any questions or a need for explanation, that will be accomplished in accordance with company procedures.

No employee will be discouraged or refused the opportunity to see any MSDS used by the company.

PROCEDURE FOR EMPLOYEE TO REQUEST INFORMATION PERTAINING TO CHEMICAL SUBSTANCES USED AND FOR MANAGEMENT TO MAINTAIN RECORD OF SUCH REQUESTS

OBJECTIVE: To provide a standard format and procedure to assure that requests for information pertaining to chemicals used are answered in a reasonable time frame, and that records are kept should they be required to confirm the request.

PROCEDURE:

1. Forms will be available in the department.
2. Employee will complete the form by indicating: the
   a. Name, Clock Number and Department
   b. Date of Request
   c. Chemical or Material in question
   d. Concern about use of the material (question)
3. The supervisor who receives the request will acknowledge and indicate date received. He will then submit to the manager designated.

4. The manager will check the appropriate MSDS, if one is part of the Chemical Inventory. If the information is available, he will make an immediate response to the employee.
5. If the MSDS is not in the collection, or the answer not obvious, the manager will request the information from the appropriate supplier.
6. Upon receipt of the information from the supplier, the employee will be informed of the answer.
7. At such time as the employee is informed, he will acknowledge by signing the response form.
8. A file will be maintained of all such requests, as part of the normal files maintained for OSHA.

NOTE: This procedure will be used only if the employee and his supervisor have read the appropriate MSDS and cannot find the information, or understand the particular question to be answered by the information contained in the MSDS.

LABELING CONTAINERS TO IDENTIFY CHEMICAL HAZARDS

OBJECTIVE: To assure that all chemical containers brought into the plant or repackaged in the plant are properly labeled to identify the hazards of the chemicals in accordance with standards that are acceptable by OSHA.

PROCEDURE, INCOMING MATERIALS

The Receiving Department will inspect all incoming drums, kits, cans, etc. to make certain that the manufacturer properly labels them.

The label must indicate the chemical packaged, and its components if a mixture, and the safety precautions for its use. A warning label will also be attached to identify the Hazardous Nature of the product.

If the product is not properly labeled, notify the manufacturer immediately. If within company policy, attach the appropriate labels before moving to a new location in the plant.

PROCEDURE, IN-HOUSE TRANSFERS OR MIXING OF MATERIALS

The mixing of solvents into blends, various color inks or paints to blend new colors, or the transfer of smaller quantities of any chemical substances requires proper labeling and the identification of the hazards involved.

If the original containers are used to hold the new blend and the labels are left intact, no additional labels will be required, considering that the hazards and protective measures are the same. The new color or identification of the new solvent blend should be written on the label.

(Transfer containers cannot be used if they are not labeled properly.)

To assure the proper identification, labels will be purchased for use in-plant to communicate the type of hazard. They will be affixed at the site when the transfer or blending has been accomplished. The following page pictures the labels that are available and will be used under the proper category.

To communicate the information and intent of the labels, bulletin boards in the workplace will identify the labels and what they mean. Where necessarily, the descriptions of the hazards and the precautionary measures will be in both English and Spanish to facilitate understanding by the employees.

ATTACHMENTS

Stock labels to be used in-house, plus samples of other labels that will by used by suppliers to identify the Chemicals, Hazards, Precautions, and First Aid measures.

TRAINING PROGRAM TO INFORM EMPLOYEES OF THE LAW REGULATING CHEMICAL HAZARDS, THE NATURE OF CHEMICALS USED AND STORED ON THE PREMISES, AND PRECAUTIONS TO TAKE IN THE USE OR IN THE EVENT OF AN OCCURRENCE WITH THE CHEMICALS

OBJECTIVES: To familiarize each employee with the law and the chemicals in his department, with the rights of the employee to know the hazards of the chemicals with which he must work, and to assist the employee in performing his job in a safe and more qualified manner.

CONTENT OF TRAINING PROGRAM

The initial training program will consist of three components.

The first session should be devoted to the regulations and the components that are provided for employee safety. This should be scheduled for a period of approximately one to one and a half hours. The content of this session is described in lesson plan I.

The basic chemical safety program is described in lesson plans II and III. Subject matter in the two lesson plans is organized for use in discussing specific hazards, or by using the overall outline to target concerns about a specific chemical or family of chemicals.

Sessions held to review items in lesson plans II and III can be held in classroom groups or on-the-job. Time will depend on the nature and scope of the subject selected for discussion.

The lesson plans are organized as follows:

I. THE HAZARD COMMUNICATION COMPLIANCE STANDARD: WHAT IT MEANS TO YOU AND TO YOUR COMPANY

II. PHYSICAL HAZARDS: RECOGNIZING THEM AND PREVENTING ACCIDENTS BY SAFE WORKING PROCEDURES

III. HEALTH HAZARDS: RECOGNIZING POTENTIAL HAZARDS AND UTILIZING SAFE WORKING PROCEDURES TO PREVENT EXPOSURE

The basic tools to be used are the Material Safety Data Sheets and the labels.

IMPLEMENTATION OF TRAINING PROGRAM

1. The training program will be conducted by the managers and supervisors from the various departments.
2. Each session will be prepared utilizing the outlines prepared for that session and materials that will be made available to the lecturer.
3. A roster of employees scheduled for the session will be posted on the Bulletin Board. Participants will sign-in to record attendance at the session. (See form – TRAINING SESSION ROSTER.)
4. The primary purpose of the training sessions is TO TRAIN AND TO TEACH SAFE HANDLING OF CHEMICALS.

    The secondary purpose shall serve to improve the ability of personnel to:
    a. Analyze and solve problems
    b. Achieve acceptance of a program or idea
    c. Elicit group discussion of issues
    d. Reconcile any conflict
    e. Discuss information essential to others

COURSE CONTENT: See lesson plans for the three sessions.

CONTINUITY

The training program will be repeated annually, unless new developments—chemical or equipment introduced—require more frequent sessions.

Guidelines to use for hazard classification when using HMIS or similar style labels.

INDOCTRINATION OF NEW EMPLOYEES

OBJECTIVE: To assure that all new employees are advised of:

1. The laws pertaining to chemical hazards and their right to know.
2. The chemical hazards in the plant (including MSDS and Labels).
3. Precautions in handling chemicals and in the event of an occurrence.
4. Location of all facilities and equipment for use in the handling of chemicals, protective equipment and supplies, and facilities for first aid or other supplies needed to treat in the event of exposure.

PROCEDURE

The first day that a new employee is reporting for work will include the following as an initial assignment:

The foreman will be assigned to instruct the employee and tour the plant with him/her.

He will give him/her the brochure on the OSHA Hazard Communication Standard, and explain what the law means and how it applies to the worker and the firm:

1. Chemical Inventory and Chemical Hazards – Health and Physical.
2. Warning Labels to alert the worker and inform him.
3. Material Safety Data Sheets – what they are and how to use them.
4. Training requirements and how the company carries them out.
5. The overall program and what it means as a commitment of management to the safety of the worker.

He will conduct the employee on a tour of the plant to show him/her the areas in which chemicals are stored and used, the labels on the containers, and the location of the MSDS files in each department.

He will also show them the various facilities for emergency care, and the exits for fire evacuation.

He will advise them of the various precautions that will safeguard the worker in the conduct of his job, i.e. Safety and Housekeeping practices, handling of chemicals and no-smoking areas, lifting properly where applicable, etc.

1. The plant manager responsible for OSHA Hazard Communication Compliance will check to see that the employee understands the information that has been presented.
2. The employee will sign an acknowledgement that the training took place. A copy of this format is attached.

TRAINING PROGRAM, LESSON I

THE HAZARD COMMUNICATION STANDARD – WHAT IT MEANS TO THE COMPANY AND TO YOU, THE EMPLOYEE

OBJECTIVES:
1. To explain the nature of the regulation, CFR 29 1910.1200.
2. To explain how the regulation affects the company and the way it conducts business.
3. Review employee rights under the regulation.

4. Describe the methods that the company will employ to comply with the regulation:
   1. Labeling.
   2. Material Safety Data Sheets/Chemical Inventory Lists.
   3. Procedure for Employee to file inquiries.
   4. Training program.
   5. New employee training.

AGENDA

A. Explain the Hazard Communication Compliance Regulation
   1. OSHA (the Occupational Safety and Health Administration) has written this regulation to reduce the incidence of chemically related illnesses and injuries among employees in the manufacturing industries. It is assumed that wider availability of information relating to workplace hazards will allow employers to design safer work environments while enabling employees to better protect themselves.
   2. Employer is required to:
      a. Compile Workplace Chemical Inventories
      b. Obtain Material Safety Data Sheets
      c. Label all Chemicals used in Workplace
      d. Inform and train employees
      e. Develop a written Hazard Communication Program
      f. Implement an ongoing Hazard Communication effort
   3. Employees rights under law with regard to "Right to Know" and access to the Chemical Inventory and MSDS Book.

B. Discuss how the regulation affects the company:
   1. All materials brought into the plant must have a Material Safety Data Sheet on file. Explain content.
   2. All containers brought into the plant must be properly labeled to indicate the hazards potential. Explain using samples to illustrate.
   3. All containers carrying chemicals that have been filled within the plant must carry appropriate labels to identify content and hazards.
   4. Information regarding the chemicals, the hazards and precautions for use or in the event of an accident, must be made available for any employee to see.

5. A procedure must be in place for employees to address questions with regard to chemical hazards and receive answers, as well as action when required.
6. A training program must be in effect to train existing as well as new employees with regard to the regulation and the chemicals in use.

C. Discuss the right of the employee under the law and the standard:
1. An employee has the right to know what chemicals he is handling and the hazards involved.
2. An employee has the right to consult the MSDS Book to obtain more detailed information than is available on the label.
3. An employee has the right to question the nature and safety of any chemical that he is called upon to use.

D. Explain the various methods of communicating chemical hazards.
1. Chemical Inventory
A listing within each department of the chemicals used, where they are stored and in what quantity, where they are used, and categories of hazards which they or components may represent.
Describe where in the department, the list will be maintained as a reference for the employees.
2. Materials Safety Data Sheets (MSDS)
Review the general components of the form so that each employee may understand where he/she can find the information required in the event of an occurrence or need-to-know situation.
   a. Manufacturer data; emphasize emergency phone number
   b. Hazardous Ingredients Information
   c. Physical and Chemical Characteristics
   d. Fire and Explosion Data
   e. Reactivity Data
   f. Health Hazard Data
      (1) How to recognize exposure/medical conditions
      (2) Emergency First Aid
   g. Precautions for Safe Handling and Use
   h. Control measures – safety equipment, clothing, work practices
3. Procedure for employees to request information:

If the Inventory and the MSDS do not satisfy the questions raised by an employee, he may use established procedures to request additional information.
Explain form and handling within company.
4. Training program – to familiarize the employees with the regulation, procedures and chemical hazards, sessions will be held every week, lasting no more than 30 minutes each, to review the various hazards, how to identify them, and what to do if an accident occurs.
5. New employee training – at such time as a new employee starts work, he/she will receive information pertaining to the law, the chemicals in the plant, safe handling procedures and other appropriate measures.

CONCLUSION

What we have done today has been to discuss your rights and what the company will do to protect you and inform you so that you can protect yourself. It is important that you understand the intent of the OSHA Regulation for Hazard Communication.

It is equally important that you each realize that by doing your job in the proper way, taking precautions in the handling and use of the chemicals, that you will prevent occurrences that can be harmful to you or your fellow workers.

TRAINING PROGRAM, LESSON II

PHYSICAL HAZARDS; RECOGNIZING THEM AND PREVENTING ACCIDENTS BY SAFE WORKING PROCEDURES

OBJECTIVES:
1. Define the physical characteristics considered hazardous in industrial materials.
2. To inform and teach the use of MSDS's and Labels as sources of information with regard to identification of physical hazards, procedures for the safe storage and use of the materials, and procedures to follow in the event of an accident/occurrence.
3. Identify the chemicals and review the specific hazards and precautions in the plant.

FORMAT:
1. Supervisors and trainers will attend an initial program, approximate time – 1 hour, in a classroom setting. This will serve as the basis for their role in training all other employees.
2. All employees will be trained in a combination of classroom and on-the-job sessions by the designated supervisor or foreman over a period of time following the initial session. Time allotted will depend on the size of the group and subject matter. It is anticipated that the contents of this lesson plan will be segmented for presentations to be made to the employees.

AGENDA

I. DEFINITIONS:
A. Definition of Physical Hazard – OSHA Standard 1910.1200, page 881
   "Physical Hazard" means a chemical for which there is scientifically valid evidence that it is a combustible liquid, a compressed gas, explosive, flammable or organic peroxide, pyrophoric, unstable (reactive) or water reactive.

B. Flammable and reactive chemicals are hazardous when they undergo reaction after a chemical event triggers them.
   1. Flammables can burn when ignited.
   2. Reactive when brought together with the wrong materials can produce heat or gases explosively.

C. There are other physical hazards which are produced by machines. Some of these hazards are:
   1. Noise
   2. Dust
   3. Heat
   4. Various types of rays or waves, i.e. X-rays, ultrasonic, lasers, etc.

II. THE MSDS, SOURCE OF INFORMATION:
A. All information concerning the materials in use are summarized in the Material Safety Data Sheets under appropriate headings:
   1. Identity – information about the chemical name and manufacturer, including emergency phone number to reach in event of need for emergency treatment or spill.
   2. Hazardous Ingredients – lists all hazardous ingredients and their threshold limits. In the case of physical hazards, it is possible for this section to be marked N/A (not applicable) and for a hazard to exist.
   3. Physical/Chemical Characteristics – technical data to identify a material by appearance and odor and other data to help you control exposure.
   4. Fire and Explosion – tells you how to prevent fires and explosions; how to extinguish; special fire fighting procedures.
   5. Reactivity – identifies reactive materials, conditions to avoid, and what materials must be kept away from each other to assure safety.
   6. Safe Handling and Use – discusses spills.
   7. Control Measures – protective equipment, and conditions required to prevent overexposure.

B. Location of MSDS books

C. Procedure for obtaining information if not clear or in question after consulting the MSDS.

III. LABELS:
A. Content of labels—information digested from MSDS—on all incoming chemical containers.

B. Need to label in-plant containers to identify hazards.

IV. FLAMMABLES:
A. Flammable substances are those that burn when ignited at or below room temperature. Combustibles must be heated before they will burn.

B. Flammable materials can be solids, liquids, or gases:
   1. Finely divided solids such as metal filings of aluminum or zinc.
   2. Solvents or fuels.
   3. Gases such as propane, natural gas.

C. Safe Handling and use of Flammables:
   1. Don't smoke.
   2. Keep work containers as small as possible.

3. Reduce surface area of all containers.
4. Use adequate ventilation.
5. Clean up spills promptly.
6. Cover containers when not in use; safety cans.
7. Store flammable soaked rags in covered protective containers.
8. Bond and ground all containers when dispensing.
9. Use explosion proof wiring and equipment.
10. Remember that flammable also pose Health Hazards.

D. Safe Storage of Flammables:
1. Proper containers.
2. Protective storage areas or cabinets.
3. Do not store in vicinity of oxidizers or corrosives—oxidizers may ignite; corrosives may destroy the containers and allow release of vapors.

E. Emergencies: Spills and Leaks:
1. Small leaks or spills should be attended to promptly:
   a. Close leak with valve, shutting down equipment, or moving and sealing the container.
   b. Turn off electrical equipment or any other machine that can cause ignition.
   c. Absorb spill with rags or Speedy Dry absorbent materials.
2. Large leaks or spills should be handled in accordance with the established contingency plan.

F. Emergencies: Fire and Explosion:
1. Explain emergency alarm and response equipment and systems.
2. Location of phones, alarms, and fire extinguishers.
3. Train in use of fire extinguishers.
4. Train in evacuation procedures.
5. Inform of the procedures spelled out in the Contingency Plan.

V. REACTIVE
A. Reactive chemicals are materials that can change violently when combined with other materials or conditions:
1. Oxidizers add oxygen to any situation where burning is occurring, making the fire more intense and difficult to extinguish.
2. Some reactives explode or give off gas and heat in air or on contact with water.
3. Incompatible materials can act like reactive, i.e. acids and bases.

B. Storage and Handling:
1. Store away from other materials.
2. Read the MSDS carefully when you see the word oxidizer or reactive. Note what chemicals are incompatible with materials you are using.
3. Be sure to use protective clothing and respiratory protection required.
4. Protect yourself against health hazards as well. Many reactive chemicals are corrosive or toxic, or both.

C. Emergencies:
1. If it is practical, shut down any electrical equipment.
2. If possible, stop the spill or leak.
3. If any doubt, leave the area and notify supervisor.
4. DO NOT TRY TO NEUTRALIZE MATERIAL OR CLEAN UP THE SPILL UNLESS YOU HAVE APPROPRIATE PROTECTIVE EQUIPMENT AND HAVE BEEN PROPERLY TRAINED IN HOW TO DO IT SAFELY.

VI. THE CHEMICAL INVENTORY AND THE MSDS BOOKS
The list of chemicals should be maintained as a content page in the MSDS collection loose-leaf book. It should be updated on a regular basis and the list periodically checked against the collection of MSDS's.

VII. SUMMARY
What we have done here today is discuss the physical hazards that exist with regard to the chemicals used in our plant. Proper handling and use of these materials will avoid the risks of potential exposure and/or emergency conditions such as fire and explosion. Using the MSDS's and labels to inform you and your fellow workers as to the specific hazards and precautions in the materials you use should help you to work safely and avoid health and bodily damage.

Think safe, work safe, live a healthy lifestyle.

TRAINING PROGRAM, LESSON III

HEALTH HAZARDS; RECOGNIZING THE POTENTIAL HAZARDS AND UTILIZING SAFE WORKING HABITS, IDENTIFYING POTENTIAL EXPOSURE AND PROCEDURES TO AVOID OR CONTAIN EXPOSURE TO HAZARDOUS CHEMICALS

OBJECTIVES:
1. To define the health hazards characteristic of chemicals and materials used in the plant.
2. To inform and teach the use of the MSDS as a source of information with regard to the hazardous nature of materials employed, identification signs to recognize the existence of chemical substances, safe working practices and habits to prevent exposure, and steps to be taken in the event of exposure.
3. To review the chemicals and materials used in the plant and the specific concerns that employees should anticipate.
4. To impart an understanding to employees that use of the communication provisions of the OSHA Standard through MSDS and labels to learn the proper way to handle chemicals will enhance the chances that they will live a longer and healthier life.

FORMAT:
1. Supervisors and trainers will receive a one-hour class to introduce them to the subject matter and how it should be taught. This will be a classroom session and will be conducted by Pro-Flex Consultants Ltd.
2. All employees will be trained in a combination of classroom and on-the-job sessions by the designated supervisors or trainers, over a period of time following the initial session. Time allotted will vary depending on the subject and the manner in which the subject matter is being presented. It is planned to break the outline into segments for presentation for ease in transferring the materials to the employees.

AGENDA

I. DEFINITION (OSHA Standard 1910.1200, page 880)
Health Hazard means a chemical for which there is statistically significant evidence based on at least one study conducted in accordance with established scientific principles that acute or chronic health effects may occur in exposed employees. The term "Health Hazard" includes chemicals which are carcinogens, toxic or highly toxic agents, reproductive toxins, irritants, corrosives, sensitizers, hepatoxins, nephrotoxins, neurotoxins, agents which act on the hematopoietic system, and agents which damage the lungs, skin, eyes, or mucous membranes. Appendix A provides further definitions and explanations.

The scope of health hazards covered by this section and Appendix B describes the criteria to be used to determine whether or not a chemical is to be considered hazardous for purposes of this standard.
Chemical Hazards are normally grouped as:
1. Flammable
2. Corrosive
3. Toxic
4. Reactive

Exposure normally takes place by:
1. Skin contact
2. Eye contact
3. Inhalation
4. Ingestion

II. THE MSDS – SOURCE OF INFORMATION:
A. Information contained in MSDS
1. Identity and manufacturer
2. Hazardous ingredients and threshold values
   a. OSHA listings
   b. ACGIH
   c. NTP
3. Health Hazard Data
4. Precautions for Safe Handling and Use
5. Control Measures

B. Location and use of MSDS Books

C. Procedure to use if information is wanted and not found or understood in the MSDS.

III. LABELS – ON SITE SOURCE OF INFORMATION:
A. What information is found on labels?

B. How internal containers are labeled and what the labels mean.

IV. THE CHEMICAL INVENTORY AND THE MSDS BOOKS

V. POTENTIAL EXPOSURES, PROTECTIVE MEASURES, REACTION TO EXPOSURE:
A. Eye Exposure:
1. Caused by splashing when pouring liquids, mixing liquids (particularly if reactive are mixed incorrectly) and by machinery mixing or moving liquids.
2. Care should be taken to:
   a. Wear safety glasses or goggles
   b. Handle liquids with care
   c. Use proper container (safety cans) to avoid splashing
   d. Have machine guards in place to contain splash
3. First Aid:
   a. Eye wash stations
   b. Flush with lots of clean warm water for at least fifteen minutes
   c. Consult physician
   d. Depending on chemical, consult MSDS; in some cases physician should be consulted immediately.
4. In addition to liquids, fine dust or pieces of metal can cause eye damage. Take the proper precautions (glasses) and avoid this type of exposure.

B. Skin Contact:
1. Can result in reactions due to corrosive chemicals, or allergic reactions.
2. Precautions – wear working gloves designed to cope with the nature of the exposure, particularly when working with corrosives or reactive chemicals.
3. First Aid:
   a. Provide wash-up facilities with proper soaps in key areas of plant.
   b. First Aid station should include lotions for skin care
   c. In event of contact, wash with soapy water and rinse thoroughly. Use skin lotions where applicable.

   d. Consult MSDS for specific action with each chemical.
   e. If irritation persists, consult physician.

C. Inhalation:
1. Concern is due to allergies as well as excessive fumes that may trigger other bodily damages.
   Corrosive fumes can do considerable damage to internal tissues.
2. Precautions:
   a. Use chemicals as specified, mixing in the right sequences.
   b. Keep all cans closed when not in use.
   c. Keep minimal amounts needed at machines.
   d. Place all contaminated rags in safety containers.
   e. Keep machine guards in place to contain fumes.
   f. Wear protective gear – facemasks or respirators where required.
3. First Aid:
   a. If allergic reaction, use an antihistamine; consult a physician.
   b. If employee has been over-exposed, remove him to fresh air. If he has stopped breathing, give mouth-to-mouth resuscitation. Get medical attention immediately.

D. Ingestion:
1. Concern is if chemical is taken into body by eating or through a break in the skin (cut, bruise).
2. Precaution should be taken by wearing gloves when known chemical hazards are being handled.
3. Wash hands thoroughly before eating or placing your hands in or near your mouth or other body orifices.
4. Protect cuts by using bandages and gloves.
5. First Aid – seek medical advice if you encounter any symptoms or knowingly find that you have ingested a hazardous chemical. Do not induce vomiting unless directed to do so by a doctor or poison control center.

E. In general, look through the MSDS's and be familiar with the materials with which you work. Learn to recognize what the hazards are, how to work safely, what to do if you recognize that exposure has taken place.

SUMMARY

Health hazards are everywhere – in your home, in the streets, in the workplace. Use good sense and safe practices to avoid exposure. Know what you have to do in the event that you are exposed. Use the tools supplied by your employer and his suppliers to be smart and live safely – read labels, read the MSDS's – don't let twenty-five years of experience fool you into thinking you know everything.

CONTRACTORS WORKING IN YOUR PLANT

OBJECTIVE: The Standard calls for contractors working in your facility to have knowledge of the hazards in the plant. At the same time, it is incumbent upon the contractor to supply MSDS's for any materials he is bringing into the plant.

PROCEDURE: The following statement should be requested of all contractors at the time a Purchase Order is issued for work to be performed.

CONTRACTOR/VISITOR NOTIFICATION FORM

I have been notified of the hazardous materials to which I and/or my employees may be exposed while working at or visiting the plant of _____ located at_____ _____.

A copy of the Chemical Inventory for the facility has been made available to me to review.

I have also been informed that I must supply a current Material Safety Data Sheet (MSDS) for all materials covered under the OSHA Hazard Communication Standard (29 CFR 1910.1200) that I and/or my employees will be using or bringing into the plant.

CONTRACTOR/VISITOR
NAME_____

ADDRESS_____

_____

SIGNATURE_____

DATE_____

NAME OF PLANT EMPLOYEE
PERFORMING
NOTIFICATION_____

A copy of this form should be attached to the Purchase Order.

RESPONSIBILITY: Purchasing Department

FIRE EVACUATION PLAN AND FIRE DRILLS

OBJECTIVE: To outline, the specific plan for evacuating the plant in the event of a fire, and to establish procedure and policy for conducting fire drills to acquaint employees with exits closest to the departments in which they work.

PLAN OF BUILDING WITH EXITS MARKED: Attached

EXITS TO BE USED BY DEPARTMENTS: Mark on layout

PROCEDURE:

1. When fire is suspected, the switchboard operator will be advised immediately.
2. The switchboard operator will announce that, "There is a potential fire on the premises; evacuate through the Fire Exit designated for your department or the area of the plant you are in." She will then call the Fire Department.
3. Foremen will assure that all employees depart the building in an orderly fashion and congregate in the designated assembly area across from the plant. Each supervisor will conduct a head count to

assure that all personnel under his supervision have left the building.

4. After being advised by the Plant Manager or other designated executive of the firm, the foreman will either have the people in his department return to their work stations, or take such action as determined in the event of a fire.

FIRE DRILLS:

Practice sessions will be conducted at the outset of this program and will be repeated once a month to assure that all employees are aware of the evacuation plans and carry them out in the proper decorum.

HANDOUT TO EMPLOYEES
INSTRUCTIONS FOR FIRE DRILLS/ OTHER EVACUATIONS

In the event of a fire, a major spill of chemicals or any other disaster in our plant or at any site at which we are working, the management wants to be sure that all employees leave the premises safely.

This memo is to advise each employee of the procedure to be followed in the event of a fire, spill or other disaster, which requires us to evacuate the building.

ALARMS: In the event of a fire, etc. there can be two types of alerts.

Fire or smoke will trigger the automatic alarm, which is connected to the sprinkler system. If you hear this loud, very obvious noise, you will know that there is reason to leave the building.

Drills, and other emergencies, will require the use of voice alarms. At such time as a fire, spill or other disaster requires you to leave the building, one, or more, of the supervisors will announce at least three times:

"THERE IS AN EMERGENCY IN PROGRESS. LEAVE THE BUILDING NOW."

EVACUATION PROCEDURE

You will leave the area, in which you work, and go to the closest designated exit door.

Designated employees will shut off all operating equipment.

Your supervisor will direct you during the evacuation. Listen to him as directions are given. He will check to see that everyone has left the building.

Walk calmly and without pushing into or ahead of other people leaving the department and building. Do not use the elevators.

When you reach the outside, go to the designated area away from the building.

Assemble so that a supervisor can check to make sure that all personnel are present and that no one has been left in the building.

The assembly area will be at:

You will be told when it is safe to return to the building, or if you are to leave the area.

COMPANY: _____

ADDRESS: _____

PHONE: _____ FAX: _____

OSHA/HAZARDOUS WASTE CONTINGENCY PLAN

OBJECTIVE: To outline the responsibilities and procedures to be taken in the event of fire, explosion or spills of hazardous materials or wastes.

EMERGENCY COORDINATORS:

A. Primary Coordinator –

   Home Phone Number

B. Secondary Coordinator –

   Home Phone Number

C. After business hours, contact

   Home Phone Number

GENERAL PLAN OF ACTION

A. FIRE OR EXPLOSION:
   1. Evacuate building (shut all power to equipment)
      Employees are to assemble at entrance to
   2. Call Fire and Police Departments
   3. Call Primary Coordinator
   4. Call Secondary Coordinator
   5. Contain fire within limits set for plant personnel until arrival of Fire Department; abandon efforts if limit is exceeded.

B. CHEMICAL SPILLAGE:
   1. Evacuate building (shut all power to equipment and stop any flow of solvents or inks)
   2. Call Police and Fire Departments
   3. Call Primary Coordinator
   4. Call Secondary Coordinator
   5. Contain spill within limits of in-plant personnel and emergency equipment

6. Call emergency environmental agency to arrange for containment and clean up in accordance with DEP regulations.

EMERGENCY ALARM AND EXTINGUISHING SYSTEMS
A. Location of all emergency alarm and containment equipment is indicated on the enclosed plant layout.

Terminology and codes are as follows:

F	– Fire Extinguishers-ABC Powder
	– Fire Extinguishers-Water
A	– Alarm bells or loudspeakers
Tel	– Telephones accessible to plant
Exit	– Exits from various departments and building (arrows indicate directions)

First Aid – location of first aid supplies.
Bathroom facilities noted.
Manufacturing and storage areas indicated

B. Fire Extinguishers
   1. Number in building – _____
                                FLOOR___ ___

      ABC Powder
      CO_2 Water
      Other

   2. Service and inspection performed by:

C. Alarm System
   1. Telephones located in administrative office and plant offices.
   2. Loudspeakers (intercom) located at central points in plant.
   3. Loudspeakers (intercom) can be activated by contacting receptionist or by dialing _____. Speak clearly into mouthpiece and message will be transmitted over the intercom loudspeakers.
   4. Alarm bells for sprinkler system will be sounded when sprinklers are activated.

Sprinkler system is serviced by:

Fire Alarm System is contracted to:

D. CHEMICAL SPILLAGE EQUIPMENT:
1. Adequate supply of absorbent rags or materials to contain and absorb minor spills will be maintained in operating departments and storage areas.
2. Respiratory equipment, gloves and goggles are maintained in designated operating departments for normal operations requiring protective gear, as well as for any emergency which may arise.
3. In the event of a major spill, outside emergency support for containment and clean-up will be provided by an authorized clean-up contractor, who will perform in accordance with NYSDEC regulations.

EMERGENCY PROCEDURES

A. GENERAL EVACUATION PROCEDURE

When fire, explosion or spillage alarm is activated, all personnel are to leave their stations and walk to the closest exit from the plant, via the assigned route from their departments to the assigned exits.

Should the assigned route and/or exit be blocked by the fire, explosion or spill, alternative means of departure will be designated by the supervisor (foreman) in area.

The employees will assemble in the designated areas outside and away from the building for the purpose of a head count to assure that all personnel are present. This will assure that employees have not been left in the plant.

Simultaneously with the evacuation of the plant, designated personnel will man the emergency equipment to contain or eliminate the emergency condition. All power will be shut off and the flow of liquid chemicals stopped.

At such time as the Fire Department arrives, or the emergency conditions exceed the ability of the personnel to contain it, the plant emergency brigades will withdraw from the scene of the incident and the building.

B. EMERGENCY ENVIRONMENTAL PROCEDURES

The specific emergency procedures as related to the exposure of chemical hazards and/or hazardous wastes are as follows:
1. Whenever there is an imminent or actual emergency situation, the Emergency Coordinator (or a designee when the Emergency Coordinator is on call) shall immediately:
   a. Identify the character, exact source, amount and real extent of any discharged materials.
   b. Activate internal facility alarms or communications systems, where applicable, to notify all facility personnel.
   c. Notify appropriate State or Local Agencies with designated response rolls if their help is needed.
2. Concurrently, the Emergency Coordinator shall assess possible hazards to human health or the environment that may result from the discharge, fire or explosion. This assessment shall consider both direct and indirect effects of the discharge, fire or explosion.
3. If the Emergency Coordinator determines that the facility has had a discharge, fire or explosion that would threaten human health or the environment outside the facility, the Emergency Coordinator shall:
   a. Immediately notify appropriate local authorities if an assessment indicates that evacuation of local areas may be advisable. This will include the Fire Department, Local Environmental Planning Committee of the NYCDEP, and any other agencies required.
      The Emergency Coordinator shall be available to help appropriate officials decide whether local areas should be evacuated.
   b. Immediately notify the New York Department of Environmental Conservation – (518) 457-7362 and the New York City Department of Environmental Protection Spill Hotline 718-DEP-HELP. A written notification will be provided to the NYCDEP within a week, addressed to:
      Department of Emergency
      Response & Technical Assessment
      NYC Department of
      Environmental Protection
      96-05 Horace Harding Boulevard
      Corona, New York 11368
   c. When notifying the Department of Environmental Conservation pursuant to subsection 373-3.4g(4)(ii) report:
      (1) Name and telephone number of reporter
      (2) Name and address of facility

(3) Time and type of incident

(4) The type of substance and the estimated quantity discharged (if known)

(5) The location of the discharge

(6) The extent of injuries, if any

(7) The possible hazards to human health, or the environment outside the facility.

4. During the emergency, the Emergency Coordinator shall take all reasonable measures necessary to ensure that fire, explosion and discharge do not occur, recur, or spread to other chemical materials or hazardous wastes at the facility. These measures must include, where applicable, stopping processes and operations, collecting and containing released chemicals and/or waste, and removing or isolating containers of chemicals and wastes.

5. If the facility stops operations in response to a fire, explosion or discharge, the Emergency Coordinator shall monitor for leaks, pressure build-ups, gas generation, or ruptures in valves, pipes or other equipment, wherever this is appropriate.

6. Immediately after an emergency, the Emergency Coordinator shall provide for treating, storing or disposing of recovered waste, contaminated soil or surface water, or any other material that results from a discharge, fire or explosion at the facility.

   All hazardous wastes produced by the incident shall be disposed in accordance with the applicable requirements of Part 372 and Subpart 373-2 of the NYSDEC Hazardous Waste Management Regulations (6NYCRR).

7. The Emergency Coordinator shall insure that in the affected areas of the facility:

   a. No waste that may be incompatible with the discharge materials is treated, stored or disposed of until clean-up procedures are completed.

   b. All emergency equipment listed in the contingency plan is cleaned and fit for its intended use before operations are resumed.

8. The owner and operator shall notify the Department of Environmental Conservation and appropriate local authorities that the facility is in compliance with subparagraph 373-3.4(g)(8) before operations are resumed in the affected areas of the facility.

9. The owner and/or operator shall note in the operating record, the time, date and details of any incident that requires implementing the contingency plant. Within fifteen (15) days after the incident, the owner/operator shall submit a written report on the incident to the Department.

   The report shall include but not be limited to:

   a. Name, address and telephone number of the owner or operator.

   b. Name, address and telephone number of the facility.

   c. Date, time and type of incident.

   d. Name and quantity of material involved.

   e. The extent of injuries (if any).

   f. An assessment of actual or potential hazards to human health or the environment, where this is possible.

   g. Assessment of the scope and magnitude of the problem(s).

   h. Description of the immediate actions that have been taken and the estimated quantity and disposition of recovered material that resulted from the incident.

   i. Provide implementation schedule for undertaking suggested measure(s) to eliminate the problem(s).

NOTE: Modify the specific data to conform with your unique requirements.

APPENDIX **XXXI**

Representative MSDS Forms

OSHA established a format for material safety data sheets (MSDS) but did not make the format mandatory. The requirement is that all information mandated must be in the MSDS regardless of format. Input from management, technical staff and legal advisors has led to many different formats. Some are a basic two pages; others may consist of many more pages.

Represented here are typical MSDSs for your information. Some are abridged to avoid unnecessary repetition. In the ink category, the MSDSs are for various formulations of the same color so that the reader may become aware of the differences between components and characteristics (hazards) for different applications, even though the color remains the same. Included are MSDSs for:

1. Inks, courtesy of Sun Chemical Corporation (pp 732–759)

2. Coatings, courtesy of Amalgamated Coatings (pp 760–761)

3. Adhesives, courtesy of Henkel Corporation (pp 762–770)

4. Fountain solution concentrates, courtesy of Printers' Service and Tower Products (pp 771–774)

5. Solvents, courtesy of Pride Solvents & Chemicals, (pp 775–779)

6. Press washes, courtesy of Printers' Service (pp 780–783)

Contact your suppliers if you do not have an MSDS for every chemical that enters your facility. Make sure a copy is in your files and in the collection that is available for plant personnel to read.

MSDS - 5265-1163

MATERIAL SAFETY DATA SHEET

Sun Chemical Corporation
631 CENTRAL AVENUE
CARLSTADT, NJ 07072

MSDS Distribution: (201) 933-4500
Regulatory Information: (201) 933-4500
Emergency Phone No.: (201) 804-8228
                              (24 hours)

1. PRODUCT IDENTIFICATION

Product Name	5265-1163
Product Description	SUNSHEEN PHTHALO BLUE
Product Category	FLEXOGRAPHIC INKS & COATINGS
MSDS Identification No.	000000000000
MSDS Date	10/24/01

2. COMPOSITION (Hazardous Components)

The components listed below are identified as hazardous chemicals based upon the criteria of the OSHA Hazard Communication Standard (29 CFR 1910.1200).

Chemical Name	CAS Number	Concentration (wt %)
Ethanol	64-17-5	28.62
n-Propyl Acetate	109-60-4	9.32
Heptane	142-82-5	7.87
n-Propyl Alcohol	71-23-8	5.01
Nitrocellulose Resin	9004-70-0	3.40
Isopropyl Alcohol	67-63-0	3.39

For further information on the individual hazardous component(s) listed above, please refer to the Toxicological Information section of the MSDS (Section 11).

3. PRODUCT HAZARDS IDENTIFICATION

Emergency Overview

Flammable Liquid and Vapor.
Material may be irritating to skin and eyes.
May cause respiratory tract irritation.
May cause central nervous system effects.

MSDS - 5265-1163

Potential Health Effects

Inhalation and dermal contact are expected to be the primary routes of occupational exposure. The following statements are based upon an assessment of the health effects associated with the components present in this product mixture.

Eye

This product may cause mild to moderate eye irritation. Direct contact or excessive exposure to vapors may cause redness, tearing and stinging.

Skin

This product may cause mild to moderate skin irritation. Prolonged or repeated exposure may result in contact dermatitis which is characterized by redness, itching, drying and/or cracking of the skin.

Inhalation

Inhalation of excessive quantities of vapors may cause irritation of the nose, throat and respiratory tract, as well as headache, nausea, dizziness, loss of coordination and fatigue.

Ingestion

Ingestion of this product may cause gastrointestinal irritation, headache, nausea, vomiting, diarrhea, dizziness, loss of coordination and fatigue.

Chronic Effects

Chronic overexposure may result in liver abnormalities.

Medical Conditions Aggravated by Exposure

Preexisting skin disorders may be aggravated by exposure to this product.

Impaired respiratory and liver functions from preexisting medical conditions may be aggravated by exposure to this product.

4. FIRST AID MEASURES

Eye Contact

In case of direct contact, flush eyes with clean water for at least 15 minutes. Seek medical attention if irritation or redness develops and persists.

Skin Contact

Remove contaminated clothing. Wash affected area thoroughly with soap and water. Seek medical attention if irritation or redness develops and persists.

Inhalation

Remove affected person away from source of exposure and into fresh air. If breathing difficulties develop, oxygen should be administered by qualified personnel. If breathing has stopped give artificial respiration. Seek immediate medical attention.

Ingestion

Ingestion is an unlikely route of exposure under normal industrial conditions. However, if appreciable quantities of this product are accidentally swallowed, seek immediate medical attention.

5. FIRE FIGHTING MEASURES

Flash Point (degree F)	Less than 73 F (Closed Cup)
Flash Point Category (OSHA/NFPA)	IB - Flammable
Lower Flammability Limit in Air (% by Vol)	1.0

NOTE : Flash point value/category has been derived from testing of products of similar composition.

Extinguishing Media

Extinguish with a multipurpose fire fighting foam, water spray, dry chemical or carbon dioxide.

Fire Fighting Instructions

The use of self-contained breathing apparatus is recommended for firefighters. Water spray may be used to cool containers exposed to heat near flame. Avoid spreading burning liquid with water used for cooling purposes.

Fire and Explosion Hazards

This product is (OSHA) flammable and may be ignited by heat, sparks, flame or static electricity. Closed containers may build up pressure and rupture when subjected to extreme heat. Vapors are heavier than air, may travel along the ground and may be moved by ventilation; flashback along vapor trail may occur.

6. ACCIDENTAL RELEASE MEASURES

Eliminate all sources of ignition. Keep unnecessary personnel away from spill area. Ventilate area of spill; use appropriate personal protective equipment.

For large spills, a multipurpose foam may be used to suppress vapors. Contain the spill by diking with sand or other inert material. Keep out of drains, sewers or waterways. Transfer product to suitable containers for recovery or disposal. Use explosion proof equipment and non-sparking tools. Do not flush area with water. If necessary, follow emergency response procedures.

For small spills, do not flush with water; use an inert absorbant material.

MSDS - 5265-1163

7. HANDLING AND STORAGE

Keep containers tightly closed. Keep containers cool, dry and away from all sources of ignition. Protect from freezing. Bond and ground all equipment when transferring material from one container to another. Use and store this product with adequate ventilation. Use appropriate protective equipment when handling this product and maintain good personal hygiene practices.

8. EXPOSURE CONTROLS / PERSONAL PROTECTION

Engineering Controls

Provide explosion proof general and/or local exhaust ventilation to maintain airborne contaminants below the established exposure limits. It is suggested that a source of clean water be made available in work area for flushing eyes and skin.

Personal Protective Equipment

Eye / Face Protection

The use of chemical splash goggles or safety glasses is recommended to prevent eye contact.

Skin Protection

The use of impermeable, solvent resistant gloves is advised to prevent skin contact. Use chemical resistant apron if splash hazard exists.

Respiratory Protection

If vapor concentration does not exceed established exposure limits, respiratory protection is not normally required.

If vapor concentration exceeds established exposure limits, use a NIOSH/ MSHA approved respirator. Respirators should be selected and used in accordance with OSHA directive 29 CFR 1910.134.

Established Exposure Guidelines

Chemical Name	ACGIH-TLV		OSHA-PEL	
	TWA	STEL	TWA	STEL
Ethanol	1000.00 ppm	N/E	1000.00 ppm	N/E
n-Propyl Acetate	200.00 ppm	250.00 ppm	200.00 ppm	250.00 ppm
Heptane	400.00 ppm	500.00 ppm	400.00 ppm	500.00 ppm
n-Propyl Alcohol	200.00 ppm	250.00 ppm	200.00 ppm	250.00 ppm (skin)
Isopropyl Alcohol	400.00 ppm	500.00 ppm	400.00 ppm	500.00 ppm

N/E = Not Established

9. PHYSICAL AND CHEMICAL PROPERTIES

Boiling Point / Range (degree F)	173 F - 215 F
Typical Density (lbs/gal)	7.69
Vapor Density (excluding water) vs. Air	Heavier
Evaporation Rate (vs. Butyl Acetate)	Faster
Appearance	
Volatile Organic Compounds (wt%)	54.70

10. STABILITY AND REACTIVITY

Stability

Stable. Hazardous polymerization will not occur.

Conditions to Avoid

Keep product away from heat, sparks, and open flames.

Incompatibility

This product is incompatible with strong acids or bases and oxidizing agents.

Hazardous Decomposition Products

By high heat and fire: carbon dioxide, carbon monoxide and/or oxides of nitrogen and sulfur.

11. TOXICOLOGY OF COMPONENTS

Information pertaining to the health effects and toxicity of the "pure" form of the hazardous components identified in Section 2 is presented below. This information reflects the known hazards associated with the component and may not reflect that of the purchased material due to concentration (dilution) effects. Review and interpretation by your Hazard Communication Department is recommended.

Ethanol (28.62 %)

Causes eye and skin irritation. Eye contact may cause stinging, watering and redness. Skin contact may cause redness and burning of skin. Skin irritation may be severe after repeated or prolonged exposure, causing drying and cracking of skin. Other effects of overexposure may include irritation of the nose and throat, irritation of the digestive and respiratory tracts, vomiting and signs of nervous system depression (e.g., headache, drowsiness, dizziness, loss of coordination and fatigue). Repeated, intentional mis-use or ingestion can cause liver damage. The International Agency for Research on Cancer (IARC) has determined that chronic exposure to ethanol through human consumption via the drinking of alcoholic beverages can cause cancer. The relevance of this finding to the exposure in the industrial environment is uncertain.

n-Propyl Acetate (9.32 %)

Causes eye and skin irritation. Eye contact may cause stinging, watering and redness. Skin contact may cause redness and burning of skin. Repeated or prolonged exposure may cause drying and cracking of skin. Other effects of overexposure may include irritation of the nose and throat, irritation of the digestive and respiratory tracts, vomiting and signs of nervous system depression (e.g., headache, drowsiness, dizziness, loss of coordination and fatigue). Repeated overexposure may result in liver damage.

Heptane (7.87 %)

Causes eye and skin irritation. Eye contact may cause stinging, watering and redness. Skin contact may cause redness and burning of skin. Skin irritation may be severe after repeated or prolonged exposure, causing drying and cracking of skin. This material can enter lungs during swallowing or vomiting and cause lung inflammation and damage. Other effects of overexposure may include irritation of the nose and throat, irritation of the digestive tract, vomiting and signs of nervous system depression (e.g., headache, drowsiness, dizziness, loss of coordination and fatigue).

n-Propyl Alcohol (5.01 %)

Causes eye and skin irritation. Eye contact may cause stinging, watering and redness. Skin contact may cause redness and burning of skin. Skin irritaion may be severe after repeated or prolonged exposure, causing drying and cracking of skin. Other effects of overexposure may include irritation of the nose and throat, irritation of the digestive and respiratory tracts, vomiting and signs of nervous system depression (e.g. headache, drowsiness, dizziness, loss of coordination and fatigue).

Nitrocellulose Resin (3.40 %)

This material is a flammable solid in a dry state. It will be less flammable in a solvated liquid mixture.

Isopropyl Alcohol (3.39 %)

Causes eye and skin irritation. Eye contact may cause stinging, watering and redness. Skin contact may cause redness and burning of skin. Skin irritation may be severe after repeated or prolonged exposure, causing drying and cracking of skin. Other effects of overexposure may include irritation of the nose and throat, irritation of the digestive and respiratory tracts, vomiting and signs of nervous system depression (e.g., headache, drowsiness, dizziness, loss of coordination and fatigue).

12. DISPOSAL CONSIDERATIONS

Dispose of product in accordance with local, county, state and federal environmental regulations. Do not introduce this product directly into public sewer systems.

Containers of this product may be hazardous when emptied. Since emptied containers may retain product residues, all hazard precautions given in this data sheet should be observed.

13. REGULATORY INFORMATION

Toxic Substances Control Act (TSCA)

The chemical components of this product are listed or have been registered for inclusion on the Section 8(B) Chemical Substance Inventory List (40 CFR 710).

This product contains a chemical which is reportable under the export notification requirements of TSCA, Section 12(B).

EPCRA Section 313 Supplier Notification

This product does not contain any substances in quantities which must be reported under the supplier notification requirements of Section 313 of the Emergency Planning and Community Right-To-Know Act of 1986 (40 CFR 372).

Clean Air Act Amendment (HAPs)

This product does not contain any substances which are defined as Hazardous Air Pollutants under Title III of the Clean Air Act Amendments of 1990.

California Proposition 65

This product does not contain any chemicals which are defined by the state of California to cause cancer and/or reproductive toxicity.

OSHA Hazard Communication Label for Product
WARNING!

FLAMMABLE LIQUID AND VAPOR
MAY CAUSE SKIN AND EYE IRRITATION
MAY CAUSE RESPIRATORY TRACT IRRITATION
MAY CAUSE CENTRAL NERVOUS SYSTEM EFFECTS
Please refer to the MSDS for more details.
Keep away from heat, sparks and flame.
Keep containers closed.
Use with adequate ventilation.
Avoid contact with eyes, skin and clothing.
Use appropriate personal protective equipment.
Avoid breathing vapor.
Wash thoroughly after handling.
FIRST AID : In case of contact, flush eyes or skin with plenty of water.
Remove contaminated clothing. Seek medical attention if irritation
develops or persists. If inhaled, remove to fresh air. If breathing is
difficult, give oxygen. If not breathing, give artificial respiration.
Seek medical attention.
IN CASE OF FIRE, use a multipurpose fire fighting foam, water spray, dry
chemical or carbon dioxide.
Empty containers may retain product residues, all hazard precautions given
on this label should be observed.

MSDS - 5265-1163

DO NOT REMOVE THIS LABEL.

14. ADDITIONAL COMMENTS

Hazardous Materials Information System (HMIS)

Health 2   **Flammability** 3   **Reactivity** 0

NOTICE : These ratings are intended only for the immediate and general identification of acute hazards. Sun Chemical is providing this information on a voluntary basis as a guide for our customers. The use and interpretation of this information may vary from company to company. All information contained in this data sheet should be considered in order to adequately deal with the safe handling of this material.

Revision Date

07/17/00

The information presented in this data sheet represents a compilation of information generated from our suppliers and other recognized sources of scientific evidence and chemical information. To the best of our knowledge and belief, it is accurate and reliable as of the date of issue. However, no warranty, express or implied, including any warranty of merchantability, fitness for any use, or any other guarantee is offered or implied regarding the accuracy of such data, the results to be obtained from the use thereof, the safety of this product, or the hazards connected with the use of this material. Since the conditions of handling and use of this material are beyond our control, Sun Chemical shall assume no liability for damages incurred by the use of the material. This information and product are furnished on the condition that the person receiving them shall make his own determination as to the suitability and completeness of this information, the safety measures necessary to handle this product, and the actions needed to comply with all applicable Federal, State, and Local Legislation.

VOLATILE COMPONENT INFORMATION

		US EPA Designate
A. Product Density:		
1.)	7.69 LB Product /gal Product	=(Dc)s
B. Nonvolatile Content:		
1.)	45.29 Weight percent of nonvolatiles in product	=(Wn)s
2.)	36.43 Volume percent of nonvolatiles in product	=(Vn)s
3.)	9.56 Density, lb nonvolatiles/gal nonvolatiles	=(Dn)s

MSDS - 5265-1163

C. Volatiles:

1.)   54.71 Weight percent of total volatiles in product   =(Wv)s
2.)   6.62 Density, lb volatiles/gal volatiles   =(Dv)s

D. Water Content:

1.)   0.01 Weight percent of water in product   =(Ww)s
2.)   0.01 Volume percent of water in product   =(Vw)s

E. Organic Volatiles, (VOCs):

1.)   54.70 Weight percent of organic volatiles in product   =(Wo)s
2.)   63.57 Volume percent of organic volatiles in product   =(Vo)s
3.)   6.62 Density, lb organic volatiles /gal organic volatiles   =(Do)s
4.)   99.98 Weight percent of VOCs in total volatiles   =(Wo)v
5.)   99.98 Volume percent of VOCs in total volatiles   =(Vo)v

F. VOC Content in Product Expressed in Other Terms:

1.) a.)   4.21 lb VOC / gal Product
1.) b.)   504.12 grams VOC / liter Product
2.) a.)   4.21 lb VOC / gal Product less water & exempt solvent
2.) b.)   504.19 grams VOC / liter Product less water & exempt solvent
3.)   11.55 lb VOC / gal total nonvolatiles

G. Volatiles: (all VOCs, HAPs, water & ammonia)

Ingredient	CAS Number	Weight Percent	Density (lb/gal)
Ethanol	64-17-5	28.62	6.62
n-Propyl Acetate	109-60-4	9.32	7.40
Heptane	142-82-5	7.87	5.87
n-Propyl Alcohol	71-23-8	5.01	6.71
Isopropyl Alcohol	67-63-0	3.39	6.55
Light Aliphatic Solvent Naphtha	64742-89-8	0.49	6.26
Non HAP/SARA Organic Volatiles		0.00	7.75
Water	7732-18-5	0.01	8.34

NOTE : The term Volatile Organic Compounds (VOC) refers only to volatile organic materials as defined by the US EPA and does not include water, ammonia, acetone or other exempt solvents. Unless otherwise stated, the VOC values reported above are based on materials of construction.

MSDS - 52217-1700

MATERIAL SAFETY DATA SHEET

Sun Chemical Corporation
631 CENTRAL AVENUE
CARLSTADT, NJ 07072

MSDS Distribution: (201) 933-4500
Regulatory Information: (201) 933-4500
Emergency Phone No.:   (201) 804-8228
                        (24 hours)

1. PRODUCT IDENTIFICATION

Product Name	52217-1700
Product Description	ULTRABOND PHTHALO BLUE
Product Category	Solvent Flexo Film Ink
MSDS Identification No.	000000000000
MSDS Date	10/24/01

2. COMPOSITION (Hazardous Components)

The components listed below are identified as hazardous chemicals based upon the criteria of the OSHA Hazard Communication Standard (29 CFR 1910.1200).

Chemical Name	CAS Number	Concentration (wt %)
n-Propyl Alcohol	71-23-8	63.10
Heptane	142-82-5	7.08

For further information on the individual hazardous component(s) listed above, please refer to the Toxicological Information section of the MSDS (Section 11).

3. PRODUCT HAZARDS IDENTIFICATION

Emergency Overview

Flammable Liquid and Vapor.
Material may be irritating to skin and eyes.
May cause respiratory tract irritation.
May cause central nervous system effects.

Potential Health Effects

Inhalation and dermal contact are expected to be the primary routes of occupational exposure. The following statements are based upon an assessment of the health effects associated with the components present in this product mixture.

MSDS - 52217-1700

Eye

This product may cause mild to moderate eye irritation. Direct contact or excessive exposure to vapors may cause redness, tearing and stinging.

Skin

This product may cause mild to moderate skin irritation. Prolonged or repeated exposure may result in contact dermatitis which is characterized by redness, itching, drying and/or cracking of the skin.

Inhalation

Inhalation of excessive quantities of vapors may cause irritation of the nose, throat and respiratory tract, as well as headache, nausea, dizziness, loss of coordination and fatigue.

Ingestion

Ingestion of this product may cause gastrointestinal irritation, headache, nausea, vomiting, diarrhea, dizziness, loss of coordination and fatigue.

Chronic Effects

No chronic health hazards are associated with the components present in this product.

Medical Conditions Aggravated by Exposure

Preexisting skin disorders may be aggravated by exposure to this product.

6. ACCIDENTAL RELEASE MEASURES

Eliminate all sources of ignition. Keep unnecessary personnel away from spill area. Ventilate area of spill; use appropriate personal protective equipment.

For large spills, a multipurpose foam may be used to suppress vapors. Contain the spill by diking with sand or other inert material. Keep out of drains, sewers or waterways. Transfer product to suitable containers for recovery or disposal. Use explosion proof equipment and non-sparking tools. Do not flush area with water. If necessary, follow emergency response procedures.

For small spills, do not flush with water; use an inert absorbant material.

7. HANDLING AND STORAGE

Keep containers tightly closed. Keep containers cool, dry and away from all sources of ignition. Protect from freezing. Bond and ground all equipment when transferring material from one container to another. Use and store this product with adequate ventilation. Use appropriate protective equipment when handling this product and maintain good personal hygiene practices.

MSDS - 52217-1700

8. EXPOSURE CONTROLS / PERSONAL PROTECTION

Engineering Controls

Provide explosion proof general and/or local exhaust ventilation to maintain airborne contaminants below the established exposure limits. It is suggested that a source of clean water be made available in work area for flushing eyes and skin.

Personal Protective Equipment

Eye / Face Protection

The use of chemical splash goggles or safety glasses is recommended to prevent eye contact.

Skin Protection

The use of impermeable, solvent resistant gloves is advised to prevent skin contact. Use chemical resistant apron if splash hazard exists.

Respiratory Protection

If vapor concentration does not exceed established exposure limits, respiratory protection is not normally required.

If vapor concentration exceeds established exposure limits, use a NIOSH/ MSHA approved respirator. Respirators should be selected and used in accordance with OSHA directive 29 CFR 1910.134.

Established Exposure Guidelines

Chemical Name	ACGIH-TLV		OSHA-PEL		
	TWA	STEL	TWA	STEL	
n-Propyl Alcohol	200.00 ppm	250.00 ppm	200.00 ppm	250.00 ppm	(skin)
Heptane	400.00 ppm	500.00 ppm	400.00 ppm	500.00 ppm	

9. PHYSICAL AND CHEMICAL PROPERTIES

Boiling Point / Range (degree F)	200 F - 207 F
Typical Density (lbs/gal)	7.39
Vapor Density (excluding water) vs. Air	Heavier
Evaporation Rate (vs. Butyl Acetate)	Faster
Appearance	Blue Liquid
Volatile Organic Compounds (wt%)	70.18

MSDS - 52217-1700

11. TOXICOLOGY OF COMPONENTS

Information pertaining to the health effects and toxicity of the "pure" form of the hazardous components identified in Section 2 is presented below. This information reflects the known hazards associated with the component and may not reflect that of the purchased material due to concentration (dilution) effects. Review and interpretation by your Hazard Communication Department is recommended.

n-Propyl Alcohol (63.10 %)

Causes eye and skin irritation. Eye contact may cause stinging, watering and redness. Skin contact may cause redness and burning of skin. Skin irritaion may be severe after repeated or prolonged exposure, causing drying and cracking of skin. Other effects of overexposure may include irritation of the nose and throat, irritation of the digestive and respiratory tracts, vomiting and signs of nervous system depression (e.g. headache, drowsiness, dizziness, loss of coordination and fatigue).

Heptane (7.08 %)

Causes eye and skin irritation. Eye contact may cause stinging, watering and redness. Skin contact may cause redness and burning of skin. Skin irritation may be severe after repeated or prolonged exposure, causing drying and cracking of skin. This material can enter lungs during swallowing or vomiting and cause lung inflammation and damage. Other effects of overexposure may include irritation of the nose and throat, irritation of the digestive tract, vomiting and signs of nervous system depression (e.g., headache, drowsiness, dizziness, loss of coordination and fatigue).

MSDS - 52217-1700

VOLATILE COMPONENT INFORMATION

	US EPA Designate

A. Product Density:
1.) 7.39 LB Product /gal Product =(Dc)s

B. Nonvolatile Content:
1.) 29.82 Weight percent of nonvolatiles in product =(Wn)s
2.) 21.54 Volume percent of nonvolatiles in product =(Vn)s
3.) 10.23 Density, lb nonvolatiles/gal nonvolatiles =(Dn)s

C. Volatiles:
1.) 70.18 Weight percent of total volatiles in product =(Wv)s
2.) 6.62 Density, lb volatiles/gal volatiles =(Dv)s

D. Water Content:
1.) 0.00 Weight percent of water in product =(Ww)s
2.) 0.00 Volume percent of water in product =(Vw)s

E. Organic Volatiles, (VOCs):
1.) 70.18 Weight percent of organic volatiles in product =(Wo)s
2.) 78.45 Volume percent of organic volatiles in product =(Vo)s
3.) 6.62 Density, lb organic volatiles /gal organic volatiles =(Do)s
4.) 100.00 Weight percent of VOCs in total volatiles =(Wo)v
5.) 100.00 Volume percent of VOCs in total volatiles =(Vo)v

F. VOC Content in Product Expressed in Other Terms:
1.) a.) 5.19 lb VOC / gal Product
1.) b.) 621.71 grams VOC / liter Product
2.) a.) 5.19 lb VOC / gal Product less water & exempt solvent
2.) b.) 621.71 grams VOC / liter Product less water & exempt solvent
3.) 24.07 lb VOC / gal total nonvolatiles

G. Volatiles: (all VOCs, HAPs, water & ammonia)

Ingredient	CAS Number	Weight Percent	Density (lb/gal)
n-Propyl Alcohol	71-23-8	63.10	6.71
Heptane	142-82-5	7.08	5.87
Non HAP/SARA Organic Volatiles		0.00	7.75
Water	7732-18-5	0.00	8.34

MATERIAL SAFETY DATA SHEET

Sun Chemical Corporation
631 CENTRAL AVENUE
CARLSTADT, NJ 07072

MSDS Distribution: (201) 933-4500
Regulatory Information: (201) 933-4500
Emergency Phone No.: (201) 804-8228
                        (24 hours)

1. PRODUCT IDENTIFICATION

Product Name	BAS-161868
Product Description	AQUASURF II G/S CYAN
Product Category	FLEXOGRAPHIC INKS & COATINGS
MSDS Identification No.	000000000000
MSDS Date	10/24/01

2. COMPOSITION (Hazardous Components)

The components listed below are identified as hazardous chemicals based upon the criteria of the OSHA Hazard Communication Standard (29 CFR 1910.1200).

Chemical Name	CAS Number	Concentration (wt %)
2-Butoxyethanol	111-76-2	5.00
n-Propyl Alcohol	71-23-8	4.00

For further information on the individual hazardous component(s) listed above, please refer to the Toxicological Information section of the MSDS (Section 11).

3. PRODUCT HAZARDS IDENTIFICATION

Emergency Overview

Combustible Vapor.
Material may be irritating to skin and eyes.
May be harmful if absorbed through the skin.
May cause respiratory tract irritation.
May cause central nervous system effects.

MSDS - BAS-161868

Potential Health Effects

Inhalation and dermal contact are expected to be the primary routes of occupational exposure. The following statements are based upon an assessment of the health effects associated with the components present in this product mixture.

Eye

This product may cause mild to moderate eye irritation. Direct contact or excessive exposure to vapors may cause redness, tearing and stinging.

Skin

This product may cause mild to moderate skin irritation. Prolonged or repeated exposure may result in contact dermatitis which is characterized by redness, itching, drying and/or cracking of the skin.

This product contains hazardous component(s) which may be absorbed through the skin.

Inhalation

Inhalation of excessive quantities of vapors may cause irritation of the nose, throat and respiratory tract, as well as headache, nausea, dizziness, loss of coordination and fatigue.

Ingestion

Ingestion of this product may cause gastrointestinal irritation, headache, nausea, vomiting, diarrhea, dizziness, loss of coordination and fatigue.

Chronic Effects

Chronic overexposure may result in liver abnormalities, kidney damage and blood disorders.

Medical Conditions Aggravated by Exposure

Preexisting skin disorders may be aggravated by exposure to this product.

6. ACCIDENTAL RELEASE MEASURES

Eliminate all sources of ignition. Keep unnecessary personnel away from spill area. Ventilate area of spill; use appropriate personal protective equipment.

For large spills, a multipurpose foam may be used to suppress vapors. Contain the spill by diking with sand or other inert material. Keep out of drains, sewers or waterways. Transfer product to suitable containers for recovery or disposal. If necessary, follow emergency response procedures.

For small spills, use an inert absorbent material. Water may be used to clean the area of the spill.

MSDS - BAS-161868

7. HANDLING AND STORAGE

Keep containers tightly closed. Keep containers cool and dry. Protect from freezing. Use and store this product with adequate ventilation. Use appropriate protective equipment when handling this product and maintain good personal hygiene practices.

8. EXPOSURE CONTROLS / PERSONAL PROTECTION

Engineering Controls

Provide adequate general (dilution) and/or local exhaust ventilation to maintain airborne contaminants below the established exposure limits. It is suggested that a source of clean water be made available in work area for flushing eyes and skin.

Personal Protective Equipment

Eye / Face Protection

The use of chemical splash goggles or safety glasses is recommended to prevent eye contact.

Skin Protection

The use of impermeable, solvent resistant gloves is advised to prevent skin contact. Use chemical resistant apron and face shield if splash hazard exists.

Respiratory Protection

If vapor concentration does not exceed established exposure limits, respiratory protection is not normally required.

If vapor concentration exceeds established exposure limits, use a NIOSH/ MSHA approved respirator. Respirators should be selected and used in accordance with OSHA directive 29 CFR 1910.134.

Established Exposure Guidelines

Chemical Name	ACGIH-TLV		OSHA-PEL		
	TWA	STEL	TWA	STEL	
2-Butoxyethanol	25.00 ppm	N/E	25.00 ppm	N/E	(skin)
n-Propyl Alcohol	200.00 ppm	250.00 ppm	200.00 ppm	250.00 ppm	(skin)

N/E = Not Established

MSDS - BAS-161868

9. PHYSICAL AND CHEMICAL PROPERTIES

Boiling Point / Range (degree F)	207 F - 336 F
Typical Density (lbs/gal)	8.82
Vapor Density (excluding water) vs. Air	Heavier
Evaporation Rate (vs. Butyl Acetate)	Slower
Appearance	BLUE VISCOUS FLUID
Volatile Organic Compounds (wt%)	9.47

11. TOXICOLOGY OF COMPONENTS

Information pertaining to the health effects and toxicity of the "pure" form of the hazardous components identified in Section 2 is presented below. This information reflects the known hazards associated with the component and may not reflect that of the purchased material due to concentration (dilution) effects. Review and interpretation by your Hazard Communication Department is recommended.

2-Butoxyethanol (5.00 %)

May cause eye and skin irritation. Eye contact may cause stinging, watering and redness. Other effects of overexposure may include irritation of the nose and throat, irritation of the digestive and respiratory tracts, and vomiting. Ingestion of significant quantities may result in red blood cell disorders. May be absorbed through the skin in harmful amounts and effects may include those described for ingestion. Exposure to excessive amounts of vapors or ingestion may cause nervous system depression (e.g., headache, drowsiness, dizziness, loss of coordination and fatigue). Repeated, intentional mis-use or ingestion can also cause liver and kidney disorders. This material has been shown to be a reproductive hazard in animal testing.

n-Propyl Alcohol (4.00 %)

Causes eye and skin irritation. Eye contact may cause stinging, watering and redness. Skin contact may cause redness and burning of skin. Skin irritaion may be severe after repeated or prolonged exposure, causing drying and cracking of skin. Other effects of overexposure may include irritation of the nose and throat, irritation of the digestive and respiratory tracts, vomiting and signs of nervous system depression (e.g. headache, drowsiness, dizziness, loss of coordination and fatigue).

MSDS - BAS-161868

VOLATILE COMPONENT INFORMATION

	US EPA Designate

A. Product Density:

1.)	8.82 LB Product /gal Product	=(Dc)s

B. Nonvolatile Content:

1.)	38.26 Weight percent of nonvolatiles in product	=(Wn)s
2.)	32.86 Volume percent of nonvolatiles in product	=(Vn)s
3.)	10.28 Density, lb nonvolatiles/gal nonvolatiles	=(Dn)s

C. Volatiles:

1.)	61.74 Weight percent of total volatiles in product	=(Wv)s
2.)	8.11 Density, lb volatiles/gal volatiles	=(Dv)s

D. Water Content:

1.)	51.68 Weight percent of water in product	=(Ww)s
2.)	54.72 Volume percent of water in product	=(Vw)s

E. Organic Volatiles, (VOCs):

1.)	9.47 Weight percent of organic volatiles in product	=(Wo)s
2.)	11.62 Volume percent of organic volatiles in product	=(Vo)s
3.)	7.19 Density, lb organic volatiles /gal organic volatiles	=(Do)s
4.)	15.34 Weight percent of VOCs in total volatiles	=(Wo)v
5.)	17.30 Volume percent of VOCs in total volatiles	=(Vo)v

F. VOC Content in Product Expressed in Other Terms:

1.) a.)	0.84 lb VOC / gal Product
1.) b.)	100.15 grams VOC / liter Product
2.) a.)	1.84 lb VOC / gal Product less water & exempt solvent
2.) b.)	220.77 grams VOC / liter Product less water & exempt solvent
3.)	2.54 lb VOC / gal total nonvolatiles

G. Volatiles: (all VOCs, HAPs, water & ammonia)

Ingredient	CAS Number	Weight Percent	Density (lb/gal)
2-Butoxyethanol	111-76-2	5.00	7.53
n-Propyl Alcohol	71-23-8	4.00	6.71
Diethylene Glycol Monoethyl Ether	111-90-0	0.35	8.25
Non HAP/SARA Organic Volatiles		0.12	7.75
Water	7732-18-5	51.68	8.34
Ammonia	7664-41-7	0.59	5.99

MSDS - BMIFW5831157

MATERIAL SAFETY DATA SHEET

Sun Chemical Corporation
631 CENTRAL AVENUE
CARLSTADT, NJ 07072

MSDS Distribution: (201) 933-4500
Regulatory Information: (201) 933-4500
Emergency Phone No.: (201) 804-8228
                       (24 hours)

1. PRODUCT IDENTIFICATION

Product Name	BMIFW5831157
Product Description	DPF-426 PHTHALO BLUE
Product Category	Water Flexo Film Ink
MSDS Identification No.	000000000000
MSDS Date	10/24/01

2. COMPOSITION (Hazardous Components)

The components listed below are identified as hazardous chemicals based upon the criteria of the OSHA Hazard Communication Standard (29 CFR 1910.1200).

Chemical Name	CAS Number	Concentration (wt %)
1-Propoxy-2-Propanol	1569-01-3	4.00
Isopropyl Alcohol	67-63-0	3.92
Propylene Glycol Monomethyl Ether	107-98-2	1.20

For further information on the individual hazardous component(s) listed above, please refer to the Toxicological Information section of the MSDS (Section 11).

3. PRODUCT HAZARDS IDENTIFICATION

Emergency Overview

Combustible Vapor.
Material may be irritating to skin and eyes.
May cause central nervous system effects.

Potential Health Effects

Inhalation and dermal contact are expected to be the primary routes of occupational exposure. The following statements are based upon an assessment of the health effects associated with the components present in this product mixture.

MSDS - BMIFW5831157

Eye

This product may cause mild to moderate eye irritation. Direct contact or excessive exposure to vapors may cause redness, tearing and stinging.

Skin

This product may cause mild to moderate skin irritation. Prolonged or repeated exposure may result in contact dermatitis which is characterized by redness, itching, drying and/or cracking of the skin.

Inhalation

This product is not expected to cause respiratory tract irritation under conditions of intended use. Exposure to high concentrations of vapor may cause headache, nausea, dizziness, loss of coordination and fatigue.

Ingestion

Ingestion of this product may cause gastrointestinal irritation, headache, nausea, vomiting, diarrhea, dizziness, loss of coordination and fatigue.

Chronic Effects

No chronic health hazards are associated with the components present in this product.

Medical Conditions Aggravated by Exposure

Preexisting skin disorders may be aggravated by exposure to this product.

6. ACCIDENTAL RELEASE MEASURES

Eliminate all sources of ignition. Keep unnecessary personnel away from spill area. Ventilate area of spill; use appropriate personal protective equipment.

For large spills, a multipurpose foam may be used to suppress vapors. Contain the spill by diking with sand or other inert material. Keep out of drains, sewers or waterways. Transfer product to suitable containers for recovery or disposal. If necessary, follow emergency response procedures.

For small spills, use an inert absorbent material. Water may be used to clean the area of the spill.

7. HANDLING AND STORAGE

Keep containers tightly closed. Keep containers cool and dry. Protect from freezing. Use and store this product with adequate ventilation. Use appropriate protective equipment when handling this product and maintain good personal hygiene practices.

MSDS - BMIFW5831157

8. EXPOSURE CONTROLS / PERSONAL PROTECTION

Engineering Controls

Provide adequate general (dilution) and/or local exhaust ventilation to maintain airborne contaminants below the established exposure limits. It is suggested that a source of clean water be made available in work area for flushing eyes and skin.

Personal Protective Equipment

Eye / Face Protection

The use of chemical splash goggles or safety glasses is recommended to prevent eye contact.

Skin Protection

The use of impermeable, solvent resistant gloves is advised to prevent skin contact. Use chemical resistant apron if splash hazard exists.

Respiratory Protection

If vapor concentration does not exceed established exposure limits, respiratory protection is not normally required.

If vapor concentration exceeds established exposure limits, use a NIOSH/ MSHA approved respirator. Respirators should be selected and used in accordance with OSHA directive 29 CFR 1910.134.

Established Exposure Guidelines

Chemical Name	ACGIH-TLV		OSHA-PEL	
	TWA	STEL	TWA	STEL
Isopropyl Alcohol	400.00 ppm	500.00 ppm	400.00 ppm	500.00 ppm
Propylene Glycol Monomethyl Ether	100.00 ppm	150.00 ppm	100.00 ppm	150.00 ppm

9. PHYSICAL AND CHEMICAL PROPERTIES

Boiling Point / Range (degree F)	180 F - 302 F
Typical Density (lbs/gal)	8.89
Vapor Density (excluding water) vs. Air	Heavier
Evaporation Rate (vs. Butyl Acetate)	Slower
Appearance	Blue Liquid
Volatile Organic Compounds (wt%)	9.79

11. TOXICOLOGY OF COMPONENTS

Information pertaining to the health effects and toxicity of the "pure" form of the hazardous components identified in Section 2 is presented below. This information reflects the known hazards associated with the component and may not reflect that of the purchased material due to concentration (dilution) effects. Review and interpretation by your Hazard Communication Department is recommended.

1-Propoxy-2-Propanol (4.00 %)

Direct contact may cause moderate to severe eye irritation with reversible corneal injury. Repeated or prolonged exposure may cause skin irritation. Ingestion of large quantities can cause central nervous system depression (e.g., headache, drowsiness, dizziness, loss of coordination and fatigue). Material can enter lungs during swallowing or vomiting and cause lung inflammation and damage.

Isopropyl Alcohol (3.92 %)

Causes eye and skin irritation. Eye contact may cause stinging, watering and redness. Skin contact may cause redness and burning of skin. Skin irritation may be severe after repeated or prolonged exposure, causing drying and cracking of skin. Other effects of overexposure may include irritation of the nose and throat, irritation of the digestive and respiratory tracts, vomiting and signs of nervous system depression (e.g., headache, drowsiness, dizziness, loss of coordination and fatigue).

Propylene Glycol Monomethyl Ether (1.20 %)

May cause eye and skin irritation. Eye contact may cause stinging, watering and redness. Can be absorbed through the skin in harmful amounts. Other effects of overexposure may include irritation of the nose and throat irritation of the digestive tract, vomiting, and nervous system depression (e.g., headache, drowsiness, dizziness, loss of coordination and fatigue).

MSDS - BMIFW5831157

VOLATILE COMPONENT INFORMATION

US EPA
Designate

A. Product Density:

1.)   8.89 LB Product /gal Product   =(Dc)s

B. Nonvolatile Content:

1.)   35.94 Weight percent of nonvolatiles in product   =(Wn)s
2.)   29.75 Volume percent of nonvolatiles in product   =(Vn)s
3.)   10.74 Density, lb nonvolatiles/gal nonvolatiles   =(Dn)s

C. Volatiles:

1.)   64.06 Weight percent of total volatiles in product   =(Wv)s
2.)   8.11 Density, lb volatiles/gal volatiles   =(Dv)s

D. Water Content:

1.)   53.83 Weight percent of water in product   =(Ww)s
2.)   57.38 Volume percent of water in product   =(Vw)s

E. Organic Volatiles, (VOCs):

1.)   9.79 Weight percent of organic volatiles in product   =(Wo)s
2.)   12.24 Volume percent of organic volatiles in product   =(Vo)s
3.)   7.11 Density, lb organic volatiles /gal organic volatiles   =(Do)s
4.)   15.28 Weight percent of VOCs in total volatiles   =(Wo)v
5.)   17.43 Volume percent of VOCs in total volatiles   =(Vo)v

F. VOC Content in Product Expressed in Other Terms:

1.) a.)   0.87 lb VOC / gal Product
1.) b.)   104.25 grams VOC / liter Product
2.) a.)   2.04 lb VOC / gal Product less water & exempt solvent
2.) b.)   244.24 grams VOC / liter Product less water & exempt solvent
3.)   2.92 lb VOC / gal total nonvolatiles

G. Volatiles: (all VOCs, HAPs, water & ammonia)

Ingredient	CAS Number	Weight Percent	Density (lb/gal)
1-Propoxy-2-Propanol	1569-01-3	4.00	7.37
Isopropyl Alcohol	67-63-0	3.92	6.55
Propylene Glycol Monomethyl Ether	107-98-2	1.20	7.69
Monoethanolamine	141-43-5	0.45	8.51
Non HAP/SARA Organic Volatiles		0.21	7.75
Water	7732-18-5	53.83	8.34
Ammonia	7664-41-7	0.45	5.99

MATERIAL SAFETY DATA SHEET

Sun Chemical Corporation
631 CENTRAL AVENUE
CARLSTADT, NJ 07072

MSDS Distribution: (201) 933-4500
Regulatory Information: (201) 933-4500
Emergency Phone No.: (201) 804-8228
                      (24 hours)

1. PRODUCT IDENTIFICATION

Product Name   FLHFV5480055
Product Description   UV FLEXO BLUE
Product Category   Energy Cured Flexo Film Ink
MSDS Identification No. 000000000000
MSDS Date   10/24/01

2. COMPOSITION (Hazardous Components)

The components listed below are identified as hazardous chemicals based upon the criteria of the OSHA Hazard Communication Standard (29 CFR 1910.1200).

Chemical Name	CAS Number	Concentration (wt %)
Trimethylolpropane Ethoxy Triacrylate	28961-43-5	10 - 30
Polypropylene Glycol Acrylate	52408-84-1	10 - 30
Tripropylene Glycol Diacrylate	42978-66-5	7 - 13
Proprietary Material	Trade Secret	5 - 10
Alkyl Acrylate Ester	—	3 - 7
Modified Acrylate Ester	—	1 - 5
Proprietary Material	Trade Secret	1 - 5

For further information on the individual hazardous component(s) listed above, please refer to the Toxicological Information section of the MSDS (Section 11).

3. PRODUCT HAZARDS IDENTIFICATION

Emergency Overview

Material may be irritating to skin and eyes.
May cause allergic skin reaction.

MSDS - FLHFV5480055

Potential Health Effects

Dermal contact is expected to be the primary route of occupational exposure. The following statements are based upon an assessment of the health effects associated with the components present in this product mixture.

Eye

Direct contact with this product may cause moderate to severe eye irritation. Symptoms may include stinging, tearing, redness, swelling and/or burning. This product contains component(s) known to cause severe irritation and/or injury to the eye.

Skin

This product may cause mild to moderate skin irritation. Prolonged or repeated exposure may result in contact dermatitis which is characterized by redness, itching, drying and/or cracking of the skin.

This product contains component(s) which may cause skin sensitization. Initial contact may go unnoticed, irritant effects can be delayed.

Inhalation

This product is not expected to cause respiratory tract irritation under conditions of intended use.

Ingestion

Ingestion of amounts incidental to normal industrial handling are unlikely to cause adverse health effects. Deliberate ingestion of excessive quantities may result in gastrointestinal irritation, nausea, vomiting and diarrhea.

Chronic Effects

No chronic health hazards are associated with the components present in this product.

Medical Conditions Aggravated by Exposure

Preexisting skin disorders may be aggravated by exposure to this product.

6. ACCIDENTAL RELEASE MEASURES

Keep unnecessary personnel away from spill area. Ventilate area of spill; use appropriate personal protective equipment.

For large spills, contain the spill by diking with sand or other inert material. Keep out of drains, sewers or waterways. Transfer product to suitable containers for recovery or disposal. Do not flush area with water. If necessary, follow emergency response procedures.

For small spills; do not flush with water; use an inert absorbent material.

If solvents are used to clean up spill, impervious gloves must be worn since solvents are known to intensify the exposure and irritation effects of UV/EB materials. Radiation curable products will not dry by evaporation. It is important that any spills be completely cleaned up, otherwise these materials will remain a continued source of exposure.

MSDS - FLHFV5480055

7. HANDLING AND STORAGE

Keep containers tightly closed. Keep containers cool and dry. Protect from freezing. Use and store this product with adequate ventilation. Use appropriate protective equipment when handling this product and maintain good personal hygiene practices.

UV/EB-curable materials are reactive and may degrade or polymerize when stored for extended periods of time or under conditions of extreme heat. In order to prolong shelf life, it is recommended that containers of these products be stored at temperatures between 40 F and 140 F.

8. EXPOSURE CONTROLS / PERSONAL PROTECTION

Engineering Controls

Provide adequate general (dilution) and/or local exhaust ventilation. It is suggested that a source of clean water be made available in work area for flushing eyes and skin.

Personal Protective Equipment

Eye / Face Protection

The use of chemical splash goggles or safety glasses is recommended to prevent eye contact.

Skin Protection

Barrier cream (applied before exposure) should be used along with impervious gloves. Do not apply barrier cream after exposure. Use chemical resistant apron and face shield if splash hazard exists.

Respiratory Protection

Respiratory protection is typically not required under conditions of normal use. However, unusually high concentrations of vapor may require respiratory protection.

Established Exposure Guidelines

No ACGIH or OSHA exposure guidelines have been established for any of the components in this product.

9. PHYSICAL AND CHEMICAL PROPERTIES

Boiling Point / Range (degree F)	559 F - Not Determined
Typical Density (lbs/gal)	9.41
Vapor Density (excluding water) vs. Air	Heavier

MSDS - FLHFV5480055

Evaporation Rate (vs. Butyl Acetate)	Not Applicable
Appearance	Blue Viscous Liquid

Volatile Organic Compounds (wt%)
For radiation curable products, the US EPA has determined that Method 24 analysis on the uncured product is inappropriate. The EPA suggests that the test be modified to evaluate cured products. Average Method 24 VOC values for the cured products are less than 1.0 %.

11. TOXICOLOGY OF COMPONENTS

Information pertaining to the health effects and toxicity of the "pure" form of the hazardous components identified in Section 2 is presented below. This information reflects the known hazards associated with the component and may not reflect that of the purchased material due to concentration (dilution) effects. Review and interpretation by your Hazard Communication Department is recommended.

Trimethylolpropane Ethoxy Triacrylate (10 - 30 %)

This material can cause severe eye irritation and moderate skin irritation. Skin contact may also cause skin sensitization.

Polypropylene Glycol Acrylate (10 - 30 %)

This material can cause severe eye irritation and moderate skin irritation. Skin contact may also cause skin sensitization.

Tripropylene Glycol Diacrylate (7 - 13 %)

May cause eye and skin irritation. Skin contact may also cause skin sensitization.

Proprietary Material (5 - 10 %)

May cause eye and skin irritation. Skin contact may also cause skin sensitization.

Alkyl Acrylate Ester (3 - 7 %)

This material can cause severe eye irritation and moderate skin irritation. Skin contact may also cause skin sensitization.

Modified Acrylate Ester (1 - 5 %)

May cause eye and skin irritation. Skin contact may also cause skin sensitization.

Proprietary Material (1 - 5 %)

May cause eye and skin irritation. Skin contact may also cause skin sensitization.

12. DISPOSAL CONSIDERATIONS

Dispose of product in accordance with local, county, state and federal environmental regulations. Do not introduce this product directly into public sewer systems.

Containers of this product may be hazardous when emptied. Since emptied containers may retain product residues, all hazard precautions given in this data sheet should be observed.

MATERIAL SAFETY DATA SHEET

AMALGAMATED INTERNATIONAL, LTD.
145 Toledo Street   -   Farmingdale, NY 11735
Phone: (631) 391 - 4577   Fax: (631) 420 - 1109
Effective Date: June 14, 2000

IDENTIFICATION

TRADE NAME: **AQUACRYL 2920**
PRODUCT CLASS: Acrylic Emulsion
MANUFACTURED BY   Amalgamated International, Ltd.
                  145 Toledo Street
                  Farmingdale, NY 11735

EMERGENCY PHONE NO.   (631) 391 - 4577

PHYSICAL DATA

BOILING RANGE °F: above 200°
APPEARANCE   milky white viscous liquid
VAPOR DENSITY: lighter than air
LIQUID DENSITY: heavier than water
EVAPORATION RATE: heavier than butyl acetate
TYPE OF ODOR: latex
PERCENT VOLATILITY   40-65%

HAZARDOUS INGREDIENTS

Ingredient:	CAS#	WEIGHT	Hazardous Data
Styrene	100-42-5	<.015%	
Ammonia	7664-41-7	< 1%	TLV = 25 PPM
Isopropyl alcohol	67-73-0	< 2%	TLV = 400 PPM
Water	7732-18-5		
VOC's (per lb./gal.)	2.4% - 3.6%		

FIRE & EXPLOSION DATA

FLAMMABILITY CLASSIFICATION: OSHA - NA
                                          DOT-NA
FLASH POINT øF: (Method Used   NA
LEL   NA
EXTINGUISHING METHOD: Foam, CO2, Dry Chemical, Water fog
UNUSUAL FIRE & EXPLOSION HAZARDS: Container may burn and leak in heat of fire.
SPECIAL FIREFIGHTING PROCEDURES: Normal

HEALTH HAZARD DATA

EFFECTS OF OVEREXPOSURE: Contact with eyes may cause irritation. Prolonged or repeated contact with skin may cause irritation.

PRIMARY ROUTES OF ENTRY: Dermal and Inhalation
EMERGENCY AND FIRST AID PROCEDURE: Flush eyes with warm water for 15 minutes. Wash skin with water for 15 minutes. I f inhaled remove to fresh air. If ingested, induce vomiting. Contact physician.

REACTIVITY DATA

PRODUCT STABILITY: Stable
CONDITIONS TO AVOID: Contact with strong acids.

SPILL OR LEAK PROCEDURES

PROCEDURE WHEN MATERIAL SPILLED OR RELEASED: Dam up. Clean up with absorbent materials and place in containers Rinse area with water.

WASTE DISPOSAL METHOD: Follow Federal, State and local laws. Solids may be precipitated from water.

SPECIAL PROTECTION INFORMATION

VENTILATION: General
PROTECTIVE GLOVES: Neoprene or rubber
RESPIRATORY PROTECTION: None
EYE PROTECTION: Splash-proof goggles
OTHER PROTECTIVE EQUIPMENT: None

SPECIAL PRECAUTIONS

HANDLING & STORING: Do not store where exposure to excessive hot or cold temperatures may exist. Material Will last through 3 freeze-thaw cycles; high temperatures may cause viscosity instability.

OTHER PRECAUTIONS: Do not puncture fiber drums or lay on side.

The information and recommendations contained in this data sheet is believed to be accurate and represent the best information currently available to us, but no warranty, guarantee or representation is made by Amalgamated International as to the absolute correctness or sufficiency of the information and recommendations in this data sheet; nor can it be assumed that all possible safety measures are contained in this data sheet or that measures may not be required under varying circumstances.

Material Safety Data Sheet

Product Name	**56-7007**	**Effective Date**	**09/17/01**
Product Use	**Polymer Emulsion Adhesive**	**Supersedes**	**01/07/97**
Manufacturer	**Henkel Adhesives** **1345 Gasket Drive** **Elgin, IL 60120** **(847) 608-0200**	**Transportation Emergency** Chemtrec: 800 424-9300 **Non-Transportation Emergency** **847-608-0200**	

Section 2. Composition and Information on Ingredients

Name	CAS #	% by Weight	Exposure Limits
1) Vinyl Acetate	108-05-4	<0.38	10 ppm (OSHA-PEL),(ACGIH-TLV) 15 ppm (ACGIH-STEL)
2) Acetaldehyde	75-07-0	<0.08	200 ppm (OSHA-PEL) 25 ppm (ACGIH-TLV) 2 ppm (ACGIH-STEL)

Section 3. Hazards Identification

Physical State and Appearance	Off-white liquid emulsion
Emergency Overview	Non-flammable liquid polymer emulsion. This product does not present significant health hazard when handled using good industrial hygiene and safety practice. Exposure may cause mild irritation of eyes, skin or respiratory tract. May cause gastrointestinal irritation if swallowed.
Routes of Exposure	Eyes Skin Inhalation Ingestion

Potential Acute Health Effects

Eyes May cause mild irritation of eyes upon contact.

Skin May cause mild irritation of skin upon contact.

Inhalation May cause mild irritation to respiratory tract.

Ingestion May cause gastrointestinal irritation

Potential Chronic Health Effects

CARCINOGENIC EFFECTS: Classified A3 (Proven for animal.) by ACGIH [Vinyl Acetate], 2B (Possible for human.) by IARC [Vinyl Acetate]. Classified None. by OSHA [Vinyl Acetate]. Classified + (Proven.) by NIOSH [Acetaldehyde]. Classified A3 (Proven for animal.) by ACGIH, 2B (Possible for human.) by IARC [Acetaldehyde]. Classified 2 (Some evidence.) by NTP [Acetaldehyde]. Classified None. by OSHA [Acetaldehyde].
MUTAGENIC EFFECTS: No known effect.
TERATOGENIC EFFECTS: No known effect.

Continued on Next Page

56-7007	Page: 2/5

Section 4. First Aid Measures

Eye Contact	In case of contact with eyes, rinse immediately with plenty of water. Seek medical attention if irritation persists.
Skin Contact	Wash gently and thoroughly the contaminated skin with running water and non-abrasive soap.
Inhalation	If inhaled, remove to fresh air. If not breathing, give artificial respiration. If breathing is difficult, give oxygen. Get medical attention.
Ingestion	Do NOT induce vomiting unless directed to do so by medical personnel. Never give anything by mouth to an unconscious person. Loosen tight clothing such as a collar, tie, belt or waistband.

Section 5. Fire Fighting Measures

Flammability of the Product	Non-flammable.
Auto-ignition Temperature	Not applicable.
Flash Points	Not applicable.
Flammable Limits	Not applicable.
Fire Fighting Media and Instructions	Aqueous emulsion is non-flammable

Section 6. Accidental Release Measures

Spill and Leak	Absorb with an inert dry material and place in an appropriate waste disposal container. See section 13 for disposal considerations.

Section 7. Handling and Storage

Handling	Avoid breathing vapors or spray mists.
Storage	Keep container tightly closed. Do not store below freezing temperatures.

Section 8. Exposure Controls/Personal Protection

Engineering Controls	Provide exhaust ventilation or other engineering controls to keep the airborne concentrations of vapors below their respective threshold limit value.
Personal Protection	
Eyes	Safety glasses with side shields.
Body	Wear overalls or long sleeved shirt and long trousers.
Respiratory	Use appropriate respiratory protection if there is the potential to exceed exposure limits.
Hands	Rubber Gloves
Feet	Chemical resistant safety shoes.

Section 9. Physical and Chemical Properties

Physical State and Appearance	Off-white liquid emulsion
Odor	Characteristic.
Color	Off-white.
pH	6 to 8 [Neutral.]

Continued on Next Page

56-7007	Page: 3/5

Melting/Freezing Point	May start to solidify at 0°C (32°F)
Specific Gravity	1.1 (Water = 1)
Vapor Pressure	Not available.
Volatility	Same as water
VOC	< 0.61% (w/w)
Viscosity	~ 800 cP @ 76 F
Solubility	See dispersion properties.
Dispersion Properties	Easily dispersed in cold or hot water.
Boiling Point	100°C (212°F)
Physical Chemical Comments	No additional comments.

Section 10. Stability and Reactivity

Stability and Reactivity	The product is stable.
Conditions of Instability	No additional remark.
Incompatibility with Various Substances	Not available.
Hazardous Decomposition Products	Not available.
Hazardous Polymerization	Will not occur.

Section 11. Toxicological Information

Toxicity to Animals	LD50: Not available. LC50: Not available.
Chronic Effects on Humans	**CARCINOGENIC EFFECTS:** Classified A3 (Proven for animal.) by ACGIH, 2B (Possible for human.) by IARC [Vinyl Acetate]. Classified + (Proven.) by NIOSH [Acetaldehyde]. Classified A3 (Proven for animal.) by ACGIH, 2B (Possible for human.) by IARC [Acetaldehyde]. Classified 2 (Some evidence.) by NTP [Acetaldehyde]. Classified None. by OSHA [Acetaldehyde]. **DEVELOPMENTAL TOXICITY:** Classified Reproductive system/toxin/female, Reproductive system/toxin/male [PROVEN] [Acetaldehyde].
Other Toxic Effects on Humans	ACGIH evaluated vinyl acetate (1993) as an A3-Animal Carcinogen. Available evidence suggests that the agent is not likely to cause cancer in humans under uncommon or unlikely routes of exposure. The International Agency for Research on Cancer (IARC) published a monograph on vinyl acetate (1995). In this monograph IARC indicates "there is an inadequate evidence in humans for carcinogenicity of vinyl acetate. There is limited evidence in experimental animals for carcinogenicity of vinyl acetate". Normally, this lack of conclusive evidence would place a substance in the IARC Category 3 classification. (not classified as a human carcinogen). However, because vinyl acetate is metabolized to acetaldehyde, which is an IARC 2B (possibly carcinogenic to humans) classification, it is also has been listed under Category 2B.
Special Remarks on Toxicity to Animals	No data available.
Special Remarks on Chronic Effects on Humans	No data available.

Continued on Next Page

56-7007	Page: 4/5

Section 12. Ecological Information

Ecotoxicity	No data available.
Toxicity of the Products of Biodegradation	No data available.

Section 13. Disposal Considerations

Waste Information	Waste must be discarded in accordance with federal, state and local environmental regulations.

Consult your local or regional authorities.

Section 14. Transport Information

DOT Classification	Not a DOT regulated material (United States).
Proper Shipping Name	Not applicable.
UN/NA Identification Number	Not applicable.
Packing group	Not applicable.

Section 15. Regulatory Information

U.S. Federal Regulations	TSCA 8(a) PAIR: Acetaldehyde TSCA 8(b) inventory: All components are listed or are exempt. SARA 302/304/311/312 extremely hazardous substances: Vinyl Acetate; Formaldehyde SARA 302/304 emergency planning and notification: No products were found. SARA 302/304/311/312 hazardous chemicals: No products were found. SARA 311/312 MSDS distribution - chemical inventory - hazard identification: No products were found. SARA 313 toxic chemical notification and release reporting: Formaldehyde <0.02%; Vinyl Acetate <0.38%; Acetaldehyde <0.08% Clean Water Act (CWA) 307: Vinyl Acetate; Formaldehyde; Acetaldehyde Clean Water Act (CWA) 311: No products were found. Clean air act (CAA) 112 accidental release prevention: Vinyl Acetate; Formaldehyde; Acetaldehyde Clean air act (CAA) 112 regulated flammable substances: Acetaldehyde Clean air act (CAA) 112 regulated toxic substances: No products were found.
State Regulations	Rhode Island RTK hazardous substances: Vinyl Acetate; Formaldehyde; Acetaldehyde Pennsylvania RTK: Vinyl Acetate: (environmental hazard); Formaldehyde: (special hazard, environmental hazard); Acetaldehyde: (environmental hazard) Florida: Vinyl Acetate; Formaldehyde; Acetaldehyde Minnesota: Vinyl Acetate; Formaldehyde; Acetaldehyde Michigan critical material: Formaldehyde Massachusetts RTK: Vinyl Acetate; Formaldehyde; Acetaldehyde New Jersey: Vinyl Acetate; Formaldehyde; Acetaldehyde New Jersey spill list: Vinyl Acetate; Formaldehyde; Acetaldehyde California prop. 65: This product contains the following ingredients for which the State of California has found to cause cancer which would require a warning under the statute: Formaldehyde; Acetaldehyde
International Lists	No additional information.

Continued on Next Page

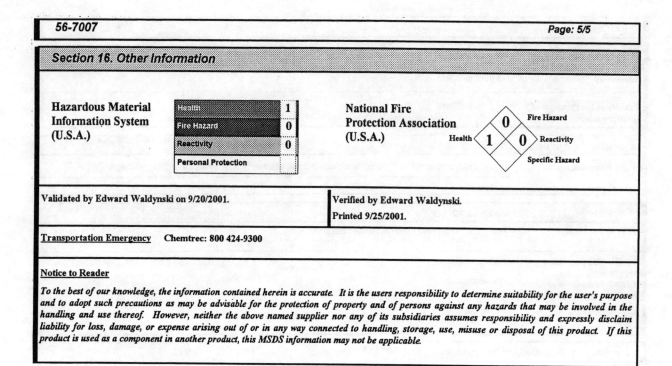

56-7007

Section 16. Other Information

Hazardous Material Information System (U.S.A.)

Health	1
Fire Hazard	0
Reactivity	0
Personal Protection	

National Fire Protection Association (U.S.A.)

Fire Hazard: 0
Health: 1
Reactivity: 0
Specific Hazard:

Validated by Edward Waldynski on 9/20/2001.

Verified by Edward Waldynski.
Printed 9/25/2001.

Transportation Emergency   Chemtrec: 800 424-9300

Notice to Reader

To the best of our knowledge, the information contained herein is accurate. It is the users responsibility to determine suitability for the user's purpose and to adopt such precautions as may be advisable for the protection of property and of persons against any hazards that may be involved in the handling and use thereof. However, neither the above named supplier nor any of its subsidiaries assumes responsibility and expressly disclaim liability for loss, damage, or expense arising out of or in any way connected to handling, storage, use, misuse or disposal of this product. If this product is used as a component in another product, this MSDS information may not be applicable.

Material Safety Data Sheet

Section 1. Chemical Product and Company Identification

Product Name	**Technomelt 80-8748**	**Effective Date**	**09/21/01**
Product Use	**Industrial Hot Melt Adhesive**	**Supersedes**	**06/16/99**
Manufacturer	**Henkel Adhesives** **1345 Gasket Drive** **Elgin, IL 60120** **(847) 608-0200**	<u>Transportation Emergency</u> Chemtrec: 800 424-9300 <u>Non-Transportation Emergency</u> 847-608-0200	

Section 2. Composition and Information on Ingredients

Name	CAS #	% by Weight	Exposure Limits
1) Vinyl Acetate	108-05-4	<0.10	10 ppm (OSHA-PEL),(ACGIH-TLV) 15 ppm (ACGIH-STEL)
2) Paraffin Wax	8002-74-2	< 30	TWA: 2 mg/m3 from ACGIH (TLV), Paraffin Wax Fume

Section 3. Hazards Identification

Physical State and Appearance	Light yellow solid
Emergency Overview	WARNING! Molten adhesive may cause severe burns. Adhesive vapors may cause slight irritation of the skin, eyes or respiratory system.
Routes of Exposure	Skin contact Eye contact Inhalation Ingestion

Potential Acute Health Effects

Eyes	Adhesive vapors may cause eye irritation. Molten adhesive may cause severe burns.
Skin	Adhesive vapors may cause skin irritation. Molten adhesive may cause severe burns.
Inhalation	Adhesive vapors may cause slight irritation of the respiratory tract.
Ingestion	May produce gastrointestinal irritation or cause diarrhea

Potential Chronic Health Effects	**CARCINOGENIC EFFECTS**: Classified 2B (Possible for human.) by IARC [Vinyl Acetate]. Classified None. by OSHA [Vinyl Acetate]. **MUTAGENIC EFFECTS**: No known effect. **TERATOGENIC EFFECTS**: No known effect.

Section 4. First Aid Measures

Eye Contact	Molten adhesive may cause severe burns. If eye contact occurs immediately cool with water. Do not remove adhesive. Seek medical attention.
Skin Contact	In case of skin contact with molten adhesive, cool skin with plenty of water. Do not remove adhesive from skin. Remove contaminated clothing and shoes. Get medical attention.
Inhalation	If vapors are inhaled, move to fresh air. If not breathing, give artificial respiration. If breathing is difficult, give oxygen. Get medical attention if symptoms persist.

Continued on Next Page

Technomelt 80-8748	Page: 2/5

Ingestion	Do NOT induce vomiting unless directed to do so by medical personnel. Never give anything by mouth to an unconscious person. Loosen tight clothing such as a collar, tie, belt or waistband. Get medical attention if symptoms persist.

Section 5. Fire Fighting Measures

Flammability of the Product	Non-flammable.
Auto-ignition Temperature	Not applicable.
Flash Points	Not applicable.
Flammable Limits	Not applicable.
Fire Fighting Media and Instructions	Use dry chemical, water spray or carbon dioxide. Qualified persons wearing full fire-fighting suits and approved/certified self-contained breathing apparatus.

Section 6. Accidental Release Measures

Spill and Leak	Use appropriate tools to collect adhesive solids and place in a waste disposal container. Discard in accordance with federal, state and local regulations.

Section 7. Handling and Storage

Handling	Avoid contact with molten material.
Storage	Keep container tightly closed when not in use.

Section 8. Exposure Controls/Personal Protection

Engineering Controls	Use process enclosures, local exhaust ventilation, or other engineering controls to keep airborne levels below recommended exposure limits.
Personal Protection	
Eyes	Safety glasses with side shields.
Body	Wear overalls or long sleeved shirt and long trousers.
Respiratory	Wear appropriate respirator when ventilation is inadequate.
Hands	Heat and chemical resistant gloves.
Feet	Safety Shoes

Section 9. Physical and Chemical Properties

Physical State and Appearance	Light yellow solid
Odor	Odorless.
Color	Light yellow
pH	Not applicable.
Melting/Freezing Point	166 °F (Softening Point)
Specific Gravity	1 (Water = 1)
Vapor Pressure	Not applicable.
Volatility	Non-volatile.
VOC	< 0.10 % (w/w)

Continued on Next Page

Technomelt 80-8748		Page: 3/5
Viscosity	~ 500 cP @ 300 F	
Solubility	Insoluble in hot and cold water.	
Dispersion Properties	Not dispersed in hot or cold water.	
Boiling Point	Not applicable	
Physical Chemical Comments	No additional comments	

Section 10. Stability and Reactivity

Stability and Reactivity	The product is stable.
Conditions of Instability	Avoid contact with strong oxidizers
Incompatibility with Various Substances	May react with strong oxidizing agents.
Hazardous Decomposition Products	Carbon dioxide, carbon monoxide
Hazardous Polymerization	Will not occur.

Section 11. Toxicological Information

Toxicity to Animals	LD50: Not available. LC50: Not available.
Chronic Effects on Humans	2B (Possible for human.) by IARC [Vinyl Acetate]. Classified None. by OSHA [Vinyl Acetate]. **DEVELOPMENTAL TOXICITY:** No known effect.
Other Toxic Effects on Humans	ACGIH evaluated vinyl acetate (1993) as an A3-Animal Carcinogen. Available evidence suggests that the agent is not likely to cause cancer in humans under uncommon or unlikely routes of exposure. The International Agency for Research on Cancer (IARC) published a monograph on vinyl acetate (1995). In this monograph IARC indicates "there is an inadequate evidence in humans for carcinogenicity of vinyl acetate. There is limited evidence in experimental animals for carcinogenicity of vinyl acetate". Normally, this lack of conclusive evidence would place a substance in the IARC Category 3 classification. (not classified as a human carcinogen). However, because vinyl acetate is metabolized to acetaldehyde, which is an IARC 2B (possibly carcinogenic to humans) classification, it is also has been listed under Category 2B
Special Remarks on Toxicity to Animals	No additional remark.
Special Remarks on Chronic Effects on Humans	No additional remark.

Section 12. Ecological Information

Ecotoxicity	No data available
Toxicity of the Products of Biodegradation	No data available.

Section 13. Disposal Considerations

Waste Information	This product does not meet the criteria of a USEPA hazardous waste if discarded in its original purchased form. Must be disposed of in accordance with federal, state and local environmental regulations.
Consult your local or regional authorities.	

Continued on Next Page

Technomelt 80-8748   *Page: 4/5*

Section 14. Transport Information

DOT Classification	Not a DOT regulated material (United States).
Proper Shipping Name	Not applicable.
UN/NA Identification Number	Not applicable.
Packing group	Not applicable.

Section 15. Regulatory Information

U.S. Federal Regulations

TSCA Inventory: All components are listed on the inventory or are exempt .

SARA 302/304/311/312 extremely hazardous substances: Vinyl Acetate
SARA 302/304 emergency planning and notification: No products were found.
SARA 302/304/311/312 hazardous chemicals: No products were found.
SARA 311/312 MSDS distribution - chemical inventory - hazard identification: No products were found.

SARA 313 toxic chemical notification and release reporting: Vinyl Acetate <0.10%

Clean Water Act (CWA) 307: Vinyl Acetate

Clean Water Act (CWA) 311: No products were found.

Clean air act (CAA) 112 accidental release prevention: Vinyl Acetate

Clean air act (CAA) 112 regulated flammable substances: No products were found.

Clean air act (CAA) 112 regulated toxic substances: No products were found.

State Regulations

Rhode Island RTK hazardous substances: Vinyl Acetate
Pennsylvania RTK: Vinyl Acetate: (environmental hazard), Paraffin Wax
Florida: Vinyl Acetate, Paraffin Wax
Minnesota: Vinyl Acetate, Paraffin Wax
Massachusetts RTK: Vinyl Acetate, Paraffin Wax
New Jersey: Vinyl Acetate
New Jersey spill list: Vinyl Acetate

California prop. 65: No products were found.

International Lists

No additional information.

Section 16. Other Information

Hazardous Material Information System (U.S.A.)		
Health		1
Fire Hazard		1
Reactivity		0
Personal Protection		

National Fire Protection Association (U.S.A.)

Fire Hazard: 1
Health: 1
Reactivity: 0
Specific Hazard:

Validated by Edward Waldynski on 9/21/2001.

Verified by Edward Waldynski.
Printed 9/25/2001.

<u>Transportation Emergency</u>   Chemtrec: 800 424-9300

Continued on Next Page

Technomelt 80-8748   *Page: 5/5*

M A T E R I A L   S A F E T Y   D A T A   S H E E T

FOUNTAIN CONCENTRATE 2351   Page: 1

PRODUCT NAME: FOUNTAIN CONCENTRATE 2351   HMIS CODES: H F R P
PRODUCT CODE: C110   1 0 0 B
CHEMICAL NAME: FOUNTAIN SOLUTION

================= SECTION I - MANUFACTURER IDENTIFICATION =================
MANUFACTURER'S NAME: PRINTERS' SERVICE
ADDRESS   : 26 Blanchard Street
                    Newark, New Jersey 07105

EMERGENCY PHONE   : 1-800-424-9300   LAST REVISION : 06/23/98
INFORMATION PHONE : 1-973-589-7800   DATE REVISED : 07/27/00
                                        PREPARER   : ENVIRONMENTAL DEPT.

========= SECTION II - HAZARDOUS INGREDIENTS/SARA III INFORMATION =========

REPORTABLE COMPONENTS	CAS NUMBER	VAPOR PRESSURE mm Hg @ TEMP	WEIGHT PERCENT
* MAGNESIUM NITRATE	10377-60-3	NO DATA NO DATA	10 - 20%
LD50-5.44g/Kg			
* 2-BUTOXYETHANOL	111-76-2	0.6 mmHg 20 C	10 - 20%
PEL 25ppm; TLV 25ppm // LC50 800ppm/8hr; LD50 1.746g/kg //HAP reportable			
* ETHYLENE GLYCOL	107-21-1	<0.1mmHg 20 C	1 - 10%
PEL 50 ppm. TLV 50 ppm // LD50 5.84g/kg // HAP reportable			
* 1-METHYL-2-PYRROLIDONE	872-50-4	0.29mmHg 20 C	1 - 10%
PEL 100 ppm // LD50 4.2g/kg			

* Indicates toxic chemical(s) subject to the reporting requirements of section 313 of Title III and of 40 CFR 372.

=============== SECTION III - PHYSICAL/CHEMICAL CHARACTERISTICS ============
BOILING POINT : 213 F   SPECIFIC GRAVITY (H2O=1): 1.10
VAPOR DENSITY : 1.099 (air = 1)   VAPOR PRESSURE : 12.2 mmHg   at 20 C
DRYING RATE   : <0.1(nButyl Acet.=1) VOC   : 0.88 lb/gal   METHOD: EPA #24
PHOTOREACTIVE : NO   H2O SOLUBILITY : 100 %
VOLATILES   : 87 %   APPEARANCE   : RED
PHYSICAL STATE : LIQUID   ODOR   : MILD ODOR
================ SECTION IV - FIRE AND EXPLOSION HAZARD DATA ==============

FLASH POINT: NONE   METHOD USED: NONE
FLAMMABLE LIMITS IN AIR BY VOLUME- LOWER: NONE   UPPER: NONE
EXTINGUISHING MEDIA: WATER. CARBON DIOXIDE. FOAM. OR DRY POWDER.
SPECIAL FIREFIGHTING PROCEDURES : KEEP CONTAINER COOL.
UNUSUAL FIRE AND EXPLOSION HAZARDS: IF BOILING POINT OF SOLVENT IS REACHED. THE CONTAINER MAY RUPTURE
EXPLOSIVELY.
======================= SECTION V - REACTIVITY DATA =======================

STABILITY: YES   IF NO CONDITIONS:
INCOMPATIBILITY (MATERIALS TO AVOID): YES
IF YES WHICH ONES: STRONG OXIDIZER
HAZARDOUS DECOMPOSITION OR BYPRODUCTS: CARBON DIOXIDE. CARBON MONOXIDE. NITROGEN OXIDES. MAGNESIUM OXIDES
ON IGNITION
HAZARDOUS POLYMERIZATION: NONE
==================== SECTION VI - HEALTH HAZARD DATA =====================
INDICATIONS OF EXPOSURE:
INHALATION HEALTH RISKS AND SYMPTOMS OF EXPOSURE: NONE
EYE CONTACT AND SYMPTOMS OF EXPOSURE: REDNESS OR BURNING SENSATION.
SKIN HEALTH RISKS AND SYMPTOMS OF EXPOSURE: REDNESS. ITCHING. IRRITATION.
INGESTION HEALTH RISKS AND SYMPTOMS OF EXPOSURE: GASTROINTESTINAL IRRITATION. NAUSEA. VOMITING AND DIARRHEA.

M A T E R I A L   S A F E T Y   D A T A   S H E E T
FOUNTAIN CONCENTRATE 2351   Page: 2

EMERGENCY AND FIRST AID:
INHALATION - NONE
EYES - FLUSH EYES WITH WATER FOR 15 MINUTES. LIFT UPPER AND LOWER LIDS. SEE DOCTOR.
SKIN - WASH WITH SOAP AND WATER.
INGESTION - INDUCE VOMITING. SEE DOCTOR IMMEDIATELY.

HEALTH HAZARDS (ACUTE AND CHRONIC):
EFFECT OF CHRONIC EXPOSURE: PROLONGED HIGH VAPOR EXPOSURE MAY CAUSE LIVER. KIDNEY. LUNG. BLOOD. AND CENTRAL NERVOUS SYSTEM PROBLEMS.
EFFECT OF ACCUTE EXPOSURE: NONE

IN ALL CASES OF EMERGENCY AND FIRST AID, WE STRONGLY RECOMMEND A DOCTOR BE SEEN

CARCINOGENICITY: NTP CARCINOGEN: No   **IARC MONOGRAPHS:** No   **OSHA REGULATED:** No
MEDICAL CONDITIONS GENERALLY AGGRAVATED BY EXPOSURE: DERMATITIS. MAY AGGRAVATE EXISTING LIVER AND
KIDNEY AILMENTS.

========== **SECTION VII -   PRECAUTIONS FOR SAFE HANDLING AND USE** ============

STEPS TO BE TAKEN IN CASE MATERIAL IS RELEASED OR SPILLED: VENTILATE AREA. KEEP AWAY FROM
STRONG OXIDIZERS. HEAT. SPARKS OR OPEN FLAMES. PREVENT SPILL FROM SPREADING BY USING AN INERT MATERIAL. SUCH AS SAND. AS A DAM.
KEEP OUT OF ALL WATERWAYS OR WATER DRAINS. DO NOT FLUSH AREA WITH WATER. FOR SMALL SPILLS USE ABSORBENT PADS. FOR LARGE SPILLS.
CALL A SPILL RESPONSE TEAM. IF REQUIRED. CONTACT STATE/LOCAL AGENCIES.
WASTE DISPOSAL METHOD: PRODUCT SOAKED ABSORBENT SHOULD BE PLACED IN SEALED PLASTIC DRUMS FOR DISPOSAL IN ACCORDANCE
WITH LOCAL. STATE AND FEDERAL REGULATIONS.
PRECAUTIONS TO BE TAKEN IN HANDLING AND STORING: DO NOT FREEZE. IF FROZEN. THAW OUT AND MIX WELL
BEFORE USING.
OTHER PRECAUTIONS: WE RECOMMEND THAT CONTAINERS BE EITHER PROFESSIONALLY RECONDITIONED FOR REUSE OR PROPERLY DISPOSED OF
BY CERTIFIED FIRMS TO HELP REDUCE THE POSSIBILITY OF AN ACCIDENT. DISPOSAL OF CONTAINERS SHOULD BE IN ACCORDANCE WITH APPLICABLE
LAWS AND REGULATIONS. "EMPTY" DRUMS SHOULD NOT BE GIVEN TO INDIVIDUALS.

==================== **SECTION VIII - CONTROL MEASURES** =====================
EXPOSURE CONTROL AND PERSONAL PROTECTION:
RESPIRATORY PROTECTION: NONE NEEDED.
VENTILATION: MECHANICAL (GENERAL) SATISFACTORY.
PROTECTIVE GLOVES: USE RUBBER OR SYNTHETIC GLOVES.
EYE PROTECTION: USE SAFETY GLASSES OR GOGGLES.
OTHER PROTECTIVE EQUIPMENT OR CLOTHING: NONE.
WORK/HYGIENIC PRACTICES: WASH SKIN/CLOTHES IF THEY COME IN CONTACT WITH THE PRODUCT. DO NOT WEAR CLOTHING WET WITH
THE PRODUCT.

========================= **SECTION IX - SHIPPING INFORMATION** ====================

GROUND SHIPMENT.   **UN No   : NONE**
D.O.T HAZARD CLASSIFICATION: NOT A D.O.T HAZARDOUS MATERIAL.
========================= **SECTION X - DISCLAIMER** ==========================
THE INFORMATION AND RECOMMENDATIONS HEREIN HAVE BEEN COMPILED FROM OUR RECORDS AND OTHER SOURCES BELIEVED TO BE RELIABLE. NO
WARRANTY. GUARANTY OR REPRESENTATION IS MADE BY PRINTERS' SERVICE AS TO THE SUFFICIENCY OF ANY REPRESENTATION. THE ABSENCE OF DATA
INDICATES ONLY THAT THE DATA IS NOT READILY AVAILABLE TO US. ADDITIONAL SAFETY MEASURES MAY BE REQUIRED UNDER PARTICULAR OR
EXCEPTIONAL CONDITIONS OF USE. WITH REGARD TO THE MATERIALS THEMSELVES. PRINTERS' SERVICE MAKES NO WARRANTY OF ANY KIND WHATEVER.
EXPRESSED OR IMPLIED. AND ALL IMPLIED WARRANTIES OF MERCHANTABILITY AND FITNESS FOR A PARTICULAR PURPOSE ARE HEREBY DISCLAIMED.

MATERIAL SAFETY DATA SHEET 05/10/99

Tower Products, Inc., 2703 Freemansburg Ave., Easton, PA 18045

SECTION 1: PRODUCT INFORMATION
Product Name: **MILLENNIUM** (Universal Fountain Solution)
D.O.T. Designation: Cleaning Liquid. Not Regulated.
U.N. Designation: Same as D.O.T.

SECTION 2: HAZARDOUS COMPONENTS/IDENTITY INFORMATION

HAZARDOUS COMPONENT	CAS No.	% WT.	OSHA PEL	ACGIH TLV-TWA	OTHER RATINGS	OSHA STEL
Propylene Glycol	57-55-6	1-2			50ppm(AIHA)	
Dipropylene Glycol Monomethyl Ether	34590-94-8	2-6	100ppm			150ppm
Glyceritol	56-81-5	2-6	10mg/m3	10mg/m3 5mg/m3(respirable)		

SECTION 3: PHYSICAL/CHEMICAL CHARACTERISTICS
Boiling Point: 212 degrees F.
Specific Gravity: (Water = 1) 1.01
Vapor Pressure: (mmHG, calculated) None
Melting Point: N/A
Vapor Density: (Air = 1, calculated) 2
Solubility in Water: Complete
pH of Concentrate: 3.8-4.2
Appearance & Odor: Blue liquid, detergent odor.
Maximum VOC Content: .3 lbs. per gal. (40 grams per liter)
Maximum VOC% : 4%

SECTION 4: FIRE AND EXPLOSION DATA
Flash Point (Tag Closed Cup Method): Greater than 200 degrees F. (TCC)
Flammable Limits (Calculated): LEL: N/A   UEL: N/A
Extinguishing Media: Water
Special Fire-fighting Procedures: N/A
Unusual Fire and Explosion Hazards: N/A

SECTION 5: REACTIVITY DATA
Stability: Stable
Incompatibility: None
Hazardous Decomposition or Byproducts: None
Hazardous Polymerization: Will not occur.
Conditions to Avoid: Avoid exposure to high heat sources, electrical and welding arcs and open flame. Also avoid strong oxidizing agents.

SECTION 6: HEALTH HAZARD DATA
Routes of Entry: Inhalation, Ingestion, Skin.
Health Hazards: Eye Contact: May lead to irritation.
    Skin Contact: May lead to dermatitis.
    Ingestion: May lead to vomiting.
Carcinogenicity (NTP, IARC, OSHA): The components of this product have not shown any evidence of carcinogenicity.
Signs and Symptoms of Exposure: Overexposure may lead to dermatitis and eye irritation.

MILLENNIUM Page 2

Medical Conditions Aggravated by Exposure: None known under recommended usage conditions.

Emergency First Aid Procedures:
For Skin Contact: Flush with large volume of water for at least 15 minutes.
                               Get immediate medical attention if necessary.
For Inhalation: Remove to fresh air. Get immediate medical attention if necessary.
For Eye Contact: Flush with large volume of water for at least 15 minutes. Get immediate medical attention.
For Ingestion: Get immediate medical attention. Do not induce vomiting.

SECTION 7: PRECAUTIONS FOR SAFE HANDLING AND USE/REGULATORY INFORMATION
Steps to be Taken in Case Material is Released or Spilled:

(Minor Spills): Absorb material with ground clay, vermiculite or similar absorbent material, then place into containers for removal.

(Major Spills): Eliminate sources of ignition. Dike and contain spill. Shut off source of spill if possible. Remove liquid by chemical vacuum, absorbent or other safe and approved method and place into containers for proper legal disposal. Flush area with water to remove residue, and remove flushed solutions as above.

(Waste Disposal Method): Dispose of all waste in accordance with federal, state and local regulations.

Regulatory Information: Reportable quantity (RQ), EPA Regulation 40CFR302 (CERCLA) Section 102: None
EPA Regulation 40CFR372 (SARA) 313: None
Product may contain components which may be further regulated by state and/or local agencies - Consult Appropriate Agencies.

Precautions to be Taken in Handling and Storing:
Keep containers closed when not in use. Empty containers can be hazardous.
Plastic or stainless steel handling and transfer equipment is recommended.

HMIS: Health Hazard: **1**   Flammability: **1**   Reactivity: **0**   Personal Protection: **B**

SECTION 8: CONTROL MEASURES
Respiratory Protection: Not normally required.

Ventilation: Local and mechanical exhaust recommended. Avoid open electrical sources near product vapor areas. Keep containers tightly closed when not in use. Store between 50 degrees and 100 degrees F. Do not reuse empty containers.

Protective Gloves: Impervious or chemical resistant gloves recommended (consult safety equipment supplier).

Eye Protection: Chemical splash goggles recommended to protect against potential eye contact.

Other Protective Clothing and Equipment: Safety shoes and aprons recommended.

Work and Hygiene Practices: Do not take internally. Avoid skin contact and wash skin after using products. Do not eat, drink, or smoke in work area. Keep away from children.

FOR MORE INFORMATION, CONSULT TOWER PRODUCTS, INC.
THE INFORMATION HEREIN IS GIVEN IN GOOD FAITH, BUT NO WARRANTY, EXPRESS OR IMPLIED IS MADE.

```
              PRIDE SOLVENTS & CHEMICALS
              6 LONG ISLAND AVE.
              HOLTSVILLE, N.Y.  11742
              (516) 758-0200
         FOR CHEMICAL EMERGENCY: Spill, Leak, Fire
         Exposure or Accident Call CHEMTREC- Day or
         Night: 1-800-424-9300

         MSDS*********MSDS**********MSDS**********MSDS
         THIS MSDS COMPLIES WITH 29 CFR 1910.1200 (HAZARD
         COMMUNICATION STANDARD ) IMPORTANT: Read this MSDS
         before handling & disposing of this product. Pass
         this information on to employees, customers and
         users of this product.
*********************************************************
PRODUCT IDENTIFICATION
*********************************************************
     Trade name: Slow Blend
     DOT Shipping name: Flammable liquid, n.o.s (nPropanol)
     Chemical Family:Solvent Blend
     DOT Hazard class: Flammable liquid
     Generic name: Solvent blend
     Co. ID NO.: Slow Blend
     CAS NO.: Mixture
     UN/NA #:UN 1993
     Packaging group: II
     Signal word: nPropanol
*********************************************************
SECTION I  HAZARDOUS INGREDIENTS/ EXPOSURE LIMITS
*********************************************************
HAZARDOUS INGREDIENTS      CAS #     TLV/PEL    AGENCY     TYPE
nPropyl Acetate            109-60-4  200PPM     ACGIH      TWA
nPROPANOL                  71-23-8   200PPM     ACGIH      TWA-SKIN

*********************************************************
SECTION IA SARA 313 LISTED CHEMICALS
*********************************************************
LISTED INGREDIENTS        CAS#              WT. % RANGE
NONE

*********************************************************
SECTION II EMERGENCY AND FIRST AID PROCEDURES
*********************************************************
EYE CONTACT:
   Move person away from exposure and into fresh air. If
   irritation or redness develops, flush eyes with clean
   water and seek medical attention. For direct contact
   hold eyelids apart for at least 15 minutes. Seek
   medical attention.
SKIN CONTACT:
   Remove contaminated shoes and clothing and cleanse
   affected areas thoroughly by washing with mild soap
   and water. If irritation persists seek medical attention.
INHALATION (BREATHING)
   Immediately move person away from exposure and into fresh
   air. If respiratory symptoms or other symptoms of
   exposure develop, seek immediate medical attention. If
   person is not breathing, immediately begin artificial
   respiration. If breathing difficulties develop, oxygen
```

should be administered by qualified personnel. Seek
immediate medical attention.

INGESTION (SWALLOWING)

This material is a potential aspiration hazard. If
swallowed, seek emergency medical attention. If person
is drowsy or unconscious, place on the left side with
head down. Do not give anything by mouth.
Induce vomiting. Seek immediate medical attention.

```
**************************************************************
```
SECTION III   HEALTH HAZARDS/ ROUTES OF ENTRY
```
**************************************************************
```

EYE CONTACT:

One or more components of this material is an eye
irritant. Direct contact with the liquid or exposure to
vapors or mists may cause stinging, tearing, redness or
swelling.

SKIN CONTACT:

One or more components of this material may cause mild
skin irritation. Prolonged or repeated contact may cause
redness, burning, drying and cracking of skin.

SKIN ABSORPTION:

Contact may result in skin absorption but symptoms of
toxicity are not anticipated by this route alone under
normal conditions of use. Persons with pre-existing skin
disorders may be more susceptible to the effects of this
material.

INHALATION (BREATHING):

One or more components of this material is toxic by
inhalation. Breathing vapors or mists may be harmful.
Effects of overexposure may include:
Irritation of the nose and throat.
Signs of nervous system depression, such as, headache
drowsiness, dizziness, loss of coordination, fatigue,
coughing and shortness of breath.
Respiratory symptoms associated with pre-existing lung
disorders (asthma like conditions) may be aggrevated by
exposure to this material.

INGESTION (SWALLOWING)

While this material has a low degree of toxicity,
ingestion of large quantities may cause the following:
Irritation of the digestive tract.
Signs of nervous system depression, such as,
headache, drowsiness, dizziness, loss of coordination
fatigue and nausea.
ASPIRATION HAZARD: One or more components of this
material can enter the lungs during swallowing and cause
lung inflammation and damage.

```
**************************************************************
```
SECTION IV   SPECIAL PROTECTION INFORMATION
```
**************************************************************
```

VENTILATION:

If current ventilation practices are not adequate to
maintain airborne concentrations below established
exposure limits (see Section I), additional ventilation
or exhaust systems may be required. Where explosive

mixtures may be present, electrical systems that are safe
for such locations must be used.

RESPIRATORY PROTECTION:
   The use of respiratory protection is advised when
   concentrations exceed the established exposure limits.
   (see Section I). Depending on the airborne concentration
   use a respirator or gas mask with appropriate cartridges
   or canisters (NIOSH approved, if available) or supplied
   air equipment.

PROTECTIVE GLOVES:
   The use of gloves impermeable to the specific material
   handled is advised to prevent skin contact and possible
   irritation.

EYE PROTECTION:
   Approved eye protection to safeguard against potential
   eye contact, irritation or injury is recommended.

****
SECTION V   REACTIVITY DATA
****
STABILITY:
   Stable
INCOMPATIBILITY (MATERIALS TO AVOID):
   This product forms combustible and/or explosive mixtures
   with air and /or oxygen.
   This product is incompatible with:
        Strong acids or bases
        Oxidizing agents
        Selected amines
        Alkali metals
        Halogens
        Anhydrides
        Isocyanates
        Acetaldehyde
        Chlorine
        Ethylene oxide
        Hydrogen peroxide
        Organometallic contaminants

HAZARDOUS DECOMPOSITION PRODUCTS:
   Thermal decomposition in the presence of air may yield
   carbon monoxide and/or carbon dioxide.

HAZARDOUS POLYMERIZATION:
   Will not occur.

****
SECTION VI   SPILL OR LEAK PROCEDURES
****

PRECAUTIONS IN CASE OF LEAK OR SPILL:
   Keep all sources of ignition and hot metal surfaces away
   from spill/release. Stay upwind and away from

spill/release. Isolate hazard area and limit entry to
emergency crew only. Stop spill/release if it can be done
without risk. Wear appropriate protective equipment
including respiratory protection as conditions warrant.
(see Section IV). Prevent spilled material from entering
sewers, storm drains, and natural waterways. Dike far
ahead of spill for later recovery and disposal. Spilled
material may be absorbed by an appropriate absorbant.
Notify fire authorities and appropriate federal, state
and local agencies. If spill/release is in excess of EPA
reportable quantity, immediately notify the national
response center.(phone # 1-800-424-8802

WASTE DISPOSAL METHOD:
Dispose of product in accordance with local, county,
state and federal regulations.

****

SECTION VII   STORAGE AND SPECIAL PRECAUTIONS

****

HANDLING AND STORAGE PRECAUTIONS:
Keep containers tightly closed, cool, dry and away from
all sources of ignition. Use and store this product with
adequate ventilation. Avoid inhalation of vapors and
personal contact with the product. Use good personal
hygiene practices. Bond and ground equipment when
transferring to another container. "Empty" containers
contain residue (liquid and/or vapor) and can be
dangerous. Do not pressurize, cut, weld, braze, solder,
drill, grind or expose such containers to heat,flame,
sparks,or other sources of ignition. They may explode and
cause injury and death. Empty drums should be completely
drained, properly bunged and promptly shipped to the
supplier or drum reconditioner. All other containers
should be disposed of in an environmentally safe manner
and in accordance with governmental regulations.
Before working in or on tanks which contain or has
contained this product, refer to OSHA or ANSI Z49.1
regulations and other governmental and industrial
references pertaining to cleaning, repairing, welding
or other contemplated operations.

****

SECTION VIII   FIRE AND EXPLOSION HAZARD DATA

****

EXTINGUISHING MEDIA:
Extinguish with dry chemical,CO2 or a universal type foam.

FIRE AND EXPLOSION HAZARD:
This material is combustible and may be ignited by heat,
sparks, flames, or other sources of ignition (e.g. pilot
lights, static electricity, or mechanical/electrical
equipment). Vapors may travel considerable distances to a
source of ignition where they may ignite, flashback or
explode. Liquid may create a vapor/air explosion hazard
indoors, outdoors or in sewers. Vapors are heavier than
air and may accumulate in low areas. If container is not
properly cooled, it may explode in the heat of a fire.

FIRE FIGHTING PROCEDURES:
  Wear appropriate protective equipment including
  respiratory protection as conditions warrant.(see Section
  IV) Stop spill/release if it can be done without risk.
  Water spray may be useful in minimizing or dispersing
  vapors and cooling equipment exposed to heat and flame.
  Avoid spreading burning liquid with water used for cooling
  purposes.

****
SECTION IX   PHYSICAL DATA
****

  APPROXIMATE BOILING POINT (DEG F):204-217
  PER CENT VOLATILE: 100
  SPECIFIC GRAVITY (68 F): 0.813
  FLASH POINT, (TCC, DEG F): 58
  RELATIVE EVAPORATION RATE (ESTIMATED): 1.2
      (nBuOAC =1)
  PERCENT SOLUBILITY IN WATER (ESTIMATED): 89
  VAPOR PRESSURE @20 C: 20 mmHg
  VOC CONTENT (g/l): 813
****
SECTION X   OTHER REGULATORY DATA
****
  SARA
      SECTION 311, 312: NONE
      SECTION 313:   NONE
  TSCA
      ALL COMPONENTS ARE IN FULL COMPLIANCE WITH THE TSCA
      INVENTORY.
  RCRA
      IF THIS PRODUCT BECOMES A WASTE MATERIAL , IT WOULD
      BE AN IGNITABLE HAZARDOUS WASTE, D001.
  CERCLA
      NONE
  HMIS
      HEALTH   1
      FLAMMABILITY   3
      REACTIVITY   0

MATERIAL SAFETY DATA SHEET

AUTOWASH 6000

Page: 1

PRODUCT NAME: AUTOWASH 6000
PRODUCT CODE: A299
CHEMICAL NAME: BLANKET AND ROLLER WASH

HMIS CODES: H F R P
            1 2 0 B

================== SECTION I - MANUFACTURER IDENTIFICATION ==================

MANUFACTURER'S NAME: PRINTERS' SERVICE
ADDRESS : 26 Blanchard Street
Newark, New Jersey 07105

EMERGENCY PHONE : 1-800-424-9300   LAST REVISION : 09/22/00
INFORMATION PHONE : 1-973-589-7800   DATE REVISED : 01/25/01
                                       PREPARER : ENVIRONMENTAL DEPT.

========= SECTION II - HAZARDOUS INGREDIENTS/SARA III INFORMATION =========

REPORTABLE COMPONENTS	CAS NUMBER	VAPOR PRESSURE mm Hg @ TEMP	WEIGHT PERCENT
ALIPHATIC PETRO DISTILLATE (C9 - C11)	64742-48-9	2.7 mmHg 25 C	70 - 80%
PEL 100ppm: TLV 100ppm // LD50> 25ml/kg: LC50 700ppm/4hr			
AROMATIC PETRO DISTILLATE (C8-C11)	64742-95-6	2.7mmHg 25 C	20 - 30%
PEL 100 ppm // LD50 4.7g/kg: LC50 3670 ppm/8hr			
NONYLPHENOXYPOLY(ETHYLENEOXY)ETHANOL	9016-45-9	NO DATA NO DATA	1 - 10%
LD50 2.4g/Kg			

CAS# 64742-95-6 contains approximately 5% XYLENE (CAS# 1330-20-7) an HAP reportable which has a PEL and TLV of 100 ppm: approximately 4% CUMENE (CAS# 98-82-8). an HAP reportable which has a PEL and TLV of 50 ppm-skin: and approximately 27% 1.2.4 TRIMETHYLBENZENE (CAS# 95-63-6). which has a PEL and TLV of 25 ppm. XYLENE. CUMENE AND 1.2.4 TRIMETHYLBENZENE are subject to the reporting requirements of section 313 OF SARA TITLE III.

=============== SECTION III - PHYSICAL/CHEMICAL CHARACTERISTICS =============

BOILING POINT : 313 F   SPECIFIC GRAVITY (H2O=1): 0.78
VAPOR DENSITY : 4.56 (air = 1)   VAPOR PRESSURE : 2.7 mmHg   at 20 C
DRYING RATE : .12(n-Butyl Acet.=1)   VOC : 6.48 lb/gl   METHOD: EPA #24
PHOTOREACTIVE : YES   H2O SOLUBILITY : SLIGHT
VOLATILES : 98%   APPEARANCE : CLEAR
PHYSICAL STATE : LIQUID   ODOR : SOLVENT ODOR

================= SECTION IV - FIRE AND EXPLOSION HAZARD DATA ==============

FLASH POINT : 105 F   METHOD USED: TCC
FLAMMABLE LIMITS IN AIR BY VOLUME- LOWER: 0.5   UPPER: 6.0
EXTINGUISHING MEDIA: CARBON DIOXIDE. FOAM. OR DRY POWDER (WATER MAY BE INEFFECTIVE)
SPECIAL FIREFIGHTING PROCEDURES : KEEP CONTAINER COOL. CONTROL COOLING WATER SINCE IT MAY TEND TO SPREAD BURNING MATERIAL.
UNUSUAL FIRE AND EXPLOSION HAZARDS: IF BOILING POINT OF SOLVENT IS REACHED. THE CONTAINER MAY RUPTURE EXPLOSIVELY AND IF IGNITED. GENERATE A FIREBALL.

======================== SECTION V - REACTIVITY DATA ========================

STABILITY: YES   IF NO CONDITIONS:
INCOMPATIBILITY (MATERIALS TO AVOID): YES
IF YES WHICH ONES: STRONG OXIDIZER
HAZARDOUS DECOMPOSITION OR BYPRODUCTS: CARBON DIOXIDE. CARBON MONOXIDE ON IGNITION
HAZARDOUS POLYMERIZATION: NONE

==================== SECTION VI - HEALTH HAZARD DATA ====================

INDICATIONS OF EXPOSURE:
INHALATION HEALTH RISKS AND SYMPTOMS OF EXPOSURE: HEADACHE. DIZZINESS. NAUSEA. VERY HIGH LEVELS OF VAPORS COULD CAUSE UNCONCIOUSNESS. SLIGHT IRRITATION OF THE MUCOUS MEMBRANE
EYE CONTACT AND SYMPTOMS OF EXPOSURE: REDNESS OR BURNING SENSATION.
SKIN HEALTH RISKS AND SYMPTOMS OF EXPOSURE: REDNESS. ITCHING. IRRITATION ON OVEREXPOSURE.
INGESTION HEALTH RISKS AND SYMPTOMS OF EXPOSURE: SEVERE GASTROINTESTINAL IRRITATION. NAUSEA. VOMITING AND DIARRHEA.

M A T E R I A L   S A F E T Y   D A T A   S H E E T

AUTOWASH 6000   Page: 2

EMERGENCY AND FIRST AID PROCEDURES

IF IN EYES: FLUSH WITH WATER FOR 15 MIN. LIFT UPPER AND LOWER EYE LIDS. SEE A DOCTOR.

IF ON SKIN: WASH WITH SOAP AND WATER.

IF INHALED: REMOVE TO FRESH AIR. IF UNCONSCIOUS. USE ARTIFICIAL RESPIRATON.

IF INGESTED: DO NOT INDUCE VOMITING. SEE DOCTOR IMMEDIATELY TO PUMP STOMACH.

HEALTH HAZARDS (ACUTE AND CHRONIC):

EFFECT OF CHRONIC EXPOSURE: PROLONGED HIGH VAPOR EXPOSURE MAY CAUSE LIVER AND KIDNEY PROBLEMS.

EFFECT OF ACCUTE EXPOSURE: NONE

IN ALL CASES OF EMERGENCY AND FIRST AID, WE STRONGLY RECOMMEND A DOCTOR BE SEEN

CARCINOGENICITY: NTP CARCINOGEN: No **IARC MONOGRAPHS:** No   **OSHA REGULATED:** No

MEDICAL CONDITIONS GENERALLY AGGRAVATED BY EXPOSURE: DERMATITIS

=========== **SECTION VII - PRECAUTIONS FOR SAFE HANDLING AND USE** ===========

STEPS TO BE TAKEN IN CASE MATERIAL IS RELEASED OR SPILLED: VENTILATE AREA. KEEP AWAY FROM STRONG OXIDIZERS. HEAT. SPARKS OR OPEN FLAMES. PREVENT SPILL FROM SPREADING BY USING AN INERT MATERIAL. SUCH AS SAND. AS A DAM. KEEP OUT OF ALL WATERWAYS OR WATER DRAINS. DO NOT FLUSH AREA WITH WATER. FOR SMALL SPILLS USE ABSORBENT PADS. FOR LARGE SPILLS. CALL A SPILL RESPONSE TEAM. IF REQUIRED. CONTACT STATE/LOCAL AGENCIES.

WASTE DISPOSAL METHOD: PRODUCT SOAKED ABSORBENT SHOULD BE PLACED IN SEALED METAL DRUMS FOR DISPOSAL IN ACCORDANCE WITH LOCAL. STATE AND FEDERAL REGULATIONS.

PRECAUTIONS TO BE TAKEN IN HANDLING AND STORING: KEEP AWAY FROM STRONG OXIDIZERS. HEAT. SPARKS AND OPEN FLAMES. DO NOT CUT OR DRILL INTO AN EMPTY CONTAINER IN ANY WAY THAT MIGHT GENERATE A SPARK. SOLVENT RESIDUE IN THE CONTAINER COULD IGNITE AND CAUSE AN EXPLOSION. KEEP CONTAINER TIGHTLY CLOSED AND OUT OF THE WEATHER.

OTHER PRECAUTIONS: WE RECOMMEND THAT CONTAINERS BE EITHER PROFESSIONALLY RECONDITIONED FOR REUSE OR PROPERLY DISPOSED OF BY CERTIFIED FIRMS TO HELP REDUCE THE POSSIBILITY OF AN ACCIDENT. DISPOSAL OF CONTAINERS SHOULD BE IN ACCORDANCE WITH APPLICABLE LAWS AND REGULATIONS. "EMPTY" DRUMS SHOULD NOT BE GIVEN TO INDIVIDUALS.

===================== **SECTION VIII - CONTROL MEASURES** =====================

EXPOSURE CONTROL AND PERSONAL PROTECTION:

RESPIRATORY PROTECTION: IF TLV IS EXCEEDED USE A GAS MASK WITH APPROPRIATE CARTRIDGES. CANNISTER OR SUPPLIED AIR EQUIPMENT.

VENTILATION: IF NORMAL VENTILATION IS INADEQUATE USE ADDITIONAL SYSTEMS.ESPECIALLY LOCAL VENTILATION. IF THE VAPOR LEVEL CAN APPROACH THE LEL - LOWER EXPLOSION LIMIT. USE EXPLOSION PROOF SYSTEMS.

PROTECTIVE GLOVES: USE SOLVENT RESISTANT GLOVES.

EYE PROTECTION: USE SAFETY GLASSES OR GOGGLES.

OTHER PROTECTIVE EQUIPMENT OR CLOTHING: NONE.

WORK/HYGIENIC PRACTICES: WASH SKIN/CLOTHES IF THEY COME IN CONTACT WITH THE PRODUCT. DO NOT WEAR CLOTHING WET WITH THE PRODUCT.

========================= **SECTION IX - SHIPPING INFORMATION** ====================

GROUND SHIPMENT.   **UN No**   : NA 1993

D.O.T HAZARD CLASSIFICATION: COMBUSTIBLE LIQUID- N.O.S.

========================= **SECTION X - DISCLAIMER** =========================

THE INFORMATION AND RECOMMENDATIONS HEREIN HAVE BEEN COMPILED FROM OUR RECORDS AND OTHER SOURCES BELIEVED TO BE RELIABLE. NO WARRANTY. GUARANTY OR REPRESENTATION IS MADE BY PRINTERS' SERVICE AS TO THE SUFFICIENCY OF ANY REPRESENTATION. THE ABSENCE OF DATA INDICATES ONLY THAT THE DATA IS NOT READILY AVAILABLE TO US. ADDITIONAL SAFETY MEASURES MAY BE REQUIRED UNDER PARTICULAR OR EXCEPTIONAL CONDITIONS OF USE. WITH REGARD TO THE MATERIALS THEMSELVES. PRINTERS' SERVICE MAKES NO WARRANTY OF ANY KIND WHATEVER. EXPRESSED OR IMPLIED. AND ALL IMPLIED WARRANTIES OF MERCHANTABILITY AND FITNESS FOR A PARTICULAR PURPOSE ARE HEREBY DISCLAIMED.

M A T E R I A L   S A F E T Y   D A T A   S H E E T

MRC-F   Page: 1

PRODUCT NAME: MRC-F   HMIS CODES: H F R P
PRODUCT CODE: A941   1 3 0 B
CHEMICAL NAME: METERING ROLLER CLEANER

================== SECTION I - MANUFACTURER IDENTIFICATION ==================
MANUFACTURER'S NAME: PRINTERS' SERVICE
ADDRESS   : 26 Blanchard Street
                     Newark, New Jersey 07105

EMERGENCY PHONE   : 1-800-424-9300   LAST REVISION : 03/02/99
INFORMATION PHONE : 1-973-589-7800   DATE REVISED   : 11/22/00
                                         PREPARER   : ENVIRONMENTAL DEPT.

========== SECTION II - HAZARDOUS INGREDIENTS/SARA III INFORMATION ==========

| | | VAPOR PRESSURE | WEIGHT |
REPORTABLE COMPONENTS	CAS NUMBER	mm Hg @ TEMP	PERCENT
ACETONE	67-64-1	186 mmHg 20 C	40 - 50%
PEL 750ppm: TLV 750ppm // LD50 9.75g/kg: LC50 16000ppm/4hr			
* XYLENE	1330-20-7	6.6 mmHg 20 C	20 - 30%
PEL 100ppm: TLV 100ppm // LD50 5.2g/kg: LC50 6350ppm/4hr // HAP reportable			
ISOPROPANOL 99%	67-63-0	37 mmHg 20 C	10 - 20%
PEL 400ppm: TLV 400ppm // LD50 5.84g/kg: LC50 12000ppm/8hr			
* 1-METHYL-2-PYRROLIDONE	872-50-4	0.29mmHg 20 C	1 - 10%
PEL 100 ppm // LD50 4.2g/kg			

* Indicates chemical(s) subject to the reporting requirements of section 313 of Title III and of 40 CFR 372. CAS# 1330-20-7 Contains approximately 20% ETHYLBENZENE (CAS# 100-41-4). an HAP reportable which has a PEL of 100 PPM and a TLV of 100 PPM. ETHYLBENZENE is subject to the reporting requirements of section 313 OF SARA TITLE III.

=============== SECTION III - PHYSICAL/CHEMICAL CHARACTERISTICS =============
BOILING POINT : 133 F   SPECIFIC GRAVITY (H2O=1):   0.82
VAPOR DENSITY : 2.5 (air=1)   VAPOR PRESSURE : 102mmHg (-Acet 21.5) at 20 C
DRYING RATE   : 3.6(n-Butyl Acet.=1)   VOC   : 3.54 lb/gal   METHOD: EPA #24
PHOTOREACTIVE : YES   H2O SOLUBILITY : STRONG
VOLATILES   : 100%   APPEARANCE : CLEAR
PHYSICAL STATE : LIQUID   ODOR   : STRONG
**COMPOSITE PRESSURE: 21.5 at 20 C
The VOC Composite Pressure is calculated as per California AQMD Rule 1171.

================== SECTION IV - FIRE AND EXPLOSION HAZARD DATA ==============
FLASH POINT   : < 20 F   METHOD USED: TCC
FLAMMABLE LIMITS IN AIR BY VOLUME- LOWER: 1.0   UPPER: 13.2
EXTINGUISHING MEDIA: CARBON DIOXIDE. FOAM. OR DRY POWDER (WATER MAY BE INEFFECTIVE)
SPECIAL FIREFIGHTING PROCEDURES : KEEP CONTAINER COOL. CONTROL COOLING WATER SINCE IT MAY TEND TO SPREAD BURNING MATERIAL.
UNUSUAL FIRE AND EXPLOSION HAZARDS : IF BOILING POINT OF SOLVENT IS REACHED. THE CONTAINER MAY RUPTURE EXPLOSIVELY AND IF IGNITED. GENERATE A FIREBALL.

====================== SECTION V - REACTIVITY DATA ======================

STABILITY: YES   IF NO CONDITIONS: .
INCOMPATIBILITY (MATERIALS TO AVOID): YES
IF YES WHICH ONES: STRONG OXIDIZER
HAZARDOUS DECOMPOSITION OR BYPRODUCTS: CARBON DIOXIDE. CARBON MONOXIDE. OXIDES OF NITROGEN ON IGNITION
HAZARDOUS POLYMERIZATION: NONE

=================== SECTION VI - HEALTH HAZARD DATA ======================
INDICATIONS OF EXPOSURE:
INHALATION HEALTH RISKS AND SYMPTOMS OF EXPOSURE: HEADACHE. DIZZINESS. NAUSEA. VERY HIGH LEVELS OF VAPORS COULD CAUSE UNCONCIOUSNESS. SLIGHT IRRITATION OF THE MUCOUS MEMBRANE

MATERIAL SAFETY DATA SHEET

MRC-F   Page: 2

EYE CONTACT AND SYMPTOMS OF EXPOSURE: REDNESS OR BURNING SENSATION.

SKIN HEALTH RISKS AND SYMPTOMS OF EXPOSURE: REDNESS. ITCHING. IRRITATION ON OVEREXPOSURE.

INGESTION HEALTH RISKS AND SYMPTOMS OF EXPOSURE: SEVERE GASTROINTESTINAL IRRITATION. NAUSEA. VOMITING AND DIARRHEA.

EMERGENCY AND FIRST AID PROCEDURES

IF IN EYES: FLUSH WITH WATER FOR 15 MIN. LIFT UPPER AND LOWER EYE LIDS. SEE A DOCTOR.

IF ON SKIN: WASH WITH SOAP AND WATER.

IF INHALED: REMOVE TO FRESH AIR, IF UNCONSCIOUS. USE ARTIFICIAL RESPIRATON.

IF INGESTED: DO NOT INDUCE VOMITING. SEE DOCTOR IMMEDIATELY TO PUMP STOMACH.

HEALTH HAZARDS (ACUTE AND CHRONIC):

EFFECT OF CHRONIC EXPOSURE: PROLONGED HIGH VAPOR EXPOSURE MAY CAUSE LIVER. KIDNEY. BLOOD. AND EYE PROBLEMS.

EFFECT OF ACCUTE EXPOSURE: NONE

IN ALL CASES OF EMERGENCY AND FIRST AID, WE STRONGLY RECOMMEND A DOCTOR BE SEEN

CARCINOGENICITY: NTP CARCINOGEN: No **IARC MONOGRAPHS:** No   **OSHA REGULATED:** No

MEDICAL CONDITIONS GENERALLY AGGRAVATED BY EXPOSURE: DERMATITIS

========== **SECTION VII** - **PRECAUTIONS FOR SAFE HANDLING AND USE** ============

STEPS TO BE TAKEN IN CASE MATERIAL IS RELEASED OR SPILLED: VENTILATE AREA. KEEP AWAY FROM STRONG OXIDIZERS. HEAT. SPARKS OR OPEN FLAMES. PREVENT SPILL FROM SPREADING BY USING AN INERT MATERIAL. SUCH AS SAND. AS A DAM. KEEP OUT OF ALL WATERWAYS OR WATER DRAINS. DO NOT FLUSH AREA WITH WATER. FOR SMALL SPILLS USE ABSORBENT PADS. FOR LARGE SPILLS. CALL A SPILL RESPONSE TEAM. IF REQUIRED. CONTACT STATE/LOCAL AGENCIES.

WASTE DISPOSAL METHOD: PRODUCT SOAKED ABSORBENT SHOULD BE PLACED IN SEALED METAL DRUMS FOR DISPOSAL IN ACCORDANCE WITH LOCAL. STATE AND FEDERAL REGULATIONS.

PRECAUTIONS TO BE TAKEN IN HANDLING AND STORING: KEEP AWAY FROM STRONG OXIDIZERS. HEAT. SPARKS AND OPEN FLAMES. DO NOT CUT OR DRILL INTO AN EMPTY CONTAINER IN ANY WAY THAT MIGHT GENERATE A SPARK. SOLVENT RESIDUE IN THE CONTAINER COULD IGNITE AND CAUSE AN EXPLOSION. KEEP CONTAINER TIGHTLY CLOSED AND OUT OF THE WEATHER.

OTHER PRECAUTIONS: WE RECOMMEND THAT CONTAINERS BE EITHER PROFESSIONALLY RECONDITIONED FOR REUSE OR PROPERLY DISPOSED OF BY CERTIFIED FIRMS TO HELP REDUCE THE POSSIBILITY OF AN ACCIDENT. DISPOSAL OF CONTAINERS SHOULD BE IN ACCORDANCE WITH APPLICABLE LAWS AND REGULATIONS. "EMPTY" DRUMS SHOULD NOT BE GIVEN TO INDIVIDUALS.

==================== **SECTION VIII** - **CONTROL MEASURES** ======================

EXPOSURE CONTROL AND PERSONAL PROTECTION:

RESPIRATORY PROTECTION: IF TLV IS EXCEEDED USE A GAS MASK WITH APPROPRIATE CARTRIDGES. CANNISTER OR SUPPLIED AIR EQUIPMENT.

VENTILATION: IF NORMAL VENTILATION IS INADEQUATE USE ADDITIONAL SYSTEMS.ESPECIALLY LOCAL VENTILATION. IF THE VAPOR LEVEL CAN APPROACH THE LEL - LOWER EXPLOSION LIMIT. USE EXPLOSION PROOF SYSTEMS.

PROTECTIVE GLOVES: USE SOLVENT RESISTANT GLOVES.

EYE PROTECTION: USE SAFETY GLASSES OR GOGGLES.

OTHER PROTECTIVE EQUIPMENT OR CLOTHING: NONE.

WORK/HYGIENIC PRACTICES: WASH SKIN/CLOTHES IF THEY COME IN CONTACT WITH THE PRODUCT. DO NOT WEAR CLOTHING WET WITH THE PRODUCT.

========================= **SECTION IX** - **SHIPPING INFORMATION** ====================

GROUND SHIPMENT.   UN No   : NA 1993

D.O.T HAZARD CLASSIFICATION: COMPOUND CLEANING LIQUID.

======================== **SECTION X** - **DISCLAIMER** =========================

THE INFORMATION AND RECOMMENDATIONS HEREIN HAVE BEEN COMPILED FROM OUR RECORDS AND OTHER SOURCES BELIEVED TO BE RELIABLE. NO WARRANTY. GUARANTY OR REPRESENTATION IS MADE BY PRINTERS' SERVICE AS TO THE SUFFICIENCY OF ANY REPRESENTATION. THE ABSENCE OF DATA INDICATES ONLY THAT THE DATA IS NOT READILY AVAILABLE TO US. ADDITIONAL SAFETY MEASURES MAY BE REQUIRED UNDER PARTICULAR OR EXCEPTIONAL CONDITIONS OF USE. WITH REGARD TO THE MATERIALS THEMSELVES. PRINTERS' SERVICE MAKES NO WARRANTY OF ANY KIND WHATEVER. EXPRESSED OR IMPLIED. AND ALL IMPLIED WARRANTIES OF MERCHANTABILITY AND FITNESS FOR A PARTICULAR PURPOSE ARE HEREBY DISCLAIMED.

APPENDIX **XXXII**

OSHA Form 300 NS Instructions for Completion

SOURCE:
O.M.B., Document No. 1220-0029

What do you need to do?

1. Within 7 calendar days after you receive information about a case, decide if the case is recordable under the OSHA recordkeeping requirements.

2. Determine whether the incident is a new case or a recurrence of an existing one.

3. Establish whether the case was work-related.

4. If the case is recordable, decide which form you will fill out as the injury and illness incident report.

You may use *OSHA's 301: Injury and Illness Incident Report* or an equivalent form. Some state workers compensation, insurance, or other reports may be acceptable substitutes, as long as they provide the same information as the OSHA 301.

How to work with the Log

1. Identify the employee involved unless it is a privacy concern case as described below.

2. Identify when and where the case occurred.

3. Describe the case, as specifically as you can.

4. Classify the seriousness of the case by recording the most serious outcome associated with the case, with column J (Other recordable cases) being the least serious and column G (Death) being the most serious.

5. Identify whether the case is an injury or illness. If the case is an injury, check the injury category. If the case is an illness, check the appropriate illness category.

An Overview:
Recording Work-Related Injuries and Illnesses

The Occupational Safety and Health (OSH) Act of 1970 requires certain employers to prepare and maintain records of work-related injuries and illnesses. Use these definitions when you classify cases on the Log. OSHA's recordkeeping regulation (see 29 CFR Part 1904) provides more information about the definitions below.

The *Log of Work-Related Injuries and Illnesses* (Form 300) is used to classify work-related injuries and illnesses and to note the extent and severity of each case. When an incident occurs, use the *Log* to record specific details about what happened and how it happened. The *Summary* — a separate form (Form 300A) — shows the totals for the year in each category. At the end of the year, post the *Summary* in a visible location so that your employees are aware of the injuries and illnesses occurring in their workplace.

Employers must keep a *Log* for each establishment or site. If you have more than one establishment, you must keep a separate

Log and *Summary* for each physical location that is expected to be in operation for one year or longer.

Note that your employees have the right to review your injury and illness records. For more information, see 29 Code of Federal Regulations Part 1904.35, *Employee Involvement*.

Cases listed on the *Log of Work-Related Injuries and Illnesses* are not necessarily eligible for workers' compensation or other insurance benefits. Listing a case on the *Log* does not mean that the employer or worker was at fault or that an OSHA standard was violated.

When is an injury or illness considered work-related?

An injury or illness is considered work-related if an event or exposure in the work environment caused or contributed to the condition or significantly aggravated a preexisting condition. Work-relatedness is presumed for injuries and illnesses resulting from events or exposures occurring in the workplace, unless an exception specifically applies. See 29 CFR Part 1904.5(b)(2) for the exceptions. The work environment includes the establishment and other locations where one or more employees are working or are present as a condition of their employment. See 29 CFR Part 1904.5(b)(1).

Which work-related injuries and illnesses should you record?

Record those work-related injuries and illnesses that result in:

▼ death,
▼ loss of consciousness,
▼ days away from work,
▼ restricted work activity or job transfer, or
▼ medical treatment beyond first aid.

You must also record work-related injuries and illnesses that are significant (as defined below) or meet any of the additional criteria listed below.

You must record any significant work-related injury or illness that is diagnosed by a physician or other licensed health care professional. You must record any work-related case involving cancer, chronic irreversible disease, a fractured or cracked bone, or a punctured eardrum. See 29 CFR 1904.7.

What are the additional criteria?

You must record the following conditions when they are work-related:

▼ any needlestick injury or cut from a sharp object that is contaminated with another person's blood or other potentially infectious material;
▼ any case requiring an employee to be medically removed under the requirements of an OSHA health standard;

▼ tuberculosis infection as evidenced by a positive skin test or diagnosis by a physician or other licensed health care professional after exposure to a known case of active tuberculosis.

What is medical treatment?

Medical treatment includes managing and caring for a patient for the purpose of combating disease or disorder. The following are not considered medical treatments and are NOT recordable:

▼ visits to a doctor or health care professional solely for observation or counseling;
▼ diagnostic procedures, including administering prescription medications that are used solely for diagnostic purposes; and
▼ any procedure that can be labeled first aid. (*See below for more information about first aid.*)

What is first aid?

If the incident required only the following types of treatment, consider it first aid. Do NOT record the case if it involves only:

▼ using non-prescription medications at non-prescription strength;
▼ administering tetanus immunizations;
▼ cleaning, flushing, or soaking wounds on the skin surface;
▼ using wound coverings, such as bandages, BandAids™, gauze pads, etc., or using SteriStrips™ or butterfly bandages.
▼ using hot or cold therapy;
▼ using any totally non-rigid means of support, such as elastic bandages, wraps, non-rigid back belts, etc.;
▼ using temporary immobilization devices while transporting an accident victim (splints, slings, neck collars, or back boards).
▼ drilling a fingernail or toenail to relieve pressure, or draining fluids from blisters;
▼ using eye patches;
▼ using simple irrigation or a cotton swab to remove foreign bodies not embedded in or adhered to the eye;
▼ using irrigation, tweezers, cotton swab or other simple means to remove splinters or foreign material from areas other than the eye;
▼ using finger guards;
▼ using massages;
▼ drinking fluids to relieve heat stress

How do you decide if the case involved restricted work?

Restricted work activity occurs when, as the result of a work-related injury or illness, an employer or health care professional keeps, or

recommends keeping, an employee from doing the routine functions of his or her job or from working the full workday that the employee would have been scheduled to work before the injury or illness occurred.

How do you count the number of days of restricted work activity or the number of days away from work?

Count the number of calendar days the employee was on restricted work activity or was away from work as a result of the recordable injury or illness. Do not count the day on which the injury or illness occurred in this number. Begin counting days from the day after the incident occurs. If a single injury or illness involved both days away from work and days of restricted work activity, enter the total number of days for each. You may stop counting days of restricted work activity or days away from work once the total of either or the combination of both reaches 180 days.

Under what circumstances should you NOT enter the employee's name on the OSHA Form 300?

You must consider the following types of injuries or illnesses to be privacy concern cases:

▼ an injury or illness to an intimate body part or to the reproductive system,
▼ an injury or illness resulting from a sexual assault,
▼ a mental illness,
▼ a case of HIV infection, hepatitis, or tuberculosis,
▼ a needlestick injury or cut from a sharp object that is contaminated with blood or other potentially infectious material (see 29 CFR Part 1904.8 for definition), and
▼ other illnesses, if the employee independently and voluntarily requests that his or her name not be entered on the log.

You must not enter the employee's name on the OSHA 300 *Log* for these cases. Instead, enter "privacy case" in the space normally used for the employee's name. You must keep a separate, confidential list of the case numbers and employee names for the establishment's privacy concern cases so that you can update the cases and provide information to the government if asked to do so.

If you have a reasonable basis to believe that information describing the privacy concern case may be personally identifiable even though the employee's name has been omitted, you may use discretion in describing the injury or illness on both the OSHA 300 and 301 forms. You must enter enough information to identify the cause of the incident and the general severity of the injury or illness, but you do not need to include details of an intimate or private nature.

What if the outcome changes after you record the case?

If the outcome or extent of an injury or illness changes after you have recorded the case, simply draw a line through the original entry or, if you wish, delete or white-out the original entry. Then write the new entry where it belongs. Remember, you need to record the most serious outcome for each case.

Classifying Injuries

An injury is any wound or damage to the body resulting from an event in the work environment.

Examples: Cut, puncture, laceration, abrasion, fracture, bruise, contusion, chipped tooth, amputation, insect bite, electrocution, or a thermal, chemical, electrical, or radiation burn. Sprain and strain injuries to muscles, joints, and connective tissues are classified as injuries when they result from a slip, trip, fall or other similar accidents.

Classifying Illnesses

Skin diseases or disorders

Skin diseases or disorders are illnesses involving the worker's skin that are caused by work exposure to chemicals, plants, or other substances.

Examples: Contact dermatitis, eczema, or rash caused by primary irritants and sensitizers or poisonous plants; oil acne; friction blisters, chrome ulcers; inflammation of the skin.

Respiratory conditions

Respiratory conditions are illnesses associated with breathing hazardous biological agents, chemicals, dust, gases, vapors, or fumes at work.

Examples: Silicosis, asbestosis, pneumonitis, pharyngitis, rhinitis or acute congestion; farmer's lung, beryllium disease, tuberculosis, occupational asthma, reactive airways dysfunction syndrome (RADS), chronic obstructive pulmonary disease (COPD), hypersensitivity pneumonitis, toxic inhalation injury, such as metal fume fever, chronic obstructive bronchitis, and other pneumoconioses.

Poisoning

Poisoning includes disorders evidenced by abnormal concentrations of toxic substances in blood, other tissues, other bodily fluids, or the breath that are caused by the ingestion or absorption of toxic substances into the body.

Examples: Poisoning by lead, mercury, cadmium, arsenic, or other metals; poisoning by carbon monoxide, hydrogen sulfide, or other gases; poisoning by benzene, benzol, carbon tetrachloride, or other organic solvents; poisoning by insecticide sprays, such as parathion or lead arsenate; poisoning by other chemicals, such as formaldehyde.

All other illnesses

All other occupational illnesses.

Examples: Heatstroke, sunstroke, heat exhaustion, heat stress and other effects of environmental heat; freezing, frostbite, and other effects of exposure to low temperatures; decompression sickness; effects of ionizing radiation (isotopes, x-rays, radium); effects of nonionizing radiation (welding flash, ultra-violet rays, lasers); anthrax; bloodborne pathogenic diseases, such as AIDS, HIV, hepatitis B or hepatitis C; brucellosis; malignant or benign tumors; histoplasmosis; coccidioidomycosis.

When must you post the Summary?

You must post the *Summary* only — not the *Log* — by February 1 of the year following the year covered by the form and keep it posted until April 30 of that year.

How long must you keep the Log and Summary on file?

You must keep the *Log* and *Summary* for 5 years following the year to which they pertain.

Do you have to send these forms to OSHA at the end of the year?

No. You do not have to send the completed forms to OSHA unless specifically asked to do so.

How to Fill Out the Log

The *Log of Work-Related Injuries and Illnesses* is used to classify work-related injuries and illnesses and to note the extent and severity of each case. When an incident occurs, use the *Log* to record specific details about what happened and how it happened.

If your company has more than one establishment or site, you must keep separate records for each physical location that is expected to remain in operation for one year or longer.

We have given you several copies of the *Log* in this package. If you need more than we provided, you may photocopy and use as many as you need.

The *Summary* — a separate form — shows the work-related injury and illness totals for the year in each category. At the end of the year, count the number of incidents in each category and transfer the totals from the *Log* to the *Summary*. Then post the *Summary* in a visible location so that your employees are aware of injuries and illnesses occurring in their workplace.

You don't post the Log. You post only the Summary at the end of the year.

OSHA's Form 300

Log of Work-Related Injuries and Illnesses

Year 20 ____

U.S. Department of Labor
Occupational Safety and Health Administration

Form approved OMB no. 1218-0176

You must record information about every work-related death and about every work-related injury or illness that involves loss of consciousness, restricted work activity or job transfer, days away from work, or medical treatment beyond first aid. You must also record significant work-related injuries and illnesses that are diagnosed by a physician or licensed health care professional. You must also record work-related injuries and illnesses that meet any of the specific recording criteria listed in 29 CFR Part 1904.8 through 1904.12. Feel free to use two lines for a single case if you need to. You must complete an injury and illness Incident Report (OSHA Form 301) or equivalent form for each injury or illness recorded on this form. If you're not sure whether a case is recordable, call your local OSHA office for help.

Establishment name XYZ Company

City Anywhere   State MA

Attention: This form contains information relating to employee health and must be used in a manner that protects the confidentiality of employees to the extent possible while the information is being used for occupational safety and health purposes.

Identify the person

(A) Case no.	(B) Employee's name	(C) Job title (e.g. Welder)	(D) Date of injury or onset of illness
1	Mark Begin	Welder	5 / 25 month/day
2	Shana Alexander	Foundry man	7/2 month/day
3	Sam Sander	Electrician	8 / 5 month/day
4	Ralph Bocella	Labour	9 / 17 month/day
5	Jarrel Daniels	Machine opr	10/ 23 month/day
			/ month/day
			/ month/day

Describe the case

(E) Where the event occurred (e.g. Loading dock north end)	(F) Describe injury or illness, parts of body affected, and object/substance that directly injured or made person ill (e.g. Second degree burns on right forearm from acetylene torch)
basement	fracture, left arm and left leg, fell from ladder
pouring deck	poisoning, from lead fumes
2nd floor storeroom	broken left foot, fell over box
packaging dept	Back strain lifting boxes
production floor	dust in eye
	.

Classify the case

Using these four categories, check ONLY the most serious result for each case:

(G) Death	(H) Days away from work	(I) Remained at work — Job transfer or restriction	(J) Remained at work — Other recordable cases
☐	☑	☐	☐
☐	☑	☐	☐
☐	☑	☐	☐
☐	☐	☐	☑
☐	☐	☐	☐
☐	☐	☐	☐
☐	☐	☐	☐

Enter the number of days the injured or ill worker was:

On job transfer or restriction (K)	Away from work (L)
12 days	15 days
___ days	30 days
7 days	30 days
___ days	3 days
___ days	___ days
___ days	___ days
___ days	___ days

Check the "Injury" column or choose one type of illness (M)

(1) Injury	(2) Skin disorder	(3) Respiratory condition	(4) Poisoning	(5) Hearing loss	(6) All other illnesses
☑	☐	☐	☐	☐	☐
☐	☐	☐	☑	☐	☐
☑	☐	☐	☐	☐	☐
☑	☐	☐	☐	☐	☐
☐	☐	☐	☐	☐	☐
☐	☐	☐	☐	☐	☐
☐	☐	☐	☐	☐	☐

Be as specific as possible. You can use two lines if you need more room.

Revise the log if the injury or illness progresses and the outcome is more serious than you originally recorded for the case. Cross out, erase, or white-out the original entry.

Choose ONE of these categories. Classify the case by recording the most serious outcome of the case, with column J (Other recordable cases) being the least serious and column G (Death) being the most serious.

Note whether the case involves an injury or an illness.

OSHA's Form 300

Log of Work-Related Injuries and Illnesses

Attention: This form contains information relating to employee health and must be used in a manner that protects the confidentiality of employees to the extent possible while the information is being used for occupational safety and health purposes.

Year 20___

U.S. Department of Labor
Occupational Safety and Health Administration

Form approved OMB no. 1218-0176

You must record information about every work-related death and about every work-related injury or illness that involves loss of consciousness, restricted work activity or job transfer, days away from work, or medical treatment beyond first aid. You must also record significant work-related injuries and illnesses that are diagnosed by a physician or licensed health care professional. You must also record work-related injuries and illnesses that meet any of the specific recording criteria listed in 29 CFR Part 1904.8 through 1904.12. Feel free to use two lines for a single case if you need to. You must complete an Injury and Illness Incident Report (OSHA Form 301) or equivalent form for each injury or illness recorded on this form. If you're not sure whether a case is recordable, call your local OSHA office for help.

Establishment name _____

City _____ State _____

Identify the person

(A) Case no.	(B) Employee's name	(C) Job title (e.g., Welder)

Describe the case

(D) Date of injury or onset of illness	(E) Where the event occurred (e.g., Loading dock north end)	(F) Describe injury or illness, parts of body affected, and object/substance that directly injured or made person ill (e.g., Second degree burns on right forearm from acetylene torch)
month/day		

Classify the case

Using these four categories, check ONLY the most serious result for each case:

Death (G)	Days away from work (H)	Remained at work	
		Job transfer or restriction (I)	Other recordable cases (J)

Enter the number of days the injured or ill worker was:

On job transfer or restriction (K)	Away from work (L)
___ days	___ days

Check the "Injury" column or choose one type of illness: (M)

(1) Injury	(2) Skin disorder	(3) Respiratory condition	(4) Poisoning	(5) All other illnesses

Page totals ▶ ___ ___ ___ ___   ___ ___   ___ ___   ___ ___ ___ ___ ___

Be sure to transfer these totals to the Summary page (Form 300A) before you post it.

(1) (2) (3) (4) (5)
Injury | Skin disorder | Respiratory condition | Poisoning | All other illnesses

Page ___ of ___

Public reporting burden for this collection of information is estimated to average 14 minutes per response, including time to review the instructions, search and gather the data needed, and complete and review the collection of information. Persons are not required to respond to the collection of information unless it displays a currently valid OMB control number. If you have any comments about these estimates or any other aspects of this data collection, contact: US Department of Labor, OSHA Office of Statistics, Room N-3644, 200 Constitution Avenue, NW, Washington, DC 20210. Do not send the completed forms to this office.

OSHA's Form 300A

Summary of Work-Related Injuries and Illnesses

Year 20____

U.S. Department of Labor
Occupational Safety and Health Administration

Form approved OMB no. 1218-0176

All establishments covered by Part 1904 must complete this Summary page, even if no work-related injuries or illnesses occurred during the year. Remember to review the Log to verify that the entries are complete and accurate before completing this summary.

Using the Log, count the individual entries you made for each category. Then write the totals below, making sure you've added the entries from every page of the Log. If you had no cases, write "0."

Employees, former employees, and their representatives have the right to review the OSHA Form 300 in its entirety. They also have limited access to the OSHA Form 301 or its equivalent. See 29 CFR Part 1904.35, in OSHA's recordkeeping rule, for further details on the access provisions for these forms.

Number of Cases

Total number of deaths	Total number of cases with days away from work	Total number of cases with job transfer or restriction	Total number of other recordable cases
(G)	(H)	(I)	(J)

Number of Days

Total number of days of job transfer or restriction	Total number of days away from work
(K)	(L)

Injury and Illness Types

Total number of . . .
(M)
(1) Injuries
(2) Skin disorders
(3) Respiratory conditions
(4) Poisonings
(5) All other illnesses

Establishment Information

Your establishment name _____

Street _____

City _____ State ____ ZIP ____

Industry description (e.g., *Manufacture of motor truck trailers*) _____

Standard Industrial Classification (SIC), if known (e.g., SIC 3715) _____

Employment Information *(If you don't have these figures, see the Worksheet on the back of this page to estimate.)*

Annual average number of employees _____

Total hours worked by all employees last year _____

Sign here

Knowingly falsifying this document may result in a fine.

I certify that I have examined this document and that to the best of my knowledge the entries are true, accurate, and complete.

Company executive _____ Title ____

(____) ____ - ____ _____
Phone   Date

Post this Summary page from February 1 to April 30 of the year following the year covered by the form.

Public reporting burden for this collection of information is estimated to average 50 minutes per response, including time to review the instructions, search and gather the data needed, and complete and review the collection of information. Persons are not required to respond to the collection of information unless it displays a currently valid OMB control number. If you have any comments about these estimates or any other aspects of this data collection, contact: US Department of Labor, OSHA Office of Statistics, Room N-3644, 200 Constitution Avenue, NW, Washington, DC 20210. Do not send the completed forms to this office.

Optional

Worksheet to Help You Fill Out the Summary

At the end of the year, OSHA requires you to enter the average number of employees and the total hours worked by your employees on the summary. If you don't have these figures, you can use the information on this page to estimate the numbers you will need to enter on the Summary page at the end of the year.

How to figure the average number of employees who worked for your establishment during the year:

❶ Add the total number of employees your establishment paid in all pay periods during the year. Include all employees: full-time, part-time, temporary, seasonal, salaried, and hourly.

The number of employees paid in all pay periods = _____ ❶

❷ Count the number of pay periods your establishment had during the year. Be sure to include any pay periods when you had no employees.

The number of pay periods during the year = _____ ❷

❸ Divide the number of employees by the number of pay periods.

$$\frac{❶}{❷} = ❸$$

❹ Round the answer to the next highest whole number. Write the rounded number in the blank marked *Annual average number of employees.*

The number rounded = _____ ❹

For example, Acme Construction figured its average employment this way:

For pay period...	Acme paid this number of employees...		
1	10		
2	0		
3	15		
4	30		
5	40		
▶ 24	20		
25	15		
26	+10		
	830		

Number of employees paid = 830   ❶

Number of pay periods = 26   ❷

$$\frac{830}{26} = 31.92$$ ❸

31.92 rounds to 32   ❹

32 is the annual average number of employees

How to figure the total hours worked by all employees:

Include hours worked by salaried, hourly, part-time and seasonal workers, as well as hours worked by other workers subject to day to day supervision by your establishment (e.g., temporary help services workers).

Do not include vacation, sick leave, holidays, or any other non-work time, even if employees were paid for it. If your establishment keeps records of only the hours paid or if you have employees who are not paid by the hour, please estimate the hours that the employees actually worked.

If this number isn't available, you can use this optional worksheet to estimate it.

Optional Worksheet

Find the number of full-time employees in your establishment for the year. _____

Multiply by the number of work hours for a full-time employee in a year. _____

This is the number of full-time hours worked.

×

Add the number of any overtime hours as well as the hours worked by other employees (part-time, temporary, seasonal) _____

+

Round the answer to the next highest whole number. Write the rounded number in the blank marked *Total hours worked by all employees last year.*

OSHA's Form 301

Injury and Illness Incident Report

U.S. Department of Labor
Occupational Safety and Health Administration

Form approved OMB no. 1218-0176

Attention: This form contains information relating to employee health and must be used in a manner that protects the confidentiality of employees to the extent possible while the information is being used for occupational safety and health purposes.

This *Injury and Illness Incident Report* is one of the first forms you must fill out when a recordable work-related injury or illness has occurred. Together with the *Log of Work-Related Injuries and Illnesses* and the accompanying *Summary*, these forms help the employer and OSHA develop a picture of the extent and severity of work-related incidents.

Within 7 calendar days after you receive information that a recordable work-related injury or illness has occurred, you must fill out this form or an equivalent. Some state workers' compensation, insurance, or other reports may be acceptable substitutes. To be considered an equivalent form, any substitute must contain all the information asked for on this form.

According to Public Law 91-596 and 29 CFR 1904, OSHA's recordkeeping rule, you must keep this form on file for 5 years following the year to which it pertains.

If you need additional copies of this form, you may photocopy and use as many as you need.

Completed by _____

Title _____

Phone (____) ____ - ____   Date ___/___/___

Information about the employee

1) Full name _____

2) Street _____

   City _____ State _____ ZIP _____

3) Date of birth ___/___/___

4) Date hired ___/___/___

5) ☐ Male
   ☐ Female

Information about the physician or other health care professional

6) Name of physician or other health care professional _____

7) If treatment was given away from the worksite, where was it given?

   Facility _____

   Street _____

   City _____ State _____ ZIP _____

8) Was employee treated in an emergency room?
   ☐ Yes
   ☐ No

9) Was employee hospitalized overnight as an in-patient?
   ☐ Yes
   ☐ No

Information about the case

10) Case number from the Log _____ *(Transfer the case number from the Log after you record the case.)*

11) Date of injury or illness ___/___/___

12) Time employee began work _____ AM / PM

13) Time of event _____ AM / PM   ☐ Check if time cannot be determined

14) **What was the employee doing just before the incident occurred?** Describe the activity, as well as the tools, equipment, or material the employee was using. Be specific. *Examples:* "climbing a ladder while carrying roofing materials"; "spraying chlorine from hand sprayer"; "daily computer key-entry."

15) **What happened?** Tell us how the injury occurred. *Examples:* "When ladder slipped on wet floor, worker fell 20 feet"; "Worker was sprayed with chlorine when gasket broke during replacement"; "Worker developed soreness in wrist over time."

16) **What was the injury or illness?** Tell us the part of the body that was affected and how it was affected; be more specific than "hurt," "pain," or sore." *Examples:* "strained back"; "chemical burn, hand"; "carpal tunnel syndrome."

17) **What object or substance directly harmed the employee?** *Examples:* "concrete floor"; "chlorine"; "radial arm saw." *If this question does not apply to the incident, leave it blank.*

18) **If the employee died, when did death occur?** Date of death ___/___/___

Public reporting burden for this collection of information is estimated to average 22 minutes per response, including time for reviewing instructions, searching existing data sources, gathering and maintaining the data needed, and completing and reviewing the collection of information. Persons are not required to respond to the collection of information unless it displays a current valid OMB control number. If you have any comments about this estimate or any other aspects of this data collection, including suggestions for reducing this burden, contact: US Department of Labor, OSHA Office of Statistics, Room N-3644, 200 Constitution Avenue, NW, Washington, DC 20210. Do not send the completed forms to this office.

APPENDIX **XXXIII**

Typical Storage Regulations by Local Agency; Suffolk County, New York

SOURCE:
Suffolk County, NY, Sanitary Code

(DE02:ART12.FI)

ARTICLE 12
TOXIC AND HAZARDOUS MATERIALS STORAGE AND HANDLING CONTROLS

Section 1201. Declaration of Policy

The designated best use of all groundwaters of Suffolk County is for public and private water supply, and of most surface waters for food production, bathing and recreation. The federal government has officially designated the aquifer below Suffolk County as a sole-source for water supply. Therefore, it is hereby declared to be the policy of the County of Suffolk to maintain its water resources as near to their natural condition of purity as reasonably possible for the safeguarding of the public health and, to that end, to require the use of all available practical methods of preventing and controlling water pollution from toxic and hazardous materials.

Section 1202. Statement of Purpose

It is the intent and purpose of this article to safeguard the water resources of the County of Suffolk from toxic or hazardous materials pollution by controlling or abating pollution from such sources in existence when this article is enacted and also by preventing further pollution from new sources under a program which is consistent with the above-stated Declaration of Policy.

Section 1203. Definitions

Whenever used in the article, unless otherwise expressly stated, or unless the context or subject matter requires a different meaning, the following terms shall have the respective meanings set forth or indicated:

a. **Aboveground**, when referring to tanks, means more than 90 percent exposed above the final ground elevation.

b. **Bulk Storage** means the loose or bagged storage of dry or semi-dry materials.

c. **Commissioner** means the Commissioner of the Suffolk County Department of Health Services.

d. **Discharge** means to release by any means or to relinquish control in a manner that could result in a release to the surface waters, groundwaters, surface of the ground or below ground Discharge includes but is not necessarily limited to the following, either singly or in any combination:

1. leaks from the failure of a storage facility;

2. spills during transport or transfer of toxic or hazardous materials;

3. disposal or storage of soils, sand or debris containing toxic or hazardous materials;

4. disposal to: storm drains, cooling water, roof drains, sanitary systems, or any other drainage system or leaching system of toxic or hazardous materials;

5. -burial, land-spreading or dumping anywhere of toxic or hazardous materials, including but not limited to landfill and scavenger facilities, notwithstanding that the material so buried, spread or dumped was containerized at the time of said burial, spreading or dumping;

6. passing of toxic or hazardous waste materials to any person;

7. abandonment of containers, tanks, pipes, vehicles or premises containing toxic or hazardous materials or residues. For the purpose of this subdivision, abandonment shall mean:

i. substantially empty and unattended, or

ii. the relinquishment or termination of possession, ownership or control without full disclosure to the new owner thereof of containers, tanks, pipes, vehicles or premises containing toxic or hazardous materials or residues, whether by vacating or by disposition thereof, and shall not depend on a mere lapse of time.

e. **Double-Walled** means constructed with more than one containment layer with space between the layers sufficient to allow monitoring of any leakage into or out of the space.

f. **Impervious** means a layer of natural and/or man-made material of sufficient thickness, density and composition as to prevent the discharge into the underlying groundwater or adjacent surface waters of any toxic or hazardous substances for a period of at least as long as the maximum anticipated time during which the toxic or hazardous substances will be in contact with the material, and sufficient to allow complete recovery of the spilled product with minimum disturbance of the containment material.

g. **New York State Discharge Standards** means standards of quality and purity and special standards, and groundwater quality standards and effluent standards, and/or limitations as found in Title 6, Parts 701-703 of the Official New York Compilation of Codes, Rules and Regulations.

h. **Pollution** means the presence in the environment of conditions and/or contaminants in quantities or characteristics, which are or may be injurious to human, plant or animal life or to property, or which unreasonably interfere with the comfortable enjoyment of life and property throughout such areas of the county as shall be affected thereby.

i. **Product-tight** means impervious to the material which is or could be contained therein so as to prevent the detectable seepage of the product through the container. To be product-tight, the container shall be made of a material that is not subject to physical or chemical deterioration by the product being contained.

j. **Properly Registered Industrial Waste Scavenger** means a person in the business of collecting industrial wastes who carries a current, valid industrial waste collector registration issued by the New York State Department of Environmental Conservation.

k. **Substantial Modifications** shall mean the construction of any additions to an existing storage facility as defined under Section 1203(m), or restoration, refurbishment or renovation which:

1. increases or decreases the in-place storage capacity of the facility;

2. alters the physical configuration; or

3. impairs or affects the physical integrity of the facility or its monitoring systems.

l. **Single-Walled** means constructed with walls made of but one thickness of material. Laminated, coated, or clad materials shall be considered as single-walled.

m. **Storage Facility** means tanks, pipes, vaults, buildings, yards, pavements or fixed containers used or designed to be used, either singly or in any combination thereof, for the storage and/or transmission of toxic or hazardous materials or for the storage of portable containers containing toxic or hazardous materials.

n. **Toxic or Hazardous Materials** means any substance, solution or mixture which, because of its quality, quantity, concentration, physical, chemical or infectious characteristics, or any combination of the foregoing, presents or may present an actual or potential hazard to human health or to the drinking water supply if such substance, solution, mixture or combination thereof is discharged to the land or waters of the County of Suffolk. Toxic or Hazardous Materials shall include:

1. each and every substance, material or waste found listed in either or both Part 116 and Part 261, Title 40 of the Code of Federal Regulations; or Title 6, Part 366, of the New York State Codes, Rules and Regulations;

2. acids and alkalies beyond the pH range of 4 to 10;

3. heavy metal sludges, mixtures and solutions in excess of standards;

4. petroleum products, including fuels and waste oils;

5. organic solvents, including petroleum solvents, halogenated and non-halogenated hydrocarbons;

6. any material listed in Schedule I, Part 703.6 of the Official Compilation of New York Codes, Rules and Regulations, in excess of the concentration standards thereof, except for iron, manganese, foaming agents and pH unless otherwise provided elsewhere in this article;

7. any substance not included within subdivisions one through six above subsequently declared to be a Toxic or Hazardous Material by the commissioner;

8. any solid or semi-solid material which, if left to stand or if exposed to water will leach out or wholly or partially dissolve forming a Toxic or Hazardous Material as defined in subdivisions one through seven above.

All Toxic or Hazardous Materials are hereby declared to also be offensive materials for the purposes of Article VB.

o. **Toxic or Hazardous Wastes** mean:

1. Toxic or Hazardous Materials as defined in subdivision (n) above, generated by or as the result of operations in or the existence of any manufacturing or other industrial or commercial establishment, which toxic or hazardous materials are not actually used in a final product for sale, and shall include those toxic or hazardous materials retained as byproducts of the operations within such manufacturing or other industrial or commercial establishment for the purpose of recouping salvage value; or

2. Toxic or Hazardous Materials generated by one in possession or control of any residential premises, for which materials disposal

is intended, and which waste is not domestic wastewater without the admixture of non-sewage wastewater from any industrial process.

3. All toxic and hazardous wastes are Toxic and Hazardous Materials.

p. **Underground**, when referring to tanks, means 10 percent or more below the final ground elevation.

Section 1204. Powers of the Commissioner

a. The commissioner may make, or cause to be made, any investigation or study which, in his opinion, is desirable for enforcing this article or controlling or reducing the potential for contamination of the waters of the county from toxic or hazardous materials.

b. The commissioner may order the owner or any other person in possession or control of any land, structure or equipment, or agent of such owner or other person, to take whatever action is necessary in the opinion of the commissioner to bring said land, structure or equipment into compliance with the provisions of this article and any standards or regulations promulgated thereunder. Such action may include but is not necessarily limited to the following, either singly or in any combination thereof:

1. ordering tank-testing or the testing of the physical integrity of pipes or any other part of a storage facility or ordering the physical testing of the integrity of an entire storage facility;

2. ordering the removal of the contents of a tank, portable container, storage facility or any part thereof;

3. ordering the removal or abandonment or reconstruction of any installation, tank, storage facility or any part thereof installed in contravention of any of the requirements of this article or any standards or regulations promulgated thereunder;

4. ordering that physical improvements be performed on any tank, storage facility or part thereof before permitting it to be returned to service including such improvements as tank lining removal and replacement, bottom and structural repairs;

5. ordering the drafting of and/or implementation of contingency plans if there is evidence that such plans may be necessary to protect the public from toxic or hazardous materials stored at any particular facility;

6. ordering the posting of a performance bond or other undertaking either prior to or subsequent to the construction or operation of a storage facility within Suffolk County on a case-by-case basis if evidence indicates such may be necessary to protect the public from the effects of operating or closing such a facility.

c. Notwithstanding any other provision of this article, if the commissioner finds a condition which has the potential for contaminating the waters of the county with toxic or hazardous materials, or which otherwise constitutes an immediate danger to public health, and determines that it could appear prejudicial to the public interest to delay action, the commissioner may serve an order upon the permit holder, or if there is no permit upon the person in charge of the facility or site, citing such conditions and specifying the corrective action to be taken and a time period of less than fifteen (15) days within which such action shall be taken.

Such order may state that a permit is immediately suspended and/or that all operations are to be discontinued forthwith.

Any order requiring certain action or the cessation of certain activities immediately or within a specified period of less than fifteen (15) days shall provide such person an opportunity to be heard, which hearing shall be scheduled for a time no more than fifteen (15) days after the date the order is served.

Section 1205. Prohibited Discharges, Transporting and Disposal

a. It shall be unlawful for any person to discharge toxic or hazardous materials in Suffolk County, unless such discharge is specifically in accordance with a State Pollutant Discharge Elimination System (S.P.D.E.S.) Permit or other permit issued by or acceptable to the commissioner for that purpose.

b. It shall be unlawful for any person to pick up, transport or dispose of toxic or hazardous waste materials in Suffolk County without having a valid and appropriate New York State industrial waste collector registration.

c. It shall be unlawful for any industrial waste collector with a registration issued by the New York State Department of Environmental Conservation to fail to maintain a copy thereof on each vehicle operated by said collector at all times.

Section 1206. Construction and Modification Permits

a. It shall be unlawful for any person to construct, install or substantially modify a storage facility, or part thereof, without a valid permit therefor issued by or acceptable to the commissioner.

b. It shall be unlawful for any person in possession of or acting pursuant to a permit issued under this section to act, allow or cause any act in contravention of any provision of the permit.

c. Any permit issued pursuant to this section shall be effective for the specified duration of time indicated thereon, not to exceed one year from the effective date thereof.

Section-1207. Permits to Operate

a. It shall be unlawful for any person to use, cause to be used, maintain, or fill or cause to be filled with toxic or hazardous materials any storage facility or part thereof without having registered all the tanks at the facility on forms provided by the commissioner, and without having obtained a valid permit to operate such storage facility or part thereof issued by or acceptable to the commissioner.

b. It shall be unlawful for any person in possession of or acting pursuant to a permit issued pursuant to this section to act, permit or cause any act in contravention of any provision of the permit.

c. No permit to operate a storage facility as required pursuant to this section shall be issued by the commissioner or shall be satisfactory to the commissioner unless and until the prospective permittee:

1. has provided a listing to the commissioner of all of the toxic or hazardous materials to be stored at the storage facility; and

2. has demonstrated that said storage facility complies with all of the provisions of this article and all regulations and standards promulgated pursuant to it applicable to said storage facility based upon submission of such written proof as is required by the commissioner.

d. Any permit issued pursuant to this section shall be effective only for the specified duration of time indicated thereon, not to exceed five (5) years from the effective date thereof.

Section 1208. Exemptions

a.   All storage facilities which meet all of the following criteria shall be exempt from all provisions of this article except those contained in Sections 1203 - Definitions; 1204 -Powers of the Commissioner; 1205 - Prohibited Discharges; 1208 -Exemptions; 1210(a) - New Storage Facilities; 1210(e) - General Provisions and Requirements; 1210(g) - Overfill Protection; 1211(a)(4) - Overfill Detection; 1211(d)(1) and (2) - Leaks; Repairs; 1213(b)(1) and (4) - Transfer Operations; and 1220 -Waivers.

1.   the materials so stored are not toxic or hazardous wastes; and

2.   the volume of the storage facility is less than 1,100 gallons; and

3.   the facility is intended solely for the storage of kerosene, number 2 fuel oil, number 4 fuel oil, number 6 fuel oil, diesel oil or lubricating oil; and

4.   the intended use of the product stored is solely for on-site heating, or intermittent stationary power production such as stand-by electricity generation or irrigation pump power; and

5.   the materials stored are not intended for resale.

b.   All storage facilities which meet the following criteria shall be exempt from the provisions of this article contained in Sections 1210(b), 1212(b), 1214, 1219, and any regulations or standards promulgated thereunder:

1.   the materials so stored are not toxic or hazardous wastes; and

2.   the volume of the storage facility is greater than 1,100 gallons; and

3.   the facility is intended solely for the storage of kerosene, number 2 fuel oil, number 4 fuel oil, number 6 fuel oil, diesel oil, or lubricating oil; and

4.   the intended use of the product stored is solely for on-site heating, or intermittent stationary power production such as stand-by electricity generation or irrigation pump power; and

5.   the materials stored are not intended for resale.

c.   All storage facilities no longer receiving the benefit of any exemption but which were previously exempted from any or all provisions of this article shall be required to appropriately conform to all of the provisions of this article

and all regulations and standards promulgated pursuant thereto by November 1, 1983.

d.   Tanks for the storage of number 6 fuel oil, or other petroleum products of equivalent viscosity, are exempt from the internal inspection and tank lining requirements. Further, storage facilities for these products are exempted from the impervious dike and enclosure around the tank requirements if, in the opinion of the commissioner, the location of the facility is so situated that a spill could not run off into storm drains or surface waters.

e.   All storage of toxic or hazardous materials in containers of five-gallon capacity or smaller where the total capacity stored at any time does not exceed 250 gallons or where the dry storage in bags, bulk, or small containers does not exceed 2,000 pounds is exempt from all portions of this article unless specifically ruled otherwise by the commissioner on a case-by-case basis.

Section 1209. Transfer of Permits Prohibited

It shall be unlawful for any person to transfer a permit issued pursuant to Sections 1206 and 1207 of this article from one location to another, from one storage facility to another, or from one person to another. Any permit transferred in violation of this section shall be deemed null and void and without any effect whatsoever as of the date of said unlawful transfer. However, upon making proper application, a new owner of a facility which was previously operating under a valid permit may continue operation under the terms of the old permit until such time as the new permit is issued or denied.

Section 1210. Underground Storage Facilities

a.   New Storage Facilities

1.   All new storage facilities used or to be used for the underground storage of toxic or hazardous materials shall be designed and constructed in a manner which will, in the opinion of the commissioner, provide the maximum reasonable protection available against leakage or spillage from the facility due to corrosion, breakage, structural failure, or other means. Double-walled or equivalent facilities are required for all toxic or hazardous materials except those with a specific gravity of less than one and which

are only slightly soluble in water such as oils and gasoline. For these floatable materials, acceptable designs for tank construction include cathodically protected steel; glass fibre reinforced plastic; steel clad with glass fiber reinforced plastic; double-walled steel or plastic; or other equivalent design approved by the commissioner.

2. Approval of design by the commissioner is required before installation, and the determination of equivalency or adequacy lies with the commissioner.

3. Design, construction, fabrication, and installation of new underground storage facilities shall be in accordance with regulations and standards as they may be adopted by the commissioner under this article from time to time.

4. A new storage facility for all facilities not previously covered by this section is one for which construction actually begins on or after November 1, 1982; subject however to the exemptions contained in Section 1208(a).

5. It shall be unlawful for any person to sell for use in Suffolk County, install, use, put into service or maintain the existence of any new underground storage facility or part thereof after November 1, 1982, if said new storage facility or part thereof fails to conform to all of the provisions of subsections (1), (2), and (3) above, and all regulations and standards promulgated thereunder; subject however to the exemptions contained in Section 1208(a).

b. Existing Storage Facilities

1. An existing underground storage facility is one for which construction actually begins prior to November 1, 1982.

2. It shall be unlawful for any person to substantially modify or cause the substantial modification of any existing underground storage facility or part thereof without complying with the provisions of subdivision (a) above and all regulations and standards promulgated thereunder.

3. It shall be unlawful to use, or maintain the existence of any existing underground storage facility beyond January 1, 1990, which is intended for use with toxic or hazardous materials with a specific gravity of less than one and which are only slightly soluble in water such as oils and gasoline, without modifying said storage facility so as to comply with all of the provisions of subdivision (a) above and all regulations and standards promulgated thereunder.

4. It shall be unlawful to use or maintain the existence of any existing underground storage facility beyond January 1, 1987, which is intended for use with any toxic or hazardous materials other than those with a specific gravity of less than one and which are only slightly soluble in water such as oils and gasoline, without modifying said storage facility so as to comply with all of the provisions of subdivision (a) above and all regulations and standards promulgated thereunder.

c. Abandonment

1. It shall be unlawful for any person to use or maintain the existence of an abandoned underground storage facility or part thereof.

2. It shall be unlawful for anyone to sell or transfer to another an improperly abandoned underground storage facility or land containing an improperly abandoned underground storage facility if there exists any reasonable evidence of the existence of such a facility, unless the purchasing party has been made fully aware of the presence of such facility or evidence.

3. It shall be unlawful for any person to repair, alter or prepare for use any abandoned storage facility without first obtaining a permit to construct from the commissioner.

4. It shall be unlawful for the owner or other person in possession or control of any real property, building or place or vehicle to fail to immediately empty of all toxic or hazardous materials and to completely fill with sand or concrete or permanently remove an abandoned storage facility or part thereof within ninety (90) days of the discovery thereof on or in said real property, building or place pursuant to the provisions of subdivision (h) below unless approval is granted by the commissioner to do otherwise.

5. For the purposes of this section, an abandoned storage facility or part thereof means one which has remained out of service for two (2) years or more, or which has been declared by the owner to be abandoned.

6. For the purposes of this section, out of service filled; or not in use, meaning no regular filling or drawing; or not being maintained, meaning lacking adherence to the requirements of this article; or uncontrolled, meaning not attended or secured; or any combination thereof.

7. For the purposes of this section, discovery means either actual discovery or knowledge of the existence of the abandoned storage facility or part thereof or possession of sufficient

knowledge of the facts and circumstances involved so that the existence of the abandoned storage facility or part thereof should have been discovered or known of.

d. Testing and Inspection

1. All existing underground storage facilities or parts thereof which do not meet the construction standards in subdivision (a) above, must be tested and inspected in accordance with the schedule set forth below. It shall be unlawful for any existing underground storage facility owner, operator or lessee to fail to test his tanks and file an acceptable certificate of test completion with the commissioner in accordance with the following schedule:

TESTING SCHEDULE FOR EXISTING UNDERGROUND TANKS
AGE OF SYSTEM BY 1980
(in years)

	1-4	5-9	10-14	15-19	20 or more
1980					
1981					X
1982				X	
1983			X		X
1984		X			
1985	X			X	X
1986			X		

ALL TANKS COVERED BY SECTION 1208(b) BY VIRTUE OF THE 1986 AMENDMENT SHALL BE INITIALLY TESTED IN 1986 IF THE TANK IS TEN (10) YEARS OR OLDER, AND/OR ALL TANKS SHALL BE TESTED ON THEIR TENTH ANNIVERSARY AND EVERY FIVE (5) YEARS THEREAFTER UNTIL PERMANENTLY CLOSED.

FULL COMPLIANCE FOR ALL FACILITIES EXCEPT THOSE DESCRIBED IN 1210(b)(3)

	1-4	5-9	10-14	15-19	20 or more
1987				X	X
1988		X			
1989					
1990					

FULL COMPLIANCE FOR ALL FACILITIES

2. If for any reason testing satisfactory to the commissioner cannot be performed, the tank must be removed from service or brought up to the standards of subsection (a) by the first scheduled test date.

3. The Final Test of the National Fire Protection Association (NFPA), Recommended Practice No. 329 or other test of equivalent or superior accuracy as approved by the commissioner must be used to comply with the testing and inspection requirement of Section 1210(d)(1).

4. Any test and inspection as required by this subdivision shall be performed by a person whose qualifications are acceptable to the commissioner, pursuant to Department standards, for performing such tests. Certificates of test completion containing the results of such tests as performed shall be prepared by the tester and shall be filed with the commissioner within thirty (30) days after completion of the testing of the storage facility. No certificate of test completion shall be acceptable to the commissioner to indicate satisfactory compliance with the testing requirements of this subdivision if the qualifications of the tester have not been accepted by the commissioner prior to the test. No certificate of test completion shall be acceptable to the commissioner, pursuant to Department standards, if the test and inspection were not performed in accordance with subsection (3) of this subdivision and in accordance with any regulations and standards which may be promulgated pursuant thereto.

5. The Certificate of Test Completion shall be filed on a form provided by the commissioner and a copy of such form, completed, shall be kept by the storage facility owner, operator or lessee and by the tester for a period of not less than five (S) years from the date of its issuance. It shall be unlawful for the storage facility owner, operator or lessee and for the tester thereof to fail to keep a copy of the Certificate of Test Completion for the required five (5) year period.

6. Certificates of Test Completion shall contain a legally authorized form notice to the effect that false statements made knowingly therein are punishable pursuant to Section 210.45 of the Penal Law.

7. A Certificate of Test Completion not properly completed and/or not subscribed by the tester shall not be acceptable to the commissioner.

e. General Provisions and Requirements

1. When an underground storage facility or part thereof is found to be leaking, the portion containing the leak must be immediately emptied of all contents therein and removed from service. It shall be unlawful to cause or permit a leaking underground storage facility or part thereof to remain in service or to continue to

retain its toxic or hazardous contents after the owner, operator or lessee of said storage facility or part thereof knows or should have known of the existence of the leak therein.

2. It shall be unlawful for any person to repair or to permit the repair, in place, of any underground storage facility or part thereof which has leaked or has otherwise failed, for the purpose of reusing said storage facility, unless:

i. such repair will result in the storage facility or part thereof complying with the requirements of subdivision (a) above and all regulations and standards promulgated thereunder; and unless

ii. such repair occurs pursuant to plans therefor previously submitted to and approved by the commissioner.

3. It shall be unlawful for any person to replace or cause the replacement of any underground storage facility or part thereof for any reason if the replacement facility does not meet the requirements of subdivision (a) above and all regulations and standards promulgated thereunder.

4. It shall be unlawful for any person to use, maintain, or put into service any underground storage facility or part thereof without first complying with the testing and inspection requirements of subdivision (d) above and regulations and standards promulgated thereunder.

f. Monitoring and Leak Detection

1. All underground storage facilities or parts thereof must be equipped with means of calculating product delivery and consumption. Accurate records must be kept of all deliveries and consumption and the figures reconciled daily in an approved manner unless a less frequent schedule is allowed by the commissioner.

2. All underground storage facilities or parts thereof must be provided with a means of monitoring frequently and accurately for any leakage and spillage that might occur. All leak detection systems and tanks shall be monitored by the facility operator at least on a weekly basis and the results recorded and kept with the product records. Leak detection and monitoring can be provided by an electrical continuous leak detection system; visually operated or float operated alarms for tanks in pits; pressure, vacuum or fluid level detectors for double-walled facilities; observation wells and collection barriers or membranes for use in high groundwater areas; for gasoline and oil facilities a perforated, properly designed U tube installation is acceptable, or other equivalent design approved by the

commissioner. Permanent records of all monitoring shall be kept for a period of five (5) years.

3. It shall be unlawful for the owner or other person in possession or control of a storage facility or part thereof to fail to comply with any of the requirements of this subdivision and of any regulations and standards promulgated pursuant thereto.

g. Overfill Protection

1. A means of overfill protection shall be provided for all new underground storage facilities or parts thereof and for all replacement underground storage facilities or parts thereof. Overfill protection shall consist of either an overfill prevention device or a product-tight containment capable of intercepting and preventing the release to the ground or groundwater of an overfill spill.

2. It shall be unlawful for the owner, operator or lessee to fail to provide satisfactory overfill protection for any new underground storage facility or part thereof in accordance with the provisions of this subdivision and any regulations and standards promulgated pursuant thereto.

h. Removal of Underground Storage Facilities From Service

1. It shall be unlawful for the owner or any other person in possession or control of an underground storage facility or part thereof, to remove it from service unless:

i. said storage facility or part thereof is declared abandoned, emptied immediately and removed within ninety (90) days of so declaring, and is disposed of as junk by first rendering it vapor-free and by sufficiently perforating it so as to render it unfit for further use; or

ii. said storage facility or part thereof is declared abandoned, emptied immediately and removed within ninety (90) days for reuse for the storage of toxic or hazardous materials after having met all of the requirements of subdivision (a) and all regulations and standards promulgated pursuant thereto; or

iii. said storage facility or part thereof is declared abandoned, emptied immediately and removed within ninety (90) days for the storage of other than toxic and hazardous materials in which case the facility shall be emptied, cleaned of all residue, and made safe and vapor-free; or

iv. said storage facility is declared temporarily out of service and maintained in accordance with subdivision (3) of this section;

v. said storage facility or part thereof is declared abandoned, emptied immediately and made inert by completely filling with sand or concrete within ninety (90) days;

vi. said storage facility is declared to be suspected of leaking and maintained in accordance with Section 1210(e).

2. Any declaration of facility abandonment or of taking a facility temporarily out of or returning a facility to service, must be made to the commissioner in writing.

3. It shall be unlawful for the owner or any other person in possession or control of any underground storage facility or part thereof to render it temporarily out of service unless said storage facility or part thereof is planned to be returned to active service within two (2) years of the placement of it temporarily out of service, and it is returned to active service within said two (2) years, it is emptied of its contents immediately, and the fill line, gauge opening and pump suction are capped and secured against tampering, and the vent line is left open. No facility in a temporarily out of service condition shall be returned to use prior to notification to the commissioner and prior to the successful completion of any tightness testing due under Section 1210(d).

4. It shall be unlawful for anyone to place toxic or hazardous materials in a facility which is temporarily out of service.

Section 1211. Outdoor Aboveground Storage Facilities

a. New Storage Facilities

1. For the purpose of this subdivision, a new aboveground storage facility shall be one for which construction actually begins on or after November 1, 1982.

2. It shall be unlawful to fabricate, construct, install, use or maintain any new aboveground storage facility or part thereof in a manner which will allow the discharge of a toxic or hazardous material to the ground, groundwaters, or surface waters of Suffolk County.

3. It shall be unlawful to fabricate, construct, install, use or maintain any new aboveground storage facility or part thereof without having constructed around and under it an impervious containment and dike enclosing the storage facility or part thereof, conforming to the following requirements:

i. The volume of the diked area shall be at least 110% of the volume of the largest tank contained therein excluding the volume below the dike level occupied by other tanks. Additional volume up to 10% of the total volume of all other tanks or vessels contained in the diked area may be required if the configuration, arrangement and spacing of the tanks and dikes do not meet National Fire Protection Association standards.

ii. The dikes and the entire area enclosed by the dikes including the area under the tanks shall be made permanently impervious to the types of products expected to be stored in the tanks. A tank cannot be switched from one product to another unless the barrier is impervious to the new material stored.

iii. Drainage of precipitation from within the diked area shall be controlled in a manner that will prevent any toxic or hazardous material from entering the ground, groundwaters or surface waters of Suffolk County.

4. It shall be unlawful to construct, fabricate, install, use or maintain any new aboveground storage facility without providing a positive means of detecting an overfilling condition therein before any spillage can occur, which detection system shall include, but shall not necessarily be limited to, both visual and audible alarms at a point on the storage facility most frequently manned. The overflow point must be clearly visible to the operator filling the facility or the operator at the receiving facility where possible. If not possible, adequate means must be provided to immediately detect an overflow.

5. It shall be unlawful to fabricate, construct, install, use or maintain any new aboveground storage facility or part thereof without conforming to all regulations and standards promulgated pursuant to this section relating to such new storage facilities.

6. It shall be unlawful to fabricate, construct, install, use or maintain any new aboveground storage facility sitting on the ground and making contact therewith or partially buried in the ground and making contact therewith, or part thereof, unless and until the exterior surface of the areas in contact with the ground are cathodically protected in conformance with a design approved by the commissioner.

b. Existing Storage Facilities

1. An existing aboveground storage facility is one for which construction actually begins prior to November 1, 1982.

2. Commencing January 1, 1990, it shall be unlawful for any person to use, maintain

or fill with toxic or hazardous materials any existing aboveground storage facility or part thereof without conforming to all of the requirements of subdivision (a) above and all regulations and standards promulgated pursuant thereto, with one exception. It will not be required to place an impervious barrier directly beneath an existing tank that is sitting on or partially in the ground and is too large to be moved. In this case, the interior bottom of the tank shall be coated with a glass fiber reinforced epoxy coating or approved equivalent acceptable to the commissioner, pursuant to Department standards. In achieving the above compliance, the following schedule shall be adhered to:

iv. said storage facility is declared temporarily out of service; and

v. the commissioner has been notified of the intended status of removal from service.

3. It shall be unlawful for the owner or other person in possession or control of an aboveground storage facility or part thereof to render it temporarily out of service unless said storage facility or part thereof is planned to be returned to active service within two (2) years of its placement temporarily out of service, and it is returned to active service within said two (2) years pursuant to the provisions of subsections (c)(6) and (7) following, and it is drained of all liquid and the fill line, gauge opening and discharge line are capped and blind flanged and secured against tampering, and the vent line is left open.

4. It shall be unlawful for anyone to place toxic or hazardous materials in an abandoned or temporarily out of service aboveground storage facility.

5. It shall be unlawful for any person to bring an abandoned aboveground storage facility back into service without meeting all of the requirements of subsection (a) above. No abandoned facility shall be brought back into service without a complete inspection acceptable to the commissioner.

6. It shall be unlawful for any person to bring a temporarily out of service facility back into use after January 1, 1990, without first meeting all the requirements of subsection (a) above.

7. An aboveground storage facility properly declared to be temporarily out of service may be returned to service prior to 1990 by written notification to the commissioner if the requirements of Section 1211(b)(2) have been met.

8. It shall be unlawful for the owner or other person in possession or control of an aboveground storage facility or part thereof to fail to empty, clean, and inspect pursuant to subsection (b)(3)(iii) above, to file Proof of Inspection pursuant to subsection (b)(3)(v) above, to leak test, and/or to recoat if necessary every seven (7) years each tank or vessel for the storage of toxic or hazardous materials within the said storage facility or part thereof.

9. It shall be unlawful for any person to replace or cause the replacement of any aboveground storage facility or part thereof for any reason without complying with the new storage requirements of subdivision (a) above and without complying with the inspection and Proof of Inspection requirements of subsections (b)(3)(iii) and (b)(3)(v), respectively.

v. Proofs of Inspection must be filed with the commissioner on a form provided by the commissioner or one acceptably equivalent thereto within thirty (30) days of each inspection and before the tank is refilled, and a copy of such form shall be kept and maintained by both the owner or other person in possession or control of the aboveground storage facility or part thereof and the inspector for a period of not less than five (5) years from the date of the inspection. The Proof of Inspection form shall be subscribed by both the owner or other person in possession or control of the aboveground storage facility inspected and the inspector. This Proof of Inspection form shall contain a legally authorized form notice to the effect that false statements made knowingly therein are punishable pursuant to Section 210.45 of the Penal Law.

4. It shall be unlawful for any person to substantially modify or cause the substantial modification of any aboveground storage facility or part thereof without complying with the provisions of subdivision (a) above and all regulations and standards promulgated pursuant thereto.

c. General Provisions

1. It shall be unlawful for any person to abandon an aboveground storage facility or part thereof without first cleaning out all residue, venting it until dry and safe and leaving all of the hatches open or with all connections severed and valves blank flanged. For the purpose of this subdivision, an abandoned aboveground storage facility or part thereof means one that has remained substantially empty and unattended for one (1) year or more without being declared temporarily out of service, or has been temporarily out of service for two (2) years or more.

2.   It shall be unlawful for the owner or other person in possession or control of an aboveground storage facility or part thereof to remove it from service unless:

    i.   said storage facility or part thereof is disposed of as junk by first rendering it vapor-free and by sufficiently perforating it so as to render it unfit for further use, and demolishing it and removing it from the site; or

    ii.   said storage facility or part thereof is demolished for sale or use elsewhere in which case it must be first cleaned and made vapor-free to be safe in transit, and such reuse shall be in accordance with all pertinent portions of this article if relocation is to be within Suffolk County; or

    iii.   said storage facility is declared abandoned; or

10.   It shall be unlawful for any person to use, maintain, construct, fabricate, modify or install any aboveground storage facility or part thereof without conforming to all plans and specifications submitted to and approved by the commissioner prior to such use, maintenance, construction, fabrication, modification or installation.

    d.   Leaks; Repairs

1.   When an aboveground storage facility or part thereof is found to be leaking, it must immediately be emptied of all contents therein contained and removed from service unless approval is specifically granted by the commissioner to do otherwise.

2.   It shall be unlawful for the owner or other person in possession or control of a leaking aboveground storage facility or part thereof to cause or permit it to remain in service or to continue to retain its toxic or hazardous contents after said owner or other person knows or should have known of the existence of the leak.

3.   It shall be unlawful for any person to reuse and repair or cause the reuse and repair of an aboveground storage facility or part thereof which is leaking or which has leaked without:

    i.   performing or having said repairs performed in accordance with a written protocol submitted to and approved by the commissioner prior to said repairs; and

    ii.   inspecting or having said leaking storage facility or part thereof inspected by a person whose qualifications are acceptable to the commissioner, with such inspection in accordance with subsection (b)(3)(iii) above and filing a Proof of Inspection in accordance with subsection (b)(3)(v) above, with such inspection

performed and Proof of Inspection filed prior to reuse of the storage facility or part thereof or filling it with a toxic or hazardous material but after repairs have been effected.

Section 1212. Piping, Fittings, Connections

    a.   New Installations

1.   For the purpose of this section, new installations means piping, pipelines, fittings, connections for use with toxic or hazardous materials for which installation or construction actually begins on or after November 1, 1982.

2.   All new installations shall

    i.   be fabricated, constructed and installed in a manner that will prevent the escape of the toxic or hazardous materials contained therein to the ground, groundwater or surface waters of Suffolk County; and

    ii.   be protected against corrosion by the use of non-corrosive materials, cathodic protection with coatings approved by the commissioner or the functional equivalent of the foregoing options approved by the commissioner; and

    iii.   be designed, constructed and installed with access points as required by the commissioner to permit periodic pressure testing of all underground piping without the need of extensive excavation; and

    iv.   be designed, constructed and installed with a simple, effective, reliable means of monitoring the new installation for leakage including a warning device to indicate the presence of a leak, spill or other failure or breach of integrity for piping installed underground or in areas where piping is not clearly visible; and

    v.   be constructed of double-walled pipe or be constructed in product-tight trenches or galleries where the piping is buried or below grade except that single-walled piping will be allowed for facilities containing products with a specific gravity less than one and only slightly soluble in water such as gasoline and fuel oil.

3.   It shall be unlawful for any person to fabricate, construct, install, use or maintain or to cause the fabrication, construction, installation, use or maintenance of any new substantial installation or part thereof for use with toxic or hazardous materials:

    i.   without previously having submitted plans therefor to the commissioner, and without having received approval of said plans; and

    ii. without complying with the plans submitted to and approved by the commissioner as required in subsection (a)(3)(i) above; and

iii. without complying with the provisions of subsections (a)(1) and (a)(2) above and any regulations and standards promulgated thereunder.

b. Existing Installations

1. For the purpose of this section, existing installations shall mean piping, fittings and connections for use with toxic or hazardous materials for which installation or construction actually begins prior to November 1, 1982.

2. Commencing January 1, 1990, it shall be unlawful to use or maintain any existing installation or part thereof in association with any underground storage facility or part thereof unless said existing installation complies with all of the provisions of subdivision (a) above and all regulations and standards promulgated pursuant thereto.

3. It shall be unlawful for the owner or other person in possession or control of any existing piping installation or part thereof associated with any underground storage facility or part thereof to fail to pressure test said existing piping or part thereof whenever the associated underground storage facility or part thereof is tested.

4. It shall be unlawful for the owner or other person in possession or control of an existing installation or part thereof when testing or contracting to test said installation or part pursuant to subsection (b)(3) above:

i. to fail to test or have said installation or part thereof tested by a person whose qualifications are acceptable to the commissioner; and

ii. to fail to test or have tested said installation in a manner acceptable to the commissioner; and

iii. to fail to test or have installation tested in accordance with a written protocol submitted to and approved by the commissioner prior to said test; and

iv. to fail to test or have tested said installation in accordance with any regulations or standards which may be promulgated under this subdivision relating to said testing; and

v. to fail to submit to the commissioner within thirty (30) days of said test a completed Certificate of Test Completion form, pursuant to Section 1210(d)t3-6) and an-y regulations and standards promulgated thereunder.

c. General Provisions

1. Notwithstanding the requirements of subsection (b)(3) above, it shall be unlawful for the owner or other person in possession or control of a new or existing installation or part thereof not to test said installation or part in accordance with the procedures set forth in subsection (b)(3) above and in all regulations and standards promulgated thereunder whenever the commissioner has determined that such a test is necessary, or whenever the commissioner has ordered that such a test be performed.

2. Whenever an existing or new installation or part thereof is found to be leaking, it must immediately be emptied of all contents therein contained and removed from service.

i. It shall be unlawful for the owner or other person in possession or control of said leaking installation or part thereof to cause or permit it to remain in service or to continue to retain its toxic or hazardous contents after said owner or other person knows or should have known of the existence of the leak.

ii. It shall be unlawful for any person to repair or cause the repair of any new or existing installation or part thereof which has leaked or otherwise failed without performing said repairs or having said repairs performed in a manner approved by the commissioner.

iii. It shall be unlawful for any person to reuse or cause the reuse of any new or existing installation or part thereof which had leaked or otherwise failed without repairing said installation pursuant to the provisions of subsection (c)(2)(ii) above and all regulations and standards promulgated thereunder.

iv. It shall be unlawful for any person to reuse or to cause the reuse of any new or existing installation or part thereof which had leaked or otherwise failed without repairing said installation or part so as to conform to the requirements of subdivision (a) above and all regulations and standards promulgated thereunder.

v. It shall be unlawful for any person to reuse or cause the reuse of any new or existing installation or part thereof which had leaked or otherwise failed without inspecting or having said installation or part inspected subsequent to the completion of any repairs but prior to said reuse by a person whose qualifications are acceptable to the commissioner in accordance with Section 1211 (b)(3)(iv) and any regulations and standards promulgated thereunder and without filing with the commissioner a Proof of Inspection prior to said reuse in accordance with Section 1211 (b)(3)(v) and any regulations and standards promulgated thereunder.

Section 1213. Transfer of Toxic or Hazardous Materials

a.   Transfer Facilities

1.   Transfer facilities means truck fill stands and/or any other facility for the loading or unloading of toxic or hazardous materials.

2.   It shall be unlawful for any person to fabricate, construct or install a transfer facility or part thereof:

i.   without first submitting plans therefor to the commissioner and without first obtaining the commissioner's approval thereof; and

ii.   without fabricating, constructing and installing said transfer facility or part thereof in accordance with the plans submitted and approved pursuant to subsection (a)(2)(i) above; and

iii.   without providing a simple, effective, reliable means of monitoring the transfer facility or part thereof for leakage or spillage, including a warning device; and

iv.   without providing a level of spill protection equivalent to that provided by a fill stand area completely paved and curbed with an impervious material and drained to a holding tank of adequate size to contain any spill that could reasonably be expected to occur from the normal operation of the facility, and roofed so as to exclude precipitation which would otherwise tend to fill the holding tank.

3.   It shall be unlawful for any person to operate, maintain or use a transfer facility or part thereof so as to permit the escape therefrom of toxic or hazardous materials to the ground, groundwaters or surface waters of Suffolk County. All holding tanks associated with spill control shall be maintained in an empty condition at all times to provide maximum storage capacity at the time of a spill.

4.   It shall be unlawful for any person to fabricate, construct, install, use, operate or maintain any transfer facility or part thereof without doing so in accordance with all regulations and standards pertaining thereto which may be promulgated by the commissioner.

b.   Transfer Operations

1.   It shall be unlawful for any person to transfer, cause the transfer or permit the transfer of toxic or hazardous materials to or from a storage facility, part thereof or vehicle, where conditions at the transfer facility are inadequate at the time of said transfer to ensure a safe transfer operation without the occurrence of spills, leaks or accidents.

2.   Failure of a transfer facility to conform and comply with the provisions of subdivision (a) and all regulations and standards promulgated thereunder shall constitute a rebuttable presumption that conditions at said transfer facility are inadequate for the purposes of subsection (b)(l) above.

3.   The transfer of toxic or hazardous materials to any storage facility or part thereof which does not comply with all provisions of this article applicable thereto and any regulations and standards promulgated under this article applicable thereto, shall constitute a rebuttable presumption that conditions at said transfer facility are inadequate for the purposes of subdivision (b)(l) above.

4.   Conditions at the transfer facility shall be deemed to be inadequate at the time of a transfer if:

i.   the transfer facility is constructed so that all possible points of overflow are not visible from the loading and unloading locations; or

ii.   the truck, storage facility or part thereof being delivered to does not have adequate capacity to contain the amount of toxic or hazardous material being transferred or to be transferred, or if a person performing or causing said transfer does not insure by some reliable means that the truck, storage facility or part thereof has adequate capacity to contain the amount of toxic or hazardous material being transferred or to be transferred.

Section 1214. Indoor Storage Facilities

a.   An indoor storage facility is specifically intended to include within its meaning all tanks, vessels and appurtenant plumbing which contain or are to contain or be used for the transmission of toxic or hazardous materials regardless of the volume of said tanks and vessels and regardless of the duration of time said tanks and vessels may contain the toxic or hazardous materials and regardless of their use.

1.   All processing baths and tanks including dip tanks and rinse tanks and tanks associated with wastewater treatment located indoors shall constitute an indoor storage facility or part thereof.

2.   All portable containers and tanks with an individual volume of greater than 80

gallons, stored or located indoors and used to contain toxic or hazardous materials, shall be deemed to be an indoor storage facility or part thereof and shall be subject to all of the provisions of this section and any regulations and standards promulgated pursuant hereto, and not the provisions of Section 1215 and the regulations and standards created thereunder.

b. New Storage Facilities

1. A new indoor storage facility or part thereof is one for which construction, fabrication or installation actually begins on or after November 1, 1982, or one consisting of portable containers and/or tanks each with an individual volume in excess of 80 gallons, for which indoor storage of said portable containers and/or tanks containing toxic or hazardous materials actually begins on or after November 1, 1982.

2. It shall be unlawful to fabricate, construct or install a new indoor storage facility or part thereof unless:

i. plans and specifications for said storage facility have been first submitted to and approved by the commissioner; and unless

ii. said fabrication, construction or installation is accomplished in accordance with the approved plans and specifications submitted pursuant to subsection (b)(2)(i) above; and unless

iii. said fabrication, construction or installation is accomplished in accordance with all regulations and standards which may be promulgated under this subdivision; and unless

iv. the fabrication, construction or installation provides for impervious secondary containment for the new storage facility or part thereof equal to or greater than 110% of the entire volume to be contained; and unless

v. said storage facility or part thereof is fabricated, constructed or installed in a manner which will prevent the release into the ground, groundwaters or surface waters of Suffolk County of any toxic or hazardous materials; and unless

vi. any open tanks or vessels containing or to contain toxic or hazardous materials within the storage facility or part thereof in a building equipped with a sprinkler system are provided with head deflectors or automatic covers or the equivalent thereof acceptable to the commissioner to prevent the overflow of the tanks by reason of flow from the sprinkler system; and unless

vii. high level alarms or other adequate means of detecting an impending overfill

condition have been provided for all tanks not readily visible by the operator controlling filling.

3. It shall be unlawful to operate, maintain or use a new indoor storage facility or part thereof unless:

i. said storage facility or part thereof has been fabricated, constructed and installed in accordance with all of the provisions of subdivision (b) above and any regulations and standards promulgated thereunder; and unless

ii. said storage facility or part thereof has been inspected prior to said operation, maintenance or use pursuant to the provisions of Section 1211(b)(3)(iii) and any regulations and standards promulgated thereunder; and unless

iii. Proof of Inspection is filed with the commissioner within thirty (30) days of the inspection conducted pursuant to subsection (b)(3)(ii) above and such filing occurs prior to said operation, maintenance or use, and said Proof of Inspection conforms to all of the provisions of Section 1211(b)(3)(v) and any regulations and standards promulgated thereunder; and unless

iv. said storage facility or part thereof is operated, used or maintained in a manner which will prevent the discharge of toxic or hazardous materials therefrom into the ground, groundwaters or surface waters of Suffolk County.

4. It shall be unlawful to repair and reuse a new indoor storage facility or part thereof without complying with all of the provisions of subsection (b)(2) above and all regulations and standards promulgated pursuant thereto.

c. Existing Storage Facilities

1. An existing indoor storage facility includes all indoor storage facilities or parts thereof as described in subdivision (a) above, not within the class of storage facilities described in subsection (b)(1) above as new indoor storage facilities.

2. Commencing November 1, 1982, it shall be unlawful to fabricate, construct, install, modify, operate, maintain or use any indoor storage facility or part thereof which does not conform to all of the provisions of subdivision (b) above and all regulations and standards promulgated thereunder.

3. It shall be unlawful for any person to operate, maintain or use an existing indoor storage facility or part thereof in a manner which will allow the discharge of toxic or hazardous materials therefrom into the ground, groundwaters or surface waters of Suffolk County.

Section 1215. Portable Containers and Tanks

a.   Storage Facilities

1.   It shall be unlawful to fabricate, construct, install or otherwise create a storage facility or part thereof for portable containers and tanks in excess of 250 gallons total capacity containing toxic or hazardous materials if the facility has to be used for more than thirty (30) days without:

i.   first having submitted satisfactory plans and specifications therefor to the commissioner; and without

ii.   constructing, installing, fabricating or .otherwise creating said storage facility in accordance with the reports and plans submitted pursuant to subsection (a)(1)(i) above; and without

iii.   constructing, installing, fabricating or otherwise creating said storage facility so as to prevent the discharge of any of the toxic or hazardous contents of the portable containers therein to the ground, groundwaters or surface waters of Suffolk County; and without

iv.   providing a chemically resistant pad on which to place the portable containers or tanks, impervious to the toxic or hazardous materials being stored in said containers and tanks; and without

v.   providing a complete impervious containment of the storage facility or part thereof sufficient to contain at least thirty (30%) percent of the volume to be stored; and without

vi.   constructing, fabricating, installing or otherwise creating a storage facility or part thereof in accordance with all regulations and standards promulgated under this subdivision.

2.   It shall be unlawful for any person to use, maintain or operate a storage facility containing portable containers or tanks for the storage of toxic or hazardous materials without:

i.   preventing the discharge of any of the toxic or hazardous contents of the portable containers or tanks to the ground, groundwaters or surface waters of Suffolk County; and without

ii.   properly securing the portable containers or tanks containing toxic or hazardous materials so as to protect them from vandalism, unauthorized access and damage by traffic, machinery or falling objects; and without

iii.   storing the portable containers and tanks containing toxic or hazardous materials indoors except where such storage is prevented by fire regulations, or where sufficient evidence is presented that physical or financial constraints of the facility make indoor storage impractical. Waiver of the indoor storage requirement shall be only by permission of the commissioner; and without

iv.   protecting any outdoor storage of portable containers or tanks containing toxic or hazardous materials from damage from heat, cold, rust and other weather-related conditions; and without

v.   complying with all regulations and standards promulgated relating to the maintenance, use or operation of a storage facility containing portable containers containing toxic or hazardous materials; and without

vi.   complying with all of the provisions of subdivision (b) below and any regulations and standards promulgated thereunder.

b.   Handling of Portable Containers or Tanks

It shall be unlawful for the owner or other person in possession or control of a storage facility containing portable containers or tanks which contain toxic or hazardous materials:

i.   to stack said portable containers or tanks more than two (2) high without using a properly designed storage rack for that purpose, or to attempt any stacking without adequate equipment; and

ii.   to store said portable containers or tanks in a manner so as to prevent all sides thereof from being available for inspection; and

iii.   to fail to maintain current inventory records indicating deliveries, consumption, sale and final disposal of all toxic or hazardous materials stored in portable containers or tanks and to maintain said records for five (5) years from the occurrence recorded; and

iv.   to fail to handle the said portable containers or tanks in accordance with any regulations and standards promulgated pursuant to this subdivision; and

v.   to store said portable containers in numbers in excess of the maximum allowed by the approved design of the storage facility.

c.   Inspections

1.   It shall be unlawful for the owner or other person in possession or control of a storage facility containing portable containers or tanks for the storage of toxic or hazardous materials to fail to have said facility or part thereof containing said portable containers or tanks inspected:

i.   prior to application for the renewal of a permit to operate a storage facility issued pursuant to Section 1207; and

ii.   subsequent to any substantial modification of the storage facility or part thereof containing said portable containers or tanks, and prior to the using or putting into service a storage facility or part thereof; and

iii.   prior to the using or putting into service said storage facility or part thereof after repairs had been performed on it.

2.   It shall be unlawful to fail to have the inspections required by subsection (c)(1) above performed in accordance with the provisions of Section 1211 (b)(3)(iii) and all regulations and standards promulgated pursuant thereto and those promulgated under this subdivision.

3.   It shall be unlawful to fail to file a Proof of Inspection with the commissioner within thirty (30) days of the performance of an inspection required by subsection (c)(1) above complying with the provisions of Section 1211 (b)(3)(v) and any regulations and standards promulgated pursuant thereto.

d.   It shall be unlawful for any person to repair or modify or to cause or permit said repairs or modifications of a storage facility or part thereof containing portable containers or tanks for the storage of toxic or hazardous materials without performing said repairs or modifications or having them performed pursuant to a written protocol previously submitted to and approved by the commissioner.

e.   At the discretion of the commissioner, Sections 1215 (a)(1)(iv),(v),(vi), and 1215(c), may be waived for temporary facilities such as spill cleanup operations.

Section 1216. Bulk Storage of Toxic or Hazardous Materials

a.   It shall be unlawful for any person to fabricate, construct, install, repair or modify any bulk storage facility or part thereof without doing so in accordance with a written protocol previously submitted to and approved by the commissioner.

b.   It shall be unlawful for any person to fabricate, construct, install, modify, repair, use, maintain or operate any bulk storage facility or part thereof without:

1.   doing so in a manner that will prevent the toxic or hazardous materials contained therein from coming into contact with precipitation

or other sources of moisture unless there is provision made for collecting and treating the leachate and runoff generated so as to prevent a discharge of toxic or hazardous materials to the ground, groundwaters or surface waters of Suffolk County and so as to prevent the development of an explosive, incendiary or other hazardous or dangerous condition; and without

2.   providing for the segregation of and without segregating potentially reactive chemicals which are toxic or hazardous materials or which may react so as to form toxic or hazardous materials, which reaction may present or cause a hazardous or dangerous condition; and without

3.   providing for and storing bagged toxic or hazardous materials on pallets, and within a roofed structure which prevents precipitation from reaching the bags; and

4.   in the case of an indoor bulk storage facility, without providing for and providing an impervious floor without floor drains with a surrounding impervious dike so as to provide containment for hazardous or toxic materials generated from firefighting within the building; and without

5.   providing for and providing adequate security so as to protect the storage facility and toxic or hazardous contents therein from vandalism and accident; and without

6.   complying with any regulations and standards which may be promulgated pursuant to this section.

c.   Road deicing salt and other deicing materials are toxic or hazardous materials. In addition to the foregoing provisions of this section, road deicing salt may be stored near the shore or other areas where no adverse environmental impact will occur without brine control so long as the commissioner's approval for such a storage facility has been applied for and received in advance.

Section 1217. Reporting; Records; Clean-Up

a.   It shall be unlawful for the owner or other person in possession or control of any storage facility or part thereof to fail to report any unauthorized discharge, spill, leak or recognizable loss of toxic or hazardous materials therefrom or the failure of said storage facility to the commissioner within two (2) hours of the time such owner or other person had sufficient evidence that he knew or should have known of said unauthorized discharge, spill, leak, loss or failure.

1. A report to the commissioner shall not be deemed compliance with any reporting requirement of any other federal, state or local law.

b. It shall be unlawful for the owner or other person in possession or control of any storage facility or part thereof to fail to keep records in writing reflecting the types and amounts of toxic or hazardous materials stored in the said storage facility or part thereof at any given time.

1. It shall be unlawful for the owner or other person in possession or control of any storage facility or part thereof to fail to keep records of the disposal or other transfer in or out of the said storage facility or part thereof, such records reflecting the types and amounts of toxic or hazardous materials involved in the transfer. The name and vehicle license and registration numbers of the transporter, and the intended destination must also be included if the material is waste.

2. It shall be unlawful for any person required to keep records by any provision of this article to fail to maintain said records available for inspection by the commissioner for a least five (5) years from the date of the event, occurrence or transaction recorded. Copies shall be provided by the owner or operator for the commissioner if requested.

3. It shall be unlawful for any person required to keep records by any provision of this article to fail to keep, record and maintain said records in accordance with any regulations and standards promulgated pursuant to this section.

c. It shall be the responsibility and obligation of any person who discharges, or causes or permits the discharge of any toxic or hazardous material to the ground, groundwaters or surface waters of Suffolk County to cease said discharge, to reclaim, recover and/or properly dispose of the discharged toxic or hazardous material and any other substance contaminated therefrom, to restore the environment to a condition and quality acceptable to the commissioner, and to repair any damages caused thereby, all to the satisfaction of the commissioner.

1. It shall be unlawful for the owner or any other person in possession or control of any source discharging toxic or hazardous materials to the ground, groundwaters or surface waters of Suffolk County to fail to cease said discharge immediately upon obtaining knowledge or notice of its existence.

2. It shall be unlawful for the owner or any other person in possession or control of any source discharging or which has discharged toxic or hazardous materials to the ground, groundwaters or surface waters of Suffolk County to fail to reclaim, recover and/or dispose of the discharged toxic or hazardous materials. Where time permits, cleanup shall be i. accordance with a written protocol previously submitted to and approved by the commissioner.

3. It shall be unlawful for the owner or other person in possession or control of any premises or place to fail to reclaim, recover and/or otherwise dispose of any toxic or hazardous materials discharged thereto, in accordance with a written protocol previously submitted to and approved by the commissioner, in the event the persons described in subsection (c)(2) above are not ascertainable or otherwise fail to comply with the provisions of subsection (c)(2). This provision shall not abridge any existing right of action in any person, nor shall it create any new right of action in any person.

4. It shall be unlawful for the owner or any person in possession or control of any source which has discharged toxic or hazardous materials to the ground, groundwaters or surface waters of Suffolk County to fail to restore the environment contaminated or damaged by the said discharge to its condition prior to the discharge, repairing any damages caused thereby in accordance with a written protocol previously submitted to and approved by the commissioner.

5. It shall be unlawful for any person required by this article or by any order of the commissioner to reclaim, recover or otherwise dispose of discharged toxic or hazardous materials and other substances contaminated therefrom and/or to restore the environment to the condition that existed prior to the discharge of toxic or hazardous materials thereto, to fail to perform said required acts pursuant to any regulations and standards promulgated pursuant to this subdivision.

Section 1218. Confidentiality of Records

a. Any information relating to secret processes, or methods of manufacture or production, obtained in the course of an inspection or investigation, or submitted to the department, shall be kept confidential except for the use and purpose of the department in the enforcement of this article and the rules and regulations promulgated thereunder.

b. In the event that a person claims to be unable to file complete reports and/or plans and specifications on the grounds that it relates to and is part of a secret process or method of manufacture or production, an affidavit signed by an authorized person must be filed with the commissioner, stipulating:

    1. location of process or equipment, specifying the building and the section or part of the building in which it is located;

    2. in general terms, the name of the process equipment;

    3. means to be employed for the control of water contaminants;

    4. nature and estimated rate of discharge of contaminants to the ground or surface waters;

    5. authority of the person signing the affidavit;

    6. a statement that the installation is related to a secret process or method of manufacture or production.

In the event any such affidavit is filed, the commissioner shall determine the extent to which an exemption should be granted. Any information relating to secret processes, methods of manufacture or production which may be required, ascertained or discovered by the commissioner shall not be disclosed and shall be kept confidential.

Section 1219. Posting and Labeling

a. It shall be unlawful for the owner or other person in possession or control of any place, building, land, vehicle or thing to store toxic or hazardous materials therein without conspicuously posting a notice threat or thereon warning of the presence of such materials and providing any safety information necessary to protect the public and assist emergency response personnel in carrying out their responsibilities.

b. It shall be unlawful for any person to use, maintain or operate any storage facility or part thereof:

    1. without clearly labeling the specific contents of each portable container conspicuously on said container; and

    2. without clearly labeling the specific contents of each indoor and aboveground tank or vessel conspicuously thereon; and

    3. without clearly labeling the specific actual, intended and possible contents of piping associated with any storage facility or part

thereof at or near the points of filling or drawing; and

    4. without conspicuously posting any permit issued pursuant to this article.

c. It shall be unlawful for any person to falsely post or label any container or storage facility or to post an invalid permit.

d. It shall be unlawful for any person to use, maintain or operate any storage facility or part thereof without complying with all regulations and standards promulgated pursuant to this section.

Section 1220. Waivers

Any requirement, mandate, prohibition or time limitation imposed by this article or any regulation, standard or order generated hereunder, may be waived or modified by order of the commissioner.

Enacted	9/12/79
Effective	1/1/80
Amended	7/28/82
Amended	8/29/84
Amended	4/9/86
Amended	1/14/87

APPENDIX XXXIV

SOURCE:
EPA Journal, Jan/Feb/Mar 1993

Risk Assessment

"The ABCs of Risk Assessment"
by Dorothy E. Patton

Risk assessment is a cornerstone of environmental decision making. Despite this role as the scientific foundation for most EPA regulatory actions, risk assessment means different things to different people—a point that comes across in subsequent articles in this issue of *EPA Journal*—and is thus a source of misunderstanding and controversy. Some points of controversy involve the interpretation of scientific studies. Others have to do with science policy issues. Still others center on distinctions between risk assessment and risk management.

The scope and nature of risk assessments range widely—from broadly based scientific conclusions about an air pollutant such as lead or arsenic affecting the nation as a whole to site-specific findings concerning these same chemicals in a local water supply. Some assessments are retrospective, focusing on injury after the fact—for example, the kind and extent of risks at a particular Superfund site. Others seek to predict possible future harm to human health or the environment—for example, the risks expected if a newly developed pesticide is approved for use on food crops.

In short, risk assessment takes many different forms, depending on its intended scope and purpose, the available data and resources, and other factors. It involves many different disciplines and specialists with different kinds and levels of expertise, representing many different organizations. Moreover, risk assessment approaches differ somewhat in line with differences in environmental laws and related regulatory programs.

Even with these differences, some features of the risk assessment process stand out as instructive principles that clarify and demystify the process for expert and novice alike. This article highlights these principles.

(Patton is Executive Director of EPA's Risk Assessment Forum.)

Risk Assessment and Risk Management

Risk assessment and risk management are closely related but different processes, with the nature of the risk management decision often influencing the scope and depth of a risk assessment. In simple terms, risk assessment asks, "How risky is this situation?" and risk management then asks, "What shall we do about it?"

Also, it is especially important to understand that *risk assessment* and *comparative risk analysis* for ranking environmental problems are not the same.

I use the term "risk assessment," as the National Academy of Sciences (NAS) and EPA risk assessment guidelines have defined it for almost 10 years, to mean the process by which scientific data are analyzed to describe the form, dimension, and characteristics of risk—that is, the likelihood of harm to humans or the environment. Risk management, on the other hand, is the process by which the risk assessment is used with other information to make regulatory decisions.

Contributing Disciplines

What specific kinds of information are used for risk assessment? For risk management?

Environmental risk assessment is a multidisciplinary process. It draws on data, information, and principles from many scientific disciplines including biology, chemistry, physics, medicine, geology, epidemiology, and statistics, among others. The feature distinguishing risk assessment from the underlying sciences is this: After evaluating individual studies for conformity with standard practices within the discipline, the most relevant information from each of these areas is examined together to describe the risk. This means that individual studies, or even collections of studies from a single discipline, are used to develop risk assessments, but they are not *in themselves* generally regarded as risk assessments, nor can they alone generate risk assessments.

One way to highlight differences between risk assessment and risk management is by looking at differences in the information content of the two processes. What kinds of information, then, are used for risk management but *not* for risk assessment? In general EPA practice, data on technological feasibility, on costs, and on the economic and social consequences (e.g., employment impacts) of possible regulatory decisions are critically important for risk management, but not for risk assessment. To the extent called for in various statutes, risk managers consider this information *together with* the outcome of the risk assessment when evaluating risk management options and making environmental decisions. (See chart..)

The NAS Paradigm

The risk assessment paradigm put forward by NAS in a 1983 publication called *Risk Assessment in the Federal Government: Managing the Process* (or more colloquially, the "Red Book," alluding to its cover) provides a useful system for organizing risk science information from these many different sources. Moreover, in the last decade, EPA has used the basic NAS paradigm as a foundation for its published risk assessment guidance and as an organizing system for many individual assessments. The paradigm defines four "fields of analysis" which describe the use and flow of scientific information in the risk assessment process.

One virtue of this system of analysis is clarity: The paradigm makes the risk assessment process accessible so that scientists, regulators, lawyers, journalists,

What's In a Number?

Risk values are often stated, shorthand-fashion, as a number. When the risk concern is cancer, the risk number represents a probability of occurrence of additional cancer cases. For example, such an estimate for Pollutant X might be expressed as 1×10^{-6}, or simply 10^{-6}. This number can also be written as 0.000001, or one in a million—meaning one additional case of cancer projected in a population of one million people exposed to a certain level of Pollutant X over their lifetimes. Similarly, 5×10^{-7}, or 0.0000005, or five in *100* million, indicates a potential risk of five additional cancer cases in a population of 100 million people exposed to a certain level of the pollutant. These numbers signify incremental cases above the background cancer incidence in the general population. American Cancer Society statistics indicate that the background cancer incidence in the general population is one in three over a lifetime.

If the effect associated with Pollutant X is not cancer but another health effect, perhaps neurotoxicity (nerve damage) or birth defects, then numbers are not typically

$$1 \times 10^{-6}$$

given as probability of occurrence, but rather as levels of exposure estimated to be without harm. This often takes the form of a reference dose (RfD). A RfD is typically expressed in terms of milligrams (of pollutant) per kilogram of body weight per day, e.g., 0.004 mg/kg-day. Simply described, a RfD is a rough estimate of daily exposure to the human population (including sensitive subgroups) that is likely to be without appreciable risk of deleterious effects during a lifetime. The uncertainty in a RfD may be one or several orders of magnitude (i.e., multiples of 10).

What's in a number? The important point to remember is that the numbers by themselves don't tell the whole story. For instance, even though the numbers are identical, a cancer risk value of 10^{-6} for the

$$0.000001$$

"average exposed person" (perhaps someone exposed through the food supply) is not the same thing as a cancer risk of 10^{-6} for a "most exposed individual" (perhaps someone exposed from living or

working in a highly contaminated area). It's important to know the difference. Omitting the qualifier "average" or "most exposed" incompletely describes the risk and would mean a failure in risk communication.

A numerical estimate is only as good as the data it is based on. Just as important as the *quantitative* aspect of risk characterization (the risk numbers), then, are the *qualitative* aspects. How extensive is the data base supporting the risk assessment? Does it

$$10^{-6}$$

include human epidemiological data as well as experimental data? Does the laboratory data base include test data on more than one species? If multiple species were tested, did they all respond similarly to the test substance? What are the "data gaps," the missing pieces of the puzzle? What are the scientific uncertainties? What science policy decisions were made to address these uncertainties? What working assumptions underlie the risk assessment? What is the overall confidence level in the risk assessment? All of these qualitative considerations are essential to deciding what reliance to place on a number and to characterizing a potential risk.   *—Eds.*

Disciplines Contributing to Environmental Decisions

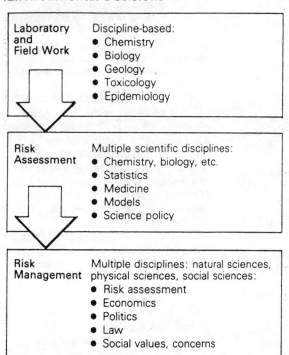

Risk Assessment Process

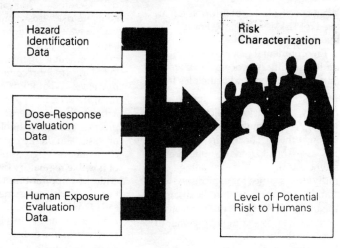

educators, and committed laypersons can use the paradigm as a relatively simple frame of reference for understanding where and how the data, scientific principles, and science policies have been used in any risk assessment developed in line with the paradigm. (Even where the paradigm is not explicitly used—e.g., certain climate issues—the same kinds of questions are studied to evaluate potential risk.)

The following discussion walks through the four fields of analysis. Note at the outset that each phase employs different parts of the information base. For example, hazard identification relies primarily on data from the biological and medical sciences. The dose-response analysis then uses these data in combination with statistical and mathematical modeling techniques, so that the second phase of the risk analysis builds on the first.

• *Hazard Identification.* The objective of hazard identification is to determine whether the available scientific data describe a causal relationship between an environmental agent and demonstrated injury to human health or the environment. In humans, the observed injury may include such effects as birth defects, neurologic effects (nerve

damage), or cancer. Ecological hazards might result in fish kills, habitat destruction, or other effects on the natural environment.

Information on the agent responsible for the effects may come from laboratory studies in which test animals were deliberately exposed to toxic materials, or from other sources such as chemical measurements in the workplace. In addition, studies on a pollutant's effects on genetic material or metabolism, and comparison of such effects in humans and experimental test systems, may be part of the analysis.

The principal question is whether data from populations in which effects and exposure are known to occur together suggest a potential hazard for other populations under expected conditions of exposure to the agent under study. If a potential hazard is identified, three other analyses become important for the overall risk assessment, as discussed below.

• *Dose-Response Relationships.* The dose-response analysis is designed to establish the quantitative relationship between exposure (or dose) and response in existing studies in which adverse health or environmental effects have been observed. The dose-response analysis is

based mainly on two extrapolations. One extrapolation uses the relatively high exposure levels in most laboratory studies (or, for example, human studies at relatively high workplace levels) to estimate the probable magnitude of the effect in the same population at lower environmental levels where little or no data are available.

The other extrapolation entails looking for the expected level of response in humans, or in animals or plants in nature, based on comparisons of data from laboratory and natural test systems. As explained later, each extrapolation involves numerous scientific uncertainties and assumptions, which in turn involve policy choices.

The number produced in the dose-response analysis—perhaps a cancer risk value or a reference dose (see article on noncancer effects on page 30)—is sometimes regarded as a risk assessment because it describes important information from animal and human studies. Under the NAS paradigm and in most EPA practice, however, risk assessment is complete only when human exposure assessment information is joined with dose-response analysis and all relevant information to characterize the risk.

• *Exposure Analysis.* The exposure analysis moves the assessment from the study of known populations (laboratory or epidemiologic) in which dose (exposure) and response occur together, to the task of identifying and characterizing exposure in other potentially exposed populations. These populations may be as general as the nation as a whole for certain widely distributed materials (e.g., contaminated food), or as limited as certain occupation or user groups (e.g., pesticide applicators). Questions raised in the exposure analysis concern the likely sources of the pollutant (e.g., incinerator discharge, factory effluent, pesticide application), its concentration at the source, its pathways (air, water, food) from the source to target populations, and actual levels impacting target organisms.

The exposure analysis relies on many very different kinds of information, some based on actual measurements and some developed using mathematical models. Measurements of the kind and quantity of a pollutant in various environmental media and, when available, in human, plant, and animal tissues are used to project expected exposure levels in individuals, populations, or both. The exposure analysis also develops "lifestyle" data to identify and describe populations likely to contact a pollutant. For example, if a chemical that causes birth defects in test animals contaminates tomatoes, the exposure analysis would consider such "lifestyle" information as the number of women of childbearing age who eat tomatoes, how often they eat this food, and in what quantities. To complete the exposure analysis, the lifestyle information is combined with information on how much chemical, probably measured at very low levels, remains in tomatoes when sold for consumption.

If the estimated exposure for an environmentally exposed population is significantly smaller than the lowest dose producing a response in the study population, the likelihood of injury to exposed humans is smaller; if the estimated exposure is significantly greater than the lowest dose, then the likelihood of injury is greater.

• *Risk Characterization.* Although each of the preceding analyses examines all relevant data and information to describe hazard or dose-response or exposure, under the 1983 paradigm none reaches conclusions about the overall *risk*. That task is reserved for the final analysis, where important information, data, and conclusions from each of the preceding analyses are examined together to *characterize* risk—that is, to fully describe the expected risk by examining the exposure predictions for real-world

conditions in light of the dose-response information from animals, people, and special test systems.

Risk characterization—the product of the risk assessment—is *much more* than a number. (See box on page 15.) While the risk is often stated as a bare number—for example, "a risk of 10^{-6}" or "one in a million new cancer cases"—the analysis involves substantially more information, thought, and judgment than the numbers express. These factors take us behind the simple structural framework that the NAS paradigm provides into a complex world of scientific uncertainties, assumptions, and policy choices. As discussed below, revisiting the NAS paradigm with these conceptual principles in mind sheds new light.

Uncertainties and Policy Choices

Scientific uncertainty is a customary and expected factor in all environmental risk assessment. Measurement uncertainty refers to the usual variance that accompanies scientific measurement such as the range (10 ± 1) around a value. Another kind of uncertainty refers to data or information gaps—that is, information needed but unavailable for any particular assessment. Sometimes the data gap exists because specific measurements or studies that would complete an assessment are missing; sometimes the data gap is broader, referring to a fundamental lack of understanding about a scientific phenomenon.

The 1983 paradigm and EPA risk assessment guidelines stress the importance of identifying uncertainties and presenting them as part of risk characterization.

In ordinary scientific practice, scientific uncertainties describe new data needs and stimulate further research, with questions remaining open until research provides needed information. Like traditional science, environmental risk assessment invariably identifies new data needs and generates recommendations for additional research.

However, "state-of-the-art" limitations on risk methods, resource limitations, and statutory timetables for regulatory decisions often require EPA as well as other participants in the regulatory process (other governmental agencies, industry, environmental groups) to complete risk assessments in the face of data gaps and other scientific uncertainties. As a result, "science policies"—that is, technically reasonable

positions assumed in lieu of scientific data—may be developed to address some of these uncertainties. Some familiar policies relate to use (or nonuse) of animal data to predict human risk, models used to quantify or project cancer risk, and the size of uncertainty factors for health effects other than cancer.

Variability, Misunderstanding, and Controversy

Variability is an often overlooked but important feature of the risk assessment process. Reasons for variability in risk assessment should be obvious from the preceding discussion. The need to use data from many different disciplines, characterized by data gaps and uncertainties, is one source of variability. Assumptions and policy choices spanning a spectrum of scientific theses about the nature of incompletely understood biological processes is another. These diverse elements can lead to diverse results, an outcome that leads to misunderstanding and seeds many risk assessment controversies.

Controversy might be less strident if practitioners and observers recognized that varying interpretations of the scientific information may lead to a range of science-based descriptions of risk for any particular situation. In addition, depending on data selected, scientific assumptions, policy calls and perspectives, different experts or organizations may describe risk differently. For example, a single data set, applied to different populations with different assumptions, may result in different numerical risk estimates for a single chemical. However, if the risk characterization identifies data and science policy choices, apparently inexplicable inconsistencies may be recognized as responsible, reasonable descriptions of different aspects of the same problem. The risk characterization process can also aid identification of less responsible, less reasonable descriptions of the problem.

Perhaps this clarifies some of the reasons for misunderstanding and controversy. Rarely is there a single "answer" to an environmental risk assessment question. The risk assessment process has an enormous capacity to expand and contract in line with the available data, science policies, and problems. When risk management information, options, and decisions are examined along with the risk assessment, opportunities for variability, misunderstanding, and controversy are even greater.

The task is to look behind the process, always keeping in mind the multiple sources of information, the several kinds of scientific analyses, and the related uncertainties and science policy choices that shape each assessment. A related task is to remember that risk assessment and risk management are equally important but different processes, with different objectives, information content, and results. ☐

Uncertainty and the "Flavors" of Risk
by Robert J. Scheuplein

If you are an average person (or even above average), you're exposed to a large amount of risk. Like ice cream, risk comes in a variety of flavors, and some people like to add nuts and berries to suit their tastes. So it is with risks. But the basic ones—the vanilla, chocolate, and strawberry of risks, if you will—are the following three: personal activities, natural disasters, and chemical exposures.

Consider first certain dangerous *personal activities* like firefighting, coal mining, skiing, motorcycling, driving automobiles, etc.—things you do for a living or for fun. Here the danger in the activity may be self evident, and the risk is ordinarily self imposed. As a class, these risks are the highest, along with risks from ordinary diseases, which personal behavior can also affect. For example, the annual risk associated with motorcycling is about 2 percent, or about 2,000 deaths per 100,000 persons at risk. Firefighting is much safer, only about 80 annual deaths per 100,000, or 0.08 percent. The annual death rate from motor vehicles is around 24 per 100,000, or 0.024 percent. This is just the death rate; of course, the accident rate and injury rate are much higher.

The risks above might be described as part of the price we pay for living in a civilized world, but the next category of risks, *natural disasters*, are not wholly our fault. The risks from floods, hurricanes, earthquakes, lightning, meteorite hits, etc., are the price we pay for our 70-year or so lease on the planet. Of course, if you want to live on an earthquake fault, you share some responsibility. These risks in the aggregate are quite small. But try telling that to the folks in South Florida who experienced Hurricane Andrew. Lightning kills 0.05 people per year per 100,000, or about 0.00005 percent. The risks from meteorite hits are about 0.000006 per 100,000, or 0.000000006 percent.

Now the last major category of risks, the "strawberry of risks," derive from *chemical exposures*. Before we discuss them, let me emphasize an important point. The risks above are real, obtained by counting victims. They are actuarial risks. They depend only on how accurately the deaths and the populations at risk were attributed and recorded. They are not based on inferences from animal data, nor on prudent extrapolations of adverse effects in animals. This distinction is essential to make because the risks from chemical exposures are for the most part based on such inferences and extrapolations.

Everyone knows about poisons, drugs, and acute occupational exposures to industrial chemicals. For many of these exposures there is human data. But for chronic low-level risk from chemicals in the environment we live in, in the air we breathe, in the water we drink, or in the food we ingest, we need to depend on animal data. These risks are ordinarily small. For example: The cancer risk from chlorinated drinking water has been estimated as 0.8 per year per 100,000 persons exposed or 0.0008 percent. While this number looks the same as the others and can be expressed in the same units, it is not the same and can be compared with the actuarial risks only if the differences are kept in mind.

What are these differences?

First, as stated above, chemical risk is based on the finding of an adverse effect in an animal study. In the case of chlorinated drinking water, it is based on several carcinogen bioassays conducted in mice using various chlorinated compounds. It is inferred that humans will be similarly susceptible to these same compounds. But this is not necessarily true.

(Scheuplein is Director of the Office of Special Research Skills at the Food and Drug Administration.)

Second, the quantitative result is a worst-case estimate sometimes called an upper-bound estimate. It is based on a mathematical extrapolation of adverse effects in animals, exposed at high dose levels, to the much lower levels anticipated for humans. Why is this done? Why not just expose the animal to the appropriate lower doses? The reason is there would be no effect at low doses, unless the number of animals in the experiment were increased dramatically—say to several thousand. The problem lies in trying to detect in a population of 100 a disease incidence that you might believe to be one in 1,000. So toxicologists need to exaggerate the animal doses and extrapolate downwards—hopefully.

To continue with our particular example, the actual amount of chlorinated hydrocarbon chemicals in drinking water, the chemical byproducts of the chlorination process, is very small, typically a few parts per billion. The doses to which the animals were exposed are very high, many thousands of times higher than human exposure levels. The high-to-low dose extrapolation is used to estimate the effect of the lower dose using various conservative assumptions. The most important of these assumptions is that there will inevitably be some cancer risk no matter how small the dose.

Third, the risk is an average attributed risk; it applies to no one in particular and to everyone on the average. If you're an average person and you drink the expected amount of water with the expected concentration of chlorinated compounds, your possible risk is no greater than the given risk number. But in no way is this intended to be a predicted risk for you individually; your particular pattern of exposure, your exposures to other carcinogens, your genes, your diet, and other factors determine your particular susceptibility.

This is the way carcinogenic risks are determined for most regulated chemicals: foods and cosmetics, pesticides, household chemicals, most industrial and workplace chemicals, air and water pollutants, and toxics and waste site contaminants. (Drugs and biologics are usually regulated with human data.)

Of course, not all chemicals present a cancer risk but they can pose other risks. There are chemical substances that affect developmental, reproductive, neurobehaviorial, and other body functions. Typically, such substances are regulated by determining "no-effect levels" in animals and applying safety factors. Numerical risk estimates are not made because thresholds are assumed. In other words, unlike for carcinogens, risk is not assumed to be present at all doses.

Cancer risks of less than 10^{-6}—one in a million per lifetime or one in 14,000 per year or 7 per 100,000 per year or 0.007 percent—are usually not considered worth regulating. (Lifetime risks are approximately 70 times higher than annual risks if the risks are similar from year to year for a lifetime.)

The inherent conservatism in estimates of the cancer risk may be illustrated the following way. Suppose you work for a regulatory agency and you are asked for the agency's official estimate of the average height of a person. You remember that the average height of an American male is, say, 5 feet, 10 inches. But that applies only to American men, and probably doesn't include modern American basketball players, some of whom are over 7 feet.

Getting the data on all the people in the world is impractical, but unless you do, you can't really give a figure without including some certain error. And the size of the error is also impossible to obtain. So in order to be absolutely clear and correct in your response you decide to give a worst-case estimate. You will cast your response in the form: "The average height of a man will in no case exceed ...."

This is a very strong statement, so to hedge your bet and to be sure you're right, you will have to make conservative assumptions. One you might make is that the average height of a person will in no case exceed the tallest person in the world. This contains the inherent reliability one likes to have when called upon to defend the regulatory decision against tall activists. Now, the tallest people you know about from your research are all less than 8 feet. But there may be giants somewhere, and there is some anecdotal evidence. (Remember the stories about "Bigfoot.") Let's assume you find a record of a 12-foot giant now deceased. On the possibility that he might have left living relatives, you assume a maximum height of 15 feet because there is plenty of data indicating that better nutrition over the last 50 years has increased the average body size by about 20 percent. So your official response, supported by several pages of data, reads:

"The average height of a person will in no case exceed 15 feet."

This statement has all the required regulatory qualities needed for the *Federal Register*. It is impeccably correct. It will withstand any legal challenge. It is prudent and does not underestimate the height. It also has at least two undesirable qualities: It is not very helpful. And it discriminates against short people. (Translation: The recasting of the regulatory problem away from *probable risk* (average height) to *worst-case risk* results in the under appreciation of risk-lowering factors.)

The linear extrapolation of rodent bioassay data embodies the regulator's credo ("It's better to be safe than sorry") far more than it does the scientist's, ("It's better to be right than wrong"). Currently the regulatory objective is often fulfilled at the expense of the scientific one.

When carcinogens were few, biological understanding of mechanisms more primitive, and analytical sensitivity in the parts per million range, the differences in these two points of view were not large and didn't really matter much. Today, for many substances, the situation has changed in each of these areas, and we face an ever-growing separation between the application of good science and credible, efficient regulation. ☐

The Role of Comparative Risk Analysis
by Wendy Cleland-Hamnett

EPA's support for using comparative risk analysis to help set the Agency's priorities has been no secret. Building on the lessons and insights gained in the 1988 *Unfinished Business* report, the Science Advisory Board's 1990 *Reducing Risk* report, and our experience in implementing strategic initiatives, we have seen how valuable it can be to have a grasp of the relative risk of various problems in narrowing our focus to the most important ones— especially as fiscal reality has dictated that we must.

Of course, other forces play critically important roles in directing policy, including statutory mandates, traditional considerations of costs and benefits, the

(Cleland-Hamnett is Acting Deputy Assistant Administrator for Policy, Planning, and Evaluation at EPA.)

state of technology, environmental equity, and, above all, public values and concerns. But comparative risk analysis, and its promise of objective, relevant, and even-handed guidance, has definitely "made it to the table" at EPA. The challenge for the Agency and its stakeholders will be in deciding the precise role it will play in delineating our priorities.

The particular ways we have tried to

use relative risk and the conditions under which we operate are not universally understood. Some think risk ranking affects our entire budget, and some think it derives from a backroom dialogue with cloistered scientific gurus. Perhaps most often it is viewed as the only factor we intend to include in our decision making. It is important to note that we have never understood priority setting to be one dimensional, where comparative risk analysis is the last word. In *Reducing Risk*, the SAB made it clear that establishing the relative risks of different environmental problems was only "one tool" that could help make integrated and targeted national environmental policy a reality. It also stressed that the "dichotomy" that exists between the perceptions of the public and the "experts" on which risks are important "presents an enormous challenge to a pluralistic, democratic country."

As good as our intentions have been over the last few years, there is ample room for EPA to do a better job in meeting the challenge of piloting the doctrine of risk through a democratic society. A quotation from Thomas Jefferson provides valuable insight:

> I know of no safe depository of the ultimate powers of the society but the people themselves; and if we think them not enlightened enough to exercise their control with a wholesome discretion, the remedy is not to take it from them, but to inform their discretion.

This piece of wisdom implies, among other things, that a democratic government operates at its peril if it becomes so arrogant that it makes important decisions without informing, involving, and taking guidance from average citizens, and it should never underestimate the citizens' ability to understand. Jefferson is warning us not to lose touch. He is not recommending that all technical decisions of a government agency be made only through town meetings. But his statement is a persuasive argument for broader inclusion of the public in the basic decisions that determine the direction of all the policy minutiae that follows.

It is becoming clearer to those involved in this debate that risk-based decision making should be based on a synthesis of inputs broader and deeper than was envisioned in the past. Risk-based priority setting will be a major element of

the kind of informed and effective dialogue that raises the quality of environmental action across the board, especially in the state and federal legislatures. To achieve this, though, we need a more participatory model of prioritization—a risk system much broader than the stereotypical one in which "experts" make their pronouncements about risks with clinical dispassion; one which is an organic part of a broad-based, decision-making process in which equity, social concerns, fiscal feasibility, technological innovation, and legislative mandates are fully considered alongside the science.

To ensure a proper place for comparative risk in developing environmental priorities, we must build the strongest possible foundation of individual risk assessments. I see three basic guiding principles in the building of that foundation. The first involves an early step in the risk assessment process, the characterization of risk. A memorandum on the subject issued in February 1992 provided that EPA needs to offer more useful information when characterizing a given risk—we need to give more accurate predictions than a single point estimate would allow, and we need to evaluate more realistic exposure situations than the unlikely worst-case scenarios sometimes used as the basis for policy. We must characterize individual risks using straightforward, consistent terminology identifying uncertainties and data gaps so that both experts and citizens can more easily compare one risk to another.

This challenge remains enormously important as more attention is focused on the need to take into account both hard science factors and societal elements in the comparison of risks. The question "What is really at stake here?" will need to be answered realistically and usefully, again and again, in terms that all can understand.

The second guiding principle is the need to bring varied expertise into the risk assessment process from the earliest stage. Our work in relative risk stands much less chance of acceptance if the common perception persists that assessments of specific risks emerge from a black box. Therefore, just as the whole enterprise of priority setting needs to be broadly inclusive, the work of our Agency professionals in working through the important issues of specific risks needs to be exposed to the critical eye of independent experts, peers, and

colleagues in their fields. This both enhances the quality of the work and maximizes the number of people who understand what the work attempts to accomplish.

The Agency's existing peer review process should be expanded as far as possible into the earliest segments of the life cycle of our risk-related work, and active peer involvement in the characterization and assessment of individual risks should become standard procedure. We are implementing the recommendations made by the SAB and an independent panel in the March 1992 report *Credible Science, Credible Decisions* by establishing science advisors for the Administrator and Assistant Administrators, and I hope future administrations build on this collegial network.

We have also participated extensively in interagency organizations such as the Risk Assessment Working Group of the Federal Coordinating Council on Science Engineering and Technology (FCCSET), mindful that cross-pollinating expertise and real coordination on cross-cutting issues with other parts of the government can improve the quality of our work. This cooperation must continue and must extend not only to specific risk assessments but also to the important guidelines that are establishing the state of the art in process and methods for cancer, noncancer, and ecological risk end points.

The third guiding principle we must observe in building a foundation of credible risk assessment is the need for basic research and state-of-the-environment data. One of the most fundamental reasons for the controversy surrounding the uses of relative risk is the persistent belief that our risk assessments are based on default assumptions rather than on hard facts. Simply put, facts and hard conclusions from data are better than estimates based on extrapolations and interpolations. Facts are what our research operations must give our risk assessors if their work is to have dependable credibility at the priority-setting table. These facts can then be brought to life through advanced computer visualizations in geographic information systems, which will allow us to target risks and develop more meaningful geographic strategies.

Even if these principles are followed and our risk assessments become more widely accepted, there will remain major legislative barriers to the widespread use of relative risk, which makes it imperative that Congress be an integral part of the dialogue. As it stands now, EPA policy makers implementing risk-based priority setting can have an impact only at the margins of funding. The two funds set up for construction of wastewater treatment plants and the cleanup of abandoned hazardous waste sites under Superfund dwarf all other EPA spending areas, accounting in fiscal year (FY) 1990 for over 70 percent of the Agency's $6 billion budget. Only 16 percent of the full budget is allocated toward the higher risk areas identified by the SAB in *Reducing Risk*. In FY 1992, for example, indoor radon, indoor air, stratospheric ozone, and climate change accounted for a little more than 2 percent of our total budget, although they were listed by the SAB as high risk.

Adding to the pressure is spending for congressional projects: In FY 1993, Congress added about 100 specific items while approving an essentially flat budget from FY 1992. These new responsibilities have to be met at the expense of both existing Agency priorities and new initiatives. To be sure, there is not always a direct correlation between funding levels and results—EPA programs such as "Green Lights" prove that rich results can be achieved through small budgetary investments. These budgetary facts do indicate, however,

that comparative risk has a long way to go before it becomes a dominant element of priority setting at EPA.

Nevertheless, there are a number of things going on within EPA to prepare the way for a more inclusive and more credible role for comparative risk in priority setting. The current dioxin reassessment sparked by new findings on the mechanisms of dioxin toxicity, has been widely praised as evidence that the Agency will practice what it preaches concerning dedication to good science and meaningful risk assessment, and has involved both extensive peer review and public participation. Agency professionals used the techniques of inclusion in the development of the forthcoming neurotoxicity and immunotoxicity guidelines, and EPA this vulnerability must be addressed if we are to bring the credibility of the information up to par with the influence that this very important database has developed since it became public in 1988. (See box, at left, on IRIS and its present reassessment.)

The Environmental Monitoring and Assessment Program, or EMAP, is a centerpiece of the Agency's enhanced focus on risks to the ecological health of regions and ecosystems. Yet the massive amounts of information gained from the environmental indicators it monitors form so broad a cut of cloth

that there is a real challenge to link this information to new, concrete understandings about risk, and then to develop indicators that measure the progress of our prevention programs. And, in the wake of the June 1992 United Nations Conference on Environment and Development in Rio de Janeiro, risk assessment will necessarily be an international issue as well, and the Agency will have a direct stake in the attempt to build upon the work of the U.N.'s Organization for Economic Cooperation and Development in coordinating risk assessment activities by scientists and governments around the globe.

Government cannot do everything, and the question of which things matter the most is inevitable. Environmental decision making in a democracy is not a math problem. As a result, comparative risk will never be the only criterion for setting priorities. But if EPA's findings are built upon a foundation of good science and the public is fully informed and involved in the dialogue, then comparative risk will be an increasingly important factor. By building integrated strategies based upon solid facts, and by harnessing the power of communities and markets, I am absolutely confident EPA can stimulate entire new generations of clean production and give new expression to the concept of "sustainable development." □

APPENDIX **XXXV**

SOURCE:

USEPA; Community Right-to-Know and Small Business; Understanding Sections 311 and 312 of the Emergency Planning and Community Right-to-Know Act of 1986

SARA Title III Inventory Reporting, Tiers I and II

Sections 311 and 312 of Title III—popularly named community right- to-know—are the focus of this brochure.

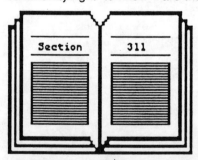

These provisions, which affect facilities where hazardous` chemicals are present, require submission of data on the amount, type and location of those substances. The collected data serve as an essential informational tool for local planners and response personnel, providing the basis for the emergency planning process of Title III.

Perhaps most important, fire departments and health officials can tap this wealth of knowledge. At present, firefighters face great risks in battling chemical blazes at factories, small businesses, hospitals, schools. Many chemicals demand special precautions and techniques. If used correctly, Title III information can provide emergency workers with vital data, enabling them to respond safely to chemical accidents. Likewise, medical personnel require ready access to such

storage data. Unusual symptoms caused by chemical spills demand immediate attention. Title III will help.

Sections 311 and 312 also create a new entitlement. The public in _every_ state now has the "right-to-know" about hazardous chemicals present at facilities located in the community. Now, any citizen can request such detailed information. Never before have data on chemical use been so accessible to the public. And never before have so many businesses been potentially affected by a reporting regulation. All companies, large or small, manufacturing or non-manufacturing, may be subject to this inventory reporting.

Since the law includes a sector unaccustomed to such reporting requirements—the small business community—special help is being offered in this brochure.

These opening pages provide a brief overview of Title III. The bulk of the brochure details in step-by-step fashion the community right-to-know requirements and allows you, the small business owner, to determine whether you must report, and if so, what. The final pages provide other help, such as an index of the terms and acronyms used in the brochure, and a

818

reference guide of useful contacts, phone numbers and addresses.

Every effort has been taken to clarify the community right-to-know reporting requirements of Title III. The goal is to assist you in complying with the law—an action serving everyone's interests. Though the reporting responsibilities will require extra effort on your part, you will gain through emergency response plans for your facility, improved relations with your community, and perhaps, better management and chemical handling practices. And compliance with Title III will save you from fines of up to $25,000 per day.

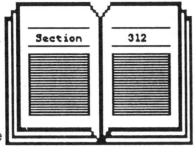

Reporting Requirements

Background - Hazard Communication Standard

The community right-to-know reporting requirements

NOTICE

Under Title III, states have the authority to go beyond the reporting requirements written in the law. Title III is the base for right-to-know reporting—it is the minimum. Since your state law may be stricter than Title III, please check wiith your State Emergency Response Commission to make sure that your submissions meet all necessary requirements.

build on the Occupational Safety and Health Administration's (OSHA) Hazard Communication Standard (HCS). The hazardous chemicals defined by the HCS are the hazardous chemicals of Sections 311 and 312. Initially, the HCS applied only to manufacturers (designated by the Standard Industrial Classification (SIC) codes 20 - 39). However, in 1987, OSHA amended the regulation to incorporate all

businesses, regardless of classification or size. As a result, your small business may now be subject to community right-to-know reporting.

Under the Hazard Communication Standard, chemical manufacturers and importers must research the chemicals they produce and import. If a substance presents any of the physical and health hazards specified in the HCS, then the manufacturer or importer must communicate the hazards and cautions to their employees as well as to "downstream" employers who purchase the hazardous chemical. The goal behind the HCS is a safer workplace—workers, informed of the hazards they encounter on the job, can create that environment.

One of the required tools of hazard communication is the *Material Safety Data Sheet (MSDS)*. These documents provide many valuable details on the hazardous chemicals regulated by OSHA. Quite likely, you are already familiar with these useful documents. If not, you must become so. The MSDS contains health and safety information for you, and due to the relationship of Title III and the Hazard Communication Standard, having an MSDS indicates that you have a hazardous chemical which may require reporting under Sections 311 and 312.

Though the Hazard Communication Standard contains no formal list of chemicals, any of roughly 500,000 products may trigger the requirement. The responsibility for issuing current MSDSs rests with chemical manufacturers, distributors and importers, but the chemical user must ensure proper and complete maintenance of MSDS files. This will help you comply fully with Title III.

Congress chose to link Title III's community right-to-know rules to the Hazard Communication Standard because both share a common goal of safety—Title III for the community and the HCS for the workplace. Understanding that connection is helpful. Although the community right-to-know rules are associated with the HCS, the Title III provisions are not redundant requirements. Instead, Title III extends the information sharing of workplace right-to-know to the entire community, especially to emergency response personnel.

Do I Have To Report?

To answer the question "Do I have to report?" you should examine four criteria—type of facility, presence of hazardous chemicals, amount present, and any applicable exemptions. As you consider each of these, the chart below will help you determine your reporting status. Simply proceed through the brochure, referring to the chart as necessary.

Note: this section details "automatic" reporting only. Facilities which are not required to report automatically must still report when citizens request data. (See page 15)

1. Facility

As noted earlier, due to the expansion of the Hazard Communication Standard, all businesses may be

1. Type of Facility

Manufacturer (Standard Industrial Classification codes 20 - 39) Follow first set of dates on page 7.		Non-manufacturer (Regulated under the expansion of the Hazard Communication Standard i.e. outside SIC codes 20 - 39) Follow second set of dates on page 7.	
CRITERIA		RESULT *	
		MUST REPORT (all "Yes")	DO NOT REPORT (any "No")
2.	Do you have a hazardous chemical (includes extremely hazardous substances) present at your facility requiring a Material Safety Data Sheet under the Hazard Communication Standard? (see page 5)	YES	NO STOP
3.	Do you have a hazardous chemical (includes extremely hazardous substances) at your facility not exempt under the five exemptions of Title III? (see page 5)	YES	NO STOP
4.	Do you have an extremely hazardous substance or other hazardous chemical at your facility with its maximum amount greater than the relevant threshold? (see pages 5-6) EHS-500 pounds or the chemical-specific threshold planning quantity, OR Hazardous (Non-EHS) - 10,000 pounds	YES All YES Report	NO STOP

* If you answer "NO" to any of the three questions (2-4), then you are not required to report automatically under Sections 311 and 312 of Title III. If you answer "YES" to all of these three questions, then you must submit the reports to your State Emergency Response Commission, Local Emergency Planning Committee and local fire department.

subject to community right-to-know reporting. However, the Sections 311 and 312 reporting deadlines for manufacturers (designated by SIC codes 20-39) differ from the deadlines facing the non-manufacturing community. The non-manufacturers' deadlines lag behind those for the manufacturers by almost one year. All the pertinent dates for the two sectors are noted on page 7.

Beyond these differences in dates, though, all facilities are treated alike. Any business with one or more hazardous chemicals <u>may</u> have to report under community right-to-know.

2. Substances

The Material Safety Data Sheet (MSDS) serves as the indicator of hazardous chemicals at your facility. If you are <u>not required</u> to prepare or keep any MSDSs, then you have no hazardous chemicals, as defined by the Hazard Communication Standard, at your facility. You do <u>not</u> need to report. The "No" in the "Do Not Report" column indicates that you have fulfilled the mandatory reporting requirements for Sections 311 and 312. On the other hand, if you must prepare or maintain <u>any</u> MSDSs, mark down a "Yes" to the question and continue reading. You <u>may</u> be required to report.

3. Exemptions

There are five exemptions from reporting requirements for community right-to-know. Some apply to specific chemicals and some to specific chemical uses.

1) Any food, food additive, color additive, drug, or cosmetic regulated by the Food and Drug Administration (FDA) is exempt from reporting. With regard to food additives, a chemical is a food additive only when in <u>use</u> as a food additive, and not when it is stored or used for other purposes, or is being sold to another business for use as a food additive.

2) Any hazardous chemical present as a solid in a manufactured item to the extent exposure to that chemical does not occur under normal conditions of <u>use</u> is exempt. For example, steel would be exempt in its solid form until you weld it, cut it, grind it or do anything else that could cause exposure to hazards such as lead, dusts or hazardous fumes.

3) Any substance used for personal, family or household purposes, or if present in the same form and concentration as a product packaged for distribution to and use by the general public. <u>Packaging</u>, not use, triggers the exemption. Regardless of actual use and intended distribution, if the substance is packaged in a similar way and in the same concentration as it is when used by the general public, then that substance is exempt. For example, a cleaner used by your business and <u>packaged for home use</u> remains exempt no matter how you use it. However, the same cleaner, packaged in bulk amounts not intended for sale to home users, must be reported.

4) Any substance is exempt to the extent it is used in a research laboratory, hospital or other medical facility under the direct supervision of a technically qualified individual. Quality assurance labs meet the exemption, but pilot testing labs, where manufacturing of a product takes place, do not.

5) Any substance used in routine agricultural operations or any fertilizer held for sale by a retailer to the ultimate customer is exempt. Again, this exemption applies only if you are the <u>user</u> of the chemical, or in the case of fertilizers, if you are a retailer holding the fertilizer for sale to the ultimate customer.

Please note, there are additional exemptions in the Hazard Communication Standard (HCS) governing the preparation and maintenance requirements for Material Safety Data Sheets. However, the five exemptions noted here are the only ones that limit the scope of the HCS. So, if <u>all</u> of the hazardous chemicals present at your facility are exempt, then insert a "No" in that column of the chart. If any of your hazardous chemicals fail to meet these exemptions, then enter a "Yes" and proceed.

4. Thresholds

To ease everyone's information management burden created under community right-to-know, the Environmental Protection Agency (EPA) established reporting thresholds for the first two years of reporting. That means that any chemical present at your facility, <u>always</u> in an amount less than its threshold level, does not need to be automatically reported (examples page 6).

In addition to the "hazardous chemicals" (those indicated by a Material Safety Data Sheet), you need to be aware of a subset of these chemicals, the List of Extremely Hazardous Substances (EHS). The extremely hazardous substances—all included as "hazardous chemicals" under the Hazard Communication Standard (i.e. all require a MSDS)—were listed initially in the November 17, 1986 Federal Register. Since then, 40 of them have been removed from the list after public comment. Revised lists can be obtained from your State Emergency Response Commission (SERC) or Local Emergency Planning Committee (LEPC). Also, you can write the Emergency Planning and Community Right-To-Know Information Line for a copy. That address and those for the SERCs are noted in the Appendices at the back of this brochure.

This list of extremely hazardous substances, consisting currently of 366 acutely toxic substances, repre-

Hazardous Chemicals designated by the Hazard Communication Standard

10,000 Pounds (unless defined as an extremely hazardous substance under Title III)

366 Extremely Hazardous Substances

500 Pounds or Threshold Planning Quantity, whichever is lower

sents the priority chemicals of the emergency planning effort. Accordingly, reporting thresholds are lower for the extremely hazardous substances than for the non-EHS hazardous chemicals, and each EHS chemical boasts its own threshold planning quantity (TPQ). The TPQ stipulates a storage level of concern for the substance if the entire quantity of that substance were released. Based on the toxicity and mobility of the chemical, the TPQ provides a reporting threshold reflecting health and safety concerns. The TPQ for each of these chemicals is noted on the List of Extremely Hazardous Substances.

When considering thresholds, you must first determine whether or not the hazardous chemical is an extremely hazardous substance. Reporting thresh-

olds vary between these two groups. Those chemicals on the *EHS list* trip the threshold if present *above 500 pounds or the chemical-specific TPQ, whichever is lower*. Those *hazardous chemicals* not on the EHS list require reporting if stored *above 10,000 pounds*. For example, if you own a dry cleaning facility and never store perchloroethylene (a hazardous chemical) in a quantity greater than 5,000 pounds, then you are not required to report because the threshold for that chemical of 10,000 pounds was not exceeded. However, a recreational swimming pool with 5,000 pounds of chlorine (an extremely hazardous substance) surpasses the relevant 500 pound threshold and its threshold planning quantity of 100 pounds. (For EHS, always use the lower of 500 pounds or the TPQ).

After determining the "maximum amount" (see page 12 of the Questions & Answers) of all your non-exempt extremely hazardous substances and hazardous chemicals, check the chart for thresholds and respond appropriately. A "No" signifies that you do not need to report under community right-to-know. A "Yes" means you may need to report.

Please note, after the first two years of Title III reporting—for manufacturers October 1989, and for non-manufacturers September 1990--these threshold levels may change. Also, since the thresholds depend on pounds of the substance present at your facility, you may need to convert the measure of some gases and liquids from volume to weight (see page 13 of the Questions & Answers). A similar discussion of mixtures can be found on page 16 of the Q & A Appendix. Again, it must be emphasized that if your inventory ever exceeds the threshold ("maximum amount" exceeds the threshold), for any length of time, then your reporting requirement is triggered.

In summary, if you answered "No" to any of the questions in the chart, then you are not required to report under Sections 311 and 312 of Title III. In other words, if you maintain no MSDSs, store no extremely hazardous substances and no hazardous chemicals above their respective thresholds, or are exempt for every reportable chemical at your facility, then you need not report automatically under community right-to-know. However, if you answered "Yes" to all of the questions, then you must report.

PLEASE NOTE: An average 55-gallon drum of chemicals weighs approximately 500 lbs., the EHS threshold.

How Do I Report?

Community right-to-know is a multi-step process for reporting, with different deadlines for manufacturers and non-manufacturers. Non-manufacturers report one year later than the manufacturers. The dates noted below highlight the timing for right-to-know requirements.

The reporting provisions of Sections 311 and 312 require submission of information to the State Emergency Response Commission (SERC), the Local Emergency Planning Committee (LEPC) and the local fire department. Both your SERC and your LEPC are newly formed under Title III. They are the heart of the system. To obtain the addresses of these groups, check the Appendix at the end of this brochure for State Emergency Response Commissions and EPA Regional Offices. The SERC should be able to supply you with the address of your LEPC. Or, you could contact the appropriate Regional Office of the Environmental Protection Agency and obtain the information on the SERC and LEPC there.

Though Section 311 requires no special forms, you are responsible for obtaining the necessary report forms for Section 312. The Local Emergency Planning Committee and/or your State Emergency Response Commission will serve as the key contacts. For Section 312 reports, you will need <u>one</u> of two

1987 October 17 — <u>Manufacturing</u> facilities subject to reporting under Sections 311-312 submit either Material Safety Data Sheets or a **list** of the reportable hazardous chemicals present at their facility to the State Emergency Response Commission, Local Emergency Planning Committee and fire department.

Beginning March 1, 1988 and continuing annually thereafter.... <u>Manufacturing</u> facilities subject to reporting under Sections 311-312 submit either Tier I or **Tier II** forms to the State Emergency Response Commission, Local Emergency Planning Committee and fire department. **1988 March 1**

Key Reporting Dates for Manufacturers
(Standard Industrial Classification codes 20 - 39)

1988 Sept. 24 — <u>Non-manufacturing</u> facilities subject to reporting under Sections 311-312 (see pages 4-6) submit either Material Safety Data Sheets or a **list** of the reportable hazardous chemicals present at their facility to the State Emergency Response Commission, Local Emergency Planning Committee and fire department.

Beginning March 1, 1989 and continuing annually thereafter.... <u>Non-manufacturing</u> facilities subject to reporting under Sections 311-312 (see pages 4-6) submit either Tier I or **Tier II** forms to the State Emergency Response Commission, Local Emergency Planning Committee and fire department. **1989 March 1**

Key Reporting Dates for Non-manufacturers
(outside Standard Industrial Classification codes 20 - 39)

annual inventory forms, namely a Tier I form <u>or</u> a Tier II form. A facility must submit only one Tier I form annually. However, if you submit a Tier II instead, entries must be made for each reportable chemical at your facility. Since each Tier II form provides room for only three chemicals, you may need several copies.

What Do I Report?

Now that you have learned of your reporting responsibility, you must choose the best method for reporting. Though Sections 311 and 312 of Title III share both a foundation in the Hazard Communication Standard and the thresholds for reporting, the two provisions entail separate reporting requirements. Section 311 involves a <u>one-time</u> submission (with any necessary updates) naming the reportable hazardous chemicals present at your facility. Section 312 remains an <u>annual</u> responsibility, demanding more detailed information on your chemical hazards and handling practices.

Section 311

Again, you need no special forms under Section 311. Instead, the Material Safety Data Sheets at your facility are your key resources. Simply compile all of these MSDSs. After taking out those hazardous chemicals exempted by Title III and those present below their thresholds, submit either copies of the remaining MSDSs or a single list of these chemicals, grouped by hazard category, to your State Emergency Response Commission (SERC), Local Emergency Planning Committee (LEPC) and local fire department.

EPA recommends that you supply the list of your reportable chemicals rather than the actual MSDSs. The list will reduce your effort by removing the necessity of copying in triplicate all reportable MSDSs. It will also enhance the capacity of the three recipients—SERC, LEPC and fire department—to manage your data responsibly and effectively. However, if you do opt for submitting the list, then when necessary, the Local Emergency Planning Committee can request substantiating MSDSs as supplemental information. You have a 30 day period to comply with such a request. As noted above, the list must also be grouped by hazard category (described on page 14 of the Questions & Answers). Despite these added steps, the chemical list should greatly ease your reporting effort.

Both the list and the Material Safety Data Sheets should include the reportable hazardous chemicals present at your facility on your date of compliance.

The list or MSDSs were first due for the manufacturing sector on October 17, 1987, and are now required for non-manufacturing businesses no later than September 24,1988. If at any time after this initial submission you obtain a new, non-reported substance, or a hazardous chemical in your inventory exceeds its threshold for the first time, then either an updated list or the relevant MSDS must be sent to the State Emergency Response Commission, Local Emergency Planning Committee and fire department. You have 3 months to comply with this provision.

Section 312

Section 312, unlike Section 311, is an annual reporting requirement and cannot be fulfilled by a one-time submission. Each year on March 1 (beginning for manufacturers in 1988 and for non-manufacturers in 1989), reporting facilities must submit reports on their inventories of hazardous chemicals. The reports,

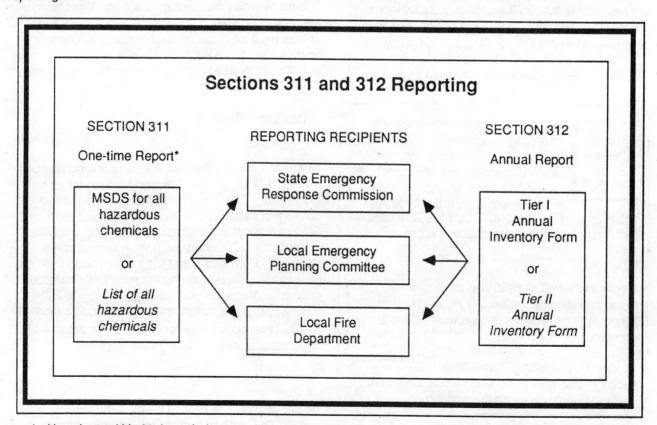

Sections 311 and 312 Reporting

SECTION 311

One-time Report*

MSDS for all hazardous chemicals

or

List of all hazardous chemicals

REPORTING RECIPIENTS

State Emergency Response Commission

Local Emergency Planning Committee

Local Fire Department

SECTION 312

Annual Report

Tier I Annual Inventory Form

or

Tier II Annual Inventory Form

* with updates within 90 days of when you obtain a new, non-reported substance or when a hazardous chemical in your inventory exceeds its threshold for the first time

which cover the preceding year, can be submitted either on the Tier I or Tier II form. Though Title III requires the Tier I submission, facilities may opt for the Tier II instead. **The Environmental Protection Agency strongly recommends submission of the Tier II.**

The Tier I and Tier II forms solicit similar information, including facility identification, types of substances by hazard category (see page 14 of Questions & Answers), and amounts and locations of hazardous chemicals in storage. Tier I simply compiles the information by hazard category, whereas Tier II asks for specific details on each hazardous chemical. The Tier II form demands more data, but actually serves as a first step to the Tier I. The Tier II offers another advantage—updating your inventory upon receipt of a new hazardous chemical builds more easily from the Tier II base than from the Tier I .

Therefore, while a Tier I report satisfies the law just as fully, you will probably choose to submit the Tier II in its place. By-passing the Tier I submission with the Tier II may save your company valuable time.

How Will This Information Be Used?

Now that you have fulfilled the reporting requirements of Sections 311 and 312, you understand the enormity of the information flow generated by Title III. With roughly 5 million facilities in the country as potential reporters, community right-to-know will create a wealth of chemical information. Effective management and use of that data must follow.

Exactly what groups and uses will community right-to-know reporting serve? As noted earlier, the **lists** (or Material Safety Data Sheets) of your reportable chemicals and your **Tier II** (or Tier I) data must be sent to three recipients—the State Emergency Response Commission, the Local Emergency Planning Committee and your local fire department. Each of these groups performs a role in Title III. The SERC integrates all the chemical-user data gathered across the state, enabling the accomplishment of state-wide goals. The LEPC, including all the affected sectors in the community (your neighbors), develops emergency response plans for the community. Fire departments, who also participate actively in the planning phase, can learn methods and precautions required in various emergencies. And public health officials, though not direct data recipients, will gain from Title III information.

HOW DO I REPORT-SUMMARY

If you must report under community right-to-know—i.e. you store, use or produce chemicals, requiring maintenance of a Material Safety Data Sheet under the Hazard Communication Standard, that are present at your facility in excess of the appropriate threshold, and are not exempt under Title III—then you must submit both Section 311 and Section 312 information.

Section 311 • copies of the MSDSs of all those chemicals requiring reporting, OR
• **a single list of all those chemicals requiring reporting, grouped by hazard category,**
must be sent to the State Emergency Response Commission, Local Emergency Planning Committee and the local fire department, one time, with updates to reflect changes in your inventory.

Section 312 • the aggregate Tier I information on all those chemicals requiring reporting, grouped by hazard category, OR
• **the chemical-specific Tier II data on all those chemicals requiring reporting,**
must be sent to the SERC, LEPC and the local fire department, annually every March 1.

Because the inventory reports involve so much effort and provide such value, a detailed Question & Answer section focusing on the Tier I and Tier II forms is included at the end of this brochure. These hints coupled with the instructions on each form should cover all of your concerns. If not, then please contact either your LEPC or SERC, or the Emergency Planning and Community Right-To-Know Information Line. All SERC addresses and that of the Information Line are noted in the Appendices.

The LEPCs' emergency response plans play the critical role in the Title III effort. These plans are  designed to identify the major chemical dangers facing communities, so in the event of an accident, full knowledge of the hazards and proper emergency preparation will be readily available to the emergency responders. Community right-to-know reporting suppports that process by collecting the essential data.

In addition to the established groups in the Title III structure, there will be another key participant—the general public. Perhaps, most important of all, Title III gave the community its right-to-know about chemical usage in the neighborhood. **Even If you have no chemicals that trigger thresholds, you, the small business owner, may be required to provide your community with Information about chemical usage and storage practices.** Anyone can request your Material Safety Data Sheets and Tier II forms by writing their Local Emergency Planning Committee and you have 30 days to respond.

Just as the public can make requests beyond Title III reporting requirements, the State Emergency Response Commissions, Local Emergency Planning Committees and fire departments can ask for extra data on your chemicals, too. Only through broad access to chemical data can public officials plan fully for accidents and chart possible long-term health problems caused by hazardous chemicals. Though such right-to-know requirements can be burdensome, the value justifies the effort of the participants.

Trade Secrets

In some manufacturing processes and business practices, strict confidentiality must be maintained as protection against competitor firms. Section 311 and 312 disclosures can threaten that secrecy. For this reason, companies can claim a chemical identity as a trade secret and modify this reporting requirement. Section 311 and 312 information must still be reported to the State Emergency Response Commission, Local Emergency Planning Committee and fire department, but the detail of the submission is reduced. A valid trade secret claim can protect the name of your hazardous chemical. Please note, since trade secrets can be claimed by suppliers, some downstream businesses may find themselves lacking the specific chemical identity information on their hazardous chemicals. In these instances, businesses can simply use the trade name of the substance in reporting under Sections 311 and 312. They will not need to make a trade secret claim.

Trade secret claims must be legitimate and must be substantiated upon submission of your community right-to-know information. This is accomplished through completion of a trade secret substantiation form, which you can obtain from EPA Headquarters in Washington, D.C. The actual trade secret claims and substantiations should be sent to the following address.

Emergency Planning & Community Right-to-Know
P.O. Box 79266
Washington, D.C. 20024-0266

In making any trade secret claims, please follow the guidelines in the Federal Register (see page 20) explicitly. Incorrect submissions will not only jeopardize your trade secret claim, but may also result in a fine. All justifications--safeguards taken to protect your secret, the harm incurred in the event of disclosure, and proof that no other federal or state law requires the information and that discovery of the secret is impossible through reverse engineering-- must be sent to the address above. There are strict rules in making trade secret claims, and your requests may be challenged by the public or reviewed by the EPA, so deny access to data only under vital and certain circumstances. Trade secret claims found to be frivolous can result in a fine of $25,000.

Conclusion

Community right-to-know reporting creates many new responsibilities and tasks for you, the small business owner--from the time involved in reporting to any emergency planning duties resulting from your storage of extremely hazardous substances. However, the value of the program justifies this endeavor.

You and your community will benefit from enhanced safety. The emergency response plans developed from community right-to-know data will serve small businesses well. Now, in the event of an accident at your facility, fire fighters can protect you better; medical personnel can treat unusual chemical symptoms faster; property and lives may be saved. Also, the communication channels between chemical users and the public will be more effective. Finally, Title III may teach you valuable lessons about the hazardous chemicals used at your business. In fact, you may decide to substitute certain less hazardous substances for those you currently store, or you may simply improve your handling practices. And you can also avoid the costly fines threatened under Title III.

Tier One

EMERGENCY AND HAZARDOUS CHEMICAL INVENTORY
Aggregate Information by Hazard Type

FOR OFFICIAL USE ONLY

C #

Date Received

Important: Read instructions before completing form

Reporting Period   From January 1 to December 31, 19 _____

Facility Identification

Name _____

Street _____

City _____ County _____ State _____ Zip _____

SIC Code [ ][ ][ ][ ]   Dun & Brad Number [ ][ ] - [ ][ ][ ] - [ ][ ][ ]

Owner/Operator

Name _____

Mail Address _____

Phone (____) _____

Emergency Contacts

Name _____

Title _____

Phone (____) _____

24 Hour Phone (____) _____

Name _____

Title _____

Phone (____) _____

24 Hour Phone (____) _____

[ ] Check if information below is identical to the information submitted last year.

[ ] Check if site plan is attached

Hazard Type	Max Amount*	Average Daily Amount*	Number of Days On–Site	General Location

Physical Hazards

Fire [ ][ ] [ ][ ] [ ][ ][ ] _____

Sudden Release of Pressure [ ][ ] [ ][ ] [ ][ ][ ] _____

Reactivity [ ][ ] [ ][ ] [ ][ ][ ] _____

Health Hazards

Immediate (acute) [ ][ ] [ ][ ] [ ][ ][ ] _____

Delayed (Chronic) [ ][ ] [ ][ ] [ ][ ][ ] _____

Certification   *(Read and sign after completing all sections)*

I certify under penalty of law that I have personally examined and am familiar with the information submitted in pages one through _____, and that based on my inquiry of those individuals responsible for obtaining the information, I believe that the submitted information is true, accurate and complete.

_____
Name and official title of owner/operator OR owner/operator's authorized representative

_____   _____
Signature   Date signed

*	**Reporting Ranges**	
Range Code	**Weight Range in Pounds**	
	From...	To...
01	0	99
02	100	999
03	1000	9,999
04	10,000	99,999
05	100,000	999,999
06	1,000,000	9,999,999
07	10,000,000	49,999,999
08	50,000,000	99,999,999
09	100,000,000	499,999,999
10	500,000,000	999,999,999
11	1 billion	higher than 1 billion

INSTRUCTIONS

Please read these instructions carefully. Print or type all responses.

You may use the Tier Two form as a worksheet for completing Tier One. Filling in the Tier Two chemical information section should help you assemble your Tier One responses.

If your responses require more than one page, fill in the page number at the top of the form

REPORTING PERIOD
Enter the appropriate calendar year, beginning January 1 and ending December 31.

FACILITY IDENTIFICATION
Enter the complete name of your facility (and company identifier where appropriate).

Enter the full street address or state road. If a street address is not available, enter other appropriate identifiers that describe the physical location of your facility (e.g., longitude and latitude). Include city, county, state, and zip code.

Enter the primary Standard Industrial Classification (SIC) code and the Dun & Bradstreet number for your facility. The financial officer of your facility should be able to provide the Dun & Bradstreet number. If your firm does not have this information, contact the State or regional office of Dun & Bradstreet to obtain your facility number or have one assigned.

OWNER/OPERATOR
Enter the owner's or operator's full name, mailing address, and phone number.

EMERGENCY CONTACT
Enter the name, title, and work phone number of at least one local person or office that can act as a referral if emergency responders need assistance in responding to a chemical accident at the facility.

Provide an emergency phone number where such emergency information will be available 24 hours a day, every day. This requirement is mandatory. The facility must make some arrangement to ensure that a 24 hour contact is available.

IDENTICAL INFORMATION
Check the box indicating identical information, located below the emergency contacts on the Tier One form, if the current information being reported is identical to that submitted last year. Chemical descriptions, amounts, and locations must be provided in this year's form, even if the information is identical to that submitted last year.

PHYSICAL AND HEALTH HAZARDS
Descriptions, Amounts, and Locations

This section requires aggregate information on chemicals by hazard categories as defined in 40 CFR 370.2. The two health hazard categories and three physical hazard categories are a consolidation of the 23 hazard categories defined in OSHA Hazard Communication Standard, 29 CFR 1910.1200. For each hazard type, indicate the total amounts and general locations of all applicable chemicals present at your facility during the past year.

Hazard Category Comparison For Reporting Under Sections 311 and 312	
EPA's Hazard Categories	OSHA's Hazard Categories
Fire Hazard	Flammable Combustion Liquid Pyrophoric Oxidizer
Sudden Release of Pressure	Explosive Compressed Gas
Reactive	Unstable Reactive Organic Peroxide Water Reactive
Immediate (Acute) Health Hazards	Highly Toxic Toxic Irritant Sensitizer Corrosive
	Other hazardous chemicals with an adverse effect with short term exposure
Delayed (Chronic) Health Hazard	Carcinogens
	Other hazardous chemicals with an adverse effect with long term exposure

- What units should I use?

Calculate all amounts as *weight in pounds*. To convert gas or liquid volume to weight in pounds, multiply by an appropriate density factor.

INSTRUCTIONS

Please read these instructions carefully. Print or type all responses.

• What about mixtures?

If a chemical is part of a mixture, *you have the option* of reporting either the weight of the entire mixture or only the portion of the mixture that is a particular hazardous chemical (e.g., if a hazardous solution weighs 100 lbs. but is composed of only 5% of a particular hazardous chemical, you can indicate either 100 lbs. of the mixture or 5 lbs. of the hazardous chemical).

The option used for each mixture must be consistent with the option used in your Section 311 reporting.

Because EHSs are important to Section 303 planning, EHSs have lower thresholds. The amount of an EHS at a facility (both pure EHS substances and EHSs in mixtures) must be aggregated for purposes of threshold determination. It is suggested that the aggregation calculation be done as a first step in making the threshold determination. Once you determine whether a threshold has been reached for an EHS, you should report either the total weight of the EHS at your facility, or the weight of each mixture containing the EHS.

• Where do I count a chemical that is a fire and reactive physical hazard and an immediate (acute) health hazard?

Add the chemical's weight to your totals for all three hazard categories and include its location in all three categories. Many chemicals fall into more than one hazard category.

3. For each hazard type—beginning with Fire and repeating for all physical and health hazard types . . .
   a. Add the maximum weights of all chemicals you indicated as the particular hazard type.
   b. Look at the Reporting Ranges at the bottom of the Tier One form. Find the appropriate range value code.
   c. Enter this range value as the Maximum Amount.

EXAMPLE:

You are using the Tier Two form as a worksheet and have listed raw weights in pounds for each of your hazardous chemicals. You have marked an X in the immediate (acute) hazard column for phenol and sulfuric acid. The maximum amount raw weight you listed were 10,000 lbs. and 500 lbs. respectively. You add these together to reach a total of 10,500 lbs. Then you look at the Reporting Range at the bottom of your Tier One form and find that the value of 04 corresponds to 10,500 lbs. Enter 04 as your Maximum Amount for immediate (acute) hazards materials.

You also marked an X in the Fire hazard box for phenol. When you calculate your Maximum Amount totals for fire hazards, add the 10,000 lb. weight again.

MAXIMUM AMOUNT

The amounts of chemicals you have on hand may vary throughout the year. The peak weights—greatest single-day weights during the year—are added together in this column to determine the maximum weight for each hazard type. Since the peaks for different chemicals often occur on different days, this maximum amount will seem artificially high.

To complete this and the following sections, you may choose to use the Tier Two form as a worksheet.

To determine the Maximum Amount:

1. List all of your reportable hazardous chemicals individually.

2. For each chemical . . .
   a. Indicate all physical and health hazards that the chemical presents. Include all chemicals, even if they are present for only a short period of time during the year.
   b. Estimate the maximum weight in pounds that was present at your facility on any single day of the reporting period.

AVERAGE DAILY AMOUNT

This column should represent the average daily amount of chemicals *of each hazard type* that were present at or above applicable thresholds at your facility at any point during the year.

To determine this amount:

1. List all of your reportable hazardous chemicals individually (same as for Maximum Amount).
2. For each chemical . . .
   a. Indicate all physical and health hazards that the chemical presents (same as for Maximum Amount).
   b. Estimate the average weight in pounds that was present at your facility throughout the year. To do this, total all daily weights and divide by the number of days the chemical was present on the site.
3. For each hazard type—beginning with Fire and repeating for all physical and health hazards . . .
   a. Add the average weights of all chemicals you indicated for the particular hazard type.
   b. Look at the Reporting Ranges at the bottom of the Tier One form. Find the appropriate range value code.
   c. Enter this range value as the Average Daily Amount.

INSTRUCTIONS

Please read these instructions carefully. Print or type all responses.

EXAMPLE:

You are using the Tier Two form, and have marked an X in the immediate (acute) hazard column for nicotine and phenol. Nicotine is present at your facility 100 days during the year, and the sum of the daily weights is 100,000 lbs. By dividing 100,000 lbs. by 100 days on-site, you calculate an Average Daily Amount of 1,000 lbs. for nicotine. Phenol is present at your facility 50 days during the year, and the sum of the daily weights is 10,000 lbs. By dividing 10,000 lbs. by 50 days on-site, you calculate an Average Daily Amount of 200 lbs. for phenol. You then add the two average daily amounts together to reach a total of 1,200 lbs. Then you look at the Reporting Range on your Tier One form and find that the value 03 corresponds to 1,200 lbs. Enter 03 as your Average Daily Amount for immediate (acute) Hazard.

You also marked an X in the Fire hazard column for phenol. When you calculate your Average Daily Amount for fire hazards, use the 200 lb. weight again.

NUMBER OF DAYS ON-SITE

Enter the greatest number of days that a single chemical within that hazard category was present on-site.

EXAMPLE:

At your facility, nicotine is present for 100 days and phosgene is present for 150 days. Enter 150 in the space provided.

GENERAL LOCATION

Enter the general location within your facility where each hazard may be found. General locations should include the names or identifications of buildings, tank fields, lots, sheds, or other such areas.

For each hazard type, list the locations of all applicable chemicals. As an alternative you may also attach a site plan and list the site coordinates related to the appropriate locations. If you do so, check the Site Plan box.

EXAMPLE:

On your worksheet you have marked an X in the Fire hazard column for acetone and butane. You noted that these are kept in steel drums in Room C of the Main Building, and in pressurized cylinders in Storage Shed 13, respectively. You could enter Main Building and Storage Shed 13 as the General Locations of your fire hazards. However, you choose to attach a site plan and list coordinates. Check the Site Plan box at the top of the column and enter site coordinates for the Main Building and Storage Shed 13 under General Locations.

If you need more space to list locations, attach an additional Tier One form and continue your list on the proper line. Number all pages.

CERTIFICATION

Instructions for this section are included on page one of these instructions.

Revised 11/99　　Important: Read all instructions before completing form　　Reporting period: From January 1 to December 31, 1999　　Page ___ of ___ pages

Right-to-Know FACILITY INVENTORY FORM TIER TWO

Facility Identification

Name _____
Street _____
City _____　State _____　Zip+4 _____
Telephone (___)　County _____
SIC Code [ ][ ][ ][ ]　Dun & Brad. Number [ ][ ][ ][ ][ ][ ]

For Official Use Only:　ID# [ ][ ][ ][ ][ ][ ][ ]　Date Received:

Owner/Operator

Name _____
Mail Address _____
Phone (___)

Emergency Contacts

Name _____　Title _____
Day Phone (___)　24-hr phone (___)
Name _____　Title _____
Day Phone (___)　24-hr phone (___)

Chemical Description | **Physical and Health Hazards** (Check all that apply) | **Inventory** | **Storage Codes and Locations** (Non-Confidential) *Storage Locations* | **OPTIONAL**

CAS [ ][ ][ ][ ][ ][ ]　[ ] Trade Secret
Name(s) of Chemical(s) _____
Check all that apply:
[ ] Pure [ ] Mix [ ] Solid [ ] Liquid [ ] Gas [ ] EHS

Fire [ ]　Sudden Release Of Pressure [ ]　Reactivity [ ]　Immediate (acute) [ ]　Delayed (chronic) [ ]

Max Amount (code) [ ][ ]
Avg. Amount (code) [ ][ ]
No. of Days Present [ ][ ]

Container / Pressure / Temperature (grid)

Check box if information submitted is identical to last year [ ]

CAS [ ][ ][ ][ ][ ][ ]　[ ] Trade Secret
Name(s) of Chemical(s) _____
Check all that apply:
[ ] Pure [ ] Mix [ ] Solid [ ] Liquid [ ] Gas [ ] EHS

Fire [ ]　Sudden Release Of Pressure [ ]　Reactivity [ ]　Immediate (acute) [ ]　Delayed (chronic) [ ]

Max Amount (code) [ ][ ]
Avg. Amount (code) [ ][ ]
No. of Days Present [ ][ ]

Container / Pressure / Temperature (grid)

Check box if information submitted is identical to last year [ ]

CAS [ ][ ][ ][ ][ ][ ]　[ ] Trade Secret
Name(s) of Chemical(s) _____
Check all that apply:
[ ] Pure [ ] Mix [ ] Solid [ ] Liquid [ ] Gas [ ] EHS

Fire [ ]　Sudden Release Of Pressure [ ]　Reactivity [ ]　Immediate (acute) [ ]　Delayed (chronic) [ ]

Max Amount (code) [ ][ ]
Avg. Amount (code) [ ][ ]
No. of Days Present [ ][ ]

Container / Pressure / Temperature (grid)

Check box if information submitted is identical to last year [ ]

OPTIONAL　I have attached a site plan [ ]

Certification (Read and sign after completing all sections)
I certify under penalty of law that I have personally examined and am familiar with the information submitted in pages one through _____, and that based on my inquiry of those individuals responsible for obtaining the information, I believe that the submitted information is true, accurate and complete.

Name and official title of owner/operator OR owner/operator's authorized representative _____　Signature _____　Date signed _____

INSTRUCTIONS

Please read these instructions carefully. Print or type all responses.

WHEN TO SUBMIT THIS FORM

Owners or operators of facilities that have hazardous chemicals on hand in quantities equal to or greater than set threshold levels must submit either Tier One or Tier Two forms by March 1.

If you choose to submit Tier One, rather than Tier Two, be aware that you may have to submit Tier Two information later, upon request of an authorized official. You must submit the Tier Two form within 30 days of receipt of a written request.

WHERE TO SUBMIT THIS FORM

Send either a completed Tier One form or Tier Two form(s) to each of the following organizations:
1. Your State Emergency Response Commission.
2. Your Local Emergency Planning Committee.
3. The fire department with jurisdiction over your facility.

If a Tier Two form is submitted in response to a request, send the completed form to the requesting agency.

PENALTIES

Any owner or operator who violates any Tier Two reporting requirements shall be liable to the United States for a civil penalty of up to $25,000 for each such violation. Each day a violation continues shall constitute a separate violation.

If your Tier Two responses require more than one page use additional forms and fill in the page number at the top of the form.

REPORTING PERIOD
Enter the appropriate calendar year, beginning January 1 and ending December 31.

FACILITY IDENTIFICATION
Enter the complete name of your facility (and company identifier where appropriate).

Enter the full street address or state road. If a street address is not available, enter other appropriate identifiers that describe the physical location of your facility (e.g., longitude and latitude). Include city, county, state, and zip code.

Enter the primary Standard Industrial Classification (SIC) code and the Dun & Bradstreet number for your facility. The financial officer of your facility should be able to provide the Dun & Bradstreet number. If your firm does not have this information, contact the State or regional office of Dun & Bradstreet to obtain your facility number or have one assigned.

OWNER/OPERATOR
Enter the owner's or operator's full name, mailing address, and phone number.

EMERGENCY CONTACT
Enter the name, title, and work phone number of at least one local person or office that can act as a referral if emergency responders need assistance in responding to a chemical accident at the facility.

Provide an emergency phone number where such emergency information will be available 24 hours a day, every day. This requirement is mandatory. The facility must make some arrangement to ensure that a 24 hour contact is available.

IDENTICAL INFORMATION
Check the box indicating identical information, located below the emergency contacts on the Tier Two form, if the current information being reported is identical to that submitted last year. Chemical descriptions, hazards, amounts, and locations must be provided in this year's form, even if the information is identical to that submitted last year.

CHEMICAL INFORMATION: Descriptions,
Hazards, Amounts, and Locations
This main section of the Tier Two form requires specific information on amounts and locations of hazardous chemicals, as defined in OSHA Hazard Communication Standard.

If you choose to indicate that all of the information on a specific hazardous chemical is identical to that submitted last year, check the appropriate optional box provided at the right side of the storage codes and locations on the Tier Two form. Chemical descriptions, hazards, amounts, and locations must be provided even if the information is identical to that submitted last year.

For each hazard type, indicate the total amounts and general locations of all applicable chemicals present at your facility during the past year.

- What units should I use?

  Calculate all amounts as *weight in pounds*. To convert gas or liquid volume to weight in pounds, multiply by an appropriate density factor.

- What about mixtures?

  If a chemical is part of a mixture, *you have the option* of reporting either the weight of the entire mixture or only the portion of the mixture that is a particular hazardous chemical (e.g., if a hazardous solution weighs 100 lbs. but is composed of only 5% of a particular hazardous chemical, you can indicate either 100 lbs. of the mixture or 5 lbs. of the hazardous chemical).

  The option used for each mixture must be consistent with the option used in your Section 311 reporting.

  Because EHSs are important to Section 303 planning, EHSs have lower thresholds. The amount of an EHS at a facility (both pure EHS substances and EHSs in mixtures) must be aggregated for purposes of threshold determination. It is suggested that the aggregation calculation be done as a first step in making the threshold determination. Once you determine whether a threshold has been reached for an EHS, you should report either the total weight of the EHS at your facility, or the weight of each mixture containing the EHS.

CHEMICAL DESCRIPTION

1. Enter the Chemical Abstract Service registry number (CAS). For mixtures, enter the CAS number of the mixture as a whole if it has been assigned a number distinct from its constituents. For a mixture that has no CAS number, leave this item blank or report the CAS numbers of as many constituent chemicals as possible.

If you are withholding the name of a chemical in accordance with criteria specified in Title III, Section 322, enter the generic class or category that is structurally descriptive of the chemical (e.g., list toluene diisocyanate as organic isocyanate) and check the box marked Trade Secret. Trade secret information should be submitted to EPA and must include a substantiation. Please refer to ´PA's final regulation on trade secrecy (53 FR 28772, July 29, 1988) for detailed information on how to submit trade secrecy claims.

2. Enter the chemical name or common name of each hazardous chemical.

3. Check box for *ALL* applicable descriptors: pure or mixture: *and* solid, liquid, or gas: and whether the chemical is or contains an EHS.

4. If the chemical is a mixture containing an EHS, enter the chemical name of each EHS in the mixture.

EXAMPLE:

You have pure chlorine gas on hand, as well as two mixtures that contain liquid chlorine. You write "chlorine" and enter the CAS number. Then you check "pure" *and* "mix"—as well as "liquid" *and* "gas".

PHYSICAL AND HEALTH HAZARDS

For each chemical you have listed, check all the physical and health hazard boxes that apply. These hazard categories are defined in 40 CFR 370.2. The two health hazard categories and three physical hazard categories are a consolidation of the 23 hazard categories defined in OSHA Hazard Communication Standard, 29 CFR 1910.1200.

Hazard Category Comparison
For Reporting Under Sections 311 and 312

EPA's Hazard Categories	OSHA's Hazard Categories
Fire Hazard	Flammable Combustion Liquid Pyrophoric Oxidizer
Sudden Release of Pressure	Explosive Compressed Gas
Reactive	Unstable Reactive Organic Peroxide Water Reactive
Immediate (Acute) Health Hazards	Highly Toxic Toxic Irritant Sensitizer Corrosive
	Other hazardous chemicals with an adverse effect with short term exposure
Delayed (Chronic) Health Hazard	Carcinogens
	Other hazardous chemicals with an adverse effect with long term exposure

---

MAXIMUM AMOUNT

1. For each hazardous chemical, estimate the greatest amount present at your facility on any single day during the reporting period.

2. Find the appropriate range value code in Table 1.

3. Enter this range value as the Maximum Amount:

Table I — REPORTING RANGES

Range Value	Weight Range in Pounds From . . .	To . . .
01	0	99
02	100	999
03	1,000	9,999
04	10,000	99,999
05	100,000	999,999
06	1,000,000	9,999,999
07	10,000,000	49,999,999
08	50,000,000	99,999,999
09	100,000,000	499,999,999
10	500,000,000	999,999,999
11	1 billion	higher than 1 billion

If you are using this form as a worksheet for completing Tier One, enter the actual weight in pounds in the shaded space below the response blocks. Do this for both Maximum Amount and Average Daily Amount.

EXAMPLE:

You received one large shipment of a solvent mixture last year. The shipment filled five 5,000-gallon storage tanks. You know that the solvent contains 10% benzene, which is a hazardous chemical.

You figure that 10% of 25,000 gallons is 2,500 gallons. You also know that the density of benzene is 7.29 pounds per gallon, so you multiply 2,500 gallons by 7.29 pounds per gallon to get a weight of 18.225 pounds.

Then you look at Table I and find that the range value 04 corresponds to 18.225. You enter 04 as the Maximum Amount.

(If you are using the form as a worksheet for completing a Tier One form, you should write 18.255 in the shaded area.)

AVERAGE DAILY AMOUNT

1. For each hazardous chemical, estimate the average weight in pounds that was present at your facility during the year.

   To do this, total all daily weights and divide by the number of days the chemical was present on the site.

2. Find the appropriate range value in Table I.

3. Enter this range value as the Average Daily Amount.

EXAMPLE:

The 25,000-gallon shipment of solvent you received last year was gradually used up and completely gone in 315 days. The sum of the daily volume levels in the tank is 4,536,000 gallons. By dividing 4,536,000 gallons by 315 days on-site, you calculate an average daily amount of 14,400 gallons.

You already know that the solvent contains 10% benzene, which is a hazardous chemical. Since 10% of 14,400 is 1,440, you figure that you had an average of 1,440 gallons of benzene. You also know that the density of benzene is 7.29 pounds per gallon, so you multiply 1,440 by 7.29 to get a weight of 10,500 pounds.

Then you look at Table I and find that the range value 04 corresponds to 10,500. You enter 04 as the Average Daily Amount.

(If you are using the form as a worksheet for completing a Tier One form, you should write 10,500 in the shaded area.)

NUMBER OF DAYS ON-SITE
Enter the number of days that the hazardous chemical was found on-site.

EXAMPLE:

The solvent composed of 10% benzene was present for 315 days at your facility. Enter 315 in the space provided.

STORAGE CODES AND STORAGE LOCATIONS

List all non-confidential chemical locations in this column along with storage types/conditions associated with each location. Please note that a particular chemical may be located in several places around the facility. Each row of boxes followed by a line represents a unique location for the same chemical.

Storage Codes: indicate the types and conditions of storage present.
   a. *Look at Table II.* For each location, find the appropriate storage type and enter the corresponding code in the first box.
   b. *Look at Table III.* For each location, find the appropriate storage types for pressure and temperature conditions. Enter the applicable pressure code in the second box. Enter the applicable temperature code in the third box.

Table II — STORAGE TYPES

CODES	Types of Storage
A	Above ground tank
B	Below ground tank
C	Tank inside building
D	Steel drum
E	Plastic or non-metallic drum
F	Can
G	Carboy
H	Silo
I	Fiber drum
J	Bag
K	Box
L	Cylinder
M	Glass bottles or jugs
N	Plastic bottles or jugs
O	Tote bin
P	Tank wagon
Q	Rail car
R	Other

Table III — PRESSURE AND TEMPERATURE CONDITIONS

CODES	Storage Conditions
	(PRESSURE)
1	Ambient pressure
2	Greater than ambient pressure
3	Less than ambient pressure
	(TEMPERATURE)
4	Ambient temperature
5	Greater than ambient temperature
6	Less than ambient temperature but not cryogenic
7	Cryogenic conditions

EXAMPLE:

The benzene in the main building is kept in a tank inside the building, at ambient pressure and less than ambient temperature.

Table II shows you that the code for a tank inside a building is C. Table III shows you that the code for ambient pressure is 1, and the code for less than ambient temperature is 6.

You enter: | C | 1 | 6 |

Storage Locations:

Provide a brief description of the precise location of the chemical so that emergency responders can locate the area easily. You may find it advantageous to provide the optional site plan or site coordinates as explained below.

For each chemical, indicate at a minimum the building or lot. Additionally, where practical, the room or area may be indicated. You may respond in narrative form with appropriate site coordinates or abbreviations.

If the chemical is present in more than one building, lot, or area location, continue your responses down the page as needed. If the chemical exists everywhere at the plant site simultaneously, you may report that the chemical is ubiquitous at the site.

Optional attachments: If you choose to attach one of the following, check the appropriate Attachments box at the bottom of the Tier Two form.
   a. A site plan with site coordinates indicated for buildings, lots, areas, etc. throughout your facility.
   b. A list of site coordinate abbreviations that correspond to buildings, lots, areas, etc. throughout your facility.
   c. A description of dikes and other safeguard measures for storage locations throughout your facility.

EXAMPLE:

You have benzene in the main room of the main building, and in tank 2 in tank field 10. You attach a site plan with coordinates as follows: main building = G-2, tank field 10 = B-6. Fill in the Storage Location as follows:

B-6 [Tank 2] G-2 [Main Room]

CONFIDENTIAL INFORMATION

Under Title III, Section 324, you may elect to withhold location information on a specific chemical from disclosure to the public. If you choose to do so:

• Enter the word "confidential" in the Non-Confidential Location section of the Tier Two form on the first line of the storage locations.

• On a separate Tier Two Confidential Location Information Sheet, enter the name and CAS number of each chemical for which you are keeping the location confidential.

• Enter the appropriate location and storage information, as described above for non-confidential locations.

• Attach the Tier Two Confidential Location Information Sheet to the Tier Two form. This separates confidential locations from other information that will be disclosed to the public.

CERTIFICATION

Instructions for this section are included on page one of these instructions.

APPENDIX **XXXVI**

SOURCE:

Section 313 of the Emergency
Planning and Community Right-
to-Know Act (Title III of the
Superfund Amendments and
Reauthorization Act of 1986)
USEPA, EPA 745-K-99-001

SARA Title III: Toxic Release Inventory Reporting, Form R

A. General Information

Reporting to the Toxic Chemical Release Inventory (TRI) is required by section 313 of the Emergency Planning and Community Right-to-Know Act (EPCRA, or Title III of the Superfund Amendments and Reauthorization Act of 1986), Public Law 99-499. The information contained in the Form R constitutes a "report," and the submission of a report to the appropriate authorities constitutes "reporting."

The Pollution Prevention Act, passed into law in October, 1990 (Pub. L. 101-508), added reporting requirements to Form R. These requirements affect all facilities required to submit Form R under section 313 of EPCRA. The data were required beginning with reports for calendar year 1991.

Reporting is required to provide the public with information on the releases of EPCRA Section 313 chemicals in their communities and to provide EPA with release information to assist the Agency in determining the need for future regulations. Facilities must report the quantities of both routine and accidental releases of EPCRA Section 313 chemicals, as well as the maximum amount of the EPCRA Section 313 chemical on site during the calendar year and the amount contained in wastes managed on site or transferred off site.

A completed Form R or Form A must be submitted for each EPCRA Section 313 chemical manufactured, processed, or otherwise used at each covered facility as described in the reporting rules in 40 CFR Part 372 (originally published February 16, 1988, in the Federal Register and November 30, 1994, in the Federal Register (for Form A)). These instructions supplement and elaborate on the requirements in the reporting rule. Together with the reporting rule, they constitute the reporting requirements. All references in these instructions are to sections in the reporting rule unless otherwise indicated.

A.1 Who Must Report

Section 313 of EPCRA requires that reports be filed by owners and operators of facilities that meet all of the following criteria.

❑ The facility has 10 or more full-time employees; and

❑ The facility is included in Standard Industrial Classification (SIC) Codes 10 (except 1011, 1081, and 1094), 12 (except 1241), 20-39, 4911 (limited to facilities that combust coal and/or oil for the purpose of generating electricity for distribution in commerce), 4931 (limited to facilities that combust coal and/or oil for the purpose of generating electricity for distribution in commerce), 4939 (limited to facilities that combust coal and/or oil for the purpose of generating electricity for distribution in commerce), 4953 (limited to facilities regulated under the RCRA Subtitle C, 42 U.S.C. section 6921 *et seq.*), 5169, 5171, and 7389 (limited to facilities primarily engaged in solvents recovery services on a contract or fee basis); and

❑ The facility manufactures (defined to include importing), processes, or otherwise uses any EPCRA Section 313 chemical in quantities greater than the established threshold in the course of a calendar year.

A.2 How to Assemble a Complete Report

A.2.a. The Toxic Chemical Release Reporting Form, EPA Form R

The five-page EPA Form R consist of two parts:

❑ Part I, Facility Identification Information (page 1); and

❑ Part II, Chemical-Specific Information (pages 2-5).

Most of the information required in Part I of Form R can be completed, photocopied, and attached to each chemical-specific report. However, Part I of each Form R submitted must have an original signature on the certification statement and the trade secret designation must be entered as appropriate. Part II must be completed separately for each EPCRA Section 313 chemical or chemical category. Because a complete Form R consists of at least five unique pages, any submission containing less than five unique pages is not a valid submission.

A complete report for any EPCRA Section 313 chemical that is not claimed as a trade secret consists of the following completed parts:

❑ Part I with an original signature on the certification statement (section 3); and

❑ Part II (Note: Section 8 is mandatory).

Staple all five pages of each report together. If you check yes on Part II, Section 8.11, you may attach additional information on pollution prevention activities at your facility.

C. Instructions for EPA Form R

Part I. Facility Identification Information

Section 1. Reporting Year

This is the calendar year to which the reported information applies, not the year in which you are submitting the report. Information for the 1998 reporting year must be submitted on or before July 1, 1999.

Section 2. Trade Secret Information

2.1 Are you claiming the EPCRA Section 313 chemical identified on page 2 trade secret?

Answer this question only after you have completed the rest of the report. The specific identity of the EPCRA Section 313 chemical being reported in Part II, Section 1, may be designated as a trade secret. If you are making a trade secret claim, mark "yes" and proceed to Section 2.2. Only check "yes" if you manufacture, process, or otherwise use the EPCRA Section 313 chemical whose identity is a trade secret. (See page 2 of these instructions for specific information on trade secrecy claims.) If you checked "no," proceed to Section 3; do not answer Section 2.2.

2.2 If "yes" in 2.1, is this copy sanitized or unsanitized?

Answer this question only after you have completed the rest of the report. Check "sanitized" if this copy of the report is the public version that does not contain the EPCRA Section 313 chemical identity but does contain a generic name in its place, and you have claimed the EPCRA Section 313 chemical identity trade secret in Part I, Section 2.1. Otherwise, check "unsanitized."

Section 3. Certification

The certification statement must be signed by the owner or operator or a senior official with management responsibility for the person (or persons) completing the form. The owner, operator, or official must certify the accuracy and completeness of the information reported on the form by signing and dating the certification statement. Each report must contain an original signature. Print or type in the space provided the name and title of the person who signs the statement. This certification statement applies to all the information supplied on the form and should be signed only after the form has been completed.

Section 4. Facility Identification

4.1 Facility Name, Location, and TRI Facility Identification Number

Enter the name of your facility (plant site name or appropriate facility designation), street address, mailing address, city, county, state, and zip code in the space provided. Do not use a post office box number as the street address. The street address provided should be the location where the EPCRA Section 313 chemicals are manufactured, processed, or otherwise used. If your mailing address and street address are the same, enter NA in the space for the mailing address.

If you have submitted a Form R for previous reporting years, a TRI Facility Identification Number has been assigned to your facility. The TRI Facility Identification Number appears (with other facility-specific information) on a pre-printed page 1 of the Form R that is attached to the cover of this Toxic Chemical Release Inventory Instructions for 1998. Please do not destroy this page 1. When completing your Form R reports for 1998, you may use this pre-printed page 1 instead of filling out a new page one.

If your pre-printed page 1 is missing information required by Form R, insert that information in the appropriate box in Part I, Section 4.1. For example, if your pre-printed page 1 contains your street address and not your mailing address, enter your mailing address in the space provided. If you receive a pre-printed page 1 which contains incorrect information, you may edit the page.

If you do not have a pre-printed page 1, but know your TRI Facility Identification Number, complete Section 4. If you do not know your TRI Facility Identification Number, contact the EPCRA Hotline (see page 4). If your facility has moved, do not enter your TRI facility identification number, enter "New Facility."

Enter "NA" in the space for the TRI Facility Identification number if this is your first submission of a Form R.

4.2 Full or Partial Facility Indication

A covered facility must report all releases and other waste management activities and source reduction activities of an EPCRA Section 313 chemical if the facility meets a reporting threshold for that EPCRA Section 313 chemical. However, if the facility is composed of several distinct establishments, EPA allows these establishments to submit separate reports for the EPCRA Section 313

chemical as long as all releases and other waste management activities of the EPCRA Section 313 chemical from the entire facility are accounted for. Indicate in Section 4.2 whether your report is for the entire covered facility as a whole or for part of a covered facility.

Section 313 requires reports by "facilities," which are defined as "all buildings, equipment, structures, and other stationary items which are located on a single site or on contiguous or adjacent sites and which are owned or operated by the same person."

The SIC Code system defines business "establishments" as "distinct and separate economic activities [that] are performed at a single physical location." Under section 372.30(c) of the reporting rule, you may submit a separate Form R for each establishment, or for groups of establishments in your facility, provided all releases and other waste management activities and source reduction activities involving the EPCRA Section 313 chemical from the entire facility are reported. This allows you the option of reporting separately on the activities involving an EPCRA Section 313 chemical at each establishment, or group of establishments (e.g., part of a covered facility), rather than submitting a single Form R for that EPCRA Section 313 chemical for the entire facility. However, if an establishment or group of establishments does not manufacture, process, or otherwise use or release or otherwise manage as waste an EPCRA Section 313 chemical, you do not have to submit a report for that establishment or group of establishments for that particular chemical. (See also Section B.2a of these instructions.)

4.3 Technical Contact

Enter the name and telephone number (including area code) of a technical representative whom EPA or State officials may contact for clarification of the information reported on Form R. This contact person does not have to be the same person who prepares the report or signs the certification statement and does not necessarily need to be someone at the location of the reporting facility. However, this person must be familiar with the details of the report so that he or she can answer questions about the information provided.

4.4 Public Contact

Enter the name and telephone number (including area code) of a person who can respond to questions from the public about the report. If you choose to designate the same person as both the technical and the public contact, you may enter "Same as Section 4.3" in this space. This contact person does not have to be the same person who prepares the report or signs the certification statement and does not necessarily need to be someone at the location of the reporting facility. If this space is left blank, the technical contact will be listed as the public contact in the TRI database.

4.5   Standard Industrial Classification (SIC) Code

Enter the appropriate 4-digit primary Standard Industrial Classification (SIC) Code for your facility.   If the report covers more than one establishment, enter the primary 4-digit SIC Code for each establishment starting with the primary SIC Code for the entire facility.

The North American Industry Classification System (NAICS) is a new economic classification system that will replace the 1987 SIC Code system. EPA will address the SIC Code change, as it relates to EPCRA, in an upcoming Federal Register notice.

4.6   Latitude and Longitude

Enter the latitudinal and longitudinal coordinates of your facility. Sources of these data include EPA permits (e.g., NPDES permits), county property records, facility blueprints, and site plans. Instructions on how to determine these coordinates can be found in Appendix E. Enter only numerical data. Do not preface numbers with letters such as N or W to denote the hemisphere.

Latitude and longitude coordinates of your facility are very important for pinpointing the location of reporting facilities and are required elements on the Form R. EPA encourages facilities to make the best possible measurements when determining latitude and longitude. As with any other data field, missing, suspect, or incorrect data may generate a Notice of Technical Error to be issued to the facility.

4.7   Dun and Bradstreet Number

Enter the nine-digit number assigned by Dun and Bradstreet (D & B) for your facility or each establishment within your facility. These numbers code the facility for financial purposes. This number may be available from your facility's treasurer or financial officer. You can also obtain the numbers from your local Dun and Bradstreet office (check the telephone book).   If none of your establishments has been assigned a D & B number, enter not applicable, NA, in box (a). If only some of your establishments have been assigned D & B numbers, enter those numbers in Part I, section 4.7.

4.8   EPA Identification Number

The EPA I.D. Number is a 12-character number assigned to facilities covered by hazardous waste regulations under the Resource Conservation and Recovery Act (RCRA). Facilities not covered by RCRA are not likely to have an assigned I.D. Number. If your facility is not required to have an I.D. Number, enter not applicable, NA, in box (a). If your facility has been assigned EPA Identification Numbers, you must enter those numbers in the spaces provided in Section 4.8.

4.9   NPDES Permit Number

Enter the numbers of any permits your facility holds under the National Pollutant Discharge Elimination System (NPDES) even if the permit(s) do not pertain to the EPCRA Section 313 chemical being reported. This nine-character permit number is assigned to your facility by EPA or the State under the authority of the Clean Water Act. If your facility does not have a permit, enter not applicable, NA, in Section 4.9a.

4.10   Underground Injection Well Code (UIC) Identification Number

If your facility has a permit to inject a waste containing the EPCRA Section 313 chemical into Class 1 deep wells, enter the 12-digit Underground Injection Well Code (UIC) identification number assigned by EPA or by the State under the authority of the Safe Drinking Water Act. If your facility does not hold such a permit(s), enter not applicable, NA, in Section 4.10a. You are only required to provide the UIC number for wells that receive the EPCRA Section 313 chemical being reported.

Section 5. Parent Company Information

You must provide information on your parent company. For purposes of Form R, a parent company is defined as the highest level company, located in the United States, that directly owns at least 50 percent of the voting stock of your company. If your facility is owned by a foreign entity, enter not applicable, NA, in this space. Corporate names should be treated as parent company names for companies with multiple facility sites. For example, the Bestchem Corporation is not owned or controlled by any other corporation but has sites throughout the country whose names begin with Bestchem. In this case, Bestchem Corporation would be listed as the parent company. Note that a facility that is a 50:50 joint venture is its own parent company.

5.1 Name of Parent Company

Enter the name of the corporation or other business entity that is your ultimate U.S. parent company. If your facility has no parent company, check the NA box.

5.2 Parent Company's Dun & Bradstreet Number

Enter the D & B number for your ultimate U.S. parent company, if applicable. The number may be obtained from the treasurer or financial officer of the company. If your parent company does not have a D & B number, check the NA box.

Part II. Chemical Specific Information

In Part II, you are to report on:

☐ The EPCRA Section 313 chemical being reported;
☐ The general uses and activities involving the EPCRA Section 313 chemical at your facility;
☐ On-site releases of the EPCRA Section 313 chemical from the facility to air, water, and land;
☐ Quantities of the EPCRA Section 313 chemical transferred to off-site locations;
☐ Information for on-site and off-site disposal, treatment, energy recovery, and recycling of the EPCRA Section 313 chemical; and
☐ Source reduction activities.

Section 1. EPCRA Section 313 Chemical Identity

1.1 CAS Number

Enter the Chemical Abstracts Service (CAS) registry number in Section 1.1 exactly as it appears for the chemical being reported. If you are reporting one of the EPCRA Section 313 chemical categories (e.g., chromium compounds), enter the applicable category code in the CAS number space. EPCRA Section 313 chemical category codes are listed below.

EPCRA Section 313 Chemical Category Codes

N010	Antimony compounds
N020	Arsenic compounds
N040	Barium compounds
N050	Beryllium compounds
N078	Cadmium compounds
N084	Chlorophenols

N090	Chromium compounds
N096	Cobalt compounds
N100	Copper compounds
N106	Cyanide compounds
N120	Diisocyanates
N171	Ethylenebisdithiocarbamic acid, salts and esters (EBDCs)
N230	Certain glycol ethers
N420	Lead compounds
N450	Manganese compounds
N458	Mercury compounds
N495	Nickel compounds
N503	Nicotine and salts
N511	Nitrate compounds (water dissociable, reportable only in aqueous solution)
N575	Polybrominated biphenyls (PBBs)
N583	Polychlorinated alkanes (C10 to C13)
N590	Polycyclic aromatic compounds (PACs)
N725	Selenium compounds
N740	Silver compounds
N746	Strychnine and salts
N760	Thallium compounds
N874	Warfarin and Salts
N982	Zinc compounds

If you are making a trade secret claim, you must report the CAS number or category code on your unsanitized Form R and unsanitized substantiation form. Do not include the CAS number or category code on your sanitized Form R or sanitized substantiation form.

Example 10: Mixture Containing Unidentified EPCRA Section 313 Chemical

Your facility uses 20,000 pounds of a solvent that your supplier has told you contains 80 percent "chlorinated aromatic," their generic name for an EPCRA Section 313 chemical subject to reporting under Section 313. You, therefore, know that you have used 16,000 pounds of some EPCRA Section 313 chemical and that exceeds the "otherwise use" threshold. You would file a Form R and enter the name "chlorinated aromatic" in the space provided in Part II, Section 2.

1.2 EPCRA Section 313 Chemical or Chemical Category Name

Enter the name of the EPCRA Section 313 chemical or chemical category exactly as it appears in Table II. If the EPCRA Section 313 chemical name is followed by a synonym in parentheses, report the chemical by the name that directly follows the CAS number (i.e., not the synonym). If the EPCRA Section 313 chemical identity is actually a product trade name (e.g., dicofol), the 9th

Collective Index name is listed below it in brackets. You may report either name in this case.

Do not list the name of a chemical that does not appear in Table II, such as individual members of a reportable EPCRA Section 313 chemical category. For example, if you use silver nitrate, **do not** report silver nitrate with its CAS number. Report this chemical as "silver compounds" with its category code, N740.

If you are making a trade secret claim, you must report the specific EPCRA Section 313 chemical identity on your unsanitized Form R and unsanitized substantiation form. Do not report the name of the EPCRA Section 313 chemical on your sanitized Form R or sanitized substantiation form. Include a generic name in Part II, Section 1.3 of your sanitized Form R report.

EPA requests that the EPCRA Section 313 chemical, chemical category, or generic name also be placed in the box marked "Toxic Chemical, Category, or Generic Name" in the upper right-hand corner on all pages of Form R. While this space is not a required data element, providing this information will help you in preparing a complete Form R report.

1.3 Generic Chemical Name

Complete Section 1.3 only if you are claiming the specific EPCRA Section 313 chemical identity of the EPCRA Section 313 chemical as a trade secret and have marked the trade secret block in Part I, Section 2.1 on page 1 of Form R. Enter a generic chemical name that is descriptive of the chemical structure. You must limit the generic name to seventy characters (e.g., numbers, letters, spaces, punctuation) or less. Do not enter mixture names in Section 1.3; see Section 2 below.

In-house plant codes and other substitute names that are not structurally descriptive of the EPCRA Section 313 chemical identity being withheld as a trade secret are not acceptable as a generic name. The generic name must appear on both sanitized and unsanitized Form Rs, and the name must be the same as that used on your substantiation forms.

Section 2. Mixture Component Identity

Do not complete this section if you have completed Section 1 of Part II. Report the generic name provided to you by your supplier in this section if your supplier is claiming the chemical identity proprietary or trade secret. Do not answer "yes" in Part I, Section 2.1 on page 1 of the form if you complete this section. You do not need to supply trade secret substantiation forms for this EPCRA

Section 313 chemical because it is your supplier who is claiming the chemical identity a trade secret.

2.1 Generic Chemical Name Provided by Supplier

Enter the generic chemical name in this section only if the following three conditions apply:

1. You determine that the mixture contains an EPCRA Section 313 chemical but the only identity you have for that chemical is a generic name;

2. You know either the specific concentration of that EPCRA Section 313 chemical component or a maximum or average concentration level; and

3. You multiply the concentration level by the total annual amount of the whole mixture processed or otherwise used and determine that you meet the process or otherwise use threshold for that single, generically identified mixture component.

Section 3. Activities and Uses of the EPCRA Section 313 Chemical at the Facility

Indicate whether the EPCRA Section 313 chemical is manufactured (including imported), processed, or otherwise used at the facility and the general nature of such activities and uses at the facility during the calendar year (see figure 3). You are not required to report on Form R the quantity manufactured, processed or otherwise used. Report activities that take place only at your facility, not activities that take place at other facilities involving your products. You must check all the boxes in this section that apply. Refer to the definitions of "manufacture," "process," and "otherwise use" in the general information section of these instructions or Part 40, Section 372.3 of the *Code of Federal Regulations* for additional explanations.

3.1 Manufacture the EPCRA Section 313 Chemical

Persons who manufacture (including import) the EPCRA Section 313 chemical must check at least one of the following:

a. *Produce* - The EPCRA Section 313 chemical is produced at the facility.

b. *Import* - The EPCRA Section 313 chemical is imported by the facility into the Customs Territory of the United States. (See Section B.3.a of these instructions for further clarification of import.)

And check at least one of the following:

c.   **For on-site use/processing** - The EPCRA Section 313 chemical is produced or imported and then further processed or otherwise used at the same facility. If you check this block, you must also check at least one item in Part II, Section 3.2 or 3.3.

d.   **For sale/distribution** - The EPCRA Section 313 chemical is produced or imported specifically for sale or distribution outside the manufacturing facility.

e.   **As a byproduct** - The EPCRA Section 313 chemical is produced coincidentally during the manufacture, processing, or otherwise use of another chemical substance or mixture and, following its production, is separated from that other chemical substance or mixture. EPCRA Section 313 chemicals produced as a result of waste management are also considered byproducts.

f.   **As an impurity** - The EPCRA Section 313 chemical is produced coincidentally as a result of the manufacture, processing, or otherwise use of another chemical but is not separated and remains primarily in the mixture or other trade name product with that other chemical.

In summary, if you are a manufacturer of the EPCRA Section 313 chemical, you must check (a) and/or (b), and at least one of (c), (d), (e), and (f) in Section 3.1.

3.2   Process the EPCRA Section 313 Chemical (incorporative activities)

a.   **As a reactant** - A natural or synthetic EPCRA Section 313 chemical is used in chemical reactions for the manufacture of another chemical substance or of a product. Includes but is not limited to, feedstocks, raw materials, intermediates, and initiators.

b.   **As a formulation component** - An EPCRA Section 313 chemical is added to a product (or product mixture) prior to further distribution of the product that acts as a performance enhancer during use of the product. Examples of EPCRA Section 313 chemicals used in this capacity include, but are not limited to, additives, dyes, reaction diluents, initiators, solvents, inhibitors, emulsifiers, surfactants, lubricants, flame retardants, and rheological modifiers.

c.   **As an article component** - An EPCRA Section 313

chemical becomes an integral component of an article distributed for industrial, trade, or consumer use. One example is the pigment components of paint applied to a chair that is sold.

d.   **Repackaging** - this consists of processing or preparation of an EPCRA Section 313 chemical (or product mixture) for distribution in commerce in a different form, state, or quantity. This includes, but is not limited to, the transfer of material from a bulk container, such as a tank truck to smaller containers such as cans or bottles.

3.3   Otherwise Use the EPCRA Section 313 Chemical (non-incorporative activities)

a.   **As a chemical processing aid** - An EPCRA Section 313 chemical that is added to a reaction mixture to aid in the manufacture or synthesis of another chemical substance but is not intended to remain in or become part of the product or product mixture is otherwise used as chemical processing aid. Examples of such EPCRA Section 313 chemicals include, but are not limited to, process solvents, catalysts, inhibitors, initiators, reaction terminators, and solution buffers.

b.   **As a manufacturing aid** - An EPCRA Section 313 chemical that aids the manufacturing process but does not become part of the resulting product and is not added to the reaction mixture during the manufacture or synthesis of another chemical substance is otherwise used as a manufacturing aid. Examples include, but are not limited to, process lubricants, metalworking fluids, coolants, refrigerants, and hydraulic fluids.

c.   **Ancillary or other use** - An EPCRA Section 313 chemical is used at a facility for purposes other than aiding chemical processing or manufacturing as described above is otherwise used as ancillary or other use. Examples include, but are not limited to, cleaners, degreasers, lubricants, fuels, EPCRA Section 313 chemicals used for treating wastes, and EPCRA Section 313 chemicals used to treat water at the facility.

Section 4.   Maximum Amount of the EPCRA Section 313 Chemical On Site at Any Time During the Calendar Year

For data element 4.1 of Part II, insert the code (see codes below) that indicates the maximum quantity of the

Figure 3

SECTION 1. TOXIC CHEMICAL IDENTITY	(Important: DO NOT complete this section if you complete Section 2 below.)

1.1	CAS Number (Important: Enter only one number exactly as it appears on the Section 313 list. Enter category code if reporting a chemical category.) **334-88-3**
1.2	Toxic Chemical or Chemical Category Name (Important: Enter only one name exactly as it appears on the Section 313 list.) Diazomethane
1.3	Generic Chemical Name (Important: Complete only if Part 1, Section 2.1 is checked "Yes". Generic name must be structurally descriptive.)

SECTION 2. MIXTURE COMPONENT IDENTITY	(Important: DO NOT complete this section if you complete Section 1 above.)

2.1	Generic Chemical Name Provided by Supplier (Important: Maximum of 70 characters, including numbers, letters, spaces, and punctuation.)

SECTION 3. ACTIVITIES AND USES OF THE TOXIC CHEMICAL AT THE FACILITY
(Important: CHECK ALL THAT APPLY.)

3.1 Manufacture the toxic chemical:	3.2 Process the toxic chemical:	3.3 Otherwise use the toxic chemical:
☑ a. Produce b. ☐ Import	☑ a. As a reactant	a. ☐ As a chemical processing aid
If produce or import:	☐ b. As a formulation component	b. ☐ As a manufacturing aid
☑ c. For on-site use/processing	☐ c. As an article component	c. ☐ Ancillary or other use
☑ d. For sale/distribution	☐ d. Repackaging	
☐ e. As a byproduct		
☐ f. As an impurity		

EPCRA Section 313 chemical (e.g., in storage tanks, process vessels, on-site shipping containers, or in waste) at your facility at any time during the calendar year. If the EPCRA Section 313 chemical was present at several locations within your facility, use the maximum total amount present at the entire facility at any one time.

Weight Range in Pounds

Range Code	From...	To....
01	0	99
02	100	999
03	1,000	9,999
04	10,000	99,999
05	100,000	999,999
06	1,000,000	9,999,999
07	10,000,000	49,999,999
08	50,000,000	99,999,999
09	100,000,000	499,999,999
10	500,000,000	999,999,999
11	1 billion	more than 1 billion

If the EPCRA Section 313 chemical present at your facility was part of a mixture or other trade name product, determine the maximum quantity of the EPCRA Section 313 chemical present at the facility by calculating the weight percent of the EPCRA Section 313 chemical only.

Do not include the weight of the entire mixture or other trade name product. This data may be found in the Tier II form your facility may have prepared under Section 312 of EPCRA.

Section 5. Quantity of the EPCRA Section 313 Chemical Entering Each Environmental Medium On Site

In Section 5, you must account for the total aggregate on-site releases of the EPCRA Section 313 chemical to the environment from your facility for the calendar year.

Do not enter the values in Section 5 in gallons, tons, liters, or any measure other than pounds. You must also enter the values as whole numbers. Numbers following a decimal point are not acceptable.

On-site releases to the environment include emissions to the air, discharges to surface waters, and releases to land and underground injection wells. If you have no releases to a particular media (e.g., stack air), you must check the "NA" box or enter zero; **do not** leave any part of Section 5 blank.

You are not required to count as a release, quantities of an EPCRA Section 313 chemical that are lost due to natural weathering or corrosion, normal/natural degradation of a product, or normal migration of an EPCRA Section 313 chemical from a product. For example, amounts of an EPCRA Section 313 chemical that migrate from plastic products in storage do not have to be counted in estimates of releases of that EPCRA Section 313 chemical from the facility.

All releases of the EPCRA Section 313 chemical to the air must be classified as either point or non-point emissions, and included in the total quantity reported for these releases in Sections 5.1 and 5.2. Instructions for columns A, B, and C follow the discussions of Sections 5.1 through 5.5.

5.1   Fugitive or Non-Point Air Emissions

Report the total of all releases of the EPCRA Section 313 chemical to the air that are not released through stacks, vents, ducts, pipes, or any other confined air stream. You must include (1) fugitive equipment leaks from valves, pump seals, flanges, compressors, sampling connections, open-ended lines, etc.; (2) evaporative losses from surface impoundments and spills; (3) releases from building ventilation systems; and (4) any other fugitive or non-point air emissions. Engineering estimates and mass balance calculations (using purchase records, inventories, engineering knowledge or process specifications of the quantity of the EPCRA Section 313 chemical entering product, hazardous waste manifests, or monitoring records) may be useful in estimating fugitive emissions.

5.2   Stack or Point Air Emissions

Report the total of all releases of the EPCRA Section 313 chemical to the air that occur through stacks, vents, ducts, pipes, or other confined air streams. You must include storage tank emissions. Air releases from air pollution control equipment would generally fall in this category. Monitoring data, engineering estimates, and mass balance calculations may help you to complete this section.

5.3   Discharges to Receiving Streams or Water Bodies

In Section 5.3 you are to enter all the names of the streams or water bodies to which your facility directly discharges the EPCRA Section 313 chemical on which you are reporting. A total of three spaces is provided on page 2 of Form R. Enter the name of each receiving stream or surface water body to which the EPCRA Section 313 chemical being reported is directly discharged. Report the name of the receiving stream or water body as it appears on the NPDES permit for the facility. If the stream is not covered by a permit, enter the name of the off-site stream or water body by which it is publicly known. Do not list a series of streams through which the EPCRA Section 313 chemical flows. Be sure to include all the receiving streams or water bodies that receive stormwater runoff from your facility. Do not enter names of streams to which off-site treatment plants discharge. Enter "NA" in Section 5.3.1. if you do not discharge the EPCRA Section 313 chemical to surface water bodies.

Enter the total annual amount of the EPCRA Section 313 chemical released from all discharge points at the facility to each receiving stream or water body. Include process outfalls such as pipes and open trenches, releases from on-site wastewater treatment systems, and the contribution from stormwater runoff, if applicable (see instructions for column C below). Do not include discharges to a POTW or other off-site wastewater treatment facilities in this section. These off-site transfers must be reported in Part II, Section 6 of Form R. Wastewater analyses and flowmeter data may provide the quantities you will need to complete this section.

Discharges of listed acids (e.g., hydrogen fluoride, nitric acid, and phosphoric acid) may be reported as zero if the discharges have been neutralized to pH 6 or above. If wastewater containing a listed acid is discharged below pH 6, then releases of the acid must be reported. In this case, pH measurements may be used to estimate the amount of mineral acid released.

5.4.1   Underground Injection On-Site to Class I Wells

Enter the total amount of the EPCRA Section 313 chemical that was injected into Class I wells at the facility. Chemical analyses, injection rate meters, and RCRA Hazardous Waste Generator Reports are good sources for obtaining data that will be useful in completing this section. Check the Not Applicable "NA" box in Section 5.4.1 if you do not inject the reported

EPCRA Section 313 chemical into Class I underground wells.

5.4.2 Underground Injection On Site to Class II-V Wells

Enter the total amount of the EPCRA Section 313 chemical that was injected into wells at the facility other than Class I wells. Chemical analyses and injection rate meters are good sources for obtaining data that will be useful in completing this section. Check the Not Applicable "NA" box in Section 5.4.2 if you do not inject the reported EPCRA Section 313 chemical into Class II-V underground wells.

5.5 Disposal to Land On Site

Five predefined subcategories for reporting quantities released to land within the boundaries of the facility are provided. Do not report land disposal at off-site locations in this section. Accident histories and spill records may be useful (e.g., release notification reports required under Section 304 of EPCRA and accident histories required under Section 112(r)(7)(B)(ii) of the Clean Air Act).

5.5.1A RCRA Subtitle C landfills — Enter the total amount of the EPCRA Section 313 chemical that was placed in RCRA Subtitle C landfills. Leaks from landfills need not be reported as a release because the amount of the EPCRA Section 313 chemical has already been reported as a release.

5.5.1B Other landfills — Enter the total amount of the EPCRA Section 313 chemical that was placed in landfills other than RCRA Subtitle C landfills. Leaks from landfills need not be reported as a release because the amount of the EPCRA Section 313 chemical has already been reported as a release.

5.5.2 Land treatment/application farming — Land treatment is a disposal method in which a waste containing an EPCRA Section 313 chemical is applied onto or incorporated into soil. While this disposal method is considered a release to land, any volatilization of EPCRA Section 313 chemicals into the air occurring during the disposal operation must be included in the total fugitive air releases reported in Part II, Section 5.1 of Form R.

5.5.3 Surface impoundment — A surface impoundment is a natural topographic depression, man-made excavation, or diked area formed primarily of earthen materials (although some may be lined with man-made materials), that is designed to hold an accumulation of liquid wastes or wastes containing free liquids.

Examples of surface impoundments are holding, settling, storage, and elevation pits; ponds, and lagoons. If the pit, pond, or lagoon is intended for storage or holding without discharge, it would be considered to be a surface impoundment used as a final disposal method. A facility should determine, to the best of its ability, the percentage of a volatile chemical, e.g., benzene, that is in waste sent to a surface impoundment that evaporates in the reporting year. The facility should report this as a fugitive air emission in section 5.1. The balance should be reported in section 5.5.3.

Quantities of the EPCRA Section 313 chemical released to surface impoundments that are used merely as part of a wastewater treatment process generally must not be reported in this section. However, if the impoundment accumulates sludges containing the EPCRA Section 313 chemical, you must include an estimate in this section unless the sludges are removed and otherwise disposed (in which case they should be reported under the appropriate section of the form). For the purposes of this reporting, storage tanks are not considered to be a type of disposal and are not to be reported in this section of Form R.

5.5.4 Other Disposal — Includes any amount of an EPCRA Section 313 chemical released to land that does not fit the categories of landfills, land treatment, or surface impoundment. This other disposal would include any spills or leaks of EPCRA Section 313 chemicals to land. For example, 2,000 pounds of benzene leaks from an underground pipeline into the land at a facility. Because the pipe was only a few feet from the surface at the erupt point, 30 percent of the benzene evaporates into the air. The 600 pounds released to the air would be reported as a fugitive air release (Part II, Section 5.1) and the remaining 1,400 pounds would be reported as a release to land, other disposal (Part II, Section 5.5.4).

Column A: Total Release

Only on-site releases of the EPCRA Section 313 chemical to the environment for the calendar year are to be reported in this section of Form R. The total on-site releases from your facility do not include transfers or shipments of the EPCRA Section 313 chemical from your facility for sale or distribution in commerce, or of wastes to other facilities for disposal, treatment, energy recovery, or recycling (see Part II, Section 6 of these Instructions). Both routine releases, such as fugitive air emissions, and accidental or non-routine releases, such as chemical spills, must be included in your estimate of the quantity released.

Releases of Less Than 1,000 Pounds. For total annual

releases or off-site transfers of an EPCRA Section 313 chemical from the facility of less than 1,000 pounds, the amount may be reported either as an estimate or by using the range codes that have been developed. The reporting range codes to be used are:

Code	Range (pounds)
A	1-10
B	11-499
C	500-999

Do not enter a range code and an estimate in the same box in column A. Total annual on-site releases of an EPCRA Section 313 chemical from the facility of less than 1 pound may be reported in one of several ways. You should round the value to the nearest pound. If the estimate is greater than 0.5 pound, you should either enter the range code "A" for "1-10" or enter "1" in column A. If the release is equal to or less than 0.5 pound, you may round to zero and enter "0" in column A.

Note that total annual releases of 0.5 pound or less from the processing or otherwise use of an article maintain the article status of that item. Thus, if the only releases you have are from processing an article, and such releases are equal to or less than 0.5 pound per year, you are not required to submit a report for that EPCRA Section 313 chemical. The 0.5-pound release determination does not apply to just a single article. It applies to the cumulative releases from the processing or otherwise use of the same type of article (e.g., sheet metal or plastic film) that occurs over the course of the calendar year.

Zero Releases. If you have no releases of an EPCRA Section 313 chemical to a particular medium, report either NA, not applicable, or zero, as appropriate. Report NA only when there is no possibility a release could have occurred to a specific media. If a release to a specific media could have occurred, but either did not occur or the annual aggregate release was equal to or less than 0.5 pound, report zero. However, if you report zero releases, a basis of estimate must be provided in column B.

For example, if nitric acid is involved in the facility's processing activities but the facility neutralizes the wastes to a pH of 6 or above, then the facility reports a zero release for the EPCRA Section 313 chemical. If the facility has no underground injection well, "NA" would be written in Part I, Section 4.10 and checked in Part II, Section 5.4 .1 and 5.4.2 of Form R. Also, if the facility does not landfill the acidic waste, NA would be checked in Part II, Section 5.5.1.B of Form R.

Releases of 1,000 Pounds or More. For releases to any medium that amount to 1,000 pounds or more for the year, you must provide an estimate in pounds per year in column A. Any estimate provided in column A need not be reported to more than two significant figures. This estimate should be in whole numbers. Do not use decimal points.

Calculating On-Site Releases. To provide the release information required in column A in this section, you must use the best readily available data (including relevant monitoring data and emissions measurements) collected at your facility to meet other regulatory requirements or as part of routine plant operations, to the extent you have such data for the EPCRA Section 313 chemical.

When relevant monitoring data or emission measurements are not readily available, reasonable estimates of the amounts released must be made using published emission factors, material balance calculations, or engineering calculations. You may not use emission factors or calculations to estimate releases if more accurate data are available.

No additional monitoring or measurement of the quantities or concentrations of any EPCRA Section 313 chemical released into the environment, or of the frequency of such releases, beyond that required under other provisions of law or regulation or as part of routine plant operations, is required for the purpose of completing Form R.

You must estimate, as accurately as possible, the quantity (in pounds) of the EPCRA Section 313 chemical or chemical category that is released annually to each environmental medium on site. Include only the quantity of the EPCRA Section 313 chemical in this estimate. If the EPCRA Section 313 chemical present at your facility was part of a mixture or other trade name product, calculate only the releases of the EPCRA Section 313 chemical, not the other components of the mixture or other trade name product. If you are only able to estimate the releases of the mixture or other trade name product as a whole, you must assume that the release of the EPCRA Section 313 chemical is proportional to its concentration in the mixture or other trade name product.

If you are reporting an EPCRA Section 313 chemical category listed in Table II of these instructions rather than a specific EPCRA Section 313 chemical, you combine the release data for all chemicals in the EPCRA Section 313 chemical category (e.g., all glycol ethers or all chlorophenols) and report the aggregate amount for that EPCRA Section 313 chemical in that category separately. For example, if your facility releases 3,000 pounds per year of 2-chlorophenol, 4,000 pounds per year of 3-chlorophenol, and 4,000 pounds per year of 4-

chlorophenol to air as fugitive emissions, you should report that your facility releases 11,000 pounds per year of chlorophenols to air as fugitive emissions in Part II, Section 5.1.

For aqueous ammonia solutions, releases should be reported based on 10% of total aqueous ammonia. Ammonia evaporating from aqueous ammonia solutions is considered to be anhydrous ammonia; therefore, 100% of the anhydrous ammonia should be reported if it is released to the environment. For dissociable nitrate compounds, release estimates should be based on the weight of the nitrate only.

For metal compound categories (e.g., chromium compounds), report release of only the parent metal. For example, a user of various inorganic chromium salts would report the total chromium released regardless of the chemical form (e.g., as the original salts, chromium oxide) and exclude any contribution to mass made by other species in the molecule.

Column B: Basis of Estimate

For each release estimate, you are required to indicate the principal method used to determine the amount of release reported. You will enter a letter code that identifies the method that applies to the largest portion of the total estimated release quantity.

The codes are as follows:

M- Estimate is based on monitoring data or measurements for the EPCRA Section 313 chemical.

C- Estimate is based on mass balance calculations, such as calculation of the amount of the EPCRA Section 313 chemical in wastes entering and leaving process equipment.

E- Estimate is based on published emission factors, such as those relating release quantity to through-put or equipment type (e.g., air emission factors).

O- Estimate is based on other approaches such as engineering calculations (e.g., estimating volatilization using published mathematical formulas) or best engineering judgment. This would include applying an estimated removal efficiency to a treatment, even if the composition of the waste before treatment was fully identified through monitoring data.

For example, if 40 percent of stack emissions of the reported EPCRA Section 313 chemical were derived using monitoring data, 30 percent by mass balance, and 30 percent by emission factors, you would enter the code

letter "M" for monitoring.

If the monitoring data, mass balance, or emission factor used to estimate the release is not specific to the EPCRA Section 313 chemical being reported, the form should identify the estimate as based on engineering calculations or best engineering judgment (O).

If a mass balance calculation yields the flow rate of a waste, but the quantity of reported EPCRA Section 313 chemical in the waste is based on solubility data, report "O" because "engineering calculations" were used as the basis of estimate of the quantity of the EPCRA Section 313 chemical in the waste.

If the concentration of the EPCRA Section 313 chemical in the waste was measured by monitoring equipment and the flow rate of the waste was determined by mass balance, then the primary basis of the estimate is "monitoring" (M). Even though a mass balance calculation also contributed to the estimate, "monitoring" should be indicated because monitoring data were used to estimate the concentration of the waste.

Mass balance (C) should only be indicated if it is **directly** used to calculate the mass (weight) of EPCRA Section 313 chemical released. Monitoring data should be indicated as the basis of estimate **only** if the EPCRA Section 313 chemical concentration is measured in the waste being released into the environment. Monitoring data should **not** be indicated, for example, if the monitoring data relate to a concentration of the EPCRA Section 313 chemical in other process streams within the facility.

It is important to realize that the accuracy and proficiency of release estimation will improve over time. However, submitters are not required to use new emission factors or estimation techniques to revise previous Form R submissions.

Column C: Percent From Stormwater

This column relates only to Section 5.3 — discharges to receiving streams or water bodies. If your facility has monitoring data on the amount of the EPCRA Section 313 chemical in stormwater runoff (including unchanneled runoff), you must include that quantity of the EPCRA Section 313 chemical in your water release in column A and indicate the percentage of the total quantity (by weight) of the EPCRA Section 313 chemical contributed by stormwater in column C (Section 5.3C).

If your facility has monitoring data on the EPCRA Section 313 chemical and an estimate of flow rate, you must use these data to determine the percent stormwater.

If you have monitored stormwater but did not detect the EPCRA Section 313 chemical, enter zero in column C. If your facility has no stormwater monitoring data for the chemical, enter not applicable, "NA," in this space on the form.

If your facility does not have periodic measurements of stormwater releases of the EPCRA Section 313 chemical, but has submitted chemical-specific monitoring data in permit applications, then these data must be used to calculate the percent contribution from stormwater. Rates of flow can be estimated by multiplying the annual amount of rainfall by the land area of the facility and then multiplying that figure by the runoff coefficient. The runoff coefficient represents the fraction of rainfall that does not seep into the ground but runs off as stormwater. The runoff coefficient is directly related to how the land in the drainage area is used. (See table below)

Description of Land Area	Runoff Coefficient
Business	
Downtown areas	0.70-0.95
Neighborhood areas	0.50-0.70
Industrial	
Light areas	0.50-0.80
Heavy areas	0.60-0.90
Industrial	
Railroad yard areas	0.20-0.40
Unimproved areas	0.10-0.30
Streets	
Asphaltic	0.70-0.95
Concrete	0.80-0.95
Brick	0.70-0.85
Drives and walks	0.70-0.85
Roofs	0.75-0.95
Lawns: Sandy Soil	
Flat, 2%	0.05-0.10
Average, 2-7%	0.10-0.15
Steep, 7%	0.15-0.20
Lawns: Heavy Soil	
Flat, 2%	0.13-0.17
Average, 2-7%	0.18-0.22
Steep, 7%	0.25-0.35

Choose the most appropriate runoff coefficient for your site or calculate a weighted-average coefficient, which takes into account different types of land use at your facility:

Weighted-average runoff coefficient =
(Area 1 % of total)(C1) + (Area 2 % of total)(C2) + (Area 3 % of total)(C3) + ... + (Area i % of total)(Ci)

where Ci = runoff coefficient for a specific land use of Area i.

Section 6.　Transfers of the EPCRA Section 313 Chemical in Wastes to Off-Site Locations

You must report in this section the total annual quantity of the EPCRA Section 313 chemical in wastes sent to any off-site facility for the purposes of disposal, treatment, energy recovery, or recycling. Report the total amount of the EPCRA Section 313 chemical transferred off-site after any on-site waste treatment, recycling, or removal is completed. Report zero for transfers of listed mineral acids if they have been neutralized to a pH of 6 or above prior to discharge to a Publicly Owned Treatment Works (POTW).

If you do not discharge wastewater containing the reported EPCRA Section 313 chemical to a POTW, enter not applicable, NA, in the box for the POTW's name in Section 6.1.B._　If you do not ship or transfer wastes containing the reported EPCRA Section 313 chemical to other off-site locations, enter not applicable, NA, in the box for the off-site location's EPA Identification Number in Section 6.2._ .

Important: You must number the boxes for reporting the information for each POTW or other off-site location in Sections 6.1 and 6.2. In the upper left hand corner of each box, the section number is either 6.1.B._. or 6.2._.

If you report a transfer of the listed EPCRA Section 313 chemical to one or more POTWs, number the boxes in Section 6.1.B as 6.1.B.1, 6.1.B.2, etc. If you transfer the EPCRA Section 313 chemical to more than two POTWs, photocopy page 3 of Form R as many times as necessary and then number the boxes consecutively for each POTW. At the bottom of Section 6 you will find instructions for indicating the total number of page 3s that you are submitting as part of Form R, as well as indicating the sequence of those pages. For example, your facility transfers the reported EPCRA Section 313 chemical in wastewaters to three POTWs. You would photocopy page 3 once, indicate at the bottom of each page 3 that there are a total of two page 3s and then indicate the first and second page 3. The boxes for the two POTWs on the first page 3 would be numbered 6.1.B.1 and 6.1.B.2, while the box for third POTW on the second page 3 would be numbered 6.1.B.3.

If you report a transfer of the EPCRA Section 313 chemical to one or more other off-site locations, number the boxes in section 6.2 as 6.2.1, 6.2.2, etc. If you transfer the EPCRA Section 313 chemical to more than two other off-site locations, photocopy page 4 of Form R as many times as necessary and then number the boxes consecutively for each off-site location. At the bottom of page 4 you will find instructions for indicating the total number of page 4s that you are submitting as part of Form R as well as indicating the sequence of those pages. For example, your facility transfers the reported EPCRA Section 313 chemical to three other off-site locations. You would photocopy page 4 once, indicate at the bottom of Section 6.2 on each page 4 that there are a total of two page 4s and then indicate the first and second page 4. The boxes for the two off-site locations on the first page 4 would be numbered 6.2.1 and 6.2.2, while the box for the third off-site location on the second page 4 would be numbered 6.2.3.

6.1 Discharges to Publicly Owned Treatment Works (POTWs)

In Section 6.1.A , estimate the quantity of the reported EPCRA Section 313 chemical transferred to all POTWs and the basis upon which the estimate was made. In Section 6.1.B., enter the name and address for each POTW to which your facility discharges wastewater containing the reported EPCRA Section 313 chemical.

If you do not discharge wastewater containing the reported EPCRA Section 313 chemical to a POTW, enter not applicable, NA, in the box for the POTW's name in Section 6.1.B._.

6.1.A.1 Total Transfers

Enter the total amount, in pounds, of the reported EPCRA Section 313 chemical that is contained in the wastewaters transferred to all POTWs. Do not enter the total poundage of the wastewaters. If the total amount transferred is less than 1,000 pounds, you may report a range by entering the appropriate range code. The following reporting range codes are to be used:

Code	Reporting Range (in pounds)
A	1-10
B	11-499
C	500-999

6.1.A.2 Basis of Estimate

You must identify the basis for your estimate of the total quantity of the reported EPCRA Section 313 chemical in the wastewater transferred to all POTWs. Enter one of the following letter codes that applies to the method by which the largest percentage of the estimate was derived.

M- Estimate is based on monitoring data or measurements for the EPCRA Section 313 chemical as transferred to an off-site facility.

C- Estimate is based on mass balance calculations, such as calculation of the amount of the EPCRA Section 313 chemical in streams entering and leaving process equipment.

E- Estimate is based on published emission factors, such as those relating release quantity to through-put or equipment type (e.g., air emission factors).

O- Estimate is based on other approaches such as engineering calculations (e.g., estimating volatilization using published mathematical formulas) or best engineering judgment. This would include applying an estimated removal efficiency to a waste stream, even if the composition of the stream before treatment was fully identified through monitoring data.

If you transfer an EPCRA Section 313 chemical to more than one POTW, you should report the basis of estimate that was used to determine the largest percentage of the EPCRA Section 313 chemical that was transferred.

6.2 Transfers to Other Off-Site Locations

In Section 6.2 enter the EPA Identification Number,

Example 13: Reporting Metals and Metal Compounds that are Sent Off Site

A facility manufactures a product containing elemental lead. Various metal fabrication operations for the process produce a wastewater stream that contains some residual lead and off-specification lead material. The wastewater is collected and sent directly to a POTW. Periodic monitoring data show that 500 pounds of lead were transferred to the POTW in the reporting year. The off-specification products (containing lead) are collected and sent off site to a landfill. Sampling analyses of the product combined with hazardous waste manifests were used to determine that 1,200 pounds of lead in the off-spec product were sent to the off-site landfill.

Therefore, the facility should report 500 pounds in Section 6.1, 1200 pounds in Section 6.2 - M72 and 1,700 pounds in Section 8.1 - Quantity Released Off Site.

Note that for EPCRA Section 313 chemicals that are not metals or metal compounds, the quantity sent to POTWs and to other off-site treatment locations should be reported in Section 8.7 - Quantity Treated Off Site.

name, and address for each off-site location to which your facility ships or transfers wastes containing the reported EPCRA Section 313 chemical for the purposes of disposal, treatment, energy recovery, or recycling. Also estimate the quantity of the reported EPCRA Section 313 chemical transferred and the basis upon which the estimate was made. This would include any residual chemicals in "empty" containers transferred off site. EPA expects that all containers (bags, totes, drums, tank trucks, etc.) will have a small amount of residual solids and/or liquids. Please see following summary of residue quantities left in drums and tanks when emptied.

If appropriate, you must report multiple activities for each off-site location. For example, if your facility sends a reported EPCRA Section 313 chemical in waste to an off-site location where some of the EPCRA Section 313 chemical is to be recycled while the remainder of the quantity transferred is to be treated, you must report both the waste treatment and recycle activities, along with the quantity associated with each activity.

If your facility transfers a reported EPCRA Section 313 chemical to an off-site location and that off-site location performs more than four activities on that chemical, provide the necessary information in Box 6.2.1 for the off-site facility and the first four activities. Provide the information on the remainder of the activities in Box 6.2.2 and provide again the off-site facility identification and location information.

If you do not ship or transfer wastes containing the reported EPCRA Section 313 chemical to other off-site locations, enter not applicable, NA, in the box for the off-site locations's EPA Identification Number (defined in 40 CFR 260.10 and therefore commonly referred to as the RCRA ID Number). This number may be found on the Uniform Hazardous Waste Manifest, which is required by RCRA regulations. If you ship or transfer wastes containing an EPCRA Section 313 chemical and the off-site location does not have an EPA Identification Number (e.g., it does not accept RCRA hazardous wastes or the wastes in question are not classified as hazardous), enter NA in the box for the off-site location EPA Identification Number. If you ship or transfer the reported EPCRA Section 313 chemical in wastes to another country, enter the Federal Information Processing Standards (FIPS) code for that country in the country field of the address for the off-site facility. The most commonly used FIPS codes are listed below. To obtain a FIPS code for a country not listed here, contact the EPCRA Hotline.

6.2   Column A: Total Transfers

For each off-site location, enter the total amount, in pounds, of the EPCRA Section 313 chemical that is contained in the waste transferred to that location. Do not enter the total poundage of the waste. If the total amount transferred is less than 1,000 pounds, you may report a range by entering the appropriate range code. The following reporting range codes are to be used:

Code	Reporting Range (in pounds)
A	1-10
B	11-499
C	500-999

If you transfer the EPCRA Section 313 chemical in wastes to an off-site facility for distinct and multiple purposes, you must report those activities for each off-site location, along with the quantity of the reported EPCRA Section 313 chemical associated with each activity. For example, your facility transfers a total of 15,000 pounds of toluene to an off-site location that will use 5,000 pounds for the purposes of energy recovery, enter 7,500 pounds into a recovery process, and dispose of the remaining 2,500 pounds. These quantities and the associated activity codes must be reported separately in Section 6.2.

Do not double or multiple count amounts transferred off-site. For example, when a reported EPCRA Section 313 chemical is sent to an off-site facility for sequential activities and the specific quantities associated with each activity are unknown, report only a single quantity (the total quantity transferred to that off-site location) along with a single activity code. In such a case, report the activity applied to the majority of the reported EPCRA Section 313 chemical sent off site, not the ultimate disposition of the EPCRA Section 313 chemical. For example, when an EPCRA Section 313 chemical is first recovered and then treated with the majority of the EPCRA Section 313 chemical being recovered and only a fraction subsequently treated, report the appropriate recycling activity along with the quantity.

6.2   Column B: Basis of Estimate

You must identify the basis for your estimates of the quantities of the reported EPCRA Section 313 chemical in waste transferred to each off-site location. Enter one of the following letter codes that applies to the method by which the largest percentage of the estimate was derived.

M-   Estimate is based on monitoring data or measurements for the EPCRA Section 313 chemical as transferred to an off-site facility.

C-   Estimate is based on mass balance calculations, such as calculation of the amount of the EPCRA Section 313 chemical in streams entering and leaving process equipment.

Figure 4
Hypothetical Secton 6.2 Completed for Two Off-Site Locations

SECTION 6.2 TRANSFERS TO OTHER OFF-SITE LOCATION

6.2. 1 Off-Site EPA Identification Number (RCRA No.) COD566162461

Off-Site Location Name: Acme Waste Services

Street Address: 5 Market Street

City: Releaseville County: Hill

State: CO Zip Code: 80461 Is location under control of reporting facility or parent company ☐ Yes ☒ No

A. Total Transfers (pounds)/year) (enter range code or estimate)	B. Basis of Estimate (enter code)	C. Type of Waste Treatment/Disposal/ Recycling/Energy Recovery (enter code)
1. 5,000	1. O	1. M^{56}
2. 7,500	2. C	2. M^{20}
3. 2,500	3. O	3. M^{72}
4. NA	4.	4. M

This off-site location receives a transfer of 15,000 pounds of toluene (as discussed earlier) and will combust 5,000 pounds for the purposes of energy recovery, enter 7,500 pounds into a recovery process, and dispose of the remaining 2,500 pounds.

SECTION 6.2 TRANSFERS TO OTHER OFF-SITE LOCATION

6.2. 2 Off-Site EPA Identification Number (RCRA No.) COD167725432

Off-Site Location Name: Combustion, Inc.

Street Address: 25 Facility Road

City: Dumfry County: Burns

State: CO Zip Code: 80500 Is location under control of reporting facility or parent company ☐ Yes ☒ No

A. Total Transfers (pounds)/year) (enter range code or estimate)	B. Basis of Estimate (enter code)	C. Type of Waste Treatment/Disposal/ Recycling/Energy Recovery (enter code)
1. 12,500	1. O	1. M^{54}
2. NA	2.	2. M
3.	3.	3. M
4.	4.	4. M

This off-site location receives a transfer of 12,500 pounds of tetrachloroethylene (perchloroethylene) that is part of a waste that is combusted for the purposesof energy recovery in an industrial furnace. Note that the perchloroethylene is reported using code M54 to indicate that it is combusted in an energy recovery unit but it does not contribute to the heating value of the waste.

E- Estimate is based on published emission factors, such as those relating release quantity to throughput or equipment type (e.g., air emission factors).

O- Estimate is based on other approaches such as engineering calculations (e.g., estimating volatilization using published mathematical formulas) or best engineering judgment. This would include applying an estimated removal efficiency to a waste stream, even if the composition of the stream before treatment was fully identified through monitoring data.

6.2 Column C: Type of Waste Management: Disposal/Treatment/Energy Recovery/Recycling

Enter one of the following M codes to identify the type of disposal, treatment, energy recovery, or recycling methods used by the off-site location for the reported EPCRA Section 313 chemical. You must use more than one line and code for a single location when distinct quantities of the reported EPCRA Section 313 chemical are subject to different waste management activities, including disposal, treatment, energy recovery, or recycling. You should use the code that, to the best of your knowledge, represents the ultimate disposition of the chemical.

If the EPCRA Section 313 chemical is sent off site for further direct reuse (e.g., an EPCRA Section 313 chemical in used solvent that will be used as lubricant at another facility) and does not undergo a waste management activity (i.e., release [including disposal], treatment, energy recovery, or recycling [recovery]) prior to that reuse, it need not be reported in section 6.2 or section 8.

Incineration vs. Energy Recovery

You must distinguish between incineration, which is waste treatment, and legitimate energy recovery. For you to claim that a reported EPCRA Section 313 chemical sent off-site is used for the purposes of energy recovery and not for waste treatment, the EPCRA Section 313 chemical must have a significant heating value and must be combusted in an energy recovery unit such as an industrial boiler, furnace, or kiln. In a situation where the reported EPCRA Section 313 chemical is in a waste that is combusted in an energy recovery unit, but the EPCRA Section 313 chemical does not have a significant heating value, e.g., metals CFCs, use code M54, Incineration/Insignificant Fuel Value, to indicate that the EPCRA Section 313 chemical was incinerated in an energy recovery unit but did not contribute to the heating value of the waste.

Metals and Metal Compounds

Metals and metal compounds will be managed in waste either by being released (including disposed) or by being recycled. Remember that the release and other waste management information that you report for metal compounds will be the total amount of the parent metal released or recycled and NOT the whole metal compound. The metal has no heat value and thus cannot be combusted for energy recovery and cannot be treated because it cannot be destroyed. Thus, transfers of metals and metal compounds for further waste management should be reported as either a transfer for recycling or a transfer for disposal.

Applicable codes for Part II, Section 6.2, column C are:

Disposal

M10	Storage Only
M41	Solidification/Stabilization-Metals and Metal Compounds only
M62	Wastewater Treatment (Excluding POTW)-Metals and Metal Compounds only
M71	Underground Injection
M72	Landfill/Disposal Surface Impoundment
M73	Land Treatment
M79	Other Land Disposal
M90	Other Off-Site Management
M94	Transfer to Waste Broker-Disposal
M99	Unknown

Treatment

M40	Solidification/Stabilization
M50	Incineration/Thermal Treatment
M54	Incineration/Insignificant Fuel Value
M61	Wastewater Treatment (Excluding POTW)
M69	Other Waste Treatment
M95	Transfer to Waste Broker-Waste Treatment

Energy Recovery

M56	Energy Recovery
M92	Transfer to Waste Broker-Energy Recovery

Recycling

M20	Solvents/Organics Recovery
M24	Metals Recovery
M26	Other Reuse or Recovery
M28	Acid Regeneration
M93	Transfer to Waste Broker-Recycling

Section 7. On-Site Waste Treatment, Energy Recovery, and Recycling Methods

You must report in this section the methods of waste

treatment, energy recovery, and recycling applied to the reported EPCRA Section 313 chemical in wastes on site. There are three separate sections for reporting such activities.

Section 7A   On-Site Waste Treatment Methods and Efficiency

Most of the chemical-specific information required by EPCRA Section 313 that is reported on Form R is specific to the EPCRA Section 313 chemical rather than the waste stream containing the EPCRA Section 313 chemical. However, EPCRA Section 313 does require that waste treatment methods applied on-site to waste streams that contain the EPCRA Section 313 chemical be reported. This information is collected in Section 7A of Form R.

In Section 7A, you must provide the following information if you treat the reported EPCRA Section 313 chemical on-site:

(a) The general waste stream types containing the EPCRA Section 313 chemical being reported;
(b) The waste treatment method(s) or sequence used on all waste streams containing the EPCRA Section 313 chemical;
(c) The range of concentration of the EPCRA Section 313 chemicals in the influent to the waste treatment method;
(d) The efficiency of each waste treatment method or waste treatment sequence in destroying or removing the EPCRA Section 313 chemical; and
(e) Whether the waste treatment efficiency figure was based on actual operating data.

Use a separate line in Section 7A for each general waste stream type. Report only information about treatment of waste streams at your facility, not information about off-site waste treatment.

If you do not perform on-site treatment of waste streams containing the reported EPCRA Section 313 chemical, check the Not Applicable (NA) box at the top of Section 7A.

7A   Column A: General Waste Stream

For each waste treatment method, indicate the type of waste stream containing the EPCRA Section 313 chemical that is treated. Enter the letter code that corresponds to the general waste stream type:

A   Gaseous (gases, vapors, airborne particulates)
W   Wastewater (aqueous waste)
L   Liquid waste streams (non-aqueous waste)

S   Solid waste streams (including sludges and slurries)

If a waste is a mixture of water and organic liquid and the organic content is less than 50 percent, report it as a wastewater (W). Slurries and sludges containing water must be reported as solid waste if they contain appreciable amounts of dissolved solids, or solids that may settle, such that the viscosity or density of the waste is considerably different from that of process wastewater.

7A   Column B: Waste Treatment Method(s) Sequence

Enter the appropriate waste treatment code from the list below for each on-site waste treatment method used on a waste stream containing the EPCRA Section 313 chemical, regardless of whether the waste treatment method actually removes the specific EPCRA Section 313 chemical being reported. Waste treatment methods must be reported for each type of waste stream being treated (i.e., gaseous waste streams, aqueous waste streams, liquid non-aqueous waste streams, and solids). Except for the air emission treatment codes, the waste treatment codes are not restricted to any medium.

Waste streams containing the EPCRA Section 313 chemical may have a single source or may be aggregates of many sources. For example, process water from several pieces of equipment at your facility may be combined prior to waste treatment. Report waste treatment methods that apply to the aggregate waste stream, as well as waste treatment methods that apply to individual waste streams. If your facility treats various wastewater streams containing the EPCRA Section 313 chemical in different ways, the different waste treatment methods must be listed separately.

If your facility has several pieces of equipment performing a similar service in a waste treatment sequence, you may combine the reporting for such equipment. It is not necessary to enter four codes to cover four scrubber units, for example, if all four are treating waste streams of similar character (e.g., sulfuric acid mist emissions), have similar influent concentrations, and have similar removal efficiencies. If, however, any of these parameters differs from one unit to the next, each scrubber must be listed separately.

If your facility performs more than eight sequential waste treatment methods on a single general waste stream, continue listing the methods in the next row and renumber appropriately those waste treatment method code boxes you used to continue the sequence. For example, if the general waste stream in box 7A.1a had nine treatment methods applied to it, the ninth method would be indicated in the first method box for row 7A.2a.

The numeral "1" would be crossed out, and a "9" would be inserted.

Treatment applied to any other general waste stream types would then be listed in the next empty row. In the scenario above, for instance, the second general waste stream would be reported in row 7A.3a.

If you need additional space to report under Section 7A, photocopy page 4 of Form R as many times as necessary. At the bottom of page 4 you will find instructions for indicating the total number of page 4s that you are submitting as part of Form R, as well as instructions for indicating the sequence of those pages.

Waste Treatment Codes

Air Emissions Treatment (applicable to gaseous waste streams only)

A01	Flare
A02	Condenser
A03	Scrubber
A04	Absorber
A05	Electrostatic Precipitator
A06	Mechanical Separation
A07	Other Air Emission Treatment

Biological Treatment

B11	Aerobic
B21	Anaerobic
B31	Facultative
B99	Other Biological Treatment

Chemical Treatment

C01	Chemical Precipitation — Lime or Sodium Hydroxide
C02	Chemical Precipitation — Sulfide
C09	Chemical Precipitation — Other
C11	Neutralization
C21	Chromium Reduction
C31	Complexed Metals Treatment (other than pH adjustment)
C41	Cyanide Oxidation — Alkaline Chlorination
C42	Cyanide Oxidation — Electrochemical
C43	Cyanide Oxidation — Other
C44	General Oxidation (including Disinfection) — Chlorination
C45	General Oxidation (including Disinfection) — Ozonation
C46	General Oxidation (including Disinfection) — Other

C99	Other Chemical Treatment

Incineration/Thermal Treatment

F01	Liquid Injection
F11	Rotary Kiln with Liquid Injection Unit
F19	Other Rotary Kiln
F31	Two Stage
F41	Fixed Hearth
F42	Multiple Hearth
F51	Fluidized Bed
F61	Infra-Red
F71	Fume/Vapor
F81	Pyrolytic Destructor
F82	Wet Air Oxidation
F83	Thermal Drying/Dewatering
F99	Other Incineration/Thermal Treatment

Physical Treatment

P01	Equalization
P09	Other Blending
P11	Settling/Clarification
P12	Filtration
P13	Sludge Dewatering (non-thermal)
P14	Air Flotation
P15	Oil Skimming
P16	Emulsion Breaking — Thermal
P17	Emulsion Breaking — Chemical
P18	Emulsion Breaking — Other
P19	Other Liquid Phase Separation
P21	Adsorption — Carbon
P22	Adsorption — Ion Exchange (other than for recovery/reuse)
P23	Adsorption — Resin
P29	Adsorption — Other
P31	Reverse Osmosis (other than for recovery/reuse)
P41	Stripping — Air
P42	Stripping — Steam
P49	Stripping — Other
P51	Acid Leaching (other than for recovery/reuse)
P61	Solvent Extraction (other than recovery/reuse)
P99	Other Physical Treatment

Solidification/Stabilization

G01	Cement Processes (including silicates)
G09	Other Pozzolonic Processes (including silicates)
G11	Asphaltic Processes
G21	Thermoplastic Techniques
G99	Other Solidification Processes

7A   Column C: Range of Influent Concentration

The form requires an indication of the range of concentration of the EPCRA Section 313 chemical in the waste stream (i.e., the influent) as it typically enters the waste treatment step or sequence. The concentration is based on the amount or mass of the EPCRA Section 313 chemical in the waste stream as compared to the total amount or mass of the waste stream. Enter in the space provided one of the following code numbers corresponding to the concentration of the EPCRA Section 313 chemical in the influent:

1 = Greater than 10,000 parts per million (1 percent)
2 = 100 parts per million (0.01 percent) to 10,000 parts per million (1 percent)
3 = 1 part per million (0.0001 percent) to 100 parts per million (0.01 percent)
4 = 1 part per billion to 1 part per million
5 = Less than 1 part per billion

Note: Parts per million (ppm) is:

- milligrams/kilogram (mass/mass) for solids and liquids;
- cubic centimeters/cubic meter (volume/volume) for gases;
- milligrams/liter for solutions or dispersions of the chemical in water; and
- milligrams of chemical/kilogram of air for particulates in air.

If you have particulate concentrations (at standard temperature and pressure) as grains/cubic foot of air, multiply by 1766.6 to convert to parts per million; if in milligrams/cubic meter, multiply by 0.773 to obtain parts per million. These conversion factors are for standard conditions of 0° C (32° F) and 760 mm Hg atmospheric pressure.

7A   Column D: Waste Treatment Efficiency Estimate

In the space provided, enter the number indicating the percentage of the EPCRA Section 313 chemical removed from the waste stream through destruction, biological degradation, chemical conversion, or physical removal. The waste treatment efficiency (expressed as percent removal) represents the percentage of the EPCRA Section 313 chemical destroyed or removed (based on amount or mass), not merely changes in volume or concentration of the EPCRA Section 313 chemical in the waste stream. The efficiency, which can reflect the overall removal from sequential treatment methods applied to the general waste stream, refers only to the percent destruction, degradation, conversion, or removal of the EPCRA

Section 313 chemical from the waste stream, not the percent conversion or removal of other constituents in the waste stream. The efficiency also does not refer to the general efficiency of the treatment method for any waste stream. For some waste treatment methods, the percent removal will represent removal by several mechanisms, as in an aeration basin, where an EPCRA Section 313 chemical may evaporate, biodegrade, or be physically removed from the sludge.

Percent removal can be calculated as follows:

$$\frac{(I - E)}{I} \times 100, \text{ where}$$

I = amount of the EPCRA Section 313 chemical in the influent waste stream (entering the waste treatment step or sequence) and
E = amount of the EPCRA Section 313 chemical in the effluent waste stream (exiting the waste treatment step or sequence).

Calculate the amount of the EPCRA Section 313 chemical in the influent waste stream by multiplying the concentration (by weight) of the EPCRA Section 313 chemical in the waste stream by the total amount or weight of the waste stream. In most cases, the percent removal compares the treated effluent to the influent for the particular type of waste stream. For solidification of wastewater, the waste treatment efficiency can be reported as 100 percent if no volatile EPCRA Section 313 chemicals were removed with the water or evaporated into the air.   Percent removal does not apply to incineration because the waste stream, such as wastewater or liquids, may not exist in a comparable form after waste treatment and the purpose of incineration as a waste treatment is to destroy the EPCRA Section 313 chemical by converting it to carbon dioxide and water or other byproducts. In cases where the EPCRA Section 313 chemical is incinerated, the percent efficiency must be based on the amount of the EPCRA Section 313 chemical destroyed or combusted, except for metals or metal compounds. In the cases in which a metal or metal compound is incinerated, the efficiency is always zero for the parent metal.

Similarly, an efficiency of zero must be reported for any waste treatment method(s) (e.g., evaporation) that does not destroy, chemically convert or physically remove the EPCRA Section 313 chemical from the waste stream.

For metal compounds, the calculation of the reportable concentration and waste treatment efficiency must be based on the weight of the parent metal, not on the weight of the metal compound.   Metals are not destroyed, only physically removed or chemically converted from one form into another. The waste treatment efficiency reported must represent only physical removal of the parent metal from the waste stream (except for incineration), not the percent chemical conversion of the metal compound. If a listed waste treatment method converts but does not remove a metal (e.g., chromium reduction), the method must be reported with a waste treatment efficiency of zero.

EPCRA Section 313 chemicals that are strong mineral acids neutralized to a pH of 6 or above are considered treated at a 100 percent efficiency.

All data readily available at your facility must be used to calculate waste treatment efficiency and influent EPCRA Section 313 chemical concentration. If data are lacking, estimates must be made using best engineering judgment or other methods.

7A　Column E: Based on Operating Data?

This column requires you to indicate "Yes" or "No" to whether the waste treatment efficiency estimate is based on actual operating data. For example, you would check "Yes" if the estimate is based on monitoring of influent and effluent wastes under typical operating conditions.

If the efficiency estimate is based on published data for similar processes or on equipment supplier's literature, or if you otherwise estimated either the influent or effluent waste comparison or the flow rate, check "No."

Section 7B　On-Site Energy Recovery Processes

In Section 7B, you must indicate the on-site energy recovery methods used on the reported EPCRA Section 313 chemical. If you do not perform on-site energy recovery for the reported EPCRA Section 313 chemical, check the Not Applicable (NA) box at the top of Section 7B.

Only EPCRA Section 313 chemicals that have a significant heating value and are combusted in an energy recovery unit such as an industrial furnace, kiln, or boiler, can be reported as combusted for energy recovery in this section. If a reported EPCRA Section 313 chemical is incinerated on site but does not contribute energy to the process (e.g., chlorofluorocarbons), it must be considered waste treated on site and reported in Section 7A. Metals and metal compounds cannot be combusted for energy recovery and should NOT be reported in this section. Energy recovery may take place only in an industrial kiln, furnace, or boiler.

Energy Recovery Codes

U01 Industrial Kiln
U02 Industrial Furnace
U03 Industrial Boiler
U09 Other Energy Recovery Methods

If your facility uses more than one on-site energy recovery method for the reported EPCRA Section 313 chemical, list the methods used in descending order (greatest to least) based on the amount of the EPCRA Section 313 chemical entering such methods.

Section 7C　On-Site Recycling Processes

In Section 7C, you must report the recycling methods used on the EPCRA Section 313 chemical. If you do not conduct any on-site recycling of the reported EPCRA Section 313 chemical, check the Not Applicable (NA) box at the top of Section 7C.

In this section, use the codes below to report only the recycling methods in place at your facility that are applied to the EPCRA Section 313 chemical. Do not list any off-site recycling activities (Information about off-site recycling must be reported in Part II, Section 6, "Transfers of the Toxic Chemical in Wastes to Off-Site Locations.")

On-Site Recycling Codes

R11 Solvents/Organics Recovery — Batch Still Distillation
R12 Solvents/Organics Recovery — Thin-Film Evaporation
R13 Solvents/Organics Recovery — Fractionation
R14 Solvents/Organics Recovery — Solvent Extraction
R19 Solvents/Organics Recovery — Other
R21 Metals Recovery — Electrolytic
R22 Metals Recovery — Ion Exchange
R23 Metals Recovery — Acid Leaching
R24 Metals Recovery — Reverse Osmosis
R26 Metals Recovery — Solvent Extraction
R27 Metals Recovery — High Temperature
R28 Metals Recovery — Retorting
R29 Metals Recovery — Secondary Smelting
R30 Metals Recovery — Other
R40 Acid Regeneration
R99 Other Reuse or Recovery

If your facility uses more than one on-site recycling method for an EPCRA Section 313 chemical, enter the codes in the space provided in descending order (greatest to least) of the volume of the reported EPCRA Section 313 chemical recovered by each process. If your facility uses more than ten separate methods for recycling the reported EPCRA Section 313 chemical on site, then list the ten activities that recover the greatest amount of the EPCRA Section 313 chemical (again, in descending order).

Section 8. Source Reduction and Recycling Activities

This section includes the data elements mandated by section 6607 of the Pollution Prevention Act of 1990 (PPA). Section 8 is a required section of Form R and must be completed.

In Section 8, you must provide information about source reduction activities and quantities of the EPCRA Section 313 chemicals managed as waste. For all appropriate questions, report only the quantity, in pounds, of the reported EPCRA Section 313 chemical itself. Do not include the weight of water, soil, or other waste constituents. When reporting on the metal compound categories, report only the amount of the parent metal as you do when estimating release amounts.

Sections 8.1 through 8.9 must be completed for each EPCRA Section 313 chemical. Section 8.10 must be completed only if a source reduction activity was newly implemented specifically (in whole or in part) for the reported EPCRA Section 313 chemical during the reporting year. Section 8.11 allows you to indicate if you have attached additional optional information on source reduction, recycling, or pollution control activities implemented at any time at your facility.

Sections 8.1 through 8.7 require reporting of quantities for the current reporting year, the prior year, and quantities anticipated in both the first year immediately following the reporting year and the second year following the reporting year (future estimates).

Beginning with the 1995 reporting year, facilities can use applicable, "NA," in Sections 8.1 through 8.7 to indicate that there is no on-site or off-site recycling, energy recovery, treatment, or release.

Column A: Prior Year

Quantities for Sections 8.1 through 8.7 must be reported for the year immediately preceding the reporting year in column A. For reports due July 1, 1999 (reporting year 1998), the prior year is 1997. Information available at the facility that may be used to estimate the prior year's quantities include the prior year's Form R submission, supporting documentation, and recycling, energy recovery, treatment, or disposal operating logs or invoices. New industries can enter NA in Sections 8.1 - 8.7 in column A for reporting year 1998 reporting only because facilities in these industries were not required to collect data for reporting year 1997.

Column B: Current Reporting Year

Quantities for Sections 8.1 through 8.7 must be reported for the current reporting year (1998) in column B.

Columns C and D: Following Year and Second Following Year

Quantities for Sections 8.1 through 8.7 must be estimated for 1999 and 2000. EPA expects reasonable future quantity estimates using a logical basis. Information available at the facility to estimate quantities of the chemical expected during these years include planned source reduction activities, market projections, expected contracts, anticipated new product lines, company growth projections, and production capacity figures. Respondents should take into account protections available for trade secrets as provided in EPCRA Section 322 (42 USC 11042) for the chemical identity.

Relationship to Other Laws

The reporting categories for quantities recycled, used for energy recovery, treated, and disposed apply to completing Section 8 of Form R as well as to the rest of Form R. These categories are to be used only for TRI reporting. They are not intended for use in determining, under the Resource Conservation and Recovery Act (RCRA) Subtitle C regulations, whether a secondary material is a waste when recycled. These definitions also do not apply to the information that may be submitted in the Biennial Report required under RCRA. In addition, these definitions do not imply any future redefinition of RCRA terms and do not affect EPA's RCRA authority or authority under any other statute administered by EPA.

Differences in terminology and reporting requirements for EPCRA Section 313 chemicals reported on Form R and for hazardous wastes regulated under RCRA occur because EPCRA and the PPA focus on specific chemicals, while the RCRA regulations and the Biennial Report focus on waste streams that may include more than one chemical. For example, a RCRA hazardous waste containing an EPCRA Section 313 chemical is recycled to recover certain constituents of that waste, but not the toxic chemical reported under EPCRA section 313. The EPCRA Section 313 chemical simply passes through the recycling process and remains in the residual from the recycling process, which is disposed. While the waste may be considered recycled under RCRA, the EPCRA Section 313 chemical constituent would be considered to be disposed for TRI purposes.

Quantities Reportable in Sections 8.1 - 8.7

Section 8 of Form R uses data collected to complete Part II, Sections 5 through 7. For this reason, Section 8 should be completed last. Sections 8.1, 8.3, 8.5, 8.7, and 8.8 use data collected to complete sections 5 and 6 of Form R. The relationship between sections 5, 6, and 8.8 to sections 8.1, 8.3, 8.5, and 8.7 are provided below in equation form.

Section 8.1. Report releases pursuant to EPCRA Section 329(8) including "any spilling, leaking, pumping, pouring, emitting, emptying, discharging, injecting, escaping, leaching, dumping, or disposing [on site or off site] into the environment (including the abandonment of barrels, containers, and other closed receptacles)." This includes on-site releases in section 5 and off-site releases (including disposal) in section 6, but excludes quantities reported in sections 5 and 6 due to remedial actions, catastrophic events, or non-production related events (see the discussion on section 8.8.)

Sections 8.2 and 8.3. These relate to a EPCRA Section 313 chemical or a mixture containing an EPCRA Section 313 chemical that is used for energy recovery on site or is sent off site for energy recovery, unless it is a commercially available fuel (e.g., fuel oil no. 6). For the purposes of reporting on Form R, reportable on-site and off-site energy recovery is the combustion of a waste containing an EPCRA Section 313 chemical when:

(a) The combustion unit is integrated into an energy recovery system (i.e., industrial furnaces, industrial kilns, and boilers); and

(b) The EPCRA Section 313 chemical is combustible and has a significant heating value (e.g., 5000 BTU)

Sections 8.4 and 8.5. These relate to an EPCRA Section 313 chemical in a waste that is recycled on site or is sent off site for recycling.

Section 8.6 and 8.7. These relate to an EPCRA Section 313 chemical (except for metals and metal compounds) or a mixture containing an EPCRA Section 313 chemical that is treated on site or is sent to a POTW or other off-site location for waste treatment.

---

[1]§8.8 includes quantities of toxic chemical released on site or managed as waste off site due to remedial actions, catastrophic events, or one-time events not associated with the production processes.

An EPCRA Section 313 chemical or an EPCRA Section 313 chemical in a mixture that is a waste under RCRA must be reported in Sections 8.1 through 8.7.

Avoid Double-Counting in Sections 8.1 Through 8.8

Do not double- or multiple-count quantities in Sections 8.1 through 8.7. The quantities reported in each of those sections must be mutually exclusive. Do not multiple-count quantities entering sequential reportable activities.

Do not include in Sections 8.1 through 8.7 any quantities of the EPCRA Section 313 chemical released into the environment due to remedial actions; catastrophic events such as earthquakes, fires, or floods; or unanticipated one-time events not associated with the production process such as a drunk driver crashing his/her car into a drum storage area. These quantities should be reported in Section 8.8 only. For example, 10,000 pounds of diaminoanisole sulfate is released due to a catastrophic event and is subsequently treated off site. The 10,000 pounds is reported in Section 8.8, but the amount subsequently treated off site is not reported in Section 8.7.

8.8 Quantity Released to the Environment as a Result of Remedial Actions, Cata-strophic Events, or One-Time Events Not Associated with Production Processes

In Section 8.8, enter the total quantity of EPCRA Section 313 chemical released directly into the environment or sent off site for recycling, energy recovery, treatment, or disposal during the reporting year due to any of the following events:

(1) remedial actions;
(2) catastrophic events such as earthquakes, fires, or floods; or
(3) one-time events not associated with normal or routine production processes.

These quantities should not be included in Sections 8.1 through 8.7

The purpose of this section is to separate quantities recycled, used for energy recovery, treated, or disposed that are associated with normal or routine production operations from those that are not. While all quantities released, recycled, treated, or disposed may ultimately be preventable, this section separates the quantities that are more likely to be reduced or eliminated by process-oriented source reduction activities from those releases that are largely unpredictable and are less amenable to such source reduction activities. For example, spills that occur as a routine part of production operations and could be reduced or eliminated by improved handling, loading, or unloading procedures are included in the quantities reported in Section 8.1 through 8.7 as appropriate. A total loss of containment resulting from a tank rupture caused by a tornado would be included in the quantity reported in Section 8.8.

Similarly, the amount of an EPCRA Section 313 chemical cleaned up from spills resulting from normal operations during the reporting year would be included in the quantities reported in Sections 8.1 through 8.7. However, the quantity of the reported EPCRA Section 313 chemical generated from a remedial action (e.g., RCRA corrective action) to clean up the environmental contamination resulting from past practices should be reported in Section 8.8 because they cannot currently be addressed by source reduction methods. A remedial action for purposes of Section 8.8 is a waste cleanup (including RCRA and CERCA operations) within the facility boundary. Most remedial activities involve collecting and treating contaminated material.

Also, releases caused by catastrophic events are to be incorporated into the quantity reported in Section 8.8. Such releases may be caused by natural disasters (e.g., hurricanes and earthquakes) or by large-scale accidents (e.g., fires and explosions). In addition, releases due to one-time events not associated with production (e.g., terrorist bombing) are to be included in Section 8.8. These amounts are not included in the quantities reported in Sections 8.1 through 8.7 because such releases are generally unanticipated and cannot be addressed by routine process-oriented accident prevention techniques.

By checking your documentation for calculating estimates made for Part II, Section 5, "Quantity of the Toxic Chemical Entering Each Environmental Medium On Site," you may be able to identify release amounts from the above sources. Emergency notifications under CERCA and EPCRA as well as accident histories required under the Clean Air Act may provide useful information. You should also check facility incident reports and maintenance records to identify one-time or catastrophic events.

Note: While the information reported in Section 8.8 represents only remedial, catastrophic, or one-time events not associated with production processes, Section 5 of Form R (on-site releases to the environment) and Section 6 (off-site transfers for further waste management), must include all on-site releases and transfers as appropriate, regardless of whether they arise from catastrophic, remedial, or routine process operations.

8.9 Production Ratio or Activity Index

For Section 8.9, you must provide a ratio of reporting year production to prior year production, or provide an "activity index" based on a variable other than production that is the primary influence on the quantity of the reported EPCRA Section 313 chemical recycled, used for energy recovery, treated, or released. The ratio or index must be reported to the nearest tenths or hundredths place (i.e., one or two digits to the right of the decimal point). If the manufacture or use of the reported EPCRA Section 313 chemical began during the current reporting year, enter not applicable, "NA," as the production ratio or activity index. Note, this is not to be

---

Example 20: Quantity Released to the Environment as a Result of Remedial Actions, Catastrophic Events, or One-Time Events Not Associated with Production Processes.

A chemical manufacturer produces an EPCRA Section 313 chemical in a reactor that operates at low pressure. The reactants and the EPCRA Section 313 chemical product are piped in and out of the reactor at monitored and controlled temperatures. During normal operations, small amounts of fugitive emissions occur from the valves and flanges in the pipelines.

Due to a malfunction in the control panel (which is state-of-the-art and undergoes routine inspection and maintenance), the temperature and pressure in the reactor increase, the reactor ruptures, and the EPCRA Section 313 chemical is released. Because the malfunction could not be anticipated and, therefore, could not be reasonably addressed by specific source reduction activities, the amount released is included in Section 8.8. In this case, much of the EPCRA Section 313 chemical is released as a liquid and pools on the ground. It is estimated that 1,000 pounds of the EPCRA Section 313 chemical pooled on the ground and was subsequently collected and sent off-site for treatment. In addition, it is estimated that another 200 pounds of the EPCRA Section 313 chemical vaporized directly to the air from the rupture. The total amount reported in Section 8.8 is the 1,000 pounds that pooled on the ground (and subsequently sent off-site), plus the 200 pounds that vaporized into the air, a total of 1,200 pounds. The quantity sent off-site must also be reported in Section 6 (but not in Section 8.7) and the quantity that vaporized must be reported as a fugitive emission in Section 5 (but not in Section 8.1).

reported as a percent (i.e., report 1.10 for a 10% increase, not 110%).

It is important to realize that if your facility reports more than one reported EPCRA Section 313 chemical, the production ratio or activity index may vary for different chemicals. For facilities that manufacture reported EPCRA Section 313 chemicals, the quantities of the EPCRA Section 313 chemical(s) produced in the current and prior years provide a good basis for the ratio because that is the primary business activity associated with the reported EPCRA Section 313 chemical(s). In most cases, the production ratio or activity index must be based on some variable of production or activity rather than on EPCRA Section 313 chemical or material usage. Indices based on EPCRA Section 313 chemical or material usage may reflect the effect of source reduction activities rather than changes in business activity. EPCRA Section 313 chemical or material usage is therefore not a basis to be used for the production ratio or activity index where the EPCRA Section 313 chemical is "otherwise-used" (i.e., non-incorporative activities such as extraction solvents, metal degreasers, etc.).

While several methods are available to the facility for determining this data element, the production ratio or activity index must be based on the variable that most directly affects the quantities of the EPCRA Section 313 chemical recycled, used for energy recovery, treated, or released. Examples of methods available include:

(1) Amount of EPCRA Section 313 chemical manufactured in 1998 divided by the amount of EPCRA Section 313 chemical manufactured in 1997; or

(2) Amount of product produced in 1998 divided by the amount of product produced in 1997.

8.10 Did Your Facility Engage in Any Source Reduction Activities for This Chemical During the Reporting Year?

If your facility engaged in any source reduction activity for the reported EPCRA Section 313 chemical during the reporting year, report the activity that was implemented and the method used to identify the opportunity for the activity implemented. If your facility did not engage in any source reduction activity for the reported EPCRA Section 313 chemical, enter not applicable, "NA," in Section 8.10.1 and answer Section 8.11.

Source reduction means any practice that:

❏ Reduces the amount of any hazardous substance,

pollutant, or contaminant entering any waste stream or otherwise released into the environment (including fugitive emissions) prior to recycling, energy recovery, treatment, or disposal; and

❏ Reduces the hazards to public health and the environment associated with the release of such substances, pollutants, or contaminants.

The term includes equipment or technology modifications, process or procedure modifications, reformulation or redesign of products, substitution of raw materials, and improvements in housekeeping, maintenance, training, or inventory control.

The term source reduction does not include any practice that alters the physical, chemical, or biological characteristics or the volume of a hazardous substance, pollutant, or contaminant through a process or activity that itself is not integral to and necessary for the production of a product or the providing of a service.

Source reduction activities do not include recycling, using for energy recovery, treating, or disposing of an EPCRA Section 313 chemical. Report in this section only the source reduction activities implemented to reduce or eliminate the quantities reported in Sections 8.1 through 8.7. The focus of the section is only those activities that are applied to reduce routine or reasonably anticipated releases and quantities of the reported EPCRA Section 313 chemical recycled, treated, used for energy recovery, or disposed. Do not report in this section any activities taken to reduce or eliminate the quantities reported in Section 8.8.

Source Reduction Activities

You must enter in the first column of Section 8.10, "Source Reduction Activities," the appropriate code(s) indicating the type of actions taken to reduce the amount of the reported EPCRA Section 313 chemical released (as reported in Section 8.1), used for energy recovery (as reported in Sections 8.2-8.3), recycled (as reported in Sections 8.4-8.5), or treated (as reported in Sections 8.6-8.7). The list of codes below includes many, but not all, of the codes provided in the RCRA biennial report. Remember that source reduction activities include only those actions or techniques that reduce or eliminate the amounts of the EPCRA Section 313 chemical reported in Sections 8.1 through 8.7. Actions taken to recycle, combust for energy recovery, treat, or dispose of the EPCRA Section 313 chemical are not considered source reduction activities.

Example 24: Determining the Production Ratio Based on a Weighted Average

At many facilities, a reported EPCRA Section 313 chemical is used in more than one production process. In these cases, a production ratio or activity index can be estimated by weighting the production ratio for each process based on the respective contribution of each process to the quantity of the reported EPCRA Section 313 chemical recycled, used for energy recovery, treated, or disposed.

Your facility paints bicycles with paint containing toluene. Sixteen thousand bicycles were produced in the reporting year and 14,500 were produced in the prior year. There were no significant design modifications that changed the total surface area to be painted for each bike. The bicycle production ratio is 1.1 (16,000/14,500). You estimate 12,500 pounds of toluene recycled, used for energy recovery, treated, or released as a result of bicycle production. Your facility also uses toluene as a solvent in a glue that is used to make components and add-on equipment for the bicycles. Thirteen thousand components were manufactured in the reporting year as compared to 15,000 during the prior year. The production ratio for the components using toluene is 0.87 (13,000/15,000). You estimate 1,000 pounds of toluene treated, recycled, used for energy recovery, or released as a result of components production. A production ratio can be calculated by weighting each of the production ratios based on the relative contribution each has to the quantities of toluene treated, recycled, used for energy recovery, or released during the reporting year (13,500 pounds). The production ratio is calculated as follows:

$$\text{Production ratio} = 1.1 \times (12,500/13,500) + 0.87 \times (1,000/13,500) = 1.08$$

Source Reduction Activity Codes:

Good Operating Practices

W13 Improved maintenance scheduling, record keeping, or procedures
W14 Changed production schedule to minimize equipment and feedstock changeovers
W19 Other changes made in operating practices

Inventory Control

W21 Instituted procedures to ensure that materials do not stay in inventory beyond shelf-life
W22 Began to test outdated material — continue to use if still effective
W23 Eliminated shelf-life requirements for stable materials
W24 Instituted better labeling procedures
W25 Instituted clearinghouse to exchange materials that would otherwise be discarded
W29 Other changes made in inventory control

Spill and Leak Prevention

W31 Improved storage or stacking procedures
W32 Improved procedures for loading, unloading, and transfer operations
W33 Installed overflow alarms or automatic shut-off valves
W35 Installed vapor recovery systems
W36 Implemented inspection or monitoring program of potential spill or leak sources
W39 Other changes made in spill and leak prevention

Raw Material Modifications

W41 Increased purity of raw materials
W42 Substituted raw materials
W49 Other raw material modifications made

Process Modifications

W51 Instituted re-circulation within a process
W52 Modified equipment, layout, or piping
W53 Used a different process catalyst
W54 Instituted better controls on operating bulk containers to minimize discarding of empty containers
W55 Changed from small volume containers to bulk containers to minimize discarding of empty containers
W58 Other process modifications made

Cleaning and Degreasing

W59 Modified stripping/cleaning equipment
W60 Changed to mechanical stripping/cleaning devices (from solvents or other materials)
W61 Changed to aqueous cleaners (from solvents or other materials)
W63 Modified containment procedures for cleaning units
W64 Improved draining procedures
W65 Redesigned parts racks to reduce drag out

W66   Modified or installed rinse systems
W67   Improved rinse equipment design
W68   Improved rinse equipment operation
W71   Other cleaning and decreasing modifications made

Surface Preparation and Finishing

W72   Modified spray systems or equipment
W73   Substituted coating materials used
W74   Improved application techniques
W75   Changed from spray to other system
W78   Other surface preparation and finishing modifications made

Product Modifications

W81   Changed product specifications
W82   Modified design or composition of product
W83   Modified packaging
W89   Other product modifications made

In columns a through c of Section 8.10, the "Methods to Identify Activity", you must enter one or more of the following code(s) that correspond to those internal and external method(s) or information sources you used to identify the possibility for a source reduction activity implementation at your facility. If more than three methods were used to identify the source reduction activity, enter only the three codes that contributed most to the decision to implement the activity.

Methods to Identify Activity

T01   Internal pollution prevention opportunity audit(s)
T02   External pollution prevention opportunity audit(s)
T03   Materials balance audits
T04   Participative team management
T05   Employee recommendation (independent of a formal company program)
T06   Employee recommendation (under a formal company program)
T07   State government technical assistance program
T08   Federal government technical assistance program
T09   Trade association/industry technical assistance program
T10   Vendor assistance
T11   Other

8.11   Is Additional Optional Information on Source Reduction, Recycling, or Pollution Control Activities Included with this Report?

Check "Yes" for this data element if you have attached to this report any additional optional information on source reduction, recycling, or pollution control activities you have implemented in the reporting year or in prior years for the reported EPCRA Section 313 chemical. If you are not including additional information, check "No."

Form Approved OMB Number: 2070-0093
Approval Expires: 04/20___

Page 1 of 5

☮ EPA FORM R

United States Environmental Protection Agency

TOXIC CHEMICAL RELEASE INVENTORY REPORTING FORM

Section 313 of the Emergency Planning and Community Right-to-Know Act of 1986, also known as Title III of the Superfund Amendments and Reauthorization Act

WHERE TO SEND COMPLETED FORMS: 1. EPCRA Reporting Center P.O Box 3348 Merrifield, VA 22116-3348 ATTN: TOXIC CHEMICAL RELEASE INVENTORY	2. APPROPRIATE STATE OFFICE (See instructions in Appendix F)	Enter "X" here if this is a revision ☐
		For EPA use only ☐

Important: See instructions to determine when "Not Applicable (NA)" boxes should be checked.

PART I. FACILITY IDENTIFICATION INFORMATION

SECTION 1. REPORTING YEAR _____

SECTION 2. TRADE SECRET INFORMATION

2.1	Are you claiming the toxic chemical identified on page 2 trade secret? ☐ Yes (Answer question 2.2; Attach substantiation forms) ☐ No (Do not answer 2.2; Go to Section 3)	2.2	Is this copy ☐ Sanitized ☐ Unsanitized (Answer only if "YES" in 2.1)

SECTION 3. CERTIFICATION (Important: Read and sign after completing all form sections.)

I hereby certify that I have reviewed the attached documents and that, to the best of my knowledge and belief, the submitted information is true and complete and that the amounts and values in this report are accurate based on reasonable estimates using data available to the preparers of this report.

Name and official title of owner/operator or senior management official:	Signature:	Date Signed:

SECTION 4. FACILITY IDENTIFICATION

4.1		TRI Facility ID Number
Facility or Establishment Name		Facility or Establishment Name or Mailing Address(if different from street address)
Street		Mailing Address
City/County/State/Zip Code		City/County/State/Zip Code

4.2	This report contains information for: (Important : check a or b; check c if applicable)	a. ☐ An entire facility	b. ☐ Part of a facility	c. ☐ A Federal facility

4.3	Technical Contact Name		Telephone Number (include area code)
4.4	Public Contact Name		Telephone Number (include area code)

4.5	SIC Code (s) (4 digits)	a.	b.	c.	d.	e.	f.

4.6	Latitude	Degrees	Minutes	Seconds	Longitude	Degrees	Minutes	Seconds

4.7	Dun & Bradstreet Number(s) (9 digits)	4.8	EPA Identification Number (RCRA I.D. No.) (12 characters)	4.9	Facility NPDES Permit Number(s) (9 characters)	4.10	Underground Injection Well Code (UIC) I.D. Number(s) (12 digits)
a.		a.		a.		a.	
b.		b.		b.		b.	

SECTION 5. PARENT COMPANY INFORMATION

5.1	Name of Parent Company	NA ☐	
5.2	Parent Company's Dun & Bradstreet Number	NA ☐	

EPA FORM R **PART II. CHEMICAL-SPECIFIC INFORMATION**	TRI Facility ID Number Toxic Chemical, Category or Generic Name

SECTION 1. TOXIC CHEMICAL IDENTITY   (Important: DO NOT complete this section if you completed Section 2 below.)

1.1 CAS Number (Important: Enter only one number exactly as it appears on the Section 313 list. Enter category code if reporting a chemical category.)

1.2 Toxic Chemical or Chemical Category Name (Important: Enter only one name exactly as it appears on the Section 313 list.)

1.3 Generic Chemical Name (Important: Complete   only   if Part 1, Section 2.1 is checked "yes". Generic Name must be structurally descriptive.)

SECTION 2. MIXTURE COMPONENT IDENTITY   (Important: DO NOT complete this section if you completed Section 1 above.)

2.1 Generic Chemical Name Provided by Supplier (Important: Maximum of 70 characters, including numbers, letters, spaces, and punctuation.)

SECTION 3. ACTIVITIES AND USES OF THE TOXIC CHEMICAL AT THE FACILITY
(Important: Check all that apply.)

3.1 Manufacture the toxic chemical:	**3.2** Process the toxic chemical:	**3.3** Otherwise use the toxic chemical:
a. ☐ Produce **b.** ☐ Import		
If produce or import:		
c. ☐ For on-site use/processing	**a.** ☐ As a reactant	**a.** ☐ As a chemical processing aid
d. ☐ For sale/distribution	**b.** ☐ As a formulation component	**b.** ☐ As a manufacturing aid
e. ☐ As a byproduct	**c.** ☐ As an article component	**c.** ☐ Ancillary or other use
f. ☐ As an impurity	**d.** ☐ Repackaging	

SECTION 4. MAXIMUM AMOUNT OF THE TOXIC CHEMICAL ONSITE AT ANY TIME DURING THE CALENDAR YEAR

4.1 ☐   (Enter two-digit code from instruction package.)

SECTION 5. QUANTITY OF THE TOXIC CHEMICAL ENTERING EACH ENVIRONMENTAL MEDIUM ONSITE

			A. Total Release (pounds/year) (Enter range code or estimate*)	B. Basis of Estimate (enter code)	C. % From Stormwater
5.1	Fugitive or non-point air emissions	NA ☐			
5.2	Stack or point air emissions	NA ☐			
5.3	Discharges to receiving streams or water bodies (enter one name per box)				
	Stream or Water Body Name				
5.3.1					
5.3.2					
5.3.3					
5.4.1	Underground Injection onsite to Class I Wells	NA ☐			
5.4.2	Underground Injection onsite to Class II-V Wells	NA ☐			

If additional pages of Part II, Section 5.3 are attached, indicate the total number of pages in this box ☐
and indicate the Part II, Section 5.3 page number in this box. ☐   (example: 1,2,3, etc)

EPA FORM R	TRI Facility ID Number
PART II. CHEMICAL - SPECIFIC INFORMATION (CONTINUED)	Toxic Chemical, Category, or Generic Name

SECTION 5. QUANTITY OF THE TOXIC CHEMICAL ENTERING EACH ENVIRONMENTAL MEDIUM ONSITE (Continued)

		NA	A. Total Release (pounds/year) (enter range code* or estimate)	B. Basis of Estimate (enter code)
5.5	Disposal to land onsite			
5.5.1A	RCRA Subtitle C landfills	☐		
5.5.1B	Other landfills	☐		
5.5.2	Land treatment/application farming	☐		
5.5.3	Surface Impoundment	☐		
5.5.4	Other disposal	☐		

SECTION 6. TRANSFERS OF THE TOXIC CHEMICAL IN WASTES TO OFF-SITE LOCATIONS

6.1 DISCHARGES TO PUBLICLY OWNED TREATMENT WORKS (POTWs)

6.1.A Total Quantity Transferred to POTWs and Basis of Estimate

6.1.A.1. Total Transfers (pounds/year) (enter range code* or estimate)	**6.1.A.2 Basis of Estimate** (enter code)

6.1.B. __	POTW Name	
POTW Address		

City		State	County		Zip	

6.1.B. __	POTW Name	
POTW Address		

City		State	County		Zip	

If additional pages of Part II, Section 6.1 are attached, indicate the total number of pages

in this box [ ] and indicate the Part II, Section 6.1 page number in this box [ ] (example: 1,2,3, etc.)

SECTION 6.2 TRANSFERS TO OTHER OFF-SITE LOCATIONS

6.2. __ Off-Site EPA Identification Number (RCRA ID No.)	
Off-Site Location Name	
Off-Site Address	

City		State	County		Zip	

Is location under control of reporting facility or parent company?	☐ Yes	☐ No

EPA FORM R PART II. CHEMICAL-SPECIFIC INFORMATION (CONTINUED)	TRI Facility ID Number Toxic Chemical, Category or Generic Name

SECTION 6.2 TRANSFERS TO OTHER OFF-SITE LOCATIONS (Continued)

A. Total Transfers (pounds/year) (enter range code* or estimate)	B. Basis of Estimate (enter code)	C. Type of Waste Treatment/Disposal/ Recycling/Energy Recovery (enter code)
1.	1.	1. M
2.	2.	2. M
3.	3.	3. M
4.	4.	4. M

6.2. __ Off-Site EPA Identification Number (RCRA ID No.)

Off-Site location Name

Off-Site Address

City		State	County		Zip

Is location under control of reporting facility or parent company?   ☐ Yes   ☐ No

A. Total Transfers (pounds/year) (enter range code* or estimate)	B. Basis of Estimate (enter code)	C. Type of Waste Treatment/Disposal/ Recycling/Energy Recovery (enter code)
1.	1.	1. M
2.	2.	2. M
3.	3.	3. M
4.	4.	4. M

SECTION 7A. ON-SITE WASTE TREATMENT METHODS AND EFFICIENCY

☐ Not Applicable (NA) - Check here if no on-site waste treatment is applied to any waste stream containing the toxic chemical or chemical category.

a. General Waste Stream (enter code)	b. Waste Treatment Method(s) Sequence [enter 3-character code(s)]			c. Range of Influent Concentration	d. Waste Treatment Efficiency Estimate	e. Based on Operating Data ?
7A.1a	7A.1b	1	2	7A.1c	7A.1d	7A.1e
	3	4	5		%	Yes ☐ No ☐
	6	7	8			
7A.2a	7A.2b	1	2	7A.2c	7A.2d	7A.2e
	3	4	5		%	Yes ☐ No ☐
	6	7	8			
7A.3a	7A.3b	1	2	7A.3c	7A.3d	7A.3e
	3	4	5		%	Yes ☐ No ☐
	6	7	8			
7A.4a	7A.4b	1	2	7A.4c	7A.4d	7A.4e
	3	4	5		%	Yes ☐ No ☐
	6	7	8			
7A.5a	7A.5b	1	2	7A.5c	7A.5d	7A.5e
	3	4	5		%	Yes ☐ No ☐
	6	7	8			

If additional pages of Part II, Section 6.2/7A are attached, indicate the total number of pages in this box ☐
and indicate the Part II, Section 6.2/7A page number in this box : ☐ (example: 1,2,3, etc)

EPA FORM R	TRI Facility ID Number
PART II. CHEMICAL-SPECIFIC INFORMATION (CONTINUED)	Toxic Chemical, Category or Generic Name

SECTION 7B. ON-SITE ENERGY RECOVERY PROCESSES

☐ Not Applicable (NA) - Check here if no on-site energy recovery is applied to any waste stream containing the toxic chemical or chemical category.

Energy Recovery Methods [enter 3-character code(s)]

1 [____]   2 [____]   3 [____]   4 [____]

SECTION 7C. ON-SITE RECYCLING PROCESSES

☐ Not Applicable (NA) - Check here if no on-site recycling is applied to any waste stream containing the toxic chemical or chemical category.

Recycling Methods [enter 3-character code(s)]

1. [____]   2. [____]   3. [____]   4. [____]   5. [____]

6. [____]   7. [____]   8. [____]   9. [____]   10. [____]

SECTION 8. SOURCE REDUCTION AND RECYCLING ACTIVITIES

		Column A Prior Year (pounds/year)	Column B Current Reporting Year (pounds/year)	Column C Following Year (pounds/year)	Column D Second Following Year (pounds/year)
8.1	Quantity released **				
8.2	Quantity used for energy recovery onsite				
8.3	Quantity used for energy recovery offsite				
8.4	Quantity recycled onsite				
8.5	Quantity recycled offsite				
8.6	Quantity treated onsite				
8.7	Quantity treated offsite				
8.8	Quantity released to the environment as a result of remedial actions, catastrophic events, or one-time events not associated with production processes (pounds/year)				
8.9	Production ratio or activity index				

8.10 Did your facility engage in any source reduction activities for this chemical during the reporting year? If not, enter "NA" in Section 8.10.1 and answer Section 8.11.

	Source Reduction Activities [enter code(s)]	Methods to Identify Activity (enter codes)		
8.10.1		a.	b.	c.
8.10.2		a.	b.	c.
8.10.3		a.	b.	c.
8.10.4		a.	b.	c.
8.11	Is additional information on source reduction, recycling, or pollution control activities included with this report? (Check one box)	YES ☐ NO ☐		

** Report releases pursuant to EPCRA Section 329(8) including "any spilling, leaking, pumping, pouring, emitting, emptying, discharging, injecting, escaping, leaching, dumping, or disposing into the environment." Do not include any quantity treated onsite or offsite.

Filing and
Tickler System for
Environmental Management

SOURCE:
P-F Technical Services, Inc.

Basic to any environmental management program is a system for maintaining records and making use of those records to evaluate progress and initiate projects. The filing and tickler system encompasses all the areas of concern for environmental and safety compliance, and acts as a reminder of when action must be taken.

The filing system provides for a logical means of filing permits, reports and correspondence in each medium, with the ability to cross-reference between them. A component is a listing of all permits with dates of issuance and renewal, regular reports and due dates, as well as other activities needed to prepare for each of these events.

The spreadsheet has been prepared in Excel 2000 and can be imported to any other spreadsheet software. Links can be established to records and reports that are being maintained on a regular basis.

Once established in your own computer, the demonstration information can be erased and replaced with the pertinent information for your facility.

A major benefit of the filing system is being able to view the file management system and coordinate broad based activities to address multiple waste streams and pollution prevention efforts.

FILING SYSTEM FOR ENVIRONMENTAL SYSTEM (Sheet 1 of 3)

THE PRACTICAL PRINTING GROUP
ENVIRONMENT AND SAFETY MANAGEMENT FILES

REGULATION / REPORT OR ACTIVITY	NUMBER	ISSUED	EXPIRES	DATE DUE REPORTS
CONSULTANTS				
GENERAL MAILINGS; ALERTS, ETC.				
PERMITS				
AIR PERMITS - NY STATE DEC				
REGISTRATION				
STATE PERMITS - PRIOR TO REGISTRATION				
EP #1 10 PRESSES- 6 EXHAUST FANS	CG3109 48000 0001		Apr-94	
EP #2 2 MARK ANDYS	CG3109 48000 0002		May-92	
EP #3 2 WEBTRONS	CG3109 48000 0003		May-92	
EP 4 EVAPORATOR	CG3109 48000 0004		May-92	
EP 6 HEIDELBERG 4 COLOR	CG3109 48000 0005		Dec-93	
EP 6 HEIDELBERG 6 COLOR	CG3109 48000 0006			
LIST PERMITS 3 YEAR TERMS:				
EP #1 6 PRESSES- 6 EXHAUST FANS	PDNY8787A		Feb-00	
EP #2 2 MARK ANDYS	PDNY8787B		Dec-00	
EP #3 2 WEBTRONS	PDNY8787C		Dec-00	
EP 4 EVAPORATOR	PDNY8787D		Feb-99	
EP 6 HEIDELBERG 4 COLOR	PDNY8787E		Dec-00	
EP 6 HEIDELBERG 6 COLOR	PDNY8787F		Oct-02	
AIR PERMITS - NYC DEP				
CERTIFICATE OF FITNESS				
AIR COMPRESSOR/JACK D. VINING	606230			
PERMIT FOR CHEMICAL STORAGE ROOM/INKS	900048	6/99	Oct-00	
AC/REFRIG>3 HP AND/OR ROOF CEIL	641599	6/99		
A/C UP TO 3 UNITS	525798	6/99		
BUILDING PERMITS				
FIRE DEPARTMENT				
USEPA HAZARDOUS WASTE ID NUMBER	NYD986899086			
HAZARDOUS WASTE ID NUMBER				

CORRESPONDENCE AND REPORTS REQUIRED

AIR EMISSIONS
NYSDEC AIR REGULATORY FEES

FILING SYSTEM FOR ENVIRONMENTAL SYSTEM (Sheet 2 of 3)

		PREPARE	DATE DUE REPORTS
THE PRACTICAL PRINTING GROUP			
ENVIRONMENT AND SAFETY MANAGEMENT FILES			
REGULATION	REPORT OR ACTIVITY		
CORRESPONDENCE WITH NYSDEC			
VOC ANALYSIS - INK/SOLVENTS	Based on periodic computation of purchases/voc content	PREPARE	QUARTERLY
REGULATIONS			
NYCDEP RIGHT TO KNOW			
1989 TO PRESENT			MARCH 1
REGULATIONS			
OSHA HAZARD COMMUNICATION			
CORRESPONDENCE AND LITERATURE			
NYSDEC HAZARDOUS WASTE			
REPORTS, ANNUAL	NYSDEC will send book if required/ LQG		APRIL 1
REPORTS, QUARTERLY	NYSDEC will send forms end of quarter		END QTR - IF
MANIFESTS	Copy of manifest must be sent to NYSDEC/STATE		ON SHIPMEN
REGULATIONS			
CORRESPONDENCE			
NYCDEP SELF MONITORING			
WASTE WATER DISCHARGE			
WATER LAB TEST			
REPORTS	NO LONGER REQUIRED		
CORRESPONDENCE			
OSHA/SAFETY			
OSHA 200 FORM ?	Ongoing record of lost time accidents		POST FEB
REGULATIONS			
CORRESPONDENCE			
TRAINING RECORDS			
LOCK-OUT/TAG-OUT			
TRAINING BOOKLETS, ETC.			
OSHA AND HW TRAINING			

FILING SYSTEM FOR ENVIRONMENTAL SYSTEM (Sheet 3 of 3)

THE PRACTICAL PRINTING GROUP
ENVIRONMENT AND SAFETY MANAGEMENT FILES

REGULATION	REPORT OR ACTIVITY		DATE DUE REPORTS
1. OSHA 200 FORM	RECORD OF ACCIDENTS		
	1. Maintain register of all incidents required in Form 200 log.	as year progresses	
	2. Post for all employees to see		2/1 to 3/1
2. HAZARD COMMUNICATION RIGHT TO KNOW	1. WRITTEN PROGRAM	review and maintain regularly	
	2. MAINTAIN MSDS'S	as new items are purchased, eliminated or modified	
	3. MAINTAIN LABELS		
	4. CONDUCT TRAINING		
	a. New employees	during first week or prior to start working	
	b. Annual group training	refresher - suggest do during a slow period at a regular time every	
	c. Fire Drills	conduct at least once a quarter.	
3. HAZARDOUS WASTE (IF LQG) MANAGEMENT TRAINING	1. WRITTEN PROGRAM	review and maintain regularly	
	2. CONTINGENCY PLAN	review and maintain regularly	
	3. LAB TESTS - WASTE STREAM	on file for existing; retest waste stream changes	
	4. TRAINING	annually	
	basics of RCRA regulations and		
	requirements of generators;		
	safety and reaction to spills, fire.		
4. LOCK-OUT/TAG-OUT	1. WRITTEN PROGRAM		
	2. PROVIDE PROPER LOCKS AND TAGS/LABELS		
	3. TRAINING		
5. PROTECTIVE PERSONAL EQUIPMENT	1. WRITTEN PROGRAM		
	2. JOB ASSESSMENT FOR EXPOSURES		
	3. FIT AND PROVIDE PROTECTIVE GEAR		
	4. TRAINING		
6. OTHER SAFETY CONCERNS	EVACUATION PLANS AND DRILLS		
	USE OF CHEMICALS AND SAFETY PRECAUTIONS		
	GUARDS ON ALL EQUIPMENT		
	FORK LIFT TRUCK TRAINING		

Source:
USEPA

Clean Air Act Stationary Source Civil Penalty Policy

I.   INTRODUCTION

Section 113(b) of the clean Air Act, 42 U.S.C. § 7413(b), provides the Administration of EPA with the authority to commence a civil action against certain violators to recover a civil penalty of up to $25,000 per day per violation. Since July 8, 1980, EPA has sought the assessment of civil penalties for Clean Air Act violations under Section 113(b) based on the considerations listed in the statute and the guidance provided in the Civil Penalty Policy issued on that date.

On February 16, 1984, EPA issued the *Policy on Civil Penalties* (GM-21) and a *Framework for Statute-Specific Approaches to Penalty Assessments* (GM-22). The Policy focuses on the general philosophy behind the penalty program. The Framework provides guidance to each program on how to develop medium-specific penalty policies. The Air Enforcement program followed the *Policy* and the *Framework* in drafting the Clean Air Act Stationary Source Civil Penalty Policy, which was issued on September 12, 1984, and revised March 25, 1987. This policy amends the March 25, 1987 revision, incorporating EPA's further experience in calculation and negotiating penalties. This guidance document governs only stationary source violations of the Clean Air Act. All violations of Title II of the Act are governed by separate guidance.

The Act was amended on November 15, 1990, providing the Administrator with the authority to issue administrative penalty orders in section 113(d), 42 U.S.C. § 7413(d). These penalty orders may assess penalties of up to $25,000 per day of violation and are generally authorized in cases where the penalty sought is not over $200,000 and the first alleged date of violation occurred no more than 12 months prior to initiation of the administrative action. In an effort toprovide consistent application of the Agency's civil penalty authorities, this penalty policy will serve as the civil penalty guidance used in calculating administrative penalties under Section 113(d) of the Act and will be used in calculating a minimum settlement amount in civil judicial cases brought under Section 113(b) of the Act.

In calculating the penalty amount which should be sought in an administrative complaint, the economic benefit of noncompliance and a gravity component should be calculated under this penalty policy using the most aggressive assumptions supportable. Pleadings will always include the full economy benefit component. As a general rule, the gravity component of the penalty plead in administrative complaints may not be mitigated. However, the gravity component portion of the plead penalty may be mitigated by up to ten per cent solely for degree of cooperation. Any mitigation for this factor must be justified under Section II.B.4.b. of this policy. The total mitigation for good faith efforts to comply for purpose of determining a settlement amount may never exceed thirty per cent. Applicable adjustment factors which aggravate the penalty must be included in the amount plead in the administrative complaint. Where key financial or cost figures are not available, for example those costs involved in calculating the BEN calculation, the highest figures supportable should be used.

This policy will ensure the penalty plead in the complaint is never lower than any revised penalty calculated later based on more detailed information. It will also encourage sources to provide the litigation team with more accurate cost or financial information. The penalty may then be recalculated during negotiations where justified under this policy to reflect any appropriate adjustment factors. In administrative cases, where the penalty is recalculated based upon information received in negotiations or the prehearing exchange, the administrative complaint must be amended to reflect the new amount if the case is going to or expected to go to hearing. This will ensure the complaint reflects the amount the government is prepared to justify at the hearing. This pleading policy also fulfills the obligation of 40 C.F.R. § 22.14(a)(5) that all administrative complaints include "a statement explaining the reasoning behind the proposed penalty."

This policy reflects the factors enumerated in section 113(e) that the court (in section 113(b) actions) and the Administrator (in section 113(d) actions) shall take into consideration in the assessment of any penalty. These factors include: the size of the business, the economic impact of the penalty on the business, the violator's full compliance history and good faith efforts to comply, the duration of the violation, payment by the violator of penalties assessed for the same violation, the economic benefit of noncompliance, the seriousness of the violation and such other factors as justice may require.

This document is not meant to control the penalty amount requested in judicial actions to enforce existing consent decrees.[1] In judicial cases,

the use of this guidance is limited to pre-trial settlement of enforcement actions. In a trial, government attorneys may find it relevant and helpful to introduce a penalty calculated under this policy, as a point of reference in a demand for penalties. However, once a case goes to trial, government attorneys should demand a larger penalty than the minimum settlement figure as calculated under the policy.

The general policy applies to most Clean Air Act violations. There are some types of violations, however, that have characteristics which make the use of the general policy inappropriate. These are treated in separate guidance, included as appendices. Appendix I covers violations of PSD/NSR permit requirements. Appendix II deals with the gravity component for vinyl chloride NESHAP violations. Appendix III covers the economic benefit and gravity components for asbestos NESHAP demolition and renovation violations. The general policy applies to violations of volatile organic compound regulations where the method of compliance involves installation of control equipment. Separate guidance is provided for VOC violators which comply through reformulation (Appendix IV). Appendix VI deals with the gravity component for volatile hazardous air pollutants violations. Appendix VII covers violations of the residential wood heaters NSPS regulations. Violations of the regulations to protect stratospheric ozone are covered in Appendix VIII. These appendixes specify how the gravity component and/or economic benefit components will be calculated for these types of violations. Adjustments, aggravation or mitigation, of penalties calculated under any of the appendixes is governed by this general penalty policy.

This penalty policy contains two components. First, it describes how to achieve the goal of deterrence through a penalty that removes the economic benefit of noncompliance and reflects the gravity of the violation. Second, it discusses adjustment factors applied so that a fair and equitable penalty will result. The litigation team[2] should calculate the full economic benefit and gravity components and then decide whether any of the adjustment factors applicable to either component are appropriate. The final penalty obtained should never be lower than the penalty calculated under this policy into account all

---

1. In these actions, EPA will normally seek the penalty amount dictated by the stipulated penalty provisions of the consent decree. If a consent decree contains no stipulated penalty provisions, the case development team should propose penalties suitable to vindicate the authority of the Court.

2. With respect to civil judicial cases, the litigation team will consist of the Assistant Regional Counsel, the Office of Enforcement attorney, the Assistant United States Attorney, the Department of Justice attorney from the Environmental Enforcement Section, and EPA technical professionals assigned to the case. With respect to administrative cases, the litigation team will generally consist of the EPA technical professional and Assistant Regional Counsel assigned to the case. The recommendation of the litigation team must be unanimous. If a unanimous position cannot be reached, the matter should be escalated and a decision made by EPA and the Department of Justice managers, as required.

appropriate adjustment factors including litigation risk and inability to pay.

All consent agreements should state that penalties paid pursuant to this penalty policy are not deductible for federal tax purposes under 28 U.S.C. § 162(f).

The procedures set out in this document are intended solely for the guidance of government personnel. They are not intended and cannot be relied upon to create rights, substantive or procedural, enforceable by any party in litigation with the United States. The Agency reserves the right to act at variance with this policy and to change it at any time without public notice.

This penalty policy is effective immediately with respect to all cases in which the first penalty offer has not yet been transmitted to the opposing party.

II.   THE PRELIMINARY DETERRENCE AMOUNT

The February 16, 1984, Policy on Civil Penalties establishes deterrence as an important goal of penalty assessment. More specifically, it says that any penalty should, *at a minimum*, remove any significant economic benefit resulting from noncompliance. In addition, it should include an amount beyond recovery of the economic benefit to reflect the seriousness of the violation. That portion of the penalty which recovers the economic benefit of noncompliance is referred to as the "economic benefit component;" that part of the penalty which reflects the seriousness of the violation is referred to as the "gravity component." When combined, these two components yield the "preliminary deterrence amount."

This section provides guidelines for calculating the economic benefit component and the gravity component. It will also discuss the limited circumstances which justify adjusting either component.

A.   THE ECONOMIC BENEFIT COMPONENT

In order to ensure that penalties recover any significant economic benefit of noncompliance, it is necessary to have reliable methods to calculate that benefit. The existence of reliable methods also strengthens the Agency's position in both litigation and negotiation. This section sets out guidelines for computing the economic benefit component. It first addresses costs which are delayed by noncompliance. Then it addresses costs which are avoided completely by noncompliance. It also identifies issues to be considered when computing the economic benefit component for those violations where the benefit of noncompliance results from factors other than cost savings. The section concludes with a discussion of the limited circumstances where the economic benefit component may be mitigated.

1.   Benefit from delayed costs

In many instances, the economic advantage to be derived from noncompliance is the ability to delay making the expenditures necessary to achieve compliance. For example, a facility which fails to install a scrubber will eventually have to spend the money needed to install the scrubber in order to achieve compliance. But, by deferring these capital costs until EPA or a State takes an enforcement action, that facility has achieved an economic benefit. Among the types of violations which may result in savings from deferred cost are the following:

- Failure to install equipment needed to meet emission control standards.
- Failure to effect process changes needed to reduce pollution.
- Failure to test where the test still must be performed.
- Failure to install required monitoring equipment.

The economic benefit of delayed compliance should be computed using the "Methodology for Computing the Economic Benefit of Noncompliance," which is Technical Appendix A of the *BEN User's Manual*. This document provides a method for computing the economic benefit of noncompliance based on a detailed economic analysis. The method is a refined version of the method used in the previous *Civil Penalty Policy* issued July 8, 1980, for the Clean Water Act and the Clean Air Act. BEN is a computer program available to the Regions for performing the analysis. Questions concerning the BEN model should be directed to the Program Development and Training Branch in the Office of Enforcement, FTS 475-6777.

2.   Benefit from avoided costs

Many types of violations enable a violator to avoid permanently certain costs associated with compliance. These include cost savings for:

- Disconnecting or failing to properly operate and maintain existing pollution control equipment (or other equipment if it affects pollution control).
- Failure to employ a sufficient number of adequately trained staff.
- Failure to establish or follow precautionary methods required by regulations or permits.
- Removal of pollution equipment resulting in process, operational, or maintenance savings.
- Failure to conduct a test which is no longer required.
- Disconnection or failing to properly operate and maintain required monitoring equipment.

- Operation and maintenance of equipment that the violator failed to install.

The benefit from avoided costs must also be computed using methodology in Technical Appendix A of the *BEN User's Manual*.

The benefit from delayed and avoided costs is calculated together, using the BEN computer program, to arrive at an amount equal to the economic benefit of noncompliance for the period from the first provable date of violation until the date of compliance.

As noted above, the BEN model may be used to calculate only the economic benefit accruing to a violator through delay or avoidance of the costs of complying with applicable requirements of the Clean Air Act and its implementing regulations. There are instances in which the BEN methodology either cannot compute or will fail to capture the actual economic benefit of noncompliance. In those instances, it will be appropriate for the agency to include in its penalty analysis a calculation of the economic benefit in a manner other than that provided for in the BEN methodology.

In some instances this may include calculating and including in the economic benefit component profits from illegal activities. An example would be a source operating without a preconstruction review permit under PSD/NSR regulations or without an operating permit under Title V. In such a case, an additional calculation would be performed to determine the present value of these illegal profits which would be added to the BEN calculation for the total economic benefit component. Care must be taken to account for the preassessed delayed or avoided costs included in the BEN calculation when calculating illegal profits. Otherwise, these costs could be assessed twice. The delayed or avoided costs already accounted for in the BEN calculation should be subtracted from any calculation of illegal profits.

3. Adjusting the Economic Benefit Component

As noted above, settling for an amount which does not recover the economic benefit of noncompliance can encourage people to wait until EPA or the State begins an enforcement action before complying. For this reason, it is general Agency policy not to adjust or mitigate this amount. There are three general circumstances (described below) in which mitigating the economic benefit component may be appropriate. However, in any individual case where the Agency decides to mitigate the economic benefit component, the litigation team must detail those reasons in the case file and in any memoranda accompanying the settlement.

Following are the limited circumstances in which EPA can mitigate the economic benefit component of the penalty:

a. Economic benefit component involves insignificant amount.

Assessing the economic benefit component and subsequent negotiations will often represent a substantial commitment of resources. Such a commitment may not be warranted in cases where the magnitude of the economic benefit component is not likely to be significant because it is not likely to have substantial financial impact on the violator. For this reason, the litigation team has the discretion not to seek the economic benefit component where it is less than $5,000. In exercising that discretion, the litigation team should consider the following factors:

- **Impact on violator:** The likelihood that assessing the economic benefit component as part of the penalty will have a noticeable effect on the violator's competitive position or overall profits. If no such effect appears likely, the benefit component should probably not be pursued.
- **The size of the gravity component:** If the gravity component is relatively small, it may not provide a sufficient deterrent, by itself, to achieve the goals of this policy. In situations like this, the litigation team should insist on including the economic benefit component in order to develop an adequate penalty.

b. Compelling public concerns

The Agency recognizes that there may be some instances where there are compelling public concerns that would not be served by taking a case to trial. In such instances, it may become necessary to consider mitigating the economic benefit component. This may be done only if it is absolutely necessary to preserve the countervailing public interests. Such settlement might be appropriate where the following circumstances occur:

- The economic benefit component may be mitigated where recovery would result in plant closings, bankruptcy, or other extreme financial burden, and there is an important public interest in allowing the firm to continue in business. Alternative payment plans, such as installment payments with interest, should be fully explored before restoring to this option. Otherwise, the Agency will give the perception that shirking one's environmental responsibilities is a way to keep a failing enterprise afloat. This exemption does not apply to situations where the plant was likely to close anyway, or where there is a likelihood of continued harmful noncompliance.
- The economic benefit component may also be mitigated in enforcement actions against nonprofit public entities, such as municipalities and publicly-owned utilities, where assessment threatens

to disrupt continued provision of essential public services.

c. Concurrent Section 120 administrative action

EPA will not usually seek to recover the economic benefit of noncompliance from one violation under both a Section 113(b) civil judicial action or 113(d) civil administrative action and a Section 120 action. Therefore, if a Section 120 administrative action is pending or has been concluded against a source for a particular violation and an administrative or judicial penalty settlement amount is being calculated for the same violation, the economic benefit component need not include the period of noncompliance covered by the Section 120 administrative action.

In these cases, although the Agency will not usually seek double recovery, the litigation team should not automatically mitigate the economic benefit component by the amount assessed in the Section 120 administrative action. The Clean Air Act allows dual recovery of the economic benefit, and so each case must be considered on its individual merits. The Agency may mitigate the economic benefit component in the administrative or judicial action if the litigation team determines such a settlement is equitable and justifiable. The litigation team should consider in making this decision primarily whether the penalty calculated without the Section 120 noncompliance penalty is a sufficient deterrent.

B. THE GRAVITY COMPONENT

As noted above, the *Policy on Civil Penalties* specifies that a penalty, to achieve deterrence, should recover any economic benefit of noncompliance, and should also include an amount reflecting the seriousness of the violation. Section 113(c) instructs courts to take into consideration in setting the appropriate penalty amount several factors including the size of the business, the duration of the violation, and the seriousness of the violation. These factors are reflected in the "gravity component." This section of the policy establishes an approach to quantifying the gravity component.

Assigning a dollar figure to represent the gravity of the violation is a process which must, of necessity, involve the consideration of a variety of factors and circumstances. Linking the dollar amount of the gravity component to these objective factors is a useful way of insuring that violations of approximately equal seriousness are treated the same way. These objective factors are designed to reflect those listed in Section 113(e) of the Act.

The specific objective factors in this civil penalty policy designed to measure the seriousness of the violation and reflect the considerations listed in the Clean Air Act are as follows:

- **Actual or possible harm:** This factor focuses on whether (and to what extent) the activity of the defendant actually resulted or was likely to result in the emission of a pollutant in violation of the level allowed by an applicable State Implementation Plan, federal regulation or permit.
- **Importance to the regulatory scheme:** This factor focuses on the importance of the requirement to achieving the goals of the Clean Air Act and its implementing regulations. For example, the NSPS regulations require owners and operators of new sources to conduct emissions testing and report the results within a certain time after start-up. If a source owner or operator does not report the test results, EPA would have no way of knowing whether that source is complying with NSPS emissions limits.
- **Size of violator:** The gravity component should be increased, in proportion to the size of the violator's business.

The assessment of the first gravity component factor listed above, actual or possible harm arising from a violation, is a complex matter. For purposes of determining how serious a given violation is, it is possible to distinguish violations based on certain considerations, including the following:

- **Amount of pollutant:** Adjustments based on the amount of the pollutant emitted are appropriate.
- **Sensitivity of the environment:** This factor focuses on where the violation occurred. For example, excessive emissions in a nonattainment area are usually more serious than excessive emissions in an attainment area.
- **Toxicity of the pollutant:** Violations involving toxic pollutants regulated by a National Emissions Standard for Hazardous Air Pollutants (NESHAP) or listed under Section 112(b)(1) of the Act are more serious and should result in larger penalties.
- **The length of time a violation continues:** Generally, the longer a violation continues uncorrected, the greater the risk of harm.
- **Size of violator:** A corporation's size is indicated by its stockholder's equity or "net worth." This value, which is calculated by adding the value of capital stock, capital surplus, and accumulated retained earnings, corresponds to the entry for "worth" in the Dun and Bradstreet reports for publicly traded corporations. The simpler bookkeeping methods employed by sole proprietorships and partnerships allow determination of their size on the basis of net current assets. Net current assets are calculated by subtracting current liabilities from current assets.

The following dollar amounts assigned to each factor should be added together to arrive at the total gravity component:

1. Actual or possible harm

a. Level of violation

Percent Above Standard[3]	Dollar Amount
1 - 30%	$ 5,000
31 - 60%	10,000
61 - 90%	15,000
91 - 120%	20,000
121 - 150%	25,000
151 - 180%	30,000
181 - 210%	35,000
211 - 240%	40,000
241 - 270%	45,000
271 - 300%	50,000
over 300%	50,000 + 5,000 for each 30% or fraction of 30% increment above the standard

This factor should be used only for violations of emissions standards. Ordinarily the highest documented level of violation should be used. If that level, in the opinion of the litigation team, is not representative of the period of violation, then a more representative level of violation may be used. This figure should be assessed for each emissions violation. For example, if a source which emits particulate matter is subject to both an opacity standard and a mass emission standard and is in violation of both standards, this figure should be assessed for both violations.

b. Toxicity of the pollutant

Violations of NESHAPs emission standards not handled by a separate appendix and non-NESHAP emission violations involving pollutants listed in section 112(b)(1) of the Clean Air Act Amendments of 1990[4]: $15,000 for each hazardous air pollutant for which there is a violation.

c. Sensitivity of environment (for SIP and NSPS cases only).

The penalty amount selected should be based on the status of the air quality control district in question with respect to the pollutant involved in the violation.

1. Nonattainment Areas
i. Ozone:

Extreme	$18,000
Severe	16,000
Serious	14,000
Moderate	12,000
Marginal	10,000

ii. Carbon Monoxide and Particulate Matter:

Serious	$14,000
Moderate	12,000

iii. All Other Criteria Pollutants: $10,000

2. Attainment area PSD Class I: $10,000

3. Attainment area PSD Class II or III: $5,000

d. Length of time of violation

To determine the length of time of violation for purposes of calculating a penalty under this policy, violations should be assumed to be continuous from the first provable date of violation until the source demonstrates compliance if there have been no significant process or operational changes. If the source has affirmative evidence, such as continuous emission monitoring data, to show that the violation was not continuous, appropriate adjustments should be made. In determining the length of violation, the litigation team should take full advantage of the presumption regarding continuous violation in Section 113(e)(2). This figure should be assessed separately for each violation, including procedural violations such as monitoring, recordkeeping and reporting violations. For example, if a source violated an emissions standard, a testing requirement, and a reporting requirement, three separate length of violation figures should be assessed, one for each of the three violations based on how long each was violated.

Months	Dollars
0 - 1	$ 5,000
2 - 3	8,000
4 - 6	12,000
7 - 12	15,000
13 - 18	20,000
19 - 24	25,000
25 - 30	30,000
31 - 36	35,000
37 - 42	40,000
43 - 48	45,000
49 - 54	50,000
55 - 60	55,000

---

3. Compliance is equivalent to 0% above the emission standard.

4. An example of a non-NESHAP violation involving a hazardous air pollutant would be a violation of a volatile organic compound (VOC) standard in a State Implementation Plan involving a VOC contained in the Section 112(b)(1) list of pollutants for which no NESHAP has yet been promulgated.

2.   Importance to the regulatory scheme

The following violations are also very significant in the regulatory scheme and therefore require the assessment of the following penalties:

Work Practice Standard Violations:
— failure to perform a work practice
    requirement: $10,000 - $15,000

Reporting and Notification Violations:
— failure to report or notify: $15,000
— late report or notice: $ 5,000
— incomplete report or notice: $5,000 - $15,000
(See Appendix III for Asbestos NESHAP violations.)

Recordkeeping Violations:
— failure to keep required records: $15,000
— incomplete records: $5,000 - $15,000

Testing Violations:
— failure to conduct required performance
    testing or testing using an improper test
    method: $15,000
— late performance test or performing a
    required test method using an incorrect
    procedure: $ 5,000

Permitting Violations:
— failure to obtain an operating
    permit: $15,000
— failure to pay permit fee:
    See Section 502(b)(3)(c)(ii) of the Act

Emission Control Equipment Violations:
— failure to operate and maintain
    control equipment required by the
    Clean Air Act, its implementing
    regulations or a permit: $15,000
— intermittent or improper operation
    or maintenance of control
    equipment: $5,000 - $15,000

Monitoring Violations:
— failure to install monitoring equipment
    required by the Clean Air Act, its
    implementing regulations or a
    permit: $15,000
— late installation of required monitoring
    equipment: $ 5,000
— failure to operate and maintain
    required monitoring equipment: $15,000

Violation of Administrative Orders[5]: $15,000

5. This figure should be assessed even if the violation of the administrative order is also a violation of another requirement of the Act, for example a NESHAP or NSPS requirement. In this situation, the figure for violation of the administrative order is in addition to appropriate penalties for violating the other requirement of the Act.

Section 114 Requests for Information Violations:
— failure to respond: $15,000
— incomplete response; $5,000 - $15,000

Compliance Certification Violations:
— failure to submit a certification: $15,000
— late certifications: $ 5,000
— incomplete certifications: $5,000 - $15,000

Violations of Permit Schedules of Compliance:
— failure to meet interim deadlines: $ 5,000
— failure to submit progress reports: $15,000
— incomplete progress reports: $5,000 - $15,000
— late progress reports: $ 5,000

A penalty range is provided for work practice violations to allow Regions some discretion depending on the severity of the violation. Complete disregard of work practice requirements should be assessed the full $15,000 penalty. Penalty ranges are provided for incomplete notices, reports, and recordkeeping to allow the Regions some discretion depending on the seriousness of the omissions and how critical they are to the regulatory program. If the source omits information in notices, reports or records which document the source's compliance status, this omission should be treated as a failure to meet the requirement and assessed $15,000.

A late notice, report or test should be considered a failure to notify, report or test if the notice or report is submitted or the test is performed after the objective of the requirement is no longer served. For example, if a source is required to submit a notice of a test so that EPA may observe the test, a notice received after the test is performed would be considered a failure to notify.

Each separate violation under this section should be assessed the corresponding penalty. For example, a NSPS source may be required to notify EPA at startup and be subject to separate quarterly reporting requirement thereafter. If the source fails to submit the initial start-up notice and violates the subsequent reporting requirement, then the source should be assessed $15,000 under this section for each violation. In addition, a length of violation figure should be assessed for each violation based on how long each has been violated. Also, a figure reflecting the size of the violator should be assessed once for the case as a whole. If, however, the source violates the same reporting requirement over a period of time, for example by failing to submit quarterly reports for one year, the source should be assessed one $15,000 penalty under this section for failure to submit a report. In addition, a length of violation figure of $15,000 for 12 months of violation and a size of the violator figure should be assessed.

3. Size of the violator

Net worth (corporations); or net current assets (partnerships and sole proprietorships):

Under $100,000	$ 2,000
100,001 - $ 1,000,000	5,000
1,000,001 - 5,000,000	10,000
5,000,001 - 20,000,000	20,000
20,000,001 - 40,000,000	35,000
40,000,001 - 70,000,000	50,000
70,000,001 - 100,000,000	70,000
over 100,000,000	70,000 + $25,000 for every additional $30,000,000 or fraction thereof

In the case of a company with more than one facility, the size of the violator is determined based on the company's entire operation, not just the violating facility. With regard to parent and subsidiary corporations, only the size of the entity sued should be considered. Where the size of the violator figure represents over 50% of the total preliminary deterrence amount, the litigation team may reduce the size of the violator figure to 50% of the preliminary deterrence amount.

The process by which the gravity component was computed must be memorialized in the case file. Combining the economic benefit component with the gravity component yields the preliminary deterrence amount.

4. Adjusting the Gravity Component

The second goal of the *Policy on Civil Penalties* is the equitable treatment of the regulated community. One important mechanism for promoting equitable treatment is to include the economic benefit component discussed above in a civil penalty assessment. This approach prevents violators from benefitting economically from their noncompliance relative to parties which have complied with environmental requirements.

In addition, in order to promote equity, the system for penalty assessment must have enough flexibility to account for the unique facts of each case. Yet it still must produce consistent enough results to ensure similarly-situated violators are treated similarly. This is accomplished by identifying many of the legitimate differences between cases and providing guidelines for how to adjust the gravity component amount when those facts occur. The application of these adjustments to the gravity component prior to the commencement of negotiation yields the initial minimum settlement amount. During the course of negotiation, the litigation team may further adjust this figure based on new information learned during negotiations and discovery to yield the adjusted minimum settlement amount.

The purpose of this section is to establish adjustment factors which promote flexibility while maintaining national consistency. It sets guidelines for adjusting the gravity component which account for some factors that frequently distinguish different cases. Those factors are: degree of willfulness or negligence, degree of cooperation, history of noncompliance, and environmental damage. These adjustment factors apply only to the gravity component and not to the economic benefit component. Violators bear the burden of justifying mitigation adjustments they propose. The gravity component may be mitigated only for degree of cooperation as specified in II.B.4.b. The gravity component may be aggravated by as much as 100% for the other factors discussed below: degree of willfulness or negligence, history of noncompliance, and environmental damage.

The litigation team is required to base any adjustment of the gravity component on the factors mentioned and to carefully document the reasons justifying its application in the particular case. The entire litigation team must agree to any adjustments to the preliminary deterrence amount. Members of the litigation team are responsible for ensuring their management also agrees with any adjustments to the penalty proposed by the litigation team.

a. Degree of Willfulness or Negligence

This factor may be used only to raise a penalty. The Clean Air Act is a strict liability statute for civil actions, so that willfulness, or lack thereof, is irrelevant to the determination of legal liability. However, this does not render the violator's willfulness or negligence irrelevant in assessing an appropriate penalty. Knowing or willful violations can give rise to criminal liability, and the lack of any negligence or willfulness would indicate that no addition to the penalty based on this factor is appropriate. Between these two extremes, the willfulness or negligence of the violator should be reflected in the amount of the penalty.

In assessing the degree of willfulness or negligence, all of the following points should be considered:

- The degree of control the violator had over the events constituting the violation.
- The foreseeability of the events constituting the violation.
- The level of sophistication within the industry in dealing with compliance issues or the accessibility or appropriate control technology (if this information is readily available). This should be balanced against the technology-forcing nature of the statute, where applicable.
- The extent to which the violator in fact knew of the legal requirement which was violated.

b. Degree of Cooperation

The degree of cooperation of the violator in remedying the violation is an appropriate factor to consider in adjusting the penalty. In some cases, this factor may justify aggravation of the gravity component because the source in not making efforts to come into compliance and is negotiating with the agency in bad faith or refusing to negotiate. This factor may justify mitigation of the gravity component in the circumstances specified below where the violator institutes comprehensive corrective action after discovery of the violation. Prompt correction of violations will be encouraged if the violator clearly sees that it will be financially disadvantageous to litigate without remedying noncompliance. EPA expects all sources in violation to come into compliance expeditiously and to negotiate in good faith. Therefore, mitigation based on this factor is limited to no more than 30% of the gravity component and is allowed only in the following three situations:

1. Prompt reporting of noncompliance

The gravity component may be mitigated when a source promptly reports its noncompliance to EPA or the state or local air pollution control agency where there is no legal obligation to do so.

2. Prompt correction of environmental problems

The gravity component may also be mitigated where a source makes extraordinary efforts to avoid violating an imminent requirement or to come into compliance after learning of a violation. Such efforts may include paying for extra work shifts or a premium on a contract to have control equipment installed sooner or shutting sown the facility until it is operation in compliance.

3. Cooperation during pre-filing investigation

Some mitigation may also be appropriate in instances where the defendant is cooperative during EPA's pre-filing investigation of the source's compliance status or a particular incident.

c. History of Noncompliance

This factor may be used only to raise a penalty. Evidence that a party has violated an environmental requirement before clearly indicates that the party was not deterred by a previous governmental enforcement response. Unless one of the violations was caused by factors entirely out of the control of the violator, the penalty should be increased. The litigation team should check for and consider prior violations under all environmental statutes enforced by the Agency in determining the amount of the adjustment to be made under this factor.

In determining the size of this adjustment, the litigation team should consider the following points:

- Similarity of the violation in question to prior violations.
- Time elapsed since the prior violation.
- The number of prior violations.
- Violator's response to prior violation(s) with regard to correcting the previous problem and attempts to avoid future violations.
- The extent to which the gravity component has already been increased due to a repeat violation.

A violation should generally be considered "similar" if a previous enforcement response should have alerted the party to a particular type of compliance problem. Some facts indicating a "similar violation" are:

- Violation of the same permit.
- Violation of the same emissions standard.
- Violation at the same process points of a source.
- Violation of the same statutory or regulatory provision.
- A similar act or omission.

For purposes of this section, a "prior violation" includes any act or omission resulting in a State, local, or federal enforcement response (e.g., notice of violation, warning letter, administrative order, field citation, complaint, consent decree, consent agreement, or administrative and judicial order) under any environmental statute enforced by the Agency unless subsequently dismissed or withdrawn on the grounds that the party was not liable. It also includes any act or omission for which the violator has previously been given written notification, however informal, that the regulating agency believes a violation exists. In researching a defendant's compliance history, the litigation team should check to see if the defendant had been listed pursuant to Section 306 of the Act.

In the case of large corporations with many divisions or wholly-owned subsidiaries, it is sometimes difficult to determine whether a prior violation by the parent corporation should trigger the adjustments described in this section. New ownership often raises similar problems. In making this determination, the litigation team should ascertain who in the organization exercised or had authority to exercise control or oversight responsibility over the violative conduct. Where the parent corporation exercised or had authority to exercise control over the violative conduct, the parent corporation's prior violations should be considered part of the subsidiary or division's compliance history.

In general, the litigation team should begin with the assumption that if the same corporation was involved, the adjustment for history of non compliance should apply. In addition, the team should be wary of a party changing operations or shifting responsibility for compliance to different groups as a way of avoiding increased penalties. The Agency may find a consistent pattern of noncompliance by many divisions or subsidiaries of a corporation even though the facilities are at different geographic locations. This often reflects, at best, a corporate-wide indifference to environmental protection. Consequently, the adjustment for history of noncompliance should apply unless the violator can demonstrate that the other violating corporate facilities are under totally independent control.

d. Environmental Damage

Although the gravity component already reflects the amount of environmental damage a violation causes, the litigation team may further increase the gravity component based on severe environmental damage. As calculated, the gravity component takes into account such factors as the toxicity of the pollutant, the attainment status of the area of violation, the length of time the violation continues, and the degree to which the source has exceeded and emission limit. However, there may be cases where the environmental damage caused by the violation is so severe that the gravity component alone is not a sufficient deterrent, for example, a significant release of a toxic air pollutant in a populated area. In these cases, aggravation of the gravity component may be warranted.

III. LITIGATION RISK

The preliminary deterrence amount, both economic benefit and gravity components, may be mitigated in appropriate circumstances based on litigation risk. Several types of litigation risk may be considered. For example, regardless of the type of violations a defendant has committed or a particular defendant's reprehensible conduct, EPA can never demand more in civil penalties than the statutory maximum (twenty-five thousand dollars per day per violation). In calculating the statutory maximum, the litigation team should assume continuous noncompliance from the first date of provable violation (taking into account the five year statute of limitations) to the final date of compliance where appropriate, fully utilizing the presumption of Section 113(e)(2). When the penalty policy yields an amount over the statutory maximum, the litigation team should propose an alternative penalty which must be concurred on by their respective management just like any other penalty.

Other examples of litigation risks would be evidentiary problems, or an indication from the court, mediator, or Administrative Law Judge during settlement negotiations that he or she is prepared to recommend a penalty below the minimum settlement amount. Mitigation based on these concerns should consider the specific facts, equities, evidentiary issues or legal problems pertaining to a particular case as well as the credibility of government witnesses.

Adverse legal precedent which the defendant argues is indistinguishable from the current enforcement action is also a valid litigation risk. Cases raising legal issues of first impression should be carefully chosen to present the issue fairly in a factual context the Agency is prepared to litigate. Consequently in such cases, penalties should generally not be mitigated due to the risk the court may rule against EPA. If an issue of first impression is litigated and EPA's position is upheld by the court, the mitigation was not justified. If EPA's position is not upheld, it is generally better that the issue be decided than to avoid resolution by accepting a low penalty. Mitigation based on litigation risk should be carefully documented and explained in particular detail. In judicial cases this should be done in coordination with the Department of Justice.

IV. ABILITY TO PAY

The Agency will generally not request penalties that are clearly beyond the means of the violator. Therefore, EPA should consider the ability to pay a penalty in adjusting the preliminary deterrence amount, both gravity component and economic benefit component. At the same time, it is important that the regulated community not see the violation of environmental requirements as a way of aiding a financially-troubled business. EPA reserves the option, in appropriate circumstances, of seeking a penalty that might contribute to a company going out of business.

For example, it is unlikely that EPA would reduce a penalty where a facility refuses to correct a serious violation. The same could be said for a violator with a long history of previous violations. That long history would demonstrate that less severe measures are ineffective.

The litigation team should assess this factor after commencement of negotiations *only if* the source raises it as an issue and *only if* the source provides the necessary financial information to evaluate the source's claim. The source's ability to pay should be determined according to the December 16, 1986 *Guidance on Determining a Violator's Ability to Pay a Civil Penalty* (GM-56) along with any other appropriate means.

The burden to demonstrate inability to pay, as with the burden of demonstrating the presence of any other mitigating circumstances, rests on the defendant. If the violator fails to provide sufficient information, then the litigation team should disregard this factor in adjusting the penalty. The Office of Enforcement Policy has developed the capability to assist the Regions in determining a firm's ability to pay. This is done through the computer program, ABEL. If ABEL indicates that the source may have an inability to pay, a more detailed financial analysis verifying the ABEL results should be done prior to mitigating the penalty.

Consider delayed payment schedule with interest: When EPA determines that a violator cannot afford the penalty prescribed by this policy, the next step is to consider a delayed payment schedule with interest. Such a schedule might even be contingent upon an increase in sales or some other indicator of improved business. EPA's computer program, ABEL, can calculate a delayed payment amount for up to five years.

Consider straight penalty as a last recourse: If this approach is necessary, the reasons for the litigation team's conclusion as to the size of the necessary reduction should be carefully documented in the case file.[6]

Consider joinder of a corporate violator's individual owners: This is appropriate if joinder is legally possible and justified under the circumstances. Joinder is not legally possible for SIP cases unless the prerequisite of Section 113 of the Clean Air Act has been met—issuance of an NOV to the person.

Regardless of the Agency's determination of an appropriate penalty amount to pursue based on ability to pay considerations, the violator is always expected to comply with the law.

V. OFFSETTING PENALTIES PAID TO STATE AND LOCAL GOVERNMENTS OR CITIZEN GROUPS FOR THE SAME VIOLATIONS

Under Section 113(e)(1), the court in a civil judicial action or the Administrator in a civil administrative action must consider in assessing a penalty "payment by the violator of penalties previously assessed for the same violation." While EPA will not automatically subtract any penalty amount paid by a source to a State or local agency in an enforcement action or to a citizen group in a citizen suit for the same violation that is the basis for EPA's enforcement action, the litigation team may do so if circumstances suggest that it is appropriate. The litigation team should consider primarily whether the remaining penalty is a sufficient deterrent.

---

6. If a firm fails to pay the agreed to penalty in a final administrative or judicial order, then the Agency must follow the procedures outlined in the February 6, 1990 *Manual on Monitoring and Enforcing Administrative and Judicial Orders* for collecting the penalty amount.

VI. SUPPLEMENTAL ENVIRONMENTAL PROJECTS

The February 12, 1991 *Policy on the Use of Supplemental Environmental Projects in EPA Settlements* must be followed when reducing a penalty for such a project in any Clean Air Act settlement.

VII. CALCULATING A PENALTY IN CASES WITH MORE THAN ONE TYPE OF VIOLATION

EPA often takes an enforcement action against a stationary source for more than one type of violation of the Clean Air Act. The economic benefit of noncompliance with all requirements violated should be calculated. Next, the gravity component factors under actual or possible harm and importance to the regulatory scheme which are applicable should be calculated separately for each violation. The size of the violator factor should be figured only once for all violations.

For example, consider the case of a plant which makes laminated particle board. The particle board plant is found to emit particulates in violation of the SIP particulate emission limit and the laminating line which laminates the particle board with a vinyl covering is found to emit volatile organic compounds in violation of the SIP VOC emission limit. The penalty for the particulate violation should be calculated figuring the economic benefit of not complying with that limit (capital cost of particulate control, etc., determined by running the BEN computer model), and then the gravity component for this violation should be calculated using all the factors in the penalty policy. After the particulate violation penalty is determined, the VOC violation should be calculated as follows: the economic benefit should be calculated if additional measures need to be taken to comply with the VOC limit. In addition, a gravity component should be calculated for the VOC violation using all the applicable factors under actual or possible harm and importance to the regulatory scheme. The size of the violator factor should be figured only once for both violations.

Another example would be a case where, pursuant to Section 114, EPA issues a request for information to a source which emits SO_2, such as a coal-burning boiler. The source does not respond. Two months later, EPA issues an order under Section 113(a) requiring the source to comply with the Section 114 letter. The source does not respond. Three months later, EPA inspects the source and determines that the source is violating the SIP SO_2 emission limit.

In this case, separate economic benefits should be calculated, if applicable. Thus, if the source obtained any economic benefit from not responding to the Section 114 letter or obeying the Section

113(a) order, that should be calculated. If not, only the economic benefit from the SO_2 emission violation should be calculated using the BEN computer model. In determining the gravity component, the penalty should be calculated as follows:

1. Actual or possible harm

a. level of violation—calculate for the emission violation only

b. toxicity of pollutant—applicable to the emission violation only

c. sensitivity of environment—application to the emission violation only

d. length of time of violation—separately calculate the time for all three violations. Note the Section 114 violation continues to run even after the Section 113(a) order is issued until the Section 114 requirements are satisfied.

2. Importance to regulatory scheme

   Section 114 request for information violation—$15,000
   Section 113 administrative order violation—$15,000

3. Size of violator

a. One figure based on the sourse's assets.

VIII. APPORTIONMENT OF THE PENALTY AMONG MULTIPLE DEFENDANTS

This policy is intended to yield a minimum settlement penalty figure for the case as a whole. In many cases, there may be more than one defendant. In such instances, the Government should generally take the position of seeking a sum for the case as a whole, which the defendants allocate among themselves. Civil violations of the Clean Air Act are strict liability violations and it is generally not in the government's interest to get into discussions of the relative fault of the individual defendants. The government should therefore adopt a single settlement figure for the case and should not reject a settlement consistent with the bottom line settlement figure because of the way the penalty is allocated.

Apportionment of the penalty in a multi-defendant case may be required if one party is willing to settle and others are not. In such circumstances, the government should take the position that if certain portions of the penalty are attributable to such party (such as economic benefit or aggravation due to prior violations), that party should pay those amounts and a reasonable portion of the amounts not directly

assigned to any single party. If the case is settled as to one defendant, a penalty not less than the balance of the settlement figure for the case as a whole must be obtained from the remaining defendants.

There are limited circumstances where the Government may try to influence apportionment of the penalty. For example, if one party has a history of prior violations, the Government may try to assure that party pays the amount the gravity component has been aggravated due to the prior violations. Also, if one party is known to have realized all or most of the economic benefit, that party may be asked to pay that amount.

IX. EXAMPLES

Example 1

I. Facts:

Company A runs its manufacturing operation with power produced by its own coal-fired boilers[7]. The boilers are major sources of sulfur dioxide. The State Implementation Plan has a sulfur dioxide emission limitation for each boiler of .68 lbs. per million B.T.U. The boilers were inspected by EPA on March 19, 1989, and the SO_2 emission rate was 3.15 lbs. per million B.T.U. for each boiler. A NOV was issued for the SO_2 violations on April 10, 1989. EPA again inspected Company A on June 2, 1989 and found the SO_2 emission rate to be unchanged. Company A had never installed any pollution control equipment on its boilers, even though personnel from the state pollution control agency had contacted Company A and informed it that the company was subject to state air pollution regulations. The state had issued an administrative order on September 1, 1988 for SO_2 emission violations at the same boilers. The order required compliance with applicable regulations, but Company A had never complied with the state order. Company A is located in a nonattainment area for sulfur oxides. Company A has net current assets of $760,000. Company A's response to an EPA Section 114 request for information documented the first provable day of violation of the emission standard as July 1, 1988.

II. Computation of penalty

A. Economic benefit component

EPA used the BEN computer model in the standard mode to calculate the economic benefit component.

_____

7. Note that a penalty is assessed for the entire facility and not for each emission unit. In this example, the source has several boilers. However, the penalty figures are not multiplied by the number of boilers. The penalty is based on the violations at the facility as a whole, specifically the amount of pollutant factor and length of violation factor are assessed once based on the amount of excess emissions at the facility from all the boilers.

The economic benefit component calculated by the computer model was $243,500.

B. Gravity component

1. Actual or possible harm

a. Amount of pollutant: between 360-390% above standard—$65,000

b. Toxicity of pollutant: not applicable.

c. Sensitivity of the environment: nonattainment—$10,000

d. Length of time of violation: Measured from the date of first provable violation, July 1, 1988 to the date of final compliance under consent decree, hypothetically December 1, 1991. (If consent decree or judgment order is filed at a later date, this element, as well as elements in the economic benefit component must be recalculated.) 41 mos.—$40,000

2. Importance to regulatory scheme.

No applicable violations.

3. Size of violator: net assets of $760,000—$5,000.

$243,500 economic benefit component
+120,000 gravity component
$363,500 preliminary deterrence amount

C. Adjustment Factors

1. Degree of willfulness/negligence

Because Company A was on notice of its violations and, moreover, disregarded the state administrative order to comply with applicable regulations, the gravity component in this example should be aggravated by some percentage based on this factor.

2. Degree of Cooperation

No adjustments were made in the category because Company A did not meet the criteria.

3. History of noncompliance

The gravity component should be aggravated by some percentage for this factor because Company A violated the state order issued for the same violation.

Initial penalty figure: $353,500 preliminary deterrence amount plus adjustments for history of noncompliance and degree of willfulness or negligence.

Example 2:

I. Facts:

Company C, located in a serious nonattainment area for particulate matter, commenced construction in January 1988. It began its operations in April 1989. It runs a hot mix asphalt plant subject to the NSPS regulations at 40 C.F.R. Part 60, Subpart I. Subpart I requires that emissions of particulates not exceed 90 mg/dscm (.04 gr/dscf) nor exhibit 20% opacity or greater. General NAPS regulations require that a source owner or operator subject to a NSPS fulfill certain notification and recordkeeping functions (40 C.F.R. § 60.7), and conduct performance tests and submit a report of the test results (40 C.F.R. § 60.8).

Company C failed to notify EPA of: the date it commenced construction within 30 days after such date (February 1988) (40 C.F.R. § 60.7(a)(1)); the date of anticipated start-up between 30– 60 days prior to such date (March, 1989) (40 C.F.R. § 60.7(a)(2)); or a date of actual start-up within 15 days after such date (April, 1989) (40 C.F.R. § 60.7(a)(3). Company C was required under 40 C.F.R. § 60.8(a) to test within 180 days of start-up, or by October 1989. The company finally conducted the required performance test in September 1990. The test showed the plant to be emitting 120 mg/dscm of particulates and to exhibit 30% opacity.

Company C did submit the required notices in November 1989 in response to a letter from EPA informing it that it was subject to NSPS requirements. It did negotiate with EPA after the complaint was filed in September 1991, and agreed to a consent decree requiring compliance by December 1, 1991. Company C has assets of $7,000,000.

II. Computation of penalty

A. Benefit component

The Region determined after calculation that the economic benefit component was $90,000 for violation of the emissions standard according to the BEN computer calculation. The litigation team determined that the economic benefit from the notice and testing requirement was less than $5,000. Therefore, the litigation team has discretion not to include this amount in the penalty consistent with the discussion at II.A.3.a.

B. Gravity component

1. Actual or possible harm

a. Amount of pollutant:

i. mass emission standard: 33% above standard—$10,000

ii. opacity standard:
50% over standard—$10,000

b. Toxicity of pollutant: not applicable

c. Sensitivity of the environment:
serious nonattainment—$14,000

d. Length of time of violation
1) Performance testing: October, 1989–September 1990: 12 months—$15,000

2) Failure to report commencement of construction: February 1988–November 1989: 21 months (date of EPA's first letter to Company)—$25,000

3) Failure to report actual start-up: April, 1989–November 1989: 7 months—$15,000
4) Failure to report date of anticipated start-up between 30-60 days prior to such date: March, 1989–November 1989: 8 months—$15,000

5) Mass Emission Standard Violation: September 1990–December 1991: 15 months—$20,000

6) Opacity Violation: September 1990–December 1991: 15 months—$20,000

2. Importance to regulatory scheme:

Failure to notify 40 C.F.R. § 60.7(a)(1)—$15,000
Failure to notify 40 C.F.R. § 60.7(a)(2)—$15,000
Failure to notify 40 C.F.R. § 60.7(a)(3)—$15,000
Failure to conduct required performance test 40 C.F.R. § 60.8(a)—$15,000

3. Size of violator: Net current Assets: $7,000,000—$20,000

$ 90,000 Economic benefit component
 224,000 gravity component
$314,000 preliminary deterrence amount

C. Adjustment factors

1. Degree of willfulness/negligence

No adjustments were made based on willfulness in this category because there was no evidence that company C knew of the requirements prior to receiving the letter from EPA. Specific evidence may suggest that the company's violations were due to negligence justifying an aggravation of the penalty on that basis.

2. Degree of Cooperation

No adjustments were made in this category because Company C did not meet the criteria.

3. History of noncompliance

The gravity component should be aggravated by an amount agreed to by the litigation team for this factor because the source ignored two letters from EPA informing them of the requirements,

Example 3:

I. Facts

Chemical Inc. operates a mercury cell chlor-alkali plant which produces chlorine gas. The plant is subject to regulations under the National Emissions Standard for Hazardous Air Pollutants (NESHAP) for mercury, 40 C.F.R. Part 61, Subpart E. On September 9, 1990, EPA inspectors conducted an inspection of the facility, and EPA required the source to conduct a stack test pursuant to section 114. The stack test showed emissions at a rate of 3000 grams of mercury per 24-hour period. The mercury NESHAP states that emissions from mercury cell chlor-alkali plants shall not exceed 2300 grams per 24-hour period. The facility has been in operation since June 1989.

In addition under 40 C.F.R.§ 61.53, Chemical Inc. either had to test emissions from the cell room ventilation system within 90 days of the effective date of the NESHAP or follow specified approved design, maintenance and housekeeping practices. Chemical Inc. has never tested emissions. Therefore, it has committed itself to following the housekeeping requirements. At the inspection, EPA personnel noted the floors of the facility were badly cracked and mercury droplets were found in several of the cracks. The inspectors noted that the mercury in the floor cracks was caused by leaks from hydrogen seal pots and compressor seals which housekeeping practices require be collected and confined for further processing to collect mercury. A follow up inspection was conducted on September 30, 1990 and showed that all of the housekeeping requirements were being observed.

Chemical Inc. will have to install control equipment to come into compliance with the emissions standard. A complaint was filed in June 1991. The equipment was installed and operational by June 1992. A consent decree was entered and penalty paid in February 1992. Chemical Inc. has a net corporate worth of $2,000,000.

II. Calculation of Penalty

A. Economic Benefit Component

The delay in installing necessary control equipment from June 1989 to June 1992 as calculated using the BEN computer model resulted in an economic benefit to Chemical Inc. of $35,000.

B. Gravity Component

1. Actual or possible harm

a. Amount of pollutant: 30% above the standard—$5,000

b. Toxicity of pollutant: $15,000 for violations involving a NESHAP

c. Sensitivity of the environment: not applicable

d. Length of time of violation:

1) Emissions violation: 22 mos.—$25,000

2) Work Practice violation: 1 mo.—$5,000

2. Importance to regulatory scheme.

Failure to perform work practice requirements—$15,000

3. Size of violator: net worth of $2,000,000—$10,000

$35,000 economic benefit component
+75,000 gravity component
$110,000 preliminary deterrence amount

C. Adjustment Factors

1. Degree of willfulness/negligence

It is unlikely Chemical Inc. would not be aware of the NESHAP requirements. Therefore, an adjustment should probably be made for this factor.

2. Degree of cooperation

No adjustments made because Chemical Inc. did not meet the criteria.

3. History of Compliance

No adjustments were made because Chemical Inc. had no prior violations.

X. CONCLUSION

Treating similar situations in a similar fashion is central to the credibility of EPA's enforcement effort and to the success of achieving the goal of equitable treatment. This document has established several mechanisms to promote such consistency. Yet it still leaves enough flexibility for tailoring the penalty to particular circumstances. Perhaps the most important mechanisms for achieving consistency are the systematic methods for calculating the benefit component and gravity component of the penalty. Together, they add up to the preliminary deterrence amount. The document also sets out guidance on uniform approaches for applying adjustment factors to arrive at an initial amount prior to beginning settlement negotiations or an adjusted amount after negotiations have begun.

Nevertheless, if the Agency is to promote consistency, it is essential that each case file contain a complete description of how each penalty was developed as required by the August 9, 1990 Guidance on *Documenting Penalty Calculations and Justification in EPA Enforcement Actions*. This description should cover how the preliminary deterrence amount was calculated and any adjustments made to the preliminary deterrence amount. It should also describe the facts and reasons which support such adjustments. Only through such complete documentation can enforcement attorneys, program staff and their managers learn from each other's experience and promote the fairness required by the *Policy on civil Penalties*.

APPENDIX **XXXIX**

Small Business
Incentive Program

SOURCE:
USEPA, Fact Sheet, May 20, 1996

BACKGROUND AND PURPOSE

- This Policy is intended to promote environmental compliance among small businesses by providing them with special incentives to participate in compliance assistance programs or to conduct environmental audits, and to then promptly correct violations.
- This Policy is one of the 25 regulatory reform initiatives announced by President Clinton on March 16, 1995, and implements, in part, the Executive Memorandum on Regulatory Reform, issued on April 21, 1995. This Policy also implements Section 323 of the Small Business Regulatory Enforcement Fairness Act of 1996, signed into law by the President on March 29, 1996.
- This Policy sets forth how U.S. EPA expects to exercise its enforcement discretion in deciding on an appropriate enforcement response and determining an appropriate civil penalty for violations by small businesses.
- This Policy expands upon EPA's August 12, 1994 policy for Clean Air Act Section 507 Small Business Assistance Programs by

applying the same principles to other environmental programs.

SCOPE OF POLICY

- For purposes of this Policy, a small business is defined as a person, corporation, partnership, or other entity who employs 100 or fewer individuals across all facilities and operations owned by the entity.

CRITERIA FOR PENALTY ELIMINATION OR REDUCTION

★ EPA will eliminate the entire civil penalty if a small business satisfies all four of the criteria below:

1. <u>The small business has made a good faith effort to comply with applicable environmental requirements</u> as demonstrated by either:
a. receiving on-site compliance assistance from a government or government supported program and the violations are detected

during the compliance assistance and, in the case of confidential assistance programs, disclosing the violations to the appropriate regulatory agency; or

b. conducting a voluntary environmental audit and promptly disclosing in writing to the appropriate regulatory agency all violations discovered as part of the audit.

2. <u>First violation</u>. In the past three years, the small business was not subject to an information request, warning letter, notice of violation, field citation, citizen suit or other enforcement action or received penalty mitigation pursuant to this Policy for the current violation. And, in the past five years, the small business has not been subject to two or more enforcement actions for environmental violations.

3. <u>Corrections Period—the business corrects the violation and remedies and harm associated with the violation within six months of its discovery</u>. Small businesses may have an additional six months, if necessary, to correct the violation if pollution prevention technologies will be used.

4. Lack of harm and no criminal conduct. The Policy applies if:
a. The violation has not caused actual serious harm to public health, safety, or the environment, and
b. The violation is not one that may present an imminent and substantial endangerment to public health or the environment; and
c. The violation does not present a significant health, safety, or environmental threat; and
d. The violation does not involve criminal conduct.

★ If a small business meets all of the criteria, except it needs a longer corrections period than provided by criterion 3 or, in the rare instance where the small business has obtained a significant economic benefit from the violation(s) such that it may have obtained an economic advantage over its competitors, EPA will waive up to 100% of the gravity component of the civil penalty, but may seek the full amount of any economic benefit associated with the violations.

APPLICABILITY TO STATES

- EPA will defer to State actions that are generally consistent with this Policy.

EFFECTIVE DATE

- This Policy is effective June 10, 1996 and supersedes the June 1995 Interim version.

Contacts: David Hindin at 202 564-6004 or Karin Leff at 202 564-7068.

A. INTRODUCTION

This document sets forth the U.S. Environmental Protection Agency's Policy on Compliance Incentives for Small Businesses. This Policy is one of the 25 regulatory reform initiatives announced by President Clinton on March 16, 1995, and implements, in part, the Executive Memorandum on Regulatory Reform, 60 FR 20621 (April 26, 1995).

The Executive Memorandum provides in pertinent part:

To the extent permitted by law, each agency shall use its discretion to modify the penalties for small businesses in the following situations. Agencies shall exercise enforcement discretion to waive the imposition of all or a portion of a penalty when the violation is corrected within a time period appropriate to the violation in question. For those violations that may take longer to correct than the period set by the agency, the agency shall use its enforcement discretion to waive up to 100 percent of the financial penalties if the amounts waived are used to bring the entity into compliance. The provisions [of this paragraph] shall apply only where there has been a good faith effort to comply with applicable regulations and the violation does not involve criminal wrongdoing or significant threat to health, safety, or the environment.

This Policy also implements section 323 of the Small Business Regulatory Enforcement Fairness Act of 1996, signed into law by the President on March 29, 1996.

As set forth in this Policy, EPA will refrain from initiating an enforcement action seeking civil penalties, or will mitigate civil penalties, whenever a small business makes a good faith effort to comply with environmental requirements by receiving compliance assistance or promptly disclosing the findings of a voluntarily conducted environmental audit, subject to certain conditions. These conditions require that the violation: is the small business's first violation of the particular requirement; does not involve criminal conduct; has not and is not causing a significant health, safety or environmental threat or harm; and is remedied within the corrections period. Moreover, EPA will defer to State actions that are consistent with the criteria set forth in this Policy.

B. BACKGROUND

The Clean Air Act (CAA) Amendments of 1990 require that States establish Small Business Assistance Programs (SBAPs) to provide technical and environmental compliance assistance to stationary sources. On August 12, 1994, EPA issued an enforcement response policy for stationary sources which provided that an authorized or delegated state program may, consistent with federal requirements, either:

(1) assess no penalties against small businesses that voluntarily seek compliance assistance and correct violations revealed as a result of compliance assistance within a limited period of time; or
(2) keep confidential information that identifies the names and locations of specific small businesses with violations revealed through compliance assistance, where the SBAP is independent of the state enforcement program.

In a further effort to assist small businesses to comply with environmental regulations, and to achieve health, safety, and environmental benefits, the Agency is adopting a broader policy for all media programs, including water, air, toxics, and hazardous waste.

C. PURPOSE

This Policy is intended to promote environmental compliance among small businesses by providing incentives for them to participate in on-site compliance assistance programs and to conduct environmental audits. Further, the Policy encourages small businesses to expeditiously remedy all violations discovered through compliance assistance and environmental audits. The Policy accomplishes this in two ways: by setting forth a settlement penalty Policy that rewards such behavior, and by providing guidance for States and local governments to offer these incentives.

D. APPLICABILITY

This Policy applies to facilities owned by small businesses as defined here. A small business is a person, corporation, partnership, or other entity who employs 100 or fewer individuals (across all facilities and operations owned by the entity).[1] This definition is a simplified version of the CAA §507 definition of small business. On balance, EPA determined that a single definition would make implementation of this Policy straightforward and would allow for consistent application of the Policy in a multimedia context.

This Policy is effective June 10, 1996, and on that date supersedes the Interim version of this Policy issued on June 13, 1995 and the September 19, 1995 Qs and As guidance on the Interim version. This Policy applies to all civil judicial and administrative enforcement actions taken under the authority of the environmental statutes and regulations that EPA administers, except for the Public Water System Supervision Program under the Safe Drinking Water Act.[2] This Policy applies to all such actions filed after the effective date of this Policy, and to all pending cases in which the government has not reached agreement in principle with the alleged violator on the amount of the civil penalty.

This Policy sets forth how the Agency expects to exercise its enforcement discretion in deciding on an appropriate enforcement response and determining an appropriate civil settlement penalty for violations by small businesses. It

---

1. The number of employees should be considered as full-time equivalents on an annual basis, including contract employees. Full-time equivalents means 2,000 hours per year of employment. For example, see 40 CFR §372.3.
2. This Policy does not apply to the Public Water System Supervision (PWSS) Program because the PWSS Program already has an active compliance assistance program and EPA has a policy to address the special needs of small communities. See November 1995 *Policy on Flexible State Enforcement Response to Small Community Violations.*

states the Agency's views as to the proper allocation of enforcement resources. This Policy is not final agency action and is intended as guidance. It does not create any rights, duties, obligations, or defenses, implied or otherwise, in any third parties. This Policy is to be used for settlement purposes and is not intended for use in pleading, or at hearing or trial. To the extent that this Policy may differ from the terms of applicable enforcement response policies (including penalty policies) under media-specific programs, this document supersedes those policies. This Policy supplements, but does not supplant the August 12, 1994 *Enforcement Response Policy for Treatment of Information Obtained Through Clean Air Act Section 507 Small Business Assistance Programs.*

E. CRITERIA FOR CIVIL PENALTY MITIGATION

EPA will eliminate or mitigate its settlement penalty demands against Small businesses based on the following criteria:

1. The small business has made a good faith effort to comply with applicable environmental requirements as demonstrated by satisfying either a. or b. below.

a. Receiving on-site compliance assistance from a government or government supported program that offers services to small businesses (such as a SBAP or state university), and the violations are detected during the compliance assistance. If a small business wishes to obtain a corrections period after receiving compliance assistance from a confidential program, the business must promptly disclose the violations to the appropriate regulatory agency.

b. conducting an environmental audit (either by itself or by using an independent contractor) and promptly disclosing in writing to EPA or the appropriate state regulatory agency all violations discovered as part of the environmental audit pursuant to section H of this Policy.

For both a. and b. above, the disclosure of the violation must occur before the violation was otherwise discovered by, or reported to the regulatory agency. See section I. 1 of the Policy below. Good faith also requires that a small business cooperate with EPA and provide such information as is necessary and requested to determine applicability of this Policy.

2. This is the small business' first violation of this requirement. This Policy does not apply to businesses that have previously been subject to an information request, a warning letter, notice of violation, field citation, citizen suit, or other enforcement action by a government agency for a violation of that requirement within the past three years. This Policy does not apply if the small business received penalty mitigation pursuant to this Policy for a violation of the same or a similar requirement within the past three years. If a business has been subject to two or more enforcement actions for violations of environmental requirements in the past five years, this Policy does not apply even if this is the first violation of this particular- requirement.

3. The business corrects the violation within the corrections period set forth below.

Small businesses are expected to remedy the violations within the shortest practicable period of time, not to exceed 180 days following detection of the violation. However, a small business may take an additional period of 180 days, *i.e.*, up to a period of one year from the date the violation is detected, only if necessary to allow a small business to correct the viola-tion by implementing pollution prevention measures. For any violation that cannot be corrected within 90 days of detection, the small business should submit a written schedule, or the agency should issue a compliance order with a schedule, as appropriate. Correcting the violation includes remediating any environmental harm associated with the violation,[3] as well as implementing steps to prevent a recurrence of the violation.

4. The Policy applies if:
a. The violation has not caused actual serious harm to public health, safety, or the environment; and
b. The violation is not one that may present an imminent and substantial endangerment to public health or the environment; and
c. The violation does not present a significant health, safety or environmental threat (e.g., violations involving hazardous or toxic substances may present such threats); and
d. The violation does not involve criminal conduct.

---

3. If significant efforts will be required to remediate the harm, the Policy will not apply since criterion 3 is likely not to have been satisfied.

F. PENALTY MITIGATION GUIDELINES

EPA will exercise its enforcement discretion to eliminate or mitigate civil settlement penalties as follows.

1. EPA will eliminate the civil settlement penalty in any enforcement action if a small business satisfies all of the criteria in section E.

2. If a small business meets all of the criteria, except it needs a longer corrections period than provided by criterion 3 (i.e., more than 180 days for non-pollution prevention remedies, or 360 days for pollution prevention remedies), EPA will waive up to 100% of the gravity component of the penalty, but may seek the full amount of any economic benefit associated with the violations.[4]

3. If a small business meets all of the criteria, except it has obtained a significant economic benefit from the violation(s) such that it may have obtained an economic advantage over its competitors, EPA will waive up to 100% of the gravity component of the penalty, but may seek the full amount of the significant economic benefit associated with the violations. EPA retains this discretion to ensure that small businesses that comply with public health protections are not put at a serious marketplace disadvantage by those who have not complied. EPA anticipates that this situation will occur very infrequently.

If a small business does not fit within guidelines 1 2, or 3 immediately above, this Policy does not provide any special penalty mitigation. However, if a small business has otherwise made a good faith effort to comply, EPA has discretion, pursuant to its applicable enforcement response or penalty policies, to refrain from filing an enforcement action seeking civil penalties or to mitigate its demand for penalties.[5] Further, these policies allow for mitigation of the penalty where there is a documented inability to pay all or a portion of the penalty, thereby placing emphasis on enabling the small business to finance compliance. See *Guidance on Determining a Violator's Ability to Pay a Civil Penalty* of December 1986. Penalties also may be mitigated pursuant to the *Interim Revised Supplemental Environmental Projects Policy* of May 1995 (60 F.R. 24856, 5/10/95) and *Incentives for Self-Policing: Discovery, Disclosure, Correction and Prevention of Violations Policy of December 1995* (60 F.R. 66706, 12/22/95).

G. COMPLIANCE ASSISTANCE

1. Definitions and Limitations

Compliance assistance[6] is information or assistance provided ,by EPA, a State or another government agency or government supported entity to help the regulated community comply with legally mandated environmental requirements. Compliance assistance does not include enforcement inspections or enforcement actions[7].

In its broadest sense, the content of compliance assistance can vary greatly, ranging from basic information on the legal requirements to specialized advice on what technology may be best suited to achieve compliance at a particular facility. Compliance assistance also may be delivered in a variety of ways, ranging from general outreach through the Federal Register or other publications, to conferences and computer bulletin boards, to on-site assistance provided in response to a specific request for help.

The special penalty mitigation considerations provided by this Policy only apply to civil violations which were identified as part of an on-site compliance assistance visit to the facility. If a small business wishes to obtain a corrections period after receiving compliance assistance from a **confidential** program, the business must promptly disclose the violations to the appropriate regulatory agency and comply with the other provisions of this Policy. This Policy is restricted to on-site compliance assistance because the other forms of assistance (such as

---

4. The "gravity component" of the penalty includes everything except the economic benefit amount. In determining the appropriate amount of the gravity component of the penalty to mitigate, EPA should consider the nature of the violations, the duration of the violations, the environmental or public health impacts of the violations, good faith efforts by the small business to promptly remedy the violation, and the facility's overall record of compliance with environmental requirements.

5. For example, in some media specific penalty policies, if good faith efforts are undertaken, the penalty calculation automatically factors in such efforts through a potentially smaller economic benefit or gravity amount.

6. Compliance assistance is sometimes called compliance assessments or technical assistance.

7. Of course, during an inspection or enforcement action, a facility may receive suggestions and information from the regulatory authority about how to correct and prevent violations.

hotlines) do not expose a small business to an increased risk of enforcement and do not provide the regulatory agency with a simple way to determine when the violations were detected and thus when the violations must be corrected. In short, small businesses do not need protection from penalties as an incentive to use the other types of compliance assistance.

2. Delivery of On-Site Compliance Assistance By Government Agency or Government Supported Program

Before on-site compliance assistance is provided under this Policy or a similar State policy, businesses should be informed of how the program works and their obligations to promptly remedy any violations discovered. Ideally, before on-site compliance assistance is provided pursuant to this Policy or similar State policy, the agency should provide the facility with a document (such as this Policy) explaining how the program works and the responsibilities of each party. The document should emphasize the responsibility of the facility to remedy all violations discovered within the corrections period and the types of violations that are excluded from penalty mitigation (e.g., violations that caused serious harm). The facility should sign a simple form acknowledging that it understands the Policy. Documentation explaining the nature of the compliance assistance visit and the penalty mitigation guidelines is essential to ensure that the facility understands the Policy.

At the end of the compliance assistance visit, the government agent should provide the facility with a list of all violations observed and report within 10 days any additional violations identified resulting from the visit, but not directly observed, e.g., results from review and analysis of data or information gathered during the visit. Any violations that do not fit within the penalty mitigation guidelines in the Policy—e.g., those that caused serious harm—should be identified. If the violations cannot all be corrected within 90 days, the facility should be requested to submit a schedule for remedying the violations or a compliance order setting forth a schedule should be issued by the agency.

3. Requests for On-Site Compliance Assistance

EPA, States and other government agencies do not have the resources to provide on-site compliance assistance to all small businesses that request such assistance. This Policy does not create any right or entitlement to compliance assistance. A small business that requests on-site compliance assistance will not necessarily receive such assistance. If a small business requests on-site compliance assistance (or any other type of assistance) and the assistance is not available, the government agency should provide a prompt response indicating that such assistance is not available. The small business should be referred to other public and private sources of assistance that may be available, such as clearinghouses. hotlines, and extension services provide by some universities. In addition, the smell business should be informed that it may obtain the benefits offered by this Policy by conducting an environmental audit pursuant to the provisions of this Policy.

H. ENVIRONMENTAL AUDITS

For purposes of this Policy, an environmental audit is defined as "a systematic, documented, periodic and objective review by regulated entities of facility operations and practices related to meeting environmental requirements." See EPA's new auditing policy, entitled *Incentives for Self-Policing*, 60 F.R. 66706, 66711, December 22, 1995.

The violation must have been discovered as a result of a voluntary environmental audit, and not through a legally mandated monitoring or sampling requirement prescribed by statute, regulation, permit, judicial or administrative order, or consent agreement. For example, the Policy does not apply to:

1) emissions violations detected through a continuous emissions monitor (or alternative monitor established in a permit) where any such monitoring is required;
2) violations of National Pollutant Discharge Elimination System (NPDES) discharge limits detected through required sampling or monitoring; or
3) violations discovered through an audit required to be performed by the terms of a consent order or settlement agreement.

The small business must fully disclose a violation within 10 days (or such shorter period provided by law) after it has discovered that the violation has occurred, or may have occurred, in writing to EPA or the appropriate *state or local government* agency.

I. ENFORCEMENT

To ensure that this Policy enhances and does not compromise public health and the environment, the following conditions apply:

1. Violations detected through inspections, field citations, reported to an agency by a member of the public or a "whistleblower" employee, identified in notices of citizen suits, or previously reported to an agency as required~by applicable regulations or permits, remain fully enforceable.

2. A business is subject to all applicable enforcement response policies (which may include discretion whether or not to take formal enforcement action) for all violations that had been detected through compliance assistance and were not remedied within the corrections period. The penalty in such action may include he time period before and during the correction period.

3. A State's or EPA's actions in providing compliance assistance is **not a legal** defense in any enforcement action. This Policy does not limit EPA or a state's discretion to use information on violations revealed through compliance assistance as evidence in subsequent enforcement actions.

4. If a field citation is issued to a small business (e.g. under the Underground Storage Tank program[8]), the small business may provide information to the Agency to show that specific violations cited in the field citation are being remedied under a corrections schedule established pursuant to this Policy or similar State policy. In such a situation, EPA would exercise its enforcement discretion not to seek civil penalties for those violations.

J. APPLICABILITY TO STATES[9]

EPA recognizes that states are partners in enforcement and compliance assurance. Therefore, EPA will defer to state actions in delegated or approved programs that are generally consistent with the criteria set forth in this Policy. Whenever a State agency provides a correction period to a small business pursuant to this Policy or a similar policy, the agency should notify the appropriate EPA Region. This notification will assure that federal and state enforcement responses are properly coordinated.

K. PUBLIC ACCOUNTABILITY

Within three years of the effective date of this Policy, EPA will conduct a study of the effectiveness of this Policy in promoting compliance among small businesses. EPA will make the study available to the public. EPA will make publicly available the terms of any EPA agreements reached under this Policy, including the nature of the violation(s), the remedy, and the schedule for returning to compliance.

---

8. The Underground Storage Tank (UST) field citation program provides for substantially reduced penalties in exchange for the rapid correction of certain UST violations for first time violators. See *Guidance for Federal Field Citation Enforcement,* OSWER Directive 9610.16, October 1993.

9. States includes tribes.

APPENDIX **XL**

SOURCE:

EPA, Office of Enforcement and
Compliance Assurance, effective
May 1, 1998

Excerpts from EPA Supplemental Environmental Projects Policy Pertaining to Penalties

A. INTRODUCTION

1. Background

In settlements of environmental enforcement cases, the U.S. Environmental Protection Agency (EPA) requires the alleged violators to achieve and maintain compliance with Federal environmental laws and regulations and to pay a civil penalty. To further EPA's goals to protect and enhance public health and the environment, in certain instances environmentally beneficial projects, or Supplemental Environmental Projects (SEPs), may be part of the settlement. This Policy sets forth the types of projects that are permissible as SEPs, the penalty mitigation appropriate for a particular SEP, and the terms and conditions under which they may become part of a settlement. The primary purpose of this Policy is to encourage and obtain environmental and public health protection and improvements that may not otherwise have occurred without the settlement incentives provided by this Policy.

Statutes administered by EPA generally contain penalty assessment criteria that a court or administrative law judge must consider in determining an appropriate penalty at trial or a hearing. In the settlement context, EPA generally follows these criteria in exercising its discretion to establish an appropriate settlement penalty. In establishing an appropriate penalty, EPA considers such factors as the economic benefit associated with the violations, the gravity or seriousness of the violations, and prior history of violations. Evidence of a violator's commitment and ability to

894

perform a SEP is also a relevant factor for EPA to consider in establishing an appropriate settlement penalty. All else being equal, the final settlement penalty will be lower for a violator who agrees to perform an acceptable SEP compared to the violator who does not agree to perform a SEP.

The Agency encourages the use of SEPs that are consistent with this policy. SEPs may not be appropriate in settlement of all cases, but they are an important part of EPA's enforcement program. While penalties play an important role in environmental protection by deterring violations and creating a level playing field, SEPs can play an additional role in securing significant environmental or public health protection and improvements. SEPs may be particularly appropriate to further the objectives in the statutes EPA administers and to achieve other policy goals, including promoting pollution prevention and environmental justice.

2. Pollution Prevention and Environmental Justice

The Pollution Prevention Act of 1990 (42 U.S.C. § 13101 et seq., November 5, 1990) identifies an environmental management hierarchy in which pollution "should be prevented or reduced whenever feasible; pollution that cannot be prevented should be recycled in an environmentally safe manner whenever feasible; pollution that cannot be prevented or recycled should be treated in an environmentally safe manner whenever feasible; and disposal or other release into the environment should be employed only as a last resort ..." (42 U.S.C. §13103). Selection and evaluation of proposed SEPs should be conducted generally in accordance with this hierarchy of environmental management, i.e., SEPs involving pollution prevention techniques are preferred over other types of reduction or control strategies, and this can be reflected in the degree of consideration accorded to a defendant/respondent before calculation of the final monetary penalty.

Further, there is an acknowledged concern, expressed in Executive Order 12898 on environmental justice, that certain segments of the nation's population, i.e., low-income and/or minority populations, are disproportionately burdened by pollutant exposure. Emphasizing SEPs in communities where environmental justice concerns are present helps ensure that persons who spend significant portions of their time in

areas, or depend on food and water sources located near, where the violations occur would be protected. Because environmental justice is not a specific technique or process but an overarching goal, it is not listed as a particular SEP category; but EPA encourages SEPs in communities where environmental justice may be an issue.

3. Using this Policy

In evaluating a proposed project to determine if it qualifies as a SEP and then determining how much penalty mitigation is appropriate, Agency enforcement and compliance personnel should use the following five-step process:

(1) Ensure that the project meets the basic definition of a SEP. (Section B)

(2) Ensure that all legal guidelines, including nexus, are satisfied. (Section C)

(3) Ensure that the project fits within one (or more) of the designated categories of SEPs. (Section D)

(4) Determine the appropriate amount of penalty mitigation. (Section E – not included.)

(5) Ensure that the project satisfies all of the implementation and other criteria. (Sections F and I partial)(G, H, I partial and J not included)

4. Applicability

This Policy applies to all civil judicial and administrative enforcement actions taken under the authority of the environmental statutes and regulations that EPA administers. It also may be used by EPA and the Department of Justice in reviewing proposed SEPs in settlement of citizen suits. This Policy also applies to federal agencies that are liable for the payment of civil penalties. Claims for stipulated penalties for violations of consent decrees or other settlement agreements may not be mitigated by the use of SEPs.

This is a settlement Policy and thus is not intended for use by EPA, defendants, respondents, courts or administrative law judges at a hearing or in a trial. Further, whether the Agency decides to accept a proposed SEP as part of a settlement, and the amount of any penalty mitigation that may be given for a particular SEP, is purely within EPA's discretion. Even though a project appears to satisfy all of the provisions of this Policy, EPA may decide, for one or more reasons, that a SEP is not appropriate (e.g., the cost of reviewing a SEP proposal is excessive, the oversight costs of the SEP may be too high, the defendant/respondent may not have the ability or reliability to complete the proposed SEP, or the deterrent value of the higher penalty amount outweighs the benefits of the proposed SEP).

This Policy establishes a framework for EPA to use in exercising its enforcement discretion in determining appropriate settlements. In some cases, application of this Policy may not be appropriate, in whole or part. In such cases, the litigation team may, with the advance approval of Headquarters, use an alternative or modified approach.

B. DEFINITION AND KEY CHARACTERISTICS OF A SEP

Supplemental environmental projects are defined as environmentally beneficial projects which a defendant/respondent agrees to undertake in settlement of an enforcement action, but which the defendant/respondent is not otherwise legally required to perform. The three bolded key parts of this definition are elaborated below.

"Environmentally beneficial" means a SEP must improve, protect, or reduce risks to public health, or the environment at large. While in some cases a SEP may provide the alleged violator with certain benefits, there must be no doubt that the project primarily benefits the public health or the environment.

"In settlement of an enforcement action" means: 1) EPA has the opportunity to help shape the scope of the project before it is implemented; and 2) the project is not commenced until after the Agency has identified a violation e.g., issued a notice of violation, administrative order, or complaint).

"Not otherwise legally required to perform means" the project or activity is not required by any federal, state or local law or regulation. Further, SEPs cannot include actions which the defendant/respondent is likely to be required to perform:

(a) as injunctive relief in the instant case;

(b) as injunctive relief in another legal action EPA, or another regulatory agency could bring;

(c) as part of an existing settlement or order in another legal action; or,

(d) by a state or local requirement.

SEPs may include activities which the defendant/respondent will become legally obligated to undertake two or more years in the future, if the project will result in the facility coming into compliance earlier than the deadline. Such "accelerated compliance" projects are not allowable, however, if the regulation or statute provides a benefit (e.g., a higher emission limit) to the defendant/respondent for early compliance.

Also, the performance of a SEP reduces neither the stringency nor timeliness requirements of Federal environmental statutes and regulations. Of course, performance of a SEP does not alter the defendant/respondent's obligation to remedy a violation expeditiously and return to compliance.

C. LEGAL GUIDELINES

EPA has broad discretion to settle cases, including the discretion to include SEPs as an appropriate part of the settlement. The legal evaluation of whether a proposed SEP is within EPA's authority and consistent with all statutory and Constitutional requirements may be a complex task. Accordingly, this Policy uses five legal guidelines to ensure that our SEPs are within the Agency's and a federal court's authority, and do not run afoul of any Constitutional or statutory requirements.

1. A project cannot be inconsistent with any provision of the underlying statutes.

2. All projects must advance at least one of the objectives of the environmental statutes that are the basis of the enforcement action and must have adequate nexus. Nexus is the relationship between the violation and the proposed project. This relationship exists only if:

a. the project is designed to reduce the likelihood that similar violations will occur in the future; or

b. the project reduces the adverse impact to public health or the environment to which the violation at issue contributes; or

c. the project reduces the overall risk to public health or the environment potentially affected by the violation at issue.

Nexus is easier to establish if the primary impact of the project is at the site where the alleged violation occurred or at a different site in the same ecosystem or within the immediate geographic area. Such SEPs may have sufficient nexus even if the SEP addresses a different pollutant in a different medium. In limited cases, nexus may exist even though a project will involve activities outside of the United States. The cost of a project is not relevant to whether there is adequate nexus.

3. EPA may not play any role in managing or controlling funds that may be set aside or escrowed for performance of a SEP. Nor may EPA retain authority to manage or administer the SEP. EPA may, of course, perform oversight to ensure that a project is implemented pursuant to the provisions of the settlement and have legal recourse if the SEP is not adequately performed.

4. The type and scope of each project are defined in the signed settlement agreement. This means the "what, where and when" of a project are defined by the settlement agreement. Settlements in which the defendant/respondent agrees to spend a certain sum of money on a project(s) to be defined later (after EPA or the Department of Justice signs the settlement agreement) are not allowed.

5. a. A project cannot be used to satisfy EPA's statutory obligation or another federal agency's obligation to perform a particular activity. Conversely, if a federal statute prohibits the expenditure of federal resources on a particular activity, EPA cannot consider projects that would appear to circumvent that prohibition.

b. A project may not provide EPA or any federal agency with additional resources to perform a particular activity for which Congress has specifically appropriated funds. A project may not provide EPA with additional resources to perform a particular activity for which Congress has earmarked funds in an appropriations committee report. Further, a project cannot be used to satisfy EPA's statutory or earmark obligation, or another federal agency's statutory obligation, to spend funds on a particular activity. A project, however, may be related to a particular activity for which Congress has specifically appropriated or earmarked funds.

c. A project may not provide additional resources to support specific activities performed by EPA employees or EPA contractors. For example, if EPA has developed a brochure to help a segment of the regulated community comply with environmental requirements, a project may not directly, or indirectly, provide

additional resources to revise, copy or distribute the brochure.

d. A project may not provide a federal grantee with additional funds to perform a specific task identified within an assistance agreement.

D. CATEGORIES OF SUPPLEMENTAL ENVIRONMENTAL PROJECTS

EPA has identified seven specific categories of projects which may qualify as SEPs. In order for a proposed project to be accepted as a SEP, it must satisfy the requirements of at least one category plus all the other requirements established in this Policy.

1. Public Health
A public health project provides diagnostic, preventative and/or remedial components of human health care which is related to the actual or potential damage to human health caused by the violation. This may include epidemiological data collection and analysis, medical examinations of potentially affected persons, collection and analysis of blood/fluid/tissue samples, medical treatment and rehabilitation therapy. Public health SEPs are acceptable only where the primary benefit of the project is the population that was harmed or put at risk by the violations.

2. Pollution Prevention
A pollution prevention project is one which reduces the generation of pollution through "source reduction," i.e., any practice which reduces the amount of any hazardous substance, pollutant or contaminant entering any waste stream or otherwise being released into the environment, prior to recycling, treatment or disposal. (After the pollutant or waste stream has been generated, pollution prevention is no longer possible and the waste must be handled by appropriate recycling, treatment, containment, or disposal methods.)
Source reduction may include equipment or technology modifications, process or procedure modifications, reformulation or redesign of products, substitution of raw materials, and improvements in housekeeping, maintenance, training, inventory control, or other operation and maintenance procedures. Pollution prevention also includes any project which protects natural resources through conservation or increased efficiency in the use of energy, water

or other materials. "In-process recycling," wherein waste materials produced during a manufacturing process are returned directly to production as raw materials on site, is considered a pollution prevention project.

In all cases, for a project to meet the definition of pollution prevention, there must be an overall decrease in the amount and/or toxicity of pollution released to the environment, not merely a transfer of pollution among media.

This decrease may be achieved directly or through increased efficiency (conservation) in the use of energy, water or other materials. This is consistent with the Pollution Prevention Act of 1990 and the Administrator's "Pollution Prevention Policy Statement: New Directions for Environmental Protection," dated June 15, 1993.

3. Pollution Reduction

If the pollutant or waste stream already has been generated or released, a pollution reduction approach—which employs recycling, treatment, containment or disposal techniques—may be appropriate. A pollution reduction project is one which results in a decrease in the amount and/or toxicity of any hazardous substance, pollutant or contaminant entering any waste stream or otherwise being released into the environment by an operating business or facility by a means which does not qualify as "pollution prevention." This may include the installation of more effective end-of-process control or treatment technology, or improved containment, or safer disposal of an existing pollutant source. Pollution reduction also includes "out-of-process recycling," wherein industrial waste collected after the manufacturing process and/or consumer waste materials are used as raw materials for production off-site.

4. Environmental Restoration and Protection

An environmental restoration and protection project is one which enhances the condition of the ecosystem or immediate geographic area adversely affected. These projects may be used to restore or protect natural environments (such as ecosystems) and man-made environments, such as facilities and buildings. This category also includes any project which protects the ecosystem from actual or potential damage resulting from the violation or improves the overall condition of the ecosystem. Examples of such projects include: restoration of a wetland in the same ecosystem along the same avian flyway in which the facility is located; or purchase and

management of a watershed area by the defendant/respondent to protect a drinking water supply where the violation (e.g., a reporting violation) did not directly damage the watershed but potentially could lead to damage due to unreported discharges. This category also includes projects which provide for the protection of endangered species (e.g., developing conservation programs or protecting habitat critical to the well-being of a species endangered by the violation).

In some projects where a defendant/respondent has agreed to restore and then protect certain lands, the question arises as to whether the project may include the creation or maintenance of certain recreational improvements, such as hiking and bicycle trails. The costs associated with such recreational improvements may be included in the total SEP cost provided they do not impair the environmentally beneficial purposes of the project and they constitute only an incidental portion of the total resources spent on the project.

In some projects where the parties intend that the property be protected so that the ecological and pollution reduction purposes of the land are maintained in perpetuity, the defendant/respondent may sell or transfer the land to another party with the established resources and expertise to perform this function, such as a state park authority. In some cases, the U.S. Fish and Wildlife Service or the National Park Service may be able to perform this function.

With regard to man-made environments, such projects may involve the remediation of facilities and buildings, provided such activities are not otherwise legally required. This includes the removal/mitigation of contaminated materials, such as soils, asbestos and lead paint, which are a continuing source of releases and/or threat to individuals.

5. Assessments and Audits

Assessments and audits, if they are not otherwise available as injunctive relief, are potential SEPs under this category. There are three types of projects in this category: a. pollution prevention assessments; b. environmental quality assessments; and c. compliance audits. These assessments and audits are only acceptable as SEPs when the defendant/respondent agrees to provide EPA with a copy of the report. The results may be made available to the public, except to the extent they constitute confidential business information pursuant to 40 CFR Part 2.

Subpart B.

a. Pollution prevention assessments are systematic, internal reviews of specific processes and operations designed to identify and provide information about opportunities to reduce the use, production, and generation of toxic and hazardous materials and other wastes. To be eligible for SEPs, such assessments must be conducted using a recognized pollution prevention assessment or waste minimization procedure to reduce the likelihood of future violations. Pollution prevention assessments are acceptable as SEPs without an implementation commitment by the defendant/respondent. Implementation is not required because drafting implementation requirements before the results of an assessment are known is difficult. Further, many of the implementation recommendations may constitute activities that are in the defendant/respondent's own economic interest.

b. Environmental quality assessments are investigations of: the condition of the environment at a site not owned or operated by the defendant/respondent; the environment impacted by a site or a facility regardless of whether the site or facility is owned or operated by the defendant/respondent; or threats to human health or the environment relating to a site or a facility regardless of whether the site or facility is owned or operated by the defendant/respondent. These include, but are not limited to: investigations of levels or sources of contamination in any environmental media at a site; or monitoring of the air, soil, or water quality surrounding a site or facility. To be eligible as SEPs, such assessments must be conducted in accordance with recognized protocols, if available, applicable to the type of assessment to be undertaken. Expanded sampling or monitoring by a defendant/respondent of its own emissions or operations does not qualify as a SEP to the extent it is ordinarily available as injunctive relief.

c. Environmental compliance audits are independent evaluations of a defendant/respondent's compliance status with environmental requirements. Credit is only given for the costs associated with conducting the audit. While the SEP should require all violations discovered by the audit to be promptly corrected, no credit is given for remedying the violation since persons are required to achieve and maintain compliance with environmental requirements. In general, compliance audits are acceptable as SEPs only

when the defendant/respondent is a small business or small community.

6. Environmental Compliance Promotion

An environmental compliance promotion project provides training or technical support to other members of the regulated community to: 1) identify, achieve and maintain compliance with applicable statutory and regulatory requirements or 2) go beyond compliance by reducing the generation, release or disposal of pollutants beyond legal requirements. For these types of projects, the defendant/respondent may lack he experience, knowledge or ability to implement the project itself, and, if so, the defendant/respondent should be required to contract with an appropriate expert to develop and implement the compliance promotion project. Acceptable projects may include, for example, producing a seminar directly related to correcting widespread or prevalent violations within the defendant/respondent's economic sector.

Environmental compliance promotion SEPs are acceptable only where the primary impact of the project is focused on the same regulatory program requirements which were violated and where EPA has reason to believe that compliance in the sector would be significantly advanced by the proposed project. For example, if the alleged violations involved Clean Water Act pretreatment violations, the compliance promotion SEP must be directed at ensuring compliance with pretreatment requirements. Environmental compliance promotion SEPs are subject to special approval requirements per Section J.

7. Emergency Planning and Preparedness

An emergency planning and preparedness project provides assistance—such as computers and software, communication systems, chemical emission detection and inactivation equipment, HAZMAT equipment, or training—to a responsible state or local emergency response or planning entity. This is to enable these organizations to fulfill their obligations under the Emergency Planning and Community Right-to-Know Act (EPCRA) to collect information to assess the dangers of hazardous chemicals present at facilities within their jurisdiction, to develop emergency response plans, to train emergency response personnel and to better respond to chemical spills.

EPCRA requires regulated sources to provide information on chemical production, storage and use to State Emergency Response Commissions (SERCs), Local Emergency Planning Committees (LEPCs) and Local Fire Departments (LFDs). This enables states and local communities to plan for and respond effectively to chemical accidents and inform potentially affected citizens of the risks posed by chemicals present in their communities, thereby enabling them to protect the environment or ecosystems which could be damaged by an accident. Failure to comply with EPCRA impairs the ability of states and local communities to meet their obligations and places emergency response personnel, the public and the environment at risk from a chemical release.

Emergency planning and preparedness SEPs are acceptable where the primary impact of the project is within the same emergency planning district or state affected by the violations and EPA has not previously provided the entity with financial assistance for the same purposes as the proposed SEP. Further, this type of SEP is allowable only when the SEP involves non-cash assistance and there are violations of EPCRA, or reporting violations under CERCLA § 103, or CAA § 112(r), or violations of other emergency planning, spill or release requirements alleged in the complaint.

8. Other Types of Projects
Projects determined by the case team to have environmental merit which do not fit within at least one of the seven categories above but that are otherwise fully consistent with all other provisions of this Policy, may be accepted with the advance approval of the Office of Enforcement and Compliance Assurance.

9. Projects Which Are Not Acceptable as SEPs
The following are examples of the types of projects that are not allowable as SEPs:
a. General public educational or public environmental awareness projects, e.g., sponsoring public seminars, conducting tours of environmental controls at a facility, promoting recycling in a community;
b. Contributions to environmental research at a college or university;
c. Conducting a project, which, though beneficial to a community, is unrelated to environmental protection, e.g., making a contribution to a non-profit, public interest, environmental, or other charitable organization, or donating playground equipment;

d. Studies or assessments without a requirement to address the problems identified in the study (except as provided for in § D.5 above);
e. Projects which the defendant/respondent will undertake, in whole or part, with low-interest federal loans, federal contracts, federal grants, or other forms of federal financial assistance or non-financial assistance (e.g., loan guarantees).

H. FAILURE OF A SEP AND STIPULATED PENALTIES

If a SEP is not completed satisfactorily, the defendant/respondent should be required, pursuant to the terms of the settlement document, to pay stipulated penalties for its failure. Stipulated penalty liability should be established for each of the scenarios set forth below as appropriate to the individual case.

1. Except as provided in paragraph 2 immediately below, if the SEP is not completed satisfactorily, a substantial stipulated penalty should be required. Generally, a substantial stipulated penalty is between 75 and 150 percent of the amount by which the settlement penalty was mitigated on account of the SEP.

2. If the SEP is not completed satisfactorily, but the defendant/respondent:
a) made good faith and timely efforts to complete the project; and b) certifies, with supporting documentation, that at least 90 percent of the amount of money which was required to be spent was expended on the SEP, no stipulated penalty is necessary.

3. If the SEP is satisfactorily completed, but the defendant/respondent spent less than 90 percent of the amount of money required to be spent for the project, a small stipulated penalty should be required. Generally, a small stipulated penalty is between 10 and 25 percent of the amount by which the settlement penalty was mitigated on account of the SEP.

4. If the SEP is satisfactorily completed, and the defendant/respondent spent at least 90 percent of the amount of money required to be spent for the project, no stipulated penalty is necessary.

The determinations of whether the SEP has been satisfactorily completed (i.e., pursuant to the terms of the agreement) and whether the defendant/respondent has made a good faith, timely effort to implement the SEP should be reserved to the sole discretion of EPA, especially in administrative actions in which there is often no formal dispute resolution process.

I. COMMUNITY INPUT

In appropriate cases, EPA should make special efforts to seek input on project proposals from the local community that may have been adversely impacted by the violations. Soliciting community input into the SEP development process can: result in SEPs that better address the needs of the impacted community; promote environmental justice; produce better community understanding of EPA enforcement; and improve relations between the community and the violating facility. Community involvement in SEPs may be most appropriate in cases where the range of possible SEPs is great and/or multiple SEPs may be negotiated.

APPENDIX **XLI**

SOURCE:
P-F Technical Services Inc.

Return on Investment Worksheets

Expenditures for equipment have to be justified. The economics of any purchase require consideration of the impact the new or modified equipment will have on the cost of manufacture or the ability to increase sales. Either option will add to the profitability of the firm.

The ratio of savings or increased income to the cost of the equipment is termed "return on investment" (ROI). Each firm will establish the comfort level with which it can finance, based on the ROI. A rule of thumb that existed for many years was a payback of three years was adequate to proceed with a project. In tighter economic conditions, many firms now look for a two year or less ROI.

The spreadsheets consist of two components:

1. A data collection form to prepare all the information that will be needed to compute the ROI.

2. The ROI spreadsheet in which the various costs are detailed, increased sales estimated, and the final numbers used to determine a ratio, based on the cost of the equipment.

In the example shown, monitoring equipment is being added to the press to reduce waste and increase speed. The anticipated savings come from the lower waste and its conversion to saleable product. Material is only one component of the cost and the savings; labor and machine time must also be taken into account.

Use of this simple form can help plant management determine the value of a project and gives them a tool for assigning priorities when considering a number of different projects.

902

PRIME FLEXIBLE PACKAGING LTD.

PROJECT: PURCHASE AND INSTALL WEB INSPECTION EQUIPMENT

A. SAVINGS DUE TO REDUCTION IN WASTE

MATERIAL COST

CURRENT WASTE PERCENTAGE (printing and converting)	25.00%	%
CURRENT WASTE PERCENTAGE (attributable to printing)	10.00%	%

ANNUAL MATERIAL PURCHASES	5000000	pounds/footage
AMOUNT PRINTING WASTE GENERATED	500000	pounds/footage
COST OF MATERIAL PURCHASED	$0.75	per pound/m feet

ANNUAL COST OF WASTE MATERIAL	(amount waste x cost)	$375,000.00

PROCESSING COSTS

AMOUNT OF WASTE (POUNDS/FOOTAGE)	PRESS	500000
(50% OF WASTE AFTER PRESS)	CONVERT	375000

RATES TO PROCESS WASTE	PRINTING	700	lbs/hour
	CONVERTING	300	lbs/hour

TIME TO PROCESS WASTE	PRINTING	714	hours
	CONVERTING	1250	hours

MACHINE RATES FOR ESTIMATING	PRINTING	$400.00
	CONVERTING	$150.00

COST TO PROCESS WASTE	PRINTING	$285,714.29
	CONVERTING	$187,500.00

COST OF LABOR AND OVERHEAD DUE TO WASTE	$473,214.29

TOTAL COST - MATERIALS, LABOR & OVERHEAD	$848,214.29

B ANTICIPATED SAVINGS FROM EQUIPMENT MODIFICATION

PERCENTAGE REDUCTION IN WASTE   50% %

AMOUNT OF WASTE SAVED (POUNDS/FEET)   437500 pounds

DOLLAR VALUE OF WASTE MATERIAL SAVED $328,125.00

TIME SAVED THROUGH REDUCTION IN WASTE

TIME TO PROCESS WASTE (POUNDS OR FEET/HOUR)

	PRINTING	CONVERTING	TOTALS
HOURS SAVED	625	1458	2083
MACHINE COSTS	250000	218750	468750

LABOR & OVERHEAD SAVED WITH WASTE REDUCTION $468,750.00

TOTAL SAVINGS - MATERIALS, LABOR & OVERHEAD $796,875.00

C COST OF MACHINE MODIFICATION   2 UNITS $500,000.00

ROI (COST OF MODIFICATION VERSUS SAVINGS PER YEAR)   0.627

year

DATA COLLECTION FORM FOR ROI

Date: _____

Company _____

Address _____

Phone: _____ Fax: _____

PRINTING:

1 Press Manufacturer: _____ Model: _____

2 Substrates Printed   a. _____ b. _____ c. _____

3 Number Colors   _____ Stack, CI, In-line   _____

4 Ink Transfer System   a. Doctor Blades   b. Chamber Blades   c. Two roll

Stations

5 Graphics Printed - %   Line _____ %   Screen _____ %   Process _____ %

6 Web Width   Maximum   Average   Minimum

7 Maximum Print Width   _____

8 Repeat (Cut-off)   Maximum   Average   Minimum

9 Graphic Quality Level   High   Average   Low

10 Average Ink Coverage   _____ %

11 Average Speed   _____ Maximum Speed   _____

12 Average Change Time   _____ Maximum Change Time _____

13 Working Week   _____ days   shifts   hours

14 Percent Actual Printing   _____ % Estimated Run Hours   _____

15 Average Number of Jobs Run Per Day_____   Per Week_____   Per Month_____

16 Average length of orders

17 Percent Waste at Press_____   Percent Waste Converting_____

COST FACTORS

18 Cost of Substrates: Substrate | $/LB |

a. _____

b. _____

c. _____

DATA COLLECTION FORM FOR ROI

19 Cost of Inks (Average)   White _____   Black _____   Colors _____

COST FACTORS (continued) _____

20 Cost of Waste Removal   Substrate _____   Hazardous Waste _____

21 Amount of Substrate Waste Shipped per Month _____ Per Year _____

22 Amount of Hazardous Waste Shipped per Month _____

CONVERTING FACTORS

23 Converting Operations: Laminations   Bags   Boxes   Corrugated   Slit to Rolls

24 Converting Cost Per Hour _____   25. Converting Units/Hour _____

26 Additional Material Costs in Laminating _____

27 Additional Material Costs in Converting _____

28 Percent Waste in Converting Operations: Laminations: _____

                                                       Other _____

29 Major Reasons for Waste in Converting: _____

_____

_____

MOST COMMON PRINT DEFECTS - REJECTIONS/CUSTOMER COMPLAINTS

Errors in copy accuracy	Registration	Repeat Variation
Color Off Color	Color Light	Color Dark
Distortion of Copy	Bar Code Scan	Too Much Impression
Streaks	Dirty Print	Others (describe)

_____

_____

_____

COMMENTS:

_____

_____

_____

_____

APPENDIX XLII

Introduction to Environmental Accounting: Key Concepts and Terms

SOURCE:
USEPA, EPA 742-R-95-001

A. Introduction

The term *environmental accounting* has many meanings and uses. Environmental accounting can support national income accounting, financial accounting, or internal business managerial accounting. This primer focuses on the application of environmental accounting as a managerial accounting tool for internal business decisions. Moreover, the term *environmental cost* has at least two major dimensions: (1) it can refer solely to costs that directly impact a company's bottom line (here termed "private costs"), or (2) it also can encompass the costs to individuals, society, and the environment for which a company is not accountable (here termed "societal costs"). The discussion in this primer concentrates on private costs because that is where companies starting to implement environmental accounting typically begin. However, much of the material is applicable to societal costs as well.

B. Why Do Environmental Accounting ?

Environmental costs are one of the many different types of costs businesses incur as they provide goods and services to their customers. Environmental performance is one of the many important measures of business success. Environmental costs and performance deserve management attention for the following reasons:

(1) Many environmental costs can be **significantly reduced or eliminated** as a result of business decisions, ranging from operational and housekeeping changes, to investment in "greener" process technology, to redesign of processes/products. Many environmental costs (e.g., wasted raw materials) may provide no added value to a process, system, or product.

(2) Environmental costs (and, thus, potential cost savings) **may be obscured in overhead accounts or otherwise overlooked**.

(3) Many companies have discovered that **environmental costs can be offset by generating revenues** through sale of waste by-products or transferable pollution allowances, or licensing of clean technologies, for example.

(4) Better management of environmental costs can result in **improved environmental performance and significant benefits to human health** as well as business success.

(5) Understanding the environmental costs and performance of processes and products can promote **more accurate costing and pricing** of products and can aid companies in the **design of more environmentally preferable** processes, products, and services for the future.

(6) **Competitive advantage** with customers can result from processes, products, and services that can be demonstrated to be environmentally preferable.

(7) Accounting for environmental costs and performance can support a company's development and operation of an overall **environmental management system**. Such a system will soon be a necessity for companies engaged in international trade due to pending international consensus standard ISO 14001, developed by the International Organization for Standardization.[2]

---

[2] See ISO 14001: *Environmental Management System Specification* (Committee Draft, February 1995). ISO 14000 guidance document *General Guidelines on Principles and Supporting Techniques* (Committee Draft, February 1995) adds that tracking environmental benefits and costs can support the appropriate allocation of resources for achieving environmental objectives.

907

EPA's work with key stakeholders leads it to believe that as businesses more fully account for environmental costs and benefits, they will clearly see the financial advantages of pollution prevention (P2) practices. Environmental costs often can be reduced or avoided through P2 practices such as product design changes, input materials substitution, process re-design, and improved operation and maintenance (O&M) practices. For example, increased environmental costs may result from use of chemical A (e.g., a chlorinated solvent), but not from chemical B (e.g., an aqueous-based solvent). This is true even though chemical A and chemical B can be substitutable. Another example: some environmental compliance costs are required only when use of a substance or generation of a waste exceeds a defined threshold. A company that can reduce chemical use below such thresholds or employ substitutes for regulated chemicals can realize substantial cost savings from design, engineering, and operational decisions.

In two of the most thorough reports on the subject of pollution prevention in the industrial community, the not-for-profit group INFORM[3] studied 29 companies in the organic chemical industry in 1985 and again in 1992. This research found that chemical "plants with some type of environmental cost accounting program" had "an average of three times as many" P2 projects "as plants with no cost accounting system."[4] The study also showed that the average annual savings per P2 project in production facilities, where data were available, were just over $351,000, which equalled an average savings of $3.49 for every dollar spent. Not only were substantial savings and returns on investment documented for P2 projects, but an average of 1.6 million pounds of waste were reduced for each project.

Results like these have highlighted the potential benefits of environmental accounting to the business community. For example, responses to a questionnaire administered by George Nagle of the Bristol-Myers Squibb Company at the Spring 1994 Global Environmental Management Initiative (GEMI) Conference showed that corporate professionals are placing a high priority on environmental accounting.[5] Of the 25 respondents to the informal survey, half stated that their company had some form of a tracking system for environmental costs. All but two reported that they believed environmental accounting issues would be more important to their companies in the near future. In addition, the Business Roundtable expects to turn its attention to environmental accounting issues in 1995, and companies of all sizes in the U.S. are beginning to consider implementing environmental accounting in their facilities.[6]

C.   What Is Environmental Accounting?

Different uses of the umbrella term *environmental accounting* arise from three distinct contexts:

Management accounting is the process of identifying, collecting, and analyzing information principally for internal purposes.[7] Because a key purpose of management accounting is to support a business's

---

[3] *Cutting Chemical Wastes* (1985), INFORM, New York, NY; *Environmental Dividends: Cutting More Chemical Wastes* (1992), INFORM, New York, NY.

[4] *Environmental Dividends*, at page 31.

[5] "Business Environmental Cost Accounting Survey," *Global Environmental Management Initiative '94 Conference Proceedings*, p. 243, March 16-17, 1994, Arlington, VA.

[6] *See Green Ledgers: Case Studies in Corporate Environmental Accounting*, edited by Daryl Ditz, Janet Ranganathan, and Darryl Banks (World Resources Institute, 1995) and *Environmental Accounting Case Studies*, EPA 742-R-95-00X (forthcoming).

[7] "Management accounting is the process of identification, measurement, accumulation, analysis, preparation, interpretation, and communication of financial information used by management to plan, evaluate, and control within an organization and to assure appropriate use of and accountability for its resources...." Institute of Management Accountants Statement on Management Accounting, No. 1A.

forward-looking management decisions, it is the focus of the remainder of this primer. Management accounting can involve data on costs, production levels, inventory and backlog, and other vital aspects of a business. The information collected under a business's management accounting system is used to plan, evaluate, and control in a variety of ways:

(1)   planning and directing management attention,

(2)   informing decisions such as purchasing (e.g., make vs. buy), capital investments, product costing and pricing, risk management, process/product design, and compliance strategies, and

(3)   controlling and motivating behavior to improve business results.

Unlike financial accounting, which is governed by Generally Accepted Accounting Principles (GAAP), management accounting practices and systems differ according to the needs of the businesses they serve. Some businesses have simple systems, others have elaborate ones. Just as management accounting refers to the use of a broad set of cost and performance data by a company's managers in making a myriad of business decisions, environmental accounting refers to the use of data about environmental costs and performance in business decisions and operations.

Type of Environmental Accounting	Focus	Audience
(1) national income accounting	nation	external
(2) financial accounting	firm	external
(3) managerial or management accounting	firm, division, facility, product line, or system	internal

National income accounting is a macro-economic measure. Gross Domestic Product (GDP) is an example. The GDP is a measure of the flow of goods and services through the economy. It is often cited as a key measure of our society's economic well-being. The term environmental accounting may refer to this national economic context. For example, environmental accounting can use physical or monetary units to refer to the consumption of the nation's natural resources, both renewable and nonrenewable. In this context, environmental accounting has been termed "natural resources accounting."

Financial accounting enables companies to prepare financial reports for use by investors, lenders, and others. Publicly held corporations report information on their financial condition and performance through quarterly and annual reports, governed by rules set by the U.S. Securities and Exchange Commission (SEC) with input from industry's self-regulatory body, the Financial Accounting Standards Board (FASB). Generally Accepted Accounting Principles (GAAP) are the basis for this reporting. Environmental accounting in this context refers to the estimation and public reporting of environmental liabilities and financially material environmental costs.

D.   What Is An Environmental Cost?

Uncovering and recognizing *environmental costs* associated with a product, process, system, or facility is important for good management decisions. Attaining such goals as reducing environmental expenses, increasing revenues, and improving environmental performance requires paying attention to current, future, and potential *environmental costs*. How a company defines an environmental cost depends on how it intends to use the information (e.g., cost allocation, capital budgeting, process/product design, other management decisions) and the scale and scope of the exercise. Moreover, it may not always be clear whether a cost is "environmental" or not; some costs fall into a gray zone or may be classified as partly environmental and partly not. Whether or not a cost is "environmental" is not critical; the goal is to ensure that relevant costs receive appropriate attention.

Identifying Environmental Costs

Environmental accounting terminology uses such words as *full, total, true,* and *life cycle* to emphasize that traditional approaches were incomplete in scope because they overlooked important environmental costs (and potential cost savings and revenues).[8] In looking for and uncovering relevant environmental costs, managers may want to use one or more organizing frameworks as tools. This section presents examples of environmental costs as well as a framework that has been used to identify and classify environmental costs.

There are many different ways to categorize costs. Accounting systems typically classify costs as:

(1) direct materials and labor,

(2) manufacturing or factory overhead (i.e., operating costs other than direct materials and labor),[9]

(3) sales,

(4) general and administrative (G&A) overhead,[10] and

(5) research & development (R&D).

Environmental expenses may be classified in any or all of these categories in different companies. To better focus attention on environmental costs for management decisions, the *EPA Pollution Prevention Benefits Manual* and the Global Environmental Management Initiative (GEMI) environmental cost primer use similar organizing frameworks to distinguish costs that generally receive management attention, termed the "usual" costs or "direct" costs, from costs that may be obscured through treatment as overhead or R&D, distorted through improper allocation to cost centers, or simply overlooked, termed "hidden," "contingent," "liability" or "less tangible" costs.[11] Exhibit 2 lists examples of these costs under the labels "conventional," "potentially hidden," "contingent," and "image/relationship" costs.

Conventional Costs. The costs of using raw materials, utilities, capital goods, and supplies are usually addressed in cost accounting

---

[8] See, for example, Paul E. Bailey, "Full Cost Accounting for Life Cycle Costs --- A Guide for Engineers and Financial Analysts," *Environmental Finance* (Spring 1991), pp. 13-29.

[9] Manufacturing or factory overhead typically includes indirect materials and labor, capital depreciation, rent, property taxes, insurance, supplies, utilities, repairs and maintenance, and other costs of operating a factory.

[10] General and administrative costs may be pooled with sales costs (i.e., SG&A) or as part of "technical, sales, and general administrative" costs (i.e., TSGA).

[11] The EPA's *Pollution Prevention Benefits Manual* (October 1989) introduced the terminology distinguishing among usual, hidden, liability, and less tangible costs. This framework was largely adopted in *Finding Cost-Effective Pollution Prevention Initiatives: Incorporating Environmental Costs into Business Decision Making* (1994, Global Environmental Management Initiative (GEMI)), which uses the terms direct, hidden, contingent liability, and less tangible costs.

EXHIBIT 2
Examples of Environmental Costs Incurred by Firms

Potentially Hidden Costs		
Regulatory	**Upfront**	**Voluntary** (Beyond Compliance)
• Notification	• Site studies	• Community relations/ outreach
• Reporting	• Site preparation	• Monitoring/testing
• Monitoring/testing	• Permitting	• Training
• Studies/modeling	• R&D	• Audits
• Remediation	• Engineering and procurement	• Qualifying suppliers
• Recordkeeping	• Installation	• Reports (e.g., annual environmental reports)
• Plans	***Conventional Costs***	• Insurance
• Training	Capital equipment	• Planning
• Inspections	Materials	• Feasibility studies
• Manifesting	Labor	• Remediation
• Labeling	Supplies	• Recycling
• Preparedness	Utilities	• Environmental studies
• Protective equipment	Structures	• R & D
• Medical surveillance	Salvage value	• Habitat and wetland protection
• Environmental insurance	**Back-End**	• Landscaping
• Financial assurance	• Closure/ decommissioning	• Other environmental projects
• Pollution control	• Disposal of inventory	• Financial support to environmental groups and/or researchers
• Spill response	• Post-closure care	
• Stormwater management	• Site survey	
• Waste management		
• Taxes/fees		

Contingent Costs		
• Future compliance costs	• Remediation	• Legal expenses
• Penalties/fines	• Property damage	• Natural resource damages
• Response to future releases	• Personal injury damage	• Economic loss damages

Image and Relationship Costs		
• Corporate image	• Relationship with professional staff	• Relationship with lenders
• Relationship with customers	• Relationship with workers	• Relationship with host communities
• Relationships with investors	• Relationship with suppliers	• Relationship with regulators
• Relationship with insurers		

and capital budgeting, but are not usually considered environmental costs. However, decreased use and less waste of raw materials, utilities, capital goods, and supplies are environmentally preferable, reducing both environmental degradation and consumption of nonrenewable resources. It is important to factor these costs into business decisions, whether or not they are viewed as "environmental" costs. The dashed line around these *conventional costs* in Exhibit 2 indicates that even these costs (and potential cost savings) may sometimes be overlooked in business decision-making.

Potentially Hidden Costs. Exhibit 2 collects several types of environmental costs that may be potentially hidden from managers: first are **upfront environmental costs**, which are incurred prior to the operation of a process, system, or facility. These can include costs related to siting, design of environmentally preferable products or processes, qualifications of suppliers, evaluation of alternative pollution control equipment, and so on. Whether classified as overhead or R&D, these costs can easily be forgotten when managers and analysts focus on operating costs of processes, systems, and facilities. Second are **regulatory** and **voluntary environmental costs** incurred in operating a process, system, or facility; because many companies traditionally have treated these costs as overhead, they may not receive appropriate attention from managers and analysts responsible for day-to-day operations and business decisions.

The magnitude of these costs also may be more difficult to determine as a result of their being pooled in overhead accounts. Third, while upfront and current operating costs may be obscured by management accounting practices, *back-end environmental costs* may not be entered into management accounting systems at all. These environmental costs of current operations are *prospective*, meaning they will occur at more or less well defined points in the future. Examples include the *future* cost of decommissioning a laboratory that uses licensed nuclear materials, closing a landfill cell, replacing a storage tank used to hold petroleum or hazardous substances, and complying with regulations that are not yet in effect but have been promulgated. Such back-end environmental costs may be overlooked if they are not well documented or accrued in accounting systems.

Exhibit 2 contains a lengthy list of *"potentially hidden" environmental costs*, including examples of the costs of upfront, operational, and back-end activities undertaken to (1) comply with environmental laws (i.e., regulatory costs) or (2) go beyond compliance (i.e., voluntary costs). In bringing these costs to light, it also may be useful to distinguish among costs incurred to respond to *past pollution* not related *to ongoing operations*; to control, clean up, or prevent pollution from *ongoing operations*; or to prevent or reduce pollution from *future operations*.

Contingent Costs. Costs that may or may not be incurred at some point in the future -- here termed *"contingent costs"* --can best be described in probabilistic terms: their expected value, their range, or the probability of their exceeding some dollar amount. Examples include the costs of remedying and compensating for future accidental releases of contaminants into the environment (e.g., oil spills), fines and penalties for future regulatory infractions, and future costs due to unexpected consequences of permitted or intentional releases. These costs may also be termed "contingent liabilities" or "contingent liability costs." Because these costs may not currently need to be recognized for other purposes, they may not receive adequate attention in internal management accounting systems and forward-looking decisions.

Image and Relationship Costs. Some environmental costs are called "less tangible" or "intangible" because they are incurred to affect subjective (though measurable) perceptions of management, customers, employees, communities, and regulators. These costs have also been termed *"corporate image"* and *"relationship"* costs. This category can include the costs of annual environmental reports and community relations activities, costs incurred voluntarily for environmental activities (e.g., tree planting), and costs incurred for P2 award/recognition programs. The costs themselves are not "intangible," but the direct benefits that result from relationship/corporate image expenses often are.

Is It An "Environmental" Cost?

Costs incurred to comply with environmental laws are clearly environmental costs. Costs of environmental remediation, pollution control equipment, and noncompliance penalties are all unquestionably environmental costs. Other costs incurred for environmental protection are likewise clearly environmental costs, even if they are not explicitly required by regulations or go beyond regulatory compliance levels.

There are other costs, however, that may fall into a gray zone in terms of being considered environmental costs. For example, should the costs of production equipment be considered "environmental" if it is a "clean technology?" Is an energy-efficient turbine an "environmental" cost? Should efforts to monitor the shelf life of raw materials and supplies in inventory be considered "environmental" costs (if discarded, they become waste and result in environmental costs)? It may also be

> The goal of environmental accounting is to increase the amount of relevant information that is made available to those who need or can use it. The success of environmental accounting does not depend on "correctly" classifying all the costs a firm incurs.

difficult to distinguish some environmental costs from health and safety costs or from risk management costs.

The success of environmental accounting does not depend on "correctly" classifying all the costs a firm incurs. Rather, its goal is to ensure that relevant information is made available to those who need or can use it. To handle costs in the gray zone, some firms use the following approaches:

- allowing a cost item to be treated as "environmental" for one purpose but not for another,

- treating part of the cost of an item or activity as "environmental," or

- treating costs as "environmental" for accounting purposes when a firm decides that a cost is more than 50% environmental.

There are many options. Companies can define what should constitute an "environmental cost" and how to classify it, based on their goals and intended uses for environmental accounting. For example, if a firm wants to encourage pollution prevention in capital budgeting, it might consider distinguishing (1) environmental costs that can be avoided by pollution prevention investments, from (2) environmental costs related to remedying contamination that has already occurred. But for product costing purposes, such a distinction might not be necessary because both are costs of producing the good or service.

E. Is There a Proper Scale and Scope for Environmental Accounting?

Environmental accounting is a flexible tool that can be applied at different scales of use and different scopes of coverage. This section describes some of the options for applying environmental accounting.

Scale. Depending on corporate needs, interests, goals, and resources, environmental accounting can be applied at different scales, which include the following:

★	individual *process* or group of processes (e.g., production line)
★	*system* (e.g., lighting, wastewater treatment, packaging)
★	*product* or product line
★	*facility*, department, or all facilities at a single *location*
★	*regional/geographical* groups of departments or facilities
★	corporate division, affiliate, or the entire *company*

Specific environmental accounting issues or challenges may vary depending on the scale of its application.

Scope. Whatever the scale, there also is an issue of scope. An initial scope question is whether environmental accounting extends beyond conventional costs to include potentially hidden, future, contingent, and image/relationship costs. Another scope issue is whether companies intend to consider only those costs that directly affect their bottom line financial profit or loss (e.g., see examples of costs listed in Exhibit 2 above), or whether companies also want to recognize the environmental costs that result from their activities but for which they are not accountable, referred to as societal or external costs. These latter costs are described in Section F.

Thus, the *scope* of environmental accounting refers to the types of costs included. As the scope becomes more expansive, firms may find it more difficult to assess and measure certain environmental costs. This is illustrated by Exhibit 3.

EXHIBIT 3

The Spectrum of Environmental Costs

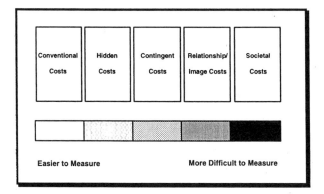

| Conventional Costs | Hidden Costs | Contingent Costs | Relationship/ Image Costs | Societal Costs |

Easier to Measure   **More Difficult to Measure**

F.   What Is The Difference Between Private Costs and Societal Costs?

Understanding the distinction between private and societal costs is necessary when discussing environmental accounting, because common terms are often used inconsistently to refer to one or both of those cost categories. Exhibit 4 provides a graphical representation of the important difference between private and societal costs. It also shows that many private costs are not currently considered in decision-making. This perspective can apply to a process, product, system, facility, or an entire company.

EXHIBIT 4[12]

• Private and Societal Environmental Costs

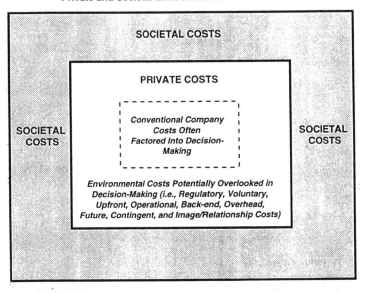

SOCIETAL COSTS

PRIVATE COSTS

Conventional Company Costs Often Factored Into Decision-Making

SOCIETAL COSTS   **SOCIETAL COSTS**

Environmental Costs Potentially Overlooked in Decision-Making (i.e., Regulatory, Voluntary, Upfront, Operational, Back-end, Overhead, Future, Contingent, and Image/Relationship Costs)

---

[12] Adapted from Allen T. White, Monica Becker, and Deborah E. Savage, "Environmentally Smart Accounting: Using Total Cost Assessment to Advance Pollution Prevention," *Pollution Prevention Review* (Summer 1993), pp. 247-259.

The innermost box labeled *"conventional company costs"* includes the many costs businesses typically track well (e.g., capital costs, labor, material). Many of these costs may already be directly allocated to the responsible processes or products in cost accounting systems and be included in financial evaluations of capital expenditures. The larger unshaded box includes all of the potentially overlooked costs a business incurs. Examples of these costs are shown on page 9 at Exhibit 2. Together, the unshaded area represents *"private costs,"* which are the costs a business incurs or for which a business can be held accountable (i.e., legally responsible). These are the costs that can directly affect a firm's bottom line.

The outside shaded box labeled *"societal costs"* represents the costs of business' impacts on the environment and society for

> **Life Cycle Perspective Can Help to Identify Private and Societal Costs**
>
> The life cycle of a product, process, system, or facility can refer to the suite of activities starting with acquisition (and upfront pre-acquisition activities) and concluding with back-end disposal/decommissioning that a specific firm performs or is responsible for. This life-cycle perspective can foster a thorough accounting of private costs (and potential cost savings) in addition to facilitating a more systematic and complete assessment of societal impacts and costs due to a firm's activities.

which business is not legally accountable. (These costs are also called "externalities" or "external costs.") Societal costs include both (1) environmental degradation for which firms are not legally liable and also (2) adverse impacts on human beings, their property, and their welfare (e.g., employment impacts of spills) that cannot be compensated through the legal system. For example, damage caused to a river because of polluted wastewater discharges, or to ecosystems from solid waste disposal, or to asthmatics because of air pollutant emissions are all examples of societal costs for which a business often does not pay. Because laws can vary from state to state, the boundary between societal and private costs may differ as well. At present, valuing societal costs is both difficult and controversial; nevertheless, some businesses are attempting to address these costs and EPA supports their efforts. A major North American power utility, Ontario Hydro, has made a corporate commitment to determine external impacts and, to the extent possible, value societal costs in order to integrate them into its planning and decision-making.[13] EPA urges businesses to address all private environmental costs shown on Exhibit 2, including hidden, future, contingent, and image/relationship costs, to the extent practical. Companies are also encouraged to move beyond consideration of private costs to incorporate societal costs, at least qualitatively, into their business decisions.

G.   Who Can Do Environmental Accounting?

Environmental accounting can be employed by firms large and small, in almost every industry in both the manufacturing and services sectors. It can be applied on a large scale or a small scale, systematically or on an as needed basis. The form it takes can reflect the goals and needs of the company using it. However, in any business, top management support and cross-functional teams are likely to be essential for the successful implementation of environmental accounting because:

- Environmental accounting may entail a new way of looking at a company's environmental costs, performance, and decisions. Top management commitment can set a positive tone and articulate incentives for the organization to adopt environmental accounting.

- Companies will likely want to assemble cross-functional teams to implement environmental accounting, bringing together designers, chemists, engineers, production managers, operators, financial staff, environmental managers, purchasing personnel, and accountants who may not have worked together before.

---

[13] See *"Full Cost Accounting" at Ontario Hydro: A Case Study*, EPA 742-R-95-00X

Because environmental accounting is not solely an accounting issue, and the information needed is split up among all of these groups, these people need to talk with each other to develop a common vision and language and make that vision a reality.

AT&T is one example of a company that has combined senior management support and use of a cross-functional team for its environmental accounting initiative.[14]

Companies with formal environmental management systems may want to institutionalize environmental accounting because it is a logical decision support tool for these systems. Similarly, many companies have begun or are exploring new business approaches in which environmental accounting can play a part:

- Activity-Based Costing/Activity-Based Management

- Total Quality Management/Total Quality Environmental Management

- Business Process Re-Engineering/Cost Reduction

- Cost of Quality Model/Cost of Environmental Quality Model

- Design for Environment/Life-Cycle Design

- Life-Cycle Assessment/Life-Cycle Costing

All of these approaches are compatible with environmental accounting and can provide platforms for integrating environmental information into business decisions. Companies using or evaluating these approaches may want to consider explicitly adopting environmental accounting as part of these efforts.

> Environmental accounting can be an important component of overall corporate environmental management, quality management, and cost management.

Small businesses that may not have formal environmental management systems, or are not using any of the above approaches, have also successfully applied environmental accounting. As with larger firms, management commitment and cross-functional involvement are necessary.

H. Applying Environmental Accounting to Cost Allocation

An important function of environmental accounting is to bring environmental costs to the attention of corporate stakeholders who may be able and motivated to identify ways of reducing or avoiding those costs while at the same time improving environmental quality.

This can require, for example, pulling some environmental costs out of overhead and allocating those environmental costs to the appropriate accounts. By *allocating* environmental costs to the products or processes that generate them, a company can motivate affected managers and employees to find creative pollution prevention alternatives that lower those costs and enhance profitability. For example, Caterpillar's East Peoria, Illinois, plant no

> **COST ALLOCATION**

longer dumps waste disposal costs into an overhead account; rather, the costs of waste disposal are allocated to responsible commodity groups, triggering efforts to improve the bottom line through pollution prevention.[15]

Overhead is any cost that, in a given cost accounting system, is not wholly attributed to a single process, system, product, or facility. Examples can include supervisors' salaries, janitorial services, utilities, and waste disposal. Many environmental costs are often treated as overhead in corporate cost accounting systems. Traditionally, an overhead cost item has been handled in either one of two ways:

(1) it may be allocated on some basis to specific products, or

(2) it may be left in the pool of costs that are not attributed to any specific product.

If overhead is allocated incorrectly, one product may bear an overhead allocation greater than warranted, while another may bear an allocation smaller than its actual contribution. The result is poor product costing, which can affect pricing and profitability. Alternatively, some overhead costs may not be reflected at all in product cost and price. In both instances, managers cannot perceive the true cost of producing products and thus internal accounting reports provide inadequate incentives to find creative ways of reducing those costs.

Separating environmental costs from overhead accounts where they are often hidden and allocating them to the appropriate product, process, system, or facility directly responsible reveals these costs to managers, cost analysts, engineers, designers, and others. This is critical not only for a business to have accurate estimates of production costs for different product lines and processes, but also to help managers target cost reduction activities that can also improve environmental quality. The axiom "one cannot manage what one cannot see" pertains here.

> **Steps in Environmental Cost Allocation**
> 1. Determine scale and scope
> 2. Identify environmental costs
> 3. Quantify those costs
> 4. Allocate environmental costs to responsible process, product, system, or facility

There are two general approaches to allocating environmental costs:

(1) Build proper cost allocation directly into cost accounting systems, or

(2) Handle cost allocation outside of automated accounting systems.

Companies may find that the latter approach can serve as an interim measure while the former option is being implemented.

[15] Jean V. Owen (senior editor,) "Environmental Compliance: Managing the Mandates," *Manufacturing Engineering* (March 1995).

[14] See *Introducing "Green Accounting" at AT&T: A Case Study,* EPA 742-R-95-00X

APPENDIX **XLIII**

Emissions Reduction Credits: An Asset for Growth

Planning for the future as a viable and profitable entity requires that a printer continue to evolve and grow with the demands of the market. Often this means purchasing and operating larger and faster presses. In the current trend for higher quality printing, the decision to expand calls for presses with more and more print stations. Ten- and 12-color presses are coming into the market every day. The more colors, the wider the press, the faster the press—all of it means using more ink and more solvents for cleaning or as diluents. Just how does one cope with the demands for reduction of pollutants under the burden of environmental regulation.

Congress has provided a tool to promote growth while reducing pollutants in the air. The name given to this tool is Emission Reduction Credits, where every credit is equal to one ton of emissions. While originally created as a concept to allow older, polluting utilities to buy credits from neighboring utilities which had built new, more effective plants, as part of the effort to stem acid rain, the concept has spread to cover most emissions by a variety of industries. As an example, the new source regulation for New York State (Part 231) provides for emission

offsets, stating "An applicant for a permit to construct for an air contamination source project . . . must provide emission offsets as part of the application. Emission offsets are required for any air contaminant for which the area is designated as a nonattainment area if the net increase in annual actual emissions of that contaminant exceeds the deminimus emission shown . . . in this Subpart." Every state has a similar provision in its air regulations.

The concept of trading emission credits was conceived as a means of reducing air emissions while encouraging the growth and modernization of business. Sustainable development could come at a price that would, in effect, reduce the emissions of air pollutants. In essence, a facility may use credits for exceeding the acceptable increase in emissions, as defined by New Source Review to offset the anticipated (actual or potential) emissions from the planned growth of a source. For every ton of emissions that will be introduced, a higher amount will be required to offset the new source. As an example, in a severe area such as the broad Metropolitan New York region, for every ton of emissions introduced, credits for 1.3 tons must be provided. In essence, for every new 2,000 pounds there will be a reduction of 600 pounds. If a plant is to need 100 tons to open, it will be responsible for retiring 30 tons of existing actual air contaminants.

Some of these credits may be acquired from past and planned efforts of the facility to go beyond compliance. Pollution prevention programs can bring the facility benefits beyond the anticipated safer, cleaner operation. If a facility uses safer chemistry, more effective working practices and newer, more efficient equipment, it can exceed the standards required of it by law. These excesses can be used to apply and register emission reduction credits. For example: A flexographic printer has been using solvent-base inks and is working with a limit of 20 tons per year. The printer converts to water-base inks, which have a much smaller requirement for allowable VOCs, and is able to use even lower VOC inks than required by RACT, further reducing the amount of his emissions. This is termed "going beyond compliance." The printer can file for credits for the difference between his old actual emissions and the new level of emissions. The operating air permit for the facility will be amended to reflect the new, lower emission level.

Putting away the credits for the future

Emission reduction credits can be "banked." The credits are registered with the state and acknowledged as certified credits. The printer can retain the credits and use them for subsequent growth, the opening of a new facility, or modifications that will add to the emissions from the plant. Use of emission reduction credits in these cases is known as "netting." Credits are applied within the permitting application process, protected from any agency policy that would transfer a portion of the credits to the state.

More often, the credits may be acquired from other facilities that have "banked" their reductions or have shut down all or a portion of their operations. A lively commodity market has developed to handle the trading of emission reduction credits. A facility may register the tonnage and make them available to other facilities that are expanding or erecting installations but do not have their own credits. Shutting down a facility or a portion of a facility that has emitted pollutants can also be registered for credits.

What are ERCs?

Emission reduction credits (ERCs) are certified reductions in air emissions of volatile organic compounds (VOCs), nitrogen oxide (NOx), and, in some areas, particulates and carbon monoxide (CO), which exceed the current regulatory standards. They are part of an economic incentive approach to reduce pollutants as an alternative to traditional command and control methods. ERCs are aimed at giving industry more choices for compliance, opportunities for economic savings, achievement of better environmental protection, and an encouragement to engage in innovative pollution prevention alternatives.

The emissions must be real, permanent and enforceable to the satisfaction of the government agencies, and have occurred within the previous five years prior to the date of submittal for certification. Only reductions which lower actual air emissions from a source beyond levels prescribed by the applicable emission standards of the regulations can be used as offsets.

How do you quantify ERCs?

Emission reduction credits are calculated as the difference between prior actual annual emissions and future potential emissions, using a baseline established from the most recent five years actual experience. The spreadsheets that each firm must maintain to verify its status under an existing air permit will provide the data necessary for computation of emission reductions.

Emissions will be based on either purchases or usage of ink, solvent, cleaning materials, etc. Emissions will be computed using:

- Stack tests for any add-on control system,
- Manufacturers' guarantees,
- Published emission rates, such as the EPA's AP-42,
- Material Safety Data Sheets/Air Quality Data Sheet,
- Continuous emissions monitoring,
- Other environmental reports, such as hazardous waste or SARA Title III,
- Best engineering judgement.

Of the five years reviewed, the two most representative years will be selected as the basis for applying for the emission reduction credits. Once registered, the ERCs represent an asset to the business, a reserve that can be tapped to raise funds for growth and development.

Other than over-control, how are the ERCs created?

Given the changes in the printing industry, there are a number of avenues to generate ERCs other than its efforts to go beyond compliance:

* Shutdown of a facility: Many businesses that have had to close due to the pressures of landlords and real estate agents are no longer emitting air pollutants.
* Shutdown of equipment, reducing the production and emission of air pollutants,
* Replacement of traditional equipment with non-polluting equipment,
* Source reduction and pollution prevention.

There's gold in them hills

At one time, the cost of registering credits versus the value of the credit in the marketplace was a disincentive for printers to consider filing. That scenario has changed. Registering can be done at a lower cost and the value of the credits is moving upwards. A Wall Street emissions credits commodity broker has announced that VOC ERCs in the states of New York, Pennsylvania and Connecticut can command from $3,500 to $5,800 per ton. The cost of registering can run as low as $2,500.00. Even for a firm that closed down or curtailed an operation in the tune of three to four tons, we are talking about a significant amount of money.

Making your move

While the concept has received a mixed reception by the various stakeholders having an interest in the environment, it has provided a means for allowing facilities to be expanded or built. The credits have also created a new investment market, where credits can be registered and held as an asset for sale in a commodity marketplace. Printers should review their usage and emissions, look at their business plans, and decide how emission reduction credits can help fulfill plans for growth. Those printers who have shuttered their plants or have drastically reduced their operations should look at the records to ascertain what kinds of assets they may be sitting on that are not working to their advantage. If you need guidance, contact the Small Business program in your state.

Bibliography

The Bureau of National Affairs, Inc., "The Clean Air Act Amendments: BNA's Comprehensive Analysis of the New Law,' Washington, DC, 1991.

Clean Air Council, "Grasping for Air . . . The Small Business Guide to Key Federal and State Air Regulations," Clean Air Council funded by the United States Environmental Protection Agency Region III, Philadelphia, PA, 2000.

Commercial Clearing House, Inc., "Clean Air Act, Law and Explanation," Chicago, IL, December 1990.

Jones, Gary A., *Air Pollution Engineering Guide for the Graphic Arts Industry*, Graphic Arts Technical Foundation, Pittsburgh, PA, May 1993.

MECA, "A Guidebook, Catalytic Control of VOC Emissions," Manufacturers of Emission Controls Association, Washington, DC, 1997.

MEGTEC Systems, *The Clean Air Compliance Handbook*, DePere, WI, 1998.

United States Environmental Protection Agency, "The Clean Air Act Amendments of 1990, A Guide for Small Business," EPA 450-K-92-001, September 1992.

———. "Graphic Arts" An AP-42 Update," EPA-450/4-79-014, September 1979.

———. "Risk Management Planning: Accidental Release Prevention, Final Rule: Clean Air Act section 112(r) Factsheet," EPA 550-F-96-002, May 1996.

Clean Air

917

———. "Study of Volatile Organic Compound Emissions From Consumer and Commercial Products, Report to Congress," EPA-453/R-94-066-A, March 1995.

Environmental Accounting

United States Environmental Protection Agency, "An Introduction to Environmental Accounting as a Business Management Tool: Key Concepts and Terms," EPA 742-R-95-001, June 1995.

———. "Environmental Cost Accounting and Capital Budgeting," EPA 744-B-96-001, September 1995.

———. "Environmental Cost Accounting and Capital Budgeting for Small to Midsized Manufacturers," EPA 744-B-96-002, March 1996.

———. "Pollution Prevention Benefits Manual," EPA/230/R-89/100, October 1989.

Environmental Management Systems

Iowa Waste Reduction Center, "The Small Business Environmental Assistance Site Visit Manual," University of Northern Iowa, undated.

United States Environmental Protection Agency, "Aiming to Encourage Stewardship and Accelerate Environmental Progress," EPA 100-R-99-006, July 1999.

———. "Environmental Management Systems: An Implementation Guide for Small and Medium-Sized Organizations," EPA 832-B-96-007, November 1996.

———. "Integrated Environmental Management Systems, Company Manual Template for Small Business," EPA 744-R-00-012, December 2000.

———. "Integrated Environmental Management Systems, Implementation Guide," EPA 744-R-00-011, December 2000.

———. "Second Edition, Environmental Management Systems: An Implementation Guide for Small and Medium-Sized Organizations," EPA 832-B-01-001, January 2001.

———. "The Small Business Source Book on Environmental Auditing," EPA 233-B-00-003, May 2000.

General Environmental Regulations

Lee, Marvin R., "CRS Report for Congress, Summaries of Environmental Laws Administered by the Environmental Protection Agency," Congressional Research Service, The Library of Congress, 93-53 ENR, January 1993.

United States Environmental Protection Agency, "Environmental Assistance Services for Small Businesses, A Resource Guide," EPA-231B-00-001, December 2000.

———. "Environmental Compliance and Pollution Prevention Technical Assistance Directory for Printers, New York City," EPA 903-B-97-001, February 1997.

———. "Environmental Protection Agency, April 2000 Agenda of Regulatory and Deregulatory Actions," EPA 230-Z-00-001, April 2000.

———. "EPA FACT Sheet, EPA Activities Related to the Regulatory Flexibility Act as amended by the Small Business

Regulatory Enforcement Fairness Act (SBREFA)," EPA 233-F-99-001, June 1999.

———. "Federal Environmental Regulations Potentially Affecting The Commercial Printing Industry," EPA744B-94-001, March 1994.

———. "Revised Interim Guidance for EPA Rulewriters: Regulatory Flexibility Act as amended by the Small Business Regulatory Enforcement Fairness Act," Regulatory Management Division of EPA's Office of Policy, March 1999.

———. "Terms of Environment, Glossary, Abbreviations, and Acronyms," December 1997.

Pollution Prevention

Business for the Bay, Chesapeake Bay Program, "Pollution Prevention Workbook, A Waste Reduction Guide for Facilities in the Chesapeake Bay Watershed," United States Environmental Protection Agency, EPA 903-B-00-02, August 2000.

Fricke, Robert and Angela Alexiades, E.S. Millenium, LLC "Compliance Assistance and Pollution Prevention Workbook for Printers," #7000-BK-DEP2338, Department of Environmental Protection, Commonwealth of Pennsylvania and USEPA Region III, Philadelphia, PA, 2000.

The Illinois Waste Management and Research Center, "Pollution Prevention for the Printing Industry," Chicago, IL, February 1997.

Institute of Advanced Manufacturing Sciences Inc. and Printing Industries Association of Southern Ohio, "Improve Efficiency and Reduce Waste Through Process Control in the Lithographic Printing Industry," funded by United States Environmental Protection Agency, 1997.

Iowa Waste Reduction Center, "Pollution Prevention Curriculum for Lithographic Printers," University of Northern Iowa, 2000.

———. "Pollution Prevention Manual for Lithographic Printers," University of Northern Iowa, 1995.

United States Environmental Protection Agency, "Designing Solutions for Screen Printers, An Evaluation of Screen Reclamation Systems," EPA744-F-96-010, September 1996.

———. "EPA Solutions for Lithographic Printers, An Evaluation of Substitute Blanket Washes" EPA 744-F-96-009, September 1997.

———. "Facility Pollution Prevention Guide," EPA/600/R-92/088, May 1992.

———. Region I, "Fit to Print, An Environmental Compliance and Pollution Prevention Manual for New England Lithographic Printers," EPA-901-B-97-001, May 1997.

———. "Guides to Pollution Prevention, The Commercial Printing Industry," EPA/625/7-90/008, August 1990.

———. "Partnerships in Preventing Pollution, A Catalogue of the Agency's Partnership Programs" EPA 100-B-96-001, Spring 1996.

———. "Preventing Pollution Through Regulations, The Source Reduction Review Project, An Assessment," EPA-742-R-96-001, February 1996.

Printing Inks, Chemistry and Materials

Apps, E.A. B.Sc., *Inks for the Major Printing Processes*, Leonard Hill (Books) Ltd., London, England, 1963.

Bureau, William H., *What the Printer Should Know about Paper*, Graphic Arts Technical Foundation, Pittsburgh, PA, 1982.

Eldred, Dr. Nelson R., "Chemistry for the Graphic Arts, Third Edition," Graphic Arts Technical Foundation, Pittsburgh, PA, 2001.

Flick, Ernest W., *Printing Ink and Overprint Varnish Formulations, Recent Developments*, Noyes Publications, Park Ridge, NJ, 1991.

———. *Printing Ink and Overprint Varnish Formulations, Second Edition*, Noyes Publications, Park Ridge, NJ, 1999.

Foundation of the Flexographic Technical Association, *Flexographic Inks: A Process Approach*, FFTA, Ronkonkoma, NY, 1998.

Laden, Patrick, *Chemistry and Technology of Water Based Inks*, Blackie Academic & Professional, London, U.K, 1997.

Owen, David J. B.A., *Printing Inks for Lithography*, SITA Technology, London, England, 1990.

Stillwell, E. Joseph, R. Claire Canty, Peter W. Kopf, and Anthony M. Montrone, *Packaging for the Environment, A Partnership for Progress*, American Management Association, New York, 1991.

United States Environmental Protection Agency, "Cleaner Technologies Substitutes Assessment: Screen Printing, Use Cluster: Screen Reclamation," EPA744R-94-005, September 1994.

———. "Cleaner Technologies Substitutes Assessment, Lithographic Blanket Washes," EPA 744-R-95-008, July 1996.

———. "Flexographic Ink Options: A Cleaner Technologies Substitutes Assessment," Volume 1 , EPA 744-R-00-004a.

———. "Flexographic Ink Options: A Cleaner Technologies Substitutes Assessment," Volume 2 , EPA 744-R-00-004b.

Printing Technology

Adams, J. Michael; David D. Faux; and Lloyd J. Rieber, *Printing Technology*, Delmar Publishers Inc., Albany, NY., 1988.

Cogoli, John E., *Photo Offset Fundamentals*, McKnight Publishing Company, Bloomington, IL, 1973.

DeJidas, Lloyd P., and Thomas M. Destree, *Sheetfed Offset Press Operating*, Graphic Arts Technical Foundation, Sewickley, PA, 1995.

Foundation of the Flexographic Technical Association, *Flexography: Principles and Practices, Fifth Edition*, Ronkonkoma, NY, 1999.

Gravure Association of America, *Gravure, Process and Technology*, GAA and Gravure Education Foundation, Rochester, NY, 1991.

Stevenson, Deborah L., *Handbook of Printing Processes*, Graphic Arts Technical Foundation, Pittsburgh, PA, 1994.

United States Environmental Protection Agency, "Printing Industry and Use Cluster Profile," EPA 744-R-94-003, June 1994.

———. "Profile of the Printing Industry," EPA 310-R-95-014, September 1995.

Bailey, David S., Esq. and Selena Mendy, Esq., "Communities Using the Law to Combat Environmental Racism, Environmental Justice Community Handbook," The Lawyers' Committee for Civil Rights Under Law, Washington, DC, August 1997.

Center for Compatible Economic Development, "A Citizen's Guide to Achieving a Healthy Community, Economy & Environment," The Nature Conservancy Center for Compatible Economic Development, Leesburg, VA, 1996.

James A. Coon Local Government Technical Series, "Conducting Public Meetings and Public Hearings," New York State Department of State, Tug Hill Commission, Watertown, NY, September 1995.

New York State Department of Environmental Conservation, Division of Environmental Remediation, "Citizen Participation in New York's Hazardous Waste Site Remediation Program: A Guidebook," Albany, NY, 1997.

United States Environmental Protection Agency, "Chemicals in Your Community," EPA 550-K-99-001, September 1988.

———. "Community Based Environmental Protection, A Citizen's Handbook for Protecting Ecosystems and Communities," EPA 230-8-96-003, September 1996.

———. "Guide to Environmental Issues," EPA 520/B-94-001, September 1996.

———. "Hazardous Substances in Our Environment, A Citizen's Guide to Understanding Health Risks and Reducing Exposure," EPA 230/09/90/081, September 1990.

———. "People, Places, and Partnerships, A Progress Report on Community-Based Environmental Protection," EPA-100-R-97-003, July 1997.

———. "Public Involvement in the Superfund Program," WH/FS-87-004R, 1997.

———. "The Layman's Guide to the Toxic Substance Control Act," EPA 560/1-87-011, June 1987.

Public Participation and Risk Assessment

King County Local Hazardous Waste Management Program, "Screen Printers Waste Management Guide," King County, WA, May 1994.

New York State Department of Environmental Conservation, "Waste Reduction Guidance Manual," Albany, NY, March 1989.

United States Environmental Protection Agency, "Business Guide for Reducing Solid Waste," EPA/530-K-92-004, November 1993.

———. "Little Known but Allowable Ways to Deal with Hazardous Waste," EPA 233-B-00-002, May 2000.

———. "Notification of Regulated Waste Activity," EPA Form8700-12 (Rev 7/90).

———. "Onsite Solvent Recovery," EPA/600/R-94/026, September 1993.

———. "RCRA In Focus, Photo Processing," EPA530-K-99-002.

RCRA— Hazardous and Solid Waste

———. "RCRA In Focus, Printing," EPA530-K-97-007, January 1998.

———. "Understanding the Hazardous Waste Rules, A Handbook for Small Businesses –1996 Update," EPA530-K-95-001, June 1996.

Safety and Health—OSHA

"Code of Federal Regulations, Labor 29, Parts 1900-1910, Revised as of 1998, The Office of the Federal Register, National Archives and Records Administration, Washington, DC.

"Code of Federal Regulations, Labor 29, Parts 1910 To End, Revised as of 1998, The Office of the Federal Register, National Archives and Records Administration, Washington, DC.

Gloss, David S., and Miriam Gayle Wardle, *Introduction to Safety Engineering*, John Wiley & Sons, New York, 1984.

Harrison, Lee, *Environmental, Health and Safety Auditing Handbook*, McGraw-Hill, Inc., New York, 1994.

Slote, Leonard, *Handbook of Occupational Safety and Health*, John Wiley & Sons, New York, 1987.

U.S. Department of Labor, Bureau of Labor Statistics, "A Brief Guide to Recordkeeping Requirements for Occupational Injuries and Illnesses," O.M.B. No. 1220-0029, April 1986.

———. "OSHA Handbook for Small Businesses," OSHA 2209, 1990 (Revised).

Superfund, Sara Title III

United States Environmental Protection Agency, "Chemicals in Your Community, A Guide to the Emergency Planning and Community Right-to-Know Act," September 1988.

———. "Community Right-to-Know and Small Business, Understanding Sections 311 and 312 of the Emergency Planning and Community Right-to-Know Act of 1986," September 1988.

———. "Emergency Planning and Community Right-to-Know Act Section 313 Reporting Guidance for the Printing, Publishing and Packaging Industry," EPA 745-B-00-005, May 2000.

———. "Title III List of Lists, Consolidated List of Chemicals Subject to the Emergency Planning and Community Right-to-Know Act (EPCRA) and Section 112 of the Clean Air Act as Amended," EPA 550-B-98-017, November 1998.

———. "Title III Section 313 Release Reporting Guidance, Estimating Chemical Releases from Roller, Knife and Gravure Coating Operations," EPA 560/4-88-004, February 1988.

———. "Toxic Chemical Release Inventory Reporting Forms and Instructions, 1999 (Revised Annually)," EPA 745-K-99-001.

———. "When All Else Fails!, Enforcement of the Emergency Planning and Community Right-to-Know Act, A Self Help Manual for Local Emergency Planning Committees," EPA 20S-0002, July 1990.

Flexographic Technical Association
www.fta.ffta.org

Graphic Arts Technical Foundation
www.gatf.org

Gravure Association of America
www.gaa.org

Printer's National Environmental Assistance Center
www.pneac.org

Screenprinting and Graphic Imaging Association
www.sgia.org

United States Environmental Protection Agency
www.epa.gove

Web Sites

Index

How to Use the Computer Disk

The accompanying disk is intended to provide templates and models for a number of the tools and reports that are described in the text. They have been designed to enable the reader to structure the programs, records and reports that will be essential for a reasonable environmental and safety management program, including the periodic reports to the government.

To simplify the task of the reader, the templates and models have been constructed for either Excel spreadsheets or in Word. The edition for both Excel and Word is Microsoft Office 2000. A few government reports have been scanned or taken directly from the appropriate web sites.

The disk will contain a short Word description prior to each item. It will introduce the model and will describe particular concerns in personalizing the content for your facility. In addition, the model programs will contain hints as to what should appear in the blank spaces; the spreadsheets will have a few examples to demonstrate the contents and formulas in a more graphic format.

In general, the reader will have to modify the various references to governmental regulations to fit those of the state or local agency. Descriptive information relative to the facility and its products, the chemicals used, and the proportions of the formulations of the chemical products will be required. Formulas to compute emissions, wastes, etc. will be included and can be copied to new entries. The sources of information will be described for each of the models and templates.

The government forms that have been scanned into the text and disk can be found at the USEPA or OSHA web sites. The Internet addresses will be included in the heading of the document on the disk.

If you encounter problems in understanding the use of any of the models or templates, you can write to Fred Shapiro, 3200 North Leisure World Blvd., Apartment 515, Silver Spring, MD 20906.

A NOTE OF CAUTION

At time of publication the author and publisher have made every effort to make certain that all data, information, interpretations and forms shown in this book are completely current and up to date. However, such data, information, interpretations and forms are subject to continual change, correction, modification and reinterpretation. The contents of the book are recommendations and are for information and guidance only; they do not constitute instructions.

The reader is cautioned to make certain that all forms and interpretations of local, state, federal, or other jurisdictional rules and regulations are adhered to properly and are complete and up to date. Forms which are required for reporting on a periodic basis should be verified and proper copies obtained. Forms which appear on the computer disk should be verified before use to ascertain that they are the proper documents that are required for providing necessary information to the appropriate regulatory agenc(y)ies. In some instances it will require use of the Internet to obtain the latest forms, instructions and interpretations.

The author and publisher have created what they believe is the best media for the purpose of meeting the various applicable rules and regulations and will not be responsible for damages in the event of misuse of the information provided herein or misuse of the computer disk that may lead to damage to the user's equipment.